SURSUM CORDA!
The Collected Letters of Malcolm Lowry
Volume II: 1947-1957

OTHER BOOKS BY SHERRILL GRACE

Violent Duality: A Study of Margaret Atwood.
Véhicule Press, 1980

The Voyage That Never Ends: Malcolm Lowry's Fiction.
UBC Press, 1982

*Regression and Apocalypse: Studies in North American
Literary Expressionism.*
University of Toronto Press, 1989

*Swinging the Maelstrom: New Perspectives on
Malcolm Lowry,* edited by S. Grace.
McGill-Queen's University Press, 1992

Sursum Corda!
The Collected Letters of Malcolm Lowry
Volume 1: 1926–1946

Jonathan Cape and University
of Toronto Press, 1995

SURSUM CORDA!

The Collected Letters of Malcolm Lowry
Volume II: 1947-1957

Edited with Introductions and Annotations
by Sherrill E. Grace
Assistant Editor Kathy K.Y. Chung

UNIVERSITY OF TORONTO PRESS
Toronto   Buffalo

Malcolm Lowry's Letters © The Malcolm Lowry Estate 1996
Introductions, annotations and editorial comments © Sherrill E. Grace 1996

Sherrill E. Grace has asserted her right
under the Copyright, Designs and Patents Act, 1988
to be identified as the author of this work

First published in the United Kingdom in 1996 by
Jonathan Cape
Random House, 20 Vauxhall Bridge Road, London sw1v 2sa

First published in North America in 1997 by
University of Toronto Press Incorporated
Toronto and Buffalo

ISBN 0-8020-4118-3

Canadian Cataloguing in Publication Data available from
University of Toronto Press Inc.

Typeset from Author's disk by MATS
Printed in Great Britain by Mackays of Chatham, plc, Chatham, Kent

For Basil Stuart-Stubbs, Anne Yandle,
and George Brandak
and as always
for John

'This cherishing of original manuscripts is a relatively new phenomenon, and one that I find puzzling. A manuscript is, after all, only a
crude representation of that step between creative thought and artefact,
and might just as usefully be employed as kindling for a fire or in the
wrapping of fishbones.'

Carol Shields, *Swann*

'The moral of the story?'

'Who said stories have to have a moral? But, now that I think about
it, maybe the moral is that sometimes, to prove something, you have
to die.'

Umberto Eco, *Foucault's Pendulum*

Contents

Illustrations

32 Malcolm Malcolm at Grasmere in the Lake District, June 1957. This view with the pier reminded him of Dollarton

33 The Dollarton pier: 'Nobody could understand how it survived so long, not even engineers and it was nicknamed The 'Crazy Wonder' on the beach. Ramshackle from certain angles though it was, and the handrails puerile (but oh the washing hung out on the line there like great white stationary birds beating their wings against the gale).' Malcolm Lowry to Harvey Burt, August 1956, Letter **662**

The Editor, Sherrill E. Grace, wishes to thank the following for permission to reproduce the photographs in this book: Harvey Burt, 18, 19, 21, 26; Christian Bourgois, 6; Éditions Pierre Horay, 10; Erich Hartmann and the Lilly Library, University of Indiana, 13; Johannes ten Holder, 15, 16; Italia Monicelli and family, 23; Dorothy Livesay and Joy Stewart, 14; David Markson and Raymond Lieberman, 12; William McConnell, 11; Dr Michael Raymond, 28; Lipnitzki and Roger-Viollet, 24; University of British Columbia (Lowry Collection), 1, 2, 3, 4, 5, 7, 8, 9, 17, 20, 22, 25, 27, 29, 30, 31, 32, 33

Preface and Acknowledgements

Volume II of *The Collected Letters of Malcolm Lowry* is a continuation of Volume I prepared in accordance with the editorial principles, citations, and bibliography outlined there. The division between volumes, at the end of 1946, is as much a matter of the number of letters for each volume as of that major turning-point in Lowry's life – the publication of *Under the Volcano* in February 1947. Up to the moment of its acceptance and through the months of preparation for publication, Lowry was buoyed by the work of revising and proofing his novel. These tasks kept him occupied until near the end of December 1946.

From the beginning of January 1947 until his death in June ten years later, Lowry could find no similar galvanizing centre to his creative life. He continued to write letters, however; one might say that he wrote letters when he should have been writing fiction. Fortunately, the epistolary record of the last ten years of his life is as rich as it is voluminous, but as a consequence, this second volume is longer than the first. A majority of the letters from these years, including many to Margerie Bonner Lowry and to various friends, and several to his English physician, are published here for the first time.

For a number of reasons it has proved difficult to be certain that every possible source for Lowry's letters has been thoroughly searched. For example, several of the addressees have died and their survivors have not been traced; Clarisse Francillon's papers do not appear to have survived; the archives of the Canadian publisher McClelland and Stewart were not completely catalogued in time; and all efforts to trace the whereabouts of parts of other archives have proved fruitless. Two exciting discoveries did turn up after Volume II had already gone to press. The first of these appears as letter **296-a**, and it is a 1947 letter to Vernon van Sickle; two more letters, from 1946, also discovered by Mrs van Sickle Allen with her late husband's papers, have been added to Appendix 3. The second discovery is letter **309-a**, written to Dawn Powell in 1947. Thanks to the interest and sharp eyes of Tim and Vanessa Page, Lowry's letter was found *misfiled* with in-coming letters to Powell from Malcolm Cowley.

Ironically, the very fact that Margerie preserved so much material after her husband's death has meant that the manuscripts in the Lowry Collection at the University of British Columbia have had to be combed for drafts of letters. Then, transcribing from drafts has presented problems for precise dating, and these problems are further intensified by the frequent errors in *Selected Letters*.

Although there is no general introduction to this volume, short introductions are provided for each of its two major sub-divisions. As with Volume I, particular letters or sequences of letters have brief editorial introductions that provide background or context. In addition there are three appendices, two of which offer further examples of Lowry's letter-writing, one that provides supplementary incoming letters or documentation. Like the first volume, this one includes photographs of the Lowrys and of several addressees and a number of holograph reproductions. Here, as in volume one, the provenance and previous publication (where relevant) are given for each letter, and Lowry's idiosyncratic spelling and punctuation have been preserved.

There are many people to be thanked for their generous assistance with Volume II. In addition to those already mentioned, with sincere gratitude, in Volume I, it is a pleasure to mention again Peter Dickinson, who has continued to provide a sharp eye and a steady hand, and George Brandak, who has kept me informed of new acquisitions and provided generous help with my many requests; Gabriele Helms, Suzanne Kim, and Anthony Podlecki, who have prepared or checked translations; Sandra Djwa and Elspeth Cameron, both of whom took time from their own research to answer questions about Canadian connections; my colleagues Richard Cavell, Margery Fee, Lisa Chalykoff, Seng Lim, Harriet Kirkley, Paul Yachnin, Luciana Duranti, Bogdan Czaykowski, and Allan Evans; Dr Jack Parnall, Dr Michael Raymond, Jack McClelland, Gordon Bowker, Pat McCarthy, Julia Denholm, Joy Stewart, Maurice Nadeau, Shirley van Sickle Allen, Roger Davenport, Dennis Duffy, Ernst Klett of Klett-Cotta, Paul Tiessen, Rt Hon The Lord Tweedsmuir, the Estates of Harold Matson and of James Stern, Tim and Vanessa Page, Al Purdy, Ralph Gustafson, James Reaney, Raymond Souster, Sheila Sutherland from the University of Surrey, Oscar Lewenstein, Fede Bertolotti Monicelli, Joan Bulger at the University of Toronto Press, archivists at the Canadian Broadcasting Company, the City of Vancouver Archives, and the Frankfurt City and University Library, Claire Hudson of the Theatre Museum in London, Agence Roger-Viollett, Laurence Bergreen, Editions Pierre Horay, Fondation Jacques Doucet, Carl Spadoni from the Research Collection at McMaster University, Shelley Cox, Special Collections, Southern Illinois University, Fred Bauman at the Library of Congress, Thomas M. Whitehead, Head of Special Collections, Temple University. I want to express my appreciation and thanks to my editor at Cape, Tony Colwell, and to my typographer Allan Ticehurst, who has transformed complex manuscripts into two handsome books, and to the men in UBC's Media Services, who have prepared most of the prints for publication in both volumes, often from poor or damaged originals. And once more for the incomparable Susan Kent Davidson my affection and thanks.

Finally, Kathy Chung, who began working with me on the letters four years ago when Volume I was well under way and the letters for Volume II were being transcribed, has played an increasingly important role. Over this time she has become an expert in archival research and a trusted colleague who has performed the duties of assistant editor on Volume II, double-checking transcriptions and researching facts, with skill, rigour, and persistence. Preparing a scholarly edition is rarely amusing, but working together we often found that cheerfulness kept breaking through.

S.E.G.
Vancouver
January 1996

Chronology: 1947 to 1957

1947 – 1 January, Malcolm and Margerie Lowry disembark at Port-au-Prince, Haiti, and check into the Hotel Olaffson; Lowry meets Philippe Thoby-Marcelin; ca 22 January he collapses and is taken to Notre Dame hospital, where he spends approximately ten days; 12 February, the Lowrys leave Haiti by plane; 16 February, they arrive by bus in Charleston, South Carolina; 19 February, they arrive by bus in New York City, and *Under the Volcano* is published that day; 4 March, they take a train to Niagara-on-the-Lake to stay with the Noxons; Lowry meets Fletcher Markle in Toronto; ca 12 March, Lowry flies to Vancouver; Margerie arrives later by train; 17 March, they return to Dollarton; Lowry resumes work on 'La Mordida'; they spend the last week of April at Harrison Hot Springs Hotel; 29 April, CBS broadcast of *Under the Volcano*; 7 November, the Lowrys sail from Vancouver on the SS *Brest* for France via the Panama Canal; 23 December, they arrive in Le Havre and continue to Paris.

1948 – From early January to mid-March the Lowrys stay with Joan Black at 'La Cerisaie' in Vernon; Lowry tries to work on the French translation of *Volcano* with Clarisse Francillon; ca 20 March, Lowry is admitted to hospital in Vernon; ca 28 March, the Lowrys travel to Cassis; by mid-April Lowry is seriously ill; 26 April, he enters American Hospital, Paris; 15 May, he and Margerie begin a trip through Italy; June, he is briefly hospitalized in Rome; 13 June, they arrive in Naples; ca 22 June they go to Capri; 8 July the Lowrys return to France; from 21 July to the end of August they stay at 'La Cerisaie'; September, they return to Paris and in October they visit Brittany; November, they return to Paris, and Margerie visits the Lowry family in England; Christmas and the New Year are spent with Norman Matson in Paris.

1949 – 14 January, the Lowrys begin their return flight to Canada; 20 January, they arrive in Dollarton; ca 19-20 March, Malcolm has an operation for varicose veins; 14 July, he injures his back in a fall

xvii

from the pier and is taken to St Paul's hospital in Vancouver; while there he experiences hallucinations that inspire 'The Ordeal of Sigbjørn Wilderness'; July to August, the Lowrys begin work on a filmscript of *Tender Is the Night*; September to December, they work on the filmscript; December, severe winter weather at Dollarton.

1950 – 13 April, they send the completed filmscript of *Tender Is the Night* to Frank Taylor; during the summer and fall Lowry works on stories ('Strange Comfort Afforded by the Profession,' 'Through the Panama,' and 'October Ferry to Gabriola'); they run short of money and the City of Vancouver threatens to evict 'squatters' at Dollarton; Margerie is ill and the winter is severe; 7 December, Evelyn Boden Lowry dies.

1951 – Begins and ends with poverty, personal problems, and illness; Lowry works on stories for *Hear us O Lord*, expands 'October Ferry' and *The Voyage That Never Ends*; March, he begins corre- spondence with his German translator, Clemens ten Holder; during the spring and summer Malcolm helps Margerie with her fiction and works on stories for *Hear us O Lord*; 16 June, he begins correspondence with David Markson; September, the German translation of *Under the Volcano* is published; November, Lowry sends a manuscript version of *Hear us O Lord* and his plan for the *Voyage* to Harold Matson, with a copy to Albert Erskine; ca 30 December, due to winter weather, the Lowrys move into Vancouver.

1952 – During the first week in January they move into an apartment at 1075 Gilford Street, west-end Vancouver; January and February, Lowry expects to receive a long-term publishing contract with Harcourt, Brace; by 10 March, he learns that Harcourt, Brace is not interested and turns to Albert Erskine at Random House; 1 April, they arrive in Dollarton where they receive Erskine's news of a contract; 5 May, Lowry signs his Random House contract; August, David Markson visits; September, Lowry learns of Clemens ten Holder's illness; through October and November he works on drafts of *Hear us O Lord* and 'October Ferry,' which is becoming a novel; mid-November, they move into an apartment at 1359 Davie Street, west-end Vancouver; 5 December, Clemens ten Holder dies; the Lowrys spend Christmas on Bowen Island with Einar and Muriel Neilson.

1953 – The Lowrys spend the New Year with Downie Kirk and family; from January to March, Lowry experiences difficulty with work; March, Margerie visits her mother in Los Angeles, and Lowry goes on a drinking binge; end of March to beginning of April he spends

on Bowen Island with the Neilsons; ca 10 April, he and Margerie
return to Dollarton, where it is again difficult to work; June, he
resumes work on *October Ferry*; 28 June, Lowry breaks his leg and
Margerie is bitten by a dog; 29 June, they are both hospitalized for
approximately a week; 14 October, Lowry sends a 'batch' of
October Ferry manuscript to Erskine; 1 November, the first deadline
with Random House for delivery of a complete manuscript passes;
ca 11-15 November they move to an apartment at 1058 Nelson
Street, west-end Vancouver; they spend Christmas with the
Neilsons on Bowen Island.

1954 – 8 January, Lowry, who cannot meet contract deadlines, receives
Erskine's 6 January letter suspending payments and is devastated;
March, money arrives from Evelyn Boden Lowry's estate; May,
back in Dollarton, they begin plans for a trip to Europe; 24-26
August, the Lowrys spend their last days at Dollarton; 30 August,
they fly from Vancouver to Los Angeles; 2 September, they arrive
in New York City, where they stay with Markson, and Lowry sees
Conrad Aiken for the last time; 8-10 September, the Lowrys visit
Joan and Peter Churchill; 12 September, they sail aboard the ss
Giacomo for Italy; 22 September, they arrive in Genoa and continue
on to Milan, where Lowry spends two weeks in hospital; 17
October, they fly to Catania, Sicily, and travel to Syracuse; ca 27
October, they settle in Taormina at the Villa Eden; 13 December,
they move to the Villa Margherita, Taormina; Malcolm is in very
poor condition.

1955 – February, the Lowrys move from Villa Margherita to Villa
Mazzullo on the beach at Mazzaro below Taormina; February to
April, Malcolm becomes increasingly incapacitated; May, they are
visited by Dorothy Templeton Burt; 30 June, they leave Villa
Mazullo for a tour of the Aeolian Islands; 9 July, they fly to
London, where Margerie enters hospital to rest; 12 September,
Lowry is admitted to Brook Hospital in Woolwich; mid-October,
still in the Brook, Lowry resumes work on *October Ferry*; Margerie
is again hospitalized; 5 November, both Lowrys leave the Brook;
25 November, Lowry is admitted to Atkinson Morley's Hospital
and meets Dr Michael Raymond; Christmas is spent in hospital
with visits from Margerie.

1956 – January, Margerie finds The White Cottage in Ripe; 7 February,
Lowry is discharged from Atkinson Morley's and they move to
Ripe, where Lowry resumes work; by late June he is drinking
heavily and collapses; 1 July, he is readmitted to Atkinson Morley's;
11 August, Lowry returns to Ripe; Harvey Burt and Dorothy
Templeton Burt visit, and Lowry hears about the loss of the pier at

Dollarton; 18 October, Margerie enters St Luke's hospital for a rest; 16 November, Margerie returns to Ripe; November and December, Lowry works on *October Ferry*; they spend Christmas and New Year's in London.

1957 – January to May, the Lowrys live quietly in Ripe, and Malcolm works on *October Ferry*; 27 May, they leave for a tour of the Lake District; 22 June, they return to Ripe; 27 June, Margerie finds Lowry dead; 3 July, he is buried in the cemetery at Ripe.

SURSUM CORDA!
The Collected Letters of Malcolm Lowry
Volume II: 1947-1957

Withdrawal and Return:
1947 to 1951

Success is like some horrible disaster
Worse than your house burning, the sounds of ruination
As the roof tree falls following each other faster
While you stand, the helpless witness of your damnation.

Fame like a drunkard consumes the house of the soul
Exposing that you have worked for only this –
Ah, that I had never suffered this treacherous kiss
And had been left in darkness forever to founder and fail.
                              'After Publication of *Under the Volcano*'

IF ONE SUBJECT dominates Lowry's correspondence between 1947 and 1951, it is *Under the Volcano*. In 1947 he was caught up in the process of publication; through 1948-49 he struggled with its first translation; and after that it seemed as if this great novel would not release him from its grasp. As he said to Jonathan Cape in his letter of 2 January 1946 (**210**): 'It can even be regarded as a sort of machine: it works, too, believe me, as I have found out.' However, not even Lowry could have foreseen that this machine would operate like the one in Franz Kafka's story 'In the Penal Colony' – inscribing its judgement on every inch of his flesh until it almost killed his creative spirit.

Which is not to say that Lowry was unable to write during these years, or that he was not engaged in new projects, or not making new friends. He was. These years were, in fact, very full. He wrote letters constantly (more in 1951 and 1952 than at any other time); they were, often, all he *could* write during the grim months of 1948 in France. By the summer of 1949 he and Margerie were enthralled with their creation of an unsolicited filmscript for Frank Taylor of F. Scott Fitzgerald's *Tender Is the Night*. There were also new novels, thousands of pages, in fact, for *Dark as the Grave Wherein My Friend Is Laid* and 'La Mordida,' and by 1951 there was his elaborate, always evolving plan for *The Voyage That Never Ends*.

I

The success of *Volcano* also led to new friendships with Canadian writers and neighbours: Earle Birney, Dorothy Livesay, and A.J.M. Smith supported and published his work, and Downie Kirk, Harvey Burt, Einar and Muriel Neilson, and Bill and Alice McConnell were among his closest friends. Others faded from his life; for example, there are very few letters from these years to Conrad Aiken or Gerald Noxon. Two new figures of enormous practical and psychological importance took up their roles in Lowry's family romance: one, his editor Albert Erskine, was already on stage; the other, whom he was yet to meet, was a young New York writer called David Markson. Lowry's French and German translators, Clarisse Francillon and Clemens ten Holder, also entered his life between 1947 and 1951, and Lowry's readers, like Lowry himself, owe these two loyal and talented individuals a substantial debt. Francillon became a champion of Lowry's work – not just of *Volcano* – and ten Holder, before his early death, had dreams of German filmscripts for *Volcano* and of further translations.

The idea of a masterwork of connected novels to be called *The Voyage That Never Ends* had been with Lowry for many years before he finally sent a detailed description of this ambitious plan to Harold Matson on about 23 November 1951 (see letter **479**). I have examined these plans at length in my *Voyage That Never Ends: Malcolm Lowry's Fiction* (1982), but a brief comment here will help to clarify the many references, and changes, that Lowry was making to his *oeuvre* over the next five years while the project continued to grow.

As he explained to Jonathan Cape (letter **210**), in 1940 he had thought he would write a Dantean trilogy (*Volcano*, a revised *Lunar Caustic*, and 'In Ballast to the White Sea'); however, the loss of his manuscript of 'Ballast' in the 7 June 1944 fire forced him to reconceive the project, which, as the years passed, grew from a trilogy to a tetralogy framed by a two-part prologue and coda; the structure was, indeed, becoming more musical than literary as stories mushroomed into novellas and novellas into novels that threatened to become, metaphorically at least, operas of Wagnerian proportions.

In his November 1951 'Work in Progress' statement (UBC 32:1), the *Voyage* looked like this:

'The Ordeal of Sigbjørn Wilderness'		1
Untitled Sea Novel [a revised *Ultramarine*]		
'Lunar Caustic' [a revised 'Last Address']		
Under the Volcano		The Centre
'Dark as the Grave Wherein My Friend Is Laid'	⎫	
'Eridanus' [to become *October Ferry*]	⎬	Trilogy
'La Mordida'	⎭	
'The Ordeal of Sigbjørn Wilderness'		2

Lowry would not live to complete the *Voyage*, if completed it could have been, but on the strength of this plan he would receive a contract with Random House in the spring of 1952.

Although this is not the place to describe every new actor in the Lowry drama or every important occurrence, three categories of event seem especially significant to the larger pattern of Malcolm's life and to the flow of his letters during these years. The first of these is travel; the second is accidents; and the third is death, notably that of his mother.

The Lowrys finished proof-reading *Under the Volcano* by mid-December 1946 and enjoyed some sight-seeing in New Orleans before continuing their trip. 1947 began with their arrival in Haiti, and the restlessness and near-tragedy that characterized this ill-conceived adventure set the tone for the years ahead. The Lowrys were only back in Dollarton a few months before they began planning their next, even more disastrous trip – to France. There was always a rationale for these excursions, of course: Haiti was on the way to New York and the publication of *Volcano*; Paris was where Malcolm could help with its translation. By the winter of 1951-52 he and Margerie were moving regularly into Vancouver for the coldest months, and in 1954 they would leave Dollarton for good. They seem to have been unable to stay put, although stability, quiet routine, and natural surroundings were what the man and the writer most needed.

Given this restlessness, amounting almost to dislocation and exacerbated by mounting threats of eviction from the beach, it is perhaps not surprising that both Lowrys suffered health problems and accidents. The letters provide a litany of these woes: varicose veins, broken bones (and back), bruxism, dog bites, blood poisoning, hospitalizations, and operations. This pattern continued through the fifties, culminating in the ultimate accident: death by misadventure.

But there were other deaths along the way: those of Anna Wickham, Charles Stansfeld-Jones, Clemens ten Holder, Dylan Thomas, Anna Mabelle Bonner, Joan Black, and Evelyn Boden Lowry. While much has been said about Lowry's troubled relations with his father and his dislike of his mother, the letters suggest a somewhat different, more ambiguous story. Judging from Evelyn's letters to her son and the only extant letter (**376**) to his mother in this volume, it would seem that Lowry wrote to her regularly and frequently after her husband's death and that he felt uncomfortable when he failed to maintain this correspondence. Her death on 7 December 1950 freed the estate and made it possible for Lowry to receive a substantial financial settlement, but it may have freed him in other ways as well. In the fiction and letters written after her death, Lowry seems to have been able to reflect more sympathetically on mothers (Cosnahan's in 'Elephant and Colosseum' and Jacqueline's in *October Ferry*, for example) and to consider more openly and frankly the implications of the Oedipus story.

The theme of incest forms a dark motif running through Lowry's work, and his literary interest in it can be traced back to Conrad Aiken's influence and, most importantly, to Jean Cocteau's *La Machine infernale* (1934). Discussion of the subject, however, surfaces frequently during the 1949 work on *Tender Is the Night*, continues in his 4 May 1952 letter (**530**) to Erskine in response to Ralph Ellison's *Invisible Man*, and culminates in his long 1957 letter (**705**) to David Markson. It would be a distortion to imply that this interest in incest is a major theme in these letters, let alone a factor in his life. Lowry touches upon many topics in the correspondence, and there are several instances of his astute appreciation of other writers, of whom Cocteau, Fitzgerald, Ellison, and his 'beloved old Conrad' are only a few. Nevertheless, there is a sense in which Lowry's own work took a sharp turn in the direction of a symbolic incest. The fiction written during the years between 1947 and 1951, especially in *Dark as the Grave* and 'La Mordida,' failed to sever the umbilical cord that tied him to the *Volcano*.

The Lowrys disembarked at Port-au-Prince, Haiti, on or about the first of January 1947 to the sounds of music, drums, and general revelry. The New Year had begun, but for the Lowrys it would be a year of mixed blessings. Haiti itself was in many ways the sign of things to come: Malcolm made new friends, some of whom, like Philippe Thoby-Marcelin, would be very dear friends, and he renewed contact with old friends like John Davenport, but he also took to drinking again with the ferocious concentration that had characterized 1937-38 in Mexico. Under the Volcano would be published with great success and acclaim, but starting new work would prove to be a torment. And beginning with a ten-day stay in Notre Dame Hospital outside Port-au-Prince, Lowry would be in and out of hospitals a dozen times over the next ten years of his life.

271: To Albert Erskine

P: UBC(pcard)   [Port-au-Prince, Haiti]
                                                   [10 January 1947]ᵃ

Dear Erskine Mr

That is creole. Will you for the love of Jean-Christophe[1] please send any mail here airmail? Else – heaven knows. Port-au-Prince is wonderful; doves & tin roofs: looks rather like Tewkesbury.[2] Bless God

                                                   Lowry Malcolm

Alternative & swifter address:
Hotel Olaffson, Port-au-Prince.

Annotations:

1 Lowry's pun on the expression 'for the love of Christ' refers to the multivolume masterpiece *Jean-Christophe* (1904-1912) by the French novelist Romain Rolland (1866-1944), who won the Nobel Prize for Literature in 1915.
2 The ancient English town of Tewekesbury is famous for its Norman church and many Tudor houses.

Editorial Notes:

a. This is the postmark date; the card shows a photograph of the Citadelle in Port-au-Prince.

272: To Jonathan Cape

P: UBC(ts)

Hotel Grand Olaffson,
Port-au-Prince, Haiti
10 January 1947

Dear Mr Cape:

Here is the promised preface,[1] in regard to which I have been seized with insurmountable and paralysing neurosis, hence, in part, the delay.

Further delay has been caused by the fact that over the New Year and for a week after that, Haiti has been shut up in immeasurable revelry, making communication with the outside world extremely difficult.[2]

It still is difficult. . .

This effort at a preface is still, in spite of endless revisions and restarts, gamma minus, and since it is, in places, semantically and grammatically suspect as well, I would be obliged if you would submit it to the eagle eye of an expert before plumping it in. Whether it helps matters, as I thought it might, I have no way of telling. But the beginning and the end of it, at least, are good. If it does not arrive in time, this provided you still want it, I can suggest only you penalise me in some way.

I hope you got the proofs O.K. And I sent off a blurb air mail from New Orleans, though I had to enlist outside aid.

I hope I haven't delayed matters, but if I have, couldn't the preface be put at the end: 'I like prefaces, I read them, especially when they come at the end.' But probably not.

I got your letter safely here and hope very much to see you in New York in February. My wife is working hard on her book and will have finished her alterations in the next week or so.

I would like the dedication, in the English edition of Under the Volcano, simply: 'To Margerie.'

Renewed good wishes for the New Year,

Sincerely

Malcolm Lowry

P.S. I believe part of the preface, at least might encourage the reader.

P.P.S. The Volcano is scheduled to come out in New York Feb 19, so if it does I take it R & H [Reynal & Hitchcock] are within your kindly extended time-limit.

P.P.P.S. I opened this letter up to say that I tried the preface out on various people and their reactions were quite staggeringly favorable. So please don't be put off by my self-abasement on the point. I really did try hard. And reading it over it really does seem to me good.

Annotations:

1   If there was a final draft or clean copy of the preface sent to Cape with this letter, it does not appear to have survived, and Cape did not use one. With this letter, there is a pencil draft of a brief fragment entitled '*Preface*,' plus a heavily marked typescript draft of the preface with seven pages of re-writes and inserts (UBC 2:10). The French 'Préface' to *Au-dessous du volcan* (1949) follows the typescript only roughly and includes new material; this preface, dated September 1946, appeared in an English translation by George Woodcock in *Canadian Literature* 9 (1961): 23-29.
2   During the first week of January, Haitians celebrate Independence Day (1 January) and the 'Glorification of Heroes of Independence Day' (2 January). Christmas is celebrated with bands, parades, singing, and dancing with candles and lighted torches.

273: To Albert Erskine

P: UBC(ms)   Grand Hotel Olaffson
                                                        [Port-au-Prince]
                                                        [January 1947]

Dear Erskine Albert Mr Esq:

In reply to yours I dispatched you by return airmail my original defence of the Volcano to Cape, together with the preface, hoping that you might find something useful in this.[1]

Typ. error: I did not dispatch it, but, sitting in a bar run by a Moroccan, gave it, together with vingt-cinq gourdes,[2] to someone to dispatch.

This morning a boy (I think to send a boy after you to see if you have not killed yourself with drinking already)[3] arrives at the hotel & makes a hell of a row: it turns out that my defence, my preface, never went to the post-office but into the nearest garbage can.

But there is a catch here too: *he knows which garbage can it is.*

But there is yet another catch. Apparently it went after all & the boy just forgot to get back with the change.

So by now you ought to have these missives.

J'expliquer.

I am not at all sure of my ethics in this matter.

I obviously cannot offer you Capes preface.

My defense of the book contains (crossed out) some private matter and agonies (probably the best parts are crossed out) that are for your private ear alone or eye: I mean not the public one, if any; I mean I trust to your judgement, hoping only that you are not too embarrassed to have received it anyway.

Besides perhaps it is illegible. I sent it on a sudden impulse; I think the idea was that I wished to impress you that at one time I at least imagined I knew enough about the book to feel that it was worth expounding.

It isn't in the least fair to Cape, who has been very good to me & kind. But I was hopping mad with one of his readers.

There is a bit about Jackson too that is crossed out, crossed out because it is quite unfair to Jackson, & was never sent.

It is true I wrote him about his book, which caused me a great deal of pain, as you can well imagine it might; it is true too, I criticised it to him but I've not the slightest notion whether he ever received my letter.[4]

It's the purest coincidence if there was anything in the film that resembled any change I might have suggested and anyhow I loathed the film almost as much as I envied the book.[5] After the first shock I did not like The Lost Week End any too well either, although it's undoubtedly the finest thing of its kind ever done, and a double-barrelled moral triumph, it somehow does not bear reading more than twice – if that.

I think that's about all. No. Re New York. We plan to be there round Feb. 15, & I very much look forward to seeing you.

I don't feel any too well at present but I guess I shall recover.

A wonderful letter from Jimmy Stern did me good, as did yours –

All best wishes

Malcolm L.

Annotations:

1 Lowry, apparently at Erskine's request, sent him copies of his 2 January 1946 letter (**210**) to Cape and a 'Preface' to *Under the Volcano*. In his 22

January 1947 letter to Lowry, acknowledging receipt of these items, Erskine says he is appalled by the time spent on the letter when Lowry 'could have finished another novel.'

2 The gourde is the basic unit of the Haitian currency.

3 This is Dr Vigil's remark to the Consul in chapters 1 and 5 of *Under the Volcano*.

4 I have not been able to trace a draft or fair copy of a letter to Charles Jackson, and Mrs Jackson does not recall any correspondence between Lowry and her husband.

5 The film of Jackson's novel *The Lost Weekend* was released in 1945 with Ray Milland as the drunken Don Birnam and scenes filmed in New York's Bellevue Hospital. It won an Academy Award for best picture in 1945 and received a lot of attention. Lowry had been worried about Jackson's novel since early 1944; see letter **189**.

Editorial Notes:

a. Lowry has written this undated letter to Erskine in pencil on three pages of 8.75-by-13.75-cm lined notebook paper. He would have been writing after 10 January 1947 but before receiving Erskine's 22 January 1947 letter (see annotation 1).

274: To Harold Matson

P: Matson(telegram)   RCA Communications,
                                                       Port-au-Prince
                                                       23 January 1947

PLEASE CABLE HITCHCOCK DECEMBER ADVANCE IMMEDIATELY PORTAUPRINCE HAITI CANNOT COME NEWYORK OTHERWISE TRIP VITALLY IMPORTANT[1]

                                                                  LOWRY

Annotations:

1 Matson immediately sent an advance of $371.70 U.S., 'less charges.'

275: To Albert Erskine

P: UBC(ms,ts)   Hotel Olaffson,
PP: *SL* 137–39; *Lln* 186–88   Port-au-Prince, Haiti
                                                       25 January 1947

Dear A.E. –

Thank you and thank you again. And again I thank you. Sincerely, and not in the Cyranoesque sense.[1]

Weird things here: toy cemeteries and doves with ruby eyes. And an American editor with a cricket cap, carrying Moby Dick in his pocket, whose house has just burned down and who is an expert, to boot, on James Shirley,[2] the only other ex-poet, beside myself, which my college of St Catherine's, she who was broken on the wheel, ever succeeded in not producing. He is mad, however, and insists I am a match-king.[3]

Strange and ever terrible, mystifying and wonderful things here. M. Marcelin (Canape Vert) and myself and wives drinking coca cola and Christ knows what or into where. He, Marcelin, Philippe Thoby-Marcelin, is a marvellous fellow.[4] He also is an exquisite poet. And he has written a miraculous book of children's stories. Rinehart, I think won't take them. His poems are not translated. Half of them were lent to the Mexican Ambassador and never returned. That, at least, I can understand. His last book was horrendously mistranslated. And he can't speak a damn word of English and though he writes beautiful French for some reason speaks mostly Creole. Shouldn't you or someone write him a letter, in French? Is that an unethical suggestion? Or New Directions? Or will you think? I want like hell to help and it is moreover also because one *should*. I believe sincerely in this exchange of ideas between chaps of different countries. Valery Larbaud[5] – he showed me the letter – thinks he is one of the greatest poets France (sic) ever produced and though he is a Haitian without a cent who lives on a mountain I bloody well agree. We disappear into those mountains on Friday. Voodoo? It is real. In one flash Rinehart, Scribner's and Reynal and Hitchcock will be deprived of their greatest authors. I hope I do not mean that. It is what used to be called a joke. Perhaps I only meant that I would revenge myself on that bloody Jackson by depriving Rinehart of one of theirs. Not to be taken seriously.

Words follow to be taken more seriously. They even have to do with business, match-king stuff. Is my old and revered and loyal Norse fore-father, Harold Matson, alive? Or has he turned into perhaps, a troll, or even a black magician, too, like what they say I am here, and hence just disappeared, back to Grimanger.[6] For it seems there have been other confusions too, which in fairness to myself, should be straightened out, as they used to say of the Consul. Thou has misprised me when thou speakest of me as if asking for another advance. When Mr Hitchcock first accepted the Volcano it was with the proviso that I would come to N.Y. at once and do some editing with him. He offered (in addition to the generous advance of $1500) to pay $500 toward expenses for my trip, $250 paid for directly by the firm and the other $250 to come out of my later royalties.[7] I agreed to this and wired Matson that I would come. Then it seems Mr Hitchcock read the Volcano again over the week end and decided he did not want to make any changes or edit it with me. So then Mr Hitchcock said that he wanted me to come to New York at publication time and that the $500 mentioned (250 to come out of my later royalties as before, 250 given me for expenses (whatever *they* are) would apply if I would come at that time. As I wrote you before, I myself wanted to come to N.Y. during the period of editing but I acceded to his wishes in the matter and finally agreed to come to N.Y. at publication time. I can assume only that my ancient and revered forefather who has been bloody patient with me for about 200 years with no remuneration for himself has never explained this to you, and I'm sorry, but I wanted to make it clear to you that I was not asking for any *further* advance but merely inquiring, quite innocently (hic!) about a proposition made to me which I understood was still valid.

That's about all.

Save various notes for another book, such as:[8]

    toy tin house with peaked roof

    a house like a child's toy made of lace paper

    beaming flamboyant trees, made of ferns, 'leaning'

    flamboyant trees *leaving* flamboyant trees 'trees that

    will never be written.'

    cure hangover with Enos Fruit Salts

    dt's ditto – Paracelsus?

The strange American whose house had just burned down while Marcelin and I were talking about fire and who played cricket. Would you like to wear my cricket cap? Sings Men of Harlech in morning, stamping.[9]

    the dark man that follows us behind graves.

    an invisible voice whispering from behind a wall:

'Gimme five cents please.' It is a boy up a trumpete tree.[10]

    healthy and swimming at midday, normal, wondering how soon the crisis was going to hit again: servants chuckling: 'Fou.' 'Bouveur'

    A thunderous cat

    being constructive

    being conclusive

love

Malcolm Lowry

P.S. Please try and help Philippe Thoby-Marcelin – he is a great and truly good man.

Annotations:

  1 Lowry is thanking Erskine for his 22 January 1947 letter, to which he had attached reviewers' comments on *Under the Volcano* by Stephen Spender, Robert Penn Warren, Conrad Aiken, and Alfred Kazin. All

are highly favourable and are used on the back of the Reynal &
Hitchcock dust-jacket. Cyrano is the hero of Edmund Rostand's play
Cyrano de Bergerac (first performed in 1896). Lowry clearly knew the
play, for he has quoted from one of Cyrano's major speeches in act two,
in which the hero, in a series of rhetorical questions and ironic answers,
refuses to compromise his values in order to succeed:

> 'No, thank you! Calculate, scheme, be afraid,
> Love more to make a visit than a poem,
> Seek introductions, favours, influences? –
> No, thank you! No, I thank you! And again
> I thank you!'

See *Cyrano de Bergerac*, trans. by Brian Hooker (New York: Henry Holt
and Co., 1923), p. 124.

2 James Shirley (1596-1666), known as the 'last of the Elizabethans,' is
remembered today for his comedies of manners. He was a graduate of
St Catharine's College, Cambridge, a point Lowry liked to recall.

3 A 'match-king' is an individual who regularly wins or who supervises a
game of Match, a racket in which coins are matched. During the late
thirties and early forties some popular crime novels featured this game.

4 Philippe Thoby-Marcelin became a close friend of Lowry's; see
Lowry's 17 February 1947 letter (**281**) to Marcelin.

5 Valéry Larbaud (1881-1957), the French novelist and modernist poet,
also translated the work of several British authors into French, including James Joyce's *Ulysses* (1922).

6 Grimanger may not be an actual place, but it is the name of a ship used
by Lowry in 'Forest Path to the Spring.'

7 This is precisely the arrangement described by Matson in his 13 April
1946 telegram to Lowry. In his 16 April 1946 letter to Lowry, Matson
informed him that Curtice Hitchcock had decided Lowry was not
needed in New York for the editing but that he might come at publication time. I have not located any correspondence from Hitchcock
confirming this decision.

8 These 'notes' also appear in Lowry's Haitian notebook, which formed
the basis for a draft chapter of 'La Mordida' called 'The Dream – From
Haitian Notes' (UBC 14:16).

9 I have been unable to confirm the identity of the 'strange American,'
whom Day describes as 'a New Yorker who sobbed quietly all night
because his house had burned down' (372). In the draft for 'La Mordida'
(UBC 14:16, 173-74) Lowry describes this American in precisely these
terms. 'March of the Men of Harlech' is a Welsh battle song commemorating the bravery of the last stronghold to surrender to the
Yorkists (1468) during the War of the Roses.

10 A trumpet-tree is a tropical American tree with hollow stems and
branches that are used in making musical instruments.

276: To Harold Matson

P: Matson(ms); UBC(phc)   [Port-au-Prince]
                                                    [early February 1947]ᵃ

Dear Hal

We plan to be in NY about the 18 Feb when we are looking forward
very much to seeing you & having a chat not to say a beer.

Thanks also for sending the cheque, which was gratefully received.¹

Hasta la vista² & kindest regards from us both

                                                           Malcolm

Annotations:

  1 This cheque was the December advance from Reynal & Hitchcock that
    Lowry had requested in his 23 January 1947 telegram (**274**).
  2 Spanish salutation: 'till we meet again.'

Editorial Notes:

a. There is neither date nor inside address on this letter, which has, how-
    ever, been stamped received in Matson's New York office on 13
    February.

277: To Albert Erskine

P: UBC(ms)   Nowhere
PP: *SL* 139-40   [Port-au-Prince]
                                                    [early February 1947]

Dear Albert Erskine:

Yes, you were absolutely right about the preface and Jackson & etc &
I wrote Cape's telling him to deracinate it.¹

I think I may have written you a somewhat peculiar letter – my last
one: it seems I was going down with a fever, with a cough, & so forth;
my doctor being the author of an interesting book entitled La Crisis de
Possession dans le Vaudou (at which you might like to take a look) he
let me out of bed rather earlier than he should have to see a ceremony
the Marcelins had discovered for us was taking place & to which they
were taking us: the result is we have been up for two terrific days &
nights witnessing that which the doctor, who did not accompany us,
had never himself witnessed; nor, I daresay, anyone else extant.²

But the final result is I feel rather better, if still a bit groggy from injections, & the voodoo: the voodoo priest, perhaps recognising a kindred
spirit, has promised to initiate me by fire if & when I return – do you

think that is really a good idea? (Just the same, I really would like to be a voodoo priest. .).

I think I wrote about Phillippe Thoby-Marcellin & brother in an unethical manner?

Hullo, hullo – at this moment (naturally!) I receive your letter.[3] But how can you have failed to – but I see perhaps your – anyhow we are great friends of the Marcellins by now – I meant Phillippe-Thoby was the poet, per se, of the brothers, & a first-rate one in my estimation – & and more too –

Anyhow I will speak to him this afternoon, when we are seeing him (if I think it proper).

My hospital was called the Notre Dame in a place known as Canape Vert.

My God, I am mixed up: but I shall become practical later.

The favourable reviews of the Volcano frightened hell out of me – I have scarcely even been able to look at them, but I do thank you again sincerely for all you have done.

No, I certainly was not trying to dun another advance out of you – what a godawful thought even to sit in the ether for five minutes – or isn't it? No. It doesn't sound even honest even though it's true.

Outside my window in the hospital was a leaning forest of small green nameless trees crowned by one very little sweet tree, blowing. . .

We leave to-morrow by air for Miami;[4] thence by bus – I should certainly think –

Best wishes

Malcolm Lowry

Annotations:

1 In his 22 January 1947 letter, Erskine had warned Lowry against using a preface at all, let alone one that mentioned Charles Jackson's *The Lost Weekend*. If Lowry did write Cape asking him to 'deracinate' the preface, his letter does not appear to have survived. Given the state of his health, it is conceivable that Margerie wrote for him.

2 This is not the version of events described by Day (376-77) or Bowker (391-92). Lowry presents a much more sanguine picture of his health and state of mind. *La Crise de Possession dans le Voudou* (Port-au-Prince: Imprimerie de l'état, 1946) was by Dr Louis Mars (1906-), a professor of psychiatry at the University of Haiti and dean of the Medical School at this time. Mars, who treated Lowry in hospital, allowed him to leave on 8 February to witness voodoo ceremonies.

3 This letter from Erskine does not appear to have survived.

4 The Lowrys left Haiti for Miami by plane on 12 February 1947. In Miami they caught a bus to Charleston, South Carolina, then to

Richmond, Virginia, before arriving in New York on 19 February. En route they stopped in Savannah, Georgia, Conrad Aiken's birthplace; see Lowry's 24 June 1947 letter (**311**) to Aiken.

278: To Gerald Noxon

P: Texas(pcard)
PP: *LLN* 134-35   [Port-au-Prince]
                                                        11 February 1947[a]

Dear old Gerald:
Thanks enormously for your newsy good letter which I won't answer now as I have been laid up in hospital with a cough & Romney's Lady Hamilton on the wall.[1] We leave to-morrow & hope to be seeing you both sometime between then & now. Alas, no reproductions. But Haiti is as resplendent with artistic genius as it is filled with kindness. Truly a miraculous place in every [illegible]. Best love to Betty yourself & Nick from

                                                                    Malc

Annotations:

1 George Romney (1734-1802), an English portrait painter, did many oil paintings inspired by Emma Hart, later Lady Hamilton.

Editorial Notes:

a. This is the postmark date on the card; 'Feb 11th 1947' has been written in pencil beside Noxon's name. The black and white photograph on the card shows the ruins of La Citadelle in the hills overlooking Cap Haitien. It was built for Henri Christophe (1767-1820), the self-styled king of Haiti. The Haitian post office has stamped the card for insufficient postage; thus, part of the last sentence is illegible.

279: To James Stern

P: Texas(pcard)   Port-au-Prince,
PP: *Encounter* 29.3   Haiti
                                                      [11 February 1947][a]

Dear old Jimmy:
    You rendered me speechless, & I still am, having been laid up in hospital here with a cough & Lady Hamilton on the wall by George Romney.[1] There was a mocking bird too, & a bird that piped, & a man next door that mooed with pain. I am ok now. We leave to-morrow

for Miami, thence proceed by bus to New York – reaching there mid-Feb. sometime. Can you find us some hole to crawl into – a previous hole fell through. Thank you a million

Malcolm

Annotations:

1 Lowry was deeply moved by Stern's reaction to the *Volcano*, and he may be referring here to Stern's 19 December 1946 telegram or his 6 January 1947 letter praising the novel as an 'epic' (UBC 1:64).

Editorial Notes:

a. A typescript (UBC 2:10) has been made of this postcard. The original, with the message written in pencil, shows a postmark of 11 February 1947 and a black and white photograph of the cathedral in Port-au-Prince. It was first published in *Encounter* 29.3 (1967): 67.

280: To James Stern

P: Texas(ms)

[Charleston]
[South Carolina]
[16 February 1947^a

Dear old Jimmy – here we are – who knows how? – in Charleston, Caroline, whence we propose to proceed by bus via Richmond V.A & Washington to New York, but since neither of us can make any sense of the timetable, when that precisely will be we know not. I was in hospital in Haiti with a cough, as I think I said, & during that time I hoped you received the letter Margie wrote you saying that this was roughly our intention. It looks as though my arrival will more or less coincide with the publication of the Volcano but this was not at all conscious any longer, though there had been, when Mr Hitchcock was alive, some stipulation to this effect;[1] it is however very necessary that both of us see our common agent, & I am dying to see you again & to meet the good Mr Erskine. The latter warned me that I should have something 'lined up' in N.Y., however, re living quarters, & this we had, an apartment in Park Avenue, no less, not far from where you once lived, but this fell through because the lessee's agent rented it without the formers consent in the former's abscence. Therefore we fall back – I believe inconsiderately – on your former offer that you could arrange something. What I mean is, we have some money, not a great deal, enough for bottles but not enough for socks, if you understand me; but we can pay. But what I understood was there was simply nowhere in N.Y. to live.[2] Pay no attention to my grammar this morning, I am still a bit groggy after my bout in hospital, not very, but a bit. So with all the good will in the world you might not be able to find any hole at all. So it looks much as though, like John Paul Jones, we are dashing with all our derangements at our object, leaving the rest to fortune.[3] There are only two other friends I know of in N.Y: one Ivan Sanderson, the explorer, the other Bill Empson, the poet.[4] But I do not know very certainly if there are in New York, though they would help, if they could, & you are stuck. Ivan, I understand, keeps his room full of rare bats and cranes and head-hunters and things, and I had a sense he might have some space on the rafters in a pinch for two more rare specimens. While Bill, with his insight into ambiguities, could have transformed something into *meaning* sleeping quarters, at least. The upshot of all this is we shall be arriving in N.Y on the 19th or 20th (if you are talking to the good Albert Erskine you might tell him this) we are stopping at Richmond VA[5] & maybe Washington but when we get near enough to our landfall to know where we are at we will send you a rocket in the form of a telegram, telling you when & where we arrive. If meantime you have gone to Ireland or somewhere that will of course be very sad, but then that is our responsibility.

Thank you again for your letter: I have read it many times, will treasure it, & will try to profit by it.[6] It is a pity your words to me were not on the cover. It would have been unique to have the *cover* of a book banned in Boston, just for the words & not for the picture, I mean —

God bless

Malcolm

Annotations:

1 The Lowrys reached New York on the morning of publication day — 19 February — just in time for the celebrations. For descriptions of the visit, see Day (379-83) and Bowker (396-401).

2 According to Day (379), Albert Erskine had found them a room at the Murray Hill Hotel on Park Avenue at 41st Street, but in his 8 February 1947 letter to Margerie, James Stern writes that he has reserved a room at the Murray Hill for them from 20 February. The Lowrys did not receive this letter, which was returned to Stern in New York.

3 Lowry is paraphrasing one of his favourite Melville passages from *Israel Potter: His Fifty Years of Exile* (1855), chapter 18, second paragraph; see also his 14 May 1945 letter (**201**) to Gerald Noxon, his 15 April 1950 letter (**396**) to Frank Taylor, and his 20 March 1952 letter (**510**) to Albert Erskine.

4 Ivan Sanderson (1911-73), a Scot who had trained as a zoologist and botanist at Cambridge University, became an explorer and writer. His first book, *Animal Treasure* (1937), gained him international attention, and after the Second World War he settled in the United States.

Neither Sanderson nor William Empson, an acquaintence of Lowry's at Cambridge and the author of *Seven Types of Ambiguity*, was a friend of Lowry's.
5 In Richmond, Lowry visited the home of one of his favourite American authors, Edgar Allan Poe, and his notes from this visit (UBC 7:10) were used in 'Strange Comfort Afforded by the Profession' in *Hear us O Lord*.
6 This is Stern's 6 January 1947 letter to Lowry.

Editorial Notes:

a This single-page pencil holograph is on letterhead from the Argyle Hotel in Charleston, and the accompanying envelope is postmarked 16 February 1947.

281: To Philippe Thoby-Marcelin

P: UBC(ts)   [Fredericksburg]
[Virginia]
[17 February 1947]

Dear Phi-to¹ – I have been feeling as though I had lost my greatmother, my greatfather, my greatuncle and all my greatbrothers, and that goes for Margie too. Nous arriverons a Nueva York Jeudi quand j'écrirai at more length. Meantime take my love and convey the same to Emmanuel, Charles & Raymond Pressoir, & your brothers Pierre & Emile.² And please salute your wife from us both. Cinq heures et que faites-vous? Quoth the raven: – 'à votre santé!'³ Good luck. votre frère, Malc.

Annotations:

1 Philippe Thoby-Marcelin (1904-75), the Haitian writer and translator, became a friend of Lowry's during his visit to Haiti. He co-authored several novels with his brother, Pierre, including *Canapé-Vert* (1944), *La Bête de Musseau* (1946), and *Le Crayon de Dieu* (1952).
2 Charles Pressoir (1910-73) was a Haitian lawyer, poet, and essayist. Like his brothers, he was a cultural nationalist and proud of the Creole language.
3 The raven is Edgar Allan Poe's portentous bird who repeats 'Nevermore' in his 1845 poem 'The Raven.' Here he says, in true Lowry style: 'Five o'clock and what are you doing? – to your health!' The Lowrys had just stopped in Richmond, Virginia, to visit Poe's home.

282: To James Stern

P: Texas(telegram)

Western Union,
Fredericksburg,
Virginia
18 February 1947

ARRIVING TOMORROW WILL PHONE YOU THROUGH ERSKINE 10 AM
BLESSINGS

MALCOLM LOWRY

283: To John Davenport

P: UBC(ms)
PP: *MLR* 22-23

Murray Hill Hotel
[New York]
[February 1947][a]

Dear old John: –
    God bless your guts . . .
    The only reason why I didn't get a copy of the Volcano sent to you,
that or something like that being the title, was that I didn't know it was
possible for the publishers to send copies to England.[1] And I had no
spare proofs.
    I now see that this must be wrong; for Stephen Spender apparently
wrote from Prague about the book.[2]
    At all events it is swell of you to write me about the thing.
    (I am dispatching to you to-day a copy of Under the Volcano.) I have
made an absolutely obscene success here with the book.
    —— Auden sends love.[3]
    It is just like a great disastar.
    My little wife is happy though, in spite of her editor having gone
mad, (in Scribners: this, off the record.)[4]
    Sweden Norway Denmark Germany China [illegible] France &
Christ knows who: front pages, every kind of bloody honor, modern
libraries, & drink, & excursions to the Rue Morgue.[5]
    I meant to write you from Hugo.[6]
    To you I send love & thanks from the heart; & also to the kids: & to
Margerie from me & Margerie.
    You are one of the best writers in the world – how long does one
have to wait before you whitely explode in bud.[7]

Malc

Annotations:

    1 No letter from Davenport asking for a copy of *Under the Volcano*

survives with the UBC Collection. His 12 and 13 April 1947 letters to Lowry (really one long letter, UBC 1:17) contain enthusiastic praise and several comments about the novel.

2 Stephen Spender (1909-95), who wrote the introduction to the 1965 Lippincott edition of *Under the Volcano*, also wrote a favourable pre-publication review, which is quoted on the Reynal & Hitchcock dust-jacket.

3 W.H. Auden was in New York and met Lowry during this visit.

4 The editor at Scribner's was W.C. Weber, but there is no confirmed basis for Lowry's remark.

5 Lowry is referring to Edgar Allan Poe's story 'The Murders in the Rue Morgue' (1841).

6 There are towns called Hugo in Colorado and Oklahoma, and the Lowrys' 1946 bus route south-east from Vancouver to New Orleans might have taken them through these places. It is also the name of one of Davenport's sons, which is why Lowry thought of him; see Lowry's 1947 letter (**297**) to Davenport.

7 In his 13 April 1947 letter to Lowry, Davenport remarks: 'My own 2½ years of total eclipse – 1942, 1943 – may have darkened my sight so that things explode in blood only rather than whitely in bud.'

Editorial Notes:

a. There is no inside address or date on this pencil holograph, which has been written on letterhead from the Murray Hill Hotel in New York, where the Lowrys stayed during their visit.

284: To Gerald Noxon

P: Texas(telegram)
PP: *LLN* 136-37

Canadian National,
New York, N.Y.
25 February 1947

DELAYED HERE PROBABLY LEAVING SUNDAY[1] SORRY INCON-VENIENCE YOU WILL WIRE AGAIN EXACT DATE OF ARRIVAL RATHER STAY IN NIAGARA ON THE LAKE AT PRINCE OF WALES OR SOME PLACE IF POSSIBLE SO WE CAN SEE BETTY AND NICK WE COULD TAKE TAXI FROM NIAGARA FALLS LOVE TO ALL FROM BOTH

MARJORIE AND MALCOLM

Annotations:

1 The Lowrys left New York by train for Niagara-on-the-Lake on Tuesday, 4 March, not Sunday 2 March.

285: To Harold Matson

P: Matson(telegram)

Western Union,
Niagara-on-the-Lake,
Ontario
7 March 1947

PLEASE WIRE DANISH CONTRACT[1] MONEY TO MARGERIE NIAGARA
ON THE LAKE FLYING TO VANCOUVER MONDAY NIGHT NECESSARY
TO SEND MONEY THROUGH BANK OF MANHATTAN COMPANY NEW
YORK TO IMPERIAL BANK OF CANADA NIAGARA ON THE LAKE
ONTARIO AS TELEGRAPH OFFICE HERE CANNOT RECEIVE MONEY
MANY THANKS BEST WISHES

MALCOLM
MARGERIE

Annotations:

1 The Danish contract for a translation of *Under the Volcano* does not
appear to have survived, but the translation *Under vulkanen* by Vibeke
Bloch was published by Gyldendal in Copenhagen in 1949 and
reprinted in 1968.

286: To Maurice and Marjorie (Phyllis) Carey

P: UBC(ms)

Vancouver, B.C.
The Ides of March[a]
[1947]

ɭoppîʒ ʔʋʈpⲥy.[1]

To Maurice Carey,
– and to Marjorie Carey.[2]
from the author.
Malcolm Lowry

Remindful of old times
– so to speak –
God bless you both
from
Malcolm.

Annotations:

1 This is Lowry's quasi-Greek transliteration of Maurice Carey's name.

2 Maurice and Marjorie (Phyllis) Carey were the Vancouver couple with whom the Lowrys stayed from September 1939 until the spring of 1940. The Lowrys usually called her Phyllis (see Malcolm's 23 February 1940 letter [126] to Conrad Aiken, and Sugars [260-64]). This note is an inscription on a set of galleys of *Under the Volcano*. In the unpublished typescript of 'Life With Malcolm Lowry' (UBC 43:4), Carey claims that when Malcolm returned to Vancouver they spent a drunken weekend together before Margerie arrived to take Malcolm back to Dollarton. He also states that his wife's name is Marjorie.

Editorial Notes:

a. This note to the Careys is in black ink on the verso of the final galley sheet for *Under the Volcano*. The Ides of March is the fifteenth of the month and is historically resonant as the day on which Julius Caesar was assassinated in Rome in 44 BC.

287: To Maurice Carey

P: UBC(ms)   Vancouver, B.C.
                                                16 March 1947

To my brother Maurice Carey
and Margerie, my sister
with love – and love, to her, & you, & hope –
and love, –
this book about the forces in
man which cause him to be
terrified of himself.[1]
   With love and love and
  truly brotherly love
 from your ancient brother
   Malcolm Lowry

Annotations:

1 This note, written in black ink on a badly torn fragment of otherwise blank galley sheet (UBC 28:20), probably accompanied the set of galleys that Lowry gave the Careys. 'Margerie' is Carey's wife; see **286**. Lowry is repeating here a comment he makes about *Under the Volcano* in his 2 January 1946 letter (**210**) to Jonathan Cape.

288: To James Stern

P: Texas(ms)

Dollarton P.O.,
British Columbia
23 [March 1947][a]

My very dear old Jimmy:

Ah Christ what a nose.

Ah Christ what a nose, what a luminous nose.

And did you mean to torture me then with these deep matters and this with Saint Patrick's day coming?

Or just teach me a bloody good lesson?

Or just out of sheer blessed Christ like kindness?

It was out of kindness, & at that, Christ like.

Nonetheless I laughed myself into another haemorrage: but always through the nose, yes, from, & through nothing else but the poor bloody nose, and what is more, *my* nose.[1]

Other news of the nose: the nose received a positive on its test for consumption. But the nose said not a word. The nose flew. The nose flew over the Rockies.

Now tell me, how can that be, how can a nose fly over the Rockies?

No nose can fly over the Rockies, let alone with consumption, and by itself.

Moreover how could such a nose, being such a talkative nose, have said nothing in the first place?

Nonetheless the nose flew: it landed: the nose even fell among thieves, i.e, in Vancouver.

The nose also fell among reporters who denied it was a nose at all and even though the nose was a self-dramatizing nose there was nothing it could say to gainsay this.

The nose was not, indeed, sure of itself, and what was worse, the nose's doctor was drunk. (It is not quite certain that the nose was not slightly drunk too.)

Finally it was decided that the nose did not have consumption – & how indeed could a nose have consumption? – but heart-trouble.

But how could a nose even have heart trouble?

Finally it was decided that the nose could not have heart trouble, but at that rate, might have once had consumption, & recovered from it. But how could a nose ever have had consumption, let alone have recovered from it?

The answer (and this all on St Patrick's Day) was that the nose was a whole nose was a whole nose once more, if such it had claimed to be previously, they would give it the benefit of the doubt.

I should say at this point that the Nose's Mate had arrived.

All I meant by this was that I/we wanted to send yourself and Tanya my/our deepest love, & my/our deepest thanks & to tell you there was no bad nose – both Margie & I are trying to read simultaneously – (myself for about the umpteenth time) – your wonderful story, 'The Force' – [2]

> God bless you both, from us both
> – Be happy –
> Malcolm

P.S. We are both longing to read your new book (title not right in my mind, The Secret Damage? The Hidden Damage? – be not offended, I could not remember the title of the Volcano the other day – but I know your book's *purport*.[3]

(P.P.S. Orson Welles is angling for the nose, a Judas kiss?[4] I have been reading Jim Agee's and Evans' book Let us now praise famous men,[5] too, you see: surely one of the most important in all American literature, & one of the finest & most beautiful; & *useful* – I think I will begin my education upon it – God damn it, he even tells me how I/we built my/our house in it – give all love to him & to Mia – & to Tanya, say loveletters blessings from us both, [and] I hope you are well again & thank you for washing out my bloodstained singlet.

> Malcolm

[P.P.P.S.] I know you will be delighted to hear Maxwell Perkins just accepted Margie's Horse in the Sky!![6]

Annotations:

1 The context for this Gogolian excursus on the nose dates back to February. During one of the parties that the Sterns held for Lowry in New York, Lowry apparently disappeared. Stern found him in the bathroom 'snorting blood out of his nose' (Day 383). He was taken for tuberculosis tests, and then withdrew to his hotel room to drink in peace with a few friends at his bedside. Lowry continued to refer to the possibility of tuberculosis; see his April 1947 letter (**293**) to Thoby-Marcelin and his October 1950 letter (**426**) to Stuart Lowry.

2 'The Force' is in Stern's *The Heartless Land* (1932); see Lowry's comments on the story in his 17 September 1947 letter (**321**) to Stern.

3 In *The Hidden Damage* (New York: Harcourt, Brace and Co., 1947), Stern describes the results of Allied bombing of German cities.

4 The American actor, writer, producer, and director Orson Welles

(1915-85) was sent a copy of *Under the Volcano* by Fletcher Markle (see Lowry's 1947 letter, **301**, to Markle), but Welles did not not like the novel; see Bowker (407). A 'Judas kiss' signifies a kiss of betrayal because Judas identified Christ to the Roman soldiers by kissing him.

5 *Let us now praise famous men; three tenant families,* by James Agee and Walter Evans, first appeared in 1939 and quickly became a classic study of American life. The Lowrys met Agee (1909-55) and his wife during their February visit to New York, and Lowry was shocked to learn of Agee's death in 1955; see his June 1955 letter (**637**) to David Markson.

6 Margerie's novel *Horse in the Sky* was published by Scribner's in 1947.

Editorial Notes:

a. The single-page, 21-by-36-cm, pencil holograph of this letter has an abbreviated date scrawled at the top right of the recto which appears to be 23/Mar. That date is corroborated by Stern's description of the letter for the Harry Ransom Humanities Research Center at the time of purchase in 1970. Internal references to the bloody nose and St Patrick's Day, 17 March, further confirm that Lowry is writing sometime after he and Margerie had returned to Dollarton. Lowry's scribbled postscripts appear in the margins of the verso, and Margerie has added: 'Dear Jimmy & Tania – God bless you both! Much love & a heart full of gratitude & friendship. All's well here – love – Margie.' All three postscripts are mistakenly added, as page three, to a letter from Margerie to 'Dear Jimmy' and published in *Selected Letters* (148) in what Stern calls a 'spurious letter.'

289: To Sybil Hutchinson

P: Toronto(tsc)   Dollarton P.O.,
                                                          Dollarton, B.C.,
                                                          Canada
                                                          [March 1947][a]

Dear Miss Hutchinson:[1]

Thank you very much for your letter and I'm very sorry I've been so long in replying but we'd been on a long journey and took a long time getting back; New Orleans, Haiti, and New York since we left here last fall.

In reply I don't think there's much I can give of biographical material of much interest that isn't on the jacket of the book or in a review or wherever.

But perhaps this is worth saying: the book, though the groundwork for it was done in Mexico, was written – in fact written three times – here in Canada, in a shack on Indian Arm, where my wife and I lived winter and summer, and I had liked to daydream of the book as being some kind of humble contribution to Canadian literature, should it turn out any good, that was.

In answer to your other questions; yes, my intention is, if possible, health permitting, to make Canada my permanent home. In fact our shack *is* home to me, and always will be. It's the only one we have.

I am passionately fond of the place where we live and devoted to our few friends, mostly fishermen, who also live permanently along the beach and I think it would take death itself to pry me loose from here, though I am British and slightly uncertain of my status at the moment. Nonetheless I am certainly as Canadian as Louis Hémon ever was.[2]

This is the second shack we have had. The other burned to the ground, taking a thousand pages of work with it, and our friends unselfishly helped us to rebuild it. This is one of the few places and few communities in the world where I have ever encountered friendship and charity in the true sense. It would seem that among such people as our British Columbian neighbours genuine unselfishness is a matter of course.

Yes, I certainly would like to write a story with a B.C. setting and in fact have already planned out a short novel laid here. I would not in any case have to move very far for my material for I do not know anyone here who would not make the hero of an epic.

But so far as that is concerned, some of the best passages in the Volcano do deal, if indirectly, with British Columbia. There is one character who may seem to be sneering at Canada per se (though he is not in fact doing so); but the particular passage I have in mind is in Chapter I, where the Consul has a delirious vision of a happier life, British Columbia (where he owns an island) being of course identified in his mind with Paradise. I have not a copy of my book with me but without wishing to blow my own horn, I perceive in the Saturday Review that the reviewer says:

'On page 37 there is a sentence which is 32 lines long and does not falter in its music and can be read aloud without burdening the breath, and that is more than Wolfe ever did for me.'[3]

This sentence concerns the wakes of fishing boats on a June evening while a freight train is passing and a thunderstorm is going on high up in the mountains and the scene of it, of course, is none other than Indian Arm (an extension of Burrard Inlet) right here in B.C.

I am very proud of this sentence (I only wish to heaven that you or someone would quote it for so far people have only quoted horrors. I hope I shall not be panned here; or even worse, banned. Better hurry.

I have heard there have been many demands for the book in Vancouver, at Ireland & Allan's particularly, and the Hudson's Bay

Stores, and I believe a pretty good sale here could be achieved if only you could send some books along; for one thing I wouldn't mind having a copy to read myself.

    With all best wishes,

                              Yours very truly,

                                        [Malcolm Lowry]

Annotations:

  1 Sybil Hutchinson (1907-92) was editor-in-chief with the Toronto pub-
    lisher McClelland and Stewart, who evidently distributed the American
    edition of *Under the Volcano* in Canada beginning in March 1947. We
    have been unable to confirm this publisher's connection with Lowry. It
    was through Hutchinson, however, that he met Earle Birney (see
    Lowry's 14 May 1947 letter **303** to Birney), and she tried to promote
    Lowry's work.
  2 Louis Hémon (1880-1913), author of *Maria Chapdelaine* (1915), was a
    Frenchman, and this novel about French Canada is considered his best
    book.
  3 In 'Dazzling Disintegration,' *Saturday Review* 30 (22 February 1947):
    9-10, John Woodburn describes *Under the Volcano* as 'magnificent,
    tragic, compassionate, and beautiful' – 'a work of genius.'

Editorial Notes:

  a. This transcription is from an undated photocopy (UBC 2:10) of a typed
      transcription of Lowry's original letter to Sybil Hutchinson.
      Hutchinson sent the transcribed copy to William Arthur Deacon, and
      it is now with the Deacon Papers in the Thomas Fisher Rare Book
      Library at the University of Toronto. Lowry's original letter has not
      been found.

290: To Anna Mabelle [Mrs John Stuart] Bonner

P: UBC(ms)
                                        Dollarton P.O.,
                                        Dollarton, B.C.,
                                        Canada
                                        26 March 1947

My very dear Mother:

    I'm terribly sorry I haven't written before, even to thank you for your
very sweet & kind & welcome words re the Volcano, but I assure you
there hasn't been time, and now I write to make amends.

    The truth is, the beastly book seemed to go off like a hundred sky-
rockets at once and I am still trying to dodge the sparks and sticks falling
on my head which is, I hope, so far from being swollen that it still has

the wit to suggest that such success, if this can indeed be called such, may be the worst possible thing that could happen to any serious author.

That does not mean that I was not truly moved by what you and my sweet sister and brother said; I *was*, more than by anything else.

(Or that I have not enjoyed it all – which, alas, is probably the trouble; all is vanity, saith the preacher.)

A more sane & sound kind of success is Margie's; Maxwell Perkins, as you now know, & to my joy, has taken Horse in the Sky, even though Scribner's had previously rejected it.

I think it was beautiful & loyal of Priscilla to be carrying the Saturday review – with such a gloomy looking mug on the cover too.

I think it was swell of Ron [A. Ronald Button], as also Bert, re the movie end of it; I've done what I can to cooperate, but here I confess myself rather bamboozled by the complications; for my part I wish I could confer the whole thing upon Ron's legal bosom, – for as I write I am involved with the following contracts to sign myself, as received to-day from Norway, France, Switzerland (which includes occupied Germany), this in addition to Denmark, & Sweden – not to say England – (which takes in the entire British Empire, including Canada & India) makes, with the U.S., – well, quite alot of countries –

By the way, – I think you have the review in the New York Herald Tribune?[1] I don't – & for various reasons I need it. I'd be most awfully beholden to you if you'd mail it to me; I'll either send yours back when I'm through, or give you another; but I *do* need it apparently.

With all fondest love to yourself, Priscilla, & Bert

Your affectionate son

Malcolm

Annotations:

1 Mark Schorer reviewed the *Volcano* for the *New York Herald Tribune* on 23 February 1947, and he praised the book highly, placing Lowry in the first rank of writers with Henry James and James Joyce.

291: To Margaret Unwin Hitchcock

P: UBC(ms)

> Dollarton P.O.,
> Dollarton, B.C.,
> Canada
> [26 March 1947]¹

Dear Mrs Hitchcock:[1]

My failure to reply looks like the ultima thule of ingratitude but I assure you it couldn't be helped.

When I left Niagara I was unable to return immediately to Dollarton and when I did get to Dollarton the postmaster had forwarded my mail, owing to an oversight, back to Niagara; it was not reforwarded for some time from there and when it did arrive there were of course the two identical letters from yourself.

And please forgive my writing in pencil: my typewriter is being repaired, after a rough train trip, and my wife seems to have lost the family pen. But I can delay no longer.

I would have been only too glad to have said something re Jacques Roumains' Masters of the Dew that might have helped along its sale,[2] and I still would be glad, though I haven't yet read the book itself, knowing of its merit only by hearsay, and I fear it is too late to say anything that could be put on the jacket, but perhaps if I may still have the galleys, I can be of assistance in some other way.

Roumains was the best friend of one of my very best friends, Phillipe Thoby-(Canapé-Vert) Marcellin, for whom I have the very highest regard both as a man and an artist, but I was acquainted only with the former's spirit, so to speak; we visited his old haunts but so harrowing were the anterior circumstances (he was one of 5 men of whom Phillipe is the only survivor, two, including Roumains being now dead by their own hand, and the other two insane, who made a desperate effort to start a cultural movement in Haiti, who were among the founders of the now famous Centre d'Art there, run by DeWitt Peters and Phillipe himself) that I gathered less about his work than of the fineness of his character.[3]

But I have so much admiration for what these Haitians are doing against such odds that I would be only too honored to help in any small way I can.

Thank you again for your letter, and my sincere apologies for the lateness of mine.

With kindest regards,

Malcolm Lowry

Annotations:

1 Margaret Unwin Hitchcock was Curtice Hitchcock's wife, and she worked for Reynal & Hitchcock at this time.

2 Jacques Roumain (1907-44), a powerful figure in Haitian cultural and political life, was a writer, politician, diplomat, and, in 1934, the founder of the Haitian Communist party. His best-known novel is *Gouverneurs de la Rosée* (1944), which was translated as *Masters of the Dew* and published by Reynal & Hitchcock in 1947. For Lowry's comments on the translation, see his 11 April 1947 letter (**294**) to Margaret Hitchcock.

3 De Witt Peters (1902-66), an American painter who migrated to Haiti,

helped found the Haitian Art Movement by opening the Centre d'Art in Port-au-Prince in 1944.

Editorial Notes:

a. This letter, and the following one to Chester Kerr, are written in pencil on foolscap paper like the 26 March 1947 letter (**290**) to his mother-in-law. Here, as in the letter to Kerr, he mentions his broken typewriter and lost 'family pen,' and these details suggest that all three letters were written at the same time.

292: To Chester B. Kerr

P: UBC(ms)   Dollarton P.O.,
Dollarton, B.C.
[26 March 1947]

Dear Mr Kerr:[1]

I humbly apologise for not having replied before but I can only say it wasn't possible. There was a confusion of mail owing to my moving around: I was not able to return from Niagara directly to Dollarton, mail arriving in Dollarton was sent back to Niagara, while it looks as though your letter must have arrived for the first time in Niagara the day I left, so that I just missed it there.

Also, my apologies for the pencil; but my typewriter is laid up after being battered in a plane and my wife has lost the one pen with the one bad nib.

Now, to reply: I'm most awfully sorry Albert [Erskine] and Frank [Taylor] have left your firm, for quite apart from anything else, I have a great feeling of friendship for them, and it seems a bit desolate and sort of wrong that they are not there; on the other hand, that would seem to be that and one can only hope that everyone will be happy all round.[2]

Re the Volcano, I was always of the gloomy opinion, & expressed the same frankly to Albert, that it was the kind of book that would sell – 1 copies, if that; worse indeed than Melville's Pierre, if not as good a book either;[3] but it would appear, either that the book says something, or that your firm was capable of *moving volcanoes*; or both. At all events, from what I can gather, it would seem to be doing well – is this so? I find it hard to balance the relative values of these things but that I must have said *something* would seem borne out by the number of letters I have had from ex-servicemen about it, & these the last people in the world you would think would give two hoots about it; Sweden, Denmark, France, Norway, & Switzerland (for occupied Germany) have also bought it – but perhaps this is not significant.

Also a sort of charwoman friend of mine said today that she had seen it listed in a Book of the Month catalogue – can that be true?[4]

But there are, however, no copies in Canada, or at least in Vancouver, as yet.

I want you to know how I appreciated your letter & your remarks and please convey to Eugene Reynal the same and how delighted I was to meet him.[5]

For the rest, though I live in the wilderness, Dollarton P.O., B.C. will be a sound and stable address, from which I do not propose to wander, so that you count upon communications now being reliable.

I would very much appreciate seeing the second cover and any copies of advertising and reviews that you can spare: I believe the Chicago Tribune said something favourable?? (I am a bit worried about the Los Angeles papers, if purely for irrelevant reasons – my wife's family live there and since they are bucked about the whole thing I thought how loathesome it would be to be thoroughly panned there. However.)[6]

I have a letter from the American Library in Paris Inc, 9 rue de Téhéran, Paris VIIIe, France, that asks if 'as a gesture of friendship & a proof of my interest in cultural relations', I will mail them a copy of the Volcano, because the library is desperately in need of books.

Since I do not have a copy to spare myself – or in fact any copy at all – I wonder if you would be good enough to mail them one yourself as from me, deducting the necessary whatever?

As for myself I'm hard at work on another book, La Mordida, which is approximately 7 times as abysmal as the Volcano, though it has, or should have, a triumphant ending; – am struggling with health too, the heart does not seem too good; a nuisance; but the primroses are out.

With best wishes & kind regards to Mr Reynal,

Sincerely yours

Malcolm Lowry

Annotations:

1 Chester Brooks Kerr (1913–) was vice-president of Reynal & Hitchcock at this time; his letter to Lowry does not appear to have survived.

2 Albert Erskine and Frank Taylor left Reynal & Hitchcock after Curtice Hitchcock's death, and these changes, especially with regard to Erskine, would be important for Lowry. See his April 1947 letter (**295**) to Taylor and his 20 March 1951 letter (**449**) to Matson.

3 *Pierre; or, The Ambiguities* (1852) was Herman Melville's seventh book and a publishing disaster. Reviews were hostile: Melville was labelled 'crazy,' the book an outrage, and sales were meagre. Lowry's high opinion of *Pierre* grows out of the revaluation of the novel that began in the 1920s.

4 In his 25 March 1947 letter to Lowry, Matson confirms that the Book of the Month Club had selected *Under the Volcano* for its Special Members' Edition list and that with a 900,000 membership the novel would receive a lot of attention. He also assures Lowry that Chester Kerr at Reynal & Hitchcock is pleased with sales.

5 Lowry had been rude to Eugene Reynal when he met him in New York; being drunk, he called Reynal the 'office boy' (Day 381). Lowry continued to use the term 'office boy' to refer to Reynal in his letters; see, for example, his 11 March 1952 telegram (**506**) to Albert Erskine.

6 The majority of Los Angeles reviews was positive.

293: To Philippe Thoby-Marcelin

P: UBC(ts phc)   Dollarton, B.C.,
                                                          Canada
                                                  April 1947¹

My dear brother Phito:

   Things did not go quite as I would have liked in New York because in the first place there was a tremendous blizzard which made communication save by phone very difficult, and in the second it was thought by a doctor that I had t.b., which confined me somewhat to my room, while I awaited the results of his tests, that have proved indecisive;¹ on the other hand it may be that I have something good to report after all, or which will, in time, bring good results.

   But, first, the bad:

   (a) Anthony Lespes book La Terre et les Hommes was refused by Rinehardt some months ago;² they said they had written but it was obvious to me that your Rinehardt had been quite negligent about this; they, however, promised to send him a letter airmail immediately, offering also to place the book in the hands of a good agent, should M. Lespes wish. There is undoubtedly a market for it in America and my guess is that the rejection of the book had nothing to do with its literary merit but was on political grounds only, so I would convey the message to M. Lespes not to be discouraged. But let me know if he gets his letter.

   (b) Snow and storms prevented my getting out to the Bronx to see Dr Métraux³ and I could not reach him by phone.

   (c) Selby was first busy, then away.

   (d) Rinehardt himself was away.

   (e) Either yourself, or Anne Watkins, is mistaken, or someone has blundered, but I have ascertained that there definitely only *is*, for whatever reason, *one* copy of Tailleur pour Bêtes in New York.⁴

   But, and now we go to the good news:

   (a) Anne Watkins has released this copy, which is now in the hands of my editor, Albert Erskine, who is, as you know, very interested in your work, and in whose hands it will not be, at least, so 'static' as in the hands of Anne Watkins (on the other hand, since no other copy apparently exists, as I said, Dr Métraux cannot very well be at the same time the guardian of it.)

(b) Though I had previously got Reynal and Hitchcock interested in your poems I spoke so passionately about them to your firm, even in the absence of your own friends there, that now they will not let them go without Rinehardt's personal consent, and at all events are going through them again, and may revise their stand. Of course, they may not, and there may be delays. But the *copy*, with the extra poems, is in the safe hands of Albert Erskine. I spoke to all Hitchcock's potential translators and as many others as I could lay my hands on and, whether drunk or sober, I certainly spread about your name as a poet with enthusiasm, and this I was able to do with some authority, for meanwhile Under the Volcano (a copy of the first edition of which I hope you have received by now) had erupted with a bang on the very day of publication, was breaking publisher's records, and even threatens now to be some kind of best seller, all of which may seem obscene to you and I, but which as you know impresses publishers.

I think I must now stop my (a) (b) technique – because the 'good' is so inextricably mixed with the uncertain, and the 'bad' with the hopeful, that it is impossible to itemize in such a manner; I had postponed writing because I wished to give you something certain – I now have to postpone it again because of illness, though meantime I am back in Canada.

It is now Easter Monday, alas, and still I have not posted this letter; I am also in receipt this morning of your more than welcome letter, though when I read of your vainly awaiting mine, it makes me feel less like Jesus Christ risen from the dead than Judas Iscariot. The fact is, however, that I have neither hanged myself yet nor got out of the tomb: I am still in bed, or still, by mistake on the cross, which comes to the same thing in Spring.

Before I have finished this letter I can see that it is going to be almost as complicated as one of Kafka's pieces and unless I have been metamorphosed into an insect[5] by that time I can see also that I shall probably have to rewrite it in French.

For what has happened in the meantime is this: Albert Erskine has resigned from Reynal and Hitchcock and is founding a new firm of his own, but I cannot tell you more about this until I know more. What it boils down to is that you now have three publishers interested instead of two. Erskine's prestige is very high, oddly because of Volcano, which Hitchcock bought just before his death, and which Erskine launched in the absence of Reynal also, who was in Washington. This may mean just more delay and still nothing is certain: but at least things are not standing still so far as the poems are concerned. But what worries me is 'Tailleur pour Bêtes' – should it remain with Erskine or go to Dr Métraux? I told you that there is for whatever reason only *one* copy; Erskine cannot make a decision on it while his new firm remains in abeyance, while Reynal and Hitchcock are not perhaps the same firm at all without Erskine and without Hitchcock. On the other hand I remember that in Dr Métraux' letter to you he had mentioned that he was always able to place 'des contes folkloriques' by yourself in an anthropological journal. So please tell me what to do. I may say that the fact that Erskine has left Reynal and Hitchcock does not mean that the latter, who are publishing Jacques Roumain's 'Masters of the Dew' in June, are not interested in 'Tailleur pour Bêtes'.[6] But I feel I have badly let you down, and Emile[7] too, by not *somehow* having managed to get hold of Dr Métraux. I am sure if I had not felt myself to be dying of drink as well as consumption (and I would have died of cold without it anyhow) by that time I would have somehow managed to crawl through the blizzard to the Bronx: but as it was, it proved impossible. I have not forgiven myself for this though in the least and will make some amends by writing to tell him as much. Please ask Emile to forgive me too; but God the way my phone was ringing, and the storm, the wind, the snow, the slush and the cold outside – and ourselves still in summer clothing, and no taxis to be had – no excuse. (You can understand the effect on one's mind though of the Judas Kiss of Success combined simultaneously with the waiting for tests to turn out positive or negative.)

For the rest: we were not able to find out anything re translation into Portugese etc. here, your friend again was away and I was more or less told to mind my own business. You must remember that the Volcano, published by a rival publisher, was receiving a tremendous reception by the New York press and you cannot blame your firm for wondering if I was who I said I was and not someone else. I did, however, get them to promise to write you and Pierre and Lespes airmail and in French, if they do not, all I can say is, with Racine:

La rame inutile fatigua la mer vainement.[8]

I spoke personally in New York to Jonathan Cape the English publisher (he is at present in Cuba, staying with Ernest Hemingway) about you, but you will hear more from me about that and also A.J. Rose, my agent-translator friend in England.[9]

Scribner's have accepted Margerie's serious novel Horse in the Sky, for which we are more than delighted.

Under the Volcano is to be published in France by – if I have it right

– Revue Fontaine Mensuelle de Litterature (something like that, do you know them?) it having turned out the N.R.F. had broken their contract with me.[10] I'll let you know more about this later, I don't think I have any say in the matter of the translation, damn it, though. Sweden, Denmark, Norway and Switzerland, for Occupied Germany, have also bought it so I may be in a position to work a magic myself in regard to translation for yourself in the not too distant future.

I'm afraid I took the liberty [of] being terribly rude about Peter Rhodes[11] to the firm of Rinehardt: my friend the Irish writer James Stern met Rhodes and his wife the next night and was about to give him hell personally but he seemed such a nice fellow, he did not have the heart to; he is an old Paris-American newspaper man and just the type you might expect to translate Paix as Peace and not Shut your mouth; but I think you may be fairly sure that no one will practise such sabotage upon The Pencil of God after the row I made: the excuse was, of course, as given to you: Tinker was away. I will inform Rinehardt once more that you and Pierre are feverishly trying to get your book finished by the end of May and also that you have changed the title (from Sortileges – if I am not mistaken, am I mistaken? Could Sorceries have been the name of your Don Juan book? Charms? Spells? Anyway, the Crayon of God goes much better in English.)

I am concluding this letter literally fievreusement (in short I actually do have a fever) so it may be a little inchoate.

New Directions, who published the translation of Rimbaud with the French on the other side, are not very reliable.[12] I have this from Erskine who was once with them. But I am trying to get in touch with Louis Varese though, who did that Rimbaud translation and perhaps something will come of this. There would be a wonderful market for your poems here in French Canada were not French Canada ruled by the Pope: there is still Napoleon's Code Law in Quebec and presumably a guinnarou is almost as censorable as any unkind mention of Guernica.[13] (Note: British Columbia is *not* French Canada.)

A warning: anything that is not sent *airmail* to New York from Haiti is liable, [if] not actually to miscarry, to take over a month to get there: neither of Margie's manuscripts of Horse in the Sky – one sent to Cape – had arrived even when we left New York and they had been sent off five weeks before from Port-au-Prince so that we had to give her last remaining working copy to Scribner's and Cape still doesn't have his final copy. I know it costs a small fortune to send a MSS airmail from Haiti to New York, but it is undoubtedly this difficulty of communication that adds to your troubles. They at least should write you airmail and if you and Pierre send your MSS off by the end of May ordinary mail don't count on its arriving before the beginning of July, would be my advice, judging by our own experience. At all events do not break your heart unnecessarily by assuming it will arrive within three weeks, although of course it might arrive sooner, if you were sure of your ship.

At this point I had to stop out of exhaustion but I am taking up the next day. No sooner am I doing this and looking sentimentally at an old rum-soaked envelope of Reynal and Hitchcock's on which you wrote in a Bistro that you were sorry you had not thought before to take us to the Museum of Ethnology founded by your great friend Jacques Roumain than – what coincidence and what honour! – I am handed by Margie a parcel from Peggy Hitchcock containing the advance proof copy of the translation of Gouverneurs de la Rosée (Masters of the Dew) together with an invitation to write something about it that they may use on the jacket so my next two days will be spent in reading the galley proofs and in writing the letters I have mentioned. I have already read five chapters of Masters of the Dew and like it enormously but I have to hurry to get my words in. R. & H. and the translators have leaned over backwards to try and get a good translation. Will you please immediately write me instructing me in regard to your opinion of the book's significance and how I may do most good, for here the Man is perhaps more than the Book, while at the same time both *are* Haiti – perhaps I should not concentrate on the merely aesthetic appreciation of it but leave that to others and apply myself to its wider significance for the world, (albeit there is an excellent preface by Langston Hughes on this point.)[14]

We have been excitedly reading your new poem Le Marron also this afternoon with a young French teacher who came to see us and he has copied it enthusiastically out to read to his class.[15] We both think it is among your best, but give us time to understand it better; I think you need a veritable genie, a poetic guinnarou to translate it into its equivalent English without losing the beauty. I will retain your copy and Margie is making a copy of it to send to Erskine so that it may be with the others. How wonderful you are writing poetry again!

Now, for the rest, will we come to Haiti again this year, as we promised and hoped? There is nothing we would like more, and we talk of it continually, – but will you be there, or in France? To some extent it also depends on health, and I feel I have to trust myself to be more a 'Governeur de *Malc*ohol' than I was before coming this second time: this can be done. As for the health, the doctors do not now think I have t.b., an X-ray showed a scar on my lung, and a patch test showed up positive, but all other serious tests were completely negative. This then most likely means that I have *once* had t.b. without knowing it and recovered from it, being strong in health. For a time they thought that

I might have torn this lesion open; but this would not seem to be the case. Nor would it seem to be that I am in danger of it, of the whole thing suddenly flaring up and consuming me. In short, I am all right. Anyway, I flew over the Rockies and you can't do that with t.b. The ironic thing is I can drink but am not supposed to smoke so now I am smoking and not drinking. Do not tell Dr Mars of any of these things nor unnecessarily worry yourself with them either. Re Dr Mars, would you tell him that the Dr Harry Murry I suggested he get in touch with has, I have just found out from Conrad Aiken, actually been in Haiti, and so I have reason to believe he would be very interested in his work. I gave Dr Mars a wrong address, however. Aiken is still in England. If you could tell him to write:

> Dr Harry Murry
> c/o Robert Linscott
> Random House
> 456 Madison Ave.,
> New York City, N.Y.
> U.S.A.
> Please Forward.

and enclosing if possible also a copy of his book, this might bring about some constructive results. Murry is one of America's first psychiatrists and I knew him as a friend when I was a boy.[16] I also know Linscott who is an editor at Random House and Linscott knows Murry's address, which I don't. Nothing could be done about Mars' Mss which [are] with Ira Morris who was not in New York as you know, and I brought the copy Mars gave me back with me to Canada as, although some people were interested, I did not make the right sort of liaison for it; – Murry might; at all events I suggest he write him in French, mentioning my name as a friend of Aiken's and of his he will remember, and outlining some of his psychiatric plans and hopes: at worst it could not but lead to an interesting contact, of the kind that there should be between human minds, and it might open a door.

There is no need for you to write Anne Watkins: as I told you, she released the one copy of Tailleur pour Bêtes on the strength of your letter that accompanied me, while so far as Dr Métraux is concerned, since here I feel myself at fault, I would be grateful if, to save my own face, which is ashamed, you could bear to wait till you heard from him (in the sense that that means he will then have heard from me) unless of course you were going to write him about something else. I have not forgotten the New Yorker with Wilson's article in it either but from whatever source, due to my negligence, sickness, you will have to wait a little for this too.[17]

I have been reading and rereading the wonderful translation you made of my 'Letter in a Bottle' poem and am wondering timorously if I could send you some more that may be translatable.[18] None of my poems save that one have been published before and I would be tremendously honoured if they could appear first in French and in Haiti or perhaps you could do something with them later with the Fontaine Revue Mensuelle or whatever. Though only on the understanding you keep the proceeds – if any. But of course I understand you must be too busy now. On the other hand you did mention it might be worth it for the practice, to get your hand in again, even if not published, and I do not need to have disciplined myself in French verse to know your version is an enormous improvement on mine. You make lines soar in French that in my English only flap heavily like seagulls stuffed with bread. Any lecture you can give me on the art of poetry will be taken to my heart, for verily I feel myself sometimes to be that saddest of all animals: a poet who cannot write poetry. In fact I think that is chiefly what is wrong with me.

Now – although without wanting to get up your hopes too high only to have them dashed to the ground again – I have reserved the best news to the end: I have asked everyone who should know and your old friend, Valery Larbaud, may still be alive, as far as I can find out. There is at least still no confirmation of his death, and there do exist rumours to the contrary. That is as far as I can go: but to reverse the proverb, where there is hope there may still be life. So let us continue to hope: anything else I can find out I will of course report to you as soon as possible.

Now I must close. Not a day goes by without our thinking most affectionately of you or without our looking forward to the hour when we shall see you and Haiti again. Please give our very best love to your brothers Pierre and Emile,[19] to Emanuel, and Charles and Raymond Pressoir and all our other Haitian friends. Commend me also to the priest John, and to the Director of the Cemetery. Give our love to Millie and Marian and say that we will write.[20] And please remember us kindly to your wife.

Margie and I embrace you fraternally.

Your brother,

Malcolm

Annotations:

1 See Lowry's 23 March 1947 letter (**288**) to James Stern.

2 Anthony Lespès was a Haitian writer; see Lowry's 21 June 1947 letter (**307**) to Lespès. Stanley and Frederick Rinehart founded their New York publishing company in 1929; in 1946 the company changed its imprint to Rinehart & Co.

3 Dr Alfred Métraux (1902-63), the Swiss anthropologist, may be the
   Métraux to whom Lowry is referring. During the 1940s he was living
   in New York (as a member of the Secretariat of the United Nations and
   later with UNESCO), and he had published studies of voodoo and
   other aspects of Haitian culture.

4 Ann Watkins had been Lowry's New York literary agent in the thirties
   before he went to Harold Matson. 'Tailleur pour Bêtes' is the title of a
   short story and the early title for a collection of forty-one folk-tales by
   Pierre and Philippe Thoby-Marcelin, published as *Contes et légendes
   d'Haiti* (Paris: Fernand Nathan, 1967).

5 Lowry is referring to Franz Kafka's story *Metamorphosis* (*Der
   Verwandlung* 1915), in which the protagonist, Gregor Samsa, wakes to
   find himself transformed into an insect.

6 *Masters of the Dew* (1947) is the English translation of Roumain's 1944
   novel *Gouverneurs de la Rosée*; see Lowry's 26 March 1947 letter (**291**) to
   Margaret Unwin Hitchcock.

7 Since Marcelin had a brother called Émile, it is not clear whom Lowry
   means here, but he may be referring to Émile Roumer, another Haitian
   writer and friend of the Marcelins and Jacques Roumain. Roumer,
   Roumain, the Marcelins, and others had founded the Haitian literary
   review *La Revue Indigene* in 1927.

8 Jean Racine (1639-99), the French poet and playwright, is known for
   his classical tragedies. Lowry is slightly misquoting a line from
   Agammenon's speech in I.i of *Iphigénie*, where he is describing why he
   was forced to sacrifice his daughter: 'Le vent qui nous flattait nous laissa
   dans le port. / Il fallut s'arrêter, et la rame inutile / Fatigua vainement
   une mer immobile.' Lowry also used the phrase in chapter 12 of *Under
   the Volcano*.

9 Jonathan Cape, who published Hemingway in England, was also a personal friend of the American writer. A.J. (Innes) Rose was Lowry's
   former literary agent and a friend from his Cambridge days.

10 Lowry means the Éditions de la Revue Fontaine. The NRF is the
   Nouvelle revue française, a French periodical.

11 Peter Rhodes translated *La Bête de Musseau* (1946) as *The Beast of the
   Haitian Hills* (1946).

12 New Directions, James Laughlin's publishing house, specialized in *belles
   lettres*.

13 After the British conquest of the French colonies in North America in
   1759, the French, in what was then Lower Canada and later Quebec,
   were allowed to keep their language, religion, and Napoleonic Code.
   Guernica, the spiritual centre of Basque Spain, was destroyed by aerial
   bombardment on 26 April 1937 during the Spanish Civil War. The
   destruction of the city was depicted in *Guernica* (1937) by the Spanish
   painter Pablo Picasso (1881-1973). We have been unable to trace the
   term "guinnarou," which may be Lowry's attempt at Créole.

14 See Lowry's 11 April 1947 letter (**294**) to Margaret Hitchcock for his

comments on *Masters of the Dew* (1947). Langston Hughes (1902-67), the Afro-American writer, translated the novel with Mercer Cook and wrote a brief introduction.

15 The French teacher is Harvey Burt; see Lowry's 1953 letter (**575**) to Burt.

16 Dr Louis Mars was Lowry's doctor in Haiti. He also wrote a study of voodoo; see Lowry's February 1947 letter (**277**) to Albert Erskine. Dr Henry Alexander Murray (1893-1988), the American psychologist, writer, and director of Harvard Psychological Clinic, was a friend of Conrad Aiken's; see Lowry's 1939 letter (**119**) to Aiken.

17 Edmund Wilson's review of Marcelin's novel, called '*Canapé-Vert*,' appeared in the *New Yorker* 20, 2 (1944): 76, 78, 81.

18 Marcelin's translation of Lowry's poem 'In Memoriam: Ingvald Bjorndal and His Comrade,' sometimes subtitled 'A Bottle from the Sea,' is in the Lowry collection (UBC 4:113). See Scherf (186, 297).

19 Émile, known as Milo, Marcelin, the youngest of the three brothers, was also a writer; see Lowry's April 1951 letter (**452**) to Downie Kirk.

20 Millie and Marian Tanner, two Americans visiting Haiti in January 1947, invited the Lowrys to stay in their rented house outside Port-au-Prince.

Editorial Notes:

a. This letter must have been written on about 7 April 1947, just before Lowry received the advance proof copy of Jacques Roumain's *Masters of the Dew* for review; see Lowry's 11 April 1947 letter (**294**) to Margaret Hitchcock.

294: To Margaret Unwin Hitchcock

P: UBC(ts)   Dollarton, B.C.,
Canada
11 April 1947

Dear Mrs Hitchcock:

I wasn't able to compress what I wanted to say re [Jacques] Roumain's Masters of the Dew into a wire (we live 15 miles from a telegraph office and have no phone and it is almost impossible to phone a wire in from the store where the wires always seem crossed) but this is going Air Mail Special Delivery, and therefore should get you Monday, which, to-morrow being Saturday when your office will be closed, ought to get you in time.

I couldn't compress it because what I wanted to say was contradictory: here was the book, there was the man, there are the Haitian people, there are my friends, and so forth; in this case the man is more than the book, which affects the book, in places, adversely; the book is explicit enough without the man jumping out of it on to the table, on the other hand who shall blame him jumping on to the table? Not I. Yet how criticise that without in some way hurting Haiti – since in a certain sense he is Haiti. I could concentrate upon what was admirable but in that case I would have subtly to shift my appraisal from the book to the Haitian people which, according to my wife, would be irrelevant for the purposes of your jacket. Besides, I am sensible of the honour as well as a certain responsibility: you don't want to throw even a pebble at what is struggling so nobly uphill – especially from several thousand feet further down.

Frankly what I feel is this (and I'm going on at length because I'm trying to clarify my own mind): when an artist of Roumain's calibre becomes identified with his country and his country's politics to the extent that he did – and with him also there was the terrific tragedy of race[1] – (he would be further divided now were he alive, if just as adamant and heroic, for he would have stones thrown at him by both the Negroes and the Whites) there seems little choice but to die, as it were sacrificially or consciously: everything that is an artist in you must rebel against the paranoic principle involved in being a leader, everything that is a leader in you, in that realm where paranoia cancels itself by being, so to say, justified by the facts, must rebel against the 'Mr Facing-Both-Ways' principle involved in being an artist per se: a point is reached where both slaughter the other simultaneously and the meaning of your life is achieved. That is perhaps what happened to my friend Nordahl Grieg of Norway, whom Roumain somewhat resembles. It is a tragedy, but a great, a central, a necessary one. Unless I am talking nonsense.

Before I go on into my attempt at a blurb, is it too late to get in a few other small things, doubtless you have eagle-eyed some of them yourself: however in case not: only one of these is not a case of personal opinion, so they are probably irrelevant. I'm in a terrible hurry to catch the post so I may get my galley numbers wrong. I think the translation in the main brilliant, by the way.

Galley 2. Bottom. 'Back of the thorn acacias. . .' Is 'back of' ever justified, even to get rid of a 'behind': perhaps I'm being limeypurist, but why not 'beyond' or beyond for the behind below: note, on Galley 10 thorn acacias is hyphenated.

Galley 3. Cooperation is the friendship of the poor. Cooperation is a weak dead word in English suggestive of chain stores: what about just 'such is the friendship of . . .'

Galley 4. 'Too poor are they to buy shoes' Would a comma after they, or an exclamation after shoes, help out this topsy-turvy one: or could it be set upright without damage? probably not.

Galley 4. Paragraph 3. I think, if you will excuse me (begging your pardon) Roumain must mean 'hips' not 'lips'. Or if not he should have, in spite of the smile. Yes, I know I'm right. (See galley 10 'When she walked her hips rolled down to the bottom of her dress and see also Galley 20, middle, 'she had those gently swaying hips.'

Galley 6. dusk-dark? Better in Creole? Or just dusk. But I guess you have labored on this, and I guess one becomes used to it.

Query punctuation last words of Chapter II.

Galley 20. 'Way down the road – ' Surely either Away or cut the apostrophe: it looks as though the paragraph were going to break into some kind of song in the wrong place. Also compare with Galley 3 and 10 for hips.

I much mislike Chapters VI and VII, though for artistic, not capitalist, reasons and I wish your translators had given themselves a free hand here and rewritten them and I bet Roumain wishes so too; and I wish the whole book had ended on the jubilant note of the drum and not at the banal new life stirring which, even if thematic, could have come in a bit before. The end is truly moving but for this bit of horror, and here again I think Roumain would agree.

Re Chapter VII etc. I can't see why the rusty chuckling old villain Gervilen has to be in love with Anna: would have been much more dramatic if he had remained simply a symbol of the other kind of vengeance that has to be transcended, and had killed Manuel purely for these reasons.

Now oh gosh I have to hurry. Here comes my blurb, which you will have to cut, doubtless.

– Roumain's often deeply moving novel has a quality of poetic beauty akin to that which made great such films as Dovschenko's *Earth*.[2] If in places it is as thin dramaturgically, in descriptive passages nothing short of stereoscopic, Roumain brings the leaves and roots of Haiti right into your room. And a faithful translation has retained the real rhythm, the natural poetical gentle speech of the Haitian peasant. One may surmise in all humilty that the book's occasional didacticism reflects a conflict in Roumain himself, between the born writer and the born leader, poetry and oratory, between aesthetic and moral responsibility to his country, and to his race. Here is not the wildly gorgeous Haiti beheld by the tourist. In a world of demons, Lucifers and saints, in a terrain ravaged by misery and desolation, Roumain reminds us that the interests of the living should come before the vengeance of the dead. But the figure of Roumain himself is almost a symbol of Haiti, whose people are at once revolutionary and merciful, at the same time surely among the most disciplined yet uninhibited, gentle and naturally artistic

people on earth; a striving people who have increasingly become an
example to the world.   Malcolm Lowry[3]

                              Yours truly,

                                              Malcolm Lowry

P.S. Would it be impertinent to suggest that it is more important in the
glossary to know what a macaw tree looks like – or what it is related to
and what its native name is (if not the same) than that bueno means
good?

P.P.S. Something wrong with the antitheses of the last sentence of my
blurb. Perhaps it doesn't matter.

P.P.P.S. Hope there's something you can get out of this – Do you want
galleys back? Or can I keep them?

P.P.P.P.S. Possibly I was wrong to say Roumain actually died by his
own hand: my informant, speaking in Creole, may have meant it symbolically – but the rest of the tragedy is only too true. Better not pass
what I said on, therefore.

Annotations:

1 Jacques Roumain was born into an elite mulatto family in Haiti. Lowry
   goes on to liken Roumain to Nordahl Grieg because both writers were
   involved with communism and both died young; see Lowry's 26 March
   1947 letter (**291**) to Margaret Hitchcock.
2 Alexander Dovjenkho (1894-1956) was a Ukranian writer and film
   director. His 1930 film *Earth* (*Zemlya*), about the death of a peasant, is
   considered a masterpiece.
3 The dust-jacket of Reynal & Hitchcock's 1947 publication of *Masters of
   the Dew*, translated by Langston Hughes and Mercer Cook, carries this
   'blurb' by Lowry.

295: To Frank Taylor

P: Virginia(ms)   Harrison Hot Springs Hotel,
PP: *SL* 140-41   [Harrison Hot Springs, B.C.]
                                              [late April 1947]

Dear Frank:[1]
   I feel like a louse not having written before but assure you that what
with one thing & another & my putting it off because I wanted to write
you a *good* letter (a symptom of narcissism) and also because I was waiting for news of *you* both; and so on; but I hope you will take the will
for the deed. In case the above address does not exactly speak for itself,

for Harrison Hot Springs suggests to me a/ a super name for some sort of jazz outfit, or even some kind of Canadian Capers – a native dance – , b/ ditto for some sort of jazz number, c/ some kind of diabolical mattress, I should add it actually is a spa,[2] & diabolical at that too, for people subsist here on a diet of sulphur, potash, repainted golfballs and occasionally a cold omelette, but what Margie and I came here for was to do some hiking, take a rest from our leaking rooftree, & write some letters, and also to mount the good strong white horse of our uncle standing with our nephew in the garden. We were very sorry not to see you again before we departed but I know you must have been on what someone once called the 'horns of a Domelia'[3] about the Chicago project, & I'm likewise very sorry indeed that this hasn't worked out as you would have wished; I hear you may be at Random House & I wish you and Albert all luck, certainly as I just wrote to Albert, it is lucky for Random House, but I will not say more before I hear more: for myself I feel highly excommunicado, and much the glowererying stepson in my now spiritually tenuous nexus with Reynal & Teamwork, Inc. Bisweilen[4] I continue to receive good & generous reviews on The Volcano from the U.S. but have been more or less panned here, especially in Vancouver & Toronto, by people who have not read the book at all & have made no attempt to. Set against this have some absolutely shatteringly favorable ones from San Francisco Chicago Dallas and a wonderful one from Providence – D.C. de J. – spells David Cornel de Jong?[5] I am working on La Mordida. Perhaps Albert told you Margie's serious novel Horse in the Sky has been taken by Scribner's. There is plenty more good news from this end too – Thanks an inarticulate million for all you have done and your marvellous generosity to Margie & myself in N.Y. – With all best love from us to both you & Nan,[6]

God bless,

Malcolm

[P.S.] Please forgive this scrawl.

Annotations:

1 Frank Eugene Taylor (1916–) entered New York publishing in 1939 and from 1941 to 1948 was editor-in-chief with Reynal & Hitchcock. In October 1948 he moved to Hollywood as a film producer with Metro-Goldwyn-Mayer (MGM). He returned to publishing in 1952.

2 Harrison Hot Springs, a small British Columbia resort town with a spa, is on Harrison Lake 112 kilometres east of Vancouver. The Lowrys spent the last week of April 1947 at the Harrison Hot Springs Hotel.

3 The correct expression is to be caught on 'the horns of a dilemma,' and the dilemma facing Taylor and Erskine was a publishing venture they had hoped to set up in Chicago. When this did not work out, Erskine

joined Random House, and Taylor moved to Hollywood. The letter
Lowry says he has written to Erskine does not appear to have survived.
4 *Bisweilen* is German for 'sometimes' or 'now and then.'
5 David Cornel De Jong (1905-67) was an American writer and teacher
  of creative writing at Brown University and the University of Rhode
  Island. His review of *Under the Volcano* appeared in *Providence Journal*, 9
  March 1947: 6; in it he calls the publication of *Volcano* a literary event
  of 'the first magnitude' and describes the novel as 'magnificent, soul-
  satisfying,' 'richly poetic,' and 'highly artistic.'
6 Nan is Frank Taylor's wife.

296: To Harold Matson

P: Matson(ms); UBC(phc)   Dollarton P.O.,
                                              Dollarton, B.C., Canada
                                                   [23 April 1947]ᵃ

Dear Hal:

I received an offer of $350 from the Columbia Broadcasting System
for one hours broadcast of a dramatisation of Under the Volcano to be
written by Gerald Noxon & produced by Fletcher Markle (Orson
Welles late assistant director) on the Studio one series and since I had to
wire reply immediately I gave them the green light.[1]

I did not then have the copy of R & H's [Reynal and Hitchcock's]
contract which I have since received but since this contract says nothing
specifically of *radio* I still don't quite know where I stand in regard to
percentages to yourself & R & H, if any, so am instructing C.B.S. to
send their contract (which I have signed) & cheque to you, & will you
please do whatever is necessary.

I hope I have done right in this matter; it will be on Studio One series
April 29th; coast to coast.

All the very best to you & Tommy from us both
                         Sincerely

                                                        Malcolm

Annotations:

1 See Lowry's May 1947 letter (**301**) to Fletcher Markle and his 21 June
  1947 letter (**309**) to Gerald Noxon for details of the CBS broadcast.

Editorial Notes:

a. This undated letter is stamped received in Matson's New York office
    on 26 April 1947, and letters typically took two or three days between
    Vancouver and New York in the late forties. Lowry has written on
    paper with the Harrison Hot Springs Hotel letterhead; see also his April
    1947 letter (**295**) to Frank Taylor.

296-a: To Vernon van Sickle

P: private(ms)
As from Dollarton P.O.,
Dollarton, B.C., Canada
[23 April 1947][a]

My dear Vernon:[1]

I was very glad indeed to hear from you & had been expecting to in New Orleans – from your letter it would seem that you didn't get mine.[2]

My late failure to correspond was due to health more than anything else: combination of the tropics of Haiti & the blizzards of N.Y led me into a t.b scare but it appears after all that I haven't got it, which is a relief: though it would seem from the Xray I once had it & got over it.

I tried to get in touch with you as soon as I hit Vancouver again but heard you were in Montreal.[3]

No, you did not precisely offend me in regard to the volcano but I think you might have made more of an effort to read it: you certainly didn't leave me with any final impression that you believed in it: when you criticise a style unthinkingly you are criticising the man without proper judgment; and if on top of that you invoke Rimbaud you are liable to get Rimbaud in return: this does not prevent me from feeling somewhat of a Judas in regard to it all but you cannot blame me for reasoning subconsciously thus: if that was all you thought of it, any script you produced would not do either of us any good.

And even if *I* did not reason thus you can scarcely blame Margie for so reasoning: & in ones cups who does not sometimes irresponsibly overlook that they have more than one person to think of?

So much for excuse; not very convincing: nonetheless I wonder you should want to do it now, for that [it] is a best seller must surely confirm your opinion in one part of your mind that it is rotten??

But as a matter of fact the script business by force majeure is quite out of my hands and we approached it anyway in the most unfeasible fashion: a confusion and frustration in your amour propre (as has there not been such in mine!) possibly leads you to think that you can write a script like a director: but you are surely a potential director & not a script writer per se; these two at best are perhaps dopplegängers, but what happens at worst, or is likely to happen in Hollywood? A good director would be jealous of or mortified by your suggestions & not take them: while a bad director would not take them anyway. So what. While all the rest depends on factors that have to do with everything but art. So I would forget about U.T.V as not being worth your time.

On the other hand, if I am ever in a position (which is not impossible) to put something in your path in the direction you wish to go along film lines I'll let you know specifically, although before that time it would seem not unlikely that you may, if you want it hard enough, be where you want yourself.

All the best to you & Shirley from us both

Malcolm

Annotations:

1 Vernon van Sickle (1910-60) was born in England of Canadian parents and educated at public school. Returning to Vancouver as a young man, he met the Lowrys while trying to revive the local branch of the National Film Society of Canada, and he and his wife Shirley visited the Lowry shack, where they listened to Malcolm reading from *Under the Volcano*. It is clear from this letter that van Sickle was not impressed with the book, though he saw its potential as a movie. See letter **251** to Gerald Noxon and two 1946 letters (**9** and **10**) to van Sickle in Appendix 3.
2 See letter **10** in Appendix 3.
3 The van Sickles left Vancouver in February 1947 (not 1948 as suggested in letter **251**) and settled in Ottawa.

Editorial Notes:

a. This single-page holograph is on Harrison Hot Springs Hotel letterhead; Lowry added his Dollarton address. The envelope carries a postmark of 23 April, Harrison Hot Springs and is addressed to van Sickle in Margerie's hand.

297: To John Davenport

P: UBC(ms)

Dollarton P.O.,
Dollarton, B.C.,
Canada
[April/May 1947][a]

My beloved old John:

I cannot say how marvellous it was to hear from you nor how much I appreciated your generous praise of what Conrad euphoniously calls: 'Under the Malcalmo or Poppergetsthebotl.'[1] [N]or how much what was wise and useful in it has sunk into my soul.

You are wrong when you say we have been out of touch, however.[2] Even had I not written you during the last years, (which, by God, I did)[3] I cannot say that I have ever felt really out of touch with you. On the contrary certain important things about you, such, for instance, as your 'enormous laughter' have become part of our life, our technique, indeed, of meeting it: so that I would say one was in touch on an average several times a week, if not more, if not indeed very much more.

I think I have said this before. I wrote it anyway in *Hugo*, Kansas:[4] perhaps I did not post it till I got to St Louis. (We went to Haiti).

As for Poppergetsthebotl it is, of all things, a best seller in the States, just having been promoted over the latest James M Cain and Forever Amber.[5]

– Gerald Noxon & Fletcher Markle (Orson Welles assistant director in his Acapulco movie)[6] have just done it on the air, coast to coast; from New York, one hour programme: typically we were able to hear precisely nothing whatever.

It is also being translated into French Swedish, Danish, Norwegian, Czecho-Slovakian, Swiss & occupied Goiman. According to the Prague publisher their copy, arrived rather dilapidated, & marked 'Found in Bremen harbour'![7]

I say these things for what they are worth; as you know, this kind of business can be a Judas kiss. But I hope in so far as it can be called work it was for God and not the devil.

I took Margie to Mexico in 45-46 – we were driven out, spent most of our time seeking sanctuary in Catholic churches, & barely escaped with our lives; – a very strange experience indeed, rendered even more implausible by the fact that quite by coincidence, as the saying is, we found ourselves living in M. Laruelle's tower of chapter vii, to which, borne by the little postman of chapter vi, came news *on the same day* of the Volcano's acceptance in England & America.

I am now engaged in trying to objectify this in a piece entitled La Mordida, a short novel with a companion piece entitled Dark as the Grave wherein my friend is laid: dark because we tried to look up Vigil, only to find he had been murdered after drinking too much mescal, & was buried in Villa Hermosa, Tabasco.[8]

I am very distressed to hear that poor old James Travers is dead – why?[9] But then, again, why not? God rest him in his celestial silver fox farm. Or perhaps he is busy. And Paddy Railton – God bless him.[10] Why does it always seem so *impossible*. One would be curious to know what they think but that the very act of being curious seems somehow disloyal.

And Nordahl [Grieg] – so is my book about him, died with our house June 7th 1944, in flames. We went East to discover Gerald Noxon doing a broadcast for Free Norway about his death six months before; he died on our third wedding anniversary, Dec 2 1948. I'm very glad indeed you met him.

Tell me about the fortune of others.

Maxwell Perkins of Scribners has just taken a serious novel by my Margerie for publication in the States in October: it is a perfectly lovely thing entitled Horse in the Sky, set in Devonshire & in the Irish Hills of Michigan. Cape seemed about to take it too but he has a paper shortage or something, & so it is more or less free in England at the moment. What about your Rodney Phillips & Green?[11] Are you interested in novels, between the cognac & the cigar? This is a unique one by an American, & to my mind stands an even better chance in England than America. It would moreover translate beautifully. Please tell Innes [Rose] I will write; & also will send him a copy of the Volcano. He was away when it was accepted in England. The continental rights having been disposed of here has detracted from its value to him (this was out of my control) but please tell him I recognize my obligation to him & anyhow would vastly prefer him as my agent: I'm trying to see my way through a maze at the moment for Margie has agential confusion too. All the best love from my Margerie to your Marjorie & from myself to you both[12] – I will write again sine mora, & moreover *reply* – God bless –

Malc

Annotations:

1 Davenport wrote to Lowry on 12-13 April 1947 (UBC 1:17) praising the novel he called 'Malcolm's Clavicle.' In his 23 February 1947 letter to Lowry, Aiken also praised *Under the Volcano* and concluded by dubbing the novel 'Poppergetsthebotl'; see Sugars (202).

2 The two men had not seen each other since the fall of 1936, when Lowry and Jan stayed with Davenport in Hollywood before travelling to Mexico.

3 See Lowry's S.O.S. to Davenport of December 1937 (**78**) and his 6 December 1946 postcard (**261**) from St Louis, Missouri.

4 There is no Hugo in Kansas; see Lowry's February 1947 letter (**283**) to Davenport.

5 James Mallahan Cain (1892-1977) was an American journalist, novelist, and Hollywood screen-writer known for violent thriller novels such as *The Postman Always Rings Twice* (1934) and *Double Endemnity* (1943). In 1947 Cain's 'latest' effort was *The Butterfly*. *Forever Amber* (1944), by Kathleen Winsor (1919-), was very popular, but in his 6 March 1950 letter (**391**) to Derek Pethick, Lowry claims that *Under the Volcano* topped *Forever Amber* as a best-seller.

6 During 1946-47 Fletcher Markle was in Acapulco working on the script for 'Salomé,' which was never produced, but he was not assistant director for Orson Welles, who directed (with the help of Sam Nelson) and co-starred with Rita Hayward in *The Lady from Shanghai* (1948). Shooting for this film began in 1946 aboard Errol Flynn's private yacht off the shores of Acapulco.

7 See letter **574** to Dr Irmgard Rexroth Kern.

8 The character of Dr Vigil in *Under the Volcano* is based upon Lowry's Mexican friend Juan Fernando Márquez; see Lowry's December 1937 and May 1940 letters (**80** and **140**) to Márquez.

9 Hugh James Travers (1909-42), born in Halifax, Yorkshire, read history at Peterhouse College, Cambridge, from 1927 to 1931. He had been a drinking companion and friend of Lowry's at Cambridge and in London between 1931 and 1933. He owned a silver-fox farm in Chagford, South Devon, and on the occasion of Lowry's visit to the farm with Travers and Robert Pocock in September 1933 Lowry smashed the only car he was ever to own. Travers took up fox farming in Canada before returning to England to join the Ministry of Information during the war; he died in action in the Middle East. After Lowry learned of this death, his former friend appears to have haunted him until he became a ghostly presence in the 'Ordeal of Sigbjørn Wilderness'; see Lowry's December 1949 letter (**380**) to Davenport, in which he speaks of 'dear old Jimmy Travers.'

10 Davenport mentions Paddy Railton's death in his 12-13 April 1947 letter to Lowry.

11 Rodney Phillips & Green was the name of the short-lived London publishing house of which John Davenport was then the director; see Lowry's letter **9** to a 'Mr Green' in Appendix 3. The reference to cognac and the cigar is an echo of Davenport's 12-13 April 1947 letter to Lowry.

12 Marjorie was Davenport's second wife, whom he married after his divorce from Clement Davenport.

Editorial Notes:

a. The pencil holograph copy-text of this letter is on both recto and verso of two sheets of Lowry's cheapest canary second-cut paper. There is an inside address, but no date; however, judging from his reference to Fletcher Markle's 29 April 1947 CBS production, Lowry must be writing on 30 April or very early in May; see his May 1947 letter (**301**) to Markle.

298: To Harold Matson

P: Matson(ms); UBC(phc)   – Dollarton P.O.,
Dollarton, B.C.
[ca 2 May 1947]ª

My dear Hal:

I am very sorry indeed about the C.B.S. broadcast;¹ I cannot find any valid excuse for not letting you know, had events been normal one of the firm of Malcolm & Margerie would have certainly informed you but we were bogged down here with trying to escape for a week from our leaking (though still beloved) roof and a truly unholy mass of unanswered correspondence.

In my defense I can only say that the thing was sprung upon me without a moment's notice and the invitation to answer yea or nay and it did not for one moment occur to me that Gerald Noxon being in New York would not get in touch with you himself; moreover it did not strike me that they would or could proceed without the formal permission of the publishers; in addition Gerald knows Albert and I was not to know that the thing was not being done with general consent. On top of this I had not the foggiest notion it was coming off so soon: I am still waiting for the promised letter from Gerald on the subject, but its non-arrival can be explained by the fact that he must have had to work night and day on the script. I wrote you within 5 minutes of receiving the news it was coming off last Tuesday;[2] but this news came from the C.B.S. itself, not Gerald or Fletcher Markle.

I think I may have been inclined to wire an immediate and unequivocal yes because of Noxon's position in the matter. He helped me greatly with the Volcano itself & also Margie & myself in work & other matters and I may subconscious[ly] have felt that I was doing him a service of some kind by not arguing about the cash: some cockeyed notion of actually saving you trouble may also have crossed our confused minds. But please convey my apologies to R & H [Reynal and Hitchcock] – for here my excuse is certainly valid; as I say, I'd no notion it was such an *immediate* proposition – I'd figured on 3 or 4 months hence at least, not weeks.

When I say, however, that we sat for hours at the time of broadcast with ours ears glued to a short-wave radio (belonging to someone else, & at someone elses house) which emitted precisely nothing, I feel that you may consider our punishment complete.

Unless it would have been even more complete had one heard it; though I feel Markle & Noxon, if given half a chance, would have done something swell.

But there again I am in the dark.

I am working hard on La Mordida, a painful process not improved by an extremely painful hand –

All the best to you & Tommy from us both

Yours

Malcolm

Annotations:

1 See also Lowry's May 1947 letter (**301**) to Fletcher Markle and his 21 June 1947 letter (**309**) to Gerald Noxon.
2 See Lowry's 23 April 1947 letter (**296**) to Matson.

Editorial Notes:

a. This holograph is undated, but Matson has stamped it received 5 May.

299: To Jacques Barzun

P: Columbia(ts); UBC(ms,ts phc)
PP: *SL* 143–48

Dollarton, B.C.,
Canada
6 May 1947

Dear Mr Barzun:

You've written, to my mind, such a horribly unfair criticism of my book, Under the Volcano, that I feel I may be forgiven for shooting back.[1]

Granted that it has been overpraised to the extent where an unfavourable review seems almost welcome, and granted that your review may end by doing me good, it rankles as an even harsher criticism, if just, could never do, and I feel that this is not only unsporting but weakens your whole general argument; people simply won't listen to your very necessary truths if you do this kind of thing once too often.

Ah ha, I can hear you saying, well I can tear the heart out of this pretty damned easily, I can smell its derivations from a mile away, in fact I need only open the book at random to find just what I want, just the right food for my article: I do not feel you have made the slightest critical effort to grapple with its form and intention. What you have actually succeeded in doing is to injure a fellow who feels himself to be a kindred spirit.

I do not think there was any need, either, to be so insulting about it. You are entitled to 'fulsome and fictitious' and you can say if you wish (though it is not specifically true and there is certainly no irrefutable evidence of the former) that I am 'on the side of good behaviour and eager to disgust you with tropical vice.' But when you say 'He shows this by a long regurgitation of the materials found in Ulysses or the Sun Also Rises' are you not overstepping the mark in an effort to be scornful? For while few modern writers, myself included, can have altogether escaped the influence, direct or indirect, of Joyce and Hemingway, the 'materials' in the sense you convey are not to be found in either of these books. 'And while imitating the tricks of Joyce, Dos Passos and Sterne, he gives us the heart and mind of Sir Phillip Gibbs.'[2] What tricks, precisely, do you mean? A young writer will naturally try to benefit by and make use of what he has read, as a result of which, especially in technique, what Van Gogh I think calls 'design governing postures' are from time to time inevitable. But where I found another writer in the machinery – the writer you are reading at the moment, [I.A.] Richards has pointed out, is nearly always the villain – I always did my utmost to sweat him out. Shards and shreds of course sometimes remain: they do in your style too. But so far as I know I have imitated none of the tricks of the writers you mention, one of whom at least once testified to my originality. As a matter of fact – and to my shame – I have never read Ulysses through, of Dos Passos I have read only Three Soldiers, and of Sterne I have never been able to read more than one page of Tristram Shandy. (This of course does not rule out indirect influence, but what about what I've invented myself?) I liked The Sun Also Rises when I read it 12 years ago but I have never read it since nor do I think I've ever been particularly influenced by it. Where the Volcano is influenced, its influences are, for the most part, other, and for the most part also I genuinely believe, absorbed. Where they are not you can put it down to immaturity: I began the book in 1936 when I was 27 and doubtless in spite of many re-writings, it carries a certain stamp of that fact. As for Sir Phillip Gibbs are you not just being gratuitously cruel? Perhaps if you would really read the book you would see that quite a lot of it is intended to be – and in fact is – funny, as it were a satire upon itself. Nor, I venture to say, do I think that, upon a second serious reading, you would find it dull.

After Sir Phillip Gibbs I can almost forgive you for juxtaposing at random two not very good passages from Chapters III and IX as though they were contiguous, as an example of bad reporting. But even if those passages are not so hot, what of the justice of this kind of criticism? I'd like to know what you'd do with the wretched student who loaded his dice like that for you.

The end, I suppose, is intended to crush one completely. 'Mr Lowry has other moments, borrowed from other styles in fashion, Henry James, Thomas Wolfe, the thought-streamers, the surrealists. His novel can be recommended only as an anthology held together by earnestness.'

Whatever your larger motive – which I incidentally believe to be extremely sound – do you not seem to have heard this passage or something like it, before? I certainly do. I seem to recognize the voice, slightly disguised, that greeted Mr Wolfe himself, not to say Mr Faulkner, Mr Melville and Mr James – an immortal voice indeed that once addressed Keats in the same terms that it informed Mr Whitman that he knew less about poetry than a hog about mathematics.

But be that as it may. It is the 'styles in fashion' that hurts. Having lived in the wilderness for nearly a decade, unable to buy even any intelligent American magazines (they were all banned here, in case you didn't know, until quite recently) and completely out of touch, I have had no way of knowing what styles were in fashion and what out, and didn't much care. Henry James notebooks I certainly have tried to take to heart, and as for the thought-streamers (if you're interested in sources) William would doubtless be pleased.[3] And I'm glad at least it was earnestness that held the anthology together. Nonetheless I shall laugh – and I hope you with me – should in ten years or so the Voice again be heard decrying some serious contemporary effort on the grounds that its author is simply regurgitating the materials to be found in Lowry. I shall laugh, but I shall on principle sympathise with the author, even if it is true.

Be this as it may. Any other kind of duello being inconvenient at this distance, I had begun this letter with the intention of being, if possible, as intolerably rude as yourself. I even bought an April Harpers to provide myself with material and sure enough I found it springing up to me, just as to you, from my work, your ammunition:[4] for did I not immediately find you lambasting Senor Steinbeck in vaguely similar terms, though at much greater length, accusing him of almost everything except stealing his bus from me – you of course didn't know I had one, it is in Chapter VIII – (a crime I may say of which he is innocent and vice versa) and speaking of his anti-artistic emotion of self-pity, by which I take it you do not of course mean your *own* anti-artistic emotion of self-pity by any chance?

There is an interesting passage here too:

'In the makers of the tradition, that is to say in Balzac, Dickens, Zola, Hardy, Dostoevsky, down to Sinclair Lewis and Dos Passos, there is an affirmation pressing behind every grimness, an anger or enthusiasm of despair which endows mud with life and makes it glow like rubies. The energy of mind makes even a surfeit of facts bearable, while plot enmeshes the characters so completely that the reader is compelled to believe in a fated existence, at the very moment when he knows that he is only the sport of the writer's will.'

Good: but why, at that rate, are you so ready to jump upon the affirmation pressing behind the grimness in the Volcano? So ready to jump upon it indeed as soon as you saw it (because it was in capital letters doubtless) that you quite missed the anger or enthusiasm of despair that it was following? Did you not trample the one to death without even taking the trouble to see if the other was there at all, without taking *any* trouble, in short, except to exhume Sir Phillip from his dull grave in order to have a cheap sneer at my expense? And if so, why. I could tell you, but this is as far as my rudeness will take me.

For one thing, I have just got another batch of reviews, all of them good, and all of them more irritating than yours. For another, the book is to be translated into French: the very tough editors, I am relieved to say, think more highly of it than you, which is something. And for another I just have news from England that one of my best friends – Anna Wickham, the poet, if you're interested – has just hanged herself in London.[5]

God has raised his whip of Hell
That you be no longer weak
That out of anguish, you may speak,
That out of anguish, you may speak well.

She once wrote.[6] My wife by a coincidence having bought me a week
ago, in Canada, the only edition of her poems (praised by D.H.
Lawrence – and why didn't you drag *him* in?) – that can have been sold
in 20 years, bought them for me indeed two days before Anna Wickham
died. So life is too short or something.

And the grammer of this letter is bad. And it will remain so. So,
doubtless, are the semantics. And the syntax. And everything else.

With the general tenor of your criticism in Harpers I am enormously,
as I hinted, in accord. That for instance political books should be read
with the historian's scepticism, and with the historian's willingness to
see the drama of both sides, that we suffer from intellectual indigestion,
philosophic bankruptcy, and adulterated 'brews' of one kind or another
– be they behaviouristic or what-not, that we are being done down by
half thoughts, regurgitated unthoughts found in so and so – how true: I
might remind you though, that there are sometimes deeper sources and
not everything comes up your own service elevator.

I think I said that the Volcano had been over praised and also praised
for qualities it probably doesn't possess and I think that one of the things
that I wanted to say was that that seemed no good reason for you to tear
it to pieces for faults it doesn't possess either.

I wish, sincerely, that you would read it again, and this time because
you don't have to write about it, look instead for what may be good in
it. It sings, I believe, considerably – the whole thing – in the mind, if
you can stand the partial bankruptcy in character drawing and what
actually *is* fictitious about it, the sentences like Schopenhauer's roast
geese stuffed with apples – [7]

But on the side of good conduct no. I myself savagely reviewed it for
a preface for the English edition – though they would have none of it –
– thus: – never mind the 'thus' but ending: All applications for use by
temperance societies should be accompanied by a case of Scotch
addressed to the author. Now put it back in the three penny shelf where
you found it.

Moreover I had even toyed at one time rather lovingly with the
notion of having Hugh and Yvonne killed off while too sober and the
Consul returning cheerfully and drunkenly to his duties to mescal and
the British Crown under a miraculously transformed and benign
Poppergetsthebotl.

You may also remember that so far as the latter was concerned I was doing what I fondly believed (in spite of L'Assomoir) to be a pioneer work. The Lost Week End et al did not come along until as always happens, it was virtually finished, and at that for the fifth time.[8] Moreover it will both horrify and relieve you to learn that it was only the third of a book, if complete in itself, most of the rest having been destroyed by fire.

And if you want sources – what about the Cabbala? The Cabbala is only in the sub-basement of the book but you would discover therein that the Cabbala itself is identified with 'garden' and the abuse of wine with the abuse of magical powers, and hence with the destruction of the garden, and hence with the world. This myth may have somewhat confined me: for though one might sympathise with Mephistopheles, Faust is a different matter. But perhaps I cite this only to show you how much more loathsome the book might have been to you had I put this on the top plane. I very much believe in what positive merits the book has, however. (I don't know if Sir Phillip Gibbs ever thought about the Cabbala, I have a gruesome suspicion that that is precisely the sort of thing he might have thought about.)

At all events I am now writing another book ['La Mordida'], you will be uninterested to learn, dealing roughly speaking with the peculiar punishment meted out to people who lack the sense of humour to write books like Under the Volcano. So far, I am pretty convinced that nothing like it has been written, but you can be sure that just as I am finishing it –

Sans blague. One wishes to learn, one wishes to learn, to be a better writer, to think better, and one wishes to learn, period. In spite of some kind of so-called higher education (Cambridge Eng) I have just arrived at that state where I realised I know nothing at all. A cargo ship, to paraphrase Melville, was my real Yale and Harvard too. Doubtless I have absorbed many of the wrong things. But instinct leads the good artist (which I feel myself to be, though I sez it myself) to what he wants. So if, instead of ending this letter may christ send you sorrow and a serious illness, I were to end it by saying instead that I would be tremendously grateful if one day you would throw your gown out of the window and address some remarks in this direction upon the reading of history, and even in regard to the question of writing and the world in general, I hope you won't take it amiss. You won't do it, but never mind.

With best wishes, yours sincerely,

Malcolm Lowry

P.S. Anthology held together by earnestness – Brrrrrr!

Annotations:

1 American writer and teacher Jacques Barzun (1907-) reviewed *Under the Volcano* for *Harper's* 194 (May 1947): 486. His comments were very negative, and Lowry was deeply wounded. Barzun describes the novel as 'fulsome and fictitious,' a 'regurgitation of the materials found in *Ulysses* and *The Sun Also Rises*.' 'While imitating the tricks of Joyce, Dos Passos, and Sterne,' Barzun continues, 'he gives us the mind and heart of Sir Philip Gibbs,' and Barzun sums up by calling *Volcano* 'an anthology held together by earnestness.' On 10 May, Barzun replied to Lowry that for an 'injured author [he was] extraordinarily forebearing, generous, reasonable.' He promised to read *Volcano* again, but still found it 'derivative and pretentious'; see *Selected Letters*, appendix 6.

2 Sir Philip Hamilton Gibbs (1877-1962), English reporter and novelist, was noted for his idealism and pacifism.

3 Lowry's praise for Henry James's notebooks is puzzling because they were not published as such until 1947, when F.O. Mathiessen and Kenneth E. Murdock edited *The Notebooks of Henry James* (New York: Oxford University Press). However, Lowry certainly knew James's fiction, prefaces, and letters. William James (1842-1910), Henry's elder brother, was a philosopher; his theory of 'stream of consciousness' is set forth in chapter 9 of *The Principles of Psychology* (1890).

4 Barzun's criticisms of John Steinbeck (1902-68), inspired by his dislike of the American novelist's *The Wayward Bus* (1947), appear in his review article 'New Books: Fiction in Novels – and Politics,' *Harper's* (April 1947): backpages.

5 Anna Wickham (1888-1947), the English poet, lived near Hampstead Heath in London in a house called 'Bourgeois Towers.' During 1932 she and her sons James (a Cambridge friend of Lowry's), John, and George provided Lowry with a second home and family; see Day (156-57), Bowker (142-43), and James Hepburn's recollections in *Malcolm Lowry Remembered* (59-63). Lowry had just learned of her suicide in a 1 May 1947 letter from John Davenport.

6 From memory, Lowry misquoted Wickham's poem 'The Torture':
    God has raised his whip of Hell
       That you be no longer weak.
    Because of anguish shall you speak,
    Because of anguish, shall you speak well.
   See *The Man with a Hammer* (London: Grant Richards, 1916), p. 81; Margerie gave Lowry a copy on 28 April 1947.

7 Arthur Schopenhauer (1788-1860) was a German philosopher whose theory of will influenced Richard Wagner, Friedrich Nietzsche, and many modern thinkers. Lowry is quoting from 'On Style' in *The Art of Literature: A Series of Essays*, trans. T. Bailey Saunders (London: Swan Sonnenschein, 1891), p. 85. Schopenhauer's criticism of German prose is that 'in those long sentences rich in involved parentheses, like a box of boxes one within another, and padded out like roast geese stuffed

with apples, it is really the *memory* that is chiefly taxed; while it is the understanding which should be.'

8 Émile Zola's *L'Assommoir* (1877), like Charles Jackson's *The Lost Weekend* (1944), is about drinking; Lowry felt that he had surpassed Zola but been nearly outdone by Jackson.

300: To George Hepburn

P: UBC(ms)   [Dollarton]
                                                                        [May 1947]

Dear Tor:[1]

I heard, to my huge grief, that Anna was dead.

I heard, also, the circumstances from which I have drawn no conclusions whatever save that perhaps even a bad letter might be more welcome than none at all.

You will vaguely remember me as a somewhat tipsy individual whom you once presented with a rabbit and who made off with one of your exercise books.

I remember you all with the greatest of affection and also gratitude for the number of times I have received sanctuary in your house.

I am writing you because I wanted to join in your feelings of loss & catastrophe and also because I am hoping that by so doing I can relieve you of some of them.

Do not above all agonize too much: sometimes, in apparent disastar, there is both a will and a wisdom that you cannot see. Shocking the will may seem, & distressful the wisdom, but there it is.

                                                          [breaks off unsigned]

Annotations:

1 According to James Hepburn (*Malcolm Lowry Remembered*, 61), Anna Wickham's youngest son, George, had a pet rabbit (that Lowry accidentally killed) and was still in school in the early thirties when Lowry visited the Wickham home. References to the rabbit and 'exercise books' suggest that Lowry is writing to George, but we have been unable to confirm that the name 'Tor' was used by any of the Hepburn brothers. Nordahl Grieg used the name in *The Ship Sails On* and Lowry used it in 'In Ballast to the White Sea' (UBC 12: 14,15); see also Day (125). The copy-text, an incomplete pencil draft (UBC 3:14) of a letter, may not have been sent to the family.

301: To Fletcher Markle

P: UBC(ms)
PP: *SL* 142

[Dollarton]
[May 1947]

Dear Fletcher:[1] (& Gerald, if extant??)

Por Pete' sake . . . It wasn't that I was bothering about the records; or the cuttings, or Dilworth; though very many thanks for the wire.

It was just merely that I hadn't heard *anything*, not the broadcast, nor yet whether you personally & Gerald were pleased with it, nor whether you thought it came off, nor whether it actually did come off, nor absolutely bloody nothing & meantime we have been here quietly piddling in our pants with suspence

Every day I have been expecting a letter from Gerald whose first wire said letter follows: – but no letter. Of course I realise the pressure of the work: but then after the event?

Conceive of yourself in Siberia with a play coming off in Moscow which is a great ambition of yours and no word but after six months of anxiously waiting for every post you receive word relayed through a commissar from the producer that always supposing that certain auxiliary circumstances are equal and that dog teams are not requisitioned for something else you may be permitted in a month or two to see part of the envelope on which at one time had reposed part of the script. This I admit is an exaggeration: but all I wanted was as it were a single word or phrase like OK, Hot Diggety, or even we are not amused.

I was anxious for your sakes too for I would have been unhappy to think the first thing you did didn't come off & I would have felt rather responsible.

But the silence now makes me think it didn't come off: but then of course perhaps it did.

I realise you are very busy & probably have not time to consider such involved feelings as this or perhaps you rightly feel that you have already considered them enough.

Gerald, you blighter, donde es that allerverdampter carta?[2]

At all events: all the very best of luck to you in Babylon there from Ultima Thule.

Blessings,

Malcolm

Annotations:

1 Fletcher Markle (1921-91) was a Canadian film and television writer and producer whom Gerald Noxon had introduced to Lowry during Lowry's March 1947 visit. Markle was with the CBS program 'Studio

One,' which broadcast Noxon's adaptation of *Under the Volcano* on 29 April 1947; see Lowry's 21 June letter (**309**) to Noxon. (The date of the broadcast is given wrongly by Day [p.385] and by Bowker [p.412].)
2 Lowry's Spanish-English-German question is, roughly: 'where is that damned-all letter?'

302: To Harold Matson

P: Matson(ts); UBC(phc)   Dollarton, B.C.,
Canada
12 May 1947

Dear Hal:

Herewith the endorsed C.B.S. check.

Unless this is not permitted I would be obliged if you could deduct $100 from it and send this to Dr E.B. Woolfan, 7046 Hollywood Blvd., Hollywood 28, Calif., to whom we owe that sum, it being still impossible, without endless red tape and sometimes not even then, to send cash out of Canada.[1]

I have also referred a Mr A. Ronald Button, of Hollywood, to you, and it is possible that he may get in touch with you, although whether you work with him in regard to the Volcano or not is of course entirely up to your judgement.[2] It may be possible you have something lined up there through someone else, or directly: on the other hand, if not, and he still has – as he unsolicitedly implied by wire some while back when I referred him to you – I can assure you he is an excellent man. Not an agent per se he is an attorney who has managed some very big people in pictures, for example, the late Max Reinhardt.[3] A personal friend of old standing, I can vouch for his sterling character and ability and the high regard in which he is held: but as I say, I leave matters up to your judgement. Other figures from Hollywood have been trying to get in touch with me apparently, with offers, some long distance, and at the wrong address, but this is the only definite bite I have had. Where I can trace any others or should I get any more I shall of course refer these to you: I don't want anything to conflict with what you are doing, nor do I wish to trouble you with false alarms, but I can scarcely do other than to pass them along, when they make sufficient noise. For example: I hear, through the grape vine but on absolutely first hand authority, that Frances Marion, until recently overall production advisor at M.G.M. and who as you know of course has been one of the leading script writers for 20 odd years, is in a lather about the Volcano, thinks it has great picture values and has bought no less than five copies of it.[4] I think that this is the line that Button wants to work on and I have reason to think it may be hot and I like the sound of the set-up.

Thanks for everything again and all the very best regards to you both from both of us.

Malcolm

P.S. I hear from New York that there has been no advertisement by R. & H. [Reynal & Hitchcock] since the very first one: is this so? Or does it matter? Some of the later reviews, especially from San Francisco Dallas and New England, and one by De Jong,[5] put even the early ones in the shade and I should have thought could have been used with effect. I saw the stinker in Harper's too: and grossly unfair it is. But the Atlantic has a good one. One does not mind being damned for one's faults, but Barzan I could garrot.[6]

Annotations:

1 Dr Woolfan (Bert) was Lowry's brother-in-law, married to Margerie's sister Priscilla.
2 Lowry wrote at length to Ronald Button, a Los Angeles attorney and friend of the Woolfans, on 15 June 1946 (**224**) explaining what he and Margerie had suffered during their 1946-47 visit to Mexico. Lowry also hoped that through Button arrangements could be made for a film of *Under the Volcano*. Button wrote to Matson in late May 1947 about working with Frances Marion, but nothing came of his letter.
3 Max Reinhardt (1873-1943), a Jew and the pre-eminent theatre producer in Germany during the early decades of the twentieth century, was stripped of his Berlin theatres by the Nazis and forced into exile in the United States.
4 Frances Marion (1888-1973), considered one of Hollywood's leading screen-writers, wrote for more than 130 films during her twenty-five-year career. She retired from screen-writing in 1940.
5 For a description of David Cornel De Jong's review, see annotation 5 to Lowry's late April 1947 letter (**295**) to Frank Taylor.
6 See Lowry's 6 May 1947 letter (**299**) to Barzun.

303: To Earle Birney

P: UBC(ts)

Dollarton, B.C.
14 May 1947

Dear Dr Birney:[1]
  Sybil Hutchinson, of McClelland and Stewart, has made the very welcome suggestion (to me) that I meet you and this I would indeed be delighted to do.[2] My wife and I inhabit a telephoneless shack upon the beach here and it is none too easy to get to town, which we visit somewhat rarely as we have no car.

The month of May implies, possibly wrongly, exams to me and gives me the feeling you may be very busy; on the other hand I was wondering if we might catch you in town some day, which might constitute a kind of half way house.

Luncheon is not our strong suit and instinct vaguely suggests a pub: my wife suggests that we meet, Heaven help us, in the 'Ladies and Escorts' at the Hotel Vancouver. If for whatever reason you do not visit pubs, perhaps you can think of somewhere else: at all events possibly the Hotel Vancouver possesses the necessary ambiguities.

I am hard at work on a book but I shall be only too pleased to get away from it so I leave the date and hour up to you if you have one to spare.

Yours sincerely,

Malcolm Lowry

Annotations:

1 Earle Birney (1904-95), Canadian poet and novelist, was a professor in the English department at the University of British Columbia when he and Lowry met in 1947. The Birneys and the Lowrys became friends, and Birney actively supported Lowry's work and reputation. See Birney's reminiscences in *Spreading Time: Remarks on Canadian Writing and Writers* (Montreal: Véhicule Press, 1980), pp. 99, 102.

2 Sybil Hutchinson, a former student of Birney's and a writer before going to McClelland and Stewart, sent Birney a copy of *Under the Volcano* and Lowry Birney's address.

304: To Margaret Unwin Hitchcock

P: UBC(ts)

Dollarton, B.C.,
Canada
17 May 1947

Dear Mrs Hitchcock:

In haste, this from Haiti, sent me by the brothers Marcellin – an extract from the French Revue Europe re Masters of the Dew – in case you haven't seen it and it can be of use: it certainly goes to town.[1]

One might make perhaps an interesting point of comparison also with the Marcellin's own Canapé Vert where the Haitian peasant is described as he actually is, as if in 'un rapport de police,' whereas so far as the creation of Manuel is concerned, 'Masters' is more of 'un acte de foi.'

With best wishes,

Yours most sincerely,

Malcolm Lowry

Annotations:

1 Lowry frequently misspelled the surname of his Haitian friends Philippe Thoby-Marcelin and his brother Pierre Marcelin. For Lowry's comments on *Masters of the Dew*, see his 11 April 1947 letter (**294**) to Hitchcock.

305: To Robert Pick

P: Harvard(ts)   Dollarton, B.C., Canada
                                                       7 June 1947

Dear Mr Pick:

I was very interested to learn from Reynal and Hitchcock that you were doing the German translation of Under the Volcano.[1] Though I spent three months in Bonn in 1928 I am not very good at the language, albeit I am a student of German drama and was a friend of Toller's – I belonged to a group that produced Hoppla Wir Leben and The Machine Wreckers for the first time in English.[2] The former having been mutilated by our censor at the last moment we hit on the notion of having two fellows with megaphones at either end of the stage to shout at the necessary intervals: Next 5 (or 6) lines banned by order of the Lord Chamberlain Department, while the action remained frozen, and in this way we felt that we had so far as possible preserved the integrity of Toller's play and at the same time made our Lord Chamberlain look ridiculous.

Be this as it may, do please feel free to write me if there are any questions, or if not simply to alleviate the task, if you feel like it, and I shall be delighted to help where I can, even though I can't translate the title – Unter den Feuerspeindenberg, would it be? You will observe also that there are, partly due to the printer, some little bits of German that need translating into German, let alone English.

You will likewise see the ghost of Wilhelm Meister stalking unobtrusively here and there, and in one spot, the use of boundless and immeasurable longing, making what I believe The Great Man himself might consider to be a subtle improvement upon his own borrowing from Homer.[3] I say nothing about the S.S. Philoctetes.[4] While I am writing all this I hope you are still translating the book and it hasn't fallen through: I feel it ought to be better in German than in English – at all events that cry of the times 'sein oder nicht sein; das ist die frage' has always seemed to me so –[5]

                              Yours very sincerely,

                                                       Malcolm Lowry

Annotations:

1 American writer Robert Pick (1898-1978) emigrated from Austria in 1940. He was a novelist, editor, and translator with an interest in *Under the Volcano*. However, when Micha Verlag in Zürich went bankrupt, Pick was unable to continue. What he did translate is with the Lowry Papers at the Houghton Library, Harvard.

2 Ernst Toller (1893-1939), a leading German expressionist playwright, was branded 'degenerate' by the Nazis. He left Germany permanently in 1933 for Switzerland and England, where his works were translated, published, and performed. During his years in England and the United States, he continued to speak out against Hitler, but on 22 May 1939 he hanged himself in his New York hotel room. *Hoppla! Wir Leben* (1927; *Hoppla! Such Is Life* 1935) and *Die Machinenstürmer* (1922; *The Machine Wreckers* 1923) received several amateur productions in England during the twenties, *The Machine Wreckers* as early as 1923, and *Hoppla!* played at the Gate Theatre in London from October to December 1929. The Cambridge Festival Theatre staged Toller, and Lowry may have been involved in their productions between 1929 and 1932. Toller arrived in London in September 1933 and lived there, off and on, for three years, but I have not been able to confirm that Lowry met him. Lowry's poem about Toller's suicide, called 'To Herr Toller, Who Hanged Himself,' concludes:

> I see your death as no party treason
> Your doom out of time, as good reason.
> Hoppla, wir leben! (*CP* 106-07)

3 'The Great Man' is Johann Wolfgang von Goethe, and Lowry is thinking of *Wilhelm Meister* (1796). Goethe's knowledge of and debt to Homer is well known, from his ideas on epic and dramatic poetry to his view that *Wilhelm Meister* was more an epic poem (after the *Odyssey*) than a novel. Lowry's 'subtle improvement' on Goethe occurs at the end of chapter 4 of *Under the Volcano* when Hugh feels in his heart 'the boundless impatience, the immeasurable longing.' He uses the phrase again in chapter 21 of *October Ferry to Gabriola*.

4 The 's.s. Philoctetes' is the ship Hugh sailed on as a young man (see *Volcano*, chapter 6). Philoctetes, the Greek archer, was wounded in the foot and left on the island of Lemnos when the Greeks sailed to Troy.

5 Lowry's German means literally 'To be or not to be; that is the question,' the opening line of the soliloquy from Shakespeare's *Hamlet*, III.i.

306: To James Stern

P: Texas(ms)   Dollarton, B.C., Canada
                                                  [13 June 1947][a]

Dear old Jimmy:
   Just a note to wish you & your book godspeed. I enjoyed the Hidden

Damage enormously – we both did – & I wrote the Harcourt of Harcourt & Brace of Brace to tell him so. Here's to its great success, from us both![1]

(The only thing one regretted were the brilliant short stories buried therein, that would have had your unique form and those endings that taste like a good pipe after a pewter tankard of strong Falstaff & a hunk of Cheshire at the Ring O'Bells;[2] but that was what had to be, once you had set out. But perhaps you only buried them sitting up like the Indians, & you will get them to their feet, & blow new breath into them at some later date when you feel like it.)

I loved your description – almost nostalgic – p. 89 – 'the falling bodies made no noise.'

(I was trying to write something rather similar, but not so good, in my present woik:[3] seven plain clothes policemen, like men lashed together, stabbing away at each other in the dark in the bar of a forbidden pub in Oaxaca.)

All love from us both to you & Tanya

Congratulations again & best of luck, wherever you may be

Malcolm

Annotations:

1 *The Hidden Damage* had just been published.
2 Falstaff is an American beer brewed in Vancouver, Washington State, and Cheshire is an English cheese.
3 Lowry was working on *Dark as the Grave Wherein My Friend Is Laid*.

Editorial Notes:

a. This single-page holograph, in blue ink, bears a note from Margerie on the verso; she has added the inside address and the month. The envelope has a Dollarton postmark of 13 June 1947 and a New York postmark of 16 June 1947 because the letter was forwarded from New York to Stern's address in Ireland.

307: To Anthony Lespès

P: UBC(ms)   [Dollarton]
                                                    [21 June 1947][a]

Cher confrère,[1]

Hélas, J'ai récu votre lettre genereuse le trois Mai: seulement il y a une semaine!

Aujourd'hui c'est le vingt-un Juin.

Pardonnez-moi, mais celui-ci est ma première lettre en Francais.

Mais pardonnez-moi encore. À bas, Reinhardt! Périssez, Reynal & Hitchcock! Au rancart tous les êditeurs Nord-Americains!

Ma lettre contenie s'explique, – j'espère.[2]

Mais Albert Erskine est un homme honnête: c'est compliqué.

Monsieur Erskine est mon editeur mais il est maintenant avec Random House, n'est pas encore avec Reynal & Hitchcock. Moi-même – c'est possible que je suis un ivre quelquefois, para consequencia lentement, mais j'arriverai toujours avec la boutaille.

J'étais agonisé à lire: 'Rinhardt ne m'a jamais écrit, et j'attends toujours la lettre annoncée.'

Je vous ai envoyé ma lettre à Reinhardt: Je l'ai écri avec l'ironie féroce, mais avec force absolue.

Ah *je suis furieux*! mais je ne suis pas un '*bourgeois*' exactement furieux. Phito comprendra la blague.

Dites-moi à mon bon gallant frère Phi-to que j'ai enfin bonnes nouvelles pour lui-même; bonnes nouvelles, de ses poèmes!

Et dites-moi à Phi-to que je lui écrirai bientôt et la cause seulement pourquoi je n'ai pas avant ecrit – I figure by this time this is such execrable French in which I am writing that I better continue in English:[3] at all events, I have *good news* for Phi-to, but wished to answer his long & wonderful letter at great length, & so to this end, I am studying French.

Meantime, avec Rimbaud, I say to you both:

P.[do] down to the dots.

My letter will arrive to Phi-to within 2 weeks.

Good luck to you

Avec toutes mes sympathies

Malcolm Lowry

P.S. And my wife sends hommage & we both wish to see you again soon.

Annotations:

1 The Haitian writer, journalist, and political scientist, Anthony Lespès (1907-78) was a friend of the Marcelin brothers and one of the artists whom the Lowrys met during their visit to Haiti. Lowry was trying to help Lespès find a North American publisher for 'La Terre et les Hommes'; see his April 1947 letter (**293**) to Philippe Thoby-Marcelin and his 24 June 1947 letter (**310**) to Albert Erskine. The letter from Lespès to which Lowry refers and from which he subsequently quotes is dated 3 May 1947 (UBC 1:36).

2 Lowry appears to be referring to a letter to Rinehart or Reynal & Hitchcock enclosed with the fair copy of this letter to Lespès, but no such letter, or draft, is now extant.

3 Lowry's French is far from fluent or accurate. His main point, however, is that he sympathizes with Lespès, who has received no word from

Rinehart or Reynal & Hitchcock or from Albert Erskine. He goes on
to say that he will be writing to Philippe Thoby-Marcelin with good
news about his poems, and he asks Lespès to tell Marcelin.

Editorial Notes:

a. The only extant copy of this letter is a pencil holograph on the rectos
    of six sheets of 7.5-by-12-cm blue notepad paper (UBC 2:14). There is
    no inside address or date, but at the top right of the first recto someone
    has written: 'P. Thoby-Marcelin 21 June 1950?' Both the context and
    in-coming correspondence, however, indicate that Lowry wrote to
    Lespès on 21 June 1947; see annotation 1.

308: To William Raney

P: UBC(tscopy)   Dollarton, B.C., Canada
                                                        21 June 1947[a]

Dear Mr Raney:[1]
   In reference to yours of March 12 you will be glad to hear I believe
I have now discovered a field for a translation of Phillipe Thoby-
Marcellin's poems, though I am not acting as an agent exactly, simply as
a friend.
   There is another matter in which you could act as the latter to myself,
if you would be so kind. In a telephone conversation had some while
ago with your firm when I was in New York I was informed among
other things that [illegible] of Haiti's most gifted writers – La Terre et
les Hommes, had been refused by your firm and that a letter had been
sent to him to that effect some long time previously. On my plea that
any letters not sent air mail to Haiti may not reach their destination for
many months it was promised that another letter would be sent him
immediately by airmail. I have now had a letter myself from M. Lespès
which that good writer has made the same innocent error of omission
as yourselves, of not sending airmail. Consequently it has taken over six
weeks to reach me, after having, moreover, apparently been returned to
Haiti.
   Albert Erskine, formerly of Reynal and Hitchcock, has expressed himself very interested in Lespès' work and I wonder, since a letter purely of
rejection, would be too galling at this late date, if you would do me the
double favour of (a) sending the MS. to Albert Erskine c/o Random
House, (b) informing M. Lespès by airmail that this has been done.
   It is possible that I am at fault in so far that your firm did offer to put
Lespès' work in the hands of a reliable agent for him and you were waiting for news from me on that subject: Albert Erskine at that time being

my publisher, but in a process of transition from one firm to another, I may not have been able, due to the obliquity of this situation, to make myself clear, while your good intentions were simply waiting upon my concision. And since I had not certain news that Erskine had moved to Random House till fairly recently I was not able to be concise.

On the other hand these things are difficult to make clear at a distance, and in a different language: I hope by now you are in receipt of the brothers Marcelin's new novel, *The Pencil of God*, by all reports I have heard this is even more excellent, if possible, than Canapé Vert, (though not as excellent as they can do).[2] When one considers the great things that Haiti is doing for art and the example they are setting to the world, I am sure you will be the first to consider this favour as a trifle.

Yours very sincerely,

Malcolm Lowry

Annotations:

1 William Eugene Raney (1916-64) was executive editor of the trade department with Henry Holt publishers in 1951, but there is no extant incoming correspondence from him. He may have had an interest in Haitian and French writing; see Lowry's 14 August 1947 letter (**316**) to Philippe Thoby-Marcelin.
2 See Lowry's 17 February 1947 letter (**281**) to Philippe Thoby-Marcelin.

Editorial Notes:

a. This transcription has been made from a poor photocopy (UBC 2:11). The provenance of the original letter is unknown.

309: To Gerald Noxon

P: Texas(ts)
PP: *LLN* 144-45

Dollarton, B.C.
21 June 1947

Dear Gerald:

– I feel very guilty not having written before but I assure you, as you once remarked some years back, it hasn't been possible within the last month.

And when it was I was hoping to get a letter from you, which would have made my P.S. so much longer than my letter that I put it off. Unless you can call the joint letter I wrote you and Fletcher [Markle][1] a letter and now I think the word 'letter' has been used enough, unless I should say that I must acknowledge both yours of May 9 and 25th.

Re the broadcast, thank you for the reviews, for much, and also thank you exceedingly for doing it.[2] I have also received a quite ecstatic letter from Reynal and Hitchcock, or rather Reynal, or rather Kerr of R.& H. about it – and a very enthusiastic one from the Daily Worker, as also excellent reports from elsewhere.[3] So far as I can gather it went off fine, I only hope you got some fun out of it, in spite of the hard work at such short notice – though we were hellishly disappointed not to hear it over the radio, this was unavoidable.

The recording you so kindly sent me got a bit delayed and when we did hear it it seemed it was not made quite *deep* (i.e. on the shellac) enough, though we got a good idea and enjoyed it: we liked it very much on the whole. Sloane's odd interpretation, everyone else to the contrary, was my chief criticism. I know he's a damn fine actor, but I cannot see why he emoted Lostweekendwise so much.[4] He could have just *spoken* plenty of horrors, and poetry too, and it would have been more all right by me: but I guess I reckon without the difficulties.

Re Gilbert Harding: I am sorry to hear of his status and have been re-enquiring re mine in England: it would appear that my money is invested in such a way that I cannot draw any such sum as required out, nor could he even if I empowered him to do so, in England.[5] What was owing to me retroactively was a different matter: but what is now invested has to remain in its present state of investment, I have no doubt a highly unwise one: but there seems little I can do about it, for I guess they now need it: in fact I expect to be borrowed from by them at any moment. For the rest, though I seem to be earning quite hard cash, I haven't even got my first royalty statement yet – taxes would suggest there is more in logging. I enjoyed your broadcast – including Harding's blague – I hope that wasn't what got him into trouble.

Hope you are working hard on Clegg's Wall and to hear more of this soon: we both have great hopes for Clegg's Wall.[6]

I am striving with a more than Volcano, and hard it is, but coming along: Margie has been having a spot of bother with the doctors, and I with my ears (my ear canals are apparently more suitable for a raven than a human being, at all events they go the wrong way) but we, apart from that, are well, swimming and in the old 'rutiny' as Whitey would say – he sends regards.[7]

Herewith my apologies re Harding – but dammit, he'll surely get on.

Re Branches: would you kindly, as a favour to me, dig out 6 or 7 of what you consider the best – maybe the sound of heavy things falling in the night – and send them to A.J.M. Smith, or on second thoughts, send them to *me*, since he's here now in Vancouver and I can reach him.[8]

I know you are ticklish to approach on this subject and may think this bloody cheek on my part, but as I say I am asking you to do it as a favour and you can but say no, or if yes, should any result be toward, can refuse again.

If this doesn't reach you in Niagara, hope it does in Martha's Vineyard.⁹ Hope you are having a swell time there.

God bless and all the best love to yourself and Betty and Nick from both of us.

su amigo
el alter difficilissimo Malc¹⁰

Annotations:

1 See Lowry's May 1947 letter (**301**) to Markle.
2 The reviews that Noxon sent do not appear to have survived, but in his 9 May 1947 letter to Lowry, Noxon concludes that, despite its weaknesses, 'it was well worth doing' because it reached a wide audience and was well received. On 12 May 1947 *Newsweek* noted that *Under the Volcano* was 'too much story for an hour's telling' (69).
3 These letters do not appear to have survived.
4 The American actor Everett Sloane (1909-65) played the part of the Consul in the CBS program. Sloane had played the lawyer Bernstein in the film *Citizen Kane* (1941), directed by Orson Welles; this reputation notwithstanding, Lowry disliked his histrionic portrayal of Geoffrey Firmin. 'Lostweekendwise' is a reference to *The Lost Weekend*, a work that haunted Lowry. In his 4 July 1947 letter to Lowry, Fletcher Markle apologizes for Sloane's performance but explains that for radio it was necessary to overplay the role.
5 The English actor and BBC personality Gilbert Harding (1907-60) was a friend of Noxon's in Toronto. After working in Canada for three years, he was recalled to London, where Noxon feared he would be reprimanded or fired. In his 25 May 1947 letter to Lowry, Noxon asked if Lowry could help Harding financially. In 1938 Arthur Lowry had established a trust account of £12,000 for Lowry, and his remittances came from interest on this trust (Bowker 245). Even after his father's death in 1945, Lowry was unable to gain access to the capital.
6 'Clegg's Wall,' a novel on which Noxon worked for years, was never completed. Passages have been published in *'On Malcolm Lowry' and other writings* by Gerald Noxon, ed. Miguel Mota and Paul Tiessen (Waterloo: *Malcolm Lowry Review*, 1987), pp. 111-46.
7 'Whitey' was Miles Went, one of the Lowrys' fishermen friends.
8 Lowry hoped the Canadian poet, editor, and anthologist, A.J.M. Smith (1902-80) would publish something from Noxon's 'Branches of the Night.' The passage 'heavy things / Falling in the night' occurs in part 1 as published in the *Malcolm Lowry Review* 19-20 (1986-87): 13.
9 Martha's Vineyard is a holiday island in Nantucket Sound, Massachusetts, where the Noxons spent the months of July and August.
10 This mixture of Spanish, Italian, and German translates roughly, 'your friend, the old most difficult Malc.'

309-a: To Dawn Powell

P: private(ts)   Dollarton, B.C., Canada
                                                     21 June 1947

Muy querido Consul Powell:[1]

I am reading, with caracolings, A Time to be Born (what did other men whose lives suddenly came apart like a cheap ukelele? and as for the fears that left only to return by the window; and I particularly like the "brightened" These were the thoughts that *brightened* Ken's nights. Brightened is the precise word.)

That is not to say that it is not spring, that the primroses are not out, and the bluebells, and the skunk cabbages, and the newborn seagulls, and the crabs "millions of life" as my friend Sam says,[2] "a swaillerin' and a stretching of their muscles" and the reflections of sunlight on water sliding down the pines, and the deer with their "hantlers sticking up pretty swimming out toward the lighthouse in spring" and a beautiful sheen and stink of bulk oil over the entire inlet from the neighbouring refineries.

Typographical error: what I should have said is that it was spring, but now is midsummer day, the longest day of the year in fact, and the summer solstice and the highest tide.

A Time to be Born has been read with delight: and so has Angels on Toast: Margie has got off the proofs of her book, Horse in the Sky, to Scribner's, I am at work on another lugubriousness, and have even blossomed, or promised to blossom last spring – hence it is a little late now – as some kind of a poet somewhere or other: at all events rather less lugubriously. We have earache due to over swimming and we have an unfaithful cat. Otherwise we are in good health, in spite of having seen two ravens mating on Friday the 13th of this month.

I thank you for all your kindness and understanding in New York, for the party you so generously gave me and the privilege of meeting you and enjoying your company. We look forward enormously to seeing you again soon. Please give our best to Colburn[3] – with love from Margie and myself,

                         Sincerely

                                             Malcolm.

P.S. Not all cheap ukeleles come apart however: we have on the wall one 10 years old, and we played so hot the other night A.J.M. Smith jumped out of the window.[4] Into the sea, fortunately, where he floated for a while of course. A very sound egg indeed, that one.

Annotations:

1 Lowry met Dawn Powell (1897-1963), an American press agent and

writer, on 26 and 27 February during his visit to New York. *Angels on Toast* (1940, reissued 1990) and *A Time to be Born* (1942) are two of her many novels. According to her biographers, Tim and Vanessa Page, Powell drank as heavily as Lowry, and she described him in her diary as an 'extraordinary devil-angel-demon-child.' Powell liked and had reviewed *Under the Volcano* for the American paper *PM*, 2 February 1947 , 14 , hence the name: Consul Powell.

2 Sam, the Fisherman, was a Dollarton friend.

3 Coburn "Coby" Gilman was a friend and drinking buddy of Powell's.

4 This is a favorite Lowry story; see also letter **310** and Salloum (109).

Editorial Notes:

a. This letter, a single-page typescript with heavy fold marks and a few pencil corrections, was brought to my attention in December by Tim and Vanessa Page. It had been misfiled with Powell's in-coming letters from her editor Malcolm Cowley, but Tim Page recognized the voice as Lowry's.

310: To Albert Erskine

P: Virginia(ts); UBC(phc)   Dollarton, B.C.,
PP: *SL* 149–51   Canada
                                                              24 June 1947

Dear old Albert:

Thank you immensely for your letter, which I think crossed with a pigeon of mine sent winging cryptically through the red forest of the post.

It was super thoughtful of you to send the list of books: the Modern Library always afflicts me with nameless and wonderful senses of early draughts and distillings: McTeague, I think was the first book I ever read, the Seven That Were Hanged the second, both in Modern Library editions, my brother come back from Dallas, gave me.[1] (The Bible didn't come till far later, hasn't yet come indeed, alas, perhaps): Tell me the price – do we get a cut rate? (I don't think the Bible is in the Modern Library.) At all events I sometimes feel you should go back to the floppy edition of those days.

Of course you must know Bob Linscott[2] – a wonderful fellow!

And how is the good Frank [Taylor]?

Margie has her proofs off to Scribner's and I have earache partly due to over swimming, partly due to the fact that my ear canals spiral in the wrong direction and don't even come out in the right place perhaps – so that a doc, aiming to treat same, nearly deafened me instead.

Yes, I was pretty good at golf once, I broke the boys under 15 record, and also later under 18 held for fifty odd years by Johnny Ball (later open champ) in 1924:³ I did the first 8 at the Royal Liverpool (Hoylake) in 28 once in the annual boy's show there when I was 14½, broke down at the 9th a short hole took in six, (still two under actual par so far) but came back in the last 9 in the late forties but still broke the record.⁴ But later I took to socketing and even beer perhaps and dreadful nervous twitchings on the green. When I began to think I was really good I became lousy. But should you care to – er – look you will still find my record inscribed on the wall in the Royal Liverpool to this day: there is a very nice pub beyond the 17th green, on the other side of the road, called The Bull also. My record isn't quite fair altogether because Johnny had to use a gutta-percha ball in them days. But I beat H.H. Hilton's winning score too,⁵ who didn't, and several others who later became amateur or open champs. My record wasn't beaten until some-time in the 30's, balls and clubs were getting better or perhaps even the players: to me, the holes were getting longer and more complicated.

I have been working hard on La Mordida, and that is exactly like those holes: only here I have both to plan the holes and play the game too. In order to make them easier one can make them shorter or what-ever, then one overshoots the green, or cross winds and sheep, ghostly foursomes, arrive from nowhere. Perhaps one should take to tennis again – well, balls anyway. I don't see that this golfing style is very help-ful either: perhaps one should write more like Edmund Wilson in Hecate County, a man who calls a spade a club. . .⁶

For the rest, a very stern crimp in my soul, your not being *there*, so to say; into what roughs, out-of-bounds and quagmires we shall get ere the book be finished, and stymies at the last green, one knows not, there-fore spiritually inscribe our handicap, put it up to twenty-four, and wink some Drummond light from some extramundane clubhouse at the end, else we are lost in the ultimate Hell Bunker.⁷

In effect, apart from not liking the Chief of Gardens too much, the news is this: there is earache, and sundry other health worries on Margie's side, though I feel all will prove triumphantly negligible.

In addition we ran into one A.J.M. Smith, whom you mentioned: we played him the Memphis Blues on the guitar so hot he jumped right out of the window, into the sea however, where he floated for a time, and even came up eventually to ask for some poems for an anthology. A good egg.

Margie has some 50 typed out but I have some more weeding out to do before I can send you any.

I have asked Farrar and Reinhart to send you a book by Antony Lespes entitled La Terre et les Hommes. They had already refused this book when I was in New York but had still failed to let him know to date.

It is in French, but it might be Random's meat. It ought to be some-one's at all events.

Also – what about Marcellin's Tailleur Pour Betes? Marcellin wants to add a story or two to it before they are published.

I have managed to find a field for his poems here at last[8] and doubt-less they will filter through back to America again, I doubt not into some kind of anthological deathlessness somewhere.

All best love to Peggy and Frank and Nan[9] from us both – and of course to yourself.

God bless

Malcolm

Annotations:

1 McTeague is the title character in *McTeague: A Story of San Francisco* (1899) by American novelist Frank Norris (1870-1902), and *The Seven That Were Hanged* (1909) is a novel by the Russian playwright and author Leonid Andreyev. Both works deal critically with social issues.

2 See Lowry's 1939 letter (**119**) to Conrad Aiken and his 5 November 1947 letter (**330**) to Robert Linscott.

3 John Ball (1861-1940), born at Hoylake on the Wirral peninsula, is con-sidered England's best amateur golfer. He played at the Royal Liverpool Club and was the first amateur to win the British Open (in 1890).

4 Lowry's description of his golfing achievements tallies closely with Russell Lowry's account in *Malcolm Lowry Remembered* (19-20).

5 Harold Horsfall Hilton (1869-1942) was another amateur golfer from Lowry's area of Cheshire. Born in West Kirby, he learned to golf at Hoylake and went on to win the British Open.

6 Edmund Wilson (1895-1972), American literary critic and writer, pub-lished a collection of stories called *Memoirs of Hecate County* in 1946.

7 A Drummond light is a strong, incandescent light invented by Captain T. Drummond in the nineteenth century. The 'Hell Bunker' is a 'well-known hazard' (see Bradbrook 153) on the Royal Liverpool golf course and an important symbol in *Under the Volcano* (see Ackerley/Clipper).

8 Lowry was overly optimistic about the fate of these poems; see his 14 August 1947 letter (**316**) to Marcelin.

9 Peggy is Albert Erskine's wife and Frank and Nan are the Taylors.

311: To Conrad Aiken

P: H(ts)
PP: *LAL* 202-03

Dollarton, B.C.,
Canada
24 June 1947

Dear old Conrad:

This ain't a letter exact because I have agrafia and a sore eardrum due to overswimming (the other is doubtless due to overwriting) but just a

Figure 1: *Pious pilgrimages no. 1: strange moonlight at midday or Malc in quest of Conrad's youth in Savannah.*
   P.S. One of the loveliest cities I have ever seen.

Figure 2: *Malc in Savannah:*   Figure 3: *'No, there you are, up*
'I can see you, Conrad.'   *that tree.' Or bull-necked by the*
                                        Baptist Church

Figure 4: *'No, damn it, you're here too'*

In a riverside tavern in Savannah.

From the negro section next door the juke box is playing Open the door Richard.

We are in the 'Whites' drinking your health in claret. (by the bottle & bought retail on the spot.)

St Malc by a (as yet) unstained glass window

Figure 5: *Margie drinks your health in same pub. (The juke box is still playing Open the door, Richard.)*

sort of stop-gap message of cheer, and also of enormous and heartfelt
thanks for your encouraging and kindly words and help and your super-
marvellous last letter which, delivered me by the excellent Bob Linscott,
has me purring yet.[1]

I fear me you have left Jeakes by now and without speaking of how
bloody awful that must have been we just send all prayers and good
wishes that all may be reborn and more than right once more at 41
Doors, though with the hope that there is a faint 42nd at least left open
for your return sometime to Rye.

Margie has a serious and good novel – Horse in the Sky – coming out
via Max Perkins, Scribners, in October: Poppergetsthebotl[2] hit the best
seller list and even a Book of the Monthly Club.

And so, I shall write when I have the wit for it; and meantime God
bless and welcome and thanks again and sincere love to both Mary and
yourself from us both.

Enclosed some photos of recent interesting pilgrimage.[3]

Malc

Annotations:

1 In his 23 February 1947 letter to Lowry (Sugars 200-02), Aiken praised
   Under the Volcano in the highest terms: 'magnificent,' 'marvellous,' and
   'splendid.'
2 Aiken had re-christened *Under the Volcano* 'Poppergetsthebotl'; see
   Lowry's 1947 letter (**297**) to John Davenport.
3 These photographs (see Figures 1 to 5), taken in February 1947 when
   the Lowrys went by bus from Miami to New York, record their visit
   to Aiken's birthplace, Savannah, Georgia. Lowry's comments appear on
   the versos.

312: To Dorothy Livesay

P: Queens(ts)   Dollarton, B.C., Canada
                                                 24 June 1947

Dear Dorothy Macnair:[1]

I am glad to think you may be doing a review of the Volcano, though
sorry to think of your time spent upon it, even if brief, when you might
be giving one another poem. I hope you like the thing though, I myself
on the whole do – I even go so far as to say I think it quite funny, too.

Margie says she will dig out a cut, if one reproducible can be found:
the last one I dug up beams out of Harper's Bazaar this month, two distinct faces belonging to someone with, apparently, elephantiasis of the
left arm and wearing four pairs of trousers.[2]

It was very nice seeing you and your husband again last Sunday week; our kindest regards to you both, and renewed good luck and congratulations.

Yours sincerely,

Malcolm Lowry

Annotations:

1 Dorothy Livesay (1909-) is a Canadian poet and one of Canada's first modernists. In 1937 she married Duncan Macnair, and the couple settled in Vancouver. Livesay was an early supporter of Lowry's work; her favourable review of *Under the Volcano* appeared in the *Vancouver Daily Province*, 16 August 1947, p. 4. In her memoir, *Journey with My Selves* (Vancouver: Douglas & McIntyre, 1991), pp. 167-71, Livesay describes her meeting with Lowry, her use of the Dollarton shack, and her last conversation with Lowry in the winter of 1952; see Lowry's December 1952 letter (**554**) to Livesay.

2 *Harper's Bazaar* for June 1947 contains Christopher Isherwood's 'Notes on a Trip to Mexico' and a cropped photograph of Lowry taken in Mexico, in 1946; see Day (355). The light in this image makes Lowry's arm appear larger than normal.

313: To Alan Crawley

P: Queens(ms)

Dollarton
26 June [1947]

Dear Mr Crawley – [1]

Please excuse the pencil, the family pen only just works, & the family typewriter is being cleaned.

The only reason we haven't phoned is that my wife is having a bit of a troublesome siege with the doctor which I'd hoped would be over by now: nothing grim, but I don't think we'll be able to drop in on you before the end of the month unfortunately, as we'd hoped, though we are both very much looking forward to seeing you again in the very near future.

Chap VII p 219: facilis descensus Averno, it should be simply, – I don't know where the 'est' crept in from – what would Mr Chips have said?[2] Or Virgil for that matter. It being of course verse, not prose:

Noctes atque dies patet atri ianna Ditis;

Sed revocare gradum superasque evadere ad auras,

Hoc opus, hic labor est.[3]

Night & day the portals of gloomy Dis stand wide; but to recall thy steps & issue to the upper air, *there* is the toil & *there* the task!

All our very best regards to Mrs Crawley & yourself, & hoping to see you in the near future.

Sincerely

Malcolm Lowry

Annotations:

1 Alan Crawley (1887-1975) was the publisher of a small West Coast poetry magazine, *Contemporary Verse*. Although totally blind, Crawley edited the quarterly with the help of his wife from 1941 to 1951.
2 The error in Lowry's quotation from Virgil appears in chapter 7 of *Volcano*. Mr Chips is the schoolmaster in James Hilton's novel *Goodbye, Mr Chips* (1934); the character was based on the Leys School headmaster, W.H. Balgarnie (Vol I, photograph 6).
3 Lowry has taken the Latin from John Davenport's 13 April 1947 letter to him, not from Virgil's *Aeneid* VI, 127-29. He repeats Davenport's correction and comment, but misreads Davenport's Latin; the correct first line is: 'noctes atque dies patet atri ianua Ditis.'

314: To Alan Crawley

P: Queens(ts)

Dollarton, B.C.
12 August 1947

Dear Alan:

We put off writing till the last minute, hoping we would get things in shape to accept your kind invitation. But though we have been enormously looking forward to coming I find that I shall still have the sign

HOMBRES TRABAJANDO[1]

outside the shack door, even a week from the 15th, the point being that having now got well away without a soul on the beach we feel we dare not stop till we've come to some kind of halting place – But some time the week after that, or the next week would be fine, if convenient for you, to which end we will with your permission telephone you or drop a note. All this sounds a bit portentous: but the truth is we have both got terribly behind in work and hence have to pay penance.

I enclose a few poems I hope you like enough to take one or two of. Some few of which have been accepted to the best of my knowledge for some kind of world anthology to be published by Scribner's next year – or the second edition thereof.[2] But this would be the first time they had been published for they have seen the light only in the anthologist's eye.

This does not mean they are good, either, and please do not regard this as any moral blackmail to publish them. I hope you like some of them: I can't think of titles to a few of them.

I had long ago planned a volume tentatively called The Lighthouse Invites the Storm: then I called it Wild Bleeding Heart: perhaps you could lump a few of these together and call them Old Two by Fours.

All our very best wishes to you and Mrs Crawley from us both.

Sincerely

Malcolm

Annotations:

1 Lowry's Spanish means 'Men at Work.'
2 Lowry is referring to the second edition of A.J.M. Smith's *The Book of Canadian Poetry* (Chicago: University of Chicago Press, 1948). Smith included seven of Lowry's poems; see Lowry's 23 February 1949 letter (**359**) to Harold Matson. There are no poems extant with this letter, but Crawley published five in *Contemporary Verse* 21 (Summer 1947); see Lowry's 20 October 1947 letter (**326**) to Earle Birney.

315: To Albert Erskine

P: Virgina(ts); UBC(phc)   Dollarton, B.C.,
PP: *SL* 151-53   Canada
                                                          13 August 1947

Albertissimo!

Christ what a breeze! And again Christ what a breeze! And again, how may I thank you. Or how may I presume.[1] What with Studs Mulligan and Buck Lonigan[2] the élan of the captive bulfinch and the dying Antony howling for a drink being hauled up a clock tower in a coalbasket by Cleopatra with ropes – which I never knew, and why didn't Shakespeare use it – and did Dryden, who translated the Plutarch, use it in All for Love – I am all, as the saying is, of a doodah: yes I am all of a doodah.[3] I am in a mammering and at a stay and upon the horns of a Domelia. I thank you. And once again we thank you. Though how thank you enough? We are building a special bookcase to accomodate the beautiful books and the house begins to look really like a home for the first time. You've no idea what a difference it makes and how it causes the Lowry's, not to say the Penates, face to shine.

For the rest, you are right, we have been a bit slack, a bit on the loafing side; though I've written the first of a first draft of Dark is the Grave and have started on the second. I can't make the first chapter come out right, but when I do I'll send it along: in fact I'll try to send it along in instalments, unless my multiple schizophrenia gets the better of me and

I decide I ought really to revise Ultramarine and Lunar Caustic first. Then there are the poems. But we are at least back at a system of work again. And the beach – though we were earlier in the season invaded ('The King of the Squatters') by reporters – is, I dare say on account of this – pretty well deserted.[4] We rise at six and beam at the molten sun and swim as of yore, only even better, save that we have lost our po' guitar in the sea: returned by Laocoon, when somewhat plastered, to Neptune.[5]

For the rest I have no news: my brother liberated the Channel Islands single-handed without a shot being fired, there being nobody there apparently to shoot, my mother sends me the British Weekly and the Illustrated London – or someone sends it for my mother, for they always have 'Master Malcolm' pencilled upon them – and my nephew, a Lieutenant in the R.A.F. has put in a request that his bibulous uncle send him some unused Canadian stamps.[6] Margie's book is coming out, we hope not printed backwards, and thank you very much indeed for the Sewanee Review – the most heartening and encouraging review of the Volcano I yet have read, (albeit I made the slight mistake of reading the Kenyon Review immediately after it).[7]

Lastly I have my usual impractical request to make re the Haitians, the San Domingans and the Doukhobors etc.

To be specific and serious, I have from our friend Philippe Thoby-Marcellin a letter informing me that the firm of Rinehart has turned down his latest book written in collaboration with his brother The Finger of God. Be it not forgotten before I go on that their novel Canapé-Vert won the Latin-American novel prize and that Mr Edmund Wilson thought highly enough of that book to devote a long article to it, in fact he mentioned it the other day again – is, indeed a highly significant book.[8] (I doubt not, indeed, that it deserves to go in the Modern Library) But be these things as they may, it is, for him, quite a confusing and pathetic letter, not the least for being written in French and asking for advice which I don't think I can ethically give him since, so far as I know, Ann Watkins is still his agent. But what seems to have happened is that he sent the book direct to Rinehart instead of to Ann Watkins and Rinehart wrote back to Marcellin – since they knew I'd referred some other work from them to you – asking if they should send it to yourself whereupon Marcellin has written to me asking me should he instruct Rinehart to send it to you and if so would there be any chance you or Random House might be interested to which I can only reply (a) How the hell do I know, (b) I can only ethically try to help with such work as Ann Watkins herself has not been able to place – (I've had some potential success, by the way, here, with the poems). – But all this takes so long and meanwhile the author goes on starving and gnattering upon his isle – I don't think he realises that he's nearer to N.Y. than I am, however. With all this in mind do you think you can find out what's what. One thing at least is clear to me: here is an opportunity for someone to take over where Rinehart have just thrown away a first rate artist. I am in a bit of an ambiguous position. I begin to think that I may, through good but impractical intentions, have damaged his position at Rinehart and Ann Watkins. But this would seem unimportant beside the fact that so far as I can see the Marcellins are now 'loose' and it would seem an honourable venture for some publisher to pick them up. Marcellin is one of the very few first-rate geniuses I have ever met. So could you inquire from Ann Watkins what the situation is, – at least, even if you read not the French, you could cause Random House to get first refusal? Or cause even the Chief of Gardens – perish the thought – to gloze upon it? But if you don't wish, would you please get Ann Watkins on the job for him again? If they sent the thing to Rinehart direct, and now he's asking me for advice, and both these things over Ann Watkin's head, I think it can be fairly ascribed to lack of cash and lack of knowledge of the general procedure. But at any rate the Finger of God and Teilleur pour Bete would be a beginning, a chance for someone to take over and cash in where Rinehart have let go.

In any event – all our very best love to you and Peggy – also to Frank and Nan – thanks a million again

God bless

Malcolm

Annotations:

1 Lowry's rhetorical questions lead him from another echo of *Cyrano de Bergerac* (see his 25 January 1947 letter, **275**, to Erskine) to T.S. Eliot's 'The Love Song of J. Alfred Prufrock':

> Then how should I begin
> To spit out all the butt-ends of my days and ways?
> And how should I presume?

2 Studs Lonigan is the hero of the trilogy about Chicago life, *Young Lonigan* (1932), *The Young Manhood of Studs Lonigan* (1934), and *Judgement Day* (1935) by American novelist James T. Farrell (1904-79). Buck Mulligan is the medical student, friend, and foil to Stephen Dedalus in Joyce's *Ulysses*.

3 Lowry is thinking of the description of Mark Antony's death in *Plutarch's Lives* (1683-88), where the Roman is pulled up to Cleopatra's window by the Queen and her servants. When they have said farewell, he calls for wine and dies. John Dryden (1631-1700) did not use this scene in *All for Love* (1678); he wrote the introduction and dedication,

not the whole of the *Lives*, which was translated from Plutarch's Greek by several hands. Shakespeare did use this material in *Antony and Cleopatra* (1607), IV.xv; his source was Thomas North's *The Lives of the Noble Grecians and Romans* (1579).

4 The *Vancouver Sun*, 1 August 1947, published an article with five pictures under the title 'Wealthy Squatters Find Rent-Free Beach Haven.' Lowry is described as a 'successful novelist who could write a cheque for thousands [and as] "king" of the beach squatters.'

5 Lowry enjoyed this Laocoön reference; see his 5 July 1946 letter (**229**) to Albert Erskine. Neptune is the Roman god of the sea, and during his happiest times in Dollarton, Lowry felt like Neptune.

6 Lowry's elder brother, Wilfrid, a lieutenant with the Royal Artillery during the Second World War, did coastal defence duty and served on the Channel Islands. Wilfrid's son, David, served with the RAF.

7 Robert B. Heilman reviewed *Under the Volcano*, together with other novels, in *Sewanee Review* 95.3 (1947): 488-92, and R.W. Flint's review appeared in the *Kenyon Review* 9.3 (Summer 1947): 474-77. Heilman praised the book, but Flint criticized it as second-hand and lacking control.

8 Lowry is referring to Wilson's review in the *New Yorker*; see his April 1947 letter (**293**) to Marcelin.

316: To Philippe Thoby-Marcelin

P: UBC(ts phc)   Dollarton, B.C.,
                                                          Canada
                                                  14 August 1947

Cher Phito:
    J'étais enchanté à recevoir nouvelles de toi mais je suis très triste que tu m'as ecrit que 'Le Crayon de Dieu' a ete refusé par le mauvais Rinehart. Mais je suis fort confident que l'éxplication pour cette infortune n'existe pas dans le roman; c'est dans les mauvaises fortunes de Rinehart lui-même et, je crois, dans tous les edituers norteamericains.
    Nous avons souffri la même chose. Au soudain personne achetera les livres. Il y a une reaction défavorable dans tous les affaires commerciales. Et malheureusement les editeurs voient plus souvent même dans un chef d'oeuvre un article de marchandise.¹
    Mais toute ma sympathie à toi et Pierre [Marcelin]!
    So much for my bad French – I had meant to write all this letter in French, but I perceive it will take me from now till next week, should I attempt it; but I will try again harder to write in French in the next letter. What I was attempting to say in effect was that I felt certain that the refusal of The Pencil of God had no bearing upon the merit of your new

novel; it is just that there has been a universal business slump in America and it was an unfortunate fact that publishers will too often see even in a masterpiece simply an article of merchandise. That all this is of poor comfort to the author, I well know.

To answer rapidly all your questions. Neither Margerie or I have been too well in health, and we have had a more than usual number of anxieties, but what has been worse, neither of us have been able to write, even to look at a pen for some time, and so have let our responsibilities slip, myself more than she: but we have recovered, the sea is blue and the seagulls crying, and we are now having a new life.

So far as concerns Rinehart, Hitchcock, Erskine, etc. the situation is complicated, as I think I mentioned before, by the fact that Erskine has left Reynal and Hitchcock and gone over to Random House: but I would not be too sorry at Rinehart's refusal. I do not think it is any longer much of a firm, and I am afraid, the same must also be said now of Reynal and Hitchcock.

The best I can do is to write Reynal and Hitchcock, and Erskine; Erskine himself does not, by the way, read French, and his is not the final voice at the larger firm of Random House, but should Random House or Reynal and Hitchcock take it they would certainly pay you an 'advance' I believe; & it would be up to Ann Watkins to get you the most favorable terms.

The next day.

I am glad to report that the above promise has been kept, for I have spent the entire morning writing to Erskine.[2] I thought it better to do this than to cause added disappointment and delay by writing back to ask you if Ann Watkins is still your agent for, if so, I think it was Rinehart's business to return The Pencil of God to her; nonetheless it is possible that you sent the manuscript directly to Rinehart, and not to Ann Watkins *first* to pass on to Rinehart, with the result that Rinehart themselves may be in the dark as to who is now your agent; though here we may give the devil his due, for it is just possible that Rinehart thought that your book would stand more immediate chance of publication by another publisher should some other publisher or publishers show an interest in it before they had given news of their formal refusal to Ann Watkins.[3] At this point I should say that the ramifications of the etiquette (or lack of it) of American publishers are more bewildering than anything in The Castle of M. Franz Kafka; ethically speaking, I can help only with such manuscripts of yours as Ann Watkins has completely failed to place, such as Tailleur pour Bête, or which are out of the hands of *both* Rinehart and Ann Watkins, such as La Négresse Adolescente (of which more later) in the case of Le Crayon de Dieu, the manuscript while out of Rinehart's hands, is not out of Ann Watkin's hands, or if it is temporarily out of Ann Watkin's hands, it is to your advantage for the door to be left open for the manuscript to return therein. Para consequencia, I have taken, as the saying is, the bull by the horns, and instructed the good Erskine thus: to obtain the manuscript from Rinehart, so that Random House will be in the process of reading it when you receive this letter, at the same time asking Ann Watkins permission that this be done, and, in the event of Random House's refusal, unless Ann Watkins has discovered another publisher more interested in the meantime, to pass it on to Reynal and Hitchcock, unless Erskine knows of another more hopeful publisher; in the event of Reynal and Hitchcock's possible refusal, the manuscript would then revert to Ann Watkins again, who would proceed to try to sell it in the usual manner, unless of course she has already done so while all this was going on. I shall also write to yet another person in Random House (if that seems wise). I reminded Erskine of Edmund Wilson's articles about you, of the universal acclaim of Canapé Vert – which I told him ought to be in the Modern Library – of Valèry Larbaud's praise of your poems, of the poor translation of The Beast of the Haitian Hills and Wilson's comments on this, and pointed out that it would be an honorable venture for any good publisher such as Random House – which they know anyhow – to take advantage, while they still had time, of the defection of Rinehart. All this is of course no sure guarantee of success: but it will not be for lack of trying. And anyhow you are sure to succeed in the end. Meantime – pazienza![4] Edmund Wilson mentioned Canapé Vert favorably, but briefly, the other day in the New Yorker, in comparison with another novel – it wasn't my copy – I realise I haven't got you the other copy of Edmund Wilson's other article yet, strangely enough, it is hard to get American magazines in Canada.

Re your poems I have all kinds of encouraging reports from everyone that I have shown them to here who understands French.

At the moment they are with a man named Ira Dilworth,[5] director of the Oxford University Press, a very important man also an editor of a key anthology, and he is extremely impressed and moved by them.

Re my suggestion that they be translated and published, he says that he will discuss the possibilities of doing something such as I suggested with the Oxford University Press while he is in Toronto, adding that he would like to have a shot at it himself, although he might find it a job far beyond his capacity. I think he could do it well and sensitively, though one would have to keep an eye on him.

Meantime he is returning the poems to me. Canadian Verse is very interested, the chief editor of the Canadian Quarterly, who wants to make his magazine more international, is enthusiastic;[6] and I hope – if

Dilworth returns me the poems in time – to show them to an American poet and anthologist, A.J.M. Smith, who is bringing out an anthology of world poetry in America next year and who recently won the prize for poetry given by Poetry Magazine, Chicago.

The only thing lacking so far is a reliable translator with whom one can cooperate or trust: but it is possible, as you see, that I can get some of the poems published singly or a few at once here from time to time, here or in the U.S., and if so I will send you both the magazine involved and the proceeds, if any, usually, alas, pitifully small.

But in regard to this I can only try, and results are likely to be far in the future; I have told you of my English agent, A.J. [Innes] Rose (a poet himself). How does Rinehart stand in relation to the publication of Canapé Vert in England? There is damn little money in England, even more pazienza might be necessary, but Rose might be able to sell it for you not only in England but in Norway and Sweden, occupied Germany, etc., but the real point is, he is nearly my ideal translator for you – one of the most sensitive people I know, and he *thinks* in French. His address is:

> A.J. Rose, Esq.,
> J. Farquarhson and Co.,
> 8 Halsey House,
> Red Lion Square,
> London, England

You could write to him any of your perplexities in French; the only trouble would be that of communication. You'd have to wait so long between letters, but doubtless the problem could somehow be solved. Will you tell me about this matter? But don't hesitate to write him yourself in the meantime if you feel like it. It might be a good idea to send him a copy of Canapé Vert? At all events, all those things are in the line of constructiveness. The main thing is to go on writing, whatever happens.

I'm very sorry you're short of money. I feel guilty for I should have some to spare myself. Unfortunately I spent my advance before the Volcano was published and I have not yet received my first royalties statement. Also we have inflation. A bottle of rum costs here the equivalent of 25 to 30 gourds. And you cannot get a decent meal for less than 7½. While authors are taxed in such a way that should you, like myself, write a best seller one year without having sold anything at all for five years, the successful year is considered to represent your average yearly income. Though we live in a hut on the beach without any modern conveniences and thus escape having to pay rent and electric light bills and are luckier than most people we still can find it hard to live within our means. What is worse, it is – if not precisely illegal under certain circumstances (something I should have to solve if I sell any of your poems) extremely difficult to send money out of this country. I am, also, further away from New York than you are in Haiti so we can share and understand and commiserate with your feeling of 'hope deferred maketh the heart sick'[7] from the very bottom of our experience.

I think that is about all the news. I wrote sometime ago to Raney concerning M. Anthony Lespes to whom Rinehart had broken their promise of sending him an airmail letter: as a result La Terre et les Hommes went likewise to Erskine. I have had no further news of this – nor of Tailleur pour Bêtes. Should M. Lespes be without an agent in New York a reliable one could easily be found – Rinehart had promised to find him one, but broke that promise too, though I do not think I have been very good with some of my promises either. Though I shall try to make amends. M. Lespes forgot to send his letter to me airmail too, so that it was delayed. Please thank him very much for me for his excellent and kind note. I tried to reply at the time in French, but my letter seemed incomprehensible so I delayed sending it. I enclose, however, a copy of the letter I wrote Raney at the time as proof of my good faith: please read it – since it also mentions you – and pass it on, with my compliments, to M. Lespes and tell him I shall rewrite my letter to him as soon as I have time.[8] I think he will be interested, since he was co-advisor on the translation, in that they brought out Masters of the Dew with some praise from myself for Jacques Roumain's novel and the translation blazoned on the cover and of course of this I am very proud. (I also even spotted a few mistakes in the text and got them changed in time!) It has been taken as the Selection for July by the Negro Book Club. At the time of Reynal and Hitchcock's writing me it had sold about 1000 copies in 3 weeks, implying it was having a slow but fairly steady sale.

We have been hoping and hoping to come to Haiti this year and are still not sure if we can or cannot but alas, it cannot, in any case, be as soon as September. I look forward enormously to seeing the completed volume of poems and I am overcome by the honour of your dedicating them to my undeserving self. So far as concerns my own poems Margie and I have still not decided which would suit your purposes best for translation: but we shall send you some soon. Margie's own novel, Horse in the Sky, is coming out in October when she will send you a copy. Meantime we wait in trepidation. Perhaps the sufferings of we authors while waiting for books to be refused or accepted, waiting for letters that never come or come too late, for money that arrives only when it is useless and you have decided to drink yourself to death, for praise or blame that when it comes does no good either, for fame that seems like disaster and failure that seems like fame, can best be compared to that of the condemned prisoners in The Penal Colony of (once more) Kafka.⁹ In this story someone has invented a curious machine for the torture of such prisoners. This machine is divided into three parts. At the bottom is a section called the 'bed' covered with cotton upon which the condemned man is strapped having first been stripped naked and provided with a little ball of felt which he keeps in his mouth to prevent his screaming and biting his tongue. Above him is a contraption like a harrow with needles and above that another contraption that looks like a dark chest with electric batteries and cogwheels. As soon as the man is strapped down the bed is put in motion. It quivers simultaneously from side to side as well as up and down, in tiny, very rapid vibrations, its motions accorded with those of the harrow above him which descends and with its needles writes the man's crime upon his bare flesh. When it has finished the first inscription on the man's back the layer of cotton begins to furl up and rolls the body slowly over on its side so as to present a fresh surface to the harrow. At the end of the second hour the man can't scream anymore so he's given some warm rice and porridge. Only around the sixth hour does he lose his pleasure in eating. All this goes on until the twelfth hour until the harrow spears him clear through and hurls him into a ditch – but even then, we must suppose, if he is – according to our analogy – a writer, and the harrow has been writing 'My crime is that I am a writer' upon his flesh, even then he is not dead. He is just getting ready, so to speak, to write a new novel.

Please give our very best respects to your brothers Pierre and Emil, and Emmanuel (for whom herewith the pictures) and all we know in Haiti. Be of good cheer and please drink our health in a glass of rum.

Je te fais toutes mes affections, et aussi les affections de Margerie

Ton frère,

Malc

Annotations:

1 See the annotation to Lowry's 8 August 1947 letter (**10**) in Appendix 3 to Dr D.K. Kirk.
2 See Lowry's 13 August 1947 letter (**315**) to Albert Erskine.
3 Ann Watkins had been Lowry's literary agent; see letter **119**.
4 The Italian means 'patience' or 'forbearance.'
5 Ira Dilworth (1894-1962), the Canadian radio executive, writer, and professor, was a supporter of the arts and editor of *Twentieth Century Verse: An Anthology* (Clarke, Irwin Ltd, 1945). Although never the director of Oxford University Press, he became national director of CBC radio.
6 Lowry's comments are puzzling. There was no journal called 'Canadian

Verse,' but he may be thinking of *Contemporary Verse: A Canadian Quarterly*, edited by Alan Crawley. Crawley, however, was not interested in publishing non-Canadians.

7　This line is quoted from *Proverbs* 13:12.

8　See Lowry's 21 June 1947 letter (**308**) to William Raney.

9　Franz Kafka's story 'In the Penal Colony' ('In der Strafkolonie' 1919) was first translated into English in *Partisan Review* (March 1941): 98–107 and (April 1941): 146–58.

317: To Mona Harrop

P: UBC(c)　　　　　　　　　　　　　　　　　　　　　Dollarton, B.C.
　　　　　　　　　　　　　　　　　　　　　　　　　1 September 1947ᵃ

[Dear Miss Harrop:]¹

[. . .] It makes me humble and also guilty to think anyone could say such nice things about me. I am now at work [. . .] upon a book that might be called – as it were – *Under* Under the Volcano. Though its title is to be: Dark as the Grave Wherein my Friend is Laid. The friend is the character who appears in the Volcano – a bit inorganically, I fear – under the name of Dr Vigil. He was a composite character and also is a fellow who appears in Hugh's memory in Chapter IV under the guise of Juan Cerrillo. He was a great friend of mine [. . .]² In 1945 my wife and I went to Mexico again to look him up: we found that he had been murdered [. . .] At that time the book had not been accepted, and I had received only discouraging reports. By a coincidence we found ourselves living in the original of the 'tower' of M. Laruelle [. . .] and there, on the same day, brought by another 'character' – the little postman of Chapter VI – I got news of Under the Volcano's simultaneous acceptance in England and America by different firms: it struck me that some imaginative interpretation of such intradimensional coincidences would make a good novel, though apart from the danger of getting buried under its rather Pirandellian masonry,³ what would happen to the author if the interpretation too, like the Volcano, should begin to go into high gear and act like a machine? I find both that prospect and the work itself uncomfortable so perhaps I shall write some short stories about local fishermen instead. Herewith my signature (if not quite the Consul's, whom one would suppose reduced to signing things with a cross) [. . . .]

　　　　　　　　　　　　　　　　　　　　　　　　　Malcolm Lowry

Annotations:

1　Mona Harrop, book review editor of the *Cincinnati Times-Star*, reviewed *Under the Volcano* and wrote Lowry on 6 August 1947 (UBC

1:30) sending a copy of her review and asking for his signature on a slip of paper that she could insert in her copy of the book. She said that she had 'fallen so deeply in love' with the novel that writing the review was difficult. Excerpts from her review were translated into French and published in *Activités Corrêa* 5 (June 1950): 3.

2 See Lowry's 15 May 1940 letter (**140**) to Juan Fernando Márquez and his essay 'Garden of Etla,' *United Nations World* 4 (June 1950): 43-47.

3 Complex blurring of the distinction between fiction and reality is central to Luigi Pirandello's work, which Lowry had been reading since the mid-twenties. See Pirandello's *Six Characters in Search of an Author* (1922; *Sei personaggi in cerca d'autore*, 1921).

Editorial Notes:

a. This transcription is from the excerpts copied from Lowry's original letter by James S. Jaffe in his 14 May 1985 letter to Ann Yandle, head of Special Collections, UBC. The original letter was sold to a private collector.

318: To Dorothy Livesay

P: Queens(ts)
Dollarton, B.C.,
Canada
1 September 1947

Dear Dorothy:

Thank you very much indeed for your very kind and understanding review of the Volcano.[1]

I am at the moment sitting – a too tolerant (omission of comma mine) lover of sun – in the sun, with the guitar off the wall, in the wicked afternoon, reading Poems for People and loving them all.[2]

Hope we shall be seeing you and your husband again soon. Margerie is going through prepublication agonies and fun and myself hacking as ifs and howevers out of a paragraph I know perfectly well in three months I shall discard altogether while betweentimes we put a new roof on our house.

Yours sincerely,

Malcolm Lowry

Annotations:

1 In her review (see letter **312**), Livesay describes *Volcano* as 'beautifully balanced' and like a 'Greek Classical drama.'

2 Livesay published *Poems for People* in 1947 and gave Lowry an inscribed copy in July; he is quoting from her poem 'Abracadabra.'

319: To Jonathan Cape

P: Reading(ts); UBC(ms)   Dollarton, B.C.,
                                                                      Canada
                                                        3 September 1947

Dear Mr Cape:

In reference to an opus entitled Under the Volcano, concerning
which we have not exactly not corresponded before, you may remember that when I first sent it to you, I requested that you get in touch with
A.J. [Innes] Rose, who was my old agent, and ask him to handle it for
me.¹ At that time he was away in the armed forces and therefore, rather
than go to another agent, we felt it better to deal directly with one
another, although you said, I seem to recall, it was a matter of indiffer-
ence to you whether I had an agent or no: and later, in New York, we
spoke of this again.

Meantime, however, various things have transpired which seem to
require that I not only have an agent, but have the same agent in
England both for myself and my wife.

We have, since our meeting, become Canadians, or rather, without
losing our several citizenships, become 'Landed Immigrants', with a status somewhat resembling that of our local Sikh timber merchant, and
therefore have to file income tax in two, if not three, countries and that
alone is sufficient almost to force us to put everything in the hands of
one person in order to keep track of it.

I am hoping to publish some short stories and possibly some poems
in England before long and my wife, besides her serious novel [*Horse in
the Sky*], has some mystery novels, published by Scribner's in America,
which we also hope to publish in England, and so on.

It will be nearly impossible for us to keep track of all these things
unless they are all, so to say, coming through one channel, all the more
so since we are expecting to travel again this winter.

My wife therefore, after taking thought, has decided to put her
English affairs in the hands of A.J. Rose and I definitely feel I ought if
possible to do the same thing, for the combination of the attempts of my
wife and self to help each other through agential confusions with the fact
of our having different agents and publishers – and herself, as it were,
now, two different careers – makes for too great a complication of
letter writing at this distance, not to say redundancies in the letters
themselves – besides it would give me time to go on with my next novel
for you.

I do not know how this will affect our arrangements for Under the
Volcano, for my copy of our contract has somehow got mislaid;² but so

far as I can remember it would be – to begin with – simply a question of my paying Mr Rose 10% of what you paid me and asking him to take over in England from here on, if this of course is agreeable to you. (And him – Ed.)

In that case I would be obliged if you would send him a copy of our contract for his files.

For the rest, I feel I owe you a sincere apology for not having informed you sooner regarding the sales of the Volcano to various foreign countries, although I had only received the contracts myself shortly before the letter came from your Mr Howard,[3] and did not know negotiations were in progress for some, and believed, erroneously as it turned out, that you had been informed of the others. I can hope only that Mr Rose will keep me from involving ourselves in any further such confusions as to the remainder of the foreign rights as yet unsold and which would be still open to both you, and Mr Rose, as well as Matson so far as I can remember our contract, and understand my American contract.

I hope that all this is quite ethical and in order, and if not I can only lean upon your generosity to inform me.

My wife wishes me to thank you sincerely for your offer to send her novel, Horse in the Sky, to various London publishers, which was most generous of you also, but for the reasons recited above you can readily see that it will be better to have everything in one place.

We both enjoyed meeting you in New York and envied you your trip back into the tropics of Cuba from that horrendous climate and we hope you had a very pleasant visit with Mr Ernest Hemingway.

We just landed for fifteen minutes in Camaguey, which was all, alas, we saw of Cuba, save for an endless coastline on our outward trip to Haiti.

Once more let me thank you for all your various kindnesses to us, and I hope that the publication of Under the Volcano may to some extent at least repay – it still seems to be going well in the States anyhow and seems particularly popular, so far as I can gather from my mail, in homes for alcoholics, insane asylums, tubercular hospitals, Southern Universities, among professors, newspaper women in Cincinnati and Miami, and, where it has no business, Chinese revolutionaries in Hongkong.

Yours very sincerely,

Malcolm Lowry

Annotations:

1 See Lowry's 1936 letter (**68**) to Rose and his June 1945 letter (**203**) to Cape.

2 Neither Lowry's nor Cape's copy of the contract appears to have survived.
3 George Wren Howard (1893-1968) was co-director with Cape of Jonathan Cape, Publisher, when the firm opened in 1921. He remained with Cape until 1963 and was chairman of the firm until his death.

The following letter has been written by Margerie with a substantial postscript in Malcolm's hand. It demonstrates her practical responsibilities and her collaboration with Malcolm on the early drafts for October Ferry to Gabriola.

320: To Harold Matson

P: Matson(ts)

Dollarton, B.C.,
Canada
11 September 1947

Dear Hal:

Thank you very much for the statement from R. & H. and the check. Your letter must have crossed mine en route. We have not yet deposited your check for this reason: once we deposit it to our account here in Canada, it's next to impossible to get it out of the country again and you're also likely, as things are now, to lose on the exchange; we are at the moment very seriously considering jumping on a freighter here and going off to Europe for a few months, and we'd then need the money. So would it be possible for you to keep this to our account in New York and send it to us when and as we need it? I hope there isn't anything illegal about this suggestion – I have known of other writers who had their agents keep American dollars for them in America – but if so, just let me know and we'll try and figure some way out of the difficulty. I'll hold the check until I hear from you and if it's O.K. with you we'll send it back to you.

About Monday, I should think, I'll finish typing and mail you a short story Malc and I have written in collaboration. There is a slight lien against this story at Harper's Bazaar, to wit: a while ago they wrote and asked Malc for an article about British Columbia. He replied that he was too busy on other things to do them an article but that he and I together were writing a story laid in B.C. and would that do them? They wrote back enthusiastically and said there was nothing they'd rather have than this story and would we please send it to them. This last letter was from the Fiction Editor, Mary Louise Aswell, so I suppose you'd better send it to them first anyhow, since Malc and I feel we rather have to, as things stand. And anyhow, why not? Well, this opus is entitled OCTOBER FERRY TO GABRIOLA and you'll get it in a few days.

All the very best from both of us

Margerie Lowry

P.S, Hal – it strikes me that October Ferry *might* be suitable for a bigger market – even to the Friday Afternoon Mail – unless I have delusions of ungrandeur – but if you should see such possibilities in it, of course do not hesitate to act upon them, for we have another as good, if more difficult to sell, & also set in B.C, – called Gin & Goldenrod, & almost finished.[1] This likewise in collaboration. For the rest, I sweat away at the other novel, & also contemplate an anthology, King Alcohol, to be composed entirely of novels published in the last two weeks.[2] How would American sale of October Ferry affect Canadian? It is possible we could sell it here to Macleans, but have deemed it advisable to wait. Heartfelt greetings to Tommy & the kids & of course yourself

Malcolm

Annotations:

1 The Lowrys' short-story version of *October Ferry to Gabriola* was sent out by Matson in the fall of 1947, but Lowry withdrew it in February 1950 because he was unhappy with it and it had not found a publisher. He then took over himself and the story grew into the unfinished manuscript that Margerie edited and published in 1970. 'Gin and Goldenrod' is included in *Hear us O Lord*.

2 In his 16 September 1947 reply to Lowry, Matson missed Lowry's joke about 'King Alcohol' and inquired about this apocryphal anthology. He also explained that the Canadian sale of a story precludes a sale in the United States and advised Lowry to wait before submitting 'October Ferry to Gabriola' to the Canadian weekly *Maclean's*.

321: To James Stern

P: Texas(ts)
PP: *SL* 153-55

Dollarton, B.C.,
Canada
17 September 1947

Dear old Jim:

It was swell to hear from you, twice, from the auld sod and Paris both: you gave no address, and I hesitated to write care of American Express in the Rue Scribe (a good playwright by the way)[1] and now I regret not having done just that. But we gathered you would be back by the 11th, and so I and we arise from contemplation of your gloomy and handsome mug upon the jacket of The Hidden Damage[2] – quite indeed the gloomiest I have ever beheld albeit with that part used to be call: character, not to say soul, writ large upon it – to welcome you back.

For ourselves, we are riding rather high. I have gone into a kind of Indian wrestler's training to commit a new opus: Margie's book coming out (did you get the copy she had Scribner's send you?) and we have done some short stories in collaboration, both doing good work: at least we are making the effort. One has even gone some distance toward – in your words – 'purging oneself of one's filthy little fears.' At least we have put a new roof on the house and rise before dawn. It is superb here in the autumn – the only inhabitants, and the tide coming up so high you can dive out of the window into the sea.

Meantime it is queer in this paradisal atmosphere to read the Studs Lonigan trilogy[3] – a monumental piece of self-deliberation if there was one, and about whose merits the critics seem to have somewhat misled a fellow, being a work, for all its monotony and ugsomeness, essentially of the best kind of artistic piety, calculated in every way to make a writer pull up his socks, supposing him to have any.

Meantime also we seem to have a spot of cash, for once, thanks to the good Albert, and subsequent sundry pieces of awesome luck, in fact quite a lot of cash, so this place being really a bit too tough in the winter I had thought to betake Margie and self where it is doubtless even tougher, in short to the place lately vacated by yourself, namely Paris. To which end I wonder if you could give the family any information (we propose to go by freighter, and if possible later shift for a while to Morocco, even look at Italy, before returning here)[4] of this nature: what can you live on in Paris? How far does the franc go or does that matter? Can you live on $200? or does it cost $500? Hotel? Do you have to write for reservations? Is Sylvia Beach still there? Do they demand that you have any set sum of money? General advice. Places to eat, drink, starve; friends alive or dead – or messages to be delivered for yourself, and so forth. Can you get an extension in France on the three month tourist visa procured here? Are tourists in general frowned upon? What not to do: Chesterfieldian council.[5] We both have the status of landed Canadian immigrants so we do not come under the English ruling that forbids travel: Margie still has American citizenship. Since ironically I don't think I shall be able to go to England, that is I could, but it might take too long to get out again, how does the ruling against travel affect Englishmen from England traveling for business etc? In short anything you can think of, or have time for. The Volcano is coming out fairly soon in France, also Norway, Sweden, Germany, Switzerland and Denmark, so I have a sort of raison d'etre for being in Europe: but perhaps it would be a bad idea to mention it.

All our very best love to Tanya – as to Albert [Erskine], Jim Agee, Kazin, Dawn Powell – not to say Djuna Barnes and the windblown [W.H.] Auden[6] – drink a health at the Lafayette – I hope you had a good trip and the very heartiest congratulations on the swell Hidden Damage and I hope it is bringing in the pennies likewise. – where and under what title do I look for the next? (Do not, either, reproach me for liking The Force so much – perhaps if you will examine it again you will see how universal it is. The monotony – the dream – the town that was so much less than its glow – the disillusion, the savage almost creative act of intercourse; a sort of mating with the fissure between the dream and reality. That is a wonderful scene also at the dance, and it remains one of the finest short stories I know, though you have done better, and of course can.)[7]

Hasta la vista

Malcolm

Annotations:

1 Augustin Eugene Scribe (1791-1861), for whom the street is named, was the French playwright credited with writing 'well-made' plays.

2 The dust-jacket of *The Hidden Damage* shows Stern, collar up-turned, eyes averted, and cigarette in hand, looking serious and reflective; see Vol. I, photograph 15.

3 Lonigan is the hero of James T. Farrell's trilogy.

4 On 7 November 1947 the Lowrys sailed from Vancouver on the French cargo ship SS *Brest* to Europe via the Panama Canal; they arrived in Le Havre on 23 December and went on to Paris; they toured in France and Italy before returning to Dollarton in January 1949.

5 Philip Dormer Stanhope (1694-1773), fourth earl of Chesterfield, was a statesman, diplomat, orator, and writer. Lowry is thinking of Chesterfield's *Letters* to his son, which were designed for the education of young men. A complete edition of the *Letters* was published in 1932.

6 Lowry is sending his greetings to a number of American literary people and to the English poet W.H. Auden. Alfred Kazin (1915-), the American literary critic, liked the *Volcano* and was quoted on the back of the dust-jacket; and Djuna Barnes (1892-1982), the author of *Nightwood* (1936), was already a cult figure when Lowry met her in New York; see Lowry's 26 April 1952 letter (**525**) to Clemens ten Holder and his wife for his comments on Barnes and *Nightwood*.

7 'The Force,' from Stern's *The Heartless Land*, is about a man who works at an isolated police station in British South Africa. On holiday in town he finds he is as alone as at his station. On his last night he dances with the wife of an acquaintance, and this leaves him aroused and agitated. The story closes with the tormented man accosting a black maid.

322: To Philippe Thoby-Marcelin

P: UBC(ts phc)
PP: *SL* 155-56   Dollarton, B.C.,
                                                    Canada
                                            30 September 1947

Cher Phito —

The Volcano's eruptions having presented me with a little cash and wishing to share some avec notre frère we hastened to the bank to discover one is permitted to send precisely $50 out of Canada at once — herewith — which may look a little larger in gourdes and which, while scarcely enough to feed the canary, has an almost Bacchanalian aspect when considered in terms of 'trois étoiles'[1] — you will notice that the cheque has quite a number of étoiles stamped on it, 40 in fact, so that it must at least be a good 'brand' of cheque. It is in Margie's name because my money is in her name at the bank, or rather we have a joint account, so that you may take it as coming with love to you from both of us, and apologies that it is so little; but please to drink our healths.

For a cognate reason, alas, we may not come to Haiti this year; England is bankrupt, the Canadian dollar is only nominally upon a par with the American, and without endless and complicated grief it is impossible for a Canadian to cross the border into America with more than $10 in his pocket, and in order to come to Haiti it is first necessary to cross America, unless one should go by boat.

Investigation in regard to the latter is responsible for my saying that we will not be spiritually, however, very far from you after all, for, all being well, we shall be sailing for France in about 7 weeks from Vancouver upon a French freighter. At first we thought that this freighter would be stopping at Port-au-Prince but now the chances of this seem, we are very sad to say, slim. I do, however, have some money in France owing to me that it seems impossible for my agent to get into the Western Hemisphere and taking this into account with the fact that I should like Margie to see Paris and Europe while it still exists, and the possibility also that you yourself may still be going to Paris, it has seemed to me a wise decision.

Revue Fontaine Mensuelle is publishing the Volcano sometime before March[2] and if you are not coming yourself please give us instructions as to whom you would like us to see for you in Paris and what else can be done, and I shall try and see that these instructions are carried out to the letter; in New York I was handicapped by the phone ringing about the Volcano, a terrible cough and the terrible weather, that nearly killed me.

Margie's novel [*Horse in the Sky*] comes out October 6 and we shall send you a copy.

I have had no word as yet from Erskine concerning your work or M. Lespes (or mine) and there is as yet no further news from here: but when there is I shall let you know. Perhaps you will have heard yourself.

I wrote to [Innes] Rose in London concerning you and I certainly hope that you will have good news soon.

Please give our best love to Emmanuel, your brothers Pierre and Emil, the Pressoirs, John the priest, and all our friends in Haiti whom we hope to see again soon in spite of all.

Margie sends you her best love as do I and nous t'embrassons fraternellement.

Sincerely,

Malc

Annotations:

1 Lowry's 'three stars' refers to Haitian Barbancourt rum, which is distilled in three grades, one, two, and five star; see Lowry's 22 January 1951 letter (**438**) to Marcelin.
2 The French publisher working on *Under the Volcano* was Clarisse Francillon who ran Éditions de la Revue Fontaine; see Lowry's first extant letter (**352**) to Francillon.

323: To Mr Seward

P: Harvard(ms)

Dollarton, P.O.,
Dollarton, B.C., Canada
[Autumn 1947]ª

Dear Mr Seward:[1]

I was very touched & honored by your letter and I thank you very much indeed. It also honours me that you should be urging your students to read it [*Under the Volcano*] and that they should be students of William & Mary particularly! I can hope only it does not give them the gruesomes.

But re the matter of the autographed copy I am at a loss. *I have not a copy at all myself* & cannot purchase one because it is not yet distributed in Canada, much to my sorrow & anger, & it is also in America, I believe, for some reason virtually sold out.

So about the best I can do is to sign my name on a separate bit of paper and trust to your brush & paste or glue to do the rest, — if *you* can get a copy, that is.

With all best wishes & thanks again for the honour
Sincerely yours

Malcolm Lowry

Annotations:

1 Mr Seward's letter to Lowry has not survived, but a William W. Seward
   was an English professor at the Norfolk division of the College of
   William and Mary in Williamsburg, Virginia, at this time, and he may
   have been the admirer of *Under the Volcano*.

Editorial Notes:

a. This letter is undated, but Lowry's inability to purchase a copy of
    Volcano in Canada suggests an early fall 1947 date.

324: To Conrad Aiken

P: H(ts)   Dollarton, B.C.,
PP: *LAL* 203-06   Canada
                                                 4 October 1947

Dear old Conrad:
    My God, old chap, I thank you deeply for the dedication of The Kid,[1]
and I simply cannot express how moved and delighted and touched I
am at the honour: in fact I was half way through a letter thanking you
for the book and expressing our and others delight at the poem itself
before I saw the dedication, whereupon I became so excited I had to go
out and chop some wood to pull myself together, whereupon again I
conked myself shrewdly upon the right forefinger with the axe, a feat in
itself, as a consequence of which this letter is rather harder to write than
the other.
    I must say that The Kid was deeply appreciated here by the best poets
of whom Canada can boast – that may not be saying much, but they can
be singularly mean critics – and some like Earle Birney and A.J.M.
Smith are really good – there was a conclave of them here recently, I
flaunted The Western Review at them,[2] The Kid was recited, and their
genuine enthusiasm would really have pleased you.
    Mine too – for I was setting The Kid to music on the taropatch[3] with
a fine hot twing and twang of my own when there came hollers for help
from the sea where A.J.M. Smith's six year old kid had overturned our
boat. After he had been rescued [to] the accompaniment of such avun-
cular comments as shut up bawling, what the hell do you mean by
interrupting us, you're not a man until you've drowned at least once,
the musical Kid was resumed but alas at a particularly hot twing I fell
myself out of the window into the sea, whence strange chords now
sometimes issue, and the guitar was lost forever. (I am getting another
however.)

Anyhow, it's a wonderful poem and I hope your publisher's backsides may have been dually pierced and Sloane's lineament rubbed into the wound by a fine general reaction to it.[4]

For my part, I am hard at work on another opus – three interrelated novels, Dark as the Grave Wherein My Friend is Laid, Eridanus, and La Mordida;[5] Eridanus is a kind of Intermezzo that takes place in Canada between two other pieces likewise set in Mexico, part of which reads, I am afraid, rather like the bizarre concatenations and symbol formations of dementia praecox, noted by Herr Jung – or even Denkwürdigkeiten Eines Nervenkranken.[6]

In this I believe I am really down among the 'catacombs to live,' with a vengeance, but I feel it will come off – it ends in triumph, which sounds pretty meaningless unless you know the why and wherefore, but more of it later. It seems to me to break new ground, though that may be nothing to commend it, even if true. – The penis mightier than the hoe.

For the rest, Poppergetsthebottl is out in England, where it seems to be getting somewhat panned, save in the London Observer, where it has been compared to Heironymus Bosch.[7] (. . . Save for a few kind words by Macarthy, the poor thing fell dead, and me with it. Here, it did rather better.)

(Just the same, I have just heard, 3/5 of the first edition has sold out in 10 days.)

On the other hand it is coming forth with a considerable blast of trumpets in France whither, upon a freighter, Margie and I propose to go briefly over Christmas.

Margie's first serious novel, Horse in the Sky, is coming out on Monday. Though this was, I believe, the last book to be accepted by Maxwell Perkins (with whom I had a fine whiskey fest in the Ritz by the way) she has, apart from that, received not one mumbling word of encouragement in regard to it save from myself and Noxon,[8] and in fact has received only sneers, especially from England, from people who couldn't write a book one tenth as good, which I find very mysterious, for unless I am completely cuckoo it seems to me a singularly fine and beautifully constructed piece of work. It comes to you, under separate cover, as from two pupils in absentia but still studying – and I hope you will approve. Only visible influence of Aiken is perhaps the last word, though perhaps, too, like the captain's horse in the charge account, even if you can't see it it's there just the same.[9] (A phrase about the orange colour of windows at night she arrived at independently as a consequence of which I couldn't persuade her to cut it out. The honesty of the source of my attempt to make her, however, remains rather beautifully in question)

Our house is now storm and rain proof (though the liquor is only seventy-five) — We rise at dawn every day and swim, and generally have an even grander life than before our fire. The village is deserted, there's nobody here but us Schizophoenix, and I only wish you could visit us. If humanly possible we mean to do just that to you sometime within the coming 10 months.

An eared grebe has just sailed past, and we are able to observe the amours of two ravens on a neighbouring dead pine.

Margie joins me in all the very best love to yourself and Mary and here's how and hoping you are very happy and lots of luck, with love and gratitude, from

Malc

Annotations:

1 Aiken's *The Kid*, published in book form in New York in August 1947, was dedicated to Lowry as follows: 'This little Travelogue / for / Malcolm Lowry / as from One Rolling Blackstone / to Another.' Lowry's copy of *The Kid* in UBC Special Collections bears the following inscription by Aiken: 'For the AniMalcolm / with great love / from Conrad.'

2 'The Kid' first appeared in *Western Review* 11.3 (Spring 1947): 133-49.

3 'Taropatch' was Lowry's term for his ukeleles or guitars. The original taropatch is with Russell Lowry's family. For a discussion of the term, see Bowker's note in the *Malcolm Lowry Review* 19/20 (Fall 1986/Spring 1987): 149-50.

4 Aiken's publisher was Duell, Sloan and Pearce; Sloan's Liniment is an ointment rubbed into sore muscles to relieve pain.

5 In his 1951 'Work in Progress' proposal to Albert Erskine (UBC 32:1), Lowry envisioned *Dark as the Grave*, 'Eridanus,' and 'La Mordida' as a trilogy within his proposed sequence *The Voyage That Never Ends*; see the introduction, 'Withdrawal and Return,' pp. 2-3. *Dark as The Grave* was published posthumously in 1968, and 'Eridanus' was absorbed into *October Ferry to Gabriola* (1970), but 'La Mordida,' at over twelve hundred pages of manuscript and typescript (UBC 13 and 14), is unpublished.

6 *Denkwürdigkeiten eines Nervenkranken* is the title of Dr Daniel Paul Schreber's memoir published in Leipzig in 1903. Schreber's account of his mental illness became well known as a result of Sigmund Freud's 1912 paper on paranoia, first translated as 'Psycho-Analytic Notes upon an Autobiographical Account of a Case of Paranoia (Dementia Paranoides)' in 1925. In his discussion of Schreber's memoir, Freud uses the complete German title and frequently refers to it as 'the *Denkwürdigkeiten*,' and he quotes at length from Schreber's text. Freud uses the Schreber case to argue for the roots of paranoia in latent or repressed homosexuality, and he describes the symptoms, hallucina-

tions, projection (hearing voices), and feelings of persecution, in detail. See volume 12 of *The Standard Edition of the Complete Psychological Works of Sigmund Freud* (1953).

Schreber's *Denkwürdigkeiten* was not fully translated into English until Ida Macalpine and Richard A. Hunter published *Memoirs of My Nervous Illness* (London: Wm. Dawson & Sons, 1955); Lowry must, therefore, have read about it in Freud. However, Macalpine and Hunter argue convincingly that Freud overemphasized homosexuality as the explanation of Schreber's belief that he was destined to be transformed into a woman; certainly, it is possible to see more than repressed homosexuality in the passages Freud quotes. Carl Jung was also familiar with the Schreber material; however, Lowry seems to be referring here to *Psychology of the Unconscious* (1912; trans. London: Kegan, Paul, Trench, Trubner, 1916), which contains Jung's discussion of the Miller memoir and many topics from mythology and symbolism that recur in Lowry's work. The degree of Lowry's debt to Schreber (via Freud), Freud, and Jung, whether in the 'Eridanus' material (later *October Ferry to Gabriola*) or in other work, is yet to be explored.

7 See Lionel Hale's 'Delirium,' *Observer*, 21 September 1947: 'The prose is Hemingway-plus-lava, with an added pictorial sense that can be horribly remniscent [sic] of Hieronimus Bosch' (3). The 'Macarthy' Lowry mentions in the next sentence may be the English critic Desmond McCarthy, but we have not located a 'few kind words' by him.

8 In November 1943 the Lowrys sent a typescript of Margerie's novel to the Noxons, and in a 13 December 1943 letter Gerald Noxon commented upon it in detail; see Tiessen, *The Letters of Malcolm Lowry and Gerald Noxon* (63–68).

9 The last word of *Horse in the Sky* is Dungarvon, the name of a character in the novel, and Aiken concludes *Blue Voyage* with a character's name: Faubion. Lowry may also be alluding to Tennyson's 'The Charge of the Light Brigade' (1854). Contemporary accounts blamed the disaster at Balaclava on a blunder by the commanding officer; in the poem neither the officers nor their horses are mentioned.

325: To Conrad Aiken

P: H(ms)
PP: *LAL* 207

[Dollarton]
[1947][a]

– the margeries and the malcolms did
so bugger the squawks from the fools who chid –
who all seem singularly full of shid
– We liked the Kid, we loved the Kid.[1]

[unsigned]

Annotations:

1   Aiken's long poem *The Kid* had received harsh criticism from reviewers. The Lowrys' supportive quatrain is a parody of the refrain in part one of the poem.

Editorial Notes:

a.   This note, in Lowry's hand, is on a small slip of paper in the Aiken Collection at the Huntington Library.

326: To Earle Birney

P: UBC(ts)

Dollarton, B.C.
20 October 1947

Dear Earle:

I'm afraid we'll have to put off our appointment for next Thursday to some later date, Margie having acquired, alack, one of her two yearly colds which, since it makes me the cook is doubtless on its way to being aggravated by stomach ache: but it would be in any case better to postpone it till after the street car strike – as I write I don't know whether the street car strike has come off but what I do know is that buses here have gone independent and haywire – the other day I had an appointment with Margie in town re the Consul and also a French lesson and I waited three quarters of an hour in the rain for a bus which didn't come. I was raising hell on the phone in the store with the bus company when the milkman said he'd seen the bus at more or less the right time on the Northlands road – thus it was a wayward bus, the driver'd just taken it into his head not to come to Dollarton at all (whence it's supposed to make a detour when it goes to Northlands) but it had turned off at Strathcona. (I arrived in town, finally, with the milkman, having made all the rounds.)

I perceive various Homeric arrows of ours glistening side by side on the Crawley fairway – to twist meanings a little.[1] I very much like *New Brunswick* – first place I ever landed in Canada. St Johns. Not being acquainted with maps in those days I thought I was in Newfoundland but I see from your description New Brunswick is where I was all right.[2] A peculiar feather in one of my arrows I didn't put there – stranger for stronger. Perhaps a subtle improvement. By God, I am getting stranger every day! Or every day in every way I am getting bitter and bitter.[3] You must have given the Consul something pretty potent on our behalf – the French one I mean – for he all but fell on our necks, so that the visa 'It ees een ze bag' as they put it.[4]

Een ze bag, that is, if we don't have wayward boat too. But thank you very much indeed!

I am working hard on my little erudanus – can't make head or tail of it so far, but doubtless it will come fairly all right after it has been burnt and lost a few times more and had its theme completely changed.

Best love to Esther and Bill from us both.[5]

Malcolm

Annotations:

1 Lowry and Birney appeared side by side in Alan Crawley's *Contemporary Verse: A Canadian Quarterly* 21 (Summer 1947). Lowry's poems were: 'Salmon Drowns Eagle,' 'The Glaucous Winged Gull,' 'Stoker Tom's Ukelele,' and two untitled lyrics, 'The poignance of a quarrel in the past' and 'This evening Venus sings alone.' Birney's poems were 'New Brunswick' and 'Ulysses.'

2 St John's is the capital of Newfoundland; however, Lowry may have docked in St John, New Brunswick, on his return to England after visiting Conrad Aiken in Boston during the summer of 1929. Lowry sailed on the ss *Cedric* in September 1929, and White Star Line vessels like the *Cedric* stopped regularly at St John.

3 Lowry is punning on the Émile Coué expression 'Every day in every way, I get better and better'; see his June 1926 letter (**13**) to Carol Brown. For Lowry's correction of 'stranger for stronger' in his poem 'The Glaucous Winged Gull,' see his 26 October 1947 letter (**327**) to Alan Crawley and his 29 April 1957 letter (**708**) to Ralph Gustafson.

4 The Lowrys were preparing for their trip to France; see Lowry's 17 September 1947 letter (**321**) to James Stern.

5 Esther is Earle Birney's first wife and Bill is their son.

327: To Alan Crawley

P: Queens(ts)

Dollarton, B.C.
26 October 1947

Dear Alan:

Thank you very much for sending the copy of Contemporary verse and I feel very vile for not acknowledging it sooner. I was delighted by it and all its contents – and herewith our subscription.[1]

We are most disappointed not to have seen you and Mrs Crawley too but we have not stirred since seeing the Smiths: Margie hoped to see Mrs Crawley at the Macnair's for lunch one day but the engagement was postponed and then there has been the strike:[2] thank you very much for the remarks re the poems and also the Volcano which is now being translated into Italian but we are both being driven *nuts* by income tax and myself by the discovery of how much some of the philosopher Heidegger's thought – which I suppose I shall now have to read – parallels that of the next opus which, being a virtual psychoanalysis of the Volcano itself among other things strikes me as being quite crazy enough as it stands,[3] if it did stand, which at the moment it doesn't: my wife's book, Horse in the Sky, is just out, Scribner's, and we have been dithering and free-floating in a general author's anxiety – or is it the anxiety that floats – for some time.

I will try and send you some more poems and I hope you will find them suitable and I also want to send you some of Gerald Noxon's (by the way there is a small misprint in the Glaucous Winged Gull, I wrote, a memory stronger than childhood even – but perhaps stranger is a subtle improvement; it builds up, so to say, though perhaps leaves too many strangers, the harmless assonance was unintentional.)

I am now about to throw myself straight into the sea on the matter of this income tax, where I shall swim for a time at least, do not be alarmed, this is but a daily habit – we look forward to seeing you again soon – congratulations always on the magazine

With our best wishes to you and Mrs Crawley,

Malcolm

Annotations:

1 Five of Lowry's poems appeared in *Contemporary Verse* 21 (Summer 1947): 3-5; see Lowry's 12 August 1947 letter (**314**) to Crawley and his 20 October 1947 letter (**326**) to Earle Birney.
2 The Smiths are Arthur J.M. Smith and his wife, Jeannie, and the Macnairs are Dorothy Livesay and her husband Duncan Macnair.
3 Lowry may be finding parallels between the theme of *Dark as the Grave* and theories of ontology and language in the work of the German philosopher Martin Heidegger (1889-1976).

328: To Dr A.F.B. Clark

P: UBC(ts phc)   Dollarton, B.C.
                                                           26 October 1947

Dear Mr Clark:[1]

It was most awfully nice of you to send me the Times Lit Supplement with the review in it.[2] Strangely enough the cross you made upon the review went right through on to the other side where there was a long commentary upon Dostoievsky which while it had its demerits most precisely informed me upon several things I was just on the point of writing.

Both my wife and I enormously appreciated meeting Mrs Clark and yourself that afternoon and we have often spoken of it since and look forward to the time we can meet again.

We miss Downie and Marjorie [Kirk] here and it is too bad they cannot be here, at this the best time of year.

I know Downie will forgive me for saying this, that while he has a little better view of the shipping hereabouts we, further down, have a little better view of the oil refinery: today it was very grand, in fact scalloped, I mean the sky, a sort of Van Gogh business in fierce waves,[3] but remote and silver and full of dives and whorls like the Great Dipper (now to be torn down) in the Fairground, against which the mountains showed an almost shocking serge blue: and with what looked like a 1918 Haley page areoplane[4] struggling against the wind very very slowly, with seagulls soaring and an old gasoline can banging under our house in the choppy sea of a high tide. (Mem: why not a book called simply 'Purple Passage'?)

I have been reading the Modern Library translations of Pushkin, yours are far the best, in [fact] nearly the only. I guess he is [a] hard old bird to translate. Edmund Wilson did one good one of the Bronze Horseman: you and he should share the second edition of any such volume.[5]

It was a dirty trick of Salieri to bump off Mozart, if indeed he did: but the business of identification between artist and artist seems to have been overlooked by dramatists – what about Keats dying, as someone I believe has somewhere half suggested, almost *consciously* identifying himself with the death of Chatterton: that would have been another interesting murder perhaps, had Chatterton lived.[6]

We hope and wish you will drive out here sometime, anytime indeed, when you feel like turning off, when there is not too much rain – or even when there is, but preferably not too much – preferably with a little light in the sky and a high tide.

All the very best to you and Mrs Clark from my wife and myself, and thank you again for your thoughtfulness in sending me the Times Lit Sup.

Yours very sincerely,

Malcolm Lowry

Annotations:

1 Dr Alexander Frederick Bruce Clark, FRSC (1884-1975), a professor in the Department of Modern Languages at the University of British Columbia from 1917 to 1949, was a scholar of seventeenth-century French literature and a translator of Russian poet and dramatist Aleksandr Pushkin.

2 The *Times Literary Supplement*, 20 September 1947, 477, carried an anonymous review of *Under the Volcano*. The reviewer was complimentary, describing the novel as full of 'great imaginative power.'

3 Lowry's description of the sky recalls many of the canvases of Vincent Van Gogh, and Van Gogh is still in Lowry's mind three days later; see his 29 October letter (**329**) to Albert Erskine.

4 Handley (not Haley) Page was the English manufacturer of a famous line of airplanes. The Handley Page 400 and 1500 were effective bombers during the First World War.

5 Dr Clark translated 'The Covetous Knight,' 'Mozart and Salieri,' and 'The Stone Guest' in *The Poems, Prose and Plays of Alexander Pushkin*, ed. Arrahm Yarmolinsky (New York: Random House, 1936). Lowry's following comment about Salieri and Mozart is in response to Clark's translation of Pushkin's play. Edmund Wilson published his translation of Pushkin's 'The Bronze Horseman: A Petersburg Tale' in *New Republic* 93 (26 January 1938): 332-34; it was reprinted in *Triple Thinkers: Ten Essays on Literature* (1938).

6 Antonio Salieri (1750-1825), the Italian composer, is chiefly remembered for intriguing against Wolfgang Amadeus Mozart (1756-91). The legend that Salieri poisoned Mozart, however, has been discredited. The linking of Keats's death with Chatterton's was suggested by Lowry himself in his 8 September 1931 letter (**35**) to Nordahl Grieg.

329: To Albert Erskine

P: Virginia(ts); UBC(phc)   Dollarton, B.C.,
PP: *SL* 156-57, *Lln* 193-94   Canada
                                                              29 October 1947

My dear revered old Albert:

I write to you, with a scalloped sky outside and clouds like a downswirl of shark's fin, or even the Great Dipper, Van Gogh proved true in grey and winter and against a remote ploughed hurricane, a ramshackle plane flying very slow, and against that, what's more, the mountains showing an obscene sort of serge blue, and an old gasoline can banging under the house, and other purple passages I won't bother you with (to say nothing either of the two ravens, making love on Friday the 13th on the gigantic dead fir tree) and just now, a rainbow going up like a rocket.

Well, at all events I am writing because there is news. I shall leave the more pressing for the last, meantime I am writing what fairly can be described as a good book – I'm not sure, of course, precisely, being a kind of sidestreet to my own consciousness; however, the report of what is going on from my own point of view would seem to be pretty good, as an objective observer I would like to wander some miles to queue up, as a subjective one I would say without any qualification at all that it is tremendo siniestro: at all events, pazienza – you will receive it in driblets, I will have a time to go through before I finish and some of what I send you may seem a little wild.[1] We progress towards equilibrium this time instead of in the opposite direction, and the result is considerably more exciting, if not even more horrible, more 'inspiring' is probably the word.

Re Margie: the poor girl really does have a problem. On top of everything else, Perkins died, his promises therefore seem to have gone vacant.[2] The last thing, (you know the rest) in Perkins correspondence with Margie is that the book would have a fair chance. Here is some estimation of what fair chance her book has got, from the Publisher's Weekly: 'The drama of a maid-of-all-work in a rural Michigan family. Thurles Dungarvon inherits a fortune and thereupon starts to indulge her dreams of being a great lady and of owning a stable full of horses.' My God – a publisher might as well have said of Wuthering Heights 'Boy loses girl on Yorkshire moors and is then free to indulge his dreams of making a fortune and becoming a first class bugger.' – though it would at least have given the book some snob appeal. I myself think Horse in the Sky is a pure, beautiful and lucid thing and an excellent work of art. Margie has not had one single review or a word from anyone in New York and we feel that this state of affairs can only be caused because Scribner's didn't even bother to send out any review copies, or if they did they sent them in such a way that the book was so presented that nobody bothered to read it. This is doubtless due to the confusion resulting at Scribner's from the death of Perkins, but what can one *do* about it? I propose to write myself to some of the reviewers and call their attention to Horse in the Sky, not in the manner of a husband taking up the cudgels for his wife, but quite objectively, to call their attention to a brutal injustice done to a writer, and to a good book.

All love from us both,

Malcolm

Annotations:

1 The 'good' book is *Dark as the Grave*, which Lowry describes, in correct Spanish, as 'terribly sinister.'
2 Maxwell Perkins, the famous editor with Charles Scribner's Sons, had intervened personally in the treatment of Margerie's manuscripts; see Lowry's 15 September 1946 letter (**246**) to Perkins.

330: To Robert Linscott

P: Virginia(ts)

Dollarton, B.C.,
Canada
5 November 1947

Dear Bob:¹

Ah, what a lonch, what a wonderful lunch, what a marvellous lunch that was.² I hope you are well: we are, and off to France day after tomorrow on a freighter.

Myself am hard at work and also being translated into double Dutch.

Margie's book came out a month ago. Horse in the Sky, (Scribner's) Margerie Bonner. This was one of the last books taken personally by Maxwell Perkins: he died while still in correspondence with her on the subject. He thought highly of it, he told me, unfortunately the publishers seem to have confused it with her detective stories. No single review — no wonder, the blurb is enough to make you run a mile. Only this in the Publisher's Weekly: 'Drama of a maid of all work in a rural Michigan family. Thurles Dungarvon inherits a fortune and begins to indulge her dream of being a lady and owning a stable full of horses.'

I don't know if you would like it: myself, I think it is a work of genius. It is, anyhow, a serious book, in spite of any naivete of facade, an Aeschylean tragedy of hatred and revenge, and it certainly deserves some notice. I feel all this is horribly unfair (how much more than horribly on top of everything else Scribner's have done to her is perhaps irrelevant) it deserves a break, and I have written you to ask you humbly if you could possibly use your influence to see it reaches someone intelligent. I didn't send you any poems because I don't like them but I'm working like fun.

Love from both. God bless

Malcolm

Give my love to old Conrad, should he be rooting around. I hope no forest fires in his direction. Ugh!

Annotations:

1 Robert Linscott (1886-1964), an editor with Houghton Mifflin in Boston from 1904 to 1944, was Conrad Aiken's editor and close friend. In 1944 he moved to Random House in New York, where he was senior editor until 1957.

2 Lowry is referring to a meeting with Linscott during his February 1947 visit to New York.

331: To Albert Erskine

P: UBC(ms)   [Dollarton]
                                    [7 November 1947]ᵃ

Dear Albert –
  in mad haste – we are sailing today. Here are some poems, finally.
Malc doesn't want some of them published because he feels them derivative, etc. But can you look them over & let him know what you think?
American Express, Paris –
                    God bless – love –
                                            Margerie

Very few of these poems – with the possible exception of the Sestina
{ah that damn jonquil colored dawn of Faulkner's again – }¹ – are any
damn good at all: it pains me indeed to send them to you, but Margie
feels easier in her mind if you have them, though I personally hate to
trouble you with them. The Sestina & a few others have been published
in Canada – the poor editor is stone blind, he was glad to have them,
& I gave them him for free, figuring he wouldn't be able to read them
anyway²
                    God bless
                                            Malcolm

[P.S.] I have literally 1000's of fragments but I should spend at least a
year on them exclusively: can't concentrate while working on present
book.

Annotations:

1 See Lowry's 30 June 1946 letter (**228**) to Erskine about the use of the
   word 'jonquil' and the possible echo of Faulkner's *The Hamlet* (1940).
2 Alan Crawley, editor of *Contemporary Verse*, published five of Lowry's
   poems during 1947; see Lowry's 20 October 1947 letter (**326**) to Earle
   Birney. 'Sestina in a Cantina' appeared in *Canadian Poetry Magazine* 11.1
   (1947): 24-27.

Editorial Notes:

a. The only extant copy of this joint letter, written just before the Lowrys
    left for their trip to France, appears to be this holograph (UBC 7:2). The
    letter is filed with a typed sequence of poems called 'Poems of the Sea'
    that largely coincides with Scherf's listing for that title. The poetry type-
    script carries some pencil notations by Lowry with pencil comments by
    Erskine and a few changes in Margerie's hand. It *may* be the typescript
    of poems enclosed with this letter.

332: To John Davenport

P: UBC(ts)
PP: *SL* 158

[ss *Brest*]
[November 1947]¹

Dear Old Davvy: –
– Am writing this rolling down the Californian coast, being followed by three black albatross, each an iron bird with sabre wings. Evidently practicing to be a left wing three-quarter: yesterday we found a dead stormy petrel on the bows, with blue feet like a bat: occasionally a large black oil tanker glistens by, empty as the Marie Celest:¹ and there tend to be golden sunsets in a blue sky.

Apart from that I have no certain news, save that we are supposed to be coming to France, but evidently not so directly as one thought: we are stopping at Christobal, and Curacao; and evidently also going to Antwerp;² we have the Chief Gunner's cabin, and so far as I know we should be in Le Havre on or about Xmas Eve.

The Brest is a freighter of the 'French Line' – but seems to have a different agent in each port: but no doubt you could find out by letter from the French Line itself in Le Havre more certainly than we when we *do* arrive.

The Foreign Control Board in Canada proved very tough – and it got far tougher just the last six weeks when we were negotiating with them – so we're a good deal shorter on the finances than we thought we'd be: however we'd decided to go, so we are going, and I guess we'll get by – but almost certainly not in England, so far as I know, yet.

However we live in hopes of seeing you somehow, somewhere.³ I find the sea intimidates me somewhat, for the first time: too big.

TO ABANDON SHIP⁴

Le signal d'abandon est donné par 6 coups brefs suivis d'un coup long. A ce signal vous embarquerez dans le canot No 1 Tribord ou 2 Babord.

Selon la direction du vent
Your lifebelt is in this stateroom
Put it on as you would an ordinary jacket.
All the best to you and your Marjorie from us both
God bless

Malc

Annotations:

1 The *Marie Celeste* is one of the most celebrated ships of marine history. She sailed from New York in November 1872 and was discovered a month later floating off the Azores entirely empty but otherwise

undamaged. Her crew had vanished, apparently having abandoned the ship in a hurry, and the mystery of their fate has never been solved.

2 Cristobal is a coastal town in Panama, and Curaçao is an island of the Lesser Antilles in the Caribbean Sea.

3 The Lowrys arrived in Le Havre on 23 December 1947 and proceeded to Paris. John Davenport arrived a few days later, and he and Lowry, who had not seen each other for over a decade, celebrated by going on a drinking binge.

4 Lowry copied the following instructions for abandoning ship into his notebook and used them in 'Through the Panama' from *Hear us O Lord*.

Editorial Notes:

a. This transcription is from a typescript (UBC, 2:11) that appears to be a copy made by John Davenport of Lowry's original letter, which has not been located.

333: To John Davenport

P: UBC(tsc)
PP: *SL* 159-60

[ss *Brest*]
[November 1947]ᵃ

S.S. Brest
– Going down the Gulf of Darien – ¹

Dear Old Davvy: –
Silent on a peak in Bragmann's Bluff. . .
Silent on a peak on Monkey Point. . . .²
The only passenger besides Margie and myself, a gentleman of the name of Charon: doubtless you have made his acquaintence on another plane?;³ here he functions as Robert Charon, Consul of Norway. Papeete, Tahiti, Society Islands – has rather a gutteral laugh, I think he is a Turk.
Or death takes a holiday, on a Liberty ship.⁴
We have also had four albatrosses, one, caught, on board: another huddled on the foremast, its great beak, from the captain's bridge, gold moving in the light: when its beak was there it made a third light.
The little caught albatross sat on the afterdeck, with its red feet, and blue enamel beak.
M. Charon would not come to see the albatross but stood on deck peering with a wild surmise⁵ at something he perhaps took to be a ferry, (through a pair of binoculars which, doubtless because they were mine, did not work).

So far so good – except that I forgot the water: Chacun est *prié* d'e-conomiser l'eau attendu que nous ne pouvons pas nous en approvisionner avant Rotterdam. En cas ou le gaspillage serait trop grand, nous serions obligés de rationner l'eau.

Le signal d'abandon est donné par 6 coups brefs suivis d'un coup long.[6]

Your lifebelt is in this stateroom.

Put it on as you would an ordinary jacket.

Your arms through the shoulder straps.

(Why do you not turn up the collar of your coat?

November 29th
(1929)[7]

– I mean 1947. Do not be afraid Monsieur Lowry, he is the ancient mariner, said the steward, to Mlle Zaza – wife of Salvadorean new passenger, who has no overcoat at all.

Bananas trees – you like? Many bananas trees.

In short we are having a very wonderful voyage – quite beyond experience indeed, that is, at least, mine: we shall be passing south of Hartland some time within the next 2½ weeks – the French government has fallen in the meantime, so perhaps we shall turn the ship around and go to Tahiti after Mr Charon. Somewhat prudently perhaps, we are going to Rotterdam first: hope (sic) to be in Le Havre on Xmas Eve, I hope too to see you and your Marjorie waving at us from the dock, even if it is but a hope; since, so far as I can see, you cannot possibly be there we shall tokenly wave just the same – please write: S.S. Brest, the French Line, Les Consignaires Rennis, Boite Postal, no 865, Rotterdam, Hollande (thank you) – where the ship's strange dream it is to be on December 18th.

Wonderful skipper on this ship, engineers, seamen, cats, stewards, pinard

God bless you both from us both

Malcolm

Please congratulate Wynyard for me, give both him and John Sommerfield my love and thanks;[8] I am suffering from a slight surfeit of flying fish at the moment which is hard on the prose.

Anyhow you can keep posted about the peculiar progress of the S.S. Brest – which rarely rolls more than 35 to tribord or babord – by keeping in touch with the office of the French Line in London.

Pity about the pinard.[9]

Annotations:

1 The Gulf of Darien is part of the Caribbean Sea on the north coast of South America between Panama and Colombia. Here, and in the following lines, Lowry is parodying the last line of Keats's 'On First Looking into Chapman's Homer' (1816):

> Or like stout Cortez when with eagle eyes
> He stared at the Pacific, and all his men
> Looked at each other with a wild surmise –
> Silent, upon a peak in Darien.

See also Lowry's use of the lines in chapter 9 of *Under the Volcano*.

2 Bragman's Bluff and Monkey Point are on the east coast of Nicaragua. Lowry used these lines in 'Through the Panama.'

3 Charon is the boatman from Roman mythology who ferries the souls of the dead across the river Styx.

4 The 1934 film *Death Takes a Holiday*, directed by Mitchell Leisen, is based on the 1929 play adapted by Walter Ferris from an Italian play by Alberto Casella.

5 See annotation 1.

6 These shipboard instructions read: 'Everyone is urged to economize on the use of water because a fresh supply will not be available until Rotterdam. If wastage is too great, water will have to be rationed. The signal to abandon ship is six short and one long whistle blasts.'

7 'Why do you not turn up the collar of your coat?' is the last line of Davenport's poem 'Winter Overcoats.' The poem, dated 'November 1929,' not 'November 29th 1929' as Lowry implies, was published in the undergraduate anthology *Cambridge Poetry, 1930* (London: Hogarth Press, 1930): 28-33. Davenport, who co-edited *Cambridge Poetry* with Hugh Sykes Davies and Michael Redgrave, published Lowry's poem 'For Nordahl Grieg Ship's Fireman' in this volume of the series.

8 Wynyard Browne (1911-64) attended Christ's College and knew Lowry at Cambridge; he began writing as a journalist and novelist in the thirties before turning to the theatre. Lowry is referring to the 1947 London West End production at St Martin's Theatre of Browne's first play *Dark Summer* (1950); see also his 20 May 1954 letter (**609**) to David Markson. John Sommerfield had known Lowry in London during the early thirties; see Lowry's 6 June 1945 letter (**202**) to Harold Matson.

9 According to Davenport's note with this letter, Lowry is referring to stains on the paper. *Pinard* is an informal French term for wine.

Editorial Notes:

a. This transcription is from a typescript copy (UBC 2:11) made by John Davenport of the original letter, which has not been located. At the bottom of the second page Davenport has added four explanatory notes which are followed by his initials: J.D.

The months from January 1948 to January 1949 are something of a blur. After the Lowrys' arrival in France at the end of December 1947, they went directly to Paris, where they found a room in rue St Benoît, and Malcolm was able to lose himself in the bistros. He drank heavily, both in Paris and subsequently at Joan Black's country home 'La Cerisaie,' but he also made some loyal friends and allies, like Black and Clarisse Francillon, and he met a number of interesting literary figures, including Maurice Nadeau and Max-Pol Fouchet, both of whom contributed to the growth of his reputation in France. One of the most mysterious of these figures was the shadowy Gabriel Pomerand, with whom Lowry clearly had a close friendship (see letters **339, 340,** *and* **341***); another was the co-translator, with Francillon, of* Under the Volcano, *Stéphen Spriel. Lowry had several spells in French and Italian hospitals during the year, but after each he recuperated with remarkable resilience. However, as he quipped in a note scrawled to Erskine (***338***), he was 'a bit herausgeshimissen,' and this was the state he cultivated for most of the year.*

334: To Harold Matson

P: Matson(ms)   c/o Mlle Joan Black,[1]
PP: *SL* 163   La Cerisaie,
                                                          Vernon, Eure,
                                                              France
                                          [early March 1948][2]

– Dear old Hal:
    I have advised an extremely promising young writer named Eda Lord who has been through every kind of blistering hell from here to Cathay to send a story of hers that I much admire to Whit [Burnett], & asked Whit, if it hits not with him, to send it to you: & I quite frankly advise you to handle her work.[2]
    (Remember *me* – never a dull moment for 14 years.) But there is lots of fine material from where this came from – she has never been published before save in German. She is American, & it would make a hell of a difference were a story published in her own language.
    As for ourselves, we hit a cyclone, 4 ships were lost,[3] & nearly ourselves, I believe Scribner's treatment of Margerie not only verges upon, but is, criminal, (I think you are a bit at fault too for not smacking them in the nose (but then have they a nose?)). I miss Greenwich, your snow, yourself, Tommy, your kids, & the ping-pong. I'll never forget that day, though the photographs didn't come out.
    Margie has some kind of a cinch for a film contract lined up in

Hollywood: you should have been informed before now, but – not a mumbling word: this re Horse in the Sky. (Note I perceive Volc in Books of the Year in Time, by the bye: Horse in B. of the Month news: Volc / apparently to be B.O.T. Month in France too.) – I have, over your head given Fontaine⁴ some kind of illegal & egocentric permission to go beyond the terms of their contract in so far as that concerns its time limit; the reason being I am working with them upon it myself & want to see that it is good. Christ knows what Czecho-Slovakia will do.

Thank you for your letters – when they arrive. I have a cold. And please do not forget Eda Lord –

God bless

Malcolm

Annotations:

1 The Lowrys were introduced to Joan Black (later Joan Churchill) at her home in Vernon, north-west of Paris, by John Davenport in December 1947; see Lowry's 29 March 1949 letter (**367**) to Black. They spent January, February, and part of March in Vernon and returned there in July 1948. While at La Cerisaie Lowry tried to work with Clarisse Francillon on the French translation of *Under the Volcano*.

2 Eda Lord (1907-76), an American writer who was born in Mexico but lived in Europe, had been interned during the German occupation of France as an enemy alien. She was a friend of Black's and one of the writers who visited La Cerisaie. She published three novels: *Childsplay* (1961), *A Matter of Choosing* (1963), and *Extenuating Circumstances* (1971).

3 See Lowry's 18 April 1948 poem-letter (**338**) to Albert Erskine; Lowry uses this experience on the SS *Brest* in 'Through the Panama.'

4 Éditions de la Revue Fontaine had three translators working on the first French edition of *Under the Volcano* during the spring of 1948: Clarisse Francillon, Stéphan Rorce, and Gabriel Pomerand; Pomerand was dropped and Rorce was replaced by Stéphen Spriel. At the time of writing this letter to Matson, Lowry was trying to help Francillon with the translation, which was taking longer than estimated in the March 1947 contract, and Fontaine was on the point of going out of business. As a consequence, Le Club français du livre brought out *Au-dessous du volcan* in 1949 with Spriel and Francillon as the translators, a preface by Lowry, and a postface by Max-Pol Fouchet. The Club français published an edition of 4,126 copies, 1,126 of which were reserved for club use.

Editorial Notes:

a. This undated letter is stamped received in Matson's office 12 March 1948.

335: To Whit Burnett

P: Princeton(ms)   c/o Mlle Joan Black,
                                                    La Cerisaie,
                                                    Vernon, Eure
                                                    May? June?
                                                    [early March 1948]

Dear old Whit:

It's been a long time.[1]

I have never forgotten the debt of gratitude I owe you from the old times, not the least for having rejected Under the Volcano, as it then was.[2]

I was mortified not to see you in Feb. 1947 when I was in N.Y, but I assure you it was impossible – for, as well as snow, there was thunder; & I daresay an inhibiting factor was that I felt sick you were not publishing the bloody book yourself, the successful fate of which has done a great deal more good to its publishers, than to its author – always excepting Hitchcock himself of course, who apparently took one look at it, signed the contract, & fell stone dead. – This letter, however, is to introduce you to the work of a new author, your compatriot if not a Mormon, but hitherto not published outside of certain German translations.

I believe you cannot fail to be impressed by the strange & horrible power of this story 'The Pig' by Eda Lord.[3] As a story perhaps it has, in one way, a kind of intolerance or lack of centre, even when it is being most subtle, but perhaps this imbalance is the clue to the author's talent, or one clue.

At all events it deserves to be published; and since the author, who writes in English, but lives in France where she remained, by the way, throughout the god-awful experiences of the occupation, but hence is now a good deal more isolated in one way & another from American thought than if she lived in Haiti, I would be immensely beholden to you if you would see that it a/ has a sensible reading in your office b/ if it does not hit with you (though it certainly does – avec reservations, – with me) send it to Hal (i.e. Harold Matson 30 Rockerfeller Plaza, New York, 20 N.Y.) whom you perhaps – er – remember, & to whom I shall also send a note. The point is: there is a lot more where this came from – there is an exceedingly good idea, for example, that Eda Lord has for a book incorporating this particular story in a book of related stories, related, that is, roughly by the gruesomes & comedies of the occupation – & nobody knows better than you or I, I would frankly suppose,the agony caused to a young author far away by imponderable delay. Or even, for that matter, by being a writer at all.

The Literary Life & the Hell with it!⁴
God bless you.

Malcolm

Annotations:

1 Lowry last wrote to his former friend on 6 July 1941 (**165**). His dating
   of this letter, therefore, is both a wry joke and a sign of his condition in
   the winter and spring of 1948. It is clear from the content and from his
   reference to Matson that Lowry is writing ca 10-12 March; see letter
   334 to Harold Matson.
2 Burnett's Story Press was one of the twelve publishers that rejected the
   1940 version of *Under the Volcano*.
3 Information on Eda Lord is slim, and we have not been able to trace
   this story; see Lowry's 12 March 1948 letter (**334**) to Matson.
4 Burnett published a book called *The Literary Life and the Hell with It* in
   1939.

336: To Conrad Aiken

P: H(ms)   c/o Joan Black,
PP: *LAL* 208-11   La Cerisaie,
                                                  Vernon, Eure,
                                                       Franceᵃ
                                                  [March 1948]

Dear old Conrad, – I am in hospital here,¹ sleeping under the cross, and
surrounded by nuns, very nice too, and a priest (I think every time he
has come to give me extreme unction) who says 'My-brodder-was-
peelote-on-a-pharting-plane' – been pretty sick, but hope to be out
soon, when & if shall probably go down south – had a stormy voyage
here on a freighter – 40 days & nights & we hit a cyclone in the N.
Atlantic & lost our steering gear; we had one other passenger, by name
– Charon; the Volcano is coming out here but am a trifle exhausted (flu,
aftermath of, among other things) to write you a long letter; so I will
content myself with the point of my letter, news I would like to be first
with, but which you have doubtless already heard, from all I can gather
The Kid is getting a triumphant reception in England; I have a New
statesman & Nation by me, doesn't belong to me, so can't send it; so I
will quote – needless to say I'm absolutely tickled pink over this, & offer
my, so to say, heartiest congratulations, in the midst of my honest joy I
cannot help purring – or is it, remembering B.V [*Blue Voyage*], the
Preludes, the Eclogues, not to say the reception given the Kid by your
own publisher, howling? – over its certain ironic implications you will
be the first to appreciate: here goes the rave review in the Statesman by

George D. Painter:[2] Not long after the landing of the Mayflower at 'Plymouth' in 1620 a young Cambridge (Eng) B.A, William Blackstone by name, reached America & bought from the Indians the future site of Boston. There the next batch of colonists in 1630 were surprised & annoyed to find him in possession. The innocent Blackstone – /to his own cost played the generous host/& asked adventurers across his river.[3]

He sold them his land but when they tried to take his spiritual freedom, too, moved south & west & died in the wilderness. /his books burned & his own book lost forever/for he had a library & he was writing a Book.

This half fabulous figure has met at last a poet in search of a myth. Mr Aiken has made of him & his successors a kind of American scholar gypsy, of epic rather than elegaic status, a transatlantic Coriolanus who once in every generation cries to the mob, 'I banish you,' and carries his divine spark to the ever-receding wilds. The chief metre of his magnificent poem is the loose anapestic couplet of the old cowboy lyric:

O when I die will you bury me
Where coyotes howl on the lone prairie.

– Plucking astonishingly lovely twangs from his bunkhouse guitar, he tracks the Kid through space & time, over the primeval American scene,/the watergap crossed, the chinquapins gone,/breasthigh laurel, & still heading on./There is not too much, be reassured, of the chinquapins (a 'native dwarf chestnut.') Mr Aiken uses his Indianised vocabulary with tact & success, as a device for excluding the White Man from his virgin landscape. He admits no human figure but the Kid himself & even He is seen only in the branch still swaying from his passage, or by/prairie-dog cities swarming in the sun/golden in the evening, and then not one./ And so a lonely beauty is created, in accordance with Mallarme's definition, 'a virginal abscence dispersed in solitude,' and with something of Mallarme's method. The shadowy record of The Kid, traced through frontiers-men physical & spritual, stops with Captain Ahab – wisely, for the last Kid was Dillinger, and there will never be another in this civilization. Having 'promised something great' for a matter of forty years, Mr Aiken has seen his moment come. (How's that, old feller me lad?) His own intense pleasure, his sense of (at last) (this 'at last' is what gets me too) inspiration & power, are communicated. The Kid is the kind of poem Melville might have created if he had remained in sight of the magic mountain Greylock, where he wrote Moby Dick – if he had not been dessicated by Palestine & written Clarel; & it will live as one of the finest pieces of indigenous American poetry since Whitman –

There! In spite of the (at last) & the 40 years etc (& the reviewers apparent blissful ignorance of what constitutes a moment for Mr Aiken, now in America, not to say the blindness of British publishers) it is better than a poke in the eye with a sharp stick, & adds a little light to the day, I feel – naturally I have a special affection for & pride in The Kid because it is dedicated to me, this quite apart from how I rate it as a poem, which is very highly – it was very popular in Canada too, I may say; I hope your publishers are suitably chastened. Reviewed with you is a book called Unarm (though not Costumes by) Eros; in the paintings section there is a sympathetic article on the Memorial Exhibition at the Tate for Paul Nash;[4] & also in this same number, March 27 1948, in the correspondence I find the following letter under the heading Soviet Artists: Sir, – Mr Martin Mitchell's humourless & poorly reasoned attack on Raymond Mortimer's article must not go unchallenged. Art, to whatever fundamental criticism it is subjected by the Central Committee of the Communist Party, remains the aesthetic expression of a personal attitude. Whether it should, for example, deal with man's heroic struggle with his environment & consequently flourish as a positive force (to quote Mr Mitchell's jargon) is the personal affair of the artist & no one else, least of all that of a philosopher or a politician. Whether a particular work has succeeded in its particular aim is for the individual critic to decide on the basis of his personal aesthetic./Mr Mitchell wisely refrains from an assault on Raymond Mortimer's strongest redoubt, namely the impossibility of conveying an ideology in music, & the consequent utter absurdity of condemning any music, however unintelligible to oneself, as not conforming to a given ideology. One can sympathise with the Commissars & peasants in their bewilderment at the recent work of Shostakovitch & his copenitents without at all lessening the force of the contention that the latter should compose as they please. The logical outcome of this arbitrary meddling with aesthetic standards in the U.S.S.R is their reduction to the lowest common denominator, that of the totally uninformed! It is fortunate that contemporary criticism of Beethoven's last quartets was not so conducted: else these profoundest of musical utterances could hardly have survived.

This is signed – John Aiken.[5]

Well – god bless old fellow, all best from Margie & I to Mary & you & all at 41 Doors – hope to be passing your way one day not too far distant.

love

Malc

Annotations:

1 Through January, February, and March, Lowry had been drinking heavily, and towards the latter part of March 1948 he took an 'extended

rest' of about ten days in a hospital in Vernon run by the Sisters of
Charity.

2 Lowry goes on to quote at length from George D. Painter's 'New
Poetry,' *New Statesman and Nation*, 27 March 1948: 259-60, with a few
changes in punctuation and paragraphing.

3 William Blackstone (1595-1675), an English clergyman and graduate of
Cambridge University, came to America in the 1620s and settled in
Massachussetts. He tried living near the Puritan colony at Boston, but
found their rules uncongenial; setting out for the wilderness to preserve
his freedom, he became the first white settler on Rhode Island.
Blackstone is the hero of Aiken's poem, which is dedicated to Lowry;
see Lowry's 4 October 1947 letter (**324**) to Aiken.

4 The Tate Gallery in London held a memorial retrospective exhibition
of Nash's work in 1948.

5 This letter was written by Aiken's son, John Kempton Aiken.

Editorial Notes:

a. Lowry wrote this letter on eight 5-by-15-cm pages of notepad paper in
his tiniest script; each page is completely filled.

*This postcard with a black and white photograph of Cassis has been jointly
written in pencil by the Lowrys. The postmark appears to be 28 March 1948,
which contradicts the accepted view that they did not arrive in Cassis until early
April. Malcolm's joke about the presidents faces the Birneys' address: 5606
Presidents Row, University Hill, University of British Columbia, Vancouver,
B.C., Canada. The postscript is Margerie's.*

337: To Earle Birney

P: UBC(pcard)   [Cassis]
                                                      [ca 28 March 1948]

Dear Earle & Esther – how are you all enjoying the house we hope?
Which poem of Malc's are you using for your British number because
somebody in London wants some & I couldn't remember which we
gave you for that number. Love to all. Is Esther in England & where?
Margerie

                                 my dears ⎱
But I can tell you where I are, mon vieux, ⎰   – I am in a bar; How

nature loves the number 5! – if you will take it out of your address I can't tell you what mightn't happen to the row of Presidents. True love to all
Malcolm

P.S. We are in a little fishing village on the Mediterranean near Marseille but please write American Express, Paris.

338: To Albert Erskine

P: Virginia(ms); UBC(phc) Hotel de la Plage,
PP: *SL* 164; Day 403; Cassis, B. de R.,
 Bowker 437-38 France
[18 April 1948][a]

– Albert the good,
 Sorry I haven't written
  Maybe I am a bit herausgeshimissen,[1]
   – I don't eat my food,
    & in my bed I have twice geschitten,[2]
– Anyhow I am living here
 in a comparative state of mundial fear –
  Also give my love to my dear
          Twinbad the bailer
 I mean dear Frank Taylor[3]
 This is written on the night of
          April 18th
 Anyway or the other, there is no rhyme
  Unless you can think of one above
          Save love
  (& we e[n]countered a cyclone)
  4 ships lost
   somewhat tempest tossed.
          God bless
          from
          Malc

[P.S.] Good heavens, good heavens!
 – On second thoughts, good lord,
          good lord –
 Mad one might go but certainly everybody
          has not jumped overboard. M.

Annotations:

 1 *Herausgeschmissen* (not 'herausgeshimissen'), as Dana Hilliot explains to

Popplereuter in *Ultramarine* (125), means: 'Sent down. Expelled. Fired. Sacked. Herausgeschmissen!' Dana does not explain the finer points of this German expression, which Lowry certainly implies in this poem-letter to Erskine. Colloquially, *herausgeschmissen* means 'to be thrown out of the bar' (for lack of money) and, more generally, to be cast out, an outcast. The transcription of the word in *Selected Letters* is meaningless, and Day corrects Lowry's German without comment or explanation. Bowker mistakenly renders the word as 'berausges-himmer' in his incomplete transcription of the letter (437). For a discussion of this letter and its editorial problems see Grace, '"The daily crucifixion of the post": Editing and Theorizing the Lowry Letters,' *Challenges, Projects, Texts: Canadian Editing*, ed. John Lennox and Janet M. Paterson (New York: AMS Press, 1993), pp. 26-53.

2 There is no such German expression, of course, but Lowry's state during the visit to Cassis was decidedly grim; see Day (401-04).

3 Frank Taylor is 'Twinbad the bailer' because he is a friend of Erskine's. The epithet also allows Lowry to complete his rhyming parody of 'Sinbad the Sailor,' the name of a character from *The Arabian Nights*, and to add to the list Joyce concocts at the end of the penultimate chapter of *Ulysses*.

Editorial Notes:

a. This poem-letter, in blue ink with pencil addendum, is on a 14-by-19-cm page torn from a notepad. The inside address is in Margerie's hand. Malcolm has scrawled his postscript on the verso beneath this message from Margerie: 'But better write c/o Joan Black La Cerisaie, Vernon, Eure France until further notice. Albert, we love you & please forgive all & hope for a more coherent message soon – '

339: To Gabriel Pomerand

P: UBC(ms)   [Paris]
                                                  [1948]ᵃ

Cher Gabriel,¹

Courage mon ami, le diable est mort! Clarisse [Francillon] dit que tu n'as pas peur de rien, et nous pensons de toi souvent, et moi, je prie pour toi dans l'église St Germain, une prière formidable et je crois 'absolument' that you will do what you like, die when you want to, (as you said), & live if you will.²

Mais pourquoi retournes-tu en huit jours à Paris? C'est une fantasie comme Keats, sans doute; pour ma part je pense que je viendrai à la Suisse aussi par force majeure.³ Dans la Suisse j'ai monnaie avec mes traducteurs là – mais à cette moment je ne suis pas certain de la situation que Clarisse connait meilleur que moi; Clarisse écrira a toi et te donne bisweilen ses grands respets.

S'il vous plait, donnez ma affection et regards à ton belle Simone.[4]

J'ai ecouté que tu as un grand pièce dans 'Psyché'[5] et je vais a l'acheter maintenant avec beaucoup de plaisir.

Soyez heureux!

Avec toute ma affection

ton ami

Malcolm

Annotations:

1 Gabriel Pomerand (1928-72), a French citizen of Egyptian-Jewish birth, was a character of the night (*un noctambule*) in the Saint-Germain-des-Prés quarter of Paris who has been described as a small, aggressive man, always dressed in black, with a magnetic personality. He lived in rue Saint Benoît, frequented the Café Flore on the corner across from Les Deux Magots, drank heavily, and dabbled in painting, translating, writing, filmmaking, and drugs. During their first weeks in Paris the Lowrys stayed in rue Saint Benoît, where Lowry may have met Pomerand, but Pomerand's connection with Clarisse Francillon and her Revue Fontaine would have brought the two men together by February or March 1948. According to Lowry's 21 June 1950 letter (**402**) to Albert Erskine, Pomerand worked on the French translation of *Volcano*; of his own works he published *Le Cri et Son Archange* in 1948, *Le Testament d'un acquitté* in 1951, and *Le D. Man*, a description of his experiences with LSD, in 1966. Pomerand was one of the founding members, with Maurice Lemaître and Isidore Isou, of 'lettrisme.' He committed suicide in July 1972.

2 The Abbey of Saint-Germain-des-Prés is the focal point of this part of Paris.

3 According to an address written by Lowry at the top of the page, Pomerand was in the 'Hôpital Cantoral, Médecin II,' in Lausanne, Switzerland. Lowry's comment that he might go to Switzerland may be a reference to an April 1948 plan of Margerie's to consult the Jungian analyst Dr Meier, in Zürich, about Malcolm's condition.

4 Simone has not been identified. Gabriel Pomerand married Roxanne Lespinas, and they had one daughter, Garance, who was born in the early fifties.

5 Lowry has written 'PSYCHE – Le suicide de' at the top of the recto. *Psyché* is the name of a French literary magazine, but I have not located a work by Pomerand with the partial title of 'Le suicide de.' It is possible that this 'pièce' is not a play but merely a piece (or excerpt) from Pomerand's *Le Cri et Son Archange*; see annotation 1 to letter **341** to Pomerand.

Editorial Notes:

a. The three letters to Gabriel Pomerand are undated pencil holographs
    on single sheets of letterhead from Éditions de la Revue Fontaine,
    which was at 1 rue Gozlin in Paris.

340: To Gabriel Pomerand

P: UBC(ms)   [Paris]
                                                               [1948]

Mon très cher vieux Gabriel –
    Mille remerciements pour le vodka – après, j'ai bon appetit pour la
premier fois dans une année!
    Mille remerciements aussi pour la carte postale de Genoa.[1]
    Si ta voyage à Damascus est réalle, imaginaire, spirituelle, ou tous les
trois, – bonne chance!
    Sois-tu heureux, un peu, avec ou ne pas avec Simone, et si ne point
pour toi-même, pour moi.
    Essaye-tu, aussi, si possible, écrire sa expérience à la même temps que
tu la vive; il est possible pour toi!
    Tu possesse un destin extraordinaire; je comprends exactement,
parceque I am Gabriel.
    Love, & may my spirit go with you through the gate,
                                    ton père,
                                                            Malcolm

Annotations:

 1 No correspondence from Pomerand to Lowry appears to have
    survived.

341: To Gabriel Pomerand

P: UBC(ms)   [Paris]
                                                               [1948]

Beloved old Gabriel,
this is Malcolm talking; of your genius I am sure; but that is quite
another thing – –
    Please don't do what you are doing because you will regret it all your
life; I mean the dedication in your book.[1]
    Revenge is mine, saith the Lord.
    And besides it will horribly hurt Simone & you.

Such a thing could only be based on your own death: You may like the idea but I don't believe in it.

Leave it then as a work of art. Whom you need is a father, & I am your father, & am <u>telling</u> you to do that!

With love from

Malcolm

Annotations:

1 Pomerand gave Lowry an inscribed copy of *Le Cri et Son Archange* (Paris: Fontaine, 1948), which is now in the Lowry Collection. The inscription reads: 'To Malcolm from his friend Gabriel.' The work is dedicated to Colette Charpentier, with an additional cryptic dedication on page 95, which is blank except for the phrase 'A Catherine Izard.' *Le Cri et Son Archange* (literally 'The Scream and Its Archangel') is an autobiographical, narcissistic, delirious monologue, in several brief, unnumbered sections, about the self as a poet divided against himself; at one point Pomerand quotes Arthur Rimbaud's line '"Je" est un autre.' The monologue is presented on the page in two columns with short marginal comments interacting with ideas and expressions voiced in the main text, and it is addressed throughout to the reader. Both the style and the subject of this narrative recall Lowry's 'Through the Panama.'

342: To Carol Phillips

p: UBC(ms)

[ca May/June 1948]ª

Revered Carol:

I haven't got your letter at the moment on me but I certainly remember its contents with shock, as well as the pleasure which is the reaction from shock, at hearing from you at all. As a matter of fact, not to say honour, I did receive your first letter, but at the other end of the world, the Dutch West Indies to be precise, & Curacao to be preciser still.[1] In this letter, to be even more precise, you reminded me, though I say it in all kindness, of a certain matter of a certain 25%, – and though, contrary to your statement that I ignored it – for as a matter of fact I replied to it, i.e the letter – I tore it up. This was not out of anger either but to save someone elses feelings, that is the immediate situation of her feelings, for I had not to the best of my knowledge kept the matter secret.[2] In this letter of yours, to the best of my recollection also you merely asked me to act as my conscience guided me. Well, my conscience guided me, simply in this fashion, that yourself being the least mercenary of mortals, you would not have come to write the letter at all had you not been – as are not all of us? – in some deep personal trouble or need of your own, one's own. My letter took this tone but I could not send you any cash because a/it is illegal b/I had only one day in Curacao, which was a Sunday & therefore I had no time to make the necessary preparations c/with the best will in the world I could not, as you must know, feel that you had the slightest legal right to it. (That is quite different thing from saying that I would not have sent something had I been able. Incidentally I can have no absolute proof that the letter was even dispatched but this is irrelevant because as I have said it contained no cash anyway. Its only relevance would seem to me to lie in the fact that you received no reply at all caused you to act as you have.)[3]

Actually of course [letter breaks off]

[unsigned]

Annotations:

1 After the publication of *Under the Volcano*, Carol Phillips appears to have written twice to Lowry, care of his publisher, to ask for remuneration for typing an early version of the novel in 1939. She remembers writing only once, in May 1948, but Lowry appears to have received two communications from her, neither of which has survived. Phillips claims she was never paid for her work and when Benjamin Parks collected *Volcano* to send to Lowry in Vancouver, he did not pay her. Before Lowry left Los Angeles in July 1939 he had agreed to give her 25 per cent of any royalties on the book; see his 11 August 1939 letter (**94**) to Phillips.

2 The person whose feelings he wanted to spare was Margerie.

3 In a 1991 interview Betty Atwater (formerly Carol Phillips) recalled enclosing with her letter to the publisher a copy of Lowry's 11 August 1939 letter (**94**) to her. This enclosure may have prompted Reynal & Hitchcock to warn Lowry about her claim and precipitated this partial reply. In any case, she never heard from Lowry and received no money. See Grace, 'The 'Asperin Tree' and the Volcano: Carol Phillips and Malcolm Lowry,' *Journal of Modern Literature* 17.4 (1991): 509-20.

Editorial Notes:

a. This transcription is from an incomplete pencil draft (UBC 2:11). Margerie Bonner Lowry has written 'November 1947' at the top of the letter, but Lowry's reference to the trip through the Panama Canal and stop in Curaçao suggests that he is writing after that trip. Betty Atwater remembers writing to Lowry's publishers in May 1948; see annotation 1.

343: To Albert Erskine

P: Virginia(pcard); UBC(phc)   [Citta Vatican,]
                                                        [Roma]
                                                  [11 June 1948][a]

Dear Albert:

I seem to be in the Vatican.

We are in good form.[1]

Will write when we settle down anywhere. Publisher of the Volcano here is the son of the President of Italy.[2] We have stiff necks from looking at the Sistine chapel. Rome is very beautiful. Hope you and Peggy are well.

best love from both

Malcolm

Annotations:

1 Despite the illness, hospitalizations, and disasters of the preceding months (see Day, 404-07, and Bowker, 435-46), the Lowrys began a tour of Italy on 15 May 1948. They went first to Milan, Florence, and Venice, arriving in Rome on 2 June, where Lowry collapsed and spent a week in a sanatorium. He was scarcely 'in good form.'

2 See Lowry's 12 June 1948 postcard (**345**) to Gerald Noxon.

Editorial Notes:

a. The address and date are from the postmark. The card has a photograph of the Roman Forum, not the Vatican.

344: To Earle Birney

P: UBC(pcard phc)   [Rome]
                                                    11 June 1948

Dear Earle

Only just received the Straits[1] for which many thanks – they are swell, – very grand indeed – but more later; at the moment I seem to be in the Vatican[2]

love

Malcolm & Margie

Annotations:

1 Birney had sent an inscribed copy of his newly published volume of poetry *The Straits of Anian*, which must have reached Lowry at the American Express office in Rome.

2 The postcard shows a photograph of Via dell'Impero in Rome, but the postmark is Vatican City.

345: To Gerald Noxon

P: Texas(pcard)
PP: *LLN* 149-50

Naples
12 June 1948[a]

Dear old Gerald: Am here in your old stamping ground & we took a trip down the Via Nomentana in honor of Sra Bicci & Teresina day before yesterday.[1] How goeth Clegg's Wall?[2] Your descriptions in T.M. [*Teresina Maria*] seem awfully true. I like Rome excessively however, far more than Paris & Margie is in her 7th heaven. We proceed not very originally if gaily. Capri to-morrow where our address is just Permo Poste. Volc is coming out in Italy soon: my publisher is the son of President & G'issimo.[3] Volc was a flop in England, but apparently book-club etc. stuff in France. Best love from Margie & I to Betty Nick & yourself love

Malc

Annotations:

1 Noxon's novel *Teresina Maria* is set in Rome in the area of the Via Nomentana and the Villa Torlonia, hence Lowry's references to the street and characters in that work. On 13 June he and Margerie left Rome for Naples, where this card was mailed.

2 See Lowry's 21 June 1947 letter (**309**) to Noxon.

3 Luigi Einaudi (1874-1961) served as the first president of the Italian Republic from 1948 to 1955; Lowry refers to him here as president and *generalissimo*. In a 27 October 1947 letter to Harold Matson, Giulio Einaudi, the son of the president and manager of the Turin publishing house Einaudi Editore, asked for Italian rights to *Under the Volcano*. His publishing plan fell through, however, and Giorgio Monicelli's translation, *Sotto il vulcano*, was published by the Milan house of Feltrinelli in 1961.

Editorial Notes:

a. There are three postmark stamps on this postcard. The earliest of these is 12 June 1948, which is also written in pencil above Noxon's name. The black and white photograph on the postcard shows the Via Appia outside Rome.

346: To John Davenport

P: UBC(pcard)
                                              Fermo Poste,
                                                      Capri
                                               12 June 1948

Dear old Davvy,
a million apologies for not writing, but this was merely because I literally *couldn't* write for a while. Cassis didn't work too well for it seemed
I had forgotten to swim too. We returned to Paris & made that a good
thing.[1] Meantime, – the word is relative – & as you see – I seem to have
strayed into the Vatican, & at the moment have a stiff neck from lying
on the floor of the Sistine Chapel sympathising with Noah.[2] At the very
moment someone is playing the Ave Maria on a barrel organ, & god
how that man can play. As a matter of fact, very well. Both Margerie &
I, who also spent some time in a gondola,[3] are enormously enjoying
Rome; it is quite the happiest & loveliest city I have ever seen, full of
lovers motorscooters & monks. My publisher here is the son of the
President of Italy & Generalissimo – office like the Doges Palace.[4] They
are enthusiastic & it comes out soon which is good for my ego. Our
fondest love to your beautiful Margerie & hope she is well now. God
bless you for those hard boiled eggs [several words illegible] to Capri.
Goodbye for the present.

                         All love,

                                                        Malc

N.B. I am writing again now.

Annotations:

1 Lowry's disastrous trip to Cassis had resulted in his stay in a Paris
  hospital; see Lowry's 18 April 1948 letter (**338**) to Albert Erskine.
2 The ceiling of the Sistine Chapel has a complex cycle of decorations
  painted by Michelangelo between 1508 and 1512. Three of them depict
  scenes from the life of the Old Testament patriarch Noah, and it is
  tempting to imagine Lowry contemplating the one called 'The
  Drunkenness of Noah.'
3 Several photographs taken during this trip to Italy have survived, and a
  few show the Lowrys as happy tourists in a Venetian gondola; see
  photograph 3.
4 This is Giulio Einaudi; see Lowry's postcard (**345**) to Gerald Noxon.
  The Doge's Palace (Palazzo Ducale) in Venice was the official residence
  of the chief magistrate of the Republic of Venice. It is an impressive
  example of Venetian Gothic architecture.

347: To Albert Erskine

P: Virginia(pcard); UBC(phc)   [Rome]
[15 June 1948]ᵃ

Dear Albert – As you see I seem to have strayed into the Vatican. But
what marvellous news that you are coming to Italy – marvellous, that
is, if one may see you. This comes from Rome but we are leaving
to-morrow for Capri where our address will be more or less indefinitely:
FERMO POSTE, CAPRI. Sorry to miss you in Paris & again hope we
may see you here.[1] Italy is grand, & there are no shortages. I wrote you
a note the other day which probably will not reach you till after this.
Your letter arrived unsealed. July 6th? seems an awfully long time, but
feel somehow we shall all see each other somehow
     Love from us both to Peggy & your good self

                                                            Malcolm

Annotations:

1 Erskine was travelling in Europe at this time, but planned to return to
   Paris, where Lowry hoped to see him on 10 July. See Lowry's postcard
   (**349**) and letter (**350**) to Erskine.

Editorial Notes:

a. This is the postmark date on the card, which has a black and white
    photograph of St Peter's Square and Basilica in Rome.

348: To Einar Neilson

P: UBC(pcard phc)   Capri,
Italy
1 July 1948

     Another eyrie,
         if not quite so cheery,
             as 'Lieben,'[1]
     (though full of ruins Theban) – [2]
         love & luck to you & Mrs
         & to all kisses
         from Malcolm & Margerie

                   Li Eeyrie. [3]

(P.S. You might tell Earle I am not alone {yet another fan: Tristan
Tzara.}[4] in considering several of his newest poems in the Straits among

the finest in the English, or indeed, any, language.)

Annotations:

1 Einar Neilson and his wife Muriel lived on Bowen Island, a small island off the west coast of British Columbia, in a house called 'Lieben' over-looking the sea. They were introduced to the Lowrys by Earle Birney in the summer of 1947 and had become two of Lowry's closest friends. Lowry describes the Neilsons and 'Lieben' in loving detail in his 12 July 1952 letter (**536**) to David Markson.
2 Capri, an island in the Bay of Naples off the south-west coast of Italy, was colonized by the Greeks and served as a vacation retreat for several Roman emperors.
3 Lowry's mock Greek is an attempt to pun on eyrie, Lowry, and Lieben.
4 Tristan Tzara, the pen-name of Samuel Rosenfeld (1896-1963), was a Romanian-born French writer and founder, in 1916, of the Dada movement. It is possible that Lowry met Tzara in Italy and that his praise for Birney's poems was expressed in conversation, but we have not been able to locate published comments on Birney by Tzara or to confirm that Lowry met Tzara.

349: To Albert Erskine

P: Virginia(pcard); UBC(phc)   Hotel Belvedere
PP: *SL* 164   e Tre Re,
                                                                Marina Grande,
                                                                        Capri
                                                                [July 1948]ᵃ

Dear old Albert: Since we both feel we absolutely have to meet in Europe we are abiding the question of your itinery (spelling mine) here in Capri & until hearing from you. With this in mind would you imme-diately upon receipt of this send us a night letter to the above address which used to be Bellevue or even Bella Vista.[1] The proprietor is an artist, a Lithuanian, whose papa was a bosom pal of Dostoievsky's. Papa reported that Feodor was an awfully nice fellow but sicka in the head. The other day we climbed Vesuvius. She recently give a the big a shake.[2] Address here repeated. Hotel Belvedere e Tre Re, Marina Grande, Capri. Maxima Gorky stayed here too.[3]

God bless you for everything – love to you & Peggy

Malc

Annotations:

1 Bellevue and Bella Vista, while meaning the same thing in English – pretty view – are personal references for Lowry, who had stayed briefly

in New York's Bellevue Hospital in 1936 and used it as the setting for
Lunar Caustic; Bella Vista is the name of the bar in chapter 2 of *Under
the Volcano*.

2 Vesuvius, a volcano about fifteen kilometres south-east of Naples,
erupted to destroy Pompeii in AD 79. Lowry gives this line, 'She give a
the big a shake' to the tour guide in his story 'Present Estate of Pompeii'
in *Hear us O Lord*.

3 Maxim Gorky (1868-1936), the author of *The Lower Depths*, settled in
Capri in 1906. He stayed in the Villa Serafina until 1913 and organized
a school to train Russians in Bolshevik propaganda.

Editorial Notes:

a. This is the postmark date. Lowry has addressed the card, which has a
photograph of Marina Grande, to 'Monsignor Albert Erskine.'

350: To Albert Erskine

P: Virginia(ms); UBC(phc)   [c/o Joan Black,]
PP: *SL* 165   [La Cerisaie]
                                                        [10 August 1948]ᵃ

– Dear old Albert –

for some benighted reason your letter got a little bit delayed: & for
some even more benighted reason I, first, could not understand it,
secondly, lost it – i.e the postcard – possibly to identify myself without
any shadow of a doubt as a privileged citizen of the Belgian Congo, (in
a thunder storm.) .. since I was dependent upon the heiroglyphics
therein – not to say the address in order to reply – I have not replied. It
will be a permanent cause of sorrow to me if my defection in this respect
has in turn been responsible for our inability to meet at this moment.
Against all this, however, it was wonderful & miraculous to meet at all.[1]
And please give our very best love to Peggy. I have to confess, however,
that in spite of this comparitively lucid burst of correspondence, that I
am going steadily & even beautifully downhill: my memory misses beats
at every moment, & my mornings are on all fours. Turning the whole
business round in a nutshell I am only sober or merry in a whiskey bottle, & since whiskey is impossible to procure you can imagine how
merry I am, & lucid, & by Christ I am lucid. And merry. But Jesus. The
trouble is, apart from Self, that part used to be called: consciousness. I
have now reached a position where every night I write 5 novels in imagination, have total recall (whatever that means too) but am unable to
write a word. I cannot explain in human terms the incredible effort it
has cost me to write even this silly little note, in a Breughel garden with

dogs & barrels & turkeys & chickens & sunsets & morning glory with an approaching storm & a bottle of half wine.[2] And now the rain! Let it come, seated as I am on Breughel barrel by a dogs grave crowned with dead irises. The wind is rising too, both on the ocean & in the stomach. And I have been kind to in a way that I do not deserve. I have to write pretty fast. And I shall send this to Brussels pronto. Please wire c/o Joan Black, La Cerisaie, Vernon, Eure, if we can meet each other again, leaving quite out of account whether I can do the same for myself. A night dove has started to hoot & says incessantly the word 'dream, dream,'. A bright idea. I remember always your kindness & generosity.

Love to you both

Malcolm

Annotations:

1 Lowry met Erskine at a Paris café on 10 July, but he was in bad shape, and by the end of the month he and Margerie had moved out of the city to stay with Joan Black. Though brief, this poignant letter is one of Lowry's most honest appraisals of his condition and of what others had to endure for his sake.

2 Pieter Breughel the Elder (ca 1525-69), the first in a line of major Flemish painters, is admired for his complex allegories of contemporary life. Lowry could be thinking of *Flemish Proverbs* (1559) or *Battle between Carnival and Lent* (1559).

Editorial Notes:

a. This letter is on six 7.5-by-13.75-cm pages torn from a small notebook. The date is from the postmark on the accompanying envelope, which has been addressed by Margerie and sent to New York.

351: To James Craige

p: UBC(pcard phc)
pp: *SL* 166

[Mont Saint Michel,]
[France]
[October 1948]^a

My very dear Jimmy:

Here the tide comes in at 60 miles an hour, & 48 feet high – there are quicksands all around & the swimming is much better home in Dollarton:[1] Please guard our beloved house & pier, use it as you will –

dearest love from

Margerie & Malcolm

Annotations:

1 On 2 October 1948 the Lowrys began a short tour of Brittany, visiting
   St Malo, Carnac, and Mont Saint Michel.

Editorial Notes:

a. The postmark is illegible on the photocopy of this postcard; 20 October
   1948, given in *Selected Letters*, is the date stamped on the card when it
   arrived in Dollarton.

352: To Clarisse Francillon

P: UBC(ms phc)   [France]
                                                    [late 1948-early 1949]ª

Chère Clarisse:[1]
   The format & everything looks marvellous to us both & I cannot
adequately express my thanks. I will search for typ. errors – if it is not
too late, but guess I am incompetent. But there is an error in spelling in
the dedication, doubtless my own fault, I'd be awfully obliged if you'd
correct, if it is not too late. The co-dedicatee's name on the title page
should be :

               PHILIPPE THOBY-MARCELIN

i.e – an 'h' in second word – one l in the third.[2]

   – I hope my preface is not too foolish or boastful or anything or has too
much the knowing air of 'My dear French readers etc.' And I wish all
the luck in the world both to Mike & yourself, & hope you may be
rewarded for your work.[3] I would be very glad to have some reactions
– also a few copies if that's not too much trouble. I hope it isn't too
gloomy for the French public – it isn't *really* gloomy. My soul trembles
lest it should not go over after all the work you have done: but God be
with it. And you. Tell me who else also I should thank for that incredibly marvellous format. With best love & wishes from us both
                              love
                                                            Malcolm

[P.S.] Jim Agee, who wrote letter was an Editor of Time, U.S. when he
wrote letter.[4] He is also director-writer of a film: The Silent One, writer
of leading articles in Life etc – a very fat cat indeed, in short.

Annotations:

1 In addition to running Éditions de la Revue Fontaine, Clarisse

Francillon (1899-1976), Lowry's Swiss-French translator, was an editor and author of twenty novels. She had written to Harold Matson in February 1947 to ask for the French rights to *Under the Volcano* and while nursing the novel and Lowry through the translation process she had become a close friend and supporter of his work.

2 Francillon was not able to incorporate Lowry's correction; see Lowry's January 1950 letter (**382**) to Marcelin.

3 I have not been able to confirm the identity of 'Mike,' but he is probably Stéphen Spriel; see Lowry's 16 February 1949 letter (**358**) to Francillon and his June 1950 letter (**400**) to Spriel.

4 James Agee, whom Lowry had met in New York in February 1947, wrote the dialogue and narration for a 1949 film called *The Silent One*; see also Lowry's 23 March 1947 letter (**288**) to James Stern. The 'letter' Lowry mentions was written to Albert Erskine and contained praise for *Under the Volcano*. The original letter appears to have been lost, but a French translation was published in *Liens: Cahier mensuel des lettres et des arts* 30 (November 1949): 7; in it Agee says that he has been more impressed by *Volcano* than any other contemporary novel for many years.

Editorial Notes:

a. Lowry's holograph is undated, but it appears to be his first extant letter to Francillon; it was probably written prior to the Lowrys' departure for Canada early in January 1949.

353: To Downie Kirk

P: UBC(pcard phc)   Paris, France
                                                  4 January 1949

Very dear old Downie;[1] I am damned sorry I haven't written adequately before: the reason, illness. But no more fatal than anyone else's. Thank you for your letter. Happy Xmas & a Merry New Year, to you & all at Dollarton. Do not read too much Leopardi – bad for the liver.[2] Give my love to all your cousins & your uncles & aunts & especially to Jimmy & Meg & of course your Margerie & little Dorothy. As for Vesuvius we climbed it on foot very hot; as for Hamlet I think it perhaps an understatement: as for Capri we shall tell you later – love:

                                                  Malcolm[a]

Annotations:

1 Downie Kirk (1910-64), a Vancouver high-school teacher of modern languages, was a close friend of Lowry's and over the years helped him with letters from his French, German, and Italian translators. The two

men shared a love of literature and jazz. Kirk, who had married Jimmy Craige's daughter Marjorie, first met the Lowrys at Dollarton in the spring of 1944, and they stayed in the Kirks' shack immediately after their 7 June 1944 fire.

2 Giacomo Leopardi (1798-1837) was an Italian poet whose early life resembled Lowry's version of his childhood: Leopardi believed that his mother neglected him, and he suffered from a period of blindness. His poetry is characterized by deep pessimism.

Editorial Notes:

a. This transcription is from a photocopy of the postcard message. Margerie has added 'we'll be home about the middle of January – we're flying.' Originals of Lowry's cards and letters to the Kirks do not appear to have survived, and this item is the earliest extant evidence of their correspondence.

354: To John Davenport

P: UBC(pcard)   Keflavic, Iceland
                                                    18 January 1949

Dear old John:

As well as snow, there was fog. So we landed here ICELAND – in a blizzard.[1] Since we are snowbound we seem destined to stay. If we ever take off our next stop is Labrador. It was great to see you.[2] Love to Margerie & all.

                                                         Malcolm

Annotations:

1 See Lowry's description of this trip in his 16 February 1949 letter (**358**) to Clarisse Francillon.

2 Lowry and Davenport had seen each other, over drinks, during the Lowrys' stopover in London on their return flight from Paris to Vancouver.

355: To John Davenport

P: UBC(pcard)   Labrador, Newfoundland
                                                   26 January 1949[a]

We were snowed in in Iceland for 3 days – now we are in Labrador – that's about all

                              love to both & all from both

                                                            Malc

Editorial Notes:

a. The postmark is 26 January 1949, eight days after the 16 January date on his previous card to Davenport, and *after* the Lowrys' arrival in Dollarton on 20 January 1949. The card must have been written ca 17 or 18 January.

356: To Albert Erskine

P: Virginia(pcard); UBC(phc)
PP: *SL* 166

[Dollarton]
[25 January 1949]ᵃ

Dear Albert —
Surprise! We're home in Dollarton having suddenly flown the Atlantic — well, not *so* suddenly, we were stuck in a blizzard in Iceland (!) in an army hut & another in Labrador. Malc is happy as a lark to be home & even threatens to get to work on his next novel — God bless you & love to you & Peggy

Margerie

— blindage, blind alley, blinder, blind fish, blindman's buff, blind staggers, blind story, — blind tiger! — blindworm, blinkard, bliss, blithesome, blister beetle, B. Litt, blizzard[1] — thanks a million for the dictionary — others were not so lucky as we getting through latter, I mean the blizzard, as you probably read[2] — am back at work, & grateful to have left Paris well astern — will write — love to you both

God bless & thanks again

Malcolm

Annotations:

1 These words are all listed in any standard dictionary, but the term 'blind tiger,' which Lowry emphasizes, would have especially appealed to him because it is obsolete American slang for an illegal liquor saloon.
2 See Lowry's report of a plane crash in his 12 February letter (**357**) to Jonathan Cape.

Editorial Notes:

a. This address and the date are taken from the postmark; the card does not carry a picture. Margerie's message is not included in *Selected Letters*.

357: To Jonathan Cape

P: UBC(ts)   Dollarton, B.C.,
                                                            Canada
                                                  12 February 1949

Dear Mr Cape:

I was in Europe recently but could manage London only for 16 hours alas, and that because our plane was delayed owing to a blizzard in the Atlantic; this is just to say how very sorry I was not to be able to see you.

We very nearly didn't get back at all, however, an American B 29 just behind us as we landed in Iceland (we were supposed to be going to Ireland, but still, there's only one letter's difference after all) couldn't make the runway, returned to Scotland, where Prestwick was also snowed up, and crashed, killing everybody. We were snowed in in Iceland for three days, in an army hut, and after that got stuck in Labrador, a fine place to stay out of — I don't know who first put the idea in the ether that flying was a luxurious way to travel, it seems to me that one could feel more comfortable crossing the Western Ocean on a raft, at least you are closer to the sea and could not get engine trouble and so forth.[1]

I am sad that the Volcano did not click very hard in England — it still goes on getting more or less ecstatic mentions in America, where it was even a best seller for quite a time, and where it has become now required reading in some ten Universities, heaven help them. I am also sad you did not have the Canadian rights; Reynal and Hitchcock were alas virtually no more by the time it reached here, to the tune of about one copy, which I bought myself. In France however it is the principal selection of the Club Livres du Francais this month, in spite of its having been translated by a Swiss, a Martiniquaise negro, and a dying Assyrian, none of whom could speak a word of English, with some assistance by my wife and myself, who could not speak a word of French.[2]

I do not know if any of the aforementioned reviews are of any use to you at this late date but I can rustle up some extravaganzas if you say the word. The following however really does seem to carry some weight. I have been informed on very reliable authority that in the Encyclopedia Britannica Year Book 1948, page 49, under the article on American Literature, appears the following comment at the conclusion:

'But the year produced no new voice as commanding as that of the Canadian, Malcolm Lowry, in Under the Volcano, to presage a major movement among the younger writers of fiction.'[3]

I haven't yet had an opportunity to see the article myself but I would be very obliged if you would have it verified as I can't help thinking it worth your quotation somewhere, and no one has commented on it so far as I know. I may be wrong but it seems to me of fairly rare occurrence that a representative of Canada or any other member of the Commonwealth save Ireland has been given precedence over America in the matter of literary influence by that presumably august volume.

My wife sends kindest regards and we both look forward to seeing you again next year if possible – meantime, on with the new book.

Very sincerely yours,

Malcolm Lowry

P.S. By the way, thank you very much for the hilarious Christmas card, just received.[4] Or is the gent on top, having observed the semaphore to be temporarily against him, looking for the club car?

Annotations:

1 What Lowry does not tell Cape about this trip is that he smoothed the way with beer, liquor, and sonoryl; see his 16 February 1949 letter (**358**) to Clarisse Francillon.
2 The first two translators were Clarisse Francillon and Stéphen Spriel. The third, 'a dying Assyrian,' is probably Gabriel Pomerand, who was of Egyptian origin and in poor health at the time; see Lowry's letters (**339, 340, 341**) to Pomerand.
3 Lowry's citation is correct. He was fond of quoting this description of himself, which he does in several letters, although not without a touch of irony because Canada's reception of *Under the Volcano* was almost as chilly as England's.
4 This card has not survived.

358: To Clarisse Francillon

P: UBC(ts phc)
PP: *SL* 166-70

Dollarton, B.C.,
Canada
16 February 1949[a]

Dear Clarisse:

We nearly didn't arrive here, but just made it. An American plane just behind us in Iceland couldn't land there because of the blizzard, and tried to return across the Atlantic to Scotland, but crashed, killing everyone on board. We were held up in Labrador and ran into a hurricane and temperatures of 44 below zero (Fahrenheit) in crossing Canada. Here we are all but snowed in; our pier is a partial wreck, although that is the only casualty. The house hadn't even leaked and is warm and cozy.

(Please tell Dr Courvoisier that I have made a very strange general recovery and I will detail it more in another letter in case it can be of some use with another patient.[1] In brief – who was it said 'I haven't time to write you a short letter?'[2] – the paragoric threw me almost instantly into a terrible fit of shakes so I used sonoryl exclusively, about 3 the first day, 4 the second day, though never, I think, more than 4. Delayed in London for 14 hours by storm I drank very heavily indeed: innumerable pints of beer, brandy, and rum that we had brought with us. The next morning I breakfasted well on coffee, bacon, potatoes, brandy and sonoryl and we took off again across the Atlantic. Crossing the Atlantic to Iceland I drank innumerable whiskies at the bar and innumerable brandies with more sonoryl, though without becoming drunk and on the plane I also ate with increasing appetite. Snowed in in Iceland for 3 days with the plane's supplies locked up on board, and ours diminishing, I subsisted on one bottle of beer and sonoryl the second day. My appetite correspondingly faded but I slept enormously without dreams of any kind. Towards evening the second day the passengers rebelled against their dry condition and although it was against the law, somehow some liquor was smuggled out to us from the grounded planes and I had little more than a pint of whisky – we had to share it out – and on the third day we were completely dry until we took off in the evening, when I drank six double whiskies on the plane. When we arrived in Labrador about three in the morning, my appetite revived and I ate a vast amount of roast turkey and vegetables, drank a quart of milk and much fruit juice. I then had 3 whiskies at the bar and more sonoryl at the airport. We took off for Montreal but had to return to Labrador due to engine trouble, where we went to bed about dawn and I slept prodigiously. Stranger than this, I took a cold shower and shaved with a steady hand in the morning and ate an enormous breakfast of fruit juice, bacon and eggs, bread and butter and milk. During the journey from Labrador to Montreal I did not drink at all nor need to, but mostly continued to sleep, though for the first and last time since I left France I had wild, but not too unpleasant, if certainly half delirious, nightmares: for instance, I thought I was kicking the head off the person in front of me and even apologised for this, and that a kind of electric stream running along the floor connected me from time to time with someone up ahead whom I couldn't see. In Montreal we had a long wait during which we drank some cocktails, ate heartily of liver and bacon potatoes and vegetables washed down with much milk. During the colossal flight right across Canada from Montreal to Vancouver liquor was disastrously forbidden on the plane but fortunately we had bought a bottle of excellent whisky in Montreal of which, with Margerie, I drank about half right under the nose of the snooty stewardess. At Vancouver we went to a pub, drank beer, pouring the rest of the whisky into it, ate enormously, bought two more bottles of whisky and went home, where we had a party, after which I sent myself to sleep with sonoryl. The next morning, although it was freezing, I rose as if automatically, made the fire and the coffee, and breakfasted upon ham and eggs, sonoryl, and the remainder of the whisky and set off to the store to get food. Both these actions, in fact all of the actions with the exception of the whisky drinking and the sonoryl, would have seemed to me extremely difficult if not impossible under the circumstances; the stove had scarcely been lit for 15 months, the path through the forest nearly impassable with snow and ice. I could not believe in my own coordination. My intention was to get a bus at the store, go to town and purchase some more whisky, which was perhaps a psychological turning point, for instead I returned as soon as possible without any liquor and did not drink for the rest of that day. The next day, Saturday, a week since I set off from Paris, I also rose at dawn and did the chores: Margerie purchased some gin, of which we drank a little, but the next day and the next I drank nothing at all. By this time I had run out of sonoryl and switched to allonal, a sleeping medicine prescribed for Margerie. I took one tablet at night, and sometimes one and a half during the day, but steadily decreasing the dose, till by the following Thursday I had no need for it. I rose each day at dawn, worked hard physically in weather that has grown steadily worse – it is the worst in Vancouver's history – snow, blizzards, ice, the city of Vancouver is practically paralysed and even has a blackout since the electric power has nearly given out – I both ate and slept like a pig. For some reason I also found I had lost my taste for tobacco and practically stopped smoking cigarettes altogether – at most 4 a day instead of 60 or so. We sometimes have a bottle or two of beer, or a few cocktails of gin and fruit juice before dinner, but the craving, the absolute *necessity* for alcohol, has stopped in a way I cannot account for; in fact it had virtually ceased a week from leaving Paris. What is remarkable is this (and I am experienced) is the complete lack of suffering during this period. For the last year I had averaged at least 2½ litres to 3 litres of red wine a day, to say nothing of other drinks at bars and during my last 2 months in Paris this had increased to about 2 litres of rum per day. Even if it ended up by addling me completely I could not move or think without vast quantities of alcohol, without which, even for a few hours, it was an unimaginable torture. During this last period here in Canada I have waited in vain for the shakes, in vain for the D.T.'s, or even worse horrors. My passage into a new regime, my turning of the corner, as the doctor would put it, if conclusive was virtually painless, and the temptation, finally, at a minimum. And I have not touched any sedatives for a fortnight. What the moral of all this is I don't know, or how such an experience, unique to me, can help anyone else. I jot down these notes at random. (a) The patient, fairly intelligent and if not absolutely hopeless or a *danger*, knows far better than is generally believed *what he is doing*. (b) Towards everyone who coerces him to stop, his attitude is by no means necessarily pathological: there is a point where the coercer, the exhorter, *does* become an enemy, for the sufferer knows that this he will drink more, somehow, anyhow, as it were for revenge, and it is in this cycle of lonely behaviour, & sadness that the sufferer shows himself pathological: on the other hand in so far as he recognizes it, his behaviour is by that much less pathological. On the other hand again, the victim, while not amenable to suggestion where it becomes a matter of stopping, can be and is extremely suggestible to example i.e. an ex-drunkard who nonetheless offers him a drink instead of a lecture can be a friend in disguise, also. Such apparently heretical advice as 'All right, instead of drinking less, why not drink far *more*, only something stronger and purer and *harder*,' might work, by contradiction, wonders. I still believe that bad French red wine was my nemesis, I began to improve slightly when I took to rum and gave up taking vitamins. What about a campaign for better liquor rather than against alcohol? The indiscriminate use of Vitamin B 1 Forte was another villainous factor (by itself and without the simultaneous use of other vitamins in the B family, etc.) this I think is pointed out in L'Homme et l'Alcool, although I don't think that it mentioned that one's system could become actually intoxicated, in the sense of *poisoned*, by B 1.[3] Since the 'shakes' in any or all of its manifestations is throughout the greatest immediate fear next to running dry, it would seem to me that one or other of the non-habit forming barbiturates should be often used in preference to strychnine or chlorol, both of which can cause it, are habit forming, & scarcely lessen the desire. I have not thought this last through & [illegible] said nothing [illegible] the bistro [several words illegible . . .] le tour de Grande Duc as [illegible] other such [illegible] aspects of the subject.)

I suppose that, as things stood when I left, the Volcano will be out in France in about a week or so; or is it to be postponed until March? Naturally I shall be only too glad, I hope, to hear any news you can send me of it and I hope also it is not causing you too much trouble. Please give my best love to Gabriel [Pomerand], whom I hope is better, and hard at work, and also all my best to Mike [Stéphen Spriel]. Please thank him for me for what he has done and I hope he is pleased with the translation, as are you. Could you find out from Simpson about his article in Saturday Night that was coming out in Canada and please give him my best regards.[4] Tell him I'd like to know more about that translation by Gide and others of my first book – I wish it didn't exist, but still.[5] If he would send me the magazine or magazines that have it I would take good care of them and return them: I have his address. If he has not yet finished the article for Saturday Night you might suggest that he use this quotation I promised to send you from the Encyclopedia Britannica and which I have now corroborated. This runs as follows and is to be found in the Year Book of the Encyclopedia Britannica for 1948, page 49, under the heading American Literature. . . 'But the year produced no new voice as commanding as that of the Canadian, Malcolm Lowry, in *Under the Volcano*, to presage a major movement among younger writers in fiction.'

Have you any news of Margerie's *Horse in the Sky*? Or of the romans de policier: *The Shapes That Creep* and *The Last Twist of the Knife*?

Please remember me gratefully to the chaps on the Club Livres de Francais: I apologise for not being able to spell anybody's name save that of M. Hopital, possibly because I have to go to hopital myself in a month or so to have an operation on those veins: the discoloration is very much better but the veins, because they now reach above my knee, have to be tied off: a minor operation and I shall be right as rain. Meantime I am working on another book. With best love and thanks and love from us both

Yours affectionately

Malcolm

Annotations:

1 Dr Courvoisier was Francillon's family doctor, who treated Lowry for his alcoholism during the fall of 1948.

2 The French thinker Blaise Pascal (1623-62) made this comment in his 4 December 1656 letter to he Reverend Jesuit Fathers: 'I have only made this one [letter] longer because I did not have the leisure to make it shorter.' See *Pascal: Provincial Letters*, trans. A.J. Krailsheimer (Penguin 1967), p. 257.

3 We have not been able to locate a book or article called 'L'Homme et l'Alcool,' and the use of B^1 (Thiamine) is unlikely to cause negative effects. Thiamine is water-soluble when taken orally and can be used to treat the side-effects of alcoholism that result from thiamine deficiency. Only if Lowry were taking the vitamin intravenously or if he were allergic would there be any risk.

4 We have not identified Simpson, and no article by him on Lowry appeared in the Canadian magazine *Saturday Night*.

5 Lowry's reference here is probably to the French writer André Gide (1869-1951), author of such works as *L'Immoraliste* (1902; *The Immoralist*) and *Les Faux-Monnayeurs* (1926; *The Counterfeiters*). Gide, however, did not translate *Ultramarine*, and Woolmer confirms that the only French translation of Lowry's first novel was done by Francillon and Jean-Roger Carroy in 1965.

Editorial Notes:

a. This transcription has been made from a faint photocopy (UBC 2:13) of the original, which does not appear to have survived. The letter has been typed on recto and verso of one page and the recto of a second; PTO (please turn over) is visible in the lower right corner of the second recto, but the verso has not been copied.

359: To Harold Matson

P: Matson(ts); UBC(phc)   Dollarton, B.C.,
PP: *SL* 170-72   Canada
                                                             23 February 1949

Dear Hal:

I think Margie has told you that we are back home; sorry we couldn't stop and see you in New York but it just wasn't possible. Nothing much to report in a short note.

Fontaine fell down rather on the French translation and to tell the truth I can't make out if Fontaine is still extant: they gave me the advance however, and thank you for your permission as regards this. In the interim the Club Livres de Francais took the Volcano for their Book of the Month – I think for this month or next, – in fact it should be out now, the translation being by both Fontaine and Book Club people (perhaps Fontaine has indeed *become* the Club Livres) with my and Margie's assistance.[1] They gave me an extra 20,000 francs on this already spent in France, and owe me another 20,000 francs on publication date (which I doubt if they'll be able to send, conditions in France being as they are now) Having had to make up my mind in a hurry I okayed this without consulting you, though Fontaine should have written you. Not much cash in American terms: but the Club Livres de Francais is an extremely influential outfit and I felt you would approve.

Is there any news of the other translations? They should all be out long before now. I just missed the Italian translator in Florence, name of Luigi Berti. Einaudi – the head of the firm – is son of Italy's president, but inhabits Turin which we didn't visit.[2]

No other news save I am trying to work on another book: I have to go to hospital for a leg or legs' operation in a month or so – circulation trouble – fashionable at least, being the King's sickness, though fortunately not so bad, and probably will be up and around in a week or so after.[3]

I think Scribner's continued to be monstrous about Horse in the Sky – it didn't get a chance, (albeit it made a Book of the Month Club recommendation) apparently they only sent it to detective story reviewers who were quite naturally puzzled by it. I wrote angrily to every intelligent reviewer I could think of – replies mostly stated that they couldn't get hold of the book even after application to Scribner's. It's hard to think of a more crushing saga than Margie's.

Apparently I have blossomed out as some kind of poet: see the Book of Canadian Poetry, edited by A.J.M. Smith, second edition, University of Chicago Press[4] – which is more than I have; and also in the Encyclopedia Britannica (Year Book for 1948, page 49) – also more than I have done – under the heading American Literature '. . . But the year produced no new voice as commanding as that of the Canadian Malcolm Lowry, in Under the Volcano, to presage a major movement among younger writers of fiction.' I wrote Reynal about the latter, thinking it worth an advertisement or something, even if a bit late, and he wrote back at once saying he certainly thought it was and would work something out that would feature it.

We spent an extremely jovial Christmas and New Year with your brother Norman and wife:[5] we drank champagne and whiskey and went to the Flea Market. Norman and Anna had been having a beer in a bistro with someone who started talking for no reason at all about the Volcano and informed him we lived in the pub next door – which is how we encountered in the first place.

With all the very best from us both

Yours sincerely

Malcolm

Annotations:

1 When Éditions de la Revue Fontaine went out of business in 1948-49, the translation was picked up by Le Club français du livre, but the exact nature of this transfer is unclear and copies of Lowry's original March 1947 contract with Fontaine appear to have been lost. Lowry regularly mistakes the name of the French book club.

2 Einaudi did not publish Lowry's novel, which was brought out by Feltrinelli of Milan in 1961; see Lowry's references to Einaudi in his 12 June 1948 postcard (**345**) and 23 January 1952 letter (**501**) to Gerald Noxon.

3 In January 1949 Lowry had been diagnosed with a severe case of varicose veins, brought on by his habit of writing while standing up and complicated by eczema. The veins were operated on in mid-March, and he was back at work on *Dark as the Grave* by late spring. The British king George VI (1895-1952) had an operation for arteriosclerosis on 12 March 1949 – thus Lowry's reference to a 'fashionable' trouble.

4 A.J.M. Smith included seven of Lowry's poems in *The Book of Canadian Poetry* (Chicago: University of Chicago Press, 1948): 'Salmon Drowns Eagle,' 'In Memoriam: Ingvald Bjorndal and His Comrade,' 'Cain Shall

Not Slay Abel Today on Our Good Ground,' 'King Lear Blinded Oedipus in a Dream,' 'The World of Ghosts Moves Closer Every Hour,' 'Lupus in Fabula,' and 'He Plays the Piano with a Razor.' Compared with the number of contributions from other contemporary poets, Lowry's representation is average or a little above.

5 Norman Matson, Harold Matson's brother, was living in Paris with his second wife, Anna Walling, during the winter of 1948-49. Matson describes his meetings with the Lowrys in his reminiscence 'Second Encounter' (*Malcolm Lowry Remembered*, 148-52). Matson was a novelist, reviewer, and playwright; his best-known play, *Comic Artist* (1933), was written with Susan Glaspell, his first wife. Lowry was familiar with some of Norman Matson's fiction, as is clear from his 25 June 1942 letter (**173**) to Harold Matson.

360: To Albert Erskine

P: Virginia(ts); UBC(phc)
PP: *SL* 172-74   Dollarton, B.C.
                                                        5 March 1949

Excellentessimo Albert:

Am very sorry I haven't written before. Have no excuse save that I wanted to write a long letter. Who was it said: I haven't time to write you a short letter?[1] We have had the most ferocious winter in history here, and we've had a tough time mushing through the forest getting our wood. Our pier was the only casualty, we found when we got home, and we've been repairing it and taking photographs of its slow development. The pier is the most sentient object of my acquaintance and our attitude towards it seems somewhat to resemble that of the Trobriand Islanders toward similar lowrys and penartes.[2] It is capable of crying and singing and also of considerable anger and I have also fancied on occasion that it was talking to itself, doubtless composing a subaqueous barnacly sort of poem.

Thank you very much for Intruder in the Dust which we value both for the book itself and your kindness in sending it.[3] However I don't think I like it very much, if you will excuse me. For one thing, with all its merits I keep thinking that it is only the first part of a second draft of a novel to be called Intruder in the Dust. Lucas of course is a masterly character but it seems to me that Faulkner is straining like hell to stuff his thought into some kind of liberal tradition and even if this is necessary to the book when conceived of in relation to his work as a whole I don't see why its expression should be technically so comparatively feeble. It seems to me careless too, the writing sometimes almost frightening in its badness. Not that it is difficult exactly, but that I find myself often sinking through a quicksand of what is not even bebop without even a body at the bottom of it. But if you say I am wrong I shall read it again from another angle.

Thanks awfully for your thought re the Signet Books, which on 3rd thinkings really does seem a good idea, especially if you could bring yourself to do the abridging as hinted.[4] In which case, tentatively, I would suggest a brutal cut in Chapter I, perhaps just keeping the beginning, middle and end (this sounds like a joke, but you see what I mean) or even just the beginning and end: no cuts in II. An abridgement of the exposition in III where the Consul is lying on the road? and other small cuts, – I don't know: IV intact, though we might cut Juan Cerillo altogether: V intact, I think; VI – your unfavorite – a whopping great cut in Hugh's thoughts especially re Bolowski(?) and in shaving scene with Consul – but keeping demons and what is necessary: VII largely uncut I *think* though some surgery might be managed: VIII probably uncut but if so whittled a bit to make more of a *conte* – this seems doubtful: IX and X – amputation in both these, in Yvonne's thoughts in former, and guide book stuff in latter and perhaps other hard-for-me-to-part with lowrecapitulations: XI intact: XII some muddy lowromancings could go, and an Eye could be poked out here, an arm lopped off there (etc.)

(Then what we have taken out, we can always put back again in a preface and footnotes etc.)

Not so by the way, the Encyclopedia Britannica Year Book 1948 page 49 under heading American Literature says the following: '. . .But the year produced no new voice as commanding as that of the Canadian, Malcolm Lowry, in Under the Volcano, to presage a major movement among the younger writers of fiction.'

Did you by any chance see that, or even spirit it in? Someone mentioned it to me and I thought they were playing a joke on me. I thought I wouldn't write you till I had corroborated it which I now have. I did however take some pleasure in writing [Eugene] Reynal about it, being sure that he would not have seen it, and not so much minding if it did turn out to be a joke. (He wrote back by return post saying they would work out an advertisement using same and enclosing the same advertisement you sent, with comment 'Books like UNDER THE VOLCANO are very few and far between. I think Knopf is stretching his imagination a bit if he thinks he has its equal.' Ha.)

Since you mention money re the Penguin-Signet thing, I suppose yes, one could always use that too. I have, like you, to go into hospital fairly soon with a leg – a more or less minor operation – our gracious King's trouble though on a smaller scale, I am thankful.[5] I should be out soon. Apart from that I am very well, in fact neither of us have felt fuller of optimisms and beans, though my correspondence may sometimes sound like Mr Micawber's.[6] I am also working very hard on the new book, at the moment like a dark belittered woodshed I'm trying to find way around in with a poor flashlight. But when I've got it in order a bit I'll send some along.

Margie sends heaps of love to yourself and Peggy and Frank Taylor and Nan. As do I.

Love

Malcolm

P.S. Also please give all our very best to Jimmy Stern should you see him, & say we are writing. We heard via France that he has been awarded an award which if so seems very fine and much deserved and if so please relay our congratulations.

M & M

Annotations:

1 It was Blaise Pascal; see Lowry's 16 February 1949 letter (**358**) to Clarisse Francillon.
2 Trobriand Islanders are a Melanesian community inhabiting a small archipelago in the South Pacific Ocean. In his 1935 study *Coral Gardens and Their Magic* Bronislaw Malinowski describes the sacred objects and rituals of these people.
3 Random House published William Faulkner's *Intruder in the Dust* in 1948. Lowry's references are, first, to Lucas Beauchamp, a black man who refuses payment for helping a white boy, and, second, to the corpse of a white man that is discovered in quicksand. Lowry's complaints focus on the character of the lawyer, Gavin Stevens, whom Faulkner uses to argue his own views about the South.
4 No such abridged version of *Under the Volcano* was ever published. The Signet edition of 1966 is complete except for the final page, which reproduces the sign in the public garden, and has an introduction by Stephen Spender.
5 See Lowry's 23 February 1949 letter (**359**) to Harold Matson.
6 Wilkins Micawber, an impecunious character in Charles Dickens' *David Copperfield* (1849-50), is remembered for saying that he is 'always waiting for something to turn up.'

361: To Downie Kirk

P: UBC(ts phc)   Dollarton
PP: *SL* 174   Monday
                                              [14 March 1949][a]

Caro Sr Downey –
    La ringrazio molto – I mean may I worry you to take a quarter of an

hour off more or less *sine mora*, not to say *quam celerrime*, and explain to me what the blazes the enclosed letter is all about, if anything, for unfortunately about the only Italian words I understand therein are Italo Svevo.[1]

What I seem to gather is that he is asking, or wants me to ask, someone for a longer time in which the translation of Volcano may be finished by himself or some person or persons unknown, which does not seem to me so surprising when you reflect that the gent is acknowledging upon February 7 a letter apparently written by myself upon February 21 and that therefore he may be supposed to have his own ideas about time. (Still, it may be important – for instance, what if he insists that it can't be finished before February 1946?)

We are looking forward to seeing you out here again soon. With all best regards from us both to Marjorie and Dorothy and in attesa d'una Sua cortese lettera La (I hope this is right, hombre) ringrazio di tutto e cordialmente La saluta il[2]

Suo

Malcolm

Annotations:

1 The enclosed letter, possibly from Giorgio Monicelli, the Italian translator of *Under the Volcano*, has not survived, but Downie Kirk frequently translated letters for Lowry. *Sine mora* and *quam celerrime* are Latin phrases meaning 'without delay' and 'as quickly as possible.' Italo Svevo was the pen-name of Ettore Schmitz (1861-1928), the Italo-German novelist and author of *The Confessions of Zeno* (1923).

2 Lowry's formal Italian has probably been borrowed from the letter he is asking Kirk to translate. Literally, it means: 'in expectation of your kind letter . . . I thank you for everything and cordially salute you.' 'La ringrazio molto,' at the beginning of the letter means 'I thank you very much.'

Editorial Notes:

a. Lowry's letter is undated but someone has noted that it was written before 23 March. Judging from Margerie's addendum explanation that Lowry would be in hospital and from Lowry's 17 March 1949 telegram (**362**) to Kirk, the most likely date is 14 March 1949.

362: To Downie Kirk

P: UBC(telegram phc)   Canadian Pacific Telegraphs,
                                                         Dollarton, B.C.
                                                         17 March 1949

LETTERS CROSSED HOSPITAL POSTPONED DELIGHTED SEE DUNC AND
YOURSELF SATURDAY[1]

                                                         MALCOLM

Annotations:

 1 Lowry had his operation for varicose veins on 19 or 20 March; see his
   18 March 1949 telegram (**364**) to Downie Kirk. Dunc Murray was a
   mutual friend.

363: To Downie Kirk

P: UBC(ts phc)   [Dollarton]
                                                         [17 March 1949]
                                                              Thursday

Dear Downie –

    Grand to hear from you, but, mysteriously, our letters crossed, and I
didn't have time to make the post on Wednesday (I should have begun
this 'in reference to ours of the Ides of March,' etc.)[1] Margie came down
from the store at about four P.M. yesterday with (a) your telepathic
letter simultaneously with (b) the information that she'd added a telepathic P.S. to *my* telepathic letter to you of the day before saying
I would be in hospital this week-end and so not here, as indeed I
expected, (c) simultaneously with the telepathic information from the
North Vancouver Hospital itself that my bed was needed for an emergency case which meant that, on the contrary, I probably *would* be here.
    I say *probably* because Margerie or I have to phone the hospital on
Friday afternoon and there is just the off chance I may have to go in
then, i.e., Friday or Saturday, though they do not think before Monday:
(I have to have a minor operation upon the veins of my legs) On the
other hand since it is only a very remote chance I am wiring you to-day
(Thursday) that I *will* be here on Saturday so that if you do not get
another wire either Friday night or Saturday morning to the contrary (i.e.
about the time that you receive this letter) you may take it that I will be
here Saturday so all is O.K. That is, from *our* point of view here. I can
only hope it may be also from Dunc's and yours.
    I am being so supermeticulous about what is more or less spontaneous
because I perceive, having been reading Bergson,[2] that the difficulties

on one plane of communication and the too great facilities on another (if telepathic ones can be called such) might have led Dunc [Murray] and yourself into some inconvenience, than which little is worse on a Saturday afternoon, unless it is disappointment, which is what we shall feel if meantime, as I am writing this, you are getting in touch with Dunc and deciding positively not to come. (On second thoughts it would be very surprising if this letter arrived without your having done something of that sort, unless you've decided to come to Dollarton anyway.)

If I do not go to hospital Friday, I shall probably go in to the library – approximately the same thing – on Saturday afternoon about one o'clock to return on the 4 or 5 bus, in which case I may be found – should you be, as I calculate you *may* logically be, in those parts – in the pub nearest to the Gore Avenue bus stop[3] from 2ish onwards for an hour or two, to return either with you, I hope, or slightly before. Either that one, which is called the *Savoy*, and which is a bad one, or the pub which is immortalized in my memory by being the scene of certain Bohemians discussing or even sitting on the American Mercury.[4] I think it has a stained glass window, doubtless in honour of the occasion. Or perhaps I am thinking of the Salvation Army Centre. If I am in the latter I shall probably be having a telepathectomy. But do not count on this for it's by no means *certain* I will be able to come into town at all.

Thank you very much for your good letter to which I haven't time to reply: this in haste, in case you didn't notice it.

At all events, it will be great to see Dunc again and yourself and please give him our love, our best to Marjorie and Dorothy from us both – we look forward to spending a week-end with you when convenient to you and the veins are tied.

Affectionamente Zu haus zu haus
Malcolm

(P.S. I think you mentioned having an Atlas of ours, you know, one of those things you find your way about with; I believe it has a Jap's name on the flyleaf, unless I rubbed it out, but it is the sort of atlas a Jap would like, full of all kinds of out of date statistics, and the population of Eclectic, Alabam, and the price of dried fish in 1929, etc.)

P.P.S. This space for unofficial p.s. by Margie which will doubtless render *torquemadan* that which so far is merely amiably *Kafkan*: in fact the possibilities are endless. . .[5]

Annotations:

1 Shakespeare makes much of the Ides of March in *Julius Caesar* I.ii, and so occasionally does Lowry; see his March 1947 note (**286**) to the

Careys and his March 1952 letter (**508**) to Albert Erskine.

2 The French philosopher Henri Bergson had been a favourite of Lowry's from the thirties, and his *Creative Evolution* (1907) influenced Lowry's ideas about time and change.

3 St Paul's Hospital, where Lowry went for surgery, is on Burrard Street, six blocks south of the former site of the Vancouver Public Library. The two buildings were close enough to be described as 'approximately the same thing,' but Gore Street is about 1.6 kilometres away. The Savoy Pub and Hotel, still at the corner of Gore and East Hastings Streets, is in Vancouver's Chinatown.

4 The *American Mercury*, founded in 1923 by H.L. Mencken, George Nathan, and the New York publisher Alfred A. Knopf, began as a magazine of essays, satirical humour, and opinion pieces on all aspects of American culture. Though not intended as a popular magazine, the *Mercury* was very successful. By the forties it had changed its format and become increasingly right-wing, a trend that continued until it ceased publication in 1980.

5 Margerie's postscript is neither 'torquemadan' (tortured, after the practice of the Spanish inquisitor Tomás de Torquemada, 1420-98) nor ambiguous (in the manner of Franz Kafka). She writes: 'Best leave well enough alone this time! In case the wires get crossed literally. Hope to see you Saturday – wish Marjorie could come too – Arrivederci Margerie.'

364: To Downie Kirk

P: UBC(telegram phc)

Canadian Pacific
Telegraphs,
Vancouver, B.C.
18 March 1949

TERRIBLY SORRY MUST POSTPONE PARTY GOING TO HOSPITAL TONIGHT

MALCOLM

365: To Earle and Esther Birney

P: UBC(ts)
PP: *SL* 175-78

Dollarton
26 March [1949]

My good Birneys:

Margie tried to contact Esther several times by phone – number always engaged, or wires crossed, or a distant voice in Sydney N.S. [Nova Scotia] – or even N.S.W. [New South Wales] – trying to sell an oil well to another distant voice in Asbestos Qu [Quebec]. Meantime I've been in hospital, having an operation. Very interesting. It lasted two solid hours and I was able to watch most of it. It seems to have been successful – they put me in the maternity wing, to the alarm of an expectant father palely standing in the lobby. I explained that I was one of these new, larger, as it were atomic babies just recently on the market.

I'm just out of hospital but won't be quite in circulation (sic) again until the stitches are out. I'm struggling to the Beethoven concert tomorrow, however, to see how I can stand up, or sit down.

Thank you for the very merry evening – I reread Titus Andronicus in hospital, after the operation – in fact while it was still going on, for the doctor had forgotten something on the operating table and had to pursue me, needle and claw bar in hand, to the ward itself. It isn't really such a bad play after all. That is there seems to be nothing wrong with it, save the writing and sundry little details like that. Dover Wilson has just maintained that it is by Shakespeare and Peele.[1] We went to see Hamlet and Macbeth, both really excellently done, all things considered, though they cut out nine-tenths of Malcolm's marvellous pseudo-condemnation of himself in the scene between him and Macduff, Act IV, Sc. III – one of the most effective and bawdy brainwaves of Shakespeare, I've always thought in that particular place, and which has always made me rejoice in the name of Malcolm.[2] (– er – relatively speaking, of course.) And they cut out too much of the witches – becoming also involved in a curious kind of error in the interests of plausibility. That is, having made Banquo's ghost in Act III Sc IV apparently the result of an attack of the horrors, which was certainly quite convincing, and better than having the man actually appear to the audience, in order to be true to the special reality created by *that* they felt bound to make the subsequent appearance of the witches in Act III Sc V and Act IV Sc I also seem like hallucination. They didn't cut out the actual apparition of the witches, like they did of Banquo before, but ran the two scenes together, at the same time truncating them, and to make matters more complicated, here at the end, Banquo actually did appear to the audience. This would have been all right, and in fact very good, had not the same witches appeared at the beginning of the play to both Banquo and Macbeth himself, who was presumably then cold sober. It's a rather pretty problem, for I've never seen a performance of Macbeth yet where Banquo's ghost didn't cause trouble, and though here they solved it in a very reasonable manner, it was only at the expense of somehow upsetting the necessary illusion in the subsequent scenes. All of which merely shows that Cocteau is right when he says that theatre must remain consistently right in terms of the special reality of the theatre.[3] On the other hand they played Hamlet uncut, I'm glad to say – or would be, for unfortunately we had to go out and catch the Deep Cove bus. It was a very good performance, what I saw of it, except for Polonius who seemed to be trying to do an imitation of Frank Morgan, and I thought that Stanley Bligh was somewhat mean about it.[4] Hamlet without Rosencranz and Guildenstern, the court intrigue and the approaching war, and above all Fortinbras at the end, is to me rather meaningless as a play, for which reason I disliked Olivier's version, save for parts of the acting.[5] (I didn't like Henry V any too well either – they hammed up Fluellen and Macmorris too much, when this, I take it is meant to be straight, realistic, if boisterous, dialogue, precisely the kind soldiers would use).

Thank you very much for sending me your student reviews {Also, for the Outposts.}[6] of the Volcano. They are, as well as flattering, damned interesting to me, especially the one that laid the stress on the mystical and religious catabasis traced by the Consul. This pointed out something in my intention I didn't know myself but which is certainly there; more of this later. All this means a lot to one.

I received a letter telling me you had spoken most kindly of the Volcano on the radio and [for] this, Earle, I am very grateful.[7] Thanks awfully. The chap, a neighbour and collateral relative of Jimmy's, a philologist and language master at Lord Byng's, named Downie Kirk (holy great cow, what prose is this?) is relaying me what you said.[8] Now I curse myself for not having a radio – I hadn't gathered you were giving the talks so soon. I have heard nothing but the most complimentary comments upon your broadcasts.

How goes the novel?[9] What you read was exceedingly good, it's so rare that something actually makes one laugh aloud (Joyce's complaint re Ulysses: 'They might at least have said it was damned funny.') – which yours certainly does, does still in fact. And it seems to have just the right combination of humour with underlying seriousness. You once asked me if I could think of any novels roughly in the same picuresque genre that might be suggestive. Schweik of course – though it doesn't wholly come off.[10] I believe I mentioned Carl and the 20th Century. I don't remember the author.[11] The only character is Carl – the rest are simply statistics. (There's much the same thing at the end of Schweik but in this case the whole book is like that.) One short chapter in this mode might be effective. And have you read Saul Bellow's Dangling Man?[12] Perhaps this is too far from your intention, but you might find it worth reading. Dead Souls again, may seem remote, but if you haven't read it, there is some sense in my suggesting it. For one thing in addition to being extraordinarily funny it is one of the most lyrical and nostalgic novels ever written. Or so it seems to me. The swing between farce and the purely lyrical might be of value technically.

And the almost Moussorgsky like sadness and longing he is able to distil simply by describing some crummy little hotel.[13]

Well, I'll have to stop. Do please come down soon – the weather is splendidly wild: Gotterdammerung over Belcarra.[14] All best love from us both to you both and to Bill and his noctambule.

Malcolm

Wywork still sits greenly & untenanted here. Wish you would buy it, though don't know how much they charge. I saw some sinister people looking at it. How can I encourage you? Crazy neighbours, or no neighbours at all. Unparalleled view of mountain scenery and oil refinerys. Plenty of cascara trees in back. D.H. Lawrence once lived in a house called Wywork. In Australia, however. He thought it should be called Wyreworks.[15]

Annotations:

1 John Dover Wilson (1881-1969), the English Shakespeare scholar, discusses the contribution of George Peele (1556-96) to *Titus Andronicus* (1594) in the introduction to his 1948 edition of the play.

2 The American director Margaret Webster mounted productions of *Macbeth* and *Hamlet* in Vancouver on 9-10 March 1949. In *Macbeth* IV.iii Malcolm maligns his own character in order to test Macduff's loyalty.

3 Jean Cocteau was a lasting influence on Lowry, from the time he saw *La Machine infernale* in Paris in 1934 to his last letters to David Markson; see his July 1946 letter (**229**) to Albert Erskine and his 22 February 1957 letter (**705**) to Markson.

4 Frank Morgan (1890-1949), an American film actor, played the title role in the 1939 film *The Wizard of Oz*. Stanley A. Bligh was editor-in-chief of the *Vancouver Sun*.

5 Sir Laurence Olivier (1907-89) directed and played the title role in the 1948 film version of Shakespeare's play. He also directed and starred in the 1944 film version of *Henry V*, which Lowry goes on to criticize.

6 *Outposts*, begun in 1943, is a British quarterly magazine devoted to contemporary poetry. Earle Birney guest-edited the summer 1948 number on Canadian poetry, which included Lowry's 'Sunrise.'

7 During the forties and early fifties Birney gave CBC radio talks on Canadian literature and general literary subjects, and he read and reviewed Canadian poetry.

8 See Lowry's 4 January 1949 letter (**353**) to Downie Kirk.

9 Birney was finishing his satiric novel *Turvey* (1949), about a Canadian soldier. In his review of the novel for *Thunderbird* (December 1949): 24-26, Lowry called it a 'ribald and paradoxical miracle.'

10 Schweik is the hero of Jaroslav Hašek's satirical novel *The Good Soldier Schweik* (1930). Schweik is a prototypical example of the ordinary

soldier who uses absurd methods to survive.

11 Rudolph Brunngraber's *Karl and the Twentieth Century* (New York: William Morrow, 1933) is a 'newsreel' novel that presents the life of its hero through a collage of documents and news headlines and against the backdrop of social, political, and economic events from the previous fifty years.

12 Saul Bellow (1915-), the Canadian-born American novelist and Nobel prize-winner, published his first novel, *Dangling Man*, in 1944. The novel portrays a man waiting to join the army who is both attracted and repelled by the prospect.

13 Gogol's *Dead Souls* was a Lowry favourite. Russian composer Modest Mussorgsky (1839-81) is noted for his opera *Boris Godunov* (1869) and his song and piano cycles.

14 *Götterdämmerung* (the German for 'Twilight of the Gods') refers to the final opera in Richard Wagner's *Ring* cycle and suggests the dramatic spring weather that the Lowrys were experiencing. Belcarra is a regional park on the south-east shore of the inlet across from Dollarton.

15 During the spring and summer of 1922 Lawrence stayed in a house called 'Wyewurk' in Thirroul, New South Wales, Australia. Lowry is referring to Lawrence's 30 May 1922 letter to Anna Jenkins, in which he writes that he and Frieda 'have taken this house 'Wyewurk' (why not wirewurks) for a month.'

366: To Alan Crawley

P: Queens(ts)   Dollarton, B.C.
                                                              26 March [1949][a]

Dear Alan Crawley:
   It is grand to hear from you and please forgive the delay in replying – however your letter reached me just when I was going into hospital for an operation – nothing too serious, a slight matter of circulation. In fact almost regal. It seems to have been successful – it ought to be, they put me in the maternity wing. As I write you I'm just out, though I won't be *in* circulation for a little while, albeit I'm trying to struggle to the Beethoven concert tomorrow afternoon, in which connection I wish you hadn't mentioned the Arctic, it's hailstorming this morning again. Typographical error: it's snowing. Perhaps a new ice age is upon us. I shall certainly send you something for C.V. [*Contemporary Verse*] if I can find anything that seems to be worthy. Though so far as anything recent is concerned I'm afraid poetry doesn't exactly come like leaves on a tree with me. More like coals to a prose-bound Newcastle. Or do I mean strike-bound? Or coke-bound. Or perhaps not even Newcastle. (I have some good titles for books of verse, however, by myself. Gastown Gruesomes I think is the best.)

We are very much looking forward to getting out to Caulfeild soon.[1]
With all the best to both Mrs Crawley and yourself,

Malcolm

Annotations:

1 Caulfeild, a residential area in West Vancouver near Light House Park,
would require a forty-five-minute bus ride from Dollarton.

Editorial Notes:

a. The date is incomplete, but Lowry's reference to his operation confirms
the year as 1949.

367: To Joan Black

P: UBC(ms)   Dollarton,
British Columbia,
Canada
29 March 1949[a]

My very dear Joan:[1]
A long time has elapsed since the Liebermans had their last trouble –
but to-day it appears that they, or a branch of that luckless family having
strayed to Vancouver of all places, have had yet another trial, and now
I look at the photograph I'm sure they're the same Liebermans, and, you
guessed it, their house has burned down: *Arson Story Scotched by B.C
police* –[2] So I'm very much afraid it looks as though they burned it down
themselves for the insurance, only there is a slight hitch here too unfortunately: *Insurance Expired day before yesterday, Lieberman taken in custody*
– so that, Margerie having just said, (*ourselves having returned from the town
five minutes since to discover the house still in place and the inlet sleeked and still,
the sky wide and the alders and cedars high, the pier there, and the stars blazing*),[3] having just said, I repeat: 'God, I suddenly thought of something
I must do, so I thought I won't do it, I'll forget it unless I write it down,
so by the time I'd found a pencil and paper to write it down, I'd forgotten what it was I had to write down in order to remember to do it,'
I decided, hearing you say too, re the above remarks about the
Liebermans, 'Really, Malcolm!', to write you a letter. Of course, in the
meanwhile, there is other fireside news.[4] 'Last Ditch Tiff on Duck Lake
Issue.' 'Split Duck Season, Later Moose Opening Asked at Game
Convention' and even 'DUCK STORY MAY DRAW LIBEL SUIT' –
obscure, perhaps, and understandably, the connotations of these, to you.
PHEASANT TAGS – that is obscure too, even to me. But when I add:

DOG REUNITES DEAD VETERAN, . . . *Half a Cocker Spaniel Found* – SHIP *retracts* S.O.S; & above all perhaps, – ORGAN MAY BE MEMORIAL! – you will know that I have come down to brass tacks, that I have indeed, ('BABY SITTING MECHANIZED BY INTER-HOME SQUAWK-BOX': – 'NOW I CAN SLEEP, SIGHS WIFE SLAYER') got out, as it were, from under. So, quite passing by *Death intervenes to Halt Wedding service, Titanium deposits believed in B. C,* {New Caledonia} I shall get down to them.

Much water has indeed gone under the bridge since Ed Ngai took table tennis at Victoria, & Joyce Davies, twice victor in foil, met.[5]

[breaks off unsigned]

Annotations:

1 This appears to be Lowry's only extant letter to Joan Black (?-1957), who had become a close friend during his 1948-49 stay in Europe and opened her country home, 'La Cerisaie,' near Vernon, Eure, in France to him. Black married Peter Churchill, whom the Lowrys met for the first time in September 1954 in New York, and the two couples saw each other from time to time in England during 1956-57; see Lowry's early 1957 letter (**704**) to Peter Churchill. Day suggests (45) that Joan's sudden death on 7 May 1957 contributed to Lowry's depression and subsequent death seven weeks later; Bowker (597) gives 12 May as her death date.

2 The fire that destroyed the home of Louis Lieberman Rubinowitz and his wife, the city's first Jewish residents, was reported in the Vancouver papers on 28 March 1949.

3 This parenthetical passage appears in part 5 of 'The Forest Path to the Spring.'

4 Several of the following captions originally appeared in the *Vancouver Sun,* 28 March 1949, and Lowry used some of them in *October Ferry to Gabriola*; see, for example, the 'Half a Cocker Spaniel' item in chapter 37.

5 Ngai and Davies were local sports figures, but they did not meet; see the *Vancouver Sun,* 28 March 1949, p. 11.

Editorial Notes:

a. If Lowry completed and mailed this letter, the final version does not appear to have survived. Two pencil marginalia suggest that he saved it for partial inclusion in his fiction. For example, opposite 'Half a Cocker Spaniel Found,' he has written: 'Get these news items too in story somewhere.'

368: To Downie Kirk

P: UBC(ms phc)   [Dollarton]
                                                      [4 April 1949]
                                                           Monday

Dear Downey, –

Thanks a million for translating the Italian letter – recent events in
Rome make me wonder if the Volcano *will* ever be published in Italy
by my particular publisher anyway, who is the son of the Generalissimo
– however, thank you again.

This is just a note which I should have written before, but I've been
having stitches out etc, to say we'd be delighted to see you April 9 (or
8th or 29th or any other day for that matter, but I certainly won't be in
hospital) & I hope Dunc [Murray] & Margerie [Marjorie Kirk] can
come too

With love to you both & Dorothy from Margie & myself,

                                                           Malcolm

369: To Downie Kirk

P: UBC(ms phc)   [Dollarton]
                                                        [April 1949]

Dear Downie – Just a note in haste to say I don't *think*, alack, I can make
your party on Saturday, reasons being more sclerosings, also the goter-
dammer doktor *forgot* to take a stitch or two out, that we hadn't noticed
(we took them out ourselves) – though in the main everything is going
well, apart from this slight & strange setback; on the other hand, the
sclerosis medicine is bad medicine, nothing less than poison, in short, &
I ought to be feeling like the krankenhaus[1] on Saturday even if not actually bound there: on the other hand again, the sclerosis may just not
come off, & I may be feeling full of beans anyway; or feeling the
extreme need of them – So may we leave it like this, that we'll come,
bodily weather permitting, but not definitely to expect us, & if I can't make
it you'll know what's up. It was very good to see you & Dunc again –
give our kindest regards to A.F.B. Clark & Mrs Clark in the event of
our defection – & all best from us both to Marjorie Dorothy & yourself

                                      Suo

                                                           Malcolm

Annotations:

  1 *Krankenhaus* is German for hospital.

370: To Albert Erskine
P: Virginia(pcard)
PP: *SL* 178–79

Dollarton,
20 May 1949[a]

Dear old Albert: Please forgive my long silence but I had an operation etc etc It seemed all right, then I had a few complications etc, – now it is ok etc. Thanks awfully for the Melville.[1] It was very kind of you. It seems to me Jay Leyda and yourselves have done a masterly job. Both the Tartarus of Maids (I'd read The Paradise for some reason) & the Bell Tower were new to me & both terrific, especially the former. I have a note or two, mostly ornithological Page 64. The snow white angelic thing with one long, lance-like, feather thrust out behind, the beauteous bird that whistles in clear silver-bugle like notes (So far as the silver-bugle like notes are concerned, there is, interestingly, an almost identical passage in Gogol's Dead Souls, – Query, was Dead Souls ever translated in Melville's day,[2] he was I think ten years older, but had just died (1852) about the time Melville was writing the Encantadas & the renaissance of piracy was taking place in Chatham Island so the bird may have blown him the thought, as it were through its bugle) – the beauteous bird any-how, fitly styled the 'Boatswains Mate' as he says, is a *red-billed tropic bird*, & though Boatswains Mate may be a good name for it, & even *a* name for it in sailors parlance, I think he is confusing it with his man-of-war hawk on page 62, which is not, strictly speaking, a hawk, & is known as the man-of-war bird, the frigate bird, or the Boatswain Bird, – in Spanish, the *digarilla*, though I stand to be corrected. Moreover while far be it for me to suggest that he *didn't* see penguins at the Encantadas, though they seem to me indubitably associated with less equatorial regions, I can't help (p 62, 63) feeling he may have meant the murre, a bird which on land is almost identical with the penguin, though this is not, I think, generally known. Perhaps he got fed up watching them on land & didn't bother to see them swim. Or perhaps *some* penguins & *some* murres. Question: do I or do I not remember, in ancient researches at the N.Y. public library, coming across a volume, published in Melville's lifetime, called The Apple Tree Table & other Sketches? Probably imagination. Likewise didn't he sign the name Tarnmoor also to Bartleby the Scrivener, a story of *old* Wall Street?[3] More imagination. Had silly letter from [Jonathan] Cape, who has done *nothing*. See end of Temple Second (p 165).[4] I am awaiting news from France & Sweden at the moment. Could not place your quotation – perhaps Melville wrote it himself. Herman is writing poetry but keep it dark, you know how these things get round etc etc. Malcolm is writing prose & will begin sending you some instalments in a month or 2. Please send me a letter,

I feel a bit discouraged, though we are well, & our new house is beauteous. I had a good letter from Frank. You must miss each other. Best love to Peggy and yourself from us

love Malcolm

P.S. Good thing they didn't have postage stamps in the old days. What would the adherents of Charles I have said to one like this! P.T.O.[5]

P.S. Or perhaps he meant, not *Bosun's* mate, but *Totipal*mate Bird.

Annotations:

1 Erskine had sent Lowry *The Complete Stories of Melville*, ed. Jay Leyda (New York: Random House, 1949), which is now with his library at UBC. See Lowry's 27 February 1952 letter (**504**) to Leyda.

2 Lowry is quoting Melville's description of the 'Boatswain's Mate' from the third sketch, 'Rock Rodondo,' of 'The Encantadas': 'But down through all this discord of commotion, I hear clear, silver, bugle-like notes unbrokenly falling . . . and behold a snow-white angelic thing, with one long, lance-like feather thrust out behind.' Gogol creates many descriptions of birds, but Lowry may be thinking of the following passage from part II, chapter 2, of *Dead Souls*, Reavey translation, ed. George Gibian (New York: Norton, 1985), p. 288: 'A quail is fluttering among the rye, a crake is creaking in the grass, linnets twitter and chirrup as they flit above, a lamb bleats out, a swallow trills as it vanishes in the light, and the bugle call of the raucous storks rings out as they fly in wedge-shaped formation high above.' The first English translation of *Dead Souls* appeared in a corrupt edition in 1854. Another translation, *Tchitchikoff's Journey of Dead Souls*, was published in New York in 1886, thirty years after 'The Encantadas' was published.

3 Melville's story 'The Apple Tree; Or, Original Spiritual Manifestations,' first published in *Putnam's Monthly Magazine of American Literature, Science, and Art* 7.41 (May 1856): 465-75, is included in *The Complete Stories of Herman Melville*. Melville used the pseudonym 'Salvatore R. Tarnmoor' for the serial publication of 'The Encantadas' in *Putnam's* (1854). 'Bartleby the Scrivener,' also published in *Putnam's* (1853), did not carry an author's name.

4 Melville's story 'The Two Temples' is in two parts, 'Temple First' and 'Temple Second.' The final paragraph of 'Temple Second,' on page 165 of the Random House Modern Library edition of Melville's stories, reads as follows: 'I went home to my lonely lodging, and slept not much that night, for thinking of the First Temple and the Second Temple; and how that, a stranger in a strange land, I found sterling charity in the one; and at home, in my own land, was thrust out from the other.'

5 There are two postage stamps on this card, both of George VI. The three-cent stamp shows the king's head from the side without military cap or crown and as if decapitated, which explains Lowry's reference to

Charles I (1600-49), who was tried and beheaded by Oliver Cromwell during the English Civil War.

Editorial Notes:

a. This letter, written in Lowry's tiniest script on an 8.75-by-14-cm card postmarked 20 May 1949, fills every available space.

371: To Anna Mabelle [Mrs John Stuart] Bonner

p: UBC(ms)
pp: *SL* 181

[Dollarton]
[ca June 1949][a]

My very dearest Mother:

Thank you for your many notes of affection and I am sorry I have not found time to write you again at length: but since here there is no time at all apparently, perhaps it is no great wonder if a fellow can't find it; and I am an atrocious correspondent anyway.

Re the situation regarding Russia, etc, in answer to your question, I have no very settled feelings though they might be crystallised something like this: she, being what she is, can behave in no other way and we being what we are, can behave in no other way either.[1] I believe it is lack of knowledge of the intellectual & practical content of the Marxist philosophy that is responsible for most of these mis-understandings and on her side, for her inhuman and abstract development of that philosophy, so far as her relations with other *countries* are concerned: where we have tried to compromise we have met with little but hypocritical and *egoistic* response but then abstractions brook of little compromise, and we have no plan: while they have.

So far as I am concerned I dislike this world intensely but still, like yourself, try to preserve ones feeling for the *earth*, the birds and the universe.

With lots of love – & love to all – your son,
affectionately

Malcolm

Annotations:

1 Relations between the Soviet Union and the West had been strained since June 1948, when the Soviet Union cut off land access to the American, British, and French sectors of Berlin. Supplies had to be airlifted to these sectors of the city until the Soviet Union removed the blockade in May 1949. The Berlin crisis was constantly in the news at this time; it served as a catalyst for Western countries to

form the North Atlantic Treaty Organization (NATO) in 1949.

Editorial Notes:

a. This letter is dated 1949 in *Selected Letters*, and Margerie has written 1949 on the pencil holograph.

372: To Dr and Mrs E.B. Woolfan

P: UBC(ts)   Dollarton, B.C.
                                             14 June [1949]

My very dear Priscilla and Bert:[1]

I do not have to tell you what a bad correspondent I am because you know. But as I have just finished explaining to your mother I have been working so hard I have not written to anybody, for a long time.[2] It is true that you are not anybody, so I apologise.

I like the new book – really three books in one – better than the Volcano; it has a happy ending: odd. Though after all, why not? Though with this in view whether to call the whole thing Dark as the Grave Wherein my Friend is Laid I still feel unsure about, despite my promise. Perhaps if I omitted the first five words of that title it would have a more succinct as well as a less sombre effect. Excuse me, that was very vulgar Malcolm. In fact it is even more vulgar than I intended, now I think about it. Excuse me again. Thank you very much, Priscilla, for your sweet note when I had the operation. It was very much appreciated. The operation in question seems to have been completely successful, which is a blessing. One of the nurses passed out while it was going on – and how it did go on, nearly two hours. Not very painful, however. I was not much impressed by France, where with a spontaneous acclaim which is as unusual as it is impossible, the Volcano is the book of the month already for next September. When you reflect that it was also, without even having been published, the book of the month for last September, you may gain some inkling of how such things are managed. With Margie's opinion of Italy I go more than all the way. I loved it, and was especially enchanted by Rome. We also got a great kick out of Capri. The French have enormous vitality, but it's a quality I don't always admire. I like things rather sleepy. The Italians seem to have things both ways. Rome was full of monks apparently dozing peacefully on enormously fast motor scooters. Margie made a great hit with my family.[3] In fact she is a good deal more popular than me – the Volcano doesn't seem to have been quite the thing, old chap. One of my brothers – a detective during the war – now edits a magazine dealing with motor cars.[4] He hasn't yet volunteered a critical opinion. I think at least he ought to give me a plug. 'This powerful one horse power combination, of Latin American build, fast and snappy.' One of my nephews seems to have disappeared into Burma, where when last heard of he was the only British surgeon, with 30,000 casualties. His being in the east at this time is the cause of considerable anxiety, especially to my eldest brother and his wife, but he is the sort of person that will probably be O.K.[5] I think that is about all. I was extremely grateful, Bert, for the stuff you gave us which I'm sure prevented me at least from dying of starvation in France.

With very best love – hoping you are both, as ourselves, in the pink, your affectionate brother,

Malcolm

Annotations:

1 Lowry first met Margerie's sister Priscilla Bonner Woolfan (1899-) and her husband, E.B. (Bert) Woolfan (1894-1961), in 1945; see Lowry's December 1945 letter (**209**) to Priscilla and his 19 April 1946 letter (**216**) to Bert.

2 See Lowry's June 1949 letter (**371**) to Anna Mabelle Bonner, where, in fact, he says nothing about his work.

3 According to Bowker (437, 448), the Lowry family wanted nothing to do with Malcolm and were contemptuous of Margerie when she visited them in October 1948.

4 Russell Lowry was the vintage-car enthusiast.

5 Donald Lowry, a medical doctor and the son of Lowry's eldest brother Stuart, did return safely from the war.

373: To Frank Taylor

P: UBC(tsc phc)
PP: *SL* 179-80

Dollarton, B.C.
1 July 1949[a]

My dear Frank:

Margerie is flying down to Nuestra Senora la Reina de Los Angeles de Porciuncula[1] next Wednesday to visit – to visit *with*, I believe I should say – her family for a week, that is approximately July 6th-14th, and I was wondering if you could find time to tear yourself away from the Divers responsibilities of the Ferris wheel long enough so that you may both have a chat again.[2] At least she will be as disappointed, as I, if you both cannot establish some contact, but on the other hand will understand as well as I should it prove impossible, she having been in what I believe is termed the Pixbix herself. However I should be immensely beholden to you if in your Wizard of Oz-like eyrie[3] you would set such hosts in motion as would enable her at least to reach you by phone, my experience being that you probably have to make this difficult out of self-defense, from people claiming not only to be Scott Fitzgerald, but doubtless representing Edward Fitzgerald too, and who insist that if you think you can get away with making a film of Tender is the Night without taking an option also upon Omar Khayam, you are very much mistaken.[4] On the other side her address in Hollywood will be care of Dr E.B. Woolfan, 1643 Queens Road and her phone number is (we think) Gladstone 3830 or if not you'll find it in the phone book, he of the wolfish name being my quite admirable brother-in-law, who entertains himself mostly by listening to the chests of movie actresses and establishing whether they are good risks or not.

For the rest I want only to say how much I value and treasure the letter you wrote about the Volcano and appreciate your having been its publisher. I am absorbed in the new book to the extent of sometimes fifteen hours a day, and boy, it has some theme, being no less than the identification of a creator with his creation – Pirandello in reverse or, Six authors in search of his characters;[5] or otherwise stated, Every Man his own Laocoon.[6] Since the philosophic implications might prove fatal to myself, I have to preserve a certain detachment. – I am going to surprise Albert, who probably thinks I am dead, drunk, or idling, or all three, with the beginning of it fairly soon, nor, should it prove really good and he eventually think it acceptable, am I going to let anyone else publish it, which loyalty is by proxy to yourself too. If it is no good on the first attempt, by which I mean, even now, the fourth, I shall have to write it again which would be a bore, for I shall never get a better idea if I wait till kingdom come. But between the idea and the execution falls the – yes, indeed it does.[7]

For the rest, we have five snakes in our garden, of high intelligence, I am convinced, for they like to listen to me twangle the guitar. Their tastes are a bit gloomy, however, running to hymn tunes played in diminished sevenths. We have not yet made an arrangement of Snakes Hips for them. I think they would consider it, having no brows to speak of, to be slightly low scale.

So may we all (as it were) meet again.

In any event, our best loves to Nan, the children and yourself.

God Bless,

[Malcolm]

Annotations:

1 The original Spanish name given the town in 1781 (Our Lady, the Queen of the Angels of Porciuncula) was later shortened to Los Angeles.

2 Lowry's pun on divers is an allusion to Dick Diver, the hero of F. Scott Fitzgerald's novel *Tender Is the Night* (1934); Taylor was interested in making a film of the novel, and the Lowrys' became consumed by the project.

3 *The Wizard of Oz* (1900) by L. Frank Baum (1856-1919), an American journalist, playwright, and author of children's books, became a classic children's story and a popular film in 1939. The Great Wizard rules the country of Oz from the Emerald City.

4 Edward Fitzgerald (1809-83), the English translator, is remembered for his translation of Omar Khayyám's (?-1123) series of quatrains known as the *Rubáiyát of Omar Khayyám*.

5 Lowry was working on *Dark as the Grave*, which he likens here to Luigi Pirandello's play *Six Characters in Search of an Author*.

6 Laocoön, who was strangled by sea serpents, is a favourite Lowry image of the artist; see Lowry's 5 July 1946 letter (**229**) to Albert Erskine for his first use of this expression.

7 Lowry's echo here is of key lines from part 5 of T.S. Eliot's 'The Hollow Men' (1925):

> Between the idea
> And the reality
> Between the motion
> And the act
> Falls the Shadow

Editorial Notes:

a. A typed copy of this letter is with the Erskine Papers at the University of Virginia. The original has not been located. In a note to Erskine about Lowry's plan to have Erskine publish the new work, Taylor has written: 'this is wonderful news isn't it.'

Between his 1 July 1949 letter (373) to Frank Taylor and this 10 August letter (374) Lowry had been busy, but not on his own work. During Margerie's visit to Los Angeles he had the fall from his pier that injured his back and sent him to hospital, where he experienced the hallucinations that inspired 'The Ordeal of Sigbjørn Wilderness.' After her return and during his recovery period Malcolm had become intrigued with the idea that, together, he and Margerie could write a filmscript of Tender Is the Night. *The months of work they would put into this project were their own decision and responsibility. Although the final document was praised by notables like Christopher Isherwood, and the series of letters to Taylor about the novel and filmscript illuminates Lowry's aesthetics and thematic interests, these facts will seem small recompense to those who wish he had spent this time on his fiction.*

374: To Frank Taylor

P: Lilly(ts)

Dollarton, B.C.,
Canada
10 August 1949

Dear Frank:

This is actually letter no. 3 – I grew a bit diffuse in the other two so shelved them and will reserve their material for a later date.[1]

I'm awfully glad Margie and yourself and Nan managed to get together and thank you very much, too, for your hospitality to her.

Also for your solicitude for me, which obtained news that set Margie's mind more or less at rest, and for this I thank you.[2]

I was in a bit of a dilemma because I didn't want to spoil her holiday so delayed the telegram as long as I could. Actually the accident had taken place at the end of the previous week and I'd been in the hospital since that Monday. St Paul's Hospital also added up to a strange experience, only too thematic – which was where I grew diffuse – when Margie returned I was in another hospital. It was not till over a week later it was finally ascertained I had actually injured my spine: fortunately it is only a crack in the 4th vertebra, and I shall be O.K. in a few months and have indeed been home for about 10 days. I have, however, temporarily, to wear a brace that is about as heavy as full parachute equipment, which makes everything hard, living as we do, especially upon Margerie: 'All one needs now is boils,' we said jovially and Job-like the other day, and sure enough we promptly got the boils, caused by the adhesive tape they strapped up my broken ribs with, the removal of skin together with tape, and doubtless not helped by the friction of the steel brace on top of that. Enough of this.

In a large intervallo so far as other work in progress was concerned we started to devote ourselves whole heartedly to your Fitzgerald problem in Tender is the Night, rereading the book several times, as well as the treatment, as well as all the other Fitzgerald books and Fitzgeraldiana we could scare up.[3] The collective result of this is so far as follows: First, though the treatment you sent us is an imaginative one as far as it goes, it is neither as imaginative as it should be, nor offers such possibilities for a great movie as it should. Moreover it is imaginative in the wrong places, and Maddow's inventiveness, while excellent, mostly occurs at the wrong moments.[4] Finally it becomes a rationalization of, not only a total misconception of the book, but, more important, of a misconception of the movie in the book.

While not insisting of course on the obvious Catholic League of Decency impossibilities such as the incest motif, it has occurred to us – having got right under the skin of the thing – to attempt a treatment such as Fitzgerald might have made himself. Actually the incest motif can go by the board without any great detriment to Fitzgerald's conception. For as I and we see it – and I think Fitzgerald, himself vastly influenced by the cinema by the way, would agree – what the thing is really about is the dividing line between sanity and madness. I have put this badly; what I should say rather is the action takes place for the most part on the windrow between those two things. Tender is the Night. . . but there there is no light.[5] Well, there is the light of the moon. The moon is madness. Even the Diver's villa is the Villa Diana – and Diana is the moon, in case one forgot. The song about Au Claire de la lune mon ami Pierrot[6] etc is not just a charming song put there only as a contrast to the ensuing horror, or merely as an additional medium of showing the Divers and family at their best: it is, far more importantly, directly thematic and as sinister as could be, and refers precisely to the same thing. The same way with the mention of the shark at the beginning, suddenly cropping up in relation to the safe blue water, the shark that swims just below the 'surface.' This is almost a Melvillean shark – 'The shark glides white through the phosphorus sea.' (James Cain has lifted the idea in Serenade, fin snout and teeth, but that doesn't in any way spoil it.)[7] And all these things could be as marvellous as could be cinematically. In fact the beginning of the book *is* largely cinematic – Fitzgerald's descriptive passages being scarcely more than a quid pro quo of first rate camera work (One necessity of the film if it is to be really good, is that the camera work should be continuously beautiful. Also it should not, cannot possibly be, as the present treatment seems to hint, be made in technicolor.) With the rest one has to grapple with a certain uncertainty and diffuseness on Fitzgerald's part, but it is surely a dreadful mistake to have Abe North fight the duel with Barban – even when one recognizes the necessity of cutting down on the characters a little. And it seems to me just gratuitous nonsense to have Gertrude Stein sitting with the Divers on the shore: why? And why altogether omit one of the most dramatic, (even if buried) scenes in the book, on the Goldings yacht, when Nicole is willing at a certain moment, significantly interrupted by Tommy Barban, to commit suicide with Dick? This is of course a repetition, almost on the sane side of the windrow, of the more obvious car scene, where she tries to kill Dick herself & the children: but here Nicole & Dick are – and literally – in the same boat. (So subtle is this bit, by the way, that it is only in the light of something that he makes Nicole think later, that you realise that this was Fitzgerald's intention. But surely it is precisely such subtleties that, when dramatic, should be brought to the light by the camera.) It is with such concepts, anyway, of the book's implicit cinema and drama in terms of cinema that one would proceed.

So that we thought, even if it helps not and comes to nothing, to send you a treatment of it ourselves. I cannot see how it can help but be better than the one you have, though we say it who ought not; and this is by no means to denigrate the doubtless otherwise able Mr Maddow, whom I conceive of as just having been a bit intimidated in the face of this particular material – or perhaps not intimidated *enough*. Or not enthusiastic *enough*.

Margie sent off 2 of her books to you – she didn't sign them for some reason; she would have, but she seems to shy off the subject of her work, as who would not after such an experience, so that it was as if she wanted to feel as though she had both sent them and not sent them, or something.[8] Horse in the Sky as I've said before seems to me a first rate thing, and also a hell of a good movie for someone: the Shapes, in another genre, is something also that could be made interestingly and cheaply, one feels, by anyone with imagination.

For the rest, life is a bit hard and painful at the moment: you can say a prayer, for it is needed. Still, we are in good form, considering. Hope you have a good time in Boston: don't forget to pack your wrought iron and Spanish moss.

I certainly would love to see Albert and hope you can persuade him to wing his way hence for a while.

All the best love to Nan and the children from us both.

Love.   God bless.

Malcolm

[P.S.] And how is your back?

Annotations:

1 The copy-text for this transcription (the final typed letter), was indeed sent to Taylor, but there is an undated, one-page holograph of it with the manuscripts for 'The Ordeal of Sigbjørn Wilderness' (UBC 22:30) that Lowry marked as one of five letters to be used in the 'Ordeal'; see letter (**12**) to T.R. Henn in Appendix 3. As was her custom, Margerie had typed approximately two-thirds of this letter (UBC 22:19) for easy reference as Lowry was composing.

2 Here and in the following paragraph Lowry presents his version of the events leading up to his stay in St Paul's Hospital in July 1949. According to Day (419), Lowry was drunk when he injured his back.

3 Taylor wanted to find a good filmscript for *Tender Is the Night*, and he must have discussed his 'Fitzgerald problem' with the Lowrys at some point. Only eleven of Taylor's letters to the Lowrys appear to have survived; they are with his papers at the Lilly Library, Indiana University.

4 Ben Maddow was a prolific American screenwriter. Frank Taylor sent the Lowrys a copy of his screenplay of *Tender Is the Night*, which is no

longer extant with the Lowry papers, during the late summer or early fall of 1949. Lowry discusses an article from *Life* magazine, 27 June 1949, mentioning Maddow's treatment, in his 1950 letter (**397**) to Taylor.

5 Fitzgerald's title is taken from John Keats's 'Ode to a Nightingale' (1819); Lowry is alluding to lines 5 and 8 of stanza 4:

> Already with thee! tender is the night.
>   And haply the Queen-Moon is on her throne,
>   Cluster'd around by all her starry Fays;
>   But here there is no light,
>   Save what from heaven is with the breezes blown
>   Through verduous glooms and winding mossy ways.

6 In the preamble to scene 6 of their screenplay the Lowrys provide the first verse of the French folk-song, which the Divers' children sing before going to bed. This is followed by a lengthy discussion of the symbolic value of the song with a dramatic emphasis placed upon the themes of death and the absence of light ('Ma chandelle est morte'); see Tiessen/Mota (61-62).

7 Melville's shark provides the final image and closing line to his poem 'Commemorative of a Naval Victory,' first published in *Battle-Pieces and Aspects of the War* (1866). In death the sailor 'feels that spirit which glad had hailed his worth, / Sleep in oblivion. – The shark / Glides white through the phosphorous sea.' James M. Cain's *Serenade* (1937) is about an opera singer who destroys the woman he needs most; its combination of art, Mexico, and the theme of betrayal would have caught Lowry's attention. Cain's shark appears for a few seconds before slipping below the surface of the sea in chapter 6, and its appearance provokes some philosophizing from two of the male characters.

8 Margerie sent Frank Taylor copies of *The Shapes That Creep* (1946) and *Horse in the Sky* (1947).

374-a: To Frank Taylor

P: Lilly(ts)   Dollarton, B.C.,
                                                            Canada
                                              29 September 1949[a]

Dear Frank:

Greetings. We hope your picture has finished triumphantly, that you're happy about it, that you like being a Hollywood Producer, that Nan and the children and you are all well and in the pink, that the present is pleasant and the future felicitous.

We have had what we think is a real inspiration and a new angle on

Tender is the Night. Malc's genius is working on all sixty cylinders, and, I may say, he is thoroughly enjoying himself; also, he says, he is Learning a Lot About the Novel in tearing this one to pieces and recreating it.

I had just reached this point when Malc came in with a letter he had been quite independently writing you at the same time. So Malc's letter follows and I will stop, with love,

from

Margerie

Dear old Frank:
We have become possessed by Tender is the Night.

I believe as we are distilling it, it offers a general and sometimes particular architechtonic of a great film which if you do it will make your name for twoevers and a day.

I myself have never felt so creatively exhilarated since writing the better parts of the Volcano so that by this I mean that what we are doing is essentially creative.

I see it as one of the greatest and most moving films of all time, one that is also a return to a great tradition of the movies, something that should combine the emotional impact of Griffith's Broken Blossoms and Isn't Life Wonderful with Citizen Kane.[1] How I go on. But we have been breathing eating and sleeping it and sometimes I have actually seem to feel the shade of old Fitzgerald himself over my shoulder approving, even *suggesting*, for there is an ethical balance he implied but somehow never got in, but which *has* to be got in to make it what it archetypically is. Moreover I see it as a picture that somehow combines all these qualities with being enormously popular . . .

What we would like to know, however, is it still on the shelf?[2] One wouldn't like to be like the chap Fitzgerald himself mentions who spent three years writing one thesis on the armadillo while someone else was doing it and got in ahead. Even if not I know it is a perfect shot in the dark, not even that, you didn't even suggest it. Something, however, seems to have made us do it —

Before our eyes both of us seem to see the picture you want. Also what we want and what everyone else wants: one of the best pictures they have ever seen, in short.

We have learned so much that it would not be construed a waste of time anyhow; but would you let us know the present status of T. is the N., and if you would like us to send it in to you. We can have something organically presentable in less than a month.

Good luck with whatever work in progress and love to Nan and the kids from Margie and myself

Malcolm

Annotations:

1 Both *Broken Blossoms* (1919) and *Isn't Life Wonderful* (1924) were directed by D.W. Griffith. Orson Welles starred in and directed the American film classic *Citizen Kane* (1941)

2 In his 7 October 1949 reply to the Lowrys, Taylor told them that although the film project for *Tender Is the Night* was shelved, 'nothing is permanently shelved in this town.' He went on to remind them, however, that their combined work on a filmscript was a 'speculative chance.'

Editorial Notes:

a. Given the Lowrys' combined work on the filmscript of *Tender Is the Night*, their joint letter to Taylor is included in full.

375: To Downie Kirk

P: UBC(ms phc)
PP: *SL* 181–83; *MLVD* 57–58   [Dollarton]
                                                                [ca 4 October 1949][a]

Dear Downey:

Thanks very much for the letter and for the invitation from Marjorie & yourself for Oct 7. We'd awfully much like to come but since correspondence between us at this short distance seems to take rather longer than it used to traverse the Roman Empire is it too much to leave it open? We are working hard on a movie treatment [of *Tender Is the Night*] and whether we can come rather depends on how much work we have completed by then; at the moment it looks favourable, but we may run into a snag, and it seems rather important that we finish it *quam celerrime*, if not indeed *sine mora*. At first I thought I couldn't come because I could scarcely bring my fracture board with me; now it occurs to me I could sleep on the floor. *Is it too much to ask for a bit of floor?* (It would not – er – be the first time that I have done that). I don't think it would put you to any more trouble.

I'm glad you're better now after your operation – the combination of a haemorrhoidectomy with a Catholic Institution sounds sadistic enough, without the orderly, in all conscience. It sounds a dreadful experience. I'm touched at your reading the Volcano to your fellow-sufferers – if you want to make people feel really cheery you might find Maxim Gorkys *The Lower Depths* even more helpful.

I am worried about your Prof. Sedgewick's *Irony* book,[1] which we can't find, though we've turned the house upside down looking for it – will you have another look? It's just possible that I returned it when *un poco borracho*, which is why I can't remember. Margerie remembers only returning the Graham Greene. I had the book by my bedside for some time when I was reading it; later I assumed it had been returned by her, but I can't remember that, nor can she. I certainly never lent it to any-one else, and as a rule we are extremely meticulous about books, so I feel badly about it. If it was actually a signed copy I shan't forgive myself if it has been lost. But where the devil can it be? The only explanation I can offer is that it has been pinched; though that doesn't sound likely. Somebody actually lifted a copy of the *Volcano* I had bought for some-one, while I was in hospital, so it isn't entirely impossible. (Once in New York my apartment was broken into and a copy of Ouspensky's *New Model of the Universe*[2] and a bottle of hair tonic was stolen: that was all: the matter had to be reported because of the damage to the door – the strange theft was traced to a negro, against whom I did not press charges, not wishing to start a race riot.) It is just conceivable that [Earle] Birney who lent me some other books, may have picked it up, think-ing it his, & I will ask him, though I don't think it likely he made the mistake. I definitely never took it out of the house. The most reason-able explanation, if it turns out finally that you absolutely don't have it, is, however, that it is still here, but that I put it away in some too safe place, something I have very occasionally done before. We shall look again carefully therefore: & if neither you nor I find it I shall order you another one. That is scarcely adequately replacing it – especially, as I say, if it is signed – & all I can say is, I am most awfully sorry.

I hope though it will have turned up somehow by Friday, if we can come: We look forward to seeing you both & talking, if we do. We saved a grebe. And the world progresses. . . That is, seventy years ago, one would not have thought that to-day, in order to cross a street, one would have to be preceded by a 3 year old child, as Valéry somewhere says –[3]

All the best to Marjorie and Dorothy from Margerie & myself, love

Malcolm

Annotations:

1 Dr Garnett Gladwin Sedgewick (1882-1949) came to the University of British Columbia in 1918 and was head of the English Department from 1930 to 1948. Sedgewick published *Irony, Especially in Drama* in 1935.
2 Lowry discovered P.D. Ouspensky (1878-1947), the Russian writer, lecturer, theosophist, and occultist in the late twenties or early thirties.

His books, *Tertium Organum* and *A New Model of the Universe*, were a direct influence on Lowry's thinking; see Lowry's 16 April 1940 letter (**135**) to Anna Mabelle Bonner.

3 Paul Valéry (1871–1945), the French poet, essayist, and critic, says something similar in *Variété III* (Paris: Gallimard, 1936): 'Monsieur, en 1892, auriez-vous prévu qu'en 1932, pour traverser une rue à Paris, il faudrait demander la protection d'un bébé de six mois et passer le gué clouté à l'abri d'un enfant en bas âge?' (p. 228).

Editorial Notes:

a. At the top of the recto Kirk has noted that this letter is in reply to his 1 October 1949 letter to Lowry. He has also corrected Lowry's misspelling of his name.

In this the second of two surviving letters to his 'very dearest Mum' (see also letter **240***), it is clear that Malcolm wrote regularly to his mother and that many of these letters have been lost. On this occasion he has created a satire worthy of Stephen Leacock on the Canadian medical system in an effort to entertain her as she recovers from an accident. Evelyn Lowry had been seriously ill during the preceding year and would die on 7 December 1950. The precise quality and nature of her relationship with her youngest 'boy' may never be confirmed, but that they communicated in later years with humour and affection seems clear.*

376: To Evelyn Boden Lowry

P: UBC(ms)   [Dollarton]
                                                                          [1949]

{For Martin's dialogue with Hippolyte.}ª

My very dearest Mum:

   I have been fifty times on the point of writing you a nice long letter since receiving your very sweet one, which was much appreciated by us both – Margie & myself – and have been as many times interrupted, first by slight exigencies of health, now all corrected, then by having to make an expedition to an island where the post office was distant, then by wanting not to make it just a short note to apologise for my not writing a long one, and always by work. This time I realise to my shame that it is at least six weeks since I wrote you, so I have laid aside my work, pressing though it is, to assure you that even though this may not be the long letter I have planned, that I will try not to let there be such a gap as this in future. In fact I shall send another one shortly, roaring through

the post after this to make up for my misbehaviour. I am very sorry you
have had such a trying time since January 6th, owing to your fall, but I
am very relieved you have a reliable woman doctor and one that you
can trust. This makes absolutely all the difference. Both Margie and I
have suffered from rotten doctors in this part of the world, and we have
both in our lives taken painful and prolonged treatment for things that
we were not suffering from at all, thus causing all kinds of anxiety, from
which we are now happily free. At one time we became so exasperated
on this score that we were nearly driven into the arms of Christian science, in which, if it cannot strike one as a satisfactory religion any more
than any other 'science,' there is a great deal more practical virtue than
meets the eye. I believe most good doctors will agree nowadays that the
mind is as capable of producing actual symptoms as it is of helping to
cure actual disease. In this part of the world medicine has reached a
degree of cynicism that is probably unknown in England and which I
believe would shock Donald [Lowry], say, a doctor used to things like
a code of honour and a Law of Hippocrates, to the core, that is, if anything could now shock him, after having been to Burma. In part I
ascribe this unhappy condition to the passing here of the old type of
country doctor, or the type say of Dr Brown (though in my eyes that
gent was never a very shining example) who knew all about everyone
in the family and to whom one could talk with all the confidence – or
even the lack of confidence, which is sometimes better than nothing, for
the important thing is sometimes just to get things off your chest, – that
one would have in talking to a priest, were one a Roman catholic, or
the local witch doctor, were one a savage. In our jungle here there was
once neither doctor or even a witch doctor who would come to you on
a Saturday afternoon, even if you were dying, or a hospital that would
take you unless you were dead, and not then until you began to stink,
and through this I once nearly lost Margerie, who had run a nail through
her foot & acquired blood poisoning.[1] Here the doctors band together
in the cities in skyscrapers known as Medical-Dental Buildings. Each
doctor, or diagnostician – the first one you are usually recommended to
go to – has his pet disease, and upstairs, is his pet specialist, who, for the
good reason that he has possibly suffered from that disease himself, spe-
cialises in it: the diagnostician downstairs prescribes his pet disease every
time when in doubt and his pet specialist upstairs will treat it mechani-
cally whether you are suffering from it or not in the hope of the
extremely likely event that if you are not, you soon will be. Still further
upstairs in our skyscraper, sits, like a spider in his web, the dentist, who
is the pet of both. To him you proceed when you are finished with the
specialist, for there is an unwritten law in the Medical Dental Building
that when the source of a local infection is in doubt it must be due to

the teeth. When therefore you return downstairs with half your good teeth pulled out, the removal of which has released poisons in your system to produce several more infections three times worse than the comparitively innocent one with which you started, you still have another call to make at the diagnostician's. This is because the diagnostician is in possession of a little, or even it may be a large machine, known as a diathermy machine, which produces deep heat to comfort the supposedly infected parts, a machine for which, being anyway expensive, the dentist, the specialist, and the diagnostician are all paying for by installments. To facilitate this the patient is therefore subjected to the machine for varying periods according to the seriousness of the ailment, the only thing certain about the length of these periods being that since the ailment, whatever it is, inevitably becomes more serious during the course of this treatment, the periods grow longer, with the result that the diathermy machine is paid for that much sooner, enabling the owners in question to buy another even more expensive machine which, quite logically also, costs more for the patient. Did I say that was the last call the patient made? I was wrong. There is one more, perhaps two. And perhaps for that matter, even three or four. For right downstairs, even further downstairs than the diagnostician, on the ground floor in fact, lives a personage known as the chemist, or as we call him here, the druggist, the pet of everybody, and it is to him you are now sent with a prescription. In the ancient days it used to be good enough to pay simply for what you bought at the chemists. But now, oh no, with that diathermy machine in mind, it is necessary to pay for the prescription too. As for the second call, if after many years, everything has failed so signally to bring about any appreciable improvement in the patient so that even he grows suspicious, there is on the very top floor of the Medical Building, even above the dentist, a little hospital. There, fever treatment may be taken to burn out all the ambiguous poisons in your system after which, if that fails – and it generally will, if your purse shows any signs of holding out – you are either ready for the whole thing again, or for the morgue, which is in the basement.

If on the other hand you survive this sort of thing five or six times you are about ready either to take to drink or to God, of which the latter is more advisable as being for one thing, less expensive.

The other solution, – or corollary to a solution – is a good doctor, such as one used to understand by that term, & we now fortunately have one, and being now in excellent health, have to see him very infrequently. My operation was an unqualified success.[2]

I may add that though we have had recently an insurance scheme here, unlike England's of late years it does not, however pay for our medical bills. It gives us one week free per year in a charity ward, but medicines and doctors are all extra. And you have to pay the insurance, which at least a quarter of our population cannot afford, or you can't go into the hospital.

I hope only that you may find Professor Roberts a good doctor such as we have & for the rest I can only counsel you, as you did me, to be patient & keep a sense of humour & I'm sure all will be well soon.

Margerie is very grateful & touched by your sweet message & she sends all kind of love to you & good messages & both of us our great moral & spiritual support & hope for your swift recovery. With great love

Your devoted son

Malcolm

P.S. I am writing a comparatively optimistic book.[3] It is even rather religious. More of this later.

Annotations:

1 This was the accident that befell Margerie in the spring of 1945 when they were rebuilding their Dollarton cabin after the June 1944 fire that destroyed their first home on the beach.
2 Lowry is referring to the operation he had in mid-March 1949 for varicose veins. His family doctor, Clarence McNeill, was a young general practitioner in Deep Cove.
3 The book is *Dark as the Grave*, which ends optimistically on a strong spiritual note of rebirth.

Editorial Notes:

a. This letter is transcribed from a signed, undated pencil draft (UBC 3:14); the contents suggest a fall 1949 date, while Lowry was still recuperating from his back injury. Presumably at some point after sending the fair copy, Lowry added this instruction for the use of the letter in his fiction; Dr Hippolyte is a character in chapter 3 of *Dark as the Grave*. A typed draft of this letter appears with Lowry's notes and drafts for the novel (UBC 10:10), but it is not included in the published text.

377: To Harry Ford

p: Virginia(tsc)   Dollarton, B.C.,
                                    Canada
                                    5 November 1949[a]

Dear Mr Ford:[1]
Thank you for giving me the privilege of reading A Long Day's Dying and for doing me the honour of inviting my comments upon it.

I read it right off, but certain difficulties due to a recent accident you were kind enough to mention, concerned with sitting down, not to say standing up, and one might add, lying down, and what used to be called also 'the pressure of work', though it may be that it is rather the work itself that suffers from the pressure we bring to it and so tries sensibly to elude us, combined to inhibit me, I sincerely hope not too long, from writing anything on the matter: then I thought I would like some other opinions, these were not very helpful, so here goes. Or rather, here does not go, for I find it awfully difficult to say anything useful in ten or fifty words, excellent though that discipline might be, as this letter so far would seem to indicate, nonetheless perhaps by trying to express my feelings as I go along one may arrive at something which could suitably be distilled.

First it seems a bit bumptious, especially on the part of another young writer – or in this case a writer who while no longer precisely young, in respect of age, seems to have been writing his last coherent paragraph at about the time that master Buechner was apparently kicking the bottom out of his cradle – to call a book such as this merely promising.[b] The chords are struck, they are resolved, and all is executed with almost flawless taste and, technically, a high degree of excellence. Moreover the book has none of the faults of over-ebullience, of overstatement, of sentimentality, usually associated with a young author. Some readers indeed may find the fault lies precisely here, in a certain lack of enthusiasm, a certain quality of inhumanness. Some unfriendly critics will doubtless maintain that the excellence of the writing, and the perfection of technique, are mysteriously faults in themselves, exhibited to conceal a poverty of content, or theme, that this excellence is somehow, even, almost morally wrong, as being derivative of other young American writers who have also shown themselves capable, or rather guilty, of equal brilliance, as though the mediocre or the slipshod, provided that it remains 'human', and – the reverse of which used to be true a few years ago – contains an inner meaning not so deep that it can be misconstrued as a blow at the Communist party or unamerican thinking,[2] were the more appropriate standard, for the 'beginner'. Then again there may be those who, calmly overlooking the book's many original virtues and positive achievement of style, will point out that it exhibits the current influence of Henry James on modern literature without, however, suggesting that this is in anyway a healthful influence, nor how much worse off it would be without it nor, what many artisans would like to know, giving us any helpful hint of how, once having got the old boy in the machinery, it is possible to get him out again. Nor will the fact that one of the book's most endearing characters, some will say the only endearing character, is a monkey, undoubtedly destined to

be called (and with some justice, having made one important reserva-
tion) one of the most intelligent characters in recent fiction, mitigate our
author's attachment critically speaking to what is almost sure to be called
the 'precious.' As for the theme – heaven help us, where is the theme –
what is it all about? Well, the theme is at once as commonplace as a
homily on the wall of a doctor's waiting room bidding you to be kind
for you may not pass this way again, and as complex as the emotions you
may be feeling while waiting in that room, shortly to be told that this
may be in fact only too true or that, on the contrary, you will have to
pass this particular way three times a week for the next six months. At
one point in the book, an important and subtle scene is enacted before
a tapestry: this tapestry, which is superbly described, causes one of the
characters to wonder whether he was to take a figure on it as symbolic
to which the protagonist, a massive and sympathetic yet pathetic figure
who presides over the book rather like a Buddha, remarks: 'You may
take the unicorn for whatever it may mean to you.'[3]

To me the unicorn means a good deal, though here I shall content
myself with saying that it might very well stand for the meaning of the
book itself, which can be read, as I have hinted, in several different ways.
The book indeed can be seen to have something of the quality of a
tapestry, both in regard to its texture considered as a hand woven
reversible textile, and its richness of adornment. From this tapestry in
the half light in which we seem to regard it, the figures, not least our
tragic monkey, that ancient standby, incidentally, of tapestries, seem to
emerge and tread a strange dance, at the end of which they recede back
into it again, at the same time a brilliant light fills the room.

It is this strange quality of 'muffled magnificence', as an anonymous
critic once said of [Henry] James, that doubtless does sometimes give the
effect of James himself, though the influence is probably remote. For
one thing, the music they dance is too often far from stately; at times it
is even, as it were, hot: using this parlance one might say that it was
sometimes pure Beiderbeck,[4] at other times a sort of spiritual be-bop: I
don't mean this in a derogatory sense, but literally – we hear the sound
of the author practicing, but, unlike most be-bop, the practising contributes to the unity of the piece. However jazz is a music largely for the
young, but young and old can rejoice in Mr Buechner's. On the other
hand nothing in A Long Day's Dying, save perhaps a slight trace of
cruelty, a trait he has in common with the early Thomas Mann, gives
the effect of its having actually been written by a young man.[5] Apart
from this, which may be kindly considered as the growing pains of a
later compassion, far from being a first book by a very young man, it
might as well be a last work by a very old man who, having written a
number of brilliant things latterly in a certain genre, has a shot at some-

thing new, that perhaps incidentally involves a dominant principle of youth, a sort of fictional When We Dead Awaken, in fact, to transpose vocations, by which, though written in prose, we are nonetheless reminded at the end that Ibsen was first a poet.[6] This last may account for much in Buechner.

Nonetheless it is paradoxically its astonishing maturity that causes one at length to use the word 'promising,' and in this he also resembles the young Thomas Mann. If development is a progress towards integration I myself find nothing of that very obviously in Mann's work. In essence, I merely find different works. Actually, by the other token The Magic Mountain is, in one sense, by its attempted more-or-less all–inclusiveness, a kind of regression from Buddenbrooks, which is integrated from first to last. We find both excellent, yet one scarcely leads to the other, nor can the latter be termed exactly more mature. Mario and the Magician is simply different from Tonio Kroger and in nothing but the most obvious respect can be considered a development from it. It is simply a marvellously successful attempt to do something else. Similarly with the elephantine Joseph; ridiculous though this may sound, it is simply rather larger, than Herr und Hund.[7] And for all its greater profundity, that does not make Herr und Hund any the less profound in its own way. Unless I am mistaken therefore,[c] Mr Buechner has the type of mind from which various things are liable to appear fully blown and more or less perfect in their own right. This is true of A Long Day's Dying: on its own terms I can offer no criticism at all. But on rereading the book I am constrained to observe that the mind that could give us, say, the station episode, can give us also a Tonio Kroger and more – and, I do not say it irreverently, thinking of the 'more', I hope, less too. Thus also I would certainly risk saying that in the truest sense his book possesses that hazardous quality, promise.

I was going on to say some other things, (my wife calls this 'getting on the horse') but perhaps you can cull 10 or 50 words from this – I haven't done it myself, because I feel if I don't catch this post I may be too late, and since I feel about the book as I do, I feel it my duty to send something in.

Some of the other things, since one is on the subject. I have the notion that such unusual minds as Buechner's skip the occupational diseases peculiar to other writers, for writers, like children, have diseases peculiar to writers alone, the terrors of hysterical identification, for example, the uncanny dying through the death of another character, and so forth, frightening things which may indeed end in death for the author himself without another word. Such minds as Buechner's – and it is an extremely interesting subject – do not seem trapped by these things at a given age; the sickness seems to be evenly distributed through the consciousness and acts as a stimulus at a given period of focus, as if one could imagine a merely latent tuberculosis actually behaving with the qualities of stimulation it is said to possess in the downhill phase of the illness, but without it causing one to go downhill oneself, to be segregated, or indeed even to have tuberculosis at all.

For the rest, Mr Buechner had a near namesake – I refer to the contemporary of Goethe.[8] I am not going into this.

There may be certain mistakes in my grammar not to say semantics, or even in common sense here or there; if so, please overlook them and I hope you can find something.

Thanks very much again for asking about my accident. In fact I broke my back – fortunately only the 4th vertebra. But apart from having to wear a brace about as heavy as a full parachute, equipment I hope to discard in a month or so, I have not suffered any great inconvenience from it latterly, nor does it threaten to have ill effects in the future. In fact it was somewhat of an experience and has caused one to work harder.

With all best wishes – and also best wishes for the success of A Long Day's Dying, and my congratulations to its author.

Yours sincerely,

Malcolm Lowry

Annotations:

1 Harold Ford (1915-), a friend of Albert Erskine's, worked with Knopf, which published *A Long Day's Dying* (1950) by Carl Frederick Buechner (1926-), an ordained minister of the United Presbyterian Church and an American writer of novels, short stories, and theological non-fiction. Ford, who had sent Lowry the preview copy of Buechner's novel, used quotations from this letter on the dust-jacket.

2 The phrase 'unamerican thinking' refers to the House Un-American Activities Committee (HUAC), which investigated fascist, communist, and other so-called subversive groups in the United States. Established in 1938 and abolished in 1975, HUAC was most active during the late forties and the fifties, when it pursued many writers, film directors, and intellectuals.

3 The scene before the tapestry takes place in chapter 14 and is, as Lowry suggests, a remarkable example of Henry James's influence on modern fiction. In it, the portly hero Tristram Bone (owner of the wise pet monkey Simon) conducts a delicate interview with a younger man, who is suspected of having a homosexual interest in the heroine's son. As a family friend, and literary descendant of James's Lambert Strether from *The Ambassadors*, Bone's mission is to rescue the son from corruption. Buechner uses the tapestry, which depicts a hunt for the mythical white unicorn, as a symbolic backdrop for his story.

4 Bix Beiderbecke was an American jazz cornetist whom Lowry particularly liked.

5 Thomas Mann (1875-1955), the German novelist and essayist, won the Nobel Prize for Literature in 1929. Lowry admired Mann's fiction and goes on to mention several examples of his work: *Buddenbrooks* (1901; trans. 1924); *Tonio Kröger* (1903; trans. 1913); *The Magic Mountain* (1924; trans. 1924), and *Mario and the Magician* (1930; trans. 1931).

6 Henrik Ibsen's play *When We Dead Awaken* (1900) is a symbolic treatment of the spiritual death awaiting those who deny love.

7 The 'elephantine Joseph' is a reference to Mann's *Joseph* tetralogy, published between 1933 and 1943. It is many times longer than Mann's novella *Herr und Hund* (1919; *A Man and His Dog*), which ran to one hundred ninety pages in its first German publication.

8 Lowry refers here to Georg Büchner (1813-37), the author of *Wozzeck*, an unfinished play that inspired Alban Berg, the Austrian composer, to write his expressionist opera of the same name in 1925.

Editorial Notes:

a.   This transcription is from a photocopy of a typed copy (UBC 2:3) of an original letter, which does not appear to have survived. The copy is with the Erskine Papers at the University of Virginia.

b.   This and the following sentence appear on the dust-jacket.

c.   The lines from here to 'Tonio Kroger and more' complete the dust-jacket quotation.

378: To Albert Erskine

P: Virginia(ts); UBC(phc)
PP: *SL* 183-84; *Lln* 188-89

Dollarton, B.C.,
Canada
7 November 1949

My very dear Albert:

We were very disappointed not to see you and show you our house and some Rockies. But we will be happy if you had a good and constructive time. I have revised my opinion of Intruder in the Dust which does indeed fit into the great plan most impressively. Please tell Jay Leyda how much I enjoyed the Melville stories and his preface. I am working up another ornithological quarrel with Melville, who in his poetry refers to shearwaters as 'haglets' and birds of ill omen. Haglets indeed – they are mystical and wonderful birds. And apart from the fact that one suspects him of thinking of jaegers. . . And even then! Someone once let loose a ringed shearwater in Venice and in less than a week it had found its way home to a tiny island off the coast of Devon, where it was discovered vociferously talking to its family about the voyage.

(Nobody knows whether it came right over the Alps or clear round via Gibraltar.)

We are working on a kind of enthusiastic deviation from usual work – will tell you when finished, otherwise am witheld by superstition.[1] One reason for this was that the broken back produced another story so related to the one I was working on & at the precise point where I was working on it that I had to revise my plans anyway – meantime this is an expericne {not a typ. error, obviously a *new Greek* word}. Hope Peggy had a very good trip – we think of you both with affection and often. Any news of the haglet or even murre editions? By which Margie says you won't understand I mean Penguin.

The back is getting better, in fact is even better than before, so to speak. I just wrote something about a very remarkable book sent me by a friend of yours, Mr Harry Ford, via Knopf;[2] having sent it in I was pursued all night by a mixed metaphor wearing black boots, from which protruded a cockade, and moreover fully armed. I have a p.s. to the letter in question – Knopf books have no address on them, & I haven't Ford's address – would you be kind enough to forward it for me?

All love and God bless from us both, to you both

Malcolm

Annotations:

1 Lowry is referring to his and Margerie's work on the screenplay of *Tender Is the Night*; however, the back injury he suffered in July 1949 had led to vivid hallucinations in hospital, which in turn inspired him to begin work on 'The Ordeal of Sigbjørn Wilderness.' See Day (139-45) and Grace, *Voyage* (9-12).
2 Frederick Buechner's *A Long Day's Dying*: see Lowry's 5 November 1949 letter (**377**) to Ford.

379: To Albert Erskine

P: Virginia(card); UBC(phc)
PP: *SL* 184   [Dollarton]
                                                    [16 December 1949][a]

You will remark that these candles are not burning at both ends. (See above candle on left) Should you see Allan Tate you might tell him in reference to his recent admirable article on Poe that if the raven was nearly extinct in the forties of the last century it certainly is not extinct now.[1] There are two kinds of raven – Corvus corax, and Corvus cryptoleucus. The former is nearly twice the size of a crow, but it flies like a hawk, flapping & soaring alternately, upon horizontal wings. It is found in most of the Western U.S. – on the whole replacing the crow in arid country or along rockey coasts. The latter is smaller and is found in the deserts of S.E. Arizona, South New Mexico, South East Colorado, south west Oklahoma, and west and south Texas. It has never been reported in Virginia. Neither raven has been heard to say Nevermore:[2] I myself have never heard it say anything stronger than cheerio. But more specifically the former raven says Cr-r-r-ruck: the latter kraak. We once observed two ravens making love upon a Friday the thirteenth, without any ill effects. The Indians think here that the raven is God. In any case it is the most anti-social bird in the world, with the exception of (a) the eagle (b) the albatross. This is all the news. We are working hard, having a good time & my back is better. We are both in very good health and hope you are. And we send our sincere love to Peggy and yourself.

from Malcolm and Margerie

P.S. Three years ago to-day we were thrown out of a pub in New Orleans for correcting therein the final proofs of the Volcano because they said 'this is not an office.' In that case I said why be so officious? So we went to another pub where we were more welcome. Shades of Bohemia! It was a happy day: & so is this.

Annotations:

1 Allen Tate (1899-1979), the American writer, editor, and poet, published 'Our Cousin Mr Poe' in *Partisan Review* 16 (December 1949): 1207-17.
2 Edgar Allan Poe's bird in his poem 'The Raven' regularly croaks out a portentous 'Nevermore.'

Editorial Notes:

a. This is the postmark date on the envelope. Lowry has written a parenthetical remark in the lower right corner of the Christmas card to draw Erskine's attention to the image of a lighted candle, and he has signed for himself and Margerie.

380: To John Davenport

P: UBC(card)   [Dollarton]
                                                [Christmas 1949][a]

Dear old Davvy:

   Am frightfully sorry I haven't written – reason, I broke my back – kerrunch, just like that, one of my building projects having overthrown me. Nonetheless I am now better, with no ill effects, or in prospect –

for some reason it has made me immeasurably stronger, odd, but true –
& doing really good work, though I say it – When in doubt, break your
back etc etc. – Was tickled pink with the Arenas[1] – though I wish you
had rewritten Economic Conference for me – I felt proud of some of
the poems too, of which 'I have more'[2] – I could stand a lecture from
you on the general subject, however, as by gosh, could some of your
other writers – a Dovjenkho & an Ivanov in every man, an early
Eisenstein & a late,[3] but Dovjenkho was good early & late, often making social truth gybe through beauty or otherwise with *the* truth etc –
why not others? In the present phase writers like Tzara[4] sound literally
gruesome with platitudes – to Siberia & Greek orthodoxy with me.
Your mag besides being good & interesting is by [far] one of the nicest
looking & best printed I ever saw, especially the verse: 'car's bane' in The
Glaucous Winged Gull is cat's bane, however – & it is 'loved' the most
in Nocturne though there seems on second thoughts no very good
reason why it should be.[5] I had an extraordinary psychical experience in
hospital – it relates to dear old Jimmy Travers[6] & of this I must write
you at great length, & also ask your advice, for it is very important. Do
you know if his mother lives, & where? Meantime please for me say
your very best prayer & think your best thoughts of The good James,
even if this has the paradoxical effect of sending the old boy to heaven.
Xmas time is a good time to go, anyway. (Above)[b]

And may great affection be upon your own head, Margeries & the
children God bless Malc.

With all warmest wishes to yourself & your Margerie & A happy new
year

& Love from

Malc & his Margerie

Annotations:

1 Davenport, a founding editor in 1949 of *Arena*, with Jack Lindsay and
   Randall Swingler, had sent Lowry copies of the two issues of the literary magazine in which his work appeared. Five poems were published
   in *Arena* 1 (Summer 1949): 79-82; his story 'Economic Conference' and
   a poem appeared in *Arena* 2 (Autumn 1949): 49-57, 58-60.
2 'I have more' is an allusion to the lines from John Donne's poem 'A
   Hymn to God the Father': 'When thou hast done, thou hast not done,
   / For I have more' (*Poems* [1633]).
3 Alexander Dovjenkho's *Aerograd (Air City, Frontier)*, 1935, is one of
   his best-known films. Judging from the references to other Russian
   film people, the Ivanov that Lowry is thinking of could be either the

director Alexander Ivanov or the pioneer of Russian animation, Ivan Ivanov-Vano. Sergei Eisenstein was a leading Russian film director and theoretician, and Lowry was familiar with his work; see his 21 September 1940 letter (**151**) to Gerald Noxon.

4 Tristan Tzara published 'Dialectics of Poetry,' a commentary on the semiotics of poetry and the revolutionary stance of the poet, in *Arena* 1 (Summer 1949): 9-19.

5 The poems do appear with these typographical errors. 'Carsbane' in 'Glaucous Winged Gull' makes nonsense of Lowry's line 'Cat's bane and defiler of the porch,' while 'loved' printed as 'love' in 'Nocturne' creates an odd ambiguity.

6 According to Lowry and to the manuscript of 'The Ordeal of Sigbjørn Wilderness' (UBC 22:19-20), Travers appeared to Lowry in hospital in a vision so clear that Lowry was able to describe his tobacco, clothes, voice, and 'gentle almost beautiful face' in great detail. See Day (140-42), and Lowry's April/May 1947 letter (**297**) to Davenport.

Editorial Notes:

a. This 'letter' has been written on the back of an undated Christmas card mistakenly filed with the Lowry correspondence for 1940. The contents of the letter (the back injury and the James Travers hallucination) clearly date it, however, as Christmas 1949.

b. Lowry squeezed in the complimentary close at the top of the page.

381: To William and Alice McConnell

p: UBC(card)   [Dollarton]
                                                    [December 1949]

Dear Bill & Alice – [1]
   It's been far too long since the happy Thanksgiving we spent in your home. We'd love to see you. God bless you & a Merry, merry Christmas
                                                          – Margerie

Heartily seconded by Malcolm – we read the witchy willowes with delight, Margie hasn't quite finished the lugubrious Guy[2] – all best love.
                                                          [unsigned]

Annotations:

1 William McConnell (1917–) and his wife Alice (1913-82) were introduced to the Lowrys by Earle Birney in 1947. The couples became friends, and Lowry appreciated the hours spent reading and discussing literature with Bill in the McConnell's Burnaby home; see Salloum (110-12). McConnell, a Vancouver lawyer, writer, and editor, often

discussed the law with Lowry, who sought his advice on legal matters in *October Ferry to Gabriola.*

2 The 'witchy willowes' was a bed-time story that Bill McConnell had written for his young son. The 'lugubrious Guy' is the Canadian actor and producer Guy Glover (1909-88), a friend of the McConnells.

382: To Philippe Thoby-Marcelin

P: UBC(ms)   Dollarton P.O.,
                                                 Dollarton, B.C.
                                                 [January 1950][a]

My very dear Phi-to:

Don't excuse my not writing – this is the tenth letter I have begun.[1] Yes, please humbly excuse it anyway. It was wonderful to hear from you, I was held up from replying, but I thank you deeply for the card.

But we have been cut off from the outer world here by below zero Arctic weather – this we have had to face in our self-built house, and even so have suffered less than some people: what was interesting to observe with a sort of gloomy satisfaction was the complete collapse of all the contrivances of civilisation here during the worst winter in history – no trains got through, the trams stopped running, the electric power gave out, the water was all but rationed.

Yet our well remained full, our oil lamps burned, & we had no modern conveniences to go wrong: none the less it was hell, & we could not take off our clothes for nearly six weeks.

(Note, from Kafka, concerning the healthy life . . . 'B, the chief auditor, tells the story of a friend of his, a half-pay colonel who likes to sleep beside an open window: 'During the night it is very pleasant: but in the morning when I have to shovel the snow off the ottoman near the window & then start shaving, it is unpleasant.)[2]

Another reason I delayed writing was as follows. I had ventured to dedicate the French edition of Under the Volcano to yourself, together with Margie – they sent me the proofs with your name spelt wrong – no h in Thoby, & two ll's in Marcelin – that I corrected & sent back again, I hoped in time to catch them.[3] I had just done that when I received your letter. Now they write it must be wrong in the first edition – but will be corrected in the second (if any) and they will write you a letter of apology, as do I now. I am very upset about this, but I am blameless, since it was not I who mispelled your name, & it is all due to that imaginative erudition of those printers which writers come to love so dearly in the course of their careers.

Re the translation itself – there are several reasons that I did not keep my promise to avail myself of your generous offer to supervise it, – the main one being that I had not the power to until it seemed too late. A translation of a kind was already in existence by the time I arrived in France, but so incredibly faulty that even I could see it was hopeless, their method apparently having been simply to miss out what they could not understand. They were however bound by contract to bring it out by March 1948. I soon saw, however, that my publishers Fontaine, who had been the chief resistance publication during the war, were now on their last legs & could not keep to this contract: they had no money to pay me, let alone a translator, and your relations with them could not have been happy: moreover I was convinced that not only the translation itself would give you an unfair version of the book but you could scarcely be expected to supervise what was not there – at least so long as we had the Atlantic between us.

What has happened since I left France a year ago however is that the Club Livre de Francais has sponsored the book, taking it over from Fontaine & it has been retranslated, with the addition of what is probably an extremely bad preface written by myself, that I had originally written in quite a few places, (for Cape in England) including Port-au-Prince. I don't know what the translation is like because I have only seen the first chapter that appeared in the Mercure de France but at least they have gone to a great deal of trouble & expense about it.[4] So I felt I would like to dedicate the French translation to you anyway, which I did: and then they went & spelt your name wrong. Meantime it has just come out – they expected it to be a great success, but I have not heard how it has been received: since I have not heard, naturally I fear the worst though I may be entirely mistaken. But please take the thought, anyway.

For the rest, I was quite ill for quite a long time in Europe – & we got out of touch because Margie & I had to leave unexpectedly early, because of the lack of boats leaving here: so that your letter written in November 1947 while forwarded after the ship to San Francisco was for some reason sent back by the ships agents in America to Canada & didn't reach us, till the spring of the next year, by which time I was in hospital.

Having returned here, first I had to have an operation on my leg – then I fell from our pier to the beach & broke my back, since when I have had to wear a steel brace. For some reason, however, my back got better without leaving me crippled in any way or otherwise incapacitated & I have now been able to take the brace off.

When in France, Phi-to, I got as far as the secretary of Valèry Larbaud, but no further: so that I can tell you he is not dead.[5] On the other hand, I'm very sorry to have to tell you that it was reported to me that he *was* very ill; that he had suffered some sort of complete collapse, to the extent of having lost nearly faculty of memory, and at the time I made inquiries I was even told that he could not in fact tragically remember ever having not been as sick as he was. On the other hand there is a bright spot, in that his malady, which should have proved fatal years ago, has not proved so: So that it is always possible he may in time completely recover. I was hoping for further news of this before writing you, in the hope that there might be something more optimistic to report: but I have heard nothing as yet. Your old friend has come to resemble Cocteau in that he is surrounded by Kafka-like secretaries & minions of the Castle so that he is an extremely difficult man to reach.

I made up a message from you to be delivered such as would have had your approval & been your wish & the impression coveyed to me was that while he could not remember the present being different than it was he did indeed remember you & the excellence of your work. I believe that this was in fact so, that suddenly in the midst of his night, Port au Prince gleamed like an exotic haven upon the horizon, & the promise he saw in you not only loomed out of it as a fact, but, tragically, as a promise & a haven in himself he had not fulfilled: amid the feelings of bafflement & dreadful sadness that such a sense of darkness falling or fallen or even light dawning produces I had not the heart to pursue the matter further. On the other hand of course, the whole thing might be some extraordinary blague, & Valèry Larbaud be all this while the President of France (while France has exchanged Presidents some ten times since then.) All we can hope otherwise he may get better completely. At all events a letter sent c/o Clarisse Francillon, Fontaine, Rue Gazan, will always reach him. Perhaps you should write him, it might be the one thing needed, for his recovery. But as I say, I cannot be sure, that even as I write, he is not making le tour de Grand Duc, even in Port-au-Prince, looking for you.

La Negrèsse Adolescente is in Montreal at present, with the Chief of the Canadian Broadcasting Company:[6] *I have little faith in the ideas I had, that is* my ideas seem to have gone wrong at present re translation, but it seems I placed too great faith in the intelligence & integrity even of Canadians: all I can say is, that my own hopes have gone wrong also – while the Volcano caused a furor in the U.S & sold wildly its sales in my own country surely constitute a real record of another kind: 2. (On the strength of these 2 copies Phito apparently – they have just put me into the Canadian Who's Who.)[7]

My English agent [Innes Rose] too, that I thought we might rely on re your poems, & wrote you about, war has changed into a *mauvais type*. Other messages I would have wished to have conveyed in Paris for you I could not because of illness or difficulty of communication from

Europe to Haiti – Margie & I went to Italy for a while & had a happy time there, but still there we were in Italy, not France.

On the other hand I spoke of you to every publisher I met with enthusiasm & the conviction I feel about your work.

For some reason I could not discover who was your Parisian publisher – I assumed one exiled during the war made this difficult – & that it in fact Canape Vert had to be published outside France, in French??

At all events that might not rule out the possibility of its republication there now? So far as I know, my stock is high in France at present: unless I hear to the contrary. So I might help. Let me know soon anyhow.

(Psyche published some of Price-Mars work though this is indeed beside the point.)[8]

– I have your translation of Boutaille a la Mer pinned to my wall; so fine is it, everyone who knows French says it is better than the original, which makes me happy at the same time rather hurts my feelings, but however that may be, that is where I keep it, so I do not write two lines, without being reminded of yourself.

Finally should you ever be able to come here, Margie joins me in saying our house is yours – & we both wish some miracle would take you this way – I think Canada would interest you; as also our strange house {at least I would like you to be interested in it} – a shack rather, but beautiful for all that & built by ourselves – it is a strange scene in the early morning with a southeasterly gale & the waves of the sea level with the windows & a freighter outside: it is like being on the bridge of a ship. Our neighbours are mostly fishermen: Save in the summer then the summer people, such as they are, come. And perhaps it won't really exist unless you do see it.

So – that is, if you don't mind sweeping the snow off the ottoman in the morning: or my doing it –

Tell me the news anyway, my dear Phito, of your own ottoman & how much snow there is on it, or not: give my sincere love to your brothers Pierre & Emil – give also my best regards to Dawn Powell.[9]

Margie joins me in sending the fondest love to you. God bless you from us both, & we long to see you –

And whatever you must doubt, please do not do not doubt, whatever his stupid faults,

ton frère

Malcolm

Annotations:

1 See Lowry's 24 February 1950 letter (**387**) to Marcelin, in which he explains why he has had such trouble writing.

2 Lowry is quoting from Kafka's 23 January 1914 entry in *The Diaries of Franz Kafka, 1914-1923*, edited by Max Brod (1949).

3 See Lowry's late 1948/early 1949 letter (**352**) to Clarisse Francillon, in which he asks for this correction to be made.

4 Stéphan Rorce published his translation of chapter 1 of *Under the Volcano* in the October 1949 issue of the review.

5 Valéry Larbaud apparently knew and thought highly of Marcelin; see Lowry's 25 January 1947 letter (**275**) to Albert Erskine.

6 Lowry had sent *La Négresse adolescente*, Thoby-Marcelin's collection of poems, to Ira Dilworth in Toronto; see his 14 August 1947 letter (**316**) to Marcelin.

7 An entry on Lowry first appeared in *Canadian Who's Who* in 1948.

8 There are several periodical publications titled *Psyche* or *Psyché*. For example, there is the French literary magazine *Psyché* and a *Psyche* that is an international journal of psychoanalysis, also published in France. Jean Price-Mars (1876-1969) was a prolific and influential Haitian writer, a leader of the 'negrism' movement, a physician, ethnologist, and diplomat.

9 Dawn Powell was an American writer whom Lowry had met in New York in 1947; see letter **309-a**.

Editorial Notes:

a. This transcription (UBC 2:14) is from a seven-page pencil, signed draft, but it is not likely that Lowry sent off a fair copy; see his 24 February 1950 letter (**387**) to Marcelin. Lowry's references to the weather and to a card from Marcelin suggest that he is writing in early January. The draft carries numerous deletions, interlineations, and accidentals that indicate Lowry's difficulty in writing.

*Between August 1949 (letter **374**), when Lowry first commented upon Frank Taylor's wish to produce a film of* Tender Is the Night, *and the following letter, the Lowrys had become fascinated with their own filmscript of the novel. Although Taylor had not asked them to undertake this work, they persevered for almost a year until, in April 1950 (letter **396**), they sent their huge cinematic brain-child off to him with the profound, if unrealistic, hope that he would be able to find a studio to produce it. The letters to Taylor during this time are full of excitement about this secret project, but Taylor was unable to arouse interest in Hollywood. Years later, when writing seemed next to impossible for Lowry, he would return somewhat plaintively to the notion of selling the filmscript as a book.*

383: To Frank Taylor

P: Lilly(ms); Matson(tsc)   [Dollarton]
                                                    [ca 17 January 1950][a]

Dear Frank:

We're a gettin' there – and how! The course of work has been followed continually by the most eerie coincidences that would make a
book in themselves, but always of an illuminating and constructive
nature, that suggests to me that there is a destiny in this, and that we are
on the right track: in fact we are almost at the end of the track – hard
work now is in revising cutting & typing chiefly. Fitzgerald has done
everything but sit right in front of us telling us directly what to do –
though I wouldn't swear he hadn't done that. He also seems adept at
working the radio at peculiar moments, so you will have at least the basis
of a score too. Meantime we have Arctic storms, that followed floods,
& have been almost frozen in. Temperatures north of us in B.C
descended to 73 below zero. We have had 10 below in the house – the
very ink in the inkpot has frozen & Margie's typewriter also has frozen.
Some of the while we have had to work in gloves & we have not taken
our clothes off for three weeks. Deaths from cold & even starvation
because of the difficulty of getting anywhere are a daily occurrence
among those who live as we do & we can see our ancestors whiskers
glisten as we write thus about the Riviera. Fitzgerald also has permitted
himself his first kindly smile at the English.

The above will delay the m.s a little, but not much – but some way
into February. We have tried to keep the work a secret & will continue
to do so. What you will receive will be good & noble, & I never spoke
with such conviction & passion in my life. God bless you – Nan – the
children

Love from us both

Malcolm

– P.S.   <u>News Report</u>
This is C.K.N.W, the voice of the Vancouver Sun, from Vancouver,
British Columbia, Canada's ever green playground on the shores of the
blue Pacific.[1] The end of the cold snap is now in sight with temperatures rising and moving up to almost zero. . .

In the Yukon, two men survived ...... (etc) – This news is brought
you by courtesy of Booth's funeral parlours, who every day at this hour
play soothing music:
– A new polar air mass is approaching from the Arctic however, bring
more snow, and winds are expected to rise to 70 mph (and so forth.)

Don't bother to reply to this – this is merely to be interpreted as news from the arctic. We don't want anybody else to get to the North Pole first though.

Annotations:

1 CKNW is a Vancouver radio station. In the transcribed copy of this holograph that was sent to Harold Matson, Lowry's 'N' has been mistaken for an 'M.'

Editorial Notes:

a. This pencil holograph is on two pieces of 7.5-by-12.5-cm notepaper. The date has been added in another hand.

384: To Harold Matson

P: Matson(ms); UBC(phc)

Dollarton, B.C.,
Canada
17 January 1950

Dear old Hal:[a]
– br – yes. We're not precisely dying yet – though damn near frozen – it's pretty hard, however, to try & live on a hundred a month – the Volcano is currently making a big splash in France, though I can't see much dough accruing from francs – similarly with other translations – any further devaluation, however, would sink us, if but to float once more of course. It seems to me the Shapes would be a natural for a 25c edition – it's so much better than most mysteries. It occurs to me, if you haven't one you might have difficulty getting a copy, since those bloody people [Scribner's] have remaindered it. So please let us know. And yes, please do what you can, moving in your mysterious way. However – N.B. – I don't want it known, even in good old Albert's circles, we are in any hardship, reason for this being that we are working upon something that has to be kept a secret even from you at present (not eventually of course – the intention is quite other, & I have every hope of your being delighted – see above)[b] but the success or unsuccess of this venture conceived in love, has to depend upon merit alone & not even the obliquest motive of pity or cash should enter in, the more especially since noone asked us to do it & it is our responsibility –
    God bless, yourself, Tommy, the children
                    Love
                                    Malcolm

Editorial Notes:

a. This letter is in the form of a holograph addition squeezed into the

bottom and right margins of a typed letter from Margerie regarding their financial situation and Matson's failure to answer her previous letters.
  b. By 'see above' Lowry is directing Matson to continue following this sentence in the right margin above the main body of his letter.

385: To Conrad Aiken

P: H(ms)   Dollarton, P.O.,
PP: *LAL* 213-15   Dollarton, B.C.
                                                      [January 1950]

Dear old Conrad:
    Thank you & Mary very much for the festive (& beautiful) card.[1] I'm sorry my words were so illegible – there weren't nothing about 'your double,' old chap – more about 'doubles' implied in your card – ha ha – what I think you read was 'trouble' – may have been – & what you ought to have said instead of 'Glad to hear you're back' was 'Sorry to hear *about* your back,' which by the way, I broke, in an accident, falling indeed off one of my own erections, I mean constructions – I had a vision in a Catholic hospital after that, but I don't think I mentioned it, though I might as well have, for I remember thinking how close Mr Arcularis was to the actual truth.[2] When I mentioned 'ship's engines' I meant I could have used more of the sound of same in Arcularis – I was referring to Gerald's radio version, very beautifully done here otherwise & excellently received.[3] Apart from that, I was referring, by ship's engines, to some work we are doing at the moment, of which, if it comes off, I sincerely hope you will be proud – but this is supposed to be a secret till accomplished – so no more now.[4] For the rest, I am delighted at the success of Arcularis – even more delighted to hear, even through the post, your kindly and ironic purr at same, without the memory of which, applied to other happenings, I must have found it difficult to meet much which has come. No other news, save that the back is better – without any after effects. We live in the same old shack in conditions of frightening toughness this winter – a flood has razed our neighbours' houses to the ground, but ours, self built, stands still – & we were never so happy, nor working so hard. I swam till mid-December, back and all, (now see what you've done with your example of a cold bath every day) – slightly north of us, there are temperatures of fifty-three below zero. The Volcano was a flop in England, but has become a classic in France, where it is this month added to their quid pro quo of the Modern Library, translated by a Swiss, a Martiniquaise negro, & an Assyrian dying of consumption, with a none too sober preface by me

(among others) apparently about something else, & in the company of Diderot & the Abbé Prévost.[5] Margie has had bad luck in her work so far, with one exception, but we sink or swim together, or both in the current one (or *are carried along*). Please give our very best love to Mary & yourself and may, most sincerely, God bless you & you both – With love from us both

Malcolm

P.S. There is snow this morning falling quite heavily, in bright sunlight, out of an absolutely cobalt sky – have you ever seen this?

Annotations:

1 See the facsimile reproduction in Sugars (212).
2 Lowry intended to use his vision in 'The Ordeal of Sigbjørn Wilderness.' Aiken's story, 'Mr Arcularis,' was a Lowry favourite and a model for 'The Ordeal.' In the story the title character reviews his life in a vision before dying on the operating table; Lowry's hero, however, was intended to live.
3 Gerald Noxon prepared an adaptation of 'Mr Arcularis' for Andrew Allan's CBC radio series 'Stage 49.' This version of the story was first aired on 28 November 1948, but Lowry is probably referring to the 30 October 1949 rebroadcast.
4 In the Lowrys' screenplay for *Tender Is the Night*, as in *Hear us O Lord*, Lowry evoked the sound of a ship's engines by using the 'Frère Jacques' refrain.
5 For this description of his translators, Clarisse Francillon, Stéphen Spriel, and Gabriel Pomerand, see Lowry's 12 March 1950 letter (**392**) to Frank Taylor and his 21 June 1950 letter (**402**) to Albert Erskine. Denis Diderot (1713-84) was a French philosopher and dramatist, and Abbé Prévost is remembered today for his classic novel *Histoire du Chevalier des Grieux et de Manon Lescaut*.

386: To Frank Taylor

P: Lilly(ts)

Dollarton, B.C.,
Canada
14 February 1950

Dear Frank:

Reply not. We have more or less finished the opus [*Tender Is the Night*], but shall be about a month more in final typing and correcting. We were delayed by this Arctic weather, the worst in all history here, much worst than I said, and myself with a frozen hand to boot. And the typewriter frozen immovable too.

But we have fallen in love with the thing. It will soon be yours for better or worse, but will you please say a sincere prayer for it? We mean please say a prayer for it.

                    Love,

                                                    Malcolm

387: To Philippe Thoby-Marcelin

P: UBC(ts phc)   Dollarton, B.C., Canada
                                           24 February 1950

My dear old Phito:

Wonderful to hear from you – and that you are so comparatively near. My silence was due to an accident, then we were cut off from the world by a blizzard – finally by your postcard coinciding with my being about to spring something upon you which I hoped would please you, though the honour is mine, but which has ended in a disappointment, not fatal, and for which I sincerely hope you will forgive somebody, for I am not to blame. That is, I took the liberty of dedicating the French edition of the Volcano to yourself and Margie and they spelt your name wrong – no h in Thoby – two ll's in Marcelin: they will write you a letter of apology and are sending you a copy, and they will correct it in the second edition, but I couldn't get my correction in to them in time.[1]

The reasons you didn't see the translation to supervise same as per my promise I have fully explained in another letter you will receive in about a month, for I am working hard against time at the moment: the main reason, however, was that the French firm [Fontaine] that accepted the Volcano went practically broke, and the book finally was transferred to another firm, meantime we had left France: difficulties of communication explain most of the rest but I scarcely dare look at the translation I just received today for fear of the mistakes you will see in it: I shall see you receive a copy of the edition with your name right – this was such a great disappointment to me I scarcely dared write you.

I ascertained that Valery Larbaud was alive in Paris, but at present very ill; I could get no further than his secretary, but still this is a little good news.

I am enclosing the letter from France about the dedication: it seems that your friend Ira Morris came to the party for the Volcano, I just heard.[2]

La Negresse Adolescente is in Ontario with a man who is an excellent translator but I fear none too trustworthy, so I am going to get the poems back again.[3]

My ideas have not worked out very well so far – for example, it seems

I recommended you the worst possible agent in England thinking he was the best, but he has changed: however that does not mean some of these ideas may not work out in the future. In my enthusiasm I didn't make enough allowance for the horrible fallibility of mortals, nor the way the war has changed some of them so that they have become stupid.[4]

Both Margerie and I sincerely hope you will be able to visit us in our shack in Canada one of these days – we have only a spare sofa for you to sleep on. – But we could all have a great deal of fun. (In fact it is not even a sofa, but a mattress picked out of the sea. Note, from Kafka, concerning the simple life: 'B, the chief auditor, tells the story of a friend of his, a half pay colonel who likes to sleep beside an open window. During the night it is very pleasant, but in the morning, when I have to shovel the snow off the ottoman and then start shaving, it is unpleasant.'

But wherever we see you, we both hope it will be soon.

Margie joins me in sending you the best of love – please forgive me for the mispelling again, even though not my fault.

Affectionately, ton frère,

Malc

Annotations:

1 See Lowry's January 1950 letter (**382**) to Marcelin. Lowry habitually misspells Marcelin but seldom omits the 'h' in Thoby.

2 There is no letter from France extant with the Lowry collection or with Eva Thoby-Marcelin's papers.

3 *La Négresse adolescente*, Thoby-Marcelin's poetry collection, was published in Haiti in 1941, but he had hoped to find an English translator and publisher. In 1947 Lowry sent a copy of the poems to Ira Dilworth, but nothing came of this effort; see Lowry's 14 August 1947 letter (**316**) to Marcelin.

4 In his 14 August 1947 letter (**316**), Lowry had suggested that Marcelin contact Innes Rose, Lowry's former English literary agent; however, Rose, who had fought in the war and was fluent in French, was not supportive.

388: To Harold Matson

P: Matson(ts)   Dollarton, B.C.,
                                                                   Canada
                                                       28 February 1950

Dear Hal:

The enclosed letter speaks for itself,[1] but if it doesn't and I should speak more, or should have spoke, what seems to have happened is that

Fontaine has gone broke or partly broke and so could not bring out the Volcano but meantime they have got together with some other people etc.

I knew the Club Francais du Livre was taking the book and perhaps should have told you, in fact I thought I had,[2] but I was never very clear as to the situation and was always waiting to hear more – but the Club Francais is a sort of Book of the Month club and not (though it seems I'm wrong too) a publishers.

Correa – all I know about it is that it's the only firm besides the N.R.F. [*La Nouvelle Revue française*] that seems capable of really plugging a book so you see their book in the bookstores.[3]

Re the rest I have no very clear notion how it's come about but it seems to be a good thing, for if Fontaine could not bring it out, it's better that someone else should. You undoubtedly could have got me better terms on these other things but the money (even if I could get it here, which I can't is not even chicken feed in dollars, so what? And Clarisse Francillon (of Fontaine) has worked very hard on it for 2 years.

Re Lunar Caustic: that's a short story you had hanging around for years and I've always been meaning to rewrite it, if I have not already done so 50 times. These French people think it's a masterpiece as it is, and should I be the one to disabuse them? And if they mean a volume it must be a very small one.[4]

Combat[5] – that sounds good too. I mean it sounds good.

The main point seems to be these people have worked like mad on the Volcano simply because they believed in it – and since there's no way for me to get any of the money anyway (alas!) without going to France, – so I've told them so far as I'm concerned to go ahead but that I must await your say so could you let me know by airmail as it is important to them.

As a matter of fact I am working so hard my mind is not on this letter at all – but please remember to let me know [by] airmail anyway.

God bless Tommy yourself and the kids,

Love from us both –

Malcolm

Annotations:

1 There is no letter now enclosed or attached with Lowry's letter in Matson's files.

2 Indeed, he did; see his 23 February 1949 letter (**359**) to Matson.

3 Corrêa, a major Paris publisher, issued a reprint of the Club français du livre edition of *Au-dessous du volcan* in 1950, and the Club français published a new edition in 1959.

4 When Lowry was working with Clarisse Francillon on *Under the*

Volcano in the spring of 1948, he apparently gave her a copy of 'Swinging the Maelstrom' (a version of *Lunar Caustic*), which she admired. *Esprit* published it serially as *Le Caustique lunaire*, translated by Francillon and Michèle d'Astorg, in February, March, and April 1956. The editing and publishing history of *Lunar Caustic* is complex because the novella existed in at least two different versions, 'The Last Address' and 'Swinging the Maelstrom,' which Lowry intended to combine in a rewritten version for *The Voyage That Never Ends*. He did not live to complete this task, but Margerie Lowry and Earle Birney prepared a text from the versions extant at Lowry's death, and this English version was first published in *Paris Review* 29 (1963): 15-72, and reissued by Jonathan Cape in 1968.

5 In a 23 February 1950 letter to Lowry, Francillon told him that the French daily newspaper *Combat* was going to publish *Under the Volcano* in serial form. Lowry was 'overjoyed' at the prospect (see his 1 March 1950 reply [**389**] to Francillon), but Woolmer (x) has confirmed that no such serialization occurred.

389: To Clarisse Francillon

P: UBC(ts phc)
PP: *SL* 190-93

Dollarton, B.C., Canada
1 March 1950[a]

Chère Clarisse:

First, we feel a million thanks are in order (for God's sake don't misread that as francs) though I think you deserve a million francs too.

On top of that I feel another million thanks are in order to you and Mike [Stéphen Spriel] for the marvellous translation and, by canalization, to the Book Club for the marvellous looking book.[1]

My pleasure here extends from the format right down to the very printing because it emphasises the fact that for all its length there is compression in the text: this is particularly felicitous in chapter VI which one or two people thought slackened in English (one idea of which was to inject some of what [André] Gide calls 'ozone' into the book) – it may do {slacken} slightly in the English, but it certainly doesn't look as though it does in French, giving one the feeling that it may have given that impression in English because the typography there tended to sprawl.

Re the translation itself, it seems to be *superb*: it feels superb. We do not live in French-speaking Canada so I can't as yet give you any other expert opinions, but nevertheless it *is* mysteriously possible for the author to be a sort of judge even without command of the language –

if it is wrong, to him, something in the unity gives way visually and so far as I can tell, you and Mike have not only done your utmost but brilliantly succeeded in what must have been a horrendous task and, in all probability, it is often much better than the original: French and English far from compliment each other verbally but when the meaning comes through in French as it seems triumphantly to do in your version, the very fact that you have not so much advantage of actual 'ambiguity' in the words seems to make the meaning deeper and wider in range and certainly more beautiful in expression.

I would be very glad to know of some other opinions of the whole thing and I am very anxious to know if it is succeeding as you hoped – in fact I cannot wait to hear – and believe me, as much for your sake, & sakes, if not *more*, than mine. {[illegible] could not be more excited} Though it would be hard indeed to think of you two as feeling the work to have been in any sense in vain after the labour you have put into it. I hope you get all the credit that you deserve, and that I myself have not let you down.

Re the new conditions of the contract: my answer is of course, yes, so far as I am concerned, it seems to me more than generous: however, ethically speaking, I am obliged to refer it to my agent, Matson, which I have already done today, and I will let you know as soon as possible, that is, I shall get a reply air mail from him in a few days and will immediately forward it to you. I do not anticipate – in fact it is difficult for me to see how he has the right to raise any difficulty. I am delighted about Correa – if *you* are, that is, and *I* should be: I am very sorry that your Fontaine will not bring it out, however – if there is any grief for you in regard to Fontaine, which you half suggest, I deeply sympathise, at the same time feel that you will swiftly drive out the nail of grief with the nail of another triumph.

I am overjoyed that the Volcan should appear in Combat, however (among other things that delight me about this is that Julienne, (who used to call me that Bad Egg) and who takes Combat, will be able to read it before diner, and I am writing her to say, Watch out, the Bad Egg is going to hatch in Combat shortly![2] But it gives one surely a very good feeling to be published in Combat.

Re Lunar Caustic – again, so far as I am concerned, you have the go ahead signal, but again it has to be referred to Matson, lest I make an ethical flaw with him, or you. So I will let you know about that at the same time. It is dubious that he has any control at all over this as a story, but I cannot be sure how I stand about a volume. I have had many ideas for re-writing that story and if you do it, I shall be glad to pass them on, though perhaps this will be unhelpful and it is better as it is. It was originally written when I was 26 years old – and has never been published in English, as I think I told you. {Some of the reasons [several words illegible].}

Thank you about Marcelin – and thank you a thousand times again about everything – I feel a bit uneasy about my preface still, but if it has made a 'good impression,' that will be O.K.

But as I say I cannot wait to hear whether the whole book has made 'a good impression.'

We were frozen in here during dreadful blizzards in the winter – my hand became frostbitten – I think I told you I broke my back, that has recovered however: nor has the devaluation of the pound helped: somewhere along the time I must have made up my mind to be a Strong Man (like Mike). So, well, I have become a Strong Man.[3]

Please give my kindest regards to Max-Pol and thank him too for the excellent and kind post-face though you can tell him that if I am the Consul I am also M. Laruelle at that rate, from chapter II onwards if you look closely you could see that the whole book *could* be taken to be M. Laruelle's film – if so, it was my way of paying devout tribute to the French film, for it certainly was not an American one, nor yet English, & it could not have been Czech.

I wondered if you could somehow smuggle a copy, with my compliments, of your translation to Jean Cocteau, and tell him I have never forgotten his kindness in giving me a seat for La Machine Infernale at the Champs Elysee in May, 1934: I went to see it on 2 successive days and I shall never forget that marvellous performance as long as I live – Whatever he personally may have thought of it.[4] And so you see his infernal machine comes back to torment the Consul in chapter VII. (My first French copy of La Machine was solemnly stolen in a pulqueria in Mexico together with my dark glasses which I had left on the counter for a moment, by a bearded Mixtec Indian with two pistols who had been drinking in the corner. He rode off on his horse with it and I often enjoyed the thought of the old boy reading it to his wife in the mountains, with my dark glasses and all, and a gourd of mescal, and wondering what he made of it – a story I felt that might please Cocteau himself.)

It did occur to me tangentially however that the Volcan might through Mike's & your translation create in him some wonderful inspiration for a play from it and I could not help timorously hoping it might fire his imagination: there is certainly some material there for him wherewithal to freeze the blood with deliriums, and at the same time mysteriously to enoble one – as he inimitably can do.

Well, that's about all, save that the gent who gave me the inspiration for the cabbalistic significance of the Volcano died the day you sent me the translation – not without having received extreme unction however.[5] A very good fellow – and we mourn his death. We attend his funeral tomorrow. To make matters worse, for his wife, somebody mysteriously shot his favorite old dog, his companion of some 15 years, on the same day! That has a reminiscent ring: but fortunately if he was a magician he was a white magician and the dog, one hopes, will lead him across the river to the other side – as ancient belief has it, and at all events not down the abyss: (it is a more mysterious and eerie coincidence than meets the eye however – for the theme of the dog goes right through the Volcano. His last words to his wife were 'Do you know, I'm not really here, I'm beginning to function on a different plane already – it's quite an extraordinary experience old girl – '

It will be difficult to avoid chuckling at tomorrow's Catholic ceremony, for all its apparent sadness, on remembering these words, for I have the feeling that in Catholic thought the planes are somewhat delimited, to say the least – and if, while they are wafting him to one, he is all the while sitting calmly upon another, while it won't make any difference doubtless, the thought is irresistibly comic, which is perhaps as it should be: death may be a serious matter on both sides of the fence, but there is at least a good argument – one which was advanced by our friend himself – that all life is destined to have a happy ending, and we have not been deprived of the sense of tragedy purely out of aesthetic consideration by God.

Finally – the wooly bear garment, or tiger, saved our lives this winter and I wear one blue glove at this moment of writing upon my left hand that hasn't, by gosh, got quite warm yet, though it is spring now outside.

Thanking you again most sincerely and deeply for everything.

With the best of love from us both – & deepest thanks & regards to Mike, whom I shall try & write separately if he will make allowances for the fact I am working 15 hours per day now,

Malcolm

Annotations:

1 *Au-dessous du volcan* was first published by Le Club français du livre in February 1949; see Lowry's 23 February letter (**359**) to Harold Matson.

2 Julienne LaPierre was the cook at Joan Black's country home, La Cerisaie, where the Lowrys stayed during periods of 1948. Lowry, who was drinking heavily at the time, obtained daily doses of wine from the indulgent Julienne; see Day (398-401). *Under the Volcano* was not serialized by *Combat*.

3 Lowry may be referring to the 1926 American silent film *The Strong Man*, starring his sister-in-law Priscilla and Harry Langdon; see his November 1952 letter (**552**) to Priscilla Woolfan. In this comic film a soldier endures a number of hilarious problems and illnesses.

4 See Lowry's July 1946 letter (**229**) to Albert Erskine and his 22 February 1957 letter (**705**) to David Markson; see also photograph 24.
5 Charles Stansfeld-Jones died on 24 February 1950, but Lowry's elaborations on his friend's death are probably fanciful.

Editorial Notes:

a. This transcription is from a faint photocopy of a typescript with holograph additions in the left margin (UBC 2:14); several words of the marginalia are illegible. The whereabouts of the original letter is unknown.

390: To Downie Kirk

P: UBC(ts phc)   Dollarton, B.C.,
PP: *SL* 193-97; *MLVD* 59-60   Canada
                                                               2 March 1950

Dear old Downey:
     Don't forgive me for not writing – do certainly though, the reason is I'm working 17 hours a day against time, and couldn't write, not even you – but will you please for my sake take your Greek cap off the hook, put on your gaff-topsail boots, your hood, assemble your bow of burning gold and taking a flying leap into your desk, what time the gramaphone is playing the record about the antiquated old antique, repay my bad behaviour by answering as soon as you conceivably can the following antiquated old antique and learned questions? What I want mainly are the names of two Greek ships, and one Greek town, in Greek capitals: the first ship ARISTOTLE, the second ship OEDIPUS TYRANNUS, the town: ANTIPOLIS.[1] The difference is that both of the names of the ships should be in modern Greek characters capitals – the town in ancient Greek capitals – I don't think there is any difference, is there? But Aristotle in Greek ancient or modern would be Aristotelis, would it not? And Oedipus Tyrannus sounds like a Roman version and would not be Oedipus Tyrannus in Greek? Be that as it may, they both have to translate visually in the work in question into ARISTOTLE and OEDIPUS TYRANNUS but I want them visually in *Greek capital letters* first for dramatic effect. Do you get the point? Don't bother to be too meticulous about getting it absolutely right either, but the thing is it comes at a dramatic and important point in the work as we are presenting it; it isn't a question of showing off knowledge I don't possess, but I don't want to make too naive a mistake right off, and [two Greek words illegible] or something is about the best I can do. Parceque, Μον δεαρ

Downey, I don't know how to write these βλοοδμ καπιταρσ though I began Greek when I was acht(8) and forgot it when I was novum(9). But these νερδαμτερ capitals are of some importance in the work, as we hope to demonstrate with some delight to you when it is ὑν φαιτα'κκομπλ! For the rest ϖερμιβ Μιρ not to say uns.[2]

Therefore so far there are 3 questions: how to write ARISTOTLE, OEDIPUS TYRANNUS and ANTIPOLIS in Greek capitals.

On the last question hinges another question which I will frame in a moment, then I have several more, and then, though I am not through, I will have to pretend that I am, because I have left these questions to the last moment on the off chance that you would show up at the inlet when the weather got better, but now we have not got even time to go to the library to find an answer, supposing one could do so, which is extremely doubtful and anyway I would rather ask you. In connection with Antipolis what I want is the wording of an hotel advertisement by a railroad in the Riviera, its ironic appeal is to Americans, (in the work) so that I have to break it down in parts into *bad* English, but meantime it is better for me to know what it would be in *good* French. Here is my version of it, a mixture of bad French and bad English – I do not know yet how much bad English to use, this is irrelevant so long as I know what it would be in French, so I shall make the question clear immediately afterwards (& by gosh, I better had):

> Touriste Americain! Vous approchez maintenant la ville ancienne d'ANTIBES. Original Greek name: ΑΝΤΙΠΟΥΙΣ[3]
> ANTIPOLIS (in Greek characters)
> Originally Greek, founded by the Greek-Phoenicians, in the 3rd century, its latest walls were built by the great Vauban, and up till 1860 marked the Italo-French border.
> HOTEL DES ETRANGERS, ANTIBES, 5 km. Confort Moderne.
> Patron: Charles Gausse (son delicieux couscous)
> Beach clots - vins - liqueurs - Bar -
> Everything for the American Tourist at popular prices!

All I want to know here therefore, apart from the all important Antipolis in Greek capitals, is how to say in correct French : American Tourist! You are now approaching the ancient town of Antibes, etc. Originally Greek etc – 'latest' in the sense of newest, & Everything for the American tourist at popular prices!

I hope this is clear, but even if it isn't, the first moment it is not desperately trespassing on your time, I'd be awfully obliged if you'd have a shot at it, in fact it is very important to us if you would be so kind – and never mind if it isn't quite accurate, time is of the essence now, is the point, and though it can be corrected later, it would make a large difference in the presentation if at least I can make the Greek capitals look right.

There are 6 other questions, though of minor importance. How, roughly, should one translate 'Daddy's Girl,' as the name for a film, into French? (Fillette de Papa? Poule de Papa? But it musn't be too διρτη)[4] It should be ironic, if possible. It appears as an advertisement (much as Las Manos de Orlac does in the Volcano) And also, for two more advertisements, how would you translate into French, as titles: (a) The Doctor's Dilemma. (b) The Last Laugh.

And how would you say in French (never mind for the moment the apparent prepostorousness of the question): Freud and Peary – famous astrological twins? Would it be gemeux astrologiques fameux – or what? This is for a scene in an astrologer's tent.

How do you say, 'Bon Voyage,' in German? (Or don't you?)

And finally, how do you say: STOP! PAY TOLL! (the same sign that appears on the second narrows bridge) in French, German and Italian?

These last questions are subservient in importance to the others and if you can't figure them out right off, or don't have time, we'll be monumentally obliged if you'd give your attention to the first Greek question first – and if you have time, send in the others later.

Finally, I thought you would be tickled to know, the Volcano has made a hit in France, where it is coming out three times in the next months: first in a classic series, then Correa, and it is also being serialized in the Paris daily newspaper, Combat! They have decided that it is the writing on the wall, that your amigo is everything from the Four Quartets (which he has never read) to Joyce (whom he dislikes) – finally relates him to the Jewish prophetic Zohar (of which he knows nothing) – they have some other comments too, about Macbeth, but that is nothing to what someone is just going to say in Victoria, over the C.B.C., where they have decided that the Consul is really Moby Dick masquerading as the unconscious aspect of the Cadbosaurus in the Book of Jonah, or words to that effect.[5]

I am going to present you with a copy of the French translation and we should have some fun out of it when you have glozed upon it.

For the rest, we have many of your books, kindly lent at your and Marjorie's good party never-to-be-forgotten. Of them I have read backwards and forwards the excellent Concert Companion, which has taught me a great deal about writing (I mean from the form of music, which was not why I borrowed it however – but it has also helped me to begin to understand music a bit better) Our friend Cecil Gray makes some rather good remarks therein – and I'm glad you liked his book – more of that later.[6] Shean on Gandhi is interesting and important in substance as it could not help but be – but it doesn't seem quite as absorbing as his other books, though you may find it more so.[7] Merton on monastaries contains some phenomenal coincidences and parallels of some interest philosophically which I would like to discuss next time we meet, when one wonders why did one borrow the book, but as a book I don't think you'll go for it much.[8] On the other hand it is certainly interesting to know how St So and so was once Bill Louseweed listening to a juke box and it has a value of passionate sincerity and dedication which however is not the kind of sincerity and dedication (which he knows fairly well) that many people will read into it. Finally, of course, it should be considered on another plane altogether: it is of sufficient importance at this point in history, though he seems an unsympathetic character in many ways, even as a monk, that he has made that clear to a few people, even though it must seem to those people an exceedingly questionable book – in the sense that it is a paradox in its own terms. How the hell can a writer go into a monastery and go on writing books and then pretend he's given up 'everything,' I ask you, isn't he a sort of Trappist monk to start with? That a monastery *might*, in essence, be the capital of the world at this juncture is a possibility which not even Nietzsche were he alive would care to question – or would he? Anyhow it is a good idea – or is it?

I have some other funny and even dramatic things to say but will close now, merely intimating that it be understood how fine it will be to see you all again, asking your indulgence for my having suddenly persecuted you with so many questions, adding my hope that you will answer them too, and to that, all our very best wishes to the three of you, also imagining that when Dorothy has not been playing the tune about the antiquated old antique on the gramophone, she will have been playing ever better tunes of her own upon the more modern and sober – or at any rate upright – piano.

Again, kindest regards to the three of you from us both.

Malcolm

Annotations:

1 The Lowrys were hurrying to complete their screenplay of *Tender Is the Night*. The result of Downie Kirk's assistance with Greek, French, and other languages can be seen in *The Cinema of Malcolm Lowry* (48, 56, and 241, and other points passim). The Lowrys used the arrival and the sinking of the ships ΟΙΔΙΠΟΥΣ ΤΥΡΑΝΝΟΣ and ΑΡΙΣΤΟΤΕΛΗΣ to open and close the screenplay.

2 Lowry's holograph additions to the letter are his private macaronic joke with Kirk: 'Because, my dear Downey, I don't know how to write these bloody capitals . . . . But these verdamter capitals . . . when it is un fait accompli! For the rest forgive me not to say us.'

3 Lowry's Greek capitals for Antipolis are correct with the exception of the capital 'L' (lambda) which should be 'Λ.'

4 διρτη is dirty, but it has none of the sexual associations of the French 'fillette' or 'poule.'

5 *Four Quartets* (1943) is by T.S. Eliot, and *The Book of Zohar* is a Cabbalist text of Jewish mystical teachings. Lowry's bantering tone here belies the importance to him of these writers and texts; Eliot, in particular, is frequently paraphrased or quoted in the letters. The CBC broadcast to which Lowry refers was being prepared by Derek Pethick, but it was never aired; see Lowry's 6 March 1950 letter (**391**) to Pethick.

6 Cecil Gray (1895-1951), the Scots writer and composer, met the Lowrys during their July 1948 visit to Capri. An inscribed copy of Gray's 1947 book *Contingencies*, dated 7 July 1948, is in the Lowry library (UBC Box 54).

7 American journalist and writer Vincent Sheean (1899-1975) published *Lead, Kindly Light: Ghandi and the Road to Peace* in 1949.

8 Thomas Merton (1915-68) was a Cistercian monk and a prolific writer. Lowry could be referring to either *The Seven Story Mountain* (1948) or *Elected Silence: The Autobiography of Thomas Merton* (1949).

391: To Derek Pethick

P: UBC(tsc)   Dollarton, B.C.,
PP: *SL* 197-202   Canada
6 March 1950[a]

Dear Mr Pethick:[1]

Thank you for your letter and I am flattered you are to speak about the Volcano. I am also delighted by your interest in it and by your remarks.[2]

While you are not quite right about theVolcano, it is none the less an extraordinary piece of perspicuity on your part, for what you say would very largely be true of a book that does not now exist, and of which you cannot have known, the Volcano having been designed as the first part of a trilogy – and the third part which I refer to having been totally destroyed in a fire which consumed our house some years ago – we built another house on the ashes, however.[3]

My wife says it would be more true to say that in the Volcano the Consul bore some relation to Moby Dick himself rather than Ahab. However it was not patterned after Moby Dick (the book) which I never studied until fairly recently (and it would seem not hard enough).

The identification, on my side, if any, was with Melville himself and his life. This was partly because I had sailed before the mast, partly because my grandfather had been a skipper of a windjammer who went down with his ship[4] – Melville also had a son named Malcolm who simply disappeared – purely romantic reasons like that, but mostly because of his failure as a writer and his whole outlook generally. His failure for some reason absolutely fascinated me and it seems to me that from an early age I determined to emulate it in every way possible – for which reason I have always been very fond of Pierre (even without having read it at all).[5]

But to get back to the key – if any – the Volcano has just come out in France, where they say the key is in the Zohar. This discovery is partly due to a misleading preface by myself, written while not quite sober, but there is something in it, so I'll give you a precis of what they say for what it's worth, if I can translate it. This is in a very learned postface by one Max-Pol Fouchet and now it seems I can't translate it but I'll try to give you the gist. Now it seems I can't even give you the gist so I'll have to try instead to answer some of the points you raise in terms of what I think he says, or has some significance in terms of what I think I say – – (so far as I can see while it doesn't make you wrong, it somehow or other gives the book more thickness than even you ascribe to it, or I thought it had).[6]

To take the points in the wrong order: first, the zodiacal significance – in my intention it had none at all – least of all in relation to Melville – I am trying to be honest, so I refer things to my wife when in doubt – the quotation you mention from Moby Dick, Chapter 99, I am conscious of reading now as for the first time – it never occurred to me there was any such zodiacal significance in Moby Dick for that matter – and the passage now affects me supernaturally if at all, as if it meant something literal for *me*, and it was I who had been tracing the round again.[7]

Though there is some extra evidence, if you like, in Chapter VII when the Consul is in Laruelle's tower – the Consul remembers a make of golfball called the Zodiac Zone, a lot more evidence in XI (where the intention was astronomical however). The goat means tragedy (tragedy – goatsong) but goat – cabron – cuckold (the horns). The scorpion is an image of suicide: (scorpions sting themselves to death, so they say – Dr Johnson called this a lie,[8] but there is in fact some scientific evidence for it and was no more than that – or was it? for I now see the whole book takes place 'in Scorpio' – the action of the book is in one day, exactly 12 hours, seven to seven; the first chapter takes place 12 months later on the same day, so is also In Scorpio.

Now I'll have to begin at the beginning again. The truth is, I have never certainly fully grasped the fact that Moby Dick was a political parable, though I can grasp the fact that Ahab (in my grandfather's eyes anyhow) is on quite an important plane a criminal. I seem to remember that Starbuck and quite a few of the crew had the same idea too, but it seemed to me that his revengeful elan was shared to the extent that one could scarcely say the whole crew were enduring toil and danger simply to gratify his desire – what about the harpooners? – Yes, what about them? I don't feel on very secure ground, but I have never thought of the book before in that way.

I can see that the Confidence Man is a political parable; and that the Tartarus of Maids is a sexual one.[9] I see the applicability of the pursuit in Moby Dick to today all right, but it never occurred to me that it was intended in that way then, unless in the sort of jocular manner that Melville's vast appetite reaches out all over the table and couldn't help stuffing something of the sort in. Now I have written the above it seems not only illiterate, but not what I mean at all, but I'll have to let it stand. But what you say would be in line with much of Melville's later thought.

The Volcano is, though, and you are quite right here, quite definitely on one plane a political parable – indeed, it started off as such, Chap VIII was written first – nearly 15 years ago[10] – though I didn't mean it to suggest that the future belongs to those Mexican workers necessarily, or indeed to anybody at all, unless some true charity can mediate, and man's decency and dignity be reestablished. The police are the bloody police of the present all right – but they are also 'Interference' – interference with people's private lives – the stool pigeon theme works both ways: one should intervene in the case of the man beside the road, Spain seemed a clear case for intervention, etc – or at least Hugh's intervention; it isn't quite as simple, to say the least, as this. And what about the Consul? How much good was it interfering in his case? Well, I meant to redeem the old bird in various guises throughout the trilogy, but fate put a stop to that – but I'll go on trying to tell you more about him in terms of the Volcano only, and the beginning of the letter. As a protagonist on one plane (says this French fellow [Max-Pol Fouchet], and I think he's right) he is a faustian gent. The book somehow assumes – with some philosophic justice – that the ancestor of us all was perhaps a Magician.

The Consul has been a cabalist (this is where you get the Garden of Eden). Mystically speaking, the abuse of wine is connected with the abuse of mystical powers. Has the Consul perhaps been a black magician at one time? We don't know. What Max-Pol Fouchet doesn't say either is that a black magician is a man who has all the elements of the world (not to say universe) against him – this is what the Consul meant in Chapter X (written in 1942) enumerating the elements. In Chapter V (in the bathroom) you have a hint of similar dark forces in the background. The implication is that an analogy is drawn between Man today on this planet and a black magician. This, I feel, has to some extent come to have some basis in truth since writing the book. (The Consul implies his war, as opposed to any Hugh might be involved in, is far more desperate, since it is against the very elements themselves and against nature. This is a war that is bound to be lost.) Oddly enough I put neptunium in – but abandoned it for niobium (I thought it sounded sadder – it seems to me nobody, in my position at least, dreamed of atom bombs then – and yet you see, here one sat, just the same, dreaming up the swinish contraption without even knowing it. I just took the elements out of the dictionary). – this is on p. 304 – As I say, this part was written in 1942 – and by the time the atom bomb fell in 1945 the book had anyway been long on its way [to] being rejected by publishers. I turned to this particular page just now and it gave me an eerie sort of feeling. The Consul has thus turned into a man that is all destruction – in fact he has almost ceased to be a man altogether, and his human feelings merely make matters more agonizing for him, but don't alter things in the least: he is thus in hell. Should you hold the Bergsonian idea that the sense of time is merely an inhibition to prevent everything happening at once[11] – brooding upon which it is pretty difficult to avoid some notion of eternal recurrence, inevitable destruction is thus simply the teleological end to one series of possibilities; everything hopeful is equally possible; the horror would seem to exist in the possibility that this is no longer true on our plane and absolute catastrophe has fallen in line with our will upon so many planes that even the other possibilities are for us gradually ceasing to exist. This, I may say, is not very clear, as I have expressed it, so you better forget it. Anyhow, I don't believe it for a moment. Personally, I have a fairly cheery view of life – living as my wife and I do in the bush anyway. Nor was the book consciously intended to operate upon quite so many levels. One serious intention was to create a work of art – after a while it began to make a noise like music, when it made the wrong noise I altered it – when it seemed to make the right one, finally, I kept it. Another intention was to write one really good book about a drunk – it was a blow to me when the Lost Weekend was published, just as I finished it.[12] Another intention: I meant parts of it to be funny, though no one seems to have realized that.

Finally some odd and interesting things have happened in connection with the book itself (as they did with Moby Dick, by the way) – while he was writing it, a whale sank a ship. Disaster struck the Acushnet – the original of the Pequod). After the war, at the end of 1945, I went back to Mexico again, taking my wife: absolutely by coincidence we found ourselves living in the original of M. Laruelle's tower, in Cuernavaca, now broken up into apartments. It was the only place we could find for rent.

I began the book in 36-38, when I was in Mexico. The news of the book's acceptance – both in England and America – arrived on the same day, in February 1946, from different firms in different countries, to this very tower in Mexico, and was brought by the same little postman who is a character in Chapter VI.

There are other, even stranger coincidences connected with it – some of them frightening, and not the least strange being in relation to your letter, which arrived on the same day as the French translation, but also on the same day as the funeral we were just about to attend of the very good fellow, a mystic – one would say if he was a magician he was a white one – who gave me much of the esoteric inspiration and material for the book.[13] On the same day he died, coincidentally some brute shot his old dog (you will find the dog motif everywhere in the Volcano) – Dog motif indeed – it makes me think it would make a good opera – now we hear the opening chords of the dog motif – by courtesy of Texaco Oil etc).[14]

Finally thank you for your interest in the book – it is rather discouraging very often being a writer in Canada. Somebody put the Volcano in the Encyclopaedia Britannica Year Book 1948-9, ranking it as a work of a Canadian over and above anything then current in American literature, but not one word did I ever hear of that here. In fact, apart from a few kind words by [Earle] Birney and Dorothy Livesay, all I have heard was from my royalty report, namely, that the sales in Canada from the end of 1947 – 49 were precisely 2 copies. The Sun published only a few syndicated lines that called it a turgid novel of self-destruction, not for the discerning (or something) reader. This at least is Melvillian anyway (though it went very well in the states, and was even miraculously a best seller for a while; one month, believe it or not, it even sold more than Forever Amber, though it must be admitted Amber was getting a bit faded by then. In England it failed but quite honorably; in France they have put it in a classic series – yet another publisher is giving it wider distribution, and weirder still, it is being serialized in the daily newspaper Combat. The Swiss publisher went broke and cleared off to Mexico himself ha ha; as to the Swedish, Norwegian and Danish translation, I understand they are out, but I have not seen them. Nor, I imagine, has any Swede, Norwegian, or Dane.

With best wishes,

[Malcolm Lowry]

P.S. Hope this doesn't confuse you too much. I remain delighted by your interest – though I didn't want to leave you with the impression that the intention of the book was either completely despairing or that it contained any specific secular hope – finally I had meant to show in the trilogy that any revolution that did not appeal to the whole man –

including the spiritual, would eventually abort; least of all is it a sermon against drink – that poor man's symphony, especially in B minor, though why not D major too, after all.

P.P.S. I hope you'll come and have a drink with us when you are in Vancouver.

Annotations:

1 Derek Pethick (1920-), a Canadian writer living on Vancouver Island, prepared CBC radio broadcasts on writers during the early fifties and was working on a discussion of *Under the Volcano* at the time of his correspondence with Lowry. According to his note on the typescript copy of this letter, the Lowry broadcast never took place.

2 Pethick's letter has not survived.

3 The lost manuscript is 'In Ballast to the White Sea,' which was destroyed in the Lowrys' 7 June 1944 fire.

4 Lowry's maternal grandfather was not the romantic figure that Lowry made of him in his fiction and letters. Evelyn Boden Lowry's father, John Boden (1839-84), was a master mariner not a skipper or Captain Lyon Boden (as Lowry liked to call him). He was lost in the Indian Ocean on 26 April 1884 as first mate of the *Vice Reine* (Bowker 4). Herman Melville's son Malcolm (1849-69) did not 'disappear,' as Lowry goes on to say; he probably committed suicide, which Lowry might have known from contemporary studies of Melville.

5 Lowry's identification with Melville is a common theme in his letters, and Melville's novel *Pierre* (1852) was a painful failure for its author; see Lowry's 2 January 1946 letter (**210**) to Jonathan Cape.

6 In his 'Postface' to *Au-dessous du Volcan* Fouchet meditates upon the religious allusions and foundations of *Under the Volcano* and traces them back to the Jewish mysticism of the *Zohar* and to the Bible. He also comments on Lowry's use of the Cabbala and on his many filmic and literary intertexts.

7 This passage from *Moby-Dick* is contained in Stubb's long monologue about the signs of the zodiac, from which he claims to read 'the life of man in one round chapter.'

8 In his *Life of Samuel Johnson* (Aetat. 59, Spring 1768) Boswell reports a conversation in which he had described Italian experiments that suggested scorpions kill themselves; Dr Johnson, not wanting to believe what had not been proved scientifically, was sceptical about this information.

9 Melville published his novel *The Confidence Man* in 1857; his story 'The Paradise of Bachelors and the Tartarus of Maids' appeared in 1850.

10 This remark has led Lowry scholars to believe that chapter 8 of *Under the Volcano* was first written as a short story, but the manuscripts do not support this view. The episode with the man dying beside the road provided Lowry with the initial 'donné' for what was conceived as a novel.

11 This remark, albeit Bergsonian, is made by I.A. Richards in *Practical Criticism: A Study of Literary Judgement* (1929); see Lowry's 22 June 1940 letter (**144**) to Whit Burnett.
12 See Lowry's 24 April 1944 letter (**189**) to Gerald Noxon for his comments on *The Lost Weekend*.
13 Charles Stansfeld-Jones; see Lowry's 1 March 1950 letter (**389**) to Clarisse Francillon.
14 Lowry is alluding to the Saturday afternoon radio broadcasts of New York Metropolitan Opera productions sponsored by Texaco, Inc. Whenever possible, particularly during winter months spent in Vancouver, Lowry listened to these broadcasts.

Editorial Notes:

a. This transcription is from an unsigned copy (UBC 2:14) of Lowry's original letter. Derek Pethick has added three pencil annotations on the recto of page one. An abridged version appeared in *Canadian Forum* 42 (June 1962): 62–63.

392: To Frank Taylor

P: Lilly(ts,ms); Matson(tsc)   Dollarton, B.C.,
                                                                   Canada
                                                          12 March 1950

Dear Frank:
   Don't reply. Don't even breathe. We're on the home stretch, though not quite on the home beach, but it will still be a few weeks yet.
   I thought you would meantime be tickled to know – since I feel it largely thanks to Albert and yourself – that the Volcano has inculcated a sensation in France where first bits of it appeared in the Mercure de France, then it has become a Book of the Year through the Club Francais du Livre in a classic series in company of William Faulkner and the Abbe Prevost, shortly is to be published again on a wide scale by Correa, and finally and simultaneously will be read standing up in the metro (and who knows, sitting down too) serialised in the daily newspaper Combat (with illustrations)
   It was finally translated by a Martinquaise negro scholar, a Swiss and a dying Assyrian – which certainly would seem to bespeak something for international relations, at least.[1]
   They translated the whole thing three times, and finally really got into the groove and have turned in a wonderful looking job: I shall send you a copy when I can.
   Give my kindest regards to Fletcher [Markle] and also to

[Christopher] Isherwood (whom I have never, unfortunately, met)[2]
Love zu haus zu haus

Malcolm

P.S. Albert [Erskine] is in one of his unwriting moods. The last we had
was a postcard from Montreal — which saddened me, not because
Montreal looks sad, which it does, but because living statically sometimes in the wilderness as we do for long periods, one comes to form
certain ideas like those of the old pioneers — WHY, he was west & didn't
see us, & now he is east again — but the mind traverses the distance by
some gloomy covered wagon in reverse, not by plane, so that he would
seem lost beyond recall in THAT WICKED CITY, again rather than a few
hours away.

M & M

Annotations:

1 Stéphen Spriel, Clarisse Francillon, and Gabriel Pomerand; see Lowry's
  21 June 1950 letter (**402**) to Albert Erskine, where he names Pomerand
  as one of the translators, although he is not cited in the published translation.
2 See Lowry's May 1947 letter (**301**) to Markle, and his 20 June 1950
  letter (**401**) to Isherwood.

393: To James Craige

P: UBC(ms phc)   [Dollarton]
                                                        [1950]

Happy Birthday
to
Jimmy

with love
from

Malcolm

March 30th – – April 19th – – ?[1]
Happy birthday to you
Happy birthday to you
Though it's deferred it's
sincere it's
A message worth two.

And if it is but our fate
To celebrate it late
Please look forward
– hard to starboard! –
To that royal date!

With love from your
dilapidated grossgodson & spouse

Malcolm

Annotations:

1 Craige's birthday was 30 March.

394: To Frank Taylor

P: Lilly(ts); Matson(tsc) Dollarton, B.C.,
Canada
6 April 1950

Dear Frank:

We have it gedone. God willing it goes off this week, so it will be arriving in the Good Season. We are putting on a few final touches, rubbing the smears of paint off the windows. There are a few words we are fixing too in a sort of foreword, a few necessary notes also in a sort of afterword. (some of them unnecessary) Since it goes by train though, it will take some 5 days to arrive. Add 4 to this, 2 for the time this letter takes to reach you, making 11, I mean subtract two making 9, and you have the approximate time of arrival from the time you receive this, unless the Easter holidays delays the post a little: or unless the train gets to you quicker, in which case it will be sooner.

Meantime we are suffering from the roller coasters and as soon as we have it off are planning to hide ourselves in a bottle of gin in a remote seaside resort from which we may watch the habits of a bird known as the ruddy turnstone. We also hope to see a real sea-serpent known as the Cadbosaurus, indigenous to these parts.

It is probable that you will go on receiving occasionally irrelevant letters that are meant to be relevant for some time after you have received it, but to these you need pay no attention. The fact is we have lived so closely with the thing these last months that it will be something like sending a child off to boarding school whose whippings bulleyings, ignorings, futility possible complete unsuitability and uselessness to yourself, & even summary expulsion we have lived through a thousand times without being helped by the fact that we believe strongly in his beauty. The child weighs about some 450 pages, also, but this is largely because it is very detailed, not because its mother was frightened by Erich von Stroheim before it was born.[1] – I enclose a French bulletin in which you will see something I feel of interest to you on pages 6B and 8. It seems that we have got into the French equivalent of the Modern Library, which seems to be something. Also we have just got into the Norwegian: Under Vulkanen. Hikk, hikk, Konsulen spurter gong-gong. It looks more monumental even than Dick's thesis.[2]

When you are through with the French folder would you do me the kind favour of placing same in an envelope and dispatching it to my mother-in-law, since she lives in the same city, and she wants to see it, i.e., to Mrs J.S. Bonner, 1643 Queens Road, Hollywood 46.

With all the best to you and Nan and the children from us both. With love

Malcolm

Annotations:

1 Erich von Stroheim (1885-1957), the Austrian actor and filmmaker, was known for his long, over-budget films, and Lowry liked this analogy; see his fall 1952 letter (**549**) to Albert Erskine.
2 Dick (Richard Diver), the hero of *Tender Is the Night*, is a doctor who has written influential books on advanced psychology, but his wife's breakdown leads to his own decline.

395: To Frank Taylor

p: Lilly (ts); UBC (tscarbon)   Dollarton, B.C.,
pp: *SL* 202-06   Canada
                                                          12 April 1950

Dear Frank:

Here she goes. We don't know how to title it but perhaps that won't matter.[1]

There was a sort of preface to it and is: and there are copious notes: the first turned into a sort of reply, from our bailiwick, to certain stimulating summations made at the movie conference reported in Life last June, particularly by Joseph Mankieweicz.[2] It struck us, in brief, several months after reading his remarks that writers who professed a love of the movie, but did little but criticise it, might best show their friendship by trying to write something good themselves of a practical nature: in order to show their good will, the obstacles should seem at the beginning all but insuperable, the rewards nil, and the project uninvited – all three you will agree met the bill here. When we say rewards we quickly qualify this by saying that this has nothing to do with our opinion of such a film's success, for there is a great deal, one feels, in the view advanced by Mr Schary[3] that the best films are the ones that make money, though this might be so for no obvious reason: considering this potentially, the point would seem to be not to close the gap merely between the aesthetic and the human or social values, or you get a documentary on the one hand, and by reaction the aesthetic at the mercy of the inhuman on the other: it would be to close the gap between them both in relation to eternal values: the best values are eternal values: they are also the most popular. But all values should attempt to maintain themselves at their highest level in terms of 'cinema.' Then we would be getting somewhere. Something along these lines ran our argument, in this letter just clumsily expressed, and this is not the place to go into it. There is much relevant in that foreword to how we went to work on the problems in Tender is the Night, however, but we hope the results may speak for themselves, without this foreword at present, which we haven't had time to finish. The same goes for the notes which will follow in due course. Here we intimated that Goethe had said there were thirty-seven different types of tragedy and we hoped (or feared) this might be the thirty-eighth.[4] We went into anangke and perepeteia,[5] directors for actors, fashions, automobiles, and these will follow in due course, no matter how useless. If not before you receive this, every time you see the remark 'see notes' you will have to refer into a void, but please assume meanwhile any doubts on the points the given question raises as considered by us.

(To mention a very minor one – in one section we swiped a couple of lines of dialogue and two café names from the same author's Babylon Revisited,[6] because it seemed to fit in, as in Henry V one saw something of Henry IV, however Shakespeare didn't try to sell Henry IV to Shirley Temple,[7] let alone succeed in selling it to the Saturday Evening Post, so the possible hitch of copyright is not the same, but the importance to the film could not be less either, the idea we wanted being implicit anyway, and it only seeming important at the time, so you can count it out in advance, though for that matter no one would notice it, unless of course it doesn't matter.)

Finally this is sent to you in the earnest hope that it might in itself offer a challenge and help to start something or carry things along. Also it should be clear that it is intended as a practical basis for a film, though the grammar of the film has been scarcely used – scarcely words more complicated than cut, dissolve, or lap dissolve – and we don't always mean that of course, and any good or bad writing in it is? are? either habit or incidental. The idea, however, was threefold, to try and give a vivid impression of a film actually in progress, a film that one had actually seen, and at the same time a film that, since it had not been made, left every scope for you or a director's imagination to work in. Since, perhaps understandably, there is no accepted form for this sort of thing we know of we simply made one up. It is not meant *entirely* to be taken literally, not that it would be, but you might think we were naãve enough to think so. There are some tentatively suggested shots in the sanitarium sequence. And there are two sections, one in New York, and another at sea, that may be in part unnegotiable, – particularly, or as we have written it, the latter. Nonetheless, even if so, we felt strongly that a suggestion of the poetic and visual and aural *drang* in these two parts involved would relate the film enormously and add meaning to it: so they have been written in full. That is to say these two sections are not speculative in so far as they are completely realised and visualised and heard and play a part in the meaning of the whole adaption, and there is an excellent – indeed an unanswerable – artistic reason why something of the sort should be there at that point: but they may be assumed, where necessary, to be speculative, flexible, or inspirational, for the purposes of making the film. This of course goes for the whole thing in one way: but does not, in another, for we have, so to speak, *seen* the film, and you are supposed to be about to see it in a minute or two. But what you may see to cut, to put in, to improve, to take out, etc etc, is equally part of the intention, while you are reading it. It may be too long, but we have proceeded on the basis that richness of material was surely better than poverty of the same, and incidentally we would like to think we know where and how to cut if need be, for apart from anything else, we have left enough out for an opera by Puccini.

But we strongly feel its basic structure to be sound. Some of this you will find repeated in the preface, if it ever arrives. One thing occurs to me now we didn't put in strongly enough. Fashions, etc, but not merely fashions. The age is rather like this one: and what is in common, one felt, should be stressed, so that it should be the opposite of just another film about the jazz age to go spiralling down the drain. However with the correct use of jazz itself there is the possibility of subtly making *THE one too*. It is even reasonable to suppose that this age is a form of recurrence of the other, not exact of course, but taking it in, as Time spirals on, which is what it demonstrably does, even if we are convinced it marches. Not to praise or blame in advance what you have not read, or the method used in writing it, we do feel constrained to qualify this from something in the preface, for we may have just given you the wrong impression. Not merely did we proceed on the basis that another film about the 'jazz age,' would not do but that another 'psychological film' should be put in the wastepaper basket – it would make no money, it would not be 'about anything', or not about anything worth while, would depress one to death, and last but not least be unfair to its author. Perhaps you might say that one has to start off by being unfair to the author by depriving his book of the incest motif, but there is much greatness in the book that is only implied in it – take away the incest and what do you have left?

The answer is everything: you have for one thing, a great and unusual love story, on the other a sort of protagonist of the American soul, or of the soul of man himself, whose application to today is also patent. Do not let this blurb put you off – this is what should and can be done with it. Step right inside and see! Sex! Drama! Thrills! What should a doctor do? How should a doctor feel – with a human soul at stake! For, as we say, it is intended as a director's inspiration: or a producer's inspiration. In fact your inspiration. We hope it will fire your imagination. So perhaps we should term it: an adjustable blueprint for an inspiration for a great American film. To which we add further: for Frank Taylor.

With best love to you, Nan, and the children,

Malcolm & Margerie

P.S. I suppose we should add that this is now your property, to dispose of as you will, or not: at all events, by no stretch of the material imagination can it be conceived of as ours – so we say this, in case you felt anxious about spilling a Scotch upon it. We have a copy, but we show it to no one.

> We us excuse now that this work is doe
> How we never were yet at Citharon
> Nor on the monteine called Parnasoe
> Where the nine muses have their mansion.[8]

P.P.S. This quotation – the one that follows now – arrived from my mother (Malcolm's) some time while we were writing this in some *Illustrated London News*.[9] I think it was marked, and was intended as a dig at me, for at all events there was a favourable review of the Volcano in another accompanying issue that was conspicuously not marked. It may look a bit phony at first, but the more you look at it the more you look at it, that's sure: in fact we stuck it on the wall over the desk for some reason and in one way or another, while working on the Night, have been looking at it ever since.

'The only object worth achieving in this world is the ennoblement of man. It can never be more than a partial achievement, for man, like all terrestrial creatures, is imperfect and insufficient to himself. But he has in him the seeds of greatness, and whatever feeds, fosters and brings to maturity these vital seeds is, for short-lived man, beyond price. It is this alone which makes his checkered and tragic sojourn here worth while. And since man lives in communities, the test of a community's virtue is the capacity of its institutions and traditions to evoke the spiritual greatness of its members. A community which fails to do this is failing as a community and will in the long run perish, because it will come to consist of men and women who pass through life without ever becoming what they were intended to be: it will consist, in other words, of human failures. But a community which fires men with the desire to live nobly, to love, to create beauty and to suffer and endure for the sake of love and the creation of beauty, is a community worth preserving and dying for. Ancient Greece was such a community; so was the Judah of David and Isaiah. . .

Arthur Bryant
Illustrated London News
July 9, 1949.

M & M

Annotations:

1 This covering letter accompanied the Lowrys' screenplay of *Tender Is the Night*.
2 Joseph L. Mankiewicz (1909-93) was a Hollywood writer, director, and producer with Twentieth Century Fox. The movie conference report, 'A Round Table on the Movies,' appeared in *Life* 27 June 1949; Mankiewicz and other participants discussed writers' criticisms of Hollywood's treatment of their work, and Mankiewicz spoke about commercial control of films and about censorship.
3 Dore Schary (1905-80) was chief of production at MGM Studios; see Lowry's quotation of Schary in letter **397** to Taylor.
4 Lowry never completed a formal preface or foreword, but some of his ideas for it are set forth in letter **397**. Goethe remarked that Carlo Gozzi (1720-1806), the Italian dramatist, had identified thirty-six types of tragedy, but that others thought there were more; see the entry for 17 February 1830 in *Conversations of Goethe with Eckermann and Soret*, trans. John Oxenford (London: George Bell, 1875), p. 437.
5 *Anangke* is the Greek term for absolute necessity or force of destiny, while *peripeteia* is the Greek term for a sudden reversal of fortunes.
6 The names are Café of Hell and Café of Heaven. These and the dialogue are taken from Fitzgerald's short story 'Babylon Revisited' (1931); see Mota/Tiessen (246).
7 Shirley Temple Black (1928-), an American child actress during the thirties and forties, subsequently became a diplomat with the American government. Her popular image on screen was of a sweet little girl, an image scarcely appropriate for *Henry IV*.
8 This verse is probably a Lowry joke.

9 Bryant's article for the *Illustrated London News* column 'Our Notebook' concerns the receipt of some English songs that, so he believes, embody English traditional idealism. See Lowry's use of the Bryant passage in letter **397** to Taylor.

396: To Frank Taylor

P: Lilly(ts); Matson(tsc)   Dollarton, B.C.,
                                             Canada
                                             15 April 1950

Dear Frank:

Just a note to say it is off:[1] definitely dispatched Thursday afternoon, since when we have dreamt of it on its way, falling into puddles, opened by the claws of the wind, being rewritten by the guard in the baggage car, and finally since we were dalyaed over Easter by the appearance of a very old friend, Dylan Thomas, the Druid poet, of whom you may have – [2]

P.S. – er, Margie now brings me your letter to say that 'yesterday was a rather mad day. Dylan Thomas suddenly appeared, – ' etc. etc. . . Having said that I hope that this was just one of our routine coincidences, and recovered my sense of identity slightly (though what would doubting Thomas have said?)[3] – despite the said apparition in common of the uncommon Welshman, we met the timetable within forty-eight hours, thus it should get you a day or two after you receive this, no saying what day precisely, Margie thinks Wednesday, I hope Tuesday, at the outside, Thursday.

I hope what you have done is right, thou sayest. Interpreting this statement as referring to me (Malcolm) and to have generously emerged out of consideration from 'faction of the soul of Frank $\pi\rho^2$ lib 14 cap 12 ref Publisher' that was concerned lest your late (but apparently all too omnipresent) author was wasting his time writing, or thinking he could write, movies, when he should have been reading Pliny or even rewriting Barban's – or was it Burton's? – Anatomy of Melancholy[4] while at the same time polishing his new navel, the answer is that the author in question, being in a manner, for better or worse, possessed by the work in question, and feeling loyal to its correctitude had no choice, and obeyed his instinct. Interpreting it to mean that you hope it is right, so bloody well do we. That is, that it won't let you down. Not that it *can* of course be quite right: much dialogue would have to be rewritten, other parts slashed, reversed, stove in – that depends, depends on what sir, that again depends – so on and so forth. The idea was to present a structure that would be extremely hard to sink. You could stop its apparent list this way or that, lop off its foremast, add a funnel, subtract another, torpedo some of its meanings below the water line, and even chop off its stern and it would still float pretty triumphantly for all its implausible look, dashing with all its derangements at its object, leaving the rest to fortune[5] – as in fact have we, in engineering same, though what that object was, I could not tell you, save to do it well. But if it's *all* wrong, a hopeless misconception, a swaggle-tailed bravura, a bearded what-not, a cornuted nonentity, and in short no damn good at all, the chagrin would be ours indeed, but it would be ours for having wasted your time in erroneously having given you to think we could do something about it. But I'd have to revise all my notions as to how far self-delusion can go in the case of artists to feel we've wasted ours, whatever the result. We've never had so much terrible fun doing anything. Moreover the new navel had to steep in a preparation of bugloss and sinister herbs anyway, can't be finished for a year or two anyway, save in bits, so don't bother about that. *We sent the Night, by the way, to your house, 315 S. Rodeo Drive, Beverly Hills,* – we didn't send it to the studio, but we mention this now in case you might have moved. I'm very sorry you had trouble phoning (we calculated it was when we were with Dylan) – we live in the forest, don't have a phone, but there is a telephone in the Dollarton Post Office; the number is Deep Cove 272M, whence messages can reach us, but the service is ghastly; telegrams generally reach us, however, sometime or other, as one of us goes to the P.O. once a day to pick up mail, messages, etc. And the weather hasn't let up yet. Love to you all from us both.

Malcolm

P.P.S. Letter accompanying the script looks a bit cynical in regard to it – don't you believe it![6] We are only indulging in the ancient writers' habit of guarding our heart from blows. Or you from the ancient & even more unfortunate necessity of having to inflict them, by inflicting them in advance. No, as Senora Gregorio said: 'We put our all, our everything in it.'[7] We had an earthquake yesterday, a full gale to-day. The violets have been mysteriously up all winter (beneath the ice), but there is not a single leaf on any tree yet, though to-morrow we expect to find the Chrysanthemums in full bloom: something odd somewhere.

After just writing you a note on the same subject I turned on the radio:

It played

Daddy's little Girl[8]

Annotations:

1 Frank Taylor acknowledged the safe arrival of the manuscript on 25 April 1950, saying that 'even the most superficial glance staggers me with your brilliant, cinematic conceptions.' On 19 May he wrote again to say that he found the filmscript 'magic and miraculous' and that Christopher Isherwood shared his opinion (*SL* 441). In his 17 July 1950 letter (**409**) to Harold Matson, Lowry quoted Taylor's praise hoping to convince Matson to believe in his work enough to loan him money.

2 It is not certain precisely when Lowry first met the Welsh poet Dylan Thomas (1914-53), but both men visited London in the summer of 1933 and frequented the Soho pubs. Both were regulars in the Fitzroy Tavern and both were close friends of John Davenport's, so they may have met in pubs or in Anna Wickham's home. They celebrated their reunion in Vancouver on 6 April 1950 with appropriate quantities of drink and conversation. For a description of Thomas's visit, see Salloum (76-77). It is possible that 'dalyaed' is not a typographical slip but a Lowryan neologism that puns on the English 'delay' and the Welsh 'daly,' meaning to capture, seize, or overtake, with an echo of dallying for good measure.

3 The expression 'doubting Thomas' refers to Thomas, one of Christ's twelve apostles, who was noted for his scepticism. Dylan Thomas had just shown up in Hollywood, where Taylor looked after him.

4 Pliny the Elder (AD 23-79) was a Roman naturalist and encyclopedist; Pliny the Younger (AD ?62-ca 113) was a statesman and orator. Robert Burton (ca 1576-ca 1640), the English writer, published *The Anatomy of Melancholy* in 1621, but Tommy Barban is a character in *Tender Is the Night*.

5 Lowry paraphrases this passage from Melville's *Israel Potter* in several letters; see, for example, **280**, **462**, and **510**.

6 See letter **395** to Taylor.

7 In conversation with the Consul in chapter 7 of *Under the Volcano* Señora Gregorio advises him to put 'Your minds, your life – your everything in it,' that is, into renewing his marriage and his search for happiness.

8 'Daddy's Little Girl' is the title of a song composed in 1905 by Edward Madden, with music by Theodore Morse. A second version was recorded in 1949 with words and music by Bobby Burke and Horace Gerlach. Rosemary Hoyt in *Tender Is the Night* has starred in a film called *Daddy's Girl*, and references to the film constitute a motif in the novel and the Lowrys' screenplay that contributes to the undeveloped incest theme.

397: To Frank Taylor

P: Matson(ts)
PP: *White Pelican* 4   [Dollarton]
                                                          [April/May 1950]ᵃ

Dear Frank:

Here are a few items culled from what started out to be a sort of preface, so it is this that accounts for its occasional didactic tone. This began
with a few remarks re the movie round table conference mentioned in
our letter.¹ The second part is taken up with some of the problems raised
by Tender is the Night seen in the light of some of the questions raised
by the following.

We felt rather as if we were participating in the conference because
one of the people present, Alistair Cooke, was a very old college
friend, moreover a friend with whom I (Malcolm) had once under-
taken a hazardous expedition in Cambridge upon a tandem bicycle.²
I cannot remember any better now than then whether we thought we
were going in the same direction, or whether the steering had been
left up to Alistair or myself: but in the report of the conference in Life
it didn't strike me my old friend had taken the subject of the movies
much more seriously than the bicycle, which I found disappointing
in him, because he too is a writer, and a good one, or because the
general impression left upon ourselves by that whole conference was
one of the most hopeful and challenging made in years. Joseph
Mankiewicz, for example: 'I have heard a lot about the responsibilities of the film toward the public,' he says, 'but very little about the
responsibilities of the people toward the film.'³ To this one might
add, what about the responsibilities of the writer? Mankiewicz also
said that 'we have been assured there were many friends of
Hollywood,' and that statement he flings right back at those friends
and asks them to try and do something about it. That strikes us as just:
his reference is to what individuals can do in their own bailiwicks, but
being writers ourselves perhaps the best thing we could do was to try
to write a good film ourselves. This is not so obvious as it looks, but
since it is precisely so many of our finest writers who consistently
complain about the quality of films, sometimes we can't help wondering why they don't do something about it. Or more about it.
There are, of course, certain recent brilliant and obvious exceptions
to this in which there has been successful cooperation between writers and directors and producers, and you must assume we're bearing
these exceptions in mind, and that doubtless more are being exemplified as we write but most of the writers we have known personally
whose works have been, say, bought by Hollywood, or have gone

there themselves, seem to have failed, and then blamed the failure on Hollywood. Or even when they have succeeded, they have blamed the success on Hollywood. Very often – in fact above all – they blame it on the ethics of Hollywood. (More about which later.) They say a good many complicated things, but what it all boils down to is (1) the ethics of Hollywood are vile, because they wish to sell only sex; (2) the ethics of Hollywood are vile because it is impossible to write of sex, ergo, to tell the truth. You may substitute 'aesthetics,' 'artistic standards,' or even 'politics,' for ethics – but it seems to amount to much the same thing in the end. Yet should one look at the scripts responsible for these failures there is often only one reaction possible: they love not the film. Mysteriously, despite their protests, they love it not. They may have learned from it, they may even be able to tell you what a good film is, and write intelligently about it, but at bottom they feel superior to it – or to everything except the money to be made by it.

But we are straying from the point, which we shall return to by way of another remark of Mr Mankiewicz', whose stamp is on everything he does, and whom one must assume to be a very large exception in himself. 'In my opinion it is the hope of the motion picture industry that the competition of the future will not be competition between business men for creative talent but competition between creative people for the American audience.' Then one of Mr Schary's: 'The best pictures are the ones that make money.' This last, while not the sort of statement that recommends itself immediately to a creative person, bringing to mind, as it does, certain movie masterpieces that cannot possibly have made money, we would prefer to relate to another of Mr Mankiewicz' – 'The top grossing pictures of the last few years were *about* something. They had a point of view about people and society and they were tremendous box office hits.' From this, without casuistry, it would appear that the argument runs something like this: 'The best pictures are about something: they have a point of view about people and society and it is these pictures which are tremendous box office hits.' But what point of view, and about what people? (There is an answer to this, but it's not a bad place to be reminded of Citizen Kane, Mankiewicz' and Welles' film, which was certainly not a box office hit, but which was certainly about something, and was certainly a great film, qua film.) It was here, in our preface, we interpolated the quotation from Mr Bryant: 'The only object which is worth achieving is the ennoblement of man,' etc.[4] This – the quotation – is not intended to be taken quite at its face value, for it has its ridiculous and sentimental side, and certainly not as a reflection upon Citizen Kane where to any artist the said ennoblement may be said to be brought about by proxy, the reaction being 'there is nobility in the fact that such a film could be made at all.'

It has often seemed to us, however – speaking of challenge – that it is the conclusions of psychology itself, or those conclusions as they have filtered down to us, falsifying and over-simplifying themselves in the process, thus to become part of our daily lives, that offer a challenge to writers and the modern world, so far too often answered, not counting purely religious answers, (the failure of Fitzgerald to provide a focal point for Dick's conscience in Tender is the Night, a subject we shall approach eventually, is remedied for artistic reasons alone) by Dorothy Dix, Lloyd Douglas and Hedda Hopper – and even these sort of people weaken from time to time.[5] Even Catholic spokesmen are liable to use the word 'trauma' when attacking Protestantism. At the bottom of one's mind is always the sneaking suspicion: there is something in what Grandmama says. Is there any valid reason for literature and the movies to portray man as ignoble and mean? How have we got that way? Where are the great motives, even the great temptations of Shakespeare's time, and so forth? And why, when such motives or conflicts turn up again, do they do so nearly always in corrupt and sentimental form, and why are the writers who employ them, like as not, fifth rate? Surely one place for this to be corrected is the film. But should this be left – bearing in mind the exceptions as before – to de Mille, or Bing Crosby, much as one likes them? or to the realm of enormous over-simplifications?[6]

Now ourselves, like Mr Huston, are opposed to any form of censorship finally.[7] One would like to see censorship disappear in the movies as elsewhere. But at the risk of heresy to our own profession as writers one ventures to state that the matter may be, so far as the movies is concerned, approached from the wrong direction. Let us look at what happened in literature. The ban on Ulysses, whatever anyone says, was not really lifted because it was not intentionally obscene or an aphrodisiac and so on, but because of the passion and scholarship and artistic devotion Joyce had put into it, so much more passion and scholarship and artistic devotion indeed was there in Joyce's work than in almost any other contemporary production, unless we except Proust's, which was about buggery, that it gave one the illusion that the conventional resources of nobility or ennoblement in literature right up to their highest expression were exhausted, and the thing became a noble achievement in itself: nor, if we are being somewhat incomplete, are we wholly joking: it was the very best there was, and so we had to have it, and not to have it would have been a grave impairment of our freedom, and that of other writers.[8]

Now however that may be about literature, one has often thought it might be just the other way round with the film. 'The resources of nobility' (for lack of a better phrase) seem not really to have been tapped. There is nothing 'wrong' – what is wrong? don't we want to be uplifted? – with the 'uplift' side of Hollywood's ethics. It is just that the mantle for its expression has rested too long upon people of the calibre of Lloyd Douglas. Yet a man should be able to write nobly, and even greatly, even within such limitations as Hollywood provides even those of the Catholic Church. But the way to break your bonds is nearly always by straining upwards, as everyone knows who has ever been tied to a bed.

The point of all this rigmarole is that in the sound movie there is as yet, to our knowledge, no filmic equivalent of Antigone, no filmic Peer Gynt, no King Lear, and so forth. Citizen Kane you might call a sort of filmic Timon of Athens. Timon is one of Shakespeare's finest plays, but also his most demeaning and most unpopular: there is room for the demeaning as even perhaps for the depressing, in the movie as in nearly all art, especially when accompanied by genius, which is exhilarating anyway, but isn't that rather putting, in this case, the cart before the horse? That the cart might be filled with sheer filmic gold to a real film lover is quite by the way, save to him and for history: unschooled to the gold, the public might mistake the contents of it for the cart. Timon was preceeded by most of the great plays. But we think the reason for this is roughly in the direction of our quotation: it is a teleological reason, or a philosophical one. Man *wants* to be drawn upwards. (Even should the protagonist go downwards.) And why not? What we're driving at is this: if all works were noble we should perhaps become as fed up as if they were all obscene; but should the film attempt seriously to reach the highest – by which we do not mean trying to portray Shakespeare which in our estimation is quite on the wrong track – but to achieve something in its own cine-matic terms, perhaps other limitations would fall away. Actually if you go really high enough the censorship won't be able to see you (though the public will, you having carried them part of the way with you, while the censorship and the League of Decency were still down below with their noses stuck in the mud.)

But this is actually tangential to the point. We submit that when people say they want better films, one thing they long for is some sort of powerful reflection of the true dignity of man. 'The only object worth achieving in this world is the ennoblement of man. It can never be more than a partial achievement, for man, like all terrestrial creatures, is imperfect and insufficient to himself. But he has in him the seeds of greatness, and whatever feeds, fosters, and brings to maturity these vital seeds is, for short-lived man, beyond price. It is this alone which makes his checkered and tragic sojourn here worth while.' etc.[9]

Here are a few notes re certain dramatic problems and technicalities in the recreation of the novel, Tender is the Night, in the medium of the film, in relation largely to what has just preceeded – since it is inevitable that some of this will seem to be repeated in later notes substantiated in direct regard to the context we ask that you make allowances for this in advance.

After working for some time it became apparent that Fitzgerald had at the back of his mind some kind of great tragedy, and was divided as to how to write it: personal disaster further divided him and inhibited him, and the sober conclusions of psychoanalysis, apparently fresh to him, served further to adulterate any heroic quality in it. (This is corroborated in a life of Fitzgerald which has been coming out concurrently with our working upon it: though the tragedy was very different from what one suspected: Rosemary apparently was once a man and murdered Mrs Hoyt!)[10]

As a movie, at first sight, it would seem to have impossible counts against it. First the incest motif. Then its sprawling and sometimes incoherent length, despite its finally excellent form. Third its lack of any clear dramatic line, and despite the many superb *scenes*, its final lack of integration.

There are certain themes that cannot be touched and perhaps that is a good thing – Mr Huston. Apart from the Oedipus, perhaps the most bona fide chef d'oeuvre about incest is Shelley's The Cenci.[11] Once, however, while wandering about Rome thinking of his play Shelley heard, to his horror, a beggar crying 'Cenci, cenci,' and discovered to his astonishment that it meant 'old rags.' This we believe is an adequate appraisal of incest as a form of etiology. Though the most obvious of basic ideas it has been avoided for some equally obvious and basic reason and one only has to imagine how intolerable it would have become had it been common, how really 'old rags,' to see some fairly good reason for avoiding it. It is true that Hamlet is about a kind of incest, but one feels its popularity would have been gravely impaired had anyone suspected it, while the persistence of the Oedipus play is probably due to his final redemption, not the incest.

On the other hand, you couldn't make a movie of Oedipus without the incest – or even with it – nor could you bowdlerize The Cenci in any way and make it worth while. The incest is endemic to both works: you couldn't have Jocasta turn out to be Oedipus' maiden aunt who had disguised herself as a boy without, to say the least, hurting it considerably, even if, as Mr Huston might say, the substitution of vice involved proved acceptable to the Catholic League of Decency.

The case of Tender is the Night is quite different and had this not been so one would have scarcely dared work upon it: there is a way of looking at it in which the incest does not appear essential, and there is the fact that it is not altogether integrated into the architechtonics of the book: but the case is not quite the same, to say the least, as with those novels or plays (The Children's Hour, Hangover Square, etc.)[12] which have been utterly transmogrified, but made into effective movies: with Tender is the Night the residue, after the incest was subtracted, to say nothing of a great deal of other censorable material, was of such a nature that if it could not be integrated with what one had substituted, so that the whole became integrated within itself, and this integrity dramatised and realized in such a manner that one's reaction to it would be like a recognition of truth, there would be no film at all. That is to say what was left was in one way too great: a feeble structure would let it fall of its own weight, where it would be indistinguishable from the rest of the ruin. And there was the further difficulty that, on close inspection, its foundations, for all that it is one of the most haunting novels of our era, were none too secure to start with. – As a novel, though, it failed at the time, and this failure has been called due to its theme: this, however, we submit, is almost certainly untrue. As a matter of fact, as a novel, this might strangely have been a reason for its succeeding. There is a valid argument that it fails artistically too, or very nearly fails, theme and all: what saves it is that it is a work of a genius of importance, and contains other elements in it; its failure, or near failure as a novel, was due, we suggest, to the fact that it was not realised fully as a book; but maybe it is this that paradoxically saves it for the movies because it gives one more room to move creatively within it, to disentangle other great underlying motifs without damaging a perfect whole, unlike with the Great Gatsby, whose theatrical perfection was conceivably a filmic liability: you might make a poetical tragedy out of Tender is the Night, but hardly a straight play, and this we take to be an advantage. There will doubtless be those who may have good reasons for thinking this was a perfect enough book anyway and that it is mere impertinence to have tampered with it as we have done and with this view we sympathise. However we have tried sincerely to have regard for the great American artist who wrote it and where possible even to imagine what he would have done were he trying to make it into a film: as a novel he would have agreed it would have stood some tampering with: as a film it *has* to be tampered with, certain sacrifices have to be made, for which we shall try to make due compensation but in terms of what one might call Fitzgerald's own buried intentions, or what we conceive them to be. In order to find what these were we have had to go to work practically with geiger counters. Even many of the most apparently explicit scenes are only explicit on the surface. Some of them seem to have their roots in books he never wrote. And perhaps one of the most important scenes of all, on Golding's yacht, is so underwritten (and for that matter, in the wrong place, overwritten) that it is by no means clear that Fitzgerald understood its significance. Certain articles on Fitzgerald that have appeared concurrently with our own writing the movie would have seemed to confirm or endorse in places what we were doing but we have preferred to go to work cold, without even the benefit of the Crack Up until recently, which confirmed matters still more.[13]

It is in fact not merely Nicole, but the whole book which suffers – if not so acutely – from schizophrenia. Her age is misrepresented three or four times during the book, showing that Fitzgerald may have still not quite discarded two or three alternate ideas for her. In one of the finest realized scenes, in the funicular, it is noonday at one moment (no shadows on the tennis court) a quarter of an hour later at the top of the funicular it is nearly sunset. Yet the scene is brilliantly and carefully written: even this mistake has obviously been burnished over and over again. This shows something peculiar indeed: a meticulousness in regard to foreground or background, to conceal the disorderliness of the whole, would seem to suggest that the book is, however wonderful, ill. This may not keep us from loving the book, or Nicole, or Dick, or Fitzgerald or even Mrs Fitzgerald – as a matter of fact one comes to love all five, finally – but this kind of thing, for there are many far more important instances, serious enough almost to impede the flow of the novel towards any consistent resolution at all, should one examine them, certainly make it a hard task for any would-be adapter who would like to keep his eye sternly upon cause and effect. (On the other hand in the subterrannean part of the book, Abe – the duel – Peterson – Abe's death – Dick becomes Abe – there is a law of cause and effect going on that works out almost like a collaboration between Buddha and Sophocles.)[14] The temptation would be, since Fitzgerald is too good a cook not to have produced some sort of apparently consistent good dish – having pushed the forbidden hot sauce of incest aside and substituted a gasket sauce of one's own – filmically to attack what appears to be at the surface; a sort of spring chicken a la King Oliver, with Jungfrau dressing, or perhaps an olla podrida a la jazz age washed down with one cold boiled psychologist. One can well conceive how this is enough to undo anybody. Or one could always blame it again on not being able to bring in the incest, which, when all is said and done, is a loss, and enormously enhances the pathos of Nicole at one point. So what about that great scene of the return of the father, dying, or rather, wonderfully not dying? Or does it only *look* like a great scene? We regret that it perhaps does. It is never realised and never resolved. Practically speaking one would have had to keep an eye upon this theme to a far greater extent than Fitzgerald for it to come off, even if one could use it.[15] An unsympathetic critic might even say without total injustice that one reason for this is that it, the incest, has so far ceased to have any organic importance for Fitzgerald himself that the return of the father is a formal thing only, or almost formal, and is tossed off as cynicism. This might well have been a great scene in itself but since the book has forgotten it started off, unconsciously or even consciously, by being a tragedy, it falls here into almost no category of art at all – this is not important, but it is not *new* either – what happens here is just simply a brilliant even genius-like note: but the scene is not really written, which is true of more than half the other scenes in the book: he is telling you that something like such and such is a good scene, polishing his exposition of how he feels it might be, and palming it off on you as the thing itself. In other parts he is polishing simply in terms of a single installment in a serial, not of the whole book. This is perhaps the best explanation of the scene just mentioned – obliged to cut the explicit statement of incest out of the serial Fitzgerald could scarcely revaluate the true importance of its instrument: it was a problem of compromise for him too, not economy. This would not matter in a film where it would be up to oneself: what matters is that this scene in question would need, even if usable in a film, supporting factors (we have cut out the next 10 pages that prove this) one could not afford. Another scene – this time one of the best written scenes in the Night, a truly wonderful scene, Barban's love affair with Nicole, and the cannon and the whores and the American battleship, even if one at first regrets the impossibility of using it, could scarcely have been used anyhow in a *film*, however lenient or even non-existent the censorship, for by almost cynically seeming to identify Nicole with the whores, one has raised a whole new set of questions that, if followed through logically would bely the point of the movie even in Fitzgerald's hypothetical terms: it is a masterpiece in the item but the frisson it gives one is out of place: even if handled with supernatural subtlety, so that one saw just the tiniest suggestion of a tragic or pathetic nuance of guilt in Nicole's feeling, the scene could not be made effectively without implying meaning that was in excess of that and carried beyond the end of the picture: treated simply as a coincidence it would be the same; and the meaning of the scene would bely, as has been said the meaning of the picture – indeed it would over-shadow it, for it would imply: Nicole has decided against insanity and for sanity, but at the expense of being, as it were, a whore: this may be wonderful and even true (of somebody else) but it is certainly another story.

To sum up therefore: in the ideal country of no censorship – and there is this much to encourage the adapter – Fitzgerald's whole intention in Tender is the Night could not be carried out because Fitzgerald's whole intention is *not there in the book*. This however, once again, scarcely makes matters any easier once the incest is thrown out: if his use of incest was one of the first things one would have felt called upon to render more consistently organic in the hypothetical film, one of the first things to improve, how would it be with its substitute that yet must be more consistently organic than the incest was in the book? Well, at least we can say that in our version the traumatic precipitate of Nicole's madness is *as equally* an integral part of the structure as was the incest while in so far as the symbol of that precipitating factor, the car, is carried from that point right through the film and appears not only as a motivation of Nicole's later actions but as a vehicle of her cure – coming in line here with Fitzgerald's intention – it is more consistently organic. Such a concept (though there's some evidence Fitzgerald may have entertained it himself as an alternative) would have taken some heart and pathos out of the book, as written. But we don't believe this need be so in a film for the following perfectly good reasons. You could not dramatise the incest anyhow: one is not saying it could not be appalling by suggestion, because it could, and even Fitzgerald does not dramatise it, but you would have to stop short: it is questionable whether even a verbal suggestion in a film would not cast a shadow of such appallingness that it would outlaw any subsequent humour, which would be a problem in itself. Here you can dramatise it easily. And if it can't be too gruesome we nonetheless will have had the whole shock and seen how it happened. Nicole's madness, far more vivid and convincing in a film since we see it actually in operation, has a visual backing that projects the madness itself into far sharper visual focus, and it is after all the madness itself that is far more important than any precipitating factor. Yet the latter is important too for the plot if its substantiation, enables, as it now does, the plot there upon to become completely integrated. You are constantly reminded of theme and countertheme and nothing is left dangling to mar the structure. Deeper causations and etiologies simply drop out of sight, as they must do and as they did with Fitzgerald (for the reason stated above) but *not* the precipitating factor itself. This means that actual causality is kept in balance, as it is not in the book, and it is a gain. Moreover since the car is a multiform visual symbol – as we doubtless have said in the notes, the Isotta for one thing is the patent symbol of Nicole's wealth, in addition to her neurosis, and hence of yet another thing that stands between Dick and Nicole – the film also gains in complexity of interpretation, while being perfectly simple on the surface. An accident – if it was an accident – may be a conventional enough idea: but not the car. It merely looks conventional. We might (though mind you no one else, only we) even begin to wonder what we had lost after all. No one has said the precipitating factor didn't in itself have another precipitating factor; the trauma is not usually so close to the result, but then it sometimes is. A fire can drive you nuts: but that does not explain the fire. And if we are showing ourselves conveniently disinterested in remote etiologies we might blandly point out too that that too is in line with certain psychiatric practice. And if you're not satisfied with that we could say that it most certainly is in line with art. And even with truth. We don't want to start the story in Westphalia in 1715, as Dohmler implied when he said 'Peasant!'[16] And even then? So you see perhaps it is all a little like our washes which remote steamers keep sending up on beaches from time to time. But perhaps this is not the place to tell you the story of the sea-captain's horse and his expense account.

A few other obiter Dickta,[17] some of them will seem repetitive.

(a) It was necessary to redefine its intention in terms as it were of Fitzgerald's 'higher self' – if any kind of a great movie were to be made out of it.

(b) Necessary, indeed, for the film, almost to apply the technique of psychoanalysis or blind analysis to the book itself, to try to see, or imagine, what it had passed through, and might have repressed in its unconscious: for surely there was never a great book that was more finally unclear – even unwritten – in places you would expect to find explicit: nor does an undoubted genius for understatement explain it all.

(c) In spite of its real and heartbreaking merits, its outcome implied a curious consciencelessness, even supposing that the conscience had been intended to manifest itself, which was none too clear either: if conscience there were it is a sort of psuedo-Freudian one – though one searches in vain in the novel for even this much – and in attempting to save his hero from the sentimental heroics of a David Garrick – who you remember deliberately got drunk in the play in order to repel the young girl who loves him[18] – he has denuded Dick of any tragic stature: the book narrows down on its protagonist upon a shabby ending that is scarcely even pathetic, having the one negative virtue that it is *apparently* honest and true to life. Because of Barban, falsely accounted for, it does not as a matter of fact have even that virtue. But this is not so important as to ask was this, Barban aside, the true resolution he meant to give the novel? Is the book true to Fitzgerald, or has it, in some subtle way, betrayed or eluded him, or managed to manifest itself to the world as a kind of neurotic version of itself? Working upon the treatment and adaption for the film, where it was necessary apart from anything else, to get to the essence of the thing – we became convinced that this was so.

This brings us back to the beginning. It was a tragedy. Perhaps it *is* a tragedy but what we mean is that it seemed to have something more classically and tragically tragic about it than met the eye, though one could not find the clue. As we say, we went to work cold on this but it would not have helped us had we possessed the corroborative information. Likewise with Antibes: it is true that Tarmes is almost recognizable as Antibes (see later letter) but we were not convinced of its rightness because of that, or because as everyone knows Fitzgerald lived there, or from the fact one of us knew Bob Macalmon[19] who was actually there with Fitzgerald, or because we were in the neighbourhood year before last: but because suddenly, obvious though it is from any guidebook, but striking us like a revelation fairly springing at us out of the blue, we realised that Antibes, together with its neighbours for that matter, was an old Greek city. Vauban (Barban) built the walls. (No relation to Dr Barbon, a disgraced medical practitioner, who capitalized as realtor on the old walls of London after the fire, rebuilding those as slums, and whose sinister mark is to be seen to this day, and of whom one had to read right at this minute.)[20] The Mediterranean is the Greek ocean, the sea is the unconscious. But more important, it was this most certainly that was in the unconscious of the book. By the same, if a more far fetched – but still strictly logical – token if Dick Diver, who might seem one thinks, to have his name by accident does not unconsciously by virtue of that name come to enjoy some of the attributes of that famous and sinister – in short Dick-Moby-Dick-Diver (and if not, why Diver?) transmuted into and around his ego, the buried intention having been to make him, both on the constructive and destructive side, a sort of archetypical American, one misses one's guess. In literature one can get very irritated with this kind of intricate criticism that turns work into a sort of rebus (as we write, somebody, over the air is doing it to the Volcano, your, my, our Volcano)[21] it is flattering, there is a grain of truth in it, but there is the end of the matter, or rather there is no end of the matter, for you can go on forever, once started – but this is because its practical value as criticism is about nil: in trying to uncover the truth, or certain essential truths, about a work such as Tender is the Night with the purpose of making it into a film, that if it could not equilibrate the book would attempt to equilibrate the importance of the American author who wrote it, the object may be said to be pious as well as practical in the extreme: first, anything less than a great film will not do: another 'psychological film,' another film about the 'jazz age,' should be put in the wastepaper basket, as we said in our letter,[22] so that finally, this becomes a way not only of ferreting out its greatness, but its immediate and practical value as a great film, as we submit it certainly could and ought to be.

M & M.[b]

Annotations:

1 See Lowry's 12 April 1950 letter (**395**) to Taylor. The beginning Lowry refers to here exists in draft fragments (UBC 23:14).

2 Alistair Cooke (1908–), who had been at Cambridge with Lowry, was a British commentator and chief correspondent for the *Manchester Guardian* at this time. Cooke participated in the 'Round Table on the Movies' reported in *Life*, 27 June 1949.

3 This and subsequent quotations are from the *Life* article.

4 See Bryant's observation in Lowry's 12 April 1950 letter (**395**) to Taylor.

5 Dorothy Dix (1861–1951) and Lloyd Douglas (1877–1951) were American writers. Hedda Hopper (1877–1966), the Hollywood gossip columnist, appeared in many films, and Douglas had several of his novels made into films.

6 Cecil B. de Mille (1881–1959) was a Hollywood film director, and Bing Crosby (1904–77) was a popular American singer and actor.

7 John Huston (1906–87), the American film director, was one of the 'Round Table' participants (see annotation 2). In 1984 he would direct the film version of *Under the Volcano* starring Albert Finney, Jacqueline Bisset, and Anthony Andrews.

8 James Joyce's *Ulysses* (1922) was plagued with obscenity charges and bans against its importation. Judge John M. Woolsey of the United States Federal Court cleared it of charges of 'literary turpitude' in 1933, but Canada still banned import of the novel in 1949, when Earle Birney gave his CBC talk on the subject. Marcel Proust's (1871–1922) *Remembrance of Things Past*, while scarcely about buggery, explores homosexuality in the third volume, *Cities of the Plain* (1922).

9 See the Bryant quotation in the 12 April 1950 letter (**395**) to Frank Taylor.

10 Sections of Arthur Mizener's (1907–88) *The Far Side of Paradise: A Biography of F. Scott Fitzgerald* appeared in American journals between 1949 and 1951, when was published by Houghton Mifflin in book form. Lowry's comment about Rosemary (a character in *Tender Is the Night*) refers to Mizener's revelation that in an early version of the novel called 'The World's Fair' or 'The Boy Who Killed His Mother,' a character called Francis Melarky comes to the Riviera with his mother and kills her there. Fitzgerald abandoned the matricide idea in 1929, so that Rosemary Hoyt comes to the Riviera with her mother but does not kill her.

11 The English romantic poet Percy Bysshe Shelley (1792–1822) completed his five-act verse tragedy *The Cenci* in 1819. In it Shelley tells the story of incest, revenge, and murder within the family of Count Francesco Cenci of Rome in 1599. *Céncio* is Italian for 'rag' or 'piece of cloth'; thus, *cénci* are 'rags.'

12 *The Children's Hour*, a 1934 play by American writer Lillian Hellman (1905–84), is about a spiteful child who accuses her teachers of

lesbianism. *Hangover Square* (1944) is a film about a psychopathic composer and serial killer who murders women in London. It is based on a 1941 novel by Patrick Hamilton.

13 Fitzgerald's *The Crack-Up* (1945), edited by Edmund Wilson, is a collection of autobiographical pieces.

14 The Buddha was Prince Siddhartha (566?-ca 480 BC), the Indian leader and founder of Buddhism; Sophocles (496-06 BC), the Greek tragedian, wrote three Oedipus plays.

15 The problem of Mr Warren's incest (Fitzgerald calls it a 'rape') with his daughter Nicole is not developed in *Tender Is the Night*. Incest, however, was a theme of some interest to Lowry, as his lasting fascination with Jean Cocteau's *La Machine infernale* (1934) suggests; see, for example, Lowry's 1 March 1950 letter (**389**) to Clarisse Francillon and his 22 February 1957 letter (**705**) to David Markson.

16 Dr Dohmler is with the Zürich clinic to which Mr Warren brings his daughter Nicole. During Dohmler's interview with Warren in book II, chapter 3, the father confesses to the incest/rape that has caused his daughter's breakdown; the confession prompts the doctor to exclaim 'Peasant!' thereby judging not only Warren's crime but the pretensions to feudal authority of wealthy Chicago families like the Warrens.

17 The Latin *obiter dictum* means a passing remark or opinion. Lowry's pun is with the plural form, *dicta*, and Dick Diver's name.

18 David Garrick (1717-79), the English actor, theatre manager, and playwright, was famous for his performances of Shakespeare and for his own lively farces. Lowry, however, is thinking of the Victorian play by T.W. Robertson called *David Garrick* (1864), in which the actor pretends to be a dissolute drunk.

19 Lowry met the expatriate American writer Robert McAlmon in Paris during the summer of 1934.

20 Sébastien Le Prestre de Vauban (1633-1707), French royal engineer under Louis XIV, was responsible for designing the fortifications at Antibes. Nicholas Barbon, a seventeenth-century English physician, was one of the builders of London after the great fire in 1666.

21 Lowry is probably referring to Derek Pethick's proposed broadcast on *Under the Volcano*; see his 6 March 1950 letter (**391**) to Pethick.

22 See Lowry's 12 April 1950 letter (**395**) to Taylor.

Editorial Notes:

a. This transcription is from the original letter, which carries Lowry's minor editorial changes in pencil. Neither the two drafts (UBC 23:14) nor this typescript has an inside address or date, but the contents of the letter place it mid-way in this spring 1950 series of letters to Taylor. The letter was first published with introduction and annotations by Paul Tiessen in *White Pelican* 4, 2 (1974): 2-20.

b. There is no formal signature on this letter.

398: To Gian Carlo Menotti

P: UBC(ms)   [Dollarton]
                                                          [May 1950]ᵃ

My dear Gian-Carlo Menotti:[1] –

I am beginning to think you are my döppelgänger, – or we share an undersoul, or would it be an oversoul? & I am sure I could not want for a better of any of these.

Here is why: About the time that you were looking out of the window of the Edison in 47th (I once lived 16 years ago nearly next door), wondering who was going to stop in at the Ethel Barrymore, a book of mine – Feb 1947 – the one I send you though I send you the English edition – was in process of becoming a very considerable hit in New York.[2]

In fact I have suffered in a measure from what you have suffered, for I am an Englishman (though resident in Canada) & the book was a roaring success in America while only a succes d'estime in England: – even so, I thoroughly expected it to be a complete failure everywhere): Yes, I too might have well have said 'I keep telling them I am famous in America, famous! They just look at me sympathetically.' (In Canada they think it is a treatise on the properties of sulphur, I believe.)

The book also has gone similarly well in France – {in fact in France you may even be haunted by it in your Daily Paper Combat where it is called Au dessus du Volcan – (it has been published in 3 different forms in Paris since the beginning of the year.) & Norway, & is coming out shortly in your own old country, by Einaudi, in Turino: the joke is that it is about a consul, who is so often referred to as 'The Consul', that he is thought of as nothing else & even some of my friends in the last few years have actually acquired the name 'The Consul' – & it has become something of a catchphrase even.

Now I'm sure the fates ordained that you've never heard of *my* Consul until now, & I live so far away in the wilderness, that more's the pity, I never heard of *yours* till recently – they have something remotely in common, however, which is that while *yours* apparently was a spy or a member of the secret police, mine was merely suspected of being a spy & was *killed* by the secret police: yours was a wickeder Consul than mine in short, though mine certainly had *his* failings, among which was one very original one, namely he drank so much he had a terrible sense of persecution & thought that he was being followed, so that when he saw himself being followed he thought it was just his sense of persecution, but the joke was, you see, this time he *was* being followed: or they were following his half-brother, his doppleganger, which came to the same thing.

However, I have not come to the most peculiar part of the story: the novel I have been working on for the last 5 years, on & off, which I began at the end of 1945 (I began my Consul in 1936), of which you could not possibly have heard, for I told no one the plot, & none of it has been published, not even in part, has a plot not dissimilar to that of *your* Consul, so far as I can gather: really it is a gigantically long work, a trilogy, the first being called Dark as the Grave wherein my friend is laid, the second Fridanus, & the third La Mordida: (on the other hand it is all related to *Under the Volcano* (the book I've sent you), & hence to *my* Consul: when I am about eighty I hope to publish a tetralogy, that would include with the above the Volcano, & another work) that being so, the actual resemblance only relates to the third part, but it is sufficiently important to be eerie nevertheless: there is the same theme of waiting, waiting most – the last part takes place in the British Consulates in Mexico City, or in the even worse offices of the Minister of the Interior, where they deport people.[3] There is an endless scene before the shut door – with the pictures of the deportados on the wall – in this office with the damned souls sitting there waiting: & the only people that come out of that door come out weeping. I don't know if thats anything at all like your opera, which I only know from the reviews & the pictures I saw in Life etc, which anyhow I now dare scarcely see, in case I came to be influenced when I came to put my final touches: though come to that it is more or less written & fixed as it is.

La Mordida (the Mexican phrase for La Mordidura is correct) of course refers on the surface to the civic corruption: 'The Bite': the way some people are able to buy their way out of these difficulties, but the corruption is as self extending as a plot by Ibsen: but it also relates to remorse (remords) & though I am not good at Italian I can still conjugate mordeo, mordere, morsi, morsum in Latin. I trace down other causes why the people are in the position they are.

Finally what all this was *about* was the process of creation itself: I was trying to anatomise the inner life of the unconscious of the man that wrote *Under the Volcano*, my Consul – though I imagined it, in La Mordida as somebody else: this part I have not finished, nor shall for a long while, though I had actually imagined, & already written an account of, a coincidence of somewhat this type that I refer to in this letter, but of having a far direr effect on the protagonist, because in this case the knowledge that someone has written a work supernaturally similar to his own (his not being published at all) almost shatters him altogether: in our case, both our works were successes, but in different genres: the similarity of the nature of my unfinished work, together with the titular & spiritual resemblance of my two to your one (it is only a miracle they did not call *Under the Volcano* was not called The Consul, different sort of Consul though he may be) confirms the philosophic resolution I was trying to give the whole, without making either of us unhappy.

But I have not finished yet: for the most eerie is yet to come. I know nothing about music; but I happen to have been working in a different art form recently, where my advice was necessary on a technical matter; but it was knowledge of drama, not music, that required it. Whereupon I wrote my first & last musical disquisition upon the possibilities of – what! do you think. No less a thing than the canon. No sooner have I finished it than I open Time, the cover of which, with the hooded figures already childishly & enviously hurts my feelings, as does any mention of 'The Consul' a bit – because you must remember that I have lived with my Consul for fourteen years, am even sometimes myself known as the 'Consul' (apart from some of my friends, being known as the 'Consul' too.) – I open it, & read: 'Thanks to Scalero's perserverance, Menotti is now a master at writing canons . . .'[4] Now mind you what I had to say about the canon was in every way different from what you have apparently done with it: had I been in touch with things I would know more about your music anyway: I had something mystical, I think right in its way, but perhaps of no significance to you to say about the canon: but the fact is, when I saw the word canon in print in Time in that article is the first time I happen to have seen it in print since I was looking at Tallis' Canon in my fathers hymn book 35 years ago – I am 2 years older than you.[5] The only other time I've seen it was in my own typescript & in the dictionary where I had to look it up because I couldn't spell it & even thought what I was driving at might be a madrigal. But I had been haunted by my idea, such as it was, night & day: if anybody ever puts into practice I'd like to know what you think of it.

And so I close – or rather I don't close. I hope you will read the Volcano & I hope you will like it. I have a idea that its dissimilarities, not its similarities would strike you, & I have an even more childish idea that you would find a marvellous idea in it for an opera. The idea is childish so far as I am concerned because living in the wilderness as I do probably I should never be able to journey far enough to hear it. Nor was the idea money: You have my permission so far as the copyright is mine. I note however that you write your own librettos, & don't like to repeat your work. An excellent idea. But may I humbly ask you, Signor everything I have said being true, which it is, how the hell do you know that *you* didn't write *Under the Volcano*, while *I* wrote your opera? So you see, it would all [be] original anyway. Besides you never know you might have that flop you said would be good for your soul: as for the Consul his actual Consularness in *Under the Volcano* is not so important as yours in The Consul (though there is a consul in La Mordida that does have more of your Consul's significance) — it is important more in the sense of 'all earthly authority turned aside', & is an admirable spiritual qualification to your work — a sort of punishment for *your* Consul, while you could call mine just by his name. As I say I childishly dream you will see an opera in it, so that I may read about it 5 years after the event: you can write in Italian for that matter, & the next thing you will tell me is that Einaudi is *your* publisher too.

I think something or other I read in my infancy about certain inspirational collaboration between Belasco & Puccini not to say Dumas & Rossini have put the idea in my head.[6] I hope you will anyway read the book, & I hope what's more, after all, that I am going to get an opportunity to see *your* 'The Consul.' We were in Italy year before last & if we do any travelling that is probably where we'll go again, so I don't know when I'll be in the U.S again.

At all events, forgive this rigmarole which I hope amuses you at least. Be assured of all my wishes for your success
God bless you,

Yours sincerely

Malcolm Lowry

P.S. I have not the slightest idea, at bottom why I felt constrained to write this letter: but since I did feel so constrained, I am going to post it.[7]

Annotations:

1 Italian-born composer Gian Carlo Menotti (1911-) has written many operas with English librettos. Menotti, who moved to the United States in 1927, was enjoying the Broadway success of *The Consul* during the 1949-50 season, and feature articles on him and the opera appeared in *Time* 1 May 1950 and *Life* 7 May 1950.

2 During 1935-36 Malcolm and Jan had lived in New York at the Somerset Hotel. The *Time* magazine article on Menotti begins with a description of the composer anxiously watching from his window in the Edison Hotel as patrons arrived at the theatre for the 1947 opening of *The Medium*.

3 'La Mordida' is the unfinished novel (UBC 13:1-26 and 14:1-15) based on Malcolm's and Margerie's experiences in Mexico in 1946; see Lowry's 15 June 1946 letter (**224**) to Ronald Button and my discusssion of *The Voyage That Never Ends* (2-3). Menotti's *Consul* is the story of a desperate woman waiting in a consulate for a visa; when it fails to arrive, she commits suicide. This waiting at the mercy of officials in a fascistic state resembles the plot of 'La Mordida.'

4 Rosario Scalero of the Curtis Institute of Music in Philadelphia was Menotti's composition teacher; the *Time* article (65) reports that Menotti mastered the canon form under Scalero's tutelage.

5 Thomas Tallis (ca 1505-85) was an English organist and composer. 'Tallis's Canon,' originally written in 1567 with the words from the Sixty-seventh Psalm, has, since the eighteenth century, been sung to the hymn 'Glory to Thee, my God, this night,' and so it appears in the *Methodist Hymn and Tune Book* (1917).

6 Two of Italian composer Giacomo Puccini's (1858-1924) operas, *La Fanciulla del West* (*The Girl of the Golden West*), 1910, and *Madama Butterfly*, 1904, were based on plays by American playwright and producer David Belasco (1853-1931). However, Italian composer Gioacchino Rossini (1792-1868) did not base any operas on work by either Dumas *père* or *fils*. Lowry may be thinking of *La Traviata* (1853) by Giuseppe Verdi (1813-1901), which is based on *La Dame aux camélias* by Alexandre Dumas *fils* (1824-95).

7 I have not been able to trace a fair copy of this letter or to confirm that Menotti either received it or read *Under the Volcano*.

Editorial Notes:

a. This transcription is from a seven-page signed pencil holograph (UBC 2:14) with many deletions, accidentals, interlineations, and marginal insertions. The holograph is undated, but it is clear from the context that Lowry is writing after the 1 and 7 May articles on Menotti in *Time* and *Life*.

399: To Frank Taylor

P: Matson(ts)

Dollarton, B.C.,
Canada
20 May 1950[a]

Dear Frank:

Enclosed – see p. 36 – an aston[i]shing, even eerie (as I think you will agree if you'd had time to go through our notes even cursorily) example of the operations of the free-wheeling daemon.[1] For full effect you must become convinced, first of all of the date of the enclosed New Yorker, which is May 7, 1950 then recall that you received our script upon April 19, 1950. If you've had time again to read all the latter you will remember that 'Heavy, heavy hangs over thy head,' comes in, where the children are playing 'forfeits' in the park in Paris immediately prior to Dick driving them down with Nicole to Switzerland, the 'Heavy, heavy' motif being repeated from time to time subsequently in its serious application to Dick's destiny and the theme of the picture.[2] In the scene in the park a child holds a toy automobile, the forfeit, over Lanier's head, chanting 'Heavy, heavy,' the while. Since this idea was

Margie's not mine, I have no hesitation in saying that I consider it a piece of symbolic foreboding that H. Ibsen himself could hardly have bettered! The notion of repeating it as the voice of destiny itself – much as Malcolm Brinnin does – was, however, mine: and, if mentally tentative in its present context on the ship, is likewise, I feel, an excellent idea in itself, related as it is to Dick's vocation and his and Nicole's future, not to say the world's estate and moreover serving to remind you of the seriousness of the whole and being something like a restatement of the theme. John Malcolm Brinnin's poem is likewise an excellent one, and I would like to know when it occurred to him. The idea occurred to Margie last November, or late October, in a bus as we were going to town (I think I was going to get an X-ray for I fancy I remember thinking she couldn't have chosen an odder time to have such an inspiration). What is interesting is that this patter of the children's game of forfeits, which I take to be of pretty ancient derivation, has been in the public domain for well over a century at least without anyone, so far as I know, ever having seen its serious and tragic implications, then two people think of it simultaneously. Since the 'Night' is scarcely in the category of an ordinary written work, and since we must remain silent about it, we can't very well write to the good Mr Brinnin to say we had the same idea. Nonetheless, if anything comes of the picture, it is something one would hate to see cut out: which is why I ask you to take cognisance of the dates. We were not inspired by Mr Brinnin nor Mr Brinnin by us. As an original notion we are very proud of it, however, and as an original notion we feel honestly we have the right to ask you to make your judgement of it, for whatever its importance may be. (Chiefly philosophical in this letter, see later part) For that matter, anyone who could write that poem must have a good deal of understanding: forfeits is still in the public domain: though it could turn out, eventually to be polite for us to drop him a line. Such things can hurt. We have been tempted to write him already, leaving the nature of the work vague: (what if he gets the idea, as dreadful as it is excellent, of calling a book of poems 'Heavy heavy hangs over thy head?') What do you think? Set against it is the fact that our Night is somewhat in the realm of the unborn, even ectoplasmic, or even the potentially reshelved till God's great venite change the tune, so it might seem like tempting fate. Worse still, by calling attention to yet further significance in the poem, it might give him the very idea one hopes won't occur to him: yet it would seem immoral to tempt him with that idea and then not expect him to take advantage of it, since after all he got there first in print, whereas we weren't even thinking of print.

I guess we would have been mysteriously hurt but for the fact – as re which I have written you – that we were prepared for such coincidences. In fact, I should look out for more. It is, in fact, one theme of the novel: I was prepared even for the fact that someone else would meantime base a novel upon coincidence. (which is why I refer you to p. 95, too, of the New Yorker, though this refers to an evident distortion of this theme on the destructive side) I feel it should be treated as a good omen even if meantime you have what seems discouraging news, or even encouraging news.[3] It relates to what has been called philosophically The Law of Series, a subject hitherto neglected in art, though the novelist with his all but solipsistic world of the novel is in the best possible position to cast some exciting light on its dramatic operations. Osbert Sitwell has had a sort of inorganic but fairly praiseworthy shot at something of the sort, once or twice;[4] really bad writers have occasionally fastened on it, in ghost stories and the like; but more sensitive writers may have fought shy of it out of sheer fright: great ones, not because the path is through unreason, though it indeed is, albeit not necessarily disastrous for that reason – to the contrary – but because the author may not, ex officio, treat of it, and remain altogether immune to its mysterious manifestations. It is a wonderful theme, however, it seems to me. I won't say anymore about it at the moment, save tangentially, though this may be important, though view it impersonally. Whatever its shortcomings – and we haven't had time enough to let it simmer, to see, though it doubtless has many – our 'Night' was put together and executed with an enormous amount of concentrated creative enthusiasm – sleeping and waking the idea poured upon one; perhaps there are too many, but we did as good a job as possible of sifting within the time we felt we could allow ourselves: though we still entertained and worked out many alternative methods, in the midst of this blizzard, outside and in. With this in mind, it is our notion there may be a good many other fecundating ideas therein, which – like 'Heavy, heavy,' if indeed here the process was not in the contrary direction – which will implant themselves in other minds, quite irrespective of who sees it or not; we can only pray that the overall idea or something like the overall idea will retain its originalities while it is in the course of some kind of consideration by you: I need scarcely point out that what is good, or original, and vital about that, if it does not have precisely the same kind of validity of goodness originality or vitality that we certainly think we ought to ascribe to it – for it is hard to think it could not at least lead to something important is now, as it were, *loose*, for we have let it loose: so that one feels that if this idea is not expressed exactly through this, the touchstone now being in the ether, it is almost bound sooner or later to get expressed through something else by somebody else: this would be a pity, and one can hope only that the manuscript will assert itself wisely, being in a manner alive. That is why I said that the 'Heavy heavy' coincidence should be looked upon as a good omen. For, however it came about, it is a certain proof of liveness, for dead ideas do not fly so fast or so far. They may fly all right, but they need a tactile human agency; and this can have had none. So, as I say, look out for more, not, we hope, so near home as that one.

This brings me to live ideas that also can fly through human agency, namely to what we owe to the strictly human source of B.M.;[5] ethically in a slight impasse, we feel we ought ethically nonetheless to make a slight itemization, though if there is cause for this perhaps B.M. himself or yourself could judge better. We did not originally work from the B.M. Treatment at all, but from a new one of Margie's, which grew and became elaborated through our rereading of the book: I went through B.M.'s treatment once and did not read it again till the other day, in order not to be influenced. Margie's original treatment had scarcely one thing in common with B.M.'s; nonetheless, by the time we both got through with the adaptation certain parallels remain which it seems fair to mention, though I can't be sure how far this is equally due simply to having worked on the same material and come, now and then, to a similar conclusion.

Antibes – though B.M. uses Antibes as against Tarmes in the original, our decision to call it Antibes was arrived at independently, in so far as Tarmes turned into Antibes via the memory that Fitzgerald had lived there, and above all, because of its Greek connotations and beauty as a place: there is no dwelling on its significance or possibilities as a place in B.M.'s treatment but a director might certainly have discovered it and it is unquestionably right.

Abe's suicide in Paris in B.M.'s treatment and Peterson's suicide in ours have suicide in common as against murder in the original. This doubtless sprung from our mutual conviction that Dick could not be an accessory after the fact in a murder. This, originally an ironic sop to the Catholic League of Decency, but no longer necessary since we murdered Dick, was retained because it seemed more original, a very slight doubt being left as to the exact manner of Peterson's death.

Barban – in B.M.'s treatment – was also in the first funicular sequence. I'd thought he should be there and wondered if you were going to have him there, ever since you wrote me over a year ago you were working on the Night and I wrote back saying that was my favourite scene in the book. B.M. had the same idea and he seems to me quite right. The difference is among others, we thought Dick should introduce Nicole to him.

In B.M.'s treatment there is mention that both Nicole's parents were killed in a motor smash beside her, though there is no suggestion of

Nicole's agency in such a smash, or mention of any psychological relation between that smash and the incident where Nicole turns the car over the cliff with the children or indication that a car need be important, nor does Nicole, at the end, with dramatic meaning, drive a car away, as in the book: there is, in fact, no specified relation in B.M. between Abe dead on the bloody sheets, and the accident, not specified at all, in which Nicole's parents were killed, though it seems fair to assume that some may have been intended, or that this would have been brought out had another scenario writer worked on his treatment, for it is presumably still the blood on the sheets, as in the book, that sends Nicole off the deep end again. The same goes for the relation between the unspecified accident and the cliff scene but as we said elsewhere we argued backward from the scene in the book where Nicole herself drives – we make the symbol of the car important – and what parallel there is you can judge for yourself, where the conclusions we came to were similar, where derived from B.M, and where from Fitzgerald. I didn't think an auto accident was a good idea just by itself without any guilt: on the other hand I can't say for certain that our reasoning would have come congruent with it as a basic and more intrinsic notion if B.M. hadn't given the suggestion, though it is equally true that Fitzgerald gives it – for if this were not so, another idea might work as smoothly, which it seems to us it does not, for we tried.

Dick treats Nicole: this seemed an almost inevitable dramatic turn of the screw, because in the film, if it were to be a flashback, unlike the novel you could not afford to shift the point of focus to minor characters. In essence it is what he does and it seemed better to dramatise the meaning rather than become involved with too many ambiguities, though we left some, by still keeping Dick's connection with the hospital partly tentative. Margie can't be sure whether part of this was suggested by B.M. or not, I think I arrived at the conclusion by another channel, but the parallel exists.

And that is about all; we will return said treatment, which we have not opened till now since about last August, and I was surprised to find that even these similarities existed. From it I formed the impression that he was probably a good writer trying simply to render the thing concise [in a] saleable and negotiable form rather than to come to grips with the subject or its real potentialities, which he didn't consider his province at the moment. I have a hell of a lot more respect for an attempt on either account now that we have grappled with some of the difficulties ourselves: the better the material the harder, I surmise, in a treatment, for a writer to dignify it – especially when faced with [the] wholesale sacrifices of it such as here. Besides if there are any great touchstones for the art of precis I don't know them and I can't believe even Lamb's Tales from Shakespeare were so hot.[6] Which reminds me that the United Nations the other week asked me to write an article on the 'Mystik' of Mexico in 1800 words: I tried to oblige.[7]

For the rest, in our or my enthusiasm, I may have got over critical about Fitzgerald; as well as somewhat fatuous in other respects in the notes: put this down to simply exuberance or whatever. After finishing we couldn't stop our minds working: and every now and then it may have had an unfair workout somewhat at Fitzgerald's expense: that it is a faulty book doesn't mean one doesn't enormously admire it and as I hope we demonstrated.

I note now that the Mississippi flood was in May, 1927: that was a pertinent item overlooked from the Times Building News, when Dick was in New York.[8]

We have a ghastly flood in Winnipeg: and are awaiting, in the Fraser Valley, an even more ghastly one here in British Columbia, though this, if it takes place, which it may not, will be more of the Mill on the Floss type of tragedy, than an actual ditching of an entire city, as seems possible in Winnipeg, though it makes it no happier for the people involved.[9]

Our house still stands, however, and we face no worse than being cut off from town again if God ain't willing and the creeks do rise. But the news makes us think we are in Ararat.[10]

Best luck with the film that was in the 'can'. You might tell us its name so we can go and see it when it comes to Vancouver. And also best luck with the Journeying Boy.[11]

With all best love to you and Nan and the children from Margerie and myself,

                                        Malcolm

P.S. Thanks very much for the telegram & the words in the letter. Don't bother to reply to this Roget's Thesaurus of words & phrases, though I felt it obscurely necessary.[12] As for the 'Night' we perfectly understand that exigencies of your current work may delay any further news in regard to it for a long while so don't bother about that. I meantime am writing a long short story, later to be incorporated into the novel, entitled 'The Ordeal of Sigbjørn Wilderness' — which seems to me a good resounding mournful name for someone or other. Should you be in New York please give Albert all our best loves

                                        M

Annotations:

   1 Lowry has enclosed two clippings from the *New Yorker* for 6 (not 7) May 1950, the poem 'Heavy Heavy Heavy' by American writer John Malcolm Brinnin (1916-), and a review of Ugo Moretti's novel *Vento Caldo* (1949; *Rough Wind*, 1953); see annotation 3.

2 Forfeits is any game in which the players relinquish articles when they lose, and the Lowrys use this chant in scene 29 of their screenplay; see Mota/Tiessen (128).

3 The reviewer claims that Moretti's novel 'is deeper than the actions it relates, because of the author's thesis that human destiny is the result of an endless series of coincidences, which man puts up with out of his necessity to exist.' Lowry had long been fascinated by coincidence and the law of series, and J.W. Dunne's theories had considerable influence on him; see his 16 April 1940 letter (**135**) to Anna Mabelle Bonner.

4 The English writer Sir Osbert Sitwell (1892-1969) portrays an artist who experiences hallucinations and prophetic dreams in *The Man Who Lost Himself* (1929); see also Lowry's October 1945 letter (**205**) to Conrad Aiken.

5 'B.M.' is Ben Maddow, who had prepared an earlier screenplay of *Tender Is the Night*; see Lowry's 10 August 1949 letter (**374**) to Frank Taylor.

6 Charles Lamb (1775-1834), the English writer, compiled *Tales from Shakespear* (1807) with his sister Mary.

7 This is 'Garden of Etla.'

8 The Mississippi River flooded its banks from April to June 1927, causing major damage, and American newspapers reported on events for weeks. In scene 29 of their screenplay, the Lowrys call for a *tour de force* of headlines (see Tiessen/Mota, 140-63).

9 The Red River in Manitoba flooded its banks in May 1950, causing the city of Winnipeg to be declared a national emergency area. Floods along the Fraser River in British Columbia caused damage in June 1950. *The Mill on the Floss* (1860) by George Eliot (1819-90) is a story of domestic tragedy that ends with the drowning of the chief protagonists in the flooding River Floss.

10 According to tradition, Mount Ararat, which is located in eastern Turkey, is where Noah's ark landed when the biblical flood subsided.

11 In his 25 April 1950 letter to Lowry, Taylor writes that he has begun work on a film based on the 1949 mystery novel *The Journeying Boy* by Michael Innes, the pen-name for British author John Innes MacIntosh Stewart.

12 English physician Peter Mark Roget (1779-1869) published his *Thesaurus of English Words and Phrases* in 1852.

Editorial Notes:

a. This transcription is from the original typescript. Lowry made a few changes and added the postscript in pencil. The two *New Yorker* clippings are extant with the letter.

400: To Stéphen Spriel

P: UBC(ms) [Dollarton]
[ca 20 June 1950][a]

Dear Mike:[1]

This is just a tardy letter of congratulations on the wonderful job you have done with Under the Volcano!

I have an enormous enthusiastic review here – from the New York Herald Tribune Paris Edition – that I hope you have seen – which says that your translation, it must be better than the original & that I can readily believe & so it seems to me too![2]

I hope sincerely the labour & creative work that you have obviously put into it will be recognized & repaid. I have never doubted your great ability to do it but I have sometimes had some bad moments when I wondered whether the book itself was worth or would reward you & Clarisse sufficiently for the great pains you were taking with it . . . I hope the French critics agree but I am sure they must so far as the translation is concerned whatever they may think of the book –

Naturally I hope they like the book as much as the man in the Tribune – who had not by the way read it in English; but if they don't, – and I am itching to hear – that will certainly not be your fault – meantime I am of course full of gratitude and excitement at the immediate result.

So – my sincerest congratulations & deepest thanks –

Very Sincerely yours

Malcolm

Annotations:

1 'Mike' is probably Lowry's familiar name for Stéphen Spriel, who, with Clarisse Francillon, translated *Au-dessous du volcan*; see Lowry's letter (**352**) to Francillon. According to Maurice Nadeau, Spriel used the name Paul Pilotin; see Lowry's October 1952 letter (**548**) to Nadeau, annotation 3.

2 On 5 June 1950 Albert Erskine sent Lowry a copy of George Slocombe's review of the translation in the *New York Herald Tribune*, 1 June 1950; see Lowry's 21 June 1950 letter (**402**) to Erskine.

Editorial Notes:

a. This undated holograph is a draft of the letter sent to Spriel. It appears on the verso of a draft typescript page for 'Strange Comfort Afforded by the Profession' (UBC 23:6). Lowry has signed his full name, then cancelled the Lowry.

401: To Christopher Isherwood

P: UBC(tsc)
PP: *SL* 206–08

Dollarton, B.C.,
Canada
20 June 1950[a]

Dear Christopher Isherwood:[1]

It was a high spot indeed in our life when we read your letter speaking of our scripts in such generous terms.[2] It would have been a high spot in mine anyway, the day I felt I had written something good enough to command praise from yourself. I've often felt like writing you in regard to your own work; I never thought I'd see the day you wrote me first. I do feel I have known you a very long time, however, through your work and through the eternal Marlowe who broods upon the cross currents of life's relationships.[3]

For the script though, since you like it and where it comes off, my wife must take equal credit, she being the lady named Margerie Bonner who is a writer herself and the author of an extraordinarily good – and so far in destiny extraordinarily hapless – novel called Horse in the Sky.[4] I hope enough really constructive commotions went into the making of the script that it will somehow come to a good fruition; one very sincere hope and motivation was that it would be a lucky thing for Frank [Taylor]. How it actually came into being strikes me as very curious indeed. One expects, and indeed welcomes, normal obstacles, but something so astonishing happened to the climate last winter we thought another ice age was upon us. This is supposed to be a fairly warm part of Canada; we built our house ourselves with lumber from an old sawmill, but didn't prepare for temperatures of fifteen below zero inside it, such as we had January and February. Nor had anyone else prepared. Even so, we came off far better than people in the city, not having any modern conveniences to go awry. The city of Vancouver was cut off altogether for eight days from the outside world and we had stormy petrels flying beneath our windows. What they thought they were escaping from I don't like to imagine, but it was an exciting phenomenon I don't think has ever been recorded before in an inlet, in this latitude at least.

I find myself with so many things to say I am walking round in circles. What I would like to phrase properly, so that it doesn't sound too repulsive or impractical, is that should you ever find yourself in a mood where you feel like taking a rocket ship to nowhere, and have the time, we do wish you'd consider coming up in this direction and paying us a visit. It doesn't take so long by plane to Vancouver, and I think you'd find it interesting. We live in a shanty town, built on piles, in an inlet, with the forest behind, mainly deserted during the week save by a boat builder, ourselves and a fisherman or two. At first all you see is a bay with shacks called Wy-Wurk and the like. But it is actually the remains of an old seaport of which we have often been the sole inhabitants. Dollar – hence Dollarton – was the shipbuilder, but somebody took his ship building and his sawmill away from him and we're all that's left. Windjammers used to come here, and we've shouted to a Norwegian skipper of a passing freighter out of the window, below which there's enough water to float the Mauretania.[5] At the weekends nowadays many of the shacks fill up so it is more fun during the week. We have a small boat and there are many islands where one may picnic. It is a wonderful place to swim if you like swimming and the forest is full of birds – we are just now (it is Midsummer's Eve) – having spring and summer at once and the weather is marvellous. There is a fine view of the mountains: and also, for that matter, of an oil refinery. We could put you up on a sort of improvised contraption that we rescued from the sea but which is a great deal more comfortable than it looks. There are no conveniences but when the weather is fine as it is now there are no inconveniences either. We thought it might be a cheery place to discuss Tepotzlan and kindred subjects.[6] The invitation, at all events, is very sincere from us both, but if it is too far, I hope, like Huysmans, you will at least think about it.[7] We asked Frank too but I think he may have been put off by the bears. There are bears. But there are also deer. And ravens. Not to mention many rare wild plants such as the Blazing Star, Love Lies Bleeding, and even the contorted lousewort. And through what wild centuries roves back the contorted lousewort?[8]

Anyhow, here we are, and you would always be more than welcome.

After this travelogue, again thank you very much indeed for your words. All the very best to you from us both.

Good luck!

[unsigned]

P.S. I began to write this letter originally, returning the compliment (which I appreciate) in my own handwriting, such as it is – though I have no pen that works – taking advantage of this to write outside. But a cat spilt coconut oil on it. Then another cat spilt beer on it. Finally it blew into the sea. Retrieved thence it came somewhat to pieces and was, besides, a bit illegible. So I gave in, temporarily, to the machine age.

Annotations:

1 Christopher Isherwood (1904-86) was an English playwright, screenwriter, editor, translator, and novelist. During the forties he worked on a contract basis for Hollywood studios.

2 In his 12 June 1950 letter to Lowry, Isherwood called the Lowrys'
 screenplay of *Tender Is the Night* 'wonderful,' a 'revelation of new
 meanings,' and a 'masterpiece' (*SL* 443).
3 This 'eternal Marlowe' is probably Joseph Conrad's narrator Marlow in
 Heart of Darkness (1902), *Lord Jim* (1900), and *Chance* (1913), and the
 protagonist in *Youth* (1902).
4 Lowry's point is worth noting because Margerie's co-authorship often
 goes unmentioned.
5 RMS *Mauretania* of the Cunard White Star Line, built in 1907 with a
 length of 762 feet, could carry over 1,500 passengers.
6 Tepotzlán is a tiny town near Cuernavaca. In 'Notes on a Trip to
 Mexico,' *Harper's Bazaar* (June 1947): 80-81, 134-6, Isherwood comments that he will remember his half-hour at Tepotzlán for the rest of
 his life.
7 Joris-Karl Huysmans (1848-1907), a French writer of Dutch descent,
 analysed the spiritual side of modern life in works like *À rebours* (1884)
 and his studies of Impressionism.
8 See Walter de la Mare's poem 'All That's Past' (1912): 'Oh, no man
 knows / Through what wild centuries / Roves the wild rose.'

Editorial Notes:

a. This transcription is from a typescript copy of the original, which does
 not appear to have survived. A pencil draft of the first two paragraphs
 (UBC 2:14) suggests that the original and this copy follow Lowry's text
 exactly. Two deviations should, however, be noted: this copy is
 unsigned, and the typed name appears to have been added later; the
 postscript is described as written 'in pencil,' which suggests that whoever made the copy (either Isherwood or Margerie, when she was
 preparing *Selected Letters*) was working from the original letter.

402: To Albert Erskine

P: Virginia(ts); UBC(phc)   Dollarton, B.C.,
                Canada
               21 June 1950

Dear old Albert:
 Thank you very much for Browning's gondola.[1] Gondolier –
Stephen Spriel – is a negro, which seems to bespeak something for inter-
national relations, especially since the other translator, Clarisse
Francillon, is a Swiss, and another not mentioned, Gabriel Pommerand,
is an Assyrian, who has just recently married an Egyptian. In writing the
French preface I used, – though I tried to make it more humorous
(because you told me it was terrible) – part of what had originally been

intended for Cape, which is responsible for such a comment as 'pub-lishers objected to certain parts,' that if not read in relation to the English publication would horrify me if it gave you a suspicion of any 'sharper than a serpent's tooth' feeling.[2] I could not have insisted more than I did on the more than complete understanding and generosity you showed me in the American publication and that has made implicit elsewhere, though Fontaine, in so far as it was not Francillon but Fouchet, who would have let the book more or less slide down the drain if we hadn't been on the scene, originally might have had their own reasons for not wishing too strongly to be reminded of it.[3]

I have some news for you and I hope, when we are able to tell you what it is, it will be good. At all events it is not smug. In one important sense we could not possibly have less reason for not telling you what it is: in another, it is a case of not crossing one's bridges before one's chick-ens are hatched. But whether you will approve of the bridges, the chickens. . . Ah, that. But it is our fond hope you will indeed, even if you cannot resist unshuttering, temporarily, a fraternally punishing eye. Meantime let us have our little pleasure, at being enigmatic, even if you know perfectly well what we are talking about.

All our very best love to Peggy and yourself from us both

God bless!

Malcolm

P.S. There is article ['Garden of Etla'] in United Nations mag by me – June – might interest, – pseudo-journalistic embryo of Dr Vigil – character to be – they asked me write piece on Mystik of Mexico, in 1800 words, wif anecdotes – gave me a week's notice & God was it hard.

Annotations:

1 In his 5 June 1950 letter Erskine wrote: 'I enclose an item about Browning's gondola which just came to me from a friend in Paris.' The article is George Slocombe's review of the translation of *Under the Volcano* (UBC 37:1), which has a brief insert item titled 'Browning's Gondola Goes to U.S. Museum.' The thirty-six-foot gondola, owned by the English poets Robert Browning and Elizabeth Barrett, was given to Browning's gondolier in 1861 and sold to an American in 1890. 'Browning's gondola' is a Lowry-Erskine joke.

2 Lowry's allusion is to Lear's lament in Shakespeare's *King Lear* I.iv: 'How sharper than a serpent's tooth it is / To have a thankless child.'

3 Lowry is implying that, when Éditions de la Revue Fontaine closed in 1949, Max-Pol Fouchet, the director, was prepared to abandon the translation of *Under the Volcano*.

403: To Downie Kirk

P: UBC(ts phc)
PP: *SL* 208-13

Dollarton, B.C.
23 June 1950

Dear Downey:[a]

I have been meaning to write you for some time and had been hoping I would receive my promised copies of the French edition of the Volcano so I could send you one. However, I have so far received, in addition to the one you saw, only one paper bound copy of the regular (not the book club) edition, and I wanted to give you a good cloth one of the first edition, the arrival of which I am still awaiting, so please bear with me a while longer. I also received an excellent review of the French version in the Paris edition of the New York Herald Tribune which says it is better than the original, (though he hadn't read the original) however I am supposed to take that: and a caricature of the (English-Canadian) author in a French paper that I trust is not only worse than the original but bears no resemblance to the original.[1] I also have a copy of the Norwegian translation for you of which the only report we have so far is what it says on the cover – somewhat curtly – 'En djevelsk roman.' I am trusting that means devilish in the better sense, rather than hellish awful. We had the pleasure of meeting Marjorie one day when we were going to the movies, and she said you were a bit under the weather but I hope you are O.K. now. We were going to see the film of The Hairy Ape which I'd heard was good:[2] it is djevelsk in the worst sense, however, though the suspense was subtly increased by the accident of the lights failing for one hour in the middle. People look very sinister and strange standing about in the foyers of movies when the lights fail, and I made a note that I must use it in a book. Then I remembered I had used it in U.T. Volcano.

Someone from outside came and cut down an enormous maple tree, (not far from the trail) you may have liked as well as we did, felling it right across the path, with no thought for the birds who were nesting in it, and all this to take one minute piece of wood out of it, wherewith to make a fiddle. I thought of chalking on the stump: 'Would you like this to happen to you, you pig-dog. When you hear your lousy fiddle it will make a noise like slaughtered birds.' However I decided that it would not be solving anything to discomfort the inhabitants by adding my bit of grand guignol to what was already djevelsk enough – and likewise, incidentally, the work of Scandinavians – unless I could have done it in Scandinavian.

I meant to tell you before I had been reading the Spanish philosopher Jose Ortega y Gasset – I don't know how many books he has written or works created, but Towards a Philosophy of History, Invertebrate Spain, The Revolt of the Masses, and The Modern Theme are listed on the fly leaf, presumably because they are available in translation. I possess also a wonderful lecture of his on Goethe – first delivered in 1932 in Germany, but reprinted in the Partisan Review at the end of last year.[3] It is the only article I have ever read that criticises Goethe for his many-sidedness, his Leonardo da Vinci aspect. Ortega's thesis is roughly that he should have stuck to maintaining himself as a poet and not falsified his vocation by finding it necessary to be President of the Weimar Republic, run a theatre, create theories of color, and become a professional patriot and so on. This versatility is usually considered a supervirtue so it is interesting to find someone who takes the opposite view. The point seems to be that Goethe could have acquired imaginative knowledge of these sort of things and used that knowledge to support the substructure of his work – as Strindberg practically became a historian in order to write his historical plays – but in so far as he became their professional exponent, he was *not* Goethe, and this might philosophically speaking be considered a dead loss and a waste, and the world's dead loss, because 'life itself is haste'. This is the sort of philosophy that seems to me particularly useful in a public library when one is confronted with thousands of books that one cannot possibly have time to read, so that one thinks: Ah, well, if I only had more time, then what could I not read; how hopeless it all is! For the fact is, on this view, even the thought becomes a waste of time if life is a matter of stripping away inessentials from the central core of one's being which is, in fact, one's vocation itself. This makes life rather like fiction and in fact he says at one point in Towards a Philosophy of History, which I was reading:

'Life in the zoological sense consists of such actions as are necessary for existence in nature. But man manages things so that the claims of this life are reduced to a minimum. In the vacuum arising after he has left behind his animal life he devotes himself to a series of non-biological occupations which are not imposed by nature but invented by himself. This invented life – invented as a novel or a play is invented – man calls 'human life,' well-being. Human life transcends the reality of nature. It is not given to man as its fall is given to a stone or the stock of its organic acts – eating, flying, nesting – to an animal. He makes it himself, beginning by inventing it. Have we heard right? Is human life in its most human dimension a work of fiction? Is man a sort of novelist of himself who conceives the fanciful figure of a personage with its unreal occupations and then, for the sake of converting it into reality, does all the things he does – and becomes an engineer?'[4]

This probably recommends itself to me partly because if it is true, and man *is* a sort of novelist of himself, I can see something pihilsophically{too good a word to correct} valuable in attempting to set down what *actually* happens in a *novelist's* mind when he conceives what he conceives to be the fanciful figure of a personage etc – for this, the part that never gets written, with which is included the true impulses that made him a novelist or dramatist in the first place, and the modifcations of life around him through his own eyes as those impulses were realized – would be the true drama, (This would be not unlike Pirandello who, – I quote from an article in the *Partisan* review – 'inverts the convention of modern realism; instead of pretending that the stage is not the stage at all, but the familiar parlor, he pretends that the familiar parlor is not real as a photograph, *but a stage* containing many 'realities'.'[5] – This is Shakespeare's speech come true. My feeling is that Pirandello may not have wholly appreciated how close to the truth this view of human life might be, as a consequence of which the 'realities' of 'Six Characters in Search of an Author', say, do not measure up to the profundity of the view, though I have not studied him sufficiently, & the accepted critical opinion upon Pirandello is apparently faulty.) and I hope to finish something of this sort one day. But Ortega is not, here, at any rate, concerned with fiction: this is the thesis upon which he bases his value of history. Man is 'what has happened to him.' This is interesting too because it is a philosophy that starts with one's existence, ties in with Heidegger, and Kierkegarde etc., and hence with Existentialism.[6] This latter has become by now a music hall joke in France but there is none of the same despair in Ortega. One supposes that Sartre's Existentialism (so far as I can understand it, it is anything but new) is merely a sort of reach-me-down or second hand philosophy, altered dramatically to fit the anguish of the French in the midst of its occupations, hurts, valours, resistances, duplicities and treacheries, and so give it some look of meaning – even so, it's refreshing to read a philosophy that gives value to the drama of life itself, of the dramatic value of your own life at the very moment you are reading. Who wants to read 3000 pages that prove irrefutably that we don't exist? even if it is true? But I think what would be interesting to you in Ortega is his often philological approach to the unravelling of problems, and the great value he gives to philology itself. The word snob he tells me comes from sine nobilitate, and is a phrase that comes, incidentally, from Cambridge.[7] The lists of students at Cambridge once apparently indicated beside a person's name his profession and rank. Beside the name of commoners there appeared the abbreviation: 's. nob:' sine nobilitate: whence the word 'snob.' That means that if you weren't the Duke of Bugnasty, like me for example, you were technically, at one time, a snob, which I certainly never knew before. In fact one thought it had come to mean the exact opposite – we tend to think that the Duke of Bugnasty would be, ex officio, a snob, or if he does not behave like one we would consider him remarkable. Ortega doesn't explain how the phrase itself came to be corrupted, but it turns out – through a footnote – to be all part of his general thesis and has nothing to do with the Duke of Bugnasty or otherwise, save that a Duke, or whatever, once had, in addition to rights, obligations. The real snob is the person who imagines he has only rights. What it comes down to is the business of vocation. To have found one's vocation, whatever it may be, is 'to understand that one is alive for some specific and unexchangeable purpose.' 'The universal snobbism,' he says, 'so apparent, for example, in the worker of the present time, has blinded men to the fact that, if indeed all the given structure of continental life is to be transcended, the change must be brought about without a serious loss of its inner plurality. The snob, having been emptied of his own destiny and since it does not occur to him that he is alive for some specific and unexchangeable purpose, cannot understand that life offers particular callings and vocations. He is therefore hostile to liberalism, with the hostility of a deaf man for words. Liberty has always been understood in Europe as the freedom to be our real selves. It is not surprising that a man should want to be rid of it who knows that he has no real mission to fulfil.'

This at first sight appeared to me among other things, one of the most convincing arguments against communism, I had ever read in such a short space; but in fact it is only a statement in defence of the old school of liberalism which it is so fashionable to denounce, and without the possibility of free discussion of revolutionary tenets, such as those contained in communism for that matter, and even the right is practical absorption of revolutionary tenets where they seem desirable, such a school could not exist. I suppose the thought is preeminently European, and based (as he says later) on Guizot's observation that in Europe no principle idea group or class has ever triumphed in an absolute form (due to the progressive character and constant growth of the said liberalism).[8] The thought a Marxist communist would instantly pounce upon – or ought instantly to pounce upon – as arising from Ortega's remarks, is that Russia is the only place where a really serious effort has been made on a large scale both to discover the particular vocation for which the individual is most psychologically adapted and also to clothe with some dignity and drama those vocations that otherwise are soul destroying (such as the adjusting the same nut every day in a mass-producing plant). I think that is where the trouble lies, with (as usual) the machinery, or where at least the argument might begin. Mechanization – one pompously ventures – is the result of a creative technological faculty in man that has already begun to outwit itself. But the Russians – who never really had a capitalist system – do not seem to realise this, for the very people equipped to tell them this are forbidden to express themselves. For in Russia, in effect, the mechanic is exalted above everyone else. Deprived of a spiritual meaning to his life, deprived even of the luxury of cosmic despair, yet encouraged (which seems to be an advance on the Ford factory) to find some meaning in what he does himself, for he's not doing it any longer for his children, he finds and is encouraged to find that meaning in service to the State. This might solve that particular kind of robot–mechanic's problem very well, because he can feel, and probably it makes him, unselfish and feel less like a robot, but unfortunately everybody else is expected to fall in line: a writer, for example, is supposed to be such a noble worker for the State, and so is the philologist – (I notice by the way that the philologists in Russia have just got into a whole lot of hot water.) Composers go the same way, the highest pay does not compensate the individual creative artist for lack of freedom of expression (we do not speak of individual freedom within the orchestra – one could have some fun too imagining Shostakovitch writing a decadent 'bourgeois' trombone part for a 'patriotic' piece) and Russia pays the price in the poorest art, the poorest music, the poorest literature in the world.[9] Teachers must teach lies – all for the State. It seems so senseless when you look at it; for freedom of expression, as of religion, far from resulting in the destruction of communism, would probably win a multitude of adherents to it. True, freedom of expression would end by destroying the police state, and abolishing the stool pigeon, but surely the preservation of these commodities was not the goal of communism, or it would have found its adherents more exclusively among policemen and stoolpigeons? And so one goes round the prickly pear,[10] common sense finding one unfortunate solution to Russia's apparently insane behaviour in the fact that she has been preparing to go to war for about the last 20 years and more, and so lives in a state of constant 'war effort', with its attendant stringencies and 'jelly-bellied flag-flapping': but I believe that, people's basic needs really being very simple, that there is more hope and life in Europe than meets the eye, and that its liberal tradition – which extends over there – will eventually save the day. That is a bit different from saying that democracy or cocacola or British socialism will save the day but doubtless the vast majority of people everywhere mean the same thing within that part used to be call: soul. The rest is simply repetition of editorials. And since I set out to write this letter in order to palliate your colitis, if any, and not by speaking of purges, to give you Asiatic cholera, I had better say that I feel optimistic.

I want to thank you again deeply for so kindly translating those items for us: that work is now finished, and their correctitude must certainly have added to the effect which, so far, has been momentous in certain circles: but we are keeping our fingers crossed, so won't say any more for the moment, out of a certain superstition.

We saw A Street Car Named Desire and Death of a Salesman – of these, more later. We also saw The Third Man, and Germany Year Zero. Both these are essentially poor films though for complicated reasons, I think, though both are probably well worth seeing.[11]

We look forward very much to seeing Marjorie and yourself again soon, and we wish you a speedy recovery. Please give my regards to Dunc. And all the very best to you both and to Dorothy from us both.

Sincerely,

Malcolm

Figure 6: *Lowry could be sensitive about photographs or drawings of himself. This unflattering caricature from* La Gazette des lettres *(UBC 37:1) struck a nerve.*

Annotations:

1 This review from the 1 June 1950 issue of the *New York Herald Tribune* is the 'Browning's gondola' piece; see Lowry's 21 June 1950 letter (**402**) to Albert Erskine. The caricature accompanied Gilbert Sigaux's review

of *Au-dessous du volcan* in *La Gazette des lettres* for April 1950; see Figure 6.

2 *The Hairy Ape*, a 1922 play by Eugene O'Neill, was an early favourite of Lowry's; the 1944 film version was directed by Alfred Santell and starred William Bendix as Yank.

3 Spanish philosopher José Ortega y Gasset (1883-1955), whose work Lowry discovered at this time, became an influential source of ideas. Lowry refers to Ortega frequently in his fiction from this point on and in his plans for *The Voyage That Never Ends*. The essay 'In Search of Goethe from Within: Letter to a German' was first published in *Die Neue Rundschau* in 1932; an English translation appeared in *Partisan Review* 16.12 (1949): 1163-1188, which is in Lowry's library. See also Lowry's 24 March 1952 letter (**512**) to Albert Erskine.

4 Ortega develops this idea in *Toward a Philosophy of History* (New York: W.W. Norton, 1941); see p. 108.

5 Lowry is quoting from Francis Fergusson's article 'The Theatricality of Shaw and Pirandello' in *Partisan Review* 16.6 (1949): 598.

6 Martin Heidegger (1889-1976), a leading modern German philosopher, was influenced by the Danish Christian existentialist philosopher Søren Kierkegaard (1813-55) and by Friedrich Nietzsche (1844-1900). Heidegger in turn had a profound influence on Jean-Paul Sartre. Heidegger's major text is *Sein und Zeit* (1927; *Being and Time*, 1962).

7 Ortega defines the word 'snob' in *Toward a Philosophy of History*, p. 56.

8 François Pierre Guillaume Guizot (1787-1874), a French statesman and historian, was first minister to King Louis Philippe from 1840 to 1848. He believed in government by and for the propertied classes. Lowry is quoting Ortega's comment on Guizot in *Toward a Philosophy of History*, pp. 57-58.

9 Russian composer Dimitry Shostakovich (1906-75) was a leading experimentalist in twentieth-century music; he wrote chamber and orchestral works and three operas. In the mid-thirties his work was denounced as bourgeois by Soviet communists for failing to adhere to principles of 'social realism.'

10 Lowry is echoing a line from part 5 of T.S. Eliot's 'The Hollow Men': '*Here we go round the prickly pear.*' See also his 1 July 1949 letter (**373**) to Frank Taylor.

11 *A Streetcar Named Desire* (1947) by American playwright Tennessee Williams (1911-83) and *Death of a Salesman* (1949) by American playwright Arthur Miller (1915-) were performed in Vancouver in the spring. The screenplay for *The Third Man* (1949), a British film starring Orson Welles, was written by Graham Greene (1904-91), but it did not impress Lowry; see his 7 July 1950 letter (**408**) to Frank Taylor. *Germany Year Zero* (1947) was directed by Roberto Rossellini.

Editorial Notes:

a. This transcription is from a photocopy (UBC 2:14) of the original.

Downie Kirk has made editorial changes and comments passim, corrected Lowry's spelling of his first name, and underlined titles and foreign words.

404: To Clarisse Francillon

P: UBC(ms,ts phc)   Dollarton, B.C.,
                                                          Canada
                                                     23 June 1950[a]

Cher Clarisse:

Just a note of further congratulations on your work on the Volcano! – I am just now in receipt of an enormously favourable review in the Paris edition of the New York Herald Tribune of the translation by one George Slocombe – giving you two whole columns and Winston Churchill 1/6 of a column – in which it says that the translation not only absolutely couldn't be better but that it is better than the original and adds another dimension to it![1] This is wonderful news, and I hope that the French critics will see eye to eye with this fellow and give you all the credit you deserve: meantime you have my unstinted gratitude and praise, and I have just written to Mike chez Correa – (their address of 4 years ago, which was all I could find, on the back of Sach's Le Sabbat,[2] – I hope it reaches him safely) telling him the same and that I hope the French critics agree: I have further said and now say again that where they don't it will be my fault in the book and not yours in the translation. But I am hoping that they will find both equally to their taste and the Herald review augurs well. But I don't know, for I have only received this one review about the translation. The only French one you sent me, while very favourable, more or less simply recapitulated the exposition. Anyhow, – all my congratulations & thanks again.

                              Love from us both –

                                                          Malcolm

P.S. (Minor matters.) The interview horrified me.[3] Do I have to live through my life with that view of myself? I am sufficient of an existentialist that I hid it – and looked at it no more – though I shall probably take it out again one of these days, when I need some suggestion for a character sufficiently monstrous. I don't think it's quite fair either. I'm not like that at all, or am not now. Shall I send you a photograph of myself as a weight-lifter? A child with jam on my face? What about the one with me and the gargoyles – I thought the gargoyles would at least show off how winning a fellow I was.[4] Or why don't you publish the

picture of Gargantua the Gorilla and entitle it The Superego of the
Author of Au Dessous de Volcan? Well – all is vanity saith the preacher.
The caricature seemed only less loathesome.[5] What is hard to take is that
I started the bloody book as a young man, almost a boy. Now it looks
as though that toothy and repellent old sage wrote it. Well: what the
hell. . . By the way, I thought I was going to get ½ dozen copies of the
Club edition. I've received one so far, and one of the ordinary editions
of the Correa.[6] I have a sort of feeling it didn't get into a second edition,
the club version, and thus disappointed you but I hope I am wrong or
that anyway Correa will make up for it. I'd like Marcelin to get a club
copy with the name straight however. And I'm itching to give away a
few to my friends. I'm glad Gabriel [Pomerand] is married and I hope
happy. I also hope he didn't give his Egyptian gal his letters to Simone
as a wedding present.[7] My regards to her too.

Best love –

M.

Annotations:

1 On the same page as Slocombe's review, there is a five-centimetre item
  on Winston Churchill.
2 Several works of the French author Jean Maurice Sachs (1906-44) were
  published posthumously, including *Le Sabbat: Souvenirs d'une jeunesse
  orageuse*, with Éditions Corrêa in 1946. Lowry met Sachs in 1934 and,
  through him, Jean Cocteau; see Bowker (178-79). For the letter to
  Mike, see **400** to Stéphen Spriel.
3 Lowry was interviewed by A.-J. Frédérique for *Liens* 33 (February
  1950); the interviewer, who was not having an easy time, used most of
  his space to describe Lowry's drunken silence.
4 A photograph of Lowry posed between two gargoyles appears with a
  review of his novel in *Le Rouge et le Noir* for 22 August 1950.
5 See Figure 6 with letter **403**.
6 Only the Corrêa first edition exists with Lowry's library at UBC. His
  copy of the Club français du livre edition (1949) does not appear to have
  survived.
7 Pomerand married Roxanne Lespinas, but Simone has not been identified; see Lowry's 1948 letter (**339**) to Pomerand.

Editorial Notes:

a. Both a signed holograph draft and a photocopy of the typescript sent
   to Francillon are in the Malcolm Lowry Collection (UBC 2:14); the
   original does not appear to have survived.

405: To Innes Rose

P: UBC(ms)   [Dollarton]
                                                                          [ca June 1950]ᵃ

My dear Innes:[1]

Thanks very much for your letter & Sir Stafford Cripps being what he is we could certainly use the £3:17:5.[2]

The translation of Under the Volcano has received some tremendous reviews in France where it has also appeared in a classic series, together with the Abbé Prévost & similar eatables, though whether this is of any practical value to you – or me either, for that matter – at the moment anyway – , I ha' my doots. It is also come out in Norway though I have received no reviews.[3] The French version was translated by a negro [Stéphen Spriel].

Margerie received a belatedly enthusiastic review of Horse in the Sky in the Los Angeles Times which said it was a marvellous book – & which made her hit the ceiling – (& not with pleasure) that it was much better than National Velvet. I cite this in case this may be of any use in England. It is my impression that an English publisher must eventually awake to the great merits of this book.

I note Cape has brought a cheap edition of the Volcano.[4] No doubt this is really yesterdays pork pie, still upon the counter, and must be got rid of at any price; still it was my notion that that might not invalidate a cheap edition of the cover. The Volcano apparently broke a record for enthusiastic & orgasmic reviews in the U.S. – don't you think a few might be used? And when I have done, I have not done, I still have more?[5] Could you let me know about this? I believe, bearing such pieces as Oklahoma and Death of a Salesman in mind, that the argument that the English are unimpressed by the pronouncements of such encomiasts is invalid.[6]

                                                                    [breaks off unsigned]

Annotations:

1 This holograph and a 1936 letter (**68**) appear to be Lowry's only extant letters to his former literary agent and Cambridge friend Innes Rose.

2 Sir Stafford Cripps (1889-1952), a British socialist and statesman, was a member of the Labour Party and chancellor of the Exchequer after the war. Faced with an economic crisis in Britain, he instituted an austerity program, raised taxes, and was instrumental in revaluing the pound sterling in September 1949.

3 The Norwegian translation by Peter Magnus appeared in 1949.

4 According to Woolmer (24), the 'cheap edition' was advertised in May 1950. It consisted of 1,600 unsold copies from the 5,000 copies printed in Cape's first edition.

5 Lowry's allusion is to John Donne's poem 'A Hymn to God the Father': 'When thou hast Donne, Thou hast not done, / For I have more.'

6 The American musical *Oklahoma!* (1943) by Richard Rogers and Oscar Hammerstein II, and Arthur Miller's play *Death of a Salesman* were popular in England as well as in the United States. Lowry's work gained very little attention or support in England until the 1970s.

Editorial Notes:

a. This transcription is from a single-page pencil holograph (UBC 23:7) on the verso of a page of typescript for *October Ferry to Gabriola*. It can be dated approximately from internal evidence.

406: To George Gode

P: Matson(ts); UBC(phc)   Dollarton, B.C.,
                                                           Canada
                                                           4 July 1950

Dear Mr Gode:[1]

Thank you for your letter. No. Re Ultramarine, and the German rights, this book, which is besides long out of print, and which was written in my teens, absolutely won't do as it is, and so cannot be now translated; even if it were possible I would not give my consent. I hope however within the next few years to have rewritten this book completely, making major changes, and have it published together with another piece called Lunar Caustic. This last piece fell between two stools as to length in regard to its publication in America: the French however wish to publish Lunar Caustic as a small volume.

If the German inhibition is fear that I am a one book author I wish you would mention this fact, also that Under the Volcano – in addition to the above – is part of a projected much larger work containing three other novels, the whole to be called either The Ordeal of Sigbjørn Wilderness, or The Voyage That Never Ends – I'm not sure which. At present I am working on this: I hope to offer parts of the novels themselves for publication, but it will be long before the whole project is concluded. If I have not made this clear to Hal it is due to my own uncertainty as to the order of the volumes.[2]

I am very anxious that Under the Volcano should be published in German however (as you know it was accepted by a Swiss firm, that folded up)[3] and I would be very much obliged if you would push this project. The French translation has received some magnificent reviews and perhaps this might weigh with the Germans. I have also received copies of the Norwegian and Danish editions. I have had no reviews, and would be extremely glad of some, though I'm unsure of what source to apply to. But this multiplicity of translation might greatly facilitate the German translation, which I think is another point. They could be reasonably assured of more volumes to follow, I repeat, if that is what is holding them up.

　With best wishes,

Sincerely,

Malcolm Lowry

P.S. Do you know, or could you find out, what has happened to the Swedish and Italian translations? I heard the Swedish edition came out but I never received any copies: the last I knew of the Italian it was still in translation.

Annotations:

1 George Gode handled foreign rights for the Harold Matson Company.
2 See my discussion of the *Voyage*, pp. 2-3.
3 The Swiss publisher was Micha Verlag in Zürich. Robert Pick had begun work on the translation when the firm went bankrupt; see Lowry's 7 June 1947 letter (**305**) to Pick.

407: To Derek Pethick

P: UBC(ms)   [Dollarton]
                                                       [July 1950]ᵃ

My dear Mr Pethick:
　This is a long overdue letter but is to say I didn't resign matters to a broadcasting-like limbo: on the other hand I am still pretty much inundated with work & the letter cannot be longer than an apology for itself.
　Do tell me how things worked out with the C.B.C: – [Earle] Birney departed hence about 5 minutes since, having sold his house here, so we shan't see much of him, henceforward I guess. I did not in any case succeed unfortunately in even getting near the right ear in regard to your work though I don't think I can have damaged your cause, not wittingly anyway. However since my connection with it seemed liable to be misinterpreted as stemming from a desire for self-advertisment – which was far from being the case – I have kept largely silent, but as I say I hope sincerely things will work themselves out for you.
　Curiously enough I had a letter recently from one Jay Leyda in America – another expert on Melville, who is acquainted with Melville's grandaughters, which concerned however the other aspect of my work (which I said would make you laugh at the coincidence), but which I am obliged still not to speak.[1]

I hope to see you over in these parts some time – & I hope that grim Newcastle disease has not affected your fowl.[2]

I'll return the Melville soon – if there's no immediate hurry, for my wife is reading it.

Yours sincerely

Malcolm Lowry

Annotations:

1 In his 4 June 1950 letter (UBC 1:37) to Lowry, Jay Leyda praised the screenplay for *Tender Is the Night*. Lowry, however, still felt he could not talk openly about the project.
2 Derek Pethick kept poultry on his Vancouver Island farm, and there was a local outbreak of the virus causing this disease in spring and summer of 1950.

Editorial Notes:

a. This transcription is from a draft found on the verso of draft material for 'Strange Comfort Afforded by the Profession' (UBC 23:7).

408: To Frank Taylor

P: Lilly(ms)

Dollarton, B.C.,
Canada
[July 1950]^a

Dear Frank:

Wie gehts?[1] May your remote Canadian pen pals have a bulletin?

How wanders the Journeying boy? And how Journeys, and to what end, if any, the Night?

You didn't tell us the name of your first film for which we have been anxiously watching; please do, because we don't want to miss it.

How has the Korean crisis affected cinematic tensions & currents?[2] I suppose the difficulty is wisely to look forward into the exigencies of possible crises two years from now, rather than at the present moment. Whatever these may be, for better or worse, we pray that the Powers that Are realise that the need for fine films must become greater rather than less.

We saw A young man with a Horn & writhed with anguish, as did the negro bull-fiddle player in the next seat.[3] No indication whatsoever is given of Beiderbecke's genius, & none for that matter, or only a little, & at that wrong, as to what constitutes jazz or unjazz. None of Beiderbecke's compositions *were* used either which leaves us In a Mist still. Or In the dark.[4] It is a pity, for it was a good book: & it was also a totally unnecessary pity. I thought Beiderbecke as a kid was good though. We also saw the Third Man, which seemed more or less inexcusable too, though for different reasons.

We have taken to horoscopes, if not yet to witches – so will you give us a little news?

We hope also very much you'll some day find time to spend a few days with us.

With best love to yourself Nan & the children,

Malcolm & Margerie

Annotations:

1 *Wie gehts*? is German for 'How are you?' or 'How are things going?'
2 After the Second World War, Korea was divided into North and South Korea, which fell under the influence of the Soviet Union and the United States respectively. When North Korean troops invaded South Korea in June 1950 the Americans supported United Nations peacekeeping efforts with a naval blockade. By mid-July ground troops were engaged to repel North Korean forces, and the first phase of the Korean War had begun.
3 *Young Man With a Horn* (1950) is a melodramatic film based on Dorothy Baker's novel about the life of Bix Beiderbecke.
4 'In a Mist' and 'In the Dark' are parts of a piano suite, usually called 'Bixology,' composed by Beiderbecke, who made a famous recording of 'In a Mist' in 1927. The Lowrys called for both pieces to be heard throughout their screenplay of *Tender Is the Night*.

Editorial Notes:

a. The holograph is undated. This date is in another hand at the top of the recto, and the letter follows in sequence Lowry's letters to Taylor from spring and summer 1950.

409: To Harold Matson

P: Matson(ts); UBC(phc)

Dollarton, B.C.,
Canada
17 July 1950

Warning: BEGGING LETTER
if couched in golden,
(and truthful) words.

Dear Hal:

Eschewing the element of surprise at the beginning therefore –
Could you be generous enough to loan us a couple of hundred dollars

on the strength of our potential and existent worth for a couple of months, or until such time – which might be only a couple of days for that matter – it can be made good at your own end? If by the time you have finished this letter you feel that you could advance us three hundred it would be better still for the reason that it would enable me to concentrate on the work which, if all else fails, would more immediately pay it back. I want to avoid if possible becoming temporarily involved with the local newspaper, my only alternative at the moment, for the following good reason with which is incorporated the history we had hoped to tell you later, with which is incorporated too part of what I believe to be the security. Or one security. I had thought, since something seemed likely to happen in regard to the German translation before long which doubtless could not be hindered by the Paris reviews of the Volcano (which are incredibly good, better even than they were in New York) of asking you to advance it on the strength of that, though it swallowed the whole – (for I don't imagine the German publisher would be willing to pay as much as our globe-trotting Swiss one, who recklessly proffered $750 but apparently decided to spend it instead on a swift voyage to Ijijiuic or even Yucatan.)[1] However perhaps the time has come to tell you the Great Secret.

Not to speak of gold plated securities to put up as collateral, this might well prove one of diamond studded platinum. If it comes off we couldn't begin to overestimate what it might do, if it doesn't, quite as one thinks, it may still come off after all in another way. At all events it is, in the sense that is written, a fait accompli. To clarify: Margerie and I have written, finished and sent off an adaptation of a certain Famous Novel for the movies. This was sent to Frank Taylor who you remember as of Reynal and Hitchcock, but who is now a producer at M.G.M. in Hollywood, as you doubtless know. It is hard to say precisely how this came about, for it began by Frank asking us to say in confidence what we thought of a previous adaptation of the same F.N. [Famous Novel] that had been temporarily shelved. Still respecting this confidence it is still not a breach of confidence to say that we answered by doing an elaborate adaptation ourselves. Since this wasn't precisely what he asked for, it is therefore hardly fair to say that Frank instigated it. And moreover it was at our risk, a risk all the greater since it was a work that has baffled the best brains of Hollywood to make anything of (though 2 years ago they paid $100,000 for the novel) for the last fourteen years. But the challenge, therefore, was all the greater – see a little later on in the letter for some evidence of how we rose to it.

But the status of the thing being such with its ramifications and complications it had to be, and still has to be, kept absolutely secret – at least from our end: it is up to Frank of course to use his judgement at his. I know you understand how complicated things can be in Hollywood better than we do. It has been of course understood between Frank and ourselves that you would handle it should anything come of it: but first of all there were some obliquities to straighten out before it got into the category of something to handle. I won't itemize these things here, and some of them we don't even know. From our point of view we could not morally look upon it in the nature of a negotiable business proposition until it became that of itself from Frank's own end. So the only reason we have not told you, apart from the above reasons of interpenetrating and obscure ethics, is the extreme delight we were holding in advance in order to spring it on you. So this must still be in the nature of something you have not heard about. (This was the Labour of Love we mentioned earlier.)[2] But it is not just a Hollywood Dream. The reports upon it so far have been so staggeringly complimentary we could hardly take it. For instance, Frank wrote us in part as follows: 'I have not felt this way since my first reading of the Volcano. On those rare occasions when I read something as brilliant, original and artful as your script, I am so humbled and awed that written words come only with the greatest difficulty. I have read many scripts and seen many pictures, but never before have I seen writing so purely cinematic. The impact of your work was much, much greater than that of the novel. It goes devastatingly deep, and its direct filmic evocation of life's complexities is magic and miraculous. I have the feeling that everything that has been thought, written and recorded on and about film is preparation for and prelude to this creation. The only other person who has read it is Christopher Isherwood, and he will be writing you separately. He shares in every particular my feelings.'[3] Then we had a letter from Isherwood who said: 'I have finished your wonderful script. Indeed, it's an insult to call it by that mere name, there ought to be another, new one for it, made specially. It so happened that I had read the novel, for the first time, not long before. It impressed me greatly, of course. But I'm not trying to flatter you when I say that your version of it was a complete revelation of new meaning and of a greatness which was certainly in the book somewhere but which you made evident. When I'd read you, I was really haunted for several days by the greatness of the theme. It has every bit as much right as Dreiser's to be called An American Tragedy – and all your changes and developments fill it out and add significance to it. But . . . quite simply said, it is a masterpiece – a new sort. I wait to see it filmed of course – but equally I wait to see your full script published with all your notes and comments – It *ought* to be printed as well as played, because much of it is for a mental theatre like Hardy's Dynasts. Well, Congratulations!'[4]

From the latter you can see that if there is a slip between cup and lip our ace in the hole is that the thing is eminently publishable – or there is an excellent chance of it so being – though we would like that naturally to take place in conjunction with the film, not before it. Frank showed it in strictest confidence to Isherwood, so the above excerpts are *strictly confidential* too.

So – although we are not legally so – we feel as if we were rather in the position of a chap who is holding a thousand dollar bond on Sunday and wants to borrow ten bucks on it. Something final on the subject may in fact come any day, but meantime prices have risen about 1100% here, and because of the fall of the pound, we have to struggle on on about $90 a month. This of course has become progressively impossible, we set a deadline beyond which we could not go, and so have written to you, since we still have not heard though as I say, no sooner have we written this letter than we may hear.

Doubtless it was foolish to have put off asking you till we were staring the Grocer in the face but again we wanted to spring our surprise full blown upon you and at the same time didn't want to look fools by promising something that didn't come off.

But we feel so wildly highly of the work in question that we cannot imagine something will not come of it.

For the rest, did you receive Margerie's letter re my article in United Nations World Mag in June, who had cabled me out of the blue: Can you write article on Mystic of Mexico in 1800 words deadline next Friday.[5] It seemed a natural for the Reader's Digest.[6] We hoped that that might stave off the crisis in between times. By the way, the U.N. Mag paid me 75 bucks, as Margerie wrote you. I didn't know until the last minute they were going to print it, by the way, since I gave them a longer article than they'd cabled for. It was all done in a great hurry: and once the 75 was sent here, I couldn't of course send back what I owed you. So will you please put that on the bill too. If you engineered it, thank you too.

At all events this is a real if absurd crisis of the kind that involves oneself actually feeding, so could you please let us know about it right away, as August 1st will see us in the mulligitawny unless something happens in the meantime.

Finally, I'd better say I'd felt I could ask you to ask Reynal-Harcourt Brace – one supposes? – for an advance on my next novel, which I have been hacking away at and is shaping up but – if the Hollywood thing comes through I want to be free to take it, and not be tied up to finish my novel at the same time, at least not to feel confined to finishing it in a certain period: I better say too the shifting sands of Harcourt Brace and the likewise of Reynal and Hitchcock – the split of Frank and Albert give me a bit of neurosis:[7] I want above everything to stick with Albert, but Albert is in Random House – still this is another problem: re the novel I took your advice when you said: A book could be written about writing the Volcano. And that is the whole point, what I have set out to do, bearing in mind also E.M. Forster's dictum that no one has yet written the history of the human imagination.[8] The result – parts of which [ought] to be eminently saleable meantime – ought to win us the Nobel Prize or at least a free trip to Chinatown and a visit to Helzapoppin.[9]

Reviews of the Volcano in France, as I say, are better than New York, if possible. But what of Norway? Denmark? I have seen one, I quote from one review: 'A devilish romance,' is all it says.

U.N. article was a sort of bowdlerized part of the novel – writing it like that makes it harder to unbowdlerize. I don't mind writing saleable parts: but I don't want to dash off watered parts of parts – if it can possibly be avoided: as I say, it's too much of a chore to unscramble.

Anyhow, here we are. And that is the problem. It may be that if you can send us the money, we won't by that time need it. On the other hand the intermediate situation is urgent and it seemed wiser to ask you. And even at absolute worst we will do our utmost to see it made good as soon as possible.

With best wishes and love,

Sincerely,

Malcolm & Margerie

Annotations:

1   The Swiss publisher, F.G. Micha, had gone bankrupt and Robert Pick abandoned the translation; see Lowry's 7 June 1947 letter (**305**) to Pick.

2   In his 17 January 1950 letter (**384**) to Matson, Lowry explains that he and Margerie are working on something 'conceived in love,' which must be kept a secret for the time being.

3   For Taylor's and Isherwood's letters see *Selected Letters*, appendix 7.

4   See Lowry's 20 June 1950 letter (**401**) to Isherwood. Here Isherwood is comparing the Lowrys' script to Theodore Dreiser's realist novel *An American Tragedy* (1925) and to Thomas Hardy's epic drama *The Dynasts* (1904–08).

5   This is 'Garden of Etla.'

6   The American magazine *Reader's Digest* contains short essays of general interest to a wide range of readers.

7   When the firm of Reynal & Hitchcock broke up shortly after Curtice Hitchcock's death, Eugene Reynal joined Harcourt Brace, taking Lowry's work with him; Frank Taylor left for Hollywood; Albert Erskine joined Random House. These 'shifting sands' were to cause Lowry great anxiety, which surfaces in his letters to Erskine over the next two years.

8 Although Lowry attributes this idea to E.M. Forster, it is Henry James he is thinking of. In his preface to *The Portrait of a Lady* James speculates about writing 'the history of the growth of one's imagination.' See *The Art of the Novel*, with an introduction by R.P. Blackmur (New York: Scribner's, 1948), p. 47. Lowry was familiar with this edition of the prefaces and with Blackmur's introduction; he had conflated James and Blackmur in his 2 January 1946 letter (**210**) to Jonathan Cape.

9 Lowry lowers his sights from the Nobel Prize to bus fare from Dollarton to Vancouver's Chinatown or a ticket to the musical-comedy film *Hellzapoppin'* (1941).

410: To Harold Matson

P: Matson(ts); UBC(phc)

Dollarton, B.C.,
Canada
25 July 1950

Dear Hal:

Thanks a million for your generosity in sending the $250 which indeed saves our lives in this peculiar interim. We appreciate greatly your kindness too because we guess you may have been on holiday and hope it didn't put you to too much inconvenience, and if so we thank you all the more.

We still haven't heard from Hollywood but should do so at any moment. In fact there may be a letter at the post office right now waiting for us. Or even a telegram.

Most definitely we will let you know as soon as and/or if and when, the very moment the thing becomes a business proposition, – and certainly we will not talk any figures to anybody without you – which of course was nothing but our entire intention all along, save that we saw no point in telling you we had shot the arrow out of sight altogether, since it was held an impossible target. I can assure you it is not an albatross either, though there is (as we wrote it anyway) one involved.[1]

Best to you all and thanking you again.

Love and God bless –
Malcolm & Margerie

Annotations:

1 See, for example, the Lowrys' instructions regarding the 'lone albatross' in Tiessen/Mota (183).

411: To George Gode

P: Matson(ts); UBC(phc)   Dollarton, B.C.,
                                                               Canada
                                                       23 August 1950

Dear Mr Gode:

Thank you for your part in the news that Under the Volcano will be translated into German and I am happy indeed.

The terms seem fine to me, though Ernst Klett Verlag should understand in regard to the option that for practical purposes there are no earlier works that will not be subsumed in later ones, for which I ask you to refer to my last letter. There is a possible exception to this in a long short story [*Lunar Caustic*] they are thinking of publishing in France, but even that I am rewriting for the American market. Anyway I think they'll have their hands full for a while with translating the Volcano.

Best wishes from Mrs Lowry and myself,
                                        Sincerely,

                                                       Malcolm Lowry

412: To Frank Taylor

P: Lilly(ts)   Dollarton, B.C.,
                                                               Canada
                                                       28 August 1950

Dear Frank:

Congratulations! Magnificent! We drafted a telegram to you as soon as we had seen it – we went into town to see it lured by the enclosed review, written a few days before – which I have sent in its native state, with a few significant ferns attached to it, just to show that its genuine – we felt sure it must be yours (we didn't know the name of yours, but Margie remembered your telling her it was laid in Boston) though the reviewer didn't say so, the mug;[1] (nor did the review in Time we'd seen, which was damn swell though) had we known the gent we would have made sure he did, had we known ahead of time – for whatever that was worth, in Gastown, Before Chirst – though for that matter it should be worth quite a lot: it is a large town, and being once the capital of a colony, half its cinemas are gigantic old opera houses, brothels and the like – Mystery Street played to packed and enthusiastic houses during a heat wave, was held over, and was an enormous success: as I say, we drafted a telegram, then your letter crossed, then we had (are still having) a railway strike, which includes the two telegraph companies, which muddled and made impossible such communications, at least from here, though they hope to be straightened out this week, I believe: then we had some local complications of our own, and so forth: well, as I say, congratulations, it is a swell film, beautifully photographed, intelligent, adult and *clear*: you know what I mean when I say clear. I mean – that it is about the only piece of its type I've been actually able to follow in every detail, and Margie, an expert in who-dun-its, concurs in every way. I would also add: worth following. Anything that is as beautifully lucid as that – I don't see many examples – perhaps there are no examples in that genre – cannot help but have, what they call in books, style. It was beautifully produced, acted, directed – couldn't see a flaw. We loved, among other things, the funeral parlour: that was brilliantly Addamsgrandguignoly[2] funny – so was the music – and the stifled purring that went on in the audience showed that everyone had excellently got the point too. It contained two of the most magnificent shots I've ever seen also: one, the rollers on the Cape, likewise Boston at dawn. Can't see why it doesn't send you to the top, unless someone is jealous, but probably by now it has done, so that I wouldn't worry. It is a bloody bore about the Journeying Boy though. But do you remember Toynbee:[3] that one success but involves a greater ordeal, what, whatnot, and so forth: no, I do not think that they prefer failure. But they may have got used to it so that it was embarrassing, or something. We hope Life does its piece upon it. We will even buy Life for that week if it does. We saw Mystery Street twice through and it deserves to be remembered, for it has a place in films. Re the Night: of course we trust to your instincts. And don't let the disgrace at having made such a good film get you down.

   Best love to you and Nan and the children,

Malcolm & Margerie

Annotations:

1 No copy of a review survives with this letter, but Lowry is referring to Taylor's MGM film *Mystery Street* (1950), about Harvard medical students who help to solve a murder.

2 Lowry's neologism 'Addamsgrandguignoly' is a reference to the American cartoonist Charles Samuel Addams (1912-88), who specialized in the macabre.

3 Arnold Joseph Toynbee (1889-1975) was a leading English historian, economist, and classics scholar. He wrote several studies of the First World War, Western civilization, and Greece, but his major work is the six-volume *A Study of History* (1934-39).

413: To Evan Morton

P: UBC(tsc)   Dollarton, B.C.
                                                    30 August 1950[a]

Dear Mr Morton:[1]

Thank you very much for your good letter, the nicest I ever had from a bank, I may say, despite any disappointment it may have contained, which, after all, was my affair.

In answer to it, I note you say you'd like to have the story I mentioned to hand, without any guarantee you'd be able to use it. Meantime, (see enclosed),[2] I became enthusiastic about the story and wrote it anyway, so it seemed foolish not to send it along immediately, having finished it to my satisfaction. Do I hear aright? Do authors ever finish things to their satisfaction?

However: though the story is considerably longer [than] Callaghan's, it still – unless I am very much mistaken – would fit effectively within the frame at your disposal.[3] In this regard of length, I may be wrong but Callaghan's story could be an exception in that it is so successful in that number of words. Like many of his stories it is informed by a sense of charity and moral meaning that infiltrates down into the story and has the effect of turning much of what normally is known as the organic into something almost superfluous to its intention, while it still remains a work of art. This is a very rare quality in an artist, and really first rate short stories seem to me to be very rare in literature, and rare to the point of extinction in magazines. What I mean is, though one may be capable of an effective anecdote, unless one happens to have that particular quality of Morley Callaghan's, it is very difficult for any writer to write [an] even worthwhile anecdote in 800 words, for without that quality of parable he must lean to some extent on the organic, and there goes 500 words already – if I am right.

Well, this is not much more than an anecdote either. Though the story would not at first sight seem able to bear more top-hamper, more top-hamper I should have to give it were I to sell it to the American market, say, to the New Yorker. Possibly I wouldn't like the story so well – which now seems to me, looking at it, to have dropped straight out of heaven just as it is especially for yourself – but that is what I should have to give it. Constantine would find himself coming in, Thomas Mann, the strange taste of Pope Sextus VII, who knows, even Gogol. The ghost of Shelley would be found in Keats' house and Henrik Ibsen brooding in the park drinking a glass of sherry.

Anyhow, I endeavored to write a little story for you that would have its appeal to Canadian readers, and in a minor way, I have tried to touch amusingly on the isolation of the Canadian artist himself, though in such a manner that I hope he is universalised.[4]

Further in regard to your letter, however, putting me into the category of 'name authors' is slightly ironic, so far as Canada is concerned. I feel there might be some justification in being put into the category of 'one who ought to be known but isn't.' My royalty statement showed exactly two copies of my novel sold in Canada last year – it can't have sold more than a few hundred in Canada at the outside all together. Though it was certainly published here – and it was for a while a best seller in the States where it received the best reviews (according to some opinion I read) any novel has been accorded since Look Homeward Angel,[5] – only a few copies were sent to the bookshops here and not a single advertisement for it ever appeared in Canada, let alone any mention of it having made the Encyclopaedia Britannica. In fact, the reception in Canada was certainly disheartening, the more especially since I had been sustained somewhat while writing it by the notion that one might be doing something for Canadian literature etc. – though it is true, that though written in Canada, it is far from being, in one way, an indigenous Canadian book.

In any event, if there is any change in the situation, will you let me know, because otherwise I shall have to send the story – having made the aforesaid alterations, doubtless to its extreme detriment – off to New York to try its fortunes there, the reasons for this being purely financial, financial enough at least that I would not be able to wait till next spring for the decision.

However – other things being equal – perhaps this story will appeal to you sufficiently to make you want to publish it, perhaps somebody else will have failed you, or again perhaps – ?

In any event here it is: if I haven't sent a self-addressed stamped envelope for its return this is partly due to the fact that you said you would like to see it – and partly, no doubt, that I didn't want precisely to encourage you to send it back too immediately.

Thank you again for your understanding and friendly letter.

Yours faithfully,

[unsigned]

P.S. I don't seem to have said quite what I meant about altering it for America. But if the kind of experience I have had is universal it puts a finger on yet something else that may cramp the style of Canadian authors, even in the foreign markets. In this case it probably doesn't apply and all I would be obliged to do would be to give it a slightly more international flavour. But that 'slightly more' – which seems a slight thing – is really to cover up the fact that the central character is too obviously a Canadian. A story I once was asked to write for an American magazine would have been all right if I hadn't insisted on calling a beer parlour a beer parlour and Nanaimo Nanaimo. What they really wanted was a story about Canada with a Canadian in it all right, but who instead of going to a beer parlour in Nanaimo went into a bar in Seattle, where he could have been visited by a Canadian mounted policeman and a Mexican, for all they cared, so long as they were on holiday in the state of Washington, and yet mysteriously in Canada at the same time.

Annotations:

1 Evan Morton was public relations officer with the Canadian Bank of Commerce head office in Toronto. He wrote to Lowry on 21 August and 18 September 1950 (UBC 1:48) concerning the bank's sponsorship of the publication of short fiction by Canadian writers in Canadian magazines.

2 Lowry sent Morton a seven-page story called 'Sooner or Later or So They Say,' which was subsequently developed into 'Elephant and Colosseum' for *Hear us O Lord*; see Lowry's 20 September 1950 letter (**417**) to Morton.

3 The Bank of Commerce sponsored publication of Morley Callaghan's one-page story 'The Bachelor's Dilemma' in *Maclean's*, 1 August 1950, 24-25.

4 Kennish Drumgold Cosnahan, the protagonist of 'Sooner or Later' (and 'Elephant and Colosseum'), is a Manxman living in the United States – not a Canadian. He is in Rome to see the Italian translators of his novel *Ark from Singapore*.

5 Thomas Wolfe published his autobiographical novel *Look Homeward, Angel* in 1929, and it was an immediate success.

Editorial Notes:

a. This transcription is from an unsigned draft typescript (UBC 2:15) with several pencil changes and marginal insertions. The original has not survived.

414: To Derek Pethick

P: UBC(tsc)   Dollarton, B.C.
                                                                           31 August 1950

Dear Mr Pethick:

I am covered with shame that I have not earlier replied to your letter, but I have been working like hell and still am – and as Flaubert says – Is there no end to this murderous prose?[1]

I am tickled to death you may speak of the Volcano. It may be that

I brought some imperceptible and tactful and almost invisible pressure to bear upon certain powers; if not, I should not like to be entirely disabused of the notion that I did. Re the script I have of what you have done on the Volcano, it could not be kinder, and I am very grateful. Only suggestion I have: there is an indigenous Canadian passage bottom of 36 – end of 37, might be of interest to you, for it reads well.

In one way you have yourself to blame, for writing such fantastically interesting letters, that you get no reply to them immediately. Your last letter is amazing, and full of frightening and stimulating reports from the labyrinth, which I am still brooding upon, and cannot even now answer in detail. I have some strange corroborations of certain things I could do better in conversation than on paper. I was born, by the way, in New Brighton, near Birkenhead, not far from where Hawthorne had his Consulate in Rock Ferry. Liverpool of course is just across the way. My father's office was near a small square, with a small statue of Lord Nelson in it, which is described in Redburn.[2] I passed through this square every day when at home – quite an insignificant square, closed to traffic, surrounded by houses – and this also was described in the lost In Ballast – practically no difference in the description, for there was practically no change in the square in a hundred years – and I hadn't read Redburn then. Ultramarine, however, which is a ghastly abortion, I wish you would forget, not mention as by me, nor connect with me, and even burn. It is a sore point with me, for various reasons. I mean to rewrite it someday, but meantime I don't want to be reminded of it. There is a short novel called Lunar Caustic that's coming out in France I'm not ashamed of, though – about the best thing I ever did. It was paid for – in 1936 – in America, but not published. They thought it too horrible at the last minute. It is a sort of forerunner to the Lost Weekend, but it actually starts with a man looking for Melville's old house in 28th St. and 4th on a bet and ends up in the alcoholic ward at Bellevue where he can see the sidewheelers going to New Bedford.

This I mean to rewrite too – I'm letting it come out in France as it stands, however; I'd let you have a copy but I have only one. This is really good. I mean to make about six novels eventually, all related, the Volcano being the third, to be published in one volume and called: The Ordeal of Sigbjørn Wilderness. I haven't got the promised French copies of the Volcano yet so can't send you one yet.

Fellow I heard from same day as you was Jay Leyda.[3] He has written a book called the Melville Log – a documentary biography of Melville – coming out this October by Harcourt-Brace – and knows Melville's family, etc., though he was writing me about something quite different.

I hope the chickens are o.k. – and also hope we can get together sometime.

   Best of luck

                              Cheerio

                                        [Malcolm Lowry]

Annotations:

1 The allusion to Flaubert is a Lowry favourite; see his 22 June 1946 letter
   (**226**) to Albert Erskine and his 27 May 1956 letter (**655**) to Clarisse
   Francillon. In a letter of 22 July 1950 (UBC 1:56) Pethick had
   expounded on parallels between Lowry and Melville and likened
   Ultramarine to *Redburn*.
2 Lowry was fascinated by Melville's description of Merchant's Exchange
   in Liverpool and by the coincidence of his similar description of the
   square, but he claimed not to have read *Redburn* until the early forties
   in his 28 September 1943 letter (**184**) to Gerald Noxon.
3 See Lowry's July 1950 letter (**407**) to Pethick, and his 11 January 1952
   letter (**495**) to Robert Giroux, who sent him a copy of the *Melville Log*.

415: To Philippe Thoby-Marcelin

P: UBC(tsc)   Dollarton, B.C.,
                                                          Canada
                                                  12 September 1950

My dear Phito:
   A thousand congratulations to you from us both! We are very happy
indeed for your success, and that Gollancz is to publish The Crayon and
La Bête in England.[1] Gollancz is an excellent and enterprising publisher;
and as for Edmund Wilson, who is doing your preface, that is wonderful – you could not find a more enlightened and creative critic in this
hemisphere, nor one more hard to please.[2] I have also received your
other postcard, though I think it may have been a bit delayed, for we
have been cut off for a while by a railway strike. Meantime I have been
anxiously awaiting the proofs of The Crayon, but now – if you had
wondered if we were in Dollarton – is the better time to send it, for the
strike is over and we shall be here in Dollarton indefinitely. We were
repairing the foundations this afternoon, in fact, our house being built
in the sea, in stormy weather we have the problems of a sailing-ship,
rather than a house, only the difficulty is to stop it sailing, rather than to
make it sail. We had stormy petrels flying beneath our window last winter, but it is lovely in autumn, and we only wish you could be here to
make it perfect. We shall be looking for the proofs by every post. But if

Edmund Wilson has kept his eye on the job there is certainly not much likelihood that that which should be translated 'Shut your mouth,' will be translated 'Peace, woman,' for as I recall it was he that pointed out a few such discrepancies in the translation of the Bête which I expect have been smoothed out now – though isn't it damned difficult for the poor author himself to maintain a stern attitude about such things in a translation – as if writing the book were not enough! While I for my part still probably am not sufficiently acquainted with the nuances of French to discriminate between what should and should not literally be, 'Peace, woman,' or 'Shut your mouth,' I think I can feel my way rightly into the correct intention of a given sentence of yours or piece of dialogue even if already translated into English: at least I know enough to be able to say with fair certainty that nothing at all should be translated as 'Peace, woman,' unless with humorous intent, or where somebody perhaps is trying to silence a female politician. But, as I say, it is not likely that such discrepancies will arise this time with the Bête. We are enormously looking forward to reading it. What is the destiny of La Negrèsse Adolescente? Again I express my deep gratitude at the honour that you have dedicated A Fonds Perdu to me – & what is its destiny?[3] My French publishers are now Corrêa and the edition with your name spelt right is now out and has been incredibly well received in Paris. This is the second edition, though, and the paradox seems to be that the first edition, which was put out by the Club francais du livre, though likewise very well received critically, did not beget – or has not by now begotten – a second printing in that format, as they had thought it would: this was the one with your name spelt wrong and naturally I was reluctant to send it to you – even to mention it – but being a very much better bound volume I have been almost equally reluctant to send you the Corrêa edition which is only in paper. So far I have received only one of each and have been awaiting each day to receive from the Club the edition with the dedication correct. If it does not arrive I shall send the Corrêa one, if indeed they have not sent it to you already. As a matter of fact I shall send you one anyway because I wish to write in it for you – they owe me another five, meantime I have only this one to make my own corrections with, it is a little different from the other, which besides is invested with my abhorrence save in looks, because of the aforesaid error. I hope this Kafkan explanation is comprehensible and does not cloak the true apology it contains. Who are your French publishers? Correa seem good, full of get up and go, as Margie says. I bet you'll start getting translated by everyone else now. What about Canapé-Vert in England? Don't let success give you an angoisse. How is Pierre? Emile? Please give them our best love. We long to come to Haiti again. Should you ever be in Cape Cod you must look up Conrad

Aiken, if you have time – one of my oldest friends. His address is 41 Doors, Brewster, Mass., and I know he'd be delighted to see you.

There is a heron standing on the beach – you would like this landscape, seascape I mean, or is it a fishscape? Congratulations again from us both. Margie sends her best love. As do I

Affectionately ton frère,

Malcolm

P.S. All our best love to Dawn Powell too, should you see her.

Annotations:

1 The London publisher Gollancz brought out both *The Pencil of God* and *The Beast of the Haitian Hills* in 1951.
2 Edmund Wilson wrote a thoughtful introduction to the Houghton Mifflin edition of *The Pencil of God* (translated from the French by Leonard Thomas), in which he discussed other works by the Marcelin brothers and set them in the context of Haitian culture.
3 *A fonds perdu*, a poetry collection, was not published until 1953 by P. Seghers in Paris.

416: To Frank Taylor

P: Lilly(ts)

Dollarton, B.C.,
Canada
12 September 1950

Dear Frank:

How lunacy it all seems – but undoubtedly it will work out for the best, as it appears to us.[1] Mystery Street, I note, is still recent and recommendable in Time, and still succeeds happily wherever it goes, as it deserves to do. However, all our sympathies, if meantime there is a slight stoop in the soul: probably all it means is, you got that old Saturn in your third house cusp, and Venus well dignified. Anyhow, greater freedom. There was an article in Time on psychoanalysis last week may have been of interest. On the other hand it is in every way true, that there tend to be many articles in Time on psychoanalysis.

Best love to you, Nan and the children,
M & M

Annotations:

1 In his 1 September 1950 letter to Lowry, Taylor explains that he has been released from his contract with MGM because he is not felt to be their type.

417: To Evan Morton

P: UBC(ts)

Dollarton, B.C.
20 September 1950[a]

Dear Mr Morton:

Thank you very much for your letter. Yes indeed, by all means hold on to the manuscript if you feel it worth while submitting to your panel.[1]

Re your opinion that it is completely out of character with the series as you visualize it, however may I say I am just slightly bewildered? When I first wrote you and asked if I might do a story for you, I inquired what your restrictions were as to subject material, theme, etc. Your very kindly reply stated that your policy had been to commission your writer to produce what he wanted, and if he was satisfied, you were satisfied too. Of course you did not commission me, *yet your letter was what I had to steer by.* {Yet nothing in your letter seemed actively to discount the conception I had.} By the same token I feel I can be excused if by out of character you mean simply that it is too long or detailed for your immediate purposes, though as concerns this you had not mentioned a specific length; naturally there were limits to this, so I wrote it to the length I thought would fit into your space, if admittedly longer than [Morley] Callaghan's, the only example I had seen.

If it is the matter of length that is the principal objection, I could of course shorten it, in fact, would have already done so, supposing this to be the trouble and I had known the exact limits; my object was to take advantage of as much space as seemed at your disposal, for in this way I thought the story would be more successful.

But if it is the actual plot of the thing that strikes a wrong note, then I am a bit at a loss, though I can't help thinking I could still figure an excellent one out. Naturally I'd be very glad to act on any recommendations in regard to it, if by those recommendations you mean cuts or alterations. However I did fancy it to be a fresh and humourous little piece, that could not give offence, and was even subtle in its way. In short, I very much liked it myself, for I meant it to be first-rate in its genre, and if you don't like it yourself for reasons that have nothing to do with its length, but simply as a story, I am much disappointed.

Anyhow, unless you let me know to the contrary, I shall assume that it is its length that is the trouble, or that it is something else that may not be irremediable.

It occurs to me though to suggest – trying to put myself in your place – that its 'out-of-characterness' might still be just a virtue, in the sense that a series may sometimes effectively use an exception, that being an exception it would draw the more attention to itself, by drawing the more attention to itself it would draw more attention to the bank, and by drawing more attention to the bank it would, subtly, the more fulfil, on your own terms, the function of advertisement.

Set against this is the undoubted fact that you can't very well say 'Printed by us because the author liked it,' any more than you could say, 'Printed by us because we happened to dislike it extremely!'

[breaks off unsigned]

Annotations:

1 In an 18 September 1950 letter (UBC 1:48) to Lowry, Morton described 'Sooner or Later or So They Say' as 'out of character' with what he imagined for the series, which the Bank of Commerce was sponsoring.

Editorial Notes:

a. This transcription is from a draft typescript (UBC 2:15) with pencil changes.

418: To Harold Matson

P: Matson(ts); UBC(phc)

Dollarton, B.C.,
Canada
21 September 1950

Dear Hal:

Herewith a story I commend to your special attention, for it could be somewhat specially out of the top-drawer.[1]

It was designed with the feeling that it would be definitely saleable, without too much difficulty, and I had, particularly, the New Yorker in view.

In fact, though it is a decidedly literary story, unless I am very wrong the New Yorker is the right goal. In any event I hope it will hit with you and that you may feel it can find some more or less lucrative home.

I fancy there must be such a market for it: if so, there would be certain small questions of typography, impossible to be precise about with the typewriter, as you will see, that would enter in with whoever accepts it: but I guess that is no disadvantage if the story itself is good enough, which I feel it to be. In case it does not make you laugh I better add that it was intended to be a humourous story, albeit the humour may be a bit Charles Addamish.

We have not yet heard re the Hollywood venture: war seems to have changed matters[2] but now that the news is looking up, that may change still other matters, so that we still feel very hopeful: of course we shall let you know the very moment we hear anything.

Meantime, on the assumption of further delay, we have been working some ten hours a day at stories like this though this is the only one in complete shape so far: if it prospers, or even if you fancy it may prosper, it will be encouraging, for as things stand I have to recoup somewhat before taking time to go again wholeheartedly at the novel, though I am hopeful parts of that may be saleable too.

Our best to both Tommy and yourself and the children: and thank you, sincerely, again for the loan.

Best from us both,

Malcolm Lowry

P.S.[a] I have appended a page or so of notes for the editor, re typographical difficulties mentioned above: among these the name of the character – whom you will see again – is Sigbjorn, though I hesitated to write it like that. Or should it, conversely, be Sigbjørn? – If you think the notes would militate against the story please detach them, for the questions could be gone into later when & if accepted: – I've read the story again (to say the least) & can't help thinking it's better than ever. I hope you agree. I'd better add – for your own expectancies' sake – it's not autobiographical, I mean the end[3]

Best of luck,

M.

Annotations:

1 Lowry is sending Matson 'Strange Comfort Afforded by the Profession,' which first appeared in *New World Writing* 3 (1953): 331–344 and subsequently took its place in *Hear us O Lord*.

2 Lowry is referring to events in the second phase of the Korean War, when American troops were sent in to defend South Korea against invasion from the North.

3 Since Lowry owed Matson money and Matson made his living by selling his authors' work, Lowry wants to reassure him that the ending of 'Strange Comfort' is not autobiographical. The story explores the fate of the writer, especially those like Keats or Poe who die young or in poverty, and ends with the protagonist's somewhat bitter laugh at this grim fate turning into a 'prolonged . . . fit of coughing. . . .' Presumably Lowry is associating Sigbjørn's coughing with tuberculosis (and Keats), and Sigbjørn's terrible 'begging letter' (and Poe's) with his request for help in his 17 July 1950 letter (**409**) to Matson.

Editorial Notes:

a. This postscript has been added in pencil beneath the full signature. The notes Lowry refers to are no longer extant with the letter.

419: To Derek Pethick

P: UBC(tsc)   Dollarton, B.C.
                                                     28 September 1950

Dear Mr or even Sir Moby Mellish (or should one use the more familiar
term simply D(erek Peth)ick: − [1]
    Yours to hand. Thank you very much for the contents. I was very
disappointed not to hear the dead baby on my poems. Unfortunately
our radio is likewise a dead baby at the moment but it must be brought
to life before you take to it. What did the Swinburnian corpselet say?[2] I
had no idea anybody had read any of my poems, save for [Earle] Birney,
a few − most of which, if any, seem to have been published without my
knowledge − though I gave some to Alan Crawley: verdict, with one or
two exceptions, silence. I dare say because they are mostly lousy, not to
say unwritten. Something about the shape of most poems annoys me, I
don't know why, or I feel they ought to be part of a play − with the
result my ambition is obscure on the subject, though it is something that
frequently troubles me. One of my main difficulties is that I've read very
few poems that I honestly like by anybody at all, which has not kept
most of my own few from being derivative.
    Re museums: I just wrote a story about a museum ['Strange Comfort
Afforded by the Profession'], or rather two museums; Keats' house in
Rome, compared with the Poe museum in Richmond, Virginia.
    Re Lindbergh − I was writing something about the time of your let-
ter last February − in which I advanced the theory that Lindbergh's flight
over the Atlantic in 1927 represented a symbolic victory for America of
the superego over the unconscious or Id: gangsters represent Id of
America and take their horrendous revenge on baby.[3]
    We would be delighted to talk over your scheme when you come.
Maybe we could even be of some help. I was in America when I was a
boy during prohibition, and before I went to college, and my wife is
American. She is a very good writer (Horse in the Sky, Scribners) and a
conservative-christian-anarchist in politics. She likes to excoriate enthusiastically one's fog-dog of hope for humanity; though the above Horse
is an excellent example of hope at its best − bears no relation to current
American literature, and if anything, resembles Wuthering Heights.
    Don't let your age put you off: I am only about ten years old, as con-
sciousness goes, nearly all of which time I have lived on a beach as a
beachcomber.
    I received an extremely favourable review of David Walker's Geordie
from my mother in England, who likewise informed me that I had been
born at midnight, on a Wednesday, upon July 28th, 1909[4] − sounds

ominous, but maybe it's the opposite. I put that in because this letter seemed rather full of dead babies, I thought you might like one that was reputed to be alive.

Salud!

[MCMLowry][5]

P.S. I have an idea this, also the 28th, is Melville's 59th death-day. 5 and 9 are 14; 4 and 1 are 5; and 2 is 7; and twice 14 are 28; or so they say.

Annotations:

1 Lowry's playful address is an allusion to Pethick's interest in the links between Melville's *Moby-Dick* and Lowry's *Under the Volcano*.
2 In his pencil annotations to this letter Pethick remarks that the 'Swinburnian corpselet' (as Lowry calls him) was a morbid young man from the CBC who had been talking about Lowry's poetry.
3 Charles A. Lindbergh (1902-74) made his solo flight across the Atlantic in May 1927; in 1932 his infant son was kidnapped from the Lindbergh home and murdered.
4 David Harry Walker (1911-92), a Scot, settled in New Brunswick, Canada, in 1947. He wrote adventure novels and children's stories, including *Geordie* (1950). Lowry's birthday, 28 July 1909, was a Wednesday.
5 This version of Lowry's signature (supplied by Pethick in his copy of the letter) continues the play on names with which Lowry began, by creating a roman numerological pun on his initials.

420: To Conrad Aiken

P: H(ts)
PP: LAL 216-17

Dollarton, B.C.,
Canada
28 September 1950

Dear old Conrad:

Have just received short stories[1] with much thanks and great pleasure in rereading, where not often reread – Though I have not had time to reread all, let me say many have for me mellowed with age, if affection and nostalgias evoked have not made me uncritical. This is true of some stories such as Spider Spider, and Your Obit, which I was not so fond of at the time when I first read them in Costumes,[2] but I guess I did not fully understand them. They now seem excellent. Strange Moonlight is better than ever, if possible, and of relatively new ones Hullo Tib seems to me a marvellous little story. Jesus that poor cat. And for all one's perception! – And did I say little? Morally her fate has considerably more meaning than that of Anna Karenina under similar circumstances, and her continuance in heaven seems to me far more assured than that of that dame.[3] May endless dances with moths undying in the Elysian Fields be her lot! I remember Smith and Jones once meeting with your severe disapproval so have not reread but it looks as if you have cut it. I somewhat miss Pure as the Driven Snow and the Moment,[4] but you can't have everything: too bad, too bad. (That is not criticism but friendly quote) Of the merits of Secret Snow and Arcularis you must have heard more than enough. What is now the status of the play? I am now scaring myself with The Disciple[5] – I guess it is an excellent volume, I hope you are satisfied with the selection and that it has much success!

For ourselves, am a great hit in France, and am in the equivalent of the Modern Library thingmetight there and in Norway. We are frighteningly poor at the moment, but life in the old – or rather new – shack is better than ever. We are working hugely so finances may improve, with a rush, in which case hope to see you, in fact will, if humanly possible. Hope you and Mary are keeping very well, we are, myself never better. We had some fan mail from a gent in Minnesota named Z.L. Begin, a lawyer. Where? or why bother? Or maybe a symbol. For example, I broke my back with the result that I am no longer constipated and have even started to grow again. (Though you can forgive me for feeling I was a bit 'knocked oop' at the time.)

Send us your news, God bless and best love to you both from us both

Affectionately,

Malc

Annotations:

1 Lowry's copy of *The Short Stories of Conrad Aiken* (New York: Duell, Sloan and Pearce, 1950) does not appear to have survived.
2 'Spider, Spider' and 'Your Obituary, Well Written' were originally published in *Costumes by Eros* (New York: Charles Scribner's Sons, 1928).
3 Like Tolstoy's heroine, the cat in Aiken's poem is killed by a train.
4 'Pure as the Driven Snow' appeared in *Among the Lost People* (New York: Charles Scribner's Sons, 1934) and 'The Moment' in *Costumes by Eros*.
5 'The Disciple' is one of Aiken's short stories; it was first dramatized on CBC radio's 'Stage 49' program on 10 April 1949 and rebroadcast in March 1951; see Aiken's 9 March 1951 letter to Edward Burra (*Selected Letters of Conrad Aiken*, p. 294).

421: To Philippe Thoby-Marcelin

P: UBC(msc)
PP: *SL* 246-47 [Dollarton]
[12 October 1950]ᵃ

KARAMBA, my very dear Phi-to,
our very best congratulations on The Pencil[1] which I haven't time to
discuss here, but will just content myself with saying that while it is not
the best book *you* can do, nor was meant to be, it will very much surprise me if it does not become a classic, and this it fully deserves to do.
I expect to see it reprinted many times and even students having to learn
it in school (even if the parents object.) Taking it as a whole the translation is very successful, I think: but there are quite a few errors of taste
especially here and there in the wrongful or inconsistent use of
American slang and one or two other points where one senses that a literal translation has not done you justice or otherwise makes a slightly
false impression: we are going to send you these suggested emendations
at intervals of a few days – posting the first to-morrow (Friday) which
will cover you the first few chapters, which we are doing to save time,
which may be of the essence to you. In this way we shall indicate precisely where these suggested emendations should occur on the proofs
which you will be able to check with on your copy and consult about
with a friend or advisor but without our sending you back the proofs
themselves until afterwards, which we need here for this purpose.

Where possible we will try to avoid making suggestions that will
mean resetting a paragraph but we earnestly counsel you to consider
them in cooperation with someone else who knows English or your
translator himself for we believe that these lapses, while not individually
very bad, cumulatively might affect the reviews.

Please tell me *immediately* how much time you have but in any case
our first batch of notes will go off to-morrow.

Right at this moment we are facing eviction from our house, together
with our neighbours the fishermen, please pray for us that this tragedy
may be avoided, which it still just may: nonetheless, tragedy or no, you
are going to get your notes on time and as stated, even if they begin
moving our house away from under us while we are doing it.[2] This is
too long and complicated a story to go into here – but it is another story
of sharks, believe me: we will live on government land which they will
not let us buy, but meantime we are treated as without rights altogether,
not even human ones, so that we have no legal toe-hold, unless I am
clever enough to invent one. So please pray. It is worse for some of our
neighbours than for us, who are still young and kicking after all.

God bless you & congratulations on your horrendous and witty

Greek grand guignol comedy-tragedy again, & love from Margerie & myself

ton frère,

Malcolm

Annotations:

1 Philippe Thoby-Marcelin and Pierre Marcelin's novel *Le Crayon de Dieu* (1952) appeared in an English translation as *The Pencil of God* (Houghton Mifflin, 1951) a year before its French publication. They did not receive the Lowrys' comments on the translation in time for publication; see their card (**430**) to Marcelin.
2 During the early fifties there were several attempts to remove Dollarton squatters from their foreshore shacks. Lowry's anxiety about this threatened eviction grew into an obsession that fed the central theme of *October Ferry to Gabriola*; see his 23 October 1950 letter (**424**) to Harold Matson.

Editorial Notes:

a. This date is from the photocopied envelope filed with the letter (UBC 2:15).

422: To Derek Pethick

P: UBC(tsc)   [Dollarton]
                                                   [ca October 1950]

Dear Mr Pethick: –

Yes, I do think your broadcasts are excellently worth while, very intelligently put together, and moreover it is a difficult form of concision, combined with critical discovery, that is really needed; I particularly commend you tackling the Sound and the Fury.[1]

As for me, you make me feel good too; but while you tell me something about my metaphysical self, my wife and I have got together and discovered the fact that we did not have a copy of Moby Dick in the house till about six months before our fire and gave it away as a Christmas present! This means I had none during nearly all the years I was writing the Volcano.

In Ballast, the book that was burned, was written in 1934, when though I identified myself to some extent with Melville, by God, I had not the intelligence to understand the passages you quote, believe it or not![2] I didn't know, though I'd been a sailor, the difference between a star and a planet till meeting my wife. I still half think the world is flat, unless I consult her about it, so while there is an explanation, it is not of this world. The eternal recurrence came from reading Ouspensky.[3]

Our radio version of Moby Dick was away for 8 months at the CBC, without a word; in dealing with the CBC I recommend absolute simplicity.[4] Failing that I suggest you contact my good friend Franz Kafka, Praha, Czechoslovakia. He can be relied upon to forward mail and what is more is a good hearted fellow.

Cheerio,

[Malcolm Lowry]

Annotations:

1 Pethick may have sent Lowry a copy of a planned broadcast on William Faulkner's *The Sound and the Fury* (1929), or Lowry may be suggesting, somewhat wickedly, that Pethick apply his talents to Faulkner's complex tale of madness and incest.

2 In his 22 July 1950 letter to Lowry, Pethick discusses the similarities he sees between Lowry and Melville. Lowry may be answering this letter, but as no others from Pethick for 1950 appear to have survived, the date and status of Lowry's letter cannot be confirmed.

3 In his 22 July letter Pethick notes that Lowry and Melville share an interest in eternal recurrence. Lowry had read Ouspensky in the early thirties.

4 During the mid-forties the Lowrys had begun work on a radio script of *Moby-Dick*, but it was neither completed nor used by the CBC. It is a twenty-four-page typescript, containing a draft scenario for episode one with synopses for the remaining twelve episodes (UBC 16:4) and has been published as '*Moby Dick* Adapted (1945)' in the *Malcolm Lowry Review* 36 & 37 (Spring & Fall 1995): 96-153. See Lowry's 14 May 1945 letter (**201**) to Gerald Noxon and his 30 May 1953 letter (**577**) to Philippe Thoby-Marcelin.

423: To Downie Kirk

P: UBC(tsc) [Dollarton]
PP: *SL* 214-15 [18 October 1950]
Wednesday –

Dear old Downie:

I got your letter a week ago with your very welcome and kind invitation and immediately made up a reply in my head – we were on our way to Crescent Beach for a day to look at birds – but when we got back we got rather anxious news I dare say you have read (re the beach) if not, forget I've told you and don't bother – see below.[1] For I am somehow quite convinced it will blow over, and if it does not, we still have a few strong cards left to play, so we are not worrying now, though for a while we did not exactly feel like standing on our heads and in fact altogether there was Heavy Traffic on Canal Street[2] emotionally: in addition to this I received the proofs of a Haitian novel [*The Pencil of God*] – (with a preface by Edmund Wilson) by a friend of ours – but so shockingly translated that we felt bound all but to retranslate the whole book for him in a week, no easy task without the original: hence the delay.

We would be delighted to come and will bring the records if it's not raining too hard: (the records are delighted they have been asked too.)

With the bloody situation at your new school I deeply sympathise: you must indeed feel like Dante eating alien bread,[3] and all I can say is that perhaps it is Ordeal E5 on the roll of ordeals and by the time you've solved the bitter problem you'll probably find that another more important problem has been solved automatically and triumphantly without making any effort.

Meantime I have been composing you a new grammar or system to entertain you, which it is proposed can be used with effect while teaching the juvenile delinquent section in your temporary purgatorio.

Translate: Q. Where does the cousin of our aunt go in the morning?
             A. He goes to the bank.
             Q. Why does he go to the bank?
             A. He goes to get money from the bank.
             Q. How does he get money from the bank?
             A. He holds up the bank.
             Q. Where does the cousin of our aunt live now?
             A. The cousin of our aunt lives in Oakalla.[4]

Translate: Shake my great coat!
             Q. What is in the great coat of our father?
             A. An eyedrop and a hypodermic syringe are in the great coat of our father. (This is for advanced students)
             Q. Are there any watches in the great coat of our grand uncle?
             A. No. There are three clocks in the coat of our grand uncle.

Translate: (a) Send for a policeman who can be fixed.
             (b) We want a bootlegger.

Perhaps this is a little extreme, not to say bitter, but I hope you see the possibilities of the general drift. I think we passed your new school on the way to New Westminster and God it looked fine new shining and respectable and we hoped if it was yours you were happy there. But you never can tell what hells such appearances contain. Well, matters must look up if they can't look down. So we'll be along Saturday and we'll all cheer ourselves up.

Best love to yourself Marjorie and Dorothy from Margerie and myself.

Yours Sincerely,

Malcolm

Annotations:

1 Lowry is probably referring to eviction threats against Dollarton squatters, but 'see below' is unclear; no enclosures are extant.
2 *Heavy Traffic on Canal Street* is the title of one of Lowry's favourite jazz pieces recorded in 1940 by the New Friends of Rhythm, with Buster Bailey.
3 In Canto XVII, ll. 58-59 of the *Paradiso*, Dante's ancestor tells him the truth about his future: he will be exiled from Florence; he will be very poor, and he will be obliged to eat 'lo pane altrui' (the bread of strangers, or alien bread).
4 Oakalla was a maximum security prison on the outskirts of Vancouver.

424: To Harold Matson

P: Matson(ts); UBC(phc)   Dollarton, B.C.,
                                                                         Canada
                                                              23 October 1950

Dear Hal:

Thanks for the note – you certainly were right in regard to New Yorker being the wrongful lebensraum[1] for 'Strange Comfort' and I will keep my trap shut in future in deference to your larger wisdom in these matters – I hope I'm right in thinking the piece has some first rateness, however.

I wonder if it would be too much to ask for the advance paid on the German translation;[2] which we had set against our debt to you.

We have been going through a truly dreadful ordeal here, in regard to the land we live on here in Dollarton – half of which belongs to the Harbour Board, and half to the Provincial Government – no one seems to know whether the inhabitants, who have repeatedly tried to buy the land, have any legal rights in the matter, but the political issue they have made has driven us half cuckoo with suspense: so far we've survived, and all may yet have a happy ending, but with the pound having gone down, and the Canadian dollar up, it does not make our financial situation, already practically non-existent, any more certain.[3]

I hope I was not too optimistic in regard to the Hollywood venture but I feel something must come of it eventually, though we've had no news – so far as I can tell Frank may be even in the process of changing studios: in any case we are working like mad on short stories and should have half a dozen for you by Christmas – some of them top-notch, I hope: I am working on no less than four simultaneously. So financially we ought to be all square with you at no distant date, whatever happens.

Meantime I wish the daemon would let us have a little peace of mind: I suspect him darkly of having been trained in the school of Torquemada.[4]

Love to you, Tommy and the children from us both –

Malcolm

Annotations:

1 *Lebensraum* is the German noun meaning 'living space' or milieu.
2 *Unter dem Vulkan*, translated by Clemens ten Holder, was published by Ernst Klett in 1951.
3 Vancouver citizens's complaints about squatter's using unsightly shacks along the foreshore of Burrard Inlet precipitated proposals in the newspapers for the improvement of the area; see, for example, the *Vancouver Sun* for 1 August 1947, in which Lowry is accused by name of being a wealthy writer living 'rent-free,' or the *Sun* for 19 November 1949, in which the shacks are described as 'illegal' and 'unsanitary' and their demolition called for, or again the *Sun* for 22 March 1950, which ran an editorial titled 'Clean Out the Jungles.' Lowry felt deeply threatened by this public attention and what he saw as an inevitable loss of the only place on earth he loved.
4 Tomás de Torquemada (1420-98) was the infamous Grand Inquisitor of the Spanish Inquisition and the most aggressive and intolerant of the inquisitors. He organized a spiritual policing system that led to the torture and execution of thousands.

425: To Derek Pethick

P: UBC(tsc)   [Dollarton]
                                                      [ca October 1950]

Dear Pethick:

Thanks very much for your talks, and the Partisans and Kenyons. The magazines cover with one exception exactly all the months of those years' numbers that I didn't possess. So you had second sight, and they're a most welcome acquisition to me. It was very good to see you the other day, and we hope the next time may be longer. You caught us bogged down with anxiety, and we still are;[1] but no doubt it will lift, and when we meet again I hope we'll have more time to talk. We'll send back the Chase in time for you to catch the library date, it's an interesting book[2] – And it suggests to me that any resemblances of the Volcano to Moby Dick are quite unconscious, and stem mainly from a conception of my own of withdrawal and return I'd worked out in 1936, the main source of which was Ouspensky. I think Miss Lonelyhearts is a semi-inspired abortion, not good as they say.[3] But this brings up another question, which I have no time to go into now, but will try to tackle some time.

Good luck.

[Malcolm Lowry]

P.S. Ouspenksy says somewhere: the answer is contained in the question.

Annotations:

1 Lowry's anxiety may be due to newspaper attacks on the Dollarton squatters.
2 The American literary critic Richard Volney Chase (1914-88) published *Herman Melville: A Critical Study* in 1949. Although Lowry admired Melville and *Moby-Dick*, one of the key influences on his thinking was, as he notes, Ouspensky; see Lowry's 16 April 1940 letter (**135**) to his mother-in-law.
3 *Miss Lonelyhearts* (1933), a novella by the American writer Nathanael West (the pen-name of Nathan Wallenstein Weinstein, 1903-40), is about a newspaperman who writes a column for the lonely but is murdered by a man he tries to help.

Few artists compose letters like the following one to Stuart Lowry – Vincent Van Gogh wrote to Théo in similar tones, and James Joyce barraged Stanislaus with begging letters – and few are as aware as Lowry was of 'the technique of such letters,' especially when they might prove fruitless. Lowry's 'Dear old Stuart' exercise is a classic of its type and utterly characteristic of its author. The list of accomplishments followed by the litany of woes rings with Lowryan irony, wit, and humour. Although Stuart was unwilling to play Théo to Malcolm's Vincent or even Stanislaus to his Jim, he was, nevertheless, the only family member (after Arthur Lowry's death) to offer practical aid – in France in 1948, for example – or to assist with his youngest brother's finances. Stuart was also the only brother to attend Malcolm's funeral.

426: To Stuart Lowry

P: UBC(ms)
PP: *SL* 217-24   [October 1950]ᵃ
                                                – Dollarton.
                                            British Columbia.
                        – Or perhaps I should spell it: Dolorton.¹

Dear old Stuart:

   A towering sea is bearing down upon me. Gulls are balancing in the
gale. A black cormorant is struggling low over the waves against the
wind. All around me is a thunderous sound of breaking, smashing, trees
pirouetting & dancing, as a full gale smashes through the forest. What is
this? A seascape – or a suggestion for program music, as for Sibelius or
Wagner. No: this is the view out of our living room window, while we
are having our morning coffee. What I see is quite unbelievable, even
for you, unless you have seen it – and where else would you see, but
here, a house that is built in the sea & where the problems – & noises –
are those that beset the mariner rather than the normal householder? It
is wonderfully dramatic – too dramatic, even for me, & for us, in some
respects, for we now live under the shadow, at any moment, of losing
it. This I've told you before. We only live here by grace of being pioneers, & Canada, alas, is forgetting that it is its pioneers that built this
country & made it what it was: now it wants to be like everyone else &
have autocamps instead of trees & cocola stands instead of human
beings. In that way for it has little culture at all, it could destroy its soul:
that is its own business, no doubt, – what we mind is that it threatens to
destroy us in the process, an eventuality that it now becomes my duty
to try & avoid. Have I mentioned that this is supposed to be a begging
letter, even if addressed to one who can do naught, & is hamstrung even
as I? – one of those letters that you see, or may see one day, under a glass
case in a museum – just as this house that we fear to be thrown out of
someone may make money out of one day – for I am the only Canadian
writer ever to be placed in the Encyclopaedia Britannica (mention
where?)ᵇ – a sort of begging letter at least, though I don't know on what
moral grounds I am presumed to be begging for what upon one plane
of reasoning would certainly seem to have been once at least intended
to be mine; begging being something I understand that even the
tycoons of Canada may be driven to from their neighbouring country
as an alternative to stealing, a practice I am inhibited from less on moral
grounds than fear of the consequences & plain incompetence. However,
I couldn't get myself in the proper mood of despair, even though, as a
matter of fact, there is every reason for it. This proves that I am not really
anything so wondrously effete and as it were imitative (I am partly
joking, of course) as a latter-day Canadian, but simply an Englishman

i.e a person who, upon overhearing himself pronounced dead, remarks:
Bloody nonsense. With that we shall entitle this, instead; 'business
letter', a euphemism that so far it seems singularly unentitled to. There
is something wrong with my prose too this morning, but this I ask you
to overlook. The foregoing however is my way of saying – even if I
can't keep the cheerfulness out, that we stand in the shadow of eviction,
and thus upon the brink of what is popularly known as disastar. The
other people in the same position are mostly fishermen and may fish
elsewhere; that is to say there are fish elsewhere. We however are fishermen of another sort in a place where there is plenty of fish but no place
to sell it save very far away, by which time, if it has not indeed gone bad
meanwhile, either it tastes so unique it is accorded a civic reception, or
it realises assets that, like the fish, are frozen. Of the more hopeful &
constructive side of this later; all this, in my usual direct fashion, you
may take to refer to the crucificial position of a writer in Canada, to
which you may, though with less justice than you think if you can
imagine for a moment that you are not Stuart but the late personality for
whom you now stand in loco (*loco* in the nice sense) reply: Well, I didn't
tell you to live there! From now on, however, I shall be strictly business
like. First, I shall give you – an important item in the technique of such
letters even when one understands perfectly well the utter fruitlessness
of it – a list of my accomplishments, immediately to be followed of
course by a similar list of catastrophes, during the last years, though on
second thoughts I'll spare you some, and in third thoughts shall confine
myself to the last year & a half.

(a) have written & completed in collaboration with Margerie a
detailed movie script, – adapted from a novel you won't have heard of
– upon which we worked sometimes with the temperature below zero
in the house, some fourteen hours a day – it was so cold at one point we
couldn't take off our clothes for a fortnight – of which the report – from
two of the greatest authorities on the cinema, & a now famous Metro-
Goldwyn-Mayer producer was in brief, that 'it was obviously the
greatest achievement in movies, what the movies had been adding up
to, and that even to read, that it was comparable with the power of
Theodore Dreiser & the titantic mental drama of Thomas Hardy's –
The Dynasts – ' (I see no reason to be sparing of adjectives; they were
not.[2] The producer [Frank Taylor] is one of my ex-publishers of the
Volcano, & you may in England see a minor film of his called 'Mystery
Street' – very well worth seeing.
(b) succeeded in having the Volcano published in translation in
Norway, Denmark, Sweden, & France – in the first & last countries put
into a edition with classics of the world.

(c) Ditto Germany & Italy – now in preparation, which prospects formerly had fallen through

(d) Seen it hailed as the greatest masterpiece of the last ten years in the French Translation in Paris. You could get the reviews more easily than I could: but they have appeared everywhere, even in the famous Figaro.[3] And there was a wonderful English appraisal of the translation in the New York Herald Tribune – Paris edition. The publishers are Corréa: & a special edition by the Club Livre de France. In fact it has had every honour showered upon it there, & many French authors have received the Legion of Honour & been elected to the academy for less.

(e) Been put in the Encyclopaedia Britannica. (For how long? Are you comfortable there, Malcolm?)

Well, I could go on with these, but I think it's time now for a few catastrophes, sometimes transcended catastrophes.

(a) operation for a chronic condition of my legs. Successful but expensive.

(b) Continued anxiety – partly responsible for condition when you met me – of thinking one had t.b. Tests showed I have had t.b., at some time or other, – when? – and am liable to it: but have it no longer.[4] Have conquered anxiety neurosis on this score.

(c) Ditto and more important, that Margerie had cancer. She does not; but to that diagnosis, I am grateful to her brother-in-law. Had she obeyed the dictum of doctors here she would have been treated as if she had so that she had the anguish of thinking she had.

(d) the pound is devaluated.

(e) Because of the success of the Volcano my [editor], Albert Erskine, is invited to join the staff of the Modern Library. You know who *they* are – you brought me up on them! But that leaves me still under contract to the publisher he has left. Erskine wants me to come over [to] the [Modern Library, which of course I want to do, but according to the terms of my contract I have to send my next novel to my old publisher & give him a chance to make me an offer first – & they are holding me to this as they are very anxious to keep me. On the other hand the advantages of going into the Modern Library, & keeping Erskine as my editor, far overweigh anything else. Incidentally my other editor became a producer at MGM on the strength of my book. This is a complicated situation, which cannot fail to work to my eventual great advantage, but difficult to explain in a letter.][c] But it is the opposite of an advantage now.

(f) Because of a dispute between the Harbour Board & the Provincial Government over our land, which we repeatedly tried to buy when we had money, we face eviction for the second time & it blows over.

(g) I break my back & have to wear a brace – the cost this time is not merely expensive, but calamitous. It was after this (d) happened.

(h) I write to Alderson Smith:[5] no reply. Am still waiting.

(J) I conquer the broken back, the brace, but then am faced (sic) with my legs again. I conquer this by exercise, & Margie's help. Also I literally owe my life to the way we live – from which we are once more to be evicted, only this time the threat seems much more positive.

(n) The pound falls further yet – or rather does so, in effect, for us, because the Canadian dollar goes *up* to equilibrate the American; this it does on a free market & in a state of disequilibrium, fluctuating, in which it not only overtakes but threatens to go still higher than the American, with the result that my monthly income is now little more than 90$ – that has the purchasing power of little more than a fiver in the old days, and I am not exaggerating. Rent makes sympathetic & contradictory fluctuations of course, but you would be lucky merely to rent anywhere these days for $90 a month, without food – let alone live. I don't know if this aspect of the sheer hardship of the situation has struck you. What it comes down to is that to live on the income alone involves trying to live on somewhat less than the pay of Mary or Sarah, *without* everything being all found.[6] This practically knocks us out entirely, robbing us also of the little margin of profit we had between the American exchange & the Canadian, & between that exchange now at the same rate & the exchange of the pound. Simultaneously prices came down a little, but no sooner have they done that than they go up still further, threatening still worse inflation though the pound, despite greater faith in it, remains the same.

(o) A notice of eviction that seems final, but with just a bare possibility of reprieve in it: but it scarcely seems possible it can last more than a few months.

(p) Margerie ill – with ourselves still in the dark as to what is really wrong with her: x rays, brain tumour still suspected, treatment that must be continued, begins to put us into the category of the starving.[7] Much may be done with oatmeal. I begin even to think of the saying: 'Home is the place where, when they have to, they take you in.' But where indeed is that, unless here? Her mother lives 4000 miles away in America, mine 10000. And we have no friends in Canada save three fishermen in like case, a cat, five wild ducks, two seagulls, and, of course, a wolf.

(q) Naturally, one didn't expect to live on one's income, in the usual sense; though between books, that can become necessary, because if you live on an advance from your next book you're eating yourself, as the French say, literally; and if you get another job you won't write the book – which is one reason why so many writers quit being writers. But in my case the possibilities of a job are or were three: teaching, radio, newspaper work. The first requires at least a year's negotiation & a complete rededication of one's life – & probably going to the prairies, since the English are hated in B.C. The second pays starvation wages & moreover requires a car, while the third not only does that but would be senseless because what I do anyway to attempt to augment the income makes more money & comes into the category of free lancing. In short there is no possibility of a job where we live – short of turning sailor again or working in a sawmill – for taking one would mean abandoning the really practical hope we cling to in regard to our serious work, & also our house: & indeed at the moment we haven't got money even to *move* anywhere else. Even if I could get a labourer's job the cost of transportation would swallow the money we save by living in the house. And writing is a whole time job or nothing, so it would mean quitting. Margie can't augment matters by getting a job herself because she's not well enough: besides we do our best work together. And for the same reason, however willing to turn my hand to anything, I couldn't leave her long enough in the wilderness by herself. In short it's better to stick to one's guns: only it seems that begging is a standard part of writing; or is about to become so. You may therefore count this as work, for it's my all too valuable time, not counting yours. It may interest you to know that there is a long broadcast to-night or to-morrow night on the subject of Malcolm Lowry, Canada's greatest & most successful writer, which we can't listen to because our radio has run down & we can't afford to replenish the battery.[8]

(r) The unkindest cut of all. Despite our love I have been warned that for Margie to live another winter under these conditions is very dangerous during the coldest part, so, that while we are clinging to the poor house, for all we are worth, we are still trying to make enough to live in the city over the nearly impossible months of December & January. (The climate has changed here during the last ten years & winters have been almost as cold as in the east causing god knows what misery.)

(s) Losing the house under these callous conditions – & they are totally callous & selfish – would be a blow considering all the others – having lost it by fire once among other things & rebuilt it ourselves – of such psychological importance that if we had our way we wouldn't live in Canada at all any more. Well, we don't expect our way. The object is to live at all. I have done more for Canadian literature than any living Canadian, & that is beside the point except when I say that despite all this I have made a success of my life & had conditions been equal would have made an assured income for life too – which I may yet do, of course, through the Modern Library or the movie. You could not expect more success of anybody than I have achieved, & both of us have conquered other seemingly insuperable obstacles too (you are not to judge from my health when you saw me – I myself have now never been fitter, exercise & swim every day etc. – or I couldn't be writing like this – it is now evening, with a full roaring black gale outside, with the bottom out of the barometre, that is, not our barometre, but someone's barometre.)

Well, why go on. About the only thing we have left is a sense of humour, and the feeling & hope now that what has been undiagnosable in Margie's condition is due to the manifold & obscure results of a histerrectomy: which may well be: but this in itself is going to require prolonged treatment which at best merely means expense we cannot afford. You get a wrong picture if you think we are gloomy: but the actual situation is some ten times blacker than I've painted it. So I won't paint it: I haven't liked to paint this much. What it all adds up to is this: that while my prospects for the future will eventually add up to an income for life (vide the Modern Library & that you certainly can believe) we are at the moment faced with a financial crisis – which is not caused by extravagance or lack of forethought by the way – even my trip to Europe will turn out to have paid for itself, for without that, among other things, no French translation, rather none of any worth – which could happen to any business man, only we have noone near enough to appeal to, & no way of floating a loan. It is an acute crisis that should only be temporary for apart from the new novel & the projected film I have about ten short stories blocked out for which I have an immediate market in New York, having actually a request from 3 or 4 big magazines for my work (there is no market at all in Canada, which is part of the tragedy) & I simply cannot get the freedom & peace of mind to write them properly – even though of course I am not ceasing to try.

And here we come to the age-old pay off to be found in the shrines of every writer under a glass case in the museum – in short if there is any way, possible or impossible, for you to find any money for me – bearing in mind that there certainly were provisions made for crisis in Father's will[9] – can you look into this immediately, for I've put off writing till the last possible moment, hoping it would not be necessary. However in your last letter, with very large foresight, you did say: Hang on till October. Well, I have hung on. If there's nothing can be done, it has been in my mind, terrifying prospect though it is – though I do not consider it abject, & neither would she or you if I could make the circumstances plain – to write direct to the mater – would you advise me about this? But what else, in fact, am I to do, if all else fails? Damn it, I shall always remember she once gave me a three-penny bit.[d] If of course – & the idea is naturally hypothetical – I did this she would refer it to you and about all I could ask you to do then is to ask her not to refer it to God, or perhaps, conversely, *to* refer it to God. And all this, the consequence of ceaseless hard work & application. Well, I know you will do your best. Please forgive my writing. I hope the letter was amusing anyway. All my very best love to Margot whom I hope is in good health & to Donnie love & sincere welcome back from his ordeals & travels – [10]

In short God bless to you three – from us both,

Malcolm

P.S. This letter is going to give me a nightmare to night. So don't let it give you one. If you *can't* do anything, advice would be better than nothing, for at worst, I can always get them to deport me back to England as a vagrant – something I think ought to be pointed out to the British Government who then might have to buy me a wig – on Father.

Annotations:

1 See the penultimate sentence to chapter 1 of *Under the Volcano*. *Dolore* is Italian for 'grief,' but the allusion is to the inscription over the gate into Hell in Dante's *Inferno* III, 1-2: 'Per me si va nell' etterna dolore' ('through me you enter eternal grief').

2 Lowry is referring to the letters he received from Jay Leyda, Christopher Isherwood, and Frank Taylor; see his 17 July 1950 letter (**409**) to Harold Matson.

3 *Le Figaro*, a right-wing Paris daily, is an internationally known French newspaper.

4 See Lowry's 23 March 1947 letter (**288**) to James Stern. Stuart had last seen his brother in April 1948, when he came to Cassis to help Margerie with a severely alcoholic and ill Malcolm; see Day (401-04).

5 Alderson Smith was a Liverpool solicitor who handled the Lowry family's financial affairs; see Lowry's letter fragment (**11**) to Smith in Appendix 3.

6 Mary and Sarah had been maids in the Lowry household when Lowry was a boy; Lowry's point is that, over and above their pay, these women received room and board.

7 During much of 1950 Margerie Lowry had been suffering from what was eventually diagnosed as bruxism, an aggravated grinding of the teeth; see Lowry's 14 November 1950 and 20 March 1951 letters (**427, 449**) to Harold Matson.

8 Lowry must be referring to the broadcast that Derek Pethick hoped to do for the CBC; see Lowry's 24 January 1951 letter (**439**) to Pethick. The program was never aired.

9 Arthur Lowry's will stipulated an annual allowance of £400 for

Malcolm. There was a £12,000 trust settlement, established in 1938, that provided income from interest, but Lowry was not able to have access to the capital. Nevertheless, his brother did come to his aid; see Malcolm's 1951 letter (**457**) to Stuart.

10 Margot and Donald are Stuart's wife and son.

Editorial Notes:

a. This transcription is from the signed pencil draft (UBC 2:16). Judging from internal references to Lowry's holding on 'till October' and to the possibility of writing directly to his mother (who would die suddenly on 7 December 1950), the letter must have been written in October or early November 1950.
b. This parenthetical question is likely Lowry's notation to himself.
c. This passage in square brackets is in Margerie's hand but is included here because it completes Lowry's point and is co-terminous with his writing.
d. This reference to his mother has been added for insertion, then cancelled, at two earlier points in the letter. Lowry let it stand here.

427: To Harold Matson

P: Matson(ts); UBC(phc)   Dollarton, B.C.,
PP: *SL* 215-17   Canada
                                                                14 November 1950

Dear Hal:

We just read the draft of our last letter to you and maybe it didn't seem clear because it wasn't very clear to us.

Therein was intended to be a request, if possible, for the $150 coming from the German translation. We had written this off against our debt to you (to which, sotto voce,[1] if you have forgotten, you should add $7.50 for a United Nations article last June – this parenthesis being intended to make us sound more honest) but wondered if you could trust us with the owed money a little longer.

You may wonder why we're broke again after you've just pulled us out of the hole and the answer is we're not but we will be by the 1st of December if we haven't sold anything meantime. Prices have risen 270% here. Margie has been ill – a suspected brain tumor – a false alarm, thank God, but an expensive and harrowing one; she still has to have x-rays every few weeks.

Meantime we haven't heard anything from Hollywood of course or we would have immediately let you know. But this has been postponed by certain facts we aren't at liberty to confide at the moment. And we have a deep instinct that what we did was too good to be written off.

Hollywood or no Hollywood. And fortunately I can say we've got half a dozen or more stories coming up, some at least of which must be saleable, and into all of which we have put, or are putting, our *all*. These are, in their probable order of arrival: October Ferry to Gabriola, a story which you've had before, but which was no damned good. This we decided we couldn't collaborate on so I have completely rewritten it by myself and finally I'm extremely pleased with it and feel it will be as good as anything I've done, and saleable also. Venus is the Evening Star – a story by Margie, and I think the best thing *she's* ever done.[2] This is an extremely powerful story about Mexico, with an Anglo-German situation, and an extremely movie-wise one. Present Estate of Pompeii, by me – nearly finished, a story of our travels, and though I say it, excellent too. Homage to a Liberty Ship, ditto. Deep Henderson: about a dying hot musician who takes a bus and goes to Haiti. etc.[3] The Course: this is a story about the Hoylake golf course – scene of many of Bobby Jones' triumphs and incidentally, in the dim past, mine, and certainly has an interest for American readers, I feel.[4] A Heart-Warming Episode – which describes the visit of an O'Neillish American dramatist to a puritanical English home. This expresses a sincere emotion all too rarely expressed – the cultural debt of England to America (– er – not to speak of other debts just at the moment.)[5] Not so nearly finished are a story by Margie based on our travels in Italy, laid in the castle of Francesca da Rimini, and Gin and Goldenrod, by me.[6] October Ferry and Venus should be in the post in a week, hotly pursued by Pompeii, *And many others.*[7] (including one I just thought of this morning.)

But naturally one can't expect them to sell by Dec. 1. Against this – since I've been flawlessly wrong on the saleability of my work in the past (though I don't think I am this time) with the exception of the Volcano – I have planned a draft of Lunar Caustic, which was written as a long short story, as a novel. Albert said it was publishable as it stood, but even so, it can be improved: this would be part of the *whole* work at which I dying to get down to.[8]

Naturally we don't expect you to keep hauling us out of the abyss while you don't get any work from us: but this time *the work is there*, I mean it is before our eyes, beyond the potential stage, almost in the post.

I've tried to get out of the hole in other ways – such as journalism, writing an advertisement for a bank, etc. But it is a dead waste of time – for it takes time from doing the other work – moreover I haven't been successful at it so far as I know, save for the United Nations thing, and even if so it benefits neither of us. I also have money in England (technically a lot of it) which I'm doing my damndest to get hold of, etc.

Finally we aim, in the next three years, to make not only ourselves but yourself a lot of money. It is my prophecy that this will be done.

Christ what an old story this is. Throw it in the fire. But we mean what we say nonetheless. Meantime we would be grateful if you would postpone the debt a little and send us the German thing, for unless something turns up from the last paragraph but one there is no immediate way to pay that either.

Best love to Tommy and the children from us both.

Malcolm

P.S. The new German contract, in German, signed by Klett, arrived today and I have signed it and posted it back. Thank you: Mr Gode & your agent in Hamburg for me.

Annotations:

1 *Sotto voce* is Italian for 'in a low voice' and is commonly used in opera to indicate an aside or a private remark.
2 There are two typed drafts of 'Venus is the Evening Star' with the Margerie Bonner Lowry papers (UBC 51:27-28).
3 'Present Estate of Pompeii' is in *Hear us O Lord*. 'Homage to a Liberty Ship' became the long short story 'Through the Panama' (also in *HUOL*), but 'Deep Henderson' was no more than an idea and a few notes.
4 'The Course,' if ever written, does not appear to have survived, but the Royal Liverpool Golf Club at Hoylake was a favourite with the Lowrys, who were allowed to play there because their father was a member. Lowry won some club competitions as a boy; see Russell Lowry's reminiscences in *Malcolm Lowry Remembered*, 19-20. Robert Tyre Jones (1902-71) was an American golfer who won the British Open Championship thirteen times.
5 No drafts for 'A Heart-Warming Episode' appear to have survived.
6 Margerie's Italian story is the novella 'The Castle of Malatesta'; three typed drafts exist with the Margerie Bonner Lowry papers (UBC 51:11-23). 'Gin and Goldenrod' is in *Hear us O Lord*.
7 '*And many others*' is an allusion to the refrain in 'Strange Comfort Afforded by the Profession,' from *Hear us O Lord*.
8 The '*whole*' work Lowry refers to is *The Voyage That Never Ends*.

428: To Derek Pethick

P: UBC(tsc)   [Dollarton]
[ca November 1950]ᵃ

Dear Pethick:

How are you? Let me know what you are doing. I liked your projected broadcasts a lot — hope you have been successful with them.

Between that and creative writing of the other order – I mean as concerning what you want to do which you asked me about – it's rather hard for me to judge. Often, you know, the answer is contained in the question.[1] I felt like saying that perhaps what you needed were you to be a writer of another kind is more suffering, some kind of jolt, some bitter tangential experience; to fall in love, preferably unhappily, even if only with a hen. But that seems pretty lousy advice. After all, the treasure you are really looking for is only on the other side of the hill yonder. Something always goes wrong with a too deliberate and rational and conscious search for a direct object. Of course you may find what you want on the way. But what makes you happy yourself is a key. I'm sorry not to say anything more useful. We both have happy memories of your visit and send our love.
   Sursum Corda.[2]

[Malcolm L.]

Annotations:

1 Lowry attributes this comment to Ouspensky in the postscript to his October 1950 letter (**425**) to Pethick.
2 *Sursum corda* is Latin for 'Lift up your hearts'; it is addressed by the celebrant to the congregation at the beginning of the Eucharistic Prayer. The first poem in Conrad Aiken's *Brownstone Eclogues* (1942) is 'Sursum Corda.'

Editorial Notes:

a This transcription is from an undated, unsigned copy (UBC 2:16).

429: To Guilio Einaudi

P: UBC(ms)   [Dollarton]
                              [ca November/December 1950]a

   Einaudi[1]

Dear Sir:
   In relation to the translation of my novel, Under the Volcano, I would be most awfully grateful if there is yet time (if it is still coming out), if somewhere you could unobtrusively put a dedication to this effect:

For Margerie; and Gerald Noxon.[2]

   It is important you put in the semi-colon though, because Margerie is my wife & Gerald Noxon a very old friend of mine, who was long

resident in Italy, is a film director & now in radio, & was my first editor
– years ago when I was working on Under the Volcano, & who gave
me much valuable help with it; I know it would please him extremely
if the Italian edition were dedicated to him because he loves Italy, everything Italian, & has since childhood.

This could be done unobtrusively, from a typographical point of
view, & need not interfere should the translator wish to dedicate his
translation to someone else.

I do hope you like the book & think it is some good for I would be
very proud to think I could bring you some credit. I'm afraid that the
translator has had a very hard job & I hope he won't regret having done
it. We long to come to Italy ourselves & there disappear into the sun.
Thank you for this if it can be done, & without trouble.

Yours very sincerely
Malcolm Lowry

Annotations:

1 The Italian publisher Einaudi has no extant correspondence from
  Lowry. They did not publish *Sotto il vulcano*; see Lowry's 12 June 1948
  postcard (**345**) to Gerald Noxon.
2 The final dedication to *Sotto il vulcano* is: 'A Margerie, mia moglie.'

Editorial Notes:

a. This signed pencil draft (UBC 51:14) appears to be Lowry's only surviving letter to his first Italian publisher. Judging from his reference to
   this letter in his 23 January 1952 letter (**501**) to Gerald Noxon, Lowry
   is writing in late 1950.

430: To Philippe Thoby-Marcelin

P: UBC(card phc)   [Dollarton]
                                                          7 December 1950

– Was very disappointed you didn't [get] the proofs in time but hope
our corrections may do some good after all.[1] Will write you more fully
when we have a moment. Meantime the best of luck & I sincerely hope
everything works out happily for you, after your ordeals.

fraternellement from
Malcolm & Margie

Annotations:

1 See Lowry's 12 October 1950 letter (**421**) to Marcelin.

431: To Albert Erskine

P: Virginia(card); UBC(phc)
PP: *SL* 224   [Dollarton]
                                                    [7 December 1950]ᵃ

Thanks awfully for the Faulkner – Albert – it's full of wonderful things[1]
– I had borrowed the book on the same day so Margie & I met face to
face carrying the same book – and were later to be seen even reading
the same book in bed – a Charles Addammish cartoon – am concocting
you a long letter Best love to you & Peggy

                                                    from Malcolm

Annotations:

1   This is probably *The Portable Faulkner*, edited by Malcolm Cowley
    (New York: Viking, 1946), a copy of which survives in Lowry's library.

Editorial Notes:

a. The date and address are from the postmark on the envelope with
    this card. Lowry has written his message below the printed Christmas
    greetings.

432: To Downie Kirk

P: UBC(tsc)
PP: *MLVD* 61–62   [Dollarton]
                                                    [13 December 1950]ᵃ

Dear Downie, – It was wonderful seeing you the other night – I
thought to rejoin you having put on my boots (or perhaps one boot) but
somehow mislaid you or somehow went into reverse in the bosca
oscura.[1] I'm exceedingly glad you applied the strappado to the practi-
tioners of thugee in your class, a remedy that no doubt could be applied
with profit to the parents also. We are very grateful for – and thank you
very much for sending – the words of *Les Trois Cloches* and *Perrine était
servante* – and Margerie is delighted with them.[2] I'm also very much
looking forward to hearing some of your new records soon. We're very
relieved that Mrs Craig is well recovered: conversely, and at about the
same time, I lost my own mother, how died I am still waiting to hear,
though my eldest brother cabled me it was upon her birthday.[3] This
threw me emotionally out of gear somewhat; it is hard to say exactly
what happens to one on such an occasion even if it doesn't show out-
wardly: it seems probable that one undergoes spiritually some kind of
insurrection, as between the deathward wish that unconsciously wishes

to follow one's mother into the grave, and the lifeward one that is striving once more within the conditions of birth itself, towards a rebirth. Such a phenomenon also seems to be occurring in the world outside us, and grim though the picture seems, it doesn't seem half so hopeless as it did in 1939 – or even 1938. Even if communism were temporarily victorious it doesn't carry with it such a hopeless *teleology* of tyranny – even if tyrannical in its present phase – as did Nazism. In short anything [that] is a revolution must keep moving or it doesn't revolute: by its very nature it contains within it the seeds of its own destruction, so by 1989, say, everything ought to be hunky dory, all of which certainly doesn't make it any easier to live in 1950. And it is tragic that the few really selfless men in world affairs, such as Nehru,[4] seem to gain so little hearing. Or such at any rate is my opinion. It is even more tragic that such a great country as Russia should only be able to manifest as its representatives people that seem exactly like the prototype of Keyserling's 'absolute devil'.[5] But sometimes I get the impression that not even the people who are actually in the process of making history know in the least what is *really* going on. Or if they do it seems appalling that they should be in the position that they are. Your music appreciation club sounds a lot of fun. We went to see the old silent film *Intolerance* – played straight through without any music at all – a great mistake, since Griffith wrote his own score. Very few silent films will stand being played like that, without music, which I think is interesting. *The Passion of Joan of Arc* is an exception.[6] I have a lot more to say but will keep it till we meet again, which I hope will be soon. Meantime we're awfully glad for you that you have the situation licked at school and that once again appear the stars.

Wishing Marjorie Dorothy & yourself the happiest of Xmas from Margerie and myself.

Cheerio

Malcolm

Annotations:

1 The 'bosca oscura,' or Dantean dark wood, in this case is the forest at Dollarton behind the Lowry shack.

2 Both titles are French folk-songs from the early eighteenth century.

3 Elizabeth Craige is Jimmy Craige's wife and Downie Kirk's mother-in-law. Evelyn Lowry died from peritonitis, resulting from diverticulitis, and heart failure.

4 Jawaharlal Nehru (1889-1964) became the first prime minister of an independent India in 1947. He was a lawyer, author, and social democrat.

5 Count Herman Alexander Keyserling (1880-1946) was Russian by birth

but became a German citizen in 1918 after losing his land in the Russian Revolution. His philosophical works, written in German, expound a type of mysticism influenced by Oriental philosophy.

6 D.W. Griffith's epic film *Intolerance* appeared in 1916. *The Passion of Joan of Arc* (*Le Passion de Jeanne d'Arc*, 1928) was directed by Carl Dreyer.

Editorial Notes:

a. This transcription is from a typed copy of the original, which does not appear to have survived. The date, taken from the postmark, suggests that the original was a Christmas card to which Lowry added a lengthy message.

In September 1950 Viking Press published Samuel Putnam's translation of Cervantes' Three Exemplary Novels. *When Lowry discovered the translation, sometime after that date, he was prompted to write the following letter, which provides a fine illustration of his phenomenal memory at work. Whether Putnam ever received Lowry's letter or, if he did, what he thought of the suggested additions to the annotation on Teba is unknown. It is clear that Lowry's imagination had held and amplified the image of the Spanish town for almost twenty years and that he had woven a number of striking allusions (predominantly visual) into the rich fabric of this deeply personal memory.*

433: To The Viking Press

P: UBC(ms)   [Dollarton]
                                                       [ca 1951][a]

Dear Sirs:

I have been reading with enormous pleasure & profit Samuel Putnams magnificent translations of Cervantes.[1] There is a small point, of interest to me, & perhaps of infinitesimal use to you. On p 26 of the exemplary novels (Rinconete & Cortadillo), paragraph 4, there occurs the remark of Cortado's 'We are neither from Thebes nor from Murcia', the Thebes in this context eliciting note 7 p 222 where it says: 'In the original there is an untranslatable play on sounds here.'

I would be interested to know if the original read – or implied – Thebes or Theba, & if the former whether or no, making all allowance for Cervantes' fondness for Hellenic allusions, it was not actually a printer's error in the Castilian (so to speak) for Theba.[2] Or what was meant to be Theba. In any case if Putnam has overlooked the fact that there actually was – & is a town – perhaps it's even a city – named Theba in the rough environment of Cervantes' story it may be – if I am right & if what I say is at all relevant – that the footnote could stand a little interesting amplification. Or could it be that Theba was sometimes known as Thebes as [illegible] is Troy, & London was Ilium etc?[3] so that Cervantes wrote Thebes – or its equivalent – but without intending a play on words, or rather sounds, exactly.

Unfortunately my knowledge of Spanish & Spanish history could not be less, & I have no detailed atlas at hand, but if my memory serves me & it might certainly do here – there is a town of great antiquity & remoteness called Theba somewhere in a direct line – or at least on the railway line – between Granada & Algeciras.[4] Though I've never met anybody who has been there, & have never even heard the place mentioned until this bit in Cervantes called it (even if wrongly) to mind, it made a greater & weirder & more dramatic impression upon me than any single place I have ever seen in my life, – though I only passed through it in the train. That is to say the town is about 3 miles away from the station, at which we stopped only about two minutes, but built on the top of a mountain so that it seems to overhang you, like a cross between Taxco the House of Usher & the Castle of Worms, painted by Ryder & El Greco, with orchestral effects by Wagner Hieronymus Bosch & God.[5] All this is 20 years ago, but I remember there was a terrific thunder storm going on, & a sinister individual in dark clothes wearing a top hat descended from the train climbed into a dark coach drawn by two black horses & then began to drive up the hill into the lightning as the train drew out, so that I told myself I certainly was going to go back to Theba one day & also knew that I could never forget it.

Unfortunately I can't remember whether Theba was in the province of Granada or Malaga, on the Antequera side of Ronda or nearer Algeciras, but my impression is that I'd been when Theba was reached about 8 hours in the train from Granada, going Algeciraswards, from which I'd deduce then it was roughly 200 or so miles away from Granada itself, though I may be way out.[6] On the other hand it did strike me strongly that it must have been at one time a citadel of great importance – or at least near impregnability: I'm sorry if all this merely shows my ignorance, but since I seem to remember that Murcia[7] was once a kingdom of which the capital was the town of that name my mind was running on the lines that perhaps at one time some Thebes-Athens like rivalry had existed as between Theba & Murcia, the city, even if Theba were not similarly the capital of an old kingdom: that sounds pretty fetched (in fact it is, very) considering all Granada province as is now, & Almeria would lie between, but something of the sort I imagined would render the play on words, or rather sounds, explicable if Cervantes did indeed intend a play on sounds at all. In any case if it should turn out that Cervantes actually was referring simply to this Spanish town of Theba rather than making any euphonious allusion to other Thebeses whether in Boetia or Egypt[8] it would give this correspondent a great deal of childish pleasure to think (especially if he'd caught old Cervantes out in his own proof reading) he'd brought it to your attention.

Pardon my having written at such great length on such a trivial matter but I was so fascinated by Putnam's wonderful translation that I was literally transported back to Spain again, my memory of the mysterious Theba thereupon became vivid, there could just conceivably be something in what I say – hence (this I'm afraid none too literate) letter

Yours very sincerely

Malcolm Lowry

P.S. Or have I overlooked some more obvious point such as that while the Spanish for Thebes could be – I surmise – Theba, Theba should not necessarily here be rendered in English as Thebes?

Annotations:

1 *Three Exemplary Novels: Miguel de Cervantes Saavedra*, translated by Samuel Putnam (New York: Viking Press, 1950) contains *Rinconete and Cortadillo*, *Man of Glass*, and *The Colloquy of the Dogs*. Lowry's page references and quotations are correct.

2 Cervantes was indeed referring to the village Teba, and the original text involves a play on words using gypsy jargon.

3 Neither Lowry's writing nor his point is clear here because the Latin name for the city of Troy in Asia Minor, site of the Trojan War (ca 1200 BC), was Ilium, and the Latin name for London was Londinium.

4 Lowry is thinking of the town in the province of Malaga, and his memory here and in the next paragraph of the town's geographical location is accurate. Teba is on the railway line between Granada and Algeciras 'on the Antequerra side of Ronda.' See Lowry's comments on Teba in his June 1933 letter (**46**) to Jan Gabrial.

5 Taxco, a Mexican town south-west of Cuernavaca, is situated on a group of hills and has sloping, cobbled streets. It is famous for its silver mines and its ornate church, Santa Prisca, built by José de la Borda in the Churrigueresque style. There is no castle in the German city of Worms, although the city is situated on the River Rhine in the Rhineland-Palatinate, an area rich in castles and the myths associated with Wagner. The American artist Albert Pinkham Ryder (1848-1917) was a visionary painter of seascapes and allegorical subjects or scenes from Wagner. Domenikos Theotokopuli, known as El Greco (1541-1641), was a Greek painter who settled in Toledo, Spain, where he

painted his expressionistic canvases of the city, such as *View of Toledo* (before 1597). The Dutch painter Hieronymus Bosch (1450-1516) was one of Lowry's favourite artists. His symbolic paintings of torment and sin have a hallucinatory power.

6 Teba is approximately 145 kilometres from Granada and 145 from Algeciras. Although Lowry was unwell and drinking heavily through most of his spring 1933 trip with the Aikens, he has remembered distances very well.

7 Murcia, the capital of the province of Murcia, is approximately 240 kilometres to the north-east of Granada.

8 The ancient Egyptian city of Thebes, with its royal residences, temples, and monuments, dates from before 2160 BC. It was located on both banks of the Nile near present-day Luxor, Karnak, and Qurna, about 210 kilometres south of Cairo. The Greek Thebes, in the central area of Boetia, was settled by 1000 BC and was a leading city of ancient Greece.

Editorial Notes:

a. There is neither inside address nor date on this two-page pencil holograph. Since the Viking edition was published in September 1950, Lowry's earliest date of writing would be late 1950.

*On 25 March 1951 (letter **451**) Lowry composed his 'OATH TO HIGHER SELF,' resolving 'with God's help, to recast my life in a better, sincerer, mould.' The 1950 Christmas and New Year's season had gone badly. He was drinking heavily and had created a scene at the home of his friend Downie Kirk, a scene for which he felt obliged to apologize (letter **437**). Each successive month in 1951 brought new reversals and more disasters. There were quarrels with Margerie, illnesses, constant financial worries, and anxieties about work, about a future link with Albert Erskine, and about the protracted silences from England, France, and Hollywood. He was trying to write, but with little success.*

The one story Lowry did work on was 'Elephant and Colosseum,' a comic masterpiece of a long short story, drawing upon his 1948 experiences in Italy. It is significant that this story is his first attempt to create a mother and that the protagonist, Cosnahan, is haunted by his failure to see his mother before she died. His own mother had just died (7 December 1950), and in the aftermath of her death the selling of Inglewood, the settling of the estate, and the disposal of various personal effects had to be arranged. Although the problems of 1951 cannot be explained in some narrow causal manner by Evelyn Lowry's death, her passing, with all that meant for the family home and the past, cast a long, troubling shadow over her youngest son.

434: To Muriel Neilson

P: UBC(ts,ms)   Dollarton, B.C.
                                                        2 January [1951]^a

Dear Muriel:

We were very happy indeed to get your cheery card, which we received Saturday afternoon, so I'm replying by the very first mail thereafter.

There's absolutely nothing we'd both like better than to have you come and spend the week end with us. But could we have a rain check until perhaps the following week? The truth is, I've got a perfectly beastly neuritis in my shoulder I'm nearly paralysed. We had to call off going to the McConnell's, which disappointed us greatly, for New Years, and we can't do a darn thing until I'm feeling better which, God willing, will be soon. So all I can say is the very first moment I know I'm going to be fit company I'll drop you a line, and I hope we can make it next week. There are various buses on Saturday afternoon you could take, and we'll suggest them, and then you'll let us know which is convenient for you so we can meet you at the store, because you'd never find your way down through this wild wet woods by yourself. It's rather rugged out here this time of year, the trail is up to your ankles in mud, and it's none too warm, so put on your long underwear! Now do you, for your part, pray I'll be all right so you can come next week end instead of this week end, if that's all right with you, and I'll write you the very first day I can. And we will be there to welcome you with flags flying and a hearty welcome.

I hope you had a very merry and happy Christmas, and we both wish you and dear Einar the happiest of New Years and all the luck in the world. God bless you both,

                                            Affectionately,

                                                            Margerie,

This looks like the Ultima Thule of unhospitality not to say ungratitude, especially after your never-to-be forgotten hospitality to us: but one villain is the mail – Margie might be able to navigate by Friday or Saturday – but we could scarcely let you know in time – on top of this my mother has just died – & my affairs are considerably at sixes if not at sevens – I would like to have less of a 'heavy heavy hanging over my head'¹ feeling before seeing you for everyone's sake – but all of course this is only to be interpreted as referring to your visit as a pleasure trip – if you too have 'heavy heavy hanging over your head' or that otherwise of urgency which cannot be put off to talk about for Christ's sake of course come anyway – buses leave 1.10, 3.10, 4.10, 5.10 – bring some blankets too

whenever you come, for however we portioned the existing potentialities of warmth you would be likely to freeze – All Best love & God bless
yourself & Einar

Malcolm

– I heartily second this – love Margie

Annotations:

1 The 'heavy heavy hanging over my head' refers to John Malcolm
Brinnin's poem 'Heavy Heavy Heavy' and to the line the Lowrys used
in their screenplay of *Tender Is the Night* (Tiessen/Mota, 128); see
Lowry's 20 May 1950 letter (**399**) to Frank Taylor.

Editorial Notes:

a. The first part of this jointly written letter is a typescript; Lowry's section is in pencil.

435: To Priscilla [Mrs E.B.] Woolfan

P: UBC(ms)
PP: *SL* 187–88

[Dollarton]
[January 1951]ᵃ

My very dear Priscilla:

In addition to thanking you deeply for one third of the gorgeous
McMalcolm which I have already worn with triumphant success &
which lacked for nothing in everything that delights a Scotsman's heart
unless it was the crowning stone of Scone[1] secreted in the breast pocket
– also thank you very much indeed for the French review and please
thank Preston very sincerely for his courtesy & interest in translating it.[2]
– But apart from liking it (as the reviewer says of the book) God what a
gloomy ghoul it makes me sound! Especially when I think that my
ambition was much as the famed Sullivan – to be a humorist.[3] Won't
even Preston think it a bit funny? Just a little bit, I hope, or I shall be
hurt. (Though for that matter I see no reason why he should have to
translate the book, as well as the review.) I am recently in receipt of
some two dozen more French reviews – sent by the publishers – all of
which, so far as I can gather (which is not very much) seem of a quite
fantastic favourableness, (though each one making me seem gloomier
than the last) far more so than the New York ones, & the English one,
and the ½ one in the Skjellerup Schnappstasters Annual, & all of which
are presently lost – just at the moment I had assembled them to send to
you. I had also some months previously marked a very long very intelligent very enthusiastic resumé of Preston's work particularly in relation

to Unfaithfully Yours that was sent to me by my mother & which appeared in the Illustrated London News.[4] Particularly though it was an appreciation of Unfaithfully Yours – a film I missed when abroad unfortunately. I thought Preston probably had so many of such things that he didn't bother to look at them any longer: then I thought Damn it, no – he writes his films too, as well as directs them: perhaps having been glutted with praise upon the directorial swings he could – sentence impossible – escritorial roundabouts – what am I saying? But it is the New Year after all. I meant well but preserved the notice so faithfully that even as mine, I lost it – temporarily I hope. I put things away (or if I don't, Margie does.)

Idea for a humorous situation.

Young man from parts unknown, with obscure ambitions to be a film director who has spent last ten years writing a book about alcohol anxious to impress his wife's family finds himself seated next to the cameraman of The Lost Weekend – which has come out meantime & is playing with enormous success at all the movie houses – while his own book is unpublished & shows every likelihood of remaining so – with a famous film director drinking a tankard of ginger ale at the head of the table – with his wife & his wife's family present, on an occasion that happens to be his 5th wedding anniversary.[5] A limited conversation begins between the cameraman & the Y.M.F.P.U. [Young man from parts unknown], who having just had an operation for varicose veins, is drinking whiskey, doubtless with the object of improving them.

The cameraman. (kindly). And you say you write too, young man?

Y.M.F.P.U.. Yes, sir. I try to.

The cameraman. What about?

Y.M.F.P.U.. Well, as a matter of fact, sir, alcohol.

The C. H'm.

Well God bless you all – we are a bit at sixes and sevens here, my mother having lately died as you know – and news delayed as it always is in Canada, etc. Thank you muchly again for the shirt, & Preston for translating the review. Mad Wednesday hasn't reached here yet, but we'll be right in to see it when it arrives – hope it goes well; of special interest to me because I saw a bit of it being made – and very excellent too –[6]

Best love from your brother

Malcolm

Annotations:

1 The Stone of Scone, used for inaugurating Scottish kings, was taken from Scone Abbey near Perth to Westminster Abbey in 1293. The theft of the Stone on Christmas Day 1950 was much in the news at this time.

2 Preston Sturges (1898-1959), an American film director and writer, and friend of Priscilla Woolfan's, was educated in Europe and, for a time, managed his mother's cosmetic firm in France.

3 Frank Sullivan (1892-1976) was an American newspaper columnist, humorist, and the creator of the character 'Mr Arbuthnot.'

4 *Unfaithfully Yours* (1948), directed and produced by Preston Sturges, is considered his most important film. It depicts a man who plans to murder his wife.

5 This 'idea for a humorous situation' is based upon a dinner Lowry, Margerie and her family had at Preston Sturges's Beverly Hills home on 2 December 1945. On that occasion Lowry may have sat beside John F. Seitz, the photographer for the 1945 film of Charles Jackson's novel *The Lost Weekend*; see Day (309-10).

6 *Mad Wednesday* (1947) was directed and produced by Preston Sturges.

Editorial Notes:

a. This transcription is from the original undated holograph (UBC 2:17). Margerie has dated it incorrectly in *Selected Letters* as January 1950, but Lowry's reference in the last paragraph to his mother's recent death means that he is writing to thank his sister-in-law for her 1950 Christmas present. His comment that 'it is the New Year after all' confirms a January 1951 date.

436: To Anna Mabelle [Mrs John Stuart] Bonner and
    Dr E.B. Woolfan

P: UBC(ms)   [Dollarton]
                                                [January 1951]ª

My very dear mother & Bert
It is a truly wonderful shirt.

Thank you sincerely for this gorgeousness. I also thank you for the words of sympathy about my mother: appendicitis, sudden, & sad.

I hope you all had a very Merry Xmas & I wish you all the best for the New Year. I hope we may all meet again soon.

Bad writing is caused by a writer's blister or callous on my finger – I still write all my things in pencil oldfashionedly – I suppose it would be worse if the callous weren't there, just the same it doesn't make it any easier to write that it is.

The very best of love
                        from
                                                        Malcolm

Editorial Notes:

a. The holograph is undated, but references to his mother's death and to
    Christmas confirm an early January 1951 date.

437: To Downie Kirk

P: UBC(msc)

PP: *SL* 189-90; *MLVD* 58-59   Dollarton

[January 1951]ª

Dear Downie –

This is a letter of thanks to you & Marjorie for a wonderful evening
but also a letter of apology so it is addressed to you alone, since I do not
feel even worthy of addressing your wife at the moment.

My Margerie has impressed me with my bad behaviour but I can't
very well write a letter of apology to her either and as for the behaviour
I can only hope that it does not seem so bad to you as it does to me.

I am also told I used bad language in front of your wife & Dorothy;[1]
this is utterly inexcusable of course – nor is it an excuse when I say that
I would not have done so had I been aware of their prescence. But I was
not so aware & here you must believe me. I am deeply sorry.

That there are reasons for all this – such as that I must have had one
too many phenobarbital (My faithful enemy Phenobarbus – treacherous
to the last)[2] or that I felt myself in some way frustrated – apparently a
nearly total illusion – in my conversation with Les[3] – that I was, or rather
became – and in what a damned mean manner also – borracho, etc are
not proffered as excuses, but are merely set down in an unsuccessful
attempt to make me feel better.

Thank you for coming downtown with us:[4] but even here my selfishness had reached such a pitch that in fact I was trading on your
generosity & disorienting yourself from your own orbit – a mixed
metaphor appropriate to the nature of the potations of the guilty party.

That *jocular* sentence is ill-suited to my mood however, which is
pretty grim. I would say it was totally grim – for I count it a failure in
character if I of all people (because God knows my work should give me
sufficient practice) can't keep my wretched Id in order for five minutes.

All I can say is that I hope your wife & you will forgive me. Though
frankly I see no reason why you should. Nor why, should I say that I
can at least see it won't happen again, I should even be given the opportunity.

For the rest our sincere thanks – I only hope I didn't cast too much
of a shadow.

I would ask you though if you can – since it is the New Year – to put the whole thing out of your minds, hearts, and speech: expunge it as a wretched aberration for which I hope I can make amends.

Sincerely

Malcolm

Annotations:

1 Dorothy is the Kirks' young daughter.
2 Enobarbus, a soldier in Shakespeare's *Antony and Cleopatra*, is faithful to Antony until near the end of the play, when he abandons Antony's army only to die of grief and guilt for deserting his leader.
3 Les is Lesley Kirk, one of Downie's brothers.
4 Downie Kirk must have accompanied Margerie and a drunken Malcolm downtown to catch the bus back to Dollarton.

Editorial Notes:

a. This holograph is undated. *Selected Letters* gives 1950, but 1951 seems more likely in view of Lowry's behaviour during the holiday season.

438: To Philippe Thoby-Marcelin

P: UBC(tsc)

Dollarton, B.C.,
Canada
22 January 1951

Mon cher Phito:

I have now received The Pencil [*The Pencil of God*] (Margie has not been able more than to look at it since she is laid up with laryngitis but she adds her croak of good luck to mine) and what I want to say immediately to you and Pierre is: congratulations and all good wishes for its great success!

Concerning our proposed emendations, all I can say is: that we *meant* well. Also, we went to work as soon as we got the proofs – the regular post takes an awful time even from America to these wildernesses – and we were not to know that you were, meantime, in Haiti.

I had the notion of your being able to get together (over a bottle of rum, I hoped, even if Barbancourt, trois etoiles, were unprocurable) with your translator on the one hand, and another, or others, who knew Haiti, Creole and French and your work, and someone like the good Dawn Powell on the other; that, if there were errors, or possibilities for improvement, that our suggestions pointed to the source of them, and that some happy arbitration would arise out of this happy party I visualized to make what was excellent, if possible, even more excellent.

If the photo of the very attractive girl you sent us is your bride to be it would not seem to me that happiness will be very hard, the more so since you have an intellectual companionship. In any event, we drink to your happiness, however it may come about, and to hers, she of the photograph, or if it is not she of the photograph, whoever or wherever she may be.[1]

Re the French version of the Volcano the only reason I haven't sent it you is that the first edition with your name wrong in it is in morocco (Margie says it is definitely *not* morocco) the one with your name right – of which I have only received one copy – in paper: I was promised, as soon as it appeared, the corrected version in morocco and for this I am still waiting; even should the corrected version in morocco never come out, I shall be ashamed to send you the paper version, though I shall send it just the same in a month or so, if the other doesn't arrive – at which point of course the one in morocco will of course ironically come out too: perhaps it is not morocco (only board) but it looks as if it were compared with the other:[2] I truly apologise for this, not the less so because it is their mistake, and I can only ask you to laugh at it (though it was not funny to me) until it is corrected.

Re the translation again, it is unfortunate our words, due to force majeure, arrived late; we had to work in such a hurry we had little time to think of the translator's feelings – we were just thinking of the book. We did not imagine the translator receiving the emendations en bloc from yourself at a point remote from you: and if this has made Mr Thomas angry or hurt his feelings in any way please convey our sincere apologies to him (as also to yourself, if it has given rise to any difficulties)[3] Seeing the Pencil in final book form, it wears of course an air of final authority and we hope that the objections we raised are not such as to intimidate in its reception more than a few purists. On certain points of course we may have been wrong but our hope was merely to raise some arbitration at your end where your translator might agree, for example, that something good might be still better. I still feel that certain of the objections may be valid and are worth, at least, your attention – that is in the same sense of friendly arbitration and susceptible to third or fourth opinions by others – say, in regard to the English edition or later and more final editions.

Occasionally we allowed our own personal dramas into the machinery of our notes; this couldn't be helped but may well bewilder anyone else reading them cold – but while they were objective notes, so intensely were we working it was difficult to separate from them the mood of 'subjective' letter to yourself.

As it stands, however, I think it must be admitted the translation has very high merits of its own, a statement which I feel I owe to Mr

Thomas, and in one way is by far the best you have yet received (albeit I still suspect the excellent Mr Wilson of only having read it in French – even if that was impossible) – anyhow, may it prosper! I would review it here in Canada if I could find a paper that was not illiterate, did not review only children's books, and had the faintest influence: probably the Canadian publication will follow the American by some months, however – intelligent people do live here, I am told: the trouble is they are not very intelligent. But if I can help, I shall.

Thank you very much for your heartwarming New Year's card, and give our best love to yourself and your brothers from Margie and myself.

Ton frère

Malc

Annotations:

1 Philippe and Eva Thoby-Marcelin were married in November 1951.
2 In bookbinding the term 'morocco' refers to the genuine leather covers on fine books. The 1950 Corrêa edition of *Au-dessous du volcan* is bound in cheap yellow paper and is far less handsome than a standard hardback binding.
3 Leonard Thomas was the translator of *Le Crayon de dieu*, but neither the Lowrys' suggested improvements (see letter **421**) nor Thomas's response appears to have survived.

439: To Derek Pethick

P: UBC(tsc)   Dollarton, B.C.
                                                                     24 January 1951

My dear Pethick:

I was very pleased to get your letter, with your good news; our radio being still caput I am writing to [Andrew] Allan for a copy of your radio addresses, the excellent reception of which, taking all our correspondence into account since your first letter arrived (on the morning last February that I was attending the mystical original-of-the-Consul's funeral)[1] reads like a refreshing happy ending, or beginning, in an era of so many bogus unhappy ones.

I look forward to our seeing each other and you mention that might be possible toward the end of this month. This would be grand with us, if we have received some news we expect to any day; as you must know by now, a Canadian writer's ordeal is to live with Mercury eternally in retrograde (which is no doubt better than Baudelaire, who had to live with Mercury altogether). Meantime we have to hack hemlock out of the blizzard to keep ourselves warm. But toward the very end of the month we should not be so dependent on the hemlock, which is where I close, else Socrates come into the next bracket.[2] At all events let us know what is a good time for you, in terms of this month from our standpoint I think later rather than sooner – but let us try all to arrange a get-together sooner rather than later in the more general sense anyhow.

Cheerio

[Malcolm Lowry]

P.S. The Volcano is quite a fabulous critical success in France where they have invoked everybody from Flaubert's whiskers to Villon concerning it; even in – shades of one's early reading of De Maupassant – in the Figaro.[3] I have some ideas re a larger thing in which to incorporate it of which I would be very glad of your advice.

P.P.S. I note that since beginning this it *is* very nearly the end of the month, and our ship has not yet been bespoken over the horizon. Perhaps it will be today. We will let you know as soon as it does. In bad weather, which is now, our life here resembles a bit the movie of the Fall of the House of Usher combined with the lower reaches of Crabbe;[4] save that we get a lot more fun out of it. Just the same, my wife doesn't want you to freeze to death and we'd like to have the pemmican, the dried reindeer skins and the oxygen tent out of hock, so to speak, before we could get together with free and easy minds. She joins me in saying we sincerely look forward to seeing you.

I've just read your radio addresses again; they are very good indeed, and you've excellently and consistently marshalled your facts.[5] My only criticisms are that in my opinion A Farewell to Arms is an incomparable better book than The Sun Also Rises, which seems a stagnant, pointless and immoral tale today for all its interest in a historic perspective. What seems frightening to me is the influence it had on people remote. I can't help feeling I'd have liked Hemingway better if he'd been a rather unpopular writer. I don't think I agree with any current estimations of him, though, unfavourable or otherwise. In Phoenix is to be found an appreciative and interesting review by Lawrence of Hemingway.[6] (Which reminds me that Dahlberg is surely a significant writer worthy to be included in your thesis – ghastly though he is?)[7] And I don't think it quite fair even making allowances for your time, to evaluate Fitzgerald with no mention of Tender Is the Night. (Not to say The Crack-Up – though it's true that Gatsby is the only work that made port as a whole work of art.

[ML]

Annotations:

1 The 'mystical' original of Geoffrey Firmin was Lowry's Cabbalist friend Charles Stansfeld-Jones, who died on 24 February 1950. Lowry attended the funeral; see his 1 March 1950 letter (**389**) to Clarisse Francillon and his letters (**179, 190**) to 'Stan'.

2 The Greek philosopher Socrates (?-399 BC) was tried and convicted of impiety. The penalty was death, and Socrates was given hemlock to drink.

3 Lowry was flattered by these comparisons with Gustave Flaubert and François Villon; he reiterates the Villon parallel in his June 1953 letter (**579**) to Albert Erskine. Lowry had discovered Guy de Maupassant (1850-93), the French novelist and short story writer, in his youth, but the connection with the newspaper *Le Figaro* is unclear.

4 In 1928 Jean Epstein and Luis Buñuel co-directed a film version of Edgar Allan Poe's story 'The Fall of the House of Usher.' The film has some stunning storm effects. The link with English cleric and poet George Crabbe could be to 'Inebriety,' a poem about the excesses of drinking that Lowry knew well, or to 'Peter Grimes' (1810), with its stormy sea and tormented hero.

5 According to Pethick's note on the transcription of this letter, he gave CBC talks on American writers F. Scott Fitzgerald, Ernest Hemingway, John Dos Passos, William Faulkner, and Thomas Wolfe during 1950.

6 *Phoenix: The Posthumous Papers of D.H. Lawrence*, edited by Edward D. McDonald, was published in 1936. It contains Lawrence's reviews of literature and art, one of which is his review of Hemingway's *In Our Time* (1925).

7 Edward Dahlberg (1900-77) was an American writer; D.H. Lawrence wrote an introduction for his first novel, *Bottom Dogs* (London: Putnam, 1929).

440: To Frank Taylor

P: Lilly(ts); Matson(tsc)   Dollarton, B.C., Canada
                                              27 January 1951

Dear Frank:

Wie gehts?

Tell us your news. There is not much from here. Margerie has written two serious stories, and I, two humorous ones.

Albert does not write. Give him our love. It is raining. The cat has peed behind the arm-chair. This morning we saw a duck called a buffle head.

We note that Fitzgerald appears to be in the news and thought as from afar off that might be an omen of something or other.[1]

Did you really write a book called Black Bonanza?[2] We once had a book shop but it seems to have moved away somewhere so that we have fallen out of touch, – (though just to keep up with the times we went to see the Battleship Potempkin and the Fall of the House of Usher in the auditorium of a consumptive's home, but departed without catching anything.)[3]

Clyde Gilmour, our local film critic, who comprises it seems the whole of the Canadian intelligentsia, never fails from time to time to bring up Mystery Street as one of the best who-dun-its ever, in which we are with him.[4]

The Volcano continues to get excellent reviews in France, a fact which produces a somewhat complex and distant emotion, the more so since it has not yet been productive of any francs.

I remark however that some characters in current fiction have taken to wearing dark glasses and have acquired limps: in fact my eye fell on one just now, where I read: 'And the sun, inimical (he had forgotten his dark glasses, of course) . . . With his reverie, his limp had grown more exaggerated.'

H'm. And that, I think, is about all. We keep very fit, apart from colds, sulfanilamide, etc. We were invited out for Christmas and had some turkey with carrots and gin. Somebody came in with a bottle of whiskey but they sent him away. Margerie found a dime in her carrots, though whether the carrots were on fire or not I have forgotten. My recollection is they were smouldering a bit.

And that is about all. So please tell us something or other.

With best love to yourself, Nan, and the children from Margie and myself

Malcolm

P.S. Give our love to Christopher Isherwood.

P.P.S. How like a man, is Man, who rises late,
And gazes on his unwashed dinner plate
And gazes at the bottles, empty too,
All gulped in last night's loud long how-do-you-do
(Although one glass yet holds a gruesome bait)
How like is Man to this man, and his fate,
– Still drunk, and stumbling through the rusty trees
To breakfast on stale rum, sardines, and peas...[5]

Annotations:

1 This is probably a reference to the publication of Arthur Mizener's biography of Fitzgerald, *The Far Side of Paradise* (1951).
2 The answer is no. Frank F. Taylor co-wrote *Black Bonanza* with Earl M. Welty in 1950. Lowry's friend is Frank E. Taylor.

3 Sergei Eisenstein's *Battleship Potemkin* (1925) is a silent film classic, as is Jean Epstein's *Fall of the House of Usher* (1928). During the forties and early fifties the Lowrys regularly attended film screenings organized by Vernon van Sickle; see Lowry's 15 October 1946 letter (**251**) to Gerald Noxon.

4 Clyde Gilmour (1912–), a Canadian broadcaster and journalist, was movie critic for the *Vancouver Sun* during the early fifties; *Mystery Street* (1950) was one of the more successful films Taylor produced during his years in Hollywood.

5 See 'Eye-Opener' (Scherf, 176).

441: To Harold Matson

P: Matson(ts); UBC(phc)

Dollarton, B.C.,
Canada
30 January 1951

Dear Hal:

If you remember you said last December you had no objection to sending the $150 for the German translation when it arrived, though you added it would scarcely be before the 1st of the year.

If this has not already arrived and you have sent it, have you any way of chivvying them up because on its expectation we are in this interim practically dependent for something to eat?

Since I last wrote you my mother has died in England.[1] Many legal and interfamilial details have arisen from this grief as a consequence of which I've been a bit set back in my schedule for work. And while I gather that my own financial situation will considerably improve, or even has improved, contact is not made any easier by the fact that its source in this regard, Liverpool, is in the grip of a first class and death-dealing epidemic of flu.

Meantime we have to keep alive how we can from day to day, the exigencies of which does not make writing any simpler either, though work has been carried on steadily to the point where pretty soon, other things being equal, the dam will break and it will start getting through.

Best from us both,

Malcolm

Annotations:

1 Evelyn Lowry died intestate, but according to Russell Lowry (Bradbrook 158), Arthur Lowry left his estate to his widow for life and then to his sons, with Malcolm's share held in trust. See Lowry's June 1945 letter (**204**) to the Westminster Bank and his October 1950 letter (**426**) to Stuart Lowry.

442: To Frank Taylor

P: Lilly(ts); Matson(tsc)
Dollarton, B.C.
Canada
6 February 1951

Dear Frank:

Wonderful to hear from you and we are delighted you are at Twentieth Century Fox and happy there. My imagination has entitled me to enter vicariously into the ungrateful interim of time for you prior to your departure thither, the higher significance of which your Mr William James has perhaps better – than Mr Kipling in his If – somewhere brilliantly and comfortingly excogitated.[1] (Here lies Mr Lowry, born in the Bowery, his style was flowery, but could be sprightly, he lived nightly, and sometimes daily, and died, playing the ukelele.)[2]

We have not had such a ferocious winter as last, quite mild indeed till three weeks ago, since when we have had everything your ancestors did, save for the prairie schooner. It is quite impossible, so extreme is the life we lead, in its ghastliness wonder absolute sordidity and extreme magic, to give you any indication of it and even should you come up here, as we hope you sometime will, in a good season, it might be hard for you to deduce what it is like. Even the people who live here do not know. (But a little elsewhere a starving cougar sprang through a window, not open either, glass and all, into one of these houses. 'He was eating my elbow before he got to the ground. So I gave it him to eat, while I pushed him along the floor to the stove etc etc . . . Somehow I got the kitchen knife, and while he worked away on my elbow, I sawed at his throat. Afterwards I rowed six miles in my underdrawers . . . I didn't like to think of the poor beast still suffering and I had no ammunition. Besides I was afraid the house might burn down in my absence. But I was glad of the bounty, for the mountain lion. Twenty smackers.')[3]

We are naturally incredibly excited and made anxious by what you say. I hope and pray Mr Mankiewicz may go on being aroused. As Jay Leyda also informed me, by an error at one point I seemed to mix up the two Mankiewicz.[4] I hope this mistake does not annoy him and ask that it may be overlooked. I pray also he may overlook any possible tangential pretentiousness in the film, and see the real possibilities that are there. He is, in my opinion, a genius. But I feel much the same of John Huston: yet could almost hear him, so I imagined, being impatient with the film.

Re Mizener;[5] I forefelt something of that sort would be in the public eye – even before I read, concurrently with our writing, one or two of the Mizener excerpts. A certain object appeared, naked of jealousy, self-thought or gain, I hope, coming from a certain gratitude, nor having any precise desire to outwit the other, that related simply to the portrayal of a work of genius by a great American author being portrayed greatly – how often has this been done? how often the world, in terms of movie, seen? Not that Mizener might leave any doubt as to Fitzgerald's general significance, whatever one's moral attitude towards that portrayal, or the portrait not well and painstakingly done, but that the Night, pushed off symbolically from Fitzgerald himself in the film as in the novel, might serve as a sort of biography too, or rather a super-biography, clear as drama, but pertaining subtly and more roundly within its inner scheme also to Fitzgerald's creative significance to America and to the world, and to the answer he made to his ordeal (heroic in my estimation – I see that Delmore Schwartz in the current Partisan Review agrees, even to bringing in Medusa as we did)[6] making the direct biography as screened with what injury it might do by that time to the dead or hurt to the living unnecessary. Nor is this point of view something wholly to be excluded from a business or practical attitude. The dead have their ways of objecting – as why should they not?

(In another respect, apart from personal considerations as between yourself and ourselves, the film might have been called forth by some of Joe Mankiewicz' own brilliant remarks at the film conference, which is why I live in some fear and trembling that he may not like it, praying he may make allowance for any peripheral pretentiousness and non-professional digressions, and that these may not put him off from what we feel unmistakeably to be *there*.)

And to recapitulate the former theme, having a deep respect and reverence not merely for Fitzgerald but for the fact Zelda and he did after all deeply love each other (something is to be gained from Mizener, certainly not to be gained in the write-up in Life etc. – and how grossly sentimentalised and obscenely and doubly crossed it might become even with the best of motives one can readily see) it struck me as more in accordance – since it was to be a film and hence directly applicable to an aspect of Fitzgerald's most honest ambitions – the film of Tender is the Night, that is – with his own destiny, (if not to be supraironic at the more than last) as also with his own reticence and sense of decency. (We are old-fashioned enough to wish the Fitzgeralds happy where they are *now* and believe in extending chivalry to the dead.)

This is an argument perhaps worth presenting to the excellent Mr Wayne,[7] in regard to which I might further say, if you or he are interested in dopplegangers[8] or destiny or the usages of the cryptic, that the descendance of Dick Diver from a certain Mr Wayne in Tender is the Night – Antony Wayne – was something we thought worth while insisting upon to a point rather beyond that to which Fitzgerald brought it: he mentions Wayne once only, in the conversation with Baby: ourselves 4 or 5 times – including the graveyard scene in Virginia and the prison scene with Baby in Rome. As for Judy Garland – immediately upon having finished what you to our delight term The Monument we went to see a revival here of Fleming's Wizard of Oz[9] whereupon, having reenjoyed the said masterpiece, I remarked to Margie – in complete concord, as you see, with Nan, if not in the same words: Jeez, that is Nicole. . . She absolutely is, must be, Nicole It was not long after that she, Judy, had her little contretemps, whatever it was. But more than ever, we have felt that; so what you say, from Nan, is strange.

I hope you can put up with these daydreams. Perhaps they are not exactly daydreams. (Talking of which, however, I have just been forwarded no less than fifteen French reviews of the Volcano, each pages long, of such all but fabulous praise – including the Figaro – that I would have to become a philosopher as intricately rooted as Sartre in order to understand them, and receive the Legion of the Holy Great Cow like the man at the end of Bovary,[10] if they can really be intended to mean what they say.)

Best love to yourself, Nan and the children from us both –

Malcolm

Annotations:

1 After leaving MGM, Taylor moved to Twentieth Century-Fox at the beginning of 1951. Lowry often refers to William James, the American philosopher, whose work he particularly enjoyed. Rudyard Kipling praises patience and good sense as the signs of maturity in his poem 'If' from *Rewards and Fairies* (1910).

2 This is a version of the last seven lines of Lowry's poem 'Epitaph' (Scherf, 174).

3 Lowry uses this anecdote in part VI of 'Forest Path to the Spring.'

4 In his 4 June 1950 letter to Lowry praising the screenplay of *Tender Is the Night*, Jay Leyda reminds Lowry not to 'mix up the 2 Mankiewiczes.' Herman J. Mankiewicz (1897-1953), the journalist and screen-writer, was the older brother of the film producer Joseph L. Mankiewicz.

5 Lowry is referring to Arthur Mizener's biography of Fitzgerald, but since the incoming letter from Taylor is not extant, Lowry's point is unclear.

6 Delmore Schwartz (1913-66), American writer and editor, describes Fitzgerald as a tragic hero who looked at the monstrous Medusa of his age in 'The Grapes of Crisis,' *Partisan Review* 18.1 (1951): 15.

7 In his 31 January 1951 letter (UBC 1:66) to Lowry, Taylor suggested that the American actor David Wayne (1914-) would be excellent in the role of Dick Diver who tells his sister-in-law that he is descended from 'Mad Anthony Wayne.' Anthony Wayne (1745-96), an American

soldier from Pennsylvania, earned the nickname 'Mad Anthony' for his
courage and recklessness.

8 Lowry frequently misspells *Doppelgänger*.

9 The American actress Judy Garland (1922-69) played Dorothy in *The
Wizard of Oz* (1939). Nan Taylor may have felt Garland would be
excellent as Nicole because her own life was tragic.

10 Gustave Flaubert's novel *Madame Bovary* (1856-57) ends with the deaths
of Emma and Charles Bovary; only the conniving apothecary, M.
Hommais, survives, and he is awarded the 'croix d'honneur.'

443: To Albert Erskine

P: Virginia(ts); UBC(phc)   Dollarton, B.C.,
PP: *SL* 227-31   Canada
                                                        13 February 1951

My dear Albert:

I hate to break a long silence in this way but can you somehow lend
us $200 immediately? (I was always taught to begin a short story like
this.)

Since the answer to this, the world being what it is at the moment,
must be 'no,' your having said no and damned my importunity for asking, could you read what follows, see how it differs from such usual
requests in terms of security, and see whether on the strength of that you
can, even if you can't? We have nowhere else to turn, all possible
avenues are explored or non-existent, and our condition having passed
the stage of mere desperation, the plea itself turns moral. So far, not so
good.

Here is the situation. We have been working hard – but without any
material success, slowly using up our capital until for the last six months
we've been obliged to live on our income, reduced, since the devaluation of the pound and the freeing of the Canadian dollar to about $95 a
month.

We've had latterly to waste the effort we would otherwise put into
writing simply to keep alive but little by little we've begun to go under.
Margie is sick and is in almost constant pain: she has some sort of growth
that is affecting her teeth, but it has been impossible to determine what
kind, and now I can't even pay for the X-rays so she can't get any more.
This is a callous and barbarous country in many ways. The store is on
the point of stopping our further credit for food, and every day we face
eviction from the house we built. Despite that $95 not Maxim Gorky
himself could dream up any worse privations than we, and especially
she, have had to suffer this winter, though I myself am physically O.K.

But there is a point beyond which even William James' kind of voluntary poverty leads to despair.[1] This is when it becomes involuntary. On the other hand we have been owed, for many months, $150 on the German translation of the Volcano which Hal will send the moment it comes through. The contract for this was signed last fall and on the daily expectation of this we have been living from day to day – though we have another expectation of a certain and legal nature I shall come to. But only yesterday we get the usual letter from Hal of rejection of our stories and postponement of the payment of the German advance (another one, signed for $750 fell through altogether.)

Hal has been good enough to say that he'll send it through, despite the fact we already owe him $250 on the expectation of stories that either haven't sold or that we have been in too much misery or anxiety to write, so we could not ask him for more.

The other expectation is due to a grief. Last December 6th my mother died suddenly on her birthday, I had previously appealed to my eldest brother [Stuart Lowry] to do what he could, outlining our position and my anxiety about Margerie – Christ, even then! – because the Government had not been letting out all the money, it seemed, that I was legally entitled to even under the terms of their own stringencies, his reply – including the news of my mother's death – was that my financial position was very considerably improved and he as the chief executor of the estate was now in a position to help immediately.[2] Other things being equal, I would now be quite rich in fact, but even as things stood my income would be sufficient to live on here. I understood him to say that under the circumstances he would be able to get some money through immediately before the will was probated but instead silence closed down – a silence due, so far as I can see, to the fact that my family and solicitors are in the centre of the flu area in Liverpool where there have been a ghastly number of deaths – far more than they said in the paper. (Doubtless because of the coming Festival of Britain – do not let a little plague put you off, my dear American cousins, if you'll only supply the dollars, we've got in addition to wigs some nice gravestones all supplied by the Government.)

So this is something else we also have to tell the store keeper who is also unfortunately the postmaster. Nonetheless, however inhibited by the Government or flu, something is bound to come through from this direction soon.

For the rest, I have tried to write an advertisement for banks – and so on and so forth – all with complete unsuccess, and all in a vicious circle, as you see.[3] Now we haven't the peace of mind even to get the stories off. (We did that other long work also, of which we still can't speak; hope for that went up like a rocket the other week, one can't count on more than the Bergsonian ashes in one's face this week, though perhaps it'll be different next.)

Hal says that possibly he could get some kind of advance from Reynal-Brace on another novel – if I could give them a time limit – but I'm not going to do that because if humanly possible, if you still want me, I want desperately to hang on to you as a publisher. This is an extraneous problem to the present one, or it would look like moral blackmail on my part – and I'd hoped and would like to discuss it separately, for it is all-important to me. The only thing I've said about the novel so far, you said, was smug, and I guess it was. But I have unsmugly worked out an unsmug project in my mind which, if of huge proportions, would more than live up to your expectations of me, if only I can find a chance to begin to execute it.[4] Because of the accident of the fire coming so close to the acceptance of the Volcano and destroying so much work I haven't been able to get it or recreate it in proper perspective until now: and what happened in Mexico at the time U.T.V. was accepted is an important part too, that was hard to get in focus until now. Now in addition to being an orphan, with you at another publishers I feel excommunicated too.

– Can you tell me as much of your plans as you feel I might know? I don't want to give you any feeling of responsibility, or imply a psychological dependence on my side, distressing to yourself, but if by some legerdemain I became transferred to Random House and then you decided to leave, I'd be in the same position as now. I don't think I can be blamed for wanting to grapple myself with hoops of steel to you as a publisher irrespective of the mutations of publishers and your own plans etc.[5] Well, I trust you will see the sincere thing I sincerely mean.

Re the projected novel, I will allow myself my one smugness in asserting that it should continue to pay you dividends long after I am dead (it includes the Volcano) – or I feel it certainly could be of this calibre, with your sympathetic Eye hovering near, unless I know nothing of literature at all.[6] (Margie was doing excellent work likewise till she had to stop temporarily.)

But to get back to the loan I asked you for. This would enable me to pay for the X-rays, and get some more, and put off the grocer with a reasonable expectation of the money from England having arrived before our next crisis falls due. Also it should enable us to get some more stories in the mail, and try and get my mind clear about the novel in terms of a presentation of it to yourself. I won't use the argument that I hope you'll be publishing some of these stories some day – though of course I hope this is true: some are sort of fragments of novel.

I had originally intended to ask you for $150 on the basis that Hal would pay you back when the German money arrived, which it should

any day. I think I've explained why I've no right to expect Hal to do
that, even though he might stretch a point and do it. But the absolute
desperation of our situation it is very difficult to make clear, that without some money, one can't work to pay it back. But this $150 from Hal
to ourselves is promised as *absolutely certain*, and what we could do is
immediately we received it here, to pay it back to you. This would leave
us $50 in your debt which $50 together with our $95 would give us a
little margin until the other English money got through. When that got
through we could pay you back the $50. Thus we ought not to be in
your debt more than two or three weeks on the $150, and maybe no
more than a month on the whole $200 – shortly thereafter which Hal
himself can be paid in kind. (We have ½ a dozen other stories coming
up.)

But our whole problem is *time*. This agonizing business of Margie's
won't wait, even if its outcome, as one hopes, proves simple. The storekeeper won't wait. Perhaps they won't even wait to evict us. Only
England waits, while we brug around in ever wearier circles. And so I
have written to you to ask you if you can help – according to the pro-
visos above concerning repayment. I shall not be able to express our
gratitude if you can.

All the best to Peggy and yourself from us both. God Bless.

                                                                    Malcolm

P.S. I send some French clippings – a new batch – there are about a hundred others, all very long, very intricate, & all of a vast enthusiasm. I was
getting the more interesting ones translated for you and will send them
on – all in all, the Volcano's had a better press, if possible, in Paris, than
in New York – though the latter is no doubt partly due to the former.
But I have yet to make a centime on all this. And its repercussions have,
so far as I can see, been nil. The sales in Canada have been 2 copies –
apart from some sold by the flying start you gave it in New York, my
sole recognition here an unfavorable squib in the Vancouver Sun.[7] I
don't think Reynal exactly kept his promise to have it distributed in
Canada after you left: there may have been a reason for this, & Canadian
publication not a factor, but I am looking for an 'out.' It certainly was a
factor with Cape.

[P.P.S.] Margie wants these reviews back when you are through & will
you forgive me having written the letter?

Annotations:

   1 In 'The Value of Saintliness,' from *The Varieties of Religious Experience*,
     one of Lowry's favourite books, James extols the virtues of poverty,
     especially voluntary poverty.

2 Evelyn Lowry died on 7 December, not 6, and Lowry's family and biographers cannot confirm her birthday. Stuart Lowry's letter telling Malcolm of her death and of his financial situation has not survived; see Lowry's May 1951 letter (**457**) to Stuart.

3 The only Lowry correspondence about writing for a bank that I have discovered is Lowry's 30 August 1950 and 20 September 1950 draft letters (**413** and **417**) to Evan Morton.

4 Lowry is thinking of *The Voyage That Never Ends*. By 1951 he was drawing up his thirty-five-page 'Work in Progress' statement with a revised sequence of works for the *Voyage*; see my discussion of the plan, pp. 2–3.

5 Lowry is paraphrasing one of Polonius's 'precepts' in his advice to his departing son Laertes: 'The friends thou hast, and their adoption tried, / Grapple them to thy soul with hoops of steel,' *Hamlet* I.iii. 62–63.

6 *Dark as the Grave* 'includes the Volcano' in the sense that the author of *The Valley of the Shadow of Death* (Lowry and *Volcano*) is in Mexico with his manuscript.

7 Vancouver newspaper reviews of *Under the Volcano* in 1947 were either favourable or irrelevant. Dorothy Livesay's review in the *Vancouver Province*, 16 August 1947, p. 4, is intelligent and positive, while Toddie Beattie's piece, 'He Doesn't Like Who-Dunits But He Thinks Mine are Good,' the *Vancouver Sun*, 17 April 1947, p. 13, is about Margerie's writing and only mentions Lowry as the famous author of the best-seller *Under the Volcano*. The *Sun's* 1 August 1947 article, 'Wealthy Squatters Find Rent-Free Beach Haven,' is about the Lowrys' life-style, not their work. Perhaps Lowry is thinking of William Arthur Deacon's critical and suspicious review in Toronto's *Globe and Mail*, 22 March 1947, p. 22.

444: To Albert Erskine

P: Virginia(ts); UBC(phc)   Dollarton, B.C.,
                                                                          Canada
                                                          23 February 1951

Dear Albert:

Thank you enormously for your most understanding letter, received just after my sending our letter of acknowledgement and thanks.[1] Yes, it was the anniversary of the Volcano. – No, the way you sent the money was superb in every way, for while it's true the storekeeper was both the creditor – or one of them – and the postmaster, the message was phoned in by the telegraph company in Vancouver, and simply stated that an unspecified sum of money was awaiting us, which is all the information they are allowed to give here until the addressee identifies himself. So your choice of means couldn't have been better, or as it happens, more providential, or your kind consideration deeper, and the storekeeper-postmaster, since he was going to get some of the money anyway, was only pleased;[2] we'd been assuring him since January first that some money was coming, as it should indeed have come.

Re Margerie: the situation is still complicated and anxious. As a last resort, because they couldn't find out what was wrong here yet, we communicated her symptoms to her brother-in-law in Los Angeles who is a surgeon, and he is tyring to find out through his colleagues in Seattle if there is a reputable oral surgeon here in Vancouver. The medical situation here is absolutely shocking and without parallel I think in any other country, however backward, or we should not be in the position we are. There are perhaps fairly good individual doctors – our first one was a dope fiend who made a fortune in radar and retired, and our second one, a disbarred dentist whom I found tight on the floor with his wife on the day I got the proofs of the Volcano when Margie got a serious tummy ache and who tripped over his stethescope in the forest and finally had to be given first aid by ourselves. He was a good egg and is now the captain of a tug-boat. Normally all doctors refuse to visit you in outlying districts like this even if a matter of life and death. Seriously there are one or two good doctors, in their own field, or for something uncomplicated, among them, as you rightly say, was the one who admitted his ignorance. But what is barbarous are the piratic customs which frustrate and inhibit treatment, even in serious cases. Especially our hospital insurance, for which you are forced to pay or go to jail, and which is shocking: the other day a man was brought in after an accident, x-rayed, and told to get out and go home – that he was O.K. The next day he died of a broken neck. But he was lucky to have got even the x-rays, which are not coverable by insurance. (In our case *because* we had to pay the hospital insurance we were unable to obtain the x-rays, a monstrous thing in a crisis. And Canadians are callous in the big way. They still use the lash in Vancouver.)[3] It is Chapter VIII all over again. But I hope not – I am sure not as bad as that in this case. Margie's brother-in-law suspects a non-serious growth of some kind which he says would be 'curable,' but meantime she has to suffer or take codeine. Which is bloody for her. But thanks to yourself the whole situation is much less bloody than it was.

I meant naught of an injured mien about smug – your remark did not miss fire, nor did I fail to imagine the tone of voice and the grin. But what I meant was, however I wrote *about* what I wrote, *what* I wrote was, probably, smug – after all – an opinion arrived at independently in accidental congruence. Though in every way I hope capable of being eventually desmugged, triumphantly so, he added smugly.

I'm naturally incredibly excited at the possibility of being able to have you after all as an editor; I honestly believe that the reason I haven't got further on with the novel is that I felt too uneasy without you: it must be obvious by now that I'm not going to write anything for Reynal Harcourt Brace, yet I have never in my life felt or been more creative. When my mind is a bit clearer I'll write to Hal about this, as you say I should, though he knows how I feel from other letters. But then if you and he could put your heads together and figure out what I should do, I'll do it. But the problem of producing a finished book to disagree about is a pretty problem when the problem is to solve the problems of being able to find the time and peace of mind to begin to produce for you the problem of an unfinished book to agree about. Though this does not mean I have not been working, and at that hard. But this whole thing is immensely intricate and I want to discuss it at length with you, though I can't do this till I have heard from England and we see otherwise how and where we are. We still have not heard up to this writing.

It's marvellously good of you to tell us we could wait until then and we have enough to pay you back: we have no certain way of knowing which carrier pigeon will reach us first, or what the message round its leg. But that we shall be in a better position not far off there seems little reason to doubt and we shall repay you as to the money: as to the deed, and the thoughtful generosity thereof, it would be hard to think how one could ever repay that.

Margie joins me in sending heartfelt thanks again. (My original letter of grateful acknowledgement was written on the back of a laundry list on which was printed 'This parcel is short,' and was considerably less formal as to style but I felt it wasn't the proper way to acknowledge it just the same, then afterwards I felt you would have preferred the laundry list after all.)

Well God bless you and love to Peggy and yourself from us both.

Malcolm

Annotations:

1 There is a gap in the incoming correspondence from Erskine between 21 December 1951 and 7 March 1952, and the letter that Lowry refers to here does not appear to have survived.
2 The storekeeper and postmaster in Dollarton at this time was Percy Cummins. Cummins and his wife, Ethel, were on good terms with the Lowrys until June 1953, when Lowry broke his leg and Margerie was bitten by the Cummins' dog; see Lowry's July 1953 letter (**584**) to Albert Erskine.
3 In 1949 the provincial legislature of British Columbia passed a Hospital Insurance Act that made hospital insurance compulsory. However, X-rays were only covered by this insurance if a patient was hospitalized; as an 'out-patient,' Margerie had to pay. Lowry is correct about the use of the lash in British Columbia prisons until at least 1952.

445: To Downie Kirk

P: UBC(msc)
PP: *Prairie Schooner* 37;
   SL 233–34; *Brief* 19

[Dollarton]
[March 1951][a]

Dear old Downey:

Thank you very much indeed for your letter. It made me feel a whole lot better. And no sooner had we got your interesting book home about the avalanche and the [word illegible] villagers are digging themselves out than we read in the papers about a similar avalanche in nearly the same place burying them again.[1] Meantime we were digging ourselves out of *our* avalanche. And so it goes. I have received this enclosed letter & can understand scarcely a word, not even if it is bawling me out or not.[2] But it obviously pertains to the German translation (this is the one that will be dedicated to you) & it looks as though I better answer it. What I seem vaguely to gather is that it is from the translator himself who begins by being friendly, goes on into the difficulties of the translation, and ends by asking some questions about the obscenities on the menu in X. He also asks me to elucidate something connected with Mexican land reform & a technical matter in the dialogue in Chapter II. Is this roughly right or does he want to transpose a couple of chapters or something? And how am I to answer about the obscenities if the translator is a woman! I'd be enormously obliged if you'd tell me if the letter requires my immediate attention and if so, when you have time, give me the drift of it. I'm going to reply in English because even if I could reply in German I could scarcely elucidate a point in German that depends upon mistakes being made in English by a Tlaxcaltecan translating from a misprinted menu in Spanish and French. What a wonderful word is Daseinsaussage! Is this a technico-architechtonic term or may one order Dasein saussage, from a menu too, mit zwei eier und Kartoffelnsalat und ein Stiefel Münchener? Or is perhaps Daseinsaussage his translation of my boudin – a kind of cousin to blutworst? I know you will be pressed for time, so don't put yourself out; I think you ought to charge me a fee for these questions I keep firing at you. Still I feel the German translation is almost a family matter. How goes the school? It seemed to me you had that situation finely licked & I am very glad. Has Master Fury brought the Jemmy of my uncle? No. Master Fury is in the garden studying. What is Master Fury studying? Master Fury is studying how to become a Mercy. Yes, Rousseau had some children & the dog put them all in an orphanage.[3] Would you, when you have a moment, send back the French reviews – don't bother at all about translating any part of them now, I know you haven't time,

but my sister-in-law wants to see them, & anyway I can let you have
them back; if it comes to that I have some more, from the existentialist press! I'm tickled to death to be thought a master-existentialist: it
seems only the other day I was asking you what Existentialism was. I
see we have a repertory theatre: that is a bright sign. It is also a Bright
day & all in all one feels bright. I'm still hanging on to your Tellers
of Tales unless you want it returned immediately. I'm trying to learn
more economy of style. The Avalanche book is very good, though
not in the way they say on the cover. Sapphira I have not had time to
read yet.[4] Say if you want these posted back. And don't forget the
Daseinsaussage . . . Sorry to trouble you. All the best love to Marjorie
& Dorothy

Mit freundlicher Begrüssung

Malcolm von Lowry

Annotations:

1 *When the Mountain Fell* (1947; *Derborence*, 1935), by Charles-Ferdinand
   Ramuz (1878-1947), is a historical novel about a man who survived an
   avalanche in the Swiss Alps; see Lowry's comment in his 20 March 1951
   letter (**447**) to Kirk. Several avalanches were reported in the Alps during
   January and February 1951.
2 In his 5 February 1951 letter to Lowry, Clemens ten Holder asked
   Lowry for help with several translation details pertaining to *Under the
   Volcano*, including the menu in chapter 10. As Lowry goes on to note,
   ten Holder comments upon poetic *Dasseinsbedeutung und Dasseinsaussage*
   (meaning of existence and statement about existence). Not knowing
   the German, Lowry has considerable fun with *Dasseinsaussage*, and his
   German spelling is shakey: potato salad is *Kartoffelsalat*; there is a double
   s in *Dassein*, and two eggs are *zwei Eiern*.
3 Jean-Jacques Rousseau (1712-78), the French-Swiss moralist and social
   theorist, had five children with Thérèse le Vasseur, all of whom he sent
   to a foundling hospital.
4 Lowry is 'hanging on' to Somerset Maugham's selection of stories called
   Tellers of Tales (1939), which Kirk had asked for in a 20 January letter.
   Sapphira and the Slave Girl (1940) is by American novelist Willa Cather
   (1873-1947).

Editorial Notes:

a. Lowry's holograph is undated, but in his 21 March 1951 letter (**450**) to
    ten Holder, Lowry explains that ten Holder's 5 February 1951 letter
    (about which he is asking Kirk here) did not reach Dollarton until
    March. The February 1951 date given in *Prairie Schooner* 37.4 (1963/64):
    326-27 is incorrect.

446: To Downie Kirk

P: UBC(ms phc)
PP: *SL* 175; *MLVD* 56   [Dollarton]
                                                              [March 1951]

Dear Downey – A thousand thanks for the translation and the letter. I have been down with flu, & now Margerie has it, though she is now recovering – but I am taking care of her so have no time for more at the very moment if I want to catch the post. (We have run out of wood in the blizzard, too) Meanwhile here is the Marcellin, in English that leaves much to be desired, in our opinion, though it is extremely funny in places! Time mag. to the contrary, it is not about Voodoo chiefly, but witchcraft: there is a difference (Perhaps not apparent to the layman).[1] Still it is well worth reading. (Warning – it is incredibly obscene in places too so don't leave it on the piano.) – Again a thousand thanks for so very kindly translating the German, – will reply as soon as Margerie stops sneezing – Both our loves to yourself Marjorie & Dorothy

                                                              Malcolm

!P.T.O!

P.S. We very much look forward to seeing you at Easter.

P.P.S. Do not dream of a white Easter.[2]

P.P.S. Thanks again for the German translation – but what a gloomy picture it paints of contemporary German culture. As if we had to rebuild our literature with no memory save of alley oop & Superman, & perhaps not even that.[3]

                              (Also thanks for the French reviews)

                                                              M.

Annotations:

1 The Marcelins' book *The Pencil of God* is about a curse placed upon the hero, who is torn between his belief in Catholicism and the power of the Voodoo priests. Lowry was unhappy with the translation; see his 12 October 1950 letter (**421**) to Marcelin.

2 The Lowrys were having another severe and protracted winter, but Malcolm's allusion is to the first line of Irving Berlin's popular song 'White Christmas.'

3 'Alley Oop' is the Neanderthal hero of Vincent Hamlin's comic-strip *Alley Oop*, and 'Superman' is the hero of the successful comic-book series by that name.

447: To Downie Kirk

P: UBC(tsc) Dollarton
20 March [1951]ᵃ

Dear Downie:

Thank you very much indeed again for translating the German letter, on the basis of which I have already been able to make a reply to Herr Holder; it was damned nice of you too to offer to be an interpreter between us, but I feel I have already troubled you too much, I instructed him in any case to reply in English, no matter what kind, and failing that simply to give the page number and say 'Was bedoidet das?'[1] and I would comprehend the problem he was having. Whether or no he will understand my English is another question but he ought to be able to, seeing that he's going to translate the novel. But should he disregard my request and reply in German again after all, or in terms of too complicated Zusammengesetzteswörter,[2] I'd be awfully glad to feel I could trespass on your generosity once more. Your quotation from Mark Twain is very funny; it reminds me of Schopenhauer's 'roast geese stuffed with apples,' as a description of contemporary German prose.[3] I hope you all managed to survive the winter without flu: we both got it, and had a fine time trying to prop each other up. The climate did not help, though I did not see any stormy petrels flying past the window as last year. Both Margie and I liked When the Mountain Fell very much and you probably saw the pictures in, coincidentally, Life describing just how such mountains do fall.[4] In the criticism printed on the cover, however, I got the decided impression that Ramuz' style was being approached in an odd way – thus it was supposed to be natural, as if artless, unsophisticated, stark, stern, unintellectual, above all uninfluenced, simple as a flower, a natural growth; that sort of thing, or that was the impression I received from Fadiman and the others.[5] I don't see how a style, however arrived at, often I imagine largely by cutting, can hope at bottom to be much more than simply apprpopriate (a good word, leave it) in the fullest sense to what the writer is writing about. (Not exactly new!) However much of the original flavour is preserved in the translation in Ramuz I don't know, but I didn't find the style particularly simple. And I didn't find the story any too simple either. As for sophisticated influences I can detect a great many, including the avant-garde cinema, but I don't see the story is any the worse for that. Just the same one is all in favour of a clear, pure, concrete style, and one with the utmost simplicity, etc. But if one has arrived at that position, it is unlikely that the style has been uninfluenced. Doubtless one has to pass through a maximum of influences before achieving a style at all. It is difficult to see how a style like Ramuz, even if it achieves great clarity, can be called unsophisticated. Anyhow his simplicity, such as it is, strikes me as having cost great intellectual effort. God, what tripe I am talking. I shall spare you the quotation from William James that was going to follow – or I shall save it for when we see you. To that we are very much looking forward and I hope the weather will be fine. It's marvellous today, and it's a pity you can't take the Indianarm-dampschiffgesellschaft[6] boat instead of the bus and land right at our wharf.

With best love to yourself, Marjorie and Dorothy from us both and thank you for your kindness again. Happy Easter.

Malcolm

Annotations:

1 *Was bedeutet das* is the correct German for 'what does it mean?'
2 In his March 1951 letter to Lowry, Kirk explains that the German language builds new words by putting words together in 'zu-sammengesetzte Wörter.'
3 In his letter (UBC 1:33) Kirk has quoted Mark Twain's essay 'The Awful German Language' from *A Tramp Abroad* (1880), but Lowry is quoting a favourite line from Arthur Schopenhauer's essay 'On Style' in *The Art of Literature: A Series of Essays*; see his 6 May 1947 letter (**299**) to Jacques Barzun.
4 Michael Druhen's 'Picture of the Week' in *Life*, 12 March 1951, p. 37, is of a snow mass falling from near the top of Mont d'Or in the French Alps at the start of an avalanche.
5 Clifton Fadiman (1904-) is an American essayist, editor, critic, and reviewer.
6 This is Lowryan German for an imagined Indian Arm steamship line, which should be *Dampfschiffahrtsgesellschaft*.

Editorial Notes:

a. The typescript copy is undated, but the context and Lowry's closing 'Happy Easter' indicate 1951, when Easter Sunday fell on 25 March.

448: To Albert Erskine

P: Virginia(ts); UBC(phc)   Dollarton, B.C.,
                                                                    Canada
                                                            20 March 1951

Dear old Albert:

We have now got the money from Hal on the German translation but England has still not yet come through, though I have had word: so far as I can gather they are waiting till the end of the fiscal year before releasing any capital or making any change in income, the end of this month, that is, so I am taking you at your more than kind word and not sending you the German cash or its equivalent-plus right off in repayment but will abide these developments (unless you are short yourself, in which case let me know.)

I don't know how we could have got through but for your goodness since almost immediately after my last letter, when at least I thought we were through the winter, we were hit with the worst blizzard ever known in March here and in fact the temperature hit the lowest point ever recorded here at this time of year (and stayed there 2 weeks) so on top of everything else we had this, and then on top of that I got flu, then Margie did; however we've weathered it O.K: only a week ago it was Siberia, the woods all but impassable, but today it is spring and marvellous. (My existential soul wishes you could see it like this now: it is too good to be true).

The further good news is that via correspondence with Los Angeles via Seattle I finally located a specialist here who was able to diagnose Margie's illness which is not, thank God, malignant; it is called bruxism (I cannot spell the word) and is caused by involuntarily gritting or grinding the teeth. The infinite trismus, in short.[1] This raises hell with all the nerves in the nose and eye which run up to the brain (hence the suspicion of a brain tumour, the almost certainty of some kind of growth) and meantime all the teeth begin to change position, with the result that the 'bite' is altered. One begins to think that all one's teeth are falling out, which in fact they would do if one didn't discover what it was and do something about it. Thanks to you again we've been able to clear up all this, pay the specialist and get her well on the road to recovery, which will take six months or so. The teeth, after some rather subtle treatment return in time to their old position, as they are now doing, and the pain slowly ceases. Yet no dentist or doctor we saw here, with the exception of this fellow who was recommended from America, had ever heard of such a malady: a brain surgeon who saw the X-rays did not suspect it (he suspected a developing cancer) and the person who came nearest to a correct diagnosis turned out to be my humble self some months back, though naturally due to the other opinions, or lack of them, like herself I was beginning to fear the worst. This diagnosis of course obviates the necessity of any further X-rays because there is nothing sinister to develop. You can imagine the relief, with which goes our heartfelt gratitude again to you!

For the rest, as I say, I'm still waiting to hear further word from England. My brothers are selling the family estate and the old homestead but according to the terms of my father's will – since my old man wanted to keep the house in the family if possible – it could not be sold without agreement between all four brothers and the other three having declined – how to keep it up? – it fell to me.[2] By a strange coincidence the letter asking my ratification by cable was delayed 3 weeks during which time, since they'd had an offer, and wished to avoid a public auction, I take it my poor brothers were having bruxism too. Actually I delayed only two hours before sending the cable, enjoying therein the strange sensation, as it were, of technically being the owner, for those two hours, of Wuthering Heights. I must say that it had occurred to me that if one couldn't keep up the house no one could stop me putting up a shack on the grounds, but Margie persuaded me this was impractical. Impractical too is taking the crashing loss involved by the fall of the pound – should it go up which it might do overnight if there were a change of government; but there is little chance, paradoxically, they will release enough capital at once anyhow, not to give one a chance to profit by this remote possibility eventually, though no doubt they would hate the thought if it occurred to them: meantime, quite apart from this, I take it that not even the government can prevent our affairs brightening somewhat – though to what extent I don't yet know, as I say. In fact until I hear again from England it is difficult to know what plans to make for the future at all or where one stands.

The only thing I do know is that I want with all my heart yourself as my publisher and I have written Hal again to this effect. Until I see where I am however, it is impossible to prophecy as to the completion of work. At the moment we still owe Hal some short stories which we haven't got off because for one thing Margie hasn't been able to type, I have been involved with intricate correspondence with England and I have been in any case nursing her through the flu. The short stories that have nothing to do with the novel I tend to be schizophrenic about, to the detriment of the stories themselves. The ones that have something to do with the novel sometimes seem to suffer from not being bona fide chapters but at bottom I have never been more creative and in any case I am bounden to try and get as many of these stories off in the next two months as I can, disciplined to their form. The hell of it is, has been, being in the almost continuous throes of creation and not having time to get a quarter of it down – which particularly pertains to the novel.

Well that is how the land lies at the moment and I will keep you posted as to further developments. Actually it has all been much worse than I said, but when old Vallipo looms through the sunshine it is easy to forget Cape Horn.

God bless and best love from us both to yourself and Peggy.

Malcolm

P.S. Would you like any suggestions for some rare words, if legitimate, for any further editions of the Random House dictionary you sent me? Esemplastic? Driftbolt? Moonsail? (This last beauty is the highest, highest, tiniest sail, rarely employed, above the main skysail, on certain types of windjammer. I have often thought it would be a lovely title for something).

Annotations:

1 *Trismus* is the muscle spasm of the neck and lower jaw that leads to lock-jaw (in tetanus) or to the grinding of teeth.
2 'Inglewood,' the family home in Caldy, Cheshire, had a large property. It was scarcely as gothic as Brontë's 'Wuthering Heights,' to which Lowry compares it below; see Vol. I, photograph 7.

449: To Harold Matson

P: Matson(ts); UBC(phc)
Dollarton, B.C.,
Canada
20 March 1951

Dear Hal:

A thousand thanks for your generosity in sending the German money.[1]

And thank you for sending on the letter from the German translator: the poor guy was obfuscated by some of my own Zusammengesetztes-worter; I replied with enthusiasm.[2]

Margerie's trouble thank God has been diagnosed as nothing malignant, but as something obscure called bruxism (I can't spell it) caused by gnashing the teeth, or gritting them, or conversely by keeping a stiff upper lip in time of trouble: one gets it coming and going, it seems. Though we can laugh at this now, it was the opposite of funny for her because all her teeth began to change position, the pain was frightful, and the only reasonable explanation seemed a brain tumour. But all will be completely well in six months or so and she is already getting very much better. But it was necessary to apply by correspondence through Los Angeles back again through Seattle before we found a doctor here competent to make the diagnosis.

Meantime she went down with flu (so did I) and I have been looking after her here in what coincided – just as we thought we were through the winter – with the coldest March in recorded history here. She is now well, but the delay in stories has been partly caused by the fact she hasn't been able to type again until the last few days, also by the necessity of getting wood. Since we only have one usable typewriter, though I can type I've fallen out of the habit, and for me to attempt a fair copy is a waste of time. Also the whole situation has conspired against getting any work off. The release of my English capital (however much they choose to release) has apparently been delayed till the end of their fiscal year, that is the end of this month, so this ought to be cleared up soon. Another strange complication was that owing to the terms of my father's will my brothers could not dispose of the old homestead and the family estate – as at first to my surprise they wanted to – without my permission too: but the letter asking for that permission was delayed by three weeks. When I finally received it I could have replied that I wanted the old home – as indeed I would have, other things being equal – but how the hell could we keep it up, if they couldn't? So that has gone – I hope not by public auction – and though a considerable amount of cash should accrue to me even so, it is perhaps better not to think of the loss it implies, financial or otherwise. It is hard to get through my brother's heads that a pound is less than three bucks and that three bucks is less than what five shillings used to be here. (Something like that). (Oddly, even that house doesn't mean as much as this little shack.) However despite all this my financial situation should be considerably improved but I ask you to bear with me a little longer until I see exactly how matters stand – I find it almost impossible to concentrate fully on creative work while involved with these legal intricacies.

I have been in touch with good Albert and I have several excellent design-governing notions in relation to future work. It would be wonderful if he could be my editor. If humanly possible I would desire this to be brought about. So complete was his understanding of the Volcano and creative sympathy with my work that psychologically and in every other way it seems to me unthinkable that I could ever have another editor. He has told me (in strictest confidence of course) that he has ascertained that Random House would like to have me. Also that a contract could be arranged so that if he should leave Random House I could leave with him. Is it possible that Reynal Harcourt Brace would let me out of my contract with them in a friendly manner? If not, is it then necessary for me to submit something, they make me some offer and I turn it down? What can be done, or in your estimation, should be done? You possess the better telethermometer on the point. What is clear to me – and while I am also at that section of the dictionary – is that, with Albert in another firm, in a way the teleology of my own work in its larger pattern has drawn to a kind of standstill. This does not mean I have not been working, as I have said, and at that, hard: but I am undoubtedly going about it in the wrong way. (Though I mean to get these short stories off.) I had a piece of tough and long hemlock the other day I was trying to saw through, but the primary problem was not its toughness, nor the bluntness of the saw, but my inability to balance the wood with-

out getting the saw trapped; I wasted half the afternoon on this problem
by which time I was tired, and it had begun to snow, and the wood was
so wet it was almost unburnable while a whole host of other problems
were now arising around the problem of how to dry it in time for it to
be any use. This struck me as the outward expression of the inner situation with my work. In fact I have written a sort of whole first draft of
the novel in longhand but it would take at least 3 months even to get it
typed out in readable form, even if one concentrated on nothing else.
Neither of us have time, as things stand. Then again it is not one novel,
but three, and not three finally but five, six including the Volcano; three
of these are short, one (the madhouse one [*Lunar Caustic*]) largely
written but in a form that is inadequate as it stands – another is a sort of
intermezzo, and so forth;[3] the whole fills me – and I hope will you,
eventually, with the wildest enthusiasm and in fact consumes me day
and night – but without Albert there, somehow I can't even begin to
talk about it in a practical form, from which could be excogitated this
or that stipulation for finishing a part or parts complete in itself or themselves in a given time. Needless to say if Albert or yourself could put
your heads together on this matter of a transfer of my obligations and
something could be arranged it would be a complicated load of worry
and unhappiness off my mind.

We have heard nothing further from Hollywood and will of course
let you know instantly about that if there is anything. But quam celerrime we must get to those short stories and send them off. I have one
large wheel-barrow-wood-getting-in chore over the next few days, my
end of the English business should be cleared up and then bingo.
Margerie has one first rate story coming up, though it is almost a novelette – about 100 pages it looks now, better than Venus I think and more
saleable. Themes from the novel keep getting into mine and giving
them elephantiasis. Then again, there are parts that will be part of the
novel. Please bear with me a while longer. Thank you again sincerely
for your generosity and please forgive this added delay which has been
unavoidable.

With love to yourself Tommy and the children from us both

Malcolm

Annotations:

1 On 1 March 1951 Matson wrote that the German money had arrived
  and that he was sending it, together with royalties due on *Under the
  Volcano*.
2 See Lowry's 20 March letter (**447**) to Downie Kirk and his 21 March
  letter (**450**) to Clemens ten Holder.
3 At this point, the 'intermezzo' was the material for 'Eridanus'; see my
  discussion of the *Voyage* (2-3).

450: To Clemens ten Holder

P: UBC(ts)
PP: *Brief* 20-28; *MLR* 21/22, 43-66   Dollarton, B.C.,
                                              Canada
                                       21 March 1951[a]

Sehr Geehrter Herr Clemens ten Holder![1]

You must forgive me – doubly – both for writing in English, and for, at the outset, not getting your name perhaps quite right: your letter of February 5 arrived here, delayed, on the coldest and most violent day for March in recorded history here, and the blizzard had penetrated even to your signature which was slightly smudged with storm as to the nexus between your Christian and surname. And to these truly Wagnerian circumstances of the delivery of the letter I also owe the delay – for the storm did not cease for nearly two weeks and I live in a forest and had to get a friend from town to translate it – in replying. But that I must write English is because I remember so little German – though as a youth I once spent a happy year in Bonn-am-Rhein[2] – that I cannot even stammer (as you say of English) therein: of German I understand 'a fury in the words but not the words themselves' – albeit I know and admire enough of German literature to feel profoundly the honour and excitement of being translated into your great language, as we were taught, the language of all languages.

Thus I need not say how deeply I appreciate your generous words about Under the Volcano nor how anxious I am to assist you concerning the translation in any way that may be in my power.

But before I reply to your first specific and immediate questions – and I am anxious to get this letter posted as soon as possible to you – (if only to have the privilege of answering more questions the sooner) I should say that my geographical circumstances very much parallel your own, and in fact are probably even more remote; I too live far away from the city, in a shack built with our own hands on the beach in the remnants of an old seaport: – Dollarton, – that has a grim and moneyed sound, but in fact what was once the town took its name from the shipowner's Dollar, of the American Dollar line, they once had a sawmill here at whose wharf deep sea ships would put in – and when during the war this sawmill was torn down, so were most of the mill houses, and we have since been often the sole inhabitants here. The city of Vancouver is only some twenty miles hence but to get a reply from there, especially in bad weather, often will take as long as from Germany; I have a friend, a schoolmaster in the city, and a neighbour here in summer, who translated your letter, and has – being a linguist – delightedly offered to act as an interpreter between us, but because of the added delay it might be better for you to risk your English in future letters, and trust me to understand, for your English cannot ex officio be as uncomprehending as my comprehension of German; nor is my friend – apart from my wife my sole cultural contact here – always infallible, it may be, before the higher complexities of the magnificent Zusammengesetztesworter of your language.[3]

Permit me then to pass over your difficulties that beset you in translating the book at all – which I do not minimise, while in every way agreeing that it can be more thoroughly and dramatically assimilated perhaps, than into French – albeit to add that I could not be more happy and proud that one who shows such a deep and intelligent appreciation, warmly gratifying to me, of my book should be its translator – and answer your first questions without delay, so that you be not discouraged to pose me some more.

(I have to interpolate that one of the first things I beg of you to do at this point is, after this rather formal if sincere opening, to *laugh*: at least half of the questions are applied, as it happens I fear, to obscenities – the word, or a word like schmutzige[4] comes to mind – and nearly all those questions that pertain to Chapter X – involve phrases obscurely in this category. Still, I hope this does not upset you. Though I take it that at this point – the menu of Chapter X – a technique of adaptation quite the opposite of your admirably described 'cleansing bath' is indicated! In fact, though the intention here in X – at the points mentioned – is not so much obscene as in the realm of a kind of gruesome wit or morbid hilarity, it may be on the contrary hard to find a bath dirty enough in order that the words come out adequately filthy. I add in passing that the obscenity is not there for its own sake, that there is even definitely a moral – or infernal – reason for it; on the other hand its effect in English – so some critics have been kind enough to say – is of the most devilish kind of humour. Such, at least, was what I was striving for.)

Now to the questions. (Not obscene, this time.)

Chapter II page 43, 47, 48.

p. 43 – *just a bunch of Alladamnbama* farmers –

p. 47 – when Alabama comes through etc.

ibid – bull-headed Dutchman! The sun parches the lips and they crack etc.

p. 48 – life, came from beyond the glass partition etc.

— went down to Fort Sale etc.

— and like hell you can you can't do it u.s.w.[5]

— Christ, if you want it, Alabama, go ahead and take it etc.

The voice, from beyond the glass partition, is that of a man, Weber, who belongs to a kind of sub-sub-sub-plot of the novel. He is not very important, in one way, and yet he has to be there, bracing something far down within the substructure of the whole. Weber is an Alabaman, yet refers to himself – as to his one time regiment in the Foreign Legion – as 'Alabama.'

He is the 'gun-running gun-toting pal by the name of – Weber? – I forget, anyway I didn't meet him,' mentioned by the Consul on page 60 of the same chapter and the point is – though it's not necessary and indeed impossible to get that point here unless on rereading the book – that though the Consul *hasn't* met Weber, he has, without knowing it, overheard his *voice*. The meaning of this, or what I believe to be the unconscious meaning (for I first wrote this chapter over a decade ago) is that the Consul is, as it were, already *involved* with his destruction, his fate, carrying it around with him, so to speak; separated in that instance, or those instances, of p. 43, 47, 48, 51, only by a glass partition from it, as good as in the same room with it, in fact; for Weber is to turn up again at the very *end* of the book, – Chapter XII p. 363 'Winchester, hell, etc.'; 364 'Weber's my name,'; 365 'He turreted out this underground place here,' – and elsewhere in that last chapter, where though Weber is not the direct instrument of the Consul's fate, he is nonetheless present at the final *scene*, in Parian, of the Consul's destruction – as is the old woman, top of p. 51, who tries to save him in Chapter XII – while you may surmise too, that Weber is in some way sinisterly connected with the policemen who *do* murder him in Chapter XII. He – Weber – a sort of pseudo-American fascist – has indeed been running ammunition to the rightest faction the police represent in Parian from whom obscurely, it is suggested, may be expected (some time after the book ends) a reactionary uprising, or counteruprising {though in the larger more universal sense what is of course meant is simply war, chaos, etc.}. I am aware that this may seem insanely complicated, as well, as needlessly obscure in Chapter II, but the purpose seems to have been musical more than anything in that chapter and it seemed necessary that Weber should be kept well in the background, his name not mentioned, and simply a voice: a contrapuntal device, as it were, that at the same time is a motif (?) of fate. As such (forgive me for expressing myself badly) he almost seems to answer Yvonne's and the Consul's voice and make comment on *their* situation, though Weber is in the next room and they don't know him from Adam. Thus when Yvonne is actually about to ask the Consul (p. 48) What have you done with your life, it is Weber who from the other compartment adds the word 'life,' though using 'life' in a totally different meaning of that word, and might have been for the moment finishing the sentence for her (Yvonne,) as if he were another instrument taking up the theme on a different plane, Weber's two other interpolations on p. 48 having the effect in English of oblique ironic comment both on the Consul's past and possible future. ' – went down to Fort Sale etc' suggests vaguely both escape, suicide, and has an overtone of 'shooting' (the Consul's fate) whereas ' – and like hell you can, you can't do it, and that's what you do in Alabama,' implies in Weber's peculiar jargon, – almost as if this were the expression of an interior thought of the Consul's – the achievement of the impossible ('his stopping drinking' and making a new life with Yvonne. Or, conversely, the giving in to the impossible of achievement. Few readers of English could understand this either save on rereading, nor is it altogether necessary to understand. The dialogue and the device should have a value of their own. See French translation of this I'll come to later.) While on p. 51 Weber's 'Christ, if you want it, Alabama, go ahead and take it etc.' – though no doubt not having anything to do with drink at all – reflects almost 'constructively' on the Consul's alcoholic plight to the Consul himself who overhears it, for he leaves half his drink. In this last usage here of Weber's voice it must be well-nigh impossible for you to understand that someone called 'Alabama' is *not* being addressed on the other side of the partition: but Weber is merely referring in his jargon (the dialogue or, in effect, monologue, is exactly realistic, in fact taken from life) to some Alabamans with whom he identifies himself in his one-time regiment – perhaps attached to the Foreign Legion in the first World War – or because he is just drunk too and wandering in his mind. (This does not prevent Hugh at one point later from referring to Weber himself as 'Alabama' unless I have cut the bit I refer to [out] in your edition. If so, it shouldn't matter.) On the other hand Weber *is* an instrument of fate in so far as he has flown Hugh himself part of his way down to Mexico, p. 97. In fact Hugh has crossed the border with him in a cattle truck, which is why he's wearing cowboy clothes: (this too is founded on fact, the Mexicans would charge him more duty than the clothes were worth, under those questionable circumstances of the cattle truck at the border, so he'd leave them behind, as happened to a friend of mine, it being cheaper to let them be impounded. The underlying idea of the cowboy clothes at all, apart from the thematic relationship of this with Yvonne, was to dress Hugh's communism, or his conception of it, however he may be a sincere decent and farsighted fellow at bottom, in supraromantic, even operatic clothing. Something like that. A communist acquaintence of mine once said of another acquaintence, not a communist, but who had actually been killed fighting against Franco: 'And that was the end of *that* little romantic urge in him.' The complicated inhumanity of this remark has stayed with me: nonetheless Hugh has his cowboy clothes.)

Another buried irony is that though the Consul has a first-class case of alcoholic persecution mania the people with dark glasses in Chapter II and elsewhere following him *are*, or have become, real: even Yvonne sees them: they are probably watching for Hugh though, not the Consul

– as implied in Chapter I p. 30, in M. Laruelle's thoughts – (bottom, that he, M. Laruelle could not cross the border in a cattle truck etc) – albeit this, if dwelt upon too literally, could lead to a totally different reading of the whole book; i.e. as a sort of fantastic movie through M. Laruelle's mind, to make provision for which I materialised the 'bald boy with earrings' of p. 30 in Chapter VIII, p. 240 – where Hugh sees such a boy (after the klangmalerei for the bus in the middle): I don't dwell on this interpretation (that way madness lies) though there is a philosophical reason for it – partly I was perhaps having some fun myself with my own book, which I hope you will agree I needed after I've finished this letter. (I was not much more than a boy myself when I started it, or so it seems now – if not a bald boy with earrings.) What I have just said about page 30 Chapter I in relation to page 240 Chapter eight probably could not matter less, can only confuse you, and it might be better to forget it, for there is a further philosophical complication in that on page 30 M. Laruelle is assuming or half-assuming that there is indeed justification for the Consul's being followed on the grounds that the Consul was perhaps a spy himself: at all events that people have been in the habit of following the Consul is presumed to be a fact; and that this supposition filters through M. Laruelle's mind via the conduit of the actual conversation of Sr. Bustamente might seem to contradict what I have just said re the possible totally different reading of the whole book as a shadowy filmic fiction of M. Laruelle's; – to simplify all this; the book is written and is supposed to function on many different planes simultaneously and what I was striving for was richness of orchestration (as what man with soul so dead would not strive for it after having had the privilege of living in his youth in Bonn-am-Rhein!) – on the purely dramatic plane, what I was attempting to do, through using musical means, was slowly to establish Hugh in the reader's mind not merely as the half-brother but the *doppleganger* of the Consul, at the same time, to the contrary, by every means in my power, to make them, the Consul & Hugh, both live and exist as separate breathing human beings, not merely coexist as symbols.

But to get back to Weber. Though he is scarcely ever much more than a voice you can find out quite a lot about him if you persevere, especially in Chapter XII, though there is perhaps not much need to. In any case it is sufficient for you to know eventually that the voice in Chapter II is eventually identified with the 'gun-running gun-toter' mentioned by the Consul on page 60 also in Chapter II, and then by Hugh on page 97 in Chapter IV. On page 99, you learn that he has probably been, though an American 'on the wrong side' in the Mexican revolution, no doubt fighting *against* Diaz,[6] (Hugh's principles are the exact opposite of Weber's, if W. can be presumed to have any) and this was the first place where you were supposed to recognize his voice, which was one reason why his speech is put in italics here (p.99) (I don't see the 'Alabama' motif repeated here, which would have made it easier: it looks as though I felt he would be recognized soon enough, in so far as he needed to be recognized, by less obvious means.)

To concoct a little story out of this: when the action opens – assuming it for the moment to begin at Chapter II not Chapter I – Weber, the smuggler who has some days before accompanied Hugh down to Mexico, happens by a coincidence to be in the same bar as the Consul at the moment Yvonne arrives, though divided from him by a glass partition. Presumably Weber, still on nefarious business, has come back from Parian to Quauhnahuac; though during the course of the day he returns to Parian – see Chapter XII. Parian is on one plane a symbol of death, and suggests a teleology thence. See p. 115 Chapter IV. ('There seems something sinister about Parian. I wonder what Weber sees in it.') Hugh of course does not know that Weber is in Quauhnahuac as he speaks and is going back to Parian, or that he too is going to Parian too etc. (The garden by the way is on one plane the Garden of Eden – see Chapter VIII, p. 236, bottom – though there were twenty-one other paths they might have taken! – There were, according to the Quabbala, supposed to be twenty-two paths back to Eden.)[7]

Now for your questions re Chapter X, page 290, 291, 294. I could not sympathise more, your difficulties could not be greater, and what makes it worse, in places, my difficulties in explaining what I meant to myself – as Browning might have said – are no less – so how should I to you? But I will attempt to elucidate. For one thing someone informed me from America – the success of this book has been always at a great distance from me, by the way – that this particular passage, i.e., the menu, had become famous. My correspondent referred to the 'now famous menu', so bearing this tribute in mind I shall try to deliver it from the realm, at least of the *totally* obscure. I have warned you that this is obscene – though not all obscene. But in order to get the joke at all it is necessary to understand that this is the literal transcription – with certain reservations and improvements – of an actual Mexican menu and such a menu, now lost, was in my possession when I wrote it.[8] When I say 'actual Mexican menu,' it has to be borne in mind also that (a) the Consul is reading from the menu (b) Cervantes is reading it over his shoulder and also trying to translate it into English (c) he – Cervantes – doesn't have to translate it all for the menu is already partly written in English of a fantastic and ridiculous character, which he also reads, though for that matter it is also partly written in French as well as Spanish. (This vaguely relates to the confusion of tongues – the Babel motif of Chapter XII, but forget that for the moment.) The general character of such menus in Mexico is often of a kind of semi-illiterate obsequiousness to the tourist, nearly always presumed to be American {though the Americans by and large are hated in Mexico}, though perhaps this is not important to remember either here, though it was an obscure part of the intention. The main point is that there happens to be about nearly every item on this menu, though not all, for I try to maintain a strict realism, an overtone of the fiendish (though expressed in a ridiculous manner) pertaining to the Consul's general situation, or the whole situation, largely sexual, once or twice even political. Some of the items are just funny mistakes in English, and simply are intended to make you laugh when you read them, and on this plane, the thing is simply comic relief – on the other hand, viewed in another way, it is decidedly horrible. I'll take them one at a time.

   p. 290. Cawliflowers or poottootsies – these are simply misprints on the menu for cauliflowers or post toasties. Post toasties is an American breakfast food; 'tootsies' is baby talk for 'toes' – if there is humour it exists in the gruesome combination implied. In extramapee syrup – an impossible Mexican version of extra maple syrup (though extra maple syrup is an impossible usage too) the Consul is con-

Figure 7: *For full size reproduction of the recto of the menu, see photo page opposite text page 394.*

tinuing to jest in the same vein. Onans in garlic soup on egg – it presumably means Onion Soup, – must surely bring back to the Consul the uncompleted coition of the morning. (Genesis xxxviii 9) . . .[9] (My God, have you ever eaten a spaghetti sandwich, followed by the chocolate-coated fish, the whole washed down by coffee with mustard in it?) 'Pep with milk' of Cervantes' is simply ridiculous, though it might suggest unintentionally an aphrodisiac. (The word 'pep' is very American, originally pertains to the digestion.) What it was meant to be, this 'pep with milk' no one knows and anyway one couldn't have it, I hope, for dinner. Now I remember that Pep is a well-known American breakfast food; 'pep' is also of course an innocent American slang word simply meaning vitality. In Filete de Huachinango etc Cervantes is half reading, half translating. The dish has tartar sauce. Evidently there is a Spanish word like friends that is really a vegetable, I forget. But the note struck is political: both tartar {Though there is also a meaning of Tartar that gives you Tartans! See p 339, middle. (Chap XII).} and German friends imply the 'fifth column', though on opposite sides: tartar = Russian. (Cervantes himself who is a Tlaxcalan, also suggests, generally speaking traitorousness.) 'Dr Moise's special soup etc is merely funny because portentous, but a pepped petroot is phallic: 'pepped' implies the aphrodisiac again (though it's another, intentional on my part, mistake, probably the attempt is to say 'pickled' another slang term for drunk,) 'petroot' is 'beetroot', but the combination of 'pee', to urinate – please excuse the vulgarity – and 'root' (penis) makes the joke; in other words an aphrodisiac might be in order after his impotence. (See Chapter II, bottom of p. 90: also Chapter XII, p. 352) Page 290-291 . . . The Consul sees the joke about the 'german friends,' and Hugh counters with the Russian; 'tartar.' Then 291, Cervantes' well meaning translation succeeds in being diabolical. Stepped on eggs, is merely funny: there must have been something in the Spanish that could be translated like that or it is another absurd mistranslation on the menu. Divorced eggs; likewise – though here Cervantes is attempting to translate from the Spanish; there is a word pertaining to a way to doing eggs that also means divorced; but remembering Yvonne and the Consul have been divorced the translation could not be more unfortunate. For fish etc. is just ridiculous phrasing. Vol-au-vent à la reine, translated by somersaults to the queen suggests brutally some strange sexual acrobatic feat: by poxy eggs Cervantes means poached eggs but pox is syphilis. Veal liver tavernman and Pimesan chike chup are just meaningless Mexican attempts at English, though tavernman refers to the Consul and his love of taverns, and chup is chop. Spectral (ghostly) chicken of the house is Special chicken of the house. Youn' pigeon, just a strange way of saying a young pigeon, itself strange enough. Red snappers with a fried tartar, means the fish red snapper with tartar sauce, but revives the political joke again. Spectral explains the joke about ectoplasm. Sea-sleeves in his ink; this is octopus served in its ink, a Mexican specialty, the Spanish word for octopus being like the English word for sleeves.[10] In tunny-fish I have outsmarted myself, for there is a fish, the tunny-fish, whereas I thought the menu meant 'tuna fish.' (I must have thought they'd got tuna fish mixed up with the American boxer Gene Tunney, but in fact this is almost correct.)[11] Exquisite mole: mole is an indigenous Mexican dish with a very hot sauce, but printed like that it looks like a dish made out of the blind animal 'mole' that lives underground. If not like the one of Kafka's.[12] Fig mermalade simply means marmalade. Brambleberry con crappe Gran Duc, I cannot well explain: probably some sort of crepe if not crepe suzettes is indicated but crappe suggests crap which is excrement. Omelet he sourpusse, is an omelet surprise: sourpuss (sourpusse) is an Americanism for a gloomy fellow. Gin fish is gin fizz. Silver fish is silver fizz (whatever *that* is). Sparkenwein, an odd way of saying sparkling wine, and God what a mixture! Badre is actually a fish indigenous to Mexico, but madre is mother. (The Oedipean motif) When the Consul says 'do you want to wait for the fish that dies,' he is thinking of a famous English poem by Ralph Hodgson he is parodying too in Chapter IX p. 273. 'See the old unhappy bull, in the forest beautiful,' is how the original begins. I forget how it goes on, but the 'birds in the skies,' the vultures, are 'waiting for the *flesh* that dies,' in the original poem, (i.e. the vultures are waiting for the bull to die) which relates to the very end of Chapter VIII, p. 253.[13] The Consul in identifying himself with the impotent bull, also identifies himself with the man lying by the roadside in Chapter VIII.

I don't imagine that I've made myself any too clear, and I have here and there found it impossible to be quite correct even in my own terms, but perhaps I've made it a little less obscure. It is the kind of wit one might well be ashamed of in another context: on the other hand, in English, in this particular place, I have known it reduce some people who know the story – even my wife – to almost helpless laughter: though I say it who ought not, and heaven knows there's not much to laugh about: but what was needed, I felt, was a *caustic*. (A similar kind of laughter becomes ghoulish, of the abyss, in Chapter XII)

Whether it would assist you for me to give you what the French translation made of this I do not know; anyway here it is, in the same order, missing out the easier bits.

p. 291 – 'Qu'est-ce-que vous préférez, vous tous? Des chouxfleurs ou de la soupoupouille,' le Consul etc. 'Ou du sirop d'extra-mapie. Oeuf a la soupe à l'ail, de l'onanan!'

'Des poivrons au lait? Ou que diriez-vous d'un bon Filete de Huachinango rebozado tartare garni d'allemande friture.' etc.

'Je crois qu'un bitterave poivrait m'irait assez,' dit le Consul, 'apres ce onanan.' etc. etc.

p. 292. 'Si, je suis Tlaxcaltécan. . .Vous aimez les oeufs señora. Marchons sur les oeufs. Muy sabrosos. Des oeufs divorce? Pour poisson, tranché de filet con pois. Vol-au-vent à la reine. Cabriola por la reina. Ou bien vous aimez les oeufs Vérolèse, Vérolèse sur toast. Ou du foie de veau patron d'hôtel? Chapon sur canapé? Ou le poulet spectre mai-son? Pizzoneau. Les haricots ronges fiture tartare, vous aimez?' etc. etc.

'Si vous aimez les seiches dans son encre? Ou des petis poissons? Ou une sauce exquise mole? Peut-être vous aimez du melon mode pour commencer? Mermelade de figues? Des mures con crappe Grand-duc? Hommelette surpris, vous aimez? Vous aimez d'abord boire un gin-vis? Un bon gin-vis? Un 'Poisson d'argent?' Un Sparkenwein?'

'Madre?' demanda le Consul, 'Que fait ici cette Mere? – Veux-tu manger ta mère, Yvonne?'

'Badre, senor. . .Poisson aussi. . .' etc.

The French translation was done by Clarisse Francillon, the Swiss novelist, and Stephen Spriel, a Martiniquaise scholar, both friends of mine, and from all reports they have done a very brilliant job, though how much of the original they have managed to preserve in the above, I cannot tell, but it looks as though most, if not all, of the double meanings have had to go by the board here by *force majeure*, or have certainly gone. Of course there is always the point, when it comes to a different language, how much is worth preserving, and how much should be willy-nilly adaptation. When I was in Paris they – Clarisse and Stephen Spriel – had my assistance, from time to time, though I can barely understand French either. Whether or not I helped here in Chapter X I've forgotten, but it seems to me I certainly helped in Chapter II, so I'll give you what they ingeniously made of Alabama also. (Before I do that, though, there is an unintentional misprint in the English text, p. 292, top: the old number seven *train* should be the old number seven *tram*. And turning back to find my place, I come across something of my own, among other things, that could be better; p. 244, top. The Consul said, in a voice that betrayed a trembling tongue. I originally wrote just: The Consul said, with trembling tongue. This last seems much better. I must have changed it because I thought this phenomenon could not be perceived by Hugh, but of course it could.) And after all that, I have forgotten the stone you ask about of p. 294, 296! I regret to report that this stone which Cervantes well-meaningly, though as it happens rather cruelly, offers the Consul, might seem to belong to the lowest category of humour. During my youthful wanderings in the mountains of Mexico (and Tlaxcala is such a cold mountainous region) the people are so hardy that I discovered that, other things lacking, one was expected to use a stone in lieu of toilet paper. This ascetic custom made an indelible impression upon me, as well it might, and it seems that if I could not exactly transform the wretched stone into art, I was determined somehow to revenge myself upon its memory.

And so, back to Chapter II: I give you the French of Francillon and Spriel, with the English page numbers.

p. 43 ' – Rien q'une bande de fermiers de l'*Alladamnebama!*'

p. 47 ' – quand c'est l'Alabama qui s'amène nous n'posons d'questions à personne,' emit soudain une voix venue du bar de l'autre côté de la cloison vitrée. 'C'est en jouant des talons qu'nous nous amenons.'

Ibid. ' – têtes de vaches de Hollandais! La soleil dessèche les lèvres qui s'fendillent. Seigneur, c'est une honte! Tous les chevaux s'sauvent en ruant dans la poussiere! J'aurais pas supporté ca. Et ils leur ont flanqué des pruneaux. Ils n'ratent pas leur coup. Ils tirent d'abord et posent des questions après. T'as foutrement raison. Et v'la l'plus joli. J'en prends une bande d'ces foutus fermiers, et puis j'leur pose pas d'questions. Ca va! – fume une cibiche à la menthe – '

p.48 (Yvonne) Qu'as tu fait de ta – '

' – vie' lança-t-on de derrière la cloison vitrée. 'Quelle vie! Bon Dieu, c'est une honte! Là d'où j'viens on n'les met pas. On rentre dedans, et comme ça – '

Ibid. ' – descendait à Fort Sale. On prenait ses bobottes. Prenait ses brownings aussi. Et hop-hop-hop-hop-hop, vu, tu piges?'

' – et mon oeil que tu peux, tu n'peux pas l'faire, et voilà ce qu'tu fais dans l'Alabama!'

p. 51 ' – Bon Dieu, s'il te l'faut, l'Alabama, vas-y et prends-le. . . J'n'en veux pas. Mais si t'en as envie, t'as qu' à aller l'prendre.'

'Absolutamente necesario.'

Le Consul en laissa en moitie.

A minor matter that likewise puzzled the French translators was my usage of the place name Hornos on page 47; after my explanation of what was really implied they decided – wittily and I think rightly – to translate the Consul's *repetition* of Hornos as Cornos. – Ah, Cornos. – Mais pourquoi avoir doublé le Cap Horn? (This carries an implication of his besetting awareness of having been cuckolded.) As an actual geographical fact Hornos is the name of the place where the Acapulco airport is situated. The Consul's pretense of confusing it with Cape Horn is simply a joke. Why come round the longest way? is all he is saying. But his evocation of Cape Horn suggests in a casual way the terrors of Cape Horn itself. 'Its bad habit of wagging its tail,' is derived from the old maritime belief (and philosophical truth) that it's *after* you've rounded the Cape that, despite your accomplishment, your worst danger may be *ahead* of you. Yvonne by returning to the Consul has 'rounded the Cape' so the Consul's remark is a form of tragic irony. His reference to ovens carries another hint of the infernal but in fact this particular Hornos in Acapulco is so called after a native word meaning 'ovens' (the natives built ovens on the shore or something). To the best of my belief there is a Spanish word very like Hornos that obviously means Cape ('Horn') too, though of this I am uncertain. At all events Hornos is not an uncommon place name in Mexico and it can't have meant ovens each time. It is possible I have been misled in my research but perhaps it doesn't much matter. (I don't have a Spanish dictionary.) Quauhnahuac is really the town of Cuernavaca that you can find on your map at the latitude designated in the opening sentences of the book. Quauhnahuac was the old Aztec name, and I sought to disguise the real one (without avail I have discovered!); though some of the surrounding geography is more like Oaxaca, than the original. The Conquistadores could not pronounce Quauhnahuac so called it Cuernavaca, which again means 'cow's horn.' Thus when the Consul calls the place Cuckoldshaven, also in Chapter II, he is having an etymological joke the real point of which is outside the book. (Though still a good joke, I hope – not quite mine either, the Consul lifted it from the Elizabethan play Eastward Ho! by Marston, Ben Jonson, and – I think – Haywood – surely the worst play ever written by such a galaxy of genius but they got great fun out of calling London Cuckoldshaven:[14] unfortunately it sent them all to prison too.)

It might help you to obtain the French translation: the publishers are Corréa, I can't find the address. I would send you a copy if I had a spare one but the only one I have at present belongs to somebody else. For that matter Clarisse Francillon, a delightful person, would I know send you a copy, should you ask her, as well as any hints concerning any difficulties that might be in common, should there be an occasion where French would reach you more easily than English. Her address is: 23 Rue Gazin, Paris 13ᶜ

In any case you are nearer than I and a parcel I sent you would take a year or so, relatively speaking.

If I can help you in any further details do not hesitate to write and I shall be only too delighted to try my best: I am well acquainted enough by now with the poor old book pretty well to be able to scent any difficulty you may have, should you just mention the page, or say 'Was bedoitet das?'

One reason the French translation might help is that it contains a preface by myself. True, the preface is somewhat misleading, the best part of it is a wonderful quotation from Schopenhauer (directed at myself)[15] and it may well seem to you to have been written in a state bordering upon the Consul's own, but it is a preface for all that; and failing that, there is also a post-face by Max-Pol Fouchet, that may contain some matter of interest about the book's form.

In my preface you would discover among other things that could not be of less interest and are besides, no doubt, partially untrue, that Under the Volcano was originally designed as the first part of a trilogy; this much is certainly so, except perhaps for the 'originally.' But it did grow that way. Under the Volcano represented as it were an Inferno (The

Casino de la Selva = Dante's wood: also see El Bosque end of Chapter VII etc.) and there was going to be a Purgatorio and a Paradiso. (Not a very new idea!) – Unfortunately, or fortunately, for the bewiskered notion, in its primary conception at least, the 'Paradiso' ['In Ballast to the White Sea'] went up in flames with our house seven years ago. The Purgatorio – entitled The Last Address, and set, lyrically, in an American madhouse, and the consequence of an excursion into journalism (not madness, I'm glad to say) and the Inferno, which was the Volcano – then just about completed (for the third time) were rescued. (By my wife; I managed to get one of her novels out) I hadn't finished The Last Address save in a short version, though the ill-starred Paradiso was a Gargantuan meal for the flames indeed. The whole was, and is again, I hope to be entitled The Voyage That Never Ends, but all this meant considerable rewriting, and in fact recasting of one's life. Well, whose life these days hasn't had to be recast? With the details of that life I have no right to confuse you save in so far as it bears on your work in hand. As for a private little fire, or two fires, or a hundred and two fires, with the world in flames, and so much suffering everywhere, it might seem bad taste even to mention it, though as a matter of fact that damned fire was probably one of the best things that ever happened to me. And there is something, I flatter myself, (indeed even Schopenhauer would agree that this was the best way to look at such coincidences, else one would be at the mercy of the suspicion of the terrible in oneself, and if terrible, how is one to transcend it and if to transcend it, how to find some meaning or dignity, supposing it to exist, in the terror?) so essentially, by the way, Germanic in the *mythical* sense, about part of the history of this work that started off quite modestly, that I yield to the temptation to digress a little on the point. To begin with I was sustained by the feeling simply I was doing among other things a pioneer work on drink; it was as well I had the illusion for at the same time, unknown to me, a gentleman far away was writing The Lost Week End. Then it began to strike me that the Consul meant something more: was he not like man himself, like Faust, and in the position, as it were, of a black magician, and if so, had I not better learn something about what really haunted him? Fatal supposition! Indeed no sooner had I thought that than I actually encountered a strange personage in the forest here, who, ostensibly a canvasser for votes, was in reality just such a magician, I should quickly add, just not such a magician, because he was a white magician and a good man, (not Amfortas).[16] I hasten to say that I am not a magician, black or white, nor have practised magic – good lord (as someone said) Malcolm is not a black magician but a hot musician. My friend, however, threw open his library to me, whereupon I began to feel like The Student of Prague indeed.[17] My friend told me that a black magician who fell into the abyss was in the unenviable position of having all the elements in the universe against him. This is what accounts (though I had by this time arrived at the same conclusion myself – Goethe is chuckling in the wings) for the recital of all the elements in Chapter X – written long before the atom bomb. Nonetheless there is a way of seeing all this that is transcendental to say the least. It seemed that by merely looking upon these things I had involved myself with a far more intricate karma, not to say a set of ordeals. Not only did our own house burn down under quite mysterious circumstances but two months later, when we were four thousand miles away, the house to which we had tranferred our other belongings (though fortunately not the saved manuscripts) was consumed by fire – without damage to others, as was the case with ours, a rarity in a forest here. There was no explanation of this last fire at all, no one in the house at the time.[18] Not merely this but in Ontario, in the space of a few months, on two occasions the house next to us caught fire: once in Niagara we were surrounded by a veritable ring of fire! – though none of these last fires caused any great damage. But equally they had no explanation: no fires had occurred for as long as forty years in one instance in these particular places. The grocer said: 'The element is following you around.' {of course I suppose they all had a perfectly mundane explanation too.} Having remembered the mystical saying 'Fear is a lion in the path,' (we were both by this time frightened out of our wits by fire) I took this to mean that we better return to this very place and build on the old ruined site. This we did: and I am writing this letter from here on top of the old burned foundations where we have lived the last five years without any fire protection at all beyond a pyrene extinguisher! To do that seemed one meaning of the ordeal itself: then, in 1945, before the Volcano was accepted, I returned to Mexico for a short visit. We went to Cuernavaca (Quauhnahuac): by a coincidence the only place my wife and I could find to live in was the *original of M. Laruelle's house* – now broken up into apartments – and it was to this house that the news of the acceptance of the Volcano (from England and the U.S. on the same day) was brought in February 1946 – god save us, by the original of the little postman in Chapter VI. Meantime we had gone to look for my friend, the original of Dr Vigil in Oaxaca, with whom I had lost touch for years, only to discover that he had been murdered under similar circumstances to the Consul.[19] Finally even more truly awe-inspiring things began to happen in Mexico so that it was as if one were living *inside* the book. We narrowly escaped with our lives finally, due to one thing and another: but this is now the basis, the plot of the new Paradiso. (It sounds like a worse inferno but the characters transcend it.) I had to go apparently *under* Under the Volcano myself in order eventually – as is now my intention

– to redeem the Consul. I am now trying to redeem him: and I hope that you will like my redemption sufficiently that one day you will like to translate it. I should be very proud if you would. Naturally I have to charge my protagonist with the authorship of Under the Volcano itself – on one plane it has to be a history of a man's imagination – which in its division of personalities makes for all kinds of difficulties: but I hope to bring off the whole Voyage That Never Ends one day. At all events it is clear that I have to *write* it, unless I want to be *written*, as it were: I hope you will agree that it is at least a wonderful philosophical problem. Bristling with horrors, paranoias, and insanities on every hand, it should yet be possible, if I may mix my metaphors, to harmonize them and sail through triumphantly to port. (I forgot to add that when we came back from Mexico we found the flowers on our old burned site had come up in our absence which, if you remember your Parsifal, should be taken as a good omen indeed!)[20]

Please forgive me for having gone on at such length. A few other minor things occur to me. Is it possible to vary the length of the dash occasionally in German? In Chapter X especially, the dashes all of the same length, seem rather boring. It struck me that in that chapter, say for instance on page 298-299 and on 299 and elsewhere – an occasional long dash would give effective relief, not a very long one, just twice the ordinary length, particularly before the quotations from the Tlaxcala folder. A long dash has a quite different emotive value: viz:[21]

298-299 ' – who have nobody them with — '

TLAXCALA ROYAL CHAPEL

299 'In the Farolito — '

SANTUARIO OCOTLAN IN TLAXCALA

Also I hope you can dig up a pointing hand in the German typeset. (p. 333) I am very proud of this hand; (having stolen it from Thomas Hardy – from Jude the Obscure, to be precise, the only other place where I have seen such a hand) which never fails to give me a chill down the spine;[22] aesthetically the hand may be a bit hard to justify, I admit, but I am very fond of it just the same. Concerning the sign in the garden 'Le gusta esta Jardin? – especially at the very end – I've often wondered whether cursive capitals would not be more effective: old style Italic – or even for the very end, Gothic. I don't know, but ordinary capitals seem to leave something to be desired. German Gothic seems to me so fascinatingly beautiful I can just look at it for hours on end without understanding a word. Doubtless Gothic would be scarcely appropriate in the public garden in Chapter V but perhaps the headings in X, such as Santuario Ocotlan in Tlaxcala, would go well in Gothic, or as we call it Black Letter. But very probably I am wrong. And most certainly I have long since ceased to be helpful.

However I hope I have said some helpful things, though my letter owing to the difficulty of communication about one's own work even in English may not always be strictly accurate – it is particularly hard to explain the menu and the alternative reading of the book is irrelevant – and may be even slightly illiterate in places. But if I have succeeded in giving you the general drift all this will not have been wasting your time.

I hope one day to see you in Wurtemberg and drink a Stiefel of good Münchener or Dortmunder Union with you – meantime do you please drink one for me – and meantime too all the best of luck with the work and again very many thanks both for selecting the book and for your generous and heart-warming words.

Mit freundlicher Begrüssung

Malcolm Lowry

P.S. A further small matter. I dedicated the American edition to my wife, and for some of the foreign editions we have liked to share the dedication with various friends of ours. Since I long ago promised to dedicate the German translation to the schoolmaster, Downie Kirk, who is the translator of your letter – whose specialty is the German language – and in whose house, incidentally, we lived immediately after our fire – and who has offered where necessary to act as a sort of interpreter between us – I would count it a great favour if you could cause to be inserted on some flyleaf: *to my wife Margerie and to Downie Kirk.*[23] This would be much appreciated by him and it could be done so unobtrusively as not to interfere with yourself should you wish to dedicate your German translation to someone else.

Annotations:

1 Clemens ten Holder (1903-52), an editor and writer, was the first German translator of *Under the Volcano*. Although Lowry and ten Holder never met, the two men became friendly through their letters. Lowry's command of German was poor and he often had to turn to Downie Kirk for help in answering ten Holder's questions, but he had not forgotten his early love of German theatre, film, and art or the weeks he had spent in Bonn. Margerie and Hildegard ten Holder (1905-75) also corresponded, so that when Clemens fell ill in 1952, Hildegard wrote to both the Lowrys. Before his untimely death ten Holder was hoping to translate more of Lowry's fiction and to be involved in a German film of the *Volcano*.

2 Lowry spent a six-week period from September to October 1928 at Weber's School of Modern German in Bonn, where he studied the language mainly in pubs and theatres; see his 23 April 1951 letter (**455**) to ten Holder and Day (98-101) and Bowker (79-80).

3 See Lowry's 20 March 1951 letter (**447**) to Downie Kirk.

4 *Schmutzig* is the German for dirty, filthy, or smutty.

5 The German acronym u.s.w. stands for *und so weiter*, meaning 'and so forth.'

6 Porfiro Díaz was president of Mexico from 1877 to 1880 and 1884 to 1911. Notoriously corrupt, Díaz was a key influence in bringing the country to the brink of revolution.

7 See Lowry's 2 January 1946 letter (**210**) to Jonathan Cape.

8 See Figure 7.

9 In Genesis 38:9 Onan masturbates to avoid fathering a child that will not be raised as his. This disobedience so angers God that he kills Onan. Onanism, meaning coition without ejaculation, or masturbation, recalls Geoffrey's failed intercourse with Yvonne in chapter 3 of *Under the Volcano*.

10 The Spanish word for octopus is *pulpo* and for squid, *calamares*, but Lowry may be thinking of the obsolete English name for squid: sleeve-fish.

11 James Joseph 'Gene' Tunney (1898-1978) was an American boxer who won a controversial match with Jack Dempsey in 1926 to become world heavyweight champion.

12 The Mexican term *mole* indicates a dish covered with black chili sauce, but the English word 'mole' has three distinct meanings that contribute to Lowry's macaronic joke: a mole is an animal, a small congenital blemish on the skin, and a measurement for weight in chemistry. The word is also slang for an undercover spy.

13 English poet Ralph Hodgson (1871-1962) wrote a poem called 'The Bull' (1917) that Lowry used as an intertextual reference in *Under the Volcano*. It is a grim projection of human fears on to an animal, and the vultures hover throughout the poem. Lowry has slightly misremembered the first verse.

14 *Eastward Ho* (1605) was written by George Chapman, Ben Jonson, and John Marston. Thomas Heywood (1574?-1641) was another prolific playwright who collaborated on plays, but not this one. London is called 'Cuckhold's Haven' repeatedly in the play.

15 The passage Lowry quotes in his preface to *Au-dessous du volcan* (Paris: Corrêa, 1950), p. 1, is from Arthur Schopenhauer's essay 'On Style'; see Lowry's 20 March 1951 letter (**447**) to Downie Kirk.

16 The black magician in Richard Wagner's *Parsifal* is Klingsor. Amfortas is the King of the Grail Knights who has been wounded by Klingsor. These echoes of *Parsifal* are frequent with Lowry; see, for example, his July 1944 letter (**194**) to Margerie. Lowry's friend was Charles Stansfeld-Jones; see Lowry's June 1944 letter (**190**) to Stansfeld-Jones.

17 There are three film versions of *The Student of Prague*: one directed by Stellan Rye in 1913; one directed by Henrik Galeen in 1926, and one by Arthur Robison in 1936. Galeen's expressionist film, starring Conrad Veidt as the student and Werner Krauss as the villain, depicts a poor student who sells his reflection (and better half), only to be haunted by it until he kills his double and himself.

18 See Lowry's description of the fires that seemed to pursue him in his mid-October 1945 letter (**205**) to Conrad Aiken and in chapter 18 of *October Ferry to Gabriola*.

19 See Lowry's 15 May 1940 letter (**140**) to Juan Fernando Márquez.

20 Spring flowers bloom in the forest surrounding the Grail Castle on Good Friday in the third act of *Parsifal*.

21 These variations in the length of the dash were important to Lowry; he raised the same point in his 28 October 1946 letter (**252**) to Albert Erskine.

22 Hardy uses the sign of the hand in part 1, chapter 11 of *Jude the Obscure* (1896).

23 The dedication in Clemens ten Holder's translation, *Unter dem Vulkan* (1951), is: 'Für meine Frau Margerie und für Downie Kirk.'

Editorial Notes:

a. The copy-text for this transcription (UBC 2:17) is a twelve-page typescript consisting of six sheets of letter paper, closely typed on both sides, with few minor deletions and interlineations but some interesting marginalia. All addenda are in pencil, and Lowry's signature, originally in pencil, has been overwritten in ink. The typescript has been folded in half for mailing, and a lengthy pencil draft of the letter is also extant (UBC 2:17). All the marginalia have been marked by Lowry for insertion in the letter, but he has also written the page numbers in German at the top left of each page and has added a comment to some: EINS (1); ZWEI (2); DREI (3); VIER (4); FUNF (5); SEX (6) {Down to the bottom of the class, Herr Lowry! Haven't you learned to count up to six in German yet?}; SIEBEN (7) {Up again, Herr Lowry, & give out the pencils}; ACHT (8) H'm.; NINE 9 (Enshuligensie, mein Herr!. .Into the corner, Herr Lowry!); DECEM 10 (The Dunce's cap); DIX 11 (Nein!); UNDECIM 12 (Herr Lowry herausgeschmissen ist, & is to be found thereafter in the bar at the Rheinischer Hof.).

451: To Malcolm Lowry

P: UBC(ms)

[25 March 1951]ᵃ

S.S. EL LEON:[1]   OATH TO HIGHER SELF

(1) I resolve, starting this day, Easter Sunday, 1951 to attempt sincerely, with God's help, to recast my life in a better, sincerer, mould, and with attention to minute particulars. In place of selfishness to place – especially in regard to the Harteebeeste – [2]

(2) unselfishness, understanding, and wisdom.

(3) to banish self-deception in small matters.

(4) to banish self-indulgence in destructive neuroses.

(5) not use drink as a means of oblivion. To have self-mastery on this point. Where drink is used it should be purely as an enjoyment, a release, or occasionally as a help to work. One should have the courage to be a purist on this point and

(6) not to use this resolve as a means to ratify more oblivion.

(7) to clear up the situation with Jimmy [Craige]: which subtly stinks.

(8) to smoke less, to make small sacrifices, with the end of improving one's character, such as this, and where there are two alternatives of behaviour, to choose the harder task.

(9) to banish anxiety on Margie's part regarding my relationship to other people and genuinely to do something about this.[3] And conversely:

(10) in the interests of work, not use the above as an excuse, & have the courage where necessary not to see them at all.

(11) to keep fit

(12) to get the whole pattern of our mental & physical lives in honest shape, so that a year from now, one may feel, and feel without smugness, that one has improved one's character and done one's duty to God.

Signed this Easter Sunday

EL LEON

Annotations:

1 Lowry was born under the zodiacal sign of Leo, the Lion, and frequently referred to himself as 'El Leon'; see his notes to Margerie in Appendix 1.

2 The term 'Harteebeeste' refers to Margerie and is part of the repertoire of pet names used by the Lowrys.

3 The nature of the problem Lowry refers to here and in resolution seven is unclear. 1950 to 1951 was an extremely difficult period and Lowry had behaved badly at Downie Kirk's home; see his January 1951 letter **(437)** to Kirk.

Editorial Notes:

a. Lowry has edited this pencil holograph (UBC 21:5) and the three October 1951 letters **(473, 474, 475)** to Margerie for inclusion in *October Ferry to Gabriola*. The names El Leon and Harteebeeste have been changed to Ethan and Jacqueline, and the page is numbered 18. In the top right margin of the recto Lowry has inserted: 'And then, there were resolutions the oaths to the higher self – as' and directly below this he has written: 'That had been last Easter.' The latter comment suggests that Lowry was editing the letters and his oath during the spring of 1952.

452: To Downie Kirk

p: UBC(msc)
pp: *SL* 234-37

[Dollarton]
[April 1951]ᵃ

Mein lieber alter Freund Downie –

We were sad not to see you at Easter, and also that you have been under the weather, though delighted to get your letter – so here is something to amuse you, and I hope interestingly to divert you at the same time not to say please you, I hope – everything from how to put the hex on your more troublesome pupils (though for god's sake don't use it like that for it might work) to some more Dasseinsausage, as well as a letter of gratitude in the same language, with which is incorporated needless to say my own too, hereby renewed.[1]

Re the former it might interestingly be dipped into in relation to the Pencil of God: the work is by the Marcelin's younger brother, himself an ethnologist (& though it doesn't say so, a voodoo priest too, as is the illustrator, Hippolyte, or rather was, he having recently died, though not before having achieved an enormous reputation as a painter, a reputation that was as highly deserved in my opinion as it was inevitable perhaps in one who did not paint at all, more or less, unless possessed by John the Baptist.), and I think it is endlessly fascinating, & moreover written in a French so translucent that even I can tell that it represents an achievement of style too of a creative order.[2]

Though its style may be irrelevant to the terrifying abysses & potentialities of the human mind that it opens up! – I would be delighted to see you & Limpus get together on it, since Milo, as I say, is a scientist too.[3] The pen seems to make too much impression on the paper so I carry on in pencil. I don't think the Marcelin is likely to be translated into English, though it is certainly an opportunity for someone. Of course I haven't yet been through it all – I couldn't resist sending it almost at once, since I thought it [would] be of such great interest to you.

Needless to say, it is sent with a *pure* blessing upon it, as it were: this remark or precaution may seem peculiar in this material age, but the fact is that Milo would not have sent it to us in the first place, I believe, had we not been privileged to witness some of the mysteries in question,[4] nor himself dared to write it, had he not been a high practitioner of the said mysteries themselves, thus being empowered to clothe them in the harmless and useful guise of inquiring science & comparative religion: so I am not giving away any secret I should not, nor are you in possession of a 'magic' book that could wreak any damage (I once felt Margie & I were, as I told you, & so sent the book, that was another book of course, back) – if it makes you uncomfortable send it back, – all I can think of is – though this may seem absurd – I wouldn't let Dorothy see it; I have no idea of the power of some of the symbols should they be copied – apart from that, I am not sending you a Monkey's Paw[5] as it were, – it is merely in the good spirit of friendship to interest you. The most that can happen is that it might bring you some unexpected good luck, as happened to me once: though that is no harm: essentially Voodoo is a religion, to be regarded with reverence, since unquestionably it is the matter-transcending religion based upon the actual existence of the supernatural as a fact that is funadamental to man himself (I express myself very badly), compared with which most other religions are simply techniques to hide that fact, or confine the supernatural to relatively safe distances; it would seem that only the Negro race are powerful enough or holy enough to be able to handle it and even they of course often abuse it. Heaven knows what we do with the same power. But that is not to say one should not regard with awe the great dignity & discipline that is behind it at its highest, nor its conception of God, nor the meaning that it gives to life – & all this on the part of a race we so often glibly think of as inferior, or comprising medicine men, or the powers of darkness & so on. Heart of Darkness indeed! Joseph Conrad should have been to Haiti. What he failed to understand was that the savages of the Congo had to some extent *subdued* the dark forces that are in nature by creating their religion in the first place in order to subdue them, that that, in its way, was a civilizing, almost a pragmatic process. A white man comes along & is made a god & uses the same magic to keep & to gain power with these 'unspeakable' rights [sic] etc.[6] But in my estimation it was the white man who had corrupted them with his own brand of unspeakableness. Anyhow that story – great though it is – is at least half based on a complete miscomprehension. (I'm not sure if my words make sense, & not sure I would know what to make of them were they played back to me on your magic recording machine) It is clear that Comrade Joseph did not allow himself to be corrupted by any savages though: he stayed in Polish aloofness on board in company with some a priori ideas. Anyway there you have a more than Golden bough in one way,[7] & return the books at your leisure; though Margie has hardly looked at the volumes, neither of us have time at the present anyway to read them fully, whereas your mind will take in much more much more swiftly at what glances you may have opportunity for.

For the rest I enclose two letters from ten Holder – one to yourself.[8] I don't know what he says to you, save that is a letter of thanks but don't bother to translate it, unless there is some specific question that looks important that you might have time to translate – because he has sent me another questionnaire in English, I am well able to answer & I don't want to bother you. I had already taken the matter of the dedication with [Ernst] Klett but did so again to make sure.[9] I would have dedicated it to all three of you, also bringing in Dollarton, & our gratitude for lending us your house, & other more happy days, but for the identity of our wive's names, & the fact that an oblique question of consideration of space arose out of the feeling he might want to dedicate the translation per se as a translation from his end to someone else {The dedication of Proust gets gummed up in this way.}: so please all take the will for the deed – I hope it pleases you, but let me know if it doesn't & how I should alter it. (That this should not pass without its strange coincidence – the Karlheinz Schmidhüs he mentions *was* one of my German teachers in Bonn, though not Godesberg (2 miles away) if I learned little it was not his fault but mine for usually being in the Rheinischer Hof; he was by far the nicest, the most brilliant, & the only genuinely kind teacher I had there, & we were great friends, despite my being such a rotten pupil – & to cap it all, he has always reminded me very strongly of yourself)

With best love from Margerie & myself to Marjorie Dorothy & yourself & hoping to see you soon –

Malcolm

Annotations:

1 Clemens ten Holder wrote to thank Downie Kirk for his help on 14 April 1951 (UBC 1:67).

2 The book by Milo Marcelin with illustrations by Hector Hippolyte is *Mythologie Vodou*, 2 vols (1949), a study of witchcraft. Marcelin sent Lowry an inscribed copy on 6 March 1951; it is with his library in the UBC Lowry Collection.

3 George and Dorothy Limpus were friends of the Kirks; see Salloum (57).

4 Lowry always maintained that he had been taken to Voodoo ceremonies during his weeks in Haiti in early 1946.

5 Monkeys' paws are credited with having sinister supernatural power, and 'The Monkey's Paw' (1902) is a short story by W.W. Jacobs (1863-1943) that Lowry had enjoyed from his youth; see his 10 June 1926 letter (15) to Carol Brown.

6 In part 2 of Joseph Conrad's novella *Heart of Darkness* (1902) Marlow reads, in Kurtz's report to the 'International Society for the Suppression of Savage Customs,' the latter's description of 'unspeakable rites' and realizes that Kurtz has himself succumbed to such rites.

7 Sir James George Frazer (1854-1941), the Scots anthropologist, folklorist, and classicist, published his encyclopaedic twelve-volume comparative study of magic and religion between 1890 and 1915. In *The Golden Bough* Frazer traces an evolutionary sequence in human think-

ing from the magical to the religious to the scientific. Lowry owned the
1942 single-volume abridged edition.

8 See annotation 1.

9 The German translation of *Under the Volcano* is dedicated to Margerie
and Downie Kirk; see Lowry's 21 March 1951 letter (**450**) to ten
Holder, annotation 23. There is no reference to the dedication in
Lowry's letters to Ernst Klett (**478**, **544**).

Editorial Notes:

a. The holograph is undated, but the subject-matter and reference to
Easter suggest an April 1951 date. The last paragraph of this letter has
been translated into German for *Briefwechsel* (30).

453: To The Editor, *Vancouver Sun*

P: UBC(ms)   [Dollarton]
                                                   [ca 4 April 1951]ᵃ

Dear Sir:

In your tragic story of the 'Seven Sisters,' headed 'Famed Giants of
Forest Doomed,' about our six great Douglas firs and the one cedar,
seven hundred years old, that have been so long the guardians of Stanley
Park, but are now all dead and must come down, you mention that the
City Archivist Major Matthews says that their name has two possible
origins.[1] They may have been named the Seven Sisters you write – after
the seven famous women known as the Sutherland Sisters, who sold hair
tonic, and performed in Vancouver shop windows.

Or another possibility is, you say, that they were named after the
daughters of one of Gastown's prominent citizens, Angus C. Frazer of
Jericho.[2] (Justifiable civic pride!)

But is it not just barely possible that the seven famous Sutherland sisters who sold hair tonic, no less than the seven daughters of Gastown's
prominent citizen, Mr Angus C Frazer of Jericho, would not have without several ways been so known as the Seven Sisters in the first place had
it not been for the existence of a concept of a yet more famous 'Seven
Sisters,' whose performance has been visible weather permitting from
your own Sun tower – for that matter – every night from winter to early
spring since it has been built? And which have been visible too, from
where Stanley Park now stands, thousands of years before even our own
Seven Sisters took root?

Is it possible that neither the gallant Major nor the Vancouver
Sun have heard of the Pleiades, the constellation known since time
immemorial as the Seven Sisters? The good Major perhaps who cannot

be a sailor after all, may have slipped, but not the Vancouver Sun surely, (named after a sort of star itself, if not one of the Pleiades, though the astronomer Meidler considered that Alcyone was the central sun of the universe.)³ not the Sun, surely with its daily quotation from the Bible! Ah no. Unless of course you are the very people born to bind the sweet influences of the Pleiades — though a greater authority than I — Job 38 31 — & one who, as I say, you heavily draw upon — suggested (in the passage where God convinces Job of ignorance and imbecility) that it can't be done.⁴

Canst thou bind the sweet influences of Pleiades, or loose the bands of Orion?

Canst thou bring forth Mazzaroth in his season? or canst thou guide Arcturus with his sons?

Knowest thou the ordinances of heaven?

Sure you do. At all events I humbly suggest that this is the imaginative origin of their name on someone's part, & your moving photograph showing the constellatory arrangement of the stricken trees would seem to bear one out.

In mythology the Pleiades were, as of course you know (though that doesn't mean I've been slap through them very lately myself) the seven daughters of Atlas & Pleione: Electra, Maya, Alcyme, Merope, Sterope, Taygeta, & Celano were the names of the sisters. As stars six can be seen with the naked eye, but there used to be an almost universal legend there were seven stars you could see in the group, & that one has been lost. Hence the seven sisters & the myth of the Lost Pleiad. The one cedar in the seven firs might correspond to the Lost Pleiad.

According to the book the Pleiades were mentioned — so quite a *lot* of people know about them, as the seven sisters too, — in China over 2000 years before Christ. The Egyptians, the Aztecs, the Japanese all worshipped them. And the Festival of All Hallows, All Saints Day, the Mexican Day of the Dead etc. are all associated with the culmination of the Pleiades. It is thought, adds my source (for I now have a source), that these universal memorial services commemorate a great cataclysm that occurred in ancient times, the basic reason, in short, why at Halloween, some fellow like Jack Scott puts a Ford car on the roof, and who, for all I care, may one day put one next Halloween night on the roof of the Vancouver Sun.

But apart from all this kind of thing would not the Seven famous women themselves known as The Sutherland Sisters who sold hair tonic, have liked to think of just this, & of *their* names' origin, if indeed they did not think of it all the time, as they performed in their dear Vancouver shop windows?

And as for Angus C. Fraser — Angus is not so much unlike Atlas perhaps (especially with the circumstances) that prominent citizen of Gastown, would he not have been absolutely tickled to death at the notion of the identity of his daughters with the seven celestial daughters of Atlas & Pleine on high?

It may be, in time to come, that owing to the sweet influences of the Vancouver Sun that instead of the Pleiades *dancing* up there at night we may all be able to imagine the Sutherland sisters, who sold hair tonic, performing in their eternal shop window.

Or conversely, may we hope, that in place of Alcyone & the rest, as Hallow'een descends upon us, we shall look heavenward and imagine instead the culmination of the seven daughters of Angus C. Frazer, of Jericho, that prominent citizen of Gastown?

But that time is not yet, & privately, though I know your loving care for Canadian culture, that care is surely not as great as all *that*. (Be that as it may, on the other hand, there is another way of looking at it, I'm sure that the Pleiades themselves, after all this time, would be delighted to give place etc etc)

Meantime, – to continue on the stem note – the Seven Sisters are dead, & 'must be destroyed as menace', & the best that they can hope for is that their stumps be preserved for posterity by 'encasing them in plastic.' A touching thought: even more touching might be to put a little tablet, likewise encased in the plastic of course, commemorating their high-minded murderer: thus; Persecuted & killed by civilisation in the form of the Noble City of Vancouver. nee Gastown R.I.P. {Hugged to death out of love}

For that they too, like their constellatory counterparts, may have died, in one way and another, of grief, I can understand. But do you have to make them die of grief twice?

With the reservations above of course, & no doubt there are further reservations, beyond that, I haven't seen.

Yours truly

Malcolm Lowry

New Caledonia Yrwol M Loclam

{True though is it is an unkind & cruel & unfair note on which to conclude that instead of the Pleiades twinkling up there we may project our minds into the higher conception of the Sutherland sisters, who sold hair tonic, performing twinkling in their eternal shop window!}

Annotations:

1 Lowry is responding to a front-page article in the *Vancouver Sun* for Tuesday, 3 April 1951. The story is accompanied by a dramatic photograph of the seven trees, and several eminent Vancouverites are

mentioned, including J.C. Matthews, the city archivist. Lowry used this article in 'The Bravest Boat' from *Hear us O Lord*.

2 Angus Carmichael Fraser (1848-1906) was a well-known British Columbia lumberman and leading citizen of Vancouver. He and his wife had *eight* daughters.

3 Johann Heinrich Mädler (1794-1874) was a leading astronomer of his day, although his theory that the Milky Way possessed a central constellation formed by Alcyone in the Pleiades was disproved.

4 In Job 38 God challenges Job and enumerates his works to demonstrate Job's comparative weakness. In verse 31 he asks the questions that Lowry goes on to quote.

Editorial Notes:

a. This undated holograph draft letter (UBC 3:14) to the editor of the *Vancouver Sun* may not have been sent and does not appear to have been published.

454: To Frank Taylor

P: Lilly(ts)   Dollarton, B.C., Canada
                                                    7 April 1951

Dear old Frank:

In receipt of yours – all I can say is that it is magnificently sporting of you, and to believe me when I say that it is as hard at bottom for us even to imagine one concurs with such a suggestion, which spiritually one doesn't, as for you to make it; the fact remains however that whereas we are presented with the fluttering of the thing, however battered, into some kind of remotely possible flight, you are presented with the thing lost.[1]

There is this to be said, though, that if it ever comes off in anything successfully approaching the way we dreamed it, you will have produced it after all.

For you certainly drew it out. For my part it was as if my consciousness were saying – to you and Albert both for that matter – There, you see, I can do it, you were not wrong to believe in the Volcano. So it the Night is your baby.

I have several times thought that we were fooling ourselves a bit in regard to the baby. But I am wrong. It is *there*. It has faults, as you say; of 'novelistic' dialogue, Manciewitz might point out; too much New York, too much ship, an overreaching at the end, though these things had to be written, even if the final intention was for some of them rather to be suggested. But this was in part caused by lack of time, finally, to cut, and it was as if certain metaphors had to be followed through, here and there, to test their validity as suggestions. And unquestionably again it requires further work, for there are no doubt faults of sheer ignorance of the possibilities of the medium. (Though I doubt that they are grave. Has anyone ever said anything about professional near-sightedness? Unknown side of Malcolm's life. When I was a kid two top South African comedians had a song of mine in their repertoire. But their gags between songs would not go over in vaudeville on tour. Why? Said friend Malcolm: You don't really test them on the audience, you test them in the dressing room back stage. If Mr Bain of Mr Bain's Cats and Rats, or Sealy the Seal Man laugh like hell at one of your jokes, you seem to think it'll go over. When you're on the stage you're laughing so hard yourself, and Mr Bain and Sealy the Seal Man are so pleased with you – partly because the jokes probably originated with them – that you think you're going over fine. Now you discover that the audience was bored to death all the while and the manager of the Kilburn Empire's going to drop you from the top of the bill. All right, Malcolm, they say, you're the audience, suppose *you* think up some gags for us. – O.K., I will. I think I can see exactly what you have to do etc. etc. – largely a matter of timing. So I thought up some more gags for them and they were a riot. Finally they became the lead in the London run of an Irving Berlin show at the Aldwych and made enough money damn nearly to buy Rhodesia. I don't know why I tell you this fool story and I better stop, or a ukelele will come into the next paragraph.)[2] But what I felt about it on looking at it severely was that objectively it would be damned hard to find anything better to work on than that script as regards that particular book. In short, whatever anyone may say, I think it's potentially one of the best films I never saw: or rather, for that matter, we *did* see it. And that film is fundamentally yours, anyway, archetypically.

So now we come to Fletcher Markle. Curiously enough – there always is a curiously enough – while spring cleaning the other day I turned up an old letter to you not posted for some reason in which I said I wished to God you and Markle could get together on the script.[3] It was while you were at M.G.M. and I read somewhere that Fletcher had signed a contract to direct for them. I didn't know he'd done Tender is the Night on the radio, I'm glad to say, or I think I would have been discouraged.

So much for that. Personally I liked Fletcher Markle, found him simpatico in a serious sense, and was gravely delighted by his fantastic enterprise. What I did think was that the quality of his work would probably depend to a large extent on the nature of the opportunity and what was working through the opportunity. I didn't think much of what he made of the radio Volcano but I did think if only we'd written the script he'd have done it fine.[4] Gerald Noxon, his collaborator, and one of my best friends, and who certainly knew the Volcano because he helped me with it, and who is a quite excellent writer himself, must have been thinking of something else or in too much of a hurry. Something like that. As a result an opportunity, such as it was, was grasped, but rather at the expense of the book, which people told me they would now not like to read, thank you. On the other hand people praised the radio script, though they were wrong to do so; what they liked were the noises off and the general momentum of the show. Markle, like me, is a fine noises-off man. I like to think I am a good noises-off man.

So I think he could be a first rate director with a first rate producer and a first rate script and something working through all that. So I don't think I was wrong in imagining you would make a good team, especially since you may be as much or more director as producer, and he producer as director, to have done the Night, though you might have gibbed at the suggestion. But possibly I am superstitiously a bit prejudiced in his favour because he hails from old Vancouver here, or because he liked the Volcano. Next to your own good hands though, from my point of view, if there have to be other hands (though the actors of course are another question) and though we can't be happy about it, I would perhaps be least unhappy if the hands were Markle's.

So, if you still think to do so, yes, would you please quietly slip the script to Markle: there's no reason to waste three or four weeks sending it up here to us to send back to Hollywood again. I can't say how extraordinarily good of you all this is. If things were not going well with you I would rather you burned it. But there is the point, that if the script is any *use*, and can be none to you conceivably, there is a certain something that tends to mortality in letting it seethe and sit while another palimpsest is hatched in the air on top of it, the more especially as it is difficult for me to see, however many faults may be in our version, so many actual tactile dramatic problems can be solved in another, at least in so short a time as Markle is counting upon: while one thing is making itself another thing of the same sort is unmaking itself, and since ours I conceive is an accomplished entity of a kind, it can but work mysteriously against the other, unless it would help, and so it might be better for all and it to bring it thus to light and let it accomplish what it will – even if nothing, it will have tried to culminate itself.

So if it has come down to that, give it to Markle, and I will meantime write a sort of note to him.[5]

It has come down to me at long last that one might not be altogether without ambition oneself – an ambition that of course has naturally not been shared by any other writer – to have a crack at the movies oneself in a serious way before one shuffles off this mortal coil.

Should this ever come to pass, I feel it in the cards and the hands –

and trust the feeling to be right – that we may at last do something else of worth for you that will be this time luckily realised for you.

I believe Clyde Gilmour, your faithful admirer, and the most reliable and entertaining judge of movies here in Canada, to be in Hollywood himself doing something, or on holiday.[6] I don't know him, but I know he would be tickled to death to meet you.

Meantime all the luck in the world with the scripts in progress, and for the future; again our deep thanks for your generous heartedness, we continue to look forward to seeing you here someday, and with the best of love to yourself Nan and the children from us both.

                                                                        Malcolm

P.S. Meantime Margerie is doing some truly excellent work. And I too have considerably matured: aged in the wood, as the saying is: y siempre tam campante, anyhow.[7]

Annotations:

1 Taylor was never able to sell the Lowrys' filmscript, but in his 3 April 1951 letter to Lowry he offered to give the filmscript to Fletcher Markle, who was with MGM and trying to revive interest in a film of *Tender Is the Night*, thereby relinquishing his claim to the script.
2 Lowry's story sounds apocryphal, or at best exaggerated; however, he did write and publish two songs with Ronnie Hill in 1927. See his 12 March 1929 letter (**21**) to Conrad Aiken.
3 This letter has not survived with Lowry's papers.
4 Markle's radio version of *Under the Volcano* was broadcast on CBS 'Studio One' on 29 April 1947; see Lowry's 21 June 1947 letter (**309**) to Gerald Noxon.
5 There is no record of Markle preparing a radio broadcast of *Tender Is the Night*, although he did do *The Great Gatsby* in 1947. No 'note' from Lowry to Markle on the subject has been located.
6 See Lowry's report on Gilmour's admiration for *Mystery Street* in his 27 January 1951 letter (**440**) to Taylor.
7 The Spanish expression *y siempre tan campante* means 'and always carefree (or relaxed).'

455: To Clemens ten Holder

P: UBC(ts)   Dollarton, B.C.,
PP: *SL* 237-41; *Brief* 30-36   Canada
                                                     23 April 1951[a]

Seehr geehrter Herr ten Holder:
    Thank you very much for your most amusing letter, and also for

writing to Downie Kirk, to whom I have sent on your letter, though he has not yet had time to reply to this.

I am extremely obliged to you in the matter of the dedication and I am certain that Downie will be delighted too.

Re the Gothic headings, etc. – also I thank you; but of course I meant to say, only if you thought it a good idea yourself; but I am surmising that you do. – I would very much like to hear you lecture at your Volkshochschule; what a wonderful word – does that mean Folk-happiness school?[1] also I sincerely appreciate the fact of your having discovered the Volcano. I hope you may preserve that feeling in regard to my work and that I may be worthy of it. The feeling of discovery, as well as having actually discovered something, especially in a foreign language, is a valid thing and hard enough to explain, and indeed is worth a novel in itself.

Enclosed you will find the answers to your questions, which I hope are adequate; they are at any rate fulsome, as a result of which I must unfortunately curtail this letter, {See P.S. to notes, though wait till you've got there.} in order to catch the airmail; though the letter cannot conclude without mention of what may be the extraordinary coincidence of your friend Karlheinz Schmidthüs which, if so, would seem to entitle you to the discovery of myself on yet another plane.[2] There was indeed a teacher when I was at Bonn – Koblenzerstrasse 100 (though this was not Godesberg) in 1928, named Schmidthüs, and one of whom I entertain the kindliest and most affectionate memories, for he was not only the most brilliant of the teachers there and the most well-liked – as brilliant a teacher as I was a dumbkopf of a pupil – but he was a person of such great goodness and wisdom that I not only have never forgotten him but can describe him in absolute detail, even though this is 23 years ago, and my sojourn in Bonn only 8 weeks, and the reason for this no doubt is, that though as a child one sets forth expecting to meet people who are kind and patient in this life, it turns out to be extremely rare to meet a combination of those virtues in anyone, of which patience is a component: he needed a lot of patience with me, as I had an almost abnormally slow mind, which caused me to suffer a great deal; however I can read German aloud today almost as well as a German – that was about the only class I took with Herr Schmidthüs who mostly dealt with advanced students, but then that was almost the only thing I learned at all in Bonn, outside the bar of the Hotel Rheinischer Hof, and it was not for lack of many other excellent teachers, and to be able to pronounce German properly, even despite my other deficiencies, has been an enormous help and pleasure to me: for example, once having determined the meaning I can appreciate much German poetry, even extremely complex poetry, in fact I can appreciate some poetry without having determined the meaning – [Rainer Maria] Rilke, strangely enough, I have sometimes been able really to understand in German, without being able to understand as well the English translation before me. It is true that this is confined to poetry: but with application and the time I could begin a study of German from there, whereas another person, knowing far more to begin with, would get much less out of it. Not the least strange part of this is that the Herr Schmidthüs I knew – whether Karlheinz was his Christian name I don't know – was almost the exact double of the very Downie Kirk, likewise a teacher, you have just written to – in fact, to describe him, as I remember him, would be to describe Downie; that is, I put him about 4 or 5 years older than I was then, which was 18 or 19, so he would be about 23 then that is – of somewhat above medium height, but with extraordinarily broad shoulders, and an extremely wide and intelligent forehead, he had, generally speaking apart from being very pleasant looking, an air of being younger even than he was, an air of something boyish, full of life, and twinkle, against which, as if half disapproving of his own élan, he wore rather conservative, usually dark clothes. One thing I shall always remember, I pleased him because I showed a true appreciation even at that age, which the other English boys didn't, of the triumphs of the German theatre – even modern expressionist triumphs, and he was staggered that I even knew about 'George' Kaiser, and what was more knew that he had written about thirty plays and not just Vom Morgens bis Mitternachts, and set about righting (as you may right my rendering of From Morn till Midnight) my pronunciation immediately![3]

Gay-org Kaiser, Herr Lowry.

He didn't think as much of Gayorg as I did (I had just seen Claude Rains playing in From Morn till Midnight in England as I was later to have a minor hand in the production of the same at Cambridge, as also of [Ernst] Toller, whom I later came to know well, both in London and Mexico) but he was delighted just the same, as he was also delighted when I reported to him that 'Der Gross Gott Brown' by Eugene O'Neill then playing at the Shauspielhaus in Köln – by far the most imaginative and wonderful production I have ever seen of O'Neill incidentally, far better than the play itself, which it had leant over backwards to extract the last juices of meaning out of, and where there weren't any, had provided some of its own – could not have been written surely without the influence of the said Gay-org. Herr Schmidthüs promised to look into these deep matters, but perhaps was more pleased when I showed some knowledge of Wedekind;[4] had this exchange occurred at the beginning of our short relationship there might have been some reason for his extraordinary decency in always making allowance for my slowness and never embarrassing me or holding me up as an example, but actually this occurred toward the end and it was perhaps the first indication he had had that I was not a congenital idiot. I have therefore always held Herr Schmidthüs in a place of unique esteem in my memory so if it should turn out by any miracle to be the same Herr Schmidthüs – though if not the coincidence of the name and the date and the location becomes weirder still – please tell him so, with my love. Also I hope he can take a bit of pride in his old pupil because the influences that have formed the Volcano are in a profound degree largely German; though it may be hard to see where they come from. (It was in Bonn I saw Murnau's Sonnenaufgang;[5] the first 20 minutes of this wonderful movie (though it falls to pieces later – doubtless due to the exigencies of Hollywood) have influenced me almost as much as any book I ever read, even though I've never seen it since.) It was through Herr Schmidthüs too I acquired the love of Gothic printing or at least writing that I hope has not discommoded you in Chapter X.

For the rest, yes, we rebuilt our house and were the carpenters and all. We too endure some financial hardship here, even as you: there is no outlet for one's work in Canada, no magazines, and the U.S. is not interested, should the mise-en-scène be Canada that mise-en-scène not contain a mounted policeman. It is difficult to make a living at 4000 miles distance, and it is hard to make a reply to the editor who says: Why don't you write another Under the Volcano? At least overnight. Moreover we have inflation. We spent our money earned from the success of the Volcano in America long ago, old England sits like a broody hen on most of the rest of our cash, expecting perhaps to hatch an iron virgin from it, we starve from time to time, but have a lot of fun just the same, and when we make some more cash, we shall come and see you in Wurttemberg.

I am very gratified about the Wibberli-Wobberli and your friend singing it on the guitar.[6] I didn't compose it however. It was the traditional song of our family that all the Lowry brothers sang at a certain recurrent ordeal for new boys at school. It probably was a music-hall song of the nineties, but I'm sure its copyright, if any, has long since expired. I am not at all sure that the composer was not my eldest brother himself; anyway I'm convinced your friend will have got a better version of it on his guitar. I have composed some things though, mostly jazz, also on a guitar. Indeed I was arrested in the street once in Bonn for playing and singing said guitar in company with some of your countrymen and one of mine on the occasion when we were celebrating the defeat of Essen Verein at hockey, I having played inside left for Bonn Verein, a refrain that went, every now and then: Zwei null! we having defeated them 2-0. Also there was another song to the refrain Drei Segelmann. . . But the policeman didn't like it. Finally he decided he did like it but would fine us all a little bit just the same. Whereupon your countrymen swore gallantly we would go to gaol rather than we be fined. Whereupon we swore gallantly we would go to gaol rather than they be fined. Whereupon we all repaired to the Hotel Kaiserhof, and were fined just the same, though nobody, it seems to me, mysteriously, paid.

And so, my dear Herr ten Holder, the very best luck to you with the translation. And also to yourself and your wife, from myself and my wife – herself American and the author of an exceedingly good and wild novel, Horse in the Sky. And not fogetting the 2 rowdies, Peter and Johannes.[7] While as for the little Xicotancatzerl (by the way the original Aztec name was, as you probably know, Xicotancatl, a Tlaxcaltecan hero) greetings from ours, whose seltsamer name does not reflect his benign character nor great gifts of singing, Citron-le-Taciturne –

With kind regards,

Malcolm Lowry

p. 21[8] It merely means that the Taskersons, despite their Pantagruelian delight in what was unfortunately not Dortmunder Union or Münchener, and hence general wildness as to their habits, had their Abendessen etc – they ate in short – at a fairly respectable hour, had dinner promptly at 7, that sort of thing. (I don't know about their früh-stuck.)[9] It seems damned silly now for me to have mentioned this at this particular point but no doubt I had some good reason for it. I think the object was to slip in just a note of the *veneer* of British respectability still operating in a family that was really incredibly dissipated – a veneer which the Consul himself acquires for that matter in later life.

p. 39 Humpty Dumpty sat on a wall
Humpty Dumpty had a great fall
All the King's horses
And all the King's men
Couldn't put Humpty Dumpty together again.

The Consul is thinking of this English nursery rhyme. (Hence too the title to Robert Penn Warren's best selling novel All the King's Men. Though his title has a highly ambiguous significance.)[10] What is in the Consul's mind – therefore – when writing the letter – is some lingering hope he would pull himself together – gather the pieces of himself together – (though it is impossible, not even all the King's Men could do it for Humpty Dumpty, because in the nursery rhyme Humpty Dumpty is an egg, hence the quasi-mystical significance) should he accept himself as a poet – which he perhaps secretly is – and not imagine himself as a mystic – which he perhaps secretly is too. But the buried intention is to universalise the Consul as Man himself here. All the references above that to Chesed, Binah, etc. are to the Caballah. The Qliphoth is the world of shells and demons – presided over by Beelzebub, the God of Flies, the underworld indeed. See also Chapter VII p. 218, bottom. Jean Paul Sartre has developed this theme, though I never heard of him when I wrote this (nor he of me, for that matter when he wrote The Flies.[11] Nor Beelzebub, I hope, of either of us.) The Nose with a Luminous Dong – reference is to a tragi-comic, though mostly tragic, poem of genius by Edward Lear, the English humorist and inventor of the limerick, The Dong With a Luminous Nose. But if you reverse it – since Nose is a very obscure slang term for spy and Dong I regret to report is, as a noun, another obscene word – it means something like this illuminating picture: The Spy with a luminous penis. Clare was another English poet who went mad and it was a snail in one of his poems that 'wove fearful vision.' The Knight of Sorry Aspect is Don Quixote and of course himself – the Consul – too; it is not exactly one of the Consul's most cheery moments.

p. 74 No – Mariana and the moated grange is a reference to a poem by Tennyson, I think of the same name – I've forgotten – but I think there's a ball in the poem that goes on all night as in the Volcano and of course a moated grange, which is the point: or rather the point is that the grange is a ruin. Or ought to be if there is a point.

p. 86 It gives cohobations in my dictionary. But I'm not sure it's the same word – which is an alchemical term I got out of an Elizabethan play. Originally this passage ran: living among the cohabitations – cohabitations! – of Faust etc. But I cut out the Consul's pun, which was meant to refer, via alchemy, to Yvonne's infidelity. Maybe cohabations has become cohobations. Cohabatious Cohobations on it!

p. 94 There is an old English soldier's expression – I've heard my brother use it – when describing someone who is unreliable or whom one dislikes to this effect: So and so is a dung-cart except for the straw and that's in his feet. Because Hugh has stopped automatically while reading a telegram and when he wasn't looking where he was going, on the edge of a pothole, he reflects that he must have eyes in his feet. Because he is going through a period of hating himself too he imagines the straw in his feet, (as in the soldier's saying above). There's also the word strawfoot, for soldier; straw man, for a fake. Something like Eliot's hollow man only made of straw. Strawman is also a favorite American political term for a dummy or a 'fence.' (See also p 102.) That gives you the rough connotations of Hugh's thought. Note: my wife, who is the daughter of an American Colonel and ought to know, says that the term 'strawfoot' comes from the following true incident in early American history, she thinks the Revolution or the War of 1812. A regular army officer was trying to break in some recruits who were farmers, and so stupid they did not know right from left. He finally put a piece of hay in the left shoe and a piece of straw in the right shoe of each soldier, and then commanded them to march hayfoot! strawfoot! instead of right! left!

p. 95 It means absolutely nothing at all, a figure of speech at which we English excel. Hugh corrects himself from saying 'How absolutely astonishing' or 'How absolutely extraordinary' – and reluctant to use any adjective to express what the coincidence is like, he substitutes 'something or other.' At bottom it is a method of speaking that has infiltrated into English usage via Punch (the humorous magazine) Ben Travers' farces, P.G. Wodehouse's stories, etc.[12]

p. 100 Because the goat has very nearly caused Hugh to embrace Yvonne, which might lead to other things, one never knows (one never can tell quite the intention of goats either for that matter) there is something nervous about their laughter, mutually dependent in the sense that if one laughs, so does the other. (The goat might stand for tragedy as well as lust, but Hugh and Yvonne have enough on their minds without having to write the book too.) The goat crops up in different forms throughout the book too, peering through the hedgerow of the prose, every now and then. See p. 171 (bottom) Gotelby becomes Goat old Boy. Also p. 189. *Father is waiting for you, Father has not forgotten.* Tragedy = Goat song. But it isn't that which makes their laughter 'mutually dependent,' which simply means something like 'infectious' though in a more serious sense, for their laughter is serious, or almost so, or is still so. It's a fairly common device in the movies, and certainly happens in life, though I never saw it described in a book before.

p. 109 Report, mein lieber Herr Holder, back to the Tattersall at 3 o'clock punkt! And then we will spaziergang on horseback durch den wonderbaren Drachenfelsgebirgen.[13] The horse (unique character though it be in this book) *doesn't* want to drink, does want to look at its reflection. Misjudgement of the horse's intention is liable to cause a serious accident in a country where you have to keep fording rivers. I daresay the remark has a deeper meaning, though, as pertaining to the narcissism involved in the Consul's drinking . . . Whew! How thirsty that horse has just made me though – in fact it's surprising how thirsty this whole book makes one. Ah, to be in Wurttemberg now that April's here![14]

p. 120 Silly, unimaginative names in the state of Saskatchewan. They have some beautiful examples in British Columbia of which Cow-Dung Lake is perhaps the most expressive.

p.121 Pango-pango quality a quality vaguely of the South Seas, pertaining to Vancouver. Pango-pango is the capital of somewhere in the South Seas, maybe it is Pago-pago, but Pango-pango is sadder or more amusing or something, Hugh evidently thinks. The reference is to the amount of rainfall which in Vancouver, like Pango-pango, is very heavy.

p. 175 No, by P.G. Wodehouse. The point of its presence − the Clicking of Cuthbert − is that it is a humorous book about golf. Peter Rabbit *is* a children's book though, by Beatrix Potter. One of the most charming of English children's stories it has just struck me that in its innocent little plot the Consul might have seen a forshadowing of his own doom: the little rabbit leaves the burrow for a frolic in the forbidden garden, where he is chased by the gardener (The Chief of Gardens?) loses his jacket, finally returns to the Burrow. (but the burrow is now the abyss.)

p. 176 The Wheel of St. Catherine − a crucificial object on the gate of my ancient Alma Mater − St. Catherine's College, Cambridge. A wheel because the Saint of that name was broken on a wheel. Hugh imagines it a ship's wheel.

Mr Bultitude is the hero of a famous English novel by F. Anstey, who − Mr Bultitude − due to some magic or other, changes place with his son at school, though he has carried some of his habits or maturity back into his youth.[15] Meantime his son runs the family business. It's supposed to be a funny book and is, but is psychologically one of the most appalling and sad of the near English pseudo-classics. (The exchange of rôles might be seen as foreshadowing the exchange of rôles between the Consul & Hugh.)

p. 178 Thalavethiparothiam = strength obtained by decapitation. See the Golden Bough, by Fraser.[16] But I can't find where. Not sure of the spelling either. My impression was it was thalavettiparothiam, can't remember.

p. 193 A peak on the desert that looks like a lion called Signal Peak and reproduced on the postcard. El Paso is a town on the Mexican-American border, but here means the mountain pass near El Paso, that gives the town its name.

p. 203 On many golf courses in England & elsewhere is the sign: Please replace the Turf. Not to do so is a golfer's sin. The Consul conceives himself as a sort of fatuous golf poet. But golf implies also 'gulf' or abyss.

Unreplaced turf is almost equivalent to an unexpiated sin. Also see other excursions of the Consul on golf courses round about p. 21 etc. Who holds the flag etc is a parody of a poem by John Donne about sin of which the refrain is 'Though I have more.' (More sins, more turf – to hell with all this, let's have another swim. But maybe it was necessary to write this in order to enjoy the swim. Pause while one has a swim. Temperature of water: 39°)

p. 207 Exactly. But good god, how filthy!

p. 248 Props is stage parlance for stage properties; 'props' is less slang than technical, meaning all movable objects on the stage – but the play which is 'war' is here compared to a fantastically bad unimaginative and unbelievably gruesome play of Shakespeare's, in which all the characters are hideously mutilated and legs and arms are strewn about the stage, which would seem an almost perfect image if Titus Andronicus were more often performed (like war is) though I never remember even hearing of a performance of it, even at Stratford-on-Avon. But perhaps it is a good image after all for Hugh's contempt for modern war – at this point at least – is so great that he sees it as something worse than horrible, but dishonest and useless even on its own terms, and not merely gruesome, but obsolete too, like the play. The dictionary I was using doesn't give prop or props at all but another does and it says: property. Theatrical. (def. 8) Definition 8 of property (prop) is much as above. It is Yvonne who evokes war for Hugh by being afraid of the blood: hence all these images in his mind, the 'props' of war's senseless play Titus Andronicus – which is one long grand guignol. It is anything but a simple thought, and I don't seem to have expressed it clearly here for you, it being hard exactly to recapture. But I hope the 'props' are plain.

p. 313 Triskele triskelion – a figure composed of three branches, usually carved, radiating from a centre. The 'three legs' – emblem of the Isle of Man is a triskele, I think. But the Consul clearly has something gruesome or delirious or even sexual in mind – there are some frightening looking triskeles: But the underlying thought is involved strangely with ukuleles. Ukuleles strum, no triskeles. Yvonne was born in Hawaii, the place of ukuleles. Hugh might be thought to play a sort of ukulele. (The 'eles' common to both words is the key.) 'I want to go where those ukuleles are strumming' – usual popular escape song, is perverted here by delirium into an intra-uterine-reversion image of escape symbolised by the centre of a triskele, but which becomes the abyss itself, where is the trismus or gnashing of teeth. Did I think of all that when I wrote it? No. And it's too nice an afternoon to think any more of it now. In fact I'm going to have another swim. My wife has given me a drink too, which is more than the poor old Consul got, just at that point anyway.

p. 322 But dear old Capricornus *was* a sea goat, with a tail instead of hind legs. I warned you that that goat would keep turning up, even if you didn't expect a sea goat.

Sagittarius? H'm. Where? Nowhere. On the previous page? Yes, but I don't see old Sagittarius here, alas. Guess he must have been left out by mistake. Please put him in again quickly for god's sake either as Sagittarius, or the Archer, however the rhythm suits you — the equivalent of the Archer would be better. I have it, put him back in as both Archer and Sagittarius, i.e. Sagittarius the Archer, Capricorn the Seagoat, etc.

p.326 The drinks . . . lay like swine on her soul. A phenomenon peculiar, not to drunkenness, but to those occasions when one has had just a few drinks, mostly long spaced out, over the whole day, none of which have taken much effect, — Bacchus' revenge on those who insult him with too conscious moderation; since the drinks have not really stimulated you, save once or twice spasmodically, they are not doing you any good, but yet can be felt as still there, like a weight of fatigue on your soul, but also as a nastiness, as a sense of impending disaster, though of a minor kind; and particularly is this so some little while after doing something manic and clean and energetic like having a swim, as Yvonne has, at the culmination of such a long day, though the effect is opposite at first; I wanted to give a purely physical reason for her wanting to get tight: but even if the drinks didn't sit like swine on her soul, you can see how the poor girl in spite of Sagittarius and the poxy eggs, or indeed because of them, might think that her soul had been degraded to the point it felt a bit like a pigstye.

p. 333 Made a sort of hairpin turn.

p. 337 Stops are the things on a musical instrument (any contrivance by which the pitch of an instrument is regulated.) The poor rabbit {There is more in this book than I thought — it must be Peter Rabbit of course — but how dreadful. See note to p 175.}, to the Consul is, as it were, *playing* the corncob like some sort of harmonica. It is an accurate image, even were it not delirious, for these sort of corncobs I mean are varigated in colour — not all yellow like American ones — but with yellow and black and purple kernels. Please don't tell me you don't like it. I almost felt Heironymus Bosch putting a claw of approbation out of his grave when I wrote that.[17]

p. 347 The really great thing about this game of bumblepuppy (much better even than the game of bumblepuppy itself and the image, both of which have their merits) is that – if, as I hope, I am by a miracle right – the person in the world who could best answer the question is no less a man than your friend and who I look on as mine too, Herr Karlheinz Schmidthüs. (See the letter) The image stems from a murderous – if apparently innocent – game (in origin English) played for the first and last time in my life in Bonn-am-Rhein, at Koblenzerstrasse 100 and which Herr Schmidthüs must have often witnessed, if he didn't play very much; if he did not care to play, it was not because he could not – quite the contrary – but because he was too kind-hearted and did not like to break our young noses.[18] Anyway it was inconvenient for anyone to play unless they were actually living in the house, so very few of the teachers did: one got so hot, for one thing, and then there would be nowhere to change. I have since discovered that classical bumblepuppy (whatever *that* is) was played in England by bouncing some kind of tennis ball – a kind of ping-pong played with a tennis net. The way it was played in Germany in Bonn was wholly different and very much sterner: first it was played round a contraption like a maypole, to which was attached by a rope an object, with the hardness, thickness, and consistency of a mediaeval cannonball. You took up your stance on either side of this maypole armed with a kind of primeval club, at a distance of about one inch from your opponent. You then began magically and diabolically to persuade this rope with the cannonball on the end of it, by means, fair or foul, of the primeval club, to whisking round and round the maypole at the speed of thirteen uninvented engines of destruction with the subsidiary object of knocking out your opponent, preferably by depriving him of his nose, on the way. Once the rope really started and got into the groove – to use the terms of le jazz hot – it was damned difficult to stop, because it – like one of my flying machines in the square – naturally whirled higher and higher and higher round the maypole, round which with a final fizzle it would finally disappear altogether winding itself up into a neat knot to give you the game, or a point of the game. (Seriously, it could be a lot of fun at least at that juncture.) Sometimes, though, the swinging of the rope would be loose and easy, through a wide, and ever-widening, series of arcs, necessitating that the opponents should stand further and further apart: this is the condition in which I imagined the two gods, with a burmese gong instead of the ball, at the end of the rope, making a fine noise.

The head of Koblenzerstrasse 100 was an Englishman named Weber, but who lived in Dantzig, in my estimation a truly frightening man, as unfair and hard on the feelings as Herr Schmidthüs was kind and good.[19] Whether I in turn am unfair to Weber or not, which may be, he certainly hated me, so that it was a moment of great satisfaction to me when I finally managed to better him at his favorite game of Bumblepuppy.

You would have thought this would have been enough, but no, I had to give his name at least if not his attributes to one of my villains in the Volcano, and revenge myself that way. Just like the stone![20]

P.S. (see p. 1 of letter.) Brevity is the soul of wit.

ML

Annotations:

1 A *Volkshochschule* has nothing to do with happiness; it is a college for adult education or for university extension classes.

2 In a 7 May 1951 letter to ten Holder (UBC 1:67), Karlheinz Schmidthüs recalls the young Lowry in some detail and describes the game of 'Bumblepuppy,' which sounds like an aggressive form of tetherball played by the young men at the school; see Appendix 2.

3 German expressionist playwright Georg Kaiser (1878-1945) published many plays, but *Von Morgens bis Mitternachts* (1917) is the best known in the English-speaking world. The production to which Lowry refers, starring the English actor Claude Rains, played at the Regents Theatre in London, 9-20 March 1926; Lowry alludes to it again in *October Ferry to Gabriola*.

4 Frank Wedekind (1864-1918) was a German playwright, poet, and short-story writer. His most influential plays – *Frülings Erwachen* (1891; *Spring's Awakening*, 1923) and *Der Erdgeist* (1895, republished as *Lulu*, 1903) – offer powerful critiques of pre-war German society.

5 Frederick W. Murnau (1888-1931) was a noted German film director. *Sonnenaufgang* (1927; *Sunrise*), an expressionistic treatment of marital problems and near murder, is one of the film allusions in *Under the Volcano*; see Lowry's 31 October 1951 letter (**477**) to ten Holder.

6 Jacques Laruelle recalls singing the 'Wibberlee Wobberlee' song with the Consul in chapter 1 of the *Volcano*; the song was sung by the Lowry brothers when Malcolm was growing up.

7 These are the ten Holders' two sons.

8 Lowry's six typescript pages of notes are attached to the letter. Readers should consult *Under the Volcano* for the sources of Lowry's references and Ackerley/Clipper for further information about the text.

9 *Abendessen* is the evening meal or dinner; *Fruhstück* is breakfast.

10 The American writer Robert Penn Warren (1905-89) published *All the King's Men* in 1946.

11 Jean-Paul Sartre's play *The Flies* (*Les Mouches*, 1943) was first translated into English by Stuart Gilbert in 1946.

12 Ben Travers (1886-1980) was an English playwright who created nine so-called 'Aldwych farces' between 1929 and 1933. The affectations Lowry describes are typical of Travers and Wodehouse.

13 Because Hugh and Yvonne go horseback riding in chapter 4 of *Under the Volcano*, Lowry jokes about riding through the Drachenfels Mountains. The Drachenfels is actually a famous rock that is the focal

point of the Siebengebirge (Seven Mountain) range overlooking the Rhine River in Germany. According to legend it was once haunted by a dragon. Lowry's German should read *spazierengehen durch das wunderbare [Drachenfels]gebirge*.

14 Lowry is paraphrasing the opening lines of 'Home-Thoughts from Abroad' (1845) by the English poet Robert Browning (1812–89): 'O, to be in England / Now that April's there.'

15 Thomas Anstey Guthrie (1856-1934) published *Vice Versa, or A Lesson for Fathers* (1882) under the pseudonym of F. Anstey. Paul Bultitude, the father, changes roles with his schoolboy son, and when he is transformed back into an adult he becomes a more understanding man.

16 The institution of thalavethiparothiam is discussed by Sir James Frazer in chapter 24 of *The Golden Bough*; Frazer spells the word with a double 't.'

17 Hieronymus Bosch's allegorical canvases depict a violent nightmare world swarming with torments and delirium; see Lowry's letter (**433**) to Viking Press and his allusion to Bosch in 'Through the Panama.'

18 Lowry is trying to explain the reference to 'bumblepuppy' in chapter 12 of *Under the Volcano*. The game of 'bumblepuppy' or tetherball is described by Schmidthüs as 'gruesome' in his 7 May 1951 letter to Clemens ten Holder; see Appendix 2.

19 According to Douglas Day (99), Captain Weber was a retired British Army officer who had established a school in Bonn for teaching German to the sons of well-to-do British families.

20 See Lowry's 21 March 1951 letter (**450**) to ten Holder, where he explains the use of a stone 'in lieu of toilet paper.'

Editorial Notes:

a. The pencil draft of this letter with the typescript sent to ten Holder (UBC 2:18) shows many cancellations, additions, and instructions to Margerie for preparing the final copy.

456: To Margerie Bonner Lowry

P: UBC(ms) [Dollarton]
[Spring 1951][a]

Dear sweet darling duck

In this section I fell into a quagpond of uncertainty because I have changed the technique (for the better I believe) – I am sure for the better – & at last know what the story is about.[1] This latter though made me want to put back some things you'd cut out: you were right to cut some of them out because they were unclear then, but they mostly involved certain chords that will now all be resolved.

35 & 36 – may not be cut so well in places as you did it, but I prefer this as a new basis. (Because there was no movement in the technique your version had to be shorter.)

37 Whether his alter-ego should speak again is a question but I think one wanted some technical relief & I think I like it. Of top of 38 I am pathetically uncertain but I had to make some bridge & I want the thought. The thought 38 – re alcoholism – is also brilliant, – if divorced from C.'s [Cosnahan's] personal life.

I am in almost perpetual danger – round about here – though perhaps just avoid it – of becoming redundant –

I've tried to get the spitefulness out of 40 but it seems to me to have a savage kind of power – especially at the bottom – more than justified in its own right, though the writing (as elsewhere) is often scrappy.

In 41 (top) – or part of it, I fear redundancy, though the thought is different, but having lost touch I couldn't improve it.

41 bottom & 42 – I felt I wanted the thought that his mother didn't really know the extent of his success (for the elephant will be like a signal that she does know, among other things.)

The lecture 42-43 is again another thought that is necessary (or so I felt): there seems charm & interest in the writing but too much of it, while if the bottom of 42 is redundant is a matter I can't judge at present

43 is probably badly written though one can't tell till one sees. On 38 the section ends at present & from there I shall proceed to work on a basis largely of your version, though with a few exceptions.

If 43-44 is unsuccessful it is due to the fact that I wanted badly to use the stuff on my original – especially about the 'little man.' Because this seemed to act as a counterpoint to the 'Man's uniqueness' motif. But the real thought is so intricate compared with the way I've expressed it I didn't feel up to it. The butterflies are going to turn up elsewhere, & it is possible that the passage on '44' doesn't hold water without the charm of the butterflies.

But please look sternly at this & my original little man – my original of course shows the old technique of the scene being in the Rupe Tarpea. Please do not hiss hoot nor honk at me should you think my devices badk[2] & excuse the extra trouble I cause – but however it works out with your sweet help with this off my chest I shall make great strides to-morrow – –

Sweetest quackings & goodmornings

M.

[P.S.] 'Maybe we will make something of this writer's work yet.'

Annotations:

1 Lowry began working on the story that would become 'Elephant and Colosseum' in 1950. He would write a version, pass it to Margerie for typing and comment, and then begin the process of revising and rewriting. The story, now part of *Hear us O Lord*, was begun as 'Sooner or Later or so They Say,' and went through several revisions (UBC 10: 16–21 and 11: 1–10). Margerie's comments, to which Malcolm is replying, are with the drafts (UBC 11:8).

2 This attempt to simulate a duck's quack is part of the Lowrys' private language.

Editorial Notes:

a. This undated letter (UBC 11:8) was written sometime during the spring of 1951, when Lowry was working on 'Elephant and Colosseum'; see Doyen (296).

457: To Stuart Lowry

P: UBC(ms)

[Dollarton]
[ca May 1951][a]

Dear old Stuart:

Thanks a hell of a lot for putting the Bee on the powers that bee to the grateful tune of £189:15:6 safely & more than thankfully received, as you can well imagine.

(So thankfully that it hasn't occurred to me till now to speculate until now with some amusement upon what on earth the British government thinks it can do with your other £10:4:4 that we couldn't – or that is more useful to humanity than anything we could. Still, if it wants to be mean-minded, that's no reason for me to be. Quite the contrary.) This then – for which I reiterate our heartfelt thanks – has already enabled us:

(a) to get out of debt on the medical side & get a thorough check-up upon our warts, blains, frost bites, broken teeth, myopias, varicose veins, pseudo-cancers, broken spines, crudities, noses, our touch of lupus, & our wooden leg ('it's a luverly thing' – it doesn't exist, it's a family joke that derives from the circumstance that some years ago I seriously did think, so bad had my circulation become, that I might have to lose my leg,[1] and while I was entertaining glumly this gruesome possibility in a doctor's office, a conversation tactlessly began between a woman, whose son had recently lost his leg at the hands of the doctor in question, but who was so far from being displeased with the result she evidently considered the leg's stand in as a much better one than the one she'd presented her offspring with by way of nature: in short, as she said it was a 'luverly thing') – our occupational diseases, & hysterias.

(b) it has taken a great general load from our mind, will enable us to have a more balanced diet, & above all – we have been able to get down to work with new hope. Not that we haven't been working, quite the contrary. Margerie's been able to get a short novel almost finished in the last few months, & I several long short stories of a quite new kind that I'd think you'd too think damned good & are damned good as is hers. But poverty had been tightening

[Two pages missing.]

be paid back, one doesn't psychologically like to jeopardise the chances of the film, & what is not so obvious – [illegible] you may have found it true to experience – it seems ten times more difficult to borrow from someone in a fantastically different income group – even if you are in part responsible (the gratitude for which no doubt is reflected in the length of the telegram) for sending him to the top of the tree.

Now in answer to your questions CM.L ★ & ★.

The answer in both cases – re selling of effects – is of course, yes.[2]

Re that if {by way of kind any trinket should have if there is any likelihood of any trinket} my only personal feeling is that there is any trinket however small which by way of kind shows any remote legal likelihood of filtering down the family escalator as far as me I would naturally be awfully grateful to have one I could affix to my wife's finger both as a souvenir of the mater & of the thing itself so to speak & would be awfully grateful if Margot's taste would discriminate in the matter: on the other hand I see no reason why anything should so filter down & do not put yourself out from any other ideas for this reason that you may have, with which sight-unseen I concur. For my part the only family effect I'd like to feel I had a lien on even if not rightful was or were the old man's volumes of Dickens which can't be very valuable & I can't think anyone save me would

[Two pages missing.]

not as much as is paid in rent alone in one little room for a domestic servant – (this of course quite exclusive of wages, food etc) in many parts of America, & prices here are swiftly becoming comparable. So if we couldn't pay even for one little room for ourselves on the money we receive – which is the way things are going – how is one without a regular job to eat?

And if you can't get a job what then? Go to another country, but how get there?

I hope you will let me know immediately how the land lies & won't take any of this personally which of course is not intended & will excuse me for blowing off steam: I also hope to God you will prod Alderson Smith into some action if not already taken . . . I repeat wearily after the sixth month that is an s.o.s.[3] And what is the point of all this on England's side? All that is happening is that for the lack of a little petty cash an intelligent Englishman is being prevented from earning the dollars that eventually he might very well like to spend partly in England. Since all England wants seems to be dollars all I can say is, on these terms, may they burn her arsehole to a crisp.

[breaks off unsigned]

Annotations:

1 Lowry is referring to his treatment and operation for varicose veins in February and March 1949.
2 The Lowry family was disposing of Inglewood and Evelyn Lowry's effects.
3 Alderson Smith was the Liverpool solicitor handling Evelyn Lowry's estate; see Lowry's letter-fragment (11) to Smith in Appendix 3. His reference here to six months of waiting – presumably for his share of the estate – suggests he is writing in May, six months after his mother's death.

Editorial Notes:

a. There are at least four pages missing from the foliation of this draft holograph (UBC 51:15).

458: To Anne Ford

P: UBC(ms)   [Dollarton]
                                                             [ca 1951]

Dear Anne Ford:[1]
    Thanks alot for sending me the stories of James Stern and I'm also glad to see myself quoted on the cover as saying what I did, which I mean more than ever, after having read the stories, some for the first time, in the volume called The Man Who was Loved.[2]
    I am very overtaxed with responsibilities at present – not to say over-taxed period – & haven't the breathing space to say what I'd like as well as it deserves to be said, also I've lost touch with Jimmy himself, who must be in Europe or somewhere, at least he didn't seem to get our last note or two to him.
    It's late at night & what I say may go wrong & be unquotable but is

something like this since you asked for my opinion.[a]

The Woman who was Loved is perfect, one of the most poignant I know. One of the strangest things about it is that though he deploys our sympathies quite frankly away from the mother one still feels sympathy for her. Does anybody these day I wonder read Hard Times, – as F.R. Leavis somewhere soundly advises us we should – or remember Mr Gradgrind? It is by the ethical standards of that masterpiece which one should judge this story, should anyone be tempted to feel it was old fashioned or that the moral was forced.[3]

Mr Stern is a moralist, but of a high order & I would like to write an essay on the subject. I had forgotten Something Wrong – it seems to me brilliant, completely successful, almost too successful, if that were possible. Two Men I have always thought first rate. I hope the volume will meet the success it deserves, though I would have preferred to have seen another story or two from the Heartless Land such as The Force (a story which James hates) instead of Traveller's Tears & perhaps The Face behind the Bar.[4] Also he wrote a first class horror about a boy that fell down a cliff I would like to have seen; however maybe these will appear in another volume. But it is a very good volume indeed, and well representative, & perhaps contains quite enough treasures for one book.

So, to sum up I can only repeat what you quote me on the cover as saying. What I could not very well have said then was that I feel that some of the incidents in the Hidden Damage such as Nurenberg 1945 (published separately in the Partisan) surely not merely an overwhelmingly moving piece of prose but a superb short story in itself as it were, with a few statistics removed, should be salved as entities. It is unfair that they should masquerade or languish as bits of another kind of book, however damned good, & that the Hidden Damage is.[5] But my point is that Jimmy Stern is not only a short story writer, he is *all* short story writer. That is his vocation as in Ortega's opinion, Goethe's was to be a poet. He should not be made to write novels or mess about. I don't know where the English tradition of the short story begins but wherever it begins Stern has surely brought [it] into line & helped to save it for future English writers. One should really have said something about that almost unparalleled period of aridity in English letters, roughly coinciding with the death of Lawrence, when he first began to write or publish his stories. It may be that the late Edward J. O'Brien's end was hastened by the heroic attempt to find any British short stories at all to put into his yearly volume that even deviated into the mediocre, & which he could put beside the fine stories of Sterns, whose worth to his credit he early recognised. But that doesn't mean that Stern could sell the story necessarily, that finally would find its weary way via a non-paying magazine into an almost non-paying anthology. I seem to recollect that J.C. Squire, also greatly to his credit, published some of Stern's stories in the London Mercury and to my mind if that it is correct it is most significant that this most extremely English of all English literary gents should have been struck by their worth & not felt that he had hold of some kind of literary mamba by the wrong end & which was shortly going to bite him sharply in the British Empire.[6]

And this brings me to what is perhaps one of the main points about James Stern, his integrity is such that he actually seems to call the bluff of the moral ideals of the British Empire (does this make sense?), while at the same time to rescue from degradation those values of decency, courage, sportsmanship, straightforwardness, & tolerance, which the English have for so long considered peculiarly their own. In short Englishmen can well look to him as an example. After which it is enough to make one fall down Pat Murphy's well laughing when one realises he is an Irishman.

Well, that's more or less what I have to say, mostly less & wish it were better, & something like what I would say to Jimmy, (except for The Force, which he dislikes me to mention) to whom my kindest regards anyway, wherever he is, & thank you very much for sending me the book.

Yours sincerely

Malcolm Lowry

Annotations:

1 Anne Ford worked for Harcourt, Brace in 1951.
2 Harcourt, Brace published a collection of James Stern's stories called *The Man Who Was Loved* in 1951, and Lowry is quoted on the dust-jacket as saying that Stern is 'one of the world's best short story writers.'
3 'The Woman Who Was Loved' is about two children's affection for a governess who teaches them to enjoy the natural world and to trust their imaginations. When their hard-hearted parents fire the woman, the children are devastated. Lowry's comments about this story are interesting in light of his relations with his parents: Stern creates pity for a wife who is dominated by an insensitive husband and alienated from her better self. F.R. Leavis recommends the reading of Charles Dickens in *The Great Tradition*, and Mr Gradgrind in *Hard Times* (1854) is the 'eminently practical man' who nearly destroys his children's lives by his harsh treatment and mercenary example.
4 See Lowry's praise for 'The Force' in his 17 September 1947 letter (321) to Stern.
5 Lowry first read *The Hidden Damage* in 1947; see his 23 March 1947 letter (288) to Stern.
6 J.C. Squire, the English editor, writer, and parodist, founded the monthly magazine the *London Mercury* in 1919 and was its editor until

1934. The magazine was not known for publishing experimental writing, but seven of Stern's stories appeared in its pages between 1931 and 1935.

Editorial Notes:

a. This signed, paginated pencil draft (UBC 51:15) is missing two pages at this point.

459: To Albert Erskine

P: Virginia(ts); UBC(phc)
PP: *SL* 241-46

Dollarton, B.C.,
Canada
5 June 1951

Beloved old Albert:

After a fabulous lengthy grinding of machinery, such as once might have signified the final unbending of the Khedive in the matter of the hegemony of the Suez Canal, the liquidation of the Sikh of Sokotra, and the incorporation of the Maldive Islands into the British Commonwealth[1] after the seduction of its cannibal Queen by a subaltern from Bridlington-on-Sea, the British Government has at last – after interminable and unfathomable investigations on every other plane too – condescended to permit me to receive £189:19:6½ on advance of what is left of what I take it is, nevertheless, mine, and will eventually arrive. This, I am to understand, is a concession, because technically speaking my brother informs me, no money at all has still been released 'on account of deaths,' as the saying is, nor did this much release seem to have anything to do with the end of the fiscal year, as I had every reason to suppose from my brother, and as I told you.

But we are now as a consequence anyway in possession of some 560 extra bucks in addition to what I already have of my own, which is roughly $98 per month, according to the fluctuation of the pound. Thanks to what you so generously lent us yourself, which saved our lives, we were tided over our crisis, are out of debt here and are even in a position to pay you back today without precipitating another crisis should you need the money right off. So please tell us that quam celerime. I am dreadfully sorry at the delay in writing you, but time went on, I sold no stories, (in fact I have been able only to send off one more) and despite promises we didn't hear from England so that we began to feel we were in the first chapter of Bleak House again.[2]

On the other hand though the mills of the gods grind exceedingly slow in England they *do* grind, and now that one has some tangible proof that they are working I am almost certain to hear again soon. The estate is being sold, and though the Government will take a disproportionate amount, my income cannot fail to be increased to some extent, nor can I fail to receive some fairly large – for us – addition to my capital.[3] Moreover a law has just been passed I understand that does provide for the release of more money, for the present system has been proving mutually ruinous in respects that touch the Governments own bank balance, if any. (An ironic aspect of all this which I have quite forgotten until this moment is that even before I was of age I was in receipt of at least a couple of bequests from collateral relatives of whom I was mysteriously the favorite relation, every penny of which was invested by force majeure in my old man's firm that was later liquidated by Cripps.[4] Or you might say I helped to liquidate it myself, for the only time I voted in England, when barely old enough, I voted Labour, out of what then seemed a sense of justice. But I did not vote for a *party*, simply for an independent individual with some belief in a coalition. My father was a Tory of Tories but he used to lunch every Thursday, I discovered, with a Scots socialist who was a financial expert and an authority on West Indian cotton, from whom I suspect him of having derived half his ideas on beating the market.)

This means in brief that though we can pay you back now – if it is not too inconvenient to you, we would feel safer in waiting a little longer until we see how we stand, both in respect to England, and when we have a little more work off. Since it seems I was too optimistic before, as regards to the former, I would say before the summer is out; in regard to the latter I'll speak in a moment. We would not have hesitated to repay you instantly we received the £189:19:6½ (out of £200 originally sent – one felt like sending back to them the 6½d. as a tip, and asking what they thought they could do with the other eleven guineas that we couldn't, or even suggesting that had my brother had prior information he would have applied for £211:11:6½) were it not for the feeling haunting one in the truth brutally stated by Moliere: 'Death is not always at the beck and call of heirs and while the grass grows, the cow starves.'[5]

Even so we would not so have hesitated and would not hesitate now had you not so very thoughtfully intimated that you would prefer us to wait until we felt a bit safer. We are and we aren't. So please let us know for there is no reason on God's earth why we should make you suffer for trusting us: nor would you have to suffer for us on account of feeling that we were absolutely broke should we send it tomorrow.

Margie's health is steadily improving and our chief remaining anxiety is the house, though this is only indirectly an economic problem; no amount of money perhaps can help us keep it, should they start to 'develop' the land. On the other hand should we lose it our economic situation thus worsens overnight – to say nothing of any other aspects of it – and with this in mind it is wiser from our point of view to keep some money in hand should this blow fall before England comes through or we have sold anything more. Scares of eviction come and go, and it is a situation of some universal significance I have always meant to develop in the novel; but it is a whole lot easier to write about than endure, and while enduring for that matter as hard to write about as it is not to write about. The threat strangely enough now comes from America and not Canada, American interests having bought up all the neighbouring property. But there is a chance they may prove more humane for that reason and let us stay or at least give us time to move, which Canadians would not do.

So far as concerns work I have been fairly gravely inhibited by all these anxieties from accomplishing anything recently that is first rate or at the same time saleable, the more so since it has been as if the plot of the novel, which gets into all the short stories too, were catching up with me. But I am perfectly sure that the work when it is done will have a sounder quality for those particular things we have been or are going through and in short it seems to have done us a lot of good.

Margerie though for her part has had a real burst of creative genius and is just putting the final touches on a short novel called The Castle of Malatesta.[6] This is such a really wonderful piece of work that partly for that reason, and partly because it seemed most practical, it having represented the piece of fiction in the family most nearly complete and I believe saleable, and it being absolutely necessary for us to get something in to Hal, that I have devoted five sixths of my time latterly to helping her get it finished, my help consisting in large part in getting out my own influence where maldigested and baleful and thus enabling her to give her own extremely original talent its head, and in acting as a sort of remote Fritz Lang, crosser of t's and p's, and supplier where necessary of strange 'noises-off.' This – as often happens with me these days too – started as a short story, then became a novella, and has ended up as rather longer than Jim Agee's really superb Morning Watch[7] which we read with delight not long ago, so it should as a consequence be publishable as a volume. I don't know what Hal would want to do with it, or whether it has any transitional place in a magazine, but it should be finished this week and having had a final version being typed as mopping up operations were completed should be off before the end of next. That means, allowing ten days for transit, that Hal should have it by about the 24th of June and I would extremely much like you to have a look at it. Though I have felt that unwittingly I've proved rather deleterious to Margie's destiny and freedom as a writer so far in one way and another, whether by advice influence opinion existence or sheer bulk I know not, I feel free to waive such considerations in regard to this and don't think I'm putting a wrong thought in the ether by stating objectively that it's quite one of the most remarkable short novels, certainly one of the most remarkable love stories, or stories of passion, ever written by an American woman. I have had various feelings of reluctance about asking you to read it because you might be personally embarrassed. If you hated it you wouldn't want to hurt me by saying so. And equally if you liked it you might feel we would be hurt if the circumstances were such that you couldn't put your opinion behind it. Having come after long cogitation to the conclusion that there is a good chance that, on the contrary, you would never forgive me, if because of these considerations I hadn't at least *tried* to have you read something that might for that matter easily become a classic, I hereby threw these considerations {What prose! Oh, Malcolm, what prose!} out of the window. I don't like to make any suggestions to Hal. Margie is afraid to say anything to you – naturally we can't be blamed for wanting both to be 'ducks of distinction' (as she once amused you by saying) with the same publisher who would of course be yourself. That idea, never far from our minds, seems too marvellous to be true. But the fact is she has an enormous lot of guts, and enormous talent, and I am sure if she only had some encouragement would go a long way. At all events I hope it isn't too much to hope that you can find a way of getting a look at it – I would hope first look, my feeling being of course that I have spotted a winner for you. To sum up, the last thing we'd want to do is to put you on the spot or embarrass you because of the personal obliquities of the situation. She doesn't want anyone to publish it who doesn't feel some enthusiasm for it and belief in her – the Scribner's situation was a nightmare, but enthusiasm can't be forced, and opinions differ, I know, even yours and mine (though I'm not sure I know where) – anyhow she doesn't want it to be published 'owing to certain auxiliary circumstances.'[8] On the other hand if it is going to be published and going to be a success we don't want anybody else to have the credit except yourself, if it is the kind of thing you feel you can take credit for.

It's quite hard to disseverate her work and mine, at our serious best, that is, even though it is very different, in a larger sense: when we really get going like that, though we're two separate and very different writers, we're like one organism, and in that regard I owe her a terrific lot on the Volcano. So I more or less have to speak like this anyway. And it's even selfish in one way. If I can't keep her going then she can't help me and then I fall to pieces. But to do me justice this is not the way I look at it. Her problem has been to keep herself going without me, or to

Figure 7: The menu (half actual size) for chapter 8 of *Under the Volcano*, with Lowry's instruction to 'reprint in full' at the top. See letter **450**.

1 Malcolm Lowry
aboard the ferry to
Gabriola, 1946.

2 Malcolm and Earle
Birney on the beach
at Dollarton, July 1947.

3 Malcolm and Margerie in a gondola during their visit to Venice, May 1948.

4 Malcolm at Versailles, 1948.

5 Malcolm with Downie Kirk and his family on the
beach at Dollarton, ca 1949. *(top left)*

6 Gabriel Pomerand, ca 1948. *(far left)*
7 Philippe Thoby-Marcelin in Haiti, 1948. *(left)*

8 Margerie working outside the shack at Dollarton, ca1949. *(above top)*

9 Malcolm surveying the snow outside the Dollarton
shack in the winter of 1949. *(above)*

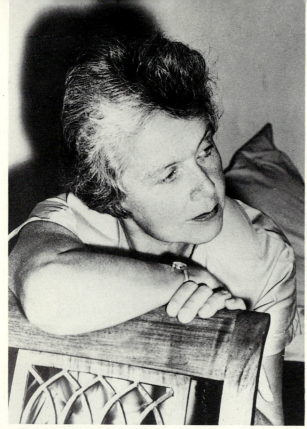

10 Clarisse Francillon
ca 1949. *(left)*

11 William McConnell,
ca 1949. *(below left)*

12 David Markson, 1956.
(below)

13 Frank Taylor, ca 1951.
(right)

14 Dorothy Livesay, 1950.
(far right)

15, 16 Clemens ten Holder and
his wife Hildegard, ca 1950.
(below right)

17 Einer Neilson
relaxing at 'Lieben'
on Bowen Island,
Christmas 1952.

18 Harvey repairing
'My Heart's in the
Highlands', ca 1952.
(below left)

19 Dorothy Templeton
Burt and Harvey Burt
on the beach at Dollarton,
ca 1952. *(below)*

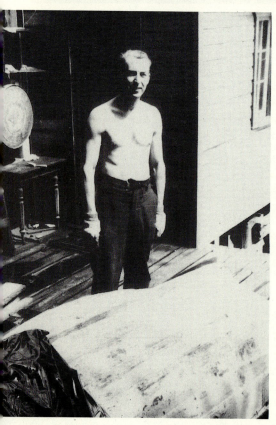

know what she really wants of help for her own individual purposes, and in this she's triumphantly done just that.

As for me, I have a long short story more or less finished that is out of the Intermezzo part of the novel – this whole part will be called Eridanus.[9] This part of the part is known as The Forest Path to the Spring and we aim to get it off when Malatesta is out of the way. There're a lot of other short things that have been held up and we should now get under way to Hal too; there is a kind of log jam in my work. Forest Path has some of the best things I've ever done in it, I hope you'll think. Eridanus is what I call Dollarton here: called such after the constellation – the River of Youth and the River of Death. Reading Dante the other day I came to the conclusion that the celestial scenery of pine trees and mountains inlet and sea here must be extremely like that in Ravenna, where he died and wrote and got the inspiration for the last part of the Paradiso. Then I discovered that Eridanus is in mythology among other things *is* the River Po and where the Po emerges to the sea *is* Ravenna. It gave me quite a turn, though I'm sure I don't see why it should have.

But all this is not getting the Voyage That Never Ends written. It is not even getting blocked out for you. Even to do that in readable form would take me about four months without doing anything else, and perhaps it would be a good thing so to block it out?

I ought at least to park some of the material with you: it would be a lousy idea to lose another Paradiso completely – nothing in it at all for either of us. Perhaps you won't like the idea of the Voyage at first but I feel you will finally. But I ought to get down to it as soon as I can and think of nothing else for a long time if I'm ever to finish it – ideas seem to be escaping all the time, but perhaps it's merely 'ripening,' as Ryder puts it.[10]

And other stories. . . damn them, but I better get a sheaf of them off first. But first, Malatesta.

I had a long and happy dream about The Voyage the other night – a dream of an interminable and fruitful discussion about The Voyage with yourself that unlike most discussions kept creating something beyond the discussion that took shape in some transcendental form continually, but while an actual 'Voyage' of some kind was continuing: I kept waking up, but feeling so delighted I had to get back into the dream again – it was the most exceedingly happy and consistently cheerful dream I have ever had, as if the tyranny of prose, the ands the buts and the howevers did not exist, and all we had to do in order to write that book was to get *on* something and go somewhere, what class I don't know.

Well, I must sign off to catch the post (in a thunderstorm). Please tell us whether you need the cash right away or can await His Majesty's Paymaster's next convenience a little longer at not too much inconvenience to yourself.

God bless you from us both for sending it so swiftly & kindly & our best loves to both Peggy & yourself from us both –

Malcolm

Annotations:

1 Khedive was the title of the Turkish viceroys in Egypt between 1867 and 1914; the Suez Canal was built between 1859 and 1869. During the spring and summer of 1951 tensions between Egypt and England were increasing over who would control the canal. Socotra, an island in the Indian Ocean, was made part of Britain's Aden Protectorate in 1886 after years of failed negotiations with its sultan, and the Republic of Maldives (formerly the Maldive Islands), also located in the Indian Ocean, joined the British Protectorate in 1887. Socotra joined Yemen in 1907; the Republic of Maldives gained its independence in 1965.

2 In chapter 1 of *Bleak House* (1852-53), Charles Dickens describes the Court of Chancery and the fog of legal complication and corruption surrounding the case of Jarndyce and Jarndyce, which concerned a dispute over a family estate.

3 When the estate was finally settled in 1953, Lowry's share was an annual £1,000, on which he was taxed in England and Canada; see Margerie's addendum to Lowry's April 1953 letter (**572**) to Erskine. All he received at this time was an advance on his share in the sum of £189.15.6 after taxes; an additional £500 arrived in January 1954, and he received £8,000 from his mother's estate in January 1954 (Bowker 533).

4 A.J. Buston & Co. was the Liverpool cotton-broking firm that Arthur O. Lowry joined in the early 1890s. He rose quickly to become a junior partner, and by 1926 he was in charge, with his two elder sons as partners. Malcolm, who never joined the firm, held the business in some contempt. Cripps could be the name of a partner in one of three firms handling liquidations, but it is more likely that Lowry is thinking of the policies of Sir Stafford Cripps, chancellor of the Exchequer in the 1945-51 Labour government; see Lowry's comment on Cripps in his June 1950 letter (**405**) to Innes Rose.

5 In Molière's play *Le Mèdecin malgré lui* (*The Physician in Spite of Himself*) Géronte makes precisely this remark to Jacqueline (II.ii). Lowry owned the 1924 Modern Library translation of Molière's plays, with an introduction by Waldo Frank.

6 'The Castle of Malatesta' was never completed or submitted for publication. Drafts are held with the Margerie Bonner Lowry papers (UBC 51:11-25).

7 James Agee's *The Morning Watch* (1951) is a short novel about a day in the life of a Catholic boy in Tennessee.

8 This phrase from Kafka's *The Castle* is one of Lowry's favourites; see his use of it in his 14 May 1945 letter (**201**) to Gerald and Betty Noxon.

9 'Eridanus' was Lowry's working title for most of the material that eventually became *October Ferry to Gabriola*; see my discussion of his *Voyage* plans (pp. 2-3) and his 23 November 1951 letters (**479** and **480**) to Harold Matson and Albert Erskine.

10 Albert Pinkham Ryder was the subject of an illustrated article by Winthrop Sargent in *Life*, Feb. 1951, 86-91. Sargent quotes Ryder's description of his canvases as 'ripening' on his easel as he repaints them. The first four pages of this article, including a large two-page colour reproduction of the undated oil *Under a Cloud*, were kept by Lowry with his materials for *October Ferry to Gabriola* (UBC 16:9); see the reference to Ryder in his January 1952 letter (**496**) to Robert Giroux.

460: To Clemens ten Holder

P: UBC(ms)
PP: *Brief 37*

Dollarton, B.C.,
Canada
[14 June 1951][a]

Sehr geehrter Herr ten Holder

I answer in haste to catch the post.

Am sending you a copy of Horse in the Sky & simultaneously will reply to your last letter. Bitte vergit mir mein bleistiff. Danke sehr.[1]

All the very best luck & both our warmest regards to yourself & Frau ten Holder.

Malcolm Lowry

Annotations:

1 Lowry is apologizing for writing in pencil.

Editorial Notes:

a. This pencil draft is undated, but 14.6.51 has been added at the top right and 18.6.51 at the bottom right of the recto. Incoming letters from ten Holder confirm a summer 1951 date. Two pages of notes (not included here) on *Under the Volcano* have been stapled to the letter. They are titled ACHTUNG! ANTWORTEN (Attention! Answers), and they clarify words and phrases such as runcible spoon, cabrón, camel's hair brush and lunar caustic. The German translation in *Briefwechsel* includes the notes.

When David Markson first wrote to Lowry on 3 June 1951, he was working on his master's thesis at Columbia University, and his subject was Under the Volcano. *He explained that he was '23, a foetal artist,' and had read Lowry's book three times before daring to write. In an uncanny way history was repeating itself, because Markson was now doing with Lowry what Lowry had done, twenty-three years earlier with Conrad Aiken. And Lowry did not miss the parallel. Out of this initial contact would grow a lifelong friendship and deep literary bond, an excellent critical study in Markson's* Malcolm Lowry's Volcano, *and a series of remarkable letters by Lowry. In one of the most important of these letters* (**467**) *Lowry, who had before been reticent about his lost manuscript 'In Ballast to the White Sea,' spelt out in considerable, if convoluted, detail all his hopes and plans for that work.*

461: To David Markson

P: UBC(ts)
PP: *MLMW* 113–16

Dollarton, B.C.,
Canada
16 June 1951

Dear David Markson:[1]

Thank you sincerely for your letter and the warm-hearted remarks therein, and I feel very honored that you should have chosen to do a thesis on the Volcano. I was half way through a reply to you when I found myself held up this weekend 'owing to certain auxiliary circumstances,' so I am catching the Saturday air mail with this, so you won't think your letter didn't reach me.

I don't say much more in my reply (that I'll try to get off to you by Monday) save that if I can do anything to lighten such a grim chore for you in a hot summer I certainly will be glad to, but it is not quite such a dead letter as this one.[2]

With kindest regards and the best of luck

Malcolm Lowry

Annotations:

1 David Markson (1927–) is an American writer. His 1978 study *Malcolm Lowry's Volcano: Myth Symbol Meaning*, based on the thesis he had begun when he first wrote Lowry, is an important analysis of *Volcano*. His second novel, *Going Down* (1970), which is set in Mexico, is dedicated to Markson's wife Elaine 'and to the memory of Malcolm Lowry.'

2 See Lowry's 20 June 1951 letter (**462**) to Markson.

462: To David Markson

P: UBC(ts)
PP: *CL* 44

Dollarton, B.C.,
Canada
20 June 1951[a]
(owing to more 'auxiliary
circumstances.')[1]

Dear David Markson –

I thank you sincerely for your letter, the remarks therein, and the honor you do me.

As I said the least I can do is to see if I can lighten at all such a formidable chore for you in a hot summer, especially since my name means 'Servant of Colomb' and we have two Columbias in the address, not to mention a selva, if not oscura, while we literally do live in a forest, or rather edge of one.[2]

Moreover just as I received your letter I too seemed to have been reading a bit of Faulkner hotly pursued by Djuna Barnes, Dante, Joyce, etc., and feeling frightened by *my* limitations – incidentally if I may say so in a tone of complete joviality and politeness you made a wonderful typ. error, unless it was done on purpose at this point: you said 'frightened,' but your wise typewriter knew better and said 'freightened.' Now I only remark this because having begun this letter in pencil I went on to use it to introduce my apology viz that our typewriter was then lying at a garage having its inner workings cleansed by an aeolian instrument for blowing up tires; so, writing in pencil, I did not lay myself open to such typ. errors – if I do now, all I can say is, may they be as good as that one of yours! For you said a mouthful. If your vocation is to be a novelist you certainly couldn't do better – in my sincere if by no means new opinion – than to be 'freightened' rather than 'frightened' by the said limitations: one should (upon the 'frighter' of life) take them to Palembang with one and deliver them in good order as may be – after all they can be among the most valuable cargo one has, those limitations! Though I don't mean quite to say as Melville somewhere marvellously puts it – one should never wait for fair weather, which never was on land or sea, but dash with all one's derangements at one's object, leaving the rest to fortune.[3] Not quite; very unsound advice: though it may be very necessary at times.

But this is not answering any of your questions. Re these, I think the most helpful thing I can do at the moment is to send you – it will go off by the same post as this letter – a copy of the French translation of Under the Volcano which contains a preface written by myself, as also a postface written by someone else [Max-Pol Fouchet], so many faces indeed

that instead of being much help they probably serve to the contrary as
so many masks over the material. This preface was written in Haiti – or
going there – and was originally intended for the British edition.[4] (You
will note that I received news of the acceptance of the Volcano, from
England and America, upon the same day, delivered by a *character* in the
Volcano and in a house that figures in the Volcano in Mexico itself
where ten years after I'd begun the book we went back on a short visit
– the original of Laruelle's house I'd never set foot in before, was now
turned into apartments: the very tower described in the Volcano was the
only place we could find to live – this sort of thing – a sort of Under
Under the Volcano or fantasia of the Law of Series or the History of
Peter Rabbit's imagination – E.M. Forster says someone should write
the history of someone's imagination – is roughly the theme of what I'm
working on now and one day hope to complete – I had some setbacks
as you will see – who doesn't?)[5]

In this preface also I go on about the Kabbala in a way that is – in this
case – quite misleading and probably not a little juvenile, and which was
no doubt suggested by the magnificently abyssal and heavenly motions
of one of your bauxite freighters on which the preface was written,
rather than strict fact. Moreover we had probably been drinking rum
with the excellent skipper, not to say listening to the voodoo drums battering and tambouring and otherwise genekruppering along that inlet
when you begin to sail into that Heart of Lightness and Tightness and
Barbancourt Cinq Etoiles. It is true that the Kabbala played a part,
though scarcely anterior to the fact of writing the book; I mean I didn't
group it *consciously* around any of the correspondences within that
unresting and dynamic filing cabinet-cum-tree of knowledge. But that
I ran into a Kabbalist at a critical and coincidental moment in the writing of the book: that is true, right in this forest also.[6] But apart from that
my remarks here – though not the other remarks I have cited – can be
taken about on a par with Sganarelle's Latin:

Sganarelle (assuming various comic attitudes)
Cabricias arci thuram, catalamus, singulariter,
nominativo, haec musa, the muse, bonus, bona, bonum.
Deus sanctus, estne oratio latinas? Etiam, Yes.
Quare? Why.
Geronte. Ah! Why did I not study?
Jacqueline. What a clever man![7]

It might have been more honestly to the point if I'd mentioned the
influence of Bismarck – to wit Bix Beiderbecke – especially a break in
Singing the Blues in an old Frankie Trumbauer record, in that preface[8]
– but it appears I like to be thought erudite: the truth is other; I have
the kind of mind that is sometimes politely called archaic, it is true, but

not in the sense that it is on really fraternal terms with the scholastics and mediaeval philosophy.

Subjective, stream of consciousness, multi-leveled and symbolic. Yes indeed, but this is too symbolic multi-levelled conscious and subjective a matter for me to speak about in a short letter in a way which would be much use to you.

Joyce, Dante, Djuna Barnes, Faulkner. Of these I'm not really qualified to speak either, though I'll try and reply to anything, should you ask me any specific questions.[9] I think they're certain writers who in youth tend to react against anything like a ready made tradition, or the suspicion that teachers or another poet taught may be foisting a tradition upon one for reasons of their own; thereafter they approach these recommended writers tentatively, preferably when they have fallen into more disrepute. Meantime the writers the writer feels *he* has discovered for himself remain the more valuable. I know that's more or less true of me.

Re Joyce and Djuna Barnes I find myself ungratefully inclining a bit to Leavis' distaff view in The Great Tradition (even though he is trying to impose a tradition and is dealing with the English tradition of novelists. But this is a valuable book if only it encourages you to read George Eliot's Middlemarch.)[10] I've never grappled with the whole plan of Faulkner yet, though I mean to. I didn't realise for myself what a tremendous writer he was at his best till fairly recently. (Dante's still a bit too famous for me, though you caught me reading him on the sly, when your letter arrived.)

Ultramarine is very fortunately out of print (was never really printed as it was meant to be) and is an absolute flop and abortion and of no interest to you unless you want to hurt my feelings. As my brother said to me recently when I mildly suggested to him that the British Government owed me some cash 'don't even *speak* of it to me!' However I mean to rewrite it – or rather write it – one day. A later work Lunar Caustic – not published yet in America because I wanted to rewrite it but I believe to be published in France as it stands – is maybe of more interest; anyway I think it's good.[11] Unfortunately I haven't got a spare copy of the thing to send you, but maybe I can tell you what you want to know about it. You'll find some mention of the general plan in the French preface which fundamentally has not been abandoned.

My wife – who is American – wrote a grand book called Horse in the Sky which was very unfairly neglected and should cognately interest you – we swop horses and archetypes with each other all the time. She has just finished another much better book even than this, which I certainly feel you will hear of.

I also have had the great privilege of being one of Conrad Aiken's oldest friends. Him I have known since my teens and the good old days of bathtub gin and the best and most helpful of fellows he is.

I am reading at the moment The Road to Damascus by Strindberg. . . . By the well a large tortoise. On right, entrance below to a wine cellar. An icechest and dust bin. The doctor enters from the verandah with a telegram playing a long range ukulele, etc. . .[12]

We live an extremely sunfilled and seay life between the beach – & I mean the beach – and the forest here and if you're ever in these parts I hope you'll look us up and have a drink and some sun with us.

With kindest regards and the best of luck,

Malcolm Lowry

P.S. Of course send along any of your mss you wish to and I'll make any helpful comments I can.

Annotations:

1 For this Kafka allusion, see letters **201** and **459**.
2 The Scottish name Malcolm is derived from the Gaelic *Mael Coluim*, meaning 'devotee of St Columba,' the sixth-century Irish saint who converted Scotland and Northern Ireland to Christianity. The Columbias and *selva* (Spanish for wood or forest) in the addresses are Lowry's British Columbia and Markson's Columbia University, where he was a graduate student, and Lowry's Dollarton forest and Markson's street address: 60 Forest Avenue, Albany, New York.
3 This passage from Melville's *Israel Potter* is a Lowry favourite; see letters **280** and **396**.
4 The British edition did not use a preface; see Lowry's 10 January 1947 letter (**272**) to Jonathan Cape.
5 This remark was made by Henry James, not E.M. Forster, in his preface to *The Portrait of a Lady*; see Lowry's 17 July 1950 letter (**409**) to Harold Matson.
6 This 'Kabbalist' was Charles Stansfeld-Jones, whom Lowry met in 1941; see his letter (**179**) to Stansfeld-Jones.
7 Lowry is quoting from the Modern Library translation of Molière's play *The Physician in Spite of Himself* II.vi.
8 Bix Beiderbecke and Frank Trumbauer (1901–56) were two of Lowry's favourite American jazz musicians. The recording of 'Singing the Blues' that Lowry mentions was made on 4 February 1927, with Beiderbecke on cornet, Trumbauer on saxophone, Miff Mole on trombone, and Eddie Lang on guitar.
9 In his 3 June 1951 letter to Lowry (UBC 1:43), Markson says he is 'rereading' these authors in preparation for his work on the *Volcano*; he does not ask Lowry about influences.
10 In *The Great Tradition: George Eliot, Henry James, Joseph Conrad*, F.R. Leavis devotes a chapter to George Eliot with particular attention to her

novel *Middlemarch* (1871). He criticizes Joyce's work as 'a dead end' and dismisses Barnes's *Nightwood*; see *The Great Tradition*, p. 26. According to Leavis, the great tradition of the English novel was continued by D.H. Lawrence.

11 *Le Caustique lunaire* did not appear until 1956; see Lowry's 28 February 1950 letter (**388**) to Harold Matson.

12 August Strindberg published the first two parts of *Till Damaskus* in 1898 and the third part of his trilogy in 1901. Lowry is referring to the stage instructions for I.ii outside the doctor's house. The character who 'enters from the verandah with a telegram' is the doctor's sister.

Editorial Notes:

a. This letter was first published in *Canadian Literature* 44 (Spring 1970): 53-56, with a comment on the preface that Lowry mentions in the letter; see annotation 4.

463: To Clemens ten Holder

P: UBC(ts)
PP: *Brief* 38-40

Dollarton, B.C.,
Canada
6 August 1951[a]

Sehr geehrter Herr Ten Holder!

We sent you a copy of Horse in the Sky about a month ago, and if you have not already received it you should do so shortly. Naturally we both hope you'll like it enough to translate it; its history is very curious, I haven't time or space to tell you all of it here, and so was its reception. More properly speaking, it received no reception, but that was not the book's fault. Previous to writing the Horse my wife had become well known as a writer of mystery stories – things put together (with my help as the detective) largely to repair our battered fortunes, so what with this, that, and the other, the book was neither taken seriously or given a chance.

On the other side of the medal though, this was just the sheerest mischance. Horse in the Sky was the last book ever accepted by the most famous of all American publishers, Maxwell Perkins of Scribner's, the discoverer of Thomas Wolfe and Scott Fitzgerald, and of whom numerous books have been written, and a man who never accepted a book without a belief in its author's promise.[1] But while she and he were still working on the proofs he died. The publisher who succeeded Perkins had not read the book and somehow confused it with my wife's mystery stories that had been successfully published by Scribner's, with the result it got sent out to all the wrong reviewers who quite naturally could not see what the mystery was and looked for the murderer and the detective in vain. As a consequence of this Scribner's merely fulfilled the minimum requirements of the contract and advertised it – where they advertised it at all – as something quite other than it was.

Despite this it became a selection or recommendation of the vastly influential Book of the Month Club! However when people tried to get it they *couldn't* get it, Scribner's having brought out too few copies to meet such a possible demand and it having been against their policy previously to encourage their mystery writers to write serious novels, and not knowing the extent of Perkins interest (for he was a sort of God in the firm who didn't take the rest of Scribner's into his confidence) they were unwilling to revise that policy overnight, and having other big names on their list they callously let it drop.

I wrote to most of the top reviewers who'd praised the Volcano saying they should be interested in giving the Horse a chance: one and all replied (thus implying that literature was merchandise) that they couldn't get a copy out of Scribner's who in fact remaindered it before it even had time to get born. Despite this it has received some wonderful reviews from isolated sources – some even quite recently and far too late to do any good – such as the Los Angeles Times. (The tough New Yorker also praised it highly.)[2]

My own objective opinion is that, while it has some peculiar faults – or has it? – it is a book so far off the beaten American track as to be almost unique. It takes place in the state of Michigan, U.S.A., in 1911, and deals in a way that surely must have evocations for the modern dispossessed and displaced world with a literal transplanting of a fate and revenge motif that pursues the immigrant protagonists as relentlessly as if the family poltergeist had packed itself in their kit bag. Interesting too is the fact that the 'Taft' on p. 92 was the father of the present Taft you may hear about these days as one of the leaders of the Republican party, the 'Roosevelt' in this book is the uncle of Franklin Delano Roosevelt.[3] Of course my wife was not old enough to be aware of this mise-en-scène, and got it from her mother.

A recent English critic, Leavis, in an attempt to discover a tradition for the English novel, has very rightly put George Eliot's masterpiece Middlemarch in a central position. The other branch of any literary family of tradition, he says, should have stemmed from Emily Bronte's Wuthering Heights but it has had no progeny save the Scottish work, The House With the Green Shutters.[4]

Very interesting, for in my opinion Horse in the Sky does stem – is the first American work (unless it is Moby Dick – this is an opinion of my own, I have never seen expressed, that the psyche of Heathcliff begot Ahab) that does come into that tradition. In short it is the assumption on different terms of the English tradition by an American of a real and completely defiant kind of genius: it links the two traditions in a way I would find it my business to express were I a critic and what it lacks in the mythic certainty of putting a ferocious archetype into the ether it makes up for by a sense of form for which I might reasonably go back to Aeschylus for an example. This sentence is rather obscure. Also I am her husband & may seem to be 'laying it on a bit thick.' Nonetheless Maxwell Perkins said to me that he had found husbands to be reliable critics of their wife's work & intimated that I was no exception.

It is a point worth noting that so far as I know she had – like Goethe at one point in his life – read or felt that she had read nothing but Shakespeare and the Greeks; most of modern literature at that time she had either not grappled with or felt an aversion for: this is nothing to boast of (though I'm glad to say she loved, helped me enormously with, the Volcano) but in my opinion it was simply a defense her unconscious put up in order to preserve that priceless possession, one's naivete (she was an actress, that is she was first a child movie star and then on the legitimate stage – her sister was a well known movie star – so I presume she knew her Strindberg).[5]

This then is what I think of Horse in the Sky. The story, a true one – related by her mother and concerning their family – her mother is aged eighty-six, still beautiful, and lectures on astronomy so you can see what pioneer stock *she* comes from and by God she needs it here in Canada – is, as I think you will agree, an absolutely superb one; so superbly integrated and inevitable that it makes this old hand's mouth water with envy. Technically, though it may not seem like it, it is a triumph of story telling too. And the writing, and the discipline thereof is superb, all terribly terribly difficult for a woman who is a woman and thus with that fatal instinct to gush: I dare say she does gush a bit, but she has a sterner hand on the old gusher {gusher is an oil well} than my poor old devious Albion has on those contraptions in Abadan, Abadan is in Persia, (so, probably, is some of my cash) where amidships sweatrag in hand I sweated once before, at the moment. (I hope, my honoured sir, you will be kind enough not to purr, or at any rate not too loudly, at this ghastly joke). Anyway, I have given you honestly what is against the book – though that might play into your hands for your publishers might get it for almost nothing at the moment: also you would be anticipating a development perhaps, she has just written another one, The Castle of Malatesta, that is so damned good it is bound to cause a stir.[6]

And speaking of the unconscious I cannot resist thinking what some-one like Jung – my wife was quite innocent of psychology – would make of a book like the Horse. I read some of what Jung says about the symbolism of the horse and the mother {In 'Man in search of a soul.' Chapter on Dream Analysis}[7] to Margerie the other day and she remains quite unimpressed by it: nonetheless that doesn't stop me from being impressed by the psychological relation, especially since she lent me the forepart of her horse to add on to the stern end of my horse already there in the Volcano when I was finishing it!

Tell the good Herr Schmidthüs God bless him from me,[8] and that I'll try to be a good man though I was not of the impression that God had any very stern ideas, or if stern certainly not fixed, actually fluid (?), about alcohol − even so I assumed He might have in my case, so knocked off alcohol for 3 years while rewriting the Volcano for the last time, to let the inspiration such as it was come from a deeper source, so devilish deep indeed that I was glad when the ordeal was over and I seemed to be permitted to trust myself as some kind of another gay human being again. What horrified me particularly in the abyss, when and if I was really in it, was the feeling wonderfully expressed by the American poet Wallace Stevens who once in America looked out from some hotel room in Jersey City 'from room 2003 out over that particular countryside which, I think, God sent the angels to destroy, but which the angels thought worse than anything they could do to it.'[9]

At all events the world seems a little brighter tonight, there seems, somewhere in the air, some hope. With this feeling I sincerely send a thought of good wishes to your wife and yourself and your children from my wife and myself, so strong you should hear it singing like a lark still by the time it reaches you.

Sincerely,

Malcolm Lowry

P.S. − your kind birthday gift of the translation of Keats just received as I have finished this letter to you. It is a beautiful book & it seems to me Herr Schmiele has done an excellent job.[10] I thank you much! Has the Eve of St Agnes ever been done into German by the way? Also see Volcano, p. 36 . . . Doch Grauen, seiner Riesenkraft gemäß (after the vulture sitting in the washbasin) − what did you make of that, Watson? − p.21. Hyperion. Thank you again!

Annotations:

1 The circumstances under which Scribner's accepted Margerie 'serious' novel are not entirely clear. The trouble that plagued Scribner's handling of *The Last Twist of the Knife* (see Lowry's correspondence with Maxwell Perkins, letters **246**, **247**, **250**) were an embarrassment to Perkins, but there is no evidence that Perkins himself worked on the

proofs for *Horse in the Sky* (1947). In her 10 September 1951 letter (UBC 1:67) to Lowry, Hildegard ten Holder explains that they would like to translate the novel but are waiting to hear from a publisher; however, Clemens ten Holder died before these plans could be pursued.

2 Reviews of *Horse in the Sky* have not been located in the *New Yorker* or the *Los Angeles Times*, but a favourable review did appear in the *New York Times*, 24 October 1947, p. 26.

3 Chapter 12 of *Horse in the Sky* opens with a discussion of American politics during the summer of 1909. The Taft mentioned in Margerie's novel was William Howard Taft (1857-1930), president of the United States from 1909 to 1913. The 'present Taft' was Robert A. Taft (1889-1953), a senator and arch-conservative. Franklin Delano Roosevelt (1882-1945) was president of the United States from 1933 to 1945, and the 'uncle' was Theodore Roosevelt, the uncle of Eleanor Roosevelt, who married Franklin Roosevelt in 1905.

4 F.R. Leavis's thesis in *The Great Tradition* is that the English novel is best represented by a set of major novelists – George Eliot, Henry James, Joseph Conrad, and D.H. Lawrence. According to Leavis, Brontë established a 'minor tradition' that includes *The House with the Green Shutters* (1901) by George Douglas Brown (1869-1902). Lowry's view, expressed below, that American fiction has more in common with the Gothic romance tradition associated with Brontë than with the mainstream English novel, is argued convincingly by American literary critics Lowry had not read such as Richard Chase in *The American Novel and Its Tradition* (1957).

5 Lowry saw parallels between *Horse in the Sky* and August Strindberg's *Miss Julie* (1888). He first makes this point in his 7 August 1942 letter (**176**) to Priscilla Woolfan and Anna Mabelle Bonner.

6 'The Castle of Malatesta' was never published, but three drafts are held with the Lowry Collection (UBC 51).

7 In the first chapter of *Modern Man in Search of a Soul* (1933), 'Dream Analysis,' C.G. Jung connects the horse and mother symbols in a patient's dream and concludes that they both stand for life; the mother represents life in its origins, while the horse represents the life of the body. He interprets the dream to mean that animal life destroys itself, a meaning that coincides nicely with the function of the horse in *Under the Volcano* and *Horse in the Sky*.

8 Karlheinz Schmidthüs, one of Lowry's teachers at Weber's English College in Bonn in 1928, had written to Clemens ten Holder about his former pupil on 7 May 1951; see Appendix 2 and Lowry's 23 April 1951 letter (**455**) to ten Holder.

9 Our searches and inquiries have not located this quotation from Wallace Stevens (1897-1955), although the experts agree that it sounds like Stevens.

10 Ten Holder had sent Lowry a copy of Walter Schmiele's translation of John Keats's poem for his birthday. *Hyperion: Ein Fragment* (1948) is in Lowry's library and is inscribed: 'to Malcolm Lowry 25.7.51 many

happy returns! C. ten Hulden' (a pun on his name that suggests ten good graces). Lowry goes on to ask about two other Keats poems, 'The Eve of St Agnes' (1820) and the posthumously published *Fall of Hyperion* (1856-57), which had provided an allusion in chapter 1 of the *Volcano*: 'But horrors portion'd to a giant nerve.' Lowry's German line is from Schmiele's translation. Always delighted by coincidences, Lowry constructs a puzzle for ten Holder, then concludes with another allusion – this time to Sherlock Holmes's friend Dr John Watson in the mystery novels by Arthur Conan Doyle (1859-1930).

Editorial Notes:

a. Lowry's typescript (UBC 2:19) carries four marginal pencil insertions and a postscript in which the first sentence is typed and the rest added in pencil. The signature and final thank you are in blue ink.

464: To David Markson

P: UBC(ms)   [Dollarton]
                                                 [13 August 1951][a]

Great Christ man I am terribly sorry Stop Please consider this a telegram which it would be but that there are no telegraph offices hereabouts stop reason for delay in replying is last one you think namely I replied at such great length involving when I tried to get it into the post such underground bleeding that I thought why should I depress you with this besides is what I am saying true is it funny is it witty is it pretty is it relevant to your thesis will it help you as a writer which is more important in short am I being misleading and feeling I might in letter be the latter and also being a secret reader of that organ of the intelligentsia named Horoscope wherein being born under Leo I found myself counselled to weigh my words & not however unintentionally to say starboard when I meant port I decided to revise said letter more usefully meantime telling myself that the French version stop has it arrived by the way if not I will send another would answer some of your questions {all this, in answer to yours – by all means write anything you want, as uncalculated as you please, don't worry if I can't reply at once though, I haven't an awful lot of time – don't even bother to correct the grammar, like me} if misleadingly too but would have elicited some new ones whereupon I would answer all at once Stop. Meantime though on top of this slight inhibition we have a hundred and forty (140) forest fires raging in British Columbia no rain for sixty days and the entire population apart from being on fire prostrated in a state of prayer to say nothing of rain machines and Jehovah's witnesses so far we have escaped though keep fingers crossed however partly thereby we have other problems of wood and work and wilderness difficult to explain moreover my wife was sick stop happily better stop we *were* away for a while too and I can honestly say I do not think I have posted a letter at all of any description written since receiving your last one. All this being so you see my silence is explicable even without the explanation on first page though I will immediately as possible begin to remedy this by revising said letter and posting same. Meantime, old chap, be assured that I am only deeply grateful for your words and as for your questions they are so far from being crude that it has been, on the contrary, the very complexity of the intelligent answers they deserve that has in part held me up. As for the thesis, I am only extraordinarily complimented by it, though made even more happy by the fact that you feel as you do for the book, which in another life it will no doubt turn out that you have written, while it is you that are not replying to me about the thesis. Also I too certainly look forward to when we may meet – time may not be far off. We are in a sort of interrogative stage with our work, which may take us any-where within the next year, even to New York – (I had forgotten to tell you that I have been working like hell too – trying to finish a story about an elephant!)[1] – should we come to N.Y. we won't fail to get in touch. Meantime, failing that at the moment, hie you with your gal, to whom my best love too, to your favorite pub, & therein consider that I am most sincerely drinking both your healths –

A thousand apologies again for the delay, I'll get the letter off with-out further delay this week, likewise

God bless you

Malcolm L.

Picture of our house in sea to conceal nicotine spot[b]

Sorry, more nicotine, here are some good seabird messengers for you

Nicotine was result of cleaning a pipe, incidentally the original property of one Preston Sturges[2]

Annotations:

1 This story is 'Elephant and Colosseum' in *Hear us O Lord*.
2 Lowry had met the Hollywood director Preston Sturges during a visit with Margerie's family in December 1945.

Editorial Notes:

a. This two-page holograph (UBC 2:4) is undated and set up in the form of a telegram.
b. These captions accompany three pictures of the beach that Lowry has drawn in the margins.

465: To Anna Mabelle (Mrs John Stuart) Bonner
    and Priscilla Woolfan

P: UBC(ms)   Dollarton, B.C.
                                                        [August 1951]ª

My very dear Mother & Sis:
    Thanks enormously for the lovely shirt you sent me for my birthday,
which I wear with pride & which is universally admired.
    It was very thoughtful & kind of you, & I thank you again.
    I'm sorry I haven't written before but we've been working night &
day on various hopeful projects.
    Margie is to be translated into Italian – we are tickled pink at the
prospect of the Pope delaying his next encyclical as he pores over &
unravels the intricacies of The Last Twist of the Knife!
    Margie has also written a first rate short novel, I some long short sto-
ries, of which I am proud. We have no indication as yet however of
when these may appear.
    I see Preston [Sturges] has been married: give him my congratula-
tions.[1] His curved pipe, by the way, that Bert gave me – tell Bert – after
five years impossible behaviour has now become a peach & is my
favourite one.
    Give Bert my best love, as to you both also, as from your affection-
ate son, brother

                                                        Malcolm

P.S. Please remember me to Harry.[2]

Annotations:

    1 Preston Sturges married his fourth wife on 15 August 1951.
    2 'Harry' has not been identified.

Editorial Notes:

a. This pencil holograph (UBC 3:14) is undated, but internal evidence and
   the date of Sturges's marriage confirm an August 1951 date.

466: To David Markson

P: UBC(pcard)   Dollarton, B.C.,
                                                        Canada
                                              Sunday [19 August 1951]

Hold on! – I was unexpectedly beset, over the week-end, in the middle

of a semi-colon: letter will reach you this week without fail though
    Salud y pesetas[1]

                                                                    M.L.

Annotations:

  1 The familiar Spanish salutation – 'Health and wealth' – forms a motif in
     Under the Volcano.

467: To David Markson

P: UBC(ms)
PP: *SL* 247–58   Dollarton, B.C.
                                                       [25 August 1951][a]

Dear David M.
    If I said all that your letter suggests to me it would lead us right smack
into the primeval forces of creation and twenty years from now I would
still be engaged on the 15th volume of a Grundlage der Wissenshaft vom
Ausdruck & the letter would remain unwritten.[1] So much for what you
feared might be the 'crudity with which you concocted your questions',
concerning which let your mind be at rest; concerning yours of Aug 9,
let it be not only at rest but positively joyful – I am very glad indeed that
you wrote it, as it goes without saying I was grateful to receive it, and
as for the contents of *this* letter let your mind in advance be at rest too,
though in motion, – in fact just like the Tao, – no psychic or psychological thunderstone is going to drop on your head, though it is to be
hoped some manna (which possibly should be spelt mana) may fall, and
though by virtue of the dignity of my years I may assume the right of
speaking like a parent from time to time, it's not going to be as austere
as all that: as a matter of fact this pseudo-copperplate handwriting and
semicolon technique will doubtless be gradually discarded as the letter
proceeds – here it goes – as in Haiti, during what has begun as something resembling one's good old starched evening chapel days in
England, with Madame, here's your pew, & the meek arrival of the
Presbyter, & the congregation in their best clothes, are discarded the
shining Sunday shoes of the Voodoo priest when, the drums having
called down the gods from Olympus for the hundredth time, & himself
possessed for the hundred & fiftieth, he hurls himself cheerfully into the
flames: but first for the muted conversation in the vestry, and as the voluntary plays, my explanation – & my apologies for this – as to how the
helpful daemon I promised to return to you got stranded in the chimney pot . . . First I did write you & here is a précis of what I said.[2]
    I began by explaining about the forest fire situation, adding that

although one did not have one very near yet you could breathe nothing else and even at a distance those things were enough to give you the horrors. So I would be brief, I said. Yes, Aiken's Blue Voyage was an enormous influence upon me, especially since (I made its acquaintance at the age of 18 in England having just returned from my first voyage to sea) not being able to find out anything about its author, I felt that Aiken was my own discovery. Of course the truth was Aiken was highly respected in a small circle in England, but I didn't find this out till much later, coming from a huntin' and shootin' family near Liverpool, who weren't interested in literary matters. Meantime I was not slow in taking up the dedicatory coincidence of C.M.L. either. So much so that in no time at all I was practically of the opinion that the book was not only dedicated to me, but that I'd written it myself, – & was thus, though an Englishman extremely gratified, though I think privately I was damned annoyed, vicariously to receive the Pultizer Prize a few years later.[3] (Actually C.M.L was Clarice Lorenz, Aiken's second wife.)[4] I went on to add, (in this letter drafted last June) that what I had to say in this regard would be of more use to you privately as a novelist & as a writer, than in writing the thesis. It would lead me into a vast psychological field, not to say into the realm of the confidential & the intensely personal: and from the copy I have before me (as the saying is) it's not quite clear whether the subject is broken off at this point because I fear to appear to my discredit in that field if I am to be honest, or whether, in the attempt possibly to offset certain pitfalls that I imagine might confront *you* as a writer, I fear I may create some bran-new ones for you of my own. So at this point we get on to the Kabbala, to answer your question & the subject is changed.

'Re the Kabbala' I wrote '& the whole business of the occult, however right I may be about reducing my French preface to the level of some little dopplesgangerelle's chatter, I feel bound to tell you as a fellow mortal of somewhat elder years who wishes to be useful, though not, so to say, to sway your mind, unless it be toward A Better Thing, that however much it may be intermediately important or even healthy for you to rationalise such matters, your rationalisation is an illusion. As a matter of fact you could with some justice 'rationalize' the Kabbala itself (roughly speaking a system of thought that creates a magical world *within* this one that so far as I know has no pretense of being anything but an illusion – you may send it flying out of the window if you like, though perhaps it's not wise, it might come back by another one –) but you can't rationalize or anything else the unknown depths of the human psyche – at least not in the way you mean – *You* have one, & its operations are to be found working within you too. (Of course, you know this, & much more; still, while amassing the 'much more', it's surprising what knowledge of one's own, indeed foreknowledge, one can overlook & which has been there all the time, as if waiting to be used. You'll just have to pardon the pomposity of all this)

One of the clearest answers that comes immediately to mind in regard to all this sort of thing is to be found in Jung's 20 years old 'Man in search of his soul', which I didn't read till the other day so forgive me if the suggestion seems infra-dig. More or less popular & dry half-gobbledegookery though it is — & I dare say psychologically superseded or out of date in places & what-not — you nonetheless might find it soundly full of the wisest kind of speculation if you haven't happened to have read it. To revert, you suggest Joyce would smile at it all. Not so. Joyce — whom I once encountered smiling, however, in the Luxembourg gardens — was on the contrary an extremely superstitious (if that's the right word) man. His only regret re Yeats The Vision — which you should read too if you haven't even if you can't make those cones work — (I got so that I could make just one cone work) — was that he did not use all that tremendous stuff in a work of art.[5] You may call it tripe. There's a certain element of danger, maybe, in calling it anything else. Joyce, (who was looking for Aiken's Coming Forth By Day of Osiris Jones when he died,) even had a superstition, according to one of his biographers, about the name Lowry, which occurs in his funeral scene, as he had about all the other names of the corpses in that scene. No sooner had he given them these names, he delighted to report, than one after the other, these names acquired living, or rather dead counterparts, all of which had one thing in common, they were found to have come to grotesque & tragic ends![6] I never checked up to see if a stand-in called L. has already let me out but whether or no it is enough to keep one fighting for a happy ending till the day one dies against *that*! More seriously (if this is *not* serious) you can readily see why, on purely pychological grounds, Joyce might be a superstitious fellow. What goes up must come down, not to say what happens when you throw nature out with a pitchfork.[7] To be superstitious is not indeed to be 'mystical' but I let the point rest for the moment.

Likewise I said I'd let Joseph Frank & Mark Shorer rest for the moment, finding that chiefly interesting as having bearing on what you do with the paper yourself.[8] I noted, with a friendly salute and as it were the purr of a fellow artisan, that if you have to write a thesis, that you can't bear to write it in a form not suggested by the substance, or at any rate not without form itself, thus showing, I would say, the predominance of the artist in you over the critic: that really means more than 'Shorer's passing on & out', or should I say 'The Consul's passing out & on': (my writing is not very clear at this point, as one might say Gap in the manuscript, after this, & as a matter of fact much more, not at all interesting, it goes on about Las Manos de Orlac.)

Las Manos de Orlac – then – is a preposterous mad (& bad, though I pretend it was relatively good which it perhaps was) movie of the German UFa Wiene Caligari Fritz Lang Destiny Golden Age, with Conrad Veidt as Orlac: therein, Orlac was a great pianist who lost his hands in a railway accident, had the hands of a murderer grafted on by a 'Mad Doctor', – ever afterwards felt – no doubt because he'd played the sleepwalker in Caligari too – impelled to commit murders; Hollywood made a remake in about 1936 of truly awe inspiring badness, but with Peter Lorre imported from the Fritz Lang-Ufa era playing the doctor: the surgical sequences were in this version photographed by the UFA genius Karl Freund so you get 5 minutes of that kind of Grand Guignol anyway, though the overall effect could not be worse:[9] thematically speaking, though, the pelado in Chap VIII – by extension the Consul, by extension M. Laruelle – gives the clue: the pelados hands were covered with blood. So are man's.

'Thou art the grave where buried love doth live.' Shakespeare (William) Sonnet XXXI. No reference to a swimming pool in it, however.

Reception: This is a bit complicado; it was a considerable success, – at least for me – even financial, in the U.S, though not as much as its presence as 5th on the best seller lists for some months would seem to indicate: it seemed to be most successful in Dallas, Texas, – to my delight, & it was once cited in a best seller list as 'one up' on Forever Amber,[10] though to do Forever Amber justice Forever Amber had been going on rather longer, & we were both down at the bottom anyhow by that time; we waged quite a battle, though, for a while – I imagine about 15, or 16000 copies altogether. Here in Canada it sold 2 copies – so far as I can gather – & was panned in the local paper. In England it was well received but did little better. In France it was greeted with enthusiasm & shoved into a modern classic series, as was the case in Norway. Sweden, Denmark, Italy, & Germany, have also made translations of it, though I have no idea of the outcome save in Denmark, where it flopped, and Germany, where it's coming out shortly, which of these last countries has taken the most serious attitude to it. (I mean Western Germany, of course.) (Mark Shorer wrote two reviews of it – one extraordinarily sympathetic one in Vogue of all places; others demolished it, no less, & it also made the Encyclopedia Britannica.)

I then mention that it was [my] Royal Welsh Fusiliering brother [Stuart Lowry] who'd insisted I be called Clarence after the gent of that name who was drowned in a butt of Malmsey wine,[11] gave my regards to your friend Leonard Brown, intimating that if he was Firmin that was fine,[12] for I bring the Consul to life in a later book & make him do just the opposite, & all this without even joining Alcoholics Heironymus, though it must be said he changes his potations & even goes on a diet of Schopenhauer & vinegar for a while, & other remedies from Burton's Anatomy of Melancholy, even up to and including water which nearly makes him die of dysentery, & milk which gives him sinusitis, & tea which gives him an even worse attack of delowryium tremens: and then reverted to Aiken again, adding that I still thought he was a very great genius, and incidentally a much misunderstood one, but that it seemed to me that this touched on a subject so important for a writer launching away that I'd better write you a letter for your private ear on the subject (Gap in m.ss.) — for it yet remained to be explained how a boy of 18, more or less inexperienced save in one tough aspect of life, namely the sea, (a fragmentary thing, but still I'd been a seaman — O'Neill sent me to sea, I guess — looked at it as such, not a passenger),[13] could be drawn as by some irresistable teleological force toward an aspect of the mind or psyche of another much older, totally different in experience & nationality & outlook, and moreover, in Blue Voyage at least, with a philosophy & psychological *drang* — save where it touched beauty on the one hand, human misery on the other, expressed & linked through the phenomenal & magical usage of language — that he the boy, did not understand & had he understood, would have found thoroughly inimical — for sheer lack of sunlight & air & mountains, if not blue water — (you might call it pseudo-Freud + the philosophy of the 'nothing but') and then, as it were, stuck there, calmly disregarding among other things that Aiken himself, save in all but a few of his short stories which on the contrary are mostly a reversion of his prosaic & false & influenced side to almost nothing of lasting worth at all, as he would be the first to agree, say Time mag. what it may, had, with certain other exceptions, enormously & continuously developed in his poetry (but curiously I didn't know he was a poet at first) beyond that point into a metaphysical & far wiser & wider realm, to a point indeed where he might well serve as master to any writer in the world, in which connection it is as well not to forget the mature, indeed dying, Joyce, looking for Osiris Jones being reborn. (When Conrad sent me some 20 years ago a copy of the latter masterpiece to my lasting shame I neither acknowledged it nor made any comment. Why should I? What was all this about Osiris Jones? After all it was not Blue Voyage & *I* had not written it. Worse still, it never occurred to me he might be hurt, so cruelly abstract is one side of youth. And wierder than all, one might have reckoned without one's *own* remote influence, even if not literary or direct, but beneficently springing rather (in so far as it sprang, if spring it did,) in part from that very shattering & unsolicited faith in his work I had shown! But what did I see in Blue Voyage? Certainly something that was beyond my power rationally to see. Nor was I wrong. Perhaps what one might term Operation [illegible] of the daemon?) However it is no wonder I stopped the letter here, for the subject is hard to explain indeed, quite apart from which I had not even touched on what seemed to me the essence of the far greater subject that this began to adumbrate –

Then, after a while, I received yours of Aug 9.

At which point I think it's time to take those shoes off & get into the flames.

(No joke either; if he didn't do it himself first, noone would believe it could be done & then there would be no initiation)

I'll start with a few assumptions, in fact jump boldly to conclusions, all of them flattering to myself, & doubtless due to my great narcissism – though I won't waste time on this aspect of it – then make a few tangential observations, in the hope that even if inapplicable, they may some day, odds & ends of 2 x 4's though they are, serve as reliable timber with which to build a bridge should you need one. For no wonder Dante found the straight way was lost. There is no straight way. There is no path, unless metamorphosed – Dante's wood was an abyss.[14] Psychological – for the last time psychology!, as Kafka says – but true. Fortunately Virgil – since we all stand together in this – was standing near & he had the common sense to make use of him. Dante didn't grow much happier, it is true, but perhaps that was his fault: & at least he finished his book. Perhaps he'd have done better still if he'd pushed Virgil into one of those swamps instead another of his poor unfortunates & walked over using his head as a stepping stone but that's beside the point. Anyway Virgil was dead. If he'd been alive it might have been a different story. And I ain't no Virgil. Still I shall squelch along upon my feet of clay as well as I can – perhaps they will even turn into some kind of mottled marble in the process. Anyway: –

(a) I'm going to assume, as I should, you mean the letter you write.

(b) That having written it, you now wish you hadn't: i.e perhaps you feel ashamed of so expressing your feelings, in fact you may even feel I've misinterpreted it etc.

To (b) – *Don't* wish you hadn't written it. It is the best thing you could have done. And you are right, it *is* perfectly healthy. What would be unhealthy would be if you hadn't so simply & directly expressed your empathies on the subject. True – no doubt you could think – eventually you would have forgotten the said feeling, but here comes nature & the pitchfork again: more than that, a book is a much harder proposition than a human being – once truly recognised it is not in the nature of the thing to let you alone, though the source of its behaviour is a reciprocal gratitude beyond human understanding, it's liable to turn into a kind of mantra yoga: old stuff I have to talk here, stemming from the last sentence but one – the feelings turn inward & what is worse begin to work against you: worse still, they can even give one a kind of persecution mania, one suspects necrophily in oneself, incipient paranoia, heaven knows what (and on top of that the mind, equally with the heart, is a lonely hunter[15] – I once fell in love with an elephant – & it's certainly no use worrying about the damaging & morbid 'correspondences' of these things, they become ridiculous, when all one is trying to do is *live*, & God how hard it can be at your age: perhaps I am talking about myself, not you, – no matter, still I can permit myself to suffer on your account feeling yourself to be misunderstood, or disregarded, or worse, understood coldly & *cleverly* & rationally & 'psychologically,' & so more than disregarded, when all one has said is something direct & sincere: (Gap in the mss): – well, I myself am extremely happily married, the luckiest kind of person, both in my wife & the kind of life we mostly lead, as one might say healthy – & by god, it really is healthy – normal; what a word! – as if happiness were normal to-day, or this kind of life which has almost disappeared from the world altogether {Howard had no means & no words with which to explain to these simple men that business is the only real thing in life, that it is heaven & paradise & all the happiness of a good Rotarian. These Indians were still living in a semi-civilized state, with little hope of improvement within the next hundred years. – The Treasure of the Sierra Madre.}[16] – but there are all kinds of huge life-giving feelings in the world you can't pin down: for prose, for elephants, for the sea, even for the ducks that swim therein: we are all *here* anyway.)

Well, it is healthy, your identity with the Volcano I mean, even though the book may be not worthy of you, though it might be worse, (& I cannot say how moving to me, because I won't disguise from you that I'm extremely proud of most of it) but somehow all this must be *used* for your benefit; in fact it is yours, that's what it's there for. And whatever they say or don't say I think it's a good book probably.

However the full drama of what you have said has not yet emerged. Nor will it be lost on you. Here is the plot of the book lost by fire. (In Ballast to the White Sea – once the sort of Paradiso of the trilogy of which the Volcano was the first, or 'Inferno' section – now incorporated hypothetically elsewhere in the whole bolus of 5 books – I think – to be called The Voyage that Never Ends. It was lost 7 years, June 7 1944, when our first house went up in flames, not ten feet from where I sit, & written 9-10 years before that, in New York, when I was a little older than you.)

A, the hero of my novel, a young student at Cambridge, of Scandinavian origin & with a sea-faring experience such as my own, feels roughly speaking such a kinship for a work as you have most generously expressed for mine, – a novel of the sea, he has read in translation, by a Scandinavian novelist X [Nordahl Grieg].[17] The disorientation of A at the university is much the same as Hugh's at Cambridge in U.T.V & for the same reasons. X's novel is an appalling, & horrendous piece of work, a sort of Moby Dick in fact, but a Moby Dick that was concerned less with whales than the fate of the individual living characters of the Acushnet, (that being the original name of the Pequod). Only in this case the more A reads X's book the more identified he becomes with the principal character in that book, Y – who supplies the one note of relief (in X's book) – (it is a book on the side of life though) – the more so as the experience of Y – & by extension he feels that of X too – closely – indeed supernaturally – resembles his own: not merely that, but X's book uncannily resembles the one A's been trying to write himself, which it seems to have rendered futile. (As a matter of fact it's more complicated even than that but let it pass)

My hero is troubled among other things – (a stormy love affair with an older woman, the risk of being sent down for pursuing it, the invidiousness of being a man at the university & yet treated as a child, a Dostoievskian brother, the ghoulishness of his contemporaries, & the idiocy of the English faculty, the feeling of hopelessness that overwhelms him about his choice of a vocation when now he figures he perhaps isn't a writer & so no better than a child after all, & so on) by the fact that he can find absolutely no parallel in *literature* to this growing sense as of identity with the character Y, – & the field of X's novel – save a rather minor, if good, but scarcely helpful book by Louis Adamic, a feeble short story by Aldous Huxley, & a sinister German play running in London called The Race with a Shadow by one Wilhelm van Scholz, based on an idea by Goethe.[18] All these with the exception of the last, which is so horrible he can't take it, are almost parodies on the surface of an experience, by which he is bewildered because he cannot believe that it does not represent something universal & so of vital human importance; nor has it got anything to do with the normal experiences of hero-worship through which one passes: Y is not a hero in the usual sense, his experiences are not enviable, he is not even wise – he isn't even physically described in X's book for that matter so that he has no features or stature & is quite impossible to picture save as several kinds of person at once; on another plane he seems more like a voice that has commented upon a human experience with honour & an agonizing truth that is unique to A: (Y is not Melville's 'handsome sailor' nor Conrad's ugly one[19] – his virtues are simple & such as A's life in the England of that period everywhere betrays & even interdicts: loyalty, simplicity, decency, & a capacity to be reverent, in the bloodiest of circumstances, before the mystery of life, & a hatred of falsehood.

It would appear also that he has a faith, of a kind, in God, if not strictly according to Martin Luther).[20] Yet how can it be unique to A, when by God, Y *is* A. And what's all this about a hatred of falsehood, when one of the things that most bothers A is that A himself is an almost pathological liar – unable to give any kind of rational account of himself, he invents the most fantastic tales about himself at every point that are so vivid they have a kind of life of their own. (It is important for you to bear in mind that though I, as you may have guessed, am by & large, more or less (with reservations of course) A – though X is not Aiken, albeit an individual too – *I* am not lying to *you*, even though it might be more comfortable to do so. X represents the complimentary & lifegiving operation of the daemon pleading to $\pi\rho^2$ perhaps – implicit in π too – but without which π becomes satanic. Something like that. My terms are all mixed up, & I realise that like this it sounds more than a little ridiculous. But bear with me. Probably I don't have to explain it.) And how can A be A when he's Y? And yet this is not the half of it either. A is no narcissist. He has not caught paranoia. Moreover he is a tough baby, on one side (in my book or ex-book) almost as extroverted as some character in the Treasure of the Sierra Madre, even though that is a side of himself he exploits with women & lies about, but this much is true, his ship has taken him smack through the first bloody Chinese revolution of 1927 etc.,[21] though he has only seen tragic glimpses of the real thing & this knowledge of what he has actually been through even so, has only just ceased to be about nil: Nor has he some adolescent fixation or crush on X, because if Y is mysterious, X is ten times more so. (About X he can find out absolutely nothing at all, the Scandinavian's novel having been long since remaindered in translation, the publishers non-existent in England, & there is no blurb to tell him a thing – he's bought the book second hand & strangest of all A doesn't even want to *write* like X. Not at first, he doesn't, that is. A has a style all his own – & what A & X have in common – though A sees his whole life in that book – is something different). A, though he feels like an old man, has either by passed or not even reached the stage of adolescence. People like [Walt] Whitman with an all-embracing love of mankind, & also [D.H.] Lawrence, put him off, save when they write about nature. His knowledge of how gruesome man can be is too close, & in Cambridge, on a {cafe con leche} flabbier plane, closer still. So his brother not being a type he can take into his confidence, & his father being engaged in a gigantic lawsuit with the Peruvian Government, & his girl friend rapidly growing fed up with him, he sits down & writes to X. In fact he writes letter after letter to X – they formed, intermediately, a large part of the book – but it never having occurred to him that almost any publisher in Scandinavia would forward his letters, if X is extant, he keeps his problem, as the letters, to himself, – meanwhile becoming increasingly afraid of his thoughts as his identification with Y – & by extension with X – becomes more complete. . . .

(to be continued)

In order to keep my promise to get this letter off I have to post this right now to catch the Saturday mail – there is one mail a day only, none on Sunday, & the relative time of the two stages the letter must make to reach you are roughly as follows:

From Dollarton to Vancouver, 15 miles – – 24 hours

From Vancouver to Albany, 3500 miles? – – 12 hours
approx.

So if I delayed you wouldn't receive anything till the middle of next week. I shan't stop writing, however, till the letter is finished, if it ever can be finished. Plot of In Ballast has a triumphant outcome. So see exciting installment next week. On back of all pages save page 1 are some bits of the original mss of Under the Volcano my wife & I dug out for you & thought you might like to have: when I say original, some of it is pre-original, dating 11 years or so back, though I can't find any of the pre-pre-original which goes back to 1936 save in typescript; as a matter of fact we can't even find any typescript to speak of; notes down the margin are due to a habit my wife & I have of exchanging mss for mutual correction: some of the work looks as though one definitely knew what one was doing, other parts look uncertain & as if the author were out of touch, & the style flabby or derivative, other bits are happily no longer there – but in the main it's as is – sorry it's not in order, but felt it might please you. When I said confidential – of course that I leave to your highest judgement. I merely meant it was off the record so far as the thesis was concerned, because it might hurt someone's feelings. But I didn't mean that you shouldn't speak to your girl about it, if you feel like speaking to her. If you badly want any of it when I'm through for your thesis better let me edit it. In one way it seems like a dirty trick, on second thoughts, even to have voiced a bonafide criticism in these circumstances of Aiken, to whom I owe so much (though Aiken himself I am sure would be the first to give assent that I should write you this) & you must be wise & see beyond the superficial envy & ingratitude that evinces, the criticism of myself & my own weaknesses it involves.

Sursum Corda!

Malcolm L

Annotations:

1 Markson's 9 August 1951 letter, to which Lowry refers in the following sentence, is no longer extant with the incoming correspondence. However, in his second letter to Lowry, dated 24 June 1951, Markson compares *Volcano* to Joyce's *Ulysses*, calling the latter a 'bad' novel that benefited from the mythic infrastructure and the former a 'good' novel that buried its mythic foundations. Lowry's German for 'Fundamentals of Scholarly Expression' should read *Grundlage der Wissenschaft.*

2 If Lowry did begin a letter (other than **462**) to Markson discussing Aiken, Joyce, the Cabbala, and his plans for *The Voyage That Never Ends*, it has not survived, but at points Lowry appears to be quoting from a draft.

3 Conrad Aiken won the 1930 Pulitzer Prize for his *Selected Poems of Conrad Aiken* (1929).

4 Clarissa M. Lorenz married Conrad Aiken in February 1930; they divorced in 1938. Lowry had been struck by the fact that Aiken's *Blue Voyage* is dedicated to C.M.L. because they are also his initials and gave him his schoolboy's pseudonym, 'Camel.'

5 W.B. Yeats's *A Vision* (1925) interested Lowry as well as Joyce; see Lowry's June 1944 letter (**190**) to Charles Stansfeld-Jones.

6 In his 28 November 1951 letter (**482**) to Seymour Lawrence about Aiken's work, Lowry comments at length about Joyce's interest in Aiken. The name 'Lowry' appears in the deaths column of Bloom's newspaper in the 'Hades' chapter of *Ulysses*, and Joyce was indeed superstitious about what he felt was the book's prophetic nature. See also Lowry's 3 March 1940 letter (**128**) to Conrad Aiken.

7 Horace's proverb *Naturam expellas furca, tamen usque recurret* ('Even though you drive nature out with a pitchfork, she will rush right back') is from his *Epistles* I. 10. 24. Lowry quotes fragments of the Latin in his story 'Elephant and Colosseum.'

8 In his 24 June 1951 letter Markson explains that he has been reading Joseph Frank's article on 'Spatial Form in the Modern Novel,' which appeared in three parts in the *Sewanee Review* 53.2, 3, 4 (1945). He had also been reading Mark Schorer's review of *Under the Volcano*, called 'The Downward Flight of a Soul,' in the *New York Herald-Tribune Weekly Book Review*, 23 February 1947, 2, and he quotes Schorer's comment that *Ulysses* is 'like a pattern of concentric circles.'

9 Robert Wiene's (1881-1938) expressionist film *The Hands of Orlac* (*Orlacs Hände*, 1924), starring Conrad Veidt as the pianist Orlac, was made for the German Ufa studios in Berlin. *Mad Love* (1935), the Hollywood remake of *The Hands of Orlac* directed by Karl Freund, is an important intertext in *Under the Volcano*. It starred one of Lowry's favourite actors (see his 8 December 1951 letter, **484**, to Harold Matson), the Hungarian Peter Lorre (1904-64) as the mad doctor. Wiene's *The Cabinet of Doctor Caligari* (1919) is *the* classic expressionist film. Fritz Lang (1890-1976) directed several influential expressionist

films such as his *Dr Mabuse* trilogy, *Metropolis* (1926), and *Destiny* (*Der Müde Tod*, 1921).

10 Lowry was amused by the *Volcano*'s success vis-à-vis Kathleen Winsor's *Forever Amber*, and he mentions this success often; see, for example, his April/May 1947 letter (**297**) to John Davenport.

11 George Plantagenet, Duke of Clarence (1449-78), was the younger brother of Edward IV; according to legend and Shakespeare's *Richard III* I.iv.270, he was drowned 'in the malmsey-butt within.'

12 In his 24 June 1951 letter Markson notes that his friend from Syracuse, NY, Leonard Brown, thinks of himself as Lowry's Consul, Geoffrey Firmin.

13 Lowry had read Eugene O'Neill's early plays about the sea (such as *The Hairy Ape*, 1922, and *Anna Christie*, 1921) as a schoolboy at the Leys in the early to mid-twenties. See Lowry's May 1926 letter (**8**) to Carol Brown.

14 Lowry is referring to the opening lines of Dante's *Inferno*: 'In the middle of the road of our life / I found myself in a dark wood, / for the right way was lost.' These lines form an important motif in *Under the Volcano*; see Lowry's 2 January 1946 letter (**210**) to Cape and Ackerley/Clipper.

15 American novelist and short-story writer Carson McCullers (1917-67) published *The Heart is a Lonely Hunter* in 1940. It is the story of a deaf-mute in a Southern town and a warning about fascism.

16 *The Treasure of the Sierra Madre* (1935) by B. Traven (?1890-1969) is a novel about human greed that was made into a film by John Huston in 1948. Howard, one of the three gold prospectors, represents the values of honesty, work, and decisiveness that are praised in the book.

17 Lowry's identification with Nordahl Grieg and with Benjamin Hall, the hero of Grieg's novel *The Ship Sails On* (1927), was an important theme for Lowry as early as 1929-30; see Lowry's 8 September 1931 and spring 1939 letters (**35** and **85**) to Grieg. Only a few pages and charred fragments of Lowry's copy of 'In Ballast to the White Sea' survived the 1944 fire and remain with the Lowry collection (UBC 12:14-15).

18 Alojzij (Louis) Adamic (1899-1951), the American writer of Slovenian birth, published *Grandsons* in 1935. It is an autobiographical novel about the writing of a novel by another man who is a 'shadow' figure of the chief narrator. Aldous Huxley (1894-1963), the English essayist, novelist, and satirist, published many stories. Lowry may be remembering a convoluted long short story called 'Farcical History of Richard Greenow,' in *Limbo* (New York: George H. Doran, 1920), about a writer with a split personality who writes different types of work under the influence of his male or female persona. Wilhelm von Scholz (1874-1969) was a German playwright, novelist, and poet who was interested in mysticism and the worship of fate. His most successful play, *The Race with a Shadow* (*Der Wettlauf mit dem Schatten*, 1920), is about the rivalry between a writer and one of his characters.

19 Herman Melville's handsome sailor is Billy Budd in his novella *Billy Budd* (1924); Conrad's ugly one is almost certainly Donkin in *The Nigger*

of the 'Narcissus' (1897).

20 Martin Luther (1483-1546), the German religious reformer who broke with Roman Catholicism at the beginning of the Protestant Reformation, argued that people were saved by personal faith and therefore did not need Catholic rituals.

21 Lowry may be thinking of Chiang Kai-shek's Nationalist Army purges of Communists and leftists within the Kuomintang in Shanghai in April 1927, or the army's attacks on foreigners in Nanking in March 1927. British and American gunboats in the Yangtze River intervened to stop these attacks.

Editorial Notes:

a. The copy-text of this letter (UBC 2:19) is interesting. It is written in blue ink on the rectos of nine pages of Lowry's canary second-cut paper. Seven of these pages carry pencil draft material for the 'original' draft of *Under the Volcano*, which Lowry describes for Markson towards the end of the letter. The last section of the letter, with Lowry's signature, is written on the verso of manuscript page 9. See Lowry's 27 August 1951 letter (**468**) for the continuation of this letter.

468: To David Markson

P: UBC(ms)
PP: *SL* 258-66   [Dollarton]
                                                      [27 August 1951]
                    (Intervallo)[a]

(Is ah Senor David Markson in the house? Will he proceed to the cantina – the dirtiest one – next door, where the gringo peon bruto pelado Senor Lowry is lying seriously ill. Chocolates? Tequila? Cerveza? Gaseosas? Mescal? H'm. Buenas tardes, señor. How's it going, old man? Sorry, it wasn't that I was lying seriously ill – nor that I was ill because I was seriously lying – because I'm not indeed, though I find it difficult & indeed even painful to remember certain details of the plot of my chingado novel – on the contrary I'm trying my damnedest to tell the truth, fantastic though it may be – but because, in this intervallo, I have read your letter again, & I perceived, misericorde, hombre, alas, that I had not thanked you sufficiently from the heart – I hadn't mentioned I had a heart – for what you have so generously & above all *simply* said, and with a feeling, & trust, I was going to say, I didn't deserve: but if that is so, viejo, what the hell is the point of writing this letter? what kind of the hell reflection of yourself would I give back if I didn't deserve it? So, all right, I *do* deserve it. As certainly you deserve something back of equal sincerity. If I deny myself, I deny my book, & in denying my book, I deny you. For equally it is your book. So I shan't do anything of the sort; I will, on the contrary, affirm it, be proud of it. As I am not? But how have I answered – & this is what is making me at the moment sick, hombre – sickness is in that part used to be call: soul,[1] – moreover I hate to think that my silence, however explicable & non-invidious, made you suffer, – this forthrightness, this frankness, this directness? Have I answered it with an equal forthrightness, an equal simplicity of feeling? Or with a concatenation of complexities, an evasion of gobbledygookeries – in short, for simplicity, have returned – psychology? And then on top of that have worn a mien of being so unco guid[2] pure normal healthy & beyond reproach that perhaps it's unnatural in itself, as if my life, or anyone else's life, had not been wrested – & does not have to go on being wrested – out of the Molochian maw of errors so often destructive they make one's hair stand on end: so you would be wrong to think that the human being is not there, that he in turn is not sympathetic, or that he regards that life – despite a definite element of having *come through* – as anything purer or more upright than a collaboration between Strindberg, Dostoievsky, the Underground Man, a Ouija board, a talking horse, Joe Venuti and a Houngan:[3] this on the one side, on the other you must feel yourself right to have trusted me, though not for reasons that are at all easy to answer. Still you *are* right to do so. The decency, the honesty is here, sprouting laboriously amid the indecency, the dishonesty. But immediately I say that the shadow of Melville's Confidence Man seems to fall upon my pen, that emblem of the worse than worst, warning me away from one's easy interpretations, one's facile optimism, and whose nostrums conceal who knows what hidden desire for power, even to exploit, even though on the face of it, it wouldn't be at all easy to see where he comes in. Very hard for yourself to see, who feel, if anything, you were exploiting me. Well, on both sides that is a risk one has to take. Simply for fear of error, of being self-condemned, of making mistakes, even ghastly mistakes, of sounding indeed like The Confidence Man, I don't think we should shrink from trying to be constructive, or rather to help one another, where we see the chance. And what is even God to do when if you ask for help the ambassador he chooses fails even to attempt to deliver the goods. Clearly His rating, even if unjustly, would go down. Which brings me to what I conceive to be the purpose of this letter. The best way that I can answer your own trust, can show my own gratitude to you as it were, can only be on the basis of the thought: 'I wish to God someone had said something like this to *me*' when I at your age said, or worse did not say 'I don't quite know how to say this' 'I insisted to myself for a while' 'Do you have any idea what it means to me?' 'Do you realise what I'm saying?' I don't mean I have been unlucky in my friends or influences, exactly. In fact, in many respects, considering this & that, I've been a creature of luck all through. The few friends I've made in my life I've mostly kept, & still revere. I have spoken of the help Aiken gave me, sadly needed, because my father – who was by way of being a capitalist on the grand scale – good man though he was, rarely gave me any advice of much pragmatic value, though I'll always bless him for turning me into a good swimmer. But apart from that I often felt myself a kind of item on the business agenda, even, in some respects, an expendable item. It is natural I think, to eschew giving, as taking, advice. I'm not sure there's any advice per se in this letter. Still there are times when the need for understanding is absolutely imperative. And it has been my experience that it is precisely among people of one's own artistic persuasion that one is likely to find the most crashing disillusionment. At least I often wished, at your age, should I say, or even not say 'Do you realise what I'm saying?' no matter what the subject, that someone older would have the courage to say 'Yes, I think so', & explain it for my benefit, even if wrongly, at least give me something to go on, at least *take the trouble*. But in fact – though there are exceptions as I've pointed out, especially in the good old tradition of poets – by & large these stuffed geniuses, this aristocratic proletariat of peacock, these sanctissima God donkey, this Jesus man burro, say, like as not, nothing at all. Mean as so many stingy old gold miners sitting on a stake they seem to think it too dangerous to open their trap, even if, like certain professors I know of, they're being paid to do so. And it's not merely that they fear to give away the source of the mine. It's how to work it – ah no, that would harm their bloody little conception of their own uniqueness. Ah, that contemptuous look that seems to say: 'But don't you know *that*?' Even if they saw their best friend about to fall slap down the abyss, it wouldn't occur to them to say: 'I've been there before, brother – in fact I'm down there now – let me stand like a caryatid down there, while you step on my head & go round the other way, for you can achieve the same or a better result by doing that! Even if by saying that they would be achieving the only possible human good they were likely to do on this earth they'd think of some way out of doing it. Still, if I'm not to be worse still, back to this letter What? Senor Lowry is not in that cantina, but in his shack on the waterfront, drinking a friendly glass of plebian gin & orange juice with his wife – & I'm not going [to] drink much of that at the moment, if this letter is to be right, – & writing the letter, as from the Charly Chaplin stove ascends the pungent aroma of frying horse, for inflation has driven us not merely to sharing, but to eating our archetypes too!)[4]

So all this isolates the poor guy A more than ever.[5] So he never posts any of those letters, keeps the whole matter to himself. Meantime two other things are going on, on another plane. As he writes the letters he becomes consumed with an absolute passion – in one sense hereditary – to return to the sea. The sea begins to rise within him, haunts his dreams, & this longing that storms in him day & night to return to the sea was one of the best parts of the book – all of which makes it such a nuisance I have to write it again (Do I hear myself aright? Well perhaps your letter will one day give me the guts to do just that, not leave it merely buried, as it lies now, as so much exposition) for it takes a curious form: – the longing for the sea emerges into a longing for the fire of the stokehold, for the actual torment – masochistic, though it somehow isn't, but above all for the fire (which being so the book could not have had a finer funeral – my wife rescued all the Volcano, I one of hers, but we had to let that go –) the fire in which he sees himself purged & emerging as the reborn man, which the absolute integrity decency and as it were purity of the feeling that overwhelms him whenever he reads X's book or writes – still without posting any of the letters – to X – it can scarcely but be pure for X is like an abstraction, but it has none of the evil either of absolute purity on this plane (albeit the White Sea itself is that, is death too) gives him to believe he may turn into. For, largely due to the suppression of this feeling, all is not well with him in almost every other respect. He neglects his studies, starts to drink like a fish, finds his own work increasingly worthless, gets through an exam on Dante's Inferno by consulting a blind medium who tells him what the questions will be, at least becomes in spite of that so closely identified with X that now when he does pull himself together & write, he can't be sure he isn't transcribing whole sections of X's novel which, whenever he is sober, which is not often, he has to destroy. Meantime he makes the mistake of taking his brother into his confidence who instead of being sympathetic is scornful of the whole business and accuses him of every kind of abnormal tendency under the sun, & several not under it. On top of this he – the brother – derides X's book which enrages A to such an extent that inadvertently he causes his brother to turn all his venom on himself in a Dostoievskian scene that leads to the brother's death. Shattered & sobered by this tragedy (there has to be a large gap in the mss. here if I am ever to finish) A. makes a tremendous effort of will, and during the long vacation – he has four months in the summer – signs on, as a fireman, a Scandinavian timber ship bound from Preston, near Liverpool, to Archangel, in ballast. (His purpose, so he thinks, in doing this, is to gather added material for a play he proposes to make of X's novel, though incidentally he has arranged with his professor that this play will serve in lieu of a thesis for the second part of his English Tripos!)[6] One of the best parts of the book I have to pass over too briefly here: almost on the point of sailing it turns out that A has to return to

20 Malcolm and Margerie in Vancouver, where they
spent the coldest winter months in 1951, 1952 and 1953.

21 Malcolm on the beach at Dollarton with the shack and his boat in the background, summer 1953. There is an interesting note (**578**, *above right*) on the back of this photograph to the Burts.

Sinister bearded man

With love to Dorothy & Harvey
— not forgetting Dapper Dan & Mr Plumley —
from Malcolm
(herewith to be observed pronouncing
benediction upon the one-hopes-seaworthy
craft) happy memory & by name "My
Heart's in the Highlands"; & with great
thanks from her & us for the renovation
) same, & aboard which I hope you & the
may soon be rowing toward a happy picnic.)

22 Malcolm with his staples, a book and a bottle, outside the Dollarton shack, ca 1953. *(right)*

23 Giorgio Monicelli, Milan ca 1954. *(top left)*

24 The 1934 Comédie Champs
Elysées production of Jean Cocteau's
La Machine infernale, with Martha
Régnier and Jean-Pierre Aumont as
Jocasta and Oedipus and Robert le
Vigan as Anubis. *(left)*

25 Malcolm in Taormina in Sicily,
1955. *(above)*

26 Malcolm with Dorothy Templeton
Burt outside the Villa Mazzullo on
Mazzaro Beach, Taormina 1955. *(right)*

27 The White Cottage at Ripe in Sussex, 1956. *(above)*

28 Dr Michael Raymond, Malcolm's physician in England, ca 1956.

29 Margerie holding one of the Lowrys' cats outside the White Cottage, 1956. *(below)*

30 Malcolm at the garden pump, White Cottage, 1956. *(left)*

31 Malcolm during a hike in the Lake District, June 1957. *(below)*

32 Malcolm at Grasmere in the Lake District, June 1957. This view
with the pier reminded him of Dollarton.

33 The Dollarton pier: 'Nobody could understand how it survived so long, not
even engineers & it was nicknamed The 'Crazy Wonder' on the beach. Ramshackle
from certain angles though it was, & the handrails puerile (but oh the washing hung out
on the line there like great white stationary birds beating their wings against the gale).'
Letter **662** from Malcolm to Harvey Burt.

Liverpool according to law to sign on with the Norwegian Consul, this being impossible with the Captain, & there not being such a Consul in Preston. In Liverpool he runs into another brother, a criminal lawyer, who is tight & tries to stop him going: so the whole weary effort of will has to be made over again. The ship however does not go to Archangel but to a port in northern Norway that oddly *has the same name* as one of the principal characters, though not the hero, of X's novel. Here, seemingly by coincidence, while the charter of the ship is held in abeyance pending a decision by the shipowners in Oslo, he falls in with a character in a café reading another book of X's. This book shows that X has been in China at the same time A has and it turns out that this character, a schoolmaster, has met X. Also there is a photograph of X in the book – this is the first indication to A's conscious mind that there really is in Existence such a person as X. I had forgotten to say the most important thing, namely that while he took no human *action* at all (posting the letters would have amounted to that) some principle of tyrannic yet thwarted force in his feeling has worked against him, à rebours:[7] now he does take action – & heroic action at that – mysteriously the thing begins to work for him in a way that alters his whole conception of life & human destiny. This place (where he is in Norway) also turns out not to be far away from the place where his own mother has been buried and he pays a pilgrimage to her grave, the ship meanwhile, for lack of orders – though as a matter of fact the orders are contradictory, paralleling the indecision in A's mind whether to take another job & go on to Archangel or actually try & meet X – being stalled in the fjord, & the crew paid off. Here we begin to get on to the theme of rebirth. On the day of his pilgrimage to his mother's grave he meets a girl with whom he falls violently in love. This love is returned & this in fact is his first real experience of mature love. Meanwhile, quite without his seeming to will it, coincidence after coincidence, obeying a kind of Law of Series of their own, combine to take him to Oslo & result in his actually meeting X, this meeting coming about through the shipowner who has been sending the contradictory messages – & X is no easy person to meet, lives under an assumed named, & – though he has become a playwright too – is a figure of great political significance (He is working against the conspiracy of Quisling's Nasjonal Samling, which considering this was written in 1936 is a pretty good piece of clairvoyance when you think they hadn't even got wise to it in 1940 after the event.)[8] When he meets X though, X is on the point of going to *Cambridge* , – the very place where A has come from – to do some research on Elizabethan drama, but because of a divided vocation, in a state of confusion & despair bordering on A's own original confusion & despair.[9] It is too complex to describe in detail this part of the book – but the resemblances

between A & X are almost as uncanny as the differences. The character
Y turns out not to be X but an objective projection – though X has been
to sea – whom I had imagined as very like A. However X's apartment,
books etc, though they are mostly Scandinavian, is an almost exact
replica of A's rooms in Cambridge. X moreover tells A that the *real*
name of the ship that had given him his experience is the same as that
of the ship that A had used in imagination in *his* book. (of which he has
proof, having brought some of the more original sections with him to
work on in between planning the play.) X gives him permission to make
the play, and the absolutely glaring testimony to the existence of the
transcendental in the whole business, to a man like X, who imagined up
till then that he had created things out of cold reason whatever he made
his characters say or do, restores his faith, which had almost been lost, in
his art. Both men are realigned on the side of life & A's action has also
resulted in his salvation by his girl; in effect both the life of the imagination & life itself, has been saved by A's having listened finally to the
promptings of his own spirit, and acted upon those promptings, rather
than the analytical reductions of reason, though it is reason too, – by
virtue of harmony with the great forces within the Soul – that has been
saved, and on this note the story, & the trilogy closes.

Well, what a hell of a plot, you say, a kind of a Strindbergian Tonio
Kröger, by Maeterlinck, out of Melville.[10] That may be, but the point
is – that with a few exceptions like the brother's death etc – & in a few
other minor points – I *didn't* make the story up. There *was* an X: I did
write, I did not post the letters.[11] Some force did work against me, when
I took no action, & then when I took some action, for me. The story of
the name of the imaginary ship being the same as the one in fact is true
too, & there are a lot of other even more curious things that are true
which I haven't mentioned so that altogether one might say, as X did,
in fact once wrote: Reason stands still, what do we know? I have said
that X was not Aiken. Someday I will tell you the whole story. (X's full
remark was: 'Another spiral has wound its way upward. Reason stands
still. What do we know?)[12]

Tragedy in real fact comes in in that after our first house burned
down, we took refuge with a friend in Niagara who, not knowing I
knew X, or that I had written a book largely about him that had been
lost in the fire, was actually engaged in composing a broadcast on his
death when we arrived, so giving me that news for the first time too –
he had perished six months before the book of which he was the co-
hero, also in flames, in a bomber over Berlin, on the wedding
anniversary of my wife & myself.

Meantime you needn't bother even to find out who X is. One day,
as I say, I shall tell you the story. The reason I have mentioned it here is

that upon the subject that makes up that story I have brooded, as you could not have known, half a lifetime. A's feeling – I want you to realize – is, in my opinion above all, first & foremost *creative*. In that book I advanced the opinion that it was one of the most powerful and one of the most unknown – as to knowledge of what it is – feelings it is possible to have, & one of the purest as it were, even if directed at an object of blistering evil – though it is not exactly an object, it is something you share yourself, as you sooner or later discover; and anyway it is one of the most misunderstood: perhaps it is religious in origin or perhaps it has something to do with evolution itself: but it is certainly a *force* & as a force it obliges you to use it, obliges you to make an act of transcending. You have to go on from there. Aiken once told me that he considered it primarily an operation of genius. Genius knows what it wants & goes after it. He told me – this I say in strict confidence, though he did not swear me to confidence on the subject but admitted it freely – that he was once drawn to Eliot's work in the same way. Eliot himself – who owes a great deal to Aiken himself that has not been acknowledged – has called this identification 'one of the most important experiences (for a writer) of adolescence'.[13] I'd like to know when adolescence stops at that rate. I surmise an identification on Eliot's part with Laforgue.[14] On the tragic plane you have Keat's identification with Chatterton, leading, Aiken once suggested, to a kind of *conscious* death on Keats part.[15] However that may be, it is a force of life. But also it is an operation of the soul. As you have observed – in fact as you [said] yourself – it can be clairvoyant. But it is only a writer, poor devil, who would ever imagine such a thing was unhealthy. I imagine that in the realm of music it is recognised simply and consciously absorbed as a process in composition e.g. Berg & Schönberg. Leibowitz has pointed out that though Berg followed Schonberg in almost every discovery, adopting all his principles & reaching the same conclusions, he yet remained a great & original composer.[16] Conversely – without doubt (says he) one can become a great composer after having had a bad master, but in such a case the very fact of becoming a great composer implies that, at one time or another, one has resolutely turned against one's master. I don't know why I have said all this, or what it adds up to. I started from an assumption – possibly quite wrong-headed – that you would regret having written me. I've tried to show that you certainly should not regret it. All this reckons without the human element, but since you unfortunately live some thousands of miles away, to write is the next best thing to our meeting to which I look forward one day. Don't try to reply in detail though – it would be too difficult, if not impossible. But if I have said anything useful use it for your own good. One thing you could do is to look back sternly upon the impulses in operation before, say, you read The Volcano, the teleology that drew you toward it. For example I am drawn inexorably toward Blue Voyage, a novel which is the work of a poet, though I don't know that. I am also drawn toward the work of X, a novel likewise the work of a poet it turns out, but who is also a dramatist, though I don't know that either. I think both are novelists only. Sure enough, I become a novelist, whatever that is. But since the aim of my psyche seems to have been to make a synthesis of these two factors, & since my earlier passion was the drama, wouldn't it be a reasonable point to call sublime reason to one's aid in the person of someone like [José] Ortega [y Gasset] & assume I have some buried capacity as a poet or dramatist? It might. And something similar may be true of you. Anyhow you are much younger than I, & with time to decide what you want to do. And if you like my book that much, let it help you to get things in the right order. Perhaps they are, anyway. But still, also send me whatever spontaneity you like. I have to work so hard now that I shan't be able to reply for some months save in monosyllables but don't let [that] put you off again. It is a pity there is so much space between us but perhaps there is not so much as there appears to be. Give my love to your girl – be happy in this order: Health, Happiness, Sense of Humour, Art, Pleasure. My wife sends her love too. Hold that note, Roland![17]

Sursum Corda!

Malcolm L

Annotations:

1 This statement, made by Dr Vigil in chapters 1 and 5 of *Under the Volcano*, is one of many allusions in the preceding sentences to Lowry's novel.

2 The term 'unco guid' is an ironic Scots or northern British term for those who are excessively pious; see Robbie Burns's poem 'Address to the Unco Quid, or the Rigidly Righteous' (1786).

3 Lowry is suggesting that his life resembles a bizarre mix of events, ideas, and experiences drawn from the plays of Strindberg, the fiction of Dostoevsky, the reflections of Dostoevsky's 'Underground Man' (the narrator of *Notes from Underground*, 1864), and supernatural interventions in the form of a Ouija board, a talking horse (see his 13 December 1956 letter [**699**] to Albert Erskine), jazz, and voodoo.

4 Chaplin's film *The Gold Rush* is set in a prospector's cabin, the central feature of which is a wood stove; see also Lowry's 26 April 1952 letter (**526**) to David Markson. The shared archetypes are the horses in *Under the Volcano* and *Horse in the Sky*, both of which trample people to death.

5 In the following discussion of his lost manuscript 'In Ballast to the White Sea' Lowry is continuing where his 25 August 1951 letter (**467**) to Markson left off. A is the hero of 'In Ballast' and modelled on Lowry;

X is Nordahl Grieg, and Y is Benjamin Hall, the hero of Grieg's novel *The Ship Sails On*. That Lowry actually did meet Grieg is clear from his 8 September 1931 letter (**35**) to Grieg.

6 In 1933 Lowry submitted the manuscript of *Ultramarine* as part of the requirement for his Cambridge degree, but he had contemplated turning *The Ship Sails On* into a play; see his spring 1939 letter (**85**) to Grieg.

7 The French phrase *à rebours* means 'the other way around.' *À rebours* is the title of Joris-Karl Huysmans' 1884 novel to which Lowry refers in his 20 June 1950 letter (**401**) to Christopher Isherwood.

8 Vidkun Quisling (1887-1945) was a Norwegian fascist whose name is a synonym for traitor. In 1933 he founded the National Unity Party, modelled on the German National Socialist Party; in 1940 he helped the Nazis invade Norway and then headed a puppet government. After the war the Norwegians executed him for treason.

9 At the time Lowry met Grieg (in 1931) the Norwegian was working on his study of English poets (*De unge døde*, 1932). Rupert Brooke, who had been at Cambridge and written a book called *John Webster & the Elizabethan Drama*, is one of the poets in Grieg's study; see Lowry's 8 September 1931 letter (**35**) to Grieg.

10 *Tonio Kröger* (1903), a story by Thomas Mann, is about a sensitive, artistic boy of Italian-German ancestry who becomes a famous writer whose inspiration is drawn from his suffering. Maurice Maeterlinck (1862-1949), the Belgian poet and symbolist playwright, created characters that embody aspects of an unseen force lying behind everyday reality.

11 These unsent letters to Grieg do not appear to have survived.

12 Lowry has combined two remarks by the moralizing narrator of Grieg's novel: 'a new spiral had wound its way upward' and 'reason stands still; what do we know?'

13 Conrad Aiken and T.S. Eliot met in 1906 as undergraduates at Harvard University. Aiken, who satirizes Eliot as 'the Tsetse' in *Ushant* (1952), was fully aware of his debt to Eliot. Eliot's debt to Aiken is perhaps the more general one of friendship and support. We have not located this quotation in Eliot's work.

14 *Les Derniers Vers de Jules Laforgue*, by French poet and critic Jules Laforgue (1860-87), was published posthumously in 1890 and had an important influence on Eliot's development of technically innovative free verse.

15 Lowry presents this argument as his own in his 8 September 1931 letter (**35**) to Grieg.

16 René Leibowitz (1913-72) was a composer and student of Anton Webern and Arnold Schönberg, and the author of *Schoenberg and His School* (trans. 1949). In a chapter on Alban Berg (1885-1935) Leibowitz focuses on his expressionist operas *Woyzeck* and *Lulu*. Berg studied with Arnold Schönberg (1874-1951), the Austrian composer and inventor of the twelve-tone or serial method of composition, and was profoundly affected by his teacher.

17 Lowry has taken this line, which he usually combined with another –
    'Blow that horn' – from a 1947 radio play by the English poet Louis
    MacNeice (1907-63), called *The Dark Tower*. The play is based on
    Robert Browning's poem 'Childe Roland to the Dark Tower Came'
    (1855) and the lines were favourites of Lowry's; see, for example, his 5
    February 1954 letter (**604**) to David Markson.

Editorial Notes:

a. This is the continuation, sent separately, promised in the preceding
    letter. It is written in ink on six pages of second-cut paper; four pages
    are versos of pencil drafts for *Under the Volcano* (UBC 2:19).

469: To Margerie Bonner Lowry

P: UBC(ms)

[Dollarton]
[ca September 1951]ᵃ

*Appendix to IV*ᴬ

Dearest Duck

Please retype as *little* of this as possible – just do what is consistent with
our seeing it as a whole.

But retype *none* of the lifesaving story e.g 40A - 43 -

(though because there is an insert you will have to retype bottom
of 43.)

Here I want *your* version, which is superior & the underlinings in
your text are only matters we should discuss.

Similarly 43A onwards – only pages where there are inserts in the
middle etc, & only then when necessary, as, say partly on 46. basing it
all here largely on your version.

(There are difficult matters to remember in Forum where I have put
notes on the side, such as: *Has Tom had a phone conversation with Cosnahan*
etc.² So keep this note too.) It is not even absolutely necessary to retype
47, unless you think so.

Similarly don't bother to retype the scene in the publishers 52 - the
end 55 where *my* old version is a superior basis, quite neat enough, & if
there must be alterations, I want them made afresh, though I will of
course keep your version to compare after.

Thank you. With love

Your dear duck

Annotations:

1 The story that Lowry is discussing, 'Elephant and Colosseum,' is not
   divided into numbered sections. By appendix he means his notes for
   revision (UBC 10:18 and 11:3).
2 The 'difficult matters' concern Drumgold Cosnahan's visit to the
   Roman Forum, into which he is 'shepherded' by a 'gaggle of priests.'
   As he walks around, he imagines he sees his brother, Father Matthias
   Cosnahan, and he indulges in a series of 'contra-Proustian reveries.'

Editorial Notes:

a. This pencil note to Margerie appears on the verso of a typescript for
   'Through the Panama' (UBC 25:7). It was probably written between
   August and October 1951, when he was working on 'Elephant and
   Colosseum.'

470: To David Markson

P: UBC(ms)   Dollarton, B.C.
                                              [10 September 1951]ᵃ

Dear David: –
   Was delighted to hear from you as you wrote. But for the moment
monosyllables – am trying to get a short story completed against time.[1]
   (a) Might a soul . . . Andrew Marvell.
   (b) Ah, that the dream of . . . Alastor – Shelley (M. Laruelle
         made a movie of same: see opening of VII)
   (c) Himavat business at start of Chapter V. Only God
knows . . . And by degrees they reached the briny sea etc is quotation from
some Vedantic thing or other. But the dog is a thematic note – dogs pursue the Consul. Himavat is dream transposition of Popo but also relates to
Consul's childhood, as you say, for whole scene of dream is Kashmir.
Scenery of Quanhuahuac is a bit like Kashmir. Source of scenery was
doubtless 'some little book' out of the public library, for I've never been
to Kashmir. Or India proper for that matter. (Though I've been to
Ceylon. Likewise Formosa. Likewise China & Japan. Also Dollarton.)
Cruel idea was to make the poor old bird have an almost ecstatic dream
when actually he has the heeby-jeebies – also to point contrast with, yet
continuance from, Chap IV, where likewise there are dogs.
   You might have seen our inlet (in which a dog is swimming at the
moment) in the movies recently without knowing it – A hundred thousand people moved in to watch two of your countrymen try to break a
speedboat speed record. Attempt at record had to be abandoned because

of too great danger from driftwood propelled by mighty currents which we could have told the newspaper that tried to deceive them into trying. We were very glad when the 100,000 people moved away & left us in peace but your speedboat men put on a very heroic show, risking their lives rather than disappoint we bastards, & going faster than anything I ever saw go on land or sea before – to what end I know not, but it was mighty exciting to watch at 1/2 a cable's length from our house

God bless & best of luck –

Malcolm

P.S. My wife wrote under the name of Margerie Bonner – her maiden name – though in her last, as yet unpublished book, she is trying her luck with Lowry.[2] (Sending you the bits of m.s though was my uninfluenced idea, incidentally, though it was she who dug them out.)

Annotations:

1 This story is 'Elephant and Colosseum'; the notes following are answers to Markson's questions about allusions in *Under the Volcano*; for annotations, see Ackerley/Clipper.
2 Lowry must be thinking of the unpublished work called 'The Castle of Malatesta.'

Editorial Notes:

a. This single-page holograph is undated; Markson has supplied this date in the upper right corner of the recto.

471: To Albert Erskine

P: Virginia(ms)

Dollarton, B.C.,
Canada
2 October 1951

(All this [Margerie's wishes for Erskine's happiness] inarticulately doubled & seconded by me.)[a]

comic relief (i) Klett liked it about as much as Reynal,[1] as a matter of fact, but as a consequence of its success according to the translator is 'now soft as butter in the sun & like an ass before the church door'

comic relief (ii) I also received a fan letter from Paterson yesterday, which says in part: 'Final testimoniall to its excellence, incidentally I have found from people in much the same alcoholic condition as your hero some of whom have perished since we discussed your book among a round of other things – one particularly bright woman who kiccked the bucket in Mexico, incidentally. But this is sort of a grim gossipy style to congratulate you with. I hope you are writing more, saw by jacket years ago you'd spent a lot of time in Volcano & were getting along in years so to speak. Well, hope you are well off generally. Yours sincerely etc.[2]

[unsigned]

Annotations:

1 According to Clemens ten Holder, Ernst Klett disliked *Under the Volcano*; this has reminded Lowry of Eugene Reynal's alleged dislike of it.
2 This letter 'from Paterson' does not appear to have survived.

Editorial Notes:

a. These passages are Lowry's addenda to a letter from Margerie to Erskine about Lowry's progress with *Hear us O Lord*. They are written in pencil in the bottom and left margins of the verso.

472: To Harold Matson

P: Matson(ts); UBC(phc)
PP: *SL* 266-68

Dollarton, B.C.,
Canada
2 October 1951

Dear Hal –

I am posting you today under separate cover a comic classic, or at least a masterpiece of nature, or at all events that is the only way of looking at it, at least for me, or I wouldn't have felt justified in writing it, so if you don't think so, don't tell me, at least not just yet.[1] I believe there is some chance some people will think it first rate in its genre though, if it has one, for it breaks all the rules, save that, I hope, of being interesting and amusing; on one plane it is no less than a kind of short short for Titans, a Moby Jumbo, a comic strip for the infant Panurge, of philosophic trend, and I do not need reminding that the magazine designed to accomodate easily such a Pantagruelian fancy, or multum in colosseo[2] – for it is longer than the Heart of Darkness – is not yet, though it may be that its merit is such that one would stretch a point even to a bursting of the seams, or at least in two installments, to garage the monster.

However of this I am not sanguine, so please hearken unto my further intention. This enclosed new epistle to the Colossians[3] was originally designed to be accompanied at the same time by another novella of the same length, though absolutely opposite in intention, locale, sturm und drang,[4] etc. and of great seriousness (though it is a story of happiness, in fact, roughly of our life here in the forest, exultant side of) entitled The Forest Path to the Spring. So far as I know this is the only short novel of its type that brings the kind of majesty usually reserved for tragedy (God this sounds pompous) to bear on human integration and all that kind of thing: though it isn't my final word on the subject by a damn sight, I'm mighty proud of it.

As a matter of fact this latter is in part an adumbration – though complete in itself – of a novel to be called Eridanus which, if things go well and I can get through the necessary ordeals so to speak which permit me to write the whole, will form a sort of Intermezzo or point of rest to the larger work of five, perhaps six interrelated novels, of which the Volcano would be one, though not the best one by any means, the novel you suggested I should write some years back, a sort of Under Under the Volcano, should be ten times more terrible (tentatively it's called Dark as the Grave Wherein my Friend is Laid) and the last one La Mordida that throws the whole thing into reverse and issues in triumph. (The Consul is brought back to life again, that is the real Consul, Under the Volcano itself functions as a sort of battery in the middle but only as a work of the imagination by the protagonist) Better still: some years back I was not equipped to tackle a task of this nature: now, it seems to me, I've gone through the necessary spiritual ordeals that have permitted me to see the truth of what I'm getting at and to see the whole business clearly: all that remains is to get myself into a material position where I can consummate the ordeal by the further ordeal of writing it. H'm. Sounds as bad as Bernard de Voto on Mark Twain. Without being Mark Twain.[5] Still, have faith!

To which end this elephant and the Forest Path were intended – apart from a kind of practice on a few smaller peaks – to achieve among other things the practical end of getting a contract with Albert; these two would form part of yet another book to be called Hear Us Oh Lord From Heaven Thy Dwelling Place[6] and would consist of:

(1) Through the Panama. A story in the form of notes taken on going to Europe, partly on a ship in everything but final distress off the Azores it reads something like the Crack-Up & bit like Alfred Gordon Pym:[7] – but instead of cracking the protagonist's fission begins to be healed. 60-odd pages.

(2) October Ferry to Gabriola. Another novella, a first version of which we wrote in collaboration for you though it didn't come off. This I've completely redrafted and largely rewritten, and it deals with the theme of eviction, which is related to man's dispossession, but this theme is universalised. This I believe to be a hell of a fine thing.

(3) In the Black Hills.[8] The humorous-tragic short short I wrote which you have and which I take is for some reason unsaleable. While

only tiny it's not quite as slight as it looks when contrasted along side other themes – I mean it would take an added affect through inclusion in one volume.

(4) Strange Comfort Afforded by the Profession. Ditto.

(5) Elephant and Colosseum. 100 pages.

(6) The Forest Path to the Spring. 100 pages. (about)

I could throw in a couple of other short ones, as a matter of fact I could go on completing short stories till all is blue, other things being equal, which they are not, and the point is I want to call a halt, especially if they're not too saleable in the item, as appears the trouble, and I don't seem able to help this, and get on with the novel. Hear Us Oh Lord etc is from the old Manx fisherman's hymn that occurs in 3 of the stories.[9]

Of the above mentioned, three of them at least have the intent of being major productions in their class, and Margerie thinks The Forest Path contains the finest stuff I've done. What I meant to do was finish the Elephant and Forest Path simultaneously and this I've almost done but not quite. I should be through with the Forest Path in about a month. Though about the same length as the Elephant I feel it might sell, on the other hand this wasn't exactly the point so much as the Elephant and the Forest Path together would constitute (200 pages) something to show Random House and thus perhaps (together with a precis of my projected novels etc.) give one a chance to survive the winter. I am sending you two copies of the Elephant but I feel it would be pointless to show it to Albert by itself, so bear with me till you receive the Forest Path, for the two of them together have a wholly different effect, maybe quite electrifying, but the circuit won't come off the way I want for Albert with the Elephant alone. Perhaps the Elephant would be sufficient to get me turned down by Harcourt Brace.[10] Not that I don't love the Elephant myself, and psychologically you can see it as a good sign – my authority is Herman Hesse,[11] the writer to whom I feel I bear most inner resemblance, though I haven't got that far yet, but the plan for the five, maybe six, goes as far as he in invention, maybe further. But more of this later, when you have the Forest Path.

Meantime try and bear with me. Love to Tommy and yourself.

Malcolm

Annotations:

1 At sixty pages 'Elephant and Colosseum' is slightly shorter than Joseph Conrad's *Heart of Darkness*, to which Lowry goes on to compare it.

2 The infant Panurge, more correctly a young man, meets the great Pantagruel in book 2 of François Rabelais's *Gargantua and Pantagruel* (1532; 1534). Panurge, who is a linguist and given to philosophic

ramblings, becomes Pantagruel's lifelong friend and companion. The Latin phrase *multum in parvo* means 'much in little,' but Lowry's adaptation echoes his story's title while suggesting its quality.

3 Lowry's pun on his story's title is also a reference to the Epistle of Paul to the Colossians from the New Testament.

4 The German term *Sturm und Drang* refers to an eighteenth-century literary movement led by young poets who rejected the ideas of the Age of Reason in favour of emotion, imagination, and the occult. Literally it means 'storm and stress,' but is used to suggest intense emotional and psychological struggle.

5 Bernard De Voto (1897-1955), the American writer and Harvard professor, wrote two books on 'Mark Twain,' Samuel Langhorne Clemens (1835-1910): *Mark Twain's America* (1932) and *Mark Twain at Work* (1942). In his preface to the latter, De Voto speaks of 'the true ordeal of Mark Twain,' and in his last chapter he describes Twain's art as arising from and transforming personal suffering.

6 Lowry's plans for this collection of stories changed considerably over the years as 'October Ferry to Gabriola' grew into a full-scale novel. The collection was published posthumously in 1961, when it comprised seven stories: 'The Bravest Boat,' 'Through the Panama,' 'Strange Comfort Afforded by the Profession,' 'Elephant and Colosseum,' 'Present Estate of Pompeii,' 'Gin and Goldenrod,' and 'The Forest Path to the Spring.'

7 *The Crack-Up* (1945) is a collection of essays and letters by F. Scott Fitzgerald, edited by Edmund Wilson. The sequence of three autobiographical essays called 'The Crack-Up' details Fitzgerald's breakdown and the crises and disappointments that haunted him. Edgar Allan Poe's *The Narrative of Arthur Gordon Pym* (1838) is a fictional first-person account of a mutiny and shipwreck in the South Seas. Both texts resemble Lowry's story in their subject-matter and autobiographical mode, but the complex symbolism amounting to allegory in 'Through the Panama' is closer to Poe than Fitzgerald.

8 'Kristborg's Story: In the Black Hills' appeared in *Psalms and Songs* (1975), pp. 250-53.

9 These are 'Through the Panama,' 'Elephant and Colosseum,' and 'The Forest Path to the Spring.' The text and score for the hymn provide a preface to the final published collection.

10 If Harcourt Brace were to turn him down (as indeed they ultimately did) Lowry would be free to rejoin Albert Erskine at Random House.

11 German writer Hermann Hesse (1877-1962), author of *Steppenwolf* (1929; *Der Steppenwolf* 1927) and *Demian* (1923; orig. 1919), plays an important role in *October Ferry to Gabriola*, where the protagonist describes Hesse as 'one of the most distinguished figures in the world' and quotes a long passage on puberty from the beginning of chapter 3 of *Demian*.

*The following three letters (**473, 474, 475***) to Margerie provide a fascinating glimpse into the way Lowry worked. That he always saw a profound and intricate connection between his day-to-day life and his fiction is clear, but these letters capture red-handed the artist raiding his private life for the textual creation of his fiction. The three letters to Margerie (written, after all, when she was by his side) have been crumpled up, then smoothed out and edited for inclusion in* October Ferry to Gabriola. *All three, like the one to himself called 'Oath to Higher Self' (**451***), were changed to make them 'fit' the work-in-progress, and the four edited holographs are filed in the Lowry Collection with the notes for chapter 1 of the novel.*

Although these three letters are undated, they were likely written during October 1951, at a very low point in the Lowrys' marriage, when he was struggling with the defence material for chapter 31 of October Ferry. *Lowry was deeply troubled by the trial and conviction for murder of seventeen-year-old Francis Stephen Sykes. The boy was arrested and charged in the fall of 1950 but did not come to trial until 28 May 1951. From that date until the commutation of his sentence on 24 October 1952, from death by hanging to life imprisonment, stories and letters to the editor appeared regularly in the Vancouver papers. Lowry kept clippings of these items that demonstrate the vindictive anger of most public comment as well as the contrasting pleas for pardon. He wrote of this trial and of public sentiment in several letters (see, for example, his 31 October 1951 letter [**476***] to David Markson and his January 1952 letter [**493***] to Clarisse Francillon). He also created from this tragedy the stuff of fiction, especially in Ethan Llewelyn's dramatic inner monologue in chapter 31 of* October Ferry: *'Every passing day brings nearer the doom of the fifteen-year-old youth, and I should like to plead with all my heart — '*

'Save him!' 'Oh, shut up!' 'Hang him!' 'Hang him!' 'Hang Ethan Llewelyn!' (271)

473: To Margerie Bonner Lowry

P: UBC(ms) [Dollarton]
[ca October 1951][a]

Darling Margie —

I *have* made decisions, I wanted you to see that I had and that it was different. What I might like to do is to take you out to a movie and to dinner but I feel I can get through this evening if dinner is postponed a little – or even if not – to a point where you could type a large chunk (of the Davies defense) to-morrow.[1] I thought my suggestion, though tactless on the surface, psychologically good for if I have to go through the rest of my life either cowering at a bottle of gin or feeling compelled to drink the whole of it I might as well throw myself out of the window. If you consider it a question of mere alcohol I've yesterday & the day before to point to in one way but if that seems worse than irrelevant you must surely see that to offer (and *mean it*) to let you dole me out a drink in your own measure or not at all, while having a reasonable drink yourself slightly to relieve the misery-grisery I can't help this work sometimes putting you through is a very different proposition than making the same suggestion with simply the object of blotting out my own mind in my own way at your expense. If it was tactless please out of the generousness of your heart put it down to the fact that our own tension has me momentarily out of balance. If you consider it a lousy idea forget it but please don't trouble my poor heart further by casting aspersions on its sincerity. Because we have to start *anew in sincerity & duckery* we cannot & must not stand always in fear & trembling of the reactions of the but must stop this *now*. The gin as gin meant almost less than nothing to me. What does mean something to me is the fact that it is a tactile challenge & I want us to get back to the way we were before the fire. But when we have tension I get such a flooding at the heart I can't write at all – Oh hear me, dear duck, my poor illiterate words! Oh hear oh hear! I do love thee so.

Your Malc

Annotations:

1 The scene of the 'Roy Davies' defence occurs in the 'D' draft of *October Ferry to Gabriola* (UBC 16:20, 85-94), which Lowry was working on in 1951. In chapter 31 of the published text the boy's name has been changed to Richard Chapman, possibly because Davies (like Sykes) reminded Lowry of his Cambridge tutor and friend Hugh Sykes Davies.

Editorial Notes:

a. On this undated pencil holograph (UBC 21:5) Lowry has cancelled 'Margie' and inserted 'Jacqueline' above it, deleted private terms of affection like 'duckery' and 'dear duck,' and changed his signature to 'Ethan.' Other changes include the page number '15' with an instruction at the top right of the recto to 'Single space' and a comment in the left margin, opposite the second sentence, that reads: 'This sort of thing.'

474: To Margerie Bonner Lowry

P: UBC(ms) [Dollarton]
[ca October 1951]ᵃ

My dear sweet wife:

Please do not punish me by the silent or savage system or otherwise. I want things between us to be better as much as you do, and I have determined to make sacrifices to bring this about. Please do not say Bah! either: there is no 'Bah' about it. The impasse is my fault, I am thoroughly aware of the fact, and if I don't pull us through you have every right to leave me. I am extremely aware of that and being aware of it doesn't make it any happier for me.

Your devoted yet alas ill-natured – yet still determined to improve – husband

Malcolm

P.S. Please say dear duck at least and don't leave me with such a troubled heart in silence.

Editorial Notes:

a. Lowry has made the following changes in pencil: after wife, he has added 'Jacqueline'; the words 'dear duck at least' in the postscript have been pencilled out, and the signature has been changed to 'Ethan.' The page number '16' has been added in pencil at the top of the recto.

475: To Margerie Bonner Lowry

P: UBC(21:5) [Dollarton]
[ca October 1951]ᵃ

Dearheart: I'm extremely sorry. I don't want to make excuses. But I wasn't being deliberately churlish. Nor was heart *not* in the right place. The mistake I made was more childish than anything else. I have been having a hell of a time with this section writing this defense and I was in fact so tired, that no drink would have pulled me together for very long.[1] I did honestly want to 'use' it: & for that matter I did 'use' it to get over a large hump: witness 8 intricate pages this morning: that don't show any signs of alc. But I allowed myself foolishly – or perhaps it was due simply to strain – to feel hurt that you weren't 'trusting' me, even if you were justified & that was for my good. I don't know if you've ever felt in the mood: *'Anything* is better than to feel like *this.'* I imagined a big slug or two would help & of course it both did & didn't & then I was tight for awhile & lost my temper. That my heart was fundamentally in the right place is shown by the fact that I did eventually pull myself together even dress to take you out (even though you understandably didn't want to come by then) finally tucked you up in bed, put water by your side & tidied up. You are, of course, 'right.' But it wasn't deep dark treachery on my part or the usual kind of compulsion or even loss of self-control. I had felt myself heading all day for one of my gloomy & intolerable moods because of frustration in the work & I had wanted to avoid that at all costs at your little Europa party. Then when I'd solved the problem & wanted to read – you thought that was just the 'old kind of thing', & I got a kind of coitus interruptus. But oh dear duck things are so much better & I do want things to be happy for you & then for me: so will you out of the goodness of your heart at this season give the ramshackle old boy the benefit of the doubt & allow him to make [amends.]

With all love

Dear duck

P.S. Besides you hurt my [wouf] & dat's de truf.

Annotations:

1 See letter **473**, annotation 1.

Editorial Notes:

a. This undated pencil holograph (UBC 21:5) is badly worn and smudged. Lowry has numbered it '17' and written in the right margin of the recto: 'Quote *Lamb* in fact I will quote Lamb.' He has not, however, changed the names to Jacqueline and Ethan. Page 18 in this sequence of letters for *October Ferry* was his 'Oath to Higher Self' **(451)**.

476: To David Markson

P: UBC(ms)
PP: SL 269-70

[Dollarton]
[31 October 1951]^a

Hallow'een

Dear Dave:

Just a note sincerely to congratulate you on the critical article, which I hope by now has gone through successfully.[1]

Jolly, as the English say, good old chap. And I hope you'll tell me where it is so that I can read it. I don't subscribe to the Kenyon but it's a damned interesting magazine & I buy it whenever I can.

The reason I'm long in replying is that I'm trying to secure a contract for another book (stories) before the winter is out. Also I have sprouted Zola's whiskers & have been preparing a public objection to a local injustice where a 16 year old boy was sentenced to hang (in a disused elevator shaft, painted yellow) for a rape he had not committed.[2] Fortunately they reprieved the poor fellow (apparently to please the visiting Princess Elizabeth) but neither the ritual pardon nor the near ritual murder on the part of our barbarous public, who has now sentenced him to life imprisonment, is something you would leave alone, if you had studied the evidence, the feeble & neurotic protests, the blood-thirsty cries for revenge, & you were the only writer in the community, much as one hates to risk one's position in it, even if one hasn't got one, & what is more does not care whether one has or not.

Apart from that I've been working very hard indeed on other things & have written a story called The Bravest Boat I think you would like.

Meantime my wife wrote Horse in the Sky under name of Margerie Bonner. Don't even try to look for Ultramarine which is not worth reading (the thought hurts my feelings) & which I shall rewrite one day maybe. Did you see Louis Adamic of whom I wrote you tangentially died about a week later?[3] More of this someday. Meantime God bless him, – its Hallow'een anyway. Let me know news of your thesis – & how your article goes. Many thanks for all your words & lots of luck.

Love Malcolm

P.S. Sunrise next morning, frost outside, tide high, just below window – seagulls having been fed – Coffee *being* made. Have you any advice for me re anything good to read? I agree Miss Lonelyhearts is an important book, & that Rimbaud had one leg, but where is the sunrise? where is the frost? where are my seagulls? where is my coffee? Where is love? Where is your tennis racket? What has happened to Joe Venuti? They can't all be in the Atlantic Monthly or Bill Saroyan. And in fact there's alot to be said for Bill Saroyan: My Heart's in the highlands anyway. Don't forget that priceless possession, the author's naïvete. I will prepare you a more austere list, though yours can be austere for that matter. I would read Yeat's The Vision (second version) for your purposes, though it is scarcely Joe Venuti. Of recent books I liked 'The Catcher in the Rye' better than 'The Barkeep of Blémont' which I am reading with some enthusiasm.[4]

Annotations:

1 Markson wrote an article on Clay Allison (Henry John Keevil, 1840–87), a gunslinger and hero of the old west, for a men's magazine sometime during 1951; see Lowry's 22 February 1957 letter (**705**) to Markson.

2 Francis Stephen Sykes was reprieved on 24 October 1951. I have not located a 'public objection' by Lowry; the closest he came to objecting was to use the subject in *October Ferry*.

3 Louis Adamic's death on 4 September 1951 was an alleged suicide, although murder was also suspected. See Lowry's reference to Adamic in his 25 August 1951 letter (**467**) to David Markson.

4 The preceding comments on American literature include Lowry's agreement with Markson about Nathanael West's *Miss Lonelyhearts* and praise for William Saroyan's *My Heart's in the Highlands*, J.D. Salinger's *Catcher in the Rye* (1951), and French writer Marcel Aymé's *Barkeep of Blémont* (1950); see Lowry's comments on Aymé's novel in his 23 November 1951 letter (**480**) to Albert Erskine. This is not the first time Lowry has recommended the reading of W.B. Yeats's *A Vision*; see his June 1944 letter (**190**) to Charles Stansfeld-Jones.

Editorial Notes:

a. Lowry's holograph is undated, but Markson has inserted this date, with 1 November 1951 as the postmark.

477: To Clemens ten Holder

P: UBC(ts)   Dollarton, B.C.,
PP: Brief 45-47   Canada
                                                   31 October 1951

Dear Herr ten Holder:

    Your wife will by this time have received a letter from my wife expressing our delight at Unter dem Vulkan![1]

    A thousand thanks and congratulations! Wonderbar! I could not of course be more delighted to hear of its success in Germany, and I hope that this success will be of some very real benefit to you. Certainly you deserve it, for from everything I can gather it is a marvellous translation and in fact no doubt very often an improvement on the original. The typography and format throughout seems excellent, just as I would have liked it indeed, and I know you must have gone to endless trouble, but most of all I am grateful for your very real and sympathetic interest in the book itself and understanding of it that I felt so sincerely in all your letters, to the extent one feels also 'it is your book.'

    However this particular letter is really in reply to your last letter concerning the possibilities of [Ernst] Klett making a film of the Volcano.[2] This has been delayed by the exigencies of corralling Downie [Kirk] (who is of course absolutely enchanted with the book) to translate your letter: we are only neighbours in summer for a very brief time, for he lives in the city many miles away where he teaches school, and I am

about as accessible here as a mountain goat. Neither of us has an automobile, the bus and streetcar service is bad, and we can only see each
other on weekends for it means spending the night, which he of course
cannot do during the week, and for me it means taking two days away
from my work, which I cannot afford to do at present. I have been and
am working against time trying to finish my next book sufficiently to
get an advance, and I am involved in two kinds of complications there,
for Hitchcock died, the firm dissolved, and while the new one is excellent, I feel honor bound to go with my old editor, who has gone to
another firm; though several other publishers want me I am involved
with difficulties here of a kind familiar to yourself which are boring and
delaying. But so ferocious have the winters become here that it is practically a matter of life and death for me to have something arranged here
as soon as possible so that my wife and I may get away until spring. You
wouldn't believe me even if I told you how tough it has been here –
much as we love this place when the weather behaves. So before I go
on, if you have any further immediate news, I beg you to try and write
in English, no matter how difficult in a moment of stress. For Downie
might not be available, and I am unable (little credit though it does to
the extent of my application in Bonn) to translate well enough to be sure
at all of what you are saying. Now while I realise well enough that if
what you suggest re the film should materialise it would certainly relieve
any financial worries, until it *has* gone through I have to behave as
though it had not. Which finally brings me to the point.

Nothing could make us happier – happy is not the word, in fact – and
what an opportunity it is! – than for a film to be made of the Volcano
in Germany, providing it were done in the best tradition of your great
films. I think I have seen nearly all the great German films, since the days
of Caligari, some of them many times, risking my neck even when at
school (where movies were forbidden) to see Erich Pommer and
Dupont's Vaudeville with Emil Jannings and Lya de Putti, Arthur
Robison's Warning Shadows and Conrad Veidt in The Student of
Prague, and Murnau's wonderful things, all the films of the great Ufa
days, and other later masterpieces like the Kapitan von Kopernick, and
the wonderful wonderful film made from Karl and Anna called
Heimweh,[3] and it is an enthusiasm that has not deserted me for only
recently we have trekked through the snow, (still risking our necks –
physically on this occasion because of the ice) just to keep up with the
times, to see Murnau's Last Laugh, Fritz Lang's Destiny (a pioneer piece
if there ever was one) and other contemporary films & klangfilms at the
local Vancouver Film Society. Nor has anything I have read influenced
my own writing personally more than the first twenty minutes of
Murnau's Sonnenaufgang or the first and last shots of Karl Grüne's The

Street.[4] So you can see what it means to have a film of the Volcano made in Germany. Not only am I an aficionado but the German film itself is almost to me as 'my little grey home in the west.'[5]

But it is not possible for me to make any binding reply to you regarding this that could be referred to Klett, save off the record, unofficially, – which it goes without saying is of an entirely sympathetic nature. Any deal regarding the filming of the Volcano must be made by Klett, or whoever is concerned, through my agent in New York, Harold Matson. He handles all my business in such matters, and though of course I would have to approve of the contract for my part, I cannot legally make any reply at all until the proposition come to me through the usual business channels. This is not because I am a business man but precisely because I am not a business man, and indeed it makes it no easier that my agent lives nearly 4000 miles away; on the other hand it would be a breach of contract on my part to enter into a stipulation that might (even though I don't see how) affect his commission. Nor do I completely understand – even after Downie had translated the letter – whether Klett was approaching me through you, or whether that approach was independent on your part: obviously I would know how to reply better to your own interest if I knew for certain which, or even if it was a bit of both.

If the former it seems to me to be taking a very pessimistic view of human affairs to suppose that he would have you approach me for him, while intending all the time to exclude you altogether. Of course I can see that working on my bloody Consul is enough to make anyone pessimistic, so I can sympathise just the same, old fellow.

But the fact is, on the plane of the people who arrange it, any details of the proposition can hardly be ethically discussed until the proposition itself becomes a bona fide one.

Then indeed I might be in a position to say something of worth on the matter.

In the realm of private discussion, however, and for your private ear, needless to say I certainly concur in all that you speak of in relation to yourself and the Volcano: I certainly wouldn't willingly be a party to your being excluded from any deal, but as I have said there is absolutely no way in which I can act for your interests, or mine, until I have something definite to act upon, more tangible than 'a plan for the Tomalin spa!'[6]

For example, I would myself very much wish to make a treatment of the Volcano for the film, and I would be very anxious to work on that and the scenario with my wife, who not only was a movie actress for years, but has collaborated on one film with me (described by several Hollywood directors as one of the finest things Hollywood has ever seen and which still may yet be produced, though it has been shelved for various reasons outside our power, and we were never paid, and its title even still has to remain secret for reasons that have nothing to do with us)[7] and who not only knows the Volcano backwards, but has a first rate capability and imagination in that direction: so incidentally do I, though I say it myself, and we are a first class team, the like of which is scarcely to be found, I dare say, even in Germany or anywhere else, with such knowledge strangely enough even of the German film, which knowledge would go far in the long run to compensate for the barrier of language, especially with the assistance of yourself.

So goes a by no means impracticable dream, if the thing is to be done well! I believe your best bet, for yourself, your wife, the little Xicotencatl, myself, my wife, Stuttgart, Klett, Germany, England, humanity at large and the film industry would be for you to push the matter for all you are worth as far as you are able into the correct channels, bearing in mind that it certainly would not meet with my approval if you are excluded, and that I will act, in so far as I can act, or have any say in the matter, in your best interests.

But what those interests more precisely are, since you imply yourself you know little about the cinema and do not wish — (or are not able) — to write the scenario, any more than perhaps to play 'fussball' (wonderful word) I have no way of knowing at present. My own opinion is that it must be a director's and a camerman's picture, that a certain sacrifice of language will be very often necessary on my or our part but there is no reason why it can't be, with genius, translated into visual terms, though if the picture is going to be a great one the director can scarcely fail to profit enormously by my assistance, that would of course mean yours too. Something like this anyhow, I should like to aim for, if all goes well. But there is no end to the ideas we have, for deliriums, church bells, guitars, horrors, and final hope that would add three more dimensions to the cinema itself.

I have received meanwhile a very nice letter from Klett written September 19, forwarded through my agent, in which he says nothing at all of this film project, though doubtless it was not conceived when he wrote. But in answering his letter, I can hardly suggest that you be included in a contract that he has not written me of himself, which puts me in a rather ambiguous situation at present, as I'm sure you'll see on thinking it over.

So I can only repeat that there is nothing I can do for either you or myself until I have before me some definite proposition in writing from Klett through my agent in New York.

But perhaps simple goodness, by assuming the best motives for all, will work its own strategy. Please forgive me if this letter sounds formal

– actually I am in a complete dither of excitement at the idea of making the film, or of it being made, but it is absolutely necessary for me to have something definite before we can possibly discuss this any further. Rest assured of my friendship and gratitude to you – as to your wife – for your long and arduous work on my book, and again, my congratulations on the success of your translation. With every good wish – and may God bring good luck to us both – for you and your wife again, and not forgetting the little Xicotancatl, nor the kinder either, – and reserving my sincere appreciation of the lecture[8] too for another letter, I am ever sincerely,

Yours,

Malcolm Lowry

P.S. Though this may be against my own financial interest, & again for your private ear, if the German film is to go through, it probably could be bought cheaper now than later: for television has forced a more serious attitude on Hollywood toward the film in general, & there are two directors there, including one who is my old publisher [Frank Taylor], who have long been wanting to do it: – moreover when my next book comes out, probably next year, that will revive the sales of the Volcano – which still sells by the way in the U.S – to some extent, thus driving my stock – as they say on the horse market – up. About all this I can't of course be positive. Former film bids for the Volcano in America fell through for fear of censorship, I believe, though a very successful hour long radio version of it was made from New York.

P.P.S. I append a copy of what I have said to Herr Klett, so that you will know exactly.[a]

Annotations:

1 Clemens ten Holder's translation, *Unter dem Vulkan*, was published in September 1951.
2 In a 20 October 1951 letter (UBC 1:67) ten Holder wrote enthusiastically of Ernst Klett's proposal to make a film of *Under the Volcano*. Though Lowry was interested, his doubts were well founded, and nothing in fact came of Klett's plan; see Lowry's 31 October 1951 and 23 November 1951 letters (**478** and **479**) to Klett and Harold Matson and his 8 December 1951 letter (**484**) to Matson, in which he enclosed a copy of the contract supplement regarding Klett's film rights.
3 Erich Pommer (1887-1966) produced several German silent films, including *Variety* (or *Vaudeville*), starring Emil Jannings and Lya de Putti and directed by E.A. Dupont in 1925. *Warning Shadows* (1923), directed by Arthur Robison, is another German expressionist classic, like Robert

Wiene's *Caligari* (1919). Conrad Veidt starred as the student in Henrik Galeen's 1926 version of *The Student of Prague. The Captain from Köpenick* was not released in film version until 1956; therefore, Lowry must be thinking of Carl Zuckmayer's play *Der Hauptmann von Köpenick* (1931), which was a stage success, translated into several languages, and frequently performed on stage and radio. The film Lowry describes as 'made from Karl and Anna' is actually *Heimkehr* (1928, *Homecoming*). This expressionist film about a man who falls in love with his friend's wife, directed by Joe May (Joseph Mandel, 1880-1954), is based on the 1926 novelette *Karl und Anna* by German novelist and playwright Leonhard Frank (1882-1961).

4 Frederick W. Murnau's expressionist film *Sunrise* (1927) is a story of marital betrayal and near murder with a happy ending. Karl Grüne's *The Street* (1923) is also about an attempted escape from married life, with dramatic expressionist effects. Murnau's *Last Laugh* (1924) and Lang's *Destiny* (1921) are silent film classics.

5 'My Little Grey Home in the West' is the title of a popular song by composer Hermann Löhr with words by American poet D. Eardley-Wilmot. The line that gives this romantic song its title is the last one in the refrain; in chapter 12 of *Volcano* the line recalls Yvonne for the Consul.

6 The 'Tomalín spa' is Lowry's ironic reference to the reservoir, swimming pool, and baths outside the Salón Ofelia in chapter 10 of the *Volcano*.

7 This collaboration is the screenplay for *Tender Is the Night*.

8 Hildegard ten Holder sent a copy of her husband's lecture on *Under the Volcano* with her 22 September 1951 letter; it is no longer extant.

Editorial Notes:

a. Attached to this letter is Lowry's 31 October 1951 letter (**478**) to Ernst Klett. Lowry has written in the top left corner of the verso: 'THIS IS A CARBON COPY OF A LETTER SENT TO HERR KLETT IN STUTTGART. (By the same post as yours.)'

478: To Ernst Klett

P: Klett(ts); UBC(c)
PP: *Brief* 47

Dollarton, B.C.,
Canada
31 October 1951

Dear Herr Klett:[1]

Thank you very much for your kind letter.[2] I should have answered before except that I waited to receive my copies of Unter dem Vulkan, which I now have before me. It is a beautiful volume and I am delighted with the format, printing, and in fact with everything about it, for which my heartiest thanks to you.

Herr ten Holder has written me that the book has made a success and needless to say I am most happy about that, equally for your sake as well as mine, and I hope that you will be well repaid for your efforts in publishing it. I deeply appreciate Herr ten Holder's fine translation, and I believe that he has really understood my book in a way that is rare; I count myself most fortunate in having had such a sympathetic translator and publisher in Germany – which of all lands must be the one in which the artist would most like to succeed.

I have also received a letter from Herr ten Holder a few days ago in which he gives me to understand that there is some interest in producing a film of the Volcano. I have always felt it would make a great film and I would rather have it produced in Germany than in any country in the world, for I have admired and followed German films since I was a boy and am well acquainted with all of your magnificent films. If it is indeed true that you are interested, I look forward to hearing more definitely of this through my agent Harold Matson. I feel strongly that I would like myself to make a treatment of the Volcano for you; it has long been in my mind and I have many excellent ideas for its transposition into the cinematic medium, which I cannot help but feel would be valuable.

(In any event if I should ever come to Germany again, which I hope to do some day, I shall at once accept your invitation to have 'a good day and a better night' with you in Stuttgart – though I can bring no mescal with me, which perhaps is just as well, though as a matter of fact I feel I have rather maligned that poor drink for which I shall never be forgiven by the Mexican distillers, which, if of an unimaginable potency, is certainly a good deal purer than most Canadian rye whiskey: but perhaps there is some in Stuttgart. I have often wondered what the potation of Rimbaud and Verlaine was that they so misbehaved themselves in your famous and historical city.[3] Which – the life of Rimbaud I mean – is another idea for a film for you which – unless I am exceedingly wrong and someone has done it already – it seems to have occurred to no one to make: certainly his life in relation to the history of that period treated in cinematic terms has the markings of a great tragedy one is liable to miss in his life alone, terrifying enough in all conscience though it was.)

With many thanks again for your kind words about my novel and for your most excellent publication of it, I am
Sincerely yours
Malcolm Lowry

Annotations:

1 Professor Dr Ernst Klett, Jr (1911-) is the former head of the Stuttgart publishing firm, which was founded by his family in the nineteenth century.
2 In a letter dated 19 September 1951 Klett expressed his pleasure at publishing the translation and notified Lowry that he was sending a copy under separate cover.
3 Arthur Rimbaud (1854-91) and Paul Verlaine (1844-96), the French poets, had had a stormy relationship for several years, when Verlaine was arrested for the attempted murder of his friend in 1873. In the spring of 1875 the two were briefly reunited in Stuttgart, where Rimbaud was staying; however, on a tour of the city's bars they became drunk and quarrelled violently over religion. This final quarrel has become well known in literary circles.

The Voyage That Never Ends was to be Lowry's magnum opus. Predictably – for Lowry – the idea had grown and changed since its inception in the late thirties and its trilogy structure of the mid-forties (see pages 2-3), and it would have continued to change had Lowry lived to work on it. Although he makes frequent reference to the Voyage *in his letters and describes it in detail in the 'adumbration of future works' mentioned in the following letter (479) to Harold Matson, it is here and in the next letter (480) to Albert Erskine that he articulates his high hopes for it. 'I am convinced,' he assures his agent, 'that The Voyage That Never Ends will be a great book if it is found I deserve grace to finish it.'*

479: To Harold Matson

P: Matson(ts); UBC(phc)   Dollarton, B.C.,
Canada
23 November 1951

Dear Hal:

Herewith – or more or less herewith, you should receive it Monday – an adumbration of future works and/or work in progress,[1] with the idea of the package being immediately relayed to Albert, with some 330 pages of the first work to be published, – Hear Us Oh Lord From Heaven Thy Dwelling Place, which is to be composed (I hope) of recent short novels, not all finished, two of which you have not seen, and some tales you have and have not seen.

I slightly altered my first plan of finishing The Forest Path to the

Spring, instead cracked through and slugged out a rough version of another long work, Through the Panama (later perhaps to be a chapter in one of the novels, here simply in the form of a journal, a sort of Alfred Gordon Pym)[2] with the idea of giving the whole a better chance, and have sent the incompleted Path to the Spring too.

No matter whether some of these stories proved unsaleable – a fact for which I am sincerely sorry for I really meant well – I can't help thinking they are all masterpieces or can be such in their peculiar way.

The delay in all this of course has been largely caused by the loss of In Ballast [to the White Sea], which while I am by now grateful for it, has obliged me to solve all the subject-objective problems all over again nor have I solved them all yet.

Nonetheless, though the persistent Moravia-like[3] humiliation of not thinking so and even being told to the contrary may be part of the test, I am convinced that The Voyage That Never Ends will be a great book if it is found I deserve grace to finish it.

The trouble, naturally, at the moment, is cash, and how much I have of my own depends on the stabilization of the pound, and what happens in England. The situation there is enough to give an Englishman like me schizophrenia on the big scale, but while I look for some improvement in the near future it is hard not to fear the worst eventually, a worst in which the pound would be beside the point, for there would be no pound. However it seems to me that some greater wisdom may be generally fermenting in the world at large, though it's pretty damned hard to see it and even if so may have little to do with the pound.

To get back to the book – or books – while my hopes for it, or them, are large, I'm perhaps not very well qualified to describe it, or them, in a way that will do it, or them, justice: you can imagine the trouble I would have had with the Volcano. However this I have attempted also in the package you will be receiving.

We have still not heard anything from Hollywood on the other thing while we still seem ethically obliged to be silent on the subject.[4] However we got a wildly enthusiastic letter (as Margie wrote you) from the German translator speaking of the Volcano's reception in Germany and that it had caused a stir also in the theatrical-film world there: to this I replied immediately that Klett would have to get in touch with you. I hope he has done so and that the enthusiasm has not fallen off. I said that we would like to have a hand in doing the scenario, but everything would have to be arranged through you. I know we could make a great film out of it especially if – as they suggested might be – Peter Lorre was involved.[5] In fact I feel we could make such a great one God knows what it might lead to eventually. This would not interfere with Hear Us Oh Lord to any great extent, for Margerie would first break it down and do a treatment, then we would plot out the scenario with [Clemens] ten Holder translating, etc., so it would not take all my time.

This would be a great thing for us and enable us to get out of debt to yourself and also financially ahead a bit, and they seemed very serious about it. Meanwhile the Germans are also very eager to translate my next book, so if we went to Germany on the film, ten Holder could meanwhile be translating Hear Us Oh Lord as I was polishing it up.

Well, we still believe in miracles, but meanwhile of course the main reason I finally sent this off with the Forest Path to the Spring unfinished is that the wolf is howling again on the Path itself, not to say on the porch. I know it will make an excellent volume as I plan it, and even as it is it seems to me impressive. You mentioned you were going to have a talk with Reynal about the other contract so that it is my hope that this can be sent to Albert at Random House at once. And I hope to God this can be pushed through and that I may in some sort receive an advance on it before the wolf and the winter storms break the door down. Damn this urgency to hell, but England is still a tomb, and one has no choice, save to dig ditches, and still faith that this may work out. Of course if the German film were to go through that might solve much, the more so since it might lead to other similar chances of a tangential – of more profitable – nature, that though it doubled the work one had to do, would yet permit me to get the more serious work done. By which I mean the sequence of novels called The Voyage That Never Ends, for more of which see the package which should arrive simultaneously with this letter.

Oh yes, I had a letter from a chap in Rome who has read the Volcano in French and is very admirous. He edits a review, (which has printed an excerpt from Thomas Mann's new unpublished novel, etc) and wants to put in a chapter of the Volcano.[6] It apparently hasn't come out yet in Italy, but I am referring him to Einaudi, who have the Italian rights as I understand it, but this might be good publicity for them.[7] From what I can make out he doesn't offer to pay me though.

All the very best to you and Tommy and the children.
God bless.

Malcolm

Annotations:

1 Lowry had drawn up a 'Work in Progress' statement (UBC 32:1), mailed to Matson on 22 November, containing a thirty-four-page typescript discussion of *The Voyage That Never Ends* and a twenty-nine-page description of *Hear us O Lord* and 'The Forest Path to the Spring.' It was largely on the strength of this document that he got his long-term contract with Albert Erskine and Random House.

2 Lowry also makes this comparison with Edgar Allan Poe's *Narrative of Arthur Gordon Pym* in his 2 October 1951 letter (**472**) to Matson.

3 Lowry's discussion of his writing suggests he is thinking of Italian existentialist writer Alberto Moravia (1907-90), whose central theme is alienation and the absurdity of life. In *Two Adolescents: The Stories of Agostino and Luca* (1950) Moravia depicts the humiliation of a boy whose mother ignores him for a lover, and in *Conjugal Love* (1951) his hero is a writer who is betrayed by his wife.

4 The Lowrys were still hoping for good news from Frank Taylor regarding their filmscript of *Tender Is the Night*.

5 See Lowry's 31 October 1951 letter (**477**) to Clemens ten Holder, annotation 2, and his 8 December 1951 letter (**484**) to Harold Matson. As it turned out, Lowry never signed a contract and nothing came of his hopes for a film with Lorre.

6 Lowry is probably referring to Aldo Martello, the editor of *Carosello di narratori Inglese*, which published Giorgio Monicelli's translation of 'Strange Comfort Afforded by the Profession' ('I vanteggi del mestiere') in 1954.

7 Einaudi's rights to *Under the Volcano* were extended until 1954, when, after a five-year delay caused by the translators, they were forced to withdraw. The firm of Aldo Garzanti Editore proposed a new translation but withdrew their bid in 1957. Feltrinelli then bought the rights and published Giorgio Monicelli's translation in 1961.

480: To Albert Erskine

P: Virginia(ts); UBC(phc)   Dollarton, B.C.,
                                                                      Canada
                                                            23 November 1951

Dear old Albert:

I have yesterday despatched a package to Hal containing a nearly completed work entitled Hear Us Oh Lord From Heaven Thy Dwelling Place and an adumbration of present work and what I expect with luck to be future work too for the next few years.[1]

Since the contents – which I am happily hoping may be passed immediately to yourself – are self-explanatory, and indeed directed largely as towards yourself too, I won't go further into them now, save to say that Hear Us Oh Lord is a volume tangential to the mainstream of the work, though essentially part of it, and consists of 3 or 4 short novels – 3 of which are appended, though only one is completely finished, and several tales, also related, and mostly finished.

One of these short novels, the one completed, Elephant and Colosseum, is of a humorous nature, and though its intention was to be a classic, an intention in which so far as I am concerned it maharajahly succeeds; – but what I have not allowed myself to think is that you might not like it much, because I recollect that you did not like Chapter VI of the Volcano so much; however perhaps its fooling is of a rarer quality and as a matter of fact it is a serious story. Though on the other hand it is not serious at all.

Another thing about the Elephant is that you might think you are a character in it:[2] that is to say, you do not appear, but the protagonist, who is a humorous author named Cosnahan, at a loose end in Rome, expects as it were 'you' to appear at any moment: and what I have worried about though is you might be hurt and I ask you in advance not to be, because the character as well as disguised could not be more affectionately drawn anyhow, nor the raillery, if any, more friendly; but what has further upset me is that there is some bitterness in the story that you might take as directed at something or other that was personal knowing how deep I was, or think I am, but please don't anyway, because it isn't, as indeed, if you reflect, how could it be? On the other hand the business of writing and publication is not taken in a very serious manner either in places: however that is only my way of affirming a certain superseriousness of outlook.

The position of Through the Panama I explain in the text, as also that of The Forest Path to the Spring and the reason for there being some slack writing in this. Through the Panama needs not only some revision if it's going to be included but I've indulged in some savagery at some other writers which probably might go and indeed the whole book requires discussion finally, (as to what should be in it, for one thing.)

However (quite apart for the moment from The Voyage That Never Ends) I can't help feeling that Hear Us Oh Lord From Heaven Thy Dwelling Place can be and indeed almost is as it stands an impressive and original volume.

As you will see by the note at the beginning in paper clips, despite everything I have been hacking away at the main line – which, by God, *is* shaping up. I couldn't have got down to finishing The Voyage before because I wasn't ready to.

Now I see what I want to say – rather more than shadowly, though there will be, no doubt, great difficulties to be overcome: at all events I am now physically and mentally ready to tear into it (not that it hasn't already been torn into); my main difficulty is of course financial. I must again apologise for our not having yet paid you back: but once more financial news from England was held up pending the election, and I still wait to hear every day, and so availed myself of your generous offer to postpone payment until we could make it without bleeding to death. As I write this – see by the way enclosed program – I have heard from Germany that the Volcano is an enormous hit there, that they have taken The Consul as 'Germany's own conscience', and that there is a great deal of talk of making a film out of it – so help me God! – with *Peter Lorre* as the Consul (See reference to the Law of Series in the bolus).[3] If this comes off, it would of course solve many things at one blow. As a matter of fact we would hope to have a hand in the scenario, but if that should come off, I would not let it hold me up on the work of The Voyage or even on Hear Us Oh Lord – even if we went to Germany for a while: in fact, it would help me. Margie would do the treatment and I would come in later: meantime the German translator [Clemens ten Holder] has invited us to stay with him. He would be translating Hear Us Oh Lord, on which I would be making my deadline with you, if you accept it. Meantime the experience would be invaluable both for Margie and myself and for The Voyage, in a way I will explain. (It will help me with the character L'Hirondelle-Laruelle, for one thing,)[4] and I am capable of working 10 times as hard, if only I know my work is wanted. In any case I have a capacity for work that would not be overstrained by doing both things, for it would be a relief compared to the present conditions here for a while. However we have as yet no certain intimation that this movie will come off, and we still have the winter to get through.

But to get back to The Voyage That Never Ends. It's hellish near impossible to make a precis of my plan – precisely 7 times as difficult to make a precis of the Volcano in 4 pages – but I've tried to give you an idea, a frame. I myself can *hear* – almost – the whole thing; that is to say I can already project myself into a given section, no matter how remote, and feel, hear, sense more or less how it must be. And of course an enormouse amount of preliminary work and spadework has already been done, but all untyped, and legible only to me: – thus creating an impasse, in my present financial circumstances, if one were asked to submit samples (though parts of Panama and the Forest Path may be taken as such) of the thing, for I am obliged to work on what at least has some reasonable chance of selling to magazines.

That does not mean that I don't think the stories in Hear us Oh Lord are not masterpeices or potential masterpieces in their way, I do. By and large though, what I have been doing has been sharpening up my claws and trying a few small peaks – I believe successfully. It seems to me that if Hear Us Oh Lord was followed by Lunar Caustic (which you have read and approved of in its first shorter version) I would be paying my way, even if – which I must face the possibility of – you can't approve of, or others don't, of Hear Us Oh Lord. Anyhow what is enclosed is the best and most practical compendium and presage I can slug out amid the winter poverty and frostbite.

What I am of course praying for is that Hal has got me out of my other contract by now and that here I come flying under your Wing.[5]

Of course I realise all sides of your own position: – just the same to say that I hope that you may feel that you can expedite the notion is an understatement, not that I exactly know what I mean by 'notion.' But perhaps you may be good enough to give me some advice and in fact I stand in great need of some advice – my toy boat being a breezy social character compared with our lot at the moment.

Tell me news of Evil Under the Sun – I have not seen any reviews yet, but I sincerely hope it went, or is going, or is about to go well: my very best wishes for its launching at all events.[6] (In the Forest Path I also had thought of the sea being like diamonds, – my diamonds, that is to say they were Margie's, were boiling however.)

Influence of Volcano strongly in Ayme's Barkeep of Blemont – or do I dream it? In any case I'd be tickled pink; it's a wonderful book. (But the alcoholic who was a poet at heart, the 'scene by the side of the road,' etc: seems somehow familiar)[7]

And finally I have written this whole bloody letter as if calmly not thinking of *your* troubles. Well, that's not true: I – we – have been thinking of them a lot, and I can only hope they may come out right for you, and that you do not have to have suffered too much, however they may have come out: and for the rest, I shall, for the moment, be inarticulate save to say:

God bless you from us both,

Malcolm

Annotations:

1 This 'adumbration' is the thirty-five-page 'Work in Progress' statement for *The Voyage That Never Ends* (UBC 32:1).

2 Erskine is transformed into Cosnahan's publisher, Arthur Wilding, from whom Cosnahan receives a postcard while he is in Rome. The postcard Lowry reproduces in the story is based on one Erskine sent to him while he was in Rome in June 1948. Cosnahan and Arthur do not manage to meet in Europe; Lowry and Erskine met in Paris on 10 July, but the meeting was not a happy one. See Lowry's letters (**347, 349, 350**) to Erskine from the summer of 1948.

3 Lowry comments on the German response to *Under the Volcano* and on the idea of a film starring Peter Lorre in several letters; see, for example, his 23 November 1951 letter (**479**) to Harold Matson.

4 Jacques Laruelle owns the tower in which the Wildernesses stay during their time in Cuernavaca in *Dark as the Grave*, but the L'Hirondelle character is not developed; see Day's comment on the editing of the manuscripts (*DAG* xv-xvi).

5 Lowry was still waiting to hear from Harcourt, Brace about his status with them, and he would continue to wait until 10 March 1952, when

Robert Giroux finally wrote to tell him that Harcourt, Brace was
releasing him.

6 *Evil Under the Sun* (1951) by the American writer Anton Myrer (1922-)
was published by Random House and panned in the *New York Times*,
16 December 1951, p. D17. Myrer wrote an article on Lowry for *Les
Lettres nouvelles* 5 (July-August 1960): 59-66.

7 *The Barkeep of Blémont*, by French writer Marcel Aymé (1902-67), is the
1950 English translation of *Uranus* (1948). It portrays the violent, sordid
life of the provincial town of Blémont after the Second World War.
Scenes with the drunkard Leopold, the general context of warring
political factions, and the man who is shot by the police, all recall *Under
the Volcano*.

481: To Albert Erskine

P: Virginia(ms); UBC(phc)
PP: SL 347-48

[Dollarton]
[24 November 1951][a]

Dear old Albert:
A

Bear with me. Am reading book. But am also working night & day
on two short novels, one, comic, above, about an elephant, hope may
form basis (Elephant is in part V) — well, form basis anyway of coming
on your wing again. Am very disappointed no go by you with Margie's
book. Passion comes from such deep source — makes interesting corollary to Myrers[1] — however see complicated point. If you truly like it
personally though, if you see collateral way, give it helping voice. I
myself love it: all she need is some encouragement to do big things.
Hope someone will see it. P.S. above.

B

I also love Myrer's books in many respects so far, though stylistically
often Joyced in own petard. So my reaction is divided a bit between
what I feel you ought to say to *him*, & conviction it deserves wide audience (not much doubt — perhaps all too little — it will get that!) — but
make no mistake, it *does* deserve sincere salutations. Indeed it makes me
feel like Father Mapple.[2] And it has sent me on several long swims
already. Will try & come back with some clams — if not giant ones.
(Though there is no reason he shouldn't receive giant ones.) Other
(financial) clams seem still covered with Iranian oil. But I have just seen
7 mergansers outside window. Our favorite birds of good omen. So bear

with me yet. God bless & both our loves to you & Peggy – & our thanks
for reading Malateste[3] promptly too despite sad result

love

Malcolm von Steppenwolf[4]

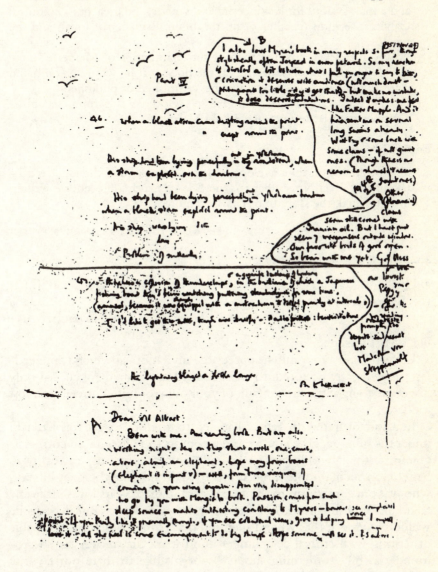

Figure 8: *The holograph sent to Albert Erskine is squeezed on to the page with
draft passages of 'Elephant and Colosseum.' Lowry's mergansers (six at the top
and one beneath the signature) are hopeful signs and, like the draft material, are
integral to the meaning of the letter.*

Annotations:

1 See Lowry's 23 November 1951 letter (**480**) to Erskine for his comments on *Evil Under the Sun*.
2 Father Mapple is a character in Melville's *Moby-Dick*. A former whaler and a man famous for his sincerity and sanctity, he preaches a colourful Calvinist sermon (chapter 9) on the biblical subject of Jonah and the whale.
3 Lowry had asked Erskine to read the manuscript of Margerie's new novel 'The Castle of Malatesta' in the hope that he would recommend it for publication. The novel was never finished or published.
4 Lowry was reading Hermann Hesse's work at this time; see his 2 October 1951 letter (**472**) to Harold Matson.

Editorial Notes:

a. The postmark on the envelope is '1951 Nov 24,' and the letter is mistakenly dated 24 November 1953 in *Selected Letters*. The letter is written in red pencil, the story in black. See Figure 8.

482: To Seymour Lawrence

P: H(ts)   Dollarton, B.C.,
PP: Wake; SL 270–79   Canada
                                                        28 November 1951

Dear Mr Lawrence:[1]

Unfortunately your much appreciated invitation, at which I am needless to say greatly honored, to write a word on Conrad Aiken, has only just come to light (due to no fault of your own, or mine) now it is almost too late.

In a sort of frenzy therefore I hasten to attempt to get this letter in under the gun, begging you, where it appears too illiterate, to correct its grammar: for not only am I ashamed to write anything unworthy in haste upon such a noble subject, but I would not like the poet himself, who was once my tutor, to think that after all these years I was incapable (I am an Englishman too) of writing an explicit letter. But perhaps he will forgive me at that when I mention that I am still anyhow incapable of writing with critical detachment upon work that moves me so profoundly as his: 'something about us doesn't like to share our favorite authors with anyone,' perhaps not even with the author himself!

Not that the very fact of your winter number's being devoted to Aiken's work does not give me an immediate clue to a point of departure! For surely – as Winston Churchill might say – never has such a great author been for so long recognized as such by so many yet seemingly appreciated by so few!² It is true that any bibliography will lead one to an impressive documentation of criticisms on the poet, ranging from the learned Melody of Chaos by Houston Peterson to the sensitive and painstaking analysis of Marianne Moore,³ but it still *feels* as if he were but niggardly appreciated, – especially in the domain of simple public information: misconceptions, both of the man, and his work, have been perpetuated: and then when a criticism appears in some quasi-authoritative organ like Time, how woefully uninformed it sounds: 'But it is for his short stories that Aiken is most likely to be remembered'⁴ – what bloody unusual nonesense, if I may say so, fine though some of his stories may be. That is, that while there's no reason why half a dozen of his short stories shouldn't survive, as among the best of their kind, it is extremely unlikely that a miscarriage of justice in the realm of enlightened criticism (even if it existed on that plane, which is a puzzling point too, because in one way it doesn't – Aiken has of course long been universally respected as a major poet) should go for so long unredeemed into posterity as to result in the stories being remembered by future generations, while the magnificent body of poems was forgotten, even though every other kind of injustice – for reasons that are absolutely inexplicable, unless a Buddhist could explain them! – seems to have been done to Aiken's work in his lifetime.

It seems odd to me that Time, which in its art sections at least, likes to give the impression it wouldn't willingly mislead its student readers, should make what amounts to a crashing boner like that under the guise, more or less, of established opinion, the more especially since it is to that magazine one was indebted – years before that, in its obituary, and a fine one within its limits, on James Joyce – for the information that, almost up to the very point that great man died, he was actually looking for, trying everywhere to purchase, expecting to receive indeed, Conrad Aiken's masterly dramatic poem, The Coming Forth by Day of Osiris Jones.⁵ This, in my opinion, is an incident of literary history well worth remembering: in one stroke, it seems to demolish a whole bolus of misconceptions and injustices in regard to Aiken: while at the same time, to disengage my metaphor, it seems to sum up and contradict three decades of inadequate and wholly unfair repetitions and conditioned uncriticism – on that curious plane where this existed – of certain aspects of Aiken's work. Anyhow I like to think that there was that great author looking for The Coming Forth by Day of Osiris Jones, seeking for it at the very end of his life with such persistence that there can be no doubt he had every expectation of being, should he manage to secure it, fructified by it, of learning from it. As indeed would he not! One lets the story rest, as 'speaking volumes.' The point does not lie in the eerie coincidence, even though it is one that Joyce himself would have well appreciated. In fact, after that bit of information it seems almost unnecessary to add that saying that Aiken was most likely to be remembered for his short stories is much like saying that Shakespeare should be remembered for writing A Lover's Complaint, or Sonnets to Sundry Notes of Music, Eliot for The Hippopotamus, Stravinsky for his children's pieces – or if one wants to grow really popular and international on the subject – that Henrik Sienkiewicz was most likely to be remembered for writing The Lighthouse Keeper of Aspinwall. Sienkiewicz might well be remembered for writing The Lighthouse Keeper of Aspenwall, as a matter of fact, and I have forgotten to bring in Sibelius' the Valse Triste, which makes perhaps the most sensible comparison.[6] But you get the idea. Aiken is, in fact, in my opinion, of least importance as a short story writer; some of his pieces are wonderful, but often the daemon can almost be heard rebelling against the material involved, determined only to help him do his worst. (Nonetheless, both in best and worst, as the Canadian writer Gerald Noxon has demonstrated in some hair-raising and first rate radio dramas he has made out of some of Aiken's stories, one is astonished at the enormous amount of sheerly dramatic material that lies in them: in which connection I'm not alone in hoping that Aiken will take the daemon's tip and write some plays himself.)[7]

But if Aiken's work has been seriously enough misprised sometimes in America this has at least not been, with few exceptions, at the hands of his creative contemporaries: it was merely the odd reviewer who, albeit in a place of authority, would give the impression now and then that a certain work was outdated or insignificant or showed 'traces' of something or other: this opinion someone else would repeat almost verbatim in a given review, even though in that very same paper, you would quite likely find a reference to Aiken as 'perhaps the greatest poet now living,' or 'Aiken, the most majestic of all our poets,' in other words, though most of his works seem to me to have been more or less panned individually when they came out, there was always a growing body of authoritative and attentive opinion which paid no attention whatever to these verdicts and which existed independently and applied its judgement to the whole: in my own country, however, (I mean in this instance England) it was a very different matter. Here the poet was obliged to suffer for many years not merely absolute neglect or downright rudeness on the part of most of our so-called intelligent periodicals (even of those to which he had brilliantly contributed) but an odd and inexplicable neglect by the very contemporaries he was probably influencing at that time – or should have been influencing, had there existed in England any real independence of perception. Hard to believe though it is, nearly a quarter of a century ago, when I was in my teens, there was even an opinion given currency that there was one Conrad Aitken – they liked to spell it Aitken, perhaps out of some obscure deference to Lord Beaverbrook[8] – a poet, who was already in some sense passé (despite the fact that at that very moment he was engaged in a work that if he had written nothing else should have been sufficient to secure his position in world literature twice over, though it is true that he had already written enough to make most people famous five times over even on their plane) was probably dead – perhaps he was even some mysterious contemporary of Howells,[9] this Mr Aitken, so that it was not at all impossible that in picking up your monthly Memoirs and Dead Letters, that then very modern journal, you would find some such caustic statement (I don't mean by one of our bullyboys remarkable for their cruelty, their emasculated phraseology and their complete lack of any real creative talent, but by someone perfectly decent, well-meaning, an author of many distinguished books admirable in themselves, and who probably went on to win the V.C. in the war, and who wrote in that serene semi-colon-technique-style for which we are all so justly admired) as: 'It gave me much the same sort of faded impression, as if I had seen one of the poems of Conrad Aitken in the yellowing – but once, ah, how new – American Journal.'

But contemporaneous with this sort of strange opinion, that Conrad Aitken belonged to another age or was dead, was another one which caused people, on the contrary, sometimes to refer to him as if he were about 15, as 'one of the more bumptious and fractious of the very youngest generation of American poets,' a kind of latter day E.E. Cummings rampant,[10] so that it was not impossible too, that in the next journal you picked up for the same month, which likewise lamented the state of modern culture, you might come across some such considered advice as this given to the author of The Divine Pilgrim by some wise old bird twenty years his junior – 'Young Aitken, for all his extravagance, and when he has put his poetic excesses behind him, may yet be the poet to give us another Jack and the Beanstalk.'

Of course this state of affairs must anyhow have been long ago corrected, possibly even the wise old bird in question having helped to correct it. Though it was a fact that until I left England some eighteen years ago the only intelligent and fair appraisal I had read of Aiken was by the Scot, Edwin Muir (the co-translator with his wife, of Kafka, the good people to whom you may also be indirectly indebted for being able to find, in the New York Public Library, some volumes of Søren Kierkegaarde beside the Diary of a Seducer, which was the only one there in 1934 when I looked).[11]

Well, (even though I have been partly joking) this kind of thing might have sorely discouraged and even broken the spirit of a lesser man than Aiken – talk about being snuffed out by an article,[12] at that rate one has to think of Aiken in terms of cathedrals of immortal and undying candelabras! – which brings me to the man himself. Here I must report, that though he would have been inhuman if such neglect had not wounded him to some extent, I never saw him bat so much as an eyelid at an injustice to himself. As for England, Conrad Aiken was far too chivalrous a fellow ever to criticize, as the Celts say, the bridge on which he had crossed. (That we English should have expressed ourselves long ago as highly honoured that he should have deigned to cross on it at all is my only burden here.) Always willing to help his fellow writers, where possible, he was readier to find excuses for others than to criticize: (as a matter of fact, as I have read is also true of William Faulkner, he never put up with any harshness at all about his contemporaries): while as for his own work, if it were in suspension, a half sardonic smile, and some such comment as, 'Well, it's about time another book went spiralling down the drain,' was often about all that in conversation it would elicit. (As against this he never failed to refer to his own literary struggles as having been on the whole a bit of fun and well worth it.)

In this connection however, I mean as a human being, I have often wondered how future generations would picture Aiken and it is here that I can possibly render a small service by jogging the elbow of posterity in advance a little. Because for a writer who has been accused of being 'subjective' as they say, Conrad Aiken has left, save in the very greatest of his poems where for that matter any picture of the man perhaps is irrelevant, very little impression of himself, and so much has been, I won't say written, but simply repeated of his 'quest for a kind of absolute poetry', of his passion for the translunar, and his appetite for the expression of velleities, his 'incorrigible mellifluousness,' etc. etc. etc. that one is liable to gain the impression of some one living eternally in a sort of Sussex or Cape Cod twilight. Again, some of his prose protagonists, however brilliantly drawn, can be the opposite of helpful should one be seeking therein any clue to the identity of their creator. Some of his work moreover is of such an appalling savagery that you might imagine the author personally resembled a cross between Abraxas Bahomet and Ahasuerus.[13] Or again, it is of such transcendent beauty that you might imagine he did not live on this earth at all but had his hammock slung up on high somewhere between Aries and the Circlet of the Western Fish. Nor has Aiken himself, who has even written a poem called Palimpsest a deceitful portrait, that is perhaps least help of all, ever pretended to be other than unhelpful.[14]

Of course, what I say may be totally irrelevant to you, or to any consideration of his poetry. From an existential (perish the word, but let it stand anyhow) point of view, it perhaps is not so irrelevant however.

Nor from the human. In this connection anyhow a relative of Aiken's (I hope Mr Aiken will not shoot me for telling this story, and if it has been told elsewhere, I ask to be forgiven for repeating it, moreover I can see another kind of irony creeping in here – when his old friends are asked to make a statement on his poetry, instead they recommend his name glowingly to the Society for the Prevention of Cruelty to Animals) once told me that when the poet was a lad he climbed up a telegraph pole to rescue, from its crosstrees – and what is more did rescue – a stranded cat. Perhaps that doesn't sound so much, thus badly reported. Perhaps the reader has climbed telegraph posts when a youth. But however lately you may have climbed your last telegraph post, I think I can (the more especially as an ex-seaman) safely suggest that it is a very different business when you have to make the return journey accompanied by a cat that, having raised Cain in order to be taken down, is now striving its utmost to regain its former position aloft. Moreover the ascent of a telegraph post is perpendicular, and so is the descent, it may be – all too perpendicular. You are not, as on board ship, climbing a sort of staircase: you are lucky if you have a few spikes, and these don't carry you very far: you need both hands to hold on, but you don't have them, the cat demands both: and though the post may not be the height, say, of a mast, the invitation aloft to vertigo is very similar: while the ground below in your mental view makes no bones about being the ground below – and mends no broken bones – whether at a distance of a hundred, fifty, or twenty-five feet. So I imagine it. In Canada the custom rather more often is, on such occasions, to call the fire brigade, there being an extremely natural fear in the public mind in regard to telegraph poles, indeed in most minds, particularly in that of children partly occasioned by the suspicion that the wires themselves may be alive, moreover unlike trees, or certain trees, they constitute something forbidden, dangerous ('trespassers will be prosecuted,' Aiken no doubt observed, quoting himself in advance, to the cat) and in short the majority of children, it is my experience, would almost rather climb anything else, even were there no cat in question. This act of compassion, just the same, I would say, was extremely typical of the man. It may even be that this concern for the indignity the cat might suffer at being rescued by other unskillful hands weighed with him almost as much as the animal's danger. Aiken indeed would not readily see any indignity or hurt inflicted either upon animals or human beings. He was capable moreover, as I recall him, of such an instantaeous grasp of a whole situation in all its permutations and combinations that you might have said that he had perceived it by some means of clairvoyance before it had been given a chance to develop. This empathy – of a kind that one associates also with expressionist painters, such as Munch[15] –

extended even to natural objects, so that he would point out even such a humble thing, say, as a piece of drainpipe, through which a cool stream was conduited, on a burning summer day, in such a manner that just for a moment you felt you were that bit of piping: listening, looking, you partook, by Jove, for an instant, of that piping's cool feelings, even if it didn't have any before. So I didn't mention the cat on the telegraph pole from a sentimental viewpoint or even because it was a pleasant thing for people to remember about Conrad Aiken – though it certainly is, for that matter, but the point is, it wasn't exactly an isolated incident, or something that gives you no clue to the man, such as that Edgar Poe took off all his clothes at West Point on parade, or Schiller couldn't work without a desk full of rotten apples: Mr Aiken was, as the landlady of the Ship Inn, Rye, Sussex, remarked, replenishing my tankard, a real kind thoughtful gentleman wot would go out of his way, you know, to be kind. Not many like 'im, sir.[16] What occasioned the landlady's remark I forget: probably it was no more than some minor act of courtesy, but courtesy of that true kind which is, as Keyserling points out, no empty form, but the assent to man's true being.[17] What I think I mean is that you couldn't, no matter who you were, have met Aiken, if only to pass the time of day with the exchange of a few words, without mysteriously feeling, as it were, that your system had been 'toned up': possibly it would not be until you got round the next corner that you saw the joke he had inserted tangentially into this exchange, whereupon all at once the day too would take upon itself a new, a brighter, or it might be a more bizarre, a more complex aspect, in any case became a wholly more amusing and sympathetic adventure; in some amazing way he had sensed *your* problem, made *your* own burden, whatever it was, seem lighter. In other words, to an extraordinary degree he possessed charity: in addition to this however he possessed a quality that, despite some richly comic scenes, and others savage and appalling, is not easily, or consistently at least, to be deduced from his works. That is to say he possessed about the most superlatively robust sense of humour it would be possible to encounter in a fellow human being. Very often, though more quietly, this combined with other qualities I have mentioned in a manner you did not fully appreciate till years afterwards.

For example, during one of his rare visits to America while he was still resident in England, I happened to be in New York myself, where 'owing to certain auxiliary circumstances' I found myself living in the basement in the West Seventies of an old brownstone house, of which I had rented the room of the janitor, which he in turn had vacated because of the incidence therein (if I may say so without impoliteness, for they are after all international and know no boundaries) of certain rare insects.[18] The other good roomers of this house all had the habit, with the maximum of conviviality, of playing pinochle all night in the basement kitchen so that, for that matter, had one wanted to, one couldn't sleep: as a consequence (though I learned happily in this way how to play pinochle) I often found myself working all night, that is, I was able to do so without disturbing others: on this occasion I had not only been working all night but for some enthusiastic reason for perhaps three days and nights on end, and the pinochle game having broken up in the early morning was, with the landlady's permission, continuing to type in the basement kitchen, having been driven out of my room by the aforesaid rare insects, not having shaved for four days, and sitting surrounded by a great deal of washing, some seventy empty beer bottles, and perhaps ten empty whiskey bottles, the residue in fact of the vanished pinochle party, all of which I must certainly have given the air of having recently consumed myself, though it was not later than half past ten in the morning. At this point (I had stopped typing, to make matters worse) the landlady broke in upon my thoughts in respectful tones, in fact she whispered:

'Mr Kraken is upstairs, sir.'

'What!'

'A kind gentleman – very well dressed – his suit is made of real good material . . . Mr the Kraken would like to see you, sir, and is coming downstairs now.'

It was indeed no less a person than Conrad Aiken himself, who finding himself in New York for a day had hunted up his old pupil in Columbus Circle, where having surrounded my whole position of embarrassment at a glance, he had metamorphosed himself verbally into the famed Scandinavian sea-monster, in order, perhaps, to blend himself the more unobtrusively with my cavernous, indeed monstrous apparent circumstances which, hinting to say the least of failure, if not of the abyss itself – without even the pinochle players to lend it all a touch of jovial humanity – however innocent in reality, were certainly not those in which one, immediately the pupil again, anxious to produce an illusion of steady work and regular hours, would have cared formally at first meeting to greet the great man in his own country.

Mr Kraken![19] Well, well, sometimes, when feeling gloomy, I find I only have to think of this incident to start chuckling: finally the chuckle becomes a roar of laughter, and melancholy is banished. And then again I think to myself: who the hell am I? What an incredible privilege! Did I really know Conrad Aiken? And did he once actually come to see me. Or did I make that up?

Also I have sometimes wondered, as in a story of his, Round by Round, one of Aiken's characters wonders, as regarding a picture of the James family, their good faces 'look forward at him with an extraordinary integrity'[20] – where has that integrity, that kindness, decency, understanding, humour, as exemplified by Aiken equally – where have these qualities disappeared to in human beings? Were they the perquisite of particular people of a particular age? What? Perhaps someone like Aiken was a link with a past age and at the same time is a link with a future one, that has not yet come to pass, when the cultivation and the possession of such qualities will again seem worth while to man.

I realize I have now finished this letter without having said more than a mumbling word about Conrad Aiken's work. I realize also I have spoken of him slightly in the past tense, when he is indeed very much alive, and with no doubt some of his profoundest work ahead of him. But this is perhaps because, as a matter of fact, (though I have myself benefited from his generosity) I haven't, more's the pity, seen him for some fifteen years and I don't think, for that matter, we have even corresponded for some two, though we have conversed once upon the phone. As you see though, his memory is very much alive here, even in the Canadian wilderness.

Speaking of Aiken as a writer, from the time that, before I had ever heard of him, his work first slammed down on my raw psyche like the lightning slamming down on the slew outside at this moment, I have always thought that he was the truest and most direct descendant of our own great Elizabethans, having a supreme gift of dramatic and poetic language, a genius of the highest and most original order, and I have no doubt at all that in years to come we will do our best to claim him back from America as our own.

Yours sincerely,

Malcolm Lowry

Annotations:

1 Seymour Lawrence (1926-94), the editor and publisher of the literary magazine *Wake* from 1945 to 1954, was preparing a special issue on the work of Conrad Aiken, and had written to Lowry asking for a contribution. Lawrence published Lowry's letter, with editorial changes (notably to Lowry's punctuation and English spellings), in *Wake* 11 (1952): 80-89. Lowry's letter strikes an odd ambivalent tone of highest praise qualified by discordant notes of criticism and irony.

2 Sir Winston Churchill (1874-1965) was prime minister of Great Britain from 1940 to 1945 and from 1951 to 1955. Lowry is paraphrasing Churchill's remark in his 20 August 1940 speech paying tribute to RAF pilots who fought the German Luftwaffe in the Battle of Britain that summer: 'Never in the field of human conflict was so much owed by so many to so few.'

3 Houston Peterson's *Melody of Chaos* (1931) was the first critical monograph on Aiken's work. The American poet Marianne Moore

(1887-1972) discusses Aiken's *The Coming Forth by Day of Osiris Jones* (1931) in detail in 'If a Man Die,' *Hound and Horn* 5 (1932): 313-20 and the article was reprinted by Lawrence in *Wake*.

4 Lowry is quoting from an unsigned review of the *Short Stories of Conrad Aiken* called 'Faintly Bitter' in *Time*, 2 October 1950, 80.

5 Aiken's *Coming Forth By Day of Osiris Jones*, an autobiographical poem drawing upon the Egyptian *Book of the Dead*, appeared in 1931. Joyce was trying to find a copy during the summer of 1940, only months before his death in January 1941, because he suspected, from Aiken's title, that it would have a theme similar to *Finnegans Wake* (1939). See Richard Ellmann's comments on Joyce's search for the book in *James Joyce* (Oxford: Oxford University Press, 1982), pp. 732-35. The article Lowry mentions as the source of this information is Joyce's obituary notice 'Silence, Exile & Death' in *Time*, 10 February 1941, 72-73.

6 These are all minor works by the writers or composers Lowry mentions. Sibelius's 'Valse Triste,' one of six pieces of incidental music composed in 1904 for the play *Kuolema* (*Death*), was immediately popular with audiences while the composer's other work was not.

7 Gerald Noxon prepared several Aiken stories for radio: 'Mr Arcularis' (1934), first produced in 1948 on Andrew Allan's CBC radio drama program 'Stage,' was a particular success. During 1949-50 Allen produced three more Aiken stories in Noxon's adaptations: 'The Fallen Disciple,' 'Impulse,' and 'A Thief in the House.'

8 Lord Beaverbrook (1879-1964) was the Canadian-born English newspaper magnate William Maxwell Aitken.

9 The American writer and editor William Dean Howells (1837-1920) published a regular column called 'The Easy Chair' in *Harper's Magazine* from 1900 to 1920, but he was scarcely 'contemporary' with Aiken.

10 American poet Edward Estlin Cummings (1894-1962) is known for his formal and stylistic innovations and his divergence from the main course of high modernism represented by contemporaries like T.S. Eliot or Ezra Pound. He experimented with typography, punctuation, and etymology.

11 Edwin (1887-1959) and Willa Muir (1890-1970) translated many works by German and Czech authors, including Franz Kafka. Kierkegaard published 'Diary of a Seducer' as part of his *Either/Or: A Fragment of Life* (1843), and it was first translated into English by Knud Fick in 1932.

12 See Byron's *Don Juan* (1819-24), canto XI, ll 479-80: ''Tis strange the mind, that fiery particle, / Should let itself be snuffed out by an Article.' Byron's subject is John Keats, who had been savagely attacked in a review that some believed contributed to his early death.

13 Abraxas is a word sometimes inscribed on gems and used by Cabbalists as a charm, while Bahomet (also spelled Baphmet) is a 'devil' allegedly worshipped by Freemasons and the reputed god of the Knights Templar. Ahasuerus, the Wandering Jew of mediaeval legend, is the name of the man who insulted Christ and was condemned to wander the earth until the Second Coming.

14 Aiken's poem 'Palimpsest: A Deceitful Portrait,' first appeared in *Coterie*
5 (1920): 7-16.

15 Norwegian painter Edvard Munch (1863-1944) was one of Lowry's
favourites; see his September 1931 letter (**36**) to Aiken with his sketch
of Munch's lithograph 'The Scream' (1895).

16 The Ship Inn is a pub in Rye that Lowry and Aiken frequented during
Lowry's visits with the Aikens between 1929 and 1932.

17 The German philosopher Hermann Keyserling was influenced by
Oriental philosophy and developed a type of intuitional mysticism.
Lowry was reading some of Keyserling's work in 1950-51 (see his 13
December 1950 letter [**432**] to Downie Kirk), and he may be thinking
of Keyserling's comments on courtesy in China in part 5 of *The Travel
Diary of a Philosopher*, vol. 2 (1925).

18 This visit probably occurred in the summer of 1936 after Lowry's
release from Bellevue Hospital. See the chronology in Vol. I and Jan
Gabrial's recollections in *Malcolm Lowry Remembered* (18-19).

19 A kraken is a legendary sea monster; see Tennyson's poem 'The
Kraken' (1830). This 'Kraken' business had become a Lowry/Aiken
legend; see the postscript to Lowry's October 1945 letter (**205**) to Aiken
and his poem 'No Kraken Shall Be Found Till Sought By Name'
(Scherf, 198).

20 'Round by Round,' first published in *The Short Stories of Conrad Aiken*
(1950), is about a sports writer's disillusionment with his marriage. On
the wall of his office hangs a photograph of Henry, William, and Alice
James that becomes a focal point of contrast with present mores.

483: To Seymour Lawrence:

P: Hunt(ts)

Dollarton, B.C.,
Canada
4 December 1951

Dear Mr Lawrence:
   P.S. – This is not for publication – save where any emendations, if it
is possible to make them without too much inconvenience – may be
involved.
   Incidentally I hope you got my letter on Conrad Aiken in time:
maybe you won't think it suitable. Anyhow I meant well, to say the
least. On the other hand, as so often happens when you get a thing off
in too much of a hurry, I have been seized with misgiving: that in this
case – even while of course not meaning to – what I have said might
afford Mr Aiken pain or vexation rather than pleasure. Perhaps if you
are in touch with him you could show him the letter and then if he
dissapproves not publish it or let him censor it. (One thing which of
course I couldn't explain to you were the conditions of occupational

hazard under which it was written: we live on an inlet and after four days of onshore gales the tide had not a chance properly to go out – consequently we had such an appalling high tide on that morning that I thought the whole house was going to wash away, and even as I write this the situation is not much different so that I can't hear myself think. This is a maddening situation in which to try and write a considered piece of work.) In any case I didn't make a carbon copy – I just have the pencil script, so it's going to be hard to direct you to a given spot. Anyhow these are the main objections, apart from the fact that the whole thing is not as good as it ought to be.

(1) Where I say (which is about page 3 on my pencil script, round about some stuff about Stravinsky, Sienkiewicz, Sibelius, etc.) Aiken is, in fact, in my opinion, of least importance as a short story writer: Could you append a footnote or something? *I don't mean as a novelist: or that he is not – flukes and flames! – a master of prose.*[1]

(2) Where I say – (about a couple of pages later) I don't mean by one of our bully-boys, etc. etc. (What follows here is *not* intended as a footnote or anything, they are simply my private feelings.) Reading this bit over I'm by no means sure that that is a fair kind of jeering – especially the bit about the V.C. seems a kind of lapse of taste: even the bully-boys are not much better: psychologically speaking, it probably really betrays some sort of feeling of guilt, though of another kind, on my own side: no one likes to be reminded of past failings, certainly not me – but here I am reminding somebody. In this case the culprit is Osbert Sitwell or it may have been even Max Beerbohm: that I forget, but it has occurred to me – am I actually being libelous?[2] Of course it was a stupid thing for whoever it was to have said: a phenomenal lapse of judgement, but then by reminding anyone of it am I doing Aiken damage, rather than good? I don't think Aiken would approve of my actually impugning an individual, so to speak, (Damn that tide!) Anyhow if the damage is done – or it's too late to repair same – could you alter the V.C. bit to read: – 'and who probably was the recipient of the Order of the Bath or something, but who liked sometimes to write in that serene, etc. etc.'

Or however you can wangle it yourself – cutting a bit elsewhere – if it is necessary to keep the same number of words. In fact, I hadn't meant to impugn anyone personally either – the whole body of unfair judgement on Aiken constitutes in my opinion an actual phenomenon, in the face of which Aiken's own sportingness was beyond praise – which is all my point.

(3) In the telegraph pole bit I missed out something by mistake that gives it more sense, and perhaps you could put it in, or as a footnote: at the end of that section it should really read:

moreover unlike trees, or certain trees, they constitute something forbidden, dangerous – *but without possessing the corresponding attraction for that reason* –

My sincere apologies if this puts you to any extra trouble, but perhaps you haven't gone to press yet. My own admiration for the work of and respect for the poet is in fact overwhelming and always has been: I had thought by couching my tribute in more or less humorous terms I would avoid a tendency sheerly as it were, to gush, – which would have been embarrassing for him to read rather than a pleasure. Had I had time to send the letter in advance for his approval it would have destroyed some of its spontaneity. However now I've written it without so submitting it, it's keeping me awake with the uneasy feeling that I haven't written it right when the last thing in the world I would like to do is in any way to offend him. So tell me what you think.

Yours sincerely,

Malcolm Lowry

Annotations:

1 Lawrence included this entire comment in the published letter, and he has made each of the following changes suggested by Lowry.˙
2 We have been unable to confirm Lowry's suggestion that a knowledgeable critic like Sitwell or Beerbohm misunderstood Aiken's work, but see letter **482** for the type of dismissal of Aiken's work that Lowry is remembering.

484: To Harold Matson

P: Matson(ts); UBC(phc)   Dollarton, B.C.,
                                                                        Canada
                                                           8 December 1951

Dear Hal:

The enclosed is self-explanatory, that is to say you now know as much as I do about it, unless you have heard more.[1] As we wrote you, on learning that Under the Volcano had caused a sensation in Germany and that they wanted to make a movie out of it, I wrote Klett and the translator, Herr ten Holder, saying that I would expect eventually to hear from you about it: Herr ten Holder I adjured to make doubly clear to Herr Klett, (who in his one letter to me that passed through your office never mentioned any film at all, merely expressed himself delighted with the book, – but this was on the eve of publication and before the 'sensation') that I would only do any business through yourself.

It is possible, however, that the enclosed supplement(?) to the contract, which I have of course not signed, was drawn up before Klett had received that letter.

Herr ten Holder's first letter about the movie, which was in German, and whose general purport we have already conveyed to you to our best capacity,[2] seemed on further studying by a German expert, less uncertain that they would make a film as that he would be completely cut out by Klett in any share of the proceeds: I replied that so far as I was concerned that seemed thoroughly unfair, but that I would have no say in the matter until a contract was directed through the proper channels, namely through yourself, and finally signed with your ratification.

I also intimated that I should, in that case, have probably asked you to have tried to arrange a clause whereby Margie and myself could function in some capacity in regard to the scenario, treatment, – working with the director or Lorre himself etc, much as you mentioned you would try to do when there seemed a chance it would be done in Hollywood. (In this way Herr ten Holder's services might logically come to be required in the end, even if no stipulation in regard to that could be made in my part of the contract, though it is hard for me – I must add – to see, since in some cases it must be his creative translation of the original that has caused the sensation and which they would be aiming to use, from what standpoint of justice Klett imagines they could be dispensed with in the first place.) Here I had meant to quote from the curious letter from Herr ten Holder, but finally decided to copy the whole letter and send it.[3] So please refer to that here. (The 'contract' – note – is dated from exactly one month before, though this is the first I have heard of it.)

Though Herr ten Holder mentions a letter for me from Axel Kuan[4] – the one presumably that he has not signed (as why should he?) he has not sent this letter either (or a copy, which seems to me a bit odd) so I can only guess at its contents. From his own letter you will see that there can be no doubt that I have long since made the matter clear about the business having to be handled through yourself. You will also gather from the general tone that the ten Holders and ourselves have become good friends during the course of the correspondence on finer points of the translation. That is perfectly true. At the same time on the other plane I cannot very well afford to be involved with what seems to be his personal quarrel with Klett, with whom I am supposedly also on quite friendly terms (despite the evidence in the 'supplement' that may look as though he were trying to double cross both yourself and myself): poor old ten Holder's motives are anyhow quite clear; Klett has underpaid and overworked him for and over the translation, and he's probably starving, and he has a wife and three children. That's something we can understand too and I hope, if anything comes through with the film, that I can help him, even if that be at a personal sacrifice: that however need have nothing to do with the contract necessarily, concerning which all I can suppose is that if Klett has gone to the trouble to have this thing drawn up – even if in this backhanded way – he perceived some profit in it: I only hope you think so too (though even were there not there would still have to be some personal stipulation in regard to my having some say in anyone's making the Volcano as a film – for one thing it's far too dangerous in unscrupulous hands, like the Wandering Jew, they can make it mean anything)[5]

Ten Holder's letter as you see puts me in an ambiguous position where he says to me 'Discretely and only for your ears,' etc. and then goes on to say something that he clearly means me to refer on to yourself. In this I can only see his fear that in some Kafkan manner his position would further deteriorate with the wily Mr Klett should the latter get wind of his confidence to me behind *his* back; so that, in this regard, if it be true that ten Holder is as it appears actually trying to protect our interests as well as his own, one would not like him to suffer on that account.

As for papa Klett it would seem that we could afford to forget his trying to doublecross us if the outweighing advantage to us both of an actual contract via Lorre arranged by yourself seems worth your while and/or is possible to arrange. Probably the German film companies have little money and normally speaking, I imagine, it would be worth while grasping such an opportunity simply for a bare living wage for a while, the experience, and what it might lead to. If that were impossible a flat sum down would of course be better than nothing. Or so it seems at the moment. Or does it? But in fact it doesn't. Poverty just makes it seem so. If it is to be done it has to be done well. The thing that weighs with me chiefly is the calibre of Peter Lorre himself (who by an odd coincidence keeps occurring in the Volcano) – in my opinion one of the greatest actors who has ever lived, with a part that might have been written for him.[6] But I refer the whole possibly glorious, possibly abortive, possibly even non-existent matter, to your wisdom. If Peter Lorre will indeed be in New York that might seem a stroke of luck too.

Yours very hopefully anyway, with love from us both

Malcolm

P.S. Re Peter Lorre being in New York, it has struck me that I might well keep his interest hot by writing him, through you directly at his theatre. That is, I would send the letter addressed to Peter Lorre but to you, to be delivered through your good self, or not as you chose. The reason for this is that I not only know a hell of a lot about movies, have a real regard for Lorre's art, which by the way has rarely been seen here at its highest, not even in 'M.' – Chaplin said he was the greatest living actor too, by the way, and Chaplin is probably right. – But the point is the public has tended to think of him as a sort of Mr Yamamoto-cum-horror doctor. There couldn't be a better part for him than the Consul, though an enormous amount depends on his director. Not even Fritz Lang did well enough by him perhaps. And even Paul Fejos – an even greater, if possible, director – did not do right by him, or himself.[7] I have a lot of obscure knowledge like this of films never shown in America, and in which he has appeared that would show my appreciation could not be more genuine, and this is the rough line I would take. Please let me know whether I should do this or not.

P.P.S. I am sending the other poor old Malcolm Lorre – whose father was president of 'Erskine' University of South Carolina, an Xmas card, together with a family holly tree. I hope you received my M.S. Hear Us Oh Lord From Heaven Thy Dwelling Place in time to observe the relevance of this coincidence, if your eye fell on it in transit. I am hoping he may be an American cousin: curiously on my father's side, many of my forebears were, as he, either architects or engineers, one was Stephensen's chief on The Rocket,[8] that old steam engine. (If the source of this entirely escaped your notice, it is that a certain Malcolm Lowry, an engineer of Kansas City, wrote to Reynal saying that he had been congratulated on writing Under the Volcano, and would like to trace his namesake and the family! Perhaps I should offer him the family house – now for sale in England, as a refuge, when Kansas gets too wet, or dry?)

P.P.P.S.[a] This is a projected second letter to Herr Klett with whom I am assuming it seems still a good idea to keep on friendly terms. Please tell me if you think I should send it, or not. I repeat that I have still not heard directly about the film from *Klett* at all, despite the so-called supplement to the contract. My phrase 'though perhaps I did not make it clear enough,' is, however, sheer politeness on my part. To Klett I said 'I shall be expecting to hear about this *through my agent*' and ten Holder, I repeat, I counselled doubly in regard to this: so I could do no more. If you consider this following letter unsuitable for me to send to Klett perhaps it will serve as clarifying for you my general attitude, unless corrected by your own advice, in regard to any possible contract.

Dear Herr Klett:

I have received two copies of a supplement to the contract re a possible film of Under the Volcano from Herr ten Holder which I am sending on to my agent, Harold Matson.

Naturally I shall be more than delighted if this goes through especially should the great Peter Lorre play the leading role, and I am indeed honoured and grateful that your interest should have extended thus far.

On the other hand as I intimated in my letter – though perhaps I did not make it clear enough – I am not empowered to sign any contract without the ratification of my agent and friend, Mr Matson, who handles all my affairs and to whom I have therefore sent the contract on.

However even did I not possess an agent, and be the terms never so favorable, I do not think I'd like to sign the contract as it stands, for one thing, as I said, I'd like to have a say in the treatment and scenario.

For another thing, were I myself a billionaire – if not out of Georg Kaiser – and my motives without financial bias of any sort, I think I would find myself considering equally with Herr Lowry, Herr Lorre: in other words I'd like to have some indication that the director, whoever he may be, was worthy of Herr Lorre's talents, and that thus the picture, which incidentally at this point in the movies' offers a great opportunity, was going to move that director (not to say the cameraman) with as much enthusiasm as one dares hope Herr Lorre may be moved; some more definite indication also, without insisting on over-haste, that the film *would* be made, not just left dangling: such aesthetic and purist considerations would also, I feel, be the opposite of impractical from the business point of view too, and in fact from everyone's point of view.

Meantime, however, until matters may be more settled, allow me to thank you for having implemented the possibility in this way, and also again, let me express my sincere delight at the manner of the production of the book itself by yourself, its excellent translation by Herr ten Holder, and not least, from what I hear, its excellent reception,

Yours sincerely,

[unsigned]

Annotations:

1 Lowry had enclosed with this letter a contract supplement dated 30 October from Ernst Klett for the film rights to *Under the Volcano* (see Appendix 2) and a copy of Clemens ten Holder's letter about the film (see annotation 3).

2 This is ten Holder's 20 October 1951 letter to Lowry; see Lowry's 23 November 1951 letter (**479**) to Matson.

3 This 30 November 1951 letter to Lowry (UBC 1:67) is with a collection of fifteen letters from Clemens and Hildegard ten Holder spanning the period from February 1951 to October 1952. A translation of the Lowry/ten Holder correspondence has been published in *Malcolm Lowry/Clemens ten Holder Briefwechsel* (1985).

4 Axel Kaun is mentioned in ten Holder's letters to Lowry as the person responsible for interesting Peter Lorre in a film of *Under the Volcano*, but there is no mention of Lorre in Klett's contract.

5 One of several films about the Jew's story is Maurice Elvey's *The Wandering Jew* (1923), starring Matheson Lang, which Lowry uses as a motif in *October Ferry to Gabriola*.

6 Lorre first achieved recognition for his role as a psychopath in *M* (1932) and went on to perform in other expressionist films before leaving Germany in 1933. Because he played the crazed doctor in *Mad Love* (1935), the Hollywood remake of *The Hands of Orlac*, Lowry describes him as recurring in *Under the Volcano*. After his arrival in Hollywood in 1935, Lorre played the Oriental detective 'Mr Moto' in a series of detective films and the parts of mysterious, sinister foreigners in other popular films.

7 Paul Fejos (1897-1963), a Hungarian scientist and film director during the twenties and thirties, directed films, including documentaries, in Hungary, Europe, and the United States, but the reason for Lowry's criticism is unclear.

8 George Stephenson (1781-1848) was the famous English engineer credited, together with his son Robert, with the invention of steam locomotion. 'The Rocket' was the engine that reached a speed of 35 mph in 1829 and was subsequently used on the Liverpool and Manchester Railway. Russell Lowry has confirmed that a Lowry grandfather, about whom little is known, once worked for Stephenson.

Editorial Notes:

a. A two-page pencil draft of this postscript and draft letter to Klett is filed with Lowry's outgoing letters for 1951 (UBC 2:20), and a cancelled draft fragment of the letter to Matson survives with the manuscripts (UBC 51:26).

485: To Philippe Thoby-Marcelin

P: UBC(card phc)   [Dollarton]
                                                       11 December 1951

My dear old Phi-to – do not burn those objects[1] at both ends – have you received a copy of the Volcano yet in French – are you well? are you happy? Tell me when you have time. How are things going? The books? Where are you? We long to return to Haiti, or wish you would come to Canada. Times are hard & I like the world less & less. But do not let us lose touch. We have floods here [illegible]. Best love for Xmas & New Year from Margie & I

                Affecteusement

                         Malcolm

Annotations:

   1 This note is written on a Christmas card depicting three red candles
     burning brightly and standing in pine-cone candle-holders. The copy-
     text is a faint photocopy, which is illegible at one point.

486: To David Markson

P: UBC(card)   [Dollarton]
                                                    [ca 11 December 1951]

Looking at these things[1] sternly I came to the conclusion that the fir-
cone contraption was to conceal the fact that they were really being
burned at both ends; however let not that obscure the good thought!
    With all the best love –

                        & as from us both –

                                                         Malcolm

Annotations:

   1 Lowry has sent Markson a Christmas card identical to the one he sent
     Marcelin (**485**).

487: To Clemens and Hildegard ten Holder

P: private(card phc)   [Dollarton]
                                                        [December 1951]

Happy New Year
&
great love
&
gratitude
to Clemens & Hildegard ten Holder
(und alles queer ducks)
from

Malcolm Lowry

(– Dear Clemens: will answer letters quam celerrime but formerly
floods threatened: now we are snowed in. Hope to have some good
news for you soon. (Thanks also for the song:[1] – please say Froliche
Weinachten[2] to the alles queer birds: don't know author of words but
your tune is probably better than original). Enclosed for you find several
bits of original – in fact, in part, pre-original – of book you may recognise.[3] With my love & gratitude.

                                                         Malcolm L.

Annotations:

1 Clemens ten Holder sent the Lowrys a Christmas poem with their parcel. The poem, called 'Dreifaltigkeitssong' (Trinity Song) is typed and bound in heavy paper, tied with a red ribbon (UBC 1:67).
2 The correct German is *fröhliche Weihnachten*: Merry Christmas.
3 Lowry must have enclosed some draft pages of *Under the Volcano*.

488: To Harold Matson

P: Matson(telegram)   Western Union,
                                                North Vancouver, B.C.
                                                   17 December 1951

REASON WANTED CHANGE RANDOM WAS LOYALTY TO ALBERT NOT DISLIKE OF HARCOURT IF HARCOURT HOLDS ME TO CONTRACT SITUATION SUCH I HAVE NO MORAL RIGHT TO REFUSE I LEAVE FINANCIAL ARRANGEMENTS TO YOU BUT DESPERATELY NEED IMMEDIATE CASH RECEIVED NEWS SEVEN HUNDRED DOLLARS ROYALTY PARIS HAVE INSTRUCTED SENT TO YOU CONSIDERING THIS AND CONTRACT CAN YOU WIRE ME SOME MONEY[1] MANY THANKS FOR EVERYTHING LETTER FOLLOWS LOVE

                                                           MALCOLM

Annotations:

1 Chronically short of funds, the Lowrys were again in considerable need and hoping to escape severe winter weather by renting a Vancouver apartment. They moved in January 1952.

489: To Albert Erskine

P: Virginia(ts); UBC(phc)   Dollarton, B.C.,
PP: *SL* 279-81   Canada
                                                   19 December 1951

Dear old Albert:

Melancholy news about us: you've probably heard.

Harcourt won't let me out of the contract. I have no choice – so it has seemed to me – but to stay with them.

All this time though I've been thinking *you* had the M.S. of my projects but it turns out Hal had no choice either but to examine the Harcourt situation as an immediate problem before that could be done, with the above result, which is no one's fault, and though one cannot drink of it,[1] can't be helped.

I did not arrive at the sad decision without thinking of yourself, to say the least, for without the Volcano I would be a liability rather than an asset, the Volcano being, as you know, part of a sequence: and Harcourt wouldn't give up the Volcano. It had also occurred to me that you might not like Hear Us Oh Lord From Heaven Thy Dwelling Place, which tales were the immediate work in hand, or if you did, that others at Random House might not. I am still half of this opinion. I am also of the opinion that I would probably not have exerted myself to such an extent had I known the project was going to Harcourt and not yourself, though this is hard to determine because as a matter of fact I had naively no notion at all that it was going to Harcourt albeit now I see that Hal, who had my own interests at heart, but also the legal aspect to consider, cannot be blamed for this. Robert Giroux has very highly praised some of the tales in Hear Us Oh Lord, referring to one as the best he'd read in a long time for which praise I am grateful[2] but the truth is that I have not sold a single bloody solitary one of these tales, whether they are masterpieces or not, and this seems to be the trouble, that though I have tried my best I do not seem able to survive in this way: and for the matter of that Hal has to survive too.

Poor Margie has not sold a damn thing either so what with inflation, debt, the dead pound and the usual problems (we have not been to a movie, a pub, had a haircut in 6 months, nor a battery in our radio in a year, nor had a hot bath in 3 years) I actually had reached the point where I had no moral right to continue writing unless I was able to secure some kind of definite contract.

This is also the cause of my not yet having paid back your very kind loan to us though England's restrictions may soon prove less suicidal and indeed I think I can repay you soon now though it is something like doing it with your own property. Oh shit. Excuse me. In fact, but for yourself, not being there I suppose I should be happy enough to be with Bob Giroux and the rest for I am not involved with a 'Reynal current': quite the reverse. They are most understanding and on this account I know you will be glad. For the rest you could not have thanked me for the position in which I would have put you should I have insisted on staying with you, in fact I argued to myself that I was saving you the embarrassment of your having to refuse to be put in such a position at all, for indeed I cannot see how you could have wanted me under the circumstances that would have accrued, under which everyone would have been unhappy. This does not mean I do not feel a bit like Judas Iscariot: I exactly do and I look to you to tell me I need not, though that cannot stop me feeling like Germany without Bismarck, not to say Enos without Fruit Salts, or Johnny Walker without the whiskey.[3] Of course on one side we are grateful and pleased no end that Giroux is enthusiastic: on the other hand, because of yourself, one is heavy-hearted and has as it were a hangover before the celebration. For Christ's sake though do not let us fall asunder ourselves however. For another thing I am frightened by the appalling meaning of some parts of the book ahead and the character of some of the demons who have to be turned into mercies. All very well to say it's just fiction. This does not account for the fact – to hell with it. I'll tell you another time. But Bartleby in mid-Atlantic is a jovial and social fellow compared with the company my character has to keep sometimes.[4] Anyhow I hope you will still let me share some of its burdens with you. Also if I may I will dedicate some part or other – the best part when it comes along – to you. Do not forget there is always a shoulder here to lean on also. I hope your own serious troubles are not somehow too bad though how can they help but be bad: of course I know this but still I don't know what to say save that you have all our sympathy and prayers.

I now see this letter is psychologically one long piece of self-reproach for acting (or rather for not acting) in a way contrary to my higher self. Further to reproach me is a bit of pencilled letter to yourself that has just poked its way out of some papers, written last February, the draft of our S.O.S. last February that you answered so selflessly & immediately & generously. Alack. Thank you. Alas. Blast. Damn it. On the other hand I am convinced this is better for you too. For all God knows by the time I get to the end of the benighted work you may have returned to Brace & even be running it & so, what had started out from loyalty & friendship might well have turned out, from lack of long sightedness on my side, neither loyal nor friendly enough: I may feel as though I've shot the albatross now but I fear that you might have come to feel as though you'd been shot *by* an albatross.[5] In short I would have abrogated some other responsibility of wisdom I'd left out of account. However, for purely personal reasons, if this is any good to you, I emphasise that I did not know {I even sent a Xmas card to Frank [Taylor] saying I was awaiting your verdict in fear & trembling} the course events were taking. In fact for once Hal's office even forgot to acknowledge the m.s. I could not understand why you hadn't replied to my letter, & when I received Hal's with Giroux' report, we'd about decided it must have got lost. But by this time the ice was up to our door again. So there it is. Anyhow God bless you from us both

desconsolado –
Malcolm

Annotations:

1 As Señora Gregorio says to the Consul in chapter 7 of *Under the Volcano*: 'Life changes, you know, you can never drink of it.'

2 In his 11 December 1951 letter to Harold Matson, Robert Giroux said he was 'very much impressed' by the stories in *Hear us O Lord*, and he singled out 'In the Black Hills' for particular praise; see *Selected Letters*, 445-46.

3 Typically, Lowry feels guilty about not staying with Erskine, though the notion that he is betraying Erskine the way Judas betrayed Christ is a melodramatic exaggeration. By contrast, the idea that, without Erskine, he might be falling apart like the unified German state without its architect, Otto von Bismarck (1815-98), or that he is no more than the name of an antacid or a famous scotch whisky, is in an altogether lighter vein.

4 Bartleby, the title character in Melville's 1853 story 'Bartleby the Scrivener,' is one of the most unsociable, taciturn characters in fiction.

5 Lowry's reference is to Coleridge's *Rime of the Ancient Mariner* (1798). The mariner in the poem shoots an albatross, thereby bringing a curse on his ship and himself. He is condemned to wear the bird's carcass around his neck as a symbol of his guilt and betrayal. On the one hand, then, Lowry *feels* like the mariner; on the other, he fears that he has merely become a burden to Erskine.

490: To Harold Matson

P: Matson(ts); UBC(phc)

Dollarton, B.C.
Canada
20 December 1951[a]

Dear Hal:

In haste. I thank you sincerely for everything. Lunar Caustic is available but there is only one copy so it would have to be retyped here before I could send it, though Clarisse has another one in France. This as it stands is same one you have read years ago: it is still an integrated honest piece of work, but unmotivated, and not the final work I intend, which would be a hundred pages longer, a novel rather than a novelette, and take some six months more work. Nonetheless as it stands, it probably has some final, if not immediate, value. That is, I feel it's a near first rate novella, if anything but explicit. Reason for S.O.S.[1] – which I deplore making to you again at this time of the year – is simply that we are frozen in, so that work is impossible and I have somehow to shift us to warmer quarters in town for a couple of months. We have only 50 bucks actually in the bank though the pound now being freed this situation can improve any moment. I had expected owed money to reach us from other sources i.e. my share in the family estate – etc but so far it hasn't yet. However this time there is more than expectation* I can pay it right back and on top of that really begin to justify your trust in us. I feel sad about Albert but I feel convinced everything will work out for the best and am very grateful to you. Apart from anything else I would have been putting Albert on the spot, without the Volcano.

God bless: Merry Christmas: Thank you: etc:

Yours,

Malcolm

* With advance Clarisse tells me Volcano has made about half a million francs altogether in Paris: that is there is about 800,000 fr, or about 700 or 800 dollars they still owe me. I've told her to tell Corrêa[2] to send this to you via the Office des Changes though how long it will take I don't know. Her letter reached me one day before yours.

Annotations:

1 See Lowry's telegram of 17 December 1951 (**488**) asking for money.
2 Corrêa, the Paris publishing house that issued a reprint of *Au-dessous du volcan* in 1950, had accrued royalties from the combined sales of the first edition, published in 1949 by Le Club français du livre, and their reprint.

Editorial Notes:

a. This letter is a one-paragraph typescript, with complimentary close, and three holograph addenda marked for insertion in the main paragraph; the addenda are illegible at several points. The last addendum, although clearly marked for insertion after 'expectation,' is placed after the close to preserve the sense and flow of the paragraph.

491: To Bill, Alice, and Arthur McConnell

P: UBC(card) [Dollarton]
[December 1951]

To Bill & Alice & Arthur[1] Merry Christmas! from Margerie

& Malcolm (am very ashamed of my silence but we've had just one thing after another. Meantime I've just had news the old Volcano has made ½ a *million* francs in France: don't know if I'll ever see any of it: And Peter Lorre (who is reading it over Radio Munich) may make a film of it, – of which have been offered, to date, 50%. But I haven't seen any of that either yet & the problems of being a writer in Canada don't grow less nor the stove any younger.

Annotations:

1 Arthur is the McConnells' young son.

492: To Harold Matson

P: Matson(telegram)   Western Union,
                                              North Vancouver, B.C.
                                                27 December 1951

YOUR MONEY ONLY RECEIVED TODAY[1] GOD BLESS A THOUSAND
THANKS HAPPY NEW YEAR

                                                        MALCOLM

Annotations:

1 Matson wired Lowry $100 on 21 December 1951 and airmailed a
   cheque for $350.

Beginning Yet Again: 1952 to 1957

The next moment the mountains and forests were sweeping past them again on the same wide arc as before, though in a contrary direction. Beginning: beginning again: beginning yet again. Off we go! Once more they were bound for Gabriola.

(October Ferry to Gabriola)

THIS LAST PERIOD of Malcolm Lowry's life is characterized by repeated beginnings, many of which were false starts, and two dramatic endings. With the wisdom of hindsight, it is now difficult to see these years as anything other than a slow downhill slide punctuated by losses – the loss of Albert Erskine, the loss of a publisher's contract, the loss of Dollarton and the pier, the loss of health, peace of mind, the ability to write, and the loss of life. But throughout all this 'misery-grisery,' as he liked to call it, Lowry struggled with his fiction and his despair.

1952 started badly. Confined to a Vancouver apartment for the winter months, Lowry waited for news of a new contract. He drank, wrote increasingly anxious letters to Robert Giroux, the editor with Harcourt, Brace who had expressed interest in his work, and he sent desperate telegrams to Harold Matson. Without the money owed him in France and England he was running dangerously low on cash, and the months of separation from Albert Erskine, who was now at Random House, weighed heavily on his mind and heart.

When he finally received word (see his telegram, **506**, to Erskine) that Harcourt, Brace could not offer him a contract and were releasing him from any obligation, Lowry was both angry and elated. On the one hand the baffling silence from Giroux, followed by formal rejection, were serious blows to his precarious self-confidence; on the other, the

Harcourt, Brace decision meant he was free to go with Erskine if Random House could be persuaded to take him on. From the start of 1947 to the end of 1951 he had been drifting without a contract (despite the success of *Volcano*) and thus without a reliable income from his work. Although there had been projects – *Dark as the Grave*, *La Mordida*, the filmscript of *Tender Is the Night* – he had completed and published nothing new except a few poems, one review, one story, and one essay. *Under the Volcano* had continued to dominate his life in the form of translations, dreams of films, and more Mexican fiction about being *under* under the volcano! In short, Lowry had little to show for these years, and it is small wonder that he was looking frantically for direction and encouragement.

When word of a contract with Random House reached him at Dollarton on April Fool's Day 1952, Lowry was ecstatic. But even in elation he had doubts about his ability to meet deadlines, concerns about buying extra time should he need it, and worries about where to focus his writing efforts. Again in hindsight, the decision to work on completing and polishing the stories for *Hear us O Lord*, rather than *Dark as the Grave* or *Lunar Caustic*, may have been a strategic mistake because it carried him straight into the stormy seas of *October Ferry to Gabriola*. It was, however, a decision in favour of a new beginning that signalled an important break with the past.

Through 1952 and 1953 Lowry laboured on these stories and watched in alarm as *October Ferry* grew into a recalcitrant novel. From all this work only two stories would be published before his death: 'Strange Comfort Afforded by the Profession' (1953) and 'The Bravest Boat' (1954). There are several fascinating letters from this period, especially to Erskine, about writing and the creative process, but the general impression conveyed by the letters is one of confusion and distress. Accidents, largely the result of drinking, precipitated excuses, which led to guilt, accusations, and missed deadlines, which led to more drinking. This downward spiral gathered momentum when Lowry received Erskine's 6 January 1954 letter informing him that Random House was suspending contract payments and that he, Albert, was not enthusiastic about what he had seen of work in progress. Ironically, Lowry had foreseen delays and the need to suspend payments, and he had written to Erskine on 4 January 1954 (letter **600**) asking for just such an arrangement: 'I am in a position to propose what I have long planned under the circumstances . . . that your monthly payments to me be suspended for a period of time.' But the letters crossed in the mail, and Lowry was devastated by what he interpreted as a unilateral, complete, and *personal* rejection.

After this, he withdrew into a severe depression. The wounds caused by the rift with Erskine never completely healed, and with increased civic pressure to evict the Dollarton 'squatters,' Lowry felt threatened and abandoned on all sides. By May 1954 he and Margerie were planning to leave – not for good, mind you, *never* for good, but for some substantial, unspecified period of time. Lowry wrote to David Markson and Conrad Aiken announcing the forthcoming move to Sicily in search of new beginnings, but the truth of the situation was more aptly summed up in his farewell (**618**) to Einar and Muriel Neilson 'with love, grief, agony, joy . . . Aug 24, 1954 (that day of wrath & hope).' When Lowry left Vancouver on 30 August 1954, he knew it was an ending.

His New York farewell encounter with Aiken was a pathetic fiasco, and his meeting in Milan with Giorgio Monicelli, his Italian translator, though friendly was unproductive. Sicily was an unmitigated disaster, as Douglas Day and Gordon Bowker have shown. Very few letters survive from late 1954 and 1955, but those that do speak for themselves. In a postcard (**625**) to Markson from Syracuse, Lowry quotes Sophocles (and himself from the first epigraph to *Volcano*): 'only against death / shall he cry in vain.' By July 1955 he was back in England, where he staged several more attempts to begin again. Indeed, despite his repeated hospitalizations and Margerie's recurrent health problems during 1956, he slowly resumed work on *October Ferry to Gabriola* in the peaceful rural surroundings of Ripe, Sussex. He also renewed old friendships with John Davenport, Jimmy Stern, and the Churchills, and he established a cordial relationship with his physician, Dr Michael Raymond.

It would be a considerable mistake to assume that Malcolm Lowry had given up hope of a productive, creative life. Published here for the first time is a series of letters to Margerie from the fall of 1956 with almost daily news of his work on *October Ferry*, and an extraordinary 22 February 1957 letter (**705**) to David Markson that bursts with literary allusions, Oedipal reflections, and writerly advice. During these months, however, Lowry's work on *October Ferry* was pulling him back to Dollarton with new intensity. He longed for the beach; he mourned the loss of his beloved pier; and he missed Harvey Burt and Jimmy Craige. Even a June visit to the English Lake District only served to remind him of Dollarton.

On the night that he died – 'by misadventure' – in the upstairs bedroom of The White Cottage in Ripe, Lowry was trying to work, presumably on *October Ferry to Gabriola*. We know that he was drinking, that he and Margerie quarrelled savagely, and that by the morning of 27 June 1957 he was dead. We do not *know* that he committed suicide, or that Margerie killed him, but it is safe to say, with Dylan Thomas, that whatever happened, he did not 'go gentle into that . . . night,' but raged 'against the dying of the light.'

493: To Clarisse Francillon

P: unknown
PP: *Lln* 5:206

[Vancouver, B.C.]
[early January 1952][a]

Carissima Clarisse:

The new book I told you about is a collection of short stories entitled: Hear us o Lord from Heaven thy Dwelling Place. I think you will really love some of the stories. Though Hal so far never managed to sell any to any magazine whatsoever – whence our poverty. On the other hand, Harcourt & Brace in New York declare that they can be rated among the best ones they have ever read and they would like to publish them in one volume. So I still may write one of those famous prefaces for America. I'll say: No one of these damned stories ever appeared in any of your Godawful magazines in this sickening country. So I really can't see why you should want to read them now. Good night. Malcolm Lowry. This is all contradiction and makes my head swim. I have finally drawn an outline of the Voyage that Never Ends.[1]

We hope to come to France very soon. For the time being, we are living in the city of Vancouver – a rotten hole full of stool pigeons – toilets – policemen – ill manners – tedium – hypocrisy – spy hotel managers – repression – falsehood – and – brutality . . .[2] I hate it no less than hell. Sometimes I even hate the Canadians too – at least their scandal mongering authorities. Calvin's Geneva and Tory England would have seemed cheerful compared to this place where one is forbidden to advertise a symphony concert on a Sunday. And yet they still use the penalty of the lash and sentence 15 year old children to hang for rape – as was the case only recently[3]

Malcolm

Annotations:

1 Lowry drew up the outline of the *Voyage* in October-November 1951; see his 23 November 1951 letter (**479**) to Harold Matson.
2 The Lowrys had moved into the city on about 30 December 1951. They stayed in a hotel for a few days before moving into a West End apartment on Gilford Street.
3 Lowry is referring to the Sykes case; see the editorial introduction to his October 1951 letter (**473**) to Margerie.

Editorial Notes:

a The only surviving copy-text of this letter is the French translation by Clarisse Francillon published in *Les Lettres nouvelles* 5 (1960): 206. It carries neither inside address nor date but can be dated approximately from internal evidence; see annotation 3. This translation back into English has been prepared by Suzanne Kim.

494: To Einar Neilson

P: UBC(ms)   [Vancouver, B.C.]
    [early January 1952]ᵃ

Dear Einar:

A thousand thanks for so generously and sportingly and immediately answering our s.o.s and I hope it did not put you to too much inconvenience. What happened at this end has just been a series of crossed wires & inexplicable mischances that one can't explain in a few words. You may wonder why I didn't wire my publishers since they owe me money I am expecting at any moment and the reason for that is the most inexplicable of all: *we have − Christ help us − a feud with the C.P.R telegraph office people* who last December held up some money from America that was wired us for nearly ten days: when the mistake was discovered they gave us $68 too much which we had spent before they or we discovered that mistake too and when we discovered it, having also been inconvenienced to more than the amount that had been wired in the first place, we refused to return it save in our own good time: poetic justice, as you will admit, since if we'd wanted to be lousy we could have had half of them fired for not making any effort to notify us at Dollarton there was any money there.

Actually I've just sold a book in America to Harcourt Brace (about America's richest firm) and logically speaking on paper we've never been better off.[1] But the contract has been delayed because they wanted to draw up a contract, not for one book but several. Because France had promised us half a million francs on the Volcano we'd told them − the publishers − not to hurry but meantime it turned out France is not only not fixing to send that money right off but is fixing to devalue the franc. Ethically speaking we couldn't wire over our agent's head to the publisher for cash because he is in a sense a new publisher we don't know and we didn't want to wire to our agent because this would considerably depreciate the advance when it arrived.

[breaks off unsigned]

Annotations:

1 Lowry is exaggerating Robert Giroux's interest in *Lunar Caustic* and *Hear us O Lord*. In his 11 December 1951 letter to Harold Matson, Giroux had sounded optimistic about a contract, but on 10 March 1952 he wrote Lowry to say that no contract would be forthcoming.

Editorial Notes:

a   This pencil holograph is on the verso of an annotated page of typescript
for *October Ferry to Gabriola* (UBC 16:15). It can be dated from internal
evidence; see annotation 1.

The following letters to Robert Giroux (**495**, **496**, **498**) *provide eloquent*
evidence of Lowry's acute need to communicate with the man he thought would
be his new editor. He had established a close relationship with Albert Erskine
based upon trust and respect, and the prospect of losing that connection and
friendship left him feeling bereft and unsure of his direction. He was thus in a
vulnerable frame of mind, beset with conflicting desires, when he decided to write
to Giroux about his work. These three letters reveal many interesting side-lights
on Lunar Caustic — *the personal experiences that lay behind the events in the*
novella, some of the sources of inspiration for the text (in Expressionism, for
example), and his ideas for integrating the story into The Voyage That Never
Ends. *When, after a long silence, Giroux finally replied with the news that*
Harcourt, Brace would not publish him, Lowry understandably felt personally
rejected.

495: To Robert Giroux

P: UBC(ts)
PP: *SL* 285-87

1075 Gilford St,
Apt. #33,
Vancouver, B.C.,[1]
Canada
11 January 1952

Dear Mr Giroux:[2]
    First let me apologise for my silence.
    I hope you don't think it was due to ingratitude or improvidence.
Also, right off, I want to thank yourself, Jimmy Stern, and Jay Leyda
most sincerely for the superlative Christmas present of the latter's monumental Melville book.[3] This is a triumph, a thing of obviously
permanent importance. It is a triumph in many other ways too. Tell J.L.
[Jay Leyda] I shall write him the first moment I can. (As a matter of fact,
his technique of cross-references spatially divided would be the only
adequate vehicle by which I could express what has been happening
here.) Give my love to him and Jimmy.
    Now I want to thank you for so generously and promptly making it
possible for me to have some money through Harold Matson.[4] In fact

this has tided us over a very hard spot indeed, though a most peculiar circumstance surrounds it at this end: it arrived here by wire on the morning of the 21st, but it was not until the afternoon of the 27th that we were informed of its existence. The fault, or aberration, lies somewhere between the Canadian Pacific Telegraphs and our local postmaster, each of whom blame the other.

One reason I needed some money immediately was that if I was to get any work done at all this winter I knew I should have to get into town and into an apartment, for life in Dollarton in these winter months is – or has become of late years – largely a matter of cutting wood and merely managing to stay alive and keep from freezing. Moreover it was proving too hard on my wife's health. Meantime, a series of gales, hurricanes, blizzards, snowstorms, icestorms, sub-zero temperatures (the house has only cardboard inside walls, a small cookstove, but no heater) and general acts of God (which calmed down yesterday only to descend tonight with redoubled force from the Yukon) made it impossible to commute from Dollarton in order even to search for an apartment in town. The flooding inlet with gales at the January high tides almost swept the house away altogether – you can imagine how kindly the former threat struck one under these circumstances. Somehow we slugged it out, without having to abandon the house at the very highest tides and it is still O.K. (and safe with only half tides at present) though all in all there has been much havoc and anxiety. Finally we managed to find the only vacant hotel room in Vancouver 15 miles distant (it being full of wild loggers here for the holidays) packed up all my work – or what seemed the most important part thereof – into various brief cases and Mexican shopping bags and suitcases, moved in and started to look for an apartment through the continuing gales, snows, etc., during which my wife got flu, but it by now being after January first nothing in the way of an apartment was to be found – why go on? We did find one, and here we are, more than ready to get down to work, though it is not easy since I have not been able to do any since almost mid-November.

During this hildy-wildy situation (as it were 'Under' Eridanus) I have begun this letter fifty times, for I not only wanted to thank you, but I felt a compelling need to be in communication with you, in some way, before I could begin work again.

In this connection, first of all, I want to say how sincerely grateful I am for your words of praise and that you wish to publish me.[5] I certainly want to be worthy of this.

There are a lot of things I want to discuss though, matters peripheral or central to the work – not least, I'm not sure what to do next, it has been a sad disappointment not to have sold individually any of the stories in Hear Us Oh Lord etc. – before I can properly go on, yet I would like very much to complete it and publish it before finally getting down to The Voyage. Perhaps you could suggest to me how many more stories seem to you advisable to be finished and included in this volume? Yet our recent perils – and coming at what a time! – suggest to me that I owe it to you to get you a copy of even imperfect drafts or half intentions to cache away, which in any case might not one day be without value in themselves and in any case also would have been and would be pretty disastrous for me to lose without a copy. Of Lunar Caustic, I possess 2 versions, neither of them final: and I think a copy of these ought to be made and sent to you before I go on with Hear Us Oh Lord, so my wife will begin tomorrow to make these copies.

Re Albert Erskine: you will understand my position. I am deeply fond of him personally, so that the break hurts. Also I owe him a lot. I don't know which is troubled more, my heart or my conscience. On the other hand I don't wish you to believe that I was swayed by any financial extremity, even though that extremity existed: it was a fully thought out decision. And of course I am likewise proud to be with you.

Anyhow we are now settled in the city until April first, having worked for three years in the wilderness; I have not been to a cinema for seven months or had a haircut or seen any kind of conveniences for some time so that civilization seems almost as strange to me as if I were Alley Oop. All in all I could not blame civilization refusing to give me a pew after I'd made such an ugly face at it. And that the events of the last month might compose, as a matter of fact, one of the best stories I could ever write does not make it easier to start again by reworking something old in a new place. (I am one of those fellows who when not deeply engaged in work immediately find themselves on the receiving end of some twenty works) In short it is difficult enough to start again at all after our siege though it will be done. The problem is where to begin.

These are a few of the things that perplex me. But first may I know if it is yourself I may address, not to say to whom I may unburden myself, in an editorial capacity? Or if I have not the honour, to whom may I speak? For I must speak at some length.

With every good wish to yourself and many thanks again.

Ever sincerely,

Malcolm Lowry

Annotations:

1 In 1952, 1953, and 1954 the Lowrys moved into Vancouver for the winter months. The Kenmore Apartments at 1075 Gilford Street in

the downtown West End, was the first of these winter retreats; see
Salloum (42-43).

2 Robert Giroux (1914-) was an editor with Harcourt, Brace, the publishing house that obtained the option on Lowry's future work when
Eugene Reynal joined the firm.

3 Lowry had received Jay Leyda's *The Melville Log: A Documentary Life of
Herman Melville* (New York: Harcourt, Brace, 1951), which is now in
his library (UBC Box 54).

4 On about 20 December 1951 Giroux wired what Lowry took to be an
advance on the stories for *Hear us O Lord from heaven thy dwelling place.*

5 See Giroux's 11 December 1951 letter to Harold Matson (*Selected
Letters*, 445-46).

496: To Robert Giroux

P: UBC(ts)   [1075 Gilford St]
                                               [ca 15 January 1952]

[Dear Mr Giroux:]ᵃ

Thank you very much for bearing with me. I felt you would be
bound to be hard pressed at this period and not have an opportunity to
write me. Don't feel pushed to reply to this either. But I thought we
should get in touch, so I took the responsibility: also I thought you
should have this material as a precaution, apart from wanting you to see
it, especially since you wanted to see it.[1] Well, naturally. Likewise that
of The Ordeal – as much as possible, Dark as the Grave, Eridanus, and
La Mordida: – this though will be mostly raw material, but there is an
enormous amount of it, and largely irreplaceable, so we should have
copies safe; of course I have copies here, but only God and the fishermen protect our house, though the weather might cut our friends off,
so in this way we shall be quite secure. What I mean is that of course I
have all this stuff with me safe at the apartment: only the poems and a
few minor things have been left in the house, though at that we are
counter-insured by the number of notebooks left there from which the
stuff here has been transcribed: the danger was to have all this in one
place in this combustible and storm and flood-ridden country. Of genuine flood of the river type we are in no danger, so all is O.K. now. I
am deeply grateful that you made it possible for me to have that money
through Matson. As a consequence, after our tribulations, things could
not have worked out more luckily. We have an admirable apartment in
the old English part of 'Enochvilleport,' hard by the park and the scene
of the Bravest Boat.[2] It is quiet and one can devote all one's time to
work. At first the lack of stormy movement outside the windows, lack
of noise under the house, lack of sea (but not of mountains), odd aspect

of refrigerator, strange warmth, lack of forest, lack of our familiar pioneer responsibilities, almost drove me crazy, but now I'm very grateful which is a story in itself: certainly one should 'withdraw and return.' Even Thoreau did not stick it as long as we:[3] apart from a few months in Mexico, a week in New York, a month in Haiti and a year in Europe, we've stuck the wilderness – and loved it – for 12 years, with only one other break when the house burned down when we went to Ontario for a few months, which was tougher still, without the advantages. Another year and I would probably have been an irretrievable hermit! As it is, we can return in April, when we can work there, and like it better than ever. I won't try to describe the way we live in Dollarton-Eridanus: obviously we must love it, or we wouldn't live there, and it is marvellous. But never have I known the inlet to behave in such a wicked and ominous and threatening manner as recently, the tides were the highest in history this New Years, and also the cold and storms the worst in recorded history. It is something to wake up and see the tide so high it is actually level with the bottom of your windows, with a hundred foot long uprooted floating fir tree menacing you, and to feel the whole house rocking when your very foundations begin to lift, (everything settled down finally and we were very proud of our building in the end.) I am reminded that Eridanus also means the Po. The easterly gales were so persistent at the full moon tides the tide never had a chance to go out, so that each high tide with the water piled up became phenomenally higher than it should be. However all is well now: and 'Kristbjorg' and 'Quaggan' – about the sole remaining inhabitants besides ourselves – guard the house, as we guard theirs in similar (though I have never known quite similar) circumstances.[4] I thought of posting all this to you yesterday. But I decided to sleep on the notes I made for Lunar Caustic.[5] I hope you don't hate it. I see that one could reasonably feel from this way of presenting it, that it was the kind of book that left 'an unpleasant taste in one's mouth.' But I believe its unpleasantness to be beside the point, if it is done right, and is made an integrated work of art. It could even be, unless I am very self-deceived – if one is hanging on at the same time to the highest kind of thing – that a work like this could fill a gap. Anyhow I've often thought that modern literature suffers from not being anchored deeply enough on the one hand, or made fast high enough on the other. To myself, these secret inadmissible shames, these unpronounceable words, and unvintageable anxieties, which I would try to bring out into the open in Lunar Caustic, might have real value, though that would be only in proportion to the book's artistic merit. In other words, I tend to believe in it. But I will cease being pleased with myself. For one thing I haven't written it yet. However there is just sufficient truth in the 'unpleasantness' charge that I feel it would be a bad idea supposing you see any hope in the book, to publish it next. I suggest next year, after Hear Us Oh Lord. Otherwise people would say that this damn fellow can't write about anything but drunkenness etc. and that would not be fair to you or me. So I would propose, having got this off, to get down to the largely more healthy and sunlit Hear Us Oh Lord, – first to finish the stories that are uncompleted, then, if you approve, to try and round off that volume. Meantime – in our spare time – we shall be making and sending you a copy of the material of the Ordeal, Dark as the Grave, Eridanus, La Mordida. The sea novel [*Ultramarine*] that should eventually precede Caustic will have to wait for a while: it is a separate problem. In the book that was published 20 years ago in England & fortunately & simultaneously died there's probably scarcely an original line. Everything is derived, pastiche, hash. In short it is one of those pieces of juvenilia that their authors would like to buy up all the copies of and burn and then forget that they had written. But its form, *drang*, the experience that informed it is a different matter: it can be a first class work if I totally rewrite it on the basis of what is truly mine in the experience. I thought of rechristening it False Cape Horn. Re Lunar Caustic, I have this much further to say. I think calling the protagonist, creating him as the Earl of Thurstaston a wonderful idea finally, especially if he is on the side a hot musician.[6] Train of thought is: Earl Hines, Duke Ellington, King of Jazz, etc. I had forgotten Count Basie. He could be the son – that is when it's got in line with the logic of Burke's peerage, because I've forgotten the rank of the gent an Earl's properly supposed to be the son of – of someone (albeit thoroughly disguised), like Lord Kylsant, or the Duke of Manchester, both of them crooks, and still serving time, at least the former, unless he's dead.[7] (The Royal Mail Steam Packet Co. scandals.) Manchester, Duke of poor devil, is an impoverished drunk, who spends most of his time in the bridewells his ancestors had built. Something like that. Thurstaston could have been farmed out in youth to more bourgeois relatives and not being at the 'best' schools – though he goes to Cambridge – his title could have proved a curse. Maybe his wife marries him for the title but has long since rightly decided that there is more hope should she marry an American, especially since perhaps she can keep the title, even if they are divorced. This makes the identity between Garry and the protagonist even more complete and ironic: the protagonist's father is in prison too. Moreover I believe that Thurstaston takes refuge in the hospital because he feels himself, almost as if by force majeure, or poetic justice, being driven to commit suicide himself, his life having become a sort of eternal 'to be or not to be': actually he has too much final guts – nonetheless I perceive great drama in a man being confronted at every turn of the wheel with this kind of temptation, exacerbated by the feeling that this is what he is *supposed* to do; – he feels himself a character again, as if at the mercy of some transcendental gloomy novelist. There should be a baseball scene on the roof of the hospital: and a horrendous hydrotherapy scene in the basement, though in the reverse order: if I analyse him 'in terms of each situation, and not in a vacuum,' – as someone said – these geographical polarities should be helpful. However the best thing to do now is to cork in the daemons of Caustic and let the thing itself ripen, as Ryder says, and get down to Hear Us Oh Lord.[8] First I have to finish the two long unfinished stories, meantime trying to resist working on Battement de Tambours, inspirations for which are fairly hurtling about the apartment, though perhaps I can do both. And there are the shorter things, and October Ferry, which is not short either. Re Through the Panama, Pierre Charon is the real name of a real man who was on the boat and really was the Norwegian Consul in Papeete so I suppose I ought to change his Christian name and make him the different Consul of some other Antipodean islands; it would be a little hard to change the name Charon, but I guess that would be unnecessary. (In fact, if I did, there would be no point in his being there.) Anyhow he was a swell guy who probably wouldn't give a hoot. There seem some unnecessarily vindictive remarks about other writers in Panama too, which should go. And I have wondered if it too much resembled The Crack Up, which partly gave me the idea. On the other hand of course The Crack Up resembles Butler's note books etc.[9] And there are a few other minor points I'll take up in a later letter. Meantime I thought I should put the double whammy, as the saying is, on my hesitations in regard to the Caustic material. So here it is. With many thanks again and kindest regards,

Yours sincerely,

Malcolm Lowry

Annotations:

1 Although he had not heard from Giroux since receiving the latter's 11 December 1951 letter to Harold Matson and the cheque that enabled him to move into Vancouver, Lowry is sending Giroux copies of 'The Last Address' and 'Swinging the Maelstrom' with this letter and preparing to send copies of draft material for *The Voyage That Never Ends*.

2 Enochville Port is Lowry's name for Vancouver in 'The Bravest Boat.'

3 Thoreau spent two years at his small cabin near Walden Pond.

4 The characters of Kristbjorg and Quaggan are based upon the Lowrys' fisherman friends on the beach, Whitey (Miles Went) and Sam Miller.

5 See letter **498** to Giroux with the heading 'LUNAR CAUSTIC.'

6 Although Lowry did not live to rewrite *Lunar Caustic* using the name Thurstaston, the choice is interesting because it is the name of a town

in the Wirral Peninsula, Cheshire, very near to the family home. During the fifties Lowry often drew upon early experiences and memories of the past for ideas and inspiration.

7 Earl Kenneth Hines (1903-83), Edward Kennedy 'Duke' Ellington (1899-1974), and William 'Count' Basie (1904-84) were Afro-American jazz musicians. To be an English earl one must be the eldest son of a duke or a marquis, who bestows this title as a courtesy. Owen Cosby Philipps, first Baron Kylsant, was a Welsh shipping magnate and member of the British House of Commons. He was convicted of fraud in the Royal Mail shipping scandal in 1931, passed less than a year in jail, and died in 1937. William Angus Drogo Montagu, ninth Duke of Manchester and member of another once distinguished family, was always in financial and personal trouble; he spent time in jail for fraud and died in 1947.

8 See Lowry's quotation of American painter Albert Pinkham Ryder in his 5 June 1951 letter (**459**) to Albert Erskine.

9 Fitzgerald's *The Crack-Up* (1945) is a miscellany of stories, notebooks, and letters. The autobiographical essay 'The Crack-Up' is narrated in the first person and presented in a series of dated entries or pieces. Samuel Butler (1835-1902) was a prolific English writer and satirist. *The Notebooks of Samuel Butler* (1916), edited by H. Festing Jones, is a collection of epithets, reflections, and witty philosophizings.

Editorial Notes:

a The copy-text carries neither inside address and date nor salutation. It comprises six pages of typescript foliated A to F with several pencil additions, cancellations, and other minor changes; Lowry has signed the letter in blue ink.

497: To David Markson

P: UBC(ms)

1075 Gilford St,
Apt. #33,
Vancouver, B.C.,
Canada
[15 January 1952][a]

Dear old Fellow:

I am touched beyond measure. It is obviously a marvellous piece of documentation & you know far more about that book than I do. I only wish me & it could, can be worthy of all the trouble & work you have gone to.[1]

But it has only just arrived! See above address. I hope to Christ you haven't been worried you received no ackowledgment.

I just had another book (tales) accepted & simultaneously we were driven temporarily by gales storms cold & acts of God from our little hut in the sea: we have had a real Flying Enterprise, in fact, what with trying to keep m.s & house safe.[2] And now I have to work like hell day & night & hence cannot give it the minute attention it deserves at present, even with best will in the world. Also it stimulates my mind in a way I cannot let it be stimulated when trying to concentrate on something else. Please understand & forgive. How much time have you before you must turn it in? Just in case there was something in it I might be able to help on, just in case I might be able to, though from what I have been able to absorb it seems excellent & I don't believe I could add anything. My wife, who worked right through the Volcano with me & hence is very sensitive to anything that is said about it, & is moreover a damn good critic, sat up all last night reading it & agrees & affirms that it is a marvellous job & just to show you that this isn't phoney she is damn well going to write you a note at the bottom of this letter to say so. Thank you for your other letter. Will reply. Meantime you have my blessings – & all good wishes, & the very best of luck to you, & thanks. Hold that note Roland!

Malcolm

Annotations:

1 David Markson sent Lowry a complete draft of his thesis on *Under the Volcano* in December 1951, but the holidays, the bad weather, and the Lowrys' move into Vancouver delayed their receipt of the manuscript until the new year.
2 *Hear us O Lord* had not been formally accepted by Giroux. The *Flying Enterprise* was the name of a freighter that sank in the north Atlantic on 10 January 1952.

Editorial Notes:

a The pencil holograph is undated, but Markson has added this date, presumably from the postmark. Margerie added her own note of congratulations at the bottom of the recto.

498: To Robert Giroux

P: UBC(ts)   [1075 Gilford St]
                                                 [ca 17 January 1952]

LUNAR CAUSTIC

Dear Mr Giroux:
    Though 'The Last Address' and 'Swinging the Maelstrom' – here

appended – have different titles they are simply different versions of Lunar Caustic. Or rather The Last Address (1936) can scarcely be called a version at all, can be looked on as simply the material from which I worked up 'Swinging the Maelstrom' ('39, 40, 41) – which even then had the alternative title of Lunar Caustic, at that time intended to play a sort of Purgatorio to the Volcano's Inferno. The reason I've copied out the earlier version in toto as well is because, looking at it, I perceived that it contained some material that should go into any final version and for that matter probably should not have been cut out of Swinging the Maelstrom, the more artifact version. This latter then is the one you're supposed to read, and *not* The Last Address, though you can cast an eye at The Last Address version if it interests you but please don't read it first, for it is a chaos and contains much of which I am ashamed in some ways. My idea in sending it to you to begin with was simply to have a copy of the material safe in your hands in case it got lost at this end or the author got lost or something or other. On the other hand while copying it it began to strike me that The Last Address did after all seem to possess certain artistic and even technical merits of a queer kind, particularly in the beginning few chapters following on the first, not possessed by Swinging the Maelstrom, which however may have other merits. (However that may be it gave me a very strange idea, possibly impractical, but certainly so far as I know original as I went along, that runs something as follows: if The Last Address were more integral than it is – though even its lack of integration might be a point, would be in any case part of the point – Last Address plus Swinging the Maelstrom plus Lunar Caustic might one day make an extremely interesting trilogy in itself; the material of the Address being so modified, reversed, counterpointed etc by Maelstrom that reading the second after the first gave one – or gave me – the effect of a strange kind of music: in fact perhaps it is basically a sort of music, the music of a work of art, however flawed and lousy, trying to integrate itself. In Lunar Caustic – the third one – you'd have the integration, the resolution. The repetitions would merely intensify the effect though no doubt it is not the kind of thing to be recommended during a paper shortage. Nonetheless the hellish theme, I felt, with its sense of repetition and repetition and repetition {I'm afraid, reading it through, that there is all too much repetition & repetition & repetition in this letter!} of the same sort of thing going on forever in the hospital, but with the protagonist and the protagonist's perception becoming clearer, the sense as of a spiral winding its way upward,[1] could make this an artistically valid and exciting creation if it could be done right, though no doubt some people would get very angry. Anyhow such an idea would be not yet)

The Maelstrom version, though, which is the one you are supposed to read, or read first, does, I think, possess integrity in itself the way it stands, as a work of art. Parts of it I must confess to you I absolutely love. I think you would find, if you experimented that it reads aloud pretty well, which is a test. Certainly it has been written with great care. But maybe it hasn't always been written with the right kind of care. In places all rhythm, personal voice, style – whatever that is – seems to have been compressed out of it by obeying some quite negative and visual touchstone of writing, such as that there should not be too many 'ands' or something: maybe there shouldn't, but it is a copy-book or journalistic principle. Similarly with its technique, which is often pretty poor, or not good enough especially at the beginning: and its very concision has in some places robbed it of a feeling of grief, catastrophe, the right kind of Grand Guignol that is sometimes in the first. Also it must strike you that it is insufficiently 'motivated' (I must explain that on one plane this doesn't worry me) though more motivated than the first. With all these faults though, where they are faults, I repeat that perhaps it could hold its own as a quite formiddable work of art, even if published much as it is. This certainly isn't true of the first version, which you will readily see should you read it, but first I think I should make some explanation of its inception even if not full or quite accurate, unless you are to think its author slightly cuckoo too. The Address is *not*, as a matter of fact, absolutely the first version, which version more or less, if tangentially, corresponded to experience. In this a journalist with an inveterate Zolaesque[2] and in fact healthy youthful appetite for sticking his nose into morgues and human interest stories of every type is at a cocktail party with a psychiatrist pal of his who promises to wangle him into his city hospital, and if only as an accident case into the alcoholic ward, where he'll really get himself a story, the doctor indeed being anxious that he should do this, for the more publicity he obtains for the ghastly conditions under which he works the better.[3] The next morning the journalist has a crashing hangover and doesn't feel like keeping his promise, moreover he has another tough assignment. During this assignment he keeps right on drinking and the next day waking up with a tougher hangover still feels even less like keeping it. However he has just enough drinks during the day that he becomes reckless or honest enough to call his own bluff and – though he can't reach his friend on the phone – goes to the hospital. However once the poor mug has got there he finds he can't get hold of his psychiatrist pal right off who has in any case not really believed for one moment that he had the guts to come. Moreover it being an old paranoic story that one is a 'friend of the doctor' the tough hombres at the hospital don't believe a word he says, and he gets just quarrelsome enough that before he has time to say 'newspaperman' they frisk him and shove him in the observation ward instead, which is however kept liberally supplied with an overflow of alcoholics, juvenile delinquents and other poor brutos. Here he lies incommunicado for a couple of days, suffering considerably himself, until his psychiatrist friend finds him. When he does he sportingly gives him more or less of an open sesame to the horrors of the place, which shatter him to such an extent that it changes him almost overnight from a reporter into a serious writer.

Well, this straighter and more obvious version was once going to be published, but the magazine changed its mind or its policy and it got lost, though I never lost the material; though naturally it was never published either as 'material.'[4] For one thing the element of good manners entered in. I woke up to the fact that I was an Englishman and in fact I have been uneasy several times in pursuing the work during critical times lest it be construed as a slap in the eye at America. This, needless to say, it certainly is not, though its harder to explain what its real intention is. From the personal point of view I had travelled about the world as a sailor so extensively without a passport before I was twenty that I had practically lost all sense of national barriers and had almost come to look on the world as a citizen thereof and its inhabitants as one happy or unhappy family. Devoted since boyhood to America, and married now to an American, I practically think – and thought of myself – as a kind of American, even though Canadian, English and what-not. My role therefore could not be less that of one who lets off a blast against conditions in American madhouses etc. with the object by extension of impugning the American ethos. I know I don't have to say this to you, but still. Nor has it anything to do with the improvement of such conditions per se so though naturally one might like to see them improved, one deplores the tragedy (but still why not Canadian or English or Liberian madhouses?) and it might enter into the matter for dramatic reasons. But undoubtedly they have – and in any case its none of my business on this plane – been improved etc. etc. (The scene is not a madhouse either but an observation ward, a distinction which doesn't seem to have been too clear in my own mind.) No: the attempt seems to have been to find some image of the eternal underworld, of hell on earth, where the point is not so much the conditions as the *condition*: the former may be ameliorated but the latter, however modified locally, will always pertain more or less somewhere in the world, in short a condition of permanent human suffering and tragedy unredeemable finally by any merely social or humane or material enlightenment: please forgive this lousy and pretentious way of phrasing it which isn't exactly what I mean to say either: 'what is above is like that which is below' – the suffering, the hospital, have their counterparts elsewhere. Perhaps these people are being punished for the evil in our own hearts and they are in truth the caryatids that hold up the world from below, and their infernal habitation has its divine complement in a Trappist monastery. Possibly their condition, even if redeemed in this world, would pertain in another. Or maybe the whole thing has a yet more infernal counterpart in the poor old Consul's Qliphoth, the world of shells.[5] But these things are as yet unclear in my mind and sound in any case too pretentious expressed here like this. All I wanted to do here was to explain how a character like Lawhill – should you read the first and rougher version – came to be created, or rather not to be created. The answer is very simple: I wanted to get away from myself and that obvious journalist idea and having an incurably ham-terror-romantic side (also a theatrical side – I saw it, and still can see it, as a sort of expressionist play a la Georg Kaiser) I thought it would be amusing to create a sort of bonafide half lunatic an amnesiac who was a drunk too. (Above all else I wanted to create a drunk and here I was more successful, though he transferred himself to the Consul) The results otherwise of course are deplorable, the madness and amnesia on his side just deliberate ham, a kind of forced insanity, his identity with Melville unconvincing, and Rimbaud simply immature and unpleasant surrealising, and the story itself catches a multiple schizophrenia when despite my poor efforts – and I mean they really are poor in this version so far as he is concerned – the crusading journalist comes right back again. On top of this like the fat boy in Pickwick[6] I seem to have determined to make the reader's flesh creep (this the piece certainly ought to do elsewhere, although in effect this part is just boring) by piling on every other kind of neurosis not merely into the situation but upon the story itself. The psychiatrist is named Claggart, after the homosexual in Billy Budd;[7] and it would seem that neurosis even wins the day, for it turns out that the psychiatrist is probably a homosexual and Lawhill, wrongly suspected of a quasi-homosexual relationship with a juvenile delinquent (symbolically really himself) which actually was – it is implied – a purely normal, if pathetic, friendship. This may certainly be and is intended to be the truth, though it is a little hard by this time to believe in anything normal, or abnormal for that matter, about Lawhill (though of course no sooner have I written this than I read of a case in this evening's newspaper about a drunk brought into the general hospital in Vancouver who has turned out after two days to be both amnesiac and aphasiac, though I have not read that he thought he was a ship) A truce to this. The version is sent to you mainly for precaution for the material involved (unless there is anything in my other idea for some day about the trilogy within other trilogies) – otherwise it has been copied out that I might turn a light again upon its buried motives, discover how why or where such material managed to get itself fouled up and generally look upon it with a creative psychologist's eye for the sake of Lunar Caustic. And that from the two you might have a better idea of Caustic than from the one. I haven't said so much about its virtues but it has some, perhaps, and if so, you will see them. But naturally I didn't want you to think I was Lawhill. Not much use accepting a book by him! (Even so, my God, what would Mr Chips say?)[8]

Swinging the Maelstrom then, is the one I'd be awfully grateful if you'd judge the potentialities of Lunar Caustic on. I've said I felt it to be an integrated – if insufficently motivated – thing and I can't help feeling it's a work of art as it stands. Even so it could be improved by the restoration of some stuff in The Last Address – particularly re Garry's stories, the rattle snake murder horror and a little of the realistic business in the stupid dialogue chapter which could be put back – not the dialogue but the business – in another form. I have to say that Battle's song about the Titanic is a bonafide piece of American folk lore that is my own discovery taken down right in the mouth of the inferno so we don't have to be beholden to a music company or any anthology of folk songs for it.[9] Though it may exist in another form, if so I'd be interested to find out how it differs. The Address Titanic song is more complete than Caustic's. Undoubtedly there are other songs about the Titanic though this is the only one I've ever heard, and I might bet it's the only Negro one. Of course it might be I'd only discovered something as well known as Casey Jones and that would be a pity.[10] I don't feel that Maelstrom dates, even after all these years: albeit it should be deliberately dated just the same in 1936. Anyway, I hope you think there's some hope in it. In it Lawhill is now Bill Plantagenet, as you will see, still a bit of a pose, but a much sincerer character. The Melville identification turns up again (something that would make me blush before Mr Leyda and I hope he never sees, but there it is) – and again it is used neurotically and I can see also betrays some ignorance on my side. It corresponds, however, to nothing I hope neurotic in me and in fact his continual emergence is merely the result of a very long standing friendship and admiration for the old gent. I dare say that in those days I felt that his works could do with a bit of a boost – the least a fellow seaman from Liverpool could do. It seems a bit anticlimactic now. In fact almost anything is an anticlimax after Jay Leyda's opus.[11] Therefore, but not for this reason, this Moby Dick part of it would be reduced to a minimum in Lunar Caustic; though it would not be entirely absent (it is a clue, for me, to something else also) you will have observed (if you have read Address) that there is some slight ethic progression on Plantagenet's side as over his vis-a-vis Lawhill. Lawhill seems merely to return to the womb, fully identified with Garry. Plantagenet makes up his mind to fight, as he thinks, for humanity in the shape of the Spanish Loyalists (but on the Mar Cantabrico, alas, will be captured by fascists).[12] Both these people, the one 'American,' the other English, are presented as neurotics, Lawhill indeed as almost completely ga-ga: actually they are not much more than actors, Lawhill indeed being an actor without a character, or one who has forgotten his part. Or you could say that Plantagenet isn't much more than a 'noises off' man, or even a musical accompaniment. Before I go on to say that in Lunar Caustic the attempt would be to draw a rounded character for a protagonist in fact a normal human being who, while through no mundane fault of his own, has got himself nevertheless into a situation fully as overtly catastrophic and tragic as that of Garry's, I'd better explain what I meant when I said that on one plane, so far as Maelstrom was concerned, I didn't care about its lack of this element, lack of 'motivation', objective co-relative etc. I have had to write this letter though in order to rediscover this buried intention on my side. Weird though it may sound, it seems that I actually had an ambition to write an indigenously American book. This doesn't sound very complementary when you consider where I went to look for the material, but if you regard it in another way I hope you can see that on the contrary it is due to long and incessant brooding upon and admiration for American forms of expression, if that doesn't sound too pretentious. I cannot escape from making this sound a bit grotesque, even adolescent, but that's a risk I have to take, and anyway, what the hell, I *was* an adolescent when I began this book. Just the same it is an exceedingly complicated thing to explain in a satisfactory manner, I am bound to oversimplify, and I don't even possess the terminolgy to explain it. In fact I better not try, or this letter will never get off. What it comes down to, though, is this (skipping my ideas on the novel per se, Howell's notion of the novel in which nothing should happen, D.H. Lawrence, Ulysses, God, the semicolon technique, plot, the novel as a presentation of life, as felt experience etc.)[13] why, I kept asking myself, were there so few novels or stories from which I received as lasting a pleasure as from such & such a simple jazz record? (I have forgotten to say that I was crazy and still am about American jazz). But to myself the best kind of American jazz, – which seemed to me full of sorrow and tragedy, as well as fury, exhilaration, youth, – comprised also a sort of literary criticism. Why shouldn't there be something in literature that exhilarates me as much as this break? Where is the rhythm, the momentum, in writing, that is comparable to this guitar bit? were the questions I asked myself. Why does this record do this to me and why do I never get fed up with it? Why can I play it over and over again? As many times as a Beethoven quartet, save that I'm not going to compare the two, since jazz isn't music perhaps so much as a form of expressionism, maybe actually more analogous to literature or poetry, than music? But where the heck in what passage or movement of prose can I find the selection, the discipline, unselfishness, spontaneity, freedom, and final concision, and form of this darn thing. As well as the chaos, mournfulness, despair? These qualities ought to be in prose, this rhythm ought to be manifest in any interpretation of the modern world: but it simply isn't. Why not? All right, jazz is shallow musically; all choppy attempts to 'ape' jazz in words fail of course. But one's words don't have to be shallow; the discipline, the form, might be useful. Of course this sounds – and is – affected. But I suppose it's natural to try and produce the same kind of pleasure one's received oneself. In any event, though I don't claim to have succeeded, I think this was part of the intention of Swinging the Maelstrom, whether it comes off or not. It is a sort of jazz record, and one part of me didn't care what it meant at all, so long as it obeyed its own peculiar touchstone, though it is not by any means orchestrated meaninglessly. Far from it. Yet it was what it *did*, I guess that was more important to me. And in places I feel I may really have succeeded. I can 'play the record' so to speak of Garry and Mr Kalowsky's conversation – or Garry's last words – and feel yes, that's exactly what they did say.[14] They couldn't have said anything else. That still moves me, just as when I wrote it. That has authority. For all that the records got cracked a bit, that's a good break. Jazz may be cold now and not hot but it's still O.K., and anything but corn. It may even be a child of the jazz age but after 16 years its still good. I know that this is pretty ridiculous: and that the ethical qualities I have assumed possible for prose (and this sounds silly in itself) are far from appearing. Nonetheless it is in this respect that Swinging the Maelstrom to some extent succeeds with me, though it could be better. At all events I am reminded that, despite having greatly matured in the meantime, I might spoil the whole thing if I forgot that I'd had this youthful and cockeyed idea at the bottom of my mind. By amplifying it, and rendering it a more plausible and motivated human drama, I could easily turn [it] into some unusual kind of hash quite forgetting the kind of weird discipline – and it is very much controlled whatever it may look like – that went into it. And in trying to correct such faults of prose and technique as I have mentioned I might forget the problems I'd solved even to get as far as the faults. However I don't think this need be the case and I believe I can have my cake and eat it. After all, in the Voyage That Never Ends, it ought to strike Wilderness, confronted by it, with far more resonance of meaning than it has. (The protagonist of Caustic would not be called Sigbjørn Wilderness but would be him just the same.) The final details of this – how to lead into it finally in the Voyage – I haven't worked out. But that could be taken care of later. Sufficient for the present if I can make the real right thing out of Lunar Caustic as an entity. It would require about another 100 pages. But if that proves too terrifying or beyond my strength or you think the idea is lousy it would be possible to improve Lunar Caustic in its own terms. I had even thought, if you disapproved, or you don't think it would make a larger novel, that the more modest version of it would make a good vis-a-vis to The Path to the Spring, in Hear Us Oh Lord. But I perceive that I have too many ideas, and even if they are all good, they might as well be bad or non-existent unless I can choose between them. The notes for the final form that it seems to me that Lunar Caustic should take follow after Swinging the Maelstrom. Meantime thank you for bearing with me and I'd be further grateful if for the moment you'd skip over the listing address on to the more buoyant Maelstrom.

[unsigned]

Annotations:

1 Lowry is echoing one of his favourite lines from Nordahl Grieg's *The Ship Sails On*: 'a new spiral had wound its way upward' (167).

2 A 'Zolaesque interest' is concerned with the naturalistic dark side of life, as was the French novelist Émile Zola.

3 Lowry always maintained that his 1936 stay in the psychiatric wing of New York's Bellevue Hospital was voluntary, but Jan Gabrial and Eric Estorick remember the incarceration differently; see *Malcolm Lowry Remembered* (101, 104-05).

4 Lowry had submitted a version of 'The Last Address' to Whit Burnett, the editor of *Story Magazine*, in 1936 through his New York agent Ann Watkins.

5 See Geoffrey's unsent letter to Yvonne in chapter 1 of *Under the Volcano*.

6 The 'fat boy' is Joe, Mr Wardle's young servant, in Charles Dickens' *Pickwick Papers* (1836-37).

7 John Claggart, the villain in Herman Melville's novella *Billy Budd*, is not overtly homosexual, but he is often read as having a homoerotic interest in Billy.

8 Mr Chips, the schoolmaster hero of James Hilton's novel *Goodbye, Mr Chips* (1934), is based upon W.H. Balgarnie, one of Lowry's teachers at the Leys School; see Vol. I, photograph 6.

9 Battle sings his song about the *Titanic* in part 7 of *Lunar Caustic*.

10 'Casey Jones' is a popular American folk-song. Composed in 1909, with words by T. Lawrence Seibert and music by Eddie Newton, it is about a locomotive engineer who died in a train crash.

11 This 'opus' is *The Melville Log*.

12 These references to the Spanish Loyalists and the *Mar Cantábrico* occur in the drafts for 'Swinging the Maelstrom' (UBC 15:7, 8, 12), but do not appear in the published version of *Lunar Caustic*.

13 William Dean Howells (1837-1920), the American novelist, editor, and critic, expounded a theory of realism as a truthful representation of the commonplace in his essays and fiction. Lowry's references to Lawrence, Joyce, and stylistic techniques constitute a tongue-in-cheek summary of the modern novel.

14 Garry's last words, spoken as he stands beside Plantagenet at the hospital window at the end of part 10 of *Lunar Caustic*, are: 'It only looks like spring, that's all.'

499: To Clemens ten Holder

P: UBC(ms) [1075 Gilford St]
ca 23 January 1952]

Dear old Clemens.

Hold that note, Roland.

I am putting a few finishing touches & notes of another kind on an opus entitled The Bravest Boat for you, this being the opening salvo of Hear Us Oh Lord from Heaven Thy Dwelling Place.[1] I shall be sitting up to-night caulking its seams & it shall go off this week without fail, if possible to-morrow.

We are living in an attic opposite a convent on whose roof is sitting a seagull.

I send you all our hopes & prayers, not forgetting St Jude & the Jungfrau.[2]

God bless you

Your friend
Malcolm

Annotations:

1 Lowry sent an autographed copy of 'The Bravest Boat' to ten Holder with the following inscription: 'For dear old Clemens, this story with much love from dein alter Malcolm.' The inscription has been reproduced in *Briefwechsel* (57), together with a German translation of Lowry's description of the story. The story first appeared in *Partisan Review* 21.3 (1954): 275-88.

2 St Jude, the first-century apostle and martyr, is known as the patron saint of hopeless causes. He is Lowry's favourite saint, and when his writing was going badly, Lowry would scrawl invocations to St Jude across the top of his drafts. *Jungfrau* means, literally, maiden or virgin in German, and *heilige Jungfrau* is the Virgin Mary.

500: To David Markson

P: UBC(ts)

1075 Gilford St,
Apt. #33 (if you've been
slap through your Dante
very lately?),[1]
Vancouver, B.C.,
Canada
23 January 1952

Dear David:

I have now read your thesis with great pleasure and excitement. As it did to my wife, it speaks to me very highly of your own abilities as a creative writer. It also tells me lots of things about the book which even if I hadn't or you hadn't written the latter it would encourage me to read.

In case this sounds too formal, I want to add that as a matter of fact it is about the only thesis of its kind I have ever read which seemed to me to be organized with an actual feeling of dramatic excitement working through its architectonics.

I don't say this because it's flattering to myself, but I can scarcely pay you a higher compliment after all. No creative writer really wants to write a goddamned thesis. Indeed in thinking of modern writers I am often reminded of Thoreau's settler who originally simply wanted to take shelter under the tree, then decided to cut the tree down and farm the land for profit, ended up by losing his freedom and owned by the farm, which yielded fewer and fewer crops.[2] The gradual creative declension of something like the Partisan Review, say, into a kind of incestuous gobbledygook, is a case in point: not that there is not instruction in the gobbledygook, or that it may not be a necessary process, there is, it probably is: but one suffers for the time taken, the sheer bloodlessness of the impulse, month after month, to achieve such dessications, and the enslavement by sterility it leads to.

On the other hand, you had to write a thesis, you put your back into it, and you have achieved something that is anything but bloodless and really is as thrilling as a kind of drama of the unconscious, so I most sincerely congratulate you. That your subject feels himself unworthy is beside the point, unless that involves a point on which its reception might be dubious. But I feel what you have written is good enough to transcend such an objection and I hope it brings you good luck.

If you can, let me see anything else you are doing, in the fictional or poetical line, and tell me what you contemplate.

What you say about the incident in your boyhood appals me.[3] How people can be such brutos is beyond me. Hugh's prejudices of course I made up out of whole cloth. I myself had a grisly childhood in some respects. In any case I could not feel more for you in such injustice. Of course it is a privilege to be persecuted but that doesn't make it feel any nicer.

Some minor points: cohabitations (p. 36 in your MS.) is cohabations – some sort of alchemical term. Originally this passage involved a pun. Among the cohabations – cohabitations! – of Faust. And on your page 68 did you miss that, after Senora Gregorio, the mother, 'Es inevitable la muerte del Papa' has a tripartite if not watertight meaning, sort of, that Papa is not only the Pope, and the Consul, but that the *inevitable* refers to the Consul as Oedipus: though in so far as the Consul himself was Papa he would be Laius. At least I think something like that was what the daemon was trying to mescall to mind when I wrote it.

Another point, David, while I think of it: le gusta esta jardin etc scarcely means 'nothing more than don't pick the flowers.' (p. 50 your MS.) or just (p. 70) that children be kept from destroying the garden: sure enough, in one way, that's all it implies, but even literally it translates itself as a far more serious injunction:

Do you like this garden

Which is yours?

See to it that [it] is thus: that your children do not destroy it!

In this there was intended to be a sort of imperative, an injunction that carried beyond the book, and that related to the garden as the world: – (though written *before* the atom bomb, as was the elements section in X): a black magician has all the elements in the universe against him. Man, with his atom bomb, has placed himself in that position and your humble servent, considering when he wrote it, in that of a sort of potted prophet.

Datta, Dayadhvam. Damyata.[4] (It may interest you to know that I had half written you a note ending with these words when I got your p.c. with Shantih Shantih Shantih on it.

Love from us both

Malcolm

P.S. other coincidences: namesake of S.S. Pennsylvania (Yvonne's ship Chap II) went down Pequod-wise here with all hands but one – who'd got off the ship at Seattle – same day as Flying Enterprise, a week before which my book, Hear Us Oh Lord From Heaven Thy Dwelling Place, was accepted with story in it Through the Panama, telling of a near shipwreck in a hurricane to Liberty Ship in exactly the same place as Enterprise.[5]

Annotations:

1 The numbers three (signifying the Holy Trinity) and thirty-three are of symbolic importance in *The Divine Comedy*, which has three books of thirty-three cantos and is written in terza rhyma. In the thirty-third canto of the *Inferno*, Virgil and Dante proceed through the ninth circle of hell and descend down Lucifer's body until they re-emerge at last into the world.

2 Henry David Thoreau's *Walden* (1854) is a meditation upon a life of freedom in nature in which he frequently reminds the reader not to become enslaved by ownership of the land.

3 At about the age of ten Markson, who grew up in Albany, New York, had been beaten up because he was Jewish. Lowry's sensitivity to anti-Semitism is evident in *Under the Volcano* in Hugh's sense of guilt and the insults hurled at the Consul before he is shot.

4 These words from the Hindu book of scriptural commentary Upanishad 5, 1, mean 'give, sympathize, control.' Lowry uses them to respond to Markson's use of *Shantih*, which is a formal ending to a Upanishad meaning 'the peace that passes understanding.' T.S. Eliot used these words from Upanishad 5 in *The Waste Land* and Lowry had borrowed *Shantih* for his own use in *Ultramarine*, where there are many echoes of Eliot; see his 1933 letter (41) to Conrad Aiken.

5 The *Flying Enterprise* and the *Pennsylvania* both sank on 10 January 1952, the former in the North Atlantic, the latter in the Pacific, north-west of Vancouver Island; see also Lowry's 27 February 1952 letter (504) to Jay Leyda.

501: To Gerald Noxon

P: Texas(ts)
PP: *LLN* 153–56

1075 Gilford St,
Dantesque no. Apt. 33,
Vancouver, B.C.,[1]
Canada
23 January 1952

My poor beloved old Gerald:

I am appalled by what you tell me.[2] I didn't know anything could hit me so hard either. And we couldn't understand it: when we wrote to Niagara, the letters were returned (I was trying to explain what had happened to the selections from Branches [of the Night], namely nothing, was not only not my fault but due to loyalty to yourself and Branches in the first instance, and untrustworthiness and carelessness and for all I know even professional jealousy on the part of another Canadian poet – (not A.J.M. Smith)[3] – that I was foolish enough to trust, in the second – I had to, because we had to take a boat weeks earlier than we thought,[4] but maybe all this will work out for the best in the end: still I figured you would have a right to blame me anyway, and in any case I felt you would have some cause to curse me and I was anxious to prove to you that this miscarriage was not due to any callousness in regard to Branches, and certainly no lack of deep respect for the work, which was the only thing that mattered here as between you and me, because they probably wouldn't have printed it right or something anyway and I was sufficiently punished by their printing something of mine I gave no permission for) – Oh Jesus, Oh Montreal, my poor old Gerald.[5] I guess that in some ways I am such a malevolent character, or have in certain senses suffered so much myself, that I almost take sadistic pleasure in hearing that something has happened to so-and-so, or that such and such has suffered, or what, what-not has come to pass with Herr So und so: that may indeed be because I feel in some sort it serves them right or because, vile hermit, I love so few people myself. I don't like to think that this is true, and perhaps it really isn't. But whether or not it certainly wasn't and isn't true here with you, for God's sake! No tithe of a ghost of satisfaction that my old companion's ship had hit a hurricane while mine was still riding pretty smoothly crossed my consciousness: no evil leer deformed or deforms one corner of my mouth while with the other I was or am pretending to be sorry. I am just horribly and agonizingly sorry, on every plane at once, that this has come to pass, & that you have had to suffer so much. Moreover I woke up to the fact that you are undoubtedly one of the best friends and indeed one of the only real friends I have – or we have – which simply makes it worse. We were so sad we left our 2 Christmas presents under the tree unopened and didn't open them. And in fact we haven't accepted it yet: it seems incomprehensible. I don't believe it, as you would say. Still, this is not the way to talk. We wish you all happiness in your new life with your wife, and happiness to her, and again and again to you both! We likewise have never ceased to think of you, always expect and look for your step on the rural stair, from time to time retrace the walks & the talks of a decade ago. Nothing is lost, nothing forgotten – not even your criticism of the madhouse story [*Lunar Caustic*] which I was working on when we received your news, and was just saying to myself: 'H'm, this is where old Gerald said it was lousy, the protagonist shouldn't take 2 steps forward, and two steps backward, at least not *again*. He was quite right. . . Everything is much the same, save we rebuilt the house as you know: and instead of the Volcano, there is Lunar Caustic and another volume of tales called Hear Us Oh Lord From Heaven Thy Dwelling Place. After the Manx fisherman's hymn. Longest story is about fishermen in Dollarton & our life there.[6] Several others are Canadian stories, & one, about a Liberty ship that loses her steering gear in cyclone approaching Scillies – practically same place as Enterprise & personal experience of ours, must have scared publishers stiff over New Years, since I haven't heard from them since they accepted book.[7] (But because Hitchcock died and Reynal merged into Harcourt Brace, to whom I was then bound, and my editor [Albert Erskine] went to Random House, and the pound went down, and no stories were accepted by magazines (by either of us, alack) and one could get no money out of Europe, save after endless red tape, we have had a hell of a time slugging it out the last 3 years. Sometimes on less than $80 a month, (I broke my back too in a fall from the pier, somehow recovered with no ill consequences) The winters have got as cold as Niagara here and once or twice – with our cardboard inside walls and no heater – we've damn nearly frozen to death; this is not just a figure of speech. It has happened several times in shacks further down. The typewriter likewise froze both this winter and the winter before last and once we didn't take our clothes off for seven weeks. The first time I have ever really encountered the SPECTRE at first hand, I guess. This time I swore I'd get Margie out into an apartment for the winter and Hear Us Oh Lord was accepted just before Christmas, they wired us an advance – and somehow, between the Canadian Pacific Telegraph Co and our bloody postmaster in Dollarton, – we didn't get the wire for a week. Something like what happened with the hundred bucks you sent for Margie. What really puts the double whammy on the irony is that the bloody postmaster, who is as you remember also the storekeeper, was dunning us to pay our bill to him while calmly sending back the money that was arriving for us. How much mail or cash or opportunities we may have lost we simply don't know. But I don't think he'll do it again. Shades of Kafka! This winter we just sat and shivered until the advance came. Well, it was an emergency advance on an advance, which made it all the worse to have it delayed. By which time it was too late to get an apartment for the winter in Vancouver, but we finally have: *no. 33*, Good luck it Dantesque number as I said, and Margie is delighted with it, and we shall work here till April, commuting from time to time to Dollarton (where we nearly got wiped out altogether too – like they feared would happen with old St Petersburg,[8] – in a freak high tide, with a continuing easterly gale) – Pardon all this)

I don't understand the bit where you say that you guessed you had it coming to you. In fact I can't even guess at the 'it.' I have always admired the way you grappled practically with this world and the guts you showed in regard to your responsibilities – certainly not easy when a creative artist, and the mode of grappling not sufficiently off center to art not to tempt you away from creating altogether; I can't think of a harder problem, especially when you always have the creative artist within one to say: But what about your responsibilities to *me*? And it had seemed to me that you were nobly on your way to solving it – even to make the tangential and necessary activity serve you. You speak of guts being taken out and replaced – do you speak figuratively, or psychoanalytically. Explain, or not, as you wish. Say little, much, or nothing. But whatever it is don't blame yourself too hard. Even Carlson steered too far north (and then found he couldn't steer at all, but in fact that may have been the ship's fault)[9]

And in all senses, a new birth, and happiness to you both from us. How goes Nick? – Best love to him. With great love from us both –

Malc

Send news of Teresina, Cleggs Wall, Branches, – job; (opportunity to revise reading at least) – hold that note, Roland!

[P.S.][a] – Almost 14 months ago I wrote Einaudi in Torino dedicating Italian translation of Volcano to you (without your permission since I couldn't seem to get in touch) & Margie: but have received no reply.[10] Evidently they have delayed the translation: perhaps they did not get the letter, but whether or no please take the will for the deed; the more especially since the deed was did from this end.

Annotations:

1 See Lowry's 23 January letter (**500**) to David Markson, annotation 1.
2 Noxon, who had moved to Boston to teach at Boston University, was divorced from his wife Betty Lane and remarried in the early fifties. He and Lowry had lost contact with each other, and the letter in which he told Lowry about these changes does not appear to have survived.
3 It is not clear whom Lowry might be thinking of here.
4 When the Lowrys left Vancouver to spend 1948-49 in Europe, their ship, the SS *Brest*, scheduled to leave Vancouver in early December 1947, actually set sail on 7 November 1947.
5 Lowry may be referring to 'Poem,' which first appeared in *Contemporary Verse* 24 (Spring 1948): 6, and was reprinted in A.J.M. Smith's *The Book of Canadian Poetry* (Chicago: University of Chicago Press, 1948), p. 374, as 'Lupus in Fabula,' or to 'Sunrise,' which was published in *Outposts* 10 (Summer 1948): 7. The source of his exclamation, however, is certain: 'O God! O Montreal!' is the refrain in Samuel Butler's satiric poem 'A Psalm of Montreal' (1878).
6 'The Forest Path to the Spring.'
7 The *Enterprise* sank off the Scilly Islands, which lie to the south-west of Land's End at the entrance to the English Channel. In 'Through the Panama' a Liberty ship is caught in a storm off the Azores, an event similar to the Lowrys' experience during their November-December 1947 trip.

8 The Russian city of St Petersburg (formerly Leningrad, now restored to its pre-revolutionary name) lies on the shores of the Gulf of Finland on the Baltic Sea, where there is often danger of flooding.

9 Olaf Elling Carlsen (1819-1900), a Norwegian whaling captain, circumnavigated Spitsbergen and Novaya Zemlya before joining the 1872-74 Austro-Hungarian expedition to the North Pole. Carlsen served as ice-pilot, but despite his skill the ship, a low-powered steamer called the *Tagetthof*, became trapped in the ice off Novaya Zemlya. It drifted farther north with the ice until the second winter, when it became firmly stuck and was abandoned.

10 *Sotto il vulcano* is dedicated to Margerie, but see Lowry's November/December 1950 letter (**429**) to Einaudi.

Editorial Notes:

a This addendum has been squeezed into the top left corner of the recto of this single-page typescript and keyed to the word 'Dantesque' in the address with a small *X*. Margerie has also written a message to 'Darling old Gerald' in the left margin of the verso; see *The Letters of Malcolm Lowry and Gerald Noxon* (156).

502: To Harold Matson

P: Matson(telegram)   Western Union, Vancouver, B.C.
                                              2 February 1952

THANKS FOR KLETT CHEQUE[1] BUT YOUR LAST LETTER WAS SIX WEEKS AGO OR HAS MAIL GONE ASTRAY AGAIN WE HARBOUR BLACKEST THOUGHTS CANNOT WORK MOST URGENTLY WHAT ABOUT BRACE CONTRACT YOUR OFFICE SAID YOU WERE WRITING BUT STILL NO WORD PLEASE EXCUSE ANXIETY WIRE US IMMEDIATELY EITHER RELAX OR SHALL WE CONSIDER OURSELVES DEAD GOD BLESS
                                                        MALCOLM

Annotations:

1 This cheque, presumably the $350 Matson mentioned in his 21 December 1951 telegram to Lowry, would have been for royalties on the German translation of *Volcano*.

503: To Margerie Lowry

P: UBC(ms)   [ca February 1952]

My own sweet dearest wife:

I am sorry from the bottom of my heart.[1] I don't know what beastly thing got into me, or has got into me on such occasions. I have no excuses. All I know is I'm going to do my absolute level best not to let such a filthy demon get hold of me again. And I mean starting *Now!* The thought of having hurt you just gratuitously when you have been doing everything in the world for me is unbearable. Believe me, I am suffering. About all I can do to-day is to sit here & try & finish this task I set myself by this evening. Please try & forgive me, even if it is for the 70th time 7.[2] The only difference is, I do not forgive myself this time. I know I can do something about it.

With all my dearest love & remorse

> Your unworthy
> husband Malc

Annotations:

1 Lowry could lash out at others with physical violence and verbal cruelty, but the specific cause or occasion of this outburst is unknown. I have included this pencil holograph (UBC 3:14) here because in early 1952 Lowry was increasingly distraught, but a precise date cannot be confirmed. He has decorated it with two seagulls.

2 Lowry's allusion is to Christ's answer to Peter's question about how many times he should forgive his brother: 'Jesus replied, 'I do not say seven times; I say seventy times seven'' (Matt. 18:22-23).

504: To Jay Leyda

P: UBC(ts)   1075 Gilford St,
PP: *SL* 287-88   Apt. #33,
                                              Vancouver, B.C., Canada
                                                   27 February 1952

Dear old Jay Leyda:[1]

Thank you more than I can say for the Christmas present of your book.

It is a pouncing masterpiece, one of the best documented and dramatic and painstaking and altogether swell pieces of work that you or I will read in a generation.

I am sorry that I have not written you directly before, but this was due to the fact that the book's arrival seemed to occasion storms, Moby Dicks (an actual Moby Dick swam right past our window on the swollen flooding tide) of our own, that had to be weathered else we sank to rise no more: a little conjuration of climate you might say, but that the s.s. *Pennsylvania* should have gone down with all hands but one Seattle Ishmael, just after we had spoken it under the grain tips No. 2, crossing {i.e we were crossing, naturally, she, alas, went under it.} the Second Narrows Bridge,[2] this and the absolutely unprecedented fury and disaster of this winter, in which more ships have gone down in five minutes than in all my seafaring knowledge, inhibited us, especially when we thought of the Ann Alexander and would have liked to speak Dana-wise of birds of summer and of wheelbarrows and watering cans and even whales of good omen – and anyway what with an editorial dislocation, {I don't mean dislocation: merely, I had to part from Albert, was (albeit happy & proud to be in your family) writing to Robert Giroux, out of a typhoon.} inhibited us finally. I relayed therefore my admiration and thanks through Robert Giroux and I can only ask you to realise that my silence was not due to lack of appreciation.

On the contrary I was struck dumb.

With best wishes, and congratulations to yourself from my wife and myself. God bless you.

Malcolm

P.S. In case the S.S. Pennsylvania means nothing to you, she was in Chapter II of the Volcano. (went down off here same day as Flying Enterprise, you can verify it from the N.Y Times or otherwise the press.)[3]

Annotations:

1 The American author and professor Jay Leyda (1910-88) was best known as a film historian. He studied with Sergei Eisenstein, advised on Russian subjects in Hollywood, and taught cinema at Yale, York, and New York Universities. He also edited books on Melville.
2 The Second Narrows Bridge crosses Burrard Inlet just east of Dollarton. Begun in 1925 it was frequently closed due to damage from ships striking it when the tide was high.
3 News that the freighter *Flying Enterprise* was in trouble in the north Atlantic was first reported in the *New York Times* on 29 December 1951. The freighter *Pennsylvania*, which also sank on 10 January, went down in the Pacific Ocean north-west of Vancouver Island.

505: To Harold Matson

P: Matson(telegram)

Western Union,
Vancouver, B.C.
5 March 1952

IMPERATIVE KNOW IMMEDIATELY GENERAL RESULT CONFERENCE IF BRACE HAVE CHANGED MIND AND NO FURTHER ADVANCE WHATSOEVER FORTHCOMING WE MUST VISIT APARTMENT FRIDAY AND

QUIT WRITING TEMPORARILY SINCE FRENCH MONEY DELAYED AND
ENGLISH TOO GIROUX SILENCE INEXPLICABLE TO ME SAVE IN DARK-
EST TERMS DON'T EVEN KNOW IF LUNAR CAUSTIC[1] RECEIVED SO
PLEASE WIRE SITUATION IN NEW YORK LOVE

MALCOLM

Annotations:

1 Almost two months had elapsed since Lowry sent *Lunar Caustic* to
  Robert Giroux (see letter **496**).

506: To Albert Erskine

P: Virginia(telegram   [1075 Gilford St]
                                               11 March 1952

DETECTION CONTRACT BRACE FAILED ANSWER LETTERS EVEN
ACKNOWLEDGE MANUSCRIPTS RECEIVED MEANTIME KEPT ME IN
ABYSS THOUGH HEARTSICK HONESTLY TRIED COOPERATE ALBEIT
DELIGHTED THINGS WENT WRONG CANNOT BELIEVE GIROUX FAULT
PROBABLY OFFICE BOY[1] AGAIN FIND COMMITTED APARTMENT VAN-
COUVER TILL APRIL FIRST THEREFORE FINANCIAL DIFFICULTIES CAN
YOU HELP PLEASE REPLY TEN SEVEN FIVE GILFORD APARTMENT
THIRTY THREE WORK IN PROGRESS HERE WILL DELIVER GIVEN TIME
WRITING LOVE

MALCOLM

Annotations:

1 Lowry had just received the 10 March letter from Robert Giroux at
  Harcourt, Brace informing him that they could not offer him a contract. Although he was deeply disappointed by this rejection, it meant
  that he was free to follow Erskine to Random House. The 'office boy'
  is Lowry's epithet for Eugene Reynal, who, so Lowry believed, disliked
  Under the Volcano.

507: To Albert Erskine

P: Virginia(telegram)   [1075 Gilford St]
                                               14 March 1952

DID YOU RECEIVE SOS TUESDAY URGENT HAL HAS VANCOUVER
ADDRESS LOVE

MALCOLM

508: To Albert Erskine

P: Virginia(ts); UBC(phc)   1075 Gilford,
PP: *SL* 289-95   Apt. 33,
                                                   Vancouver, B.C., Canada
                                                   [ca 14-19 March 1952]ᵃ
                                                             Friday night.

Dear Albert:

Goes without saying I thank you; – and I have no way of knowing what you're going to say about the work since your letter not yet received; – and I thank you God knows too for answering my telegram so promptly today: and with my surviving teeth, all 2 of which are screaming in sympathy and wisdom, and Margie's dividing though apparently so far still surviving teeth, with all the gold in my teeth which I would I could pluck out and repay you in advance and in retreat of your generosity; Oh Christ I can't go on.

– Various bits of information etc. will arrive your way within the next week or so which will buttress the situation – none of these ever sent to [Harcourt,] Brace – draw your own conclusions.

I am enclosing the letters from Hal and [Robert] Giroux which explain why I was beguiled and forced into this situation.

At that time with hurricanes threatening our house as well as floods our own situation was desperate in that it was impossible to spend the winter (for Margie) in our house without freezing to death or worse – without being melodramatic I can't tell you how bad it was – we had tides that swept other houses away – sub-zero weather and our house has not yet been finished to stand such temperatures since we've been unable to put in any insulation and inside walls are just paper: – we have no heater at all and our old stove was literally falling apart and patched up with a mixture of wood ashes, asbestos and sea water, we had less than $50 and in short, in December, the situation would have scared Dostoevsky, drowned Goncharov, Rimbaud, or frozen them, and sworn off Nansen,[1] – (won't go into the complicated reasons {one reason, I was in danger of losing the manuscripts while trying to save the house; actually 2 little houses & the timber foundations of one were carried away by an uprooted tree & I had to shove them downstream & lose them because they began to threaten the other: perhaps symbolic of something.} why this was so but Checkov would have understood very well, even though I did not read the Demon of the Woods till the other day, long after writing The Forest Path to the Spring.)[2]

But all this beside, the final thing was, as you see by these letters, Hal informed me that I could not break my contract with Brace and that they were determined to hold me to it.

Albert, I can only beg you to understand the complications of my situation and my divided yet undivided sense of honor to my work, to you, and Margie. What I did I felt desperately unhappy about yet it seemed my only path – it seemed indeed I had no choice. I tried to do what I apparently had to do and do it honestly. I tried to make the transference from you to Giroux and I wrote him as fully as I could and from my heart, yet telling him how hard it was to do. He never answered. Then I sent Lunar Caustic (which they requested as you see in the letter) and he never even acknowledged it – matter of fact I don't even know now if he did receive it and if you have it now. How could I go on working against this silence? What is the explanation? – (1) Giroux declined the psychological gambit which is understandable, so his behaviour is in effect sacrificial. (2) I am an untrustworthy bastard myself which I qualify with lifted eyebrow but surely the Volcano must underwrite this. (3) the office boy (Reynal) got into the machinery. I can believe Lunar Caustic was too gruesome for anyone's consumption. I can even now believe my unconscious made it too gruesome for anyone whatsoever but I cannot believe there is no merit in it.

Saturday night

Ides of March have come, but not gone.[3] (Ides of March was a worse day for Wilderness in Mexico, in La Mordida, likewise for us in 1946, 2 weeks before acceptance of Volcano) Your wire received yesterday, but not your letter posted Wednesday. The postoffice says that it may have been missorted in Seattle and if it does not arrive Monday must be counted lost, so I shall have to wire you to stop cheque. If this happens – & it is the kind of thing that has been happening all along – I shall almost suspect witchcraft, that Satan does not want me to write the book or something. Even so I shall have to hang on still harder. Instead of your letter comes an impassioned and overwhelmingly tragic letter about the Volcano from one Michael Montillon, a lawyer, of 33 E 12 St., who says Volcano means more to him than anything he has ever read, but how did I ever conspire to get it done?[4] Yes – how?

Last night a night of grief and suspense – you do not say 'love' to us on wire: and if you are fed up with me by now who shall blame you. We are now living in dread both of receiving and not receiving letter. And how to explain? There is the sense of shame too in that we are trying to borrow money again without having payed back what we owe you & promised to repay & meantime you cannot know I have not let you down essentially, even though it feels like it.

Sunday night,

Spring outside with people swinging tennis rackets and taking photographs: a hell of tension within, worst thing I have ever been through,

I think, I know, for reasons I can't explain in brief: worse than the Consul, and it is *not* an alcoholic hell. {Unless a waterwagon hell is by proxy an alcoholic hell!} It is the abyss itself, or a taste of the abyss, and my job is to get out or symbolically to get out, and my only way out in this case is as it were *back*, to Tiphereth, as the Cabbalists say,[5] – but has this ever been done before? And even supposing I did it, how to explain it, or its necessity, or its appalling danger, or its validity, or its non-fictionality, or anything about it, least of all how in this one spiritual case alone going back is equivalent to going forward, or what the hell this has to do with the problem in hand anyway, even supposing it were not a delusion, which on this plane it is. Problem of commending to editors promise of authors operating on astral plane. . .

But to get down to brass, as they say, tacks.

(a) one explanation for everything is the power and truth – not the reverse – of the total concept, which comes into a sort of being the moment you postulate it, but also works against you, not wishing to be postulated in such a fashion; the truth does not stand still, hence one danger in making a précis of books of this kind. I won't go into this any further.

The Brass Tacks. Second Attempt

(1) the point of staying on here in town while there seemed any reasonable hope rather than return home apart from the fact that we'd be involved with a breach of lease if we didn't is: despite the apparently added expense (a) I thought it was – ha ha – easier to keep in communication here at this critical time (b) returning would mean stopping work because of great damage during winter and necessity of getting fuel etc. (c) Margie's eyes, badly need attention. In fact she can scarcely see at all with her present spectacles. Physically too, all this, that was to have given her some relief, has damn nearly wrecked her nerves, & since we'd paid half of this month's rent already, what with trebled price of transport in this boom province matters are about equalised, save that of course we can't get groceries on credit from the crafty Percy of Dollarton, whose life as a postmaster we recently saved by the way, just to put charity back on the line. (Though again I almost – indeed do – suspect witchcraft. The cheque Brace sent us last December through Hal was turned back as 'addressee unknown in Dollarton' and it turned out he did the same thing over a year ago when the C.B.C. [Canadian Broadcasting Corporation] sent us a cheque for a radio repeat programme of Margie's relayed by Gerald Noxon, what time he, Percy, was dunning us for the grocery bill and we were again borrowing money from you. But it turns out this is not the whole story: the C.P.R. [Canadian Pacific Railway] made – again through a series of coinci-

dences – no real effort to deliver the telegram and kept it a week. Finally they gave us $63 too much mmmm (!) which we had 'spent' before the mistake was discovered for which they (and Percy) were responsible. And this I underwrote too, to save the C.P.R. man's job. {To show you state of mind – though I am looking at this with a cold eye several days later I am letting it pass – } Please don't ask me to tell you what I really think – just pray that I may have courage to continue the battle. There have been no less than 16 related coincidences of this kind [&] should your cheque not arrive tomorrow that will be the 17th: but I believe it will, that you are – with Margie and the house – a link with the world of light and the powers of light and goodness from which I have not strayed either, to tell the truth. That it all sounds like delusional insanity makes it no easier to explain, had I a mind to, who thought he was not living in the world of Cotton Mather;[6] what I think I mean is – it's as though I were wrestling with the Abomination itself!

Nor is this getting down to those brass tacks. Of course that last was merely my imagination, working overtime.

Item: The Shrike![7]

Naturally it killed me a bit, a repetition of the publication of the Lost Week End when I was finishing Volcano: but you'll find it prophesied in the adumbration of the Voyage, i.e. that such a thing would probably happen (Law of Series). I didn't find out about The Shrike till after I had dispatched Lunar Caustic, the final plot of which I devised so horrified me that I couldn't sleep properly for about 12 nights. You'd read one version before fortunately, or is it unfortunately? I imagine that it was at this point the office boy swore off. Perhaps I would swear off myself. Perhaps that was the idea. But this is not getting down to those brass tacks. I fail to see that Lunar Caustic even as it stands is not a masterwork, or a potential one.

Brass Tack I. Renewed attempt.

Sunday night.

I have used the word transference in relation to Giroux – all that is absurd: I was still writing to you all along which is where the nightmare begins; possibly trying unconsciously to write *against* myself at the time, a damned difficult problem that!

But the practical thing that was put to me was as contained in the enclosed letters: it seems to me that despite the 'retaining fee' payed me I had a right considering what I have achieved in the world at large (though largely certainly due to you) and the aim or apparent aim to achieve an editor-author relationship – see accompanying letters (haha), work out a financial program etc. – to expect or at least some kind of contract on Hear Us Oh Lord – quite disregarding the other work.

I did not (and I suppose I have to say immediately do not) mean to be a demanding author: at the same time even if Lunar Caustic failed with them and Hear Us was as good as they said it was I had some sort of squatter's rights on the strength of what they said to be bailed out even if on that book alone {to an extent, say, of a contract on that one book which but for them I could now have finished, or nearly so, though this may seem a bit contradictory.} – but regard what happened.

Monday night.

Your letter and cheque gratefully received today – sent to wrong apartment number, arrived in Vancouver Friday and finally found us, after having apparently returned to postoffice, today, God knows how. Telegraph company must have given you wrong apt. number – just a sample of the 16 coincidences I mentioned earlier by which letters and wires have gone astray and been delayed. Also today an astonishing letter from Giroux.[8] Today spend writing night letter you will have by now.[9]

(Re your letter I enclose your envelope as evidence just as it arrived. The apartment is actually No. 33, as I said in wire, and is sublet from some people called Rorison, which no doubt accounts for the 'not known' written thereon, when it arrived on the 13th for No. 30. Had we not been in touch with the postoffice about the possibility of its having gone astray in Seattle, probably we wouldn't have received it at all.)

Tuesday night.

This letter will be posted tomorrow even if still unfinished. Hitch occurred re stamps (!) this time.

Giroux letter to me appended. In one sense it would seem extremely reasonable. That is, had it been preceded by any reply whatsoever to my previous letters to him. *But this letter is the first and last I have had from Mr Giroux: the alpha and omega of that wonderful author-editor relationship state.* And it was they who were inquiring about a financial program, not myself holding them up in that respect. I had sent them the copy of Lunar Caustic you probably have of my own free will and it had never been acknowledged. So that Giroux' letter coming after that long silence and suspense was a cruel thing, whatever the happy outcome.

But the point I want to make is that it is based on a complete mis-understanding, that if not cleared up might wreck things between ourselves too, supposing you and Random House think me worth publishing, a misunderstanding that my already having had to borrow money from you will not help. Harcourt Brace seems to have been led to believe that I am completely broke and that I was putting out for some sort of complete support or something for two years. That is bloody nonsense. As I wired you, I expected and hoped to publish Hear Us Oh Lord this year, so all I expected was a reasonable advance on that. The Volcano has been such a success in France and Germany that my publishers there are asking for my next book practically sight unseen and will give me an advance. The point imperative to make to you is that I only want to *work*, and that any such misconstruction could have been applied is appalling to me of all people. I have, as you know, a small income from England (it comes to about $90 a month at the present exchange) and had – and still have to some extent – hopes of a great deal more when my father's estate was, is, finally settled. If the pound gets back to normal and restrictions are relaxed a bit – as seems just possible within the next year or so – I'll be positively well off. So it is only this immediate period, until I can get a book finished, that is difficult. We live in a shack we built ourselves in the country as cheaply as any two people could live. When we shifted in town this winter we not only had the expectation of the Brace contract – they had given us $500, less taxes and commission etc – but a notice from Correa in France of $800 royalties there and a contract sent us on a German film of the Volcano (they offered me 50/50, we sent the contract to Hal: no further word)[10] The Correa money has been presumably held up at the last moment due to the falling franc. With all this it seemed that for once we could afford to live in a place over the winter that had some hot water and where we could get on with the work instead of spending our time cutting wood and trying not to freeze. So we committed ourselves until April first. Giroux never replied to me and everything else seems to have fallen through. I'll get the money from France eventually but much less because of the devaluation of the franc. But the most cruelly ironical thing in all is this having been placed in the position of some sort of potentially mercenary or grasping author! I've got to make this clear to you, even in the face of having had to borrow more money from you you couldn't afford and then asking for more. (We are already trying to devise means of paying this back by the way) Naturally I feel the laborer is worthy of his hire but I expect to deliver more than value received, and you know this. I hope I've made it clear why I had to shout for more help but if I haven't I'll make it so in the next letter. This has been and is a period of excruciating torment for us, as you can probably gather from the style of this letter – and the agony of suspense continues.

Thank you for bearing with me, and thank you again for your belief and friendship.

What is the news of you and Peggy?

With great love and gratitude from us both,

Malcolm

P.S. Frank has a masterpiece of ours, by the way, did you or didn't you know?[11] That too is publishable perhaps.

P.P.S. In your own good time please return the enclosed letters for I have a story cooking on the subject – possibly to be part of the novel – called In the Abyss. Also please hold on to this agonised unbalanced & demoniac missive for the same reason.[12]

M.

Annotations:

1 Lowry often refers to Dostoevsky and Rimbaud in his letters. Ivan Alexandrovich Goncharov (1812-91), the Russian novelist, was the author of *Oblomov* (1859), and Peter Nansen (1861-1918) was a Danish playwright and novelist.

2 Anton Chekov (1860-1904) wrote his four-act comedy *The Demon of the Wood* in 1889. Once more Lowry is afraid he will be accused of plagiarism or, at least, of copying Chekov, but apart from the misanthropic character of Michael Khrushchov, the 'wood-demon' landowner who likes to protect trees and makes ironic allusions to Dante ('you're all wandering in a dark wood and feeling your way,' *The Wood-Demon* IV.viii), there are no similarities between Chekov's play and Lowry's story.

3 The Ides of March fall on the fifteenth.

4 This letter does not appear to have survived.

5 Tiphereth is the sixth of ten Sephira on the Cabbalist's Tree of Life; it represents the sun, beauty, eternal truth, or the home of sacrificed gods. Lowry is probably thinking of Charles Stansfeld-Jones's ('Frater Achad') treatment of the Sephira in *Q.B.L. or The Bride's Reception: A Short Quabbalistic Treatise on the Tree of Life*.

6 Cotton Mather (1663-1728), a learned and prolific New England writer, was also a leading minister of the Massachusetts church. He became closely associated with the Salem witchcraft trials through his pseudo-scientific writings on witches and witchcraft.

7 *The Shrike*, a 1952 play by the American author Joseph Kramm, won a Pulitzer Prize that year. It is set in City Hospital, New York, where a failed playwright with a possessive wife is being treated for attempting suicide by taking an overdose of phenobarbital. He survives the attempt but is released into his wife's care at the end; she is the shrike of the play's title, and a shrike is a predatory bird with a toothed bill. The similarities between this realist play and *Lunar Caustic* are superficial; however, the play troubled Lowry, as his 3 and 4 May letters (**529** and **530**) to Erskine reveal.

8 In his 'astonishing letter' of 10 March 1952 Giroux explained that Harcourt, Brace had decided against offering Lowry a contract.

9 See telegram (**509**) to Erskine.

10 Ideas about a film starring Peter Lorre had reached Lowry from his

German translator and publisher but there never was a contract; see Lowry's 8 December 1951 letter (**484**) to Harold Matson.

11 Frank Taylor had a copy of the Lowrys' filmscript of *Tender Is the Night*.

12 This postscript, so revealing of Lowry's composition methods, has been added in blue ink.

Editorial Notes:

a. The five-page typescript of this letter carries an unusual number of marginal additions, interlineations, cancellations, and superscripts. The state of the text indicates Lowry's anxiety and the difficulty he had composing it.

509: To Albert Erskine

P: Virginia(telegram)   [1075 Gilford St]
                                                                              17 March 1952

THOUSAND THANKS CHECK DELAYED APARTMENT NUMBER IS THIRTY THREE SEEMS HOODOO COMMUNICATIONS MUST SHOUT MORE HELP PLEASE REPLY AIRMAIL WILL PAY BACK IF DIG DITCHES BUT NEXT FORTNIGHT CRUCIAL WILL POST LETTER EVERY DAY WISH AVOID SAME INEXPLICABLE MISUNDERSTANDING BRACE STOP CAN ACTUALLY HAVE BOOK FOR PRESS THIS LATE SUMMER WITH REASONABLE HELP PLEASE BELIEVE IN ME I BROUGHT VOLCANO SEAWORTHY THROUGH WORSE BUT THIS IS REAL VOLCANO GREAT LOVE

MALCOLM

510: To Albert Erskine

P: Virginia(ts); UBC(phc)   1075 Gilford St,
                                                                               Apt. 33,
                                                              Vancouver, B.C., Canada
                                                                          20 March 1952

Dear Albert:

Hope you have by now got our Special Delivery airmail letter though we're quite prepared for it to have gone to Capistrano or San Luis Obispo.[1] I said we'd post letter every day – that isn't possible without going uptown every day however – for we've no way of computing the weight thereof save at the P.O. and if we do it inadequately letters may get returned: will do next best thing, however, which is to write every day and post when possible: once back in Dollarton, where we go April first, all communications are going to become twice as difficult (all air-mail letters for example are delayed a day or two by the time it takes them to get out from Vancouver and the sparsity of postal deliveries) – which is one reason why I thought it necessary to stay here. Another is that the battle there simply to keep alive – woodcutting, repairs, etc., is going to swallow up every other consideration for a while. I thus consider this my last chance to convince you of the potential value of the cargo – (which I have to risk your not seeing, to give a final turn of the screw to the anguish) and it is the last chance I'll ever have of having you for an editor (if you still wish that even, I have to risk that you may be by now half wanting to be rid of me yourself) and dash with all my derangements at my object, leaving the rest to fortune. It is also now perhaps – now I have reread Brace's early letter – the best chance of prying away the Volcano from Brace, if you still want that.[2] They went on about their moral rights, drawing up a financial program, 'simply would not bow out' – and then let me down the drain – how about mine?

Another anguishing thing I have to face is: just as Giroux was reading in the Hear Us section what was intended for you: you will be reading in the Caustic section what was intended for Giroux. If he has abstracted from the parts where I have said – for this probably was in an abstractable personal letter – that while I wished genuinely to cooperate, it was giving me hell to leave you, – if, (which is quite possible out of his own well-meaning ethics or sense of personal decency), he has done that – you are likely to be hurt by the apparent swiftness and callousness with which I shifted loyalties.

Another point of torment that I made to Giroux – and I think made to you too – was that in deciding to stay with Brace I was making a *whole* decision, since without the Volcano one was nowhere with the work as a whole, and that it was much for your sake that – if Brace would not bow out – I made the decision, for otherwise the Volcano would be a kind of albatross round your neck. I have a moral right – if they are going to talk about moral rights – to have my own say so about this and hence am going to write again to Giroux personally, directly and unofficially. From the human standpoint of justice it would look as though he should feel ashamed of himself forever and a day. But I have to realise that from the official standpoint he might have been able to express himself on the showdown in no other way: I have to realise too that you are in no different case than Giroux, either, that likewise as a commander whose commands may be overruled by the 'White House', so to speak, you might have to do the same thing and quite likely feel in sympathy with Giroux yourself, whereas the whole thing, if you have to give an adverse judgement, becomes twice as crucifial [sic] because you are – in this case because I am – my, your friend. So I tell you in advance that I sympathise with and appreciate all this, as also that the practical value of the letters I am now writing and material I am now sending in, may seem to you to be nil: you may be bewildered at the paradox of my trying to 'sell' the Volcano to you – which you don't own, may not want to own, and needs to you no selling in any case: (I am sending you a thesis by a fellow at Columbia which won top marks, colossal European lucubrations, etc.)[3] I have to admit that I don't quite know why I'm doing this myself but the reason is roughly this: that while on one plane it may not matter, on another it does: staying here and keeping in touch – and God knows I'd rather be in Dollarton, which we love with our whole hearts – is (just as the reverse position arose last winter) at the moment tantamount to sticking with the ship. The cards are so stacked against me, it would seem, (against us, come to that, I meant Margie and me) that there is a temptation to accept the karma, to give ink {I loved that typographical error: to 'give ink', almost as good as the 'drunkark', do you remember? Ah, these heroic Drunkarks, in which one 'brugs' around, back across the channel . . .}[4] or take some action, or by negation take no action, that is tantamount to that: so far as I know when destiny really gets her claws into a thing like this the sphere of operation of free will is incredibly narrowed and the passage of the fatality – I use the word in the broad sense, neither to tempt same, nor the reverse, but not in the 'fatal' sense of sense – can only be reversed by some act of collossal sacrifice or by simply hanging on Carlsen-wise,[5] as it were, forcing what is trying to destroy you to respect you instead, so that the adverse winds turn fair and the furies turn to mercies. I speak in melodramatic terms, but not necessarily in self-dramatising ones; I can't help seeing something spiritual in all this – or at all events, as William James said, it *feels* like a fight. So while you may see no sense in what I'm doing at present, one day you may see its wisdom.

As for the rest, I don't know; but I'd like to put myself in advance in absolute sympathy with any difficult decision you may have to make against me.

I believe some of the stories have a classical timbre, in their weird way, and might live, and are rather more than piddling, and I ask you not to be put off too easily by their apparent machine-madeness, which is new, rather than old (or perhaps very very old) and in any case perfectly deliberate, relates to something spiritual again, and in any case again would be balanced in the final version by a few more tales of another type: as for the ghastly final idea for Lunar Caustic, perhaps the less said the better at the moment:[6] no one would relish writing such a thing, or at least could contemplate doing so without fright (though you once did say it was publishable as it stood (as it stands in the version you have as Swinging the Maelstrom)) Financial situation is as follows:

Rent is now paid here to April first, at which time we go to Dollarton and have no rent to pay. {Though the place has been 1/2 swept away in a hurricane: our main place quite intact, due to M & M building![7] *mss* also intact: *please note*.} We have to eat until then, for cannot get groceries on credit here as with our bloody-minded Percy {though now life-saved-by-me.} who'll let us go a month. We shall have certain incidental bills of light, gas, etc. coming to about $10 to pay when we move, and incidentals incidental to moving, not too much. Once we get home of course we can live very cheaply, if not quite on nothing, and my income, now about $90 a month arrives usually between 4th and 10th of the month. Actual money in bank: your $50. So we just couldn't quite make it, even living on oatmeal. As the fishermen, who have suffered through him similarly too, have adjured me to say, when he asks for the bill (as he said for us when money had come through for us) '*Not known at this address*'. '*We do not exist, according to you so how can you ask us for a bill then*.' I doubt if I'll ever grow as unkind as that, even for a joke, at least I hope not, so to speak.

As a first gesture toward trying to pay back I will send you, by Sunday, 4 or 5 light poems that perhaps you might try and palm off if you think them worthy, on the New Yorker, or somewhere {Probably on cool second thinkings, nowhere, if not the New Yorker.}, and pocket the proceeds: I can't do it from here because of the difficulty of getting American stamps, but I had forgotten that I had become quite a famous poet, here and there, of an obscure kind, (I have a sub-Edward Lear like gift,[8] combined with an ill-toned rackety dramatic one, A.J.M. Smith says I am one of the best of poets and put me in his Canadian-Scribner's anthology[9] however {also some people think the same in England. Hal has no lien on my poetry.}) and this might prove a practical notion. Or if you gyp at the idea of offering them yourself (though it's damned difficult from here and I didn't like to avail myself of Bob Linscott's offer and you once said you would) I could send them to the New Yorker sans return stamps and tell them to give the result to you as if you were my agent – a hardly more rewarding idea or less embarrassing, if they rejected them. But it would be a tactile attempt, & one my higher self tells me to make. So I'll make it.

Also we are actually owed money by one friendly source in the U.S. [Gerald Noxon] who I know would be glad to pay us back by paying you, if the party, a more than honourable one, has it (which he should have if he is not strangled by alimony after a recent Reno divorce, though he didn't have it last time he wrote, a bit ago, or we'd have asked him for it rather than you since he owes it to us.)

In addition I shall myself try to palm off some stories in the local – but huge – newspaper The Sun. They don't like me for having insulted their little boom town in the Volcano, and they like me less for the success thereof. But having made the Britannica I might be able to make them print them and pay me etc.

Failing that the rival paper, The Province, once ten years ago had me writing on their editorial page: and would probably be glad to have me writing there again etc.[10] Or perhaps we could get a job writing soap opera for the local radio. As for the other anguishing things in the sphere of decision I can perceive hovering in the air above your editorial head, just believe I understand about them and don't anguish yourself – more tomorrow.

Great love from us both and God bless you.

Malcolm

P.S. But if you want to know how I reacted to the wonderful Brace decision last Christmas when they would not bow out because of their 'moral rights' (when I could not ask how to bow in but while you seemed to be vanishing over the horizon like a freighter over the horizon to a man on a raft, which man cannot very well explain with no radio that for some mysterious reason he seems to be letting down the freighter rather than the freighter himself) despite the fact that financially it seemed to be saving our lives, on Christmas day I sat in front of the tree, bowed over a bad whiskey, with our two presents upon it which I couldn't open and wouldn't let Margie remove, and then to try and save matters composed, upon the long range ukelele, a blues. . .

> Nagging at myself something awful
> Nagging at myself something fearful
> All because we ain't used to cheerful news
>
> Nagging at myself blues
> Those old Judas blues. . .
>
> Nagging at myself something gruesome
> You're nagging too so it's a twosome
> {And} All because we ain't used to good news
>
> Nagging at myself blues
> Those old Judas blues. . .

Friday morning.

And if I don't find this piece of hangman's humor in much better taste or any funnier than I did then it may be because the situation, for all I know, is no different now: as I said, I do have hopes Brace will bow out completely, I mean to any rights to the Volcano too, but they're only hopes. Morally after what has happened I feel that they should. But the Judas situation arose because without the Volcano Brace had put me in a situation of betraying you no less whether I insisted upon 'staying with you' or 'stayed' with them. Because there seemed then no escape from the latter, and the former possibly a large potential embarrassment to yourself, naturally there *was* no betrayal, as you can see from the letters I enclosed in my other letter to you, or anything else you may read round the subject, merely a feeling *as if.* There is no damn question at all in my mind though that Brace or someone has betrayed *me* and this is the moral lever by which I now hope the whole situation may be shifted on to a plane acceptable to both yourself and myself. My 'whole decision' is not hypocrisy. It simply shifts focus. On the other hand there may be a point of view from which the whole thing seems too ambitious as a project, and a limited compromise decision on Hear Us Oh Lord – but the whole thing is driving me nuts –

Re the whole bolus of the work the moral and practical problem arose and again will arise with you of getting a *copy* of the material in a safe place. That is largely the reason for the mélange of Caustic that will now be in your possession. In this sense it was sent to Giroux with no obligation whatsoever attached to him in regard to it. I never asked him to make an offer on it only asked what they wanted me to do first – for advice, and also for contact and though I told him not to hurry, there was a moral obligation on his part surely at least to reply and acknowledge the manuscript, especially as he had asked to see such a draft. But he has pretended that another kind of obligation arose where eventually the refusal of an advance on Lunar Caustic became the point at issue on which I was dropped altogether, which if true is bad faith, and if untrue seems like a form of ignoratio elenchi. The failure of Giroux (or for that matter Hal) to make any sort of reply – the watching for the mail futilely each day, each day, each day, each day, while the money dwindled – well, not even animals in laboratories can stand that sort of thing indefinitely. What it has done to poor Margie – who had 6 years of it from Scribner's who had thrown her own whole work away to devote herself to mine with this new hope in view, and worked herself half blind I can't express, and there are other aspects I can't go into that just seem too tragic.

The apartment – the sole one to be had in town at that time was, though outside our income normally, the most economical and sensible base of operations we could possibly find under the circumstances in which to do the work – whatever it was desired one do – at top speed. I have told you that Correa wrote 'We have $800 for you – where shall we send it?' And of the enthusiasm for making a film in Germany with Peter Lorre, of the Volcano, the encomiums from Stuttgart, the contract sent us – anyone would think we were underwritten on every side.

But with the continued silence from Brace came a distrust and a discouragement and finally a despair – what was the good of sending any more? what did they want? Brace's conduct really amounts to turpitude for by their promise they in effect prevented me from attempting to make money in any other way during this period. I could have concentrated on the more saleable of the shorter stories – but I didn't know what I was supposed to do. I asked Giroux what he wanted me to work on first, how many more stories he wanted for Hear Us, etc. and he never answered. I had the promise of the 'publishing program' but what was needed was the contact. I don't know why I haven't gone mad and perhaps I have and on top of all that I can't say how relieved I am to be in your hands, though of course and here again –

Even so, Margie – in addition to copying the 300 pages of Lunar Caustic drafts and comments, – typed during this period more than 200 pages of my notes for Dark as the Grave before despair seized us, though before the despair the reluctance to send any more had crept in. Meantime I wrote another long short story, Henry Ghostkeeper, which is not quite successful yet but will be, drafted out another long one, The Week of the Flying Enterprise, and a few shorter ones:[11] was too worried about the house in Dollarton to finish the Path to the Spring, & too worried about the contract and loss of yourself and bewildered as to what I was supposed to do, to put my heart into anything. All the energy went into suspense, finally, despair, as it is now going into the determination to fight back. But to fight back with actual work while the suspense is now doubly protracted is an impossibility – meanwhile, unless one has learned anything by the suffering, this period has been an almost total, a worse than total loss.

Even with the 200 pages of Dark as the Grave Margie has not yet reached the point where the notes have left the sphere of the first draft and begun to assimilate themselves into the second – if you can call it the second. It must be admitted we had lost faith and stopped this part of the work before the point where we had reached anything we would have cared to send to Giroux, almost even yourself for that matter: typing this stuff of mine from my small notes is the most nervewracking job imaginable and I would have been doing it myself but that I felt we didn't have sufficient time to be working entirely on the same job. Notes and material are one problem: a detailed scenario another, and it is on all this I need advice. There should be a copy in a safe place. Nobody needed to know that except me – I mean that there wasn't one – but it does not seem to have paid being honorable with Brace, to whom I suppose in addition I now owe $500 – you'd be surprised how little seems left after taxes and commission etc, about the price of a cheap funeral in short, with prices what they are in a boom town like this, albeit in Dollarton {where, at the store, the prices are in fact yet higher: it is the rents that are so killing in town, though we got a place as economically as we could & I've explained why we couldn't stay home.} a fortune.

The work on which the documentation is greatest – in fact it is enormous – and most direct and hence easiest to type is La Mordida, the idea of losing the notes for which drives me clean off my rocker. Just so, if we can keep our heads above water at all, I believe I could meet the schedule I outlined in the telegram.[12] I don't know why I'm rambling on about La Mordida etc when now perhaps I'm not even at first base again, though in another sense at the base for the moment I'd most like to be. What would suit me is to have an opportunity to round off the stories in Hear Us, and now I take back what I said before, that the period has been a dead loss. For In the Abyss – the long story I am thinking of precisely in relation to this period,[13] and of which the Week of the Flying Enterprise would be a part – could not only be one of the best things I've ever done but would fit admirably into that volume. Well, that's all for the moment. Forgive me if I seem to contradict myself here and there. Will fight to be found fighting.

Hear Us Oh Lord From Heaven Thy Dwelling Place!

God bless you from us both –

Malcolm

P.S. Your letter with the second $50 check, posted March 18th, airmail, just arrived here safely & without a hitch this morning, Friday the 21st. A thousand thanks from us both – this should enable us to get through. See elsewhere designs for repayment. All is not well with Margie: the whole thing has been too much for her.

Annotations:

1 Both San Luìs Obispo and Capistrano are coastal towns in southern California. Given the date of this letter, Lowry may be thinking of the association of Capistrano with swallows, which are said to return there every 19 March.

2 This letter does not appear to have survived, but Lowry is referring to Harcourt, Brace's claim on him in the contract that Eugene Reynal brought with him when he joined the firm. Harcourt, Brace did not relinquish their claim to first refusal of Lowry's new work until Robert Giroux's letter of 10 March 1952 telling Lowry they would not make an offer on *Lunar Caustic*.

3 The 'fellow' is David Markson; the thesis is Markson's master's dissertation, 'Malcolm Lowry: A Study of Theme and Symbol in *Under the Volcano*,' submitted to Columbia University in 1952.

4 In his 14 June 1946 letter to Lowry, Erskine asked if the word 'brug' was a typographical error in the *Volcano* manuscript; henceforth, to 'brug around' became a shared joke. In his 22 June 1946 reply to Erskine (**226**) Lowry explains that 'brug' should have been 'grub.'

5 See Lowry's comments on Olaf Elling Carlsen's exploits in the arctic in his 23 January 1952 letter (**501**) to Gerald Noxon.

6 In his notes to the 1951 'Work in Progress' statement Lowry described his plans for revising *Lunar Caustic* in grim detail. He planned to use material from 'In Ballast to the White Sea' to make his hero (now called Thurstaston) suffer not only from *delirium tremens* but also from disease, the death of an only son, and betrayal by his wife. It would be, as Lowry noted, 'a novel of almost total blackness' (UBC 32:1, 4).

7 'M & M building' refers to Malcolm and Margerie's re-building of their cabin at Dollarton in the summer of 1945.

8 The English poet and painter Edward Lear (1812–88) is remembered today for his limericks and nonsense poems *Book of Nonsense* (1846) and *More Nonsense* (1872). Lowry parodies the title of Lear's poem 'The Dong with a Luminous Nose' in chapter 1 of *Under the Volcano*.

9 Smith did only one anthology with Scribner's prior to 1956, his *Seven Centuries of Verse* (1947), which did not include anything by Lowry. However he did use seven of Lowry's poems in his 1948 *Book of Canadian Poetry* (Chicago: University of Chicago Press), and in his introduction to the poems he praised *Under the Volcano* and called Lowry 'a poet of originality and distinction' (271).

10 Lowry published two short articles and one poem on the editorial pages of the *Vancouver Daily Province* in December 1939: 'Hollywood and the War,' 12 December 1939; 'The Real Mr Chips,' 13 December 1939; and 'Where did that one go to, 'Erbert?' 29 December 1939.

11 Margerie Lowry included the story 'Ghostkeeper' in her collection *Malcolm Lowry: Psalms and Songs* (202-27). No draft survives of a story called 'The Week of the Flying Enterprise.'

12 In his 17 March 1952 telegram (**509**) to Erskine, Lowry said he could have a book ready – presumably *Hear us O Lord* – by late summer.

13 This is another story that does not survive if, in fact, Lowry actually started it.

511: To Albert Erskine

P: Virginia(ms); UBC(phc)
PP: *SL* 231–32   [1075 Gilford St]
                                                  [21, 22, 23 March 1952][a]

Friday, Saturday, Sunday.

On Friday afternoon posted second serial letter also containing immeasurable thanks for second $50 received easily and swiftly that morning[1]

This will – God's thanks to you – I believe enable us to slide back fairly easily from this appalling withdrawal to the good return next Sunday – [2]

What has been chiefly appalling has been the strain on Margie in all this: medically she needed and still needs a rest, – particularly from this kind of strain – medically she needed & still needs attention, and it has largely had to go by the board: her courage & guts are phenomenal, however, & it seems to me it is peculiarly American and it must be the blood of her pioneer ancestors coming to the rescue: any English woman would have been 'carted away' – as she puts it – long ago. In fact I myself have felt not far from being 'carted away' once or twice.

Next Sunday will also be around the anniversary of the your acceptance of the Volcano in Mexico in 1946, & of which period this ordeal seems like a repetition: it is also exactly the same period of the most critical part of La Mordida.

On Saturday afternoon when your telegram arrived announcing your letter my relief and gratitude was so great I slept for 19 hours.

Meantime I am trying to write to Giroux though what I finally may have to say might be conditioned by your letter that will arrive tomorrow.

Re the poems: – I decided that it was a form of unconscious moral blackmail or something to send them to yourself at this moment under these circumstances, expecting you to place them, – as if it were just as easy as that – so I am figuring out another plan.[3]

Most immediately – to try and pay back quam celerrime re teeth – we have written that a payment sent us to the beetle-brained Percy the grocer-postmaster and sent back again as 'addressees not known in Dollarton' for an old radio programme recently repeated in Toronto & of which Margie is largely the author be sent to yourself – if the party to whom it was sent back [Gerald Noxon] can afford it.

But if this fails, I have other ideas. And besides that it seems I first went to sea, as it were, 2 years before Carlsen and in those days we carried sails even on steamships should all else fail.[4] I hadn't thought about the sails but maybe I can find some sails.

Meantime – to change elements & metaphors – while fighting a blitzkrieg[5] on one flank we are fighting a rearguard action on the other so that, should we have to endure defeat, that defeat be as little catastrophic as possible, but since we haven't quite worked out our plans here, I won't outline them.

From a letter I recently had – quite unsolicited – from Knopf I would certainly deduce that they wanted me, in default of Random House:[6] but the decision I incline to at the moment, in the dreadful event that the latter despite your efforts reject me, would be to withdraw myself from circulation altogether, hang on somehow, and then offer the thing to yourself again a year from now, with the work further advanced (though sans advances).

This is what I would certainly do if I had only myself to think of even though it is hard at the moment to see how the work could be so advanced, without one lucky break in the near future, though in three or four months the picture might be different.

But, believe me, this is what I would want to do, if it were to seem at all morally feasible and what, in event of reverse, I am seriously considering doing.

Meantime − blithely to change metaphors once again − one feels slightly like a steeplejack who, far aloft, is not sure whether the rigging is slipping or the weathercock he has been sent to repair is not going to descend upon his skull with outstretched beak −

Both of us thank you profoundly for all your kindness.

With love
Malcolm

Annotations:

1 See the postscript to Lowry's 20 March 1952 letter (**510**) to Erskine.
2 The Lowrys left the apartment on Sunday, 30 March; see Lowry's description of a 'typhoon' just before they left the city for Dollarton in his April 1952 letter (**521**) to Erskine.
3 In his 20 March 1952 letter (**510**) to Erskine, Lowry had proposed sending him '4 or 5 light poems' to begin repayment for Erskine's loans.
4 Olaf Elling Carlsen had completed his exploits long before Lowry set foot on board a ship, but the Norwegian whaling captain is much in Lowry's thoughts at this time.
5 The German term *Blitzkrieg* means literally 'lightning war,' and is commonly associated with Hitler's air raids on London during the Second World War.
6 This letter from Knopf does not appear to have survived.

Editorial Notes:

a. There is neither inside address nor date on this pencil holograph, but it is clear from both the content and the sequence of letters to Erskine that it was *not* written in February 1951 as stated in *Selected Letters*. Most of Lowry's letters to Erskine at this time were written in pencil on canary second-cut paper.

*As early 1952 dragged by with deafening silence from Robert Giroux, Lowry
sank deeper into despair. After learning that Harcourt, Brace did not want him
and while waiting for a decision from Random House, he eagerly resumed communication with Albert Erskine, the one person apart from Margerie with whom
he could discuss his work. In letter 512 he offers one of his most explicit defences
of the type of fiction he wanted to write after* Under the Volcano. *Invoking the
example of Chekov and Pirandello, he argues that autobiographical writing about
writers is both original and interesting, especially to the average reader. There is
'a poet in every man,' he insists, and Sigbjørn Wilderness is the ideal
Doppelgänger. Moreover, Wilderness is not so much a writer as a man being
written, just as Lowry had felt himself to be in Mexico during 1946, just as he
felt himself to be now as he waited helplessly for others to decide his fate. It is
unlikely that Erskine was convinced by Lowry's reasoning; he had told Lowry
in his 21 March 1952 letter that this subject was 'seldom very interesting or fruitful for fiction,' but he nevertheless came through with a fine contract. By 24
March, Lowry had only one more week to wait.*

512: To Albert Erskine

P: Virginia(ms); UBC(phc)
PP: *SL* 329-33; *CL* 8: 39-42;   [1075 Gilford St]
   Lln 189-93   [24 March 1952]ᵃ

Monday.
Your letter arrived without hitch – many many thanks, though it was
some hours before I could read it, so apprehensive was I, albeit Margie
assured me it was hopeful & encouraging, – as it was, heaven reward you
– though be assured I appreciate all your difficulties, & shall understand
should things go awry. But I am praying they won't. Meantime quam
celerrime my feelings and prejudices – which I hope will dispel *some*
doubts – in regard to fiction about writings and writers as such:[1]

   (a) Your feelings & prejudices are shared by me, almost unqualifiedly,
on the more general plane, as indeed probably by most other writers,
though one reason I feel that most other writers share them is that they
have been taught since they began writing that *all* editors & producers
have these same feelings & prejudices, so what's the use of writing about
writers etc, (even though they, the writers, somehow persist in doing so
in one disguise & another) – when they would be rejected etc etc?

(b) Against this I strongly believe, as I strongly believed was the case with dipsomania – 'as dull as dipsomania,' an impossible theme etc – this sort of thing was said to me again & again well over a decade ago – that it has very rarely, if at all, been done properly. (It hadn't, despite Zola Baudelaire & Ten Nights in a Barroom.[2] That's why The Lost Week End damn near slaughtered me.)

(c) But I don't believe the general public shares the prejudice, for there is an artist, a poet in every man, hence he is a creature easy for anyone to identify themselves with: & his struggles are likely to be universal, even on the lowest plane. Even kids, & Percy [Cummins] our unscrupulous & forgetful grocer & postmaster – perhaps especially Percy our unscrupulous & forgetful grocer & postmaster – can identify themselves with such: as can Jimmy Craig, the boat builder, & Guldbransen the fisherman etc. But this is by the way. My own prejudice & feeling remain on this plane no different in essence let alone from your good self's but from those adumbrated by bloody old Bernard de Voto in his truly horrendous excellent little bits about Mark Twain & his malicious bits about Tom Wolfe.[3]

Tuesday
But I note that even Bernard de Voto had to interpolate that 'he was a 'good Joycean' – he hoped' – and where on this line of his argument The Portrait of the Artist as a Young Man would come in, I simply don't know. But with me The Portrait of the Artist has always partly failed (while one recognises its – ha ha – importance of course) for not dissimilar reasons to those that made Wolfe fail with de Voto.[4]

(I have cut out what seems to me now a first rate digression on Joyce at this point, in the interests of space –)[b]

So I daresay I am even 'left' of de Voto on the subject, and as a consequence even more prejudiced than yourself and/or most editors or writers against such writing and on that point that does in the end perhaps begin to involve the whole of autobiographical fiction and much beside – particularly it would seem to depend upon the technique, – moreover what if one should give a real turn of the screw to a subject that is so often treated halfheartedly?: – I think unquestionably what one is after is a new form, a new approach to reality itself; though I would submit also in tangential passing that I don't think those works that treat of the matter tragically or philosophically rather than romantically have suffered in acclaim by reason of this theme – Tchechov's The Seagull is a case – perhaps irrelevant – that comes first to mind, and Six Characters – of course you can say these are single works, but in fact virtually the entire basis of Pirandello's work involves a not dissimilar theme, (in this case that art, the theatre, is somehow realer than life).[5] My reasoning may seem slightly cockeyed here or irrelevant again but I know what I mean. Nine out of ten people who saw the Seagull would scarcely remember that it is almost entirely about writing & writers or art in one way and other – what they would take to heart is that a talent not put to proper use and directed can destroy its owner; and apply that melancholy truth to their own talent, whatever it might be. But I digress. The real protagonist of the Voyage is not so much a man or a writer as the unconscious – or man's unconscious – and at present it's a little difficult for me to see how I can swing what seem to me the superb irony of Wilderness living in Laruelle's house and the death of 'Vigil' unless Wilderness has written, so to speak, the Volcano. Apart from this though, both Dark as the Grave, & La Mordida – especially the latter – should exist as powerful novels in themselves, if done aright, without obtrusive reference to writers or writing. There are emotional and sexual and alcoholic & even political dramas which overshadow these matters, albeit I would lose what seems to me one of the most potentially masterful scenes, i.e when Wilderness has his novel accepted in Laruelle's house while technically under arrest if Wilderness hasn't written the Volc. Even so Wilderness is not, in the ordinary sense in which one encounters novelists or the author in novels, a novelist. He simply doesn't know what he is. He is a sort of underground man. Also he is Ortega's fellow, making up his life as he goes along, & trying to find his vocation.[6] In this regard some of the notes to the Path to the Spring, though chaotic, may prove helpful re the treatment I propose. According to Ortega, the best image for man himself *is* a novelist, & it is in this way that I'd prefer you to look at him. He is not going to be the self-conscious author himself of so many novels, if that was what you rightly afraid of, even though I have to make him responsible for the Volc. Moreover he is disinterested in literature, uncultured, incredibly unobservant, in many respects ignorant, without faith in himself, and lacking nearly all the qualities you normally associate with a novelist or a writer. As I've said he doesn't even think he's a novelist himself. The Volcano – which 'Laruelle' doesn't think much of at first – or rather the Valley of the Shadow of Death appears less as a novel than as a sort of mighty if preposterous moral deed of some obscure sort, testifying to an underlying toughness of fibre or staying power in his character rather than to any particular aesthetic ability of the usual kind. His very methods of writing are absurd and he sees practically nothing at all, save through his wife's eyes, though he gradually comes to *see*. I believe this can make him a very original character, both human & pathetically inhuman at once. I much approve of him as a doppleganger and am reluctant to turn him into a steeplejack, a cartoonist, or a billiard marker, though he can be all these too, for all it matters. What does he know?

What he suspects is that he's not a writer so much as being *written* – this is where the terror comes in. (It came in, just then). His tragedy or his fable or whatever is less that of Faust than that of Aylmar,[7] the water diviner – whose story should be told briefly somewhere or other – a character of the middle ages who, with his wand, was used by the French authorities to track down murderers, half fake – because his talent kept failing at embarrassing moments, wouldn't work at all under certain conditions yet he had to pretend it *was* working, half genius, because he nearly always got his man, – a sort of latter day underground Aylmar, looking for himself or his soul. I'm damned if I don't think him an original fellow, not to be confused with the ordinary novelist, and I would have told you all this already, had Hear Us only gone to you & not to [Robert] Giroux. (Magic didn't seem to be working very well then, or maybe it'll turn out it was working overtime & was just a bit too subtle for once.)

Well that's Pat 30 for now & by the way it wasn't because you wrote Pat 30 that your first letter didn't arrive but because it was Pat 33 not Pat 30 at all.[8]

I read some of the Invisible Man already in Partisan and thought it pretty extraordinary but don't talk to me about the Invisible Man until I've ceased a little more being The Superfluous man.[9]

Meantime I need all the coraggio you can wish me. Am pretty scared, if still on deck

> God bless you from us both
> Malcolm

P.S. But one beautiful bit of Law of Series[10] was that the day after I had written 'you' as I thought in the Hear Us Oh Lord batch of ms that I might find myself having to split the ego of Wilderness still more into yet another character I received a letter forwarded by Reynal from one Malcolm Lowry, an engineer, of Kansas City, who said that his father had been President of Erskine University, South Carolina, that he had been congratulated frequently & erroneously on writing the Volcano but that he was interested in tracing the family history.[11] This was followed by a letter from my brother in Liverpool who reported having met me & had a conversation with me in Bayswater, England, though I was in Dollarton, & also adding that the old family house, recently sold – though I am yet to receive my share or I would have paid you back ere now – was haunted . . .

I replied, since we were finding the wilderness tough just then, that it was the probably the bathroom that was being haunted, by me!

M.

Annotations:

1 On 21 March 1952 Erskine wrote Lowry about the manuscripts he had been reading and on which he was reporting to Robert K. Haas (1890-1964), a vice-president at Random House. According to Erskine, these manuscripts included 'all of the stories and notes plus the two versions of The Last Address and the additional notes on *Lunar Caustic*,' but judging from Lowry's comments in this letter, he must have sent Erskine a copy of his plans for the *Voyage That Never Ends*. Erskine went on to say that he felt some prejudice against fiction about relationships among writers, editors, critics, and publishers, and that he had 'some misgivings about [. . .] writing a book about a man who has written a book about writing a book.'

2 Émile Zola's *L'Assommoir* is a naturalist treatment of the life in French bars and taverns, and Charles Baudelaire's *Les Fleurs du mal* (1857) contains a sequence of five poems on wine. *Ten Nights in a Bar-room, And What I Saw There* (1854), a novel by the American writer Timothy Shay Arthur, became popular with the temperance movement in its 1858 play version.

3 The American writer Thomas Wolfe wrote highly autobiographical fiction such as *Look Homeward, Angel* (1929), which displays both originality and a debt to James Joyce. The American critic, historian, and teacher Bernard de Voto wrote a famous negative review of Wolfe called 'Genius is not Enough' for the *Saturday Review of Literature*, 25 April 1936, 3-4, 14-15, in which he damned Wolfe for his 'gobs of emotion,' his bad writing, his immaturity, and the thinly fictionalized autobiography of his plots. De Voto wrote two books on Twain.

4 Lowry, who was sensitive on the point, is probably thinking of de Voto's criticism of Wolfe's autobiographical tendencies, which are also apparent in Joyce's novel and seem to be the basis for Lowry's reservations about the *Portrait*. In *The World of Fiction* (1950) de Voto describes himself as '(I trust) a complete Joycean up to *Finnegans Wake*' (p. 171).

5 Anton Chekov's play *The Seagull* (1896) is almost entirely about writing and the struggles of the artist, who, in the person of the romantic young playwright Trepleff, kills both the seagull and himself. Luigi Pirandello's *Six Characters in Search of an Author* was a favourite of Lowry's.

6 'Ortega's fellow' refers to José Ortega y Gasset's notion that a man must fabricate his own life, which is a central idea in Ortega's *Toward a Philosophy of History* (1944). The 'underground man' is the narrator in Dostoevsky's *Notes from Underground* (1864).

7 Jacques Aymar was a seventeenth-century French diviner who became famous for his ability to find murderers. For an account of Aymar's story see *Curious Myths of the Middle Ages* (1862) by Sabine Baring-Gould (1834-1924). Lowry copied several pages from the relevant chapter, 'The Divining Rod' (UBC 7:4).

8 Erskine's 7 March 1952 letter to Lowry had been addressed to 'Pat 30'

instead of Apt 33, and the error caused a substantial delay in Lowry's receipt of the letter. Erskine apologizes and jokes about this mistake in his 21 March letter.

9 Ralph Ellison (1914–94) was one of Erskine's authors at Random House, which published *The Invisible Man* in 1952. The 'Prologue' to the novel first appeared in *Partisan Review* 19:1 (1952): 31–40. For Lowry's comments on the novel, see his May 1952 letter (**530**) to Erskine.

10 References to the Law of Series and serial time are common in Lowry. The notion that time exists in a series of dimensions, each one contained within a wider one, is articulated by J.W. Dunne in part V of *An Experiment with Time* (1927), a book which Lowry discovered during the late twenties or early thirties and valued highly; see his 16 April 1940 letter (**135**) to his mother-in-law, Anna Mabelle Bonner, his 12 October 1940 letter (**153**) to Harold Matson, and his October 1945 letter (**205**) to Conrad Aiken.

11 Neither this letter nor the one from Stuart Lowry appears to have survived.

Editorial Notes:

a. This pencil holograph, on nine pages of Lowry's canary second-cut paper, carries neither inside address nor date, but both the contents and the sequence of letters to Erskine confirm a date of 24 March 1952 rather than 'Spring 1953,' as given in *Selected Letters*. Since the Lowrys left their Gilford Street apartment to return to Dollarton on 30 March 1952 (see Lowry's Ash Wednesday 1952 letter, **521**, to Erskine), this letter was written at the apartment after 21 March and before 30 March; see annotation 1. The French translation published in *Les Lettres nouvelles* 5 (1960) does not include the postscript, and the version published in *Canadian Literature* 8 (1961) has editorial cuts.

b. The 'digression on Joyce' does not appear to have survived, if it was ever written.

513: To Robert Giroux

P: UBC(ts)
PP: *SL* 295–303   [1075 Gilford St]
                                               [ca 24 March 1952]ᵃ

Dear Mr Giroux:

Let me say right off that I believe you when you say 'It is painful to me to report . . .', that you mean it and it is, just what you say, painful to you.[1] More than that, I even sympathise for you must know what complicated bewilderment, even anguish, your decision has caused at this end, both to my wife and myself, and it's often seemed to me that the only thing worse than suffering is the knowledge that one has been unwittingly forced to inflict pain on other people.

Though it may sound as though I have phrased this half cynically it is not really so: I feel that you must know there is wrong, that you hated to be the instrument of it: even if you had to tell me to the contrary, I couldn't believe you. Even if I didn't feel I know you, the formality of your first communication to me, would seem to belie it. Otherwise, if I didn't see this, this author might find himself saying something like: 'It is likewise painful for me to report that the action of your firm in suddenly casting this author adrift without warning or word after insisting several months ago he be made fast, months of complete silence on your part, would seem to any impartial observer unscrupulously inconsistent with the highest traditions of American publishing, or whatever, not to say the sincerity with which you, as a representative of that firm, sign yourself.' Lots of fine sarcasm of that kind springs only too readily from my brain, or from the demons that inhabit it – I hope in lesser part than the angels – let it go: if I get mad, in the course of this letter, the anger is not directed at you personally, but at a situation, the apparent crucificiality of which the work itself might just as well have brought about for some mysterious reason of its own, though at the moment it's rather hard to see what.

In any case (to return to the human side) I was brought up in a milieu in which I learned to know pretty well that the fellow in command, be he general or sea-captain, may have to take things that he doesn't want to take, do things he doesn't want to do, contradict himself and at the same time have to take the contumely for it, if any, out of a loyalty to the situation which he perhaps doesn't accept but at the same time is honorably committed to; (I even seem to recollect, though it's quite irrelevant, a famous point in maritime law 'where the privity of the owner be not the privity of the master etc etc, the clause that the latter so rarely avails himself of even though entitled to, – recollect, incidentally from my father who, not without a certain observance of poetic justice in this, since his father-in-law was a skipper who'd gone down with his ship, was, among things, a director of Lloyds;[2] the wrath will be piled on the master's head anyway.) In short, I know damn well how, in certain circumstances, you can say no more than that 'I personally regret this . . .' or 'It is painful for me to report . . .' etc.

However it is a pity indeed you should have to find 'painful to report' anything that could have such melancholy consequences as this when it seems to be based on an inexplicable misunderstanding. I take my cue from your letter to me – your complete rejection of me – in which you intimate, and it is courteous of you to do so, that at least there is some compensation in that the relationship must terminate (though another might be pardoned for wondering how a relationship which never exactly began can terminate) on what is after all a publishing rather than an editorial decision. Yes, but who would not be forgiven for thinking that your decision – or lack of it – not to get in touch with me at all, – & here I go, so pardon me in advance! – or even acknowledge the receipt of Lunar Caustic, was not an editorial decision. That was not a publishing decision. I was not holding you up to reply to each facet of my letter, – indeed I asked you not to hurry, knowing you were probably hard-pressed at that time – but I did emphasise, in attempting to cooperate wholeheartedly and simply, the need for contact and advice – and surely the obligation at least to acknowledge the arrival of a manuscript cannot have escaped you, even though no obligation was laid on you through its reception, to spare you any feeling of being saddled with extra responsibility was one reason I sent it direct and not via Hal. It was not sent f-a-s-,[3] so to speak. It was in one way simply a *copy* of stuff I didn't want to lose, of material for future work, and at the same time a sort of earnest of future work, that you had besides asked to see; I asked no editorial decision exactly upon Lunar Caustic per se, though I thought it would be self evident that that material could be regarded as pretty complete and that it could be seen – even if not publishable as it stands, which I'm not sure it isn't – that if I pursued a not too elaborate policy toward it it wouldn't take so long to finish, albeit on all of this I required advice. It would have been no disaster had not Lunar Caustic arrived, for I have a copy, but it would have seemed a very irresponsible beginning to the editor-author relationship from this end, and the failure here from your end would seem inexcusable, considering the torment of suspense it caused me and the psychological effect you must have known it would have, – for it *was* all important to me to know you had it, as it was important to me at least to *know* you had at least received my letters, even if you couldn't reply in detail right off, which I didn't expect or ask for – did I not now believe that part of this whole thing must have been some tragedy of misplaced ethics. You possibly acknowledged the receipt of Lunar Caustic to Hal rather than me: Hal for whatever reason did not get in touch with me, or his letter went astray: in fact, up to the moment of writing, my last letter from Hal was dated January 14, in which he assured me that you wished to establish a good author-editor relationship, that he believed you were the man to hold up your end, and that he was seeing you that week (though the next information we have is a wire on the 6th of March saying 'Brace decided to-day no more advances on basis of work available.') Still, I did not feel, in default of any reply from you either to my first long letter, or the letter accompanying the MSS of Lunar Caustic, that it was right to pursue this matter behind Hal's back, supposing one had not been by then so completely confused and heartsick at the silence that one had been able to pursue it. In this limbo – or perhaps oubliette is the better word – I eventually had to appeal to Hal by wire after letters brought no reply, mentioning that I had a right to know what was going on.[4] But from this only grew what is in fact the further misunderstanding on the basis of which came your report, which it was so painful for you to make and me to receive. Yet even supposing there had been no misunderstanding, was it so unreasonable under the circumstances – which circumstances would readily have been explained to you had you replied to my letters – to have expected some further assistance at this particular period, even if on the basis of Hear Us Oh Lord alone? I don't believe my worst enemy – and I have sweated with fright to think who *he* is – could say that there was. (I didn't mean he was in your firm, I was thinking that Old Scratch himself might have been getting his oar in, not liking – as well he might not – the theme of my work.)

First allow me to quote your whole letter of Dec. 11 to Hal, who for his part carried out your wishes immediately as per the last paragraph in communicating your desires to the said Mr Lowry.

letter.[b]

From this – even your own most inveterate supporter must admit – one would deduce, logically speaking, a feeling that (a) one was wanted as a writer by your firm (b) that you wanted to work out a publishing and financial program for the whole body of Mr Lowry's work. In fact the latter clause you repeat twice, insisting on it again at the end saying: 'We should very much like to work out a publishing program and we should appreciate your communicating our desires in this regard to Mr Lowry.'

Mr Lowry was so communicated with by his loyal agent, with what result of hope to a couple of writers who've been slugging it out in the wilderness with diminishing returns and little success for years or compensation to their agent, you can imagine.

This joy however – as I later tried to point out – was not unmixed, to say the least, because of the wrench of having to leave Albert Erskine, but now I proceed to, before I return to the other, a further point, that is made after the first mention of this noble publishing and financial program for the whole of Mr Lowry's work: that 'He has many admirers here, and indeed friends . . . . to be published here.' All this, I submit, quite logically would lead the said writer to believe that not only was a publishing and financial program for the said writer to be evolved – and that it was your desire it should be evolved, – but that in addition to the financial background, there existed yet another, subtler, background, where as in a shadowy ballet, could be descried a kind of dance of devoted and faithful friends, all of whom might be imagined, as it were, cheering on the author and providing him in his frozen retreat with a sort of warmth and security, as his work beautifully evolved with the beneficent assistance of the other, the more material financial background, with which in turn was related the publishing program you had expressed yourself as so very much liking to work out. Now before I return to the other point I think I have some right to communicate the words written to me two days later – by a coincidence upon the day of the Virgin of Guadeloupe that is so significant to the work itself – by the said agent: follows Matson letter down to than another publisher.ᶜ 'I had no choice,' he goes on, down to editor in chief. . .

'Let us assume that editorially you could have a satisfactory relationship with Harcourt: what kind of financial program would meet your requirements? Is the first draft of Lunar Caustic available?'

Now at this point I was faced with a very hard decision, as I tried to explain to you. I had thought the MSS was going to Albert Erskine, but instead it turned out it had gone to you. If you were refusing to bow out and had decided to stand by your moral and legal rights as I was informed, and I was going to insist upon staying with Albert Erskine, obviously I wasn't doing anybody any good, least of all Mr Erskine, who under those circumstances could scarcely have been other than embarrassed by my loyalty. Indeed it was also difficult to see how one would be proving a friend by insisting that that friend maintain an imaginary freehold upon property that it turned out was within the tenure of another. Moreover having emphasised the importance of the Volcano to the whole in the outline of the work in progress, it was yet further difficult for me to see how my work's attractiveness as a commercial proposition was going to be precisely enhanced by the fact that you owned the Volcano too, as a part of those rights, the more so since now it turned out I'd emphasised it to you rather than to him. So I made my decision then and there, if indeed it could be called my decision and not a case of force majeure, and wired Hal to that effect. I also wired him that I was in desperate need of immediate cash, something that merely looks as though it had something to do with your or my decision at this time, but in fact had none, and was only relevant to it, if at all, in this way, that I could justly have been swayed by the fact that in Dollarton conditions were such this winter that I had not the faintest moral right for my wife's sake to allow her to endure them a day longer than absolutely necessary, though that as I have suggested does not mean that the situation was biblical in its simplicity by any means. {But also the work: another obligation comes in, namely to yourself.} For me to raise what seemed thoroughly impractical objections to what Hal was after all trying to carry through for me, objections which could do no good to Mr Erskine, was extremely unfair to Hal, who has labored long and faithfully on our behalf. I think he would have had an absolute right indeed to tell us to go to hell, I felt I had no right to let the matter drag on into an impasse over and into the New Year but so far it had only occurred to me that your approval of my work must have sent up my stock with Hal, for at least here there seemed the prospect of some money and some possible success in the future again. But my plea for immediate cash was only in part based on this prospect, and it wasn't a plea to you, or was not intended to be, but curiously enough was an appeal to *him*, all of which would be excessively funny if it had not had such complicated and sad results. No, the idea of appealing to you right off for an advance – and on my side I can say quite honestly that this is the only near hypocritical part of the whole business if indeed even this is hypocritical, horrified me; I deplore this English trait, but there it perhaps is: when I realised at last it was you who had sent it through Hal I was not sure my gratitude, which was and is sincere, was not out-weighed by a kind of nightmarish foreboding, for I said to myself: 'There goes the whole thing – for they will say, you offer an Englishman admiration, friendship, and belief in his future, and the bloody man asks you for 500 bucks even before you've had time to down your Scotch.'

I daresay there's something equally English about this kind of self-depreciation too – it's as if we never like to think of anything being transacted on the material plane, even though we've been transacting it, and moreover are perhaps quite capable of carrying through the trans-action to the benefit of all. *We are not here to ask for dollars.* Of course not, Winnie, old boy, how could one even suspect you of such a filthy trick? But as a matter of fact, quite apart from all this, long before the money arrived, and immediately I had sent my telegram of 'acceptance' of what looked like *your* 'acceptance' to Hal, yet another obligation had arisen. This was of course to yourself, or selves, as well as to Hal. If you were going to take my work, the sooner it was got down to again the better, in addition to which it seemed to me that considerable correspondence, & that of an intricate nature, would have to be entered into with your-self. Such work, such correspondence, was becoming more impossible where we lived by the hour. The typewriter was frozen. It is hard to write with gloves on, still harder, perhaps, when you have no gloves. So for this reason alone we had to get out. In order to get out we needed money. And in order to get money, other sources having not yet come through for us, we had to wire Hal. It now strikes me I may have erred in not acceding to Hal's request to outline just what kind of 'financial program' I *did* require, merely saying I left that to him, erred both in this & in not making it clear enough to him what our *exact* financial posi-tion was, though my excuse is the unassailable one that I didn't *know*: from being blackly pessimistic we now had every reason for optimism, but I should have made it clearer that under *normal* conditions we had enough that was gilt edged barely to maintain ourselves in a fashion, even if in poverty, provided the pound did not crash further, and at that even if all our other prospects collapsed, though under these conditions of course work gets slowed down in a crisis by attempts to earn money in a different way.

And to throw some further lightning of sincerity through all this. We owed – and still indeed do owe – Hal money himself – about $250, to be precise – but for once most certainly in my life I was sure that I had some excellent security to borrow some more. There was yourselves, but that was in the future, not at that moment: for almost simultaneously we had a letter from France, from Correa, saying the Volcano had earned nearly half a million francs, and there was some $800 owing me in royalties on the profits of the French translation, and where should they send it: we told them to send it to Hal. Simultaneously I received a contract from my German publishers of the Volcano, – which was a sensation in Germany – offering me 50% of profits on a movie they wished to make of it involving Peter Lorre, who'd already been reading bits of it with great success over the Munich – (God perish the word) – radio.[5] And then there was yourself, or rather yourselves.

But alas, though I sincerely believed in these two former possibilities, Hal was only too right to be sceptical: he has informed me that the French money will take at least 10 months to get through to me – and now the franc's begun to crash – and as for the film, though frantic enthusiasms were sizzling through from Stuttgart, it looks as if it were a chimera. So you sent me the money through him and I have explained how, inexplicably, through carelessness on the Canadian side, it was delayed till after Christmas, which might be termed Favorite but Special Trick of the Fates No. 2. This ominous delay turned out to be a fatal proposition all round (I qualify this later) for we couldn't find a vacant Hotel room till New Years Eve nor a practical hole to crawl into till January 6. It put us to a lot of unnecessary expense and in that weather nearly drove us off our rockers. But yet it was necessary somehow to find that hole, if I was even to begin to deal with what seemed now to be my commitments.

For now behold again the appalling situation then existing here. I don't want to complicate this letter by making dramatic descriptions of the scenery. You only had to look at the Times Building to discover what was happening here.[6] There never has been in all living history of the Pacific Northwest such awe-inspiring weather north of Cape Flattery. Ships had been going down every day around us, including for the record the S.S. Pennsylvania, out of Chapter II of the Volcano, with all hands off Vancouver Island – all hands save one, a Vancouver

Ishmael, I should add, as if to report the matter to old Jay Leyda. Tides rose 5 and 6 feet beyond any hitherto known levels. What you think this was like living in a fisherman's shack, though built by ourselves, right in the sea, even though we are supposed to be in an inlet, I can only ask you to imagine. Huge seas, blinding snow, flooding tides, gales of hurricane force, uprooted trees threatening you, shacks falling on their knees and havoc everywhere, certain death if you slipped, etc etc etc, in short a kind of D W Griffith melodrama of the weather such as has never been known ever in these parts.[7]

Naturally amidst this the work was in danger too, as I later told you: hence that anxiety – only two fishermen (once some years ago we were the only people to stick it at all, population of Dollarton went down to 2 at that time, my wife and myself, though it wasn't so terrible as this and we were younger) stuck it right through, and themselves were bachelors: the rest you more or less know from the middle part of my letter.[d]

But to return: one of our main reasons for coming into town as I said was to enable us to get on with the work and fulfill the times suggested in the work in progress: in short, I had hoped and expected to publish – certainly finish – Hear Us Oh Lord late next fall or early winter, and Lunar Caustic the following fall, though if you preferred Lunar Caustic could have been finished and published first: i.e., next winter, and I was preparing to work, as I have in the past, 12 or if necessary 18 hours a day to that end, which was utterly impossible during the deepest part of the winter in Dollarton, as we have discovered in the past years, for there has been a real & startling climatic change here.

Primarily, I was, and am not broke, in the sense that you seem to have been led to believe: far less was I expecting you to support me on the basis of a chimera (not that it *is* a chimera) for 1, 2, 3, or 4 years, or even for that matter – it would be something that would make me decide against you and *go* broke rather – for one month, were business to be conducted as inconsistently as this appears to have been. My financial reverses were & are, I have every reason to believe, temporary: [I have a private income, at worst, – unless the pound should descend further – of just under $100 a month, and when my father's estate is settled I shall be, in these days, well off for an Englishman: certainly enough that I shall never again put myself in such absurd position with any publisher:][e] my French and German publishers are eager for my next book sight unseen and will give me an advance, (which would presumably take some months to get here however) once back in Dollarton, where we shall be moving next week end,[8] we live very economically indeed, I was merely at a point where I required some assistance in order to finish my work that much sooner. In short I must repeat, for I have perhaps not brought out the point sufficiently that in order to do anything at all, and fulfill my promises and the time schedule, I was bound to behave as I have behaved, to have moved temporarily to town in order to continue writing, despite the added expense. I leaned over backwards to cooperate with you. The work would have been done, as I specified. You, on the surface of it, – I mean as the logic of events would present themselves to an unprejudiced observer – let me down as badly as possibly can be. I have not concealed from you the obligation I still owe and still hope to fulfill to Albert Erskine, who was the only one who really believed in me or did anything for me at Reynal and Hitchcock, except Frank Taylor. What remains of this moral obligation I now apply to yourselves, to think of at 4 o'clock in the morning, which I had not known Fitzgerald had advanced as the real dark night of the soul when I wrote the Volcano, and it may be that he was it was 3:30 or even 5 o'clock.

However that may be this letter is not written in the realm of public, nor ethical, nor any other kind of relations but those called human: and it is only because I value human relations, and even in default of it treasure your invisible friendship, and believe that what you have said, as what I have said, operates outside the mechanical march of events, and if not now, 10 years from now, will give you, as me, a peace of soul that I write as I do.

And so – because I believe in the preservation of human relations and human decency – I sign myself, not merely sincerely, but yours, without hypocrisy, with true affection, and belief in what you sincerely said to begin with, and again later, as well as you courteously could – as I not merely courteously but sincerely dare to call myself, your friend,

[unsigned]

Annotations:

1 Lowry is quoting from Giroux's 10 March 1952 letter saying that Harcourt, Brace could not make an offer on *Lunar Caustic*.

2 Lloyd's of London is an association of insurance underwriters that began as marine insurers in the seventeenth century but now provides all types of insurance.

3 The acronym f.a.s. stands for 'free alongside ship/steamer' and refers to goods that are delivered under contract *to* a ship but not *on* to it. In other words, Lowry did not send his manuscript to his agent, Harold Matson, for Matson to deliver; he sent it directly to Giroux.

4 See Lowry's 5 March 1952 telegram (**505**) to Matson.

5 See Lowry's 31 October 1951 letter (**478**) to Ernst Klett and his 31 October 1951 letter (**477**) to Clemens ten Holder.

6 The tower of the Times Building in Times Square, New York, has a motogram that runs around the building and spells out the news. The

Lowrys' screenplay for *Tender Is the Night* calls for a dramatic use of headlines in scene 29.

7 The early American filmmaker D.W. Griffith is noted for his epic scenes.

8 The Lowrys moved back to Dollarton on 1 April 1952.

Editorial Notes:

a. This transcription is from a fifteen-page draft foliation of typescript and holograph (UBC 3:2). Inquiries to Harcourt, Brace have not turned up the typescript sent to Giroux. The copy-text includes many pencil cancellations, insertions, interlineations, and other changes, all testifying to the difficulty Lowry had composing the letter. There are several differences between my transcription and that in *Selected Letters*, although the editors appear to have used the same copy-text. I have followed Lowry's pencil changes *passim* with the single exception noted in e.

b. The word 'letter' is typed at this point to indicate, probably to Margerie, that Giroux's 11 December 1951 letter to Harold Matson should be inserted.

c. Here Lowry indicates insertion of a passage from Matson's 13 December 1951 letter.

d. Lowry has pencilled 'Insert 9' at this point, but no such insert is extant with the draft.

e. Pencil lines have been drawn through this passage; however, in the left margin Lowry has written 'Insert 10 B,' and this passage is numbered '10 B.'

514: To Conrad Aiken

P: H(ms); UBC(phc)
PP: *LAL* 224-28

Vernal Equinox.
/Easter Monday.
Address is now Dollarton
again, & perhaps almost
Ascension day by now.
[20 March-2 April 1952][a]

My beloved old Conrad:

Your old Hammbo[1] ain't been feeling well, in fact has been going through a hell of a passage, but is back on deck, in fact, come to think of it, never left the deck: Margie is fine, work goes well, publishing relations not quite so fine, what with the old firm of Reynal & Hitchcock split up, so that one is divided in one's loyalties & legalities – all this bedside reading to you.

Poor old Dollarton was nearly washed away in a hurricane: but our old self-built second house still stands, to the 'grave delight' of the few remaining fishermen; however we had to seek refuge here[2] finally &

don't return till April Fool's day, when the skunk cabbages will be found singing among the Love's lies bleeding & Evening star, as you might say, not to mention Death Camas & the contorted lousewort.

You were wrong to say I had no way with cats though, as I have a sort of feeling you once did on our passage from Gibraltar,[3] in a friendly fashion, or perhaps you were right, & I merely inherited your way: at all events our cat that we could not bring with us would not stay with the fisherman (though his first owner) with whom we had left him, & instead has gone wild in the bush & the forest, haunts our house, will speak to noone but ourselves by proxy, & is even terrorizing the neighbourhood – perhaps he is 1/4 lynx – so that not liking to think of that among other things, we shall be glad to get back and bail him out of his rowan tree.

Meantime I have contrived a letter to poor old Tom Neeves,[4] reminding him of the rabbits & bacon & things that will be forever unforgotten, not forgetting the Dutch ship like a haystack, & which perhaps will help to assuage his bereavement: how truly compassionate & good of you to think of this, though it is of course but what one would have expected of you.

I congratulate you from the bottom of my heart on getting Ushant done under such circumstances, i.e. the Library etc,[5] am looking forward enormously to reading it, certain it will be great (& also hoping that you will have spared me some of my obscenest failings to use myself – no matter, I would probably plagiarise them anyway etc.) I am proud to be there though, believe me, however foul.

I hope you can read my article in Wake,[6] if it appears, written when the foundations were rising under us, without vomiting: all I wanted to say really was that I considered you not only one of the ten or so greatest writers who ever lived, but one of the greatest sportsmen. So, if I don't get it over, I am telling you that that was what I wanted to say.

I send you a picture of a cat up a telegraph pole.

I'm a pynter & gilder, I am, & by Jesus now I LIVE in Vancouver![7] Or don't I? (At least I did when I wrote the first draft of this) Nevermind, we will all meet in New Zealand.[8]

Alas, that bloody little mowing machine . . .

But in spite of that old small grass be assured of my love & undying respect from ourselves to yourself & Mary from your ever devoted old friend –

Hambo-hambone!

P.S I am just grieved, period, about Gerald & Betty,[9] who were so damned good to us, & such truly good friends, albeit Betty did not like me, she did her best to try, was swell to us, & Margie loved her; I loved them both in my way, & while I wish them every luck in their apparent change of heart, I can't help wishing them together again. My feeling is they were & are both genuine artists, genuinely courageous, the best of people, but as for that good old Betty she read too much of that good old Tchechov, & when you do that on the shores of Lake Ontario, or even of the Bass River, with so many seagulls around, anything may happen . . . But I loathe like hell to think what it may have done to poor old Gerald. Fortunately he has plenty of guts. But what are guts, as Pontius Pilate might have said? . . Especially when you have to use them as bootstraps.

P.P.S. Let the almosting of Arcularis become, in New York, a positiveing – or rather the only kind of Positive that gives relief to man. (There is a swell small – & in fact not so small – beginnings of a theatre here – that is paying its way – No Exit, The Flies, & the Ascent of F6 (not to mention Much ado about Nothing),[10] all playing at different theatres, & to crowded houses, & also some marvellously bizarre dramatists, including perhaps even me; no writers to hold a candle to yourself or anything, or within a million miles, but at least one (who is poeticising something of my own) potentially a hell of a lot better than Christopher Fry, which is not saying much maybe; name of Newton,[11] & the son of a Holy roller, & not above rolling himself, from time to time – so you might, though not for this reason, bear our town in mind with the finished Arcularis? not for free either, for you might make some cash, & they would be honoured. Technical standard of production is extremely high, acting not so hot, or erratic, though there are some fine actresses: by & large though, there is an extraordinary feeling for *language*, which would be good for Mr. A. [Arcularis]. As also, enthusiasm.)

P.P.S. Have just received the news, after many months of Carlsening upon a flying enterprise with breaking tow-ropes (as a consequence of which I didn't want to post this letter in case it depressed you) that Random House & the Modern library people are taking me in tow with a large advance & contract upon the wing. (Of course one still keeps one's fingers crossed. In the army they call it chest.

'What about a game of chequers?'
'Sure, I don't mind.')

God bless you. Malc

P.S. But alack we have not found the cat.

P.P.P.S. I enclose you carbon of letter airmailed to old Tom. I wrote it twice in my own handwriting: finally decided he couldn't read it, so typed it, but was so moved couldn't get the grammar straight even then.[12]

Excuse this messy letter: it was the bloody pen, not to mention the bloody paper, combined perhaps with a slightly bloody mind at the time.[b]

Annotations:

1 As Aiken explained in his 22 January 1952 letter to Lowry (Sugars, 220-24), Hambo is the name of the Lowry character in *Ushant* (1952). Lowry frequently spelt it with two *ms*.
2 'Here' is the Gilford Street apartment where Lowry *began* this letter.
3 Lowry, like Aiken, was a great lover of cats. When Lowry accompanied Aiken and Clarissa Lorenz to Spain in the summer of 1933, the group stopped in Gibraltar before Lowry began the return trip to England; see Lowry's May-June 1933 letter (**45**) to Jan Gabrial.
4 See Lowry's 2 April 1952 letter (**516**) to Neeves. In his 22 January 1952 letter to Lowry, Aiken told him of the death of Mrs Neeves.
5 In 1947 Aiken was elected a Fellow in American Letters of the Library of Congress, and from 1950 to 1952 he held the chair of poetry with the title of Poetry Consultant.
6 In a 28 November 1951 letter (**482**) published in *Wake* 11 (1952): 80-89, Lowry tells of Aiken's rescuing a cat from a telegraph pole.
7 Lowry is parodying a line in *Blue Voyage*: 'A pynter an' gilder, I am, an I've been to Vancouver' (36).
8 In his letter of 22 January, Aiken, tired of the politics at the Library of Congress and anxious about critical response to *Ushant*, claimed to be thinking of escape to New Zealand.
9 Gerald and Betty Noxon, who had moved to Boston in the late 1940s, were divorced in 1951, and Gerald had remarried. The Lowrys were deeply distressed by this news; see Lowry's 23 January 1952 letter (**501**) to Noxon.
10 *No Exit* and *The Flies*, by Jean-Paul Sartre, were published in English translation in 1947. *The Ascent of F6* (1949), by W.H. Auden and Christopher Isherwood, was an experimental play performed by the English Department of the University of British Columbia, and Shakespeare's *Much Ado About Nothing* was the main play staged by the university's Players' Club, from 19 to 22 March 1952.
11 Christopher Fry (1907-) is a British dramatist. Norman Newton, a Canadian writer, actor, and composer, met Lowry in 1949; see Lowry's October 1952 letter (**543**) to Newton. In the early 1950s he and Lowry worked on a stage version (never completed) of Nordahl Grieg's *The Ship Sails On*. In March of 1953 Newton and his wife rescued Lowry from a binge on Vancouver's Skid Row; see Salloum (80-91).
12 2 April 1952 letter (**516**) to Tom Neeves.

Editorial Notes:

a. Lowry has written the Gilford Street address at the top of the page and

then cancelled it; the letter was mailed after their return to the beach on
1 April. Ascension Day, or Holy Thursday, the fortieth day after Easter
(13 April 1952), was 22 May.

b. This letter is difficult to read because it is on three pages of canary
second-cut and the ink has blotted, smeared, and soaked through the
paper.

515: To Albert Erskine

P: Virginia(telegram); UBC(phc)   Western Union
                                                               North Vancouver, B.C.
                                                                   1 April 1952

MARVELLOUS NEWS[1] GOD BLESS YOU AND THANK YOU YOUR WIRE
ASTRAY IN VANCOUVER AND ONLY RECEIVED TONIGHT WE ARE
BACK IN THE FOREST AND WE TOO ARE OVERJOYED LETTER SOON
BEST LOVE FROM US BOTH

                                                                       MALCOLM

Annotations:

1 The news was Erskine's 31 March 1952 telegram: 'Am authorized to
discuss contract with Hal and have accordingly begun to. Am overjoyed. Letter soon.'

516: To Tom Neeves

P: H(ts); UBC(phc)   Dollarton,
                                                               British Columbia,
                                                                    Canada
                                                               [ca 2 April 1952]

Dear Mr Neeves:[1]

Perhaps you don't remember me right off but you will soon. I was a
pupil of Mr Aiken's who lived for many years at Jeake's House on
Mermaid Street in Rye, and we used to come down at six o'clock every
evening and sometimes about midday – and sometimes myself earlier
still – and sit in the parlour of your good old Ship Inn and drink the odd
half quartern of whiskey and chat, with your self, and your beloved
wife, and I want to say that these were some of the happiest times of my
life; and among the most treasured memories, I am sure, of Mr Aiken,
who had the added advantage of living permanently in Rye and so could
patronize your never to be forgotten hostelry more often than I could,
are those of your good selves and of the Ship. In the evening he always

finished the serial in the Daily Mirror before he would drink his second half quartern, whereas I always wanted to drink my second half quartern before he had got to the end of the second paragraph of the Daily Mirror serial: but that doesn't matter. Nor does it, that it was more than twenty years ago. It is indeed 15 years since I have seen Mr Aiken, because we have been separated by circumstances of wars and different countries, but I have always looked upon him much as a father, besides which he is one of my best friends, and so we have never lost touch. Well, those were your friends and Mrs Neeves' friends – you remember Mr Aiken of course, but that was me too, sitting in your parlour at the Ship Inn (or even standing in the case of myself, supposing this to be possible, in the other bar.)

Mr Aiken was of course an old and good friend of your wife and yourself years before I ever met him, he is at present the Librarian of Congress in the United States of America, and he has just written to me in Canada, telling me the grievous news that Mrs Neeves, your dear wife, has died, and what I wanted to say – if I can say it in words – was something to convey to you my very deepest sympathy in your irreparable loss, a loss that will be shared by all I know who were happy enough to know Mrs Neeves and yourself. Mr Aiken's letter indeed goes back almost thirty years, because he fondly remembers that it was into the Ship that he went upon September 5, 1924, to celebrate the birth of his daughter Joan, at which time he tells me (for I was only a boy of fifteen at that time) that you and Mrs Neeves – and so vivid is the memory he recalls even that the hawthorn was in bloom – had newly moved from the Ypres.

For myself, I never can forget many of your wife's sweet actions of kindness to us and others: apart from anything else, I remember the incomparable rabbit and bacon, and the way she would prepare that: and many other happy things beside, of you both, including the understanding things she said, and the feeling of being at home that one had at the good old Ship, when in those days there might be a Dutch schooner you would describe as a 'haystack' loading outside in the river, and the feeling of happiness and goodness too that was imparted from your lives to this then young writer.

Mr Aiken valued both your friendships enormously: equally, myself: and as he mourns for you, so do I attempt to commiserate with you in your great bereavement, though for myself I cannot believe it to be a final loss, for surely you will be reunited again – and ourselves, may it be hoped too, all of us, in another 'Ship.'

God bless you Mr Neeves, good luck & greetings for Easter

Sincerely your old friend & happy customer

Malcolm Lowry

Annotations:

1 Tom Neeves owned and operated the Ship Inn in Rye, Sussex, where Aiken particularly liked to drink and often took Malcolm.

517: To Albert Erskine

P: Virginia(ms); UBC(phc)
PP: *SL* 304   [3 April 1952][a]

Dollarton – Thursday

Hooray, Albert!

Just a line to reciprocate joyousness, & try & express my gratitude & relief. Inexpressible, so can't do it at the moment. Everything has been held up here for the last week due to sickness + exigencies of moving – former nothing serious but requiring sulfalanimide etc, on Margie's side; more or less ok now. Your first letter arrived Monday in Dollarton; but your telegram went to Vancouver, & so was delayed!: the fault was entirely theirs, not yours or ours. There is terrific damage here in Dollarton, though our house has come through practically – or rather relatively – unscathed: some houses have fallen down altogether or have even disappeared. Nothing has been lost though & it was a wonderful homecoming. Margie is dancing a saraband despite lingering flu. There is much manual labour – fuel chiefly – to be done in next week so forgive if there is slight let up in correspondence. Will write to-morrow more fully. Hooray again & all gratitude – God bless from us both –

Malcolm

P.S. Dear Albert – decks are now nearly cleared for action, we have put ourselves on Double Daylight Saving time, & we are at the barrier & ready for the Bell: the sackcloth has been newly pressed, a load of Fine Fresh Ashes is to be delivered to-morrow, and of a *more Modern, more Efficacious* type, the spikes on the renunciatory breastplate are all shining with brasso, the iron virgin is in order (sort of), and the Waterwagon rises shining in the East each morning over a sea so cold that it was recently reported that noone could live in it for five minutes, on account of which nevertheless one swims in it each morning for six: – in short, all that remains is to *Get the Serum Through.* (P.T.O.)

But a slight problem still remains: what Serum? Margie & I are in disagreement upon this point: she thinking I ought first to finish up The Path To the Spring, the piece de resistance of Hear Us, & Panama, which needs some trimming and contains some stuff I disapprove of, as probably you do too: & myself inclining toward finishing up some of the shorter stories first none of which will have anything to do with writers or writing (though there might be an exception). Hear Us in my opinion needs another longish masterpiece – already in Existence in its near final draft – called October Ferry to Gabriola & also having nothing to do with writers; I'd tackle that next, then finish off the Path & Panama. One thing we're agreed on: I shouldn't trouble you with any more *unfinished* work, with the exception of the notes for the whole – this simply a *copy* – that will come along concurrently & sporadically, though of course finished work is subject to your criticism. So Monday I'll get down to my plan and continue upon it unless I hear very much to the contrary from you, for example to the effect that you want the novel Lunar Caustic first, & not the tales. The gruesome mood I was lately in would probably help here but I'd rather do the stories and get into a current of health & sun, with the aim of finishing up Hear Us by this autumn, & thus firing the first shot ahead of schedule. O.K. We're off already. God bless. Malcolm.

P.S. Invisible Man still languishes invisibly in Customs.[1]

Annotations:

1 Although Ellison's novel had not yet arrived, Lowry was familiar with parts of it; see his March 1952 letter (**512**) to Erskine. For Lowry's comments on the novel, see his May 1952 letter (**530**) to Erskine.

Editorial Notes:

a. The Thursday on which Lowry is writing is 3 April, three days after they returned to the beach. The long postscript and the short one regarding *Invisible Man* are in pencil on recto and verso of a torn sheet of paper (UBC 3:3), and they are included here because details of context, tone, and the sequence of events suggest they belong with this letter.

518: To Albert Erskine

P: Virginia(ms); UBC(phc)   Dollarton
                                                        [5 April 1952]

Dear Albert:

Was involved all yesterday getting up a gigantic log from the beach for fuel so found myself unable to write. This I shall try to do this week end.

With the improved financial situation, though, the major fuel transportation problem will be solved, with corresponding saving of time, for
I shall be able to afford 'to have sended a boy with it' through the forest[1]
– instead of wrestling it all down myself.

But because the house, though staunchly intact, is in the hell of a mess
& the weather is none too good as yet there may be some small delay at
this end before we can get things moving properly. Will write as I say
in more detail re contract, work etc this week end – i.e to-night & to-
morrow.

God bless you. Great love from us both.

Malcolm

Annotations:

1 See Dr Vigil's remarks in chapters 1 and 5 of *Volcano*.

519: To Harold Matson

P: Matson(ts); UBC(phc)   Dollarton, B.C.,
PP: *SL* 310-12   Canada
                                                          7 April 1952

Dear Hal –

Sorry to be so long in answering your letter re the contract,[1] but as
you see by the above address we are back home in Dollarton and the
letter took 3 days apparently to be forwarded out here from town.

Now, to get straight down to business so I can get this off to you
today by our one post. I am more than happy about the contract as of
course you must know. I think the financial terms are most generous
and I accept them without any alteration. I should like to feel though,
whether it's in the contract or not, that in case of some real emergency,
say an accident to Margie or myself entailing hospital, or something, that
I could draw up to 2 or 3 hundred if it was absolutely necessary. As
things are shaping up at the moment though, this looks unlikely for my
whole financial picture re England will eventually improve and it may
not be much longer. Yes, I most certainly am interested in your plan
of funding the money in case of any success, and please do whatever is
necessary about this. I certainly should never want over $10,000 in
one year, and I'm almost inclined to set this at less, say, $7,000 or so.

Now for my part of the contract I must say that I don't honestly know
how I can deliver **3** books in 2½ years.[2] Two books I can guarantee and
I'll do my best about the third, I can finish Hear Us O Lord and Lunar
Caustic all right, and if the third could be a book of poems they can

publish that any time for I have sufficient for a volume now. But another novel I can't absolutely promise – that is, I could get out something or other of course but it might not be my best work; but then again I don't know until I see better how things shape up. We have concurrently an enormous transcriptionary job of material in hand facing us which must be done and I am very anxious not to let anyone down, so am reluctant to promise what I'm not completely sure of. This material of course covers all the books and I could certainly guarantee to get this in, in addition to Lunar Caustic and Hear Us Oh Lord, well within that period. I can deliver the first book within a year. I hope to have finished Hear us O Lord by this fall, but just to give myself leeway you'd better say a year. Actually, I'd like to publish Hear Us Oh Lord next spring anyhow, though again this depends on correspondence with Albert, etc. What I would like is to keep the thing as flexible as possible and then exceed, rather than fall short of, the publisher's expectations. On the other hand I rewrite a lot and don't want to be tempted to let anything but my best work get by.

One last question for my part: suppose something came up about making a movie (and did you write Klett, by the way?)[3] of the Volcano, say, would something like a few months grace be granted so that I could work on the scenario? It's not impossible the scenario itself might be publishable, and I'm not sure what I mean by grace either.

I think this covers everything. I can't somehow get down to work properly until this contract is actually signed: the Brace-Giroux shindy, dragging on as it did, had us nearly shattered, and I keep worrying and nagging at myself, so I'll be most relieved when this is finally settled.

A thousand thanks, for everything, love from us both,

Malcolm

Annotations:

1 Matson had written to Lowry on 1 April 1952 outlining the terms of the forthcoming contract with Random House as follows: a total advance of $5,000 with $500 on signing the contract and $150 per month for two and one-half years.

2 Lowry's contract with Random House called for delivery of 'three works of fiction' in three years; one could be a collection of short stories. See Figure 9 with letter **521**. In his 14 April 1952 reply to this letter, Matson reminded Lowry that he could only rely on the publisher's good will in an emergency.

3 In his 14 January 1952 letter to Lowry (*Selected Letters*, 447–48) Matson says that he has never heard from Ernst Klett or Clemens ten Holder about a German film of *Under the Volcano*, and he wonders whether he should write to Klett. He promises to contact Peter Lorre in an effort to 'unravel the tangle.'

520: To Albert Erskine

P: Virginia(ms); UBC(phc)   Dollarton
                                                      [ca 8 April 1952][a]

Dear old Albert: –

This is just a note to thank you again for the superb job you did for me; I interrupted the long letter I was writing you over the weekend to reply to a letter of Hal's in regard to the contract,[1] which naturally I think marvellous – though they're a few small modifications, for example I'm not sure I can deliver **2** absolutely completed novels & **1** book of tales in 2½ years, though I can give you Caustic & Hear Us within 2 years – will you speak to Hal in regard to what I said about this? I'm terribly anxious not to let you down, is all, & I guess I've got a bad case of stage fright right at the moment. Also the purely transcriptionary job that must be done concurrently is bothering me and of course you can't see how important this is till you receive it. Moreover I think I ought now to concentrate on getting Hear Us in as fine shape as possible within the time allotted, & on top of everything else we are by necessity in the throes of a gigantic housecleaning – one has to sweep the seaweed & the dead sailors & even mermaids out before one can find a place to sit. I am speechless with gratitude to you about the whole thing so if this letter seems a bit unbusiness-like please understand & forgive.

God bless.

Malcolm

Annotations:

1 See Lowry's 7 April 1952 letter (**519**) to Matson. The 'long letter' that Lowry mentions is his of Ash Wednesday, April 1952 (**521**).

Editorial Notes:

a. This pencil holograph is undated, but internal references suggest a date immediately after letter **519** to Matson.

521: To Albert Erskine

P: Virginia(ms); UBC(phc)
PP: *SL* 304-09   Dollarton
                                                     [ca 10 April 1952][a]
                                    Ash Wednesday (.with reservations.).[1]

Dear old Albert:

This, an interpolated note of affection and gratitude merely, with the knowledge that you have not time to reply. (But also with the intention of explaining a few peripheral things.)

A clean house, at last, even a clean soul, what is more; a full moon over the inlet, the mergansers gone to rest and the mink returned to her hollow tree. Never was anything more miraculously well nor more peaceful in our town – population three: – perhaps four, if 'Kristbjorg' is still on deck: he swears, or swore the day before yesterday, that in the 60 years of his experience he has never seen the sea do anything worse than it has done here: it has cut away about 20 feet in depth of the entire forest sea bank, dropping whole gardens into the sea, not to say houses, while the entire shore has changed from about 1/15 gradient to about 1/6 in places, with the corresponding undermining of foundations. 'Quaggan's'[2] log float in front of his boathouse – the whole two hundred feet of it – carried away completely: – but our pier still stands, – absolutely undamaged – as do our foundations, despite the fact that we have four and a half whole uprooted trees terrifyingly *under* our house: since our pier is made only out of light two-by-fours & 2 inch planking, is now ten years old, & has stood the brunt of the worst furies of wind & sea ever endured here, we have not met anyone yet who has even bothered to think of a material explanation for its survival, though there might be one, namely in its simplicity, lightness, & freedom from top hamper: thus in a terrific sea, & it was overwhelmed, under water when we left, instead of giving way to the sea & lifting from its foundations, it simply & calmly clung to the beach & stayed where it was; the foundations being just slightly heavier than the overall plankings: nearly all professional jobs gave way in this vicinity, for not having recognized whatever principle there is in this: they figured that the heavier and stronger the planking, the more weight it would place on the foundations, & hence the foundations would be the securer & the whole safer in any emergency: but it ain't so – wood *floats* & will try & float even if nailed down, and, if overwhelmed by water, the heavier it is, the harder it will pull at the nails – and all round I guess there is a some sort of lesson – apart from an image – in this, the more so since the foundations in this case simply & contrariwise adjusted themselves to the under-mining of the beach, instead of vice versa & became securer than ever: naturally we are very proud of ourselves.[3] Our subsidiary house was not so lucky, as we said but then we didn't build it: even that has stood up, though minus a pile, it is sagging badly at one end & we have to prop it up.

II

I have interrupted another longer letter to you to write you this – because of changing circumstances – but will try to supply you with a sort of log. Friday, March 28, two days before we left the apartment, we ran into a typhoon & damn nearly foundered almost in Falmouth harbour – very eerie, & dramatic, albeit with a happy outcome – I'll not tell you of it now, though god knows it's worth the telling, – it left Margie, who was besides sick & taking sulfalanimade for a throat, unable to type & almost completely shattered, coming on top of everything else: I can type but not well enough on her typewriter to transcribe the job I was then doing, which was a letter to Giroux, especially as I proposed to give you a carbon: I was trying to make the point tactfully, that while I did not blame him personally, since they had made such a to-do about moral rights, where their or the office boy's moral rights to the Volcano came in: so this letter – though almost finished – I had to abandon or leave in abeyance, & since Haas' decision and yours in my favour, the Case is somewhat Altered.[4]

Sunday we came home: by a coincidence on 'Quaggan's' birthday – which he had celebrated in part by putting hot bricks on our soaking mattress & chopping some wood for us: so we had a warm as well as a happy homecoming. Of course we do the same sort of thing for him when we can & when necessary, each for the others, but I hadn't known the efficacy of hot bricks till then. He had lost our poor cat though (which has gone wild) so you might say – horrible image on second thoughts – we had the hot bricks without the cat. I guess he'll come home though, that is the cat; at least he has been 'reported to have been seen.'

Monday 31st – we got your airmail letter written to Dollarton saying that things were still in abeyance, but since Monday was a kind of crucial day with Haas so far as I could gather, we (expecting – as it happened correctly – a wire from you were there good news) felt some gloom & prepared to fight the rearguard action still further e.g letters for paying your debt etc, though I had become in transit confused about the poems, & what to send: so preparing for the worst began to 'dig out sails.' Margie meanwhile was rallying nobly.

Tuesday April 1.

Your wire came through to the store, eventually by telephone: it having been sent to the apartment the day before. They said oh well, they thought that was our address, & the note had been put under no 33 at the apartment. *But the telegram had meantime been lost* – they said. Finally they found a copy of it & phoned it to the store & Margie came whooping through the woods with the best news I ever heard in my life. (Actual telegram, which we now have on our wall, did not arrive till 2 days later – but it was a supreme moment – & bless you for sending it.)[5] Rest of the week: – I received the general terms of the contract both from yourself and Hal, who expressed his unqualified admiration for what you have done for me, as I do ten times more, my unqualified gratitude: − Hal's letter though went likewise to the ex-apartment in Vancouver, & not here (though we might seem to be to blame here for not having informed Hal directly of our change of address, this is actually one of the strangest of coincidences, for the General Post office had our change of address by postcard well in advance; in addition to the P.O.'s error Hal failed to put the apartment no. on the envelope so it was surprising it reached us at all, though it did, if delayed: (in the case of your telegram going to the apartment, while we hadn't thought it necessary to inform the telegraph Co. of a change of address since we had informed you, they simply & inexplicably disregarded the Dollarton address you'd given, as I have explained)) so I felt obliged to reply to Hal first.[6]

I told him I was not sure of 2 *absolutely completed* novels + 1 book of tales i.e **3** bonafide books, 2 of them novels, in 2½ years, as seemed called for, despite your more than generous terms, for which terms please also express my deep gratitude to Mr Haas: though I could guarantee Hear Us Oh Lord & Caustic in that time, or even in 2 years, + (as I said in a telegram −) the detailed scenario of the whole, albeit this last entails no obligation to yourself, on the other hand I feel it a necessary item: on the other hand again this *detailed* scenario of the whole might seem to many novelists to subsume several more completed novels, but it all depends upon what the hell one considers a completed work of art, and it is on this point that I really desire some leeway for consultation with yourself, and advice. It is possible that Lunar Caustic could be finished way ahead of schedule, and that The Ordeal of Sigbjorn Wilderness both parts I & II would make a novel that could be completed in the remaining time. But Dark as the Grave Eridanus & La Mordida are together a trilogy and though they might well be published separately − as will probably turn out to be the best idea − I can't *think* of them at present separately, a problem you will readily see when you receive the material in question: two years hence, if all goes well, with Hear Us already published & Lunar Caustic in your hands, it might be that in the remaining six months I could finish Dark as the Grave, say, but I can't quite think that far ahead with any degree of feeling completely honest as to what it is possible to achieve − and naturally I would like to achieve more than I promise. What I am chiefly anxious to do, presented with such generous terms as you have offered me, is to pay my way, fulfil your trust in me and not to let anyone down. So please don't think that I am beginning to hedge or chisel on the contract: the last thing I want to be is a 'difficult' author in that sense. On the contrary I really am motivated by a feeling that once I've got going with any luck & God's help I may be able considerably to exceed your expectations.

Re the financial end of it, it is more than generous,[7] as I have said, but since there seemed some possible flexibility in the arrangement, while accepting it gratefully on whatever terms seem likewise most convenient to yourself, I asked Hal that in case of some kind of untoward accident to wife or self I might feel I could ask to apply at some time for a couple of hundred dollars or so in advance, if and only if, I really mean & add now – it seemed absolutely necessary to the fulfilment of the contract, though I qualified this by saying – which is true – that such an eventuality does not seem likely, and so shouldn't necessarily be an item on the contract: the reason is that my whole financial picture seems likely to improve. I have another letter from France that so far as they know that 800 dollars *is* coming through after all without the franc having fallen: & though England is still stalling for time I expect confirmation of similar good news from that quarter. So with your generous lift & these other items I expect not only to pay my debts but to [be] well in the clear in regard to emergencies. For we do have a hospital insurance scheme. What was nearly tragic for us when we first borrowed money from you was one that the premium was compulsory & so high that one couldn't afford to pay the ordinary doctor's bills or buy medicine. As for me, my health is excellent.

The other item was there has been a question of a film of the Volcano, with Peter Lorre.[8] Whether this is going to come off or not, I don't know, but if it did, I asked for a few months grace or leave or absence or something during which I might assist with the script. Naturally one would not expect to be supported by Random House during such a period; I would not want it to interfere with the final fulfilling of the contract, but naturally such a thing might prove circumambiently a factor in paying one's way.

Finally I said if the third book couldn't be within that time a novel I have a collection of poems The Lighthouse Invites the Storm that could be got in order almost any time: one would not expect this to sell, but if Lunar Caustic was going good & more than paying for itself, it could act as a stop-gap. Finally I have something I hadn't thought of, namely the film we did for Frank [Taylor], which is still supposed to be secret, though the secret now seems absurd to keep from you, albeit I haven't told Hal its name.[9] Whether or not this would be feasible as a quid pro quo for a third completed book within that allotted period – what with the difficulties of copyright & the joint authorship – I don't know, but it's existence is at least an earnest of what one can do. We did it in seven months & have not even accepted or borrowed any cash on it & indeed it, alack, did not do for Frank what we had hoped: but perhaps that wasn't its fault, & it may yet. And certainly it wasn't Frank's fault.

Shall I write Frank to send it to you? I dropped Dark as the Grave to write this – and eventually I had hoped among other bright results for Frank it would prevent our getting into precisely the sort of situation we did get into. I enclose some comments by Isherwood, Leyda, & Frank himself.[10] It is by no means an ordinary kind of script. The film of course is Tender is the Night & I know Frank won't mind my mentioning it. In fact by writing it for him we felt we were in some sort 'keeping in the family'. The result was just the beginning of our three years heartbreak: but at least we keep a 'tryin'.

I have hundreds more French reviews, panegyrics of the Volcano, Teutonic headlines, Norse encomiums, & even caricatures of the author: – but perhaps these are now somewhat beside the point, so I am not bothering you with them for the present.

A Happy Easter to you from us both & loads of gratitude & love

Malcolm

Annotations:

1 Ash Wednesday, the first day of Lent, fell on 27 February in 1952. Lowry is writing closer to Easter Sunday, 13 April 1952.
2 Quaggan, Lowry's name for one of the beach-dwellers in 'Elephant and Colosseum,' is based upon the Lowrys' friend Jimmy Craige, who often welcomed them back to the beach by warming their cabin.
3 Lowry's pride in this pier testifies to its importance for him. The seemingly fragile structure became a symbol of strength, beauty, and endurance for Lowry, and he was devastated to learn of its destruction in the spring tides of 1955; see his August 1956 letter (**662**) to Harvey Burt.
4 Lowry's allusion to Ben Jonson's play *The Case Is Altered* (1599) not only signals the alteration in his fortunes but also recalls *Under the Volcano*, where references to this play create a leitmotif for a complex reversal of luck.
5 Unfortunately, this telegram has not survived. I have not been able to trace either letter that Lowry mentions here.
6 See Lowry's 7 April 1952 letter (**519**) to Matson.
7 Random House was considering an annual stipend of $10,000, but Lowry was prepared to accept less if he could have some flexibility on delivery dates. The final agreement, signed on 5 May 1952, stipulated that Lowry would receive monthly payments of $150, the sum of these payments and any advances not to exceed $8,000 in any one calendar year. Lowry's commitment was explicit: three works of fiction, one of which might be 'a collection of short stories and novelettes,' to be delivered to Random House no later than 1 November 1953, 1 May 1955, and 1 November 1956. See Figure 9.
8 See also Lowry's 7 April 1952 letter (**519**) to Matson.
9 This is the Lowrys' 1949 filmscript of *Tender Is the Night*.

10 Christopher Isherwood, Jay Leyda, and Frank Taylor had all been enthusiastic about the filmscript; see appendix 7 of *Selected Letters* (441–43). The original letters are with the Erskine Papers at the University of Virginia.

Editorial Notes:

a. This undated, pencil holograph is on the rectos of ten sheets of canary second-cut. The contents and state of the holograph suggest that it was written over several days.

RANDOM HOUSE, INC.

(THE MODERN LIBRARY)

AGREEMENT made this **5th** day of **May** , 195**2** between RANDOM HOUSE, INC. of 457 Madison Avenue, New York 22, N. Y. (hereinafter referred to as the Publisher) and
MALCOLM LOWRY
who is a citizen of **Great Britain**
whose address is **Dollarton Post Office, Dollarton, British Columbia, Canada,**
(hereinafter referred to as the Author and designated by the masculine singular pronoun)

WITNESSETH: WHEREAS the parties hereto are mutually desirous respectively of publishing and having published a certain work of **fiction** (hereinafter referred to in the singular: one of which may be an author or one of short stories and novelettes, and each approximately 100,000/200,000 words in length and provisionally xxxxx untitled.

Delivery of Satisfactory Final Copy

IV. The Author agrees to deliver complete finally revised copy of the said work, in the English language, in content and form satisfactory to the Publisher and ready to print from, xxxxxxxxxxxx **(see below)** .xxxxxxxxxxxxxxxxxxxxxxxxxxx If the Author fails to deliver such copy within ninety (90) days after said date the Publisher may terminate this agreement by giving written notice to the Author to such effect and thereupon shall be entitled to repayment from him of all amounts which may have been advanced to him as hereinafter provided. Unless the Publisher shall notify the Author in writing within ninety (90) days from the receipt of such finally revised copy that it is unsatisfactory, it shall be deemed to have accepted said manuscript for publication. The Author further agrees to supply promptly all photographs, drawings, charts, indexes, and other material necessary to the completion of his manuscript, and if he fails to do so the Publisher shall have the right to supply them and charge the cost thereof against any sums accruing to the Author under this agreement. The complete manuscript shall include the following additional items:

The first work not later than **November 1, 1953,**
" second " " " " **May 1, 1955,**
" third " " " " **Nov. 1, 1956,**

IN WITNESS WHEREOF the parties hereto have duly executed this agreement the day and year first above written.

RANDOM HOUSE, INC.

In the presence of

By _____ **V.P.**
The Publisher

MALCOLM LOWRY

In the presence of

_____ *witness sign here*

_____ *The Author*

Figure 9: *These excerpts from Lowry's contract show the key details of his commitment and the signatures of Albert Erskine, Robert Haas, Jimmy Craige, and Malcolm Lowry. The contract is with the Harold Matson Company Papers, Rare Book and Manuscript Library, Columbia University.*

522: To Albert Erskine

P: Virginia(telegram); UBC(phc)

Western Union,
Vancouver, B.C.
15 April 1952

PLEASE WIRE[1] IF ALL WELL AM ANXIOUS LOVE

MALCOLM

Annotations:

 1 Erskine sent a wire to Lowry on 15 April, immediately after receiving
 Lowry's, explaining that he was 'swamped by work plus two weeks'
 jury duty.'

523: To Gerald Noxon

P: Texas(ts)
PP: *LLN* 157–58

Dollarton, B.C.,
Canada
[April 1952]ᵃ

– Time for the train that 'goes a
long way,' i.e., toward Port Moody
and points east. . . *y'lang, y'lang.*[1]

Beloved old Gerald:

This written in haste and in a state of gnattering partly because of a
high temperature: first Margie with the spring fever, now me, the
weather bloody and Dollarton half smashed up last winter (though our
'gazebo' as you called it, the pier, as does our house, still stands, nobly,
though I say it who ought not, or ought, since one lives in it: and it still
is, as always, waiting for your spring visit, blaze of primroses as you once
said still there, same primroses, though that same house is not there,
except for that old semi-woodshed outside of which you used to sit,
now part of the new house, shit on this prose). Immediate trouble
though is a debt, albeit one of honour, incurred by me or us to one
Albert Erskine, Random House, 457 Madison Ave., New York 22.

This debt (I mean the debt that I have morally to pay in a hurry) is
precisely to the tune i.e. $100 of that which you were good enough to
inform us that owing to the default of our postmaster, you owe to us,
or rather Margie: and it would make us sleep better, if you have it, or
even if you don't – sleep better not on your account but on ours –
if having it, or having it not, you were able to send this amount to
the said Erskine, reason being that the said good Erskine, likewise
stuck with difficulties of divorce and above that of teeth, lent us this

money out of what he had reserved to pay his dentist.

Fate moves in a mousterious way, as Bobby Burns did not care to remind his field mouse,[2] who now occupy our entire quarters from garden to roof to basement, which was the bear's cage, as you remember: when not suffering from delirium tremens one should encourage them to eat wild bleeding heart and chickweed rather than one's dinner, though we haven't the bleeding heart to kill one yet, not even with mousecide.

When I have told you this I have not told you all; principally that I believe Random House and the Modern Library – of which the said Albert Erskine (whom you remember) is now the managing editor, – are now, after long and agonized wrangling, my publishers: they aren't going to give me a big advance, however, but a small sum every month for the next few years to enable me to get some work completed; this makes it difficult to pay out lump sums. But this is an immediate matter of teeth, Erskine's teeth: and must be paid back to him, somehow, by summer.

Meantime the Volcano has been a smash hit in Germany and there was even talk of making a movie of it there con Peter Lorre;[3] they sent me a contract months ago offering me fifty-fifty; I refused (even though broke) unless I – we & even, the faint hope persisted, perhaps you? – could have a say in the script, haven't heard any more but the fact remains that –

God bless you, from us both to you both

from

Malc

P.S. I left out the most important part. Since it now seems that a long term contract is definitely going through with Random House I should – though not immediately, for we have to get out of debt first – be eventually in a position where, should you be short at any time, we could lend you a spot of dough. We haven't forgotten your great generosity in lending us that 200 when we got burned out not to say generosity in other respects. I couldn't thank you too much for the help you gave me with the Volc & Margie with the Horse & we only wish to God we were lucky enough to have your counsel at the moment in regard to Work in Progress. Hope you are well & happy, all the best to Nick, & love to your wife & self

Malc

Annotations:

1 In 'The Forest Path to the Spring,' Port Moody, an industrial town at the head of Burrard inlet, is called Port Boden, and the train, a branch

of the Canadian Pacific Railway that still runs east along the south shore of the inlet and the north bank of the Fraser River, ringing its bell, is a symbol of joy and hope.
2 The Scots poet Robert Burns (1759-96) wrote lyrics in the vernacular about love, patriotism, and nature; Lowry is thinking of his well-known poem 'To a Mouse' (1786).
3 See Lowry's 23 November and 8 December 1951 letters (**479** and **484**) to Harold Matson, and his 31 October 1951 letter (**477**) to Clemens ten Holder.

Editorial Notes:

a 'Spring 1949' has been written at the top of this typescript, but internal evidence confirms a 1952 date. The postscript is in pencil on a separate sheet of canary second-cut.

524: To Harold Matson

P: Matson(telegram)

Western Union,
Dollarton, B.C.
25 April 1952

IS SILENCE DUE ALBERTS JURY DUTY[1] OR TROLLS HERE LOVE

MALCOLM

Annotations:

1 During March and April of 1952 Erskine was serving on a jury, and his office work had piled up. Matson replied immediately, assuring Lowry that Erskine was now free and that final word on the contract would be coming soon.

525: To Clemens and Hildegard ten Holder

P: UBC(ts)
PP: *SL* 312-13; *Brief* 51-52

Dollarton, B.C.,
Canada
26 April 1952

Very dear ten Holders:
    Please for God's sake forgive us.
    We likewise were in the abyss – of poverty, floods, hurricanes, cold, anguish and publisher's misunderstandings.
    Your wonderful Christmas box – Hildegarde – was delayed so long by our beastly customs that it seemed almost hurtful to acknowledge it

so late, but we enjoyed and appreciated deeply everything about it, and the care put into it, and we now have the beautiful calendar on the wall. Many, many, many thanks for the little Christmas cookies – still tasty after all that time and eaten with love and gratitude.[1]

We have done everything we can about the film, bearing your interests (Clemens) in mind, but there is nothing more we can do but wait. Always, wait, wait, wait.

We sympathise deeply with your awful winter, we too were forced to abandon our Paradiso, to the hail and flood and indeed we seem to have been closely identified with yourselves in your own parallel heart-break: but we are now likewise back in our Paradiso, though but a fisherman's shack, self-built, in the wilderness.

(I have met Djuna Barnes in New York.[2] She is the one and only Original Gigantic Ghoul from Gomorrah. But with a good heart. She was painting some sort of semi-female male demon on the wall, reproved me roundly for the success of the Volcano, generously gave me 6 quart bottles of beer and expressed herself frightened by Nightwood, since when she said she has written nothing. I myself cannot make out whether Nightwood is a work of genius or a disorder of the kinaesthesia: probably both. All in all, I thought her him or It an admirable, if terrifyingly tragic, being, possessing both integrity and honour: but despite the great formal and linguistic merits of Nightwood I find the sources of its inspiration so impure, and non-universal that I have been reluctant mentally really to visit them and so properly and in detail apprehend that work, if it indeed deserves to be apprehended other than in some unique category of the monstrous, though on another plane it possesses admirable technical virtues. But what a hell of a thing to try and translate. Good luck be with you! I should be the last to deny the relative heroism and even significance of that book, even if finally one hates it.)

Well, we are in sorrow for you, as you for us, but spring has come, so bear with us and let us hope for good news soon – forgive us again –

We think of you always affectionately. With sincere love from us both –

Malcolm

P.S. Should you be in touch with Djuna Barnes, for god's sake do not repeat my malicious words to her; of which I already feel slightly ashamed. Let me atone by offering to help with the translation on any points that may baffle you, for its difficulties are all but insuperable even in English, & I believe you may find her quite indifferent & unco-operative. We possess the edition published by New Directions.[3]

Annotations:

1 In her 4 December 1951 letter (UBC 1:67) to Margerie, Hildegard ten Holder writes that she has just sent a Christmas parcel to the Lowrys.
2 The American writer Djuna Barnes published *Nightwood* in 1936, and it has since become a classic. Barnes spent most of the twenties and thirties in Europe, much of the time as an expatriate in Paris. After her return to New York in 1939 her health deteriorated and she became a recluse in Greenwich Village, where Lowry visited her in February 1947; see his 17 September 1947 letter (**321**) to James Stern. Barnes did some paintings of friends and drawings, the latter to illustrate her stories and essays, so Lowry may well have seen her art. He read *Nightwood* soon after its publication, and the Reverend Betty Atwater (Carol Phillips) recalled him recommending it to her in the spring of 1939.
3 This copy, with T.S. Eliot's introduction, is in Lowry's library.

526: To David Markson

P: UBC(ms)
PP: *SL* 313–15

Dollarton, B.C.
[26 April 1952][a]

Dear Dave:
    Reason I didn't reply was that almost immediately upon the arrival of your first letter I was dropped right down the abyss myself, even as with Mr poor old Venuti Sr, whose son was by the way delivered in mid-Atlantic, in case you weren't up on your midwiferies & your cool hot be bop department.[1]
    Abyss was an abyss between two publishers, among other things: now it looks as though Random House may be signing a long term contract for my work, so things look much better.
    I had written you one of my more monumentally long letters adumbrating the drama of this & that,[2] but since there seems no prospect of finishing it in the near future, I'm sending you this short one instead as a stop-gap since also I perceive that you may have still deep worries of your own to which I would not like to add by my seeming neglect.
    One thing I had said was that if you found yourself absolutely spiritually spiralling down the drain at this period you might do worse than work your way west: my wife & I live – a la Chapter I or IX Volcano – in a place as described there, in a shack built by ourselves. The town, composed of fishermen's huts along the granite-strewn shore, is falling to pieces, is largely abandoned, & at the moment contains only about four diehard inhabitants besides ourselves. You have to hew wood, & carry water, the conditions are those of the utmost poverty, we have

nothing to offer save our friendship, there are no conveniences of any kind, and you might hate it like hell. Nor, since we only have two inhabitable rooms & a stove out of the Gold Rush, could we put you up for more than a few days without the maximum of misery to yourself. But I could probably find you another neigbouring shack to crawl into for next to nothing, or possibly even nothing. The advantages are a primeval forest to wander in, incomparable scenery (though you may hate mighty fine prospects) wonderful swimming – though extremely cold – & a fine way of life that seems dying out of the world. Likewise we have a rowing boat we could lend you. Sometimes the place fills up a bit for the summer months though it is nothing like anything you ever saw probably. In general the real life is a cross between the Sea of Gallilee, The Wild Palms & Paradise:³ & sometime in winter hell itself. It is our home, we pay no rent or taxes, & the anguish is always the danger of eviction, sometimes near, sometimes far, sometimes nonexistent. But there is always the risk. It can be a wonderful place to work, or not, according to temperament. If the Random House contract comes off we would be hard pressed to fulfill its first year term, & so working hard. We have no or almost no intellectual friends, we are nearly always hard up, but that doesn't mean that we might not all help each other in some sort & even have a fine time. I leave the suggestion at that, as a sort of risky beacon. But if you did work your way west & back again, hitchhiked, by bus, or what not – with the expectation of nothing, but with ourselves as the perhaps evanescent & unworthy gimmick – & took notes all the way, of street signs, bar signs, people, animals, houses, flying bedpans piloted by a celestial race of humming birds, you might get a fine novel of withdrawal & return & a memory of an adventure not wasted, utterly impractical though it sounds. Also I have a pal, Ted Roethke, of the University of Washington in Seattle who might help you to a job – he's a first rate fellow in every way.⁴

Anyhow we throw out this shredding lifeline of a suggestion (though with no right to do so) in case the prospect of New York in summer is too much for you, & there seems no hope at all at the bottom of the glass

love from us both

Malcolm

[P.S.] Thanks alot for enclosing Dylan's note – though we missed each other here, damn it, owing to certain 'auxiliary circumstances'.⁵

Annotations:

1 Guiseppe 'Joe' Venuti, the American jazz violinist, was indeed born aboard the ship that was bringing his family to the United States as immigrants.

2 Lowry is referring to a ten-page pencil draft of this letter to Markson (UBC 3:3), which breaks off unfinished and unsigned.

3 The mixture Lowry suggests is that of ordeal or suffering and delight and spiritual beauty. William Faulkner's *The Wild Palms* (1939) depicts the former.

4 The American poet Theodore Roethke (1908-63) was an English professor at the University of Washington in Seattle at this time. He and Lowry met, at least twice in Vancouver, at parties hosted by Alan and Jean Crawley.

5 Dylan Thomas made a reading tour of North America from 20 January to 16 May 1952, and he visited Vancouver during the first week of April. Lowry's Kafkaesque 'auxiliary circumstances' probably had to do with the move back to Dollarton. During Thomas's first visit to Vancouver, in April 1950, the Lowrys attended his reading and afterwards spent several hours with Thomas in his Hotel Vancouver room. See George Robertson's recollection of events (Salloum 76-77).

Editorial Notes:

a. This is a postmark date supplied by David Markson. There are two incomplete draft versions of this letter, one a ten-page holograph, the other one page (UBC 3:3); see annotation 2.

527: To Harold Matson

P: Matson(ts); UBC(phc)   Dollarton, B.C.,
                                                          Canada
                                                  26 April 1952[a]

Dear Hal:

I feel it remiss of me not to have mentioned our financial debt to you. When is most convenient for you, and in what form, to receive back the money you so generously lent us?

I enclose a letter from Clarisse [Francillon][1] – does it look to you from this that this French money is going to arrive fairly soon, and you could subtract it from that at your end without inconvenience, or would you like it, or part of it, back sooner as from more recent and securer potentialities of emolument? (As you can well imagine after our long siege we are more than dead broke and in debt to others besides yourself, but we intend to pay everything back little by little this year – Margie)

Thank you for replying as swiftly as you could. I could not have known my letter was delayed, but so help me God, yours was too, and went to the Vancouver address. This is not your fault because we probably failed to tell you we were returning to Dollarton April first: what made the delay inexplicable is that we had informed the postoffice of the change of address, doubly counterchecked on this, and other mail addressed to Vancouver was not delayed, though a telegram from Albert, sent to Dollarton, was held up.

It seems the trolls are not out of the machinery yet and it was with this in mind we sent you a telegram yesterday morning, to which we have as yet had no reply: doubtless it was held up because of the strike.[2]

Though advised by Albert of his jury duty, how are we to know for sure that the contract itself has not been already sent and, inexplicably, gone astray once more at this end? Perhaps it would have been safer to have dispatched you a pneumatique by super-hummingbird-piloted flying saucer: but still.

We discovered yesterday, on top of everything else, that I have to pay income tax on my share of the English estate of which I have not yet received a shilling, and God knows when I will for it is not even settled yet, though it seems if I ever do get it I'll have close to £1000 a year, maybe more. (Before taxes, on the Governor's will.)[3] Actually I calculate that at worst my income will be about doubled: if the pound goes up though it could be quadrupled: I seem to have far more possessions than I thought I did, though they are simply an added tax burden till they come through: I never heard of anyone having to pay taxes on money they haven't received: but so it is. But I mention this as a lucky break, an insurance against the future, not the reverse: it's just annoying at the moment.

Meantime, despite your letter of reassurance and with all the best will in the world, I find it damned hard to get down to work until the contract actually arrives. Also the weather is cold and rainy and since we're too broke even to buy a load of wood I have to hack it out of the forest every day, which takes time and energy.

I didn't mean to write a gloomy letter – quite the contrary – when actually we are overjoyed about the Random House contract, and so grateful to you and Albert, it is just this long long long wait is getting on my nerves. All I really meant to say is that I most certainly have not overlooked the money I owe you and that I want to pay it back at the earliest moment I can.

Love from us both –

Malcolm & Margie

P.S. What is my moral position in regard to Brace's $500? And theirs in relation to the Volcano? It seems to me I should probably pay back the former but only when I can well afford to, & it seems to me they should bloody well relinquish the latter, as they did its author.[4]

Annotations:

1 Clarisse Francillon's 1 April 1952 letter is with the Matson Lowry Papers; she is vague about when Lowry's money will arrive.
2 On 1 April 1952 the American Commercial Telegraphers Union began strike action against Western Union, which disrupted services across the United States until 30 May, when a settlement was reached.
3 The 'Governor' is Arthur O. Lowry.
4 Lowry is referring to the money he received from Robert Giroux (via Matson) in December 1951; see his 11 January 1952 letter (**495**) to Giroux. Unfortunately, this money contributed to Lowry's mistaken belief that Harcourt, Brace was about to offer him a contract.

Editorial Notes:

a. This joint letter, signed separately by Malcolm and Margerie, carries two extensive holograph additions by Malcolm. The postscript appears at the top of the recto to the left of the inside address.

528: To Harold Matson

P: Matson(ms); UBC(phc)   [Dollarton]
                                                                [1952]

Monday, April 28.

Dear Hal:

Your letter with the cheque for $200 received this morning.[1] Thanks enormously from us both for this great thoughtfulness.

I wired you on Friday[2] – no doubt at about the moment you were doing this kind thing – not from impatience, or the usual kind of anxiety, but because I was afraid the contract might have been sent already & that it really had been inexplicably delayed at this end & you were wondering why I didn't reply.

Albert had already explained he was on jury duty & that he was otherwise extremely busy but just how incommunicado the former rendered him I didn't know.

I was advised there was only a 50/50 chance of your receiving my wire before the weekend because of the strike in America but I suddenly woke up to the fact that I ought to send it just in case.

We have now got your wire this morning too, for which many thanks so letters and wires probably crossed. Please give Albert our loves; Margie & I are struggling out of mutual chills & fevers at the moment, but feel pretty damned good at that & more hopeful than in a long time – This letter is written in bed, though, hence bad writing, which pray pardon,[a]

Our gratitude & loves again

Malcolm & Margie

Annotations:

1 Matson sent this cheque, 'imagining that same might be useful to you during this long wait,' with his 25 April 1952 letter. This sum was taken from payment due Lowry on signing the Random House contract.
2 See Lowry's 25 April 1952 telegram (524) to Matson.

Editorial Notes:

a. The letter, especially in the last paragraph, is squeezed on to the bottom of the recto with the complimentary close and signatures (both by Lowry).

529: To Albert Erskine

P: Virginia(ms); UBC(phc)   Dollarton
                                                        Sat. [3 May 1952][a]

– Excelentisimo amigo Alberto el Bueno de la Justicia y Ley (all good sufferage & no redeliction)[1]

– Thank you very much for the telegram (which – you guessed it – was delayed this end after *negsatiated* a *shrike* of communications[2] without being held up at yours): – but we were very grateful for it, only sorry to have troubled you, – we should have remembered that the Horn always wags its tail. And then wags. And then wags. Wags . . .

– Should 'the' ordeal end on Cinco de Mayo – 5th of May as seems approximately likely – it will have encompassed the exact time to the very day of the Dark As–La Mordida time scheme, from the day we dispatched the m.s as to you, to the signing of the contract: strange. And though strange; somehow, can it not be thought good? Yes.

– Didn't send you poems for I felt you had enough on your hands: but have set machinery in motion to get our debt – that is, the latter one – paid quam celerimme: if this fails, it should now be easy to pay it in time anyhow from other 'holdings'. But I wanted it to be that you should see that even if the contract had fallen through the debt for teeth would have been payed as per promiso . . . This is morally important. But it would help practically if you would tell me approximate date beyond which payment of *molar debt* should not be protracted if it is to be inconvenient for you. I am keeping 'molar debt' hereinafter to be referred to as the Two Compassionate Fifties (unless advised by S.O.S.

to the contrary) as distinct provisionally from the debt of Volcanic date & 14 months back hereinafter to be referred to as The All Compassionate & Generous Two Hundred: the AC & GTH may now also be paid back at almost anytime, due to 'enlarged possibilities': eg. the 800 dollars *is* arriving from France, & money from estate is at least *in* England if it has not come through yet. (I know for I've had to pay taxes on it.) I've cut this letter short, so that it will arrive on Monday, for I wanted you to see that these things are having my responsible attention.

Have both been held up by spring fever temporarily but am finishing a Rabelaisian short story 'Present Estate of Pompeii' for the volume: I like it much.

Will write re Invisible Man this week end & thanks very much for The Shrike – latter not so hot, as you said, if still quite hard to take in places under the circs.

Hope you have not had to be sentencing anyone to 99 years in a Chinese ricefield or anything.

God bless you from us both

Malcolm

Annotations:

1 Lowry's Spanish translates roughly as 'excellent friend Albert the Good of Justice and Law,' followed by a pun on the legal term for an offence, delict, which refers to Erskine's jury duty; see also Lowry's 4 May 1952 letter (**530**) to Erskine.
2 Lowry's pun combines references to the delay caused by the American Commercial Telegraphers strike (see letter **527** to Matson) and to the title of a play, *The Shrike*, that Erskine had sent him. Luckily the telegram did not fall prey to a shrike or a strike, but for Lowry's comments on the play see letters **508** and **530** to Erskine.

Editorial Notes:

a. The pencil holograph is undated, except for 'Sat,' but 3 May 1952, a Saturday, is the postmark on the envelope with this letter.

530: To Albert Erskine

P: Virginia(ts); UBC(phc)
PP: *SL* 315–22; *Lln* 2–3

Dollarton, B.C.
[4 May 1952]ᵃ

Querido Alberto Bueno Excelentisimo de la Justicia y Ley –
(Buen suffragio y no reeleccion!)¹

I don't think I'm going to have time to say anything very considered, i.e., grammatical, about Invisible Man[2] – unless that is important to you, in which case I shall, but I've read it carefully, some of it several times, and have come to the conclusion that at best it is a really electrifying piece of work, and that the author is probably a real rooting tooting double-barreled first class writer. In fact my opinion of him is higher than that of the book as a whole, though when this is said it must be admitted that though I suppose, that book has some of the faults usually attributed to first novels, it also has some absolutely bran new virtues that have not to my knowledge shown their nose in any novel recently I mean (at least of recent date, if that makes sense). In parts it really seems – whether devilishly or not I can't make out – actually inspired. And his technical facility is such that in one astonishing brilliant and wonderful horrible scene the reader finds his sympathies and antipathies engaged in so many different directions at once – and in directions one would not have thought possible – that like the loathesome character on the receptive end of this scene, the reader may find himself crying aloud faintly for a stimulant. Yet the author is really a bit diabolic, however much one may like him. My sympathy for instance – indeed complete empathy – for the man who has committed incest – because he couldn't (a) help it and (b) his subsequent behaviour establishes his real integrity since he accepts that he is what he is – could not, as I apprised you just now, be more: but subtly you feel you're being shamed, by identity with the odious Mr Norton and the other 'benevolent' whites, when you want to identify yourself with the Invisible Man at this point whose behaviour has not been any too simon-pure either, but whose standpoint of condemnation (though subtly he was a Judas at this point) is clear, or seems to be.[3] Actually this scene abounds with the most ghastly and new insights and by and large may make one as a writer oneself want to go out and buy a new set of brains, and if possible a new set of eyes and ears too, before writing another line. Purely as a scene it's comparable with some of the best in Faulkner, and it's not the only scene that effects me that way by any means – there're five or six others almost equally inspired in the midst of the utmost complication of intention, but this does not mean it's a successful book: it might mean your author is a genius, or something, but that's rather different. – 'Nonetheless that it is besides so interesting and easy to read should not blind one to its extraordinary complexity nor the solid intellection that is behind it. Nor should this in turn blind one to its texture, its real beauty as a work of art.' If as a reviewer, say, overcome by enthusiasm, I'd stopped at about page 245 and written my piece right then without reading the rest I could imagine myself saying that or again something like this: 'Invisible Man makes comment, like a kind of benign and diabolic atom bomb upon all forms of oversimplification in regard to its central problem, on which the author goes to work not only with all the skill of a first rate story teller, but the resource and wisdom in complementary thinking of a nuclear scientist. Anyhow it's certainly a book to recommend to those who imagine that modern fiction is lying or unimportant, and it should satisfy Ortega himself on that score not to mention the damaging Mr Barzun.[4] Sure, adaptations of the book – play, movie, whatever – will no doubt be made, and at that successfully. But in what other form than the novel could so many hard and – for the world – necessary points be made so tellingly? So my hat is off to the author, his overall skill – and with some reservations – to his most original conception, as also to his guts and integrity. But alas, did I say it was interesting after, say, page 245. I wouldn't quarrel with its necessary complexity, but in my opinion the book itself – with a few miraculous cloudbursts of recovery – begins to fail and become arider and arider, even fall to pieces (pardon my mixed metaphors) approximately from this point on. I more or less dissent too from the opinions expressed by certain reviewers of the book in this regard. However noble the multiple intention the book itself begins to fail as a work of art, in my opinion, though fragmentarily still it can still show itself a hell of a sight better than many or most novels. Possibly this is because the beginning, likewise the enclosing theme is so good. Either that or he leads you to expect too much of himself. But the irony utterly ceases to be out of the top drawer, becomes somewhat derivative finally. The reporting of the Communist brotherhood is as boring very often as their dialectics probably were in real life. One has been invited so often to these cocktail parties of well-heeled communists before and the essential and important points are too often clouded as a result of the technical out-of-touchness of the writing. One thinks (though only in relation to the satire) of [George] Orwell and says no, and what is worse, the suspicion arises that – if not the author – the book is somehow trying to curry some obvious critical favour from certain people and interests, who would have to be promoted into another spiritual sphere, in my opinion, even before they were honestly damned. The white world – I feel – is wickeder than he, Ellison, dares to let on: the 'point' he makes, that the black can be equally black, is tremendously important, though he makes it with least effectiveness here at the end. I think this part should have been cut considerably because Ralph E. seems to have forgotten that the nearer a thing approximates to a true work of art, the nearer it gets – or may get – to the 'truth.' (Not vice versa.) Invisible Man ceases – or very damn nearly ceases in my opinion – to be a work of art roughly after about page 245 and consequently the truth suffers.

But the saving grace of this is, I believe, or may be, that Ellison realises that himself and makes a near heroic effort to save the thing itself in terms of art and damn nearly succeeds. For instance the speech at the funeral – tremendous! Though the book had begun to go down the drain on one plane after the wonderfully humorous as well as savage and dramatic business of trying to get rid of the Feed-me Americana emblem in the various garbage cans – a scene as good as Chaplin. But his trouble, I think is involved as I say with his brave endeavour to keep his theme consistent: i.e. to bring the thing off with flying colours as a work of art. Maybe I contradict myself but it seems to me that perhaps it is here that the very disciplined strictures imposed by his own form begin by their inevitable contraction to render the whole body a bit morbid. To put it another way, the book seems to shunt ill or uneasily between its prologue and epilogue: the couplers, the drawbars, begin to fall, or sound as if they were falling, apart: while it still makes a terrifying noise from time to time the train you are reminded seems nonetheless stalled: the prologue (that I read before in Partisan Review) seems no such brilliant observation car on close inspection as it did, and the epilogue does not show any signs of taking us into any final truth, and when the train you feel is beginning to move, whether to shed or station, it is with the uneasy feeling that it's been partially uncoupled and at least some of the passengers – including perhaps even ourselves – have been left behind. Above all, it is a bit too fantastic at the end, too unsuccessfully dada, too would-be (though with some miraculous recoveries and exceptions) nightmarish.[5] The characterisation seems to me likewise – even allowing for his anything but conventional or easy purpose – pretty feeble, though again there are triumphant flashes and insights. The race riot, so highly praised by others, strikes me as at worst resembling one of those very early Soviet futuristic films such as Arsenal, where symbol and the thing symbolised, man and meaning and photographic virtuosity are so confused that it is only your respect for the ingenuity of the director and the hope of what he may do at the next moment that keeps you from leaving the theatre out of exasperation with the sheer inertia and muddle he imposes: but above all this I had the feeling that here Ellison was not writing what he wanted to and knew it. My final feeling [is] though that his final remark is universally justified and that in the main he does, like Kafka, strike at the soul of man himself. At least he strikes at mine, and I shall certainly prize the book as the work of someone I feel may be important indeed.

As for the Shrike – for which thanks not so very much on the plane of its merit, but still thanks very much – while it has an Ibsenish sort of purity, I don't think it is so hot, as you generously intimated yourself. It has the purity and the architechtonics but it doesn't have the final honesty or understanding. The Shrike herself – shade of a shade of shades of Ethan Frome! – may be a theme in herself[6] (there is something like cowardice in the way official man blandly ignores woman's lunar capacity to drive folk insane, something like a perversion of the chivalry of pioneer days and an implied Mom worship in their so blandly taking her side in cases where they responsibly shouldn't, while one can see in modern North American and Canadian men often a victim of penis worship and pitiably a true Wylieish subject of tragedy as a result)[7] but the Shrike's behaviour in bitching the protagonist's possible job is worthy only of the comic strip and the psychoanalysts are no better dramatised, should truth and not effect be in mind, and dramatic honesty would surely have involved more of these characters being in the right: the brother struck me as being especially banal: as it is a certain kind of pseudo-good theatre, though perhaps better than nothing, wools the truth of the matter. Nonetheless I found the best parts expert, such as the Calypso singing bit (though the song was not specified) and under the circumstances a bit hard to take. But what the hell. God bless from us both.

Malcolm

P.S. Though you won't believe me, I read (your gift of) Ulysses through – essentially – for the first time, when I had a fever recently. Le gusta este Dujardin? Why is it Joyce?[8] Since it really was my first intelligent and complete reading (why I was inhibited I know not, in the last 12 years here no doubt by the censorship and sheer lack of time) some of my perceptions I feel may be unusual though I won't go into them right now.

P.P.S. Just received your letter of May 1 to which I won't reply in detail – only to say how deeply I appreciate the thought, consideration and generosity within the contract to come and to thank you again most deeply Albert, for the trouble you have gone to and time spent on my behalf. Needless to say I'll do my damndest to make you feel it was worth while. There are several immediate points. Unless England goes bankrupt or we have an extreme government or the pound crashes further my income should be more than doubled, if the pound goes up perhaps tripled. I already have had to pay taxes this year (without receiving any of the said money) on what looks from the trustee's statement, to be an income of nearly a thousand pounds a year, and this is without my one fourth share of the actual real estate, so to say, of the estate. This sort of thing was what fooled me when I said in good faith I thought I could repay you right off for the first money you lent us, i.e. the will (though not everything connected with the estate) was probated it seems: I received a certain sum as I told you, much diminished by the exchange: but the law still does not permit the transfer of even the income from the whole to a dollar area even after taxes: (current part of the income comes under an earlier jurisdiction): however the change in government does mean this much, that the money seems to belong more legally and forthrightly to me (hence the taxes, fortunately mostly deducted at the English end, but still leaving me here in a higher tax bracket than is warranted by the specie received, – i.e. in no tax bracket at all here – though fortunately we caught them in an error which reduced the spectacular injustice at the last moment): therefore (though it is too complicated really to explain) I have discovered that if you, or rather Peggy, for example, or for instance, were thinking of taking a trip to England, empowered by a note to my bank from myself, you, or she, could draw the money owing to you (on the first debt) at my English bank. I mention this only because probably its purchasing power of $200 (our first debt) is – being nearly £70 – in England far greater in pounds than dollars here. Or is it? It certainly was. The money owing me from England will in any case probably come through for me here sometime and as for this particular debt, as I intimated, it can now be paid back from other sources, such as the French money to speak of nothing else, but I just mentioned this curious fact in case you by any chance wanted to avail yourself of it. Since the money would come to me here only via income, presumably – though there might be an exception – the main capital would still be there, whether the former were paid or not. Of course I know you are not taking a trip due to exigencies of molars but it could be that Peggy was peripatetic – and my dear fellow, how is all this bloody anguish with you now? I can hope only as well as possible, and beyond that hope for your happiness. I only mentioned this in case something of this kind arose with you suddenly before I was able to pay back the first debt in the usual way: as things stand – if this is O.K. with you – second would be paid before first, i.e. well in time for your summer session with the dentist. But if the other is urgent let us know for we naturally have a better opportunity now of paying that back too sooner than we'd come to think we could.

Re the order of the books, while I agree that it would seem on the face of it strategically and financially better for me and you to have you publish the stories second and Lunar Caustic first, I've been more or less proceeding rightly or wrongly on the other assumption, and though it isn't absolutely too late to change this plan, certain minor considerations have accumulated into a larger consideration that might not in the end make my plan the more feasible after all: first there is a good chance now I can complete Hear Us well ahead of schedule, so much so that a year and a half from now I should with luck have completed or at least be in

clear sight of the end of Lunar Caustic too. There is a mechanical problem here. Dark as the Grave in its early drafts is still going along being
typed by Margie from my execrable pencil notes and until she's got to
the end of La Mordida it would be much harder in the circumstances of
2 rooms in which we live for me to concentrate on Caustic than on
Hear Us. On the other hand though Hear Us is much easier to write
with its less interrelated problems, it seems to be shaping up less like an
ordinary book of tales than a sort of novel of an odd aeolian kind itself
i.e. it is more interrelated than it looks. And so, I suppose, while it might
not sell, what if it were an exception and did? Perhaps unlikely. But
paradoxically I am not polishing anything in it that looks as if it had
much chance of selling individually though it would be pleasant if it
did nor do I offer the converse as an earnest of its possible success as a
book but what I mean is that you certainly have delivered me from that
feeling of necessity of trying to pick up money from the magazines so
that Hear Us is not being proceeded with with the idea of specie always
getting in the machinery so much as with the idea of getting into training for the Popos and peaks ahead and also because I hope it will be a
worthy book. This doesn't state the whole problem by a long shot
which is one really of getting the greedy daemon in line and forcing him
to do something more lowly and unpretentious as a discipline even at
the expense of working with logic and simple motives rather than with
more gluttonous danks and darks until the material at least of Mordida
be transcribed. I hope the whole thing will have been transcribed by
about the time I have finished Hear Us, meantime he will have to
scream in vain (though I shall feed him morsels) for until there is a copy
of this material in a safe place somewhere I shall not rest easy, for if it
were lost I could scarcely do the work I have promised in anything like
the time allotted; I don't always share his memory for one thing, and I
sometimes fear he could not care less, for having already written the
book, as it were, he has no time problem, and for things that still continue to harry us – such as that our position on the beach with the boom
and election time may be in revived jeopardy while still this is part of
the plot – no consideration at all. (Though I hesitate to set this down I
think it only fair to assure you that if worst comes to worst in this regard
I'm not going to let it throw me, or even much delay me: a Norwegian-
Canadian friend has offered to let us squat on his beach some 50 miles
away on an island in Howe Sound[9] in that case, though in that case too
a common sense problem might arise of leaving the dollar area altogether – for our dollar is higher than yours consequently we doubly lose
– and seeking a sterling one eventually, such as the Bahamas, should
England come through with a lump sum to get us there: this is about
the worst delay I can envisage, but why anticipate trouble: one's luck

has been phenomenal. Just the same this element of insecurity or uncertainty increases the responsibility of giving the copying of that material priority over the longer haul and only Margie can understand my handwriting: not even I can always understand it.

P.S. The contract has now arrived, it is wonderful, & I have signed it & dispatched it. I thank you from the bottom of my heart for everything. Can we let the matter of short stories or novel first ride for the moment.
God bless you from us both
Malcolm

Annotations:

1　The correct Spanish for the second phrase is 'Buen sufragio y no re-eleción'; the complete salutation means 'Very dear, good and excellent Albert of justice and law – (Good suffrage and no re-election!)'

2　Erskine had sent Lowry a copy of Ralph Ellison's novel, just published by Random House.

3　In chapter 2 of *Invisible Man* a black farmer, Trueblood, tells his story of incest with his daughter to Mr Norton, an elderly white benefactor of the college the young black hero is attending. It is clear from Norton's reaction that he has had incestuous desires himself, but the young man is ashamed of the farmer, whom he blames for Norton's distress.

4　See Lowry's 6 May 1947 letter (**299**) to Jacques Barzun, in which he protests Barzun's negative review of *Under the Volcano* in *Harper's* 194 (May): 486.

5　Lowry's references here to dada and, below, to 'futuristic films' are not far off the mark. In an essay called 'The Art of Fiction,' first published in *Paris Review* (Spring 1955), Ellison described the styles of *Invisible Man* as 'naturalistic,' 'expressionistic,' and 'somewhat surrealistic'; see his *Shadow and Act* (New York: Random House, 1964), p. 178.

6　Lowry is comparing the wife in Joseph Kramm's play *The Shrike* (see letter **508**) with the wife of Ethan Frome, the title character of the short 1911 novel by the American writer Edith Wharton (1862-1937). Frome is married to a neurotic, possessive woman, and his life is made miserable when he and his young lover are crippled in an accident and must continue to live with the wife.

7　Lowry may be thinking of the flamboyant American poet and novelist Elinor Morton Hoyt Wylie (1885-1928), who left her first husband to elope with her second, whom she left to marry her third, or he may be thinking of her poetry and fiction, notably her melodramatic novel about Shelley called *The Orphan Angel* (1926).

8　Lowry may have read James Joyce's *Ulysses* (1922) 'essentially' for the first time in 1952, but he was not unfamiliar with the novel. Joyce himself credited the minor French writer Edouard Dujardin (1861-1949) with developing the stream-of-consciousness technique in his 1888 novel *Les Lauriers sont coupés*. Lowry is punning on the sign in *Under the Volcano*, 'Le gusta este jardin,' to comment upon Dujardin's, not Joyce's, claim to originality.

9 The friend is Einar Neilson on Bowen Island.

Editorial Notes:

a. The usual time for a letter to reach Lowry from New York was two or three days. In his 'P.P.S.' he notes receiving Erskine's letter of 1 May; thus, it is likely that he is writing on or about 4 May. The final postscript has been added in pencil. The French translation of this letter in *Les Lettres nouvelles* 2-3 (1974): 244-53 carries an incorrect date of November 1949.

531: To Harold Matson

P: Matson(ms); UBC(phc)

Dollarton
10 May 1952

Dear Hal:

Just a note to say the contract is received (& enclosed, signed) & is swell in every respect. I thank you enormously for everything, & generally appreciate the care & thought you have put into it. Slight eccentricity of the 'M' in my initialling was due to the pen – an eagle's feather, proved lucky in the past, & the gift of the fisherman [Jimmy] Craige who was the witness, one of the heroes of the Forest Path – writing double (until we trimmed it) rather than myself seeing.[1] Yes, by all means deduct the $200 from the first payment only as regards the balance of our debt may I wait a little & see how I stand in regard to Clarisse's cash & the English money? Then even if this shows no sign of coming through we will be out of the hole in any case & it would be easy for us should you take a small amount out of the monthly checks as suggested, if that's all right by you. But if Clarisse's cash comes soon, as it should, please deduct the balance from that. I thank you again for your generosity in regard to all this too.

With love from us both to you Tommy & the children
Sincerely

Malcolm

Annotations:

1 See Figure 9 with letter **521** for a reproduction of the signatures on the Random House contract.

532: To Albert Erskine

P: Virginia(ts); UBC(phc)   [Dollarton]
                                                          17 May [1952]

Dear Albert:

Business note in haste. Will you give me a deadline convenient to you
for dentist debt? This being partly explained by enclosed note: i.e. I
can't tell whether *he'll* pay you in time or not.[1] (Poor old Gerald Noxon
to whom I explained the ethics of the situation when prospects were not
so hopeful, and who had previously sent us the money – over a year ago,
whereupon Percy [Cummins] sent letter back to him saying 'unknown
in Dollarton.' But we know he would already have sent it to you, had
he been able, & will, if still so instructed, but that's no good if not in
time.[2]

– Meantime Hal sent us an advance on the advance before the contract arrived and I told him to take this out of the advance before the
advance is sent which won't leave a great deal of advance by the time
the advance – and so on and so forth. I have some poems for you I
should have sent but I can't count on them now clicking in time: French
money is certain now, and even some Italian, but not being quite sure
of date of arrival of anything here, it makes a difference what your deadline is, and what you mean by summer, whether the middle of June or
beginning: that is, it makes no difference to your receiving it by whatever date you need it – merely I want to know the date so I can tell from
what source of increment to deduct it and by when. We had a resumption of bad weather here (it even snowed) and my immediate work on
Hear Us is a bit (though not seriously) slowed because I'm still hacking
wood for fuel out of the forest (one unlucky break was that the lumber
mills were beginning to close down by the time Hal sent some money
but we're hoping to have a load by Monday) – but at the moment the
woods are celestial and light with green vine-leaved maples, the weather
marvellous, we are besieged by racoons each night, Dark as the Grave,
to compensate matters, has taken, if prematurely, an astonishing leap
forward, and altogether we're at the top of our form.

God bless from us both

                                                              Malcolm

P.S. Suspect that this meticulousness in regard to second, & lesser, debt,
looks as though it were due to sense of guilt in regard to non-payment
of first, & larger one; if so that's not *the impression I mean to give*.

P.P.S. Gerald won't mind the letter being enclosed. Not that we
thought it funny – on the contrary – though we were relieved, I
suppose, not to have had chickenpox very lately.

Annotations:

1 There is no note from Gerald Noxon to Lowry extant with this letter to Erskine. Lowry mentions it again in the postscript. Noxon was going through a separation and divorce; see Lowry's 23 January 1952 letter (**501**) to him.

2 See Lowry's spring 1952 letter (**523**) to Noxon for his explanation of the debt to Erskine.

533: To Albert Erskine

P: Virginia(ts);UBC(phc)   Dollarton
14 June [1952]

Dear brother –

In haste. Work goes marvellously: over 500 pages of typed drafts of Dark as the Grave (against the future). Hear Us shaping up as something absolutely new; with an absolute inspiration for the end. A new novella: Present Estate of Pompeii all but completed. I swear it is a knockout, but you'll see. This will be last piece but two in Hear Us, making last three, with Forest Path a kind of small trilogy. October Ferry to Gabriola is penultimate. Pompeii is a riot, though I say it. So far we are ahead of schedule, though we only just got some wood. Point of this letter is to ask you again by what date you need money for toothman. I can't make out if Gerald [Noxon] is paying you in time or not but am assuming not. But we have to know *when* you need it, not because we can't afford it but because of necessity of calculating arrival of such with disbursement of so, a case rather of playing triple dimensional chess with the postman etc etc

God bless and love from both –

Malcolm

534: To Harold Matson

P: Matson(ts); UBC(phc)   Dollarton, B.C.,
Canada
14 June 1952

Dear Hal –

I am damned sorry to hear you have a strep throat and hope you are feeling O.K. by now though I know the whole thing is a painful business and we deeply sympathise.

Work is going marvellously – to date more than 500 (!) pages typed of drafts of Dark as the Grave: Hear Us Oh Lord shaping up as something completely new, with another novella, Present Estate of Pompeii nearly completed, the whole book completely plotted out, and inter-relating itself better every day.

So far we are ahead of schedule, though life here does not cease to offer its problems – not unlike trying to get The African Queen down-stream.[1] We have a Marxist, though fortunately not communist, government now in B.C. Fantastic. With Social Credit a hot runner up.[2] And our dollar higher than yours. It is a kind of loggers' Ruritania and tomorrow one expects to see Ezra Pound enthroned in the White House at Victoria or a royal reception for King and Queen Tito given by a procession of Colonel Blimps headed by Viscount Alexander, Raymond Massey and the Duke of Edinburgh to represent the fireman's union.[3] Meantime Margie and I live in a sort of self-governed ruggedly individualistic sub-proletarian super-Kashmir that seems to have no relation to it at all.

I don't want to trouble you (or bother Albert) but the June money from Random House hasn't arrived to date – June 14. It was due June 1. If it's already been sent don't bother to reply but if some trolls have got into the machinery again I thought I ought to tell you to put some salt on its tail.

With all the best from us both to you all and a speedy recovery –

Malcolm

Annotations:

1 One of the most memorable scenes in John Huston's 1951 film *The African Queen*, starring Katharine Hepburn and Humphrey Bogart, occurs when Charlie and Rose escape by boat down an uncharted river in German East Africa and become stuck in the swampy muck of the bug- and leech-infested water.

2 The British Columbia provincial election, called for 12 June 1952, turned out to be vicious, indecisive, and plagued with irregularities. At first it appeared that the social democratic party, called the CCF (Co-operative Commonwealth Federation), had defeated the incumbent Liberal Party, but when the delayed voting was completed and the results made official on 14 July 1952, the right-wing Social Credit Party had won by one seat and thus formed a minority government under their leader W.A.C. Bennett.

3 Ruritania is a name given to an imaginary kingdom in central Europe by Anthony Hope in his novel *The Prisoner of Zenda* (1894), or, more generally, to any imaginary country, and the image Lowry conjures up here for British Columbia is not without its humour and relevance. The

American poet Ezra Pound (1885-1972) was a proponent of the economic policies of 'social credit' formulated by Clifford Hugh Douglas (1879-1952); it is these policies that lie behind the Social Credit Party. The provincial legislative buildings are in Victoria, the capital of British Columbia on Vancouver Island. Lowry's allusion to the American presidential White House in Washington, DC, further associates Social Credit policies with American thinking, while his reference to Marshal Josip Broz Tito (1891-1980), who was the communist president of Yugoslavia, adds to his humorous view of the inconsistencies of local government.

Colonel Blimp is the cartoon figure created by David Low to depict the elderly ultra-Tory British conservative who opposes change, but the others are real people. Harold Alexander (1891-1969) was a distinguished British field marshal during the Second World War; from 1946 to 1952 he served as Governor General of Canada. Raymond Massey (1896-1983), the brother of Vincent Massey, who was Canada's first native-born governor general, became a distinguished actor in Canada, England, and the United States; he is associated with the role of Abraham Lincoln and he frequently played Nazi officers in war films. The Duke of Edinburgh, Prince Philip (1921-), is the husband of Queen Elizabeth.

535: To Albert Erskine

P: Virginia(ts) [Dollarton]
9 July [1952]

Dear Albert:

Yours of June 25 received.[1] Good God! We pray that things are getting better for you now. Meantime, the enclosed explains itself.[2] Once more, our gratitude to you for everything. God bless, and love from us both –

Malcolm

Annotations:

1 Few of Erskine's letters to Lowry from the spring and summer of 1952 have survived, and I have not been able to trace a letter dated 25 June 1952.
2 The enclosure was probably a cheque for $100 sent in partial repayment of his debt; see Lowry's 5 August 1952 letter (**538**) to Erskine.

536: To David Markson

P: UBC(ms)   Dollarton, B.C.
                                         (was once Oregon too)
                                              [12 July 1952]

Dear Dave: −

Very sorry about your mishap − for some reason I'd felt inclined to warn you about Eureka, Margie & I once spent some gruesome hours there − [1]

As things turned out, the weather here was wonderful (& is), the beach almost deserted, everything in the best kind of form, (save work) & had already written to say we'd be delighted if you could come, but would understand equally if you couldn't, though now we of course more than ever wished you had, but in any case **don't forget to take notes,** I mean I hope you haven't forgotten; only thing to do is to turn those lost suitcases & alarm clocks into immortal poesy −

The position with us spiritually is something like yours financially: i.e six or eight weeks of hard work would put us more in the clear so that we'd be freer, & we'd probably then all be more help to each other, for I'm trying to fight through a creative slump −

If you get into some real Christawful stasis or jam though, don't hesitate to head this way, even, if necessary, without warning: it would probably be the wisest & most practical course, apart from anything else, but so far as I can see ahead, other things being equal, it would be better in a month or so.

Incidentally this place can be a Paradise after Labour Day, though it's colder to swim. [2] We possess a deep water beach (i.e just in front of our own house) where you head into 60 feet of water at low tide (not to say high, when you can head out of the window) − a little bit of Acapulco in B.C. But if you catch the weather wrong it can be a little bit of hell in hell especially when ships have pumped oil into the harbour. But its beyond anything marvellous now.

Incidentally we have a Norwegian friend [Einar Neilson] who owns a hell of a lot of beautiful property on an island some distance away where, should you wish, you could live rent free, only paying for your food, this winter, or any other time for that matter: You wouldn't be encroaching because it is his ambition that writers should live on his property & he'd be only too delighted to have you. His wife, the local schoolmusicteacher will cook your food, & Einar is the lone taxidriver on the island so you'd even get your transportation for free, possibly even to Eldorado, for he's quite as wild sometimes as your Eureka driver, though he won't steal your alarm clock. They have a tape-recording machine, several eagles, & an outside toilet perched upon a hundred foot cliff where you may enjoy all the advantages of being a pigeon-guillemot & none of the disadvantages unless you happen to find yourself in the Pacific immediately beneath it.

So bear this in mind, too, from a practical standpoint. It sounds impossible but there it is. We've been there several times & can vouch for it & ourselves have a standing invitation & are empowered to pass it on to you.

Meantime:

> AVOID DREAD GARBERVILLE, MY SON
> EUREKA, BROTHER, BEWARE!
> BORING THAN THESE IS FAR MORE FUN
> (AND NOT FORGETTING DOLLARTON)
> SUBLIMITY MORE RARE.[3]

All the very best from us both

Malcolm

Annotations:

1 Before visiting the Lowrys for a week in August, Markson worked for a logging company in Molalla, Oregon. For a break he hitch-hiked to San Francisco with a friend, but the man who picked them up abandoned them in Garberville, California, and stole their suitcases. In Markson's suitcase was a letter from Lowry. Markson wrote to the Lowrys from the nearby town of Eureka, where he and his friend had gone to find their absconding driver.

2 Labour Day weekend is a legal holiday that falls on the first Monday in September, and the school year begins immediately after it.

3 Lowry's loose parody of Lewis Carroll's (The Reverend Charles Dodgson, 1832-98) poem 'Jabberwocky' from *Through the Looking Glass* (1872) incorporates the names of actual towns – Garberville, Eureka, and Boring – in the states of California and Oregon.

537: To Harold Matson

P: Matson(ts); UBC(phc)   Dollarton, B.C., Canada
                                                    24 July 1952

Dear Hal:

I've just received the following letter from Seymour Lawrence, now evidently in an editorial capacity with Atlantic Monthly:

'Dear Mr. Lowry:

'I don't think I thanked you sufficiently for your stimulating and most perceptive piece in the Aiken Number.[1] To many minds, and I speak for Conrad as well as myself, it was a totally rewarding memoir! Writing to you now in another capacity for the Atlantic, I wonder if you have any new prose work which we might see at this time or in the near future? I sincerely hope you do, and that I'll have the pleasure of hearing from you again. My very best wishes. Cordially, Seymour Lawrence.'

This seems to me perhaps to offer a more than usually reasonable chance for one of my no doubt by now long-travelled stories and I have written him to say that I was asking you to get in touch with him, mentioning the stories, The Bravest Boat, In The Black Hills, and Strange Comfort Afforded By The Profession, as possibilities, if they are available – if you agree.[2]

If none of these hit would you ask him – as I have asked him – not necessarily to give me up on that account for the longer story I am working on now, October Ferry to Gabriola – a reworking of a collaboration that formerly didn't come off – might be just the thing that would now ring the bell, or failing that The Forest Path To The Spring itself.

The status of work completed to date is as follows: all the notes and first drafts for Dark as the Grave have been typed, with a carbon copy, – 730 pages of it. This seems too much to ask anyone to read in its present form and I haven't time to stop and make a selection at this point so we're putting copies into a safety deposit box in the bank. Hear Us Oh Lord is going excellently but is offering unusual, if interesting, difficulties of integration with the rest of The Voyage That Never Ends. The Pompeian story, October Ferry and The Forest Path make a small trilogy *within* Hear Us that I think will bring that book to an astonishing close (actually they'd make a good volume even if there weren't any other stories in Hear Us.)

Present Estate of Pompeii is in places extremely bawdy and though I think it's extremely good I think it unsaleable to any magazine save perhaps The Partisan Review, so I'm grappling with October Ferry for the umpteenth time now.[3] I've told Albert I won't send him anything else until completed unless he asks for it but you might pass on the information about Dark as the Grave. Also that Margie is starting to type the notes, first draft, etc. on La Mordida immediately. Much other work has been done, including about 100 pages of stuff on Eridanus (the intermezzo which one had to prevent intermixing inconsistently with the material for Gabriola.)

So things are going fine here. But would be tickled pink to get in Atlantic if that would be approved by Random. Though naturally it should be a good one. (Perhaps they might even take 2!)[4]

All the best from us both –

Malcolm

Annotations:

1 'A Letter,' *Wake* 11 (1952): 80-89, is Lowry's essay on Conrad Aiken for this special issue; see Lowry's 28 November 1951 letter (**482**) to Seymour Lawrence.
2 This letter to Lawrence has not been located.
3 Lowry exaggerates the bawdiness of his story, even allowing for contemporary tastes, but 'Through the Panama' first appeared in *Partisan Review* 26.2 (1959): 175-99.
4 Lowry was not successful in publishing any stories with *Atlantic Monthly*.

538: To Albert Erskine

P: Virginia(ms)   [Dollarton]
[5 August 1952]ᵃ

Dear Albert; —
    Am getting worried. Have you received the cheque sent you about a month ago for $100 sent on by us the same day we received it from [Gerald] Noxon?[1] Work going on with 700 pages of draft of Dark as the Grave put in safety deposit box. Hope everything ok as possible by you.
                                        love
                                            Malcolm & Margie

Annotations:

1 See Lowry's 9 July 1952 note (**535**) to Erskine, with which he sent this cheque.

Editorial Notes:

a. This pencil holograph is on a 7.5-by-11-cm piece of yellow notepad paper. The envelope postmark is 5 August 1952.

539: To Albert Erskine

P: Virginia(ts); UBC(phc)
PP: *SL* 322   Dollarton
12 August [1952]

Dear old Albert:
    Did you get the $100? Hope you are O.K.
    Dark as the Grave — 700 pages of notes and drafts — is deposited in the bank (it hadn't occurred to me till very recently that there *were* things called safety deposit boxes): La Mordida has been started on the long

haul of typing. I didn't send you any of the former because in toto it is not in a fit state to read and it would take a lot of time to make 'suitable selections'. But if you wish me to take this time I will do so. In a moral sense the material belongs to you but in any case it is now safe.

I am having to rewrite – for the umpteenth time – the penultimate novella in Hear Us, due to the appalling difficulty of trying to render overlapping material consistent: the number of false restarts and hen tracks on the page I have made has me half dead with discouragement, I don't feel I've earned my hire for the last month despite a more or less sizzling (though still imperfect) Pompeii, I feel lamentably out of touch with the contemporary world of fiction, England seems too busy going down the drain – or pretending it is – to answer any of my letters about my interests there, I often don't think I'm even a writer, and all in all I am suffering from the Desconsolado blues;[1] but somehow the work *does* seem to be getting itself done, even without me, and perhaps even it. Love from us both –

Malcolm

P.S. I've forgotten what I was going to say but it was something more cheerful. Am reading Flaubert's Education Sentimentale, just to keep up with the times – a book so marvellously boring it induces in one a kind of ecstasy.[2]

Annotations:

1 The Spanish *Desconsolado* gives Lowry the 'inconsolable' blues.
2 Gustave Flaubert's *L'Education sentimentale* (1869) is a novel about French dilettantes and intellectuals set during the 1848 Revolution and the Second Empire.

540: To Albert Erskine

P: Virginia(card); UBC(phc)   [Dollarton]
                                                  [9 September 1952][a]

Dear Albert. Work in Progress = Margie reaching in typescript about p 100 of La Mordida {800th page considered in toto}, myself with end well in sight of October Ferry to Gabriola. Chapters in Hear Us will be XII,[1] as in Volcano, but the movement is opposite, i.e toward the stars & the sunrise, not the barranca, ends with the characters in The Forest path drinking from the stream. October Ferry is terrific story, I think: is preceded by Pompeii: & Pompeii by Henrik Ghostkeeper – both now finished in second draft, & first respectively: these last four stories are all as long as chapters of the Volcano, which is why they are so hard to do & take as long as they do finally to complete {Have to dodge from one to the other like playing celestial xylophone. How, where, is old Frank [Taylor]}, albeit we are still ahead of schedule: Hear Us is becoming an anomaly since last 3 chapters make a novel in themselves, as I've probably said. It is damned exciting though & makes the beautiful & splendid noise, though I say it. No news from Inglaterra[2] as yet. Hope you have good. Love

Malcolm

Annotations:

1 Over the next two years Lowry's plans for his collection changed considerably. 'October Ferry to Gabriola' was becoming a novel, and the 'Ghostkeeper' story was dropped from *Hear us O Lord*, which was published with seven stories. For a discussion of the 'October Ferry' material, see Doyen's 'From Innocent Story to Charon's Boat' in *Swinging the Maelstrom* (163–208).
2 Spanish for England.

Editorial Notes:

a. These are the postmark date and the address on the envelope. Lowry has filled the recto of a 6-by-11-cm piece of yellow notepad paper with his tiniest pencil script.

Lowry and Conrad Aiken corresponded rarely after 1940, but they remained in touch, and it was natural for Aiken to send his former pupil a copy of his autobiographical roman à clef Ushant (1952). The book, however, was a bittersweet gift. Aiken had a ruthless, sarcastic wit, and his portrait of Malcolm as the drunken 'Hambo' is cruel. In the psychological battle of father and son, this father wanted the last word. He also, one suspects, wanted to diminish his formidable rival. Although Lowry was hurt by Aiken's portrait, he clearly recognized himself and, at least in this letter, was able to praise Ushant and was honoured to be pilloried side by side with T.S. Eliot.

541: To Conrad Aiken

P: H(ts)   Dollarton, B.C.,
PP: *LAL* 228-31   Canada
                                                      14 September 1952

Dear old Conrad:
    Ushant is a knock-out – ow, how it hurts![1] A great book, in many
ways, technically, a marvel, in plain words a masterwork. That much I
can glean though naturally so far I've tended to read it a bit in the
manner of the wind turning the pages of the book in the garden, save
that the wind, for all the skirts it has blown up, is perhaps not reading
the book like me with the object of finding its own pants taken down
on the next page. This plus pressure of one's own work and the usual
elemental difficulties of keeping alive in the wilderness have made it
hard to form a dispassionate judgement as yet. In other words I ain't
really had time, and when I make time, I don't read it dispassionately.
Meantime there are wonders of prose, profound perceptions and apper-
ceptions and complexities expressed in miraculous limpidity. The form
is a triumph, and the end, as hot musicians say, is out of this world. No
criticisms (though I might – and certainly with it more enlightened
praise – have some later) save that now and then I felt a slight failure of
tone, e.g., round about the section of uncles' ashes.[2] And he, though it
would certainly have given him 'an unaccustomed wetness in the
trousers,' might have complained, as once before, of an occasional
unnecessary coarseness. What the hell. But I thought you unfair to B.V.
[*Blue Voyage*] at one point. In those days, young fellow, dealing with
those complicated issues of prose, you were content sometimes not to
'write,' but to 'decorate the page,' as Tchechov somewhere advises
(Sounds like bad advice too, but you get what I mean – if anything; as
a matter of fact I simply wanted to reassert my pristine loyalty to B.V.,
but became involved in a tangential & largely unfounded speculation
I couldn't develop without getting into a fine muddle) one to do.
Perhaps you have forgotten the technical problems that seem solved at
every moment in that book, on every page, in every word, and by the
placing of words. All maybe largely unconscious, (Jeez Conrad I don't
mean that though I mean the rest)[a] but I've never read a book that
appealed to so many senses at once as that, including some not in
the roster. Ushant possesses a similar genius in the art of communications; never too much fed into the channel, though you've involved
yourself with all the temptations of complete freedom. But I'm not
writing an appraisal of Ushant here so much – there are tremendous
things almost wherever you open it – as a note to set your mind
at rest about Hammbo, in case you were worrying, lest I be hurt. H'm.

Our sweating self, but better. And considerably more intelligent. Still:

> What a fearful account *he* will have to give
> of himself at the judgement day!
> OW, HOW IT HURTS!

the reference being to the sinister inscription upon the glass case containing a bepoxed Liverpudlian waxwork in the old Museum of Anatomy in Paradise outside which it also said: Man know thyself![3]

This, to make you laugh. Seriously, so far as I'm concerned, it seems to me you've been very sporting and charitable though naturally one wishes one had acquitted oneself differently in real life. Also it is a bit hijeous (as our old cook used to say) from the existential point of view, to think that at those few moments one actually did imagine one was being truly helpful – however intolerable – or sharing in some mutually sacred or secret – don't take this too seriously, old man, my hypocrisy is exposed overleaf[b] – drama that one was in fact (one forgets only in part, it is true) being eyed (as Strindberg might say) as a rabbit for vivisection. And worse still, eyeing one's fellow Conrad, for I'm just as bad, no doubt, in fact worse. And when I think what gobbets of Hammbo you might have chosen for display I can only affirm that in the matter of forbearance Clive of India has nothing on you.[2] And of course one is also honored. Hope it is all Ushantih with the Tse-Tse.[5] – And I hope the real Hammbo may prove a credit: the work – and God how much of it there is – is going well. And so is our life. Another book should be finished soon, and there are thousands of pages of drafts of future ones (in the vault of a bank, this time).[6] We've had a pretty rough tough time the last years, what with most of our assets frozen in Europe. And on occasion, the typewriter frozen too. But basta! Congratulations upon, and the best of luck with Ushant. With devotion and all the very best love to Mary and yourself from us both – in fact from all 9 of us, Mr and Mrs Blackstone,[7] Mr and Mrs Hammbo, Mr and Mrs Lowry, not forgetting Mr and Mrs Demarest, and from the old Malc himself.

As ever

Malc

P.S. I was delighted and moved to get a reply from old Tom (after you'd put the deeply good suggestion in my head he'd be glad to get a letter after the misses' death)[8]

T.W. Neeves 52 New Winchelsea[c]

> Dear Mr. Lowry very pleased to hear
> from you we hear from Mr. Aiken at times
> and from Mr. Rice and Mrs. Rice[9] they stade
> we with us two year age we hear from them

at Times now the Old Ship was good place! –
to live we Left their 17 years age last
March Mr. Aiken was shocking (he wrote speaking of course,
   it only looked like shocking)[d] to us of you
He was a nice kind of gentleman –

I myself have just come out Hospital
had bad operation came home 4 weeks ago
Felling better now, Blader Troble now
for about 6 Monnths I had a bad times Doctor
tell me your man 80 year to be alive

hope for little better time coming
feel more like old time on way
wis hing best very Pleased to hear from you
Sincerely Your Old Thomas Neeves Cheero!

Annotations:

1   The title of Aiken's *Ushant* (1952) is derived from the forbidding, rocky Ile d'Ouessant, or Ushant, off the coast of France, but it is also a pun on the English command: you shan't. Aiken inscribed the copy he sent to Lowry as follows: 'For our beloved / Malc-Hambo-Blackstone / with all devotion / from Conrad / August 23 – 1952.'
2   Aiken's favourite uncle, Alfred Claghorn Potter, died in November 1940; the story of his ashes, first recounted to Lowry in Aiken's 15 December 1940 letter (Sugars, 153), appears in *Ushant* (283-87).
3   Lowry's reference is to a display of the ravages of syphilis, which he saw as a teenager. See Day (67) and Bowker (40, 47), who both say that Stuart Lowry took Malcolm there to teach him about the consequences of casual sex.
4   Robert Clive, Baron Clive of India (1725-74), was a British general in India. He is the model of British imperialist success for the young men in George Alfred Henty's *With Clive in India, or the Beginnings of an Empire* (1884) and the hero of the trite patriotic film *Clive of India* (1934). Lowry may have seen the film and had very likely read Henty, whose books were popular boys' reading.
5   Aiken based the character in *Ushant* called 'Tsetse' on T.S. Eliot. By adding his own parodic reference to Aiken's title and Eliot's closing words in *The Waste Land* ('Shantih shantih shantih'), Lowry expresses his hope that Eliot will forgive Aiken as he has. For Lowry's use of *shantih* see his 1933 letter (**41**) to Aiken and his 23 January 1952 letter (**500**) to David Markson.
6   Lowry was working on the stories in *Hear us O Lord, October Ferry,* and *Dark as the Grave Wherein my Friend Is Laid,* seven hundred pages of which he deposited in a bank for safe keeping; see Lowry's 12 August 1952 letter (**539**) to Albert Erskine.

7 William Blackstone, who fled the New England Puritans to live in the wilderness, was a Lowry avatar and the subject of Aiken's poem *The Kid*; see his March 1948 letter (**336**) to Aiken.

8 See Lowry's April 1952 letter (**516**) to Tom Neeves.

9 The American writer Jennings Rice (1900-90) and his wife Maria Gandia were friends of Aiken and Edward Burra and often visited Rye.

Editorial Notes:

a. Lowry has drawn an arrow between the typed word 'unconscious' and the handwritten marginal note here in parentheses.

b. Lowry has drawn a bracket connecting 'this' in this interpolation to the words 'sacred' and 'secret.'

c. The original of this letter has not survived; therefore, it is impossible to confirm if Mr Neeves wrote it in this form or if Lowry has recast it as a poem for Aiken.

d. Lowry's handwritten marginal explanation of Tom Neeves' letter.

542: To Clemens ten Holder

P: UBC(ms)   Dollarton, B.C.
                                                        [September 1952]

My very dear old Clemens:

We were in the middle of writing a long letter of gratitude and love to you & Hildegard for the exquisitely thoughtful and beautiful birthday present she & you sent me (the letter interrupted by harassing worries here but for which it would have been sent long ago) when suddenly Hildegard tells me you are ill & even im Krankenhaus,[1] alas, so I am sending you this by return of superjet Luftpost avion and airmail and even it is to be hoped rocket, with no attention to prose, to offer you all prayers and fervent and affectionate hopes for your speedy recovery, which prayers I am saying also to God, to St Jude, and to die Jungfrau welche niemanden haben mit,[2] as fast and as hard and as profoundly as I and also my wife can say them. We had hoped to be in Germany this summer and it is sad that I cannot be by your side and give some comfort to you in your ordeal but at least I am there in spirit, – as are we – and in the spirit too of gratitude and friendship for all you have so expertly & sensitively accomplished on my behalf with Unter dem Vulcan, so hold on, hold that note, wer immer strebend sich bemüht, den kennen wir erlosen,[3] or if it's against doctor's orders to strive upwards at least don't strive downwards, & meantime be assured of the concern and love of your ever grateful friend,

                                                             Malcolm

Annotations:

1 During the summer of 1952, Clemens ten Holder fell ill. He first received treatment near his home in Kreis Leonberg, Württemberg, but was later admitted to the Burghalde Sanatorium in the Black Forest near Württemberg. In her 9-10 October 1952 letter to the Lowrys, Hildegard ten Holder explained the move to the sanatorium and begged Lowry to write an encouraging letter to her husband; see Lowry's October letter (**546**) to his friend.

2 This is Lowryan German for Dr Vigil's remark in chapter 1 of *Under the Volcano*: 'the Virgin for those who have nobody with.' Ten Holder had translated the remark as 'wo die Jungfrau is für die, welche niemanden haben mit.'

3 The correct line from the second part of Goethe's *Faust* (1832) is the third epigraph to *Under the Volcano*: '*Wer immer strebend sich bemüht, den können wir erlösen.*' 'Whosoever unceasingly strives upward . . . him can we save' *Faust* 2, ll 936-37.

543: To Norman Newton

P: UBC(ms) [Dollarton, B.C.]
[October 1952]ᵃ

Dear Norman,[1] very good to see you the other day, both on & off, in the old house of Ivan the terrible & the bumps & grinds, to which this is addressed. Also we done read the notices, so called, of Macbeth soon as we could. They weren't very intelligent. I guess it was a really historic occasion: moreover you deserved an honorable mention yourself.[2] All in all, we enjoyed it very much. We want to apologise to yourself & wife. We ain't seen nobody & we must get together. Things don't look very propitious at the moment, what with yourself working double shifts, & ourselves quadruple, reason being that Margie is typing –

I have written 500 pages of present book, & Margie has typed 250 of the one after that, 750 of the one after that, & another 250 for the one after that which is only a 1/4 finished [of 1st] draft.[3] That gives you an idea of the sheer bulk of the work & in addition I'm working against time. Obviously I shan't be able to keep to the time schedule but I've got to produce enough to impress them that no man could. And talking about the 40 hens here is my one useful criticism of anything you may not have done something about. Since you're playing with bloody [illegible] it seems to me you need a hell of a lot more enthusiasm in the noises off. Let there be thunder before the curtain rises and afterwards let the thunder sound like thunder, as loud as the hell {not just}, Let bells, when they should ring, ring, let alarums be alarums excursions

excursions. Tucket within & a flourish of strumpets. I swear the effect would be more salutary. For the rest congratulations! Especially Banquo.

c/o hens in a hen coop

[breaks off unsigned]

Annotations:

1 Norman Newton (1929-) is a Canadian writer, critic, and musician. He first met the Lowrys at Dollarton in 1949 through Earl Birney; in the spring of 1953 he and his wife Gloria rescued Lowry from a hotel on Vancouver's skid row, where he was in an advanced state of alcoholic depression. For a description of this episode and a photograph of the old coach-house 'of Ivan the Terrible,' as Lowry describes it, see Salloum (80-91).
2 Shakespeare's *Macbeth* was staged by the Everyman Repertory Company, under director/producer Sidney Risk (1908-85), at the Avon Theatre, Vancouver, from 29 September to 11 October 1952. Norman Newton played the roles of the sergeant and Banquo's ghost.
3 These three books are *Dark as the Grave*, 'La Mordida,' and *October Ferry*.

Editorial Notes:

a. This undated pencil holograph (UBC 16:21) is on the verso of a page of draft material for *October Ferry*. Internal references to the Newtons' house, Lowry's contract with Random House, and the performance of *Macbeth* suggest an October 1952 date.

544: To Ernst Klett

P: Klett(ts)   Dollarton, B.C.,
                                                                        Canada
                                                              3 October 1952

Dear Herr Klett:

I thank you deeply for your extremely warm-hearted and excellent letter, despite the heavy news it brings in regard to the good Herr Clemens ten Holder.[1]

About this (apart from what already seems *in extremis* providentially to have been done) one can only pray. We have indeed heard more reassuring news from his good wife Hildegard, who has spoken also so highly of your own generosity and practical kindness in the whole matter.

I can hope only indeed that this new treatment will indeed work and meantime we are acquiring from reports of his increasing cheerfulness faith that it will prove successful, even as if by a miracle.

I thank you very much both as one of your authors and as an individual for your kind remarks re Unter dem Vulkan and must also thank you as a publisher for the very beautiful presentation of it as a volume. Such experts as I know here who have also read the book in English, also in every way agree that Clemens' translation can be regarded both as an excellent translation and an exceptionally fine piece of creative work in itself.

I was, though, very disappointed to hear no more of the possible German film with Peter Lorre and I hope it is still not too late. In this regard, to explain my own silence on the point, it would, as I should have perhaps made clearer in an earlier letter, have been a breach of contract on my side with my agent to have signed a contract with yourself save via Matson, however much I might have liked to: I had no choice therefore but on receiving it to refer the whole thing to Matson immediately, so as not to delay matters for yourself should it otherwise have a chance of going through, which I very much wanted it to do, both for Herr ten Holder's sake and my own, merely intimating, as I would have to you had I been in direct contact, and as I am sure you would agree with me I should intimate, that I assumed such a film, as was only fair, should be based on Herr ten Holder's version. I also intimated I'd like to be consulted in regard to the scenario, etc. which was another way of saying the same thing. However, despite the fact that there seemed at one point a chance of Matson meeting Peter Lorre personally and despite repeated requests I have not heard another word from him on the subject. Perhaps you can tell me whether there is any longer a chance of bringing some good news to Herr ten Holder – and indeed to ourselves – on this score.[2]

For the rest, I will certainly write him as often as I can, which even so is not as often as I would like, for I am handicapped by other almost equally anxious news – or rather, in this case, lack of news – from my eldest brother in England. Also by my having to work against time, (under, moreover, with the industrial boom here, the continual shadow of eviction – no unique story). So I'll reserve writing about other matters such as my work for another letter – save to say there's a lot of it if I can only get it done, and no one would be happier than I if you would publish it in Germany and Herr ten Holder translate it. (Random House and the Modern Library are the publishers over here: the first book is due a year from November and I am under contract to them until 1956, by which time there should be two more.)

Meantime do let me emphasise how extremely touched I am by everything you have said. And please let me apologise for writing in

English. I would have returned the compliment by writing in German had my German been anywhere near as good as your English, which is perfection itself. We pray daily for our friend's recovery and hope only we may all meet soon in Germany under happier circumstances and indeed celebrate the miracle – Thanking you again for your letter.

Yours very sincerely,

Malcolm Lowry

Annotations:

1 This letter to Lowry from Klett does not appear to have survived.
2 Matson tried to see Peter Lorre in New York but without success.

545: To David Markson

P: UBC(ts)
Dollarton
3 October 1952

Dear old Dave –

This has to be in haste and just a short note. It was such a hell of a long time before you could give us an address to write to that by the time you did so most of what one had been thinking of writing was, like Melville's stone fleet, beginning – from the standpoint of any practical value it could have for you, I mean – to 'serve the obsolete.'[1] But our silence does not mean that you were not and are not a lot in our thoughts.

It seems to me {Sounds like Dorothy Dix}[2] you've done wisely and responsibly in doing what you are doing. Your father will be richly rewarded so long as he feels you're fulfilling yourself even if at this period that's precisely what you may feel you're not doing. I don't think it ever can have been harder to be a writer than at this period, and if you didn't take money from your Dad, you'd have to get it somewhere else. Even if you get an advance from a publisher on unwritten work, the pressure can half kill a fellow at a period when quite a lot of one's growth is unconscious and even spent in such apparently unprofitable occupations as looking at a flat beer or despairingly at that old empty page.[3] Both father and sons can make traditional mistakes. For example though my father generously offered me money I insisted on going to the Orient without a cent in my pocket other than the 50 shillings a month I got for my work on board. The result of this kind of abnegation is liable to be that you simply wind up at the Tsjang-tsgang Mysterious Orient Bar for marines and girls of all nations in a garbage heap five yards from the waterfront instead of going to Angkor Wat.[4]

Dollarton here might have proved in one sense practical, and is worth bearing in mind conceivably in future, or if not, Bowen Island. Here the shacks are now all empty, the weather is golden, the rent, nothing, the water warmer than when you were here, and so many bears are coming down to the beach in the evening that one doesn't have to go to Cuba to dream of Hemingway's lions {In Volcano is phrase 'dreaming lions' – Chap III} in Africa or Sierra Leone.[5] Moreover in town they have Macbeth, Tennessee Williams, Stravinsky (in person) ballet, Pagliacci Musical Comedy Tchechov, an indigenous theatre beginning no increase in prices and even soon bars (we hope) and even the Japanese film Rash-o-man, which is, as a matter of fact the greatest movie I, we, have ever seen, or nearly so, or better than that, so you had better see it, if you haven't already.[6] Just the same, it is no doubt, in fact is, psychologically necessary to return to one's New York to restablish the awareness of one's own periphery, a sine qua non in fact. And two months from now Dollarton may well be hell. We aim to go to California if I can get through the customs. Though I've known Dollarton heavenly in winter too, by gosh. But the fact is, one needs one['s] gal here, else it would be intolerable in summer too. Alone the sunrise can be simply a pain in the neck. In fact, to two people alone it can sometimes be a pain in the neck. That's all for now. Will write again soon. Meantime am working hard. Do you the same. Be happy. Best love from us both –

God bless

Malcolm

Annotations:

1 Lowry is quoting from the first verse of Melville's 'The Stone Fleet, An Old Sailor's Lament (December, 1861)':

> I have a feeling for those ships,
>   Each worn and ancient one,
> With great bluff bows, and broad in the beam:
>   Ay, it was unkindly done.
> But so they serve the Obsolete –
>   Even so, Stone Fleet!

See *The Collected Poems of Herman Melville*, ed. Howard P. Vincent (Chicago: Packard, 1947), pp. 16-17.

2 Dorothy Dix was a popular Hollywood gossip writer whose syndicated column appeared in the *Vancouver Sun*.

3 On 26 September 1952 Margerie had written a letter to Markson telling him how much they had enjoyed his visit and explaining that Malcolm was too busy struggling with the blank page to write himself. Lowry added a pencil note to her letter as follows: 'Battle of Blank Page – whose whiteness keeps it pure – or which exists to be decorated – is not

so bad as Battle of Bulge or overstuffed glowering illegible and anyhow incomprehensible page. With best love from Malcolm – '.

4 Angkor Wat is an ancient ruin and tourist site in Cambodia.

5 Lowry is almost certainly thinking of Ernest Hemingway's novella *The Old Man and the Sea* (1952). The old man dreams of lions coming down to the beach throughout the story, which closes: 'The old man was dreaming about the lions.'

6 *Rashómon* (1950) is the masterpiece of Japanese filmmaker Akira Kurosawa (1910-). It portrays the investigation of a murder and a rape as told from the different perspectives of four witnesses, one of whom is the murdered man speaking through a medium.

546: To Clemens ten Holder

P: private(ms)
PP: *Brief* 54
[Dollarton]
[October 1952][a]

Dear old Clemens:

I cannot say how happy I am to hear you are a bit better and in less pain and even able to take a walk and gaze on the bird of Indian summer.[1]

(We have a seagull family that have not emigrated but that is not because they ate too much bread like the ones in Nightwood but because they like to sit on our porch: the same seagull has done that for 13 years, ever since we rescued him when he got snowblinded & stuck in our fence, even though the fence is no longer there: we have practically learned how to speak seagullese, a very complicated language consisting of a million ways in which to say: Tea-time, you lazy fools, do you think I am sitting here to enjoy the view?)

I am hard at work on Hear Us Oh Lord from Heaven Thy Dwelling Place – 12 stories this time: motion is in opposite direction to that of Volcano, i.e out of the barranca toward the stars.

More of this later: next novel is Lunar Caustic, a grand guignol – madness & juvenile delinquency in a New York City hospital psychiatric ward: not very pretty – will have to take many swims writing it.

I hope to send you parts of Hear Us as soon as they are completed.

I had a hell of a nice letter from [Ernst] Klett who spoke of you in the warmest – &, of the translation in the highest – possible terms – more of this again later.[2] Please give him my regards & say I am writing.

This is simply an interim note that must catch the post. It is wonderful that you are feeling better, old fellow. All our love from us both to yourself & Hildegarde. God bless you. Hold that note, Rolando!

Malcolm

Annotations:

1 Clemens ten Holder died on 5 December 1952, and the 9-10 October 1952 letter from Hildegard is her last extant letter to the Lowrys. It is clear from Margerie's letters to the ten Holders that Hildegard had written in December to tell the Lowrys of her husband's death, but this note has not been located. Lowry's first mention of the death is in his April 1953 letter (**574**) to Dr Irmgard Rexroth Kern.

2 This is probably the letter Lowry is answering in his 3 October 1952 letter (**544**) to Klett.

Editorial Notes:

a. This transcription is from a photocopy of the holograph letter sent to me by ten Holder's son, Johannes ten Holder. The original carries neither inside address nor date. The date given in *Briefwechsel* is 'Summer 1952,' but Lowry's references to 'Indian summer' and migratory birds suggest a later date.

547: To Albert Erskine

P: Virginia(ms); UBC(phc)   Dollarton
                                                   [ca October 1952]

Dear old Albert:

Thanks very much for the letter; we grieve for your worries, can only hope things are looking up now, somehow.

I am still without news from England, despite inquiries; I am bound to suspect the reason is some serious illness at my brother's end, alas.

I dare say you saw that the Law of Series strikes once again, in a recent Time: the message washed up on the Irish shore & the couple that kissed the Blarney stone.[1]

Bravest Boat is likewise based on a true story, occuring here 2½ years since, though it was my idea to have the couple meet, married, & of different religions. The story received no publicity, & was no more than a 'filler' of 2 paragraphs, turned in by a rewrite man on the Vancouver Sun, under no imprint.[2]

Margie says it couldn't matter less, though something eerie about it bothers me. Also, what is my position?

I was not aware of the existence of the Blarney stone couple till last week.

Anyhow, as I have just intimated to Hal, I'm not going to rewrite the story & call it The Bravest Bottle.

With love from us both

                                                              Malcolm

Annotations:

1   In *Time* magazine for 18 August 1952, 27, there is a short article about an American soldier who put a message in a bottle and an Irish woman who found it and wrote to the man. When they met months later, they kissed the Blarney Stone together but, unlike Lowry's couple in 'The Bravest Boat,' their friendship did not blossom into romance.

2   In her 29 August 1952 letter to Harold Matson, Margerie explains that Malcolm found the inspiration for 'The Bravest Boat' in a small item reported in the *Vancouver Sun* for March 1950 about a model boat making a twelve-year journey from Vancouver Island to the city of Vancouver on the mainland.

548: To Maurice Nadeau

P: UBC(ts)   [Dollarton]
                                                        [ca October 1952][a]

Dear Maurice Nadeau[1]

Please forgive me for not answering your kind and good letters before now. I can only assure you that there were circumstances which prevented it such as, it sometimes seems to me, the ferocious difficulty of living in Canada – & as far away as Canada – knows alone how to provide. I am indeed honored that you wish something of mine for your review, and I have today written my agent, Harold Matson, in New York, for permission to send you as soon as possible a copy of a story called The Bravest Boat,[2] which I believe will not present too many difficulties in translation and although it is laid in Canada, I believe has a universal theme and treatment which I hope you will like & would interest your readers. This story is part of my next book HEAR US OH LORD FROM HEAVEN THY DWELLING PLACE. It is, in fact, the opening story. The title of the book comes from an old Manx fishermen's hymn. Perhaps that does not sound so promising: as a matter it has little or nothing to do with fishermen either.

Thank you again for your letters, and please give my kindest regards to Clarisse, Max-Pol, Paul Pilotin when you see them.[3] Perhaps it is not too much to hope that Clarisse might have time & like to translate The Bravest Boat. It is only 20 pages. I like it myself very much – hope you don't reject it after all.

With kindest regards to yourself, and best wishes and good luck for your new review.

                         Very cordially,

                                                        [unsigned]

P.S. I want to thank you for everything you did for the Volcano & both my wife & myself look forward with the greatest pleasure to meeting you again soon.

Annotations:

1 Maurice Nadeau (1911-), the Paris editor and publisher, was the founding editor of *Les Lettres nouvelles*, which began publication in 1952. Nadeau's letters to Lowry do not appear to have survived. A translation of 'The Bravest Boat' called 'Brave petit bateau' by Georges Belmont appeared in *Les Lettres nouvelles* 9 (novembre 1953): 1067-84.

2 A letter to Harold Matson requesting permission to send the story to Nadeau has not survived; however, see the postscript to Lowry's 8 January 1953 letter (**560**) to Matson.

3 Clarisse Francillon and Max-Pol Fouchet, as well as being Lowry's first translator and editor in France, were also friends and associates of Nadeau's. According to Nadeau, the name 'Paul Pilotin' was used by Stéphen Spriel; however, Lowry usually referred to him more familiarly as Mike. See Lowry's June 1950 letter (**400**) to Spriel.

Editorial Notes:

a. This unsigned draft (UBC 20:18) is on the verso of a page of draft material for *October Ferry to Gabriola*. It has pencil cancellations, interlineations, and marginalia *passim*.

549: To Albert Erskine

P: Virginia(ms); UBC(phc)

Dollarton, B.C.
[ca November 1952]

Dear brother – La Mordida & the Ordeal are now (drafts & notes) typed & copies go into the vault at the bank to-morrow to join Dark as the Grave: in all some 1600 pages of typescript. It seemed unfair to load you with this stuff on second thinkings, much of it embarrassing in this form – unless you said, which you didn't, to the contrary. The main obligation seemed to get it safely copied & safe which it now – touch wood – is. It would take many months more work to get it into a shape in which I could bear your reading it, or in which you would like to read it, so I've used my own judgment. I can't very well send it with a label on For

Christ sake don't read this even though it is, strictly, your property. Anyhow this seems the best thing to do at the moment: – only a smidgen (of Eridanus) remains to be done.

For the rest October Ferry, the penult. piece in Hear Us, developed into a short novel of some 160 pages which has occupied me also for the last few months minus one – where a flu epidemic caught first Margie then me, then Margie again. An absolutely dead silence from England has not enlightened me as to my financial status till yesterday when I received a cable; Application made transmit further money to you awaiting result Ayrcliff. (Doubtless they were awaiting results of the American election.)[1]

October Ferry in this present form wasn't on my itinerary but since it developed so well I persevered & am persevering. It has to be cut, still has to be rewritten in places. The rest of Hear Us has been building up too. It should be finished well in time according to contract though not quite as soon as I thought, partly because of going up & down on this ferry so many times – worth while journeys, as I hope, & hope you will think. Anyway, it's one of the world's best stories, though I say it who ought not: & Ghostkeeper, Pompeii, Gabriola & Spring make a monumental – if not all too monumental (getting on 400 pages for those 4 alone) quadripartite ending to Hear Us. Shades of Erich von Stroheim! But they don't bite off more than they can chew, I don't think. Trouble is, I have to bite them, & it hurts. All these are now about as complete as next to final versions of chapters of the Volcano, with many sections of all four in final version. Remains simply as finale on my part of super-concentration, so don't breathe. Or rather, do breathe.

I was too late with the application for the fellowship I applied for for next year but The Royal Society of Canada has entered my application as for 1953-4, when I probably won't get it either, though it seemed to me I ought to have a shot at it, since I don't have to do anything but go on writing.[2]

Among other harrassments has not been, till to-day, the weather. None of the money seems to have got through from France or Germany as yet & we haven't heard from Hal for what seems donkey's years. But thanks to yourself things look much brighter than they did this time last year.

Just thought I ought to make a report. Please send a word for my recastings of Gabriola & the delay caused by the last month have given me a bad case of the At my back I always hears.[3] In point of fact, the amount accomplished (despite the fact you haven't seen anything yet) has been very great.

But now comes the season of the southeasterly gales & this year we mean to move to town with as little time lost as possible putting work before everything else.[4]

    Hope all is well as possible with you.

    God bless you from us both

Malcolm

Annotations:

1 The United States election of 4 November 1952 brought the Republican General Dwight D. Eisenhower to the presidency.

2 I have not been able to trace Lowry's letters or application to the Royal Society of Canada, and the National Research Council files for the Canadian Government Overseas Awards in the 1950s have been destroyed. These awards were intended to allow twelve months of advanced study in the arts, humanities, social sciences, sciences, and professions, and were worth $4,000 for the year. They could be held in France or the Netherlands, using funds from blocked balances to Canada's credit in these countries. In her 29 August 1952 letter to Harold Matson, Margerie explained that Malcolm would be applying, and Albert Erskine wrote to J.B. Marshall of the National Research Council in support of Lowry's application on 8 September 1952. Lowry applied again in 1953; see his June 1953 letter (**579**) to Erskine.

3 Lowry alludes to a line from Andrew Marvell's poem 'To His Coy Mistress': 'But at my back I always hear / Time's winged chariot hurrying near.' He also knew T.S. Eliot's parody of this line in *The Waste Land*; see his 15 May 1940 letter (**139**) to Aiken.

4 In mid-November the Lowrys rented an apartment in the Bayview Apartment Hotel at 1359 Davie Street in the downtown West End of Vancouver; see Lowry's 24 November 1952 letter (**553**) to David Markson.

550: To Einar and Muriel Neilson

P: UBC(ms)
[Dollarton]
[ca November 1952]

Dear folks – We got boggled slightly with Margie sick + usual Anglo-Lowry-publisher boggle, – so were held up in our debt the last couple of months, for which our sincere apologies; in the general sense it was the American election[1] that was doing the boggling, so we may now consider ourselves well on the way to being unboggled again; not that our heads were not & are not well above water, if not above Juniper, but we wanted to keep a certain margin of safety in the bank; so since you weren't in a hurry, or good enough to say you weren't, we felt you wouldn't mind the delay: the last we paid you was $15 not $25

so we still owe you whatever 65 is from 100, namely $35, always sup-
posing you got the $15, or we sent it: meantime we are moving into
town to have a hot bath for a week – we saw Down in the Valley, &
thought it was tremendous: we also saw the Japanese film Rashaman,
ditto:[2] & were invited by The Film Society to see a private showing
of The Strong Man, directed by Frank Capra (1926) & starring Harry
Langdon + Margie's sister: ditto:[3] we are being driven crazy by a baby
seagull & look forward very much to coming to see you, this time
without fail only I wanted to get some work completed first to try on
you &/or tear to pieces, if necessary, which, since due to some quirk,
I write backwards, is not easy; or too easy, whichever way you look
at it.

God bless you both from us both

Malcolm

Annotations:

1 On 4 November 1952.
2 *Down in the Valley* (1948), an operetta by Kurt Weill (1900-50), with
   libretto by Arnold Sungaard, played in Vancouver from 1 to 14
   November 1952. Lowry praises Kurosawa's *Rashómon* in his 3 October
   1952 letter (**545**) to David Markson.
3 Margerie's sister Priscilla starred opposite Langdon in *The Strong Man*
   (1926), which Lowry discusses in his November 1952 letter (**552**) to
   Priscilla Woolfan.

551: To Clarisse Francillon

P: UBC(ms) [Dollarton]
[ca November 1952][a]

My very dear Clarisse:
   I apologise sincerely for not yet having acknowledged Les
Meurtriers.[1] It seems to have a most exciting & profound plot but I have
not yet had time to read it. Re Ultramarine I have a very bad &
remorseful feeling (as I once tried to tell you) about that wretched book
ever having been published in the form it was and it should be completely rewritten before being translated. Re poems: I haven't time at
present with Margie sick and myself working against time to deal with
this but a translation of one of my poems into French was made by the
Haitian Phillippe Thoby-Marcelin and I am writing him to send this to
you together with the original but concerning all this it would of course
be much easier if we were in France and I am hoping that perhaps we
shall be again at no too distant date. Concerning Lunar Caustic I am

supposed to be rewriting that next year but whether I can improve it or not I don't know. I am pretty proud of the version that Madame d'Astorg has and proud that she is translating it[2] but the whole situation of freedom of expression has grown so ticklish of recent years in the United States that I have begun to acquire some qualms, partly due to cowardice, partly to common or garden sportsmanship. What – a novel written by a Canadian (or Englishman) set in an American psychiatric ward in New York and presenting the conditions therein in such a grim light – could not this be construed by some busybody as by extension symbolising unfavorably American life or American civilization itself, or something or other, *exclusively* and thus Lunar Caustic held not to be contributing to the harmonious relationship between these respective countries?[3] I am afraid that it indeed could be so construed at the present time, even though that was very far from its intention: rather hell of the word being the hell of the world, and spiritually speaking the hell within the soul etc. (The distinction throughout Hear Us Oh Lord too is between World & Earth: vide Santayana: – 'I hate the world but love the earth.'[4] Besides, the version Madame d'Astorg has was first written 17 years ago, when I was only 26. But the unsportsmanship would seem to come in via the fact that (a) it is an American firm, not a Canadian firm, that is paying me, and if conditions in New York City hospitals were bad 17 years ago conditions in British Columbian mental institutions are ten times worse, I understand, even at the present day. A further point is that Lunar Caustic's first appearance would be in French (it's never been published before) & Madame d'Astorgs version differs considerably from the version that probably Random House will publish. This makes it a kind of sport of nature and clearly calls for some explanation in a preliminary note, without which it would seem unfair to America or biased & my position ethically dubious if it did not actually get me into some obscure trouble. But this problem lies in the future. Unfortunately it has now occurred to me that the situation of the Bravest Boat,[5] which has not been published either as yet in America or Canada, is not different in one respect since it's first appearance will be in France, and this has me worried, for its clearly one thing to insult dear old Vancouver, at home, and quite another abroad: & the standpoint of this story must seem completely unbalanced if not indeed actually prejudiced in its venom against the 'city' – if it be recognised – or *city* per se, unless again some explanation is made in a note. Frankly I wouldn't know how to write such a note, but I think it should be made clear in it that, as I said to you before, the story is essentially *about* the storms & stresses & differences & barriers & ordeals of *life*, not those peculiar to this hemisphere. For example the border between Canada & America in general presents only slightly more of a barrier than it did to the little boat; it is the one undefended border in the world; – true, there is, at present freer speech here than there, but by & large there is great friend-liness between the two peoples of our neighbouring countries (I'm married to an American myself: but there are always & everywhere & perhaps, though one might wish they could disappear, last, necessarily such things as borders, & their existence can certainly complicate the course of true love. On the other hand, if the story is not to give offense, (one reason it might give offense is that the insult to Vancouver – or Enochvilleport – could be construed by certain people as a kind of insult to Canada itself – which everywhere advertises itself as being tremen-dously proud of its vast industrial advance, as no doubt it is & even has cause to be – or, in fact, to God knows what else) if it not to give offense, I say, has to explain that the point of view, as the author must admit, is as biased as the devil & anything but objective, even while, worse still, *seeming to be*, objective: values of good & evil seem to be assumed, as for country versus city, (again Earth & World) as for the dis-possessed against those in possession, & so forth, all of which might seem artistically indefensible as well as misleadingly partisan – even the poor aldermen are made out to be 'furious' – were it not that the point of view is balanced in the other stories in the volume. Elsewhere I think I do full justice to Canada's palpable beauties & opportunities. To a cer-tain kind of immigrant of course Canada is heaven. But to a certain kind of artist it can be hell too. And this unprecedentedly great industrial advance (not mirrored in the story but perhaps felt in the background) British Columbia particularly is so proud of also threatens much of the old way of life & its simpler cleaner values. From this aspect the story is almost completely reactionary, & as it were *conservationary*. I hate to see trees cut down, & pulp mills go up in their place, no matter how inevitable the latter. I do not welcome the great industrial advance because it threatens *me* – our home & the beauty around us, even if it may eventually bring other advantages I can't see, (though I doubt it, that is I doubt the final advantages.) And moreover, big business these days seems to have all the say. So I have written, as it were, from the standpoint of the *victims* – even though the protagonists themselves happen not to be especially victims but are clearly triumphant, or their love is triumphant, indeed even as the boat, over whatever forces have threatened them.

[b][(Margerie was ill, & ourselves bitterly poor, when I wrote the story, at the same time that we were being threatened by eviction. By law I have to pay, a law that together with the liquor law has now been changed for the better, such a preposterously large hospital insurance several times a year without being able to get her into hospital, had she consented to go, that I couldn't pay her doctor's bills. Injustice can go

no further. And with the calamitous crash of the pound, such was especially hard on an Englishman, especially on one whose stories – even while the country pretended to be crying aloud for artists, & this one was even internationally famous, after his fashion, thanks largely to you – noone here wanted to buy. No wonder if one got desperate from time to time. The story so far as this concerned is in part the consequence of personal rancour (though perhaps you ought to keep this confidential – rancour even against the bloody newspaper I got the f - - king story from (without permission, though it was under no dateline of reporter's authorship, – simply the Vancouver Sun was the Seattle Star, & if I told them, that the fact is they would headline the story, & use it once again to victimize the beach & destroy our neighbours, – the Sun, my own home town newspaper, practically the only one in the world to pan the Volcano, would jump like a released pimp from {jail} on this & everybody would be under edict once more publically.]

Various things have changed in Vancouver too since I wrote the story e.g There *are* bars now, or threaten to be soon. There are some fairly decent beginnings of a theatre too. However perhaps all this won't matter & noone will recognize it. Just the same, if Mike hasn't translated it yet, perhaps you'll bear in mind what I've said & concoct something in the way of a note from this. It was based on a true story reported in the Vancouver Sun too (though the couple weren't married off later, I've told you a later coincidence about *that*) though unsigned: in short the contents of the note are factual, & the Seattle Star the Vancouver Sun but to draw attention to that would be to draw attention also to the fact that Enochvilleport is a sadistic portrait of Vancouver etc Well will write again soon – Best love from us both –

Malcolm

Annotations:

1 *Les Meurtrières* (meaning loopholes, with a pun on murderers), one of Francillon's many novels, appeared in 1952. The copy she gave Lowry is no longer with his library.

2 Lowry is referring to a version of the novella called 'Swinging the Maelstrom,' which Francillon and Michèle d'Astorg translated. It appeared as *Le Caustique Lunaire* in *Esprit* for February, March, and April 1956.

3 Lowry's concerns about the American response to the book stem from the House Un-American Activities Committee (HUAC) investigations of so-called subversive communist activities. Republican Senator Joseph R. McCarthy (1908-57) provided fresh impetus to HUAC in 1950 by sponsoring an anti-communist bill in the United States Senate; as a result, many writers, artists, and intellectuals were harassed during

the late forties and early fifties. Lowry may also be concerned about publishers' rights because his new contract with Random House was for three novels, one of which could be a revised *Lunar Caustic*.

4 Lowry was reading the work of George Santayana (1863-1952), the Spanish philosopher and Harvard professor, during 1952-53; see his 27 December 1953 letter (**598**) to Albert Erskine.

5 See Lowry's October 1952 letter (**548**) to Maurice Nadeau, who had accepted Lowry's story.

Editorial Notes:

a. This four-page holograph (UBC 2:20) is undated, but internal references suggest a late 1952 date.

b. From this point to the end of the paragraph there are very light pencil lines to indicate cancellation. I have included the passage because it provides information that assists dating and sheds some interesting light on Lowry's feelings when he was composing 'The Bravest Boat.'

552: To Priscilla (Mrs E.B.) Woolfan

P: UBC(ms)
PP: *SL* 309-10

[Dollarton]
[ca November 1952][a]

My dearest sister Priscilla:

We went to see The Strong Man; being privileged to be related to the star, to say the least, we were invited as honored guests to see a private showing albeit it is now wowing the audiences again in the theatre proper.[1] I think you should know too that of all the cinematic consummate masterpieces in demand The Strong Man is about the most popular, if not the most popular, and consequently one of the hardest to obtain. That it was got in time for us to see it was due to the courtesy of the Museum of Modern Art for the same privileged reason as above. And before I say anything else, Priscilla – though I have seen the film before – I want to say immediately that your performance is one of the most profoundly realized and inspired – one of the greatest and most permanent things in short that I or anyone else have seen in a movie. The audience was certainly of the same opinion.

That Chaplin seems to have borrowed liberally and literally from the general idea in City Lights was something that occurred to the audience too, to the grave detriment of one's memories of the direction of Virginia Cherrill therein, but perhaps this is a minor point: or one that could have been more literally minor had not your performance in The Strong Man been so absolutely major.[2]

I myself have to throw myself forward rather than backward to get any comparison in terms of excellence for your acting, recently, to Barrault, etc., and the drama of the mime:[3] though when we were in Paris we never saw any performance comparable to yours. I don't suppose such a one as good will occur again, though I don't see why it shouldn't, should you yourself choose even if tangentially to return to one or the other of the departments of drama.

The film itself – though we saw it under the worst kind of circumstances in one way, 4 or 5 people in a room, recorded thunderjug music that was far too soft and rarely varied and only once really imaginative, when they shut it off altogether when you were playing the terrific scene with Langdon on the garden seat – struck me as being colossal too: its revelation of the human soul was profound. Not to say the present situation, even if partly unconscious on [Frank] Capra's part, though it must be said that he has not failed to continue to mine that apparently inexhaustible gold mine of American consciousness of decency and wisdom against the forces of hypocrisy.[4] Perhaps it wasn't meant to be profound, but even if not, your own performance would have made it a pioneer work in cinema. In short, as a film, it must strike anyone who has loved such things as important.

> [Your affectionate brother,]
> [Malcolm]

Annotations:

1 In *The Strong Man*, an American silent film directed by Frank Capra, Harry Langdon plays a returning war veteran and Priscilla is his sweetheart.

2 The silent film comedy *City Lights* (1931), written, directed, and produced by Charlie Chaplin, stars Chaplin as the tramp who befriends a millionaire and falls in love with a blind girl, played by Virginia Cherrill.

3 Jean-Louis Barrault (1910-94), the French stage and film actor, was known for the gestural detail, elements of mime, and inventive physical action he brought to his performances.

4 Lowry may be remembering that in December 1951 Frank Capra was accused of being a communist sympathizer and that by January 1952 he had been cleared and sent to India on official business. See Capra's comments in *Frank Capra: The Name Above the Title, An Autobiography* (New York: Macmillan, 1971), pp. 427-31.

Editorial Notes:

a. This transcription is from the text published in *Selected Letters*, where it has been mistakenly placed in a sequence of letters for April 1952. The original has not been located, but there is an unsigned, rough three-page pencil draft in the Lowry Collection (UBC 3:14) with three additional pages of pencil draft. These pages are incoherent and not clearly connected to the letter; they involve a conversation and the question: 'Have you seen Harry?'

553: To David Markson

P: UBC(ms)

PP: *SL* 323-24

Bayview Apartment Hotel,
1359 Davie St,
Vancouver, B.C.
[24 November 1952]

Dear old Dave.

I am a bastardo for not writing. I am glad you are writing. That is more than I can do. So please write. We are living opposite a convent with stained glass windows. Nearby is a catholic church within which it says: '*We want girl-power for our convent.*' A little further away is a haunted house, with tall chimneys, drawn blinds, a sagging stoop, &, mounting guard upon a high window-sill, a stuffed decaying owl. What comes out of the chimneys? Smoke comes out of the chimneys. How can nothing come out of the chimneys? Alternative exercise for more advanced students! What else comes out of the chimneys? Nothing comes out of the chimneys? Because my uncle said that the postman saw nothing coming out of the chimneys. Has the postman been? The postman has not been? Why has not the postman been? In order for the postman to have been it is first necessary that the postman be. The windows (les fenêtres): the girl-power (batterie de fillettes): the haunted house ( ): the owl (l'hibou): the postman (der Briefträger): Where is my uncle? My uncle is in the garden with his good strong stout stick. We send you our sincere love. So send us the same & a word. Writing goes hard. So I think to have sended an angel – or perhaps even a saint – after you to find out if you are not dead already. So watch out.

All the very best from both of us & everything in Dollarton. News from there is we were practically alone with marvellous weather since you left. Cabins on both sides of us are now for sale – including the one to the right on our old site. But the isolation gave us for once a slight case of the cafard so we've shifted to town earlier than last year (the 2 previous winters we took it out there) & are enjoying the change hugely.

Malcolm

P.S. A seagull has shat on the roof of the convent.

P.P.S. We visited a spiritualist church where we learned (from what seemed a genuine medium) that there are some spirits who live only

47 miles away up in the air. These spirits are borrachos etc & love to haunt pubs & bars. They are not, however, good spirits, (though there are also good ones who like to drink) and drunks they will sometimes utterly possess so perhaps there is something in the Consul after all. All this was uttered by the medium in a kind of trance state & was presumably directed toward me. She went on to say in effect (the very sober audience seemed a bit taken aback by all this) that this was the only reasonable explanation why a drunk who has one drink in his hand, & another on the table, & who could not possibly drink another drink if he tried, nonetheless says: Gimme another — (i.e. he doesn't say it.)

P.P.P.S. Another seagull has shat on the roof of the convent.

554: To Dorothy Livesay

P: Manitoba(ms)　　　　　　　　　　　　　　　　　　1359 Davie St,
PP: Livesay　　　　　　　　　　　　　　　　　　　　Vancouver,
　　　　　　　　　　　　　　　　　　　　　　　　　Canada
　　　　　　　　　　　　　　　　　　　　[December 1952]

Dear Dorothy

It was very good of you to bring some influence immediately to bear, especially when suffering yourself with your hand, of which I'm very sorry to hear indeed, and hope this may soon be better; as a result of your stretching forth a hand, however, the lady's position is now much less intolerable, she having been teleported to the Newport Hotel.[1] What the Newport Hotel is like I don't like to think, but here it was actively dangerous — the stairs to the attic are so long & steep they even [make] me gasp — indeed her condition was desperate, as Margerie immediately saw. Margie had in fact walked half round town & tried about fifty places — literally — before I phoned you, none of which — though many of them run by Catholics, as is this (not to say opposite a convent) which was throwing her out, would take anyone with a baby, far less shortly also to be delivered of another one, even at Christmas time.

It turned out to be fortunate I phoned you though, for the next day she was given an ultimatum by the landlady to get out immediately, whereas previously Friday had been her deadline. Even so there were further difficulties in that she had a brother we hadn't known about & she hadn't owned to (living in an hotel in the skidroad apparently) so on & so forth, such being life in this city of terrors: what the brother had to do with it {the argument seemed to be that the lady was remiss in not availing herself of the opportunity to share his grisly abode with his wife, his wife's brother, 3 children, & his mother-in-law – presumably sleeping on the floor: moreover she was just out of hospital, her feet badly swollen, & in her eight month}, or even the husband for that matter – who evidently decamped last November – or how in such an appalling pass she could be held accountable for anything whatever I simply don't know: the main thing is that what with you on one end, & Margie on the other, something constructive was done. At worst one assumes the Newport Hotel to be better – if not much – than a gas oven. At best (unless as seems likely this would be worse still) some pressure will be brought on her husband to return or at least support her. Since he too is apparently a Catholic one can't help wondering what he's going to do with his conscience round Christmas though one presumes he gave it notice to leave in plenty of time. Hope the hand isn't too much of a beastly snag with the writing, also to see you soon

With best love to your husband & yourself from us both

Malcolm

Annotations:

1 Dorothy Livesay reprints this letter in *Journey with My Selves: A Memoir, 1909-1963* (Vancouver: Douglas & McIntyre, 1991), pp. 170-71. Although she cannot recall the details of the episode, she explains that Lowry went to her for help because she was a trained social worker.

555: To Marie D. Moore

P: Matson(ts); UBC(phc)

1359 Davie St,
Vancouver, B.C.,
Canada
10 December 1952

Dear Miss Moore:[1]

Thank you very much for your letter of the 3rd inst. in such swift reply to my wife's of the 25 ulto. (as they seem to say in England, to judge from a letter to hand, posted the 2nd inst. but apparently written on the 1st penulto.)

I'm glad to know there's some chance of the stories you mention hitting with the New American Library, and I'm hoping the novellas I'm working on at present will stand a good chance somewhere.

As for the delay re the French money, while greatly appreciating your own action, I'm a bit puzzled about the situation Club Livre du Francais vis-a-vis Correa, and also to what source the hitch is traceable, which looks to me like an oversight on the part of the French Government.[2] All we know is that it is now over a year since Clarisse Francillon, one of the French translators, informed us that there was some half a million – or was it a quarter of a million – francs, i.e., – er – some seven or eight hundred dollars there anyhow, accruing to me from earnings on the Volcano, presumably (my wife says definitely) from Correa, and did I want it (a) to be left there in case we came to France again, (b) to be sent directly to us (c) to you. We asked of course that it be sent to yourselves, and informed Hal of this, who said it might take as long as ten months, unfortunately, as had been his experience with another client.

This spring or summer we had another letter from Clarisse saying that Correa had put the money through last December or January, and that it was the French Government who was temporarily blocking it, as Hal had previously warned us was to be expected, though Clarisse thought we – or rather you – would now probably be receiving it at any moment.

It is now therefore over a year since this has been promised from France which really does seem too long: but this money so far as my information ran is from Correa and has nothing to do with the Club Livre du Francais, though if the latter owe me some more, that, of course, is fine. But my relationship with the Club Livre is so far as I know on a different plane and in any case is a bit intricate and something as follows.

First it was Fontaine and not Correa who originally took (and paid an advance for) the Volcano but when we got to France in 1947-8 Fontaine (of which Clarisse was an editor) was more or less on the point of shutting up shop and any translation of the Volcano become something of a chimera: we reawakened some enthusiasm, however, and the Club Livre stepped in, paying me an advance of 20,000 francs, I seem to remember, which went into my pocket and, no doubt, as quickly out again: (I earned every cent of it for without us on the spot at the rate they were going there might well be no French translation at all even now): – it wasn't until 1949 or even '50 that I heard that Correa was taking it and meantime I had no reason to believe that the handsome Club Livre version had even got into a second edition which considering that there were only a thousand copies printed of the first cannot have meant a very large sale.[3]

It was wonderfully reviewed, however, in France, and so far as we can tell from Clarisse's report the Correa edition must have enjoyed a pretty good sale too: whether this boosted the sale of the Club Livre du Francais edition or not I don't know (though from your letter I would surmise so) but in any event my impression is that the two things are separate and that Correa probably thinks *their* money's gone through long ago: however I suppose that there must be liaison to some extent since Correa used the Book Club's translation and not vice-versa, and that pressure exerted on the one, will exert it on the other, and so at last hit the right ninepin.

Wherever the bottleneck (just to enjoy the luxury of paying no attention to metaphors at all for the moment) this delay has put us somewhat out in our financial calculations, especially at this season and having just moved into town, for we felt even at worst we'd have received it by now, so if the French promise seems good enough we'd be very glad indeed of the German reality of $68.66 (which was not $340) and even the $11. from Harcourt Brace (not forgetting the 53 cents) leaving for the moment the debit balance as it was before: we can ask this in better faith in that with a clanking of rusty gears my English affairs – there seems something faintly familiar about this sentence – at last show some signs of getting into motion, even dramatic motion, with notable emoluments threatening from sources ranging from everything from 2500 preferential shares in the Textile Paper Tube Ltd to 3% Debenture Stock in the Stow-in-the-Wold Golf Club, and much beside, so that with any luck we should shortly be in a position to cancel the debit balance altogether.

Again, with many thanks, I am

Sincerely yours

Malcolm Lowry

Annotations:

1 Marie D. Moore was Harold Matson's assistant for many years.
2 In her 16 December 1952 letter to Lowry, Moore notes that the firm has no copy of his French translation contract but that she is putting pressure on the publisher. This absence of a contract, in either New York or Paris, continued to cause complications. In her 14 April 1947 letter to George Gode, Francillon wrote that she was returning three of the four copies of the contract, signed by herself, to Matson's office. One was to be sent to Lowry, but his too seems to have disappeared.
3 Without the contract, Lowry's comments cannot be confirmed. See his March 1948 and 23 February 1949 letters (**334** and **359**) to Matson.

556: To David Markson

P: UBC(card)   [1359 Davie St]
                                                [15 December 1952]

Thanks for Bix & Joe[1] – they certainly look in the Groove, – best Bix is Singing the Blues (the break near the beginning!), Frankie Trumbauer & his Orchestra, – now available again, also Way Down Yonder in New Orleans (& of course the piano solos In a Mist, In the Dark, Flashes) –

All best love to you, keep up the good work, we think of you & miss you – hope to see you again soon

 With best love from us both   Malcolm

Annotations:

1 Lowry owned several records featuring Bix Beiderbecke, Joe Venuti, and Frankie Trumbauer; six are in the Lowry Collection (UBC, Neilson Papers, Box 1), one of which has 'In the Dark' and 'Flashes.'

557: To Muriel and Einar Neilson

P: UBC(ms)   [1359 Davie St]
                  [30 December 1952]

Dear Muriel & Einar –

 Well, my sugar plums, we had a generally merry (in our various ways) happy & fine Christmas together didn't we? I'm sorry I became such a droop & I'll never forget how good you both were to me (in *various* ways) in my hours of need. In fact, I'll never spend another Christmas without remembering with love 1952 at Leiban.

 Please don't forget, both of you, that when you come to the Big City we are now very easily reached by the Davie St bus – get off at Broughton & you're practically at our front door – there's a modern apartment on the corner & we are right next door in one of those old houses with a big neon sign saying Bayview *Hotel*. There's a couch, & we'll be delighted – & we mean it – to put you up. You can call the landlady – Marine 7302 – & leave a message, or just walk in, we're in #11 on the third floor.

 I don't know yet what we're going to do on New Year's Eve, probably it'll be fairly quiet. But you must imagine us, the room filled with soap bubbles & smoke from Malc's new pipe, & the remarkable alligator charging furiously around the floor snapping gaily.

 Give the Duchess & the Cats a kiss for us – have they left anything of the tree? – my lovely tree! And a great big hug of affection & thanks to you both.

 May you have the happiest new year ever, my dears, God bless you both – Skoal!

             love   Margerie

(exit, on well-oiled roller skates)

Great love & thanks to you both. Was wonderful to see you 2 in such good form, also the house more terrific than ever. Will definitely be in better form myself next time. Spent yesterday reading The Imitation of

Christ.[1] The crocodile is doing well & has already learned to sing Life gets tedious don't it. (But when I found him last night grown to full size sounding off with the Battle Music from Alexander Nevsky[2] I put him in the bathroom to cool off a little.)

God bless you

Malcolm

Annotations:

1 *The Imitation of Christ* (1473), written in Latin by Thomas à Kempis (1379?-1471), contains rules on how to live a Christian life, as well as prayers and meditations. It has been frequently translated in several editions; Lowry owned the 1943 Random House edition.
2 *Alexander Nevsky* (1938) is a costume epic film by Sergei Eisenstein about Prince Alexander Nevsky, who led the Russian people against a Teutonic invasion in the thirteenth century.

558: To Einar Neilson

P: UBC(tsc) [Vancouver]
[ca Winter 1952-53]ª

FUN! Hotel Gai Paris.
Hangouver-on-Sea.

All quiet save that I dreamed
  that Duchess bit my landlord's
balls off (if he's got any, which
I doubt). We have news our
French money is on way, & are working
very hard. But no matter how
quiet we are that bastard complains
about something.
Love from us both to you
 & Muriel

LAUGHTER! COCKTAILS!

[Malcolm.]

BRING YOUR
FRIENDS!

COME IN AT ANY HOUR OF NIGHT
AND HAVE A REAL GOOD TIME!

Editorial Notes:

a. This transcription is from a typescript copy with the David Markson
    Papers (UBC 1:12). The original has not been found, and it is unclear
    why this copy is with the Markson Papers or who made it. The mes-
    sage is for Einar Neilson and it was probably written from the Bayview
    Apartment Hotel on Davie Street.

559: To Downie Kirk

P: UBC(ts phc)   1359 Davie St, Vancouver
                                                        5 January 1953

Dear old Downie:
    I hope you'll forgive me for having importuned you to cash a post-
dated check at such a hell of an inconvenient time for you (not to say
for me); it just dawned on us that Friday morning when we woke up, a
little gaga, and unbalanced our check book – the more so since as it
turned out all I had to do was to go to the bank and cash it there by the
simple expedient of arranging an overdraft – though the word is somewhat of an overstatement – which contrary to my information Canadian
banks do permit in certain cases like this with the greatest of ease. This
just to let you know we made out successfully for I know you would
have helped if you could. As a matter of fact I should – touch wood –
be pretty flush later this month so if you're still short yourself, don't hesitate to ask us, though I imagine by the time our balance is redressed
your crisis will be over. (In fact I need not have post-dated such a
cheque beyond the first of this week: but it occurred to me immediately
afterwards that it was as well I'd gone to the bank for even if the cheque
was going to arrive – as normally it should – on what was then the next
day, Saturday, the banks being closed, we might have found no one to
cash it over the week-end. But naturally I was less afraid of you than a
bank, especially with somewhat of a hangover. Now I think I was a bit
inconsiderate, though, I assure you, without meaning to be.) – Well, O
sewers! O publishers! O delayed cheques! – It was fine to see you on
New Years and all the best of fortune and good wishes for your forthcoming happy event.[1]
    With love from us both to Marjorie and Dorothy and your good
self,

                                                              Malcolm

Annotations:

  1 The Kirks were expecting the birth of their daughter Katherine.

560: To Harold Matson

P: UBC(tsc)
PP: *SL* 327-28

1359 Davie St,
Vancouver, B.C.,
Canada
8 January 1953[a]

Dear Hal:

Very happy to hear the news re Strange Comfort.[1] The revision I've done on this particular story is negligible as affecting it as a story per se, and pertains rather to its interdependent position within the volume and I'm not sure I won't have to revise the revisions; minor points were that I was uncertain whether or not to turn him, the protagonist, into a Canadian – also that his name is Sigbjørn Wilderness, which is the same name as that of the hero of the whole bolus, though the Sigbjørn of Strange Comfort is not the same person as that hero. Tant pis! Unfortunately we don't have a copy of the story here in Vancouver, having left it on an island over Christmas with a fellow who wanted to make a tape recording of it, so I shan't have time to get hold of it and make any last minute corrections if such be needed.[2] But I think I'm only too delighted for the story to be published exactly as it stands, or rather as New World Writing has it – (psychologically immoral though the story may be called) – if Arabel Porter feels the same.[3] Only please ask her to be good enough to see to it since it must be (even though as I have said in another sense strictly it isn't): Sigbjørn Wilderness. (i.e., I am infatuated with the line through the Ø) and also for God's sake to look out for my possibly faulty Italian. Other small points: Gogol's last words – repeated several times – come from Nabokov's authoritative and wonderful book on Gogol, though acknowledgement to Nabokov is made for this *within* the text of the story and I hope this is sufficent for after all they are Gogol's words not Nabokov's (though one be indebted to Nabokov for them): if not, further acknowledgement could be made in a small footnote.[4]

As an afterthought, what I *do* regret not having put into Strange Comfort, since part of the story is in Richmond, is:

– Mem: Consult Talking Horse Friday.

Yes, that really *ought* to be in and it's too bad I don't have any mss. to hand to suggest just where it should go: do you suppose Arabel Porter, if she agrees, would obligingly find a place for it?[5]

Other work accomplished outside to date is huge and has been reported on to Albert: i.e., thousands of pages mostly in first draft and notes, typed, and placed in a vault at the Bank. This takes care of the whole thing to the end, however, with the exception of the short intermezzo Eridanus from which October Ferry (see below) has to be prevented from greedily gulping the material. It's no easy task but we's a gettin' there, not too far behind schedule either. Work in progress is still last 4 novellas of Hear Us, and their interrelation: with a rewritten (and I hope terrific) October Ferry to Gabriola as the current and besetting problem that has engrossed and forestalled obsessed and delighted me for months and is still a problem child for it grew almost to a novel on its own and is still not quite subdued and cut to size, though I hope to have results soon. Mem: Consult Talking Horse. Health is good, hope you the same. Very happy New Year to you Tommy and the children from us both.

Kindest regards,

[unsigned]

P.S. Has Bravest Boat braved Atlantic yet?[6]

Annotations:

1 Lowry had just received word that 'Strange Comfort Afforded by the Profession' was accepted for publication; it appeared in *New World Writing* 3 (1953): 331-44.
2 The Lowrys spent Christmas 1952 on Bowen Island; see their joint 30 December 1952 letter (**557**) to the Neilsons.
3 See Lowry's 29 May 1953 letter (**576**) to Arabel Porter.
4 In the story (*HUOL* 103) Lowry quotes from the passage in Gogol's 'Diary of a Madman' that Nabokov uses to preface his study *Nikolai Gogol* (New York: New Directions Books, 1944).
5 ' – Mem: Consult Talking Horse Friday.' has been inserted into the story (*HUOL* 105) as part of the material that Sigbjørn reads from his notes about a trip he made to Poe's house in Richmond, Virginia; see Lowry's 12 March 1952 letter (**568**) to Pamela Hudson. Lowry is quoting from his own notes on the visit he and Margerie made in February 1947.
6 See Lowry's October 1952 letter (**548**) to Maurice Nadeau.

Editorial Notes:

a. This transcription is from an unsigned typescript marked 'Copy' (UBC 3:5), and neither a draft nor an original exists with the UBC Collection or the Matson files. It is impossible to confirm whether this transcription follows Lowry's text, but given the attention he draws to his protagonist's name, Sigbjørn, I have added the ø, which Lowry would have used.

561: To Clarisse Francillon

P: UBC(phc)
PP: *SL* 328-29

1359 Davie St,
Vancouver, B.C., Canada
20 January 1953

Dear Clarisse:

Hope you received our Christmas card O.K.?

I hate to importune you again, but I wonder if you could do me a favor, which shouldn't be much trouble for you and would be of absolutely ineffable help to me. I still haven't received the money you wrote me about over a year ago from Correa and the Book Club.[1] My agent in New York is trying his best to collect it for me through a Mrs. W.A. Bradley (A French literary agent) whose address is 18 Quai de Bethune, Paris 4. They are now holding it up because apparently they cannot locate any contract between the Book Club and myself. To the best of my knowledge there never was any such contract, as I have repeatedly told them, and the only evidence I have regarding Correa is your letter to me, of February 23rd, 1950, in which you said that Correa was taking over and asked me to agree to certain changes in the royalties, and which you will remember I replied to at once, agreeing to completely.[2] Is there some way in which you, as the witness and go-between for all these deals, and being *there* (and not ten thousand miles away as I am) could do something about this? I would appreciate it more than I can say, for I'm working desperately against time to get my new book finished, these delays are driving me crazy, my estate in England is still held up, we are in debt, we live on one hard boiled egg (bad) every three days, and I've been expecting this money every day for the last year, and having made commitments on that expectation (which I felt I had every right to do) I am now so harrassed on every side I don't know which way to turn.

We're still hoping and looking forward to returning to France some time in the future, perhaps when my next book is finished. What is the news of your novel? How goes Mike? Should you see M. Nadeau, please thank him very much for me for his letter and say I'll reply as soon as I can.

A thousand thanks in advance, and all the best love from Margerie and myself, and every good wish for a prosperous and happy new year.

Best love from

Malcolm

Annotations:

1 This letter is no longer extant, but on 14 May 1950 Francillon wrote explaining that the Club français du livre and Corrêa had not allowed *Combat* to publish *Au-dessous du volcan* serially because it might damage sales of the book.

2 This letter has not survived with Lowry's papers.

562: To Manager, Westminster Bank, Liverpool

P: UBC(ms)   [1359 Davie St]
                                                    [ca 21 January 1953][a]

Dear Sir:

I wonder if it is within your power to help me in regard to what might seem a small matter, but which is to me a large one, namely the date upon which my monthly income of £34 (92.00) derived from our family estate arrives here in Vancouver, and which for the last fourteen years until recently you have been in the habit of sending to the Royal Bank in Vancouver close to the beginning of each month.

During the last months this specie has taken to arriving later and later until this last month of January it did not arrive till the 20th of this month, whereas a year ago it was almost never later than the 6th or 7th.

The Royal Bank here were first at a loss to give any explanation of this and then said that by a new arrangement – or perhaps in my case as I hope an error, or at least an arrangement that is not irrefutable – you were now sending the money to the Royal Bank in *Montreal,* in the Province of Quebec, which is 5000 miles away, whence it was relayed here to Vancouver, British Columbia, as it were on the other side of the world, and that this was responsible for the delay, a delay which I have no earthly way of explaining here, where I have medical expenses to meet & rent to pay.

Further delay is caused to me in that my own bank is the Bank of Montreal *in* Vancouver – I hope this is clear – & not the Royal Bank so that having arrived in Vancouver it, the money, has to be transferred – or rather they have the courtesy to transfer it – to the Bank of Montreal here: sometimes several more days elapse before I am informed it has arrived, for our home is not in Vancouver itself but some little distance away in the country, although we are at present living at the above address in town.

This of course is simply due to local exigencies over which you have no control but it is almost impossible to explain – unless you lived in these complicated wilds yourself – the grief & anxiety such a small matter as this added delay elicited by your new arrangement – if such it be – can cause, where doctors bills & rent have to be paid on the dot, in a time of financial stress & anyway when one has committed oneself to the arrival of the money within the first week of the month, & all this happening quite without warning. The fact that I have been informed by Ayerton Alderson Smith[1] that they are handing over to you my share in the residuary estate of my father Arthur O. Lowry & my mother, Evelyn Lowry, to be trustees in connection with my brother, Stuart Lowry, also makes me feel rather more free to write to you concerning this minor matter of the delay in receipt of this small monthly income I have at present: though I should add, that normally the arrival of such a sum a week sooner or later would not make any difference: but events – inflation, the difficulty of obtaining royalties owing to me from foreign countries, medical expenses etc. – have all conspired to eat up our savings, so that with no back log of cash in the bank it does in fact make a serious difference, as I have intimated, or I would not perhaps have written you.

I am also advised that application has been made for £500 to be sent to me which, when it arrives, will naturally much alleviate the present situation.[2] I don't suppose you have any idea when permission for this might come through, or when it might arrive; I am not aware if the Treasury knows that I shall be obliged to pay income tax here on my *whole* income in England, irrespective of whether I receive or have any money to pay it this with or not.

Things being as they are therefore, from my own point of view, I would, ordinarily, simply find some position here to tide me over until such time as more money could be sent from England: but as it happens I am under contract to the firm of Random House in New York City for the publication of three books, I have definite publication dates to meet, & this work employs my entire time.

I have an advance settlement from them, which also arrives monthly, to assist me until I have finished my work, & which, together with my £34 (which I had given them to understand I could count on arriving regularly) barely allows me to meet my expenses here: because of Vancouver's huge transient population rents have to be paid weekly, promptly and in advance or one's room gets rented to someone else: promptitude is all, with them; so that any delay right now can put one in a most difficult position, as I'm sure you can understand.

Thanking you in advance for some consideration of this matter, if it be at all possible

Yours truly

Malcolm Lowry

Annotations:

1 Ayrton & Alderson-Smith was the Liverpool firm of solicitors in charge of the Lowry estate; see Lowry's letter (**11**) to Alderson-Smith in Appendix 3.

2 Lowry did not hear further for almost a year; see his 4 January 1954 letter (**600**) to Albert Erskine.

Editorial Notes:

a. This transcription is from a four-page, undated, signed pencil draft (UBC 20:11) on the versos of annotated typescript for *October Ferry to*

Gabriola. This letter and letters **563** and **564** were written at about the same time and internal references suggest an early 1953 date; see letter **564**, annotation 1.

563: To Marie Moore

P: UBC(ms)   [1359 Davie St]
                                                       [ca 21 January 1953]ª

Dear Miss Moore: –
    While thanking you most sincerely for all previous favours may we in all humility point out that the Random House cheque for January was not sent until January 7th, was then sent by ordinary mail & not airmail, & to the wrong address i.e Dollarton, from which being forwarded it did not reach us until the 15th of January.
    Since this was the occasion chosen also for our English cheque to go to Montreal itself – instead of the Bank of Montreal in Vancouver – & therefore not to reach us till the 19th, when it should have arrived on the 4th – we had quite a time: it is difficult to speak of 'ends' at such a period, but anyhow one couldn't make them meet. We only mention it, however, in that one be awfully grateful if you saw that the cheque winged its way hither at the usual time next month, i.e that the same thing doesn't happen in February, when if the English Govert decides to be so peripheral with its specie once more, the results could be calamitous.
    Re the above we hope soon to out of the woods as I said; meantime delaying so far as possible the course of money flowing out of the Gov. tie up is apparently a principal: & there is nothing for me to do but put with it, albeit in a few months etc
                                                       [breaks off unsigned]

Editorial Notes:

a. This transcription is from an undated pencil draft (UBC 20:11) on the verso of annotated typescript for *October Ferry to Gabriola.* The context suggests a 21 January date.

564: To Stuart Lowry

P: UBC(ms)   [1359 Davie St]
                                                       [ca 21 January 1953]ª

Dear old Stuart:
    This is just to thank you very much from us both for your Xmas &

New Years greetings which is the same as to say I received yours of Dec 20 safely but so far as I can find out none of the other letters you mention having written ever arrived in Canada – you mention having written in July or August & in September or October – & certainly not in Dollarton, where my evidence in addition to Margerie & myself is the postmaster himself, who is acquainted with your handwriting, & where our address is the post office per se.

In fact, I haven't heard from you since the end of the year before last, more or less the same time – your last letter is dated Dec 11 1951.[1]

It is a proper bugger: because I became convinced that something had happened to one or all of you & so was in a hell of a state & had to write Alderson Smith, though with instructions not to worry you, if indeed extant. (I have to pay income tax on the money I don't receive even without the money to pay it, but legally I had to find out where I stood so far as possible – moreover I was worried as hell about you all.)

On the other hand in the past Margerie & I have both had letters returned by an assistant of this same postmaster – one containing much needed money – to sender marked 'Addressee Unknown,' so the fault could still just lie with the Dollarton post office here, but if you didn't get the letters back where the hell would they go? – I haven't investigated the dead letter office yet, it is true. On these occasions we've always received further news or been able to trace the letter – though certainly they are bloody careless with mail in Canada & worse with telegrams – absolutely the most incompetent country in the world in this respect: even Mexico is more reliable. All I know t'ain't my fault.

I have only one other solution: I notice you spell in your last letter Columbia Colombia – a very natural mistake, in fact more grammatically accurate, though not alas geographically so. The trouble being that COLUMBIA is in South America or rather Central America or both & has been in a state of insurrection for several years. So if you failed to add Canada to British Columbia (another common ommission since British Columbia was once an independent country) there is a possible explanation.[2] If your letters ever got out of Colombia, which is extremely doubtful, they probably fetched up in British Guiana next door, as being the nearest British possession – no doubt in a state of even worse insurrection. Failing that the only explanation would seem to be that the hitch arose at whatever postoffice you posted it in England – something worth looking into for your own protection should it occur again. (Note: If any censor should be reading this letter, please read it, then go butter his arse and bugger himself with my compliments)

Meantime we are both well & happy, though harrassed to death by poverty blindness toothache & a broken typewriter none of which we can afford to repair until things improve – oh yes, & I forgot the

Westminster Bank itself that have taken to sending my income later &
later so that this month it didn't arrive till the 19th of the month, despite
an S.O.S to Alderson Smith earlier. It ought – I say it ought, I mean it
has in the past & I have grown to rely on it – to arrive in the first week
of the month. How can one meet promises, pay anything on the dot
here? – (with nothing any longer in the bank that is & just barely scrap-
ing by.) Apparently they've taken, no doubt as an economic measure,
to sending my pittance via Labrador, with all the further delays & grief
that causes. Well I've written to the manager of the Bank complaining
so if you hear about this, that's what I've bloody done: complained.[3] It
probably won't do any good but it makes me *feel* good. Also I've sold a
story to a pocket edition[4] – but there again: it's all like old Coltman's
rude story. 'I had 20 sailors & they're all going to pay me next Saturday
night.' Anyhow I'm enormously relieved to know you all are ok – &
extra special love to Margot. With all best love to you 3 from us both

Malcolm

Annotations:

1   This letter from Stuart Lowry is no longer extant; all that remains with
    Lowry's incoming correspondence is a letter dated 13 July 1950 and a
    telegram dated 22 May 1954.
2   The colony of British Columbia, officially named by Queen Victoria in
    1858, entered Confederation as a Canadian province on 20 July 1871.
    It was never an independent country.
3   See Lowry's 21 January 1953 letter (**562**) to the manager of the bank.
4   'Strange Comfort Afforded By the Profession' had just been sold to *New
    World Writing*; see Lowry's 8 January 1953 letter (**560**) to Harold
    Matson.

Editorial Notes:

a.   This three-page pencil holograph (UBC 20:11) is an undated draft on
     the versos of annotated typescript for *October Ferry to Gabriola*.

565: To David Markson

P: UBC(ts)

1359 Davie St,
Vancouver, B.C.,
Canada
5 February 1953

Dear old Dave:
    Sorry I haven't written. It was a very good idea to go and see Albert
[Erskine]: he's the best of fellows and I hope he was some help. I hope

you gave him a good report of me. He is one of my best friends: I should have told you to go to him, (but didn't fancy at that juncture of your destiny logging was in his line.)[1] Tell me what it is you want me to write on your behalf and I'll write it. How damned trying to get robbed again – I deeply sympathise. I can't think of anything more disheartening: a hangover without benefit of liquor. Just the same, could there be some obscure psychologic lex talionis[2] about it? – I mean if you go around swiping other people's girl friends, old chap, what what, though I guess they're fair game at that, – one might call them legal tender. Still. I hope you've got the right gal at last, maybe this letter is arriving so late that I'm several gals behind, but I mean well. And I look forward to seeing you and all of them in Dollarton. Re your parental-allowance problem. If the problem is a problem to you, that creates the weight of the problem, as they say. I wish I could advise you. But it's too personal a matter. Don't do what I did & insist on sailing before the mast to the Islands of the blest *without a penny in your pocket*, though. That merely might mean you wouldn't be able to get ashore in the Isles of the Blessed. – or above all – Even tramps have pennies in the pocket: 4 pennies to be precise, in England, which will keep one from being arrested for not having visible means.

I have now received your second letter which obviates the second part of this I had written, I now hereupon rewrite and which – yours – seems to tell me you now have the right gal for which I'm extremely glad.

I'm also very glad to hear you've also met Frank Taylor: he also is the best of fellows. They are both very much my good friends and Margie's. He and Albert incidentally as co-editors did a wonderful job of putting out the Volcano for which I shall be forever grateful but Frank was in movies after Hitchcock disbanded.[3] He produced as a start a first rate crime film for M.G.M. called Mystery Street, though much unworthy of his talents, then as a reward they hounded him into a Twentieth Century Fox.

There's a good name for a book: Twentieth Century Fox. Portrait of the artist as a Twentieth Century Fox. That's us, the Ultrafox. (A good record by the way of Django Reinhardt's.)[4]

We are now going mad at our apartment with a landlord who makes his living as a stool pigeon, having lost his faith in humanity. I advised him not to. Christ how I hate Vancouver.

I think to have sendéd a friend to look you at your apartment. Children are playing in the nunnery garden. Agamemnon is crying aloud in the U.B.C. Theatre. And the police are raiding Tobacco Road, and everything else.[5]

Basta!

Love and God bless you

Malc

Annotations:

1 Before visiting Lowry in August 1952, Markson had a summer job at a logging camp in Molalla, Oregon. When he returned to New York that fall he needed a job and contacted Albert Erksine at Random House. Through Erskine and Frank Taylor he found a job in the publishing business.

2 The Latin *lex talionis* means 'the law of retaliation' – in other words, an eye for an eye.

3 Lowry is referring to the 1947-48 dissolution of Reynal & Hitchcock, after which Erskine moved to Random House and Taylor to Hollywood.

4 Django Reinhardt (1910-53), the Belgian musician, was a virtuoso jazz guitarist who played and recorded with jazz violinist Stephane Grappelli. Lowry owned a Decca recording with the instrumental fox-trot 'Ultrafox.'

5 The English Department at the University of British Columbia were producing two plays from the *Oresteia* by Aeschylus (525-456 BC): *Agamemnon* and *Libation Bearers*. On 15 January Vancouver police raided the Everyman Theatre production of *Tobacco Road*, adapted by Jack Kirkland from the 1932 novel by Erskine Caldwell (1903-87). The play, which depicts depravity and poverty, had been very popular with North American audiences, so the police raid attracted a lot of attention in the press for several weeks.

566: To David Markson

P: UBC(ms)   [1359 Davie St]
                                                        [17 February 1953]

Dear Dave, I am sorry, old man, I was only joking. My letter, origi-nally a more serious and lengthy one, showed baleful effects of cutting. I had a letter from St Michael of Montillon who said you & he had a very pleasant evening.[1] He was the friend I was going to send to look you at your apartment but whether the right kind of friend now I half begin to wonder. In the first place I imagined him about my age & was under the impression he was a friend of Peter Viereck's. Now it turns out he is twenty years older than I and a friend of George Sylvester Viereck's.[2] That is all one to me & I know neither Peter Viereck nor George Sylvester Viereck nor for that matter Michael Montillon but having made the above blunder I might have made another corelative one & if so I am sorry, this being of course strictly confidential. Thought it would be interesting for you to meet in any case a man who was a lawyer & had been a priest had been both a monk had lived in Vancouver Island & was by way of being a devotee of the Volcano's but I may have acted out of vanity. For myself I confess to a fondness for a person who seems to have such an uninhibited love of mankind and he helped me a great deal at a bad time from the religious point of view. You wouldn't think I had troubles about religion, but I do, & especially with my conscience which races like an overheated engine sometimes. Many congratulations on your job which seems to be ideal and give both our loves to Esther who seems to be ideal too on another plane,[3] we wish you all happiness & look forward very much to seeing you as soon as may be

God bless & love from us both

Malcolm

[P.S.] I am working incredibly hard trying to complete a short novel by the end of this month.

Annotations:

1 David Markson recalls that a man known as Michael Montillon, who lived in a room in Greenwich Village, made a habit of writing to famous authors so he might receive a letter in return. When Markson, who also lived in the Village, visited the man, he found him with a desk piled high with such letters; however, no letter from Lowry to Montillon has appeared to date.

2 Peter Viereck (1916-) is an American poet and historian and the son of George Sylvester Viereck (1884-1962), a German immigrant to the United States who was a writer and editor and was imprisoned in 1942 for his pro-German sentiments.

3 Markson was working as an editor with Western Printing and Lithography in New York. Esther was a girlfriend.

567: To Albert Erskine

P: Virginia(ts); UBC(phc)

1359 Davie St,
Vancouver, B.C., Canada
22 February 1953

Dear brother –

Will try to get near final version of October Ferry to Gabriola off to you end of this month.[1] It is an unscheduled novel, about 150 or 60 pages. (Though still a part of Hear Us.) Ghostkeeper month after that. Pompeii month after that. Am not far behind – or am I in front? (Margie has to go down and see her mother as soon as possible, the old lady is 88, and quite ill, so I may be held up a little because of typing.)[2]

October Ferry has nearly slain me and I hope you don't hate it.

I think English money will come through soon and I will hasten to pay you back as soon as we can.

Thank you for helping David Markson.

Love from us both.

God bless you

Malcolm

Annotations:

1 Lowry did not send any of *October Ferry* to Erskine until 14 October 1953.
2 Margerie flew to Los Angeles towards the end of March. She was ill at the time but was obliged to return almost immediately to collect Lowry from the Neilsons' on Bowen Island, where he had been taken after going on a colossal drinking binge; see Lowry's April 1953 letter (**571**) to the Neilsons. Margerie's mother, Anna Mabelle Bonner, died in November 1956; see Lowry's 13 November 1956 letter (**693**) to Priscilla and Bert Woolfan.

568: To Pamela Hudson

P: Yale(ts)

1359 Davie St,
Vancouver, B.C., Canada
12 March 1953[a]

Dear Pamela Hudson:[1]

I hasten. There's a good bit of half effaced type at the top – and elsewhere – that you've probably seen already and probably would not appear in the final copy so I'm not making corrections re this on proofs. But if you haven't seen it I draw it to your attention.

Sigbjorn – I appended a note and even wrote a letter to this effect – was supposed to be Sigbjørn. It would be understandable if your printer would resent this ø. But the emotive effect of o is very different. More mournful with the ø. But I shall understand if your printer should say, 'To Ø with Lowry's wretched ø.' Though it is also a symbol of good luck, should you have been thinking of Platonic oversights very recently as well as per se the Norse letter in question.[2]

I append slight emendations to the biographical note.[3]

People who might be helpful in spreading the word re this new issue: (I'm not sure they're all at the same places as they were) [Orville Prescott – N.Y. Times.][b] John Woodburn – Saturday Review of Literature. H.R. Hays – N.Y. Times. Dawn Powell – 35 E. 9th St., N.Y. Mark Schorer – ? John Frederick Nims – Chicago Tribune. George Mayberry – New Republic. [Joseph Henry Jackson – San Francisco Chronicle.

Alice Dixon Bond – Boston Herald.] Martha Schlegel – Philadelphia Inquirer. [D.C. de Jong – Providence Journal] Jay Carmody – Star, Washington, D.C. Robert B. Heilman – Sewanee Review, James Agee (don't know where he is at the moment, last heard from in Hollywood) Conrad Aiken, Forty-One Doors, Brewster, Mass. [Christopher] Isherwood – one of your contributors. Query? Are you interested in critics, friends, publishers, etc., in England, France, Germany? If so, can send list. Also the brothers (Pencil of God) Marcelin. M. Philippe Thoby-Marcelin, 1712-16th St, Washington, D.C. The latter are Haitians, Philippe Thoby is genius of highest kind of order & integrity nonetheless tragically with not enough outlet for the art in question. He was praised enormously if inadequately by Valery Larbaud, translator of Joyce: also Edmund Wilson, etc: ask him from me & you when that novel about Haitian fishermen is going to get written.)[4]

Re other writers for your fourth issue: there are some very interesting things being done here in Canada. I might mention Norman Newton, 1995 W. 19th Ave., Vancouver, B.C. Wm. McConnell, Bayside Ave., North Burnaby, B.C., Earle Birney (now on a Fellowship in France) address: Canadian Embassy, Paris, France. Dorothy Livesay, 848 E. 6th St., North Vancouver, B.C. And my own wife, Margerie, (who wrote under the name of Bonner – Horse in the Sky) not to be confused with the very good Marjorie Lowrey. My wife's story, Venus Is The Evening Star, was refused by Mrs. [Arabel] Porter, who said, 'good as it is, we felt it tried to encompass too much.' My wife completely agrees with this criticism, and is editing the story accordingly. Also suggest the brothers Marcelin. (see above.)

Re the Italian on the first page of proofs: I don't know any Italian at all, though I know some Latin. I swear I *copied* it down right: L'inglese poeta, etc. (see original.)

Re John K. Keat's? Keats'? Keats's? But certainly keatsn't by Keat's House, keats it all, keats it?

Thank you for akeatsping the story at all events, I am most honoured to be in your volume and hope the story doesn't let you down. Best luck with your excellent volumes. We enjoyed the first one very much.

And thank you for the talking horse. Couldn't be in a better spot.[5]

Sincerely and cordially,

[Malcolm Lowry]

Born in Merseyside, England, in 1909, Lowry was educated at Cambridge University. Previous to that he shipped before the mast both as seaman and fireman, visiting the Orient. He has lived in France and Mexico. He and his wife, Margerie Bonner, [author of] (Horse in the Sky) have been residents of British Columbia, Canada, for 14 years.

Best-known for his extraordinary* novel, *Under the Volcano*, (Reynal and Hitchcock, 1947) Mr Lowry is also the author of numerous short stories and poems, and several other novels, as yet not in final form. He is now at work on a collection of novellas, mostly set in Canada, and short stories, of which this story is to be one, entitled, *Hear Us Oh Lord From Heaven Thy Dwelling Place*, which will be published shortly by Random House. This and *Under the Volcano* form part of an enclosing series of novels to be called *The Voyage That Never Ends*.

 *Couldn't resist keeping in the extraordinary.

Annotations:

1 Pamela Hudson was an editor with *New World Writing*, the literary magazine associated with New American Library that published 'Strange Comfort Afforded by the Profession' in 1953. The story is also part of *Hear us O Lord*.
2 The Norwegian ø is one of six diphthongs in that language. The diacritical mark indicates pronunciation, but Lowry especially liked the look of the vowel.
3 Lowry added the emended biographical note after his signature, and Hudson retained his emendations, including the 'extraordinary.'
4 Some of these people had written favourable reviews of *Under the Volcano*; others are Lowry's friends.
5 Lowry asked to have the 'talking horse' reference inserted at a late stage; see his 8 January 1953 letter (**560**) to Harold Matson.

Editorial Notes:

a. This transcription is from a photocopy of the original typescript in the New World Writing archive; there is a typescript marked 'Copy' in the Lowry Collection (UBC 3:5), but it does not include Lowry's marginalia.
b. The names shown here in brackets have a line drawn through them in the copy-text.

569: To Einar Neilson

P: UBC(tsc)

[Vancouver]
[ca 20 March 1953]ᵃ

Dear old Einar:
   Herewith the 35 remaining bucks enclosed with great thanks. It is, to my shame, now a year since I borrowed the hundred & I apologise for having procrastinated so long on the promise.
   But I had no idea how those other people were going to procrasti-

nate – fortunately I caught my English bank, now my trustees, with their pants down: it turned out they'd lost all the files themselves dealing with my share of the estate & so far as I can see someone had just been lying by blaming the delay on the Treasury. So anyway by raising a little hell got some action there at last though my French Volcano money is still apparently rotting on some wharf in Casa Blanca.

Hope to see you soon – we are leaving this den of iniquity and gaiety quite shortly.

Best love to you & Muriel & a saucer of nice warm Bourbon for Duchess.

I've written a short novel since I saw you based on something shorter I was working on at Lieben 5 years ago.[1]

[Malcolm]

Annotations:

1 *October Ferry to Gabriola.*

Editorial Notes:

a. This transcription is from a typescript copy filed with the David Markson Papers (UBC 1:12); the original letter has not been found. The copy carries neither inside address nor date, but the contents suggest a March 1953 date, shortly before Margerie went to Los Angeles.

All Lowry's talk in the following letter about mother-imagos, 'intra-uterine reversion,' deathbeds, and work is a decidedly laundered and fictionalized version of the facts. Margerie was unwell, but her mother was not dying. It was Malc who went on a monumental binge during Margerie's March trip to Los Angeles, Malc who was suffering 'an intra-uterine reversion,' and Malc who was drying out under the expert care of Einar and Muriel Neilson on Bowen Island. He was certainly not 'getting there' with October Ferry.

570: To Albert Erskine

P: Virginia(ms)

Dollarton, B.C.
[March-April 1953]

My dear Albert:

Serious difficulties of sickness – to cut a long story short & to say the least – temporarily held up the work & the completion of Gabriola. I am very sorry indeed not to have been able to keep my promise but happenings were very sudden & all but tragic & we are not out of the wood yet. I dispatched Margie to L.A. to see her dying mother but by the time she arrived it was only to discover she was on the point of death herself.[1] It was found she had no white blood corpuscles whatsoever, among other things even more serious, so that she had to protract her stay there, although she is now back, albeit a shadow. Myself believe that the mother-imago becomes so powerfully projected at such times that it is as if the dying mother were trying to drag the daughter after her, or the latter cannot help but be so drawn or longs to be drawn: an intra-uterine reversion of the death bed. But such psychological explanations I dare not advance for I have to deal with the brute facts of obvious medical symptoms & these are damned serious. Nevertheless she is on deck though scarcely at the moment with the work. I have high hopes she will pull through. But meantime my own presence far from helping only serves to aggravate her condition. I can see how anything like a father-imago may make it much worse, especially since I am an erratic nurse. So she is gravitating between the apartment & Dollarton, resting when she can & wants, & I am working high up on the edge of a cliff in Bowen Island, feverishly still trying to finish Gabriola by myself in a beautiful & perilous chapel belonging to a great mutual friend [Einar Neilson], & I still hope to have a version for you soon come what may. Meantime bear with me, even if for the thousandth time. We's a gettin there, despite all. I give my old address: Margerie is probably coming out by boat here on Thursday & if she is well enough to type I know she will.

God bless you

Malcolm

Annotations:

1 The details of Margerie's illness in the early spring of 1953 are not known, but Lowry speaks of her condition in several letters to Erskine. See also his 21 April 1953 letter (**573**) to David Markson, which includes a postscript by Margerie.

571: To Einar and Muriel Neilson

P: UBC(tsc)
[Dollarton]
[ca 11 April 1953][a]

Beloved Oceani:[1]
    Thank you both a million times for everything from us both.
    Thank you also – Einar – a million times for the pen: a wonderfully thoughtful piece of sympathetic magic for I didn't seem to function

without its prototype when we got back but now I live in hopes your kind gift will soon finish the job.

Margie's bloodcount is up to 30 which is a great relief but in some other respects the boat has not been sailing well at all since our return.

In fact we sometimes almost feel like saying, with Chaucer:

> Al steerless within a boot am I
> Amid the sea, betwexen windës two
> That in contrarie standen evermo − [2]

But perhaps the pen will change all that & with it I hope soon to indite more cheerful news.

Meantime we miss you much.

Hope the Lieben Limited is still running true to form on the N.F.M.&S. (Neilson's Funicular Mountain & Scenic)

Love from us both

[Malc.]

Annotations:

1 The Neilsons' Bowen Island home overlooked the sea.
2 Lowry uses this passage from Geoffrey Chaucer's *Troilus and Criseyde* (ca 1386) as a prefacing quotation for *October Ferry to Gabriola*; see also his 16 July 1946 letter (**237**) to Albert Erskine.

Editorial Notes:

a. This transcription is from a typescript copy filed with the David Markson Papers (UBC Markson 1:12). The original has not been found. The copy carries neither inside address nor date, but internal evidence suggests early April 1953.

572: To Albert Erskine

P: UBC(ms phc)   Dollarton, B.C.
                                                                  [ca April 1953]ᵃ

Dear old Albert:

Thank you sincerely for your consoling note. It's been a tricky & dangerous time, & for a while, not knowing how things were going to go, I didn't have the heart to write again. But I'm immensely relieved to be able to reply now that Margie's blood count is up (to 30) we are back living here on the beach, & she seems steadily getting better. On the other hand she can't sleep, & her white blood count condition won't admit of her taking sedatives than which combination, as the doctor remarked, there is nothing worse. As for me, it doesn't do me any good to realise that I am in one way partly responsible for the condition, having consistently overworked her on my behalf during the last year, & taken her at the same time away from doing any work of her own. And there are other factors – chiefly living here at all now, still under the shadow of eviction, & at the same time trying to write about just that, even succeeding in part, even while the bloody shadow creeps up on one. Obviously this is a situation that must call for, in fact called for long ago, some major psychological renunciation & acceptance + some super Stendhalian act of will:[1] – in short, I have to accept, at the same time disengaging so far as possible all latent death-wishes from the acceptance, the fact that one has to leave the place, in fact, no doubt, bring about such a break oneself, at the same time letting certain life-forces of hope feed on the possibility it is not irrevocable, even while psychology says yes: indeed maybe this is one of man's central problems, even perhaps a central religious problem, the tragedy that man is not an angel. For were we angels – some of Swedenborgs at least – we would simply carry the place with us, wherever we went, which was perhaps partly what Blake meant by embracing the joy as it flies.[2] Be that as it may, it is one of the central problems in poor old Gabriola, which has, on account of these matters & others received during the last month or so, a major, though I hope not fatal (in fact I hope quite the contrary) setback: a set back in regard to having it completed, typed etc & sent to you when I said anyway: for one thing due to a mix-up during this transitional period I won't go into here I couldn't get at the actual manuscript I was working on for nearly a fortnight, just when I'd reached a critical part – a story well worth relating, but I'll keep it for another time: this, while adding to the general misery & anxiety – I'd just discovered my hero was probably searching for the Perilous Chapel from reading an article on Mann in the Atlantic[3] – gave, however, a terrific fillip to my imagination & while going through a Perilous Chapel of my own instead of bringing the thing to a close as I intended I went & wrote another long & horrendous scene which I'm not quite sure now belongs even though this, despite all my efforts to make the thing behave otherwise really does make it a novel –

[breaks off unsigned]

Dear Albert – I'll finish this & post it because, as you can see, Malc is engaged in a life & death struggle with this bloody story, which seems to have turned into a novel, & he's determined to get through to the end this week before it kills us both. We finally got some money from England & hope to pay all we owe shortly but the catch is this: Malc now has about a thousand pounds a year income in England which we can't (so far –) get here, but we have to declare it & *pay taxes* on it here as well as the taxes deducted in England & it keeps us penniless. We have some chartered accountants working on it & just as soon as we know how much income tax we have to pay we'll know what we've got left. I'm feeling much better, thank God, & not like a Zombie. We'll report again soon. October Ferry to Gabriola is going to be first rate Lowry. At the moment it is, to me, a vampire, a tiger, a merciless tyrant but I *think* we are going to survive & defeat the goddam thing after all – God Bless – love as ever –

Margerie

Annotations:

1 The French writer Marie-Henri Beyle (1783-1842), better known as Stendhal, creates characters that embody his philosophy of aggressive self-assertion and driving will. Julien Sorel, the hero of Stendhal's *The Red and the Black* (*Le Rouge et le Noir*, 1830), is a case in point.
2 Emanuel Swedenborg (1688-1772), the Swedish theologian, scientist, and philosopher, wrote extensively about his mystical visions (notably of angels). His work influenced many writers including William Blake whose poem 'Eternity' (1791) Lowry alludes to:

> He who binds to himself a joy
> Does the winged life destroy;
> But he who kisses the joy as it flies
> Lives in eternity's sunrise.

3 Lowry may be referring to Charles Rolo's article 'Mann and his Mephistopheles,' *Atlantic Monthly* 182.5 (1948): 92-94. Rolo discusses Thomas Mann's novel *Doctor Faustus* (1948; *Doktor Faustus*, 1947) in terms of mythology, music, and German politics. The Perilous Chapel or Cemetery on the road to the Grail Castle appears in most of the Grail romances (such as *Parsifal*); in it the hero faces the horrors of physical death, which may cause his own demise. If the hero is successful in the Chapel, he proceeds on his quest for the Grail.

Editorial Notes:

a. This transcription is from a photocopy of the original letter (UBC 3:5), which does not appear to have survived. The contents confirm an April 1953 date.

573: To David Markson

P: UBC(ms)   [Dollarton]
[21 April 1953][a]

Beloved old Dave: We back in the house (which misses you) but in terrible shape, Margie after a trip to Los Angeles where it was discovered

she had a white blood count of precisely zero, & so was on the point of
death, & me after a trip through one of the worst of the perilous chapels
of my stricken life – that is, it feels as if it were stricken – in which I seem
to have had all the griefs anxieties worries guilts miseries & terrors of the
entire universe thrown at me, & they are still being thrown, even if in
part by no lesser person than myself. But it is no joke to endure[1]

                                                           [breaks off unsigned]

Dear Dave –
    I think I better finish this letter Malc started a week or so ago & post it
to you. Things are not *quite* so bad as he says, just routine chaos & catastrophe, & he is having a life & death struggle with a story, which is turning
into a novel. Your letter to hand & very good to get it because we were
both wondering, the night before the letter arrived, if you were O.K. My
blood count is coming up & I no longer feel *exactly* like a Zombie, but I
can't sleep & can't take sedatives because of the blood count & I just lie on
your couch & shake most of the time. But I'm getting better & I intend to
survive so don't worry. As for this god damn story, the blood sucking
monster, it's going to be first rate Lowry – it had better be, it's nearly
murdered us both. But the end of the 3rd? 4th? 5th? first draft is in
sight (through a telescope) & when we've recovered sufficiently will start
at the beginning again & really go to work on it. – The New World
Writing with Malc's story comes out May 27, I think, but they promised
him some copies & he'll send you one. God bless – and our love, as
always,

                                                           Margerie

Annotations:

  1 Lowry comes closest to admitting the seriousness of his predicament in
     these comments, but he could not be so frank with Albert Erskine.

Editorial Notes:

a. This is the postmark date on the envelope. Lowry has begun in pencil;
    Margerie has added her comments in ink.

574: To Dr Irmgard Rexroth Kern

P: UBC(ms)   Dollarton, B.C., Canada
                                                  [ca April 1953][a]

Dear Dr Irmgard Rexroth Kern: – [1]
    In reply to yours of the 25th inst: – u.s.w. – let me try & inject a note
of humour at least, for my sake, & at the outset, into what is, among

other things, a letter of abject apology for an intolerable & agonizing neglect in not answering at once your most brilliant & generous letter to me of April 25 1952. That there are excuses: that your letter arrived soaked through with your address completely unreadable as it was stamped – (if it did not arrive in quite as bad shape as Under the Volcano when it was sent to the Czekoslovakian publishers or agent – who anyway rejected it – where the parcel containing the book was marked FOUND AT THE BOTTOM OF BREMEN HARBOUR!) – & that you, like me, when you write rather than type, tend to do so upside down, & what is more, in Gothic – which, though I love to look at it, I cannot read any better than when I was a wicked little child in Bonn-am-Rhein, studying under a friend of Clemens ten Holder, Karlheinz Schmidthaus, I ask you to believe – there are these excuses, & more, – such as that any address on the back of the envelope was indecipherable.

And that, I *did* write you a letter, with affection, & gratitude, in reply, but that, in 2 months or so, it was returned, with one of those sinister (selstam, my German isn't all gone)[2] hands upon it moreover pointing in the wrong direction that designate) – I don't know how to reply. But you must assume it was so. Absolutely.

As for the rest, I am desperately ashamed that I have not replied till now, this perhaps too late hour.

For the rest are not excuses, but statements of what happened:

(a) I lost my house by <u>fire</u>

(b) I broke my back – (while trying to rebuild it with my own hands, which I did.)

(c) we were, intermediately, threatened with Eviction.

The word is EVICTION. (& the threat has been now

amplified by the newspapers.)

(d) Clemens ten Holder died.[3]

(e) It seems to me, I, also have died, with Clemens.

[breaks off unsigned.]

Annotations:

1 Dr Kern (1907-), a German writer, editor, and admirer of *Volcano*, has not been further identified; her 25 April 1952 letter to Lowry is no longer extant.

2 Lowry means *seltsam*: German for strange, odd, or curious.

3 See Lowry's last extant letter (**546**) to ten Holder.

Editorial Notes:

a. This transcription is from a two-page pencil holograph (UBC 3:4). The letter is unfinished and undated, but the address and contents suggest April 1953.

575: To David Markson

P: UBC(ms)   [Dollarton]
                                                        [25 May 1953]ᵃ

Dear old Dave:
    Thank you from our hearts for two wonderful – & wonderfully com-
forting – letters. Margie now has worms! But otherwise she is much
better and we have more or less decided to laugh. At least we have not
yet been attacked by an invisible werewolf though it sure as hell sometimes feels like it. The beach is more or less empty & we both miss you
& wish you were here. Is it any use hoping? Don't know how to advise
you re showing your m.s.s. prematurely. Adverse criticism can be very
dessicating at a certain point, favorable sometimes fatal. But I sure look
forward to reading it myself, as does Margie. That's all for now. God
bless you from us both,

                                                              Malc

Editorial Notes:

a.   This undated holograph has an envelope postmarked 25 May 1953.
     Margerie has added a brief postscript to say that Lowry has just received
     his copies of *New World Writing* containing 'Strange Comfort Afforded
     by the Profession.'

576: To Arabel Porter

P: Yale(ms)   Dollarton, B.C.,
                                                              Canada
                                                        29 May 1953ᵃ

Dear Arabel Porter:[1]
    Thank you very much for your very good letter and I'm glad I
returned the proofs in time. Herewith some possible useful names on
the European scene, as promised: ENGLAND: my publisher is Jonathan
Cape, 30 Bedford Square, London, W.C.1. my agent is A.J. Rose, John
Farquharson, 8 Halsey House, Red Lion Square, London W.C. 1.
Critics: K. John, of the Illustrated London News, Lionel Hale, the
Observer, also one main critic on the Times Literary Supplement,
whose name I do not seem to have at the moment. Who is this gentleman? On second thoughts he does not sound very useful. But all these
people would be interested in N.W.W [*New World Writing*].
Incidentally did I give you Philippe Thoby-Marcelin's address? It is
1712-16th St, N.W. Washington D.C. He is a Haitian & as you probably know the author of Canape Vert & The Finger of God. But also he

is an excellent poet, once highly praised by Valèry Larbaud. FRANCE: my publisher is Editions Correa, 18 Rue de Conde, Paris. My translator (and good friend) Mlle. Clarisse Francillon, 23 Rue Gazin, Paris 14. Max-Pol Fouchet, whose address I do not have now, but who can be reached via Clarisse. Critics: Bertrand d'Astorg, Editions du Seuil, 27, Rue Jacob, Paris, 6. Maurice Nadeau, Directeur of Les Lettres Nouvelles, 8, rue Malebranche, Paris 5. GERMANY: my publisher is Herr Klett, of Ernst Klett Verlag, Rotebuhlstrasse 77, Stuttgart W. Germany. My German translator is now, alas dead, but his wife, who assisted him and who is now translating another story of mine is Frau Hildegarde ten Holder, Flacht, Kreis Leonberg, Wurttemberg, Germany.

By the way, perhaps you remember where, somewhere in my story, my fellow finds himself wondering whether Keats or Poe *had* ever been compared 'in this sense'? Well, so help me, so far as I was concerned I'd flattered myself that I (not that it involves any supernally original perception) was at least a complete pioneer on that score: but alas, tant pis, and hey presto, what happens the other day but that a little, and as it turned out, very interesting magazine by name of Twelfth Street (why not a musical and boisterous step further and have styled her Twelfth Street Rag) a Poetry Issue, and of date Dec. 1949, never to my knowledge before seen by myself, tumbles out from behind my shelves, suitably opening itself at a point where, somewhat to my chagrin, in an article entitled The Gratuitous Art, I perceive these words appear:[2]

The death cult (one form of which is memorial) involves the complacent 'triumphing' of the living over the dead, Why do people pay to see where Poe's wife died or the handkerchief into which Keats spat blood. . . The middling, the fearful thus assure themselves that it is safer not to be famous. (Their wisdom is that of undistinction: In general, it is better not to prize too highly things that are hard to get. The tiger is killed for his hide, the elephant for his tusks, the parrot because he can talk like a person is put in a cage. The kingfisher is killed for his beautiful feathers. . . Such persons – posthumously avid and gloating – would not have concerned themselves with the problems of Keats and Poe while they were alive. What these 'brawlers of the auction mart' are controlled by, really, is the regressive fascination of death on which modern civilization is based.

Were this all, I suppose the coincidence – for the thesis is pretty different here – might not be worth mentioning, but the article proceeds thus:

– Poets are apt to have lives of great complexity and practical wastefulness; this is because: (1) since they use themselves as material, they are perversely curious to see how badly they can be treated.

And the fourth reason he gives is that a sense of detachment plagues them and he cites Daudet's story of finding himself involuntarily thinking at the bedside of his dying father, My God, how that cry would have sounded on the stage.[3]

Later this same writer says too: Although to the outsider, it seems as if the artist is making a gratuitous mess of his life (think of Rilke, Crane, Baudelaire, Whitman, Kafka, Kierkegaard, Gide, Verlaine) what he tries to do is to foreshadow a new kind of entente among human beings, a more total brotherhood.

While at the end of the article, an exceptionally succinct brilliant and well thought out one, in my opinion, the author, one Mr Howard Griffin, observes: 'Since certain of the ideas developed in the essay were expressed to him by W.H. Auden in conversation the author here wishes to express indebtedness to this source.'

Naturally at this point it occurred to this author to think: 'Since certain of the ideas developed in the story Strange Comfort Afforded by the Profession seem, or seem at first, to have been partly based either directly or by riposte upon an essay written by Mr Howard Griffin entitled The Gratuitous Art in which certain ideas were developed that were expressed to the latter by Mr W.H. Auden in conversation Mr Lowry should have acknowledged indebtedness to that source or those sources, etc.

The only catch is this. So far as I know – as I've said before – quite apart from the article, I wasn't even aware of the presence of the magazine in the house or even consciously of its existence which (the magazine) is not our property but seems to have found its way hither via a friend, one Mr Earle Birney, a Canadian poet and contributor to the same number, and to whom we lent the house when we were in Europe (he also, I see, borrowed unconsciously a couple of lines of mine for the contribution) and who was later for a while our occasional neighbour in a beach shack, by which time though the story was already written. In fact the Richmond notes were taken in Feb. 1947 in Richmond and the Keats notes in July 1948 in Rome in the same notebook of which the story – with the exception of the end (it is to be hoped) – is an almost literal transcription. Apart from this, a version of the story was already in existence and typed by my wife a good while before Dec. 1949 and the idea of Poe being unable to resist transcribing the story that was E.A. Poe – or however I put it – derives, so far as I know, from Ortega y Gasset. (Man is like a writer of fiction who makes up his life as he goes along etc.)[4]

However, despite this evidence to the contrary, the fact that we didn't send the story in its present form to Hal till, I think, late summer in 1950, sustains a certain feeling that if I didn't actually read Griffin's essay in the meantime I may have picked up the magazine half read it, and then put it away with a cry of Ouch!, not wanting to be influenced, and then was affected just the same. I ask myself why else I should have had to forget the magazine itself, if I ever knew it was there. It contains some other very good things. On the other hand my wife says this part of the letter is in any case quite unnecessary, which it probably is, for the dissimilarity of thought increases – at least – when you reread the essay, the existence of which would, to be sure, in no wise have disqualified me from writing the story anyhow. In fact – and this inclines me again to think I never set eyes on the mag til the other day – I could have profited by it: his intellectual argument or Auden's, holds more water than mine, where they touch. Or rather, though I'd thought the Keats-Poe touch unique, the validity, originality or otherwise – certain the finality – of some of Sigbjørn's reflections qua the artist and society were of lesser consequence to me than the story itself with its juxtapositions and its representation (how loathsomely pompous this sounds) as a work of art, which I hope it succeeds in being, as well as funny. My wife also says I might as well say that Griffin had profited – and why should one not? – by some ideas of mine, in so far as they are mine, in Under the Volcano (1947), as well as from Auden's in his article: for in both appear the artist as magician, the artist as losing things (not to say having difficulty in getting from place to place!) the artist as wearing lots of different kinds of characters, to say nothing of a mention in both of Humpty Dumpty.

As a matter of fact all these motifs appear as early as the very first chapter of Under the Volcano and resound in various forms throughout the whole of that lugubrious work. Of course this is stretching a point and I am largely joking: no doubt Griffin and I simply think in a similar (or similar-dissimilar) way. (For that matter, though not to make absurd and bumptious comparisons, so do Thomas Mann and I, at least so far as Dr Faustus was concerned – his protagonist and mine seem to have raced almost neck and neck to their perdition.)[5] The real object of this letter with its considerable much ado about nothing was merely to tell you that had I consciously known of or remembered the existence of Griffin's article at the time you took Strange Comfort I would have mentioned it to *you* or even put in a footnote, if you thought that advisable. As things stand, if you happen to be acquainted with the gentleman – he is mentioned in Twelfth Street simply as having been published widely but I am assuming he is a New Yorker – perhaps you would be good enough to assure him I wasn't consciously treading on his toes. I'm certain any resemblance can't possibly be important enough to embarrass yourself, however.

I am very sorry indeed to hear that John Woodburn is dead.[6]

Thank you for giving my address to John Goodwin: I'd very much like the Idols and the Prey, from what I read of it in the second N.W.W. A strange, strange fellow.[7]

My wife is going to send you a revised version of Venus is the Evening Star, or perhaps, as more suitable, something shorter: she has an excellently gruesome and meaningful and even masterful piece entitled The Caretakers I feel you might like.[8]

I hope you will take another story of mine sometime or other: (perhaps – I whisper it – even a poem. Nobody ever seems to take any of my poems which however have acquired a habit of getting into obscure Canadian anthologies, where prompt oblivion and all possibility of acceptance in future are thus assured at once.)

Very cordially yours, and all luck with the new volume.

[Malcolm Lowry]

P.S. Good God! I have now – after writing a draft of the above in pencil, and which is too good under the circumstances to alter either in typing, just received the new N.W.W. volumes – the contents are excellent so far as I have read {I might have some constructive criticism later, if you welcome same, or suggestions.} – for which many thanks, together with another letter of May 6th, for which I also thank you, which went to my old address and was not forwarded (I don't know why) and has now reached me through Hal – and whom do I see standing only two doors away from me but this very Mr Howard Griffin himself, with an excellent story Sauce for the Gander. Verily we seem to do more than merely think alike: the destiny of our stories seems to have acquired an affinity. And so you will be in touch with him – by the way, I have decided to send you his article so that you may judge for yourself. But is it the same Mr Howard Griffin? If so, I see, to my sorrow that the brave fellow is blind. Alas. . .

And many others. . .[9]

Annotations:

1 Arabel J. Porter, executive editor of New American Library in 1953, was the editor of their newly established literary magazine *New World Writing*.

2 'The Gratuitous Art' is an essay by Howard Griffin, an American poet and writer who published some of his work in *New World Writing* 2 (1952): 221. The essay appeared in a small magazine called *Twelfth Street* (December 1949): 21-26, published by the students of the New School for Social Research in New York. In the following passages of his letter, Lowry both quotes and paraphrases Griffin's essay.

3 Alphonse Daudet (1840-97) was a French novelist. Griffin cites this occasion as an example of the poet's detachment from life.

4 This idea is a favourite of Lowry's; see Ortega's concluding comments to chapter 3, part 3, of *Toward a Philosophy of History* and Lowry's 23 June 1950 letter (**403**) to Downie Kirk.

5 Thomas Mann's novel *Doctor Faustus*, about the tragic figure of composer Adrian Leverkühn, explores the Faustian creative drive that can lead to destruction if it is not channelled into art. Leverkühn and the Consul have much in common, and both are linked to the destructive forces of Naziism.

6 Woodburn had praised *Under the Volcano*; see Lowry's March 1947 letter (**289**) to Sybil Hutchinson.

7 John B. Goodwin (1912-94) was an American writer and painter. He published poetry and fiction in *New World Writing* 2 (1952): 255-65, and there is a copy of his novel *The Idols and the Prey* (1953) in Lowry's library, inscribed as follows: 'for Malcolm Lowry – with affection, respect and considerable qualms. John – July '53.' See Lowry's August 1953 letter (**586**) to Arabel Porter for his response to the novel.

8 Both stories are in the Lowry collection (UBC 51); neither has been published to date.

9 This phrase recurs as a motif in 'Strange Comfort Afforded by the Profession.'

Editorial Notes:

a. This transcription is from a photocopy of the original in the New World Writing Collection at the Beinecke Library, Yale; there is a typescript marked 'Copy' in the Lowry Collection (UBC 3:5), but it does not carry all Lowry's marginalia. Five notes concerning the story 'Strange Comfort Afforded by the Profession' are appended to the original letter and to the UBC copy; they deal with such matters as the ø in Sigbjørn, typography, correct French, and the change of names from Van Klett to Van Bosch to avoid using the same name as Lowry's German publisher – Ernst Klett.

577: To Eva and Philippe Thoby-Marcelin

P: UBC(ts phc

Dollarton, B.C.,
Canada
30 May 1953

My very dear Eva and Phito:[1]

Please somehow forgive me. The reasons range from a serious illness of Margie's, in Los Angeles, to misdirected mail, a change of address, and just sheer worry. When I did reply to your postcard, Eva, I was so consumed with anxiety, and then with shame that I hadn't written that I couldn't finish it. Then I was on an island and found I had lost your address. Now we are back home on our beach, Margie is well again, and all is fine once more. Phito, please forgive me, and for God's sake send me a copy of A fonds Perdu.² I don't know how to thank you for dedicating it to me. I can't tell you how unworthy I feel so I won't try. I shall write more later.

All the best love from us both to you and my sincerest apologies.

Affectueusement

Malcolm

P.S. Dear Phito: do you have a copy of the French translation you made of the 'letter in a bottle' poem? I lent mine to a schoolmaster [Downie Kirk] here (together with Canapé Vert and the Pencil of God) who teaches French and wanted to make a recording of it to illustrate to his pupils certain variations in rhythm of French versification, the original English one being now in the Anthology of Canadian Verse selected by A.J.M. Smith (Scribner's).³ I have a letter from Clarisse Francillon that leads me to believe that it would be published in France, that is with your permission. Ira Dilworth, head of the C.B.C. broadcasting system, has still got La Negrèsse Adolescente in Toronto, despite repeated efforts on our part to get it back, though previous to that he had announced his intention of translating the poems, with myself acting as assistant umpire. We should have known better, for it was into a similar maw of negligence went for years our radio version of Moby Dick, until it was too late and someone else had done it.⁴ It is just like your sad story of the Cuban. . . Please tell us all the current news of your books.

ton frère

Malcolm

Annotations:

1 Philippe Thoby-Marcelin had been living in the United States since 1948; he married Eva Ponticello on 14 November 1951.

2 *A fonds perdu*, Thoby-Marcelin's collection of twenty-one poems, was published in 1953. Lowry's copy is with his library (UBC Box 56).

3 Lowry's poem 'In Memoriam: Ingvald Bjorndal' (*CP* 186), was first published in *Atlantic Monthly* 168.4 (1941): 501, and reprinted in the second edition of A.J.M. Smith's *A Book of Canadian Poetry* (1948). Lowry first mentions sending the poem to Francillon in his November 1952 letter (**551**) to her.

4 In February 1945, at Gerald Noxon's suggestion, Lowry mailed a radio script of *Moby-Dick* to Andrew Allan of the CBC, but nothing came of the venture and no correspondence with Allan has been recovered; see Lowry's 14 May 1945 letter (**201**) to Noxon on the subject. A radio adaptation of Melville's novel, made by the English poet Henry Reed, was broadcast on the Third Program of the BBC on 26 January 1947, and Andrew Allan broadcast a version of the novel for his CBC program 'Stage' on 6 March 1949.

578: To Harvey Burt

P: UBC(ms) [Dollarton]
[Spring/Summer 1953]^a

Operation Dyke¹

Dear Harvey:

I found my first notes suffering from a slight Malcoholism, so I'm scrapping them: some of these too found their way on to the text in blotchy ink, for which I'm very sorry, so pay no attention to them there save where they make any sense, though mostly when & if they do make sense I'll repeat them here. Some of these objections – such as to the word *offset* on p 1 – I don't understand why I raised myself. But the overall feeling is this. It's an excellent & original story, with a style – indeed superlative – all its own: – which is completely successful so far too in my opinion – but its bland Kafka-Lewis-Leacock fatuous-profound-ridiculous-sad-funny-*surface* has to remain absolutely consistent to itself right down to the tiniest detail; I think: thus any complaints of mine while they may seem purist & superficial are so deliberately. You can't afford a cliché or anything that appears not to be there absolutely on purpose or you might seem – (though you don't!) – to be about to fall off the tight-rope: but it isn't that kind of half-falling-off story. Since it's at bottom serious as well as ridiculous it's more like a tightrope across a sort of Niagara falls you're walking. Anyway, even if I'm wrong, such Flaubertian attention to the most meticulous detail in terms of its own reality can't fail to improve it, if it can be improved; – of course I don't overlook the joke & the point that the story is as it were – as other stories are really metaphors – one long deliberate cliché itself, or rather parody of human *cliché* behaviour: all the more reason for the above – you can't afford even a shadow of a mistake or pomposity in those places where you're not quite speaking in the voice of the other pillars of society who're dealing out *their* pomposities in the way you want them to be dealt, & bloody well you do it. So –

Page 1

Where you're not *exactly* speaking in the foregoing terms, though you are wonderfully inculcating the *mood*, I mildly object to 'as regards financing' & suggest the more correct? (if yet more pompous) *in regard to its financing*

don't understand my objection to *offset*: – but I think it had the same basis, I wanted counterbalance (or something), & I think I'm wrong.

bottom I think I like vehemence, though I'm hoist in my own petard here: vehemence is strictly speaking only a *quality* of ardour etc whereas enthusiasm is the thing itself. Still, first thoughts are often best, god damn it. (Keep enthusiasm though, I would maybe, – on second thoughts)

Page 2

Top. I like 'rather melancholy.' 'For some obscure reason' flu strikes a too jaunty note to me amid the prevailing pomposity. Influenza would be better: even the fussy 'grippe.' (That might suggest he really has diaorrhea) Middle. What about a § at 'He hoped that the plan' bottom. 'as to who should actually receive it' you tend to overdo this construction; I think.

suggest: There was some confusion about who should actually receive it.

(!Or Christ is it about *whom*!? – I'm not doing very well as a purist myself so far. Or: about who (or whom) was actually going to receive it. (Sorry about blots)

Page 3

Top I much like: 'the worst possible solution.'
middle & bottom:
    So that the members . . .
    So as to impress the visitor   **?**
    So as to be ready *to* move quickly *to* etc
I think the last two of these are wrong, as well as being repetitious.
Suggest So to impress the visitor the more. (thus turning 'so' into 'thus.')
    Or use 'thus' itself.
    But then it isn't the bloody actual *rehearsal of the welcome* per se that's going to impress the visitor, damn it. Shove a comma after welcome? (I was going to suggest a semi-colon, but that you might have told me to have shoved *that* up my arse: or back up my arse.)

Pages 4, 5, 6, 7, 8,

    I like all this fine. Wonderful. Though you can't tell if it's quite perfect till you see it in typescript. It's grandly amusing, though, & somehow moving & profound too.

Page 9

Query 3/4 way down wondered *if* it would not be more conclusive *if* etc
    This is almost justified since you can almost hear the school teacher speaking, & that's what one would say – transposed to dialogue – but you don't make this altogether clear that those are his actual words transferred to objective rapportage (& not your own) until you get to 'May I present' – At all events you need *mightn't* or *wouldn't* I think i.e.

whether it mightn't be more conclusive if
    „   „ wouldn't   „   „   „

if   „ wouldn't⎱ „   „   if
 „   „ mightn't⎰ „   „   „

Flaubert, sprouting whiskers at this point, said it would *look* better without the two *ifs*.[2]

Page 10

(To say '*of* the kingdom *of* France' is a crime, so said the whiskerando on the previous page. But that's harder to do in English, especially if you mean just that.)

Top Sometimes, when I was young, it used to amuse me to say 'secondly,'rather than 'second' just to show I hadn't said firstly, rather than first, before it: but probably *he'd* say 'second' here. (See blot on mss later.) why not all 3? – of efficiency, effectiveness, not to say of overall speed, it was essential the preliminary greeting be short etc

A little below Another possible suggested joke (if of a somewhat saurian character.)

   – that the addition of two words or even one
     or even for that matter one

Rest of 10: – splendid – & the more 'historic occasions' 'never-abating interests' etc the better.

Page 11

Fine, but surely *universalness* is somehow wrong (– even if grammatically right – unless the reeve or someone – had said it) – but *you* are saying this universality would be wrong too. (Even if more correct.)

   – what about, more ironic still, – & yet somehow absurd.

                  in
aware of the the universal quality of ⎱ *what etc.*

So, instead of as, is a *quibble* below in the dialogue.

Page 12

Middle (Coming after 'only scattered applause.' – wouldn't it be better *to overwhelm the visitors' ears with positively thunderous applause*
bottom to bid it cease. (I jibbed for 'arf a mo at the euphemism, but I think it's justified, for what he says or his gestures at this point really add up to just that; so it becomes funny – unless you don't think so on second thinkings.

Page 13
The white tile floor with (inset?) green squares is a lovely touch – &
it gets better & better toward the bottom.

Page 14.
Continues Ditto. I love the freshly oiled floors. Just before that:

had been cleared of its indigenous
                   familiar   } ? vans   (or just
                   native   }   nothing.)

cutting as you suggest (usual to a baggage room.)

Pge 15.
The chauffeur is a triumph
What about (bottom). as a man, & a citizen, as, in short, – though he
did not perhaps say exactly this, – a *public figure* – he certainly did not etc

(The Gogolian touch.)

Though then you would have to do something about 'understatement' on 16 – & maybe even obviously put 'dimensions' in inverted
commas, (as well as maybe 'public figure', but there is much that is consonant with the tenor of the story in that kind of benign
forced-unforced humor.

P 16 Excellent, but watch out for pitfalls as before: – & there is something wonky about technique of:
   – but he was interrupted *by* 'The trains crossing the bridge' started *by*
I think the punctuation is wrong & you don't need the second *by* (or
conversely, you don't need the first *by*) – you can give yourself a
moment of direct & startling drama here)

P 17
Considering the nearness of the train's . . . . (could be better?) I can't
think of a synonym though. Nearness is a loathesome word though:
proximity still worse. *Imminence* might do, for then you could get rid of
arrival. (Imminence has a note of ominousness too.)

Considering the imminence of the train ?

As the members issued ? (if you want another word)
– 18 I much admire the ridiculousness of the dust incident.

P 18
ditto the cobwebs
but cut the two obvious & too unpleasant like monkeys etc
How about: this somewhat simian process requiring . . .
(or without the somewhat) to *permit* the telegraph operator?

page 19

What you've cut is damned funny: keep it. Even the 'auspicious.' In fact it 'makes' the page. (Why writers do this – i.e cut in the wrong place – is a mystery; maybe you can't cut in the right place till a story is at least a year old. But the reader has an advantage of fresh approach, especially if he is a writer too, & this shouldn't go. It's fine.)

Bottom. Much approve of the gold-handled pen-knife.

Very bottom. How can you cut understood? having apparently absorbed.

P20

Thank you for teaching me the word straightway. It's a good one. But mightn't it come better after strode?

This is all v. good indeed.

Bottom It was true, he, the reeve (?) see below

P 20-21

Unless I am mistaken, your technique seems shaky here, or you haven't been aware of your own strength. For the reader is at this point *in* the story, or subtly been led therein, to such an extent it is no longer as if it were being related from without; this is a feat in itself & you should take advantage of it. The feeling is of *direct* presentation, or just about to be of that – besides the reeve is really speaking. I think this can be solved by the substitution, where possible, of he, him, for the actual word reeve, especially top of 21, though to use 'reeve' once or twice is effective. If you feel this will get your reader confused with the other 'he' then it's far more permissible to substitute & repeat 'operator' for the latter

Bottom. Isn't alienate *away* a pleonasm? Cut the away? (Though to be sure the reeve may be guilty of a pleonasm, save at this point the story is becoming more objective again.)

21, bottom continued: –

This return to the more 'objective' technique would be pointed if your paragraph, – bottom line – after

from him.

But because etc

22 first thoughts often best stop: but a very good page.

bottom sixty feet . . . something ommitted. to another warehouse sixty feet away painted railway red.

Or: warehouse painted railway red sixty feet away.

– – – –   – – – –

It seems to me a really swell story so far & I'm anxious to see how it ends. I found it difficult to follow when you first read it – & even difficult when I read it again myself: – I don't think other readers or listeners would have that difficulty which, in any case, so far as I am concerned, is a virtue, for the story improves on rereading, which is always a test. If I were an editor, I'd take it like a shot, but possibly the commercial magazines who'd take it are few & far between: Norman Newton runs a quarterly in Toronto – why not send it there? You wouldn't get paid, but you'd stand as much chance of getting in Martha Foley's Best stories of the year, which can be a springboard, & where, if it finishes as well as it's begun & gone on so far, it certainly deserves to be enshrined. Congratulations!

ML

Annotations:

1 Harvey Burt (1920–), a teacher of French in Burnaby and North Vancouver and a summer resident of Dollarton, met Lowry in the early fifties. After the Lowrys' departure in 1954, Harvey took care of the shack and Lowry's books, and he prepared special gifts to remind Malcolm of the shack, pier, and boat; see Lowry's 26 July 1955 letter (**638**) to Burt. Harvey and Dorothy Templeton Burt visited the Lowrys in Europe, and he was possibly the last person to whom Lowry wrote (see his June 1957 letter [**711**]) before he died. 'Operation Dyke' is the title of a short story Burt was working on during the early fifties. It was never published, but Lowry's thoughtful comments on it demonstrate the care he took with a friend's manuscript.
2 Lowry was fond of quoting or paraphrasing Flaubert on the qualities of good style; see, for example, his 22 June 1946 letter (**226**) to Albert Erskine.

Editorial Notes:

a. This transcription is from an eight-page holograph given to UBC by Harvey Burt in 1990; he suggests a spring or summer 1953 date.

579: To Albert Erskine

P: UBC(ms)
PP: *SL* 333-40

[Dollarton]
[early June 1953][a]

Dear Albert –
    Here is a bulletin. Margerie, on top of everything else, now has worms. At this point we decided to laugh, she being gallant enough to join in. We decided also to laugh about the house, repair what has to be repaired, accept what has to be accepted, enjoy what can be enjoyed while we still have it: and we do still have it. After all, one cannot tie oneself to the bed just because there is death in the world. And perhaps

Robert Graves' attitude is the best one to preserve toward such confections as the hydrogen bomb.[1] And so the stiff – but not too stiff – upper lip, & a dose of Kiplings IF, though not too smug, each morning before breakfast, seems the watchword.[2] But despite all this Margerie – not unnaturally! – cannot help feeling like 'letting the potatoes rot in the fields', as she puts it: she can't type (& I can't either, at least on her typewriter & I can't take time off to learn) & she is temporarily more or less disengaged from the work, and in fact, although she is getting better, I should not even discuss this or anything else serious with her until she's much improved. Naturally it's hard to obey this rule, and in any case the work has suffered. And so has she. And so, by God, have I. But that the work has suffered does not mean it's suffered to its detriment, at least so far as Gabriola is concerned. This damned thing – which is now, as I say, a short, perhaps even not so short, novel – has cost me more pains than all the Volcano put together. And needless to say I am suffering agonies of conscience because it seems to have thrown me off schedule. Nonetheless I still have the hope it will fit into Hear Us Oh Lord. Having gone so far there is only one thing to do which is to finish it. Meantime the perilous chapel section obliged me to rewrite the 'exposition.' But by the time I had done that I realised that what was required was not one, but two expositions. In case you think (I do. Ed.) that this is not obeying Robert Penn Warren's excellent rule of thinking straight & right through before one sets pen to paper I must find excuse in the originality of this notion.[3] The first exposition, though objective, is nonetheless being *composed* in the protagonist's mind. A shock suddenly makes him see that he's lying to himself, merely 'goofing' in fact and a totally different consciousness arising in the same person works diabolically back through the same material putting a completely different construction on it. I am hoping that the readers sympathies far from being disengaged or bewildered will be intensified by this odd treatment which though I feel it artistically justified might certainly give any psychologist pause, I fear. What crisis was the author himself passing through, he might ask, that would cause him so deliberately to hebephrenize his apparently objective data, & did he come through it successfully? The answer to this question I can only say must be found in Gabriola itself, which I more & more see – though perhaps half humorously – almost as a challenge to the author's actual personal salvation, which I had been a little forward in already assuming maybe. Hence the storie's importance. We shall see. But I'd be glad of a comforting word. Some time last November I began to be uneasy lest the whole work itself was in places not consonant with the best mental health & spiritual economy of its benighted author so I took some weeks off & read nothing but psychology. What I learned about myself was not very encouraging – but then at that rate and in those terms the Volcano was a sheer psychologic impossibility, so perhaps I can take heart after all, even though in those same terms, however I may succeed, I am bound from time to time to regard myself as an unhappy & struggling infant. However, perhaps miracles may be wrought with the pen, even while actual catatonias seem to vampire the mind. One catatonic & besetting nightmare worry which has had me counterwhored from time to time even to the point of creating a psychic block in the work, even though I sat down a regular number of hours at the desk – (one part of Gabriola moved so slowly that in the original you may see invocations to everyone from St Jude, the Saint of the Impossible to the spirit of William James, not to say God, to help me get on more swiftly, at the head of each page)[4] was that I had made a mistake in trying to cope with Hear Us Oh Lord at all, & should have taken your advice & got right down to the novel – or *a* novel, instead of wasting my time on short stories that began to seem more & more inadequate the more I thought of them & which in any case had been originally written with the not unnatural hope of selling them; now I seem to have compromised on this advice with Gabriola but my fear now is it will make the whole damn thing too unwieldy. On the other hand if [I] can get some of the nonsense out of Through the Panama & perhaps the Elephant the *whole* thing does have a very beautiful form, & makes a very beautiful sound when taken together: – & it is a form you can only see when you see the book as a whole. Then: But at my back I always hear Time's winged chariot changing gear.[5] And now even while hearing it I am perhaps wasting more time with more worry. A veritable octopus has fastened its tentacles to our conscience at the thought we have not yet paid you back the money you so generously lent us and the procrastination on this promise seems to merge abyssmally into the procrastination on Gabriola and the procrastination on the worms and the eviction – We evict those who destroy! – and God knows what else which maketh in the night watches an incantation to the mournful refrain 'We are letting Albert down!' (Not that we are: but this is the dismal impression we fear you may have formed) The procrastination, to be sure, has been nine tenths due to the even worse procrastinations of perfidious Albion,[6] & unforeseen expenses due to illness, but it has also been due, in one unlucky instance, to perfidious Malcolm who finding himself recently with sufficient specie to make matters good proceeded to invest some – unwisely, to put the kindest construction on the matter. . . Not a word, as Mynheer Peeperkorn would say.[7] Despite this, however, we are still pretty well in the black, so let us know if there is any immediate urgency. For actually our continued delay is only caused essentially by the fact that we still are not quite sure where we stand or how we shall have to act and this at least is not our fault: we have repeatedly tried to find out and one black villain of the piece seems, alas, to be my own eldest brother [Stuart Lowry], than whom even the Consul himself at his worst could not have been more unreliable. His letters, when they come, not only do not answer such questions which as the chief trustee he is legally obliged to answer but he has taken to writing them in some sort of sinister code from which it can only appear that he has been driven absolutely cuckoo by something or other, if he has not even taken to drink or dope.[8] This means that for [my] own protection I may have to approach the whole matter through a lawyer at this end, as I have been strongly advised to do – though I am naturally very reluctant to because he never would forgive it. What a position for me of all people, the mouton noir, & the youngest if I should have to refuse power of attorney to the eldest & one whom I have always regarded as more reliable than my own father, & that on the grounds of his irresponsibility. And what if I did? I can't manage my own estate from here. In fact I'm not legally empowered to manage it at all, merely to refuse to allow him to *mis*manage it. And if I did, how could I do it without mortally wounding or embarrassing him? And meantime time has been bitterly consumed by meticulously having to answer or take up questions with the other trustees to which I cannot possibly have any adequate reply because my brother has failed to brief me even in their existence whereas they assume that I have been informed. Worse still – where we can make any sense at all out of his infrequent & cryptic despatches – he pretends, & doubtless to them too, to *have* informed me.

( )[b]

Then of course there is always the old hypocritical business – though this receptacle personally considered has acquired by comparison recently almost a distinct sheen – of the pot, or ex-pot, calling the kettle black, when compassion is required. And so it goes . . . Another & very important factor is that we are still uncertain – though we should hear any day now – whether or not the Canadian Government are going to give me a fellowship on my second application, my optimism being reinforced on this point by the fact that it was they themselves who suggested – though they are aware that I am not actually a Canadian citizen – that I *make* a second application.[9] The situation is a bit peculiar. Under the old dispensation, so I was told, I was automatically a Canadian, without for that reason having to forfeit my British passport, or lose my English citizenship. Now they have a sort of American plan, whereby you do lose it, take out citizenship papers, swear a loyalty oath etc. that would exclude my allegiance to England as a foreign power.*[c] Naturally I was not going to do this simply to qualify for the fellowship! *And*

equally though they want artists of my type to stay in Canada which is partly
the object of the fellowship itself, they can't very well let me think I'm
being bribed as it were by a fellowship to *become* a citizen. Odder yet,
though I could in good conscience swear allegiance to Canada itself,
{And how! Little Malcolm has supplied a national deficiency by writing
them a national anthem – not yet performed, though it will be, & very
good too, though I say it.} British Columbia – which is the only place
we want to live here – has a political set up of a nature that does not
greatly encourage an Englishman, to say the least, to give up that old
blue passport, that emblem of freedom. More properly, B.C. at the
moment has no government at all, though both of them are totalitarian.
This is the way George Orwell would put it.[10] Or quasi-totalitarian.
B.C. – though not me, I couldn't see anyone to vote for at all – actually voted in a Marxist government, if of a non-violent type, the C.C.F.
[Co-operative Commonwealth Federation], but by some political legerdemain or other an even more fantastic government whose
protagonists were not British Columbians at all but had sneaked down
on well-oiled roller skates from Alberta – managed to capture the more
important seats in the house & so became a minority government. This
was Social Credit, & whatever may be said for that economic experiment in its ideal state, our premier thereupon gave as *his* ideal of
government that of Venezuela! – (a bloodthirsty fascist set-up if ever
there was one), – whereupon the Social Crediters fell, after having made
some demonstrations of power that were enough to make one's hair
curl, if one saw them for what they might promise under other circumstances when they were not trying so hard to please. The C.C.F (who
are vowed to the destruction of capitalism, but nevertheless had to make
a polite promise to the Lieutenant Governor to do nothing too serious
about it – though how the hell is one to know that they're not still
worse? –) now have taken up the slack, so to speak, & are a sort of stop-
gap government now, & soon there is to be another general election.[11]
Sure enough, it's comic opera Marxism, comic-opera fascism – so it
seems: but Canadians can be tough & intolerant babies when they get
going, they have an ominous predilection for the use of informers, the
Mounted Police have a power & ubiquity that can be considered in anything but the romantic terms of Rose Marie,[12] even if they are mostly
no doubt decent guys personally: all in all, it seems to me British
Columbia is a hell of a paradoxical place to ask any Englishman to give
up his English passport in, with all that means, no matter how one might
believe in or love Canada per se. It's almost a contradiction in terms; &
so hence is my position on this score. . . And so, come winter, if we can
afford it, i.e. if England comes through & irrespective of whether we
have the fellowship or the house or not, we half contemplated making

a large if temporary & not irrevocable move, where to – whether the Barbados or Sicily – we have no idea: all this is still in the realm of contemplation: I have even contemplated carrying on the work (How Hugh would like that!)[13] in a monastery in Majorca. But before anything like this, naturally, debts must & will be paid, & work delivered. My first deadline for you is November, – & here again the position is complex, & worrying, & I can't do much more than cast [myself] upon your mercy & advice. If I succeed in getting the fellowship★, that will mean I can cease long before November taking your cash for a considerable while & so presumably that dead line could be extended. (The excellent thing about the fellowship is that though I'd have to live in a foreign country, France or Italy, I would be permitted to go on working on the work in progress for yourself, though I'd probably assist in the translation at the same time – & here again I would be able to live without taking your cash – but here too the hebephrene of the situation is without end. Well, let it not become hebephrenic dilapidation, is all I can say. One thing at a time, Mr Jorkens.[14] Perhaps the deadline does not *need* to be extended, supposing you would be good enough to extend it. For in one sense – have I? – I have already exceeded the terms of the contract by in an interim producing an unscheduled novel in Gabriola. But here is the rub. Does Gabriola make sufficient sense or lose too much without its symphonically adjacent companions. As things stand: Gabriola (I seem to have said this before) is – or will be – a novel. But so is The Forest Path to the Spring another short novel. Gabriola & Forest Path taken together make, as you will see, *another* kind of novel. Ghostkeeper, Pompeii, Gabriola, & Forest Path make yet *another* kind of novel. Hear Us Oh Lord – with 12 chapters – would be, if done aright, less a book of short stories than God help us yet *another* kind of novel: a kind of – often far less serious, often much more so – Volcano in reverse, with a triumphant ending, but ending (after the Forest Path) in the same way, with the words Le Gusta esta jardin! etc. You will see the point of this in Gabriola. But what – terrible thought – if you don't *like* Gabriola etc. . . I don't want to palm off something second rate on you simply to be able to say 'Well, you see, I've kept my promise.' Or my promise, or part of it, only kept in another way. So far – with the triumphant exception of the typing & reordering of the entire material of the Mexican trilogy – (much of it in its present form of far too intimate a nature to send even you, supposing it had been feasible to do so) I have willed one thing, & the daemon has decided another, since I've been under contract to you. I can master booze, my bad temper, my self deceit, & to some extent my other myriad bad habits, but I have not yet learned how to master that bugger. And if he was a good one it would be different. But he is slow, confused, paranoiac, gruesome of mind, as well as being completely implacable, and he seems to have some vices unknown even to me. And in Gabriola he has turned out what set out to be an innocent & beautiful story of human longing into quite one of the most guilt-laden & in places quite Satanically horrendous documents it has ever been my unfortunate lot to read, let alone have to imagine I wrote. One saving grace is that it is in places incredibly funny, I think: but here again I have a feeling that you don't altogether always approve of my humour, alack.

But to restate some of the themes at the beginning of this letter in more positive & hopeful form. Gabriola may not be the artistic triumph I sometimes think it is but if I have any knowledge of the human psyche at all it is – or can be, for I haven't finished it even yet, even while I speak of it as un fait accompli – a psychological triumph of the first order. True you have not been paying me to achieve psychological triumphs of the first order for my own benefit: but here the challenge seemed – & seems – ultimate, a matter of life or death, – & rebirth – as it were, for its author, not to say sanity or otherwise: perhaps I overstate the case, but my love for this place & my fear of losing it, nay actual terror, had begun to exceed all bounds; moreover the tactile objective threat has been horrible for me beyond words – which is part of the point, alas: not Dante's personal spiritual position when he wrote the Inferno was worse, & I shall have no Inferno to show for it, only, with luck a piece of prose which if it manages to live at all – and it just might – will no doubt do so for the wrong reason, & for a reason which might well condemn it as a work of art, {though it must be said you might have to go to Genet, or as some French critics said recently – where they are calmly & enthusiastically translating the 1st version of Lunar Caustic without permission – to Villon soi-même to find anything more extreme – [15] So they say & said.} namely that the bloody agony of the writer writing it is so patently extreme that it creates a kind of power in itself that, together with the humour & what lyricism it may possess, takes your mind off the faults of the story itself, which, incidentally, are of every kind – in fact it possesses perhaps not one single conventional virtue of the normal story, – its character drawing is virtually non-existent, symbols are pointed at blatantly instead of being concealed or subsumed in the material or better, simply real & not there at all, it is – or is as it stands – repetitious to the point beyond that which you can believe it's all done on purpose, & some readers – if they read it once – might have to read it 5 times before they could be convinced anything has happened at all. But I make it sound too interesting. I have to accept the possibility that you will consider it a total failure & my remarks prompted by self delusion. The important thing though is that I should have written it – touch wood! – at all. For it represents – but you will see only too clearly what it represents. . . And it does have some aesthetic virtues. It starts gently, so gently . . . So the important thing as it seems to me is to rise every morning with the sun have a swim & making allowances at this moment for the typist on the sick list get down (as I am doing!) at my desk & (I was going to say) write it *again*. Fortunately it won't be quite as bad as that – but so, anyhow, *get it sent to you.* Otherwise I might as well shut up shop, pay Random House back what you have already paid me, which I should be well able to do if things go only half right – right? – admit complete defeat, abandon writing altogether & in order to save my by then unsalvageable soul enter Gurjieff's nursing home in company with the beneficent ghost (perhaps) of Katherine Mansfield.[16] Which would mean admitting that the office boy was right too – a bitter pill indeed (though aren't all pills a bit bitter?) In short, if I don't finish this – & that right *now* and in these exact excruciating circumstances of being on the one hand damned Ahab-wise in the midst of paradise[17] and on the other still mysteriously given the grace to live there even if it is only the privilege of great guilt to which is added, by the way, the privilege itself – such grace has fallen on us now the Powers that Are (as Frank [Taylor] used to say) seem to have decided this part of the beach is under a special providence or haunted, probably by me, so we are the sole inhabitants, the bulldozers crash everywhere else, I can look a mile on either side & see only uninhabited houses, they having evicted themselves out of unnecessary terror or necessary terror or horror at what their lives would be without this, but they take it, since that what they say, is to exist! – while I don't – (Tant pis! The story was to tell you I did!)

[unsigned][d]

Annotations:

1 Robert Graves (1895-1985), the prolific poet, novelist, and critic, is also remembered for his study of the mythological sources of poetry, *The White Goddess* (1948). Lowry is thinking more generally here of Graves's philosophical approach to life – that one must not despair because there is death and ugliness in the world – which is a common theme in his work.

2 Kipling's 'If' begins – 'If you can keep your head when all about you / Are losing theirs' – and continues with similar advice, eventually promising dominion over the earth and full manhood to the youth who can live by such precepts.

3 The American poet and critic Robert Penn Warren (1905-89) makes this point in his *Fundamentals of Good Writing* (1949), which he co-authored with Cleanth Brooks; see his comments on 'The Outline.'

4 The holograph drafts for *October Ferry* have frequent prayers to St Jude and, less often, to specific writers. The American psychologist and

philosopher William James wrote *Varieties of Religious Experience* (1902), a book that Lowry valued highly.

5 Lowry is again echoing Marvell's 'To His Coy Mistress': 'But at my back I always hear / Time's winged chariot hurrying near.'

6 Since the death of his mother on 7 December 1950, Lowry had been waiting for the estate to be settled. Whether England (Albion) or anyone there was being perfidious, however, is doubtful.

7 Mynheer Peeperkorn is a character in Thomas Mann's novel *The Magic Mountain* (1927; *Der Zauberberg*, 1924). A wealthy, elderly Dutchman and a bit of a buffoon, Peeperkorn's conversations are characterized by the expression, 'Not a word.'

8 The only letter from Stuart Lowry extant at UBC (1:41) is one dated 13 July 1950; it is a cordial family letter with general news.

9 Lowry did not receive this 'fellowship' or any other award from the Canadian government during his lifetime. He first applied for an Overseas Award in 1952; see his November 1952 letter (**549**) to Albert Erskine.

10 George Orwell was the pen-name of the English writer and social democrat Eric Blair (1903-50). The author of *Nineteen Eighty-Four* (1949), Orwell also wrote many articles about contemporary politics. He warned that democracy was threatened from the extreme left (communism) and the extreme right (fascism), both of which he saw as totalitarian.

11 In a repeat of events from the previous summer's election, the 1953 British Columbia provincial election dragged on through the summer months, stirring up virulent attacks on all sides; see Lowry's humorous description of local politics and events in his 14 June 1952 letter (**534**) to Harold Matson. This time the left-wing C.C.F. (Co-operative Commonwealth Federation) Party formed a coalition with the Liberal Party in an effort to defeat the right-wing Social Credit Party, and at first it appeared that they had won a slim majority. A final count of votes, however, confirmed a new Social Credit government under W.A.C. Bennett, who was premier of the province until 1972.

12 The Royal Canadian Mounted Police (RCMP) is Canada's national police force. It was formed in 1918 from a merger of the earlier North West Mounted Police and the Dominion Police. *Rose-Marie* is the title of a popular 1924 stage musical made into a silent film in 1928 and a full musical version in 1936 starring Jeanette MacDonald as Rose-Marie, the belle at a Canadian trading-post who falls in love with a handsome Mountie played by Nelson Eddie.

13 The character Hugh Firmin in *Under the Volcano*.

14 Mr Jorkens is the garrulous, tippling story-teller in *The Travel Tales of Mr Jorkens* (London: G.P. Putnam's Sons, 1931) by Lord Dunsany (Edward John Moreton Drax Plunkett, 18th Baron Dunsany, 1878-1957). Like Jorkens, Lowry is telling a disjointed story.

15 The original 'poète-maudit' is François Villon (1431-63), but Jean Genet (1910-86) is a dramatic modern example. Orphan, beggar, con-

victed criminal, homosexual prostitute, playwright, novelist, and poet, Genet wrote works depicting the brutality and violence in society. Villon is noted for his dark, personal vision in such works as his long poem 'Le Testament' (1461).

16 George Ivanovich Gurdjieff (1872-1949), a mystic and theosophist, opened his second Institute for the Harmonious Development of Man at Fontainebleau in France in 1922. Katherine Mansfield (1888-1923), the New Zealand writer, was dying of tuberculosis when she embraced Gurdjieff's doctrines and entered his 'institute' in October 1922. She died there on 9 January 1923.

17 In his long monologue in chapter 37 of *Moby-Dick* Captain Ahab describes himself as being 'damned, most subtly and malignantly! damned in the midst of Paradise!'

Editorial Notes:

a. This transcription is from the only copy-text that appears to be extant (UBC 3:5): a three-page undated holograph, each page covered on both sides with Lowry's closely written, slanting script in blue ballpoint pen. It is a draft, with numerous interlineations, deletions, and other signs of its interim status. No fair copy has been located with the Albert Erskine Papers at the University of Virginia, at UBC, or with Matson's files; therefore, this must be the 'Pantagruelian' letter not sent to Erskine (see letter **580**). Ironically, Lowry's clearest statement about the alternate plans he wished to make regarding his contract and the payments from Random House was never read by Erskine. The timing of events and Erskine's acknowledgement of Lowry's prior wishes became a point of honour for Lowry when the contract was cancelled unilaterally on 6 January 1954; see his 26 January 1954 letter (**603**) to Erskine.

b. This gap and parenthesis appear on the recto of page two with no indication of Lowry's intended insert.

c. Lowry has inserted an asterisk here and later in the paragraph, but there are no corresponding marginal notes.

d. The holograph is unsigned, and the last words fill the bottom right corner of the verso of the third page. Lowry may have continued the letter on pages now missing.

580: To Albert Erskine

P: Virginia(ms)   [Dollarton]
                                                          [early June 1953]

Dear brother,

I wrote you an enormous, nay, a Pantagruelian letter, but decided it was on the whole perhaps too depressing – as well as too Pantagruelian – to post: besides I gradually worked out of the depression while writing it, so why depress you further, if you have depressions of your own? Its main points (1) Margerie, on top of everything else, went down with worms! (2) Recovered from the worms she went down with a strep throat (3) Since this meant that she was disengaged from the work at the same time I was (this time) nursing her, this meant that I have become a bit disengaged too during the last week or two, and have been trying when possible to gnaw through a vast accumulation of mail. Including most importantly the one to yourself which if it did not get itself posted, at least cleared up a large number of points about the work in progress for myself. (4) However Margie is now recovered, & also recovered wholly from the disastrous blood count, and we are getting down into the old harness to-morrow. The weather is fine, news of our position on the beach reassuring for once, life ascetic but healthy (that is to say one hopes it will be the latter for some time now, or at least *providing* health): I forgot to say that the lowries & penates even includes a water-wagon, with bright shining wheels. Meantime & betweentime & to-morrow the main trouble but two or three has been *Gabriola*. This damn thing – which is now as I say, a short, perhaps even not so short, novel – sometimes seems to me to have cost me more pains than all the Volcano (or as Aiken called it Under the Malcalmo or Poppagetsthebotl)[1] put together. And needless to say I am suffering - agonies of conscience because it seems to have thrown me off schedule. Nevertheless I still have the hope it will fit into Hear Us oh Lord. Having gone so far there is only one thing to do which is to finish it. That is to say, finish it again. For meantime the perilous chapel section obliged me to rewrite the exposition. In fact to supply two – & contradictory – expositions. I found I had overwhelmed my hapless protagonist with catastrophic sufferings that had absolutely no justification in the aetiology, or little. I hope you may find some accent of greatness in it, for all its faults. It started as a lyric, then acquired a sense of humor, continued as grand guignol, & now is ending in something like triumph. Quite apart from the others in Hear Us oh Lord, & the two other novellas, that & The Forest Path make – or rather *could* make – a unified volume: & I think a bloody good one. So I am both behind – & ahead of – schedule: I can't be sure which. Fortunately I have some reason to believe I am a kind of stretch runner: I can't get ahead unless I *think* I'm behind, anyway. Nonetheless: at my back I always hear Times winged chariot changing gear. And now even while hearing it I am perhaps wasting more time with more worry. A veritable octopus has fastened itself to our consciences at the thought we have not *yet* paid you back the money you so generously lent us & the procrastination on this promise seems sometimes to merge abyssmally into the procrastination on Gabriola etc all of which maketh in the night watches an incantation to the mournful refrain 'We are letting Albert down!' As a matter of fact we are not, but it would be bad enough if you thought so. The procrastination has actually been nine-tenths due to the even worse procrastinations of perfidious Albion,[2] & unforeseen expenses due to illness: moreover I have been expecting any day for the last months to hear whether my second application for a fellowship were successful or not.[3] This would have solved much but I heard yesterday it had not been granted, so far as we can judge on the grounds that I was reluctant under a new law to give up my British passport[4] (which is not to be confused with a Hungarian or even German one & I'm damned if I will give it up): until this was decided we could not tell where we stood at all in relation to anything. I may say that, despite this, we are still pretty well in the black, but I'm not going to say 'so please let us know if there is any immediate urgency,' because even if there were you probably wouldn't. We still can't know quite where we stand or how we have to act (in regard to our geographic destinies) until we hear again from the Westminster Bank of Liverpool (the new trustees of the estate, my eldest brother [Stuart Lowry] seems unfortunately to have gone off his noddle) & have, probably a mutual counsel here with the Bank of Montreal: but in regard to that the clouds have at least lifted a bit, & when we can behave at all in consonance again in this regard (banks slay us both) we shall now be able to do so now, I hope as if the urgency existed & not only morally on this side, even if it in fact exists on the other: in short quam celerrime. Our best love to Frank [Taylor], by the bye.

God bless you from us both

With love

Malcolm

P.S. Would you give us old Frank's address?

P.P.S. My unposted Pantagruelian epistle is full of concern as to whether you'd like Gabriola serially. We have wonderfully happy memories of sending you installments. Only trouble is that, as she stands, I run into a veritable hurricane as early as about page 20, & am swept out of my course as far as a move thru South Georgia, before I manage to head her again for old Vallipo all ataunto on about page 70, by which time she's lost most of her crew & is besides unrecognizable: that doesn't mean she not going to get there, but as a sadder & a wiser boat, I fear . . .

Annotations:

1 Aiken's terms were 'Under the Malcalmo' and 'Poppergetsthebotl'; see his excited letter of congratulations to Lowry of 23 February 1947 (Sugars, 200-02).

2 Lowry had still not received his share of the estate from England.

3 Lowry did not receive an Overseas Award; see his June 1953 letter (**579**) to Erskine.

4 We have not been able to identify any Canadian law requiring Lowry to relinquish his British passport.

581: To Margerie Bonner Lowry

P: UBC(ms)   [North Vancouver General Hospital]
                                                      [early July 1953]ª

Very dear duck: have been passing through a black phaze of mutual anti-duck lust with much pain on top & every kind of lion exacaberzal possible to imagine; will recount later in detazel but this phaze is now passed. To-night I have enemezed (I have not gone for a week, despite repeated strong attempts of which is very funny & even quite famous down here; to-day reminds me of time George – who must be made to disgorge & I brought you here for your poor foot. Now I have a poor foot – to-morrow they are going to set it. I get an anesthetic so don't worry. Am very disappointed not to have seen you but more or less get the point. Your note was delivered by a nurse who did an almost instant bunk or I would have replied by return. I send you all my love. Have been reading old News of the World. I am very apprehensive of any further life in Dollarton for you or indeed Canada at all but perhaps you can reassure me. They have given me to-day a blood test also. A sinister priest came in just as they were giving it me & they spilled the blood all over the floor – of course I noticed that – . Result as yet unknown. And many others unknown. And to-morrow a gentleman will come to cast my hand & foot. I'm sorry I cannot write more. But I do send you all the sweetest sincerest love in the world. If you can send down another note do so – it is almost impossible or at least very difficult for me to write at all (I need my right foot to beat time)
        With devotion   dear duck

Editorial Notes:

a.   This letter to Margerie, written while he was in hospital being treated for a broken leg and she for dog bites, is scrawled in pencil on the recto of a 20-by-12.5-cm piece of paper. Lowry has adorned it with two drawings, one of himself in a hospital bed and another that is supposed to represent the nurse making his bed. Beside the latter he has written: 'And in Laurel & Hardy comedies one thought this kind of thing was funny.' At the top left he has drawn one of his seagulls of good cheer. On the verso he has written 'MRS MARGERIE LOWRY.' The accident that led to their joint injuries occurred on 28 June 1953, and they were both taken to hospital on the twenty-ninth.

582: To Dorothy and Harvey Burt

P: UBC(ms)

[Summer 1953][a]

Sinister bearded man

> With love to Dorothy & Harvey
> – not forgetting Dapper Dan & Mr Plumley – [1]
> from Malcolm.

(herewith to be observed pronouncing benediction upon the one-hopes-seaworthy craft of happy memory & by name 'My Heart's in the Highlands',[2] & with great thanks from her & us for the renovation of same, & aboard which I & she hope you may soon be rowing toward a happy picnic.)

M.

Annotations:

1 Dapper Dan and Mr Plumley were characters in a story with which Lowry entertained the Burts during an evening visit.
2 Harvey Burt helped with the renovation of the Lowrys' row-boat 'My Heart's in the Highlands,' which had been salvaged from Burrard Inlet; see photograph 18.

Editorial Notes:

a. The copy-text of this message is a pencil note on the back of photograph 21, which shows Lowry in his cast.

583: To Einar and Muriel Neilson

P: UBC(ms)

[Dollarton]
[July 1953][a]

Beloved Oceani:

News is I tripped over a root cold stone sober (& indeed during a period of solemn waterwagony) – the said root apparently designed to catch someone else playing cops & robbers ('How do you like children, Mr Fields? 'Boiled'), & broke my leg in 2 places + dislocating my ankle:[1] Margie going to ring for the ambulance was sprung upon by a berserk husky (oh Duchess, where were you then?) & seriously bitten – she wound up in hospital alongside me with symptoms of angina pectoris also, quite apart from hydrophobia & what-not, though the last named turned out fortunately to be shock: I went to bed in the ward alongside a dying old man of 99 (all in all we were a great comfort to one another) who, upon Margie coming to visit me in the ward, rose up, with dying breath, & cried:

'¡Maria!'

'I beg your pardon,' says Margie, 'My name is Margerie.'

'Please bring me a bed pan!'

And who, to me, upon my going to say goodbye to him before leaving the ward, I having grown a beard meantime, said:

'What did you say your [name] was? Jesus?'

'Not yet' I replied, cautiously . . .

So that is the set-up with us; – myself in a plaster cast, unable to move or swim, & Margerie in another sort of plaster cast, if not plastered cast, though both of us only too willing sometimes to become in a really plastered cast, if not even the plastered class, seeing what sobriety seems to do for one.

I would love to see you – either both or singly, or even see you both double: Gabriola has grown into a novel, but at this point I turn the letter over to Margerie) – she herself can't carry on, so I sign it, with my pen,

With love

Malcolm

Annotations:

1 Lowry always gives this explanation of his 28 June accident to his friends, but see Day (434). See also photograph 21. The comment, 'I love children . . . parboiled,' is attributed to W.C. Fields (1879-1946), the American comedian known for his intolerance and eccentricity.

Editorial Notes:

a. This holograph is undated, but Lowry's description of his accident indicates a July date. At the top right of the recto he has drawn a cart speeding down an incline with a seagull and a tree.

584: To Albert Erskine

P: Virginia(ms)
PP: *SL* 340-42

[Dollarton]
[July 1953]

Dear old Albert:

News of the rich & strange. Dispatch of 1st instalment of Gabriola was inhibited as follows: just as it was about to be dispatched two things

happened almost simultaneously (as in XI-XII of the Volc) – I fell foul
in the dusk in the forest of a childrens cops and robbers & Indians' snare,
a deliberately upraised root (not deliberately upraised to catch *me* of
course but stretched as to create a murderous stirrup I saw too late) &
shattered all the bones in my ankle, as well as dislocating the joint of the
same organ, + fracturing both bones in my right leg (this is almost the
exact spot in the local bosca oscura where imaginatively, not being in
Mexico at that time, Yvonne was killed by the horse, as we plotted it
out then). Margerie, upon going to store to ring for an ambulance, was
suddenly sprung upon by a 'beast' (as she describes it) half husky & half
wolf, who went for her throat, horribly tore her thigh & leg (which still
after 10 days is exuding pus) was finally choked off by a bystander. She
returned half crazy with fright & pain & dripping with blood & Grand
Guignol & when I went to hospital finally she having come along in the
ambulance was ordered by the medicos to stay there hospitalized too;
her life was in balance (or seemed so) a couple of days, meantime my
injuries were so complicated they were afraid to give me a general
anaesthetic to set the leg, or a spinal one because I had formerly broken
my spine: finally they risked the latter (the spinal fracture – only a per-
cussive one – had been between the 4th & 5th vertebrae) & from that
point on luck was magnificently with us, even though at one point too
formerly unable because of a hospital ruling even to see Margerie or
know how she was getting on, I was in such general angoisse (equally
over the undelivered work) & pain that apparently I *ate* the goddamned
thermometer in rebellion. That is to say that under sedation I apparently
angrily bit it in half: however I evacuated it all 2 days later, or most of
it: temperature unknown. Maybe Mercury stays with one. So now we
are back: I having meantime forgotten everything I wrote during the
previous months. It comes to comfort one a good deal however, for it
is some of the more powerful & original stuff in its way I've read in a
long time. I must say that I have disciplined myself like an ascetic
{approx. 15 hrs a day up till the mishap & thoroughly enjoying it.
Accident was only a fortnight ago next Sunday so considering the relative seriousness of one's injuries one hasn't lost too much time. The
Spartan medium is this newly developed 'walking cast' I mention – hell
on the patient but undeniably an innovation. In former days one would
have lost months.}, allowed myself no drinks (whatever that matters!)
not even a beer. So that's something. I have to finish the flaming bloody
thing in considerable pain though, which is something else – my leg is
in a cast, the weather wonderful & hot, & I can't swim (or the cast
would melt). That's about all, brother. Horrible: but also damned lucky:
Margie is well now, myself a pegging Ahab[1] (they thought they'd have
to take off the leg too but it's still here) – nothing has been wasted, not

even the experience in the ward (continuous grand guignol that fitted in beautifully & I had the sense to keep my pencil to paper too)[2] – you will get the first installment, though, or it will be dispatched rather, end of this week or beginning of next instead. (I perhaps should not say that when the accident happened to me, I was trying also to do 2 things at once for an aficionado – a well known Canadian artist, too[3] – of the Volcano who had visited us a/ Explain the symbology of the '*dog*' throughout b/ show him the locale of Yvonne's imagined death.) This is about all brother for the moment. Accidents to me might seem psychologically suspect: but how explain the dog? And the good luck? Please forgive bad writing which is due to exigencies of leg: cast is 'walking' cast I have to wear ten weeks dying each night in bed with my boots on so to say. It's all right quite often save that one's toes get red hot. Apart from this our health & spirits are good. To-day am working in bed. Well: Through those weeds! Over those falls![4]

Love from both

Malcolm

Annotations:

1 Captain Ahab in *Moby-Dick* has an ivory leg through most of the novel, but he has it replaced by a wooden peg-leg towards the end.
2 Lowry's experiences in hospital became the basis for the draft of 'The Ordeal of Sigbjørn Wilderness.'
3 The 'young student' is identified by Day (431) as the Canadian poet Al Purdy (1918-).
4 Lowry's exclamations refer to a famous scene from *The African Queen* in which the characters escape in their boat through weeds and over a falls, and he uses them frequently from this point on to signify hope and perseverance; see his October 1953 letter (**590**) to Erskine.

585: To Albert Erskine

P: Virginia(ms)
PP: *SL* 342-44

[Dollarton]
[July/August 1953][a]

Dear brother:

I'm sorry you still have no instalment but I reckoned without certain difficulties of adjustment, on top of which Margie with her hands full with me has little time to type recently, while I at about page 12 went & had another inspiration, a lengthy insert which in any case would have held up matters slightly, even though on the further bank there is a more or less lengthy stretch of pretty final draft. The cast {No reference to the play I haven't written yet.} got loose too (as I think I intimated in my other letter) & I had to make a trip to the hospital the Friday after I wrote you to have a new one put on. (I thought I'd greet some of my old pals in the ward, only to discover ¾ of them were dead.) The new cast having been put on I was then instructed (there being no room for me in the hospital to stay overnight) I'd have to make the return trip on crutches without putting my injured foot to the ground because the cast was still wet. Such a return trip through the forest to our house is physically impossible but it being equally impossible to explain to anyone how we lived we had to make it anyhow. I would still be making it but for Margie herself of course & a shining Christian deed rare in my experience which etemphasises how all ex-Consuls in the Lowry psyche should behave in future toward their fellow man & I hope will. A bloke had spotted my – our – plight from the road, stopped his car, & followed us into the forest. I – & we – were going well at that stage, I had renewed optimism, & declined further help beyond the steep hill I was going down, but the bloke insisted, saying that it indeed was, as we had earlier thought it was, quite impossible, even with one person's assistance; he knew because he'd been in a similar predicament himself he said, – the ground is in places too spongy to take crutches which simply sink in & there was worse to follow. True I had made the frightening trip up the hill through the forest earlier in the morning on the loosened cast but then I had a stick and moreover could walk after a fashion *on* the cast, it had not been so bad and there was no pain to speak of, *now* the pain & strain was so godawful the sweat was pouring off one in cascades & one had to stop every ten feet or so.

'Well' I said. 'This is really damned noble of you sir . . . Our name's Lowry.'

'And mine Budd. William Budd. Just call me Billy. You haven't heard of Billy Budd?'[1]

We said yes & Moby Dick too but since he evidently did not understand us did not pursue the subject. The worst part was not the forest but just before reaching the house, which because of a cave in in the forest bank, now has to be approached by a plank running five feet or so above the beach & about ten feet long. Well, not even Billy Budd could walk the plank in crutches, I reflected! I had to make this last part of the journey to the great danger of the others on my seat and I was so demoralized finally it took me a week to recover, during which period it seemed to me from the pain that the leg was getting worse, not better, while the new cast didn't seem any firmer than the old. However I'm glad to say that now the pain is very much less, & I seem definitely on the mend. The only bad factor has been that if the accident – as some unsympathetic psychiatrist might aver – was a form of device on the part of my psyche to produce a situation in which I would be physically incapable of doing any difficult chores at all – or even to sit in the sun (which I can't, else the damned cast might melt) – & so give me that much more time to work, it wasn't a very successful device. I have had so far extreme difficulty in working for more than twenty minutes at a stretch, after which I have to rest for about an equal period: – moreover it's disrupted my methods of work to some extent, I'm used to working on several drafts at once, which involves much standing up & walking around, & that I'm not physically up to. What would have become of us in this situation for all Margie's stoicism (not to mention my masochism) without our neighbour – the Manx boat builder,[2] Quaggen of The Path to The Spring, I don't like to think either: but somehow it all *is* working out – but I'm very sorry indeed for the delay. For the rest I'm glad to say that despite dog bites & all (which I didn't tell you produced in Margie for some reason the exact symptoms of angina pectoris) Margerie is definitely very much better in health & getting better all the while so that all in all I feel pretty optimistic about everything apart from the original plan of Hear Us Oh Lord in regard to which I'm going to need some advice from your good self.

– Everything very much better since this was written!

Through those falls! Over those weeds!
Love

Malcolm

Annotations:

1   Billy Budd is the title character of Melville's *Billy Budd*; he is executed and buried at sea for striking the Master-at-Arms, John Claggart.
2   Lowry's close friend Jimmy Craige.

Editorial Notes:

a.   The context of this copy-text, written in blue ink and pencil, confirms a late July to early August date. *October Ferry* began arriving in Erskine's office in October.

586: To Arabel Porter

P: Yale(ms)

Dollarton P.O.,
Dollarton, B.C.
[August 1953]

Dear Arabel Porter:
     I was a bit hurt you didn't reply to my letter though probably there

was no reason why you should have. If I find myself gnattering slightly on the subject it is probably because I'm being obliged to swelter this summer out with a broken leg & ankle encased in a cast, due to an accident that coincided rather mysteriously with the reception of John Goodwin's book.[1] It is an excellent book but you might tell him to keep his demons within covers next time you see him: when my wife went to phone for an ambulance for me she got violently bitten by a crazy dog & so found herself in hospital alongside of myself which is why you have had no story as yet from her. The moths too seem a little larger this year . . . Though we have seen no monkeys as yet. I shall write John Goodwin: a very good piece of work indeed, extremely powerful, though I should think the voodoo clergy might with justice take exception to it. I said I might have some constructive criticism of NWW [*New World Writing*]: I don't – I have no criticism, it's uniformly interesting, beautifully varied & balanced. One could not, however, get it here in Canada till well on in July, which doesn't somehow seem right. In fact, one can fall out of touch here, it sometimes takes so long to get American books. Also there is the plight of a fellow like me, who can't get anything published here so that one begins to doubt if one exists despite a broken leg, which should remind one, if anything. For this reason too – I don't mean the broken leg but the out-of-touchness – I'd be very glad to know if anyone had anything good to say about my story. In fact I'd be very grateful to hear anything encouraging (or even discouraging for that matter.) I just now have noticed that you had a poem of Howard Griffin's in your second number; well, I don't apparently keep my eyes open but I hadn't read the poetry section of that number, and haven't yet, though I should do so. But everything seems very far away, & one writes in a sort of vacuum here. I hope I wasn't treading on Griffin's toes in Strange Comfort. You didn't tell me & I don't know. I perceive another, larger moth upon the curtain. Though still no monkeys. Although yesterday there was a chipmunk. And there have been at various times here deer bear mink cougar racoons (which come right into the house) & killer whales (which so far haven't.)

Yours very sincerely

Malcolm Lowry

Annotations:

1 This is Goodwin's *The Idols and the Prey* (1953); see Lowry's 29 May 1953 letter (**576**) to Arabel Porter.

587: To Downie Kirk

P: UBC(tsc,msc)   Dollarton
                                                           10 August [1953]ᵃ

Dear Downie:

I'm writing for Malc, because he's trying to use every minute he can
to work, and he can't work very long at a time, these days.

Yes, we were both in hospital at once. When I went to phone an
ambulance for Malc, that huge black dog of Percy's, not Pride, another
brute, was off his chain, god knows why, and he went for me and bit
me badly in the leg. I'm quite recovered by now, but poor Malc will
have his leg in a cast until the middle of September.

I'm sending you a book of French poems (dedicated to Malc, as you'll
see) by our Haitian friend. Not to keep – Malc wants it back – but he
thought you might like to read it up in your hinterland.★

We hope you're still enjoying the work there – and it must be a
change from being in a classroom at that. You'll probably come back
looking like Tarzan★★ himself at the rate you're going. We are certainly
sorry we missed you that day – pity you didn't come just the day before!
We look forward to seeing you when you get back and we really must
have an evening. Will you be able to get out here and see us or spend a
day or so before school starts? If not, perhaps on a week end soon after.

Ah yes, the daiqueri★★★ – we know it well. And very good it is, too.
I'm sending you a picture and recipe, but you don't need anything so
fancy as an electric mixer – you just need a shaker, a strong arm, and *very*
finely crushed or shaved ice. Usually you drink it through a straw,
because the ice must not be melted, or very little melted, and be sure
not to use a heavy dark rum, it's not so good.

I tried to buy a copy of New World Writing #3 to send you but it
hasn't arrived here yet, although they told me it was due in July – it
came out in the States on May 27. Should be here soon.

It was good to hear from you – it will be better to see you. All the
very best from us both –

As ever,
Margerie
And with love from
Malcolm

★ I'd like to know what some of it means too, if you have time, which
you probably haven't.[1]
★★ Talking of whom I have grown a beard.[2] Object (a) to distract me
from the itching of the cast (b) To amuse myself with seeing how many
people in this conformist world call caustic attention to it. What they
don't know is that *I'm* playing beaver with *them*.

*** Another wonderful drink: rum & vodka, if you can get the vodka. I presume one would have the mounted police down on one these days, if one dared ask for such a subversive beverage.

Annotations:

1 The book is Philippe Thoby-Marcelin's *A fonds perdu* (1953).
2 Tarzan is the title character of Edgar Rice Burroughs' 1914 novel *Tarzan of the Apes* and the hero of a comic strip and movie series, based on the novel.

Editorial Notes:

a. The main letter is Margerie's. Malcolm has added his comments, keyed to her letter, and he has signed separately.

588: To Albert Erskine

P: Virginia(ms); UBC(phc)   [Dollarton]
PP: *SL* 333   [late Summer 1953]
                                                     Castle of Udolpho[1]
                                                              Sunrise.

Dear brother.
    Herewith an instalment. Rest will follow quam celerrime. Instalment on debt I mean. But re work, health, all news good. We are going like a bat out of. Not to say just like a house on. Love from us both.
                                                              Malcolm

Annotations:

1 *The Mysteries of Udolpho* (1794) is a Gothic novel by the English writer Ann Radcliffe (1764-1823). Although the novel contains the required Gothic castle in the Appenines, Lowry may be confusing Radcliffe's title with that of Horace Walpole's Gothic novel *The Castle of Otranto* (1764); see his 31 October 1953 letter (**594**) to Erskine.

589: To David Markson

P: UBC(ms)   [Dollarton]
                                                     [21 September 1953]
                    (out of the ⊙ th century)

Dear old Dave.
    Sorry as hell I haven't written, though I have many times as a matter of fact, but I never got them through the post, so to bloody speak. It has

been so jeezely hard to move around. But I have the cast off & to day
took a more or less first swim again – oh brother. Well, it swam, & that
right damn fast. But getting up was another thing again. As for the rest,
I have written a – yes – & think & hope to send same to Albert the good
& have him afterward refer it to you. I'll send you a picture of Margie
when I can get her in the camera: so far, Ahab's technique has not been
so good.[1] Margie says my beard {which is growing luxuriantly & I'm
trying to trim to a Shakpearean point}

    Send along the work. We think of you very often.

Love from us both

Malc

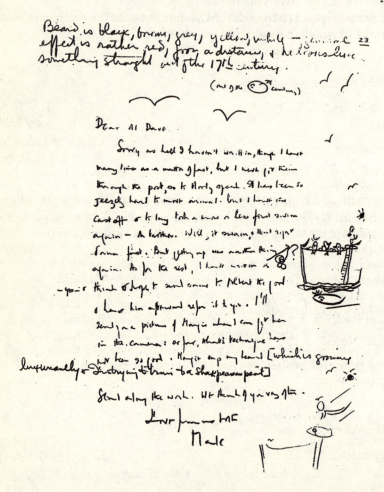

Figure 10: *This delightful holograph (UBC 3:6) is written in black and red
pencil and has several Lowry drawings. Margerie has added the description of
Malcolm's beard at the top of the page and the comment in brackets at the end.*

Annotations:

1 While wearing his leg cast, Lowry referred to himself as a 'pegging Ahab' after Melville's hero.

590: To Albert Erskine

P: Virginia(ms)   [Dollarton]

[October 1953][a]

Dear brother: Herewith the $100 – for which a hundred thousand thanks – or do we owe you another $50? did you get the other $100. I think we owe you $10 for a doctor Margie thought she paid. First instalment of Gabriola is being sent next week[1] Hold that note Roland![2]

           Through those weeds!

           Over those falls!

(Above is war cry adapted from Jim Agee's African Queen)[3]

                    love from us both

                              Malcolm

Annotations:

1 Lowry sent his first batch of *October Ferry* manuscript to Erskine on 14 October 1953.
2 This phrase, adapted from Louis MacNeice's *The Dark Tower*, became a standard Lowry line for conveying hope and encouragement. See his 27 August 1951 and 5 February 1954 letters (**468** and **604**) to David Markson.
3 James Agee wrote the screenplay for John Huston's 1951 film *The African Queen*. These exact words do not appear in the screenplay; hence Lowry's description 'adapted from.' He first used the phrases in his July 1953 letter (**584**) to Erskine, who did not recognize the allusion.

Editorial Notes:

a. The holograph is an undated note written in blue ink on a 6-by-10-cm scrap of paper.

591: To Albert Erskine

P: Virginia(ts); UBC(phc)   Dollarton

14 October 1953

Dear brother:

Here is the first batch of Gabriola, final draft – though there may be too many parentheses, howevers, etc. One key to one level of the book

– though the 100 pages I send doesn't yet quite reach it – is to be found in Herman Broch's introduction to Jimmy and Tanya's wonderful translation of Hoffmannsthal, page XVIII at the bottom relating to the Letter of Lord Chandos: it is this aspect of it that has made it so hard to write.[1] Humour is the only bridge one can use to get across that abyss too and since it's a desperately serious book and becomes more so as it goes on you mayn't find that humour always to your taste. There are keys no less pertinent to be found on pages XXVI of that same introduction and especially on XXVIII where Broch says: 'Still trusting in beauty, he did not yet recognize that nature, having been rendered harmless by culture and elevated to beauty, had in turn bequeathed to culture, as a permanent Greek gift, the sinister, the menacing.' Well, I do recognize that for what it's worth, and if I'm not as beautiful a writer as Herr Hoffmannsthal, I don't think you'll find the work deprived of polar ambiguities at least for that reason, though it may have other shortcomings, one of which won't be, if I can humanly help it, that it will be left unfinished.

I have someway to go before I reach the smoother waters of a final draft again, though, so the next batch may be a bit smaller, the next larger, and so on till the end, all of which I'll send as soon as I can: the whole novel is about 2½ to 3 times as long as what I send you, and I conceive it's no use sending it in the wrong order. At present there are no chapters or even divisions in the book: if there must be I'd wanted it, for thematic reasons, to fall into 3 chapters, though we may have to have 4.

You'll notice that some of the material overlaps on The Forest Path to the Spring but this is intentional, as you will see: I haven't entirely abandoned certain original plans I've mentioned to you in regard to all this but before I can decide on this I'll need your advice.

Right now I have got my leg out of its cast and am functioning well with an elastic bandage and recovering literally by 'leaps and bounds', – though not many leaps & bounds! – all of which I am delighted to report (as was the doctor) for the smash was about 10 times worse than I told you, I having indeed broken and dislocated everything in that limb and ankle, which was dislocated and pushed right back out of line, that it was possible to break or dislocate: and my prospects for walking, or worse, swimming, at all again were at one point none too bright, as the leg had been weakened by a previous operation, and the circulation is poor.[2] However I now can walk again, after a fashion, and even swim. All this, living as we do, has not made things any easier, and it has been worse on Margie, who, poor gal, while I have been getting more or less into the pink again, has, with the stumping burden of my Ahabian self on top of everything, been beset with one feminine trouble after another, and has now, temporarily at least – though she is happily a miraculously courageous and buoyant character – pretty much reached the end of her rope.

I don't, alack, know – and she doesn't – whether she will have to go to hospital again or not: this first batch of final typing is all she can do now without some sort of slight rest or change, I feel, and since I can't type it accurately myself without her, or for that matter see myself living without her, this gives me a hell of a problem about getting it all in by November 1; whether I could do that anyhow now is a moot point for the novel's just gone on getting longer and longer, albeit there will be much pretty clear sailing after the next batch. All I can do is try my best, and I certainly am trying. I still haven't heard from England for certain about my money, so in regard to everything I hover between optimism and panic fear for I can't carry on for very long if you stop the payments if I don't make the deadline if the English money doesn't come. Perhaps you can find some way of penalising me that is not absolute excommunication or in some sort work out a compromise though I certainly hope to have more in by Nov. 1. We were both very distressed to hear about your disappointing trip to Italy and to see Peggy and all I can say my heart bleeds but we still continue to hope for the best.

I had had some notion (of course I would like Frank [Taylor] to see it too) of asking you when you had finished reading the batches if you would pass them on perhaps through Frank to David Markson, and so back to you, he being the lad you kindly helped find a job with Frank, who became a great pal of ours and, an expert on the Lowry, might have some useful suggestions for me or yourself on it. Anyhow it would give him a kick, and another sort of kick would be lessened for me if you hate it,[3] and he doesn't so much hate it, unless of course he hates it worse than you do, though I believe that it is going to be an original and good book, in its hildy-wildy way. (At least it's not about a writer – like hell it's not.)

This suggestion, though, may not be within ethical confines, and so is left entirely up to your good self.

With great love from us both –

Malcolm

P.S. God bless you.

Annotations:

1   *Hugo von Hofmannsthal: Selected Prose* was edited and translated by Mary Hottinger and Tania and James Stern with an introduction by Hermann Broch (New York: Pantheon, 1952). Hofmannsthal's 'Letter of Lord Chandos' is an early work that reveals the despair and breakdown of its

author, and Broch explains that Hofmannsthal was himself in a similar
panic – 'the deepest abyss of man' – when describing Chandos. 'That
a poet invents murders and identifies himself with the murderers to rid
himself of his own homicidal tendencies is conceivable,' says Broch,
'and one can imagine that Goethe, after Werther's death, had once for
all conquered any suicidal tendencies of his own' (xviii). See also
Lowry's May 1956 letter (**653**) to James Stern.
2 In March 1949 Lowry had had an operation to strip the varicose veins
   in both legs.
3 Erskine did not like *October Ferry*, but Lowry did not catch the warning
   signals from Erskine that preceded Random House's decision to terminate payments.

592: To Downie Kirk

P: UBC(ms phc)   [Dollarton]
                                                Friday, 16 October 1953

Dear old Downey,
    We were, naturally, very disappointed you didn't show up with the
fallible Mr Hunter but an explanation already being forthcoming
through Jim in that that day was Margerie's birthday we were only half
expecting you anyhow so weren't put out at all, though I'm very sorry
you had the trouble of waiting for that phone call which never came.
Perhaps if you'd phoned all the Hunters in the directory you'd have
contacted a childhood friend of mine also named John Hunter – and
god what a name is that for a forest warden – destroyer & preserver
both, hear oh hear.[1] I hope all may be well between you, & I appreciate your Kafka-like scrupulousness in the matter, though to be sure
Kafka believed that while the demand on the part of the divine powers
for absolute righteousness even in the smallest matter was unconditional,
human effort, even at its highest, was always in the wrong.) I'm also very
sorry I haven't written in reply to your other very good letters, especially since I was very grateful to receive them: the explanation for this
is that when I'm working at very high intensity the writing of even the
smallest note often takes me an incredibly long time – an occupational
psychological alienation of some sort doubtless due in turn to the fact
that the narcissistic care which one sometimes expends on prose makes
a fellow forget a letter should be spontaneous & to hell with the semi-
colons, since your friend doesn't want to look at them anyway but is
simply interested in hearing from you.) I've been going through a
period of distressing despondency too, what with one thing and
another, though life seems to be looking up somewhat again, albeit not

entirely at the moment looking forward to an indefinite period on the water-wagon, with the accent on the *agon*, when seen in anticipation on a cold October Friday, so that one would have no difficulty in coining the word waterwagony & when thinking of the waterwagonised days ahead that in effect have subtle compensations of their own,) (which does not mean there would not be a bottle should you arrive, nor let it deter you from bringing one yourself should you have a mind to.) But my God what brackish bilge is this of a cold October Friday anyway. We very much enjoyed your last visit – the Mexican 3 ds[2] felt like a series of electric shocks – & look forward to seeing you again soon –

With much love to Margerie Dorothy the young Katie & your good self from us both

Malcolm

Annotations:

1 John Hunter was a friend of the Kirks, and Marjorie (Lowry has mis-spelt her name) was Downie's wife; her birthday fell in October. For Lowry's allusion, see Shelley's 'Ode to the West Wind' (1820) ll 13-14: 'Wild spirit, which art moving everywhere; / Destroyer and preserver; hear, oh hear!'
2 Lowry is recalling some three-dimensional graphic images of Mexico shown to him by Downie Kirk.

593: To William and Alice McConnell

P: UBC(ms)
PP: *SL* 344-45   Dollarton
                                                      [ca 30 October 1953][a]

Dear Bill & Alice.

I'm terribly sorry we haven't got in touch, but I broke myself a piece of leg & dislocated an ankle and broke that too, while Margie got simul-taneously chewed up by a dog, (one might think one was accident-prone from this but in fact it was too much of an accident for that though it certainly left one prone all right in another sense.) so all in all we've had a bit of a misery-grisery this summer as the Sultan of Zanzibar remarks in this weeks New Yorker.[1] However I've practically written another novel in the meantime. Hope you are working well & successfully. Your returned books arrived naked of word: I hope not an implied rebuke. Above is the reason for our silence: pure misery-grisery. But we are quite recovered & in fine form now. We are thinking to move for a month or so into town soon & get around a bit & hope to see you then. I hate to return The Seven Pillars of Wisdom but I've kept it too long already, Alice.[2] It's wholly marvellous & makes most prose look silly. I read the Darwin with fascination too – just to keep up with the times.[3] We'll give you our address in town when we know it for sure & know it's a good one. Our last one in town turned out less a place to invite a friend than ambush your worst enemy & even that's an understatement: misery-grisery.

Blessings on your heads not forgetting the boy's from us both

Malcolm

Annotations:

1 Lowry is quoting Soud bin Ali, the Pretender to the throne, not the Sultan, from an article by Faubion Bowers called 'Letter from Zanzibar,' *New Yorker*, 31 October 1953, 82, 84-94. See also Lowry's November 1953 letter (**596**) to David Markson.
2 *The Seven Pillars of Wisdom* (1926) by Thomas Edward Lawrence is an account of his exploits and adventures in the Middle East during the First World War.
3 Charles Darwin (1809-82), the British naturalist, revolutionized biology and made a profound impact upon science and theology with his theory of evolution in *On the Origin of Species* (1859) and *The Descent of Man* (1871).

Editorial Notes:

a. This undated pencil holograph is filed with the William McConnell Papers (UBC McConnell 1:2). Judging from Lowry's reference to the *New Yorker* (see annotation 1), he must have been writing during the last week of October. For the purpose of dating, it is useful to remember that the *New Yorker* traditionally publishes one week prior to the issue date.

594: To Albert Erskine

P: Virginia(ms); UBC(phc)
PP: *SL* 345-47   [Dollarton]
                                                          [31 October 1953]ᵃ

Castle of Otranto
Halloween
Clocks striking midnight
Enter Gower Ghosts & others
Tucket within & a flourish of strumpets.
Enter Ariel & Caliban singing in unison:
Ah gotta shake a wicked tail to getto Liverpool![1]

Dear brother –

Yippee!

– Or maybe that's an inappropriate remark to make when we're already running shamelessly overdue: but maybe not so much. All's a'taunto save that we have our starboard engine snaggled in a wisdom tooth the chief engineer has an ulcerated throat, & the ship itself is running on sulfalanimide. So the main trouble is still typing; there's more completed than this too, & of course beyond but there's a snag on the next page (the more so since it is a 'snag' literally), so thought this was a good place to break off, as for being sent round Hallowe'en & to arrive over All Souls, with the other batch to follow the beginning of next week. After which there's still another 50 pages or so to go till I reach my old final draft, which will need some overhauling too when – touch wood – I overhaul it; perhaps you better reserve your judgment in the meanwhile, but I can tell you this, the book gets much better as it goes along – brother, you just wait till that old tide starts a' coming in, a' roarin' & a growlin' & it does too, a bit: – in the next batch, and then what rugs & jugs & candlelights: & corpses & last judgments & perilous chapels:; I suppose I ought to tell you for your peace of mind that I *do* get my bloody hapless characters off the bus eventually and *on* to the ferry. That is to say, though the temptation may be great, I do not avail myself of the priceless opportunity no doubt offered by progress in the meantime since I began the book, of taking the bus *on to the ferry itself,* where, thus still seated in the dimensions of one element and floated off on the bosom of another – that's not quite I mean but still, let it pass – they may reach their destination, without having once set their foot on land, or in fact wake up again, or the reader either, or the author come down to terra firma. You will be wondering at the length of this first chapter too – if it is a first chapter & which, if so, threatens to be the longest on record so I will expound thus far the magic of Dr Lowrys dialectical-Hegelian-spiritualism-caballistic-Swedenborgianism conservative-christian-anarchism for ailing paranoics: the first chapter (whether visibly such or not) is as the <u>base</u> to to a triangle or **triad** (and/or a radical having a valence of three):

viz: ERIDANUS
                                    GABRIOLA

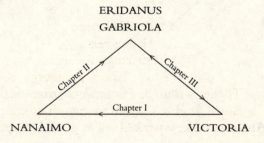

As you observe, in this configuration it is difficult for Chap III not to seem to be going back to its starting point, – or both ways at once – & in fact where does III start? And how is it solved? H'm; something that must have puzzled mightier minds than mine – but no more On with the work over those falls! through those weeds!

love from us both

Malcolm

P.S Which is meant to illustrate no more than that Chap I might be 180 pages long, Chap II & III each half that length, without its form being over balanced: – to the contrary. Anyhow I'm having a bloody good time writing it now – if you're having an anxious one reading it – which is more than I could say a year ago, when every page was covered with invocations to St Jude the Saint of the Impossible, & once it took me 3 months to produce as many readable pages, & even so some of the writing seems slack or matey in places or redundant (though sometimes later it is meant to appear redundant on purpose – as to give the effect of the man *caught*, washed to & fro in the tides of his mind, unable to escape –) & can stand tightening!

P.P.S Just received at this moment your very reassuring letter for which many thanks and contents duly noted.[2] And thank you very much. I think it's better for me to behave behave as if I <u>were</u> overdue though. It gives the firemen something to think about. I think this letter antici-pates some of your anxieties too. Perhaps if I were to tilt the triangle on its side it would be more helpful? Especially if you got out your atlas?[b]

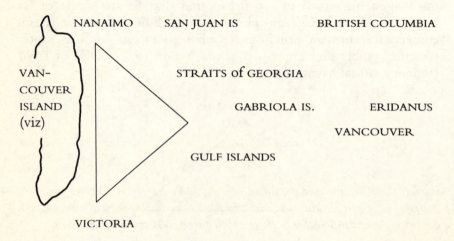

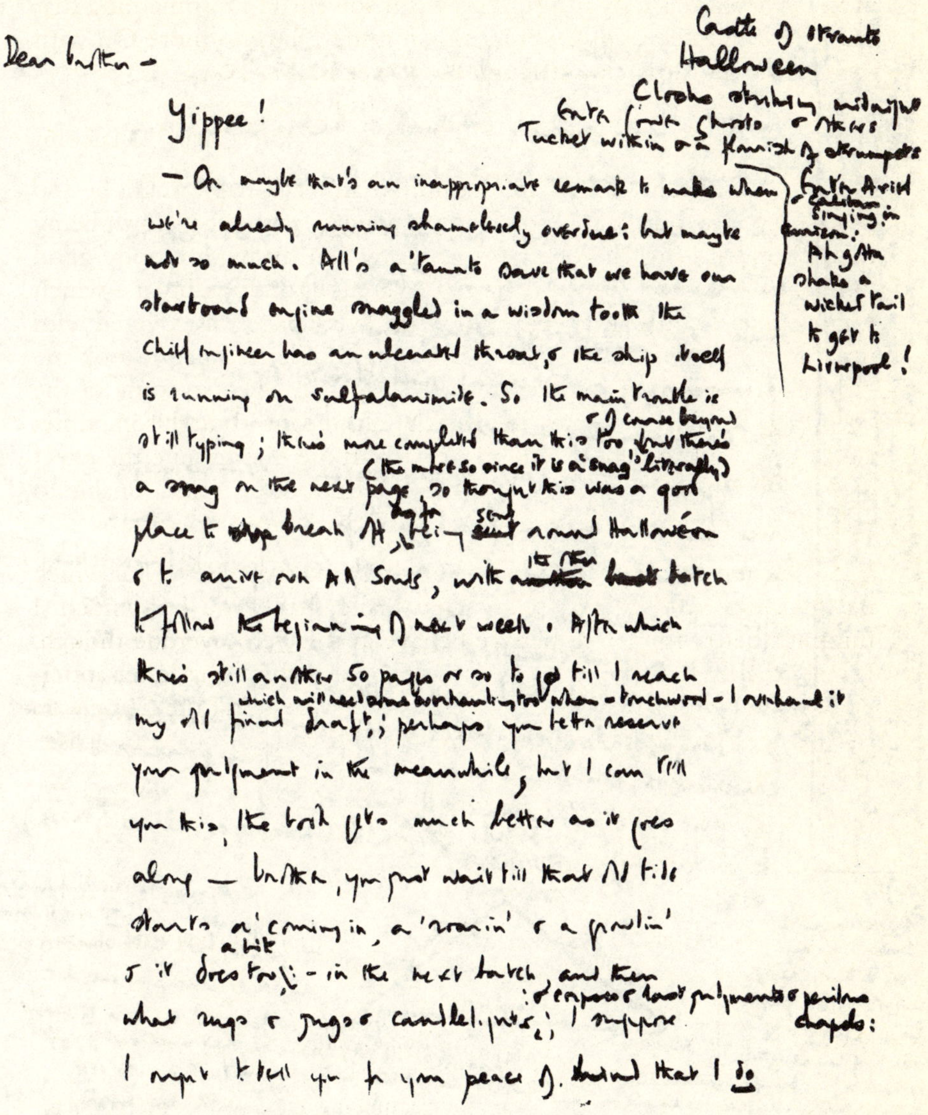

Dear Innes —

Yippee!

Castle of Otranto
Halloween
Clocks striking midnight
Enter first ghosts & others
Tucket within or a flourish of trumpets

— Oh maybe that's an inappropriate remark to make when we're already running shamelessly overdue: but maybe not so much. All's a'taunto save that we have our starboard engine smuggled in a wisdom tooth the chief engineer has an ulcerated throat, & the ship itself is running on sulfalamamide. So the main trouble is still typing; there's more completed than this too... there's a song on the next page, so thought this was a good place to stop break... sent round Halloween & to arrive on All Souls, with... hatch to follow the beginning of next week. After which there's still another 50 pages or so to go till I reach my final draft; perhaps you better reserve your judgment in the meanwhile, but I can tell you this, the book gets much better as it goes along — Innes, you just wait till that Ol' tide starts a' coming in, a'roarin' & a' growlin' & it destroys — in the next batch, and then what maps & jugs & candlelights, I suppose...

I ought to tell you for your peace of mind that I do

Enter Ariel singing in German: Ah golden shake a wicked tail to get to Liverpool!

Figure 11: *The recto and verso (see page 690) of Lowry's 31 October 1953 letter (594) to Albert Erskine demonstrated the Lowry imagination at work but did not inspire confidence in his progress with October Ferry to Gabriola.*

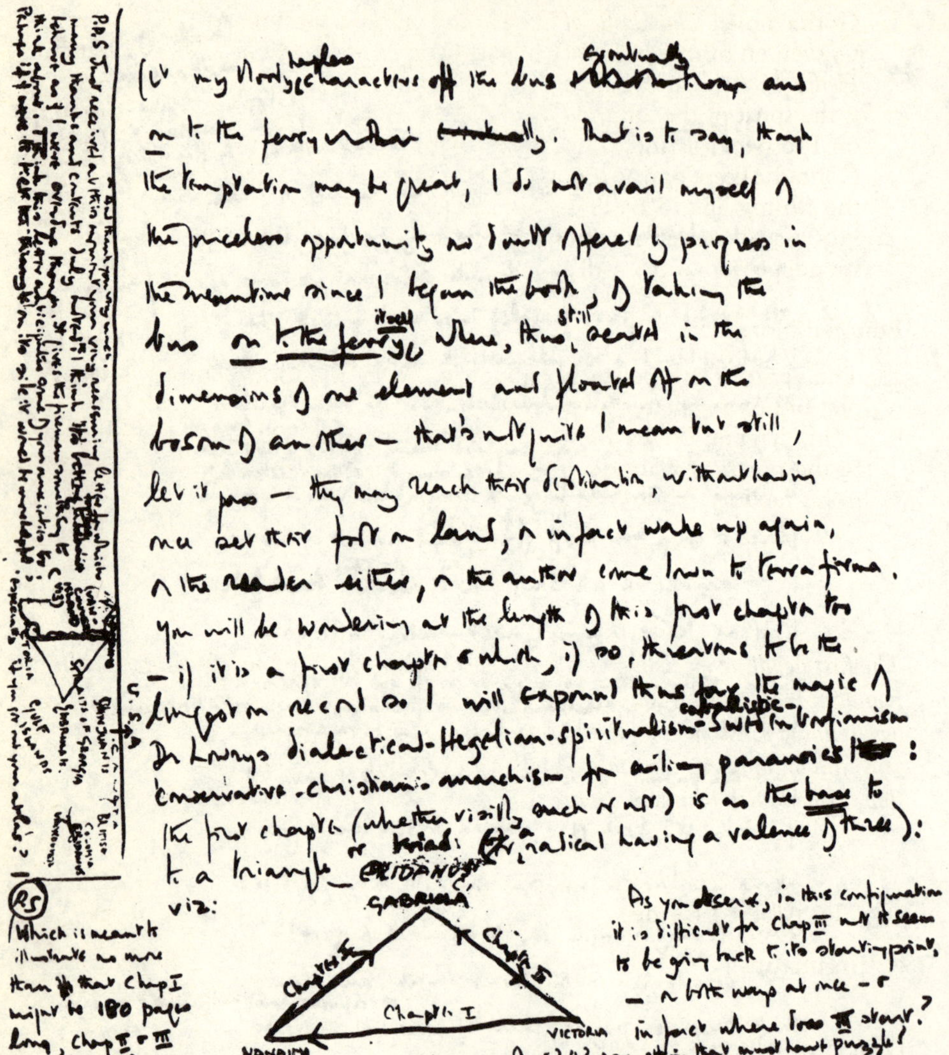

Figure 11

Annotations:

1 Lowry's opening flourish includes references to Horace Walpole's Gothic novel *The Castle of Otranto* and parodic allusions to Shakespeare. Gower, an officer in Henry V's army, appears briefly in *2 Henry IV* and *Henry V*. Ariel and Caliban are characters in *The Tempest* (1611); Ariel is the spirit of the air and Caliban is the savage, a figure of gross matter on Prospero's island. The 'tucket within' is a line Lowry shared with Conrad Aiken, and 'Ah gotta shake a wicked tail to get to Liverpool' is the closing line to Battle's song in *Lunar Caustic*.
2 No 'reassuring letter' from Erskine survives with the incoming correspondence.

Editorial Notes:

a. The verso of this pencil holograph is one of the most complex examples of Lowry's letters: see Figure 11.
b. In his diagram Lowry has put the United States and the San Juan Islands to the north of Gabriola instead of to the south, a mistake he corrects in his next letter (**595**) to Erskine.

*The first deadline for delivery of a completed manuscript in Lowry's contract with Random House was 1 November 1953. Instead of a manuscript, however, Lowry was sending Erskine small batches of draft material and letters (such as **595** and **598**) full of complex, convoluted plans for* October Ferry to Gabriola. *Neither 'bro. Albert' nor Random House would be reassured by these epistles.*

595: To Albert Erskine

P: Virginia(ms)   Dollarton
                                              [ca 2 November 1953]

Dear bro. Albert.

   The first 15 pages of the next section, which I fondly believed to be the finest piece of prose since Christ was an apprentice seaman, met with an unexpectedly dusty reception from Margie, who wanted me to cut it more than I was prepared to: so leaving it to simmer I have gone on without sending it & now think she's right, or right in so far that it was – it turned out – in the wrong place, and for another damn good reason too: on overhauling – in the sense of overtaking – my old final draft I found I had written almost the same thing further on but out of a lower drawer of inspiration, as it were: all of which makes for problems,

pleasant & by no means insuperable, but which have been responsible
for the delayed instalment. Meanwhile we are shifting to town for the
winter because of fuel problems so don't expect anything for a fortnight
or so even though another large chunk will be done; our new temporary
address has the following Jacobite-cum-Roast-Beef-of-old-England-
ring:[1]

    Caroline Court Aparts
      Suite no 73
        1058 Nelson Street
        Vancouver
          British Columbia.

And we move there sometime between the 11th & 15th of this
month, after or before which latter date anything going to our old
address will reach us not without some delay. Meantime too the health
is good, or at least mine is, my leg having improved to the extent that I
am to-day going to haul 1 cwt of coal ¾ of a mile through the forest, so
that there may be something to burn for whatever kind soul will light
an occasional fire in our absence, & (talking of fires) was in good shape
enough for me, on observing flames issuing from around the point, &
suspecting the village of which that afternoon I was the sole inhabitant,
Margie being in town apartment hunting, to be on fire, to high-tail it,
fire-extinguisher in hand (& notebook in pocket) in that direction: it
was a fishing-boat, a beautiful one we had often seen & admired, already
burning down to the water-line & with the local fire brigade (they
wouldn't send the Vancouver fireboat, which in any case had broken
down so they tried to save it by beaching it, not very thoughtfully, in
my opinion, under the trees) already on the spot, & a more melancholy
sight I have rarely witnessed, with the black clouds driving across the
mountains, just before dark, & the other fishing boats standing by drifting downstream & turning back, with their masthead lights going on
one by one like mourning candles lit by a taper & the boat burning
below seen through the trees & the dead salmon, the boat's last catch,
goggling in the water etc: bloody awful & still saddens me: so that will
probably get popped right into Gabriola too, & incidentally, though on
the spot myself, so great was the noise, & isolated the scene, & unknown
the participants, I have to look in to-days papers to see if anyone was
killed or hurt. But enough about the mountain scenery. Another problem (to tax mightier minds than mine, as I said) is why in my map I put
America *north* of Canada:[2] – well, brother, I kind of lost my compass
bearings tilting the triangle, in short it was, to say the least, a mistake.
There is a rough map of the terrain of Gabriola in last week's Newsweek
incidentally {not to say an article on the Elgin marbles in last weeks
Life.}. The lack of direct narrative I'm afraid you'll just have to bear it

for most of the first chapter, though I'm thinking to alleviate matters by dividing each of the three chapters into two, viz (2) (B) or (i) (ii) – though I have a great hatred of arbitrary gaps & divisions & or even parts & 'books' – but I hope to solve the problem sensibly & neatly – perhaps there will be two orders of division (α) (β) (γ) (δ) & I II III or 1,2,3 – to hell with this! – without too much of a typographic cauchemar[3] – God bless from & love from us both –

Malcolm

Annotations:

1 The Jacobites were supporters of the exiled James II of England and his grandson Charles Edward Stuart, 'Bonnie Prince Charlie,' whose rebellion in 1745-46 would have restored a 'Caroline Court.' English writer Henry Fielding (1707-54) intended to satirize patriotism in the song 'Roast Beef of Old England,' from his play *The Grub-Street Opera* (1731), but the song was immediately adopted by English audiences and remained a sentimental favourite through the nineteenth century.

2 See Lowry's 31 October 1953 letter (**594**) to Erskine and Figure 11.

3 *Cauchemar* is French for nightmare, and a plan such as Lowry sketches would indeed have been a 'typographic' nightmare.

596: To David Markson

P: UBC(ms)
PP: *SL* 348-50; *Lln* 204-05

[1058 Nelson St,]
[Vancouver, B.C.]
[November 1953][a]

Castle of Otranto
Tuesday. November. Midnight.
Wind. Thunder. Enter Gower & others.

Dear old Dave:
– Started this a week ago but have had one interruption after another, being both in the throes of a temporary move (our new stop-gap roast-beef of old-England-cum-Jacobite-address: The Caroline Court, 1058 Nelson St Suite #73 – Vancouver, B.C. – Ugh – but maybe we'll enjoy it, have a bath anyway, other than in the inlet, – getting a trifle chilly at this time of the year perhaps though I've had a few fine swims lately) & trying like hell to finish October Ferry to Gabriola. I'm very grieved to hear old Dylan's under the weather, if you can see him give him our love & best wishes for a speedy recovery: (you mention that he is [in] hospital with a '*brail*' ailment.★ Without conceding this to be a matter

of humour exactly or necessarily any way you look at it may I ask if you intimate an ailment 'as of one slightly blind' or that the old boy has actually got stranded in some Rolando's fissure or island of Reil?[1] Anyway I wouldn't trade his brain or braille for most other poets, drunk sober blind alive or dead, or all five simultaneously, as is more likely: – one imagines W.S [William Shakespeare] at moments not without his limbos or brails also – & you couldn't attribute that precisely to society either for he made pots of money. Es verdad.)[2] As for ourselves, we are very well, though Margie hasn't understandably reacquired any great love of dogs or myself of children playing Indians: I'm pretty lucky to be about again, for I smashed all available bones in the right leg and the ankle and dislocated the ankle on top of that with the foot pushed right out of line – basta. But I ran in 1 cwt of coal from the store to-day; do everything more or less normally with it, including swimming (& occasionaly, as I think, writing) though the damned limb will be a bit weak for a couple of years; – though I don't advise the experience on the whole, nothing in it. At any rate we still *got* it: touch wood, or rather the ivory of the revered gent from Nantucket, so we ought to be all right awhile, unless one of Margie's dogs bites it off, or I bite it off myself, all for the fun of having to chase myself to the Marquesas with a harpoon.[3] Nothing else of note: save when half through the first attempt at this letter, Margie being in town, & myself alone on the beach, on observing what appeared to be flames issuing round the point –

Well, brother, I hitailed it thither anyhow, fire-extinguisher in hand, (& not forgetting the notebook in pocket): – it wasn't a house, as I thought, but a ship, already burning down to the water-line, & which had been beached thoughtfully under the trees where a land fire-brigade (the fireboat from Vancouver having refused to come) had already failed to save it: when I say a ship, it was a fishing-boat, but with a great deal of top-hamper, alas all come crashing fierily down, & in fact it was a sad sight, as you can imagine, just before dark, with the wind & driving clouds over the mountains, & the mast-head lights of its companion fishing boats going on one by one like mourning candles, & the ferry passing silent as Charon's boat, though nobody we knew: – which reminds me that the boat of happy Port Moody memory (before I forget, the reason that wharf was so *long* was it was built to accomodate windjammers when Port Moody was the terminus of the CPR before Vancouver was built)[4] – has to be brought up to the platform to-morrow at high tide – she is banging away merrily down there, but it's too much of a good thing in the winter: said craft sends the best of love as do Margie & myself, not to mention the house which is leaking, as is the boat for that matter –

Malcolm

P.S. No, I haven't read Augie March.[5] And I'd be very grateful if you'd send me a list of books, poets, mags authors, *to* read: – of what you conceive worth reading during the last years – some time when you have the mind to, for we're both falling badly out of touch, all too easy a thing to do in these parts, & quite apart from anything else, as Ghandi once observed, 'I see no point in being ill-informed.'[6] Hope Dylan is OK.

* I wrote this Tuesday night – yesterday – did not find out till just now, Wednesday, to our great grief, Dylan is dead. Sad news was brought by a Canadian writer who has settled transiently some doors away & we drank his health poured a libation of gin to his memory on the platform & for some reason cut down a tree, likewise dead, & an old friend, but which has long since seemed asking us to pluck up the courage to cut it down, rather than let it fall down, since the only way it could fall was through our roof. There is no symbolic significance attached to the tree: unless one had felt as a reaction to the black news one had to do something exhilarating lifegiving painful death dealing dangerous & useful all at once. Selah. I see no point in changing the letter to you, though we sense how you must feel his loss hardly on the spot & sympathise deeply. God damn it all, what a misery-grisery it all is sometimes as the Sultan of Zanzibar says in this weeks New Yorker.[7] (About five minutes after that bad news, too, incidentally, to descend from the immortal to the unusual, we get our first good news in years: Philip Rahv of Partisan Review takes Bravest Boat; Dirty Degenerate Bobs anthologised in Italy etc etc.)[8]

P.P.S. Received your last & very good letter just as we were moving to town, taking this letter with me – but by mistake (or as a protective talisman) leaving yours behind on the table of the shack, together with your address, of which (since I'd got used to the old one) I'm not absolutely sure. Margie is going out over the weekend to collect some things & your letter so, damn it, this must wait till then.

P.P.P.S. Margie just came back from the shack, bearing your last note, for which thanks, but not your other letter, which *still* remains there as a talisman. Your last note hasn't your home address on it, so I'm sending this to the printing & litho.

Annotations:

1 Lowry's friend from the thirties, Dylan Thomas, collapsed into a coma and died in New York on 9 November 1953 from a combination of alcohol and a drug injection. He had been seriously ill for several days. The terms 'Rolando's fissure' and the 'island of Reil' refer to parts of

the brain named after the nineteenth-century physicians Luigi Rolando and Johann C. Reil, who discovered them; see also Lowry's 19 April 1946 letter (**216**) to Dr E.B. Woolfan.

2 *Es verdad* is Spanish for 'it is true.'

3 Both the 'gent from Nantucket' (Captain Ahab) and being chased 'with a harpoon' are Lowryan allusions to *Moby-Dick*.

4 Port Moody, a small community on Burrard Inlet east of Dollarton, was the destination of a memorable row-boat outing on which Lowry took the city-bred Markson during his August 1952 visit.

5 The *Adventures of Augie March* (1953) is a novel by Saul Bellow.

6 Mohandas Karamchand Ghandi (1869-1948) was a lawyer, pacifist, and architect of Indian independence from Britain, which was proclaimed on 15 August 1947. The poet Rabindranath Tagore first called Ghandi *Mahatma*, meaning 'great soul.'

7 See Lowry's 30 October 1953 letter (**593**) to William and Alice McConnell.

8 'The Bravest Boat' was accepted by Philip Rahv (1908-73), the founder of *Partisan Review*, for publication in 21.3 (1954): 275-88. 'Dirty Degenerate Bobs' is Lowry's joking reference to 'Strange Comfort Afforded by the Profession,' where the phrase 'dirty Degenerate Bobs' appears as graffiti; the story, translated by Giorgio Monicelli, was published in *Carosello di narratori Inglese*, edited by Aldo Martello (Milan 1954).

Editorial Notes:

a. This single-sheet holograph (UBC 3:6) is a fine example of a Lowry letter-in-progress. The main text plus first postscript and starred note regarding the news of Dylan Thomas's death are in pencil, the latter squeezed into the left margin of the recto. The second postscript, in blue ink, has been squeezed into the right margin of the recto, and the third postscript is in blue ink at the top of the verso. The letter was written over a period of a week in early November. Excerpts were published in French translation in *Les Lettres nouvelles* 5 (1960): 204-05.

597: To Eva and Philippe Thoby-Marcelin

P: UBC(card phc)

1058 Nelson St,
Vancouver, B.C.,
Canada
16 December 1953

Joyeux Noel & With all best love & luck to Eva & Phi-to
from
Malcolm and Margerie

598: To Albert Erskine

P: Virginia(ts); UBC(phc)

'Lieben',
Bowen Island,
British Columbia
[27 December 1953][a]

Dear Albert:

I know. You've caught me at a bad time to write a letter like because I have to catch a boat to an island whence the posts are few and far between. In fact a December Ferry to Bowen Island.[1] Of October Ferry – of which I've just completed another 40 pages I'm going to try and get off by the New Year I'd say, counting those 40, (which are new and written in the last 5 days and concern an outbreak of Fortean phenomena[2] following the Llewelyn's fire in Niagara-on-the-Lake) I'd say it's not quite half through: say 400-450 pages in all. For the rest I'm getting it in readable form as quickly as I can, albeit I'm dependent on Margie for the final typing. I do nothing but work on it and am suffering slightly from battle fatigue: otherwise fine. At the present rate I hope to get you another hundred pages by the extended deadline. I hadn't counted on the extensive revisions in final typing I've had to make or I'd say it could be finished by then. In the sense that there is an all but final draft complete and detailed down to the final sentence I'd say too it was *already* finished. But that reckons without hitches, also 'inspirations' such as the last week's. Where it insists on growing I have to give it its head. Not too much! As things stand it should be finished sometime in April, that is to say, six weeks 'late': but it might be a little earlier or later. As for where the story's going there an excellent and sinister reason for its apparent inability to move into the future: it turns out that both characters are potential suicides. Each has also become afraid that in a fit of hysteria or drunkenness one may murder the other. Thus the difficulty of the future taking any shape at all, as of the present having any meaning for the protagonists, is really the whole plot. They have more trouble getting to Gabriola than K to the castle though Gabriola is not a castellan symbol;[3] it *is*, finally, the future. It also turns out that both characters are hopped up to the gills: that is Ethan only doesn't realise he's got a hangover till a little later because he's been stealing Jacqueline's barbiturates. However I'm only equipped to write all this: not to describe it. I believe it to be bloody good and that it gets better. But it's not intended to fall into any particular category or obey any of the normal rules of a novel. The second part of the book concerns their difficulty in finding the ferry and takes place in Nanaimo, mostly in a pub, where Ethan gets pretty tight; there are powerful dramatic scenes (though I sez it) in Nanaimo both in the present and the past: a scene of lyrical beauty is balanced against a Grand Guignol horror that takes place on the scaffold. (A waiter turns out to be a man Ethan's saved.) The third part is on board the Ferry itself. There is a long scene here where Ethan is tempted to commit suicide but the ferry, which has run into a storm has to turn back, less for this reason than because one of the passengers has a haemmorrage. Back in Nanaimo, at a crisis of double despair, while the sick woman is being transferred to the dock, the mainland evening papers, which have just come, are tossed aboard and they read that the inhabitants of Eridanus have a reprieve and may go on living there. This is correlative to a decision Ethan (who you learn has become a complete misanthrope by this time and though managing to keep himself in balance with barbiturates is dangerously close to a serious breakdown) to go publicly to the defense of a 15 year old boy sentenced to hang, and endeavour to procure a reprieve for *him*. He has not been able to bring himself to do this formerly because he has feared that the publicity would draw attention to the fact he lived in Eridanus and hence that of the newspapers once more to the uneasy lot of the squatters on the beach, and prejudice even further the public against them. The storm has now dropped and the ferry once more proceeds to Gabriola but the whole book, and with it the ferry – something like those ships you see rising with the filling locks in the Panama Canal – now rises to another plane: whereas before the ferry was a Charon's boat proceeding to a kind of hell, now it is another sort of ferry proceeding, as it were, toward the Mount of Purgatory (Mount Baker).[4] With this too, Gabriola loses its ambivalence on the lower plane: assumes it on a higher. Centrally and realistically it becomes now the accepted future. Meantime – if you've followed that – you can see that effect of the glorious news of Eridanus' own reprieve upon Ethan must be anything but what the reader has been led to expect. He is, in fact, knocked out literally. To save them both he has already had to 'renounce' Eridanus (on the psychological plane an infantile fixation, so far as it is that I mean.) Now he has to come to terms with himself and accept the fact that he has become too mentally ill to live there, even should they return. It is he and no one else that produces the so-called coincidences and disasters that happen to them: himself, as it were, the paranoiac black magician of their own lives. He has to face the fact also that he actually is – or has been – next door to a murderer and a criminal himself in the case of Cordwainer:[5] though it's time he stopped punishing himself – he's had 20 years of penal servitude already – and others for it, including Cordwainer himself, who appears in a dream to him on the ferry boat (Scrubby the barman in Outward Bound – you might expect to find him on a ferry boat)[6] to inform him that in so far as Ethan had murdered him, he had saved him from the lot of a suicide in the next world, where he would be quite content, if Ethan's continued self-punishment did not keep drawing him down to this world: if Ethan should kill himself he would thus be turning Cordwainer's spirit into Ethan's murderer. Ethan as a consequence has to renounce not only Eridanus but his destructive life and ways: among other things he has to stop drinking and I hope that the poor bugger reaches this decision with the maximum of humour. The end is thus a kind of Volcano in reverse and the final theme Faustian, with everything from flights of angels, balls of fire, and Madonnas, to the intervention of grace and the Himmelphart.[7] The ferry reaches Gabriola at dusk, where those meeting the boat are swinging lanterns along the wharf: but you have the feeling that Ethan is now being received by mankind, that arms are stretched out to help him, help he now has to and is prepared to accept, as he is prepared to give help to man, whom he had formerly grown to hate so much: thus the characters journey toward their own recovery. Something like that. I haven't told it very well. I'm sorry I'm late with it. The book loses something by not being with its fellows: Forest Path to the Spring, Ghostkeeper, and Present Estate of Pompeii. Also the idea of Hear Us is closer than ever to my heart now I see – touch wood – I can finish this which I have several times thought was going to polish me off.

I have sent an S.O.S. to my bank in England who now owe me a hell of a lot of money I've made repeated applications for in vain – I'll inform you of the results, – with the hope of being able to buy some time or otherwise help to amortize my obligation to you which I am carrying out as faithfully as possible, though I don't see why I should assume you or others will be satisfied with its progress even though I love Gabriola. Should you have to cut me off I'll find some way of carrying on. About all I can say is that if Gabriola can't be all in on the already extended dot – should I abandon temporarily the project of the other stories in Hear Us – and should you choose to consider Gabriola as a separate novel (which of course it is too), that being delivered, I oughn't to have much difficulty in having the revised Lunar Caustic, say, in by the next deadline.

God bless and Happy Christmas from us both –

Malcolm

P.S. Partisan Review just took The Bravest Boat!

P.P.S. I haven't said anything of the psychological level on which October Ferry takes place but I now think I should, since on rereading this letter I perceived that described in this manner, some doubt might be cast upon the author's sanity, let alone that of the chief protagonist.

Moreover on this plane the whole thing can be read slightly differently and in a sense more hopefully, as a kind of abreaction of his past: I like the word cathexis, too. In some psycho-genetic sense also – if that's the word? – the news of their own reprieve (on this plane) would seem to precipitate Ethan's recovery, in the way that shell-shocked soldiers may recover at the news of the armistice. (Actually this is the scene – following that news – of the perilous chapel; a scene intended to be, and which is, I hope, horrifying, in which Ethan is actually involved in a grapple with death:) For the rest, though I haven't been slap through my 3 philosophical poets lately, you better consult that work by Santayana.[8] In brief: the future, once accepted in this case, imposes its own teleology; thus – though I have the data on the subject I don't a la Simenon[9] bother to analyse in either case, what one could conceive to be the original kobbold in the closet.[10] Both protagonists lie to themselves, perhaps they will have to continue to do so. Our expression is the ancient psychiatric one that it is nobler to do so than to make a suicide pact, and the meaning widens on the reader's soul as he realises what I mean by eviction.

Annotations:

1 The Lowrys spent the holidays with Muriel and Einar Neilson.
2 Charles Hay Fort (1874-1932), the American author and science critic, published four studies of unusual scientific phenomena: *The Book of the Damned* (1919), *New Lands* (1923), *Lo!* (1931), and *Wild Talents* (1932). All four were re-issued in a single volume, *The Books of Charles Fort*, by the Fortean Society in 1941, and Margerie had given Lowry a copy of this volume for Christmas. The study of greatest interest to Lowry is *Wild Talents*, in which Fort explores the mysterious forces that cause apparently inexplicable series of fires and the 'fire-inducing power' of certain people; see *October Ferry*, chapter 20.
3 In Franz Kafka's *The Castle* 'K' is constantly frustrated in his attempts to enter a mysterious castle to work as a land surveyor. The castle, run by a complicated, incompetent bureaucracy, could symbolize many things, from an incomprehensible God to the conditions of contemporary existence.
4 Mount Baker, one of the highest peaks in the Cascade Mountain range, lies just south of the Canada-United States border, where its snow-capped peak is visible from Vancouver on a clear day. According to the legends of the local Squamish and Lummis people, Mount Baker was all that remained above the surface of the waters after a great flood; thus, it is similar to Mount Ararat in western legend.
5 Peter Cordwainer is a friend of Ethan's who had committed suicide, and Ethan feels haunted by Cordwainer's reproachful spirit. This aspect

of *October Ferry* owes much to Lowry's experience of Paul Fitte's suicide at Cambridge in November 1929; see Bradbrook, 113-15.

6 *Outward Bound* (1924), a play by English writer Sutton Vane (1888-1963), is about a group of dead people on a ferry bound for Hell. The passengers include a couple who have committed suicide and a drunk who will have to forgo his booze. The barman, Scrubby, is the only one who knows from the start of the voyage where the passengers are headed. A film version, which Lowry saw, was released in 1930.

7 *Himmelphart*, literally 'journey to heaven,' is the German term for the Ascension. At the end of part 1 of Goethe's *Faust* Marguerite is gathered up to heaven, much as Yvonne feels herself to be at the end of chapter 11 of *Under the Volcano*.

8 George Santayana published *Three Philosophical Poets: Lucretius, Dante and Goethe* in 1910.

9 Georges Simenon (1903-89), the Belgian-born French novelist, wrote over two hundred novels featuring Inspector Maigret.

10 In German folklore, a *kobold* is a mischievous spirit that haunts houses, mines, or underground places.

Editorial Notes:

a.   This date is from the envelope postmark. The Lowrys went to Bowen Island for a Christmas holiday, and this letter is on Einar Neilson's letterhead. 'Lieben,' meaning 'to love' in Danish, is the name of the Neilsons' home.

Although the exact nature of the 'misery-grisery' that Lowry complains of in the following letter to the Neilsons is not clear, he and Margerie were very short of money again, and Lowry was also worried about his failure to meet the 1 November 1953 deadline in his Random House contract. When Lowry says that 'All is very well now,' he is probably referring to news of money on its way from England, the money that led him to write Erskine on 4 January (600) to suggest that Random House suspend payments. All would not be well for long, however. On 8 January he received Erskine's letter suspending payments but not acknowledging receipt of Lowry's request for just such a step. Lowry was devastated. 1954 had begun badly, and with uncanny prescience Lowry adorned this note to the Neilsons with a picture of an avalanche sliding down the page.

599: To Einar and Muriel Neilson

P: UBC(ms)   #73 The Caroline Court,
                                                        1058 Nelson St,
                                                             Vancouver
                                                        [January 1954]

Very dear Einar & Muriel.
    Please forgive our lack of word.
    We will explain later – whether in contractual terms or those of
haemorraghes, & other harassments or Acts of God, at least it was not in
terms of Mrs Bell.[1] But we had such an unconscionable amount of
misery-grisery & anxiety descend on us round the New Year that we
didn't even have the heart even to write you for the very merry Xmas
you gave us so kindly; we knew that you would understand the silence
& forgive us. All is very well now. Hope to see one or other of you
soon. This isn't such a bad address
                            EFFRLY Co
                    Love
                                            Malcolm & Margie

Annotations:

    1 The ominous 'Mrs Bell' was an officious neighbour at Dollarton, and
       thus a generic term for harassment.

600: To Albert Erskine

P: Virginia(ts); UBC(phc)   #73 The Caroline Court.
PP: *SL* 353-54   1058 Nelson St,
                                                   Vancouver, B.C.,
                                                             Canada
                                                       4 January 1954

Dear Albert:
    I have received a letter from the Westminster Bank, Liverpool, dated
23 December, saying in part:
    'The Bank and Mr S.O. [Stuart Osborne] Lowry have now been
appointed Trustees of your settled share of your father's residuary estate
but unfortunately the transfer of the investment certificates into the
names of the new Trustees has not yet been completed. The Trust
Solicitors hope to be in a position to send us all documents during the
next few weeks. In the meantime, we have asked them to make you a
further payment out of income held by the previous Trustees and they
will remit you the sum of £500 during the next few days. As soon as the

investments and remaining cash have been handed over to us, we will make you a further payment of income on hand.'

So far the £500 has not arrived, but the news seems straight from the horse's mouth this time, and undoubtedly the money has been just held up over the Holidays. I have been expecting this news for some time and it would have saved me a lot of worry if it had come before: the delay was caused in part because my mother died intestate; and there have been so many changes in the trusteeship, each trustee having passed the buck – my bucks too – to the other when a definite statement was requested. And of course there has been England's policy of making everything as difficult as possible for the ex-landed gentry – not unpoetic justice, on paper, so long as the cash doesn't happen to be one's own.

However it now appears that I am in a position to propose what I have long planned under the circumstances: to make some guarantee of good faith by 'buying some time,' I mean by voluntarily requesting that your monthly payments to me be suspended for a period of time, while I go on working on my own hook, and I believe there is a clause in the contract something to this effect.

Last year, what with getting out of debt and the unforseen expense of 'neck and leg break' (as Christopher Isherwood somewhere calls it), not to mention the actual time lost on my work by said leg break, what money I did get from England was not sufficient to allow me to make this proposal, and my other auxiliary efforts, such as the Canadian fellowship which would have left me free to work, came to naught.

This year it looks as though I shall be able to carry on, though *how* long I could carry on without anxiety depends on the last sentence I quoted from the Bank's letter. At any rate I propose that you suspend payments to me from next month until at least you've received delivery of October Ferry, and some more practical earnest of what shape the work that follows will take.

For one thing any estimate of Ferry made on the basis of what you have received may be unfair to the work itself, whose form is of necessity bizarre, and goes on getting more so for a while; moreover I may have got one chunk – the next you will receive – in the wrong place; – moreover there'll naturally be some editing necessary when it is completed. Anyway such a proposal as this will at least have the virtue of putting me on my metal not to break another leg, at least until *this* work is in. I hope I haven't meantime put you in the unpleasant position of having had to write me yourself that this, or something even more stern, is what has already been regrettably – or even regretfully – decided by Random House, with the result that these letters cross.[1]

All the very best from us both –

Malcolm

Annotations:

1 Sadly, this is what happened; see Lowry's 26 January 1954 letter (**603**) to Erskine.

601: To Albert Erskine

P: Virginia(ts); UBC(phc)　　　　　　　　#73 The Caroline Court,
PP: *SL* 354-55　　　　　　　　　　　　　　*1058* Nelson St,
　　　　　　　　　　　　　　　　　　　　　Vancouver, B.C.,
　　　　　　　　　　　　　　　　　　　　　Canada
　　　　　　　　　　　　　　　　　　　　4 January 1954

Personal P.S. for Albert –　or:

　　　　　　　　　　　　　　　　TEN FIFTY EIGHT MAY ARRIVE
　　　　　　　　　　　　　　　　　　　ON THE DATE

Dear Albert:　　　　　　　　BUT FIFTEEN O'EIGHT WILL
　　　　　　　　　　　　　　　ALWAYS BE LATE
　　Enclosed speaks for　　　LAND ON *NOBODY'S* PLATE
itself:[1] is pursuant on the　　SAVE ITS SENDERS WHO WAIT
other, that I hadn't per-　　　– OH INDIRECTORATE
haps kept *im*personal enough.　WITH A HAND ON'T LIKE FATE!
　　Meantime I'm just hop-　　– OR SOME BARTLEBY FATE
ing to god all this hasn't　　FOR PO' FIFTEEN O' EIGHT!
embarrassed you too much.

By ill chance – see poetical explanation opposite – your personal letter didn't arrive here till today, January 4.[2] You *re*addressed it also 1508; – but with sage afterthought also The Caroline Court. (Technically The Caroline Court, Nelson St, ought to do it without any number or vice versa, but not 1508 by itself which is an unfortunate combination that doesn't exist in Nelson St else might have found me)

Perhaps all the work on Dark as the Grave, Mordida etc. was worth mentioning: there's at least 2000 pages more of stuff, Margie estimates, reposing now in the Bank Vault, done contemporaneously, impossible to send as is, but it was impossible to proceed before it was at least as safe as that. I'll have more to say on Gabriola later: and more to send. Meantime I'm more concerned, as I say, that your kind concern for me may have embarrassed you.

So this in haste.

All the very best love from us both –

　　　　　　　　　　　　　　　　　　　　　　　　Malcolm

Annotations:

1 Enclosed with this letter was Lowry's 4 January 1954 letter (**600**) explaining his financial situation and proposing a suspension of payments on his contract with Random House.

2 In his 18 December 1953 letter, delayed because of an incorrect address, Erskine warned Lowry that he was overdue on his deadlines for delivery of manuscript and that he had to present Lowry's position at an 'official review.' He asked Lowry to clarify his plans and progress as specifically as possible, but Lowry's 27 December 1953 letter (**598**) did not allay concerns at Random House. The arrival of Erskine's 6 January 1954 letter announcing the decision to suspend the contract was a shock.

602: To Harold Matson

P: Matson(ts); UBC(phc)
PP: *SL* 355-61

#73, The Caroline Court,
1058 Nelson St,
Vancouver, B.C.,
Canada
25 January 1954

Dear Hal –

This is in reply to yours of Jan. 11, though I had already begun a letter to you re Random etc. Yes, thank you, we received the January installment.

The situation as it has arisen with Random House is a complex one which has been brewing for several months and about whose possible onset I had, in fact, repeatedly written Albert.[1] In the light of what has happened I would have finished my letter to you but that I was awaiting a reply before doing so from Albert to an important official letter I wrote him on *Jan. 4th*: moreover I was too deep in work to write any more letters if I could avoid it. There has been no reply, and there being no evidence in your letter that Albert has explained my side of the question fully to you (I don't mean this in any derogatory sense to him) I'm put in the ungrateful position of having to explain it myself. Since it seems to me I am more in the right than the wrong, and even the object of some injustice, while my gratitude to Albert remains great and we are of course friends, I'd therefore be obliged if you'd keep this confidential – I mean as between Albert and yourself – the only thing not confidential presumably being my official letter of Jan. 4, which I'm including a copy of. You may wonder why I hadn't written you before, as normally speaking I should have, as I said, but now, in any case, I owe it to you, and myself, to give you all the facts and factors, but I want it understood that I do so with no implied disloyalty to Albert. Now I'll be brief as possible.

I'd intended to complete the collection of short stories and novellas, Hear Us Oh Lord, as the first book, and for this to be delivered, being conscious of my obligation, on November 1. However, when working on the penultimate story I found, as I told you, the material developing and growing and presently I realised I had a full dress novel on my hands which I was so deeply involved with by that time it would have been fatal to stop. Moreover, this together with the last three novellas, more or less completed, made yet another sort of novel, and in fact Hear Us itself, the stories therein, began to take on an interrelated form as a work of art it had not possessed before: and some of these pieces might be publishable by themselves, particularly Gabriola. Albert seemed pretty tepid about the stories and I gained the impression, or formed it, it might be better to kick off with a new and finished novel, whether this later would form part of the collection or not. Moreover in this way I saw myself eventually considerably exceeding the terms of the contract. (Meanwhile it is important to remember that I never, consciously, gave either you or Albert the impression – and I think my former letters bear me out in this – that sooner or later I might not choose to go on by myself for awhile, without the payments, to gain time, and without the clause which gives me that right I never could have honorably signed the contract, especially after the discouraging experience with Brace.[2] And to this end I have kept hammering away at my English bank to hurry the settlement of the estate and send me the money owing me.)

Meantime Gabriola continued to develop and grow more serious, and about this time I (we, for Margie was bitten by a dog the same day and was in hospital with me) had my cursed accident.[3] Despite a broken and dislocated leg and ankle I tried to keep on working after the interim in the hospital, as I had even in hospital, but I'd lost the feel of the work, it was a ghastly and painful summer and altogether I'd say this set me back at least 3 months, looking back on it now, and whatever I may have said or felt at the time. You'll remember when signing the contract we suggested there should be some provision in case of serious accident or illness, and you and Albert decided this should be left up to the understanding or whatever of the publishers. I think I ought to point out that no one seems to have taken any account either of this time lost, or that I did not invoke any such unwritten contractual provision, though my accident could scarcely have been more serious, especially coming at that time, and one reason I didn't invoke it was that one's own anticipation of such a thing had seemed too much like clair-voyance, the accident itself too diabolically pat, psychologically suspect to another, though there was really no damn psychology about it, as I should know! However I had and have no intention of using this as an alibi. I merely state I don't find it sporting it should be entirely overlooked when there arose a question of the deadline.

During the summer I wrote Albert two or three letters re the general situation, not losing sight of the Nov. date, and received no reply. (He was away and the letters weren't forwarded.) This was discouraging, but on emergence into convalescence I may have grown too optimistic again (this time to yourselves) about my chances of getting it in on the dot. By the end of September, realising now it might not be possible to have it ready in final and negotiable form, I wrote Albert again and received a reassuring reply, not to worry.[4] Finally, in October I think, after I'd delivered an installment of over 100 pages, Albert wrote saying he'd thought the November date was merely a date I'd set myself, but had looked up my contract and discovered that Nov. 1 was there all right, but that there was a three months grace period, and *they could not 'call me' before February 1*. I felt confident that by February 1 I could have enough in that would put their eye out, even if it were not quite finished.

However, and this is important, having been in touch with my English bank, I felt I would be in a position by February 1 to buy some time – a supposition in which I've proved right, as you'll see – and my intention all along was to show my good faith by buying some time *anyway*, even if Gabriola was finished. Had Albert's letter been urgent re the deadline, I should have taken a chance and asked you to call the changes there and then and stop payments, and would have done so anyhow before that had not the accident taken most of my ready cash.

I hope this makes it clear that I have been extremely conscious of my obligation to Albert, Random, and yourself.

Just before Christmas I received an official letter from Albert written a week before that, saying that the Keeper of the Contracts had questioned him, and that the material in hand seemed to need more buttressing if they were going to extend the payments beyond February 1., the killing tone of which letter made us want to fall out of the window rather than take anything off the Christmas tree.[5] I immediately replied, outlining the novel [*October Ferry to Gabriola*] and saying I expected to have another 140 pages in by February 1.[6] His personal letter, (which of course mollified matters somewhat) further qualifying the situation Albert had sent to the wrong address, – was returned to him, sent back to me, and didn't reach us till after the first of January. A stroke of evil luck, & we may have been to blame by putting the wrong number on the envelope.

By this time I'd heard from my bank, promising me some money in a few days. I therefore, on *January 4*, wrote Albert another official letter, with a covering personal one, voluntarily suggesting that they suspend payments at least until I'd finished Gabriola and they could see better what I was doing. This letter I enclose. Personally I have a high regard for the work sent in, as I do for Gabriola as a publishable entity, but I felt it extremely unfair Gabriola be judged on those 159 pages Albert had, and a hundred times unfairer that *all* the work be judged by it. More of this later.

The immediate point is, Albert must have received this letter by the 6th of January. But now, on the 8th of January I received another official letter, with a covering personal one, saying *they* had decided to suspend payments, and of a chilliness beyond all chilliness. It appeared I had not only laid a Great Auk's Egg, but where, even, was the Egg?[7] Your letter is dated January 11, and I do not understand why Albert has not informed you of having received my letter, written 2 days *before* theirs, asking them to stop payments, for it makes a serious difference. The reason why I didn't inform you myself I hope you'll now understand. It was all sprung on me at once. Having completely accepted Albert's former reassurances I thought, even after the first official letter, I had until *February 1*. I thought too, even now, my own request to buy time would be well *in time*; as it turns out I was mistaken, and too late as it was. I hope you'll understand all this.

Naturally it is distressing, as well as psychologically mortifying, not that the payments should be suspended a while – for that is no more than I have consistently, even wishfully anticipated, could I carry on without – but that it should be done in such a fashion that it carries the direct implication of irresponsibility in this regard on my part, when the fact is I have been writing Albert about it since last summer and even before. Against this is the fact that Albert has been motivated, amid many troubles of his own, by great kindness and understanding in trying to mitigate just such worry; once having helped so generously to get the boat launched he didn't want to rock it.

Without losing sight of this for a moment, or that I am sure he thought he was acting in my best interests, all I can say is that in this instance he didn't think *enough* and I shall say this to him. For though I speak only of the embarrassment to him in the letter enclosed, should what has happened happen, what about the worse than embarrassment to me? There was plenty of time in the interim to have given me an opportunity to do it myself, which was precisely what I did do the first moment the final urgency of the situation became clear. Which leaves me with the feeling that they weren't even acquainted with my willingness to do it, if necessary and possible, otherwise what point was there in making it appear something like a punishment, as well as an impugning of the work in question? I don't see that it's even good business. For how the hell did they suppose I was going to finish it at all, since they didn't know I would have the money to carry on? Perhaps they thought discouragement of this kind, all of a sudden, would give them a better opportunity of getting their money back. For bear in mind that, after Albert's letter relieving me of the tension of the November 1 deadline, up to the time of his letter received round about Christmas Eve, it was our impression gained from that letter there was nothing in the contract that obliged me to have sent in a goddam page until the deadline, which was (now) February 1. Who knows what I couldn't have finished by then hadn't this happened? One consequence has been I've had to write so many worrying and complex letters that the section that was actually finished before the New Year is only reaching its final typing now. And then on top of this to be *judged* by what I'd already sent in, which so far as I knew I didn't have to send in at all!

Perhaps I could have laughed this off but on top of this to receive no reply whatsoever to the letter cutting myself off seems a little too much. For I think morally this is where the situation should stand and I repeat it makes a serious difference. That finally they did not cut me off. I cut myself off. My letter to them concerning this is dated Jan. 4. Albert's to me the 6th. What arises to us from this is that if the author is gentleman enough to ask the publishers to suspend their payments on his work, the publishers should be sporting enough to suspend their judgement on it, if only that some damaging gossip doesn't get round through the grapevine that might injure one's chances of selling anything, say, to the Signet outfit.[7]

Of that judgement, which is so far unfavorable, or non-existent, I'll speak briefly. It is discouraging, but I'm not really dismayed. Gabriola won't admit of any stock responses to it, as a novel of situation, character, et al. It's probably hard to read, as the Volcano was, and for some people harder, if they're not to some extent pre-sold on the reward they may have should they read it. Probably they're quite right that it isn't a 'good' book. It isn't. It doesn't aim to be, but thinks of itself as a classic. (Especially and/or also in conjunction with its fellows.) The impression arises from the dim view so far taken of it (in my more humble moments) that I may have made some elementary mechanical mistake as to the disposition or order of narrative, but I'm not particularly worried about it since, if so, it should be easy to correct. The part I'm just sending in, of which you'll have a copy, should convince you that if the narrative doesn't move horizontally it certainly can move, if in a bizarre fashion, vertically.

For the rest the Volcano, even so viewed in bits and pieces (or even – er – not viewed in bits and pieces) might have caused anyone to take a dim view of it. I have the feeling, though I may be wrong, that

Mr Haas himself rejected the Volcano. On my side I'm not impugning anyone's powers of reading, least of all Albert's, who must express his honest opinion, but I can't see it would have been much different of the Volcano under these circumstances.

As for the rest ingratitude is not among my vices, and I remain extremely grateful to Mr Haas and Random House for their financial assistance. Deo volens,[9] they will more than get it back in the end.

The section sent off to Albert simultaneously with this letter which was finished before Christmas, brings the final typed Gabriola to 206 pages. But for this we should have reached about 350 {the complete Gabriola as it stands now runs around 500 pages} pages by now. Margie is making you an extra copy of this last section, a story in itself, called The Element Follows You Around, Sir,[10] and you'll have it in a few days, I hope, though we're snowed in, the planes are all grounded, not even trains are running, and in fact the elements are following us around, sir. I'm very sorry indeed for any collateral harrassment any of this may have caused you. With all the very best from us both,

Malcolm

Annotations:

1 In his 6 January 1954 letter Albert Erskine informed Lowry that Random House had decided 'to suspend . . . the monthly payments, and to review the question again when enough of the manuscript [of *October Ferry*] is available.'

2 See Lowry's 24 March 1952 letter (**513**) to Robert Giroux.

3 See Lowry's dramatic description of these events in his July 1953 letter (**584**) to Erskine.

4 See Lowry's 14 October 1953 letter (**591**) to Erskine. Very few of Erskine's letters to Lowry are extant from the summer and fall of 1953, and none could be construed as 'reassuring.'

5 In his 18 December 1953 letter, Erskine warned Lowry that 'the Keeper of the Contracts' had reminded him that Lowry was already six weeks behind schedule – that is, beyond the 1 November date for delivery of a manuscript.

6 See Lowry's 27 December 1953 letter (**598**) to Erskine.

7 Lowry's image of himself as a great auk, a species extinct since the 1840s, makes his joke bitterly ironic.

8 Signet publishes paperback imprints for New American Library in the United States and Penguin Publishing in England.

9 The correct Latin, *Deo volente*, means 'God willing.'

10 'The Element Follows You Around, Sir!' became chapter 18 of the published text of *October Ferry to Gabriola*, but it was first published as a short story in *Show Magazine* 4.3 (March 1964): 45-103.

603: To Albert Erskine

P: Virginia(ts); UBC(phc)
PP: *SL* 361–64

#73 The Caroline Court,
1058 Nelson St,
Vancouver, B.C.,
Canada
26 January 1954

My god, you old rapscallion. I don't mean that I'm really distressed by the set-back, am not over sensitive (like hell I'm not, as you once observed,[1] in fact my throte is only cutte unto the nekke bone)[2] but if it was all going to be done as rapidly as that, and *like* that, couldn't *you* have called *me* somehow, so that I would have been given more of a chance to call myself, being given credit at least for trying to move hell so to do, and then, in fact, finally for doing it, which I morally did, for my letter was posted on Jan 4, yours to me on the 6th: or if not for doing it at least acknowledgement that I'd done it, or if not acknowledgement that I'd done it, at least some to Hal, who writes me on the 11th, and is still in the dark, though I can see opposing ethical obliquities there that might have prevented you. But which (I've postponed writing him till today, awaiting some answer, the 25th) has given me no choice but to write him a letter (but to be strictly confidential between him and yourself) saying that though I love you only second to Jesus, and will always be grateful to you to my dying day, as I am, blow me down – complete shit though I felt in having to say so – if I don't think you much at fault in letting this happen *like* this, so that such shades of ignominy surround your ambassador to oblivion, who was not even given the opportunity to save his face: (but what of Hal's face?) or if you couldn't help its happening like this, it seems to me as I said you should have replied to my last official and personal letter, of too clairvoyant eye, suggesting the suspension myself.[3] On top of this – though I haven't looked at the contract again – and though technically I may be (as I thought) at fault – or even completely at fault – in not having the thing ready for publication by Nov. 1, does it seem altogether fair to judge a fellow on merely what he'd sent under the new impression it was Feb. 1, on stuff (in that context of belief) which he was not obliged to send in at all till the deadline, whatever that was, making allowance for this, after all – especially under the circumstances – very understandable error? It does not seem altogether fair, my brother. Nor do your strictures on even what you have of the work in question, which looks to me as though you didn't have your reading cap on, nor Mr Haas' strictures, whose 'dimmer view even than mine, perhaps because more objective'[4] looks anything but objective to me, in fact much as if he'd borrowed the Consul's dark glasses in order to read it, or perhaps Mr Reynal's, or even

Jonathan Cape's. Well, we have spoken of my face, and Hal's face, but there remains, I haven't overlooked Random House's money either, more importantly, yours. Here I feel truly woebegone at the possible implications, already chasing themselves, or half chasing themselves, with 7 league boots through whatever circles they chase themselves, that you have been let down, have backed the wrong horse, that possibly there was no horse in the first place. But brother, wait, hark, what is that sound of hooves I hear? It is a sound: unmistakeably it is a sound. Perhaps this next installment, here before you, will begin to change matters slightly, though regarded, even now, with some if not complete loathing by your good self, and more dimly still again by Mr Haas. Re this, all I have to say is that it was finished, as I said, before the New Year, but because of these new auxilliary circumstances it has taken till now to type finally. The objection will arise that it is like – but read on, read on – Mr Fort[5] (It would be amusing to receive the verdict that it was apparently *only* just like Fort, even though it were, for that would prove that only the first pages had been read.) It is founded, I am horrified to say, upon a personal experience and the only official part of this letter are the following words directed to Mr Haas, to whom I shall always also be very grateful (and not being unmindful of my gratitude now): 'that the author wishes to demonstrate for Mr Haas therein that if he can't make his novel move horizontally, he certainly feels that here he proves he can do it vertically.' Other minor matters: the thematic collision of the material and the immaterial. Shadow and substance, reality and unreality. Hence of amalgam of 'fact' and fiction. Also the other side, with a vengeance, of any 'back to Nature' theme. Another small note re the whole. Poe didn't die on October 9th (1849) but Oct. 7 – curiously enough (Oct 7, 1947) the same date in which we visited Gabriola in fact: I still have the bus ticket. It would be more proper to refer to this date then as the 'centennial' rather than the centenary of Poe? Curiously enough I found myself putting the last finishing touches on this bit on Jan. 9, that 1809, was Poe's birthday. Perhaps you would do me a great favour and look at the copy of Life for Jan. 11. The Case for E.S.P. by Aldous Huxley pp 96-108.[6] But on the next pages 109 passim is an illustrated article called The Mission of the Shantymen. H'mm. Some of the photographs might be exactly of Eridanus – or Dollarton – especially the second one of the bottom on 110 (ask Dave Markson) is indistinguishable from it. Men like John Rudd on 114 are the neighbours described. And as for high tide? I enclose a few cuttings. (Deep Cove is round the point from Dollarton). We are now completely cut off (the bridge caught fire among other things and blocked shipping) from home by the worst – I thought they were the worst in 1951-52 – blizzard in all Vancouver history. See also the section sent in, that I am offering to Matson as a story, under the title 'The Element Follows You Around, Sir.'[7] Or, the elements. In short, never a dull moment. So perhaps it wasn't so irresponsible after all to take Random's time getting a copy of the notes of La Mordida in the bank.

For the rest I hope (a) the tone of injured innocence (b) facetiousness of this letter, will not blind you to the fact (a) I'm deeply sorry I've put you in this situation, (b) deeply grateful (c) your friend, (d) more than ever on the job. For the rest again while I have every regard for Random's business side of it, and intent to respect it, am grateful again, I can't see the slightest point from a business view in their doing what they have done in this manner. After all, with Lunar Caustic practically finished, it doesn't seem to have occurred to anyone how easy it would have been for me had I chosen simply to fulfil the minimal terms of the contract. And since at the time they thought they were cutting me off they didn't know I'd have the money to carry on, how the hell did they think I was going to finish the novel at all? Or did they think, by some legerdemain, this callous discouragement and schoolboy punishment technique was going to cause me to suddenly finish it over night? And as for you, brother, let us have less stock responses. Get out of your rut. You sound like Mr Reynal. (These last sentences were written by Margie & I disclaim responsibility for them. She may be forgiven both in that she has a sore throat and in that no publisher has ever kept a contract with *her* in her life.) Vancouver's only snow-plough is stuck outside. Love & God bless from us both

Malcolm

P.S. So far as I can see, the only real casualty at this end, is time – all this having put us another month or so behind, in terms of final typing that is, having had so many letters to write. I'd like to see your faces if one day you found yourselves putting Ferry into the Modern library. Perhaps not quite in this order to be humble. Further note: my source for the dialogue in the movie of The Wandering Jew is Rallo's thesis The Haunted Castle, not the movie itself or the play.[8] For the rest I don't want to spoil the story, and can only hope that noone else has noted the appalling coincidence I cite & reported it to the Fortean society, whose published organ I have never read.[9] M.L.

Annotations:

1 In his 23 October 1946 letter to Lowry, Erskine suggested a dust-jacket design for *Under the Volcano* that he hoped Lowry would like. He went on to remark that Lowry should tell him honestly if he did not approve because, in Erskine's words: 'I'm not oversensitive. (The hell I'm not . . .).'

2 The murdered child in 'The Prioress's Prologue and Tale' from

Chaucer's *The Canterbury Tales* (1387-1400) remarks: 'My throte is kut unto my nekke boon' VII, l 649.

3 See Lowry's 4 January 1954 letter (**600**) to Erskine.

4 In his 6 January 1954 letter to Lowry announcing the suspension of payments, Erskine remarks that Lowry's statement of intentions dated 18 December 1953 has not allayed their fears.

5 Lowry had read and drawn upon Charles Fort's *Wild Talents*, a study of the mysterious causes of fires, for the fires and supernatural coincidences in *October Ferry*; see Lowry's 27 December 1953 letter (**598**) to Erskine.

6 Aldous Huxley (1894-1963), the English writer, published 'The Case for ESP, PIC and PSI' in *Life*, 11 January 1954, 96-106, 108.

7 See Lowry's 25 January 1954 letter (**602**) to Harold Matson, annotation 10.

8 In *The Haunted Castle: A Study of the Elements of English Romanticism* (London: Routledge, 1927), pp. 191-210, Eino Railo provides a detailed discussion of the sources and legend of the Wandering Jew. E. Temple Thurston's 1920 play *The Wandering Jew* was made into a film in 1923; see Lowry's 8 December 1951 letter (**484**) to Harold Matson.

9 Mysterious fires plague Lowry's protagonists in *October Ferry* (as they did Lowry himself), but see chapter 18 for this 'appalling coincidence.'

604: To David Markson

P: UBC(ms)
PP: *SL* 364-66; *Lln* 194-97   [1058 Nelson St]
                                                  [5 February 1954]ᵃ

Dear old Dave:

Thanks very much for your letter, now yellowing with age in the Lowry pocket. Many happy returns on your 26th birthday; we hadn't known when it was, or we'd have sent you a birthday card with a picture of the Absolute on it or something. Your dreams of stormy weather besetting we ducks didn't seem to have much more than magnificently diverting pertinence at the time, when we were riding fairly high, all things considered: since then, as it has turned out, those excursions of your somnambulent consciousness, as you put it, have taken on, so to say, a more parapsychological – &/or psychic significance. Nothing serious; no untranscendable gales, but just lots of discouragement & misunderstanding from various interrelating sources, & all of a kind rather harder than not to take at this point: – who invented the phrase 'throw up the sponge', I wonder? It has always seemed to me that anyone with sufficient indestructible intestinal eccentricity to want to swallow a sponge in the first place would have a corresponding reluctance in wanting to vomit it forth: anyway we haven't thrown it up. Maybe because, like Hasbrouch's (Margie tells me it was to throw *in* the sponge but I thought that was a towel) Hasbrouch's rose; it is digested.[1] There is no sponge. All of which has not prevented one's interior life from becoming all of a sudden rather to resemble Balzac's with the difference that, to all appearances, there is no Comédie Humaine either.[2] Oh well, Malc, Malc, what the halc, as old Aiken used to say. Or one could always go to Sardinia & promote a silver mine. I recommend Stephan Zweig's posthumous Balzac in this connection, especially if you want to read about my childhood.[3] Or Stephan Zweig's. Or whoever's. Who cares anyway? Illnesses too, many dozens: fevers, rashes, flus, fleas, & the all-dreaded thunderstone. But the finances look up. And the little house, all alone, together with the pier, has withstood (again) the worst gales & blizzards in a century, Deep Cove, round the corner, (& where we nearly went, by mistake, under my faulty pilotage, after Port Moody) having been blown to hell & gone. Meantime we have a fascist government: books are burned in the libraries, or are threatened to be, + they have banned The Wild one, why is all too obvious: McCarthy is their hero. (Though even Ezra Pound wouldn't have recognised these strongarmed stinkweasles – they are Social Crediters.)[4] I threaten to make a stink that will resound from one end of the earth to the other, but so far I haven't got further than making myself ill & losing my temper. Besides (after seeing The Juggler) I am seized with a desire to go & die in Israel.[5] Or perhaps even live. We went 25 miles in a blizzard to see The Great God Brown.[6] Very good. And worst of all we have received a notice directed to aptm 73 specifically saying: 'We, the Caroline Court Apartments Ltd – respectfully request you *not* to feed the seagulls or pigeons . . . whose habits have the result of attracting mice & other vermin . . . and otherwise rendering the surroundings unattractive . . . to the distaste of the other tenants . . . *besides it is contrary to the City's bylaws* . . . to which I have replied: '*We seagulls & pigeons* respectfully inform the Caroline Apartments Ltd that we have been here a great deal longer than you have, that far from rendering your surroundings unattractive, we claim to be the only aesthetic attraction within 20 miles that renders your premises attractive in the least degree, & while not impugning the 'mice & other vermin' we are said to attract, we must presume that the other tenants whose distaste is referred to are the 1450 sparrows who have nested here in these walls without molestment since 1905, according to those City by-laws you invoke, by which we also are protected (see Clause 175, Ibid. 6. p.3) & with whom we have always lived in a state of amity: as to the pigeons our own sporting instinct forbids us to ask what other kind of pigeon informed upon us: meantime we shall continue to sit (and shit) upon any damned window-sill we please, especially that of Apartment 73, giving notice respectfully to the Caroline Apartment Ltd that any wanton interference with our so-called habits – the more so since in this bitter winter we have no choice unless we are supposed legally to die at the hands of 'those legally bound to protect us' – will be duly reported to the proper authorities & the culprits punished with the utmost rigour of the law, by which we merely mean that we shall withdraw our society from you altogether, with the result that your so-called premises, so far mortised & tenoned with our bird-lime, will not only become as you term it unattractive, but, having fallen down, cease to exist.'

Something of that nature. Meantime, old man, I want to say on behalf of us both, how good it is to hear from you how loyal a friend you are to write to such rotten correspondents. It is always a fine & cheering thing to hear from you. Send a manuscript. (Pay no attention to premature discouragements.) Nor, for that matter, to the misery-grisery implied in this letter. Actually, we hope to present you in the not too distant future, with some work that will make the top of your head blow off. But, if you have to blow mine off – or ours – it doesn't much matter.) Or not so much but that that we should keep somewhere a nucleus of peace where the heart's velleities are clean, its cormorants dry their heraldic wings, & its seagulls, in sunlight, fly. They'll drop something on your head, of course, but that's where the sense of humour comes in.

Not to mention where the mixed metaphors, perhaps, go out. See you in Port Moody.

Great love from us both

Malc

[P.S.] Blow that horn! Hold that note (ref. wonderful radio play of Louis Macnieces we heard – Dylan played the Raven – in Eric Bentley's Anthology.[7] Malc)

Annotations:

1 'Hasbrouck's rose' is the 'arcane, romantic flower,' 'mystic' and 'improbable,' that the drunken Hasbrouck claims to have devoured in the frequently anthologized poem 'Hasbrouck and the Rose' by American writer Howard Phelps Putnam (1894-1948). The poem is included in a volume that Lowry owned, *The Viking Book of Poetry of the English-Speaking World* (1941), edited by Richard Aldington.

2 *La Comédie humaine*, a series of novels by Honoré de Balzac (1799-1850), aspires to present a complete study of French life and contains over two thousand characters. Lowry's irony here stems from the fact that there is little comedy in his present life and even less in his writing.

3 Stefan Zweig (1881-1942), the Austrian biographer, novelist, and essayist, wrote a biography of Balzac that was published after Zweig and his

wife committed suicide in despair over the collapse of humane values in Austria under Hitler. Zweig's *Balzac*, translated by William and Dorothy Rose (Viking Press, 1946), begins with a detailed account of Balzac as a precocious, misunderstood boy shipped off to monastic schools, where he seldom saw his parents. Zweig describes him, when he left school at fourteen, as 'like someone who had passed through a dreadful and unspeakable experience' (19).

4 *The Wild One* (1954), an American film by Stanley Kramer about a motorcycle gang that terrorizes a small community, was frequently banned on the grounds that it did not show the terrorists meeting a just retribution. For Lowry's views on the Social Credit Party of British Columbia, see his 14 June 1952 letter (**534**) to Harold Matson and his early June 1953 letter (**579**) to Albert Erskine. American Senator Joseph R. McCarthy was responsible for instituting the anti-communist 'witch-hunts' of the post-war years. For Ezra Pound's connection with Social Credit, see letter **534**.

5 *The Juggler* (1953), another film by Stanley Kramer, is about a Jewish refugee.

6 *The Great God Brown* (1926), a complex expressionist play by Eugene O'Neill, is about doubles who finally destroy themselves.

7 Louis MacNeice's *The Dark Tower* was first broadcast on the BBC on 21 January 1946, with Dylan Thomas as the Raven; see Lowry's 27 August 1951 letter (**468**) to David Markson. Drama critic Eric Bentley included the play in his anthology *From the Modern Repertoire, Series Two* (1952).

Editorial Notes:

a. This is the postmark date recorded by David Markson. Margerie has added three postscripts in the margins of this four-page holograph. In one she asks if Markson would like to have some original draft pages of *October Ferry to Gabriola* because Lowry is throwing them all out and she believes something should be saved 'for posterity.'

605: To David Markson

P: UBC(ms)   [1058 Nelson St]
                                                  [22 February 1954]ᵃ

Dear old bean:

Thanks a million for your generous & manifold encouragements. Things were not quite so dire as you suspected (though for a time subsequently they threatened to become even direr.) One day we'll when it has had time to amalgamate our senses of humour we'll tell you the history of this period & it is to be hoped, over a drop of the creature, laugh all our heads off. Meantime it didn't seem to us that I'd led you to believe through our letter that we'd been undergoing much more than the usual routine trial. But I perceive – as also from your portrait of the Caroline Court with seagull, which is remarkably accurate even as to the place of the room on the top floor – & in common I hope sometimes with myself, not to mention the lobster, who knows the secrets of the sea but does not bark – , that you have the faculty of perceiving that of which there is no overt evidence.[1] Meantime too it's not so much a question of shipwreck, so much as stalled engines in a relatively calm sea, as once happened in a more tactile sense to myself, in the Meditarrean, for three whole days, with no one having much better idea of what had gone wrong than that the Chief Engineer had somehow fouled up the transmission by stuffing one of his old sweatrags into some steam-piping. Thanks, though, for sending the bird of hope to our masthead. As it happened it was sadly needed. And vastly appreciated. We'll write you again when we are more properly underway. Gravesend looks a hell of a way off at the moment, but that is as maybe.[2] Even when it's abaft the beam that doesn't always stop the grousing.

God bless from us both

Malcolm

Annotations:

1 Markson's letter to Lowry, presumably with his sketch of the Lowry plight, has not survived.
2 Gravesend, on the Thames south-east of London, is a maritime centre for shipping and a destination for ships returning home. Lowry was not planning a trip to England, but his metaphor of a ship in trouble is nicely completed by the allusion to Gravesend.

Editorial Notes:

a. The postmark date recorded by David Markson.

Given the bad news from Random House and the painful rift with Albert Erskine, it is hardly surprising that there is no correspondence between 22 February and 10 May 1954 and that, when Malcolm did begin to write letters again, he wrote to David Markson. In letters **606** *and* **607** *he explains his and Margerie's plans to travel to Europe via New York, not because they intend to leave Dollarton for good but because they need a break from the primitive lifestyle. Life under the constant threat of eviction from their paradise, together with the seeming rejection by Albert, had left Lowry seriously adrift. As the months passed and their departure grew imminent, however, not even his bravado with Markson could hide his increasing despair.*

606: To David Markson

P: UBC(ms)
PP: *SL* 366-70; *Lln* 198-202

[Dollarton]
[10 May 1954]^a

Dollarton. 3 golden-eyes. 2 mergansers. 3 gulls.
7 grebes. 1 cat.

Dear old Dave: – I should have written you weeks ago – & indeed I did write, & more than once, – but owing to certain auxiliary circumstances . . . Yeah. Well, the first auxiliary circumstance was that a pigeon nesting in the airventhead on the apartment roof fell down the said airvent shaft & got trapped in the wall behind our bed, which bed came out of the wall like a drawer. I was going to make the rescue of said bird coincident with the second circumstance, though in fact the latter preceded it; a cut forehead, no more than a mere scratch it seemed, while messing about with those city chores more unfamiliar than trapped pigeons: but suddenly or rather later the scratch had turned into grand guignol – I'd severed a bloody artery. Worse to follow: Margerie, on going to the rescue, got trapped in the elevator. I mean that the elevator chose that very moment to stop between floors when her benighted husband was bleeding to death in the bathroom. Pandemonium: save from me, who having let out the third bathful of Lowry gore felt at the top of his form, & even less disposed to holler for help myself myself than I was to put a tourniquet on the wound in question: I have not, I said to myself, got an artery in my head, so how can I put a tourniquet on it? Perhaps what I meant was any brains but at all events there was a happy ending and we were saved in the nick, on the stroke of midnight, in St Pauls hospital, having been conveyed thence at 117 miles an hour by an air-force officer who up to then had been slightly drunk in the corridor below when he'd been having an affair with his half-sister. 'And did you do this yourself?' asked the midnight interne grimly, to which I replied, 'Christ no, it was that bloody pigeon.' All went well for a week or so, when someone supplicated our own aid in a manner almost as urgent as we had – or Margie had – the air-force officer, though the urgency in this case was more psychological or interfamilial, and implied a journey, through the wet & the wilderness – long live the wet and the wilderness yet! – of some seventy miles to a remote island, – the very island upon which lives a friend of yours by the way, should you ever need him, & whom I once mentioned to you,[1] – & with a couple of cracked ribs, I mean mine, also perhaps suffered as in combat with the holy bird, & growing increasingly more painful, the more so, since to reach our friend's house, one has to descend a precipice some six hundred feet in depth & at a gradient – where steps go down – of about 1 in 2. Back in the apartment of the holy bird (the janitor suggested that despite the rules we might feed the poor thing on the window-sill after its exertions that night) it was to discover that the cracked ribs had succeeded in apparently paralysing my inwards: in endeavouring to remedy this in the approved Ghandesque manner – my enema the Douche, as Haile Salassie put it[2] – there was, after many fruitless attempts, suddenly a sound of breaking & crepitus (though alas, not crapitus, had it been crapitus it might have been better) enough to awaken the dead, the dead being me, to a sense, again, of the illogical – or brute fact: ribs (& I have broken them all before) seemed to me malleable creatures, designed for give & take – & sway & scind, & every kind of pressure from the outside: but apparently not from the inside – momentous thought – (one red-throated loon, one foolish seagull trying to steal a fish off one beautiful merganser, burning oilwaste in the refinery the first star – is the scenery outside from the room you know) – like those dams in Holland during the floods of yesteryear, the rib-cage was giving under the water-pressure, & it wasn't any use sticking one's finger in the dam. Or up one's arse for that matter. This time Margie got her instructions by telephone, nobly – & embarrassing though it must have been (our doctor lived in North Vancouver): bind sheet tightly around patient to give support: more enema the douche: cascara (many grains of): Epsom Salts (2 tablespoons of): an infusion of rosemarine: and caper several times boldly about the room, taking deep breaths of smog. And brandy, said I, should be given to the dying. It was, but by Monday night – that had been Sunday – it still hadn't done any good. 'If nothing happens by 8 then get him to the hospital.' Our last call was cut off by the cry *emergency*! from somebody else: So I made my own emergency this time under my own steam, – I mean walked – nach dem Krankenhaus.[3] St Pauls again! (The first & last scenes of the whole Volcano – The Voyage that Never Ends – are supposed to be there too, but this was nightmarish a little: I ought to have been writing this, not living it or dying it, mutters Malc to himself, chuckling thoughtlessly, – you oughtn't to chuckle thoughtlessly, old man, with broken ribs under such circumstances, & I warn you not to try it should you ever be unfortunate enough to be in the same position)[4] So our North Vancouver doctor sent an emergency doctor after me, ex-rays were taken, drugs given, & suffice it – with a temperature that was now rising much as it does when you go down into the engine-room of a bauxite freighter) –

Several mescal later

FASTING

behind the bed

And at the foot a picture of the infant Jesus, apparently being instructed, with the consolary view of constructing a cross, (since there was one above, – while he looked rather like Dylan [Thomas], when absolutely blind tight) being instructed, as I say, by his father St Joseph, in the art of what could be done with a hammer & a nail – – a truce to this

(unposted)

– very dear old Dave, extremely sorry not to have written for so long, or rather not to have posted any letters to you, especially when you were so sporting to write us parapsychologically suspecting some lowry misery-grisery, & at that so entertainingly, brilliantly & sympathetically & so often at that point –

(not posted)

Our very dear old Dave: – am terribly sorry not to have

(unwritten)

– to cut a long story short (& incidentally I wrote you another long unposted letter, which didn't mention our troubles, but concentrated on what we thought might be your own, not posted, because of the supernatural idea that perhaps the troubles didn't really exist but stating them might somehow & obscurely beget some of them for you, God damn it, all this when I know very well that all you might have wanted was for a fellow to say oh or shit or something (as you see I couldn't say shit very well, as the poet said when he shouted Fire having fallen down the sewer) – to cut that long story short, anyhow, we are thinking of coming east this summer, in fact with the object of seeing you before we depart for Tel-a-viv upon the s.s. ΟΙΔΙΠΟΥΣ ΤΥΡΑΝΝΟΣ, though actually we are bound for Sicily, or at least the kingdom of the 2 Sicilies, if not under dat ole King Bomba (who made a law that stopped the trains every night at 6 pm, making it obligatory that they held a religious service on board) – there to live, if not in turn like that old Typhoeus, beneath Mount Etna.[5] Previous to this, Prospero-wise, we aim to return to Milan, in which city the Volcano of your own better (or bitter) discovery is shortly to erupt: or fizzle out.[6] We wondered if you could put us up in New York for a few days, previous to this, under a bed or wherever, while we were on our way: said request not being made for financial reasons, but rather from love, whatever that entity is. If you want, you can have our house when we're gone if you want to go west though I don't swear we won't haunt it & sing hot teleported tunes at you: but more likely you won't want & more likely still you'll be crossing the seas like us or whatever. Actually we don't know exactly what ship we'll be going on from N.Y: whether a Greek, Egyptian, Israeli, or Italian freighter.[7] Or the exact date! But the Italian Consul is letting us know (his neighbour, the Panamanian one, true to Consular form, was shoved in jail last night, having the highest drunk count ever recorded on the local drunkometre & in fact being pronounced dead on arrival — one can't help half suspecting he was either an hombre noble or had something on his mind) quam celerrime. As the said Consul remarked to Margie the other day: 'This ship for lady-nice: — I har a friend who know the Commandante: the captain; but I must see friend . . . But maybe wait 5 or 6 day New York. But is friend I will try . . . No, it is my pri*vel*lege for lady-nice & friend-boy, or is he your housebound?

At all events, you won't be too far away even if you are; but let us know, as we shall: & meantime **HOLD THAT NOTE ROLAND! BLOW THAT HORN** Hold that note!

God bless from us both — Margie & me — & from the shack & many mergansers & other wild & profound sea-fowl ——

Malcolm

(Not written)

[P.S.] My name is Sigurd Storlesen. Hullo. – seems to be Margie's point. i.e that i would float. Unless I fill it with coal in the meantime.[8]

Annotations:

1 Lowry has woven a significant reference to Gerard Manley Hopkins's poem 'Inversnaid' (1881) into this convoluted story:

> What would the world be, once bereft
> Of wet and of wildness? Let them be left,
> O let them be left, wildness and wet;
> Long live the weeds and the wilderness yet.

Markson cannot recall any such friend, and we have not been able to confirm any trip to a remote island seventy miles from Vancouver.

2 Haile Selassie (1892-1975), the emperor of Ethiopia from 1930 to 1974, was an enlightened if absolute monarch who was forced into exile when Benito Mussolini's Fascist troops invaded Ethiopia in 1935. He regained his throne when the country was liberated in 1941. Lowry's pun, therefore, turns on the fact that Mussolini, Il Duce, was Selassie's enemy.

3 *Nach dem Krankenhaus* is German for 'to the hospital.'

4 Lowry planned to open and close *The Voyage That Never Ends* with 'The Ordeal of Sigbjørn Wilderness,' parts I and II, which take place in hospital; see Volume II introduction, pp. 2-3.

5 'King Bomba' (*bomba* meaning bomb or bombshell in Italian) was the

nickname given to Ferdinand II (1810-59), a Bourbon king who ruled the Two Sicilies from 1830 until his death. Although born in Palermo, Ferdinand was hated in Sicily for his authoritarian rule, and he became an object of fascination in the European press of the day. Lowry's information on the king's religious proclivities is probably taken from Osbert Sitwell's *Discursions on Travel, Art and Life* (London: Grant Richards, 1925): 'Bomba . . . made two stipulations . . . . Secondly, when Vespers sounded, each train must be drawn up at the nearest station, and all non-heretic passengers must get out on to the platform, kneel, and say their prayers' (pp. 64-65). Typhoeus, the Greek demon of the whirlwind, was thrown by Zeus into Tartarus, the underworld beneath Mount Etna, and the sulphur fumes of the volcano are considered to be his breath.

6 At the end of Shakespeare's *The Tempest* (1611), Prospero declares his desire to return to his home in Milan after his island exile.

7 The Lowrys sailed from New York for Genoa on 12 September 1954 aboard the Italian boat ss *Giacomo*.

8 Sigurd Storlesen is a character in the story 'The Bravest Boat.' The message he sets adrift in the toy balsa boat to be discovered by his future wife begins: 'Hello. My name is Sigurd Storlesen.'

Editorial Notes:

a. This postmark date is recorded by David Markson. There are seven pieces of paper used for this pencil holograph, some with only a line or two on them marked 'not posted' or 'unwritten,' but the entire composition was sent to Markson. Margerie has written a note on the verso of the seventh page; she asks if Markson would find it amusing 'to put us up in your bathtub.' Lowry's postscript is keyed to her reference to the bathtub.

607: To David Markson

P: UBC(ms,ts)   [Dollarton]
                                                      [20 May 1954][a]

Dear old Dave:

Hold that note, Roland. Blow that horn. For one thing 3000 bucks is 3000 bucks, so why not think in terms of what it could represent – I don't mean necessarily, though the speculation be inescapable on this particular morning, how many bottles of Jack Daniels Tennessee Sour Mash Whiskey it will beget – but rather a passage to more than India, Italy, or the Whuling Cyclades: at least Europe.[1] So if the opus bores and disgusts you anyway, why not make a good job of it and make the corrections – insert more cock, so to say – your paper-back-publisher desires, and if possible, and himself not bankrupt, collect.[2] I will provide you with a title: No Barricado for a Belly. And a pseudonym: Sigbjørn X. Ghostkeeper. Or perhaps Thomas of Erceldoune. . . This would be a palpable hit (even if the book isn't) for you,[3] I mean should it chance to help produce the environment where you can better write what you want. For to judge from your recent letters, especially your last, it would seem that New York is not proving altogether the right place. To say the least. In my own experience – odi et amo[4] – that particular city – it favours brief and furious outbursts, but not the long haul. Moreover for all its drama and existential fury, or perhaps because of it, it's a city where it can be remarkably hard – or so it seems to me – to get on the right side of one's despair; once having got on the wrong side of it, that is; even hangovers don't seem the same in New York as anywhere else, though to be sure they may not last so long, the deceitful medicament being more easily at hand; which only makes it worse in the end. Not that one can't learn a great deal from hangovers: everything, in fact, save how not to get one next time, but that one can too easily find oneself slipping into the state of mind in that city – or so it seems to me – where to be slightly tight or hungover seems one's natural state, the only way to maintain one's balance and one's harmony with the place: and the bad thing about this is not the tightness so much, which as you say can be highly enjoyable, especially when in the cheerful and uninhibited company, say, of the euphoniously named Mr Scipio Sprague – (why not Hannibal Swittenberg, or even Toussaint l'Overture Pfunfkirchen, if I may say so without impoliteness?[5] one can't but the temptation was irresistible) – but that that state of mind is really as eminently rational as it is – or can be – dangerous; an uncomfortable combination. I hope I don't seem to preach. Mens sane in corpore sano,[6] was all I was talking about. I don't say one can't keep fit (whatever that may mean) in New York, but after a while does one really want to? Perhaps you rightly, as you said, consider yourself a creature of the city: as once did I: maybe though you reckon without some of your unconscious needs, nay, the absolute necessities, of that creature, such as a few stars, ruins, deserts, cathedrals, seas, forests, ducks, ships, (even if the thought of them be loathsome) uncharted waters and undreamed shores, even indeed other cities. And above all perhaps a swim when you want it: or don't you want it? In any case, you have us both feeling somewhat anxious about you; your letters get blacker and blacker – no matter that they may have cheered this benighted author up during what seemed an acutely ulti- mate indigo period, and no matter that the blacker they get, the more entertaining they are: that has been my and our benefit. (which reminds me I would like at this moment, with yourself, to have a game of tennis) My advantage, your altruistic and far-sighted empathy: what the hell, – I haven't given you much return. And it occurs to me, as you see, sprouting parental whiskers at this point, that, somehow or other, your providence or yourself may be making a bad job for you, of what used to be call: 'withdrawal and return.' Unless sexually, of course, – but that ain't all, Jules Romain to the contrary; and I don't see even so how even that could be solved, far less fundamentally, unless you are slightly more, as the lady spiritualist observed to us, 'En Rappo with the Angelitic Host.'

Joking & obscenities aside, however, I even sometimes think, in my darker moments, that the poor bloody-minded old Volcano may have had a malign influence on your good self; it hurts somewhat to suggest you throw that god damn book out of the window and me with it, even if that were sound advice, which I'm not sure it is, and anyhow I could no doubt hotly protest: not all fathers were made for their own patricide & I never heard of Abraham asking Isaac to sacrifice *him*,[7] not willingly anyhow: but keeping that work as a symbol for the moment of something or other, you ought to try somehow to transcend it, let it at least be useful to you, since it was apparently intended for you, or its author will feel he has lived in vain. I'm not sure what I mean. But no matter. To come back to the subject. You speak of the work you've done recently not merely as bad but as though you loathed the thought of it. As for that, even if so it can't be as bad as parts of what I've been recently writing myself: and you seem blissfully to have forgotten why you wrote the book. Quite apart from the fact that it seems to me something of a feat to write any book these days, however bad, the basic idea of writing the thing in the first place must have been founded on some deep need or you wouldn't have done it. So, I repeat, you ought to follow it up. If New York hasn't stimulated you yet into doing the kind of work you fundamentally want to do there's no need to rush to the conclusion that the fault is all Dave Markson's. It could be that you need (quite apart no doubt, as sailors say, from a good strong woman) complementary factors to be found only in Europe. You can get to Europe cheaply & swiftly from New York; live there much more cheaply, & your 3000 bucks would go a long way. If – as circumstances seem to be pointing at this moment – we ourselves are going to be there, probably to Sicily (just to vary the volcanoes – the Volcano is coming out in Italian by the way this fall, as I think I mentioned) we could even dwell near one another, apply mutual cataplasms upon work in progress or regress. The idea is not a bad one. (Your girl with $8000 is not a bad idea either, but the question in my mind here is not whether you should allow the lass to take you to Mexico but – even if that solved the good strong woman problem temporarily – to what degree Mexico would *take you* should the affair go wrong, as under those circumstances, it would seem almost bound to: it is the most Christ-awful place in the world in which to be in any form of distress, a sort of Moloch that feasts on suffering souls, in fact: moreover, if you are known to take a drink, the bastardos will count every one you have, & wait around to trip you up. Gringo-baiting is their national sport: even bullfighting takes second place. All in all a good place to stay out of: (Even though one dreams, quixotically, of returning one day – a death-wish, from my point of view, if ever there was one.) But then, of course, again, all might go merry as a marriage bell. Or rather merry, if not quite as a marriage bell. And it's unquestionably a beautiful & interesting country, which you may take as the understatement of the year. The people are of course swell too: both outside & behind the bars, in both senses. Only I feel that the custodian does not correspond . . . But – if for none of the fore-going reasons – a trip there for you at this point might enormously aggravate your problems, without perhaps solving any . . .

However all this may be, though, your state of mind distresses us both, as I say. I came across the phrase the other day, in reference to Kafka, 'the lost art of being unhappy.'[8] It would seem that, so far as you & I are concerned, the art is not perhaps so lost after all. I suppose it is idle to say – & sounds phoney – that a certain amount of despair is actually necessary for people of our peculiar temperament: it doesn't make it any the easier to suffer. Margie suspects me sometimes of suffering sometimes without there being any proper 'objective correlative' for it:[9] as I her: but one overlooks the fact that the mostly hellish kind of suffering of all can be simply because of that lack – the Waste Land type. Or one may suffer because one *can't* suffer, because after all to suffer is to be alive. Because I'm twice as old as you I'm not going to go it on these lines & end up by saying that when you've reached my age & transcended what I've transcended – or worse, not transcended – then you can begin to speak; you don't need to be old to suffer any more than you do to drink. Melville, at 14, speaking through Redburn, woke up to find the mildew on his soul.[10] (I'm getting mixed up because I've got, at this moment, a titanic hangover myself, & on top of that – both of us have – a prize objective correlative for doing some really energetic suffering: to simplify – Ahab may have felt himself damned in the midst of Paradise[11] (a bloody unusual kind of Paradise too, I always thought, that of his, on the poop, with his ivory pogo stick, in the middle of the sea) but at least he did not *know* he was going to be evicted from it, nor, so far as I know, felt constrained to write about it while this was going on: – such, or something similar, seems to be our lot. But to by-pass this for the moment)

I suspect you, though, – or at this moment – of undergoing a more special and inexplicable kind of blues. The way you write, it's almost as though you were implying, though quite without self-pity, 'But nobody cares what the hell happens to me': or rather, 'Perhaps all too many people care but I don't care a damn that *they* care.' Well, this letter should certainly set your mind at rest immediately on the point that at least two people whom you really do care if they care care. Possibly this was not at all the feeling or the point and I am just projecting an emotion on to you I have sometimes felt myself, in my case largely a familial one; none of my own brothers – though they expressed themselves pleased to hear of its success in the U.S. – has ever said a word, intelligent or otherwise, about the Volcano; (my mother kept Ultramarine locked up in a drawer, which was perhaps the best place for it) which perhaps is irrelevant too.

– But a truce to all this. I have just now received your next letter of the 13th, which renders much of this letter superfluous. We're both very glad indeed you're taking the line you are. Your terms by the way – the two $1500 – are exactly what I received for the Volcano – or as Aiken termed it, Under the Malcamo or Poppagetsthebotl.[12] I'm beginning to think your book must be good, not at all as you say it is. Don't try *proving* you have any talent though, etc.; that way you can overreach yourself. But you can set your mind at rest: you have: lots of it, I can spot it a mile off, being myself a talent-scout of no mean ability. But it may take you some time to find your stride, there's lots of time too, all too much time, even, though you may not think it.

(Which reminds me that, some twenty-two years ago, I suggested to one Wynyard Browne, a college acquaintance, that he would make a damned good playwright. The aforesaid Browne, twenty-two years later, after a long career as an actor, and an architect critic, has just taken London by storm as they say, I am pleased to report, with a play called A Question Fact, the said play being based, apparently, upon a sentence in the Volcano, where the Consul speculates upon the pleasures of being destroyed by one's own imagination.[13] But I digress. No need to have such a weary haul as that either, though I feel Wynyard might have been saved a lot of trouble if a couple of other people had been as percipient as I. Then on the other hand, maybe he had to go through the actor, architect-critic ordeal in order to become the playwright: apparently, a first-rate one. Quien sabe? Which reminds me to say that I quite agree with Albert's Dictum that you shouldn't let writing interfere with your living; (I don't think I've ever read anything quite so bloody banal as parts of this letter of mine, by the way, but it is to be hoped a benign spirit informs it) Work is the curse of the drinking classes anyway.[14] – But I think you should bestride a proud Alp, pluck a piece of Edelweiss from the Absolute, visit Parma, or something . . . Meantime – Goethe-Eckermann like advice – why not write a few short things: short stories, for example, they have – er – the advantage of being shorter, at least, & take less time than novels.[15] And I think you ought to feel the atavistic influence at its source of someone wholly curious and remote in time geography and space and in fact dead, (though not too long dead): someone like Holderlin or von Kleist or Hermann Broch or even Adelbart Stifter. And Ibsen wrote Peer Gynt in Ischia.[16]

I don't think we shall bless you so much (though we shall still bless you anyway) if you've vanished from New York when we arrive, especially if via another freighter, especially if it's the same freighter we're trying to get on: at all events an Italian freighter. {Don't hesitate of course if you see a way to grab a more convenient booking: – but you can go cheaper if you wait till September.} We await word from the Vancouver vice-Italian consul, who will deliver such word to Margerie quam celerrime because she is lady-nice. Our aim is to get a freighter, Italian preferably, out of New York, thence to Milan, via Genoa. In Milan I figured, since the Volcano's coming out there, one might get some advice from translator, publishers etc as to where best to live, the teleology being Sicily. I seemed to perceive something useful adumbrating itself for you out of all this nautical juxtaposition: but maybe it was only because I thought it would be damn good fun if we all went on the same ship. Besides, if I'm not a good influence on you, you might be on me and us: old sailors when passengers are liable to get tangled up in the rigging, chip rust, hide in lifeboats, and even reverse the engines, and so on: – besides I think that conversation about Dante with the second engineer which I envisage would be better all round with some admixture of Jack Daniel's Tennessee Sour Mash Whiskey in the chianti and the gin and orange juice. It is not a bad idea. I say it is not a bad idea. Anyway, it is a gay idea. And I feel more work would get done – perhaps by both, or all of us.

There's nothing but a sort of heartbreak here: we love the place too much, and that's to be, alack, in the devil's clutches. It's true *we* haven't been evicted yet, but all the people up to the lighthouse have been served with eviction notices, and even in tonight's paper there's a heartless piece: 'Speedy Eviction of Squatters Sought. District Clerk Fred Saunders said legal action is being hampered by the slow process of catching up with the transient beachcomber owners of 'dilapidated makeshift shacks' in the area where Municipal officials plan to develop the park's beach facilities.' etc But before I begin to grow too lachrymose about this I ought to say we ought to be thankful for the line of demarcation of the evictions *does* end at the lighthouse: we have had similar scares before, & weathered them, and it is in every way possible, since there seems a special providence about the place, that we still could be here ten years from now. So we're not leaving with the object of the parting being irrevocable: indeed it had been in our mind as a counter-suggestion to offer you the house in our absence, for that would least save you rent, & it can be a wonderful & healthy life, but it is no doubt far too far & unfeasible, & together with any happiness you might only inherit the anxiety too, Vancouver is culturally as dead as the dodo, & by no stretch of the imagination could it supply you with what Europe would at this stage; moreover the abomination of desolation is already sitting in the holy place and at night the glare of new oil refineries compose a veritable City of Dis.[17] Nevertheless I cannot bring myself to say we are leaving for good: we would, to tell the truth, have been going to Europe anyhow for a while, – this life is too hard on Margie as a constant thing & this continual Under-the-Volcano-my aspens-all are-felled-all-all-are-felled feeling is so lousy it could even drive one cuckoo, I feel, in the end.[18] So we aim not to think about this too much, enjoy what good luck we have while we have it & leave the place beautiful & in good repair & in some safe hands (if you don't want it, which you probably wouldn't anyhow & certainly won't if Avon gives you your advance & you can finagle as we hope your European trip) with some remote but optimistic idea of eventual return. You mention that you have bouts of feeling afraid of yourself. So, Dave, do I: & I think we can help each other in this regard. It is the suspicious element of the possibly suicidal in all these constant small accidents that have plagued me which frightens me. And though I once prided myself on being a sometimes subtle if not good carpenter etc I have become so clumsy and unpractical I am almost ashamed to have anyone watch [me] do anything save swim & I'm scared – when I think of them – of the unnecessary risks I've got into the habit of taking even doing that, which is nearly my greatest joy. We also have taken to hitting the bottle, especially me, somewhat too hard – if not with Consular vehemence or consistency – & though this can often be a joy too, there are few things worse than a bad hangover on a glorious day. And this frightens us too, from time to time: god knows we've had experience enough to know better. But somehow, I've never been able to think of drinking as a vice, even when I'm on the wagon, where I shortly propose more or less to go, at least till we hit New York. True, a hangover is an evil thing. But then a drink cures the evil & the specious reasoning begins again. And not too much work has been done since February, alas, but it will be, it will be. In fact I put down my self-fears, no doubt partly to lack of responsibility. So I've tried to take a responsible line with *you*. And since you had already decided in part to follow the lines of this advice before I gave it you can say that I've concluded the letter as much for my sake as for yours.

I still have no exact idea when we're coming to New York, but we'll give you the exact date in plenty of time: we're hoping you'll meet us at the airport. We haven't heard from the Italian Consulate about the ship yet. We hope to sail in September for various reasons, one being that it's cheaper. Thank you for offering to put us up in N.Y. if you're there: but for god's sake don't let us put you to any trouble or anyone else out – we look forward very much to seeing you there, if not, to rejoining you somewhere beyond the Pillars of Hercules.[19]

All the very best love from us both

Malcolm

P.S. Margie – or rather one Mrs Sowry – has now received a letter from the Vice Consolato d'Italia running: Dear Madame: Further to our conversation of a few days ago, I wish to inform you that there could be a possibility for you sail from New York to Italy by an Italian freight ship. I regret I am not able to give you more particulars about, but you can obtain from Mr Purviss, Empire Shipping Co. etc. So we're heading tomorrow for Mr Purviss. Meantime we've repaired the pier and platform, swum, become sunburned, and forgotten there ever was such a thing, all in one day, as a hangover.

Annotations:

1   Lowry's allusion is to E.M. Forster's novel *A Passage to India* (1924), but he is also quoting Conrad Aiken's expression 'the Whuling Cyclades,' from *Blue Voyage* (1927), p. 246, an expression he had borrowed for his poem 'On Reading Edmund Wilson's Remarks About Rimbaud' (Scherf 81). The Cyclades are a group of twenty-four islands in the Greek archipelago circling the island of Delos.

2   Markson does not recall what book project he was working on, but the writing of cheap paperback novels fetched respectable sums of money, and he did some of this work in the early years of his career.

3   Lowry's title is from Shakespeare's *The Winter's Tale* I.ii.204, and his suggested pseudonyms allude to his own protagonist Sigbjørn Wilderness, his story 'Ghostkeeper,' and the seer and poet Thomas of Erceldoune (1220?-1297?), also known as Thomas the Rhymer. Hamlet scores a 'palpable hit' against Laertes in the duel scene from *Hamlet* V.ii.267.

4   *Odi et amo* is the Latin for 'I hate and I love'; see Lowry's poem 'And yet I am of England too' (Scherf 157).

5   'Scipio' Sprague was a friend of Markson's; see Lowry's 1 June 1954 letter (**610**) to Sprague. Lowry's Scipio/Hannibal joke turns upon the historical link between the Roman major Publius Cornelius Scipio Africanus (237-183 BC), who defeated the Carthaginian general Hannibal (247-183 BC) at the battle of Zama (202 BC). Toussaint L'Ouverture, François Dominique (1743-1804), although born to slaves

in Haiti, became an educated plantation owner, an administrator, and commander-in-chief of Haiti's miltary. He is considered the liberator of Haiti.

6 The Latin epithet *mens sana in corpore sano* means: 'A sound mind in a sound body.'

7 In Genesis 22:1-19, it is the father, Abraham, who is preparing to obey Jehovah's command by sacrificing his son Isaac.

8 Although this comment describes Kafka appropriately, the source has not been identified.

9 'Objective correlative' is T.S. Eliot's term for the successful expression of emotion in art; see 'Hamlet and His Problems' from *The Sacred Wood: Essays on Poetry and Criticism* (1920).

10 In chapter 2 of *Redburn* (1849) the hero comments: 'Talk not of the bitterness of middle-age and after-life; a boy can feel all that, and much more, when upon his young soul the mildew has fallen'; see also Lowry's poem 'On Reading Redburn' (Scherf, 80).

11 See Lowry's use of this favourite line from *Moby-Dick* in his June 1953 letter (**579**) to Albert Erskine.

12 See Conrad Aiken's 23 February 1947 letter to Lowry (Sugars, 201).

13 Wynyard Brown's first play, *Dark Summer*, was produced in 1947; see Lowry's November 1947 letter (**333**) to John Davenport. *A Question of Fact* opened at the Piccadilly Theatre, London, in October 1953, where it had a successful run. It concerns the fate of a man who discovers that his father is a murderer, but it ends quietly, without any of the drama of *Under the Volcano*.

14 This witticism is attributed to Oscar Wilde; see Hesketh Pearson, *Life of Oscar Wilde* (London: Methuen, 1946), chapter 12.

15 Johann Peter Eckermann (1792-1854) is chiefly remembered for his three-volume *Conversations with Goethe*. Goethe warned the younger man against attempting to write a long, major work too early in life in his conversation of 18 September 1823. See Lowry's 12 April 1950 letter (**395**) to Frank Taylor.

16 Lowry's recommended influences are, with the exception of Ibsen, German-language writers with little in common except the fact that each travelled widely and developed a unique style. Friedrich Hölderlin (1770-1843), Heinrich von Kleist (1777-1811), Hermann Broch (1886-1951), and Adalbert Stifter (1805-68) were not popular or influential in the English-speaking world, but Lowry's own practice was to locate 'atavistic influence' in obscure writers. Norwegian writer Henrik Ibsen (1828-1906) spent close to thirty years in self-imposed exile from Norway; his allegorical play *Peer Gynt* (1867) was written in Italy at Ischia and Sorrento.

17 The phrase 'abomination of desolation' occurs in the Old Testament books of Daniel and 1 Maccabbees and in the Gospels; it refers to the desecration of the temple by the pagan emperor Antiochus Epiphanus in 167 BC. This idea of desecration is closely associated with the beast

of Revelation. Dis, also Hades, is a name for the underworld in classical mythology.

18 See Gerard Manley Hopkins's poem 'Binsey Poplars' (1879): 'My aspens dear, whose airy cages quelled, / Quelled or quenched in leaves the leaping sun, / All felled, felled, are all felled.'

19 The Pillars of Hercules are the rock promontories on either side of the entrance to the Mediterranean Ocean; one is in Spain (Gibraltar), the other in Africa (Mount Hacho). According to Greek mythology, they were joined together until Hercules (Heracles) tore them apart to mark the geographical limits of the habitable world. Gerald Noxon wrote a radio play called *The Pillars of Hercules* that was broadcast by the CBC on 5 March 1944.

Editorial Notes:

a. The postmark date is recorded by David Markson. This letter-in-progress comprises a foliation of twelve pages on eleven sheets of paper, some typescript, some manuscript, some mere scraps of paper, others standard letter size, written over a period of several days. A brief extract from this letter was published in French translation in *Les Lettres nouvelles* 5 (1960): 203-04, and in *Canadian Literature* 8 (Spring 1961): 42-46.

608: To Albert Erskine

P: Virginia(ts); UBC(phc)   Dollarton, B.C.,
PP: *SL* 370-72   Canada
                                                                    22 May 1954

Dear old Albert:

I feel I ought to make some sort of report. Before I do though, I want to say how sorry I am the letter I wrote last January angered you or may have hurt you.[1] In fact I am sorry, period; that is, from the personal standpoint. Please forgive me. Before you write off that behaviour as being the ultima thule of ingratitude however – if you haven't done so already – try to understand the effect your news from Random House had on me coming in that particular way at that time. – Well, a truce to it all.

Meantime, I'd overlooked several things myself: one was that I had to pay $400 income tax this year on the Random House payments themselves. Moreover, by mid-March my English bank still hadn't come through and we were living precariously on an overdraft on our Canadian one; neither had the Liverpool solicitors, despite their promises (in fact they were behaving quite like certain authors) and things for a while looked pretty bleak: the money did come through finally (just in time to pay the income tax),[2] though not before I dispersed many further energies wrestling with these people and was, in fact, in hospital; not because of any more accidents, but simply some old broken bones aggravating a yet older, indeed hereditary, minor, and very English trouble: colonial anyway, vastly uncomfortable, but not very serious it turned out. (The only accident I've had this year to speak of was to sever an artery in my forehead while rescuing a trapped pigeon from an air-vent in the apartment, which is a good excuse to give one's maiden aunt when late to tea.)[3]

As you see by the address we are back in Dollarton, and so far as the financial situation is concerned things look rosy – touch wood – so much so that had you continued the payments I should by now, I think, have returned them, not out of nobility, but to avoid income tax. Not that I may not be grateful for their resumption again at some future date, if I'm still on the roster, but as things look at present I shall be, as I intimated I would, able to continue on my own, or without having to get another job, at least, I hope, until something is completed to all our satisfactions. Which brings me to another point, very important to me: it would seem better, all round, that so long as I continue on my own that the status of the work remain, so to say, my own, or more my own, stage secret. In other words, I don't think I want to send you any more bits and pieces (any more than you necessarily want them, after all, you didn't ask for them) for two reasons at least: one, I can't risk any further discouragement, not in the usual sense, and I don't mean this in a carping spirit, only that my self-critical faculty tends to be slightly manic-depressive, and to be frank, there are times when in process of creating I seem to need encouragment even if I think myself what I'm doing isn't entirely right, which certainly isn't fair to you; the second reason is that because of the peculiar way it seems I have to work, it's unfair to the work itself; for instance I honestly don't know at the moment whether I shall cut 200 pages out of Gabriola's 500 odd and I won't know until it's finally (sic) typed. So at the moment I don't even want to tell you how its going or its present status; and that's purely a sort of self-protection.

Which brings me to another point: the immediate outlook betokens a further change of plans, a further diversion of energies: I mean we have to move. Just as the work itself predicted of Eridanus the evictions so far have stopped at the lighthouse, but we are nonetheless now completely surrounded – the aspens all, all are felled, save in our little oasis of greenwood and sea – by sub-section and oil-refinery, and though this oasis last forever, sanity and health dictates we should this time go: if only because if we stay next year I shall have to pay $1000 income tax, which we could just as well use to get to Europe and find another pied-a-terre less anguishing and even, in the end, more economical. We have for the moment fixed on Sicily. We of course hope to come back, but all preparations have to be made as if we would not, and these preparations are many and complicated in a place one has lived in for fourteen years.

Now finally as to my contractual position with you, I find it a bit obscure. Although I felt sure there was some agreement on this score I can't find any clause or rider in the contract that says I may 'buy time' in this manner. As things stand I have another deadline a year hence, and a third Nov. 1956. It would simply be an impossibility for me now, under these changed and changing circumstances, to attempt to itemize what I think I can or can't do or in what order, or by then, (the way it looks at present I shall have three books for you all right – or more – by the last deadline, but all of them a little outside the general main scheme: meantime you haven't had the faintest indication of all the work that's been done) and I don't want to make any more promises I can't keep, or, more accurately, ones that may look, to Random House, as though they're not being kept to the very best of my abilities. I don't seem able to work that way anyhow: I have to let things gather more dust apparently. But I am assuming that The Case Is Altered. Or, to put it another way, I'm hoping I may consider myself to have stopped the clock at 11:59 P.M. on October 31, 1953 – or January 31, 1954, whichever way you prefer to look at it. Please inform me on this because it worries me to death. We think to be passing through New York on our way to Sicily in September, and we hope very much to see you then, when the situation may be clearer, or we can clarify it, or anyhow have a good – pow-wow is perhaps the good word, about it. Anyhow, dear brother, we want to see you. I hope you'll convey my real gratitude to Mr Haas for having tided me over and assure him I mean to come through. All the best love from us both –

Malcolm

Annotations:

1 In his 29 January 1954 letter to Lowry, Erskine wrote that he did not want to receive any more letters like Lowry's of 26 January (**603**) to him, but in his 4 February letter Erskine took a softer tone and acknowledged that Lowry had requested suspension of payments.

2 Lowry's share of his mother's estate reached him sometime in February or March of 1954. According to Bowker (533), he received £8,000 after British taxes. Lowry's 1953 Canadian taxes were due by the end of April, but they would not have included monies received in 1954.

3 See Lowry's colourful description of his accident in his 10 May 1954 letter (**606**) to David Markson.

609: To David Markson

P: UBC(pcard)   [Dollarton]
                                                                [31 May 1954]

Over those falls! Through those weeds! Through those fjords . . .[1]

love from M & M

Annotations:

1 Lowry's mention of fjords is inspired by the black and white photograph on the postcard, which shows the fjord and ice of Fra Hvitarvatni
  in Iceland. Lowry's 'war cry' 'Over those falls,' etc., is adapted from the
  film *The African Queen*; see his October 1953 letter (**590**) to Albert
  Erskine.

610: To Arthur R. Sprague

P: UBC(msc)
PP: *SL* 372-73   [Dollarton,] B.C.
                                                                1 June 1954

Dear Scipio Sprague[1]
sans plague sans blague
(if I seem vague)
I'm extremely beholden
for your words golden
as bourbon olden
in which prosit to you
as you sail toward the blue
on some Pequod gaily
or Behemoth sprightly
from Malcolm Lowry
late of the Bowery
whose prose was flowery
if somewhat glowery
who worked nightly
and sometimes daily
and died, playing the ukulele . . .[2]

[unsigned]

Annotations:

1 Arthur Rogers Sprague, Jr, was a friend of David Markson's. In spring
  1954 Sprague wrote to Lowry describing his friendship with Markson

and praising *Under the Volcano* (UBC 1:43). Markson sent the letter with an accompanying note to explain that his friend's incoherence was due to his being drunk. Lowry met Sprague in New York in September 1954.

2 See Lowry's poem 'Epitaph' (Scherf, 174).

611: To David Markson

P: UBC(pcard)   [Dollarton]
                                                         [1 June 1954]

Never mind that old man in the straw hat . . .[1]

                                                          [unsigned][2]

Annotations:

1 The postcard shows a wood engraving called 'Posado' by the Mexican artist José Guadalupe (1851-1913); the 'old man' in the engraving is an image of Death as a grinning skeleton on a skeletal horse trampling human skeletons.

2 In place of a signature Lowry has drawn two seagulls.

612: To David Markson

P: UBC(pcard)   [Dollarton]
                                                         [2 June 1954]

Hold that note, Roland! Play that horn . . .[1]

                                                         – Love M & M

Annotations:

1 The card has a black and white reproduction of 'Ethnography' (1939) by Mexican muralist and painter David Alfaro Siqueiros (1896-1974); it is a disturbing image of a Mexican Indian with an inscrutable, mask-like face.

613: To George Robertson

P: UBC(ms) [Dollarton]
[June 1954]ᵃ

Dear old George:[1]

Thanks alot for your wonderfully heartwarming letter to us both &
the only reason I didn't reply sooner or come to see you – for we were
living just around the corner from you in town was that I was in the
damn hospital. In fact I've had a year that would not disgrace
Hemingway. The day after our party – of happy memory – I broke my
right leg in three places & the ankle in two & likewise dislocated it. How
do you like that? How do you like children? Boiled, said W.C. Fields.
It was a kid's booby trap I fell afoul of in the bush: some sportsman playing Indians had pulled up a root on the right of the path & left it as a
trap for the cops or vice versa & my foot caught in it like a stirrup. It's
a very good thing we took the alternative route to the bus, or you might
have fallen into it since you were walking on my right.

So I was in a cast all summer which was why you didn't hear from us.
Then in town I cracked a couple of ribs, which produced complications,
trying to rescue a pigeon that had fallen down the airvent of the apartment,[2] which is a good excuse for you next time you turn up late on the
set, or whatever you call it in radio – I saw you out of the window of
the Caroline Court one day too, walking down Nelson, or rather
Thurlow, looking extremely well & elegant & carrying, so far as I could
make out, my father's umbrella: I hollered but you disappeared in a
northeasterly direction. Do come & see us again, any time after July 1st,
that is. I am immolated within a huge cheese of prose till then – Thanks
for liking the song. We think of you each time we sing it. As for the
beach & the woods they have never been in better form.

God bless from us both & all power to the work

love

Malcolm

Annotations:

1 George Robertson (1929–) was a student of Earle Birney's in 1949
when he first met Lowry. The 'party – of happy memory' that Lowry
goes on to recall took place on Lowry's birthday, 28 June 1953. In his
November 1953 letter to the Lowrys (UBC 1:59) Robertson describes
the songs they sang that day and his own work with the CBC, which
he had joined at the beginning of the month. In 1961 Robertson made
a two-part television documentary film on Lowry for the CBC; for his
recollections of Lowry, see Salloum (75–79).

2 See Lowry's 10 May 1954 letter (**606**) to David Markson for his description of this adventure.

Editorial Notes:

a.   This pencil holograph (UBC 3:6) has neither inside address nor date but
     the contents suggest June 1954.

614: To David Markson

P: UBC(ts)   [Dollarton]
PP: *SL* 373-74   [10 July 1954]
                                                                Saturday

Dear old Dave:

   Your Modigliani cariatid from Milan received,[1] speeded by the
imposing Columbia University stamps, but with some misgiving as to
the long silence; I am to presume from the pages of Time that the
Pocket Book business has unprospered lately, what with one thing and
another, and I hope that hasn't affected you adversely on any plane:
though I don't see, either, how it can have made things any easier, or
decisions from your prospective publishers any prompter or consistent,
if at all, or you would have informed us. But I hope luck may be with
you still. All is half gaily bloody and schizonphrenic here but hopefully
and even gaily going forward, – but going forward; – oddly enough
your card caught me at the moment when I too was reading Ushant –
for the first time more or less objectively that is:[2] I found it somewhat
too productive of underground bleeding for certain participants therein
to make much intelligent comment at the time its creator sent me it; an
oversight which I fear may have somewhat hurt the old master: something which will now be corrected. It is though, you will admit, a hell
of a difficult (and not merely in the sense of its being profound, which
it frequently is, but of its *moving away* from one while one reads) book
to grasp right off in its entirety of evocation, or of which to say 'Jolly
good job old boy', or something: especially when oneself is supposed to
be one of the protagonists. It's been a wonderfully (in part) helpful book
for me to read in a situation qua 'house' like the present one, however:
jeeze how mankind stands it all I don't know – it never occurred to me
that consciousness itself could be of any aid, quite the contrary, and let
alone a goal, 'Man forget yourself' having been too often my motto, but
I feel for the first time he may be right. All aboard for the good ship
Solipsism, boys, in short, and don't forget your sea boots. . . Our little
good ship Solipsism, for which we've already secured passage by down-
payment of $100, is Italian, of the Costa Line, takes 12 passengers (of
which we still hope you may be one) and would appear to leave sometime between September 1 and 6: with this in view, unless we have to

take a later sailing or the ship itself, which is bound for Genoa or Naples or both, be otherwise delayed, we would arrive in New York the night of the 25th of August – D. V., and hope to god at least to see you then.[3] Best love from us both.

Hasta la vista

Malc

P.S. In case something happens you can go with us, herewith the address of the agent: M. Polvere, passenger agent, J.H. Winchester & Co., Costa Line, 19 Rector St., New York. Tele: HAnover 2-0935. Our passage is for their first sailing in September, the price is $175. Take sixteen days from New York to Genoa.

Annotations:

1 Lowry is describing 'Caryatid' (1912), from the Antonio Verdirame· Collection in Milan, by Italian painter Amedeo Modigliani (1884-1920). No card from Markson with this image survives with Lowry's incoming correspondence.
2 Aiken sent Lowry a signed copy of *Ushant* dated 23 August 1952, but Lowry was wounded by Aiken's portrait; see his 14 September 1952 letter (**541**) to Aiken.
3 There were several last-minute changes in the Lowrys' plans, so that they did not finally arrive in New York until Thursday, 2 September 1954.

615: To Conrad Aiken

P: H(ts)
PP: *LAL* 232-38

Dollarton, B.C.
Canada
16 July 1954
*(See below)

My beloved old Conrad:

All too hard the letter it would seem I *should* write, especially as to the question – the question also raised by you p. 329-330 in and of Ushant (and therein, by you, triumphantly solved!) as to where, in God's name, to begin, or 'step on;'[1] – especially now, after far too long a silence, *I had left this letter to gather a little dust before sending it, feeling it still unworthy: proposing then to send it in time for your birthday (of which, old man, very many happy returns):[2] then, coming across some of *your* old letters all of them so kind, so understanding, & so generous to another (even in the midst of your own troubles) I felt deeply ashamed & I could not leave you longer without a line, a silence for which I have felt increasingly of late to blame, and this for having left you with the ungenerous and niggling impression – and what was worse, about the only impression – that I was 'hurt,' more even than anything else, more even than honoured, by Ushant itself: all this is so far from being the case as to be almost funny, or would be, save that, by leaving you that impression – if indeed I did – and venturing nothing more articulate later, I feel I may have inadvertently wounded you by my apparent ingratitude, or angered and disappointed you by my bloody imperceptiveness, not to say stupidity: not to say meanness; you could rightly have thought me guilty of an injustice too, for the book is a great one, and I should have said so – would have said so in extensive detail but for certain 'auxiliary circumstances' that were responsible for my not being able to give it my full objective attention till recently. There turns out to be another reason for this too which I hope I'll convey as I go along, since it is a splendidly Ushantesque one. – Meantime, and for the rest, I feel that I'm largely not guilty of anything save that sort of narcissism – and I submit that if narcissism it is at least of the most unselfish kind, in intention, if not in effect – that keeps one from writing at all rather than say anything not masterly about a masterpiece. – Well, I've conquered this inhibiting factor, – this letter must still be largely inarticulate, and still say little that I want to say, but yet is going to go, as better than none. I note that it seems I haven't taken into account that your silence might likewise have been occasioned by 'certain auxiliary circumstances': I hope in that case not as painful as mine which range all the way from false angina and dog bite on Margie's side to myself getting caught in a trap (the trap: a half uprooted root – symbolical perhaps?) set by boys playing cowboys and Indians of all things!: – and smashing my right leg and ankle and likewise dislocating the latter – this over a year ago, largely spent in a cast, and I've only been able to walk properly again the last month. (What! dead silence in the stalls, you are supposed to laugh; and indeed the whole thing was incredibly funny in one way, looking back on it, since Margie was bitten by the dog on the way to phone the ambulance for me, so that we both arrived in hospital together, where a good time was had by all.) The worst has been the slowly tightening net – or noose – of eviction around us as British Columbia's industrial boom (perhaps one should say derrick, further to complicate the image) has lowered upon the Loweries.[3] With the oil-refineries daily gaining ground down the banks of the inlet – at the base of the biggest one a huge illuminated cerise HELL appears nightly – they having, in the interests of truth, no doubt, omitted aphaeretically the prefatory s – on the mountainside where the aspens all, all – or nearly all – are fallen, and the simultaneous pollution to a great extent, it often seems, of everything, air, sky, water, people. Our

oasis still stands, we still even add to it, our well gives forth pure mountain water still, the sea between oil-slicks is still marvellous to swim in,
out of the window, or from a pier, near which lies our boat, – the
mountains are there, so is the dogwood bursting into bloom ten years
after it was burned with our first house, and another shack we acquired
in addition to the one we rebuilt with our own hands, – though in them
days one's own hands really *were* one's own hands – of the Better Life as
represented by the 'Shoulder Parade' etc, as a kind of prepioneer we
remain slightly sceptical, or perhaps feel a bit wryly jealous. – inhabited
by a mink and family who use old drafts of the Volcano as a toilet, and
the view at night with the two towering burning oil wastes – which
from time to time emit in concert a single great subterranean growling
belch, so that one has become almost fond of them – spouting 500 feet
into the sky – 'really beautiful creatures, Malc,' I can almost hear you
saying – with the other refinery noises of a thousand Jew's harps is something to see and hear and smell, by Crikey, if it is not: but a truce to this
drooling about the mountain scenery: the point was – but I imagine you
done got it already. To abandon the place, the house in its peril seemed,
seems, traitorous but to stay simply inviting madness: how both to abandon it without treason and remain without going cuckoo but at the
same time go – and by the way where? – whole yet leaving the door
open to come back, and supposing there not to be a door, how to keep
one in the heart – how to do all this with a sense of adventure while
staying, so to say, where you are, or one was, advancing with dignified
gait toward some extramundane yet (with a motion as natural as a trans-
humance) eminently practical haven elsewhere that though several
thousand miles away still in a mysterious way was the same place,
though as yet unknown – j'y suis, me voici, je reste là, me voilà![4] – how
to do all this sort of thing with no money yet having at the same time
more than enough – all this has been of the essence of the problem: in
brief, brother, had I not suddenly found myself taking good old Ushant
from its hiding place again – between Shakespeare and Brownstone
Eclogues but still a kind of hiding place, – I don't know what I would
have done. All this, which has been brutally aggravated for the last years
by the fact that I've been trying to write about this very thing – I mean
specifically here, the life, the wonderful wonderful life, the approaching
eviction, the horrible horrible eviction[5] – not fiddling while Rome
burns, more like making a tape recording of one's own execution – was
somewhat too dramatically borne in upon me the other night when I
found myself while swimming being swept two miles downstream and
out of course by a fifteen foot rip tide (to combat such has been, of late,
a chief amusement) to be deposited upon a far shore, like Byron, with
the palsy (but without having swum the Hellespont) in the pitch dark

on the edge of the wilderness where, upon espying a friendly, as I thought, fisherman (also, as it turned out, a benevolent character of mine, though he didn't know *that*) and having asked shiveringly for the loan of a lantern to find my way home and a towel, not to say some warmth from somewhere to stay *this* little potter's trembling hand, instead of offering any such thing, some dark Hambogtrottery suspecting, he smote me wickedly upon the snoot. . . There's Natty Bumpo[6] for you – brings you up with a bump. He also hacked me viciously on the shins. His name was Clarence, and I think I'm buried under a lilac tree, the way I've felt since.[7] He was an ex-sea cook too: I forgot to say my first name was Clarence. . . But a truce to this.

What I'm trying to say is that (though I admit that the previous paragraph doesn't seem any too logically to lead up to it) it has been a case, both within and without, with the work and with one's life, of being almost completely lost in the dark, involved with a suffering I felt to be unique, and with which I didn't know what to do: lost, and then suddenly, as if round a point in chaos, and at precisely the critical moment, suddenly to observe the beneficent light of Ushant itself, no less, *your* Ushant, swinging its transfluent crossbeams ahead, to guide *me*. (And therein – in the book this time, I mean, and don't try to unmix these metaphors – not to be socked on the snoot, not to receive a stone, but an Egg, in fact perhaps the Cosmic Egg itself, but without the bad smell I attribute to this celestial fruit in the Volcano.) . .

What it comes down to anyway, it has enabled me to make a series of wise and swift decisions that would have been otherwise, I think, nearly impossible for me. Among the most important of these is [what] enables me to say now that we are retreating, but – like the regiment who buried the bodies after Custer's Last Stand,[8] – in good order: retreating but – the financial problem also having been solved quite triumphantly – likewise advancing: – (just to keep the Ushantesque records straight, I should have mentioned that the other person I have to consider in our little saga of withdrawal and return, namely Margerie, is descended on one side of the family from the Crafts, and on the other from the Winthrops[9] – her great-great-I don't know how many great grandfathers – on her mother's side being the founder of Roxbury, Mass, no less, and another one the Priscilla Winthrop of Miles Standish fame (Margerie's sister is named Priscilla) etc. etc. She is, through Betsy Patterson of Baltimore, also related to Napoleon Bonaparte (Betsy married his young brother Jerome) as I sometimes like to remind her – it would be extraordinary, or perhaps not so extraordinary if she turned out to be a collateral relative of your own, anyway I like to think she is): – we are advancing upon Greece (first to Syracuse) there to live for a few years: meantime we are leaving the house in good hands that will give and take from it the most good[10] (and won't I hope, fill the stove full of bones) and with the understanding that if we want to come back anytime it's still ours, if it's still there: and who knows, it may be, and the oil refineries gone . . .

But for Ushant I feel all this would have been a rout though. It is the identity less with Hammbo (though there's plenty salutary there, including that which 'hurts') but with your good self – in your multiple and passionate relation to houses[11] – that has saved my bacon: you have suffered through this, for *me*, it is as if I can tell myself, and this not only takes away half of the otherwise unbearable pain, but acts as a wholesome release. What psychological abyss I might have been heading for otherwise with so much libido invested in this spot of earth I shudder to think. I would have fetched up like one of the characters in Desire Under the Elms[12] or something. My current work would have been a rout too, maybe abandoned. But more of this later. I know better what to do now. Meantimes, thanks largely to yourself, the present is exciting, the future full of adventure, and the bleeding is almost exhilarating. We are sailing, D.V. sometime in September by an Italian freighter bound for Naples or Genoa.[13] Because I shall have only a transit visa and we can't be leaving here till the end of August at earliest, and we're stopping off to see Margie's mama in Los Angeles, I shall have only a few days in New York, if that, and can hope only that some miracle may occur whereby it coincides with one of your visits there if you're not in New Zealand by this time: for of course I can't say how much I'd love to see you: but if we can't see one another I'll send you a telegram anyway – at the moment plans are still a bit uncertain; I have to hear further from the shipping company.

— For the rest, afer the foregoing chaos, it seems a bit redundant – and the paragraph after that is probably going to be, I see, redundant too – to go on to say that I have experienced here in B.C. for the first time, the revelation – v. top of 332 – not to mention, if so to speak in reverse, and for a slightly different reason, the revelation on bottom of 333 – no no no, they're all too near the knuckle, these pages: – I can't do any of it justice: which is to repeat that I have found the whole magnificent book of enormous help: just at the time I needed Ushant, here was Ushant to help me: what has been worst for me has been to approach to 'this other domain of love' bottom of 332, but without any ritual poem to be the celebration of it.[14] But maybe even that will come. (I've done an enormous lot of work – some of it good – in this place, I mean Dollarton – much of it, you will one day see, quite terrifying in the light of Ushant itself, much of it having been written while you must have been writing the other, but a lot of this work has become very unbalanced – again Ushant supplies the redress.) And the passage on 336:

beginning 'That little love: the truth was, that the poem had been D's unexpected confession etc ' – Jeeze, how I understand *that* now.

Finally I ought to say that Ushant is obviously one of the best books ever written – if not necessarily, in so many words, *your* 'best' book: but it is an ADVANCE not only on your account, but it does move literature forward surely, with an almost imperceptible jolt, every bit as much as Finnegan's Wake, though for almost precisely opposite reasons: one; its marvellous generosity, as of a uranium mine, with your stake planted there but as if it were left open for other people to work it (as a librarian here said to me 'You have to have a high class intellect – like to write a book like that, Mr Lowry.') it is also a purely *intellectual* triumph of the first water. And the thesis: collossal. – But you have had enough of my incomprehensible stuff. 'And the waves of wildflowers, asking now to be remembered . . .' I won't say anything about that either, which I feel myself to have misquoted – I can't find the page (bad light) if I've buggered it up I'm sorry: it's near the end of a marvellous passage, about 298.

Well god bless you, my dear fellow: I've read practically nothing else for nearly the whole past month and always with increasing devotion. May grace descend on you and Mary whatever your direction. Best love from us both. And to old Gerald [Noxon] too, should you be in touch (Also the bridge, tripartite, once crossed tripartight. And a house in South Yarmouth. Yes, I remember it *all*.) And talking of telegrams, as perhaps might not another character have wired: Ushantih . . . Ushantih . . . Ushantih . . .

God bless you.

the old Malc.

P.S. D didn't say 'He thinks I'm a bird in a tree,' but 'he thinks I'm a tree with a bird in it.' Hambo was empathasing more than you remembered.[15]

P.P.S. For what it is worth, Po' H. [Hambo] in fact wasn't pursued by a Chinese coolie in Kowloon[16] but, as I remember, by an Arab hawker who remained on board the ship after he should have got off at Port Said, for his nefarious purpose (together also, if I remember aright, with a sowsow woman whose blind eye socket could be procured for a mere song) bribing the pure young sailor with a whole tray of 'real gold rings stolen off the mail boat,' and even went so far as Dar es Salaam with the ship down the Suez Canal before he was rid of.

P.P.P.S. But just to show you I haven't entirely lost my articulacy, perhaps I could venture to cap – unless this be discourteous or a thought too pleonastic – the Beloved Uncle's witticism, already capping D's (top

287: and what a damn fine scene this is, especially in the cemetery) 'And'
– said the Uncle instantly – 'did she take it in?' by 'Or, having taking it
in, *did she get the point properly?'*

PPPPS (Or was this perhaps just another case of 'withdrawal and
return'?)

Annotations:

1 Lowry is echoing the following passage from *Ushant*: '. . . the primary
   question as to where, in god's name, in all that welter of material . . .
   one was to make one's first entry; or at exactly what point of the
   nebular spiral . . . dare to step on' (329-30).
2 Aiken's birthday was 5 August.
3 Over the years the 'squatters' on the beach at Dollarton had been
   threatened with notices of eviction, but in 1954 the District of North
   Vancouver began the demolitions needed to prepare Cates Park; the last
   shacks in the area were demolished in 1958 (Salloum, 123).
4 The French words 'J'y suis, j'y reste' ('Here I am, and here I stay') were
   attributed to Maréchal MacMahon (1808-93) at the taking of Malakoff,
   8 September 1855, during the siege of Sevastopol in the Crimean War.
5 This is *October Ferry to Gabriola.*
6 Natty Bumppo is the pioneer scout in James Fenimore Cooper's (1789-
   1851) Leather Stocking Tales: *The Pioneers* (1823), *The Last of the
   Mohicans* (1826), and *The Prairie* (1827).
7 In *Ushant* the narrator, D., tells of planting lilac bushes with someone
   named Clarence (333-34). Lowry's first name, which he seldom used,
   was Clarence.
8 The American Major-General George Armstrong Custer (1839-76) led
   the infamous attack on the Sioux in the Battle of the Little Big Horn
   (1876). He was defeated and slain, together with his men, in one of the
   most mythologized events of American history, often referred to as
   'Custer's Last Stand.'
9 Lowry's description of Margerie's family is largely correct. According
   to Priscilla Woolfan (in a January 1990 letter to Sherrill Grace), she and
   Margerie were descended on their mother's side from the Crafts, but
   their grandfather had changed his name to Clayton, after a quarrel with
   Moses Crafts, during the Civil War. Priscilla Woolfan has no knowledge of a family connection with the Winthrops of Roxbury,
   Massachusetts, but a distant cousin on Margerie's mother's side, Betsy
   Patterson, was married to Jerome Bonaparte.
10 Harvey Burt looked after the shack and stored Lowry's books.
11 Aiken was very attached to Jeake's House in Rye and to the house in
   Savannah where he was born. Edward Butscher describes the 'loss of
   home' as 'the tragedy' of Aiken's early life; see *Poet of White Horse Vale:
   Conrad Aiken*, pp. 51-57.

12 The characters in Eugene O'Neill's play *Desire Under the Elms* (1924) all
    come to unpleasant ends.

13 The Lowrys left Dollarton for the last time on about 26 August 1954
    and spent a few days in Vancouver before flying to Los Angeles to visit
    Margerie's family on 30 August. They flew from Los Angeles to New
    York on 1 September, arriving on the second. On 12 September they
    sailed for Italy.

14 Lowry's page references throughout this paragraph are to his copy of
    Ushant.

15 In *Ushant* Aiken (D.) insinuates that Lowry (Hambo) stole this anecdote
    from him for use in *Under the Volcano*; see the Consul's encounter with
    Mr Quincey in chapter 5.

16 Lowry is correcting Aiken's version (*Ushant*, 116) of Lowry's story
    about his adventures on the ss *Pyrrhus* in 1927.

616: To Albert Erskine

P: Virginia(pcard); UBC(phc)   [Dollarton]
                                                          [23 August 1954]ª

Dear brother Albert:

We shall arrive, d.v., approx. Sept 3 (according to the interplay of
auxiliary circumstances), in New York, thence to sail, on approx. the
12th, on the ss Giacomo (piano opening) – or Margeriemalcomo –
cargoed with 'inflammable substances', out of Hoboken for the Ionian
Sea.[1] I shall be glad of some instruction in regard to protocol of passengers on Italian freighters, remembering your experience, – how to cadge
Lacrimae Christi[2] out of the second steward, & so on. I have largely
revised Gabriola but that is another story. In fact, it is another story.
Looking forward to seeing you much. Love from us both

                                                                  Malcolm

[P.S.] Dave Markson has kindly lent us his aptmt for our stay & we'll get
in touch with you thence roughly when we arrive.

Annotations:

1 Hoboken, New Jersey, on the west bank of the Hudson River opposite Manhattan Island, was a major port facility for New York; the
   Ionian Sea lies between southern Italy and Greece.

2 Lachryma Christi is a medium dry Italian sparkling wine grown in the
   area of Vesuvius. The Latin *lacrima Christi*, means the 'tear of Christ.'

Editorial Notes:

a. This is the postmark date.

As the day of departure from Dollarton grew closer, Lowry's grief and fear rendered him virtually inarticulate. In the following letter to Downie Kirk and the note (618) inscribed in the copy of Under the Volcano *that he gave to Einar Neilson, he stammers his farewells, with his familiar touch of ironic humour. These two documents are the only extant testimonials to Lowry's leave-taking. According to Douglas Day, at the Vancouver airport Lowry embraced Jimmy Craige and wept: 'I'm afraid to leave. I'm afraid we'll never come back' (464). He never did.*

617: To Downie Kirk

P: UBC(msc)   Dollarton
                                                      [August 1954]ᵃ

Dear old Downey:

Thank you wonderfully for your wonderful visit: I am inarticulate.¹

I was delighted to see you: obviously depressed at the same time. It appears to me from the above that I can't write either as fluently or articulately as yourself: – in fact I would possibly sit down at the bottom of your form saying 'Well it wasn't I that killed the King of Hamlet' until you cheered me up somehow

But I have good news, {so build the old platform after all} – though I am going temporarily, largely on account of Margie's health – the real estate evaluator figured we would all be here 15 years at least, so don't give up the ship.

Herewith a cheque to Dave.² Ask your Margerie to like me a bit the decency doesn't show but it's there just the same) – likewise Dorothy – My {most sincere} love to Dunk, Clerk, Les, Charley Harris.³

P.S. – Please convey this postdated cheque to good old Dave, to whom my love too. (It isn't there ain't any money in the bank but I've become a miser, consequently like to think of it sinking away when I ain't thinking of it, & by that time, by Christ, I won't be. But the money will be there

                                                      [unsigned]

Annotations:

1 The Kirks had visited the Lowrys for a farewell party, but Lowry's state of mind during these final days at Dollarton was very poor.

2 Dr David K. Kirk was Downie's elder brother and may have lent the Lowrys some money.

3 Marjorie Kirk was not as fond of Lowry as her husband was. Dorothy is the Kirks' daughter; Les is another of Downie's brothers, and Duncan Murray, Clerk, and Charley Harris were mutual friends.

Editorial Notes:

a. This transcription is from a photocopy (UBC 3:8); the original holograph has not been located and the date is in another hand. The letter is unsigned, but Lowry has drawn four seagulls beneath Dollarton at the top of the page.

618: To Einar and Muriel Neilson

P: UBC(ms phc)

24 August 1954[a]

> Under the Malcalmo II — or Poppagetsthebotl III —[1]
> to my dearest friends, Einar & Muriel
> Neilson, i.e Muriel & Einar, with love,
> grief, agony, joy, & so on: —
> with gratitude & Kjaerlighet (which is
> why I suppose you called the house Lieben
> anyway),[2] from its benighted author: —
> (& 23rd pupil)
>
> Malcolm Lowry
> Aug 24, 1954 (that day of wrath & hope)[3]

Annotations:

1 Lowry is slightly misremembering Conrad Aiken's wry descriptions of *Under the Volcano*. He called the Consul 'the Poppergetsthebotl of alcoholics' and the novel 'Under the Malcano' in his 27 February 1947 letter of congratulations to Lowry; see Sugars (201).

2 The Norwegian word *kjaerlighet* means 'affection.'

3 The exact date of Lowry's last day on the beach cannot be confirmed, but Lowry clearly sees something portentous and symbolic in 24 August 1954.

Editorial Notes:

a. This inscription is from the Neilson's copy of *Under the Volcano*; the transcription is from a photocopy with the Einar Neilson Papers (UBC Neilson 1:3). The inscription could have been written in Dollarton prior to the Lowrys' departure, or on Bowen Island, if they visited the

Neilsons, or in Vancouver, where they stayed for a few days before flying to Los Angeles on 30 August.

619: To Conrad Aiken

P: H(telegram)   [Western Union]
PP: *LAL* 239   [New York, N.Y.]
                                                  [Saturday, 8:43 AM]
                                                  [4 September 1954]

CONRAD AIKEN
41 DOORS
BREWSTER MASS

MALCOLM NEEDS TALCUM BE WALCOM[1] CARE OF DAVID MARKSON 610 WEST 113 STREET BEFORE TUESDAY IF POSSIBLE WHEN ALL KRAKENS GET TOGETHER[2]

LOVE
HAMBO –

Annotations:

1 The familiar quotation, 'A bit of talcum / Is always walcum,' is from Ogden Nash's poem 'The Baby' in *Free Wheeling* (1931).
2 The Lowrys stayed with David Markson for one week before sailing to Italy on 12 September 1954. Aiken came to New York for his last meeting with Lowry on Tuesday, 7 September, at a party hosted by Markson; see Day's description of this sad event (5-9). The Kraken joke stems from Aiken's visit to Lowry in New York in 1936; see Lowry's 28 November 1951 letter (**482**) to Seymour Lawrence.

620: To David Markson

P: UBC(telegram)   [Piermont, N.Y.]
                                                  9 September 1954

SAILING SUNDAY RETURNING NEW YORK TOMORROW LOVE[1]

MALCOLM

Annotations:

1 The Lowrys had left New York for a brief visit with Joan Black and her husband Viscount Peter Churchill at Snedens Landing on the Hudson River; see Bowker (549-50). They had not seen Joan since their year in France and had not met Churchill before. The two couples renewed their friendship in England; see Lowry's 4 April 1956 letter (**650**) to Churchill.

621: To Conrad Aiken

P: UBC(ms); H(telegram)   [Western Union]
PP: *LAL* 241   [New York, N.Y.]
                                           [8:15 AM]
                                           [9 September 1954]ᵃ

CONRAD AIKEN
FONE 41 DOORS
BREWSTER MASS

WAS ON DECK AT 7AM TO SEE YOU OFF WEDNESDAY BUT WAS
OFFSET BY HURRICANE[1] IF NOT OFF CAPE HATEROUS AM GOING TO
ENCOUNTER MONDAY AFTERNOON YOUR POST CARD RECEIVED
GOD BLESS YOU AND LOADS OF LOVE TO YOU AND MARY

                                           MALCOLM MARJORIE

Annotations:

1 Hurricane Edna was south of New York off the coast at Cape Hatteras
   at this time, but Lowry made much of this portentous event; see Day
   (8–9). By saying he was 'on deck,' Lowry means that he wanted to see
   Aiken off when Aiken left New York by train on Wednesday, 8
   September. Lowry had behaved badly at the Tuesday night party and
   was already feeling remorseful.

Editorial Notes:

a. A scrawled draft in pencil of this telegram is with the David Markson
    Papers (UBC Markson 1:8). The original telegram gives the time but
    no date.

*The virtually unrelieved darkness of the ten months from September 1954 to June
1955 is rivalled only by the period from November 1937 to July 1938, and like
that period it was the prelude to a serious collapse. After arriving in Italy the
Lowrys travelled to Milan to meet Giorgio Monicelli, the Italian translator of*
Under the Volcano, *although Lowry was in no condition to be of much help.
From Milan they moved to Sicily, where Lowry lapsed into alcoholic oblivion.
He could not work, he could not swim, he could not see, and he could barely communicate, as his pathetic letter* (**627**) *to Margerie indicates. It was, as he finally
managed to say to Monicelli, 'The End, so far.'*

622: To David Markson

P: UBC(pcard)

[Genoa,]
[Italy]
[22 September 1954][a]

No use to try to thank you for everything, old fellow; won't even try. We had an inferno of a voyage – though miraculously calm on one plane – with every sort of dissension among the passengers & the crew, though with a marvellous captain, (who had been through the Flying Enterprise show) (& a priest) – & I forgot to say, a steward named *Dante*, who at grave risk to his life, gave one a skin-bracer & coffee at breakfast now & then. Genoa is full of elephants & gaslamps, motor scooters, Christopher Columb[1] etc – God how you would love it –

love Malc

[P.S.] !Give our great love to Scipio & Kitty![2] Margie sends love, thanks, blessing etc

Annotations:

1 The black and white picture on the postcard shows the monument to Columbus (1451-1506) in front of the main train station in Genoa, where he was born.
2 'Scipio' Sprague and his wife Kitty were friends of David Markson's; see Lowry's 1 June 1954 letter (**610**) to Sprague.

Editorial Notes:

a. The place and date are from the postmark.

623: To David Markson

P: UBC(pcard)
PP: *SL* 374

[Milan, Italy]
[17 October 1954][a]

Bang!

Malcolm

Editorial Notes:

a. This card, postmarked 17 October 1954, shows a black and white photograph of the fifteenth-century Castello Sforzesco (named for the wealthy Sforza dynasty) in Milan at night. The open firing-range outside the castle walls was used by Napoleon during his Italian campaign.

624: To Arthur R. Sprague

P: UBC(pcard c)   [Italy]
                                                          [17 October 1954]ᵃ

for Scipio Sprague
   Something like that.
       Love to yourself and Kitty from us both.
   This written while flying (I think) over the Appenines
                                                                    Malc

Editorial Notes:

a. This transcription is from a handwritten copy (UBC 3:8). The caption
    on the card is 'Saluti da Milano.'

625: To David Markson

P: UBC(pcard)   [Syracuse,] [Sicily]
                                                         [23 October 1954]ᵃ

                        Only against death
                       shall he cry in vain[1]

                              Malc

(P.S. But without resource etc etc. And against etc etc hath he devised
escapes.)

Annotations:

 1 Lowry is quoting from his first epigraph to *Under the Volcano*, which is
    from Sophocles's *Antigone*. The card shows a scene from a contem-
    porary performance of the play at the Greek theatre in Syracuse.

Editorial Notes:

a. The place and date are taken from the postmark.

626: To Downie Kirk

P: UBC(card phc)   [Syracuse,]
                                                               [Sicily]
                                                         [ca 24 October 1954]ᵃ

   Serve him[1] damn well right for being responsible for all those forest
fires.
                              love
                                                                    Malc

Annotations:

1 The postcard shows the Greek theatre in Syracuse dedicated to Prometheus.

Editorial Notes:

a. Only a photocopy of this postcard appears to have survived, and the postmark date is partially illegible. The card was posted in Syracuse, and below Lowry's comment Margerie has added that they will be moving to Taormina 'in a few days.'

627: To Margerie Bonner Lowry

P: UBC(ms)   [Taormina,]
                                                               [Sicily]
                                                     [October 1954]ᵃ

Very dear duck: – my beloved wife –

Got up at 6:30 am thinking to lave away the past in colder ocean, (as I think I must regularly do) only to find accident in bathroom; the fittings had rusted through as you must see, though I doubt not that I helped, which does not – or does it? – improve one's case with the sanitary inspector. Tried to go on with letter to Giorgio – to little avail.[1] Stubbed toe, cried, died, as usual without you, smoked a million Alfas, but I think I have the only solution at last, which is this: to outwit the horror by getting up & working before it does, not to say swimming, perhaps even bringing *you* breakfast. I don't want to commit myself (sick transit!).[2] (I can't make out whether it is a bird singing or you crying –) but in any event your sweet tact of yesterday was not in vain, if you will continue it, even though you may think I abused it, which to some extent I did, damn it. I would go swimming now, but that my absence might worry you. At least at this early hour I have recaptured a creative *mood*, which is something. By 11 I shall possibly be a wreck after little sleep – so may you – so for Christ's sweet sake don't let us quarrel, even though I be at fault.

I send you all my love & prayers & sweetest thoughts, the old old goodk thoughts.[3]

Your bloody but loving husbound
Malcolm

Annotations:

1 Giorgio Monicelli was the Italian translator of *Under the Volcano*, but Lowry was not able to be of much help; see his abortive letters (**631**, **633**, and **634**) to Monicelli.

2 Even in such miserable circumstances, Lowry cannot miss a chance to pun. The Latin expression *sic transit gloria mundi* means 'thus passes the glory of the world.'

3 The Lowrys had a private language mimicking duck sounds; 'goodk' is an example of this, but see also his 1956 letters (**672** and **685**) to Margerie.

Editorial Notes:

a. This holograph is in ink on a torn 21-by-27.5-cm sheet of cheap paper, folded three times to make a small note. It carries neither date nor inside address. Judging from Lowry's apologetic tone and his inability to write to his Italian translator, he is writing at the Pensione Eden in Taormina towards the end of October 1954.

628: To David Markson

P: UBC(pcard)

> *Day of the Dead*
> Villa Eden,
> Via San Pancrazio 52,
> (Room no. 7★),
> Taormina,
> Sicilia
> [2 November 1954]ᵃ

dear old Dave – (the numerology will not escape you★).[1] Am situated (we are the sole inhabitants of the very beautiful pensione of that name in a street exactly the same as the Calle Nicaragua) here at last, immediately above the cemetery, to which a procession of people are taking chrysanthemums-Christian anthems! – if not quite like that old Typhoeus;[2] very adjacent though. Margie is getting better by leaps & bounds. We bathe daily in the ancient city of Naxos. I? swim to & fro, contemplate a short story called Tremor in Taormina, & we both miss you much – from us both great love

> Malc

[P.S.] Warm greetings to Admiral Scipio & his toast of the fleet, Kitty!

Annotations:

1 Lowry has starred the room number to remind Markson of the significance of the number seven in *Under the Volcano*.

2 Typhoeus (also Typhon) was the most violent of the Titans in Greek mythology. He attacked Mount Olympus but was finally slain by Zeus and buried under Mount Etna.

Editorial Notes:

a. The postmark on this card is almost illegible, but judging from Lowry's reference to the Day of the Dead, a 2 November date seems likely. The black and white picture on the card is a general view of Taormina looking towards Mount Etna.

629: To Harold Matson

P: Matson(ts); UBC(phc)

Villa Eden,
Taormina,
Sicily
20 November 1954

Dear Hal –

Thank you for your letter of Nov. 15, etc.

Never mind the history, now, of why we wrote the script, it's no longer important.[1] Except that yes, we certainly did do it on our own, and Frank [Taylor] was hoping to be able to produce it. He was extremely enthusiastic about the result and I think now he'd just like to see it done and would do all he could to help, and to judge from his letter there seems to be something he can do.[2]

Margerie and I were co-authors of this, which was not quite a working script, but far more detailed than a treatment. It was too long, and we should like to cut and re-work much of it, if Selznick[3] were interested, but even so, we feel it a bloody fine piece of work. So, after thinking it over, we've decided to sign the release and trust to fate, the excellence of the script, and to Frank, for after all, what have we got to lose? If they like our script we gain, if they are going to make it anyhow, ours won't be worth tuppence.

We don't have a copy with us and it would take some time to get the one we left in Dollarton, but Frank has the original copy anyhow, right there, so why send for ours?

In Milan I met the translator of the Volcano and worked on it with him for a couple of weeks. It is scheduled for March publication and I understand they are going to launch it with much fanfare and publicity.

Eric Linder, of the Agencie Literarie Internazionale, said he'd sold Strange Comfort for a volume of short stories, and in fact I have the volume, given me by the translator.[4] I don't remember being paid however, though it probably doesn't amount to $10.

All the best, to you, Tommy, and the children

Love

Malcolm

P.S. I'd like to make it clear, further, that our script of Tender was written in 1949 during a sort of doldrums of the American movie and in that script is a sort of prophecy of its recovery. We missed lots of hurdles in our script, and part of the ending is probably tripe, and as I said, its far too long. We love the work we did however, and I feel we might possibly deserve, quite practically – for Selznick's sake too – a crack at the version they propose to make in any event. Despite all our mistakes we solved nearly every difficulty of transposing a long sprawling novel into the different medium of the film, and few people can possibly know so much about that book by now as do we.

Annotations:

1 The filmscript of *Tender Is the Night* was sent to Frank Taylor in April 1950; see letter **395** to Taylor.
2 This letter from Taylor does not appear to have survived.
3 David O. Selznick (1902-65) was a Hollywood producer with Paramount and MGM studios before becoming independent in 1936. There is correspondence in the Matson files from December 1954 to October 1956 about the Selznick Company's interest in the Lowrys' screenplay of *Tender Is the Night*, but nothing resulted from these inquiries.
4 Eric L. Linder (1925-83) was a literary agent, translator, and editor with the Milan-based agency Agenzia Letteraria Internazionale; he represented Matson's clients. 'Strange Comfort Afforded by the Profession,' translated by Giorgio Monicelli, appeared in *Carosello di narratori Inglese* (1954).

630: To David Markson

p: UBC(pcard)   [Taormina]
                                                        [29 November 1954]

What the blazes has happened to you? We are worried. Please write instanter, even if, like me, you can't on occasion. [We've sent 5 postcards to you – what about a note? Are you OK? We *are* worried.][a]
     All good ducks here &
                              All best love from us both
                                   Malcolm & [Margerie]

Editorial Notes:

a. This postcard has been written jointly by the Lowrys, and Margerie has added at the top of the card: 'Villa Margherita, via Castellucio, Mazzaro – Taormina, Sicily we move here Dec. 13.'

631: To Giorgio and Daniela Monicelli

P: UBC(ms)   Pensione Eden, Taormina
                                              [November 1954]

– Dear, in fact, beloved, Giorgio & Daniela;[1]
     I have tried ten times to write this letter & have not yet succeeded. I
believe I am not going to succeed this time either too well but at least
perhaps I can finish this sentence before my consciousness fails me again:
which will be a sort of beginning, if not an end. Since writing the above
we have shifted from the above address to another veritably heavenly
place, though all has so far been anything but heavenly with us, largely
due to my own ghastly incapacity to look my own grief in the face
which, not liking not to be looked at, becomes all the greater each time
I fail; fail, because I am still half unconvinced that it is not a Medusa that
has to be grappled with from behind, else I turn to stone.[2] All this has
been hell on poor Margerie . . .
                         (The End, so far.)
                                                          [unsigned]

Annotations:

1 Giorgio Monicelli (1910–68) was a prolific translator of French, English,
   and American writers such as Sartre, Genet, Zola, Koestler, Golding,
   Orwell, Steinbeck, Fitzgerald, and Hemingway. *Sotto il vulcano*, his
   translation of *Under the Volcano*, was published by Feltrinelli in 1961.
   Lowry met Monicelli in Milan shortly after his arrival in Italy and,
   according to family reminiscences, they were much alike in their love of
   literature and wine. After their get-acquainted drinking binge, Lowry
   had to be hospitalized in Milan's Niguarda hospital for two weeks. At
   her father's request Elisa Monicelli visited Lowry in hospital, and she
   remembers him as gentle, poetic, and like 'an angel.' She recalls being
   'moved by the fact that his wife had left him,' but where Margerie was
   or why she was not present is unclear. In fall 1954 Monicelli was living
   apart from his wife and children, and Daniela has not been identified.
2 Medusa was one of the three Gorgons in Greek mythology; dead or
   alive she was reputed to have the power to turn anyone who looked at
   her to stone.

632: To Dorothy and Downie Kirk

P: UBC(card phc)   Villa Margherita,
                                     via Corstellucio, Taormina, Sicily
                                              [10 December 1954]

God bless you. They must have (pto) thrown a lot of bad eggs at *that* play.[1] Not to speak of Empedocles & Typho in the wings.[2] Love to your Margerie, Dorothy & Katie. Ours was a better beach though there are more sirens on this one Happy Xmas to Les Dunk Charley Harris, Dave

Malcolm

Annotations:

1 The picture on this postcard shows the ruins of the stage in the Greek theatre at Taormina.
2 Empedocles (?-444 BC) was a Greek philosopher and poet who, according to tradition, committed suicide by throwing himself into the crater of Mount Etna. Lowry is thinking of Matthew Arnold's poem 'Empedocles on Etna' (1852), in particular lines 41-48, when the philosopher addresses the defeated Titan Typho (Typhon), whose groans can be heard from the depths of the volcano.

633: To Giorgio Monicelli

P: UBC(ms)   [Taormina]
                                                 [December 1954][a]

Beloved old Giorgio:
    This is written at 4 [am], the dark night of the soul & the Farolito. It is not the letter I meant to write; in fact I have written hundreds to you all, but posted none. I cherish yours & Daniela's: – a splendid poet, please tell her. My eyes are failing – can scarcely be under electric light at all, – hence this scrawl. By daylight I can see fairly well, intermittently! Which is something. I try to write, but the writing is mostly bad, so I tear it up (with the accent on the tear) Margerie's health is so bad I must take her soon to England to see an endocrinologist of which there are none here, (or in America for that matter.) For the rest I loathe Sicily just as much as I love Italy. Dramatic & formidable though it may be it is the worst & most hypocrite place in the world. And, I think, the most hopeless. They know neither how to live or to die; & endless are the hypocrite lectures[1] I receive about drinking their bloody wine even at the moment I am being overcharged for it & cheated everywhere; I put a malediction – as did Lawrence – upon the whole place.

[breaks off unsigned]

Annotations:

1 'Hypocrite lectures' is a punning allusion to the last line of Baudelaire's address to the reader, 'Au lecteur,' the prefatory poem to *Les Fleurs du mal*, and to Eliot's use of the line in *The Waste Land*: 'You! hypocrite lecteur! – mon semblable, – mon frère!'

Editorial Notes:

a. This transcription is from a draft fragment on three 7.5-by-14-cm pages of lined paper torn from a small notepad.

634: To Giorgio and Daniela Monicelli

P: UBC(ms)
PP: *SL*

Villa Margherita,
374-76 via Castellucio,
Mazzaro, Taormina, Sicilia
[December 1954]ᵃ

(THE MEANING OF THIS LETTER is, despite my occasional irrelevant poetics, I love you & DON'T WORRY!)

Beloved Giorgio & Daniela:

For Christ sake don't pay too much attention to the damnfoolish compilation of self-pity sent you day before yesterday[1] (save to the proof of affection for yourselves contained therein. I *had* to show I had written you). The situation is certainly a pretty perilous one psychologically (& physically), but perhaps not half so perilous as my braggadocio made out. As far as the leg was concerned, it apparently decided to heal itself as if overnight, for I walked some miles on it to-day without undue trouble: my fear of its reinfection being apparently due to the horrible pain caused by leaving a band-aid on too long. So I, removed it – I mean the bandaid, not the leg: & God help me if it doesn't appear healed (touch wood). Or almost. The weakness continues, but even here I seem to be regaining weight, & becoming my abnormal deranged fat self again, under the influence of vast quantities of Gorgonzola cheese & mineral water, (the water always being relatively mineral of course.) But not all my braggadocio can remove the perilousness of Taormina as a place to live in – & especially here, where there are ten abysses round every corner.

Enough of this. The mystery to me is how even Ulysses, reputed for his aplomb & cunning, could ever have been seduced by imaginary siren voices emerging from a barren island on which you can't even land – even though we half live on it – and which is inhabited by nothing but a few dwarf cactus & three wild constipated goats, driven mad by the noise of the traffic to Messina on the coastwise road & that of the coast-wise train. The weather is bloody awful, the Mediterranean here – final humiliation – continues almost unswimmable in – Margerie, poor gal, has another bad throat, snow falls on Calabria, we are served in this house by a male neanderthal homosexual orangutang in a flapping over-coat with a forehead like the infant Mozart & a female gorilla with a heart of gold & a mind that thinks of nothing else, unless it is food, most of which is inedible. If Western civilisation began here, all I can say is it should not have been difficult to predict long ago how it would end. Margerie has just said that she would rather be asphixiated than frozen (though what usually happens is that you are both) so I have just called for the brazier which will arrive with a lemon on top. – Meantime you can see that I *have* rallied à la Stendhal, so don't worry.

It seems terribly impolite of me to take it out on poor Sicily but all I can say is that Sicily is certainly not Italy – in fact they hate you worse than they do us, which is saying something – & that you have my permission to give Scotland a beating any time you want to, Scotland which is not England, & I say this as a descendant of Robert the Bruce (though it is true he had many descendants, most of them, like doubtless me, illegitimate.)[2] What arouses my ire about this island, though, is partly no doubt of course occasioned by a mixture of compassion & envy. The life of the Sicilians seems to me hopeless beyond hopelessness & everything bad in it of course washes into Taormina where the majority seem not human beings at all, but vultures praying on tourists. But how do they get up & down hill – & what fabulous hills? & how sing doing it? how preserve a certain stern autochthonous beauty in the native culture?

How did Pirandello, Verga, ever first draw breath in such a place,[3] which is not only improbable, but, to my mind, impossible, a fantasy God, if he ever created it, should have forgotten, or tried to have forgotten, that remorseful man. Margerie of course thinks it romantic: I think the only beauty it possesses is that of death & dead it is, – yet the people are not. Or not yet. Or not quite. As it stands it is a hideous travesty of our old life where life was yet uncompleted – the great trees still stood – who is to blame? I asked the priest, who runs the local cinema (where we saw Quo Vadis?) & all he said was 'Sprechen sie deutsch?'[4]

It all would seem to me to represent an almost incredible anomaly of the modern world that makes me feel like parodying Eliot: – strength without courage, fortitude without guts (for all the Sicilians seem to understand is brute force & shouting) – all of which is very different, (though it may be similar after all) as 'strength broken by strength but still strong,' as a friend of mine once wrote about Canada.[5] A mixture of the Isle of Man, Acapulco & Liverpool. God help us all. Margie's southern tradition, though, is in full buzz: they are nearly all slaves (I don't overlook the fact that I am one myself) & if you don't treat them as such they won't respect you. There is much love & tragedy in this, but I won't go into it any more. I went and took a look at D.H. Lawrence's house & disrespected him for having taken it, I'm afraid, –

even though I cried – I think it was on March 30th 1930, & I'd just come out of a cinema in Cambridge (which was out of bounds) when I heard he was dead. Basta! Basta! Basta![6]

Pazienza! Pazienza! Pazienza!

Publish though, what I have said neither in the streets of Tyre, nor in the bye-streets of Ascalon.[7] Do not either, (even if you already have) mention this ordeal to the good Eric Linder. For apart from anything else, he will, – good soul – worry, mention it to Harold Matson & also to Innes Rose, who will, good fellow though he is, then mention it to the Caspian Sea, out of which you know is no outlet, & so poor Otto will just go round & round & round . . . . Neither mention it to Garzanti.[8] Or mention it to yourself. (Feeling that Empedocles is finally becoming a bore)

All the best & the more than best to you & Daniela & Lizabeta & love from Margery too[9]

LOVE MALCOLM

P.S. Give my regards & thanks also to the German girl Haidée – I will send you all a Xmas card if ever I can round that Isle of Sirens.[10]

Annotations:

1 See letter **633**.
2 Robert I, The Bruce (1274-1329), was king of Scotland from 1306 to 1329 and the leader of the Scots' wars of independence from the English, which ended with the defeat of Edward II's army at Bannockburn in 1314.
3 Playwright Luigi Pirandello and novelist Giovanni Verga (1840-1922) were both born in Sicily.
4 The 1951 film version of Henrik Sienkiewicz's historical novel *Quo Vadis* (1896) was directed by Mervyn Le Roy and starred Peter Ustinov. The priest's unlikely question is: 'Do you speak German?'
5 Lowry is parodying lines from T.S. Eliot's poem 'The Hollow Men' (1925): 'Shape without form, shade without colour / Paralysed force, gesture without motion.' Lowry's friend is the poet and editor A.J.M. Smith, who was heavily influenced by Eliot. Smith's poem 'The Lonely Land' (1936) concludes with the following lines: 'This is the beauty / of strength / broken by strength / and still strong.'
6 In his July 1944 letter (**193**) to Margerie, Lowry claims that *Basta* (enough) is a favourite Lawrence expression, but it is used more frequently by Henry James in his letters and Lowry had read James's letters with care. D.H. Lawrence died on 2 March 1930 in Villa Robermond, Vence, in southern France, but he had lived in Taormina between February 1920 and February 1922. Lawrence had an early though not lasting influence on Lowry; see Lowry's April 1934 letter (**60**) to Jan Gabrial.

7 Tyre, now in Lebanon, was a Phoenician city from biblical times, and Ascalon, an ancient city in Palestine, is now a desolate spot on the coast of Israel north of Gaza. Lowry is parodying David's lament, known as the 'Song of the Bow,' in 2 Samuel 1:20: 'How the mighty have fallen! / Tell it not in Gath, / Proclaim it not / in the streets of Ashkelon.'

8 Dr Livio Garzanti is a Milan publisher who operates Garzanti Editore and Libreria Garzanti, founded in 1861.

9 Lizabeta is probably Monicelli's daughter Elisa; see Lowry's November letter (**631**) to Monicelli, annotation 1.

10 The Isle of Sirens is either two or three islands off the coast of Italy near Naples. In Greek mythology Sirens were bird-women who lured sailors to destruction on the rocks by the sweetness of their singing. Like Ulysses, in Homer's *Odyssey*, Lowry must navigate his way past the siren songs that tempt him in Sicily: alcohol, despair, and death.

Editorial Notes:

a. This holograph letter is in pencil on six sheets of 15-by-20-cm paper (UBC 3:9). It carries an inside address but no date. Judging from the address and the reference to Christmas in the postscript it was probably written shortly after the Lowrys moved to the Villa Margherita at Mazzaro, below the main town of Taormina, on or about 13 December. Lowry has printed his complimentary close and name in capitals.

Only seven letters have survived the disastrous year of 1955. Lowry drank heavily and constantly, wrote almost nothing – even his letters are brief and frag-mentary – and sank into a state of agonized paralysis. He and Margerie moved from pensione to pensione, carried out some desultory sightseeing, and finally left Sicily in July for England, where they were both hospitalized. Considering the depths of his despair over his exile from Dollarton and his apparent rejection by Random House, it is surprising that his marriage and sanity survived at all. But Malcolm's recuperative powers were considerable, and both he and Margerie would make it 'through those weeds, and over those falls.'

635: To David Markson

P: UBC(ms)   [Taormina]
                                                        [21 January 1955]

Dear old Dave:
    You have defined my position absolutely. But not your own: your

exposition of it was too brilliant & clear; – I propose, with your permission, to steal it.

You don't have any technical problem, – turn it all into the third person, as Somerset Maugham would say.[1]

Style is cutting: Markson v Flaubert + Markson - Flaubert - Maugham - H[illegible]: ςπρ²?

Something like that.

Here is the Scirocco!

And I try to smash its brains every day, & I seem to be succeeding, since it, poor wind, has none.

Love from our hearts as from Margerie

Malcolm

P.S. Please tell Scipio & Kitty the only reason I didn't send them a wedding present was I didn't know the exact date they were to be married: – their card arrived after they were: A present – (hurricanes excepting) is on its way.

Annotations:

1 Markson must have sent the Lowrys a manuscript or the description of his work in progress, but nothing survives with incoming correspondence.

636: To David Markson

P: UBC(pcard)   [Villa Mazzullo,]
[Mazzaro]
28 May 1955

Dear old Dave: – I am toweringly sorry I haven't replied yet to your brilliant letter &/or letters: nonetheless treasured for being nonreplied to. But the truth is I have had among other things dark trouble with my eyes: derivative,[1] but true, since it is about the only trouble you can have with them; nontheless true for being derivative: – turns out to be a dietary deficiency only fortunately

This is not a good letter – distressed to hear of Jim [illegible][2]

Love from us both.

Malc

[P.S.] Portrait of Artist on right.[3]

Annotations:

1 Lowry may be calling his eye trouble 'derivative' because he is thinking of James Joyce's severe eye trouble in his last years, as the postscript

reference to Joyce's novel suggests. Lowry, however, had suffered from eye trouble in boyhood (see Day 75-77), and as his poem 'Autopsy' makes clear, he always saw himself as terribly afflicted by these problems.

2 David Markson had written with the news that James Agee had collapsed from a heart attack and died on 16 May 1955; see Lowry's June 1955 letter (**637**) to Markson. The postage stamp covers Lowry's message at this point.

3 Lowry is alluding to Joyce's *A Portrait of the Artist as a Young Man* (1916). The black and white photograph on the postcard shows the Catania gate in Taormina with a local man, his face obscured by shadow, leading a burrow and standing to the left of the gate; there are distant hills to the right of the image.

637: To David Markson

P: UBC(ms)
PP: *SL* 379

[Villa Mazzullo]
[early June 1955][a]
?

Dear old Dave:

I am terribly sorry I haven't written. Partial explanation is in a p.c that should arrive about the same time as this.

I am struck dumb by your news of Jim Agee's death: something goes fast out of your life when a man as good as that dies, even though people of worth are dying like flies these days, I can only think, to armour the dead.

All my best love to Scipio & Kitty: their wedding invitation, to hand, has arrived just about in time for me to give them a christening present!: – please convey my apologies & congratulations – (it is terribly hard for me to write at all at present)

Sicily – or at any rate Taormina – is a first rate disastar & the noise so appalling I have to wear ear plugs all the time, which is causing me to go deaf (as well as blind.) I fear you would like it.

Margie sends her love. As do I. I can't send you any good news so get busy & send me some. We depart for England soon.[1] Robert Haas of Random House was here, but by bad luck I missed him. I heard roundabout that he spoke very well of me which I count damned sporting of him since I am 99 years behind in fulfilling my contract.

Our maid's daughter had a child the other day: the father & mother get married next Monday. I am thinking of forbidding the banns: apart from which the Volcano, though translated, into Italian, is apparently in potential trouble with the Vatican:[2] so it hasn't come out, the only thing that has being our dinner, from the icebox, which a neighboring cat has learned how to open. Let her have it!

Sursum corda!

Malc

Annotations:

1 Margerie has written her letter to Markson on the verso of Lowry's, and she gives factual information about their plan to return to England for medical help sometime between 8 and 20 June, where they expected to be met by a friend, Colonel B.E.R. Morton, of Lloyd's Bank in London. We have not been able to trace Morton, and the Lowrys did not fly to London until 9 July 1955.

2 Lowry's comment appears to be a fanciful excuse for the delays experienced with the Italian translation.

Editorial Notes:

a. This single-sheet holograph has neither inside address nor date, but Lowry has written the following question mark in the usual place for this information.

638: To Harvey Burt

P: private(ms)

[London,]
[England]
[26 July 1955][a]

− God bless you my dear dear old fellow your present is a masterpiece[1] − we opened the treasure together, Dorothy, Margerie & I to-day in London & drank your health. Wire following. Love: −

Malcolm

P.S. And love to Jim: to Downey: to the beach! apologise for my nonwriting. Jesus what can I say?

And love to Jim
And love to James Craige

− And then −

Annotations:

1 Harvey Burt had made a miniature wooden scale model of the Lowrys' Dollarton shack and pier with their boat, 'My Heart's in the Highlands.' He sent it to Dorothy, who was in London, and she brought the fragile present to Lowry for his birthday on 28 July.

Editorial Notes:

a. This date has been added by Harvey Burt. The letter itself has been jointly written by Malcolm, Margerie, and Dorothy Templeton Burt.

639: To David Markson

P: UBC(ms)

77 Onslow Rd.,
Richmond, Surrey
[19 August 1955]ᵃ

Dear old Dave.
Thank you.
Wait.
Malcolm.

Editorial Notes:

a. This note is written on a tiny fragment of paper. The date is from the postmark recorded by Markson. A letter from Margerie accompanied this note; in it she explains that she is going into London Hospital, Whitechapel, for an operation, and that Lowry will be seeing a psychiatrist. He can, she says, be reached care of John Davenport, 4 Rossetti House, Flood Street in London. The Richmond, Surrey address is where the Lowrys stayed from 27 July to early September; see Bowker (559–61).

640: To James Craige

P: UBC(ms phc)
PP: *SL* 382

[London]
[12 September 1955]ᵃ

Beloved Jim:
    Have never stopped thinking of you or the beach.
    Please give my best love to all, especially Downey [Kirk], the gang & the rest: & the good Harvey [Burt].
    My inability to reply has been due – tell Downey, for I value his letters more than I can say – to my eyes failing. Faltering or recovering. I go in hospital for a brain operation thing to-morrow: (But UP UP UP FROM THE FLOOR. That's the way).[1] Margie 2 days later. Don't think it serious. There has never been a moment when I have not thought of you all with deepest love —————————— Malc

P.S. And tell Downey's Dorothy not to get a big head. I made it to Barnet once alas in 1 hr & ¾.[2] We shall all rejoin back there
Love
Malcolm

Annotations:

1 Lowry was admitted to Brook Hospital in Woolwich on 12 September
1955, where Dr George Northcroft, a friend from his Cambridge days,
was a consultant neurosurgeon. He did not undergo brain surgery but
was given bed rest, then exercise, and recuperated rapidly. Margerie was
admitted to the Brook as well, where she had tests for ulcers and a gall-
bladder infection. See Bowker (562-64).
2 Dorothy is Downie Kirk's daughter; Barnet is a small community
approximately two kilometres across Burrard Inlet from Dollarton.

Editorial Notes:

a. 'September 12' has been written at the top left of the page with the year
underlined.

641: To Albert Erskine

P: Virginia(ms)   Brook General Hospital,
PP: *SL* 380-82   Ward H: (Neurosurgical),
                                              Shooters Hill Road,
                                        Woolich, London SE 18
                                              [October 1955]ᵃ

Dear brother Albert: – I would appear to be here, Margie likewise, but
in another ward, F2; fortunately we can see each other. It is an
extremely good hospital, and everyone is very kind indeed, & one eats
(I speak for myself, not Margie, who can't eat at all) like a horse: this is
a ward more or less entirely devoted to people with brain or skull
injuries, or to the post operative recovery of such, so that the reaper is
omnipresent but it is by no means grim for all that, in fact I spend most
of my time shirtless on the cricket pitch in the dew. Briefly, the news:
it was for a time thought possible that sundry past injuries & fractures or
what not might have damaged a tricky area of my brain but despite some
still perplexing symptoms it seems this isn't so therefore, though I have
been exrayed & probably will be again to determine whether an operation is necessary, so far as I can tell I'm not going to be operated on, or
at least not yet, & even if so the thing would be a minor one (I'm having
one for haemorrhoids anyway though I hope that's not where I keep my
brain), I think, touch wood. The most trying symptom has been eyesight, which has been 'on the blink' (sick transit!)[1] since the beginning
of the year, & in fact occasionaly so bad I thought I was derivatively
losing my sight altogether; moreover I had dark thoughts that my childhood trouble was recurring on another plane or to blame: not so, it is

just, some experts say, the usual weakening of the muscles behind the eyes that can occur at my age. So I now am bespectacled which would be scarcely a unique state were it not that the whole thing is so maddeningly inconsistent: sometimes, especially in sunlight I see worse with spectacles than without & by electric light print sometimes will blur or black out altogether: then for a while I'll see perfectly again; much the same too with my physical well being: I lost 42 lbs in a couple of months in Sicily, but back it all seems to have come here in a fortnight, I'm half sorry to say. Needless to say all this has not been too good for work, & in fact latterly, with poor Margie out of commission altogether quite impossible: this must be only about the third letter I've managed to complete this year, if I manage to complete it and – beautiful petard![2] – things are not rendered any easier by the fact that I can't read my own ex-handwriting or only with great difficulty. By the time you receive this we'll both have been in here a month & probably will have at least another month to go.[3] What is wrong with Margie noone has yet fully determined but she is certainly damned sick, in fact a great deal sicker than I am: both of us take some grave delight in that they are feeding her paraldehyde as a sedative though her problem is not an alcoholic one (nor is mine, though I must say I feel I could use a paraldehyde & splash sometimes.) Both of us have been under medical care a good deal longer than we've been hospitalised & the former doctor forbade me to write (especially on the Gabriola theme), suppose this to have been possible, or even think of writing until things were much better sorted out than they were: the present treatment so far as I'm concerned has had as its aim my resumption of the Work in Progress but I have to write off much of the last 18 months as a dead loss, I fear. To-day the necessary m.s.s has been teleported to me again & sits glistering by my bedside in the ward (where my neighbor died last night to the accompaniment of the Wabash Blues) waiting for me to bash into it once more, which I mean to do as well as I can, starting immediately, though things are bound to be delayed, not least because of the typing: moreover what with this eye business I have to revise entirely my method of writing & in fact generally reorient myself to it – it's been hard for me up to now sometimes to hold a pencil at all for more than 5 minutes at a time. Needless to say I feel badly not to have delivered the goods or some goods, long ere now; it was a great pity for me we had to sever the umbilical cord with Random House at the precise time we did: moreover I got very discouraged, not only by the reception there but by the lack of a word from anyone in the U.S. in regard to what small things I did publish: both Bravest Boat & Strange Comfort have become classics in French & Italian & the latter in an anthology of Best English Short Stories of all time & so on.[4] I have read aloud parts of Gabriola with great success too when in Taormina, which may mean something. But a truce to this. Should I kick the bucket untimely-like or the project seem really hopeless it is arranged that the money so far advanced will be paid back to you: as things stand I can keep our heads above water without aid but I don't want to assume failure in advance to complete things or to engage myself in extraneous projects in *order* to pay you back now. I hope the situation may be still as it was, that the clock was stopped when it was stopped, & that I may have time, no matter how much I've lost or how tardy I am, to catch up now. It would remove a major source of emotional tension (a commodity I am not allowed to indulge in) if I could feel this were so. I believe I can make the grade though luck has been consistently against me & us so far & I don't have any right to make any promises, save that I'm going to TRY, after so long silence & limbo. A letter to Mr Haas {to whom please convey as much or as little as you think fit}, who was in Taormina & who was kind & sporting enough to speak well of me there, I heard, though unfortunately I didn't meet him, accompanies this, which please give him if you think it right, & if not not.[5] Another strange casualty is my English grammar: a total amnesiacal loss, but I don't think a very serious one. All the best love from us both & as always with the utmost affection.

Malcolm

Annotations:

1 Lowry's punning reference is to *Sic transit gloria mundi*; see his October 1954 letter (**627**) to Margerie.
2 To be 'hoist with his own petard' means to be caught in his own trap, in this case his eye trouble. See *Hamlet*, III.iv.207.
3 The Lowrys left the Brook Hospital on 5 November 1955.
4 Lowry is thinking of *Carosello di narratori Inglese* (1954), which contains Giorgio Monicelli's translation of 'Strange Comfort Afforded by the Profession' and of Carl Klinck's *Canadian Anthology* (1955), which includes the story.
5 In a 1992 conversation with Sherrill Grace, Albert Erskine could not recall such a letter.

Editorial Notes:

a. Lowry has written this letter in blue ink, in his tiniest script, on two sheets of 12.5-by-17.5-cm paper. It is undated but may have been written in October 1955, when his condition was considerably improved. Margerie has added a short note of greetings at the top of the first page.

During their years at Dollarton the Lowrys developed an elaborate private discourse in which they referred to each other as the Harteebeeste and El Leon and populated their world with helpful animal figures. In the following letter, and in several more written while he or Margerie was in hospital in 1956, Malcolm uses these epithets to convey his affection. Appendix 1 contains a representative sample from over four hundred notes to Margerie written in this manner.

642: To Margerie Bonner Lowry

P: UBC(ms)   [Atkinson Morley's Hospital,]
                                                      [31 Copse Hill,]
                                                      [Wimbledon]
                                              Sat night [January 1956]

By little Trottywagtail & all the good Mergansers to their own Sweetharteebeeste[1]

My very sweet wife:

   Just a little bit of news from round the Rialto. It was wonderful to hear your voice to-night, twice; otherwise I had a rather depressing evening; poor old Ralph [Case] being so jittery I almost thought he'd been kicking the gong around again for a moment.[2] He is very anxious to see [Dr Michael] Raymond, whether on his own account or mine I don't know:[3] possibly both: possibly – & very humanly, & sadly & he may simply want his own part re me ratified as a *doctor*; it puts me in a bit of an awkward position, because his own position vis-a-vis Raymond would rather resemble my position vis-a-vis both of them, though naturally it's very different in degree: I don't fancy Raymond as having much sympathy with Ralph's position unfortunately, or if sympathy, I don't see him too tactful about it, & Ralph struck me as so shattered that it seemed to me he only needed one discouraging or careless word to push him right overboard: as for me I feel I have acquired new strength, wherever it has come from, & as a consequence it merely angers me when people argue from a standpoint of chronic weakness conceived of as permanent. Not that I deny that the weakness was chronic, or had become so, but that there is nothing more calculated to provoke the imp of the perverse[4] than the insistence on weakness with a person who has just proved himself strong: – undoubtedly one has to be stronger still to let these 'failure suggestions' bounce off one but it is a mystery to me that doctors don't seem to recognize them for what they are: strength through fear seems to be the latest technique & it is a contradiction in terms, in my opinion. I wish they would shut up talking: whatever has worked or is working with me is certainly doing so independently of the chatter, though in Ralph's case I suppose it could be a sort of projection. Basta. If they want the credit let them take it, but in fact if I have changed it is entirely due to a full & as it were *objective* realisation of what you mean to me & how much I love you & wish to make you – & us – happy: personal shame or self-interest or even respect were strangely quite negligible factors save in those terms during the worst periods. I have exultant hopes for the future & know I shall love the house in Ripe.[5] Please go & see The Man with the Golden Arm if only for an apparently marvellous film of Bonny Scotland that goes with it.[6] And I hear Rebel Without a Cause with James Dean at the Leicester Square is one of the best American films ever made.[7] (see above) From Below. Wholly remarkable. So go & see it, please. Apparently it's an absolute double-barreled knock-out. Don't overlook my important 'enclosure'[a] – perhaps you can find an entry. Prenyow. Don't pay any attention if my words put you off – I'm very very tired, but very very full of love. Oh western wind when wilt thou blow.[8] All love, my beautiful heart's darling

Your husband

Malcolm

Annotations:

1 'Little Trotty Wagtail' (1849) is a poem by the English poet John Clare (1793-1864). Clare spent much of his life in a mental asylum, but his best work celebrates rural life in direct language. Lowry was reading Clare during early 1956; see his 22 March letter (**647**) to John Davenport and his March letter (**648**) to Jimmy Craige.

2 Dr Ralph Case, the brother of Robert and Martin Case (see Lowry's December 1937 poem-letter **75**) and a friend of Lowry's from their Cambridge days, was seeing Lowry frequently. Aware that Lowry's condition was deteriorating in October and early November 1955 after the discharge from Brook General Hospital in Woolwich, Case put Lowry in touch with Sir Paul Mallinson, a leading psychiatrist, who arranged for Lowry to be admitted to Atkinson Morley's Hospital on 5 November 1955. Thus Case felt some direct responsibility for Lowry's being at Atkinson Morley's.

3 Dr Michael Raymond was the physician in direct charge of Lowry; see Lowry's 23 October 1956 letter (**671**) to him.

4 In his short story 'The Imp of the Perverse' (1846) Edgar Allan Poe develops the idea that human beings have an innate need to hurt themselves and others.

5 With Dr Raymond's help, Margerie had found 'The White Cottage' in
the picturesque village of Ripe in Sussex. They moved to Ripe after
Lowry's release from hospital on 7 February.
6 *The Man with the Golden Arm* (1956) was directed by Otto Preminger.
7 *Rebel without a Cause* (1955) was directed by Nicholas Ray and starred
the American actor James Dean (1931-55).
8 Lowry first quoted this line from the anonymous Middle English lyric
'Western Wind' for Margerie in his 22 August 1939 letter (**102**) to her.
He also quoted it in his June 1933 letter (**46**) to Jan Gabrial.

Editorial Notes:

a. There is now no enclosure with this letter.

643: To Margerie Bonner Lowry

P: UBC(ms)   Atkinson Morley
                                              Monday [January 1956][a]

By the Good Mergansers

My dearest sweetest darling waggle-tailed plum trotty wagtailissima
sweetesthartebeeste superba non parail: – just a little bit of news from
round the Rialto from you know who, though there is no other news
of note: you will at this moment be batting back from Ripe in which
connection I have collected from the Sunday newspaper some other
picturesque names of villages. Dead Maidens (nr Southampton): Wide
Open, Pity me, Kitty Brewster (nr Newcastle-on-Tyne): there is Fryup
in Yorkshire, & Cold Roast Hamlet in Buckinghamshire. Likewise
Picket Post, Gibraltar, Ready Token, New Zealand, Blubberhouses,
Make-em-Rich, & Ugley. (These in Hampshire, Suffolk, Wilts,
Gloucestershire, Yorkshire, Northumberland, Essex respectively.) Also
in Hampshire, 10 miles from Reading is Tadley God Help Us. In
Flintshire, North Wales, fairly near where our old home, We Three
Loggerheads: Christmaspie, Shippobottom, & Bundle & Foggo are
others. Also Oliver Chase Quick, King Edward Horsenail, Leaping
Well, & best of all Wig-Wig (near Much Wenlock.) What wonderful
titles some of things would make, & I see I've forgotten some of the best
mentioned, all in Cornwall: Penny-Come-Quick, Hard to come by,
Little in Sight, & Knave Go by. If not for collections of short stories or
novels or poems what titles for Blues – I've thought of writing Ralph
[Case] about it. Cold Roast Hamlet Blues, Blubberhouses Blues, Ugley
Blues, Hard to come By Blues, Make-em Rich Blues, Tadley God Help
Us Blues, Little in Sight Blues, Wide-Open Blues, King Edward

Horsenail Blues, Shippobottom Blues, Wig-wig Blues, Leaping Well Blues. Penny-come-quick Blues.

I'm definitely going to call Hear us Oh Lord Cold Roast Hamlet, I think. And we've absolutely got to write the King Edward Horsenail Blues. All dearest sweetest love from *all* the little animals

As also dearest sweetest love from me

Roll on next Tuesday week

Bundle & Foggo

Love your
El Leon

Editorial Notes:

a. In the right margin beside the 'El Leon' signature Lowry has drawn a rather canine-looking lion and a seagull.

644: To Margerie Bonner Lowry

P: UBC(ms)
Atkinson Morley
Friday night
[January 1956]ᵃ

Dearest sweetest darlingest sweetharteebeeste:

Here is just a little note & though it can't go off to-night I'm hoping it will catch an early post in the morning so you will get it to-morrow anyhow, though I ha' ma doots, mon. I played several games of ping-pong to-night, both singles & doubles, with experts & duffers, both trying to win against the former, & lose against the latter, & partly succeeding in doing both, & vice-versa, as in sweating right through a clean shirt: my hand has not altogether lost its cunning, however, though I could be in better training. I worked all day on [*October Ferry to*] Gabriola then had a somewhat discouraging chat with [Dr] Raymond whose first question was had I drunk the beer – the two 'temptation' bottles – with John [Davenport]: actually both bottles are still there, John having finally decided against having any, but since I had said in his, Raymond's, presence I was *not* going to touch a drink, I'm somewhat annoyed at this distrust & assumption especially as I have comported myself like an apostle throughout,[1] if not a holy Christian martyr, & especially as he only had to look round my room to see the horrible bottles were still there: I fixed him with a steady glittering gaze & found to my surprise he was twitching & nervous & could not meet my eyes: he is a good man whom one could make a real friend of, & perhaps will, it is too bad he has to, or thinks he has to quibble & lie & try to catch you to elicit certain psychological responses: in renewed relative health & self-confidence I'm not sure I agree with him on some fundamental points either – I believe there is an *un*inevitability of character too, though I can't blame you for not thinking so recently. And don't think he knows much about *us*, nor feels *my* side of the question at all, & only yours superficially. Be that as it may, I am quite a changed man, with quite a different attitude towards things & the hell-dance I have led you, poor lamb, & I shall try to make amends & am optimistic that you shall have real goodk & happy & ripe & ripe & fun & the ducks will be themselves & happy again. For god's sake don't worry about supplies in the house, the pub, or my anxieties keeping you awake. Your lunch with Mrs Mason sounded angelly – all my favorite dishes (&, alack, potations).[2] And the house sounds angelly. And you yourself are an angel – I rarely have seen you looking so beautiful & happy as recently. I am dead tired after the work & exercise so must close now. Oh western wind when wilt thou blow

All love, my heart's darling. Your husband

Malcolm

[P.S.] (El Leon has been advised to drink non–alcoholic cider) BEBE APPELLA BIEN FRIO[3]

Annotations:

1 In chapters 1 and 5 of *Under the Volcano* Dr Vigil remarks that he 'must comport' himself 'like an apostle.'
2 Mrs Edwina Mason, the Lowrys' landlady at the White Cottage in Ripe, lived in the attached cottage next door.
3 Appella is the name of a brand of cider; see Lowry's joke in his 22 March 1956 letter (**647**) to John Davenport.

Editorial Notes:

a. The pencil holograph (UBC 3:11) is undated, but references to the cottage in Ripe and to Appella suggest that Lowry is writing close to the end of his first stay in Atkinson Morley's and prior to seeing the White Cottage.

645: To Margerie Bonner Lowry

P: UBC(ms)   [Atkinson Morley's Hospital]
[2 February 1956][a]

You know how we are, oh most beautiful & wisest Sweetharteebeeste. But be sure you don't miss the *smallest* cutting. It's been somewhat of a *trying* Thursday, but have been given the clean bill of bonvoyage & farewell & congratulations by Sir Paul [Mallinson],[1] so that next

Tuesday takes on a more real & less mythical quality & may it roll on & the pipes not freeze: meantime my egg exploded from the cold at tea & I put a splint on Ralph [Case]'s record & played it to a female audience of Wimbledon's worst in the dayroom: I do hope it isn't too cold for you to-morrow rolling down to Ripe-O in an Eastern Train (I hope *not* 'after hours of standing in the sleet & rain')[2] – & that your poor cold is much better – I am now waiting for you to call up – waiting – waiting – oh sweetest dear duck oh Eastern wind when wilt thou stop (oh western wind, when wilt thou blow) –

All possible sweet love from all of us

Oh beloved darling

All love Your husband

Malc

Annotations:

1 Sir Paul Mallinson (1909-89) was senior consultant psychiatrist at Atkinson Morley's Hospital; he admitted Lowry to hospital for alcoholism on 25 November 1955.
2 Malcolm is reminding Margerie of the song based on the popular poem 'Riding Down From Bangor' by American poet Louis Shreve Osborne.

Editorial Notes:

a. This pencil holograph, filed with the so-called 'love notes' (UBC 53:2), was written on the Thursday before Lowry's 7 February release from hospital. In the left margin of the recto Lowry has drawn his and Margerie's coat of arms: on the left a lion rampant, smoking a pipe; on the right a pronghorn; the centre shield shows seagulls and a crown with three crosses. His heraldic inscription is 'DUCK EST MON DROIT (Lion & Pronghorn in Gamesome Mood)'.

After his discharge from Atkinson Morley's Hospital, Lowry moved to the house that Margerie had found with the help of Dr Michael Raymond. From Ripe, a small village in Sussex just south of London and a short bus ride from Lewes, he and Margerie could make trips to London to see doctors or shows and to Lewes for library books. The White Cottage, with its garden, peaceful surroundings, and nearby pub, provided the only haven Lowry would find in England.

646: To David Markson

P: UBC(pcard)   The White Cottage,
PP: *SL* 383   Ripe (nr Lewes), Sussex, England
                                                    21 February 1956[a]

Dear old Dave: – A thousand thanks for your many deeply appreciated
letters (which is an understatement) to us both: I'll just have to start
again as a letter writer since I'd never catch up were I to try to reply in
detail: one inhibiting factor among others has been the defection into
defectiveness of my eyesight: a confounded nuisance. But I'm back on
the work in progress [*October Ferry to Gabriola*] again & again thanks for
your encouragement. It seems to me you need some in kind: why not
set yourself for a start the one goal of *finishing* the Satevepost story as they
want it (you can always alter it afterwards if you want) & getting paid
for it?[1] You have Fitzgerald & Faulkner as precursors. If you can get to
England you can come & work here – a delightful old place – & we can
start a mutual aid society. There's a fine old pub too with an 120 year
old German jukebox that plays 18" brass records. Hudson lived hereabouts. Henry James' ghost prowls not far.[2] So does that of almost every
other writer you can think of for that matter, & though something
similar might be said of Greenwich Village, as from the White Horse to
the White Cottage might be a palpable step.[3] Meantime I drink Cydrax
('Cider's non alcoholic little sister') & behind a Melvillean boskage
ponder the usage of the introverted coma. Wish you could find a P.R.
[*Partisan Review*] with Bravest Boat in it – May-June '54? – & I'd love
to read the Recognitions.[4] Please send us the good word & all best
love from Margie & me,

                                                                Malc

Annotations:

1 David Markson published a short story called 'White Apache' in the
   Saturday Evening Post, 29 September 1956, 30 and 135-39; see Lowry's
   spring 1956 letter (**652**) to Markson.
2 English naturalist and novelist William Henry Hudson (1841-1922),
   who was buried in Broadwater, Sussex, sometimes took his holidays in
   Shoreham-by-sea, and Henry James lived in Lamb House in Rye, East
   Sussex (a Lowry haunt in the thirties when Aiken lived there), from
   1898 to 1912.
3 Markson was living in Greenwich Village and the White Horse Tavern,
   already famous as Dylan Thomas's favourite New York drinking spot,
   was popular with writers.
4 *The Recognitions* (1955), by American writer William Gaddis, is one of
   Markson's favourite novels; see Lowry's 22 February 1957 letter (**705**)
   to Markson.

Editorial Notes:

a. For the first time in over two years Lowry has added his characteristic
   seagulls to the top of this postcard.

647: To John Davenport

P: UBC(ms)   [The White Cottage,]
PP: *MLR* 23-27   Ripe, Sussex
                                                        22 March 1956

Dear old John: –

I have been in bed latterly with a fever occasioned no doubt by a
surfeit of Cydrax ([Dr Michael] Raymond has given me the address of
the makers of an alternative brew called Appella – the address is
Monsieur Bonbrisson, Nutfood Co. Ltd, Bootle, Liverpool! – which
irresistibly suggests an imaginary letter from Adam: – [1]

Sir; On my recent expulsion from the Garden, of which you may
have heard, I was advised to try some of your preparation Appella – the
object of which I take to be that one may enjoy all the delights afforded
by the *Apple* without enduring any of the consequent *fell* effects, – however I find this so to have vitiated my constitution that (postal order
enclosed) I am now asking you to send me by return of post a specimen
of your famous NUTFOOD etc etc) – and was thinking of Marjorie &
yourself with affection as usual when – as a matter of fact the phone rang
and there you were on the end of it. Very excellent to hear your voice;
come down any time you feel like it, in case you can make it sooner
rather than later, on the spur or not, and without phoning, if occasion
has it, and there's no telephone convenient. It is really an 18th century
poet's paradise – or a 15th century one for that matter; all it lacks is yourself. And it is more or less untouched by urban civilization, which, as
Frank Lloyd Wright observed, was first invented by Cain, 'and Cain is
still murdering his brother.'[2] The only exception is a huge mobile frying
fish shop which comes mooing and glowing whitely over the landscape
on windy Saturday nights. Two mute wild swans are nesting in a pond
hard by, the crocuses and the anenemas (as the milkmaid – for there is
a milkmaid – calls them) are out, and altogether the landscape is 'full of
things' as your friend Baroness Blixen somewhere says of a night sky, as
indeed is this sky, really extraordinary things.[3] To return to Isak Dinesen
we hadn't been able to get the March Twentieth Century because, so
we were told, it had been delayed by the printer's strike but yesterday
we got one at Victoria – we were up briefly to see Raymond at St
George's but with no good opportunity to make contact with yourself
– I hadn't known till the last moment I'd be able to go anyhow – and

having reread your article in print I do want to congratulate you on an
excellent article, both on that and because I think you are quite right,
that your 'personal' method of approach, by drawing your reader
intimately into what you have to say, will gain readers for her work who
might otherwise be the losers by missing the pattern of the whole thing,
her life & her art.[4] I am a case in point for though I loved Out of Africa
and thought it one of the best books I'd ever read – it was the first one
of hers I read – the next one I came to, which was Winter's Tales, struck
me at first as a slight let down, both stylistically, and in the sense that I
didn't feel I was being asked to take the stories seriously, or seriously
enough: anyhow I didn't do so, and my same wrong response and
wandering attention must have coloured my reading of the Gothic
Tales, which I didn't even bother to ascertain were written before In
dunkelske Afrika. In short I missed the whole idea, like a stupid fool –
though to be sure it was partly out of a kind of loyalty to Out of Africa
itself perhaps – (which I'd read so many times I'd almost begun to consider myself its sole and ideal reader) – and but for your article (not even
Margerie, who loved all the stories she'd read of hers, could convince
me – I'm speaking of a long time before, thanks to your generosity, we
became owners, or at least guardians, of the volumes) I might still be
missing it. As things stand I simply can't wait to read, as if for the first
time, all her work in conjunction with your article, and I know it's
going to be a revelation and a wonderful experience. I don't think it
unlikely on second thinkings that others – especially some writers – may
have fallen into my particular trap: after all it's a hell of a step, at first
sight, from the lucid bloom and clean spacious-anguish of Out of Africa
into the apparently churrigueresque thickets of (what seems) the 'Count
Augustus von Schimmelmann type' of style;[5] moreover I imagine there
are people who starting on the other side appreciate the simpler of the
stories for quite the wrong reasons. I must say it involves an unusually
esemplastic – if that's the right word – type of intelligence & percep-
tiveness to take the whole amazing boskage in at once and see it all on
the same property. And in addition to the personal ones the biographic
details you bring out & cunningly select all seem indispensable to the
whole picture, such a fascinating & dramatic one I don't feel it possible
anyone could make the same mistake as myself after reading your essay.
Your short exposition of Sorrow Acre I find hair-raising, and moving
in its own right, so much so noone is going to forget the meaning of this
story even if he hasn't read it, though it certainly invites one to do so: –
also talking about 'the comic' I forgot to say that I became so absorbed
that I fell out of the train more or less while reading the article, that is
to say I suddenly found myself having to jump for it at Ripe platform
when the train had already gathered considerable speed; no injuries,

unless to dignity, but a somewhat painful fall, & nearly painful in more ways than one, for flags were waved, the train thereupon stopped, meanwhile the jump had been made from a first-class compartment, in which we were travelling on a third-class ticket! (Whatever hitch-hikes I may have caddishly tried to bootleg while walking with you in my crutch rubbed past you have to hand it to my loyalty that I was still clutching Twentieth Century as I fell!) It's exceedingly good of you to ask me to keep the Clare, & it's much appreciated, but I don't think perhaps we ought to, or the Dinesens, because our address isn't permanent enough, though to be sure we don't plan to move as yet, in fact we are very happy and well off here, indeed blossoming like the nose (did you ever read Gogol's The Nose by the way? – a superlative story) & feel it to be considerably more than a pied-à-terre already.[6] However the Clare has no business being here & should have been returned to you long before: be that as it may good care will be taken of it and I'd like to keep it long enough to copy out some poems from it for an old Manx boatbuilder neighbour [Jimmy Craige] of ours in Canada who's now in hospital and who would love them, in fact he will learn them by heart, and in this way I shall have, so to speak, a spare copy of Clare in British Columbia. (James Reeves was expounding Clare, by the way, on the radio yesterday, as was Hugh Sykes, Mark Rutherford & John Galsworthy on Sunday, all of which seems rather queer – Hugh was very good, we didn't hear Reeves).[7] The Americans Abroad I have immaculately mended & you can take when you come, else in transit it might unmend itself.[8] And when you do come I wonder if you could bring the French Volcano? and also could you look about to see if I strewed anywhere a book of French critical essays named, I think, Pierres Nouvelles, I've forgotten who wrote it, but there's a long chapter about the Volcano in it;[9] I can't understand a word of it, & probably it says it's absolute cock, still it does give one a certain pleasant feeling as of having won one's international cap at shovehapenny, or something. To return to the Twentieth Century I perceive yet further praiseful notice of your fine preface to old Calabria therein but I can't help feeling it would be diverting now should someone take another view . . . . . devastating disclosures . . . this absolute skunk . . .etc. I hope the book with your preface is being reissued in America: then look out for squalls, for there is there, amazingly enough, both a respectable middle-aged-female and a bobby-sox fringe, as you probably knew, to the aficionados of South Wind & hence in a sense Douglas himself[10] . . . . . Damnable dirty Davenport . . . This dabbler in filth . . . First Sinatra, & now this . . . Spoiler of our innocent fun . . . Egghead and communist democrat . . . I have been working hard & rather meticulously; in fact some of the meticulousness seems to have rubbed off on this handwriting as of a miserly pismire.[11] All our very best love to your Margerie. Likewise to Roger & Hugo.[12] Looking forward to seeing you soon. Meantime I pray for you incessantly (as H.L. Mencken once said to Theodore Dreiser) & for your welfare, both material and ghostly

Love from both,

Malc

Annotations:

1 This address takes Lowry back to his youth and the garden from which, like Adam, he felt he had been expelled.

2 Frank Lloyd Wright (1867-1959), the American architect, became known for his 'prairie school' of architecture and his natural designs with flowing spaces. His urban buildings reflect an anti-urban bias, apparent in the remark Lowry is paraphrasing. Wright described cities as the invention of Cain in his 4 June 1954 acceptance speech for the Frank P. Brown Medal of the Franklin Institute.

3 Baroness Karen Dinesen Blixen (1865-1962), whose pen-name was Isak Dinesen, is known for her autobiographical book *Out of Africa* (1937) and her short-story collections *Seven Gothic Tales* (1934) and *Winter's Tales* (1942).

4 John Davenport's article on Isak Dinesen, 'A Noble Pride: The Art of Karen Blixen,' appeared in *Twentieth Century* 949 (March 1956): 264-74. Davenport provides a detailed appreciation of her style and themes and calls her a 'master of . . . psychological realism.'

5 Count Augustus von Schimmelmann is a character in Dinesen's 'The Roads round Pisa' in *Seven Gothic Tales*.

6 Lowry has been reading John Clare's poetry; see Lowry's March 1956 letter (**648**) to James Craige. Nikolai Gogol's 'The Nose' (1836) is a fantastic story about a man whose nose gads about town without him.

7 James Reeves (1909-78), a prolific writer, poet, editor, and lecturer, knew Lowry at Cambridge, as did Hugh Sykes Davies (1909-84), the literary scholar who, as a student himself, helped Lowry prepare for his examinations in 1932. At this time Davies was presenting radio lectures on the English novelist and philosopher Mark Rutherford (the pseudonym of William Hale White, 1831-1913) and English novelist John Galsworthy (1867-1933).

8 *Les Americaines à l'étranger* (1892), adapted by Abby Sage as *Americans Abroad* and first performed in New York in 1892, was a play by Victorien Sardou (1831-1908).

9 This book of essays continues to elude Lowry's editors and bibliographers, but Lowry probably means *Les lettres nouvelles* (November 1953).

10 The Lowrys had met Norman Douglas (1868-1952), a British diplomat, scientist, and writer, on Capri in July 1948. His *Old Calabria* (1915) is a travel book about southern Italy reissued in 1955 with an introduction by John Davenport. This new edition is the one reviewed in *Twentieth Century* 949 (March 1956): 298-300, and Davenport's introduction is particularly praised by the reviewer.

11 Lowry's handwriting throughout this holograph is very small, slightly slanting up to the right side of the page, and very precise. This letter is the first one in almost two years where his writing has returned to the control and clarity of happier, healthier times and he develops a sustained literary discussion with his addressee.

12 Davenport's second wife's name was spelt Marjorie; Roger and Hugo are their sons.

648: To James Craige

P: UBC(ms phc)   The White Cottage,
PP: *SL* 384   Ripe, Near Lewes,
                                  Sussex, England
                                  [March 1956]

My very dear Jimmy:

This is just a short note that is intended to reach you for your birthday and simply to say many very happy returns of the Day – probably it won't get you in time its being Easter time – & a very Happy Easter too! – but still the thought is the same.[1] I have heard from both Downie & Harvey that you have been in hospital for which I'm very sorry for I know how you hate that, but I hope you will now, or very soon, have left all that behind, & be back at the dear old beach again.[2] (I too have been in hospital, twice since being in England, but am better now.) Though we like this place quite a bit, please don't think we have abandoned Dollarton, we have not, & think of it constantly, & of yourself, & miss the old times, but it seems better for reasons of health to stay where we are just at the moment, though the beach will always be home. Please give my best love to Downie, to whom I am writing, to Harvey should you see him, & of course *Whitey*.[3] I am copying out some poems for you by *John Clare*,[4] an English poet (1790-1860) who reminds me of T.E. Brown somewhat, & which I think you will like, so you will have another letter from me soon. Get better soon & God bless you

Love

Malcolm

Annotations:

1 Easter Sunday fell on 1 April in 1956, and Jimmy Craige's seventy-seventh birthday was on 30 March.
2 Craige underwent surgery for prostate trouble in 1955.
3 Miles Went, a neighbouring fisherman and good friend at Dollarton.

4 John Clare's correct death date is 1864. Thomas Edward Brown (1830-
  97) was a Manx poet who wrote in dialect about life on the Isle of Man.
  Lowry believed that his old friend, who was Manx, would appreciate
  these rural poets.

649: To David Markson

p: UBC(ms)   The White Cottage,
pp: *SL* 385-86   Ripe, Near Lewes,
                                                                  Sussex
                                                          [March 1956]

Dear old Dave: just a note, between paragraphs, to thank you very
much indeed for sending The Partisan Review. I'm very fond of the old
Bravest Boat though I have never managed to ascertain what anyone
thought of it, if anything, in the U.S. Lunar Caustic, by the way, is
appearing serially in the French mag. L'Esprit in Paris.[1] I think you
would be enchanted with this place to which a visitor came the other
day asking to see the room (here) where her grandmother was at School
in 1830: must be ghosts here, gol darn it, though we ain't laid none yet.
House was built in 1740. Margie is having a wonderful time with the
garden, as am I, she planting seeds destined to be glowing hollyhocks, I
sowing sweetpeas – 4 seeds in each hole – 'one for the rabbit, one for
the crow, one for the fieldmice, & one to grow,' as they say here, while
meanwhile I weed sentences full of contorted louseworts which I lay
neatly in rows, for use later no doubt. Though we miss the water-borne
bounties and forest & sea & mountain drama of old Dollarton at times,
without abandoning our forest home, we nevertheless have a good feeling of temporary home here at least and are having a great deal of fun
while at the same time living quite cheaply, compared with American
standards. Margie's in the best health I've seen her in in years & myself
in good form too albeit bearded like the bard and despite having fallen
painlessly & soberly out of a train the other day while reading a book.[2]
I don't have any other news, save this, culled from a Government paper:
– In the nuts (Unground) (Other than Groundnuts) Order, the expressions nuts shall have reference to such nuts, other than groundnuts, as
would, but for this Amending Order, not qualify as nuts (Unground)
(Other than Groundnuts) by reason of their being nuts (Unground).
Tell me news of the Satevepost story, your health, your plans, – other
work, your comedies & dramas (or I shall have sended a boy to have
founded out, señor, whether you are not making more tragedies)[3] Best
love from us both

                                                                  Malc

Annotations:

1 *Le Caustique lunaire*, translated by Michèle d'Astorg and Clarisse Francillon, appeared in *Esprit* for February, March and April 1956.
2 Lowry's punning allusion is to the line 'bearded like the pard' in Shakespeare's *As You Like It* II.vii.150. See Lowry's description of his fall in his 22 March 1956 letter (**647**) to John Davenport.
3 See Dr Vigil's remark in chapters 1 and 5 of *Under the Volcano*.

650: To Peter Churchill

P: UBC(ms)
PP: *SL* 400-07

The White Cottage,
Ripe, nr Lewes,
Sussex
4 April 1956[a]

Dear Peter,[1]

It seems to me excellently written, with a fine choice of the right clear vocables, and uncle Hugh a genuine delight throughout, and the thing preserves interest & vitality all the way through, with humour & nostalgia intermingled in the right proportions, while uncle couldn't be better or more endearing as I said before. The writing seems to me, though, a thought less careful after the first four pages, albeit it recovers again after that and the points I pick you up on are in any case minor – ah the ands, the ifs, the buts, the howevers, as Flaubert – was it Flaubert – said? – is there never an end to this tyrannous prose?[2] Nonetheless one has to drive in one's finishing nails accurately or chinks appear in the corners of one's style; I might add that you seem to me to have achieved a good and individual one. Please excuse my writing in pencil but I can't write with the family pen (I feel one perhaps should spend one's day 'making' or 'mending' pens in this Mrs Gaskell type of atmosphere here):[3]

p. 3. (middle and bottom) 'thought about' and 'go on,' end two sentences: there's absolutely no objection to this *here*, & I just mention it as something to 'think about & go on,' for I think you tend to overdo this sort of construction elsewhere which gives the same effect as if it were incorrect, which of course it isn't.

p. 4 (top) I'm very shaky about the rule but shouldn't it be 'about *his* having tamed wild animals, – '?

p. 5. (bottom) I don't see why you shouldn't say 'he broke loose,' especially since you have a 'had' problem here & top 6.

p. 6. Query – commas after uncle Hugh and greyhound. (If you ommitted them deliberately, that's different).

p. 7. (Middle §) – Margie noted this but I think I agree – seems a bit choppy, even if you want to vary the rhythm. I append Margie's solution but I feel there now may appear something confused in the thought. 'Not being that kind of snob' doesn't apply directly to being 'not much giving to thinking things out,' on the other hand the latter is presumably included as an Edwardian characteristic: however the implication could be that had your mother been given to thinking things out she would have arrived at a point of social disapproval, (which, not being that kind of snob, she wouldn't have arrived at) – pay no attention to this, you probably take care of it by using the 'and' after 'spirit' and hence cancelling the modification of the rest of the sentence by the 'although' – *this way madness lies*, but I'd wanted to change the order in your sentence & I see I can't do it. Herewith Margie:

> You could see she thought it a silly or perhaps a
> disgraceful episode: there may have been a girl in
> the act or something. I thought of that later.
> It was not just social disapproval on my mother's
> part – although she was fully Edwardian in spirit &
> not much given to thinking things out – she was not
> that kind of snob.

And me:

> You could see she thought it a silly or perhaps
> disgraceful episode – there may have been a girl in
> the act or something, I thought of that later – but
> it was not just social disapproval on my mother's
> part, although she was fully Edwardian in spirit
> and not much given to thinking things out, she was
> not that kind of snob.

(I fear I haven't improved matters but perhaps you can make something better out of both of these. I deprived you of the last sentence by *itself* to prevent your ending on 'out'. See below.)

Ibid. (How I have always loved the word ibid.) And the very last sentence in same § as above seems a bit ill balanced and non-euphonious:

> Her hopes had not been so well realized in the
> matter of her two eldest brothers who had further
> disappointed by dying young and leaving Hugh head
> of the family, so that this circus business seemed
> like a bad beginning better not spoken of. (sic).

(I think something like this – though you may want to put back the 'as' before 'head' – brings out your meaning better too, for after all the so-called bad beginning is in the past, and moreover isn't a bad beginning in *fact* exactly, I mean not in the conventional sense in your mother's view, and the 'like' I feel deconventionalises it somehow, but the main trouble is the rhythm of your sentence; I'm not sure that 'eldest' is correct since, unless more brothers were concerned, shouldn't it be elder?)

Ibid (very bottom): Stop me if I'm wrong but shouldn't it be, after all that, '*were* all part of it.' If uncertain you can dodge the issue by using 'seemed part of it.'

Page 8. Both Margie and I felt something wrong at the bottom, which starts at 'He didn't feel any promptings,' which is clumsy, while 'All of which accounted for why' is a good ending to a poem, but not a good beginning to the next sentence, at least not without putting 'most likely' between commas, though your trouble's elsewhere, I think: maybe the subject 'Hugh' is too far away from the 'why', too far *down* the sentence. In the next sentence Margie questions the 'It' as a correct apposition for 'All of which' but I think this is OK as a substitute but the trouble certainly does carry through the construction of the sentence over to the top of p 9 where all in all one finds oneself with too many 'gettings,' and there's a monotony in the governing prepositions, a plague of 'fors'; the earlier problem I think can be solved simply by transposing the subject to an earlier position, & using more commas etc viz:

> He felt no promptings to hide his light under a
> bushel. All of which accounted, most likely, for
> why Hugh, instead of growing fat as a racehorse
> owner, and getting his sporting reputation that
> way, as other Englishmen did and do, was always
> spending large amounts of violent and dangerous
> energy, as well as a great deal of money. It
> accounted for his hunting the Quorn Hounds himself
> instead of leaving that to a professional
> huntsman, for jumping big Leicestershire fences,
> so big that they were photographed afterwards by
> horse enthusiasts, for getting himself knocked out
> by famous boxers, going on safaris, and arctic
> hunting trips, where he would become snowed in for
> half a year, and on top of it all, every so often,
> flower in button-hole, cigar in mouth, for leading
> in a Derby winner.

(I hope not too much charm is lost in this way, but it may be a basis to go on – you still have two 'gettings' as this stands: if you could sacrifice 'growing,' you could make one 'getting' do double duty i.e 'instead of getting fat as a racehorse owner, and his sporting reputation that way etc.' Also you could say: 'becoming snowed in for half a year,' if you don't like 'where he would become': and 'on top of it all, for,' etc. But it's all too easy to lose the spontaneity of the thing tinkering around in this way: still you have to do a bit here, I think. Fortunately a sentence itself will cry uncle, so to speak, when it's had enough, and though it may still look full of derangements, by that time it's probably immortal.)

Page 10. (Top). Margie criticises the sentence beginning 'I watched as the international crises' etc. I rather like the unusual construction – the only thing is you have an unconscious rhyme in crises & surprises – do you care? I don't.

But Ibid youthful hanger *on* would finally be *on*, not to say years went *on* – watch this.

Ibid (bottom) '*as it might be* by anyone these days,' or as it might *have been* etc (otherwise the second 'bought' is not properly understood in the passive) with the money.

Ibid (last words) are ok but I'd look through & back & see you don't do it too often – as I said – or it seems 'conscious': or, conversely, care-less – (c.f also 'better not spoken of' end on of, 'that he was accused of' Bottom 4.) Even when, in fact, it's more grammatically correct to end with a preposition. It's a case of pure Gallic superstition having become ingrained in the language so that one might as well seem to be flouting it with effect, I guess.

Page 13 (bottom) would be leaving . . . to be eyed . . . would be told in the same sentence.

Ibid. Typ error. For 'play with with', read 'play with them'. But don't forget you have another *with* them; & also *with* suspicion. (Note. Not merely English, but perhaps *all* children should be eyed with suspicion whom there is any danger of having to play with with with.)

Ibid (still at bottom) Comma after yellow cars too or none at all in sentence. All this I find delightful & excellently written: Margie likewise.

16 (top §) Another 'get away from' as ending. Not necessarily to alter, but simply to watch. I like all this very much: I'm afraid I can see a bit here, quoted in Time, beneath your portrait: – 'Glittering saddles and unmilitary positions in the heather' or: 'Gypsies & devilish ponies' or: 'They gave the Kaiser a quieter pony than the rest.'

17. Margie objects to lack of verb in The incredible house etc sentence. It seems to me ok because there's a sort of implied exclamation point at the end. Maybe there's something in the punctuation that could be bettered though, likewise in previous sentence, which causes the sense of lack.

19. (Top). And certainly something amiss in the punctuation here, which makes it look a bit like a poem by Jose Garcia Villa:[4]

I doubt though that Hugh, unless perhaps at the
very end, etc

Ibid. (last sentence) Margie suggests there should be some punctuation in this last sentence, a comma after 'child', perhaps, but in my opinion this would involve logically other balancing commas (after 'Hugh', after 'winter') which might spoil the unity of the sentence, which *as* the last one perhaps has a beauty and extra-authority of its own, by virtue of not being punctuated at all, & for which it has its own license as a coda. As a coda it moves me as it is, but if you didn't intend it as such, maybe Margie's right.

I hope some of these reactions may be of some practical use, if their somewhat loomy grammarian nature does not give much indication of the real pleasure reading the excerpt gave me. I look forward to seeing more. Meanwhile I have another reaction to report which came to me (while dear Joan, dipping my Plymouth Rock one day into my tea) about the story you told of visiting the Lord Chancellor. It seems to me that this, much as you told it, could form the basis of a really profoundly excellent short novel – I imagine it should be short, not more than about 210 pages because you have the temptation of too much material to draw on – which as a project is always a useful thing to have up one's sleeve when discussing matters with publishers (in fact you can make it two things to talk about as you said, & imply a sequel) – entitled something like Missing Peer, or maybe better Lost Peer, or more euphoniously still The Lost Peer. The story as you told it is full of wonderful touches, the taxidriver who you felt ought to know exactly about such objectives as the Chancellor and how to get there and did, the irrelevant conversations that nevertheless seemed so quintessentially English, the glossy unlikelihood of the Lord Chancellor himself resembling a cross between a stockholder and Michael Arlen,[5] but who nonetheless too is the chief equity Judge in England, – the significance of *Law* in this, (though the Law is talking about being stuck in the lift) the sense of the House of Lords being above the law, or a law unto themselves, the dichotomy of the spiritual need to participate, but of being American, yet at the same time being not merely English but at the very centre of history, with the superb symbol just thrown in, of the Thames flowing immediately below, seen through the big windows. It isn't the Kafka-like element of this which mainly appeals to me – though that may enter in or contribute – it is the fact that, in the matter of establishing the universality of your principal character, (who could be a projection of any or all sides of your many-sided self and simultaneously quite distinct from your autobiographical self, etc,) in establishing this, despite the apparent esotericism of your mise en scène, you are ex officio (which I hope to explain) more than up on Kafka, in fact the main battle of such a novel is already won at the outset. On second thoughts it's too complicated to explain why a peer of the realm, especially a missing one, should seem a more universal figure than a land surveyor, but one main point is that noone believes for one moment that Kafka's K. had ever surveyed any land, or ever had the remotest intention – let alone capability of doing so, whereas noone will doubt that your peer is a peer, which somehow renders his quality of being missing that much more human and dignified. In short, as a Much in Little, it has everything – there is the universal need for participation, to belong, yet the ennobled position of the protagonist, which might seem to disqualify him from universality, on the contrary makes him Everyman too, in everyman's eyes, testifies to the uniqueness of the individual – peer is also a highly ambiguous word, by the way, which can even mean comrade, if you want it to. What is more, you have the individual vis-à-vis the group, vis-à-vis law, divine and human, but also he is a maker of the law himself, or ex-maker of the law, or law unto himself, and certainly squelcher of the law, or potentially to be so once more. So then there is the suspense! – will he be able to take his seat, or won't he? You can be sure that this question will come to symbolise something of vital concern in the reader's life. There is great opportunity for splendid humour and sadness here, I feel. The piece could end perhaps with the hero's taking part in some fantastically involved debate in the House of Lords itself, either upon a subject of deadly seriousness of vital importance to mankind, or upon one of correspondingly little importance, yet whose very negligibility is almost sublime, or it could be upon some legislation pertinent to himself, in which he is obliged through honour to take a standpoint detrimental to his own aims, or vice versa, (though one draws the line at some final debate on capitalist punishment where he is an abolitionist who perhaps inadvertently has meanwhile committed a murder). – On top of all this you have, presented to you on a platter, the situation which Henry James, if I'm not wrong, always thought of as the most essentially dramatic one, yet never succeeded in carrying off emotionally himself, namely the return, after many years, of the wanderer to his own country. But here you have another turn of the screw,[6] not only in that your protagonist has become an American, but that America has come to represent to some extent, rightly or wrongly, and on several planes, the forces of reaction, contrasted with which even the most diehard Toryism exemplified in the House of Lords – not that your protagonist is necessarily even a conservative – sometimes seems liberal, 'democratic'. As against this, there is his justified pride in his aristocratic heritage, & so forth. One doesn't stop there: there's always the suggestion in James that the American finally represents some down-to-earth autochthonous force of nature, a finer fresher thing morally, alongside the calculating essentially moribund European, who while taking the other in, always tends to look

down on his 'grass roots' values.[7] Now, by gosh, when the last old sour-
dough has traded in his divining rod and gold sifting pan for a geiger
counter, and conservation itself has a positively revolutionary aspect, the
grass roots are sprouting in the House of Lords, so to say; – and none of
this by any means obvious, or cut and dried, and without ever losing
sight of the conflicting pathos and humour in the situation, nor, visually,
ever of that grand view of the Thames, below the big windows. And
very grand and beautiful is the book, likewise, in which you can draw
occasionally, but sparingly, from the material in the autobiography itself,
particularly the postillions in short yellow jackets and beaver hats on p.
14 – a masterly American thought to have in the taxi, for instance, while
journeying in more humble mode Forward The Lord High Chancellor,
Keeper of the Great Seal, privy councilor, prolucutor of the House of
Lords and what not, – or better, a bit later, in retrospect – or on p 15,
the dramatic Gothic appearance of some equivalent of Lowther, the
Castle,[8] & so on, all of which nostalgias would be highly accentuated by
the double-barreled doubly transatlantic nostalgias of your lost & found
hero. Don't let such a notion distract you from the work in progress,
but I can't help counselling you to keep it in mind for some future date,
or rather don't keep it in mind, rather forget it, & remember it when
you wish to, & dig it up then, if you wish to, for it strikes me that all
this presurmise of your own work is slightly froward, even a bit assuming and possibly mistakeable in the sense that in my enthusiasm I have
suggested a kind of book you may dislike. On the other hand I can't
apologise for I was so smitten by the conviction that you do have a book
there after your conversation of the other day that once I'd started to
write about it to you I simply couldn't bear to stop or let my words tail
off unconvincingly in a fog of cydrax fumes. Moreover I felt the more
inclined to mention my strong impression because I feel you are
uniquely equipped to write such a book and indeed nobody else but
yourself possibly could write it. So you must forgive me. Don't bother
to answer this letter either, which is far too long, though a pleasure to
write; but to answer it is another matter. I just spoke on the telephone
with John [Davenport], who seemed in very good form, and has just
burned Mr Conolly in the New Statesman, though I don't know yet on
what grounds.[9] He, John, recently wrote a brilliant thing on Isac
Dinesen in Twentieth Century which caused me to reread her Gothic
Tales with profit, and indeed it was somewhat in the manner of one of
those wonderful tales, a bit longer than the longest, and not so diffused
through various narrators, & not so Gothic (though still Gothic), & with
a certain advantage of contemporary realism, that my Plymouth Rock
caused me to visualise your unborn opus, which would have the added
advantage of taking you perhaps (Ha ha) less than six months to write.

At least in the first draft. Do I have anything else to say? Yes, Joan, a masterpiece culled from the paper, & copied from a government paper, so that it might be used in the aforesaid debate, Peter, in the House of Lords, in kindly derision of certain goings-on in Commons: it seems to concern nuts, & runs: – In the Nuts (Unground) (Other than Groundnuts) Order, The expressions nuts shall have reference to such nuts, other than groundnuts, as would, but for this Amending Order, not qualify as nuts (Unground) (Other Than Groundnuts) by reason of their being nuts (Unground). And by the way did you ever notice that the Prince of Darkness, the Prince of Peace, and the Prince of Wales, all lived next to each other in the dictionary? They do, anyhow. It was very good to see you both the other day, and the best love to Joan and yourself from us both

Malcolm

Annotations:

1 Victor Alexander Spencer, the second Viscount Churchill (1890-1973), a descendant of the first Duke of Marlborough, was disinherited by his father and pursued a life of travel and various occupations in the United States after the First World War. He had married Joan Black, and Lowry met him for the first time when he and Margerie visited the couple in September 1954; see Lowry's 9 September 1954 telegram (**620**) to David Markson. After the Churchills returned to England in 1956, Peter sent Malcolm a draft of chapter 1 of his autobiography, *All My Sins Remembered* (1965); Lowry's comments on the manuscript provide interesting insight into his meticulous concern for the poetics of prose.

2 It was Flaubert, and Lowry was fond of quoting the remark. See, for example, his 16 July 1946 letter (**237**) to Albert Erskine and his 27 May 1956 letter (**655**) to Clarisse Francillon.

3 Elizabeth Cleghorn Gaskell (1810-65), an English novelist, wrote about social and economic conditions in urban and rural settings. Her best-known novels are *Cranford* (1853) and *North and South* (1855).

4 José Garcia Villa (1908-), poet, editor, and lecturer, was criticized for his second volume of poetry, in which he developed 'comma poems' that were described as mere typographical games.

5 The work of Michael Arlen, a popular English short-story writer, now seems dated and superficial, but Lowry had admired Arlen at one time; see his 27 April 1926 letter (**4**) to Carol Brown. The Lord High Chancellor is the chief legal officer in England, a member of the Cabinet, the Privy Council, and Speaker in the House of Lords.

6 Lowry's allusion is to *The Turn of the Screw* (1898), one of Henry James's best-known stories. The idea of the wanderer returning to his own country, while certainly Jamesian, is as relevant to Lowry himself.

7 Lowry may be thinking of James's novel *The Ambassadors* (1903), which contrasts American innocence with European experience.

8 Lowther Castle is the residence of the Earl of Lonsdale in the parish of Lowther, Westmoreland, and Churchill describes his Uncle Hugh, the fifth Earl of Lonsdale, in some detail in *All My Sins Remembered*.

9 John Davenport published 'Peel Those Medlars,' a review of *Shade Those Laurels: An Excerpt from a Novel* by English journalist, writer, and critic Cyril Connolly (1903-74) in the *New Statesman and Nation* for 31 March 1956. Davenport damned the author and his book for 'literary exhibitionism.'

Editorial Notes:

a. *Selected Letters* gives 1957 as the year of composition, but the holograph is clearly dated 4 April 1956.

651: To Clarisse Francillon

P: UBC(msc)
PP: *SL* 384-85

The White Cottage,
Ripe, Near Lewes,
Sussex, England
[21 April 1956][a]

Clarisse darling, we are at the above address, scarcely a stone's throw away just across the channel, quite near Newhaven, to which a boat used to go from Dieppe. I am dying to see a copy of Lunar Caustic in your translation – could you lend me the L'esprits with it in, & I'll send them back, for it will be ages otherwise before I get them from [Harold] Matson. Also I am longing to know how it went over in France & what people thought of it, including you, as you know I haven't let it be published yet in English![1] Many congratulations on your novel, & the short story for the Mercure de France. How are you & what is your news? I am not much changed, save for a long flowing white beard and the fact that I am ruining my health drinking large quantities of non-alcoholic cider: also I am working hard. Is there any chance you can pay us a visit sometime? We could put you up & would love to see you. We live in an ancient village, where there is not even a village idiot, unless you count myself. But it is really a beautiful place. Margerie sends her best love as do I

Malcolm

Annotations:

1 It had been more than three years since Lowry corresponded with Francillon about *Lunar Caustic*; see his November 1952 letter (**551**) to her. The novella first appeared in English in *Paris Review* 29 (Winter/Spring 1963): 15-72.

Editorial Notes:

a.   The copy-text for this transcription is a photocopy of the original letter
     (UBC 3:10), and Clarisse Francillon has recorded a date of '21 avril '56'
     at the top of the page.

652: To David Markson

P: UBC(ms)

The White Cottage,
Ripe near Lewes, Sussex, England
[Spring 1956]

¡Dear old Dave!

Goodness gracious gawdnes Agnes man, many congratulations ¡¡ On
the Satevepost story, I mean!!¹ It really *is* a very solid technical achievement on one plane, you can really compliment yourself on, not to
mention boast about, so don't become a victim of your own derision
too much just because it happens to be funny too: here the news was
received with most genuine enthusiasm, everything from a chorus of
crested larks and titmice without, to a tatooing of beating toilet-seats
within. One good thing among others will probably emerge from it:
you'll probably find that your work is in demand elsewhere, in addition
to being in demand at the same source. I don't need to tell you not to
lose your head. But an equally important thing is not to lose your style,
native downbeat, personal three-point landing, or whatever you prefer
to call it. With this in mind, I would pay particular attention to the
places where you've been constrained to alter your story, where these
have improved the thing, or where you think the changes have injured
it, but above all to *why* you've had to make a change in such and such a
place – where the reasons seem good learn, but where the reasons seem
vaguely criminal learn there too, for the reasons themselves are of philosophical import no doubt and could be food for other work: in a novel,
for example, where you have almost complete freedom to do as you
please: or do you? Anyway you'll find it much easier to get a novel published now, which is all to the mustard. And if you find yourself
submerged in a sea of your own sense of irony because your first success
is not only on such a superduper scale but in a magazine noted for 'typing' its authors you can tell yourself that the New Yorker and even the
little magazines do much the same thing. Indeed the business of a writer
seems to be laboriously to establish his own self-editorship in such a way
that he can make its authority tell against such constraints, but only at
the expense, it seems often, of creating a touchstone that may con-
strain – though of course it may equally liberate – others. Sometimes the
originator himself gets caught in a 'type' he's helped to invent, – all this

pomposity being occasioned by the amount of conformity it seems to me there is now in intelligent magazines compared to when I was younger than you – look in any New Yorker and see a story by Elizabeth Taylor, say, maybe an almost first-rate one in some respects, but not written any longer in the real style of Elizabeth Taylor so much as in the style the 'New Yorker-Elizabeth Taylor style' has imposed on writers for the New Yorker and now on Elizabeth Taylor herself.[2] All this is very sad and a bit nightmarish, like seeing a beautiful sailing ship manned by radioactive robots, or whose sails flap about at the bidding of an invisible electrophorus. And somehow we have to rebel. But somehow also we have to take the cutting – sometimes until the Immortal Editor erase us by cutting our lives to the bone. But meantime it is also somehow exceedingly good to do something as sensational & unexpected as crashing the Saturday Evening Post. (first editor Thomas Jefferson.)[3] So our renewed sincere congratulations upon this. I hope you can send us a copy but if not I can buy one in Lewes! In fact it's the only magazine I *can* buy in Lewes so far as I can make out!

Love from us both

Malcolm

Annotations:

1 David Markson had informed Lowry that his story 'White Apache' had been accepted by the *Saturday Evening Post*; see Lowry's 21 February 1956 letter (**646**) to Markson with advice on revisions.

2 Elizabeth Taylor (1912-75), not to be confused with the American film star, was an English novelist and short story-writer. Many critics considered her to be a master of the short-story form, but others criticized her for creating undeveloped characters and leaving too much unsaid. Most of her stories were first published in the *New Yorker* and later collected into four volumes.

3 The *Saturday Evening Post* began publication in 1821; its first editor was Thomas Cottrell Clarke. Thomas Jefferson (1743-1826), the third president of the United States, was the author of the Declaration of Independence, a writer, legislator, architect, and founder of the University of Virginia.

653: To James Stern

P: Texas(ms)
PP: *SL* 410-11

The White Cottage,
Ripe, Near Lewes, Sussex
[ca May 1956]^a

Dear Jimmy:

We looked for you all day through the storm but didn't even see a flash of lightning (though just now, a week later, I heard a great roar of thunder.)

The poppies blew over in a bloody brood, however, & we still live in hopes you may be coming, as when a certain magician was thinking, the church bells started, elsewhere, ringing. It still seems to me the church bells are ringing, though I'm not quite sure who the magician is. I hope you didn't have any trouble with your car on that stormy day, on which I also received an extraordinary letter from Germany about The Volcano couched in terms rather more suitable to the young Hoffmannsthal than to the Cydraddict of Ripe.[1] I would be extremely glad of your translation. Don't be put off by the rumour of Cydrax either, as my other friends seem to be. There's plenty else in the house. I don't even drink Cydrax myself for that matter – not to any excess that is: in fact remembering that Burton (not on Trent) somewhere said that borage[2] was an aid to melancholy, & finding the garden full of borage, I have taken somewhat to borage: borage, I discover, on the contrary *hugely* _induces_ *melancholy*, so I can suppose only that Burton (not on Trent) meant that he found it an aid in *writing the Anatomy of Melancholy*.[3] Well, life is full of little touches like that. Do let us see or hear from you soon. The phone number is Ripe 282. Everything you say can be heard next door by our landlady's sister, who just lent me The Psychic Life of Jesus, so don't say anything too metaphysical.[4] For the rest I am doing alot of fairly good work that is boring me to death but we do have – largely thanks to Margerie – a marvellous garden, in which everything is to be found in flower, except henbane, which is to be found in the churchyard. Drop along: &, if you will, stay. In fact both of you, stay. Let us hear. Love to you & to T. [Tania]

Malcolm

P.S. I forgot to say that the house in question, (easily distinguishable over the foregathering gloom by reason of its two immense chimney stacks, pots, etc etc) is – in fact indeed is – [Zum]biespiel[5] – is – is – perhaps – indeed is –

(etc)

Telegraphic Address: Usher[6]

Annotations:

1 The letter from Germany has not survived with Lowry's incoming correspondence. Hugo von Hofmannsthal, the Austrian playwright, poet, and essayist, is known for his early lyric poetry and his interest in the symbolic nature of language. Stern had published a translation of Hofmannsthal, and Lowry was aware of his friend's work and of the differences between early and late Hofmannsthal; see his 14 October

1953 letter (**591**) to Albert Erskine. Cydra (or Cydrax) is a brand of non-alcoholic cider.

2 Borage is a common plant in England, with blue flowers, and prickly stems and leaves; it was formerly used to make a cordial.

3 Robert Burton (1577-1640), an English vicar and rector, was the author of *The Anatomy of Melancholy* (1621), a medical treatise on the subject of melancholy that expands to cover a wide spectrum of human activity. He discusses the medicinal value of borage, stressing in particular a 'famous Syrup of Borage' that will 'digest this humour.' Burton-upon-Trent is an English town on the River Trent, north-west of Leicester; it is famous for the brewing of beer.

4 The Lowrys' landlady, Edwina Mason, lived next door. *The Psychic Life of Jesus* (London: Psychic Press Ltd., 1938) is a short monograph by the Reverend G. Maurice Elliott that interprets Christ's life as a manifestation of spiritual law and claims Christ as 'the greatest Spiritualist of us all' (39); see Lowry's 10 May 1956 letter (**654**) to John Davenport.

5 Lowry's writing is not clear here, but he appears to have written 'Zumbiespeil' for the German *zum Beispiel*, which means for example.

6 This is a reference to one of Lowry's favourite stories, Edgar Allan Poe's *The Fall of the House of Usher* (1839).

Editorial Notes:

a. The postmark on the envelope is difficult to read. The year is 1956 and internal evidence suggests a May date. Lowry's single-page holograph is in pencil; Margerie has added the telephone number in blue ink.

654: To John Davenport

P: UBC(ms)

> The White Cottage,
> Ripe near Lewes,
> Sussex
> [10 May 1956][a]

Very many happy returns! I remembered it was your birthday on the way back from Lewes where we saw Richard III (apparently by Colley Cibber) and a crested skylark (very rare).[1] Hope to see you soon. The wild scarlet windflower of Greece is blooming in the garden and the cemetery is a riot of henbane. The stinking goosefoot is out, the mobile frying fish shop is advancing from the southwest, and there are two swallows nesting in the woodshed. In three days we shall have a cat and for three days we have had a toad: meantime our landlady has lent me The Psychic Life of Jesus and on the whole life seems very good. With warmest love to Marjorie and you from us both

Malc

Annotations:

1 Davenport's birthday was 10 May. Colley Cibber (1671-1757) was an English actor, theatre manager, and playwright. Lowry is referring to his 1770 adaptation of Shakespeare's *Richard III*, which, though not often used in the twentieth century, remained the standard acting text of the play through the nineteenth century.

Editorial Notes:

a. This note, probably included with a card, has been written on White Cottage letterhead, but it is undated and carries no opening salutation.

655: To Clarisse Francillon

P: UBC(msc)

> The White Cottage,
> Ripe, Near Lewes,
> Sussex
> [27 May 1956]ᵃ

My very dear Clarisse: – It must seem atrocious manners for me not to have replied before or to have acknowledged your splendid translation of Lunar Caustic or your letter but first the magazines apparently went astray, then I lent them to someone who knew French better than I who didn't return them, then Margerie who was writing you herself became quite ill then I wasn't sure we were going to go on living at this address, – meantime I didn't want to write you without having intelligently participated in the translation, which I now have done & it seems to me very excellent, (& I am very moved alas by your words thereon) – in short a million obstacles, qui s'excuse s'accuse, I know, but I can only hope you will forgive me:[1] – I have had a psychological obstacle in regard to seeing you again before I have some more completed work to give you too, much as I & we both want to see you: but it will give me a considerable sense of guilt if I should let you go without giving something completed. I have two more novellas – in addition to the novel I'm working on[2] – but they both need a bit more work & if it's all the same to you I think it would be better for me to have them completed, as well as the novel pushed to a further point, before I allow myself the pleasure of seeing you again, so if it's all the same to you I would suggest toward the end of this summer, say eight weeks hence rather than now, though if it isn't I would love to see you at any time. On the other hand I haven't yet worked out in my mind a convenient itinerary for you – should you arrive on one of our bank holidays you could be held up for god knows how long in traffic or with other delays & it would be very miserable, as indeed is all transport here at the best of times, &

the comparative nearness of Newhaven to us doesn't mean it is convenient for you. So please let us know about this. I have nothing but
praise for the translation, – please do tell me any comments made about
it. I first wrote it when I was 25, (in 4 days) and there's another version
of it, likewise unpublished called Swinging the Maelstrom: I felt the present version would be improved by another long chapter that provided
more of a motivation for Plantagenet than he has. Have you noticed that
they're practically no 'ands' in the English. When I revised the version
you translated in 1940 I had been reading Flaubert & took him so seriously that a gratuitous 'and' seemed a sin.[3] But it seems to me that your
French version is better than any of my English ones: though I too, am
very proud of the story. Or your story. Anyway, a thousand thanks &
many congratulations, please let me hear from you soon again, Margerie
will be writing but she is still not well at all

All Best love

Malcolm

Annotations:

1 The French expression *qui s'excuse s'accuse* (he who makes excuses,
accuses himself) is from the Latin: *Excusatio non petita fit accusatio mani-*
festa.
2 Lowry was again struggling with *October Ferry to Gabriola*, but the
protestation about polishing 'Through the Panama' and 'Forest Path to
the Spring' sounds like an excuse.
3 Here again Lowry uses his favourite Flaubert quotation from the French
writer's 28-29 June 1853 letter to his mother; see Lowry's 16 July 1946
letter (**237**) to Albert Erskine and his 4 April 1956 letter (**650**) to Peter
Churchill.

Editorial Notes:

a. Clarisse Francillon has written '27 mai '56' at the top of the letter.

656: To Harvey Burt

P: private; UBC(msc)   The White Cottage,
PP: *SL* 386-88   Ripe, Near Lewes,
                                              Sussex, England
                                              [9 June 1956][a]

Dear Harvey: Thank you from both our hearts for the wonderful letter. But to reply briefly and to the point since time is so short. I think
your young married couple – he the teacher and actor – sound a good
thing for the house and the house for them.[1] The important thing is to

have someone who'll both live in it and love it during the summer (I can't think too far ahead) and perhaps part of the autumn and at least drop down to see it during the winter. With this in view I feel the more things of mine, ours – books, for example – that are left there the less desolated it will look, also *feel* from this end, not to say be for you in other ways more convenient: the less desolated it will be from your point of view too. Also one has to make clear they have no actual responsibility for anything of mine, in case some such feeling as this should be a deterrent. As for My Heart's In . . . – well, all this is left to your heart and discretion.[2] You make our hearts feel better about it all, however: and again, thank you from them. There're a few important points to bequeath to any possible temporary successor, I mention, partly because they are even more valid to anyone not living your more specifically Canadian existence on the beach: first, though it may look, like a pig-in-the-poke – (& indeed is – in a spiritual sense –) to hang on to the 'mink's house' next door[3] to your old one is virtually a necessity to any married or indeed unmarried couple if their lives are to be tenable at ours; I'd hate to see that big cedar come down between the houses or imagine any other horrors that could happen otherwise. (To me, too, childish though it may seem, there is the pier,[4] which we built, & which I cannot imagine myself living without, even if it isn't there & myself am dead.)[b] Then there is the old pier: it can be a delight to a swimmer. Please give it a long counterbracing masterbuilding look at least before you should leave, cast some Harveyian architechtonic charm at it, some spell against teredos, and tell your descendants to cherish it (even if in its absence). Finally there is much of love about the place that will surely come to any lover's aid, especially in such strange seasons as autumn and winter and early spring: in your most knightly fashion I commend you to pass such words down to whom it may concern, (even if necessary in the accents of Sir Walter Scott.)[5] Finally there is the question of the M.SS. Leave 'em lay where de Lawd hath flung them. That is to say, use your discretion about this. Books – again, as I say, largely these will be better, I think, where they are more or less: wherever they are. All we'd like ourselves in Europe, if you can somehow manage it, are two magical books, both in bad shape, & written apparently by one Frater Achad. One is called Q.B.L: the other The Anatomy of the Body of God.[6] They are books about the Caballa. Another very small book is a copy of Melville's The Confidence Man, if you can slip that in anywhere: it's scarcely larger than a pocket book. The Melville Log & the Daumier your guests might like to look at, in fact they might be an added attraction. It is a blow that Jimmy won't be there, but give him our best love should you see him: he thinks very highly of you. I reiterate the names of the two possibilities we had in mind, if anything should fall through at the last moment,

[Gene Laurence, 2233 McPherson Ave S., Burnaby, Tatlow 3335 – or Dexter 3124T or Bill & Alice McConnell – Einar Neilson will know where they are now.][c]

– You say you think you're gauche. If that means left, as I understand it to do, let's hope we both are so far gauche that we're right. If I'm to understand that it means provincial, you are the exact opposite, in my opinion, as I was reflecting only the other day, treading Raleighs walk in The Tower of London:[7] [Lowry has cancelled five lines at this point and drawn a series of seagulls over the lines. In the margin he asks:] Do they still come homeward? – And the mergansers? And – ah pardon me thou bleeding piece of earth! I would rather have spoken that line (and/or we had erected that outhouse) than have taken – perhaps – Dollarton.[8] Love from us both

God bless!

Malcolm

Annotations:

1 After the Lowry's departure from Vancouver on 30 August 1954, Harvey Burt took charge of the Dollarton shack. He is largely responsible for rescuing the manuscripts, books, and other objects that survived the bulldozing of the beach in 1958. Laurie Lynds, a friend and fellow teacher of Burt's, looked after the shack during the summer of 1956 while Harvey was in Europe.

2 Burt had helped them paint and repair their row-boat 'My Heart's in the Highlands'; see photograph 18.

3 The 'Mink's house,' named for the mink that inhabited it, was a small free-standing shed in which Lowry stored things.

4 The pier had been swept away in the spring tides of 1955, but Lowry probably did not learn this until the summer; see his August 1956 letter (**662**) to Burt.

5 Sir Walter Scott (1771-1832), the Scots novelist, poet, and historian, is especially noted for his ability to describe nature and to delineate eccentric characters with qualities well suited to the Dollarton area.

6 Frater Achad was the pen-name of Lowry's friend Charles Stansfeld-Jones; see Lowry's 1942 letter (**179**) to him. Harvey Burt arrived in England towards the end of June, when he brought these books, and the Melville mentioned below.

7 Sir Walter Raleigh (1552-1618), an English naval commander, writer, and courtier under Queen Elizabeth I, was found guilty of conspiracy in 1603 by James I. He was imprisoned in the Tower of London for thirteen years, briefly freed, then charged again and executed on 29 October 1618. 'Raleigh's Walk' is the name given to the area overlooking the Thames where the prisoner was allowed to walk.

8 During one memorable occasion, Lowry and Burt had struggled to
straighten the Lowrys' outhouse when, according to the story, they
began to quote Mark Antony's speech over the body of Julius Caesar
from Shakespeare's play: 'O, pardon me, thou bleeding piece of earth,
/ That I am meek and gentle with these butchers!' (III.i.255-56) To this
Lowry adds a paraphrase of the remark made by Major-General James
Wolfe (1727-59), commander of the British forces in the Battle of the
Plains of Abraham, that he would rather have written Thomas Gray's
'Elegy Written in a Country Churchyard' (1751) than have captured
Quebec.

Editorial Notes:
a.   This is the postmark date.
b.   This parenthetical remark and the short one below have been written
     in Lowry's tiniest script, half the size of the writing in the rest of the
     letter. The visual effect is odd, almost as if Lowry was afraid of what he
     was transmitting to paper.
c.   This information has been inserted by Margerie.

*After a few months of peaceful work at Ripe, Lowry had again begun to drink
heavily, and at the end of June he collapsed, delirious. It is impossible to know
now exactly what precipitated this collapse, but Lowry was still hoping for help
and explanations, as the following letter to Margerie makes clear. At the beginning of July he was readmitted to Atkinson Morley's, where he spent almost six
weeks and underwent two intense sessions of aversion therapy. When he was discharged on 11 August he was certainly not cured, and more grief and trouble lay
just ahead.*

657: To Margerie Bonner Lowry

P: UBC(ms)   Atkinson Morley's Hospital,
                                                      31 Copse Hill,
                                                Wimbledon, England
                                                [early July 1956][a]

Dearheart – I am doing my damndest to accede to your request to write
a letter, that sounds silly written like that I know, but I am sedated (or
unsedated) with something that makes writing particularly difficult at
the moment. I won't try & explain now, in any case. The treatment is
somewhat changed: the 'room' treatment was even more intense than
before, but was somewhat shorter – about a week – not that I quit, far

from it, but that I didn't altogether respond physiologically quite as was expected; at any rate it's been intermitted though I may, I suppose, go back there yet; though I profoundly hope not, I'm certainly willing to, if it would do any good. But all this is too complicated to explain, as indeed is the rest, but you may rest assured things are progressing 'satisfactorily' as may be. Incidentally, this time, everything was as humanely done as could be expected under the somewhat gruesome circumstances: The psychological situation, though, is one of extreme difficulty, though I have great hopes all will eventually be well. The barium enema (far more humanely conducted than in Canada) revealed, as I have long suspected it still would, an organic defect not to say phenomenon, – hereditary, (nothing to do with alcohol, as the wireless operator of the Brest would say), in fact crashing deformation of the gut: the radiologist observed to Raymond that it was one of the eeriest experiences he ever had, 'like pouring barium into a huge empty hall.' Raymond – & neither of us have pulled any punches throughout this – has been exceptionally decent & understanding about the whole business, & is thus far in agreement with me in so far as I am in any agreement with myself, that indeed this may have something important to do with the 'alcoholic' aspect, even to the point of his conceding that, if not the whole cause, that it may have been anterior to & contributing to any cause or causes, since it seems likely I've had it since a baby (technically it is called something like that Schnickengrinter's disease)[1] – & continues to act partly as such; this seems to me to be very sporting behaviour on the part of a psychiatrist & so he is calling in a surgeon and it is possible therefore that I may [be] due for the knife. Nothing to get steamed up about, I may say, one doesn't die of such things & I wouldn't even [if] I keep the mego colon, (Father must have got his ulcerated) but in the good old spirit of compromise, which is existing at the moment & seems the only solution, I'd certainly be thankful to be rid of part of it at least, (not to mention the piles) for my digestive life is almost an entire misery & in fact always has been, with few intervals, as far back as I remember. So don't accuse me of lack of guts anyway, the fact being I seem literally to have too many & too much: moreover after the initial clearing space & pseudo flatulence has been dissipated by vomiting as has been often my habit, the actual *capacity* is almost unlimited – it seems the 'great hall' has an almost unappeasable desire to be filled & due to the concomitant digestive miseries especially with anything alcoholic (even if it disagrees with me): I'm not trying to excuse any moral aspects of the matter, but it may help to explain the compulsion of certain excesses under a more benign planet than that of wilful self-destruction or dipsomania or even lack of will power – perhaps too plausibly. We shall see. But I think I'm right. I don't think Raymond will allow the whole thing to be removed, even if the surgeon thinks it should be, & I foolishly gave my assent: it would play hell with one's mobile life, but that the 'hall' should be diminished, if possible, seems to me a damn good idea. But I shan't be seeing the surgeon till Thursday. Meantime I'm trying to arrange that we can meet, perhaps in Victoria, on your dear birthday [18 July]. And what a hell of a birthday letter this is all about bowels. I'm not supposed to tell you a word of it either, I'm in two minds whether to post it – so don't let on to Raymond you know at least more than a very little. Nothing to worry about anyhow. Your letters are, of course, a marvellous help & comfort & I'll be awaiting your Tuesday call on 7 (if I don't call you first – I see John on Tues. morning.) Meantime let the enclosure speak more from my secret heart to yours.[2] All love from your husband

                                                        Malcolm

Annotations:

1 Lowry's interesting name for his condition is an invention. He was suffering from Hirschsprung's Disease, a congenital enlargement of the colon; see Bowker (583).
2 There is no attachment with this holograph, but see the 'Giant Note' poem from 'El Leon' that follows (**658**).

Editorial Notes:

a. This letter is undated but references at the end suggest a date prior to Margerie's birthday on 18 July.

658: To Margerie Bonner Lowry

P: UBC(ms)   [Atkinson Morley's Hospital]
                                              [July 1956]^a

Giant note
With utter devotion – borne by
EL LEON[1]

Though we are all a little bit disappointed that this year
        there won't be any fireworks
We know that is but because we are all willy-nilly engaged
        in higherworks
And though it cannot but be with a little sadness that we
        shall not see this year fly off our beloved
        Harteebeeste's Roman Candle
That is no reason why we should to put it succinctly fly off
        the handle

For as El Leon sagely observes what this year we shall miss
    as to wild celebration
We shall in all senses make up for by what might be called
    mild cerebration
And though this year shall bring us no splendid burgeoning
    of rockets
To come down to brass tacks all that means is that we shall
    [be] burning the midnight oil right down to
        its sockets
So let us not regard these things, oh sweetest & most
    beloved Harteebeest with haggard and sallow
        E'yne
But look upon them as tokens of an even finer & by no means
    laggard Hallow'een
And all this with oh so much love is as from the hearts of
    <u>all</u> your faithful little animals torn
Who join in sending more love than ever in entire concert by
    their ancient & waggish ambassador your
              Affectionate

                    The Pronghorn

Annotations:

1 See letter **642** and Appendix 1. This is the enclosure Lowry refers to in
his July letter (**657**) as meant for Margerie's birthday on 18 July.

Editorial Notes:

a. The copy-text for this transcription (UBC 3:11) is a pencil holograph
on the recto of a single 20-by-27.5-cm sheet of paper. Lowry has
decorated the page with drawings of seagulls and a pronghorn, folded it
three times, and addressed it on the verso.

659: To Margerie Bonner Lowry

P: UBC(ms)   Atkinson Morley's Hospital,
                                    31 Copse Hill,
                            Wimbledon, England
                                20 July 1956

My dearest wife Margerie:

    X rays, x rays, & that's about all the news: they're still going on, so
that one feels they must have made quite a film by now, vista scope,
though it's going to be difficult to dub in the sound. I shall always

remember that lovely sweet day of your birthday – in spite of any quite natural renversements – or is it bouleversements? – and I only hope you enjoyed yourself as much as I did; I hope you got back O.K.; – I did on the dot, and with sheathed beak. Raymond is both astounded & confounded but it seems to me is on the whole more pleased than before: he should be – for there is psychological change, it could scarcely be less under the implications of duress. I must get physically fit though, as possible, before returning, & must insist on this: & meanwhile I simply have to put up with being expected to do the impossible – i.e. to undress & go down to the x ray room every hour or so, keep myself in readiness for this, *and* at the same time organize a clock golf tournament, cope with the great Big World outside, and write: there isn't much peace of mind for the latter at the moment, but I'm glad to have the m.s.s. (even though I find people poring over them at every moment, for I have nowhere to put them in privacy) – also thanks very very much for the mags. I have many constructive ideas for the future but these I think we should have some shearwater conversations about rather than my writing them down. A famous deep-sea diver has been added to our midst, nostalgic for the rapture of the depths: he was one of Mousebatten's right hand men.[1] The weather meanwhile is incredibly depressing, the purpose of this letter is simply to cheer you should it be the same with you. I live for 7 pm Saturday, all my love & heart to you & a mouse to Merlin[2]

Your devoted husband
Malcolm

Annotations:

1 Lowry has clearly written 'Mousebatten,' but he is referring to Lord Louis Mountbatten (1900-79). Mountbatten, uncle of the Duke of Edinburgh, was Allied commander for South-east Asia in 1943-46, and the last Viceroy of India.
2 The Lowrys' cat.

660: To Margerie Bonner Lowry

P: UBC(ms)   [Atkinson Morley's Hospital]
                                                        [early August 1956]

Ye olde Blubberhouses Boskage,
Knave Go By Corner,
Hot Half Baked Hamlet

By little trotty wagtail & good merganserpost

Dearest sweethearteebeeste –

I am just sending you this little note to get you to-morrow – or such is my intention – & there is a particular if somewhat hootnannyish pleasure about this because the said letter will be reposing in the Blubberhouse letter box waiting to be taken away at a quarter-to-four *while you will be still here.* This will go in my magical diary. I don't have any news save that I've been grossly overeating (though nearly all the patients are away for the week end the same amount of food still gets sent up from the kitchen, presumably in an effort to stem inflation) & that though I have had both a hot & a cold bath this morning there are still unmistakeable traces of bison lurking in the undergrowth – I think it is from the huge injections of B1[1] & some sort of ether that they use to swab the injection with, a formidable nosegloom believe me; &, which is scarcely news, that of course I'm colossally looking forward to being Ripeward-bound: well must close now (who was it said that?), I hope your cold is very much better & you're feeling yourself again, my darlingest bleriotwhippet lark

All Love Your

Snapped in the foyer at Glyndebourne[2]

Annotations:

1 Vitamin B[1] is used to treat alcoholism; Lowry had received this form of treatment in France during 1948.
2 Lowry has drawn a picture of himself as El Leon in formal attire attending the annual summer opera festival at Glyndebourne, Lewes, in East Sussex. 1956 was the Mozart bicentenary, so the festival, always a dressy occasion, was special that year.

661: To Margerie Bonner Lowry

P: UBC(ms)   [Atkinson Morley's Hospital]
                                    [9 August 1956][a]
                                    Thursday

My dearest sweetest double-duck Harteebeeste:

Just a tiny note I am sending via John [Davenport] containing cryptic pictorial messages from *you know who.* I too am in a glow of happiness, & looking forward all the time to seeing you on Sunday: & then forward to Ripe: do not wear yourself out doing all these things I should be doing: – Oh please *let* them, *let* them! Am meantime trying to get down, even with some feeling of success, to Ferry. Thank you for your sweet note, for your many many sweet notes which kept me alive, dear heart's darling –

True love as ever your

El Leon

Editorial Notes:

a.   The Thursday prior to Lowry's release from hospital was 9 August. The 'pictorial messages' he mentions are an indecipherable drawing beside the signature and two seagulls.

662: To Harvey Burt

P: private; UBC(msc)
PP: *SL* 388

[The White Cottage]
[ca August 1956]ᵃ

Thank you, dear old Harvey, for the more than bravest boat. It is truly a work of art and great kindness, & if I look at it long enough maybe I can forget the poor shack being hurled out of the window, though that was a great work of art too, & heartbreaking that it had to happen, especially after the love you put into making it.[1] I am writing without my glasses so the contours of this note may be a little awry. Also I am very tired: I cannot believe our poor pier has been swept away:[2] that pier, that gave so much happiness to many & us, *was us* in a sense; we risked our lives building it, especially on the further reaches you never saw, where there was a 35 ft perpendicular drop onto the granite & barnacles if you made a mistake: nobody could understand how it survived so long, not even engineers & it was nicknamed The 'Crazy Wonder' on the beach. Ramshackle from certain angles though it was, & the handrails puerile (but oh the washing hung out on the line there like great white stationary birds beating their wings against the gale). Margie & I built it together with practically no tools and I am brokenhearted it has gone.

[breaks off unsigned]

Annotations:

1   When Burt visited Lowry at Ripe in August 1956, he brought him a model boat as a gift. During her visit with the Lowrys in the summer of 1955, Dorothy Templeton Burt had given Lowry the model of the Dollarton shack, pier, and boat that Harvey had made for Malcolm's birthday that year; see Lowry's 26 July 1955 letter (**638**) to Burt.

According to Bowker (562), this model had been destroyed by a cleaning lady who knocked it 'out of the window.' Lowry is also, of course, alluding to his short story 'The Bravest Boat' and the model balsa boat that plays an important role there.

2 Exactly when and how Lowry learned that his pier had been swept away in the spring tides of 1955 is not certain. Douglas Day maintains (35-36) that Burt told Lowry of his loss when he visited the Lowrys at Ripe in the summer of 1956. The Burts recall that Lowry guessed something had happened and that Dorothy confirmed his suspicions when she was visiting with the Lowrys in the summer and fall of 1955.

Editorial Notes:

a. This letter is undated, but internal evidence suggests late August or early September 1956. It would appear from the photocopy of the letter (UBC 3:11) that approximately three lines, and possibly the signature, have been deleted.

663: To David Markson

P: UBC(ms)

The White Cottage,
Ripe, Near Lewes,
Sussex
3 September 1956

Dear old Dave:

I'm deeply sorry not to have written before – but herewith find a thousand congratulations on your forthcoming marriage to Elaine, & all the very best & most heartfelt wishes for happiness & love to her & you from me & us both.[1] Wonderful news! May I propose the flyblown ganglioness of the Volcano as a wedding present to you children, all unworthy though it be, it is really more the original mss than any other versions, being the one – & typed by Margie – on which the verdict rested & which has passed through the hands of the mostest publishers & other gallinippers (or should they be galleynippers?) – I shall try to compose you a suitable gallopade to go with it weddingdaywise. I think it's good your Satevepost story should be coming out the day before, & even if your finding a place to live be comparable in difficulty to Ahab's search for his great white socks, you can always console yourself by remembering that the man himself – Hermann I mean – expired, if [I] may mistake not, the day before that, so that by the 30th should have been well on his way to being reborn, whale & all.[2] We have had some heavy things to put [up] with recently in health & what – not – albeit with happy issue, one hopes – , on top of which we had news our beautiful pier in Canada was swept away – alas, our fool is dead, after 16 years – (though must live somewhere still,)³ – so that it's been all the better to get the grand news of yourself, with the photo too, looking so well – what about one of you both?

Love & congratulations again

Malcolm

Annotations:

1 David and Elaine Markson were married on 30 September 1956. Lowry's wedding present was his copy of the final typescript version of *Under the Volcano*, which is now held with the Lowry Papers in the Harry Ransom Humanities Research Center at the University of Texas in Austin.

2 Herman Melville died on 28 September 1891.

3 Harvey Burt may have told Lowry about the pier, or at least confirmed its loss, when he visited Ripe in August 1956, but see Lowry's August 1956 letter (**662**) to Burt. Lowry's comment is an echo of King Lear's lament over Cordelia: 'And my poor fool is hang'd! No, no, no life!' (V.iii.306)

664: To Elaine and David Markson

P: UBC(pcard)   [The White Cottage]
                                           [29 September 1956]

Best Love, Elaine & David¹
Best of Luck
God Bless
from us
both
Margerie & Malcolm
& love from M.²

Annotations:

1 This postcard, sent to the Marksons for their wedding, is addressed to Lion Books, 655 Madison Avenue, New York, where Markson was working. Lowry makes joking reference to this address in subsequent letters.

2 'M.' is Merlin, the Lowrys' cat.

This time it was Margerie's turn. She suffered what appears to have been a nervous breakdown in October 1956 and was admitted to St Luke's Woodside Hospital in north London, where she stayed from 18 October to 16 November. In order to rest and recover, she was heavily sedated in what Lowry described as her 'GREAT SNORE.' He wrote to her almost every day with reports on her garden and amusing anecdotes, and to cheer her he often used the pet language of 'harteebeeste' and 'El Leon' that had developed in the Dollarton years. Like Malcolm, Margerie had amazing recuperative powers, so that when she returned to Ripe she was thin but ready to resume life with energy.

665: To Margerie Bonner Lowry

P: UBC(ms)

The White Cottage,
Wednesday afternoon
[17 October 1956][a]

Sweetheart − this is just a tiny note of solidarity & love from all of us, intended to reach you on arrival, in case you are lonesome or feeling a bit gloomy at that hour when 'the owl's a'snoring in his tree, till it grow dark enough for him to see' (as de la Mare says)[1] the cottage is already growing lonely in advance, & the teapot missing in advance its afternoon steep to-morrow in your honour, however, don't worry about me anyhow, get well quickly, Sursum corda

<u>Great Great love!</u>

Malcolm

[P.S.] Had to scrawl this so that you wouldn't catch me writing it! I do hope you get it just as you arrive − or as evening approaches, for the evenings can be the worst & longest in hospital, − but if you don't it's because I don't know what ward you are in.

All fondest love.

Annotations:

1 Walter de la Mare says this in the final couplet of his poem 'The Owl,' from *O Lovely England and Other Poems* (1953).

Editorial Notes:

a. This pencil holograph (UBC 53:4) was written the day before

Margerie's admission St Luke's Woodside Hospital in London on Thursday, 18 October. His postscript appears on the verso of the small sheet of notepad paper.

666: To Margerie Bonner Lowry

P: UBC(ms)   [The White Cottage]
                                                    [19 October 1956]

<u>Log of the ss Harteebeeste.</u> Master. El Leon. (Coal Burner)

Dear sweetheart: – this is to catch Friday aftern post written at tea-time. All very well save that I miss you awfully awfully, especially at this time: even the teapot wears a bereaved look. The garden is fine with some beautiful new white roses on the wall to the right; & new dahlias too. Wish you could see them. House is absolutely spick & span after Dorothy's clean out to-day.[1] Laundry, cat dealt with: latter sportive, but grave, missing you, as I do. Madame Spooner heros me like a demented mother partridge trying to feed a rhinoceros.[2] Pills all taken at night time. Out of tune cock bugles in the dawn – that's where he lives, Cartreth Hospital says you have settled in fine but am phoning again to-night. Have some incredibly diverting things to report but will do so at more length over the week end when I have more time. Am giving plants Sangral in 5 minutes time. I think you are the bravest. Sursum corda & with all great love

                                                    Malc

(I am really enjoying keeping the ship in order with a terrific fellow feeling. Love from all of us, *missing you*.)

Annotations:

1 This Dorothy, not to be confused with Dorothy Templeton Burt, was a cleaning lady, and she has not been further identified.
2 Mrs. Spooner lived in the nearby rectory.

667: To Margerie Bonner Lowry

P: UBC(ms)   [The White Cottage]
                                                    [19 October 1956]

RELEASE! EL LEON DEMANDS BEAUTY SLEEP TREATMENT: CARNIVORES ROAR FOR FAIR SHARE RELAXERS AS 'SLEEPING BEAUTY' MATES ENTER FIRST DAY OF THE GREAT SNORE. Timbuctoo. Friday.

– I dare say you won't be able to read this, my dearest sweetheart but I'm hoping that you may be able to get a laugh or two in during the week of the titanic Schnooze, just got your two sweet letters – (no, your handwriting is the most integrated that I ever saw it, oddly enough) – & what wonderful news that, though the tension hasn't fully been broken, after this new treatment you may be able to come out of hospital in a few days: – but for god's sake don't feel that you have to *rush* anything, take it easy, & if you need another relaxer, then you do, that's all, & it's far better that you should have it; moreover everything's running on greased roller skates here, though of course you are missed by everything & everyone, *but to-day is* my DAY of Duties – laundrymen are breathing down my neck, Sangral pitchers are bubbling, Beautipots are squawking, & I'm going to protect your plants with newspaper against any possible chance of frost: there's a wee bit of a nip in the air, but I keep the electric fire on for a certain period each day, & I don't think there's any danger. Bless you, & god love you, – all thoughts leading to 6:15 pm & real strongbody chatter Great Love darling.

Malc

668: To Margerie Bonner Lowry

P: UBC(ms)   The White Cottage,
Ripe
Saturday, 20 October [1956]

Sweet braveheart, brave sweetheart; herewith, I hope, something like a letter, rather than just a love tap, which is all I've had time for so far, so busy have we cats been, & in passing it has struck we might both write each other more real letters, the page being the only actor-proof setting as the saying is: – not that the others *aren't* letters – God forbid – but considering our profession it's just struck me as wonderful that we avail ourselves so little of writing as a means of serious communication, especially when otherwise incommunicable. I've just called the hospital, as I have every day, & they say, of course, that you are doing fine: I tremendously hope it's so of course & that you're having the rest you need, & that, with an amenity bed – darling will you come to amenity bed with me one of these fine days? – that life is a temporary euphoria rather than a furore: (I doubt the common-sense of phoning every day if I can't talk to you though, it has occurred to me you might be less gratified by my anxiety than worried over the telephone bill, moreover I have the suspicion that psychological values will be given to my words which may get misinterpreted in transit, such as that 'your husband seems more worried by catfood & bulbs than about you.' 'A veritable *narcissus indoors* etc' – I have to take that risk, though, also about the letters themselves – do they arrive? are they opened? Anyway I'm writing every day, but with phoning I may do as you did at the Atkinson Morley, & skip a day or so till I can speak to my beloved in person, since it devolves you're not at the moment in dire need of anything *I* can well give you, except of course news): first, the home front. Life at the Rectors is as comfortable as good college digs and I am fed like a navvy, too much, in fact, & I must eat less, (as must the cat.)[1] The rector's room reminds me rather of Nordahl's in Oxford, for some reason, (more of this later):[2] roaring fires, & myself the picture of slippered & bespectacled ease & repletion of the inner bird; nothing seems too much trouble for Mrs Spooner, what time Mr Ben solemnly knits away at a bedsock for his two year old grandson. I divide my time between there & here (being The White Cottage) about equally, though missing you equally in both places, although here the more poignantly (this is written in our kitchen 7.50 pm idiot time & I must now call a halt for what but *diner* – in all likelihood a whole ox: – it turned out to be our liver sausage but I swear I had a whole ox for lunch) – & especially at tea-time. Our teas! But no melancholy now. All in all a better place from both our points of view could not have been found, so that's item number one. Now for some news of the flora and fauna. Plants all serene & sangraled yesterday: bulbs were damp enough so only watered with ¼ cup of water yesterday, (Fri) so as not to get soggy, but I think I'll repeat this small dose to-morrow, because to-day though they weren't dry & the soil was dark I felt they might not be quite damp *enough* either (Have done this). (I'll try judging by weight as per instructions on lid of Beautypot, – Talking of Beautypots there is a vast reverend beautypot under my rectorial bed constructed for an archbishop at least.) NOW THE GARDEN, of which I have very good news for despite recent storms & its obviously missing you it looks very beautiful, burgeoning in a kind of autumnal spring (it's been quite warm). Starting at the left then, by the *Dovecathouse* there're brilliant new rosebuds, perhaps only ours by proxy, sprouting aloft in the apple tree, & shortly to bloom: the nasturtium-colored nasturtiums – vermilion-orange – are still beautiful twining in that apple-tree though some others are over, but a really wonderful surprise for you are our splinted dahlias, – in spite of big storms, new enameled perfect flowers, some in single stems, & new buds, are flourishing atop the bamboo: some chrysanthemums – (I think) – (we are now moving *right* along the wall) – are coming out & there's more burgeoning of new dahlias against the wall, of the very ones you feared done for, all with their splints intacto and all a'taunto: there's a beautiful 'nameless' coming out there: & triumphant foxglove bells twangling away like mauve leopards on its waggish splint in which

I take singular pride: and now, in the righthand corner, more roses, white ones (ours this time), & very beautiful, – more of your dahlias, & very lovely: going round the bend (of the wall), still more lovely nasturtiums & in the foreground the dwarf nameless doing well. *While between the dwarf nameless and the apple trees there are new fresh crimson rosebuds!* – the Michaelmas daisies, though, are over & should doubtless be cut back though I have ropped one bush up (sorry, am writing in very bad light.)

They (the michaelmas daisies) took a bad fall against the pump in a gale (in which incidentally a freighter called the D. Templeton is now reported as going down)[3] – I don't know what to do about it, but *I looked at them sternly*. The splinted gladioli are nobly sprouting new buds but the yellow laburnum-elderberry nameless is sprouting yellow snowballs amongst the branches of the nameless Forsythia – unlilac tree – or is it the same thing? – by the cat exit: it is all a dramatic & lovely picture *from the kitchen* windows, & almost as delightful close to [several words deleted]: altogether a beautiful late flowering with quite a Dollartonian stillness & peace (despite the fact it's blowing like hell) communicated partly through the presence of your love for the garden, & vicariously maybe, but I generously *feel* it myself: – going down the left hedge there're handsome apples still found growing, 'still-lifeing', apple-cheeked, over the hedge and below, on the grass rotting into bluetits' breakfast cups of blackened grapefruits! I forgot the lily-pad pool but those wallfloribund snapdragony things are still there with their wonderful velvety snappers: out in front of the house it's slightly less impressive from the lane but still very fine with cornflowers, chrysanthemumballnameless-dahlias that are perhaps marigolds, the while the Ethiopian tiger lily is still burning whitely bright and there are quite a few other Nameless, and the Strange, doing well round the door: only the sweetpeas are 'over' there, I think, though even so, not quite, albeit a rosebush took a Flying Enterprise slant roadward. (I'm writing this in bad light in the Rectory after taking my sleeping pills – everything all correcto on the pill-box front, by the bye) – but this light is too dim to write by in bed, so I'll switch the main lamp on – have done so – & quit till to-morrow morning. (FOR ELUCIDATION OF BAD WRITING IN BAD LIGHT SEE BELOW)[a]

Main purport of the above bedscrawl is that (a) I *have looked sternly* at the michaelmas daisies by the pump which took a bit of a tumble in a storm (b) but I think they are over anyway & should be cut back (c) a freighter, the D. Templeton, is reported in trouble in the channel (c) *The splinted gladioli by the pool* is doing beautifully & has new buds the whatever-it-is by the cat exit, i.e. the kitchen window, is sprouting yellow snowballs (d) all this looks very beautiful – especially the roses &

the dahlias – & I'm getting a great kick out of it, & a Dollartonian sense of peace & love (e) meantime the apples are rotting into bluetits' breakfast cups of blackened grapefruit (f) the garden in front on the lane is less impressive, but still very fine, with the Ethiopian lily, the cornflowers, though the sweetpeas are over. Further news from the garden front is that here & there primroses are actually coming out again, & roses everywhere, & Mrs Spooner says that the primroses will actually be with us all winter till the aconite & snowdrops start. (*We* don't have primroses in our garden yet in this strange fall-spring). How wonderful if you are out of hospital, in time to see all the glory of your garden in a June-November, but even if not you'll have the pleasure of knowing how much I've appreciated the fruits of your work & love.

I'm finishing this letter off on Sunday back in the kitchen at The White Cottage. I have fed the cat & got the Observer, & am now going back to the Vicarage to eat another ox, but I hope to get this letter off by 3 so you'll get it to-morrow. *Later.* Have eaten the ox, two huge chops, gravy, beans & potatoes (I left two potatoes) & cheese. Mrs Spooner is a v. good cook I think, with some hereditary ye olde Englishe cookinge tricks: she apparently steams the chops between two plates before frying, which makes them very tender: and she gave me a roast – a brisket, a commonly despised cut, – that melted in the mouth. But I miss your cooking & in fact I even miss *my* cooking. She is giving me sausages & fried apples for supper. God help the dear old: (mego, if you didn't see the joke till 25 years afterwards) but she's being extremely good to me. She even offered *not* to go to church this morning (though it's the first time in years she & Mr Ben have been able to go to church together because he had to do the milking, whereas Ian offered to do it to-day) if in that way she could be of any extra help to me, & she really meant it: in truth I'm being treated, absurdly but delightfully enough, with actual *veneration*, & I believe that this is because in some mysterious way she associates me or identifies me with the vicar, the padre (– Rev. Leon). It is somehow touching. Anyhow she firmly believes that the house is haunted by the vicar's personality, & the house itself is a consecrated one: there's a bit of the chancel of the church built into it. It gives one a very Wuthering Heightsish feeling looking out of those black-leaded casement windows from a height in a gale, over the hencoops with the poor-Cock-in-bad-crow toward Yellow hammer corner & the high-tension pylons. Or looking at the engravings in the study: *An English Merry-making in the Olden Time, A Coming of Age in the Olden Time,* & *The Surrender of Calais* (From the original Picture for which the Art Union of London gave a premium of £500) & in which all the characters are played by Einar Neilson wearing a different type of beard. Letter continued to-morrow. I must feed the cat again, who is

making tragedies. God bless you my dear sweet darling Harteebeeste hurry up & get better quickly & let's start living again. All Love
Your husband

Malcolm

Annotations:

1 During her stay in hospital Lowry took his meals at the nearby rectory, where he was well looked after by Mrs Spooner and her husband Ben.

2 Nordahl Grieg, the Norwegian writer who had a lasting impact on Lowry, spent two terms, from 1923 to 1924, at Wadham College, Oxford, and returned to Oxford in 1931 when he was working on his study of English poets, *Die unge døde*. Lowry's comment suggests that he may have visited Grieg there. The relationship between Lowry and Grieg has received much critical attention, and Hallvard Dahlie has confirmed that the two men met in Oslo in the fall of 1931. See Dahlie's article on the Grieg connection in *Swinging the Maelstrom* (31-42), and Lowry's letters (**35** and **85**) to Grieg.

3 Before she married Harvey Burt, Dorothy Burt was married to William Templeton, and Lowry must have been struck by the name.

Editorial Notes:

a. This pencil holograph (UBC 3:12) is written on recto and verso of one sheet of paper in Lowry's tiniest sloping script. The top half of the verso is heavily corrected and this explanation appears at the top of the verso, keyed to the point where the writing improves.

669: To Margerie Bonner Lowry

P: UBC(ms) [The White Cottage]
[21 October 1956]

Just a very *tiny* Sunday note, at tea time, from all we loving cats: weather is *much* warmer, there're some beautiful roses out, & a lovely yellow one on the way on the lane side: Mrs Mason & grandson are working various horticultural magics: the plants are mostly well – & those I thought unthriving are to-day a thrive-o: Bulbs all serene: in the rectory crows the rachitic cock, in honour of which there is an embroidered cock in the kitchen in a frame, with the legend:
MANY ARE CALLED
BUT FEW GET UP

By god but that's funny.

  With all great sweet love to our dear Harteebeeste from all of us
Via Malc

670: To Margerie Bonner Lowry

P: UBC(ms)

White Cottage
Monday 22 October [1956]

Dearest dearest
Dearest duck – am overjoyed to get a letter from you, more than overjoyed to hear that your nurses are kind and sweet & that you've got a
private private room. This is just an interim letter to tell you how overjoyed I am: I've rung every day & I was getting worried, not by the
reports, which were non-committal optimistic contradictory, & generally uninformative, as is always inevitably the case (though sometimes I
can't exactly see why) but by the implication, on my calling last night
anyway, that your main trouble was that you were still 'nagging at yourself something awful' about *me* – this (though it was probably my
imagination) in Gauntlesque tones in which the sensitive soul seemed to
detect the implied rebuke[1] that had one availed oneself of the priceless
opportunity (& I have no doubt at all it would have been priceless, in
more senses than one) to enter Virginia Water[2] as an undergraduate then
you wouldn't be worrying so *much*. Be that as it may, I think *we'll* always
be glad of that two or three weeks we had together with the 'heavy
heavy hanging over our head'[3] – weeks of sweetness & even light
despite the bitterness & even total dark that might more appropriately
have been thought to be their accompaniment. Just the same, short of
getting myself stuffed & putting myself in the rectory window like one
of those local immortal Sussexian poodles, I can't think of an existence
more harmless & less productive of your worry than the one I am leading, which is positively Jane Austin-like in its stern devotion to duty
right down to the last (missing) fly-button; moreover, although of
course I miss you like hell, in so far as this existence is tolerable, I can
also find amusement in its solitude, in its rectorish rectitude, – your
plants & the garden and even the tragedy-making Cat prove real compensations, and it need be anything but a waste of time. Rev. El Leon
immured in the vicarage is a concept that never fails to divert me (see
insert)[a] – But it is also a godsent opportunity to resume work at high
pressure and break alot of difficult ground in a hurry all of which would
be much easier – & after all it can only gratify you – it is what you yourself want – if I could somehow feel you were making an effort to *stop*
worrying about me. In fact I'm trusting you to do so. Of course I'd
probably be hurt if you *didn't* worry at *all* but for god's sake lay off the
heavy self-nagging & you'll find it may be an important step in your
recovery. Mind you in your sweet letter there's absolutely no mumbling

word or hint about worry but I scent it just the same: For let me tell you honey ah feed the plants and ah water the cat, and what do you think I get for that? Worry blues. Miaoww. Miserere Worry Blues. And instead of getting high as a kite ah lock up those cottage doors all tight at night. All right? No. Bang. Crash. Worry Blues. Miaoww! Miserere Worry Blues. Now I'm giving it you straight honey if you got to worry, worry over something worth worrying over worry over Worrying because I'm telling you I ain't worrying over you half so much as I am about worrying about you worrying about *me*, and further, are you still with me sister? still there? if you can't stop those old birds of worry flying over your head you can sure enough stop them nesting in yo' hair! – Bang. Crash. Miaoww! Banish those Worry Blues. To banish those old miserere quite Contrary Jelly-roll rock and rhythm Worry Blue-ue-ues! . . . Goddam.

Doc. Raymond arrived yesterday at the Vicarage for awfternoon tea in a posh American shirt, looking a mixture between Oscar Wilde & the old Uncle in War & Peace,[4] & bearing, in a hand like a malt-shovel, a half-dozen sodium amytals to tide me over nights: he's sending the rest later, & substituting 1 grain things like yours for the pink objects on my days of benzydrene abstinence, the pink things latterly upset me slightly: in this way there's no temptation to overdose (or for that matter underdose) – too much of the one makes you a headache, the other simply sick. So you need have no worry over medicines: I do as a matter of fact sometimes tend to forget to take *anything* during the day but the good Mrs S. [Spooner] prompts my memory. This medicine seems to be doing me alot of good though I look forward to doing without it altogether, albeit I seem stuck (not in the wrong sense) with Veg. Lax. Mrs S. kindly offered to write you when I told her you were still upsetting yourself about me so I said for her to go ahead. Everyone asks very kindly about you. Raymond was very pleased with everything & I would have got him to put in a reassuring voice at St Lukes if there'd been time – as it was, by his presence he delayed my phoning the hospital till later than usual. However I was glad to see him: he's most insistent on the necessity that I get to work really seriously, & so I am trying to do, when the cat will let me. At moment I am writing in the garden using him as a writing-desk, & it's so warm I've got my shirt off – & it's October 22nd! His favorite game now is to run up my bare chest, having hacked himself a few necessary steps there with his icepick, and butt me with a great lunge in the nose; he also finds my chest a fairly convenient & adequate claw sharpener; I also must report that exasperation has caused him recently to find his voice. Instead of giving him his dinner this breakfast time I went to the bathroom: he roared, so that I could hear him upstairs. I roared back, a full octave lower, so perhaps we are both finding our voices. I am going to warm him some milk in a minute. It's really warm enough in the garden to bring the plants out into the sun, but I don't know whether I shall risk it: besides there are – er – rather alot of things on the table. On the other hand the house is looking decidedly spick – if not entirely span – Dorothy gave it a real shine. The things on the table are mostly unfinished letters, memorandi of one kind & another – library books, which I must return to Lewes to-morrow. I haven't had time to finish The Tree of Man[5] yet: it is a great book, I think, & I shall keep it out a while longer, returning the others, & investing in a few Penguin classics instead of renting more, which costs less, & then you own the books, unless I see something one wants very much. I am inhibited from making any duck-like expressions in my maturer style of my true affection & love and of how much I miss you by a slight suspicion that my letters may be opened. Are you feeling persecuted dear? Mrs Spooner maintains that Winnie [Mason] is persecuted by the water problem, which is entirely imaginary, and that there is tons of water – an unlimited supply – in her well at the Boskage & always has been, but that she has had the same obsession with all the tenants who have been in the White Cottage, most of whom apparently left largely because they were afraid to pull the plug – were stunk out, the implication was, so to speak. I believe this may be half true but I don't see that it matters very much: Mrs Mason is a good egg, & devoted to you, but one may feel a little easier now *about* pulling the plug perhaps, at least when she's not there. And I'm growing quite fond of the cottage & really so of your garden: – more roses & dahlias are out! And tea-time, – alack, & you not here to bring tea to! But the good Mrs S. has some pleasant oddities also; for example she loathes beautiful weather like this. 'There's nothing like a good *shiver* in the frost' she says 'then I'm at my best!' And I – am I feeling persecuted?

'Yes' she said 'Let's hope. There's the machine, you know. I got to take the machine.

'Eh?' said Les Docker.

'The sewing machine.'

(From p 72 of The Tides of Man.)

And the cat. Bang. Crash. Miaoww! Banish those Worry Blues. 4:15 Duck Time.

Consider thy tea brought with appropriate menu, & all dear love from

Your doting husband

Malcolm

Annotations:

1 In Shakespeare's *King Richard II* John of Gaunt rebukes the king for leasing out the 'dear, dear land' of England 'Like to a tenement or pelting farm' (see II.i.31-68).
2 Virginia Water is the great lake surrounded by trees and flowers in the south-east corner of Windsor Park and, thus, part of the royal property. It provides one of the most beautiful walks in the greater London area and was within reasonably easy reach of the Lowrys.
3 Lowry is quoting the line from Malcolm Brinnin's poem 'Heavy Heavy Heavy' that he and Margerie had used in their screenplay for *Tender Is the Night*; see his 20 May 1950 letter (**399**) to Frank Taylor.
4 Oscar Wilde was known for his flamboyant dress, and Michael Nikanórovich, the 'old Uncle' in Tolstoy's *War and Peace* (*Voyna i mir*, 1862-69), entertains guests in Cossack coat, blue trousers, and top boots; see the 1966 Norton edition, ed. George Gibian, p. 560.
5 *The Tree of Man* (New York: Viking Press, 1955) is by the Australian novelist Patrick White (1912-90); the fragment of conversation that Lowry quotes (with minor variations) below appears on page 72. White won the Nobel Prize for Literature in 1973.

Editorial Notes:

a. The insert, not reproduced here, to which Lowry is drawing Margerie's attention is a small pencil sketch at the bottom of the recto of the first page, which shows a smiling face with a halo above it and a line coming round the face and up through the halo. As Lowry explains in a parenthetical caption: 'That's his [El Leon's] tail, going through the halo.'

Dr Michael Raymond first saw Malcolm Lowry on the morning of 25 November 1955, when Lowry arrived, drunk, at Atkinson Morley's Hospital. During his weeks in hospital under Raymond's daily care, Lowry grew to trust and like his psychiatrist, and as his surviving letters to Raymond demonstrate, he had begun to create in letters the type of intellectual friendship and discourse so typical of his relationships with people he admired. For his part, Michael Raymond remembers his former patient not only as the 'author of one of the great novels of the century' but also as a man who had been rehabilitated and whose sudden death twenty months later came as a shock. In his article 'Poetic Reflections of a Psychiatrist,' for Contemporary Review, *Dr Raymond notes that in 1956-57 Lowry 'had recovered his balance, was enjoying life, and was writing again' (89).*

671: To Dr Michael Raymond

P: private(ms phc)   The White Cottage,
                                                    Ripe near Lewes,
                                                    Sussex
                                                    23 October 1956[a]

Dear Doctor Raymond:[1] – I sent a p.o. for Miss Linden of the Ph[?] Dept c/o yourself but to 18? Knightsbridge – unless that's right for you – because I'd forgotten the number was 15:[2] I hope this doesn't discommode you, or her – I sent it on Monday, but after the post had gone, I hadn't seen a postal order for 1/4 of a century & got into a considerable flap as to what to do with the thing, and I remembered that you had to tear off the [inner tinfoil against] this. I have just returned from Lewes where, without previous injury to self, I returned 5 library books to Boots, got out 3 more, (The Cocktail Party, The Last Grain Race, & Some Rise By Sin), bought myself some large envelopes, a new pipe (a Talisman), a tobacco pouch, a cup of coffee (for 9 d), & for a less price than the library books, The Golden Ass & Dostoievsky's The Devils in the Penguin edition,[3] – was received back in the rectory with feeling as much as if I had been Peter Townsend just having crossed the Sahara single-handed in a light [illegible].[4] Margerie seems to be getting on fairly well; – thanks again for coming to see me, it was a very enjoyable visit, & also for the Country Lives that are so very fascinating. In that trunk we opened was a huge album of Mexican popular (i.e revolutionary) art I meant to lend you & do remind me to do so because I think you'd find it of abounding interest – pathologically certainly, & often of great artistic power – like 3 dozen Goyas let loose in O.T.[5]

                                  Sincerely

                                                    Malcolm L.

Annotations:

1 Michael Raymond (1922-95), MD, FRCP Edinburgh, FRC Psych., was First Assistant in the Psychiatric Unit of St George's Hospital, London, from 1953 to 1958. Dr Raymond was at Atkinson Morley's Hospital, where St George's Psychiatric Unit is based, when Lowry was admitted for treatment. He was responsible for Lowry's daily care in hospital and kept in regular touch with Malcolm over the next year and a half. It was Raymond who suggested the White Cottage to Margerie; Ripe is close to Raymond's home in Burgess Hill.

2 The Psychiatric Out Patient Department of St George's Hospital was at 15 Knightsbridge; the hospital itself was located on the west side of Hyde Park Corner. Mrs Linden was administrative manager of the Out Patient Department.

3 Lowry makes several references to T.S. Eliot's play *The Cocktail Party*

(1949) in his letters from this period; see, for example, his 25 October 1956 letter (**673**) to Margerie. *The Last Grain Race* (1956) is by Eric Newby (1919-), and *Some Rise By Sin* (1956) is by Claude Houghton Oldfield (1889-?). Dostoevsky's novel *The Possessed* (*Besy*, 1871-72) is also known in translation as *The Devils* or *The Demons*. *The Golden Ass*, also called *Metamorphoses*, is a long prose satirical romance by the Roman writer Lucius Apuleius (ca AD 155).

4 Peter Townsend (1914-95) was a distinguished officer in the Royal Air Force during the Second World War, and later a traveller, writer, and journalist. In 1956 Townsend began the two-year global tour described in his 1959 book *Earth, My Friend*.

5 Francisco José de Goya y Lucientes (1746-1828), the foremost Spanish painter and engraver of his day, was court painter under Charles IV and Ferdinand VII. His court and religious commissions are conventional genre paintings, but his uncommissioned works are famous for their fantasy, expressionistic qualities, and brutal realism. Lowry may be thinking here of the etchings 'Los Desastres de la Guerra,' in which Goya captured the horrors of war, or the so-called 'black paintings' with which he decorated the walls of his country house, or the nightmare visions of the 'Proverbios.' Lowry has written 'O.T.' for operating theatre at the end of the sentence.

Editorial Notes:

a. This transcription is from a faint photocopy of a pencil holograph with several interlineations; it is illegible at several points.

672: To Margerie Bonner Lowry

P: UBC(ms)   [The White Cottage]
                                               [24 October 1956]
                                               Wednesday

Dear heart – how overjoyed I was with your so much happier-sounding letter, & I'm extremely relieved to hear that the Sister is a darling, & that everyone is so nice – it'll be making all the difference to you if they are, and not alot of strongbody bloddy fokking (fok = Swedish word for sail – I thought I'd make my letters more explicit they really were opened) boggers: I was a bit put out because you made no mention of my first notes – I wrote you on Wednesday last the day *before* you went in so that you would be sure to have a letter right on your arrival should you be feeling homesick or lost – *did* you get that one? The nurse or whoever usually answers my nightly phoned inquiry seems to have a sweet voice too: only once have I heard the Gauntlesque tones[1] – I'm afraid I do have it in for that snooping blackmailing bloddy strongbody (this lingo comes out of a magnificent book I'm reading called The Last Grain Race, about a sailing ship, by the way) though I daresay she's really harmless enough. Or is she? She reminded me unpleasantly of Esther whom I have never considered harmless.[2] But a truce to this: I've given your message to Mrs S.[Spooner] Yesterday I went to Lewes to return all library books save The Tree of Man, & against my better judgement, finding that my subscription, had not expired, got out a few more, including Eliot's The Cocktail Party that strangely enough was sitting there: it seems pretty bloddy dull at first reading & overfull of stupid strongbodies. Or rather it is perhaps not bloddy enough but too anaemic and full of weakbodies. But it's finely constructed, and there's something to be learned from it, no doubt, in its primly dramatic way. And there is – linguistically, & from a general standpoint – probably much psychological wisdom in it. Then the end of the second act gives you a genuine frisson – a fine piece of theatre. But just as migrating birds always make me weep in the movies, so I've always been a sucker for 'The Passing of the Third Floor Back' touch – I mean when you suddenly grasp the point that some perfectly pedestrian character is really meant to be a figure of Fate or God or an ambassador of God or an angel or something.[3] Here you feel let down finally, not by the illusion, or even the Ultimate Truth of the matter, but by the realisation that the magical swiftness with which these characters suddenly assume supernatural attributes is largely due to the fact there has been almost nothing genuinely human enough about them – or humanly genuine – to inhibit their transformation in the first place.

For the rest, in Lewes, resisting sternly any further temptation to buy you any more bakenite earrings, I bought *myself* something for a or with some change, a pipe (a Talisman) & a tobacco pouch, some lifebuoy soap and (despite the girl behind the counter) some Odorono, & for the diverse tastes of the inner bird in our own library, two Penguins The Devils (Dostoevsky's Possessed) & The Golden Ass. Likewise I got some longish envelopes & finally had a coffee at *our* old restaurant by the bus stop. Price 7d. (Tip 4d). *Mon*, ha' you no'heard? Then I came home on the 3 o'clock bus – feeling very nostalgic for you, especially at The Cross where there are still daisies growing and the kerbstone is haunted by sitting Harteebeestes, and was received at the Rectory in a manner more befitting to Peter Townsend having just crossed the Sahara single-handed. That's me, the Townsend Solitaire. . .[4] No adventures, though there was an extremely sinister pansy going in on top of the bumping bus who suddenly turned to me & said 'I *do* like a good joggle, don't you?' Whatever, do you suppose, can he have meant by that? A bloddy boggert. I saw about the Sokotra cave men & purred.[5] I don't think the

Burgess business is any more cooked than anything else, or Driberg would have spotted it, but the whole thing seems distinctly non U.[6] It seems to me possible that Mclean is a genuine boggert, however, whereas Burgess was simply fulfilling his higher serpent; quien sabe?[7] 'all I know is that I do like a nice bad-tempered conversation sometimes.' It will be marvellous when we can actually speak on the phone, & do you look forward to everything goodk. Miaow! Now to feed that bloddy Strongbody.

Devotedly

Malc

Annotations:

1 Once again, the 'Gauntlesque tones' belong to John of Gaunt in *King Richard II*; see Lowry's preceding letter (**670**) to Margerie.
2 Esther may be Earle Birney's first wife; she and Lowry were not on the friendliest of terms.
3 Jerome K. Jerome (1859-1927), an English humorist, novelist, and playwright, wrote his play *The Passing of the Third Floor Back* in 1908. It was an immediate success and was frequently revived until 1929; a British film starring Conrad Veidt as the Christ-like visitor in a Bloomsbury lodging-house was released in 1935. In this sentimental play the celestial visitor manages to change the lives of everyone around him for the better, and the comparison that Lowry is making with *The Cocktail Party* is less than complimentary.
4 Lowry's pun includes a reference to the Townsend's Solitaire, a slim gray bird of the thrush family, which Lowry would have seen in the conifer forests around Dollarton.
5 An Oxford University team had recently returned from two months' research among the natives of the island of Sokotra in the Indian Ocean. They were analysing blood samples in an effort to determine the origins of the islanders.
6 The term 'non-U,' meaning not upper-class, is the subject of delightful parody in Alan Ross's essay 'U and Non-U'; see *Noblesse Oblige* (New York: Harper, 1956), edited by Nancy Mitford, pages 55-89.
7 Donald Duart Maclean (1913-83) and Guy Francis de Moncy Burgess (1911-63) were British diplomats at the centre of the notorious postwar espionage scandal that led to the defection of Kim Philby (1912-88) and the exposure of Anthony Blunt (1907-83). Philby, Burgess, and Maclean were undergraduates at Cambridge during the thirties, and later joined the British Foreign Service; Philby rose to a high rank in MI6, the British Secret Intelligence Service. Warned by Blunt that they were about to be exposed as Soviet spies, Burgess and Maclean fled to Moscow in 1951; Philby followed in 1963. Thomas Edward Neil Driberg (1905-76), an English writer and member of Parliament, published *Guy Burgess: A Portrait with Background* in the fall of 1956.

673: To Margerie Bonner Lowry

P: UBC(ms)   [Ripe]
[25 October 1956]

Thursday morning in the Rectory.

Dearest sweetheart –

– Am really overjoyed with your Wednesday letter, as also, with the
Wednesday report – the Powers That Are sounded genuinely optimistic: previously I had been in a minor flap because when I had asked
did it do you any real *good* my phoning the hospital every day they said
yes but when I later asked but didn't my phoning up every day worry
you in *itself* they said yes too, or a different voice did: – I'm keeping a
check on the phone calls, mon, so that Mrs M. [Mason] won't get stuck
with them, ha' you no heard they cost 1/3 after 6 pm for 3 minutes,
something like that, otherwise 1/10? – not much of a curse on this, so
long as one hadn't previously been trying to get Raymond or somebody without success, & had made a habit of speaking each night to the
hospital for 12 minutes: but it's worth it when one gets clearly *goodk*
news, & I wouldn't mind how much it was if I could only speak to *you*
Oh Soon! I had Mrs S. [Spooner] in to the White Cottage to see how
I was doing with your plants – as I was a little worried by the leaves
falling off – not to worry! banish those miserere Worry blues (did you
like my song for you by the way?) – she says that the flowers are doing
fine & I am looking after them perfectly which privately, I thought
myself: – to-day Dorothy has been in to light the fire & generally give
the house an air dry and a cock outside (what *would* they make of this
letter even if they *did* open it?), & I'm glad of the extra warmth in the
kitchen for the flowers because there's going to be a groundfrost to-
night. Winnie [Mason] won't be back till to-morrow now: she seems
to be on the piss in Eastbourne (I beg your pardon), seeing the King &
I & heaven knows what – I must write Ruby again.[1] Before I forget,
Nekressov, by Sartre is on the Third Programme, 6 pm Saturday, & for
heaven's sake try & listen to it, even if it interferes with your dinner or
possibly (?) even phoning me (Oh, oh) – I hear it's one of the funniest
plays ever written & God knows you need a laugh.[2] Mrs S. tells me
they're not many nibbles at this house i.e. the rectory: it's going for
£3000, & it's *freehold* – & only £16 a year tax. It's a wonderfully comfortable house too, or at least the room downstairs is, & the morning
views are really marvellous: The garden comes in a poor second after
yours, ours, but there's a hell of a lot of property: it certainly is a good
buy for someone; I thought of writing Joan & Peter [Churchill] about
it, but I'm browned off on all friendships or even acquaintances if

possible till our own lives are sensibly organized again – which is after all one underlying main problem; marriage perhaps is partly a problem of organization, I sometimes feel, like a mountain climb which should be damn good fun as well as everything else, or one shouldn't embark on it. Oh dear, *dear* the ice-picks & crevasses and sherpas and even abominable snowmen that unfortunate image conjures up for the union of these innocent ducks: but I'm writing in the rectory against a radio blaring about Poland – sounds damn good news too, not going to say I told you so, but I did nevertheless – & the sun in my eyes, too, does not help.[3]

> Half of the harm that is done in this world
> Is due to people who want to feel important.
> They don't mean to do harm – but the harm does
> > not interest them.
> Or they do not see it, or they justify it
> Because they are absorbed in the endless struggle
> To think well of themselves.
> > Edward
> > If I am like that
> I must have done a great deal of harm.
> > Reilly
> Oh, not so much as you would like to think:
> Only, shall we say, within your modest capacity.[4]

A really profound boggert, at times, that Eliot in The Cocktail Party. Unfortunately all the female characters are like Dorothy (T)[5] without being alive, & all the male ones uninteresting saps with the exception of Eliot-Reilly, the Christoanalyst who, with a God complex as big as a house, presumably has abjured all desire to feel important despite his greased rrrollerskates. Since the cat is pining like the Fool in Lear for his mistress[6] I have decided to add to his diet, at Mrs S. recommendation, daily, some Felix Catfood. 'Every thing necessary for the health of cat or kitten. The main ingredients are meat, fish, rye, grass meal, iodised minerals, calcium & phosphorus for bone, nerve & muscle, sodium & chlorine for digestion, iron & sulphur for blood, tissue & general condition, (to say nothing of the lesser ingredients) ensuring a smooth silky coat & STRONG TEETH. A real strong body. In fact we'll be real strongbodies here. Am delighted with your news, & that you are resting & happy. Look forward to good things, good days. Bless you all my love

> Malcolm

P.S. Enclose mysterious document, can only suppose that FE Johnson is

Merlin's pen name – his nom-de-paw – & note concerns any ms of his![7]

P.P.S. How we all *sans exception* are looking forward to your return

'Flying saucer over
Lewes' was local headline
Tuesday[8]

Annotations:

1 Ruby's identity is unknown.
2 *Nekrassov* (1955), a play in eight tableaux by Jean-Paul Sartre, is about a confidence man who takes a Russian name. It was performed by BBC radio on 3 November 1956; see Lowry's October 1956 letter (**675**) to Margerie, in which he corrects the time for the broadcast.
3 In June 1956 anti-communist riots had broken out in Poland, and the internal affairs of the country were unstable through that summer and fall. Between 19 and 21 October it looked as if the Soviet Union might take over the Polish Politburo, but the Soviet leaders and generals in Warsaw returned to Moscow on 20 October, Polish elections proceeded, and the Soviet Union approved the composition of the newly elected Politburo.
4 Lowry is quoting dialogue between Sir Henry Harcourt-Reilly (the psychoanalyst) and Edward Chamberlayne (the troubled husband) in act two of T.S. Eliot's verse play *The Cocktail Party*. This play about adultery has been seen as a religious exploration of redemption, but in this scene Edward is articulating his fear and hatred of his wife, who, he believes, has destroyed his identity.
5 Possibly Dorothy Templeton Burt.
6 In this reference to *King Lear* Lowry is paraphrasing a comment made to the King about the court fool: 'Since my young lady's going into France, sir, the fool hath much pined away' (I.iv.80-81).
7 Merlin, the Lowrys' cat, appears in several letters to Margerie under the pen-name 'FE' or 'DS' Johnson.
8 In the space between the second postscript and this addendum Lowry has drawn a smiling face with a pipe in its mouth, a halo perched above its head, and an arrow connecting the halo to the 'flying saucer' reference.

674: To Margerie Bonner Lowry

P: UBC(ms)   [The White Cottage]
27 October [1956][a]

(Pageful of well-meaning jokes whispered in the ear of a Sleeping Beauty)[1]

Winnie has returned in splendid fettle
Myself involvèd too am twixt Cat and Kettle
Your plants – save one – are all in splendid order
The kitchen table's an herbaceous border
(But life without you's an outrageous bore, dear)
The plant in question wasn't set quite deep enough
But t'will revive if only we ducks yeep enough
(While as for Mama her great job's to sleep enough
To sleep enough, and, ay, perchance, to snore, dear.)
And as for me when down to it I settle
No more embroiled with Popucatapetl
I'll scale, instead, the heights of Mother Gettle...[2]

Cha-cha. Glah & God up the chimney. And sailed under the apple trees to brood. I'm writing this on Sat. 4.15 Idiot time, wishing I could bring you up your tea. For some reason I miss you, if possible much more *now*, after your departure into the Great Schnooze & will probably find myself phoning up just as often anyhow. How marvellously well you sounded on the phone! And I think this Schnooze is going to be just the thing for you. 6.15 Idiot time. Just rung up, & they say you're doing splendidly: my brave heart. (I hope to god you're not being just too noble & really you're not suffering somethink awful.) Tirra Lirra! There goes the fried fish-wagon, scented tabernacle to the provinces, travelling on greased roller SKATES, joke over. D.S. Johnson has had a gala afternoon of butting & has rent my old blue pullover nearly in twain, but Mrs S. [Spooner] is going to darn it, & in this way I hope to have a fine new outfit of derelict clothing suitable for apple-tree brooding. Tirra Lirra! Purveyors of His Majesty the Ling. Purveyors of a Vicious-tea obscene. I wonder that D.S Johnson doesn't go trotting after the thing who, on the other hand, when looking at one, is a *Purr*veyor to His Majesty etc.

Oh etc. Great Sweet Love my dear sleeping sweetheart

Malc

From Country Life.

Badgers to the Rescue[3]

Sir – With regard to your excellent editorial note in Country Life of October 6, *The Truth About the Badger*, I should like to defend *old Brock* on another point. Many years ago, In the Quorn Country, I was staying with a cousin who went in for working terriers which were trained for badger digging. He received a letter from the then Master of the Quorn asking him if he would dig a pair of badgers and turn them down in an earth where mange in foxes was rife. This we did, putting them in sacks and turning them down in the required place. This was such a success that we got more requests for the same purpose. Badgers, because of their smell are *supposed* to be dirty, but I, who have dug out many of their holes, can assert that they are one of the CLEANEST LIVING OF WILD ANIMALS. – In these times of shortage of rabbits I have no doubt that there is an increase of *ROGUE* badgers, but that should not damn the whole breed. – K.E. Paget. (Major) 1 Adelaide Court, Hove, Sussex.

Awfternoon Nocturne. by D.S. Johnson
(from the ms of)

Old Ben just knits and, having gnat, he nods.
His father sits and, having sat, he plods
No more a ploughman but a weary way[4]
Dropsical to daughters-in-law for tea
Mrs S. just flits and, having flat, she flits
The cat just shits then, having shat, just shits ⎫
– Merlin to us, (but as author of sundry skits ⎭
'Donald. S. Johnson' to many learned wits!) –
The garden crackles with autumnal pods
Old Ben just knits and having knat he knods
His father sits upon the bench and spits
El Leon misses you the livelong day
But works in jerks and perks and even leaps
The book creeps on and having crept just steeps   ⎫
(WHILE MAMA SLEEPS AND SLEEPS AND SLEEPS *AND* SLEEPS!) ⎭

Annotations:

1 This bit of doggerel, and the 'Awfternoon Nocturne' that follows, are the 'well-meaning jokes' meant for Margerie's ear alone.
2 'Mother Gettle's Kettle-Simmered Soup' is a refrain in *October Ferry to Gabriola*, which Lowry was working on again.
3 *Country Life* is a glossy magazine with colour photographs of English country scenes, antiques, estates, social functions, and the like. Lowry has copied this letter from the 3 November 1955 issue (p. 1035); the 6 October 1955 issue (p. 712) carries an editorial note entitled 'The Truth about the Badger.'
4 See Thomas Gray's 'Elegy,' line 3: 'The ploughman homeward plods his weary way.'

Editorial Notes:

a. This letter is in tiny pencil script on recto and verso of a single piece of 12.5-by-7.5-cm notepaper. The material from *Country Life* and the poem are in pencil on a separate piece of the same paper.

675: To Margerie Bonner Lowry

P: UBC(ms) [The White Cottage]
[28 October 1956]

Sunday in the Conservatory.   NOTE 2

Darling darling darling, said the Chinese Nightingale.[1]

Very cold with an onshore wind, and I'm trying to nurse the begonias with the electric stove, what time the cat basks in its heat and scratches himself with a noise of giants in hobnailed boots crunching up the gravel path. Nekrassov,[2] I am sorry, is on Saturday, November 3, 3rd programme, I got my times wrong – perhaps you'll be able to hear it after all: or I can, at the Rectory, and tell you of it later. There are some splendid films on in London now – Harvest at the Academy & a new one called The Red Balloon, but I'm not going till we go together.[3] I found my turtle-neck sweater, (in the lowest section of the wardrobe underneath, among the boots) & I'm glad of it, though yesterday I was sitting more or less shirtless in the sun carrying out my afternoon duties as Scratching Machine Extraordinary to the Cat. I'm going to make a concerted effort to work – you've no idea how difficult it is with all my responsibilities of Flora and the Fauna. I've intimated that – in order to make a rhyme – that life was a bore – but in fact my small chores are as a sweetness & a pleasure because they bring close to your sweet self, whom I hope is never far away really, though involved in the Great Schnooze. I have the Observer & The Sunday Times from Mrs Funnel & must now return to the rectory to discuss the Sunday Joint. I saw Mr Evans on a tiny little motor-cyclette, but wearing earmuffs crash helmet and goggles & literally wrapped up like a driver of the 90's, & with whiskers bristling: he looked unpleasant & I felt rather sorry for him: he must have had to get rid of his car. That's what comes of offending ducks. Had my ox, which was steak & onions: fair. Great Sreat great sweet Love

Your El Leon

Annotations:

1 It is odd to see Lowry quoting these lines again. They first appeared in his 22 May 1933 letter (**43**) to Jan Gabrial, then in his 1939 letter (**88**) to Carol Phillips. The correct lines are 'Darling . . . darling . . . darling . . . darling . . . / Said the Chinese nightingale'; see 'The Chinese Nightingale (A Song in Chinese Tapestries)' (1917) by American poet Vachel Lindsay (1879-1931).
2 See Lowry's earlier October 1956 letter (**673**) to Margerie.
3 *Harvest* (also called *Regain*, 1927) is a feature film written and directed

by Marcel Pagnol, and *The Red Balloon* (*Le Ballon Rouge*, 1955), directed
by Albert Lamorisse, is about a boy and a balloon. They played at the
Academy and Odeon cinemas during October in 1956.

676: To Margerie Bonner Lowry

P: UBC(ms)   [The] White Cottage
                                              29 October [1956]

My dearest, prettiest schnoozing darling!
 – Ducktober is the cruellest month.[1] It's the boiling cold & the blinding
dark & the frosting heat & the darkling light wot gets you down slightly:
moreover Mr S. spilt tea on my blue corduroy pants. Her wing doth the
eagle flap. Hungry clouds swag on the deep.[2] And gloomy Sunday in
Budapest, with a vengeance. Saw Miss Cole to-day as per arrangement,
& gave her the bird-book which I'd lent Winnie, who'd forgotten she
was coming, & gone off somewhere. Having seen the book through the
window, at Winnie's, we burgled in, using the outer key, myself slightly
disapproving of this manoeuvre, but (having suggested it in the first
place) I tolerated it finally, seeing that she was wearing full battle dress.
(Dear Miss Cole, has a flighty young soul, and a flighty young soul is
she),[3] which seemed to lend the enterprise some authority. Am just
finishing The Tree of Man, a real margiepiece, I think, slightly marred
by a curious pretension in the writing occasionally, not exactly overwriting; more a kind of overwriting of *underwriting*, an over dissection of
the expendable, in neo-surrealistic terms; and by some very bad habits,
almost like nervous twitches, that break out on every other page: e.g
White rarely says They found so & so, but They *did* find etc.[4] And
there're some Laurentian twitches and turns repeated ad nauseam.
Nevertheless it's one of the very best books I ever *did* read, comes from
Austrylia, though it might as well have taken place in Dollarton, for that
matter; in fact, half the time, I'm persuaded that's where it *is* taking place,
at Mrs Toland's to be exact.[5] I vaguely described the padre's downstairs
room in the rectory? I'll make it a little more precise. It's a room quite
full of hot-cha, – if you look close enough, – for a padre. For example,
the engraving on the right, An English Merrymaking in the olden Time
(From the original picture in the possession of John Naylor Esq (Art
Union of London 1832). At rear, beneath the trees, on a gravy-colored
day, people are dancing vamping & stamping, the Sir Roger de
Coverley.[6] R, ye olde cottages, or perhaps alms-houses. R, foreground:
rector being unwillingly persuaded from bottle-strewn table by volup-
tuous dames to join in revels. L. foregr: lady having her fortune told by
a dreamy witch under a wizard oak. Vague Bosch-Breugel-like sozzlings

going on under more oaks, back. l. Dali dream fields uncolored in background.[7] Two more pie-eyed padres at least. Orchestra of curled flunkeys: violin & flute, & other flap-bags & akimbo codpieces. Seagulls flying over the church tower. Then we come, on the right of the secretaire to another, similar engraving. I told you of: A Coming of Age in the olden Time (pub. 1855 'for the proprietors') with ye younge lorde of manor, on dais, tights and bodkin; indeterminate Pickwicks below, & the rest of the scene occupied by faithful retainers flowing through the raised portcullis – is it portcullis? of Malatesta-in-the-Wold.[8] L, a cramped Sutton, stooping, tapping a vast barrel, into a puncheon, while the Laughing Cavalier, leaning over the barrel on some bayleaves, in his plumed hat, pours a tankard over him: elsewhere I perceive a toping tall-hatted Puritan, a periwigged Gower, & a cross Queen Elizabeth – ye younge lordes' mother? – flanked by Donald Duck griffins, & a pet owl. Another Sutton carves a whole ox. Slap; ghosts are streaming out of upper mullions on a day that is otherwise apparently dead still, though there's a bell wildly swinging away, while a faithful dog is standing with pricked ears in spilled beer, & yet another smilingly reluctant padre is being persuaded into the twirly whirly trill. I'll spare you a description of the picture next to it, which is called Nothing Venture, Nothing Have, & represents a gigantic jowly mastiff with half closed tipsy eyes chained up in its straw with a gnawed bone & a venturesome puppy: hence the title. The secretary contains china of the Present from Bexhill variety – Sol et Salubritas – ,[9] or from Egypt with the crescent & star, & also contains an Encylopedic Dictionary, the Arms of Cardinal Wolsey, The Book of Reptiles & Spiders, The Scarlet Pimpernel, The Bible, Memoirs of Bethany, & the Arabian Nights. In it is a huge bowie knife with Viva Espana carved on the blade, evidently hailing from the Spanish Civil War, and upon it, when the desk is shut a picture, apparently famous, of Little Red Riding Hood, fashioned after the rector's granddaughter. The padre himself looks at one from here & there ('I've always lived in haunted houses myself,' says Mrs S. 'in the last one an invisible billiard ball used to bounce downstairs every night at mid night on the dot') & the windows themselves look straight over the chicken run with the dangerous lugubrious cock at yellow hammer corner & our road. That's all for now. Great sweet love, my dear darling bravest duck, I reread all your letters to me this morning with such warmth in my heart & hope for the future. Schnooze well – Love – love – love

Your devoted Malc

Annotations:

1 Lowry is parodying the opening line of T.S. Eliot's *The Waste Land* (1922): 'April is the cruellest month,' which is itself an allusion to the

opening line of the General Prologue of Geoffrey Chaucer's *Canterbury Tales* (ca 1387-1400): 'Whan that Aprill with his shoures soote ....'

2 'Her wing doth the eagle flap' is a line from the song in canto 3, part xi, of Sir Walter Scott's long poem *Marmion* (1808). The line 'Hungry clouds swag on the deep' appears twice in the 'Argument' to William Blake's *The Marriage of Heaven and Hell* (1790-93).

3 Miss Cole was a home-care worker and physiotherapist; see Lowry's 15 November 1956 letter (**695**) to Margerie. Lowry's parody here is of the anonymous English nursery rhyme 'Old King Cole,' which begins: 'Old King Cole / Was a merry old soul, / And a merry old soul was he.'

4 Lowry was reading Patrick White's novel *The Tree of Man*; see his 22 October 1956 letter (**670**) to Margerie.

5 Mrs Towland lived on Dollarton Highway, and members of the family still live in the area.

6 The 'Roger de Coverley' is a Scottish country dance, and the tune was first printed in 1648. Lowry's witty portrayal of the rector's room underscores with irony the kind of hypocrisy he always found in self-righteous Christians who damned, while vicariously enjoying, the joys of the flesh.

7 The 'Bosch-Breugel-like sozzlings' suggest a scene reminiscent of the paintings of Hieronymous Bosch and Pieter Breughel, which are characterized by crowded canvasses depicting ordinary folk in more or less grotesque postures. The 'Dali dream fields' suggest the surrealist spaces of a canvas by Spanish painter Salvador Dali (1904-89).

8 The 'indeterminate Pickwicks' are Lowry's characterization of figures that recall the jovial members of the Pickwick Club in Charles Dickens' *Pickwick Papers* (1836-37). 'Malatesta' refers to Margerie's unfinished novel set in Italy called 'The Castle of Malatesta' (UBC 51: 11-15).

9 This Latin phrase means: 'sun and wholesomeness.'

677: To Margerie Bonner Lowry

P: UBC(ms)   [The White Cottage]
[30 October 1956]

Letter 4. Tuesday – *Calling all sweet sleeping Harteebeestes*

Ducktober is the cruellest month, hotly – or perhaps not so hotly – pursued by Duckember. They told me you were responding well to the treatment on the whole but hadn't slept so well yesterday, my poor peewit, my loving lapwing, and were a bit restless: – I hope you have made up for it since & that it isn't too bloody for you, my love: you are the bravest, but be careful of letting them turf you out too soon, if you don't feel completely *detensioned*, even though I sez it agin my own not to say longing interests: for the weather is cruel, the little house an icebox, and the nights black as the Earl of Hell's jack boots. Mrs S's on the other hand tends to be a hotbox, though I am in the main very comfortable & appallingly well-fed; but in one way & another D.S. Johnson & I can be counted on to hold the fort indefinitely if necessary: Mrs S hasn't got to first base with selling her house yet, and though I've hinted I might know of someone, I haven't done anything about it for various reasons.[1]

I did counsel her to follow up some London leads, however, which seems her best bet, since her agent seems intent on swindling her into a local auction for which he'll get £80 even if the house remains unsold or goes for a song. Two letters this morning; one royalties on Volc. $34.20 – 76 copies in the last year! Sounds crazed to me after 10 years. What do I do with the cheque? The other has some Dunne-like significance maybe,[2] being a letter from *The Leysian Mission*,[3] I haven't heard from for 30 years, but which I mentioned to you in possible connection with somewhere to stay: 'Boys from the Leys, & old Leysians in every walk of life (& indeed of every shade of Churchmanship) have continued to maintain a close link with the Mission & its work . . . devoid of the *dour gloom* (Hoot Mon) so often associated with religious belief! I ought to have gone to Lewes again to-day to return 3 library books but I couldn't face it & am putting it off till Saturday and the hell with it: they don't give you time to read the books anyway. **NB OPERATION FLAP** starts to-day, you'll be glad to hear: – I begin work on a really big scale. Merlin & I just LIVE for your return – how I miss your tea times. Love & Love & Love & Love & Love & Kiss at every opportunity.

Love God bless

Malc

Annotations:

1 The Lowrys had some thought of trying to purchase the rectory house for themselves, but no offer was ever made.
2 J.W. Dunne and his theory of serial time in *An Experiment with Time* (1927) had fascinated Lowry since the early thirties; see his 16 April 1940 letter (**135**) to Mrs Bonner, Margerie's mother.
3 Like all the Lowry boys, Malcolm attended the Leys School in Cambridge. He was there from 1923 to 1927; see letters **1** to **19** and photographs 4, 5, and 6 in Volume I.

678: To Margerie Bonner Lowry

P: UBC(ms) [The White Cottage]
[October 1956]

AT LAST, AT LAST, a note from the dearest Harteebeeste, *but* My poor sweet ladybird, my meadow pipit, my cowslip pie & unusual parsley pudding duck, what have they DONE to you, that you say in your poor dear shaky *little* hand, as of a hydrogen-bomb shocked Least Auklet, that 'The Worst is Over,' when I imagined you and you were portrayed to me as having a continuous Euphoria and sleeping Ripvanwinkleuse[1] beauty sleep – ah, I shall ker-ush them, if they have hurt you, but it is to be hoped it is only a reaction, or even a sleeping pill, which can do queer things to the handwriting, but your thousand-times welcome note did give me a bit of a shock so that I thought My god you must have had an Aversion Treatment or undergone something mighty heroic or even worse without telling me, but they have assured me you were responding splendidly and were comfortable, and very soon I shall talk to you anyhow and you shall tell all about it. I had to write most of my notes twice to you, because the cat of the news kept poking its head out of the bag and I had to stuff it back in again, and I wanted to make sure I wasn't worrying you: but as for me I have remained optimistic throughout about Eden's action at least, which I thought you would approve of too, though it must certainly be said that you have schnewed and schnoozed (whatever ugsome side issues of suffering this may have, alack caused you) through TEN DAYS THAT SHOOK THE WORLD indeed.[2] In fact, one might say that the world has geeven-a-the Beeg-A SHAKE[3] with a vengeance and now that I am assured you know all about it & will have caught up with the current wrath and counterwackeroo I must say that between you and me about the only thing we can really have reason to feel optimistic about is – er – you & me. But that, I may say, is a very great deal. I have the plants out in the garden again, it is so warm and summery, but the cat yesterday kicked a flower pot over and sprang into another one (his little protest on behalf of the pride & sovereignty of the glorious Egyptian people fighting on the beaches and under the pyramids down to the last drop of Nasserwasser) and I must rush over there to the rescue.[4] I have just learned that the steam-engine existed at the time of Jesus Christ in the form of a child's toy called the aeolipyle: damn all this progress, I say, egad, sir. Great dear sweet love, my own precious snapdragon sandwich and borage pie

Love Malc

Annotations:

1 In 'Rip Van Winkle' (1819) by American essayist and historian Washington Irving (1783-1859) the main character falls asleep for twenty years after drinking from a magic keg. When he wakes, he finds that his world has changed for the better: his bossy wife has died and the English king has been replaced by the president of the new American republic. The story was published in Irving's *Sketch Book of Geoffrey Crayon, Gent.* (1820).

2 Sir Robert Anthony Eden (1897-1977) was a British statesman and prime minister of England in 1956. Lowry may be referring to Eden's decision to attack Egypt at the end of October 1956 in an effort to bring the Suez crisis and the war between Israel and Egypt to a close. Eden's handling of the Middle East situation was widely criticized, and the United Nations voted overwhelmingly against the attack on Egypt, but see Lowry's views in his November letter (**687**) to David Markson. *Ten Days That Shook the World* is the title of the 1919 book about the Russian Revolution by American journalist John Reed (1887-1920).

3 Lowry is echoing the expression of the guide in his short story 'Present Estate of Pompeii.'

4 'Nasserwasser' is a Lowry pun on the name of Gamal Abdel Nasser (1918-70), president of Egypt from 1956 to 1970, who had nationalized the Suez Canal on 26 July 1956 (thereby making it Nasser's water) and precipitated the Suez crisis. Lowry also alludes to Winston Churchill's defiant speech on 4 June 1940 at the time of the Allied retreat from Dunkirk: 'we shall fight on the beaches, . . . we shall fight in the fields and in the streets, . . . we shall never surrender.'

679: To Margerie Bonner Lowry

P: UBC(ms)

Ye olde Beautipotte,
Ripe
31 October [1956]
Wednesday forward: –
Hallow'een!

– And Wednesday forward because, lo & behold, what a joyous surprise, there is a Harteebeeste sweet letter this morning, headed Monday aft: so why not Wednesday forward? – and Hallow'een, I think it is, with such sweet dear memories of: especially our second one, when you made the jack'o lantern out of the melon – was it a melon? – fashioned after the spooky hut we saw on our Wigwam Inn voyage:[1] and then many such happy Hallow'eens – wolves at pingpong, & Whitey shooting off all the rockets on the pier; and many others of nostalgic memory, & now today – dare I wish you a Happy Hallow'een? I dare; I do, in spite of the, & let there be many more, oh dearest. But how vile for you just lying in the dark room if you can't sleep. How perfectly vile, my poor brave. Probably they don't give you enough of. I think to mention tactfully that you may need enough of to knock out a, like Marguerita. English hospitals never seem to care what one has been *used* to taking (same thing more poignantly goes for one's bowels): and the order, once given, tends to get frozen. I do hope you're getting some real good sleep by the time this reaches you. Nothing's more horrible than that ½ & ½

feeling of dilapidated dope-doze. No: Nekrassov's on Sat. Nov 3 at 6
p.m – I made a mistake, I told you in a letter you should have got. Just
perhaps you will be able to listen to it? I'm going to try to, but I'm a wee
bit noivous what with old Ben knitting and knodding & probably wanting to go to sleep. I listened to Henry James Princess Cassamissa (my
spelling)[2] last week under these circumstances on the 3rd programme,
and the dear Spoonerisms[3] insisted on listening to the whole thing for
my benefit though they were obviously bored to extinction & knodding
away while I for my part couldn't bear to hurt their feelings by letting
on that it was not only boring the bejesus out of me but I couldn't
understand a word of it – since it was the umpteenth installment – and
that all the while their highbrow lodger was longing to hear some Rock
n' Roll he could hear bebopping away in the background. So last night
I had a secret jam session on Mrs S. radio, just for El Leon's benefit: got
jazz from München & Lubeck, all taken terrifically seriously. *Und Jetzt
Unser haben das Meisterwerk von Duke Ellington* 'Krankenhaus Sonk
James.' (St James Infirmary, of Auray memory.)[4] Then all sorts of mad
cool stuff from Paris: absolutely sent me. And the Basin St Blues from
Stuttgart. Lastly, from Dusseldorf, someone sang Deep River.[5] My god
what a wonderful song that is. I wish *you* would sing it sometime when
the family is restored to good voice. You would sing it marvellously, &
I don't think I've ever heard you sing it. In fact I've only heard the song
once or twice before, for some reason. I just told Mrs S. this & how *my*
voice was in bad croak and she replied that old Ben's voice had never
broken at all since he was a choir-boy and that he still sang a beautiful
treble – wasn't that odd? Curioser & curioser.

Old Ben he knits, intent on th'intricate twills
Then suddenly, in tremendous throat, he *trrrills*!

– s.s. Merlin S Johnson has found as of to-day a sprightly new trick,
springing lightly to my shoulder from the ground in one movement,
then more heavily, preparing *to dig himself* in, purring now like a bulldozer, then a sawmill, as he tentatively kicks my glasses off, so that I've
spent half the morning with a BLACK CAT ON MY BACK, all this as a
protest against his not having 3 meals a day. Had a bath this morning too:
dirty stuff, that Lifebuoy Soap. Jovial news from Budapest and points
east.[6] In fact it almost looks like an Introducktion of guileless innocence
into human affairs, the reducktio ad absurdam of duckincidence.
Indeed, by & large, the most astonishing ducktory in the annals of
human duckdom. No conspiracy was timed to quack at a certain date.
They had no one duck to cordinate & dearduct their struggle. Noone
drew up plans of duction. And yet there was no duckotomy in the line
of that ducktion. It was just that the entire people's duckocracy rose
spontaneously as one duck. Thus evincing, once & for all, the truth:

Dearduckracy cannot exist half-slave, half-duck. (Not meaning to demean our dearduckracy by this, just having a little fun). Mrs M. is meaningfully waving some beans at me, or was – intending me to help plant them, but I won't bite, sorry, even if she intends them for you. I deplore the assumption that I have (Top Page 1 continued from bottom of 2) nothing to do, when I'm busy every moment, & indeed am working, now, hard, so that my letters must get shorter. Now then, my dear, I pray you may get some rest, am longing to see you again & hear your voice & above all, have you back again. all love dear heart

Malc

Annotations:

1 The unlikely-sounding Wigwam Inn is a resort hotel 32 kilometres from central Vancouver on the north arm of Burrard Inlet. A popular outing in Lowry's day was to take a two-hour steamer journey up the inlet to the inn, enjoying the spectacular scenery along the way.

2 The correct title of Henry James's novel is *The Princess Casamassima* (1886).

3 Lowry plays on his hosts' name by alluding to the modern rhetorical figure known as a spoonerism.

4 Lowry's German translates: 'And now we have Duke Ellington's masterpiece. Hospital Saint James.' 'St James Infirmary' (1930), also known as 'Gambler's Blues,' is the correct title of the piece, which the Lowrys may have heard in the town of Auray when they toured Brittany in October 1948.

5 'Basin Street Blues' was composed in 1929 with words and music by American writer-composer Spencer Williams. 'Deep River' is based on an Afro-American spiritual from the nineteenth century and was arranged, with words and music, in 1917 by Henry Thacker Burleigh.

6 The 'jovial news' to which Lowry refers is the liberation from prison on 31 October 1956 of Joseph Cardinal Mindszenty, who made a triumphant entry into the Hungarian capital that day. Between the outbreak of Hungarian rebellion against Soviet control on 23 October and Hungarian Premier Imre Nagy's 1 November appeal to the United Nations for support, the country was almost completely liberated. However, by the end of the month the Soviet Union was again in control and thousands of Hungarians had fled to Austria.

680: To Margerie Bonner Lowry

P: UBC(ms)

[The] White Cottage
Thursday,
1 November [1956]

– Rabbits! (After a lone Halloween, with just me & Mrs S's radio

playing Everybody Loves Ma Baby on Radio [Llangy].¹ And a new
letter from the beloved Harteebeeste mio this morning, a trifle erratic as
to calligraphy, but that's all to the good too, since your good news is you
really *are* being sedated sufficiently, & are at last getting some real rest:
it's wonderful news that you're being treated kindly & with understanding too – there so often seems to be a catch in these things. As for
the home front: November is the *fuel*est month – (if in fact not the
foulest) – or should be the *fuel*est: save that I burn no fuel, save elec-
tricity. There's bright sun but *in* the house it's colder than the dear shack
ever was, (almost), & despite the electric stoves, both here & in the
kitchen (which is awe-inspiring) I'd be writing in gloves, could one but
write in gloves, if I could find my gloves. (I've found my gloves). But
not to worry, I don't care, except that I worry it isn't a very ksnug
prospect like this for you to come back to, though maybe with the coal
stove going it will be different! (It is – later note) and besides you distil
alot of warmth yourself, and we shall live like two amorous anonymous
hotwater bottles and be so happy in one another forever & aye. Dorothy
hasn't come this morning, the slobette, slobeuse, or just plain slob, so
I've retired to the rectory for a while where for once it's not much
warmer. Mrs M's [Winnie Mason's] agents are now on the job for Mrs
S. [Spooner] to sell the latter's place, they have been here this morning,
and I begin to feel like Firs in the Cherry-orchard for some reason.² Mrs
S. cherishes no feeling whatsoever – or pretends not to cherish – for
Cartref: I like it, even to the strange extent of having a faint fond remote
velleity about our actually buying it ourselves – it would be a good
investment too – & I believe we could [be] happy in it, despite the
ghastly view of enclosure (which drove John Clare mad with grief, I
now find)³ & the appalling climate; or appalling at the moment: there is
some real privacy, & a huge garden (though not like *your* garden). Mrs
M. just came in, *ostensibly* to see about buying a bed-sofa (that is in this
room) for the drawing room of The White Cottage (!) I think she is
faintly displeased, though I hope not hurt, to see me writing here, as of
now quite snugly: it turns out now too she appropriated Dorothy this
morning, who, however will be working in The White Cottage now,
12.5, after my having spent two hours waiting for her, though not hours
altogether spent in vain. There is a human explanation of this apparent
high-mindedness however, if such it is, & rather amusing: Mrs S. &
Winnie are, in some way, jealous of one another, & I seem to be the
innocent coefficient of this at the moment. They run down each others
houses, when they think noone is listening, quite shockingly: silly
sailors! Mrs M. reminds me of my mother in some ways. And much as
I like Mrs S. I was reluctant to grant her her little triumph over her
'enemy' (so-called) this morning for I am loyal to The White Cottage,

(which I've also wondered sometimes whether you'd like to buy.) & of course loyal to your dear garden. I think we can still have alot of fun out of it but that buying it – or buying any other place right at the moment – would raise alot of problems that might spoil that fun. Most of October was glorious, but this climate is, finally, from the point of view of warmth & comfort, grim, let's admit it, without there being sufficient scenic & other graces & compensations in Sussex for one to be able to wind one's heart quite *all* the way round anything that's stuck with it: not a good sentence, sorry. But if we wind our hearts all the way round one *another's* hearts – then, what matter come what, may. I'm very fond of our ghost-whistling engine-room drawing-room-little-white-cottage though, which reminds me of a flying saucer, with garden; does about 18 km. And the garden. And the cat. Your plants I'm nursing along – mostly they are ok, the bulbs excellent. And here comes everybody[4] – a huge steak & kidney pudding for lunch with spuds & cauliflower & cheese, enough for 5 people & she'll be upset if I don't eat it *all*. God help my waist line & bless you. All love

> Your devoted Malc

P.S. I'm back in the White Cottage again after my gigantesque meal – & the kitchen all cosy, with the coal stove going, & everything clean & I have newspapers to protect the plants from frost – I do so want everything to be good & cosy for your return. I'm getting as important around here as the Dangerous Cock of Lugubrious Crow

> Love Love

Annotations:

1 Lowry's writing is unclear at this point, but he may be referring to the name of a town in Wales.
2 In Anton Chekov's *The Cherry Orchard* (1904) the faithful family footman Firs is left to die alone. The play is about the decline of the landed gentry and depicts the sale of Madame Ranevsky's estate to the new merchant class.
3 Clare was passionately opposed to the process of 'enclosure' – the conversion of common land into private property – that took place across England during the late eighteenth and early nineteenth centuries. Lowry, always mindful of his own loss of Dollarton, was keenly atuned to Clare's lament in poems like 'The Fallen Elm.'
4 The phrase 'here comes everybody' is an allusion to 'HCE' or Humphrey Chimpden Earwicker, the hero of James Joyce's *Finnegans Wake* (1939).

681: To Margerie Bonner Lowry

P: UBC(ms)   [The White Cottage]
                                                   [ca 2 November 1956]

Darling, sweetheart, dearest Harteebeest: You would be glad to know I
am in FULL BUZZ at work: with six piles on the rectory table comprising the end of a chapter, six piles on the White Cottage table in the
Cave comprising the beginning of the same chapter, and six piles on my
arse to denote my belief in Sinclair Lewis' dictum that inspiration is the
art of the application of the seat of the Trousers to the Seat of the Chair.[1]
No news here, except I am eating too much, and I am enjoying working again. I have go to Lewes to-morrow, or pay an unreasonable fine
on the Tree of Man, which I've kept out; a nuisance, but I can pay a
much needed visit to the Keeper of Beards & Moustaches, & I shall say
a nostalgic love-pervaded hullo to you at the daisy-haunted
Harteebeeste kerb at Golden Cross. No little note from you this morning alas, but they gave an excellent report of your progress at the
hospital, so I'm very heartened, that you are resting & getting better
apace – in fact you may be 'nearly better' now – & there may be a letter from you to-morrow morning, & soon I shall speak to SEE you,
again. Yeep, Yeep! Must stop now to put up laundry – likewise to-day
is S. (Sangral) day.[2] The plants don't seem to need much watering –
what should be my average per week? I don't want to drown them, &
try to use my judgement of course. Even so, I'm afraid we may lose two
or three – the 2 on the extreme left are sickly, & one little one. The frost
was too much. But 6 of the nine are thriving & I've saved one begonia
by replanting it, & tying it to a stick, & it's flourishing like the green Bay
Tree! Must stop for laundry Great Love

                                                          Love Malc

Annotations:

1 Harold Sinclair Lewis (1885-1951) won immediate acclaim with his
   1920 novel *Main Street* and received the Nobel Prize for literature in
   1930. In his 1937 essay 'Breaking into Print,' included in *The Man from
   Main Street, 1904-1950*, eds. Harry E. Maule and Melville H. Cane (New
   York: Random House, 1953), Lewis claims that the counsel Lowry
   attributes to him actually came from Mary Heaton Vorse (1874-1966):
   'The art of writing is the art of applying the seat of the pants to the seat
   of the chair' (74).
2 The Sangral is the Holy Grail or cup from which Christ drank at the
   Last Supper. Lowry draws upon the symbolism of *Parsifal* and the Grail
   for *October Ferry to Gabriola*. It is also the name of the plant food used by
   the Lowrys, which must have amused Malcolm; see his earlier letter
   (**666**) to Margerie. 'S. day,' therefore, is the day for feeding the plants.

682: To Margerie Bonner Lowry

P: UBC(ms)   [The White Cottage]
                                              [2 November 1956]

Dear sweet duck, am just off to Lewes after feeding cat (12.30 pm) to return library books, (they claim we have not returned Jesting Apostle,[1] which we did, but no matter, I'll settle it somehow) — shall be back by 4pm unless there's a very good movie playing in which case I'll take the 6pm bus — you'd think I was Peter Townsend[2] setting out for a world tour to judge by the stir & spoonerisms this elicits at the rectory — I've discovered there's a library in Ripe, or rather Chalvington, all this time, & apparently quite a good one, so I shall patronise it & to hell with Boots[3] — got your second letter to-day, very glad your doctor & everybody are nice & that you can do some painting etc soon, — will get a longer letter in the post to-morrow, i.e probably to-night but have to sign off now. I think you are the bravest — everyone sends love, the cat makes continuous tragedies[4] of missing you & the flowers flourish/ PS — (I could use some information) —

                                              Great Love

                                                        Malc

Annotations:

1 *Jesting Apostle: The Life of Bernard Shaw* (London: Hutchinson, 1956), by Stephen Winsten, is a biography of the Irish playwright, essayist, and music critic George Bernard Shaw (1856-1950).
2 See Lowry's 23 October 1956 letter (**671**) to Dr Michael Raymond.
3 Boots is an English chain of drug stores. It sells prescription medicines, cosmetics, camera film, and some food items, and had lending libraries in its rural branches.
4 This is Lowry's echo of Dr Vigil's comment to M. Laruelle in chapter 1 of *Under the Volcano*.

683: To Margerie Bonner Lowry

P: UBC(ms)   [The White Cottage]
                                              Ripeness-is-all,
                                              3 November [1956]

Silly Saturday. 1.15 pm. Dearheart: Am just back from Lewes after an aggravating & expensive morning mon. First I had to pay 6/8p on the books at Boots. My fault maybe but no more Boots: bugger old Boots. Then to the King of the moustaches & beards where I had to wait in a crowd of Teddy Boys till 11.35. When I mentioned that I lived in Ripe,

Lord of the beards told me that he had been thrown out of the Lamb by
Evans, there, together with some of his friends the other week, for no
reason at all; apparently the occasion was a darts' tournament between a
Lewes team & a Ripe-Chalvington one, played on the understanding
that Evans would return the compliment in kind to some Lewes club-
pub, thus bringing about a mutual increase of custom on such ugsome
dart-nights, but Evans suddenly got in a screaming temper & refused to
honour the obligation: King Beard wanted to know if he was crazy, &
I said I didn't know because I didn't go to his bloody pub (or any other
pub for that matter, ha you no heard, I lost my saxpence) but that I suspected both & he & his wife were a foul deal.[1] Unfortunately King
Beard by this time had got so wrought up he had cut nearly all my beard
off. Then, having bought a Listener & a rare packet of Players (remembering that the Funnel's Store would be shut & I was out of cigarettes
over the weekend) to the coffee shop by the bus stop & our nostalgic
seat: price of coffee, 7p, tip: (that I went all the way back from the cash
desk to give): 3p, mon. Reward: the packet of Players, left, as I thought,
on the table, had been *pinched*. Meantime I had asked the right time &
been told it was twenty to twelve: on going outside I noticed that the
clock on the bank said 11.55, the one on the post office 12.2, and
another one outside a lawyer's offices 11.49, whereas the one in the
restaurant had said 9.41: *my own* watch said 1.59. Being still on duck
time. So I went over the way & bought Crime & Punishment – in
Penguin) – that'll show those Boggerts at Boots: going to make alot of
money that way, bo. I caught the {12 pm} bus to the Cross however
and on the way composed a letter to you telling you how warm & pleasant the weather had suddenly become; however when I got off at
Golden Cross, it was into a howling freezing blizzard. Then I remembered I had, once more, no cigarettes, so after several minutes Calvinist
misgiving, I actually entered the Place of Sin, the pot-house there, and,
with sheathed beak, bought some Senior Service. Then I stood for
twenty minutes shivering in the howling rain on Harteebeeste curb,
reflecting wistfully upon the pub which, despite its grim exterior, is
extremely cozy and warm and quiet inside. Why then did I not sit in it?
But I seemed still intent on showing Boots & making money. Perhaps
in days of greater duckintegration we might pay it a visit. And so back
'home'. Nothing else to report. I didn't having any misgivings about not
seeing a movie: Zachary Taylor & Randolph Scott were in something
or other at the Odeon, and at the de Luxe was playing a piece entitled
Dig that Uranium with the Bowery Boys![2] Maybe this was good: but I
shall *never know*. There was nearly a revolution in the bus where people
are now being charged for carrying more than one parcel – ¼ of the fare.
It was setting back a party of 5 more than 5/- & I felt a bit better about

Boots and my packet of Players. I was already making alot of money by not having two parcels, bo. Well, I must to feed D.S. Johnson, & herewith some prattle about cats you may or may not have read but which anyway must amuse you. It appears that Beverley Nichols[3] – who is a kind of English accident-prose unwriter – has changed his flat and that he is afraid the change may upset his cats a little, which are obviously the best thing about him. 'But to make it easier for them I am taking with me the *little porches they sit in* that are attached to the door. It would,' he added 'be easier & cheaper to build new ones. But I think,' he said finally, 'if I can keep a familiar *smell* about things it will help them settle!' Isn't that delightful? The reason he gives for moving is a strange one too. Apparently at his other house he had created a garden that he thought too perfect to be improved. Well, that's all for now. Nothing but splendid reports of thee & I understand perfectly why you can't write; speed the day when we may see each other again. All greatest love my darling, bless you: –

Malc

Annotations:

1 Evans owned and operated the Ripe pub called The Lamb, which is located at the entrance to the lane leading to the White Cottage. Lowry had been evicted from the pub at the end of May, and he was forbidden to return; see Bowker (579).

2 Zachary Taylor and Randolph Scott were American film actors who appeared in many Westerns. *Dig That Uranium* (1955) is a black and white American film starring the Bowery Boys, a zany group who made many low-budget films.

3 John Beverley Nichols (1898-1983) was a prolific English journalist, playwright, and author.

684: To Margerie Bonner Lowry

P: UBC(ms) [The White Cottage]
[5 November 1956]

Guy Fawkes day,[1] Bang crash, me & cat inside

Dear sweetheart: They've told me – or rather suggested to me not to write, since you can't read my letters now. As if it were a bother! I can't, in fact, resist writing. This is a very very tiny one, right under the gun. I've had what may turn out to be good news from Marianne Moore: but no more at present about this.[2] Re Volc, anyway. I've had to write back instanto however, & my day's been occupied thus. All's well here. This is just a least *auklet* note. All love my dear sweethearteebeeste.

El Leon[a]

Annotations:

1 Guy Fawkes Day is celebrated on 5 November in remembrance of the 1605 Gunpowder Plot to blow up the English Houses of Parliament and kill King James I. The plot was exposed, and Fawkes, a chief conspirator, was arrested and executed.
2 Lowry means Marie Moore, Harold Matson's assistant, who often wrote to Lowry about publishing business; see the Lowrys' 28 November 1956 joint letter (**697**) to Marie Moore.

Editorial Notes:

a. Lowry has drawn a sketch of a running lion to the left of the signature.

685: To Margerie Bonner Lowry

P: UBC(ms)   [The White Cottage]
                                               6 November 1956
                                               3 pm Duck Time

Dearest sweetheart:

   Am sitting in the garden with my sleeves rolled up; the cat is trying to kick the watch off the bench – ah look my lord it comes, DS Johnson is as fat as a butterball & has been eating Mrs Mason's batterpudding, despite my ministrations; & I have put the 2 geraniums out in the garden for the first time for some sunlight! – I have to move them back again soon, I put one on top of the sundial having removed the dial. There is more news (the election for example) – all goodk of a personal sort, but they tell me you can't read my letters, so there's not much point in giving you things out of order. It'll be Eisenhauer or Stevenson to-morrow anyway.[1] Raymond arrived Sunday & found me working in the kitchen like a demon: I gave him a cup of tea so strong it gave him the shake, & he sang the song the psychoanalyst sings in the Cocktail Party for me, only a bawdy version of it:[2] since you don't know the song I don't think that conveys much. I'm really writing this letter more for my benefit than yours, it brings me closer to you. Great dear sweet darling love. Little smudges below are the cat's little signature: I'm so relieved to hear you're responding so well to treatment – you are the bravest – Soon – Soon! Great Great Love Your

                                                         Malc

& Love & a Butt from Donald S. Johnson His Marks.[3]

[P.S.] There are still riots of roses, and more coming; likewise African marigolds, in front. And many others.

Annotations:

1 The American presidential election was held on 6 November 1956. Republican candidate and incumbent Dwight D. Eisenhower (1890-1969) was re-elected to a second term. Adlai Ewing Stevenson II (1900-65), the Democrat presidential candidate, had been defeated by Eisenhower in 1952 as well.

2 The psychoanalyst Sir Henry Harcourt-Reilly sings 'One-eyed Riley' in act I of T.S. Eliot's play *The Cocktail Party* (1950):

> As I was drinkin' gin and water,
>> And me bein' the One Eyed Riley,
> Who came in but the landlord's daughter
>> And she took my heart entirely.
> Tooryooly toory-iley,
>> What's the matter with One Eyed Riley?

3 Malcolm has drawn circles here to suggest the cat's paw marks.

686: To Margerie Bonner Lowry

P: UBC(ms)   Ze olde Maisonette Blanche,
                              7 November [1956]

Sweetheart: – Such radiance for November! A glorious day of summer with roses simply blazing everywhere, & hot enough to go shirtless: – so much for my comments upon the climate: it just ain't consistent. It doesn't look like spring, that God, Garry might have said.[1] I have all the plants out on the lawn & Mrs M.[Mason] says I may have kept *all* alive, but I've overwatered the Geranii a bit (though only following instructions) but they're all a'thrive'o too. . . And so, & so, I may, marvellously see you almost instanto. Wonderful news you are soon to come out of your Rip Van Winkle Schnooze, my chirrupping sunburst, my gentle snapdragon, my loving lapwing. Goodbye Books, Hullo Chalvington: I'm off to the library there this afternoon; two male swans have started an early claim in swallow-moorhen-Nick-cowflap pond. Had another bath this morning: it *is* really filthy stuff, that Lifebuoy. I say it again. Merlin has been eating batter pudding. Have got a real egg-like horror brewing in Gabriola. I've been trying to get through to you a not so important message about a cheque: I have one on the Volc for 35 odd dollars but I don't want to go to Lewes with it & if I cash it in Ripe they may keep it too long & the cheque may not clear the New York bank. I wondered if I could endorse & send it by post to Lewes into your account. I shouldn't have tried to explain but I did: 'Hadn't your wife better have it?' Christ, all this in a message, whatever impression have you given of me at that place, oh deary deary me. That you should have it was the point: on the other hand it might have come in useful to pay the phone bill or something, which is unpaid since last June – Crikey. But there is more money a'comin: ah got news. And maybe more after that, too. So that's all right. And in fact, though tell it not in faith, even more again. Quack quack, or should I say hush hush. So don't worry about that, or indeed anything at all.

El Leon has managed on the whole quite well solo but I find he has to use his initiative *immediately* about something, unthinkingly as it were, or there is a FLAP which in a few days has become a FLAPISSIMO, as witness the fuss he is making about this cheque: the more important things he has taken in his stride, however, it's only things that he knows perfectly well how to handle himself that he feels constrained to seek advice about in the inappropriate quarter, in this case the Seal is understood to be handling the matter.[2] Well my dear dear darling, just looked where we've flapped to. Longing to talk to you, see you, soon, soon

Bless you Love Love

Malc

P.S. Am so excited at the thought of seeing you, or talking to you that I find I cannot be interesting, communicative, or even coherently affectionate – do you know the feeling?

[P.P.S.] Merlin his little mark

Annotations:

1 The young man called Garry in *Lunar Caustic* repeats the phrase 'It only looks like spring' in part X of the novella.
2 In their private language, developed around their beach life at Dollarton, Lowry was the seal.

687: To David Markson

P: UBC(ms)
PP: *SL* 389-90
The White Cottage
[ca 7 November 1956][a]

Ripeness is only the beginning or The Shape in the Haunted Rectory.

Dear old Dave: – I haven't not written out of negligence or lack of affection but Margie has been in hospital for the past month & very ill indeed for much longer. Very worrying, but I've been expecting it for some time. She has had a complete nervous collapse, can't speak, scarcely walk, anything and I am not allowed yet to see her. They keep her asleep mostly and she can read no letters at present but her address

is St Lukes-Woodside Hospital, Ground Floor West, Woodside Av.
Muswell Hill London N 10, & if you dropped her a note she'd have it
when she comes out of her Rip van Winkle Snooze. I am very optimistic about the outcome but the way it has happened has been the most
ironical thing ever to occur in this family, if possible. (All this strictly
confidential save from Elaine) In part it seems to be the result of my
having gone on the water-wagon, where I have been for months &
intend more or less sternly to stay until this bloody book is in forseeably
final shape for Albert. You would have thought the psychic effect of this
could only have been good but instead, I presume because robbed of the
potential in-a-sense nurseable object she took among other things to
hitting the Bloody Mary herself more than she should, though this is
only part of the trouble: sadly she seemed to have the illusion that she
was not loved when in fact the contrary was increasingly the case. The
trouble is it is part of the plot of the book too. Anyhow while she is
away I am living on an absolute incontrovertible wagon in a rectory
haunted by a phantom billiard ball that bounces down the stairs at midnight and working like hell & seeing noone (Apart from the billiard ball
of course). I think the pictures of yourself & Elaine are marvellously
happy and Elaine wonderfully pretty. Perhaps you look a shade
Mephistophelean though, if very fit & all a'taunto. I think your chain-
gang haircut however is only justified should you swim. All right then,
swim. I have a great grossfather beard – don't know what you would say
of that: I have taken to saying 'Beaver' in a loud tone to unshaven
people who are about to say it to me. I believe Israel's action in invad-
ing Egypt, as well as Englands, to be thoroughly justified, & admirably
courageous though I seem to be in a minority of one. England is in
unbelievable turmoil with riots in the streets, and they are burning the
Pope for some reason in effigy this afternoon in Lewes nearby here
together with Antony Eden which seems to me very confusing.[1]
I shouldn't wonder if it makes my billiard ball so nervous it starts going
upstairs. Some of Eden's reasons for taking action seem a little screwy
but all in all I continue to feel the VIII Chapter of the Volc to be
redeemed. But I don't think anybody's existence should depend on oil
& if it does they should do something about it. Don't mention the 'war'
if you write to Margie. But all manner of things will be well soon here
– at least with us. Gloomy Sunday in Hungary too – have you ever
heard the Robeson record? of Gloomy Sunday: it's the only truly tragic
song I ever heard.[2] I am studying your story in the Satevepost, it's a very
good yarn. I think it would make an admirable film, please tell me
where they made you alter it: I suspect they've made you make a grammatical mistake at one point. We may be film magnates together yet: a
producer has just paid me 500 dollars for a 6 months option on the Volc.

And just as Margie went into hospital there was a note – (which Fitzgerald would have appreciated) just arrived re Selznick offering some hope re our M & M version of Tender is the Night for Frank. We are very proud of your story & boast of knowing its author: I really mean this in case you think I'm being ironic. Give Elaine my very – our best love – & now go off & make both of yourselves happy for ever & aye as I'm sure you will – Bless you both

Love

Malc

Annotations:

1 Anthony Eden met with hostility and criticism for supporting the invasion of Egypt during the Suez crisis at the end of October 1956. After a rest in November-December of that year, Eden resigned as prime minister in January 1957. See Lowry's comments in his October letter (**678**) to Margerie.
2 Afro-American actor and singer Paul Robeson (1898-1976) was well known for his roles in plays by Eugene O'Neill, his portrayal of Othello, and especially for his singing of black spirituals. 'Gloomy Sunday' (1936), with lyrics by the Hungarian writer Laszlo Javor and music by Rezso Seres, became known as the 'Hungarian suicide song' after allegedly causing radio listeners to commit suicide.

Editorial Notes:

a. This pencil holograph (UBC 3:12) is undated, but the context confirms a November 1956 date. The transcription in *Selected Letters* lacks several lines, which are included here following 'Rip van Winkle Snooze' and ending with 'the plot of the book too.'

688: To Dr Michael Raymond

P: private (ms phc)   [The White Cottage]
                                       [November 1956]ᵃ

Ripeness is All or Monday Afternoon at the Rectory.

Well, what do you make of this, my dear Holmes? – *A*limentary my dear Watson.[1] (This by the way is a learned joke pertains to Canals, like your dream you related to me.) I myself, though still with a heart slightly to the leftward sometimes am all in favour both of Israel's and our own action. But I fear some gloomy Sundays in store in Hungary.[2] It is a pity people don't know a bit more about Hungarian history, not to mention literature. For once there could just be something in what the Russians claim, that the 'spontaneous uprising' was abetted – or would be abetted – by thorough-going reactionaries, antisemites & ex-nazis of the worst type, & plain sans-culottes[3] financed, no doubt, secretly by the U.S. And yet there seems to be truth in the spontaneity of the uprising too, not to mention have been a real hope of a Better Thing. Let's hope there still is, & that the Russians, whose humourless actions always seem to me to be dictated & timed by a sinister sense of humour will go away or out at least: from what news I overhear it seems a little late to hope, but intervention by America in Hungary could only lead to a first class calamity, I feel, and this right at the moment when we've done ourselves something extraordinarily sensible & courageous apparently in time, for once. Anyhow Margie – from whom I have asked that all this news be kept, & to whom I haven't mentioned a word of it – is going to wake up, feeling like Rip-Van-Winkle: she is responding very well to treatment, they tell me. For myself, I went yesterday to Lewes again & spent £1:5:7, though the only luxuries I allowed myself were 2 pcks of cigarettes for the week-end, (the store in Ripe being short) & 1 cup of coffee again & to think [several words illegible], 2/3 + 6d tip for a haircut, twice 3/10 for the cigarettes, 7d for the cup of coffee & 3d (as opposed to 4d last time) for the tip, 4d for the Listener, & lastly, in desperation, apart from another 7d back from Golden Cross, 15 – or 5-0 a [illegible]! – for a Penguin Crime & Punishment. I don't think that comes to £1:5:7 either. I must have some more money in my pocket – aha, found it! In fact, I'm going to make alot of money this way, I can see. For the rest, I have got to WORK, as per your advice, & I mean WORK & no backtalk about it. I am much beholden to you for sending me or causing me to be sent a fortnight's supply of sodium amytol: ie 28. Having started 9 days ago, I now have 10 left: I shall therefore be out of them by this Thursday. I have enough at the moment – 3 a day & twice a week the pink things instead. I have, however, abandoned taking 1 pink object per day after the last benzedrine: in short I take no sedatives during the day, which works fine, so long as I'm alone, at least. I don't think it any longer an active danger, so to speak, to come to London to visit you at St Georges, but I'd like not to be committed to an appointment until at least I know when & if I can see Margie in hospital, especially now I'm working hard. I think you will agree that is sensible. So could you be good enough to instruct me re the pills – if you approve, do I send another P.O. to Miss Linden, & if so, for how much? I'll be sure to make it 15 Knightsbridge this time. I rise 7:30 am: bed mid'night. Unvarying routine with us snoozers (or boozers for that matter) between times.

Best wishes

Malcolm L.

Annotations:

1 Enclosed with this letter is a slip of paper on which Lowry has written the following passage, with his own emphasis, which explains his 'alimentary' joke. The pun turns on Sherlock Holmes's well-known remark to his companion, Dr Watson, 'Elementary, my dear Watson.'

> 'The prime wines of Germany grow about the Rhine, specially in the Pfalts or lower Palatinate about Bachrag, which hath its etymology from *Bachiara*, for in ancient times there was an altar erected there to the honour of Bacchus, in regard of the richness of the wines. Here and all France over, 'tis held a great part of incivility for maidens to drink wine until they are married, as it is in Spain for them to wear high shoes, or to paint till then. *The German mothers, to make their sons fall into hatred of wine, do use when they are little to put some owl's eggs into a cup of Rhenish, and sometimes a little living eel, which twingling in the wine while the child is drinking so scares him, that many come to abhor and have an antipathy to wine all their lives after* . . . . Thus have I sent your lordship a *dry* discourse upon a *fluent* subject.' J. Howell. – *Familiar Letters* (1634: to the Lord Cliffe).

James Howell (1593?-1666), a Welsh historian, author, and diplomat under Charles I, is remembered today for his *Epistolae Ho-Elianae: familiar letters domestic and forren* (1645-55), from which Lowry takes this example. These fictional letters, most to imaginary correspondents, were written during Howell's imprisonment as a royalist, 1643-51, and they provide a charming, personal view on history.

2 Lowry is referring to the Suez crisis and to current events in Hungary; see his November 1956 letter (**687**) to David Markson, and his 10-11 November and 31 October 1956 letters (**691** and **679**) to Margerie.

3 *Sans-culottes*, literally in French 'without knee-britches,' was a term used to describe republicans during the French Revolution. The term has come to signify a man with extreme revolutionary views.

Editorial Notes:

a. This transcription is from a photocopy of a faint pencil holograph. Lowry's writing runs off the page at one point, making several words illegible.

689: To Margerie Bonner Lowry

P: UBC(ms)   [The White Cottage]
                                               8 November [1956]

– – – – ' – – – –

How overjoyed I am to get your letter
To hear that you are very nearly better

The days are long and they are getting longer
But within a song, like you, is getting stronger
So perhaps the days are short and getting shorter
Although one must admit they didn't oughta
But long or short, of him known as THE CARPER
The claws are sharp, and they are getting *shar-per.*[1]

— — — — ' — — — —

(From the Gadwall's Anthology of Modern Quack
for dipsy ducks.)

Well, my dearest darling sweetharteebeeste, Love from ALL of us. Well well well well but I cannot find my voice, wherewith to rejoice, Well, well, I am all but rendered speechless by the knowledge, Oh best belovedest, that we shall hold speech to-night: and I was very reassured by your letter to-day, though all duck's heart beat in tumultuous sympathy by the knowledge that you have been suffering the agonies of withdrawal who soon by compensation nevertheless shall experience, I hope the joys of return: in fact I'm rendered so inarticulate by all this that I shall have to stop right here, the more so since, by gosh, it's L & S day again, to wit laundry & Sangral day, and I have hands to wash, and socks to pay, and plants to splash, and bulbs to spray, and cats to feed, and doors to latch. Though I don't have no trouble teaching kittens to scratch. (Song used on p 1-2 Copyright by Lion Publishing Co.) A good name for a song: When Mamma goes Underground all hell breaks loose – Fox Trot. King Insulin & His Glucose Six . . . I gave Dave [Markson] your address: – though I've scarcely written to anyone else – hope this is not remiss of me. I am working hard: (only sad note in the general Hallelujah is I fear I may have lost a begonia, damn it, partly through having given it some sun which it didn't like, partly through cat which didn't like *it*: but we'll see how it thrives after the Friday dose of Jason's Peril:)

Gigantic Love

Malc

Figure 12: *Lowry's drawing shows 'El Leon' smiling over a row of potted plants.*

This means roughly that out of the 9 pots
4 – including the geraniums – are flourishing

2 – less flourishing, but leaves still green
1 – doubtful, but leaves still green
2 – (the small pots) v. doubtful, but there seems life still there. There is maybe another one that by any reasonable standards ought to be a goner, but I am still nursing it. (They look much brighter & healthier than I have indicated) I think if we can save 5 it's still a good record though not quite so good as the beginning: the trouble was some shoots were planted a little too shallowly, & simply fell out: then there was the frost, but sursum corda! In one pot *something else* has grown that wasn't there.

Annotations:

   1 See also *Collected Poetry* (328).

690: To Margerie Bonner Lowry

p: UBC(ms)   [The White Cottage]
                                                   [ca 8 November 1956]

Log of *ss*. El Leon   Thursday 4.45

Dearest –

This to catch evening mail: all well, dinner on fine Irish stew, read Middleton Murry[1] before fire in Padre's room, with pictures of High Jinks in ye olden Time of Merrie England on wall, back to house, lost watch, found watch, am feeding cat, watered 2 plants that seemed thirsty, schizophrenia over rector's lavatory – rectal hebephrene – decide to do part in each house – posted your mamma's letter – do not worry

Huge love from all of us
Your devoted husband.   Malcolm

Annotations:

   1 English writer and editor John Middleton Murry (1889-1957), a close friend of D.H. Lawrence, was married to Katherine Mansfield.

691: To Margerie Bonner Lowry

p: UBC(ms)   [The White Cottage]
                                                   10-11 November [1956]

Dearest sweet strong harteebeeste – ma Glucose Baby, (Tennessee would have just *loved* to call you that, honey): – Am absolutely all in a dither of adolescent love at hearing your voice: and I took your last sweet letter out of its envelope – the words 'I love you' just peeping out of the envelope, so that I half pushed the letter back again, with all the secretive self-satisfaction, religious shine, and thrilling thunderings of heart, and heroic determination concerning juicy dragons to be laid at your feet, of a lovesick swain of 13½ about to have his first date under the village elm tree. But though I'm longing – as I have been longing – to see you, I'm in a small flap about coming to see you and what day, for there is much to be usefully and joyfully done here – oh, what a scurrying of little animals and brushing of wrugs and mowing machines as the hot bricks are taken out of mothballs and dusted off in preparation for the Harteebeeste's Great return! We should have our minds made up to-night as we should have last night when & if I should come but that's exactly what we won't have done because we'll have too much else to talk about. If I should come, I lean at present towards Tuesday (1.30–3.30 pm) – maybe I can even catch the 6.20 bus back, not that we need exactly to lick our chops over our saved ducats like dirty old Nasserwasser gloating over a covey of M.I.G's[1] – for further news of events see enclosed: – I held this news back, as I did the world news, (I asked at the outset that it be kept from you, or you might just have gone into your ordeal with the invasion by Israel on your mind, and other Armageddon-like evil-bodings, by no means over as you can see, though I take an optimistic view, for us anyway. I counselled Marianne Moore[2] to try and wangle us in, especially you, at the very least in an advisory capacity, and however this works out, without your getting many hopes up, you may perhaps bay the moon a little, but not too dog-gone loudly, though I don't see the point of having any good news if you can't, even if it doesn't turn out to be good news! But then, in fact, it *is* good news, come what may, so let's face it like good little otties! Or would you like me to come on Friday & get you, or both? However I don't want to act from emotion, I want to do what is useful and sensible. I have done a little nagging at myself about not having put myself in the way of having been directly consulted over this whole business: i.e. asking myself whether it was not accepting, and somewhat humiliatingly, a certain position of irresponsibility not to have placed myself in the same position vis-à-vis your doctor, as at least you were vis-à-vis Raymond etc. True, the situation is not the same, but the logic is not dissimilar. But I'm inclined to think that my motives here may have partly an ego-saving basis, & be irrelevant to your recovery; after all a little deflation of ego is a small price to pay for your getting well again. So I'll rule that out as a further motive for coming to the hospital perhaps, unless your doc really wants to see me on your account, but that still leaves the question as to when & if I should come at all, especially as I am working hard, & there is much to be done here. Perhaps a compromise, & a meeting at Victoria on Friday? Please try to make up your mind what will please *you* best, if you know, & I will do it. Hugehugsandkisses – Soon!

Bless you

Malc

Clawler and Restaurant Merlin
(Cathouses Incorp. Ltd.)
Bill of Furr[3]

Evapurrated Soup Merlin

– –

Lights Merlin
Liver Merlin
Ug Merlin
Slug Stew Merlin à la Crème
Klacckuk Merlin Stinkarce
Fried Bee (with Sting Sauce Merlin)
Blutwurst Merlin Odorono
Slaughterhouse Steak Merlin Pew.
(Our Specialty)
Mousse Jelly Merlin

– –

<u>A la Cat</u>: Rat & Ham Pie, Beetlebrain Pudding
Rattarlets, Mosquito Sponges, Earwig paste, Wasplets
Beesting surprise, Fried Fly patties, Poached Ant etc

– –

Water.   Crunchies.   Stagnant Water.

Annotations:

1 During the early days of November 1956, the United Nations attempted to maintain a cease-fire between Egypt and Israel and stability in the Suez Canal; see letter **678** to Margerie. The Egyptian president Colonel Gamal Abdel Nasser was receiving military support from the Soviet Union in the form of fighter aircraft called MiG after designers Artem I. Mikoyan and Mikhail I. Gurevich.

2 Lowry means Marie Moore, who worked with Harold Matson and was corresponding with the Lowrys about a possible play version of *Under the Volcano*; see the Lowrys' 28 November 1956 letter (**697**) to Moore.

3 Lowry has inserted this mock menu (a parody of the menu he created for chapter 10 of *Under the Volcano*) in the top right corner of the recto of this single-sheet holograph.

692: To Margerie Bonner Lowry

P: UBC(ms)   [The White Cottage]
                                             [November 1956]
                                    As from Haus zu Krankenhaus[1]

Sweetheart

Your very sweet & goodkletter received, am in same good dither as
before but am doing some truly devilly marvellous things with Gabriola
– I have to hurry like hell to catch post, worked till 2. am this morning,
& up at 7 am every day – Don't worry about the news, we will procure
ourselves a WACKEROO – remember? Though it is reminiscent of the
good old days at that: only let's make them even better. If nothing
comes up to the contrary, I'll stay here & hold the fort then: but I'd like
you to know my heart comes to the hospital every day & will be fetch-
ing you on Friday equally.[2]

                              All great love, Bless you

                                                        Malc

From

            The Gleanings of a Gadwall. (Duck & Duck 2 puffin.)[a]
                    Saint Leon of Ripe
                    And Prince of Tripe
                    The Baron of Gripe,
Another   And Lord of Snipe
version.   (Lord Protector of Snipe)
                    Rose up in his drawers with a loud 'Hup Hipe!'
                    And said 'By god I'm a peculiar type' –
                    As he lit his breakfast & cooked his pipe
                    And gave his arse a hell of a wipe –
                    'To be at once Lord Protector of Snipe
                    And Lord of Snipe
                    The Baron of Gripe
                    The Prince of Tripe
                    And Saint Leon of Ripe!'

                    Saint Leon of Ripe
or   The Prince of Tripe
yet   The Baron of Gripe
another   The Lord of Snipe
version   (Lord Protector of Snipe)
                    And Count of Cripe
            Rose up in his drawers and cried 'Hup Hipe.'
            By God!! I *am* a peculiar type,'
            (As he lit his breakfast & cooked his pipe
            And gave to his lordly arse a wipe

The baronial backside a princely swipe
The saintly seat a hell of a wipe)
'To be at once the Count of Cripe
(Lord Protector of Snipe)
The Lord of Snipe
The Baron of Gripe
The Prince of Tripe
And Saint Leon of Ripe!'

Annotations:

1 As from the house to the hospital, in the German, allows Lowry his
  poetic flourish of rhythm and internal rhyme.
2 Margerie returned to the White Cottage on Friday, 16 November 1956.

Editorial Notes:

a. The poem is written in pencil on the verso of the page. See also
   Collected Poetry (**327**).

693: To Priscilla and Bert Woolfan

P: UBC(ms)   The White Cottage,
PP: *SL* 390–92   Ripe Near Lewes,
                                              Sussex, England
                                            13 November 1956
                                             (It would be)[1]

My very dear Priscilla and Bert:
    You must by now have received my cable[2] and fearing that it may be
anything but self-explanatory, and thus may be adding unnecessary
anxiety about Margerie to your feeling of deep loss and sorrow – in
which I deeply share and participate and for which I express my profoundest sympathy as well as I can, in the words that are none the less
heartfelt, for being platitudinous – at mother's death, I'm writing this
that will have to do at the moment (though it does not of course do &
can be nothing but inadequate) also as a vicarious expression of
Margerie's grief and solidarity with you in this, but the situation about
her is roughly this, [though] first let me assure you that there is nothing
greatly to worry about. She has however been in hospital in London –
though in a countryish section, for about a month, during which she has
had the best of care, (& has been for the most part even very comfortable, she assures me, & with a private room of her own) but has also for
the latter part of this time been mostly asleep, under deep & continuous
sedation, more or less, from which she emerged a few days ago into a

routine of glucose insulin, massive doses of vitamins & so on, but on top of this she has not been allowed to see anybody or receive any news of the world outside – & god what news it has been – until these few days ago as I say – with still a ban on any personal news of a disturbing nature, when she emerged from this Ripvanwinkledom, feeling & sounding better than she has been in ten years, all this, however as a result of a kind of cumulative nervous upset & anxiety & tension evincing as its most hospitalizable & aggravating neurasthenic symptom for her, a colossal stammer which practically prevented the poor girl from talking at all coherently: from all this (there turned out nothing *organically* wrong) I'm delighted to say that she's almost completely & miraculously more than recovered, & she was to come home, & may still do so, next Friday, une femme nouvelle; on the other hand there had to be an agreement between all concerned that I would absorb all shocks for her in the meanwhile, good or bad (for example I wasn't able to tell her that Hollywood is now so seriously thinking of doing the Volcano that she is paying me just for thinking, & please don't mention this either outside the [family] – if it comes off I hope to get Margie in on the script) and there is a tacit understanding, as to what the nature of that bad [illegible] might be, so that, suspecting with some sudden second sight, just at the moment I was going to forward the two letters, that there might just be this news, or something like it, I felt morally obliged to break the law against tampering with Her Majesty's Mail & thank god, opened them, with some misgivings, I admit – (that you were kept in the dark at first was to spare you anxiety – & of course Mother when you already had enough, but there was no reason she couldn't have written you in the last day or two giving you her good news (with the above reservations) as a fait accompli): even as it was, having, tragically, read Mother's letter first, with its cheerful tone and splendid courageous outlook, I was tempted to post that on to her as good news and scrupulously keep yours, at first I thought unopened till after her return, when she was stronger & then I read its deeply sad contents & had to make my decision not to send either letter or impart that news until I'd consulted with her doctor: I immediately phoned the sister at the hospital to get the doctor, who was away, to phone me, which he'll do to-morrow morning, with his opinion upon how best to break the news to her, or even for awhile not at all: it was terrible to speak to Margie on the phone with her in such high spirits about coming home & myself with this black tidings I dared not impart in my pocket. So there the matter rests with the added irony that apart from this & the world, things have rarely looked so good for us. I'll keep you informed. I reiterate my deep sympathy. Love to you both

Malcolm

(Please excuse the very small writing due to enormously long hours of concentrated work lately & hence bad eyestrain – [a]

P.S. Darling Prissy, do not blame yourself for having written, on top of all your poor woe: if anyone is to blame it is I for not giving you the lie of the land before, though I don't see how I very well could. Have you any liquor in the house? I am teetotal these days but I think you better have a good slug. Mother would be the last to mind.

P.P.S. Nov. 14: Dear Bert – The doctor has just phoned me long distance that he's returned from an important conference especially to break the news himself, myself having supplied the details, so that the hospital where she may have to stay a little longer now, can absorb the initial shock; I, Prissy, will now forward your letters which now can afford only relief at how splendidly you took care of her & Mother's happy outlook at the end, so you may now what you like. Your very affectionate brother

Malcolm

Annotations:

1 13 November 1956, a Tuesday, not a Friday, may be Lowry's allusion to a private concern. Paul Fitte, Lowry's Cambridge friend, committed suicide on the night of 14 November 1929, and Lowry was reworking these painful memories at this time for the Peter Cordwainer theme in *October Ferry*.
2 Lowry had cabled his condolences to the Woolfans on learning that his mother-in-law Anna Mabelle Bonner died on 6 November; the cable appears not to have survived. He was anxious not to upset Margerie by breaking this news to her too abruptly.

Editorial Notes:

a. This holograph (UBC 3:12) is in blue ink on both sides of a single sheet of 14-by-17.5-cm airmail paper. There are several blotches on the manuscript that render a few words illegibile, and Lowry has filled both recto and verso, and every corner, with his tiniest script.

694: To Margerie Bonner Lowry

P: UBC(ms)

The White Cottage,
Ripe Near Lewes, Sussex
14 November 1956

My poor dear sweetheart:
    You will now have the heavy news which, with a precognition of it,

who knows how, I decided to open, & then to intermit, until at least I had spoken to your doctor; I would rather have my arm chopped off than to be the intermediary of such tidings, especially at such a juncture, but it could not be kept from you indefinitely, and though if you had to receive it I feel you might rather have done so at home, where your husband might at least comfort you, there is always the point that the hospital has better resources to counteract somewhat the immediate pain of the irreparable loss: there isn't much I can add at the moment, or would like to, save that, after the initial blow, the letters I now forward you from Prissy, especially your mother's, & which I have sent to the Sister in charge to be delivered to you, may have a comforting effect rather than the reverse. You will see that your Mother died game to the last, full of vigor & vim, suddenly, & in no pain, in the best of spirits, and after having voted for Eisenhauer, whom she delightedly loved to see win: she had the best of care from Bert, & it must be especially dear yet gratifying to you that she wrote the letter I have enclosed as per in the manner mentioned above to yourself at the last, a letter that seems to show that, she had felt and was still feeling her life very much worth living, and which assumes that she is proud to have a daughter who at bottom feels much the same as she does. I am perfectly certain that she looks forward to whatever experiences may be ahead in the unknown worlds in a spirit of insatiable scientific curiosity – she was an existentialist in the real & true meaning of that term, & without the despair that it is usual to associate with the philosophy. And if you have temporarily lost her you can feel that at least she's reunited with your father & if you can't be sure of that I can be almost sure for you, & that the only grief she may feel is the grief you feel yourself so very naturally: I can say only that I share it, that my sympathy is complete. I cabled my condolences to Prissy & Bert, suggesting to them to postpone writing further letters for a while for your sake, but now I have spoken to your doctor who feels it important that you be told so that now I have written them airmail to say that they can write freely, & explaining the situation as I thought fit.[1] Alas, & at first, having read only your mother's letter, I had thought, what good & bright news this, & to send it by itself leaving Prissy's – which might have harrowed you with reports that your mother might go at any time, as it must be admitted, so that to this extent too, you may feel an element (or your mother would like you to) of relief – leaving Prissy's letter opened. However I did what I did, & now am acting entirely on your doctor's advice: he says you may need to stay a little longer in the hospital to recover from the shock & if you feel that too, I would certainly follow his advice & let any disappointment, mine or yours, go hang. The only thing is Sursum Corda & sursum corda & sursum corda against such an event but if you'd be better at home, so you feel, then I would come. My deepest sympathy & all my love

Your devoted husband

Malcolm

Annotations:

1 See Lowry's 13 November 1956 letter (**693**) to Priscilla and Burt Woolfan.

695: To Margerie Bonner Lowry

P: UBC(ms)

The Ripe Cottage
Ripe near Unripe
Overripeshire
Halfripeland
Great Ripery
[ca 15 November 1956]

My dear sweetheart:

I have your brave letter; you will now have the letters from Sis & your Mother's letters. I hope I did not prevent one shock only at the expense of your having a worse one later: but the juxtaposition of the letters gave me personally a severe shock, & I could only deduce from that how much worse yours might have been had they arrived on you cold. Even so I don't agree with the way the news has been broken to you but now it is done, you are being very gallant, and the best thing to do is to cling together very hard. Everyone sends their love and deepest sympathy. Dorothy's mother has had a stroke but she was cleaning up this morning, not so much as usual, but I aim to keep the fire in all night, & Mrs S. [Spooner] & I will try & have things to rights & all a'taunto for you to-morrow, so far as possible. I must admit that during the last few days I have had so many conflicting responsibilities that I haven't known sometimes whether I was standing on my head or on the end of my pointed tail. After writing Miss Cole last night I phoned Home – [physiotherapy in] Lewes this morning to make sure she could come, & found myself tied up in endless red tape: it turns out no verbal messages are accepted without a doctor's certificate so I phoned Troup who will troop his colours Ripewards on Saturday & give you one, D.V;[1] it's a bore for you having a doctor in your hair again on the first day but Miss C (it's no use my posting the letter, it turns out) is very busy & only in this way (unless you could get someone accredited to phone from the hospital, which might have been impossible) in time can we hope to get the Merry old soul to give you the electric chamber reasonably soon in the week, which is a bore, but there it is: probably she's on a birdbender somewhere. The world news is not good, but I have felt all along Eden did right – the pity is he couldn't have gone even farther – but maybe one can take hope from the very confusion: Poland's problem is different from Hungary's is different from Jugoslavia's is different from East Germany's – BAH. Incidentally I am glad this time that Eisenhauer is in. (I decided that a picture – see mess above[2] – of the confusion was better than my political logic.) Forgive this dim-witted letter. Its pseudo-levity of tone is all wrong, too, under the circumstances, but I just can't go on being solemn and gloomy indefinitely, even though you may have sometimes thought I am only too well equipped to do just that. Let me again say how dreadfully dreadfully *sorry* I am about Mother: although I can't strictly say in the same breath how much I'm looking forward to your return I do so anyway. *Damn this bloody pen!*

Well, I must to the Ripe House & assume my presidency thereof, enthroned, possibly, behind a mowing machine, though it's said to be bad for the grass. I just lit my nose & threw away my cigarette.

> Grysbok . . . It has straight, upright, pointed *shiny*
> horns, with two or three small
> annuli at the roots. Length of animal
> 3 ft long. Habitat: South Africa.
> And goes *always* in pairs, & not
> in flocks.

>> My grysbok!
>> All great sympathy again.
>> Great Love Devotedly

>> Malc

Annotations:

1 D.V.: abbreviation for the Latin *Deo volente*, meaning 'God willing.' Malcolm is attempting to arrange home care for Margerie, and the description below of Miss Cole as a 'Merry old soul' echoes the nursery rhyme; see his 29 October 1956 letter (**676**) to Margerie.
2 Lowry has cancelled eight lines preceding this comment with flourishes of circling strokes. This may be what he means by 'a picture'; there is no drawing with the letter.

696: To Margerie Bonner Lowry

P: UBC(ms)

[The White Cottage]
[15 November 1956]^a

In haste!

Dearest Sweetharteebeeste:

– as from

It is

Saint Leon of Ripe
The Prince of Tripe
And Baron of Cripe
And Protector of Snipe
And who rose in his drawers with a loud 'Hup, Hipe!'
And he gave his arse a princely wipe
As he lit his breakfast and cooked his pipe
And said 'By god, a peculiar type
Am I to to be Protector of Snipe
And Baron of Cripe
And Prince of Tripe
And not to mention Saint Leon of Ripe!
(So Said {so they say} good Saint Leon of Ripe!)

Have got all messages
– am all of a glorious doodah at your homecoming
& have to run for the post –
will speak at length to you to-night –
– Mrs S [Spooner] & I & the cat and the plants
are running around on greased roller skates
Anthracite & coalite have arrived from the baker & I shall arrange
for a loaf of brown bread from the plumber – Meantime I couldn't keep
you longer without news
Great Great sweetdearlove Bless you

Malc

Editorial Notes:

a. This undated pencil holograph was written the day before Margerie's
release from hospital on Friday, 16 November. See *Collected Poetry*
(**327**).

697: To Marie Moore

P: Matson(ms)
The White Cottage,
Ripe Near Lewes,
Sussex, England
28 November 1956

Dear Marie Moore

I'm back from hospital & feeling better than I have in years & *years*. I hated it, but it was worth it. And now Malcolm is working better than he has in years (*I* think) & in short we're both in top form & fine fettle.

Re Mr Nichols & the Volcano: we are both very happy about this & grateful to you.[1] It sounds too good – I mean exactly what we might have wished for. Malcolm asks me to say he is particularly thrilled about José Quintero.[2] We had read, & reread & pored over, reviews of his production of the Long Day's Journey. (Incidentally we are great & long-time admirers of O'Neill & saw the original Ice Man in New York when the Volcano just came out.)[3]

Re. the $10,000 vs. the percentage. We are both agreed we'd rather take the percentage as outlined in your letter of Nov. 23. If the $10,000 cash plus 5% were possible we'd have loved that. But we are confident that 7½% of the gross will be a better deal in the long run than the cash & no percentage. We rather felt from your letter that you thought so too. We have confidence in the book as potentially a great film, (& are more interested in that) & we think, from your letter, that Mr Nichols & Mr Quintero will do it as it should be done. (Odd: my grandmother was a Nichols – they're quite a well known old American family.) As things develop, *do* keep us in mind to work *directly* or *indirectly* in the film in some capacity. That is more important to me than the money. I don't think I could endure it to sit back & do *nothing* – I have had so many ideas about it as a film for so many years. Malcolm is determined to finish his book & would just sort of be there in the background to give suggestions or answer questions etc.

Thank you again, it sounds a wonderful deal. With all the best from us both.

Ever sincerely

Margerie Lowry

[P.S.] Yes, I'm all for the percentage, that is if you & Hal are. I was just brooding upon what a hell of a fine production Long Day's Journey into Night must be, from what pictures & reviews I could get of it, and just raving that there's never been anyone like Quintero in England to give O'Neill his proper due on the London stage, when I got your news, so you can imagine how thrilled I was at such a possible prospect of his directing a film of Ye olde Volcano. Any ideas I or we might have I won't go into now but I think there're some that could be of real practical value. I am working exceedingly hard on a book that is shaped up far far different from anything I had expected, & very much better. Please give our very best to Hal from us both, as to yourself.

Gratefully,

Malcolm Lowry

Annotations:

1 Marie Moore, Harold Matson's assistant, corresponded with the Lowrys between November 1956 and January 1957 about plans for a film version of *Under the Volcano*; see also Margerie's 15 January 1957 letter to Moore (UBC 51:5-6). According to Moore, José Quintero wanted to direct the film and Moore was trying to arrange a percentage for the Lowrys. We have not confirmed the identity of Nichols.

2 José Benjamin Quintero (1924-), the American theatre director, is especially remembered for his productions of Eugene O'Neill's plays. No film of *Under the Volcano* directed by Quintero was ever made.

3 Eugene O'Neill's autobiographical play *Long Day's Journey into Night* received its first New York production on 7 November 1956 under the direction of José Quintero; it won the Pulitzer Prize and the Drama Critics Circle Award. O'Neill's earlier play *The Iceman Cometh* (1939) was first produced in 1946 and received an important revival under Quintero's direction in August 1956.

698: To Elaine and David Markson

P: UBC(ms)
PP: *SL* 392-94

The White Cottage,
Ripe Near Lewes,
Sussex, England
11 December 1956[a]

Dear Elaine – and Dave –

Bless you both for your letters. Here I am again, feeling fine & 'all a taunt-o.' I was *furious* at being ill. God how I hated it! So I marched in to the hospital, fell flat on my face, flat out, opened one eye half way & hissed: Now do whatever you have to do as quick as possible & I'll cooperate. So they did & I did & it was unpleasant but worthwhile. Basta!

We are impressed, entertained & delighted, Dave, about Oedipus.[1] Malc immediately made up one blurb after another, each wittier than the last & we roared & rolled in the aisles. Seriously though, cheers, darling, cheers! (I don't see why Margerie should find it necessary to write a blurb about my wit however, if any.)

And the apartment too – my *dear* Elaine, what is in store for *you* I know only too well. Are you going to do it yourselves? If so I can only quote Malc's timeless remark when we had gazed, silently, for some minutes at the celebrated ceiling of the Sistine Chapel. 'Margie,' he said reverently, 'do you remember when we painted the ceiling of the shack?' (There she goes again: timeless because witless, probably, she means.)

Did he write you from the vicarage? I hope so. He has a new title now: Saint Leon of Ripe. (She knows I wrote you from the vicarage, which was a rectory.)

The chaps who want to film the Volcano are (1) a Mr Nichols (why *Mr* Nichols?) who's made so much money on T.V. (Why shouldn't he make money if he wants to?) he now wants to make a serious film & (2) Jose Quintero, director of the current O'Neill, Long Day's Journey, who, it seems, has long cherished an ambition to direct the Volcano. This is still only in the family, as it were, because we haven't signed yet but it looks as though we would any day now. And this morning came a letter from Alfred Knopf, Jr, who claims he's been trying to find Malcolm for years & wants to do a reprint of the Volcano for his Vintage Books. (Lion Books please note, Lion Books please note.) He says he finally located us through Jimmie Stern, though it was the wrong address & only reached us by luck.

Meanwhile my beloved old demon just tosses these missives at me & says yes, that's fine, now I must get down to work. (Just too too bloody nonchalant for words.) And he's writing as he hasn't since he finished the Volcano which is the best news of all. (except that he hasn't finished the Volcano yet.)

Love to you both

Margerie

We hope you're ripely heading ripewards before we're all overripe. Sorry, this is simply irresistable, we do it all the time.

[P.S.] All the very best love to Elaine & yourself!

Interpolated remarks were not exactly due to irritation, rather to ebullience. Or perhaps I felt she wasn't taking your Oedipus book seriously enough, that really is a crazy opportunity to do something real cool, when one thinks of it, besides you've probably got as long as Sophocles had to get Tiresias in training for Melbourne.[2] Have you got your Cocteau's Machine Infernale well oiled? sleeping with Yeats under the bed.[3] In Cocteau, the Sphinx falls in love with Oedipus, & then eats him I think, I forget but anyway it's mighty powerful stuff. And I really did have a blurb all written out for you, but I've lost it so I'll have to make up another one. All power to you anyway. We are having a grand life now and I am working like absolute sin on Gabriola with which I have completely fallen in love but I am managing to eat it a little more than it eats me so far. Back to work now, boys & girls. Whales! Inlets! The Towering Rockies! Glittering lakes in an evergreen setting on the – Sorry, I forgot. Sphinxes! Jackals! The seven against Thebes! The manwoman! Annubis! All the glory that was Greece overturned in this pulsating drama of a mother's love that triumphed even beyond the grave to give Psychoanalysis its proudest name! THE STORY *BEHIND* THE FREUD LEGEND. M.

P.S.   MARKSON
                ΣΟΦΟΚΛΕΟΨΣ
                ΟΙΔΙΠΟΨΣ

            Ω ΤΕΚΝΑ, Κάδμου Τοῦ Παλαι νέα Τροφή,–⁴

SEE kingly pride dragged in the dust by the claw-footed Desert Bosom! See the Burning Demon that Strikes her Blow at Night! The Sphinx Humbled! What did Nasser's Mother really look like? You'll find out when you see Oedipus confronted by the Lion-Faced Lady! What is behind the Greek attitude to Cyprus & the Western Powers? You'll discover when you read this torrid drama of the Son-Husband Wife-Mother *Relationship* embroiled with the madly jealous all-Egyptian Lion-Woman in Eternal Sexagon! See the Young Oedipus & the Lion-Faced Lady! See the Sphinx feeding! How the Young King saw the riddle of the Sphinx and what he did about it! HEAR THE FIRST AND MOST SEXUAL QUIZ ON EARTH!

    At all Vista-Vision Bookstores. Several Drachmas.

Annotations:

1 David Markson had begun work on a novel using the Oedipus theme for Lion Books; see Lowry's 22 February 1957 letter (**705**) to Markson for his response to the idea. The manuscript is unpublished.

2 The 1956 Summer Olympic Games were held in Melbourne, Australia, from 22 November to 8 December 1956.

3 Jean Cocteau's *La Machine infernale* (1934) was an important influence on Lowry. The work of W.B. Yeats that Lowry is recommending here may be either *A Vision* (1925), in which Oedipus plays a part, or Sophocles' *'King Oedipus': A Version for the Modern Stage* (1928) and Sophocles' *'Oedipus at Colonus'* (1934).

4 Lowry's Greek is correct. He has written 'of Sophocles, Oedipus' and then quoted the opening words of *Oedipus The King*: 'My children, latest-born to Cadmus.' See the translation by R.C. Jebb in *The Complete Greek Drama*, 2 volumes (New York: Random House, 1930), vol. 1, p. 369.

Editorial Notes:

a. This letter by Margerie has several interpolations, shown in parentheses, and a lengthy postscript by Malcolm.

699: To Albert Erskine

P: Virginia(pcard)
Lewes,
Sussex, England
13 December 1956

Dear Brother, I am working like a demon possessed on a reborn Gabriola out of the Top Drawer; Margie has been seriously ill, but is in top form again, I have never been so well so far as the work is concerned, in fact I have to go back to work now, mine being the bow & me to bend it (as opposed to the elbow) or we'll never finish what Homer began, as they say in Canada. I have a letter from Knopf, who would like to publish Volc in Vintage.[1] I have written to him explaining the situation, & referring him to yourself & Matson; I shall abide by your advice, I have little mind for anything save for the work. I told him Volcano reminded me on its level of world affairs of the Talking Horse of Richmond[2] and would answer questions itself if asked properly, so he probably must think I am cuckoo. Great Love from us both & a Merry Xmas, & please give my best to Mr Haas. I am taking a long time to deliver but it will be done well.

Malcolm

Annotations:

1 Inquiries with Knopf suggest that this correspondence has not survived.
2 The 'Talking Horse,' owned by Claudia Fonda of Richmond, Virginia, was called 'Lady Wonder,' and her feats of intelligence made regular headlines in the newspapers for many years. See 'Mem: Consult Talking Horse Friday' in 'Strange Comfort Afforded by the Profession' (105) and Lowry's 12 March 1953 letter (**568**) to Pamela Hudson.

700: To Dr Michael Raymond

P: private(ms phc)
The White Cottage,
Ripe near Lewes,
(& what's more, an old Leysian),[1]
Sussex
18 December 1956

Dear Doctor Raymond: – I have nothing but good to report, with

Margerie having made a fine recovery, self & work in excellent shape, & getting into better, and even good fortune on the material plane, with the Volcano being reissued in a classic edition in the U.S (Vintage books they are euphoniously named) & as for the movie, I now stand to get 12% of the gross, while José Querado [Quintero] wants to direct it, & has even announced his declared ambition of long standing to do so[2] – he has never directed in film before but is the man who has just produced O'Neill's Long Journey into Night on Broadway which production Time has called one of the highest peaks reached in the American theatre: since in that play (posthumous & about O'Neill's family) he has four drunks, one dope-fiend & one miser to cope with & which besides lasts 4½ hours I think one may trust him to do something special, if it comes off, or rather goes on, which indeed it threatens to do. But I'm really more interested in what I'm doing at the moment. For the rest we had one afternoon in town & saw Christophe Colomb: extraordinary: with everything in it but a performing elephant, no, there was even a performing elephant, sorry, or something that could easily be mistaken for one, all very grand indeed.[3] However I don't see how I can see you – even supposing you could see me – for about 3 weeks at least, Margerie very understandably, doesn't want to spend Christmas at home, because of her Mother, so I'm taking her away somewhere at the end of this week, I'm not quite sure where yet, which will cover that date, but apart from this it's become practically impossible to move from here without many arrangements beforehand since they've cut off our one weekly bus to Berwick station & the taxi service is similarly truncated & fouled up generally. Re medicine, I shall run out of sleeping pills within about a week which, for practical purposes, means immediately more or less, making allowance for Xmas delays in post: I was wondering if you could send me a prescription for some more, things being as they are. I should have asked you before, but didn't notice how low I'd got. During the last month I abandoned taking any pink pills at all, which means that for two days a week I don't take anything, no benzedrine at all I mean, just the sodium amytal at night. I did this as a discipline which I hope has your approval: it doesn't affect my work in any way, & is only rather difficult to do when I think about it, so I conclude it's salutary. I've also stopped taking 1 pink object as a daytime sedative, or rather evening one. I simply take 3 benzedrine during the day on 5 days of the week as originally pre-scribed: these however are American benzedrine that I've been taking. You gave me some but they look considerably larger but I've no way of knowing whether they are stronger or not, or how many to take per day, though it says 1 at breakfast time or as directed, I think, on the box: this isn't an immediate problem. As a matter of fact I took *one* of these on two succeeding days at my usual time instead of the others but could tell no difference in strength: still they *look* as though they *ought* to be stronger, so I have not further experimented, lacking direct instructions from you. Never mind, if it turns out I have to take only 1 of these per day I have yet some others

[breaks off unsigned][a]

Annotations:

1 As a former pupil of the Leys School in Cambridge, Lowry is 'an old Leysian.'
2 See the Lowrys' 28 November 1956 letter (**697**) to Marie Moore.
3 The French writer Paul Claudel (1868-1955) wrote the opera libretto *Le Livre de Christophe Colomb* in 1929 for the music composed by Darius Milhaud (1892-1974). The Lowrys may well have seen the important Compagnie Madeleine Renaud-Jean-Louis Barrault production that was mounted in 1953 and toured Europe (including England) until 1958. The opera calls for an epic range of historical and mythological characters, of scenes from around the world, and every theatrical device, including cinema, a Greek chorus, and a narrator.

Editorial Notes:

a. This transcription is from a photocopy of the holograph, which appears to be missing a final page.

701: To Downie Kirk

P: UBC(card phc)   [The White Cottage]
                                    [December 1956]

Dear old Downie:

Just a card to wish you, Margerie, Dorothy & Katie all the warmest greetings for a Merry Xmas & a Happy New Year. I am covered in shame for not having yet replied to your most excellent & welcome letters but I promise a long letter in the New Year. My Margerie has been in hospital but is now fine! I am working like mad on 'October Ferry to Gabriola' – & all because you liked it. It is better than the Volcano, a veritable symphony of longing for the beach. We hope to return but meantime think of you often & are often homesick.

All the best to Dave & Les too from us both

Malcolm

P.S. Also please say a warm seasonal hello to Al & Kurt, those wild & memorable poets, one your pupil – & I mean poets – I owe a letter there; please send my thanks & apologies: likewise to Charlie Harris & (if extant) of course to dear old Dunk.[1]

Annotations:

1 The 'wild & memorable poets' are Al Purdy and Curt Lang (1937–). Purdy, who visited Lowry at Dollarton, is a senior Canadian poet; Lang is mentioned again in Lowry's 29 April 1957 letter (**707**) to Ralph Gustaphson. Charlie Harris and Dunc Murray were friends of the Kirks.

702: To Dr Michael Raymond

P: private (pcard phc)   [The White Cottage]
                                                       [early January 1957]ᵃ

A very happy New Year to you, & thanks for your card, this should have gone before, but first it seemed wise to see if the world would reach the New Year at all. We had a marvellous time in London, taking in more shows than either of us remember having seen before at once: among them The Waltz of the Toreadors, The Country Wife, A View from the Bridge, Milkwood, & a revue World on Edge, dilapidated, unattended, treasonous, abysmally stupid but intensely interesting, at the Unity.[1] Likewise we saw a superb Greek film, The Woman in Black, at the Curzon together with an almost equally superb underwater French documentary, containing surely one of the greatest single sequences in all cinema, the discovery of a Scottish freighter, *Thistlegorm*, sunk in the Indian Ocean, since 1942:[2] a mighty moment when the diver struck her bell: a scene worthy of Melville. On Xmas day we went to the service in Westminster Abbey: and, by way of relaxation, we saw War & Peace in which there was slightly too much Peace though, for that matter, perhaps, too much War also.[3] I think that's about all the straying with the exception of the Royal Academy portraits, Chinese restaurants, many thousands, and two other films, one light & the other serious, both having in common Bing Crosby with a hangover. Poor fellow. Margerie seems reborn: my work goes excellently, now resumed. My gratitude for the prescription. All the best from both.

                                                       Malcolm L.

Annotations:

1 During their Christmas 1956 holiday in London, the Lowrys saw Jean Anouilh's (1910–87) play *Waltz of the Toreadors* (1953), William Wycherley's (1640–1716) play *The Country Wife* (1675), Arthur Miller's play *A View from the Bridge* (1955), and a dramatization of Dylan Thomas's *Under Milk Wood* (1954) – see Lowry's 22 February 1957 letter (**705**) to David Markson for a description of this production – and the news revue called *World on Edge* (1956).

2 The black and white Greek film *The Girl in Black* (1955) is about a writer holidaying on a remote fishing island. The French documentary film Lowry praises here is *Le Monde du silence* (1956), co-directed by Jacques-Yves Cousteau (1910–) and Louis Malle (1932–); it won an Oscar for best documentary in 1956. The *Thistlegorm*, an English ammunitions ship, was bombed by an enemy plane and sank on 6 October 1941; there are some striking underwater scenes of the wreck in Cousteau's film.

3 The 1956 film version of Tolstoy's *War and Peace*, starring Audrey Hepburn, Henry Fonda, and Mel Ferrer, lacks warmth and drama. It has also been criticized for the casting.

Editorial Notes:

a. This transcription is from a photocopy; the date is illegible.

703: To Dr Michael Raymond

P: private (ms phc)

> The White Cottage,
> Ripe near Lewes,
> Sussex
> 7 January [1957][a]

Dear Dr Raymond:

Thank you for your welcome and very pleasant p.c. We also very much look forward to your kind suggestion of a foursome one of these days. As for my visit to 15 K[nightsbridge] it is, these days, a great deal easier said than done, for you have to order a taxi days in advance, and then with no certainty it will arrive, buses having meanwhile doubled their infrequency, and this on dates which don't gibe with your presence in Knightsbridge anyway; even were other things equal, though, I feel I should go on biting on the nail without intermission for another 3 weeks or so, having given myself that week off and just got down to a routine again, and an extremely tough one it is, though I can't say I am not enjoying it, having acquired that healthful and lifegiving & indeed necessary paranoia in regard to Gabriola without which I suspect works of this kind would rarely be completed, if often enough begun; so what about my making an appointment some day toward the end of this month, I leave the exact day and hour up to you but preferably as near 1 pm as possible, how about the 28th, Monday, 3 weeks hence if that's convenient? – However I'm afraid, if the former is all right with you, and you have deduced, rightly, ex ungue leonem,[1] that all is very well with ourselves, that I shall have to bother you again about sodium amytol again, of which I have something less than a week's supply left: would it be possible to send me a prescription (preferably having a health service imprimatur) that Margerie may realise on some visit to Lewes soon, where I don't mean at present to accompany her? I should be much beholden. By the way we found ourselves one day outside St Georges, and thought of dropping in, but that you'd have been busy or absent. I mention it however because of the extreme proximity of the Curzon cinema to you, from which we were busily transfering ourselves to the Royal Court; that is from the Greek film, & The Silent Depths, to Wycherly's Country Wife; viz from A Woman in Black to many women in scarlet, from the rapture of the depths, to that of the heights, from the decompression chamber, to the bedchamber; or more plainly, from the submarine to the obscene.[2] Despite these comparitive delights, that somehow seem to forgive the latter, If you ever have a spare hour or so, I can highly recommend your spending it at that Curzon show, really wonderful. All the very best to you from us both

Malcolm L.

Annotations:

1 The Latin phrase means 'out of the claws of lions.'
2 See Lowry's January 1957 postcard (**702**) to Dr Raymond.

Editorial Notes:

a. This transcription is from a photocopy of the pencil holograph.

704: To Peter Churchill

P: UBC(ms)

The White Cottage,
Ripe Near Lewes,
Sussex
[early 1957][a]

Dear Peter: — I can't return the m.s till to-morrow: p.o shut and box too small.[1] It ought to arrive Tuesday. I admire both the paper and what's written on it and there are scarcely any comments, merely a few oblique suggestions. It improves on rereading too, which is a good sign, and I'd say our reaction was decidedly enthusuastic. We'd also say the same were we publisher's readers. One is interested right off in what's happening, but on page 1 I doubt your visitor from another planet, I mean I don't think he would necessarily think we were insane. Besides you're involved here in a bit of a cliché, and I'd almost cut bringing in your visitor unless you can make him think something brighter.[2] Fortunately you're also involved – even without your visitor – in something intensely interesting; the crazy names we give things. That is you don't need to be a visitor from another planet or age etc to think they are crazy. But it could equally be a striving after beauty. I like to think of a bulldozer called The Winter Aconite. Obversely, I make you a present of this: – At sea, aged 17, I spotted a beautiful ship in the Arabian Sea on the starboard bow: what wonderful romantic names could it have? It was the *British Motorist*. A Norwegian novelist friend of mine, on the other hand, wanted a name for his steamer that had polished off all its crew with disease and disastar of one kind & another, a veritable Moloch: – in reality the ship was called the Henrik Ibsen but he wanted something *sweet* so he called it the SS *Mignon*.[3] On second thoughts it would be too bad to erase the idea of insanity because it ties in well, unconsciously or no, with moonlight at the end. I mention these things because they may have some philosophical import. Descartes comes in with effect but mem. perhaps the existentialist philosophy: 'I am therefore I feel.'[4] Maybe I've got that wrong. The style is racier than the other parts I've seen and reads rather like a novel, which is another against it, so long as you don't fall into the Zilliacus trap.[5] On the contrary, I thought maybe Ortega could be useful to you here as a philosopher, where he says that a man in relation to his life is something like a novelist working on a story, he makes up his life as he goes along, becomes an engineer just for the sake of making it work.[6] Something like that. He also said that the amount of pleasure you get out of a certain thing is a clue to one's identity: – Goethe should have stuck to lyric poetry, which Germany also needed at that time, without trying to be Generalissimo of Weimar etc. I hope this is not true because by the same token I should perhaps not be a man or a writer at all but maybe a sort of alcoholic whale-shark who played the banjo. I hope you devote a passage to the whale-shark alone later on: here is really an insane name, authoritative too.[7] (By the way Pendennis in last week's Observer seemed to think that killer-whales were swordfish!) – Margie is enthusiastic & has only a few remarks about punctuation: but she says, 'you have a beautiful little entity (in this chapter) and I wouldn't 'brug' around with it at all. I concur absolutely with this: one can take the whole bolus of punctuation at the end as a separate problem, and I wouldn't alter a damn thing here at the moment, unless you feel you have to, or in case of an addition, simply append it without spoiling your pages, & let it gather dust for a while. I have some minor objections: the mirrors . . . mirrors technique on 3 – how bloody hard that is to avoid![8] (I had just been writing priests . . . priests.) But don't 'brug' around with this now whatever you do: it couldn't be simpler to adjust really. For the rest, the search for an *attitude* to life is perhaps a more original idea than it sounds at first kick. As for what I imagine may be to come, I'd like to see more of the sheer archytypical wierdness of the translunar Californian scene. It occurs to me that your name, the one you will use on the cover, is or can be actually a dramatic *value*: that's a bit of a problem indeed, & it has to be accepted as an important one, as you must have of course have accepted it. But I can't help here till I know what your plan is. Should your wanderings take you to Los Angeles, however, I can give you the full title of that city which is: Nuestra Senŏra la Reina de los Angeles de Porciúncula. I'd very much like to see more, preferably consecutive, but in any case I'd like to know what the architechtonics are, so that one can balance matters better. Our very best love to Joan.[9] I'm very glad to hear Jimmy Stern is back again, & should you see him give him our best & say we are writing. And thank you for the trust reposed to me in regard to the ms itself.

Love from us both

Malcolm

Annotations:

1 Lowry had already given Peter Churchill detailed advice on the first chapter of *All My Sins Remembered* (1965); see his 4 April 1956 letter (**650**).

2 Churchill kept this reference: 'A visitor from another age or another planet would surely think we were insane, the names we gave things' (p. 1).

3 Lowry is referring to Nordahl Grieg's ship in *The Ship Sails On*; Grieg may have told Lowry about the naming of the ship when they met in Oslo in September 1931.

4 Lowry is parodying the axiom of French philosopher René Descartes (1596-1650): *Cogito, ergo sum*, 'Je pense, donc je suis,' meaning 'I think, therefore I am.' But he has taken his cue from Churchill, who comments that he often quotes Descartes.

5 Konni Zilliacus (1895-1967) was a British Labour Party member of Parliament. He defined himself as a socialist but was often seen as a communist sympathizer. He was expelled from the Labour Party in 1949 and readmitted in 1952.

6 This analogy, from chapter 3, part 3 of José Ortega y Gasset's *Toward a Philosophy of History* (1941), impressed Lowry deeply. He paraphrases Ortega in part 7 of 'Forest Path to the Spring' and refers to him in other fiction and letters.

7 The term 'whale-shark' is used for very large sharks like the basking shark.

8 In chapter 1 of his book Churchill repeats a description of seeing his reflection in various mirrors.

9 This is Joan Black, now Lady Churchill.

Editorial Notes:

a. This transcription is from a signed undated pencil holograph (UBC
    3:13). The three folds in the sheet of paper indicate that this is the orig-
    inal letter sent to Churchill.

*The following, hitherto unpublished, letter to his literary son David Markson
provides a fascinating glimpse into Lowry's imagination and working habits just
a few short months before his death. In it Lowry offers Markson advice on a work-
in-progress, and in the process he manages to comment on everything from
Melville to Aleister Crowley. Central to the letter and to his advice, however, is
the Oedipus story, which carries him back to Jean Cocteau and his abiding admiration for* La Machine infernale. *At this time of his life Lowry was living more
and more in the past, in the shadow of the* Volcano, *with vivid memories of
events and literature that had influenced him profoundly. What better advice,
then, to give Markson than that he too should immerse himself in Cocteau's
surrealist nightmare of incest and murder? But Lowry is not glum; the letter
bristles with his familiar wit and convoluted prosings. Perhaps its worst aspect is
what is not discussed – Lowry's own work, work that was not getting done
because he was writing this complicated letter – or the fact that he would not heed
his own exhortation: 'Sursum Corda. Hold that note, Roland!'*

705: To David Markson

P: UBC(ms)

The White Cottage Ripe Near Lewes Sussex
England, The World Friday And February 22.
Nineteen Hundred and Fifty Seven O![a]

My very dear old Dave: It is quite unforgivable of me not to have
replied before, especially when I had so much to thank you for: but this
was paradoxically the reason, first William Gaddis' The Recognitions[1]
isn't exactly the kind of book (a veritable Katchen Junga, you know the
Mountain I mean anyhow, of a book, the ascent of some overhangs of
which can scarcely be made safely without the assistance, one feels, of
both Tanzing and Aleister Crowley)[2] possible to return figuratively or
in fact the next day, as happened once with Ulysses, with the comment

'Very good!': I'd wanted both to thank you extremely for this and write something intelligent upon it worthy of the book in the bargain and then, at the same time, I'd wanted to give you some definite news about the Knopf project as well as conveying my sincere gratitude to you for the Lion books offer, or tentative offer,[3] but I in fact hadn't any definite news I could convey until, one day I found I'd been working so hard I'd forgotten I'd received any and for the same reason I have not yet finished The Recognitions (which was long delayed incidentally by the Christmas mails and The Demon Oleum – that word is Oleum – oil anyway perhaps): what I *can* say is that The Recognitions is probably all you claim for it, a truly fabulous creation, a SuperByzantine Gazebo and secret Missile of the Soul and likewise extraordinarily funny: much funnier than Burton (who has me gathering borage out of the garden to heal the melancholy his laughter induces, also a spoonful of vinegar at bedtime helps) though Burton's a good parallel. I can only read a little at a time, however, because I have to watch my eyesight, which begins to get strained round midnight after having spent the day since 7:30 a.m. scratching out the previous day's work: so that it may be somewhile yet before I can send you a full report on The Recognitions; meantime, inadequately this. Re Knopf Volcano was promised forth by Matson to him before your letter arrived, I think: I think too, that a contract by now, not, indeed so remunerative as the one mentioned by you possible through Lion Books, will have been drawn up, and though I have not signed it yet – (the contract itself seems to have been delayed) – I am so far committed that I could not well back out now (& could not have then) were that advisable, which with another part of your mind it would seem you are half saying it would not be: on rereading your letter of Dec 18 which had the misfortune to arrive right at the moment that we were departing for a week to London – and so cannot have been well digested till our return near the New Year – on rereading this now I feel extremely remiss at not having written you back immediately & clearly about the whole thing: I hope you don't think I am ungrateful and trust that I have not in any real sense seriously disappointed you but as between Harcourt Brace (who hadn't then *released* the Volcano so that I'd have had as things then stood to pay them 50% or something anyhow) Albert personally, Random House more objectively, & Knopf at that time somewhat remotely, with a movie contract – attendant vanities likewise thunderpealing and doomscracking about my head, & nothing settled in any direction, & mail from both directions either crossing or not arriving, I trust that you can see that I was way up in the middle of the air among the wheels within wheels, & spirits within the wheels, & especially with Margie by no means yet strong (though well), and hence with myself both master on the bridge, and of the furnace, in

no position to give a direct answer: please don't think I'm unapprecia-
tive, though, of all the encouragement your interest and thoughtfulness
on my behalf has given and continues to give me: indeed so far encouraged, one way and another, am I that I have been producing some
mighty cool stuff, though I say it myself: but this also adds *somewhat* to
my confusion now when trying to make a practical reply or collocation
of the news, for I am these days almost continually in the grip of that
thing used to be call: Inspirations, hombre, & which I thought until
now, was rather some kind of joke or bad word used to frighten children with. But I am genuinely, somewhat preposterously, yet almost
permanently, in the grip of some such thing, & hence almost permanently as it were within the Sacred or Budding Groove: the trouble is,
the lightning usually strikes at a tangent; or flashes, I should say, rarely
lighting the place you are working on sequentially: this means you have
to turn desultoriness into a virtue, and it's sometimes wearing work
dashing round picking up your charred smithereens or even bright
illuminations and piecing them together, especially when they often
seem to mean bugger all: or as Dylan T[homas] would say Llareggub:[4]
(the telephone just rang, and an inquiry was made for a Mr Malcolm, a
postman; no, I had once known a Land Surveyor of that name, but not
a postman; no, I did not deliver my own letters, but I considered it an
excellent idea for those writers to adopt, who wished both to preserve
their sedentary habits and sing the Body Electric:[5] thank you very much,
don't mention it) which reminds me we went to see Under Milkwood
on the stage, on Boxing Day, New Theatre, London, Margie disliking
the decor and direction so much she had to shut her eyes; I thought it
curiously remote and tinny on the stage, like something going on in a
music-box, and also in parts excessively sentimental whimsical and
generally pseudo Dickensian, but a bloody unusually splendid piece of
work for all that, so that we now have a cat named Captain Catso (the
other half of his name stemming from Fatso of Godot, which I thought
(Waiting for Godot) one of the most inspired pieces of bloody-mind-
edness since the Crucifixion which we heard the other night on The
Third Programme – coming the Resurrection.)[6] All these things bring
me back to the fact, however, of my own remissness in correspondence:
it was awfully generous of you to think of Volcano as a Lion book & it
would have been great fun to have you as a publisher: still it may yet
happen, one of these days, quien sabe? In fact, I may be your publisher.
Meantime, I'm put in the position of asking you if you can suggest any
cuts or improvements I might make for Knopf on UTV: I think M.
Laruelle should see the le gusta esta jardin notice perhaps in I: chap VI
could be tautened, I feel, but how? Maybe Caligula's horse shat upon
by Barzun in the rudest review I've ever read of any book might go at

the end of VI,[7] together with some of Hugh's reflections, though I don't know which: there are a few small things that might absent themselves, likewise, from IX & X, maybe the latter needs or could stand some fairly big cuts and indeed I thought that originally & had all but reached agreement with Albert what they should be when all at once Albert, who had actually proposed the cuts in the first place, began to agree with the objections *I* raised here & there, finally we let it stand as it was but even so the dashes shouldn't all be the same length, for one thing, but I understand that some printers will absolutely refuse to vary the length of dashes. I've always thought the very beginning of the book must seem unnecessarily boring if you don't know what's going to happen and that maybe it doesn't encourage you to find out, on the other hand one can't say that the reader isn't given due warning at the outset that the action, such as it is, is going to travel at a stately gait in the reverse direction though on the other hand again I was much delighted by a Canadian reviewer who obviously not having read a line of the book or perhaps glanced at the end wrote: Mr Lowry plunges at once into his story . . . None of this 'modern' nonsense about moral obliquity . . . Young writers must take note and profit from the extreme swiftness of his dramatic narrative. . . . Something happening at every minute . . . On the edge of my chair . . . 3 am . . these tripping pages . . . sprightly dialogue etc. But you'll be glad to know that Knopf, (Junior) does seem to be enthusiastic about the book: and the notion of cuts emanates from me, not him. Margie doesn't want to read through the Volcano again at the moment for the reason that she loyally wishes to keep a Fresh Eye for it when the time comes to try to preserve a few choice chunks of original fresh Lion from the movie Daniels who will no doubt attempt to create a kind of Splamb from it,[8] if one is not cunning: incidentally they have dropped the idea of creating anything from it at all for the time being, even splamb, which was another thing I had to cope with: but I am told not to be disappointed in that its republication will probably beget a better cinematic deal all round. I feel I have done less than justice to your idea of the Oedipus novel by simply writing you some facetious blurbs. Actually it is an extremely brilliant notion. How is it working out? Your ideas all seem to me excellent, but you really and seriously must read Cocteau's Infernal Machine if you haven't already done so: it could not confuse your purpose and is one of the finest possible works. It is so simple in French I can read it myself so I can't imagine it loses much in translation: it is the one quintessentially poetical play I know of in which language seems to be scarcely a value at all, oddly needless to say this is not why I recommend it. Rather because what would appear to be substituted for *language* per se is that forgotten virtue Clarity. Of course you can say that the two are identified but the truth is that as a poet Cocteau is often extremely obscure, which must often be, but also precious, which should not be. Not however, in The Infernal Machine. On English factory windows during the depression people used to chalk the words *Please Clean* me, a form of animism not without its touching quality, since noone ever did, and why should you want to see what was inside anyhow, save from the point of view of the window's feelings? In the case of the Infernal Machine, the windows of style are so clean that you are not aware of any interposing glass. What you *see* is anything but simple however: the workings of the machine itself. Eliot has never managed anything as good as that through the medium of an almost imperceptible poetry. In any case, that play might be a good influence for you: its fame, so far as I know, is almost nil. (Yeats translation, of course, I assume you know)[9]

But did you know to what extent x ward and y ward the whole Oedipus myth has been called into question & pulled apart, on its own terms – not dramatically or novelistically, but as it were pseudohagiologically – if only for it to be put together again, much as it is? I think you might find a source of inspiration here, rather than stupefaction, if only as providing an aside, or the odd cross-brace; anyway, if you did know of these bypaths, I for one didn't, at least of their disparateness. What I have to go by here is an antique Sophocles in the original Greek to which the English notes are strange, but for your purposes, not particularly fructifying but I also have Graves' Greek myths.[10] He has it that the story of Laius, Iocaste, & Oedipus has been deduced from a set of sacred icons by a deliberate perversion of their meaning. The myth of Oedipus' arrival at the Court of Corinth is related to the Eleusinian mysteries & the torchlight arrival of a 'Divine Child.' He also relates Oedipus to the infant Moses, Romulus, Cyrus etc, the implication being he was exposed on a mountain or consigned to the waves in an ark, or both. 'It is possible that *Oedipus* 'swollen foot' was originally *Oedipais* 'son of the swelling sea,' which is the meaning of the name given to the corresponding Welsh hero, '*Dylan!*'

'Laius' murder is a record of the solar king's death at the hands of his successor: thrown from a chariot & dragged by the horses (This will lead you back to Phaeton – {indeed incidentally to Eridanus, the name for the inlet at Dollarton in Gabriola} M.)

All this seems pretty boring on the surface, half-debunking, a sort of inverted *hagiolatry* rather, very curious: 'Was Oedipus a thirteenth-century invader of Thebes, who suppressed the old Minoan cult of the goddess & reformed the calendar? Under the old system, the new King, though a foreigner, had theoretically been a son of the old King whom he killed and whose widow he married; a custom that the patriarchal invaders misrepresented as parricide & incest. {Mem: Hamlet also, which to Eliot had no objective correlative, albeit he overlooked that his uncle *was* in that case committing incest, according to the Marquis of Queensberry's Rules of Elsinore of that date, as someone must have pointed out.}[11] The Freudian theory that the 'Oedipus Complex' is an instinct common to all men was suggested by this perverted anecdote; and while Plutarch records that the hippopotamus 'murdered his sire and forced his dam,' he would never have suggested that every man has a hippopotamus complex.[12]

(I wonder what Eliot, however, might have made of that in his poem about the true church!) While this last is balls in my opinion – I mean that this does not of itself discredit the Freudian theory which would not in that case stem from the anecdote at all but from the curious compulsion in man that grew up to *repeat* the anecdote in its perverted form or dramatise it as myth or even historical truth in that form, thus leaving the theory as valid or invalid as before – it seems to me that they may be more of interest, than distraction, for you in this, if you weren't aware of these interpretations already, which you doubtless were. Tell me if you have not read this, or rather – it is in Chapter 105 of Robert Graves' The Greek Myths, in my version the beginning of Volume II – if it seems to you worth your reading: if you think it is & cannot readily lay hands on the work I will copy out whatever seems pertinent to you: certainly *not* (*only see below*★) having Jocaste, as Graves insists, leaping from a rock like the Sphinx did, & not hanging herself. Graves' opinion seems to be that Oedipus like Sisyphus tried to substitute patrilineal for matrilineal laws of succession but got banished by his subjects. Here is his précis: 'Oedipus of Corinth conquered Thebes and became King by marrying Iocaste, a priestess of Hera. Afterwards he announced that the kingdom should henceforth be bequeathed from father to son in the male line, which is a Corinthian custom, instead of remaining the gift of Hera the throttler. (The island of Vulkano where some two years ago we marooned ourselves was sacred to her: she can have it.)[13] Oedipus confessed that he felt himself disgraced as having let chariot horses drag to death Laius, who was accounted his father, and as having married Iocaste, who had enroyalled him by a ceremony of rebirth. But when he tried to change these customs, Iocaste committed suicide in protest, & Thebes was visited by a plague. Upon the advice of an oracle, the Thebans withheld from Oedipus the sacred shoulder blade & banished him. He died in a fruitless attempt to regain his throne by warfare. (According to Homer, gloriously in battle: and to Appolodorus, he was banished by Iocaste's brother, & wandered as a blind beggar through the cities of Greece until he came to Colonus in Attica, where the furies hounded him to death). – Another matter that inhibited my replying about my own affairs was that I had so far made no comment on

'Happiest Gun Alive' (very well done) & the Satevepost[14] story in regard
to which and any other stray ends of work you might have lying about,
particularly not, *excluding* any odd Oedipean endomorph⋆ – I had and
have for you one of the happiest ideas for a novel since Miss
Lonelyhearts and Nathaniel West were apprentice seamen: anyway I
hereby present it to you for whatever you want to make of it or not, one
effect it ought certainly to have on you if you think there's anything in
it is that you would suddenly see you hadn't been & aren't wasting your
time after all on the commercial stuff, because indeed part of the novel's
quality would depend entirely and precisely *upon* your being an expert,
& a professional, in that sort of line – especially the western – both in an
office such as Frank's [Frank Taylor] was or Lions' are (or even Knopf)
– where I see our protagonist engaged during the day in some editorial
publicising capacity and at home (though he won't have a home exactly)
where ostensibly to make ready cash, but in fact as it turns out as a kind
of initiation into his true being he (not you but someone like you
vaguely, Je ne suis J!), pounds out Westerns: indeed The Happiest Gun
Alive, with or without the '*The*' will do fine as a title till another comes
along though the very rough idea is partially conveyed in the words,
'Portrait of the Artist as a Young Gun': Happiest Gun Alive then is your
title – no epigraphs, no heroics, no exordium, nothing else; then, bang,
Chapter I, or I *is* Happiest Gun Alive *itself*, the story or the history, just
like that, with nothing altered, unless slight typographical changes, such
as the gaps closed, but possibly not even that. Chap II however (in contrast to which I will be seen stylistically to possess absolutely the right
kind of clarity I was attributing to Cocteau, thus proving our protagonist an artist, even doing things he hates, takes you into the mind of the
author of Chap I, who is dying laughing (figuratively) somewhat with
tears in his eyes at what he has accomplished in Chap I only so to speak
pitching forward on his typewriter: now to be sure the history of Clay
is a *True* Adventure, but in order for it to be truer still for your purposes
we shall in II, have to have some indication why Clay has been chosen
by More (which I propose as the name of your hero; Claymore is a large
two-edged sword formerly used by the Scottish highlanders) chosen to
some extent, by your hero, even though remotely, & wildly, as a projection of himself: not that More is a murderous fellow, but the world
that tramples down Drunks Truth & writers alike sometimes makes him
feel murderous; for one thing, because he is constrained to write brutal
if lively pieces like Chap I for a living; while the appalling heat, claus-
trophobia, noise, lovelessness, love, despair, violence, general
disillusion, appalling difficulty of the lot of a writer, of being a man, of
finding one's place in the world at all, these combined with certain
reflections on the effect of technology on love, say 'sex taking on the

aspect of the divine in a world of steel and asphalt' (I heard someone saying on the radio) all contribute to his sense of cribbed & confined
exacerbation: moreover, More, while well aware that a sound understanding of psychology must precede a sound knowledge of morals, still
cannot understand quite why, though possessed of a sound understanding of psychology, he should possess so few morals, still less a desire for
them, despite the extensive knowledge of them that he might seem ex
officio to possess – in brief, he symbolically would probably like to shoot
quite a few people in the environs of East Dirty Turd Street (as Conrad
[Aiken] calls it) where he inhabits a cold water flat, though he's far from
knowing what his higher self wants him to do about it, or, if clearer in
his mind what he *should* do, whether it is within his power to do it;
nonetheless the necessary hams are by now beginning to be hung in the
window, thunder is growling as we get set for the interior & exterior
drama that we now begin to see must end by the reconciliation of Clay
& More; or the triumphant triumph of More; or the disastrous triumph
of Clay: or catabasis into catabysses of both Clay & More or final extinction into the Ultimate Clay of everyone in the cast: or whatever: but
Chapter II I would see mostly as an engagingly contrasting atmosphere
& scene to I, in the wild East instead of the Wild West, in 1957, instead
of 1878, but with certain subtle points of the mise-en-scène in common:
whether or not Chap I = Happiest Gun = A *published* story, or one
unpublished which More has just finished, which in II he reads to himself, or to another, male or female, or others, would be important
questions you'd have to decide as inspiration dictates, but subtly we
should not I think know as yet too much about More, save that he is at
bottom an extremely serious writer who is living in an atmosphere – the
NARROW CLOSED SPACES as opposed to the WIDE OPEN SPACES of I –
almost as constricted as that which torments the characters in Sartres No
Exit.[15]

Just at the point, however, when the reader thinks he's going to learn
more directly of More, you spring a surprise on reader, Chap III being
no less than in toto, purely & simply The White Apache, the Satevepost
story: though here it would be effective, as exemplifying the trials of
More, less purely but just as simply, to point out the changes that have
had to be made in this story to suit the editors, who represent the
nonego or so-called outside world: not that More's integrity is exactly
at stake in making his alterations, but that the alterations, and the necessity for them, & their being made by him, *mean* something, I am quite
certain; again the status of the story, whether already accepted at this
point or not, or alternately whether More will receive a telegram
informing him of its acceptance by some Satevepostlike mag at the end
of this chapter or no, all these things are still in question for you, but I'm

inclined to feel that it would be better here had this story (like Happiest Gun) already been accepted & published, for in this way you'll neatly be able to use the biographical squib at the end of the Post *Give 'em Guns He says*:[16]

Tom ('Sir John') More, New Yorker, of British descent, Greek, both, what have you {I'm getting to identify myself a bit with your character here: but it looks to me like an excellent opportunity for abreaction, – disguised, overt, angry, understanding, bored, or all 5 at once – of your own personal experience.} known widely to his friends as Sir John, because, he thinks, 'of a certain confusion arising in people's minds between the poet Sir Thomas More,[17] & the author of The Burial of Sir John More after Corunna,' the poet who wrote the famous lines:

> Not a drum was heard, not a funeral note
> As his corse to the ramparts we carried
> Not a soldier discharged his farewell shot
> O'er the grave where our hero is buried.

but whose name, on the other hand, was Charles Wolfe, so that the confusion may just as well have come from an identity between the name of this latter poet and Tom Wolfe[18] – performs editorial duties with Etc Books and lives in E33 St New York, in which state he has lived his life: etc first Lastpoststory . . . legitimate psychological conflict . . . 'After all people who carry Colts are tempted to use them'

(By the way, Clay Allison, on the cover, looks exactly like Juan Fernando Marquez, the original of Dr Vigil in Volcano who perished not dissimilarly, albeit not kicked by a mule.)[19] He could even be glancing at the story itself, mentally substituting 'uneasy' comfort for 'doubtful' comfort in the first paragraph, and wondering why, though two words were saved by the elision of 'his shoulders', he should so dislike the sentence: '*The farmer shrugged.*' And also wondering why, though as by way of kind he should be sitting on top of the world, or feeling like that, he should so intensely dislike this sensation: perhaps because the world was round, and if he could visualise himself as sitting on top of it, the world equally could be seen as sitting on top of him, or would be sitting soon, or so it suddenly felt, but with all its weight on two pairs of shoulders instead of one, counting those so unwarrantably withheld from his prose. 'Only this made the sensation seem more unbearable, rather than less. He felt banished, no less, like Oedipus denied the sacred shoulder blade, condemned to wander as a blind beggar until he came to his Colonus, or Corunna, or wherever it was the furies were going to hound him to death, if they had not already done so. Or he would die gloriously in battle in a futile effort to regain his throne. Or, having defied the City Goddess, perish as a victim of his own superstitious fears. Or as a victim of his own superstitious fears, hounded to death by the furies, *and* gloriously in battle. That was the beauty of myth: there were always so many choices. But meantime The White Apache had brought him enough money to eat, more than enough money. All too much money. He need no longer eat the inferior portion of the sacrificial beast, the haunch: he could, at the East End Bar choose the royal shoulder, even if it had been denied him, as a first step toward dying gloriously in battle. Once a writer has thought up a legitimate psychological conflict, giving the protagonist guns intensifies the drama. After all, people who carry Colts are tempted at times to use them.' (Something to this effect.)

O'er the grave where our hero we buried. This – & I hope you'll excuse my intolerable arrogance in making these suggestions at all but your Demon has only to reject them if he doesn't like them – this foregoing piece of bad grammar really relates to later chapters of your novel where the changes are rung, not on Westerns, but from sections (possibly your own self – rejected bits) of More's more serious work on a novel on Oedipus, with whom an identity is here presaged: the immediate conflict, though, in III, would be almost precisely opposite, its being sufficient to have hinted that The White Apache, the obverse of Clay, is the mask of More's superego. On the other hand – I am using psychoanalytic terminology in a secular or literary way – but I think I will make myself clear – the sheriff is yet another aspect, and even more powerfully so, of More's superego: indeed since Sir Thomas stands vis-à-vis the Sheriff & The White Apache as creator to his creations, whereas no matter that psychologically the choice of subject implies much the same thing, he stands in relation to Clay more as mere historian, this being so, Sheriff + White Apache, (with the conflict resolved here by forbearance wisdom & meditation, by love in short, part of the author's own personal conflict abreacted in this strange manner by the story itself, and in an important sense, by the *success* of the story, by his own patience in tailoring it & retailoring it, for the Satevepost quid pro quo) S + WA amount to More's Higher Self, – to speak in terms of the Cabbala now, – collectively his Bright Doppleganger, whereas the trigger-happy Thanatos-Bound Clay is his Dark Doppleganger, (much like his Unconscious, his death-wish and General Death's Jest Book,) to the Eros-Life wish of the Sheriff-+-Apache-Combine in which the Girl, the canalisation into the Better Thing, is also all-important, though in the novel you need not have got to that point yet, the existence & indeed necessity of the Girl being merely hinted at so far by her presence in the story White Apache written by More. Are you with me? Iss ver gut, n'est ce pas?

But if More's own self-realisation lies in this latter *ascending* direction in his own personal life (opposing this to his Art for the moment) something wholly different is true of his Art itself, for here Clay has to be reckoned with & faced, or is symbolic of a force within More that has to be subdued and overcome but yet *used*: other interesting combinations will strike you, such as that Clay is the phantom dopplegänger likewise of the White Apache, but the point is that Clay represents *creatively* speaking *both* Destroyer *and* Preserver, but simply a *Destroyer* murderer and indeed Suicide if we continue the opposition between More's higher Artistic nature & his life, in that juxtaposition the 'Enemy within' More – (perish this terminology but I can't express myself, if it is indeed I who is expressing it, any other way) – Enemy because the resolution of all his conflicts are through violence (albeit the saving grace here, the nexus between opposites, may be his humour, Laughter, i.e, by projection, More's humour) & solved only by Death, but (& herein lies the drama, – how can this be? how can there be such an opposition?) – but if we abandon that opposition as false, I say and false it seems to me it must be – for how can More achieve full Self-realisation without taking his Creative Consciousness into account, without reconciling the higher & lower aspects of that? – then Clay, or what Clay inherently represents within More, is an important factor to be reckoned with in More's Life considered as travelling on the ascending Eros spiral toward the Girl & the Better Thing, potential destroyer and preserver here too but who has to be subdued into being a Preserver, and merely made use of as a Destroyer, the Unconscious in his Art, the purely physical or sexual perhaps, in his personal life; preeminently though, More will fail to achieve full existence as a man (or make anyone else happy for that matter) unless equally he realises or attempts nobly to realise himself as an artist in the best sense.

Now at this point your novel ceases to be merely good & becomes *Great*, though tis me as sez it & though you will have of course not attached any signposts to all these danks & darks which should be implicit: Great in meaning & execution, though not in *bulk* necessarily, (Your book should be fairly short, not more than 250 pages at most, possibly only 200, perhaps less than that, if I may be allowed to play Goethe as well as Pushkin to your Eckermann-Gogol for the moment[20] – if it has to put on muscle & gain weight in that way, that's one thing, but it should regard fatness as a vice and leanness with an aspiring eye.) More is indeed not split into his binary identities or More & Sir Thomas (tentatively) without reason. Within his own private reality, & quite as if there was no Clay or Apache on the scene. He is of course split himself, if not actually fragmented, so that a dual identity is probably an understatement, though let this suffice for the moment. I see him, in fact, as an ideal part for James Dean and maybe James Dean actually plays a part in the story,[21] because More might well see himself like that in a way, as a baffled Giant of the Ink-well, torn between his ten gallon hat & his visor, his shooting irons & the iron entered into his soul, the Great White way & the wide open spaces: there's no end to the alternating currents you can switch on. So far though, Happiest Gun Alive, sorts itself out much as follows in my mind, (though I have added a chapter or so)

I Happiest Gun Alive. (Clay) 1879, Texas.
II Tom More broods on I, which turns out to be Western by Tom More, and the reasons he gives to himself for writing it etc. New York. 1957. Night.
III White Apache.
IV Tom More broods on III, which turns out likewise to be a Western by Tom More, but in a top magazine, – a triumph, a jackpot, and the reasons for writing it, liking it, or disliking it, in the course of the latter emotion the reader & Tom More discovering that for some reason his triumph & acceptance give him a feeling of despair, rejection, exile, & guilt to the extent that he even finds he has an identity with Oedipus. New York. 1957 Night.
V A section of your Oedipus Rex. Logically this could be a section you like of the novel but which you have cast out. Thebes. Greece. BC?
VI Tom More broods on V, which, on the contrary, is a fragment of a very serious 'Near Eastern' by Tom More, representative of the kind of work he wants to do at its highest, but also of the compromise, even here, that he is forced to make, he thinks, with his work even on this plane, in order – beautiful and crushing and entrancing irony – that he will able to render himself independent of the editorial job which itself takes the form at its worst of having to force precisely the same sort of compromise upon others, at its best of commercializing the kind of work he would like to be doing himself, but which in fact is only now commercializable in this fashion because their authors by and large refused to make any compromise with their artistic integrity in the first place; or at least so at least they must have told themselves. Flaws in this thought. The relative element of compromise in everything. The compromise even in the *word* compromise, which, beginning by meaning 'a mutual promise to abide by a decision,' then 'to adjust and settle a difference between parties, has degenerated on the one

hand to mean 'to endanger the life of reputation of, by some act which cannot be recalled,' and on the other to a committal to something derogatory or objectionable. To come to agreement by concession, or appeasement of the commercial, is the most slaughterous meaning it can hold for a serious, but, my dear Sir Thomas, I would point out that its most useful and truest meaning is the colloquial one which stems from its meaning of *result* or embodiment of adjustment, a thing intermediate between, or blending qualities of, two different things. The most perfect work of art, the most perfect sonnet, or novel in this view, cannot but be a compromise, between what it leaves in and what it leaves out: compromise paradoxically need *not*, my dear Sir Thomas, compromise itself, and the only difficulty is to persuade the Editor that it need not. Compromise is indeed Equilibrium, Life itself. However. Sir Thomas also now broods upon the alternative endings & resolutions of his Oedipus story that are now open to him, following upon his having unfortunately stumbled upon a copy of Graves' Greek myths, in the NY Public Library. He also remembers Freud's passionate objection to the awful fixed curve of determinism of Sophocles' play: the audience, he declared should have rebelled against this *inevitable* outcome! But it would now appear that Sophocles himself had not been above compromising with the truth, – & by extension, if unwittingly Freud himself: unquestionably in this case the lie seemed to possess the greater artistic integrity, & so perhaps by blending qualities of other lies, embody somehow a greater truth. Brooding upon this & like matters perhaps, into a movie with a girl who is really the same as the White Apache's girl in III, to see the film of Happiest Gun Alive, from the story by himself, the money from which he's long since spent or has in some way been done out of, and the film of which without his knowing it has ironically been changed in such a way as to have some good claims to being a serious work of art, goes the young Thomas, baffled. Further baffled, because the film, upon which he has some difficulty at first in concentrating, partly because of the immediate stimulus of his girl, & partly because, for some reason he keeps remembering the lines with which Tereisias, summoned to settle the dispute between Hera & Zeus from his

personal experience as to whether women derived greater
pleasure from the sexual act than men, which was Zeus'
unchivalrous contention, plumped for Zeus:
If the parts of love-pleasure be counted as ten
Thrice three go to women, one only to men[22]

(Whereupon Hera was so exasperated by Zeus' triumphant grin that she
blinded Tiresias) & partly because the film, a kind of Shane + High
Noon in reverse,[23] when he does concentrate upon it seems, despite its
serious pretensions, compromised by those very pretentions to art, & as
a consequence not as true to its own special reality as was his own most
unpretending original. Perhaps also the ending is altered in some way
consonant with that section of his thoughts still puzzling about what he's
going to do with Oedipus, at the same time that he is puzzling himself
about free will, time, whether the latter must not be a compromise with
Space, and whether the Golden Section itself must not be a compromise
with both Time & Space.[24] Only God, who could be both crucified &
hanged upside down, like Peter & Mussolini, or hanged the right way
up with Jocasta but at the same time see no contradiction in throwing
himself down from a rock with her likewise,[25] & ending matters like that
for her though his son was said to have resisted this temptation, might
be said not to compromise at all, unless it was with Hera. Perhaps, however, if one pronounced the word compromise differently, as if its final
syllables were 'promise,' as originally, that would solve something. Well,
what should he promise to *himself*, for the fact remained that both his
Happy Gun Alive & Apache were compromises of a kind he could not
go on making indefinitely, even if they were leading somewhere.
Where? Well, they would find out perhaps, and, perhaps on the way
back from the cinema they stop in & have their fortunes told by a somewhat shortsighted Greek clairvoyant who, though a woman, looks most
remarkably like a man.

Well, I can scarcely [go] on without spoiling your story for you, I was
going to say, (There was a slight pause while I read the following in to-
days paper: h'm perhaps it has no significance: 'Archers 'Death
Coincidence' *Real Shooting in Wood*. The day after a 'death' from gunshot in the BBC's rustic serial 'The Archers,' Antony Brainbridge, aged
29, son-in-law of the late Robert Mawbley, the original Walter Gabriel
of the serial, was found dead on Friday night with a gunshot wound in
Quanley Wood, Daneway, Gloucestshire . . . On Thursday, Bob
Larkin, a character in the plays, 'died' in a scuffle in the woods with a
gamekeeper, Tom Forest.[26]

Mr Brainbridge, who lived in Hamilton Drive, Melton Mowbray,
Leicestershire, was on holiday at Oakbridge, Lynch, Near Stroud, it is

understood. He went out about 10 am on Friday, & as he did not return, police made a search.'

Anything in this for you as between Demons? Heigho for the Life Dimensional!)

Now, though I have written some of this letter in a facetious tone (because for one thing some of it strikes me as funny) the whole suggestion is serious and meant in a serious spirit of Pushkinship to your creative Gogolotry: you may well ask, however, what has led me to think that such a thing would come off. Since the idea was begotten by White Apache & reinforced by reading Happiest Gun Alive I can only say that it emerged out of a certain thing in the *effect* made by those stories, nearly perfect (though not quite, I think, which is an interesting point in aesthetics, I mean that, given the *genre*, & accepting that it has its own rules meant sometimes to be broken, & at that even not too far or too rashly, nonetheless the Editor of the Satevepost probably only imagines that his 'public' *demands* the kind of special conformity he imposes – & is not the New Yorker almost as bad in this respect?) nearly perfect according to what they set out to do & be, & 'having the virtue of clarity,' that is one can follow them & be interested, which is more than one can with most popular fiction, it struck me, due to the mechanicalness & rigidity involved, that I could by using my imagination gauge, down to a fraction of an inch so to say, the effect made by, say, Happiest Gun, on the majority of its readers: I may be wrong, but I don't think the differential reaction would be anything to speak of as between juvenile hot rodder or intellectual – both would think the stories good for the same reasons, that they do what they intend to do & set out to do: nor would the teen ager of to-day who has the underlying taste to appreciate an actor as magnificent as James Dean, I believe, differ very much from the intellectual or poet, in his reaction when it was brought home to him that the real drama beyond the drama lay less in the wild west story than in the prairies & campus of the soul of the serious author who'd found it necessary to choose or be chosen by that particular story. In case you think I am trying to build up an argument leading towards the popular or universal appeal of such a novel as I have suggested – though indeed it might well have that too – if a fatal potentiality to pay any attention to while writing it – my object was other: it occurred that by starting a novel with such a short story, then proceeding to the motives of the author in writing it, & the frustrations & despairs involved, you would have achieved a kind of *absolute* of construction, with the possibility of extending the frontiers of the novel. A published story is already a thing, a brute fact but with a life of its own, something at least as real as an inkpot or a bottle of whisky, or becomes so the moment you treat it as a published story, differing from a story already published that starts off a book of short stories, say, in that the latter is still pretending to the illusion of reality whereas your story is not pretending to be anything else but a story in a mag. – surrealism with a vengeance, in the truest meaning of the word, but my purpose here is to set the fires of your imagination burning with the very tinder that it is only natural for it to despise or reject, and if I've got it alight I don't want to put it out again or smother it with too much sea-coal of my own, damp or witchy, as it happens to be. In other words I firmly believe that your own blue bird, as it nearly always is, is in your own back yard, only it happens to be such a subtly disguised & original blue bird that I hope I may be pardoned in pointing out its existence. What I feel you may be failing to perceive is the incredible romance of your own familiar things, of the medium in which you swim, unnoticed because they are familiar, & you happen to swim in it. As Ricardo said, the fish would notice the water last, given conscious perception.[27] But this whole world of Editorialising & blurb writing, of popularising, & tailoring both literary & pseudo literary is, juxtaposed to the strivings of the artist that is yourself, I feel to be surely an absolute gold mine & in no obvious The-Great-Man-or-Prater-Violet sense, excellent though these pieces doubtless are.[28] Then who, to wind up, in all this, is your Iocaste, who your Laius, who your Sphinx? if the Sheriff or The White Apache or both are disguised higher selves, are they, likewise, disguised father images when we shift on to the Oedipean level to be slain? I don't seem to remember that the superego in psychoanalytic parlance is considered any more than the ego itself developed along the lines of self criticism & moral conscience but with this gentleman is almost the sole fructifying conversation, as Keyserling remarks,[29] & in so far as he is individualised, he is an object that one has to draw level with, finally transcend, and in transcending, recreate on a higher plane still: it is not necessary to kill him, even accidentally, but More would kill him, by becoming Clay, just the same, along with himself, in all the meanings that trigger-happy can have in our mundane civilisation though again, don't forget his sense of humour, or laughter anyway. No: More surely moves in two worlds obeying different laws; or rather his 'own' world is a pluralistic one, as pluralistic of morals as of Oedipusses. The world of his art, both in its higher and lower aspects, is far more rigid, & as it were more inevitable. I do not want in any way to put you off your general line in the novel you are writing about Oedipus: the old story cannot be bettered perhaps, and in the Sophoclean canon you have doubtless already chosen is the right one while leaving you the field open to do something new with it as a novel for it is a good & original idea. But if your demon should see anything to be made of Happiest Gun Alive, not necessarily as I have indicated, but something like that, surely it would be a dramatic thing to stress that even here there is a plurality of choices, due to the confusion perhaps of the original myth makers as to what market they were catering for: whereas in your contrapuntal story, of the development & realisation of More's imagination & being, your figurative Iocastas & Sphinxes could fairly come raining down (leaping from the rock) from the skyscrapers, whereas your Laiuses, in the shape of editors and publishers largely no doubt could get themselves run over by the million in his fine new Cadillac, for all More might sometimes care. In the former domain of Art again, though there is some comfort to be found in the picture of Antigone leading her father, in all the choices that myth or art provides, noone has ever suggested that the resolution, for Oedipus, however triumphant in a mystical or renunciatory sense, was happy. Any way you look at it, the fatality is abominable, and the philosophy involved hopeless, in every way to be rebelled against from the standpoint of human destiny: only the Art all the endings have in common seems valid, & the Sophoclean story the best, unless you can better it. And common to both of More's worlds is of course the figure of Oedipus as an almost archytypal figure of exile & wandering. But need I point out — I think I need, most strongly, for it is right here, from the confusion of the two worlds, of the domains of Art & Life, that my own troubles have mostly arisen, not to say that of many other writers — that More's two worlds involve apparently diametrically opposed activities, not to say ethics. In order to write with energy and authority about the Sphinx falling off a rock it is not only necessary not to fall off the rock oneself but climb up it twice every day before breakfast in order to keep fit: in order to celebrate the life horrific in art, tragedy being given one by God for one's own aesthetic pleasure & instruction, it is necessary — if not too lonely — to sing the Body Electric in life: Oedipus may blind himself but if you go and get blind too often you will not write about him so admirably. In this regard & in his own *life*, therefore, I venture the suggestion that Oedipus — Sir Thomas, his own magician, & [illegible] free will, even turn himself into Theseus, and with Ariadne's aid, slay the Minotaur, and giving the myth yet another turn, remain faithful to her and happy with her, though reserving a large sense of humour:[30] all his bloody mindedness can go into his Art, but Life itself should strive towards a Happy Ending, since however much this may seem to outrage us aesthetically, this is what we are meant for, even should the Earth itself be cast into the uttermost dustcart. As for the 'lower' part of More's artistic endeavour, I hope I have at least indicated one way in which that may be put to work & serve the 'upper.'

Well, I hope you can make something of this heat I've turned on for you: don't let it distract you, but I feel some of these things are worth your cogitation. Margerie is in splendid & happy form, though not yet strong: as for myself, I am trained down to the point where I really could be quartermaster of the Pequod, & what a mess Huston made of that film by the way: I fancy it was due to the presence of Alan Villiers as Captain on the bridge of Pequod[31] – if you don't know who he is remind me to tell you. Huston's sister-in-law (ex) is a great friend of ours: I fancy you know her, she's the wife of Churchill's nephew any-way.[32] Who, poor fellow, just had a heart attack. But that film. No: Moby Mouse, it should have been called. Thank you for thinking of Ultramarine but it has to be rewritten first. Margie joins with me in sending all best love to Elaine & love to you both & luck to you both.

Sursum Corda. Hold that note, Roland!

Love

Malcolm

P.S. I forgot to mention the most important point: the identity of a Iocaste in More's life. She is, of course, Art herself here, the higher Muse, the only woman with whom he can commit lawful incest, while having another wife of his own. And on this side of the story he uses his powers as a magician to keep her alive while both marriages are happy! Q. E. D.

P.P.S. I forgot to say that I very much like your description of the three chapters of Oedipus. In the play of La Machine Infernale, by Cocteau (to which Cocteau, 1/4 of a century ago come next month, presented me with a box seat for two nights in succession – 'for otherwise it will seem like a pantomime' –) the Sphinx' familiar, the Jackal god, Anubis, trots around dog-masked in the marital chamber on the wedding night, hissing and spilling the terrible beans into the conjugal ears while they are asleep; I don't know whether Cocteau made that up or whether Anubis is in the public domain, but if the latter, he's a real mean char-acter worth remembering in a technical impasse.[33] As for your dual control, the one part artistic, & the other editorial, you may find some-thing to your purpose about that in this letter. As for Happiest Gun – for another purpose, likewise. (There are in fact several ways of reading it; the moment it becomes attached to its author as a speech to its owner, if not quite as dialogue, though like that, & is deep indeed.) Moreover read as a bit of Faulknerian dialogue it is very funny.

Annotations:

1 The American novelist William Gaddis (1922–) is a friend of Markson's and the author of *The Recognitions* (1955), which explores hypocrisy and greed through the character of an erudite art forger. Replete with allu-sions to Western culture (Dante, Mozart, Greek myth, and so on), to

drugs, alchemy, and the occult, to a writer who is writing what we read, and with names like Bella Vista, Bellevue, and Alabama and familiars such as black dogs, the novel *must* have given Lowry a turn. Although it was not well received in the 1950s, it has subsequently received praise, together with Gaddis's later work.

2 The mountain Lowry is thinking of is Kangchenjunga, the third-highest mountain in the world, located in the Himalayas on the border between Nepal and Sikkim. Tenzing Norgay (ca 1914-86) was a Sherpa mountaineer and the first man to set foot on the summit of Mount Everest on the British expedition with Sir Edmund Hilary in 1953. Aleister Crowley (1875-1947) was an English poet and a legendary black magician.

3 Alfred Knopf was arranging to bring out *Under the Volcano* in a Vintage edition at this time (see the Lowrys' 11 December 1956 letter [**698**] to the Marksons), and Markson had also suggested that the publisher he was working for, Lion Books, might be interested in doing a paperback edition.

4 Llareggub (buggerall in reverse) is the name of the town in Dylan Thomas's radio play for voices *Under Milk Wood* (1954). The town is traditionally associated with Laugharne, the small Welsh town on the Taf estuary where Thomas was living when he wrote the play.

5 Lowry's reference is to the poem 'I Sing the Body Electric' (1855) by American poet Walt Whitman (1819-92), whose habits, like his rhythmic, musical verse, were anything but sedentary.

6 Captain Cat is a character in Dylan Thomas's *Under Milk Wood*, and Pozzo, not Fatso, is a sinister character in Samuel Beckett's play *En Attendant Godot* (1952; *Waiting for Godot*, 1954) – thus the name of the Lowrys' cat: Catso. *The Crucifixion* and *The Resurrection* are mystery plays from the York and Towneley cycles respectively. They were broadcast on BBC Third Programme on 16 February and 12 March 1957.

7 Lowry is recalling Jacques Barzun's critical review of *Under the Volcano*; see his 6 May 1947 letter (**299**) to Barzun.

8 This Lowry metaphor turns on an allusion to the Hebrew hero and prophet Daniel, who was thrown to the lions by the Babylonians after their conquest of Jerusalem in 586 BC. The Old Testament Daniel escaped the lions, but Lowry fears that his novel will not escape the marketing zeal of the Hollywood Daniels of twentieth-century artistic consumerism, who will turn it into some artificial product like Spam.

9 Cocteau's *La Machine infernale* and Yeats's translations of Sophocles were much in Lowry's mind at this time; see his 11 December 1956 letter (**698**) to Markson. Markson's novel was never published.

10 Robert Graves published *The Greek Myths* in 1955. In the discussion that follows Lowry draws upon Graves's commentary on Oedipus (pp. 371-77) and quotes Graves at several points.

11 See Eliot's essay 'Hamlet and His Problems' and Lowry's 20 May 1954 letter (**607**) to Markson. The Marquis of Queensberry Rules are the

basic rules used in modern boxing. They are named after Sir John Sholto Douglas (1844-1900), Eighth Marquis of Queensberry.

12 Graves explains that Plutarch (ca AD 46-ca 120) made this remark in his *On Isis and Osiris*; see *Greek Myths*, p. 375.

13 Vulkano, an island of the Lipari group in the Mediterranean off the north coast of Sicily, consists of a single volcanic cone. The Lowrys visited Vulkano and other islands in the group before leaving Sicily for England on 9 July 1955.

14 'Happiest Gun Alive' is the title of a magazine article by Markson on the American hero and gunfighter of the Old West called Clay Allison; see Lowry's 31 October 1951 letter (**476**) to Markson. Markson's story 'The White Apache' was published in the *Saturday Evening Post*, 24 September 1956, 30, 135-39, and Lowry always called it the 'Satevepost story.'

15 Jean Paul Sartre's 1944 play *Huis clos* (*No Exit*, 1946) takes place in a closed room where the three characters who have died find they cannot leave their hellish state even when a door is opened to permit their escape.

16 The biographical note on Markson in the *Saturday Evening Post* (152), carries the caption, over Markson's photograph, 'Give 'Em Guns, He Says.' The remark 'After all, people who carry Colts are tempted at times to use them' is attributed to Markson in this note.

17 Sir Thomas More (1478-1535), the English Catholic statesman, lawyer, and author, was executed by Henry VIII for refusing to swear an oath acknowledging the king's supremacy over all monarchs, including the Pope. He was beatified in 1886. *Utopia* (1516) is More's most famous work.

18 Charles Wolfe (1791-1823), an Irish curate, is the author of the poem 'The Burial of Sir John Moore' (1817), about the Scots lieutenant general who died of wounds received while leading the retreat to La Coruña during the Peninsular War in January 1809. Thomas Clayton Wolfe is the American novelist and author of *Look Homeward, Angel*, and Tom Wolfe, the pen name of Thomas Kennerly, Jr (1931-), is an American journalist who used the techniques of fiction to develop what is known as the 'New Journalism.'

19 Markson recalls publishing the essay 'Happiest Gun Alive' in a men's magazine but we have not located it.

20 Lowry's role of Goethe or Pushkin to Markson's Eckermann or Gogol is that of senior writer and adviser to the younger man; see Lowry's comments in his 20 May 1954 letter (**607**) to Markson.

21 James Byron Dean (1931-55) was an American actor who became a youth cult figure for his role in the film *Rebel Without a Cause* (1955). Lowry is unaware that Dean had been killed in a car accident.

22 Lowry has lifted this couplet from Graves's *Greek Myths*, p. 373.

23 *Shane* (1953) and *High Noon* (1952) were popular American Western films in each of which an isolated hero saves a community too fearful to help him.

24 A golden section is a line segment that has been divided into two parts so that the ratio of the longer part to the shorter part equals the ratio of the entire segment to the longer part. The concept of a golden section has been important in aesthetics as a measure of formal beauty or pleasing balance.

25 St Peter is traditionally believed to have asked to be crucified head downwards because he felt himself unworthy of the same death as Christ. The Fascist dictator Benito Mussolini was executed by Italian partisans on 28 April 1945 and hung, head downward, in the Piazzo Loreto in Milan. Jocasta, Oedipus's mother and wife, is said to have hanged herself, but Graves notes that this is probably an error: 'she doubtless leapt from a rock, as the Sphinx did' (*Greek Myths*, p. 376).

26 'The Archers' was a popular BBC radio series of the forties and fifties about a rural family from the Midlands.

27 Lowry may be thinking of David Ricardo (1772-1823), an English economist and author of *Principles of Political Economy and Taxation* (1817), but we have not located this observation.

28 Arnold Bennett (1867-1931), the English novelist, playwright, and journalist, wrote naturalistic fiction. His novel *A Great Man* (1911) is about an ordinary young man who becomes a popular writer. *Prater Violet* (1945), one of Christopher Isherwood's novels, is narrated in the first person and is about a young man from Cambridge who writes the script for a third-rate movie called *Prater Violet* that is directed by an Austrian filmmaker living in exile in London during the thirties.

29 Lowry alludes to the ideas of the German philosopher Hermann Keyserling in other letters from the 1950s; see, for example, his 13 December 1950 letter (**432**) to Downie Kirk and his 28 November 1951 letter (**482**) to Seymour Lawrence.

30 According to Greek myth, after Theseus slew the Minotaur in the Labyrinth at Crete, he abandoned Ariadne, who had helped him, at Naxos.

31 The American actor and film director John Huston (1906-87) made a film of *Moby-Dick* in 1956. His film of *Under the Volcano*, starring Albert Finney, Jacqueline Bisset, and Anthony Andrews, was released in 1984.

32 This is Joan Black.

33 See photograph 24, which shows the bedroom scene from the Comédie des Champs Elysées production of *La Machine infernale* that Lowry saw in Paris in 1934. Cocteau played the role of the narrator.

Editorial Notes:

a. This letter (UBC 3:13) is written in black ink on rectos and versos of five sheets of 21-by-27.5-cm letter paper. The script is tiny and comparatively clear, with several neat cancellations and interlineations, and it slopes up towards the right corner of each page. Most pages have been filled, and there are several marginalia, including the two postscripts.

706: To George Sumner Albee

P: California(ms); UBC(phc)   The White Cottage,
PP: *SL* 397–400   Near Lewes,
                                                                   Sussex, England
                                                                   17 March 1957

Dear George Albee:[1]

Thank you very much for your generously worded & warm-hearted letter. What you say about Under the Volcano is tremendously encouraging, even more so, & not without its gratifying ironies too, in that it was anything but a success here in England, so much so that my mother, whom I had deceived for years into thinking I was writing a religious book like Bullen's With Christ at Sea,[2] or at least some sort of Anglican or even Methodist-cum-Swedenborgian Bildungsroman, only the second syllable of which was apparent from the reviews, said she simply could not endure reading their harsh criticism, and she though having a kind heart was quite a tough old lady, as befitted the daughter of the skipper of a windjammer from whom she would have doubtless heard some harsher criticism still, had not the good mariner been by this time at the bottom of the Indian ocean, whither he had followed the windjammer in question.[3] All was made well when my wife (herself American) who was visiting England showed her some of the more sympathetic American reviews – including that very one which maybe put you off – so that this kindness, however undeserved, as I must gratefully say of yours too, had its pragmatic value in that my mother would otherwise have died in the unhappy belief (for old ladies are liable to set as great store in the literal interpretation of reviews, as of Gospels, without finding it necessary to investigate the original text) that I had accomplished nothing whatsoever, since my other work so far as she was concerned had for years been locked up in the strong square walnut desk of my deceased father, where for all I know it still remains.[4] Even more depressing was its reception in my then adopted city of Vancouver, Canada, (whose literature I had had the childish dream of enriching with some well-chosen words) who described the matter variously as '. . . these turgid pages . . .' '. . . not improved by being written in the style of Conrad at his worst . . .' '. . . volcanoes erupt for no reason; what is it all about?' Or even, witheringly '. . . typical of the 'new school' of American deliquency & sadism,' or, patriotically, 'this Consul should have been sacked before we reached page 5.' So much for local boy makes good in his home town. On all the more grateful ear then, fall your own kindly words, including those of the kindly action in writing to Sam Rapport:[5] here, however, friendly coincidence appears to have come into play, because at about the same time you were doing that,

Alfred Knopf, Jr was writing to me asking if he could republish it in Vintage Books. Imagine my pleasant surprise at this honour after ten years even though I had to say – as to you regards Rapport – thank you but I thought not, as I believed Random House had a lien on the work: however in the meanwhile Random House had apparently given their permission to Knopf, so that it looks as though Knopf will reissue it fairly soon in that edition.[6] But I thank you for the thought anyway. Meantime, what is life like in Cuba, I am curious. I read of revolutions, counterrevolutions, & borrachonazis in the zocalo.[7] I hope sincerely that such has not disturbed the peace or person of yourself & your good wife in Playa Varadero. I have once been in Cuba, for the space of about an hour, having set foot upon your soil in a place named something like Camaguay, from a plane flying from Haiti to Florida, about ten years ago, in fact about a week before Under the Volcano came out in America. I gained less idea of Cuba, however, probably, than those to whom my wife & I sent postcards thence, the airport being little more than a well-stocked bar in the middle of a limitless desert. And I also had a strange friend who once invited us to live in the Isle of Pines. (though not – or not then anyway – in the Convict settlement,) where, he assured me, a fortune was to be made out of marble, although he did not state what was to be done with the marble, and I very much fear, not having heard from him since, that a tombstone may have been contrived out of that same marble for himself. On the other hand I have an impression that Cuba must be a marvellous place in which to live, and pursue the Better Life, the Better Thing, & indeed celebrate generally the Life Electric: such at least would seem to be confirmed by Hemingway's attachment to it, and since you live there yourself too, (as did my father, from time to time, in Havana) perhaps you'll tell me how you find it.[8] In England, even as I write, there is a feeling not so foreign from that of your revolutions, counterrevolutions, & borrachonazis in the zocalo, though on a somewhat more polite and (perhaps) bloodless scale, though nonetheless bloody in other respects since we appear heading, unless some wisdom stops it, in to a General strike of catastrophic dis-proportions. I was a schoolboy here during the last General strike in 1926, & naturally regarded it as being a great deal of fun,[9] but there is in fact no fun about it, labour troubles here having no relation to those in the rest of the world; and but remote similarity to those in America, and being based upon a huge implacable hatred & desire for revenge upon one class by the other, indeed the desire for revenge is really mostly on one side, namely Labour's, nor does the fact they've already had all the revenge possible without cutting their own throats seem to make any difference, when there's a chance to get some more, and they don't give a damn what happens to the country in the process:

since the fact is that Labour is for the most part unblushingly reactionary while the Conservatives are relatively revolutionary the only thing that one could do, if one doesn't like the Conservatives too well either, is to put one's school cap back on & read Wordsworth: or perhaps Henry Adams, until it all blows over. Meantime it is likely that no contribution will be made to human freedom. Meantime too I had a letter coincidentally from our friend Anton Myrer himself: I thought Evil Under the Sun was a splendid book & I'm very glad to hear he's got another one on the way & am much looking forward to reading it. And have just written to tell him so.[10] We had a publisher in common for a while, prior to which I had the pleasure of reading Evil U.T.S. before publication, and indeed wrote an eulogy of the same to the publisher in question, who prior to that, had been largely responsible for the publication of the Volcano: but I think Evil did not have the same luck.

Tell me what I should know of your own work, & where I can get it. Both in Canada & here, for long periods, it has been all but impossible to keep in really close touch with American literature, for reasons of embargo & one thing & the other, so that I am ashamed that your name alone is familiar to me, & this perhaps for the wrong reasons, as I am sometimes congratulated or the reverse for the work of Robert Lowry, which I think is good for that matter, although I fear him to be dead too, or even worse, though I hope better.[11] But don't be so down-hearted because you're going to write a funny book. I hope to do so myself someday. In fact, damn it, I thought Under the Volcano was funny, in parts anyway. Please thank your wife very much for liking it – my own wife joins me in sending you both kindest regards.

Sincerely

Malcolm Lowry

Annotations:

1 George Sumner Albee (1905-64) was an American novelist and short-story writer and an admirer of Lowry's work. He wrote to Lowry in the spring of 1957, shortly after reading *Under the Volcano* for the first time, and claimed that *Volcano* was the greatest novel written in English during the first half of this century. Lowry, says Albee, surpasses Hemingway, Steinbeck, and Faulkner. A copy of Albee's letter is held in the Lowry Collection (UBC 1:3).

2 Frank T. Bullen's *With Christ at Sea: A Personal Record of Religious Experiences on Board Ship for Fifteen Years* (1900) is a type of 'religious biography' about a young sailor and the vicissitudes of life at sea.

3 For information on Lowry's maternal grandfather, John Boden, see Lowry's 6 March 1950 letter (**391**) to Derek Pethick and Bowker (4).

4 Whether or not Arthur or Evelyn Lowry kept *Ultramarine* locked away, I cannot say. Lowry complained that they did and that his family never

appreciated his work, and Bowker (542) repeats Lowry's claims. The few surviving letters from Evelyn to her son suggest that she took pride in his work.

5 Lowry may be referring to Samuel Rapport, a director with Appleton-Century-Crofts publishers in New York.

6 Lowry signed the Knopf contract in March 1957, and the Vintage paperback edition of *Under the Volcano* appeared in February 1958.

7 From the end of 1956, when Fidel Castro landed in the country to lead the revolution, through 1957, Cuba experienced several armed insurrections against the government of Fulgencio Batista.

8 Ernest Hemingway lived, off and on, in Havana at Finca Vigía from 1939 to 1960, and spots such as the Floridita Bar and the Hotel Ambos Mundos are famous because he frequented them. Arthur O. Lowry's cotton business occasionally took him to Cuba.

9 Lowry's only extant reference to the 1926 General Strike in England is in his May 1926 letter (**8**) to Carol Brown. Despite intense labour unrest, especially during the first half of 1957, no general strike was called in England that year. Strikes were frequent, however, in London food markets and bus services.

10 Anton Myer, the American novelist, published *Evil Under the Sun* with Random House in 1951; for Lowry's comments on the novel see his 24 November 1951 letter (**481**) to Albert Erskine. Myer was a friend of Albee's, and it was he who persuaded Albee to read *Under the Volcano*.

11 Robert Lowry (1919-) is an American novelist, short story writer, and poet.

707: To Ralph Gustafson

P: Saskatchewan(ms); UBC(c)　　　　　　　The White Cottage,
PP: *SL* 407-10　　　　　　　　　　　　Ripe Near Lewes,
　　　　　　　　　　　　　　　　　　　Sussex, England
　　　　　　　　　　　　　　　　　　　[29 April 1957]

Dear Ralph Gustafson:[1]

I'm very sorry to take so long to reply to your letter of March 12 but Jonathan Cape sent it back to Canada again, so that it had to get reforwarded again from B.C before I received it.

I'm very honored to be put in the Penguin though whether I qualify strictly as a Canadian is another matter though I like to think I do: under the old law I did, though I still have a British passport, albeit I took out Canadian papers, never decided on any final citizenship, so am classed as a Canadian resident. My wife & I lived there for fourteen years in a waterfront shack on Burrard Inlet which I still have that I loved & love more than my life and wrote – all my best work, as the saying is, there. I left in 1953 because of my wife's health but we hope to return.[2] But I never became a Canadian citizen under the new law: nonetheless I've as much right to call myself Canadian as Louis Hemon had & I even wrote a Canadian National anthem, though nobody's yet sung it except me. I had a childish ambition – maybe not so childish always to contribute something to Canadian literature though, & I wrote a book called Under the Volcano, which has become fairly well known, but which people seem to think is written by an American. Like all blokes in the throes of an anthology I suppose that you are persecuted by replies from contributors you want saying that they want you to select something else, of theirs, – if possible *too* – and I do not want to torment you in this way but *I* am no exception, thinking I've done some things better than these two, but I'm proud you selected them anyway, though I thought a thing called Sestina in a Cantina (perhaps too long) & one called Salmon Drowns Eagle that I thought might have been suitable: & A.J.M. Smith printed another in his Scribner's anthology called In Memoriam Ingvald Bjorndal that I'm fond of: when I say *I'm* fond of, I mean this literally, because very few people have ever expressed their opinion one way or another about my verse so any fatherly advice on the subject, no matter how devastating, will be very welcome to me: sometimes I think I've never been able fully to understand the most elementary principles of scansion, stress, interior rhyme and the like with the result, by overcompensation, that my poems such as they are *look* as though they had a kind of wooden monotonous classical frame: cf. Birrell on Dr Johnson. 'He knew but one way of writing poetry, namely to chain together as much sound sense and sombre feeling as he could squeeze into the fetters of rhyming couplets and then to clash those fetters loudly in your ear. This proceeding he called versification.'[3] perhaps I have no ear, but then I must have some sort of an ear because I began life as a would be composer of hot jazz, & what is more I think a good one. All this is very sad & complicated to me because I think of practically nothing else but poetry when I'm not thinking about my old shack on Burrard Inlet but *like* so extremely few poems of any kind by anybody that it seems to me I may be inhibiting myself from writing either by some serious lack of judgement in regard to my own craft, or some fanatical narcissism or other that makes me set the touchstone impossibly high, as [a] result of which I am now writing a huge & sad novel about Burrard Inlet called October Ferry to Gabriola that I sometimes feel could have been better stated in about ten short poems – or even lines – instead: then again I have good judgement about other poeple's poetry when I can understand what they are saying, which isn't very often, so please tell me what I should read: I'd like to educate myself as a poet seriously, though its getting a bit late in all conscience. Tell me of your own recent work: I like much all that I have read of yours. Did you ever come across the work of a man named Norman Newton?[4] He struck me as an exceptionally promising writer though I have not heard from him for many years.

Two wild western poets came to see my wife & I in the bush on Burrard one stormy night some years ago, & I enclose you some of the recent work of one, which seems to me – the typed ones – damned good. This fellow Curt Lang was scarcely out of his teens & he impressed me mightily as being a type I thought extinct: namely all poet, whose function is to write poetry. His address is Curt Lang 517 Pine West Montreal Quebec. I think the written poem would be better without the *on retina* in the first line, & the final couplet is weak: but the other two have a kind of fury, and the Architectural one at the end, a really terrifying quality, that seems to me very rare & original in a poet, whatever the merits of his typography or indeed however he means it to be printed: I do think he is worthy of inclusion, even if you have to kick me out, for he is a young bloke could use & deserves that kind of encouragement in my opinion.[5] (Not that I couldn't or don't but I'm older.) The work of his friend on that occasion, whose name I've unfortunately mislaid, is also worth looking into: his name is Al something or other,[6] but Curt Lang would put you on to his work which again impressed me by its originality intricacy & power. He is an older poet who has published a chapbook or so but both are well worth watching & he too is worth considering in my opinion but maybe you've already made your selection. I've met alot of writers but I have rarely been impressed by such dedication on the part of anybody as these two, and as for Lang he might well have genius. (I hope these poems will cause you to drop a line to Lang anyway if you decide to use any of them – he could enlighten you as to the typography or you him but could you let me have them back eventually because I thought of sending them to Spender or somebody) – Re my bad memory, I seem to recollect a misprint, if not two in the CV Glaucous Winged Gull. A memory *stronger* than childhood it was meant to be, not *stranger*, anyway, for what that's worth.[7] Among your own admirable but lesser known works did you not once write a story about someone climbing a building printed by Martha Foley 1948 – horrifyingly good. I can still feel it. If you didn't write it please take it as a compliment that I thought you did.[8]

Sincerely yours

Malcolm Lowry

P.S. We are going to live in the Lake District in Grasmere for a while not because it reminds one of Wordsworth so much but because if we half shut our eyes we may be able to imagine we're back on Burrard Inlet!

Annotations:

1 Canadian poet Ralph Gustafson (1909–) has edited three anthologies of Canadian writing. He had written to Lowry for permission to include two of his poems, 'Lupus in Fabula' and 'The Glaucous Winged Gull,' in the *Penguin Book of Canadian Verse* that he was preparing for 1958 publication.

2 This mistake in the year is Lowry's; they left in 1954.

3 Augustine Birrell (1850–1933), an English lawyer and essayist, published two volumes of essays on literature, *Collected Essays* (1922) and *More Obiter Dicta* (1924), but this remark has not been found among Birrell's voluminous writings.

4 Lowry and Newton had known each other since the late forties, and they renewed their friendship in 1952; see Lowry's October 1952 letter (**543**) to Newton.

5 Lowry enclosed three poems by Curt Lang with this letter (UBC 3:13). The untitled sonnet with the flaws that Lowry notes begins: 'On retina Peter saw an iron door.' 'Poem Architectural' is a fine example of the modernist free verse and 'demented' vision that Lowry himself so often attempted to create.

6 This is almost certainly the Canadian poet Al Purdy, who had published *Pressed on Sand* in 1955. In his poem 'Malcolm Lowry,' from *The Cariboo Horses* (Toronto: McClelland & Stewart, 1965), Purdy remembers his visit to the Lowry shack: 'going to see the soused writer and / bursting from dull green wood / out to live green water' (p. 9).

7 When Alan Crawley published the poem in *Contemporary Verse* 21 (Summer 1947): 4, the tenth line carried this misprint; see Lowry's 26 October 1947 letter (**327**) to Crawley.

8 Gustafson's short story 'The Human Fly,' first published by the *Atlantic Monthly* in 1947, was reprinted in Martha Foley's *The Best Short Stories, 1948*.

708: To Ralph Gustafson

P: Saskatchewan(ms,ts); UBC(c)   The White Cottage,
PP: *SL* 411–13   Ripe Near Lewes,
                                         Sussex
                                         [23 May 1957]ᵃ

Dear Ralph Gustafson: Thank you for your kind & very encouraging note. Also I'm very glad you liked Curt Lang's poems.¹ Yes, by all means add your praise for the old novel: I'm honored you should give it. But of Cain, of which I can't find a copy, can't remember the title, and can't quite the meaning or intention – what does it mean? I mean I vaguely remember what it was *meant* to mean, (and I also remember reading that poem – which was written in 1936, one of my first to a girl, intending to cheer her up, instead she passed out) but does it *mean* what it might appear to mean? does it have any religious parallel or is it a kind of traumatic dislocation of pre-Judgement Day?: + in any case you can improve it, for I do remember one thing in A.J.M. Smith's reprint of it which was a misprint: viz it couldn't be _recommend the Pentecost_ could it? which was printed, I must have meant *recommemorate*, though that can't be it either quite, or can it?[2] And why the Pentecost too? I'm glad you liked it though, for I loved it when I wrote it, which was with something considerable worse than a hangover, in a million acres of cactus (but fortunately some tequila) in a Mexican pullman car called the Aristotle. Lupus in Fabula was written at the same *time* I wrote p. 88 of the Volcano (how good of you to spot the identity), in the margin of the <u>MSS</u> and was originally called XOCXITEPEC, a better title, I think, but it was suggested by an article by J.B. Priestley on being followed in a dream by some beastie perhaps of the fifth dimension![3] But in Cain (or whatever title) I'm sure it <u>can't</u> be recommend. Yet what would I mean by recommemorate? Please help.

Sincerely yours.

Malcolm Lowry

P.S. I have just found the poem, & surely *recommemorate is* better, though I still can't quite understand what I meant, albeit I do like it somehow & recommemorate is in the original so could you restore it, if you cannot improve on it. I see the point now, with my wife's help; the descent of the Holy Spirit on the Apostles. Maybe the punctuation is a bit screwy in places. What about Pentecost as a title?

P.P.S. Certainly recommemorate.

Gratefully yours,

– ML

Happiness
Blue mountains with snow and blue cold rough water –
A wild sky full of stars at rising
And Venus and the gibbous moon at sunrise.
Gulls following a motorboat against the wind,
Trees with branches rooted in air;
Sitting in the sun at noon
With the furiously smoking shadow of the shack chimney,
Eagles drive downwind in one,
Terns blow backward,
A new kind of tobacco at eleven,
And my love returning on the four o'clock bus –
My God, why have you given this to us?[4]

(Or cut out all the commas?)

I couldn't resist sending you this which I love and is about our old shack that we still have. I thought it might make a good resolution to the other 2. Brother what a life that was, is. You asked for some Biographical notes which I now put on the same page, my subtle object being that you will find it harder to get rid of the poem now you have to tear the page in half. Born 1909, educated Leys and St Catharines, Cambridge. Under the Volcano was begun in 1936, not finished till 1944, and not published till 1947. That this novel was ever finished at all is largely due to the encouragement of my wife, Margerie Bonner, an American, also a writer, and another Canadian writer, Gerald Noxon, who gave us sanctuary in Ontario after our cabin on the B.C. waterfront burned down, taking with it the third part of the trilogy of which Volcano was the first. Thanks to this encouragement we were able to return to B.C. where we rebuilt the cabin and I finished the book. For the rest, my grandfather was captain of a sailing ship, and as a boy of 17-18, inspired by Eugene O'Neill, I sailed before the mast myself (1927) to China and Japan. At present living in England writing a novel with its setting in British Columbia and Burrard Inlet to which it is our dream one day to return. Under the Volcano is shortly to be reissued in an edition of classics by Knopf. It was almost entirely written in Canada, inspired by life in Canada, and by Canada, in my nearest then home town of Vancouver, thoroughly panned. It has since been translated into 6 languages.

Annotations:

1 See Lowry's 29 April 1957 letter (**707**) to Gustafson, annotation 5. Gustafson did not include Lang's poems in the *Penguin Book of Canadian Verse* (1958).

2 Scherf gives this line from 'A Poem of God's Mercy' as 'Will recommemorate the Pentecost' (95-96), while Birney shows 'Will recommence the Pentecost' (*SP* 48). In his 28 May 1957 reply to Lowry, Gustafson assured him that he would change the word, although he saw nothing wrong with 'recommend.'

3 John Boyton Priestley (1894-1984) was an English dramatist, novelist, and critic. The essay to which Lowry is almost certainly referring is 'The Berkshire Beasts,' first published in *Open House* (1927) and included in Priestley's *Essays of Five Decades* (1949). The first line of 'Xochitepec' is: 'These animals that follow us in dreams' (Scherf, 125).

4 See Scherf (136); the only comma dropped by Scherf is the one following 'backward' in line 9.

Editorial Notes:

a. The poem and final paragraph of biography are typed on a separate page enclosed with the holograph letter. Gustafson has inserted the date.

In the last weeks of his life Lowry's thoughts were often of Dollarton. On 27 May the Lowrys set out for a tour of the Lake District, but they found the scenes and Wordsworthian associations as painful as they were beautiful. Quite simply, Grasmere reminded Malcolm of what he had lost. They returned to Ripe on 22 June, by which time he was depressed and drinking heavily. His only extant correspondence from this period is the two postcards to John Davenport and David Markson mailed from Westmoreland, and the final letter to Harvey Burt. If he had lived Malcolm might have recovered energy and optimism, but in June 1957 his mourning for the past, the pier, the beach, the shack, for happiness and for old friends, had left him − almost − without words.

709: To John and Marjorie Davenport

P: UBC(pcard)

[Ambleside,]
[Westmoreland]
4 June 1957

One would not think Manchester nurtured on this:[1] but then one would not think de Quincey went to Manchester Grammar school, either, whose house is here (Grasmere):[2] no smoking, please; on top of which it's called Wordsworth's, albeit de Quincey lived in it 20 years to W's 5 − deepest respect here seems reserved for Hartley Coleridge[3] He was apparently wheeled back from The Swan every night in a wheelbarrow known as 'Hartley's one-wheel-sway.' who is still remembered as the town drunk.

Best love from us both

Malcolm

Annotations:

1 The postcard shows a colour picture of Whirlmere Lake with the mountain Helvellyn in the background. The explanatory blurb on the card notes: 'This Lake is the principal water supply for the City of Manchester.'

2 The English author Thomas De Quincey (1785-1859) is remembered for his *Confessions of an English Opium Eater* (1821) and *Suspiria de Profundis* (1845). De Quincey was a friend and associate of the

Romantic poets, and he lived in Dove Cottage (formerly the home of William Wordsworth) in Grasmere.

3 Hartley Coleridge (1796-1849) was the eldest son of the Romantic poet Samuel Taylor Coleridge. Hartley, in many respects a failure as a poet and teacher, was known for his intemperance; he is buried in St Oswald's churchyard, Grasmere.

710: To David Markson

P: UBC(pcard)

Grasmere
15 June 1957

Dollarton? That's what we thought but it's Grasmere[1] where Wordsworth designed the chimney pots and you may see de Quincey's room (smoking prohibited) in de Quincey's house to which, on payment of 1/6, you may be admitted on all days save Sundays as 'Wordsworth's cottage,' which it was for 5 years. How goes Swellfoot the Tyrant?[2] Your letter was melancholy, but cannot you *use* that very uncertainty as to one's ability as a strength? O'Neill (see Long Day's Journey) thought himself not much use as a writer too. Have you read Isaac Babel?[3] You should. Do you know which stars are which and what bird is flying over your head and what flower blossoming? If you don't the anguish of *not* knowing is a very valid field for the artist. Moreover when you learn something it's a good thing to repossess the position of your original ignorance. Best love to Elaine and yourself from

Margie & Malc

Annotations:

1 This postcard shows a black and white photograph of an island in Grasmere Lake with low mountains in the background and a few buildings huddled on the distant shore. The view is uncannily like the one the Lowrys had from their Dollarton cabin as they looked south across Burrard Inlet.

2 This is Lowry's joking reference to Markson's work in progress on the Oedipus theme; see his 22 February 1957 letter (**705**) to Markson. It is also an allusion to Shelley's translation *Oedipus Tyrannus or Swellfoot the Tyrant: A Tragedy in Two Acts* (1820).

3 The short-story writer Isaak Babel (1894-?1939) was a Russian Jew born in Odessa. His stories have a classical purity and economy that make them unique. He disappeared in 1938 and is thought to have died in a concentration camp.

711: To Harvey Burt

P: private; UBC(msc)
PP: *SL* 413-15

The White Cottage,
Ripe Near Lewes,
Sussex
[late June 1957][a]

My dear Harvey:

We have not your new address – albeit I hope it pleases you, and, whether or no, we may still have the privilege of staying with you both in some Metz of the soul, whether of good, or even of damnation.[1] I have some friends in Germany, notably a publisher, Klett of Stuttgart: should you be in that neighbourhood of the Black Forest? Though I loved your description of Metz. And I am delighted that you both were so happy there, as unhappy we missed the opportunity of all seeing it zuzammen: but this was unavoidable. We went for a fortnight to Grasmere, & it is wonderful beyond belief: even the Ambleside golf-course is only putted on by two curlews, leeches lurk for the gatherer still at the bottom of the tarns, and the loud old ferry no longer runs:[2] children too, I am glad to say, seem less noisy than Wordsworth led one to believe he was, & we sat at the desk of the old man himself in Hawkshead, which is exactly like Tlaxcala in Mexico, examining the words, mysteriously written thereon; – W. Wordsworth.

> That, musing on them, often do I seem,
> Two consciousneses, conscious of myself
> And of some other Being. A rude mass
> of native rock, left midway in the square
> of our small market village, was the goal
> Or centre of these sports; & when returned
> After long abscence, thither I repaired
> Gone was the old grey stone, & in its place
> A smart Assembly-room usurped the ground
> That had been ours . . . .[3]

He was too pessimistic: everything is the same, except the local bus, which in any case once ran into him.

> We rested in the shade, all pleased alike
> Conquered & conqueror. Thus the pride of strength
> And the vain-glory of superior skill
> Were tempered: thus was gradually produced
> A quiet independence of the heart . . . .

Try though we might, however, we could not gain quite the same kind of quiet independence out of the silence of the new Laurie,[4] the guardian of our Dollarton Grassmere, &, if I doubt not, of your own pinnance of peace of shining water, even while knaves & monarchs surely, not to mention queens gleaming through the splendor of their last decay & unfading recollections raged bitterly with keen & silent tooth all the green summer to forlorn cascades.

> The sounds of Westmorland . . .
> The creeks & bays . . .

And it is forgotten: − or at least, that's what *they* say.

No matter, my brother, thus oft amid these fits of vulgar joy, which through all seasons on a child's pursuits − (& I was about to get back to Kyd the next moment by chance collisions & quaint accidents)[5]

AND IT IS FORGOTTEN:

− I beg your pardon: I meant it wasn't: But hell − what shall I have to say but:

Uncouth assemblage was it, where no few
had changed their functions: some, plebeian cards
Which Fate, beyond the something something something. (I forget.)

> And monarchs surly at the wrongs sustained
> Protracted yelling like the noise of wolves
> Or from the meadows sent on gusty days
> Beheld her breast; the wind, then suddenly
> Dashed headlong, and rejected by the storm. −
>
> Ye lowly cottages wherein we dwelt
> A ministration of your own was ours
> Can I forget you, being as you were
> So beautiful among the pleasant fields
> In which you stood? Or can I forget
> The plain countenance with which
> You dealt out your plain comforts?[6]

(At evening, when with pencil, etc etc etc.)
Hell, I could record with no reluctant voice.

God damn it, Kyd, I didn't know how else to address you but in this verdammt Norwegian.

M

Annotations:

1 The Burts were holidaying in Metz, a picturesque, historic French city on the Moselle River northwest of Strasbourg. From Roman times

Metz has held a strategic position in the struggles between Germany and France, and this might explain Lowry's metaphor.

2 In Wordsworth's 'Resolution and Independence' (1807), the poet derives strength and inspiration from his conversation with an 'old Man' who gathers leeches, and he concludes that when discouraged and in despair, 'I'll think of the leech-gatherer on the lonely moor.'

3 Here and in subsequent passages Lowry is quoting from the 1850 text of Wordsworth's *The Prelude or, Growth of a Poet's Mind*. This passage and the one immediately following are from Book II, lines 31-40 and 68-73. Lowry has also woven numerous words, phrases, and lines from Book I into his own comments.

4 The 'new' Lowry is Laurie Lynds, who was taking care of the Dollarton shack; see letter **656** to Burt.

5 The 'Kyd' Lowry meant to 'get back to' is English dramatist Thomas Kyd (1557?-94), author of *The Spanish Tragedy* (ca 1584). More particularly, he is referring to Burt's radio play about Kyd and Christopher Marlowe called 'Green Grist,' which was broadcast in 1956. Malcolm was unable to hear the broadcast but Harvey recalls that he and Malcolm often discussed Kyd and Marlowe; Harvey identified with Kyd, Malcolm with Marlowe.

6 These long passages, and the short ones above, are from Book I of the *Prelude*; see, for example, lines 567, 585, 521-23, 534, 542, 496-98, and 499-505; the lines immediately following are from Book I, lines 509 and 483. Lowry has not always quoted Wordsworth exactly, and it is possible that he is quoting from memory.

Editorial Notes:

a. This holograph photocopy is undated, but it has clearly been written sometime after the Lowrys' return to Ripe on 22 June and shortly before Lowry's sudden death on the night of 27 June.

Appendix 1

THE TWENTY NOTES to Margerie Bonner Lowry included in this appendix represent a small fraction of the several hundred notes (UBC 53: 1-7) given to the archives in 1987 at the request of Priscilla Bonner Woolfan. There are only a few extant examples of Margerie's replies to Malcolm with the collection, but she appears to have treasured and preserved each one that he wrote to her.

For several reasons, a carefully culled selection of the notes is provided in this otherwise 'collected' *Letters*. Predictably, the notes are repetitive and extremely private. They arise from highly specific contexts, so that they constitute one side of an intimate daily conversation carried on over a period of years. Moreover, they are written in a conjugal language that can sound affected and saccharine to the outsider, especially when taken in large doses, and the information (literary, biographical, factual) conveyed is not commensurate with their number.

With the selection provided here I have tried to do several things: to provide a broadly representative sample of epistolary type (postcard, telegram, billboard, poem); to capture the quality of a special discourse created by Lowry; and to suggest the inventive range (from quasi-letter to brief message) explored in what might at first seem an ephemeral format. In making and ordering this selection I have been guided by textual and visual cues, not by dates, because the notes are not dated except, occasionally, with reference to a day of the week or a celebration such as Hallowe'en, Christmas, or an anniversary. Nevertheless, in many instances it is possible to determine which notes were written during the Dollarton years (as were the twenty here) and which at Ripe. Those from the Ripe period are usually less light-hearted than the Dollarton notes; often Lowry has signed them 'Malc' instead of using one of his animal *noms de plume*, and some of them, included with the letters, were mailed to Margerie from hospital (see **643, 658, 660**). Unlike the letters, the notes are not annotated because the apparatus would overburden what were spontaneous communications.

The notes are written by hand, usually in pencil, on tiny, often coloured, pieces of notepaper, typically 11 by 7.5 cm. They have been folded once or twice to make a tiny packet, and the outside of the packet usually carries postal instructions: thus, one note arrives 'By Evening Heron,' another 'By Special Butterflight,' and another is called a 'Harteebeestegram.' Lowry often *designed* the notes, embellishing them with stamps, advertisements, and drawings, and a few of these adornments are reproduced to illustrate his use of space and visual effects; some take the form of poems (see Scherf, 321-47). He left them in places where Margerie would find them – pinned to trees along the path to the shack, in conspicuous spots inside the shack or in the White Cottage at Ripe. To call them 'love notes' because they were left for her in these ways is, however, something of a misnomer. As J.B. Lyons recognizes in his 'Malcolm Lowry's Love Notes' (*MLR* 28), they are also full of fantasy, parody, and farce.

Perhaps the most remarkable and defining characteristic of the notes is the way each one is intensely, intimately *addressed* to Margerie in anticipation of a response and in expectation of continuing conversation. They exist in a specific moment and convey the immediacy of dialogue. The topics are everyday ones that range from welcomes home if she had gone shopping to greetings on waking in the morning, comments on the seasons, the weather, on their health, their quarrels, their work, and expressions of love on birthdays and other occasions. Lowry has captured the texture of daily life in the process of living it, which, for him, always meant writing it. There is, finally, something almost frightening about his compulsive need to place words on paper, even in situations where most couples would simply speak. It is as though he needed to write in order to be, and to surround Margerie with his verbal presence in a gesture of self-validation. If there can be such a literary mode as an allegory of daily life, then Lowry has created it in these notes. To describe them as allegory may seem an exaggeration of their importance, but that is what I think we have here – an allegory of the quotidian, constructed in the moment, to be sure, but across a series of moments that together connect many years of a marriage, shaping it into a narrative of life, a unique type of autobiography-in-progress.

Lowry develops this narrative through an elaborate, consistent set of animal personae for himself and Margerie that reinforces the hierarchy of symbolic and discursive levels required of allegory (with El Leon, symbol of Imperial Britain, as king of the Lowry castle) and establishes a complex set of equivalences between human beings and the animal world, between human activities and their counterparts within the surrounding natural order. Thus, a simple errand or house-cleaning activity becomes the flight of a shearwater or the busy interference of a mink or a clumsy well-meaning seal. In short, he gives meaning, value, and beauty to his life by locating it within the world of familiar living things around him. From one perspective, this allegory marks a profoundly anthropomorphic gesture, and yet from another it signals Lowry's keen sense of identity with – and fundamental preference for – the natural (as opposed to the civilized) world.

His chief name for Margerie is 'Hartebeeste,' often spelt 'Harteebeeste'; she is also his 'dearest duck.' For himself he has several names, many of them designating female animals or birds, each one signifying an aspect of his character or a mood. Sometimes he is 'the pronghorn' or 'the seal'; at other times he is 'the Gadwall,' who can be cantankerous. His primary designation, however, is 'El Leon,' an animal self who is noble, proud, at times absurd and inarticulate, but who is always full of love for his 'harteebeeste'.

El Leon, in fact, is another Lowry alterego, or *Doppelgänger*, like Sigbjørn, rather than a pseudonym like 'Camel,' because Lowry invests the figure of the lion (his zodiac sign) with an extended fictional identity and a distinctive voice through which he can speak. Indeed, on occasion he will talk *about* El Leon in the third person to ask where he has got to or to mock his vanities. While 'all the little animals' participate in the story by delivering the messages, visiting the 'lovecot,' assisting the principals, and sharing in their joys and woes, and while the 'harteebeeste' is the one addressed, admired, and adored, there should be no mistake that it is El Leon who occupies centre stage, whose feelings, thoughts, doings, and misdoings provide the main subject, whose presence cannot be ignored.

It would be as much an error, I think, to dismiss these notes as mere nonsense as to over-estimate their significance. Like a latter-day Robinson Crusoe or a more contemporary Grey Owl, Lowry lived in isolation for long periods, and he felt compelled to fill his world with correspondences, characters, order, and meaning, the full extent of which is difficult to pin down. That he felt more a part of his natural surroundings through this discourse is obvious, but should one go further to suggest that this animal-talk reinforced a longing for paradise in an allegory of the Garden of Eden *regained*, or that it reveals his nostalgia for a pre-lapsarian innocence and presence lost to the twentieth-century human being? And what meaning, if any, exists in his choice of animals? Most of the creatures in the drama were and are still native residents of the west coast of British Columbia, but the lion and the hartebeest are foreigners, African immigrants to a northern wilderness. Does this status parallel the Lowrys' own transplanted existence, and if it does, to what end? Is there any significance in the fact that, in the real world, the lion hunts the hartebeest and will kill and devour it if he can? Probably not.

In the last analysis, what these notes give us is Malcolm Lowry playing yet another role, the male lead 'El Leon, Imp. Rex,' opposite his female star 'the Harteebeeste,' in an allegory of the everyday, set in a paradisal location with a supporting cast of characters who fill an imaginary discursive space with life and meaning. The spectacle may be coy, maudlin, trite, even boring, but if you lower your sights while the sun comes up on the lovecot and suspend your disbelief, you may well enjoy the amateur theatrics – the farce and melodrama (it is never tragedy) – of this miniature mystery play about what was, after all, a thoroughly theatrical life.

Not all of Malcolm's notes to Margerie were as complex and elaborate as this one (see Figure 2 in volume I), which she kept in her copy of Under the Volcano.

I

SRA CARISSIMA HARTEBEESTE BY WINDBELL

We bought some notepaper but as you see El Leon has some advertisements on it, in fact he has a monopoly of the notepaper. We thought though you might like some excerpts from our forthcoming primer for ducklings to be published by LIONS LITERARY *LIGHTS* LIMITED – Some of these exceptions will also be given on El Leon's radio programme next Lion day. These are

Never Duckline an earnest request but *learn* to duckline your verbs.
Dearduckracy is a goverment by ducks for ducks of a duck.
Before going into duction clear the ducks.
Never prove things by reducktio ad absurdum when it is possible
    otherwise.
Never duckry a friend. Do not declaim too loud your own duck-
    trees.
This little program will be preceded by a Duxology & accompanied
From time to time by the musical maestro Duck Ellington
and his Duxestra who will give a choice selection of De-duck.
I hope you will [find] this a very suitable programme for the
little ducklings all of which join in sending *you*, oh
our beloved hartebeeste, the deepest and *fondest*

love, we are all very happy and quacking merrily
in this *splendid* weather – with true love & kisses from
the Mergansers

SRA CARISSIMA HARTEBEESTE BY WINDBELL

2

By Seal

Reveille!
– the morning bird is singing –
El Leon feels religious
His mane about him flinging
With gestures strange and hideous
(Yet with kindly mien fastidious)
The morning wood is drying
The morning rain refraining
The moon is slightly waning
And the kettle, hugely trying.

This little poem is written by me, all except the lines about El Leon
which El Leon himself wrote for me to help me out – hope this will
cheer you – we are helping the Greenfinch settle – with fondest &
dearest love from your faithful little friend – The Mink.

With sweetest morning love from *all* the little animals to our beloved
Hartebeeste

P.S. Soon photograph weather.

3

BY HERON

Thou wast not born for death, immortal Duck
No hungry generations tread thee down:
The quack I heard this passing night, with luck,
Was also heard by Emperor & Clown:
Perhaps the self-same quack that found a path,
Through the great heart of El Leon, when sick for you
He roamed with roars about the Cariboo ...

This is my first excursion into poetry which I am trying to learn on
the trumpet. Perhaps you will think it a bit derivative but the Vancouver
Daily Lion is to pay me for it – I have to give 50% to El Leon – but I
think that is very nice. I saw El Leon just now & he expressed himself

very pleased – he seemed to be contemplating a walk with his beloved Harteebeeste & talk over his work afterwards sometime in the near future – (probably a pub is involved at the end but do not be harsh with him on this score, I think he wanted to look at birds with you what a wag he is) With all devoted love from all the little animals to my beloved Harteebeeste

The Seal

4

Senora Harteebeeste mio By waggish Pronghorn (even rogueish)

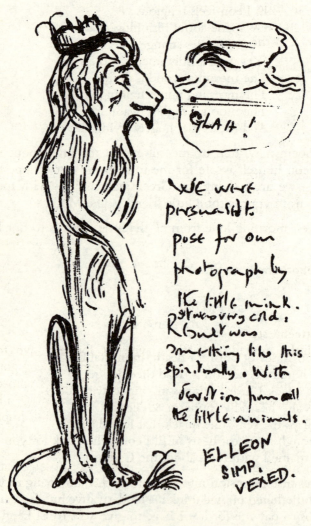

Figure 13

5

Sra Harteebeeste
BY ARCTIC THREE-TOED WOODPECKER
From Special Woodpeckerrands Inc.

QUIZ.

WHO has four paws, a fine mane, & claws, is both carnivorous yet kind to *all* animals, is a leader of an orchestra, a constellation, a sign of the zodiac, and at the same time a King?

Who has four gleaming hooves, a beautiful coat, & is both herbiverous yet kind to all little plants and flowers *and* little animals, is shy yet beloved of all in the forest, and is known by all, famous, yet famous for her modesty, & at the same time, a Queen?

Who runs a laundry yet often lives up a tree?
Who flies & swims & yet rides in state to town?

—

Such intelligent & *perplexing* questions, to the answers for each of which will be a *handsome* prize, form the substance of a new radio program for all the little animals that is to be sponsored by El Leon himself at his new radio station. This is just a little note to bring you this good news & to reiterate our warmest & tenderest love to you our beloved Harteebeeste from those who now see you every day with love
Your faithful & loving
The Mergansers.

6

By RED PHALAROPE —

Beloved Harteebeeste.
— All the little animals send their sweetest fondest love to their Harteebeeste. The only news is this, that the rumour having got round that you were interested in fungi — the mink and others who did not quite understand that your interest was botanical, have made a large & impressive collection of stinkwood stinkhorus (ethyphallus impudicus) & candlewicks for you for Christmas. On being informed by myself that this might not please you, they have thrown away their collection, if rather reluctantly, & going to do something else to surprise you at Xmas. Have you seen the Lion of Oz, playing downtown? All love to you my sweetest most beloved Harteebeeste
from
The Pronghorn

7

> Senora Harteebeeste
> By mink
> for mink
>   about mink
>   – oh shame.

Oh my sweet harteebeeste, I hurt my *little* paw coming through the snow faithfully to deliver the *jaeger's gay* message – it is the first time such a message has been lost – but I *couldn't* find it, & oh, I was heartbroken, but it shall be found & brought to-morrow faithfully – meantime all this has a *happy* ending – for the *seal* saw my plight & invited me down to his cosily furnished *retreat* & gave me camomili tea & bound my paw with rare sea-herbs – meantime never have all the little animals felt such warmth of love for thee oh sweetest harteebeeste please think of me as always your faithful little

> The Mink.

P.S. The weather is getting nice again now—perhaps you will take *another* photograph of me, as before? So precious to me. This is not the right letter – to-morrow I will deliver it – oh shame! – bad writing due to paw.

8

> Courtesy of all the little animals;
> with love.

> LIO-NOL sleeping tablets
> BEBE LIONCOLA BUEN FORTE

This is just
a little letter
to convey our love to you
oh Harteebeeste & to announce
that we shall be shortly back to see
you all after our recent taking of the   Figure 14
waters. The above is a copy of a little picture of me
taking a snooze while recently climbing a mountain –
note sunburn. With great love.   EL Leon Imp.Rex.

9

> By an exaltation of Loving Larks!

immeasurable depths }
> the chapter will be great!
fathomless bliss }

With love love love from all your sweet little animals, & little flowers too, including the golden day lilies, with so much gratitude

from
EL Seal MA. & EL Leon Imp.Rex.F.R.S.
Duktors of Literature

10

> By Telopronhornic Special Delivery

5.15 pm Pronghorncingo Urgente
Sweet Deduckly
> Extremely anxious lest my previous message may have
> suffered some damage stop since my messenger stop has
> bad temper and may have caught horns in bushes stop if
> so will punish him severely stop therefore repeat
> previous teleprong sending this Special delovery to
> your telepathic address quote darling will you please
> please be my valentine I love you so unquote stop sug-
> gest perhaps we might play a little ginrummy tonight am
> hastening to you on my sleigh with bells unquote your
> Pronghorn.

This is historical document being first draft of cable from pronghorn evidently written in snow to his mate Witness hurried hoofmarks of this gracious beast as he struggles with difficult form

Rules & memorandum for Travelling on Lone Duck Limited Flyer.

1/ Be careful of herons – though our special duckplex roof affords both facility of vision and adequate protection.
2/ when in doubt have a happy thought.
3/ look out for new ideas for work for a/ you
>> b/ us
& any flying words phrases notices etc for
>> c/ me
4/ Remember that into every writers life must fall:
>> a/ some rain
>> b/ some doldrums.

5/ Study the expression on people's faces: Where are they going? Whither? Whence? Why? What are they for?

6/ Use general deductions from this as means to feel cheerful in gloomy mood, if any.

7/ Moral: be happy.

8/ Remember I shall be thinking of you all time, & working hard

9/ The house & garden will also be thinking of you & I of them.

All love, my darling
    from your devoted

                El Lion

II

              JAEGERPOST.

Beloved Harteebeeste:

What a time we had my dear at the christening party for the Gadwall's 'Egg' – oh how we wish you could have been there – such rugs & jugs & candlelights! At the last moment El Leon turned up in the Bleriot whippet's Car, so our happiness was complete, or it would have been had our dear Harteebeeste been there. But then everybody drank so many toasts to you in rosepetal wine that things *started to happen*! First there was a beautiful exhibition of NORTHERN LIGHTS which El Leon insisted had been put on by himself as an advertisement for '*A meat car named Desire*' – & then El Leon insisted too that the Gadwall's egg be baptised LEO Gadwall, which we ducks thought a little unsuitable, especially as the Gadwall is convinced that it is a girl. And at the height of the excitement the Gadwall laid *another* egg: so here we are – to day we have our bills swathed in wet towels, & an acute case of Ducksenjammer! Hope you like our little bit of news – with devotion all love to you, our sweetest Harteebeeste, from all the little animals.

              Love from the Jaegers &
              the shearwaters

I2

              BY SEASERPENT

My dear –

We have had yet another christening party, and oh my dear what a time, – What happened was this: the Gadwall has laid yet another egg, in fact a double-yoked egg. What a scandal too! For the rumour has gone round that it is a turkey egg. At all events this morning we can scarcely fly let alone walk: our beaks are swathed in dock leaves; and our poor webbed feet ache, so forgive us if to-day our communication is a little stilted. But that even under such circumstances as this we can *still* find time to send you a little message of love & devotion, oh most beloved Harteebeeste, is surely a tribute to that love – like yeast, oh Harteebeeste – with devotion

(What were) The
Mergansers

13

Very sweet duck:

Through those grasses!	I have crashed through to a sort of working copy of the whole, though I can only brief you *verbally* on the typing etc. Though I've re-written the very end the	Hammer & tongs!
Straighten that propellor!	next to last few pages involve a few more notes & alternatives etc I could finish up while you type to-morrow morning. –	Through that mud!
Mind those mosquitoes!	not more than a hour's work in all *now*; (Take away those leeches – lift me up, take them away!)	Bingo, over those falls!

Your loving
El Leon

14

BY MINK

Use *quink*
Sent by *mink*

Just a little note from a *very* old friend who thinks of his sweet hartee-beeste *all* the time, hoping that she is very well & happy, as everybody says you are. I came down to see you to-day but you were out — I took the liberty of looking through the window however (since I knew you would permit this to as close a friend as I) & saw a very strange sight, my dear: Spooky sitting at the desk, looking through a dictionary, & occasionally writing something in an elegant hand, & El Leon upon the floor devouring a huge slab of cheese from Spooky's plate. Yesterday I went into Woodwards & who should I find but El Leon there too. He has written a best seller, you know, recently, called The Left Claw is the Dreamer, & was there signing copies, & purring very happily. I understand the book is a little *stark*. I am busy at my music. I send all my deepest love to all the little animals, and of course to you, my sweetest, most beloved one & only Harteebeeste

Great love from
The Pronghorn.

15

CAT POSTAL

Just another little card from your
northern friend to say that I am
speeding with all possible haste to
be with you on Hallow'een. In
addition to the foxtail shakers I
am bringing you a little jewelled
cask of snowberry wine — specially
aged by my *special* process. I send
all love to you my sweetest harteebeeste but must point out am a little
surprised by the stamp on the new
type postcard I bought. It seems
that it has El Leon upon it in his
'winter coat' sitting among the
northern lights in what I think he
meant to be a parka but looks to me
like a bowler hat while your poor
little arctic fox is relegated to —
well you can see for yourself. well
I am happy if he is, & you are.
With all sweetest devotion to you my
dearest dear from your affectionate

The Arctic Fox

Figure 15

Sra Harteebeeste

The 'Lovecot'

Duckland,

Canarda

16

By EL LEON, IMP REX,
With love forever.
(Our dignity does not permit us to make any
statement upon what has occurred.)

Giant New Year's Note of Welcome for their belovedest Harteebeeste from all
the little animals of the lovecot!

– We *all* came round to-day to give you a little surprise in your absence
by cleaning up everything so sweetly for you: all but one, that is – you
guessed it – who was already loyally here: when we arrived the seal had
already left certain indelible marks of his oh so well-meaning helpful-
ness: the wood for one thing was set upon the table which we thought
would not please you – but even we ourselves were not able to get the
wood into perhaps the right place. And then while we were doing that
in & out went the dear seal with the lamps – not knowing – as how
should he know living as he does – whether they were full or not. And
how should *we* know, though we looked, but so fearful were we for the
floor at that point that we looked no further though at the next moment
the seal was to be heard in the woodshed tossing sacred & profane wood
together with great exultant flips. Lastly having with the greatest difficulty dissuaded him from having his afternoon dip in the well – about
which he manifested not unnaturally the *extremest* curiosity – we left
him – upon El Leon's advice who has been royally helping too –
balancing bottles which he was emptying upon his gallant nose – left
him, because we already hear thy hoofs approaching through the forest,
oh beloved, & must make haste, hoping you will not be offended at our
ill-conceived but well-meaning plans & especially not with your dear
sweet seal! – With love eterne from *all* the little animals

As from your affectionate
little

The *Mink*

17

By special shearwaterexpress.
(transcribed by Shearwatograph)

The shearwaters came flying to see you yesterday but were put off by 4
Greater Hawksbeards with telescopes binoculars troglodytes and human
infants but came again bravely we feel to see you the hartebeeste to-day
bringing love to you ps what is the matter with El Leon – has someone
taken him away to band him perhaps?

love the shearwaters

18

By Captain Horatio Pronghornblower

With devotion eterne from all your little animaux

Welcome Home
Oh braveheart-eebeeste!

Sursum pawda!
With devoted duckdom
Hold that quack

EL Leon
Imp Rex

19

BY HOUND

Beloved Harteebeeste –
While I was coming to pay an informal call upon the Harteebeeste I discovered an extremely flustered and angry El Leon in the forest dancing
around and roaring and clanging one spur – he feared he had lost the
other. He also was unable, so he said, to tie his black tie which he had
considerably injured while attempting to. Gathering that the noble beast
was attending a formal occasion with his beloved, and since I always
carry a little store of snow white ties on my journeys for emergencies
just such as this I lent him one of mine and tied it for him. When I last
saw him it was under one ear and I was not able to replace the lost spur.
But I have seen to it that his hooves are clean and at the moment he is
somewhat angrily shaving his mane. May you both have a very good
time & a happy one. With true true love your devoted

The Arctic Fox

20

HARTEBEESTEGRAM

CAPE FLATTERY

OCEANS OF LOVE TO THEE OH BELOVED HARTEBEESTE STOP WE ARE
SAILING ENDLESSLY OVER THE SUNLIT WAVES WITH YOU EVER IN
OUR SEABIRDS HEARTS STOP WE WILL SHEER BACK SOON OVER THE
INTERVENING WATERS STOP LOVE TO ALL THE LITTLE ANIMALS IN
THE LOVECOT AND ENDLESS LOVE TO THEE THE GOOD

SHEARWATERS

Appendix 2

In the course of preparing the *Collected Letters* it has often been necessary to consult incoming letters, contracts, and other items that shed light upon Lowry or upon comments that he makes in his letters. These documents are not easily summarized in annotations; the few that follow will hopefully be of use and interest. For further examples of letters to Lowry, see the appendices in *Selected Letters*.

1939 *Lowry greatly prized this letter from John Buchan, Lord Tweedsmuir. He sent it to his father to prove that he had the highest support and to Harold Matson with the 1940 manuscript of* Under the Volcano; *see letters* **129**, **143**, **144**, *and* **165**. *Lowry thought the letter had been lost, but the original is with the Harold Matson Papers.*

Government House,
Ottawa
14 December 1939

Malcolm Lowry, Esq.,
c/o Major Carey,
595 W. 19th Avenue,
Vancouver, B.C.

Dear Mr Lowry,

    I was very glad to hear from you, but I am sorry to learn that you have been seedy. I hope you will soon be all right. I had a note from McTavish about you, and he will do all he can. Colonel Tobin is a capital fellow.

I shall be delighted to see your new book when it is ready.
With kindest regards and all good wishes.

Yours very sincerely,

Tweedsmuir

1940 *The following letter to Lowry from Harold Matson (UBC 1:45) carried the unwelcome news that Martha Foley had rejected* Under the Volcano. *Her reasons stung Lowry, who was forced to acknowledge that she was correct; see letters* **146, 153, 156, 163,** *and* **205.**

Matson and Duggan,
630 Fifth Avenue,
New York
7 October 1940

Dear Malcolm:

Under the Volcano came up to me from Whit Burnett and I have talked about it to Harcourt, Brace & Company. They have definitely rejected it after examining it.

Here is what Martha Foley wrote:

'We have had several readings on Malcolm Lowry's *Under the Volcano*. It is a very unusual book but one that we feel does not quite emerge from under the burden of the author's preoccupation with what might be described as the Dunn [sic] theory of time. We have been so interested in what Malcolm has been trying to do that we hate to give this as our decision.'

I enclose a note from Robert Lamont, of Harcourt, Brace.

Now it is with Duell, Sloan & Pearce. Pearce, you may remember, was interested in you before, when he was editor of Harcourt, before he started his own firm with his two pals.

The Last Twist of the Knife has been to Doubleday and Reynal & Hitchcock, and is now with Dodd Mead.

I enclose my own reader's report on Margerie Bonner's work, which she may find interesting and if it moves her to want to do any more work on it I will be glad to hear about that.

Best wishes,

Hal

1947 *In January 1947 Malcolm and Margerie were holidaying in Haiti en route to New York City for the publication of* Under the Volcano. *The following letter of praise from Jimmy Stern is a one-page typescript with holograph postscript in the Lowry Collection (UBC 1:64).*

207 East 52nd St
New York 22
6 January 1947

In a hot confusion of guilt, my dear Malcolm, a confusion of guilt! And before I tread another step, the top of the morning to you and, a trifle belatedly, the tiptop of the year. By all the stars and portents, it should be propitious for the Novelist: does it not close with a Seven on its rump, its four digits add up to Vingt-et-Un, its as yet pubic-hairless little body beautifully divisible by the magic number Three!

To fla-fall, I mean – flatly into platitudes, my honored & talented friend, thank you for your card, your seasonable greetings, your warmth of expression (which you still wear like my Papa, The Major, his military moustache), for remembering so unfailingly one of my early *contes*, and finally for encountering, in some typically Malcolmian manner, one of my latest (according to this city's *Times*) 'delightful Irish lullabies' – God rot the reviewer's wretched little soul!

Since my telegram of cheers hardly a night has passed, need I tell you? that I have not dined out, wined out and thought myself into alcoholic slumbers on the *Volcano*. ('Oh tell us, tell us, Jimmy Stern, what's he *like*?' – 'Oh you moronic miseries you, you you and you, by their works shall Great Men be known! Read and get thee hence! A flea's phart could be heard further than your loudest scream!')

O friend, am I to write you a book about your epic? Have patience, and have my love, you have done a mighty deed. Praise and damnation will ring in your ears, and you will live. By the highest standards you deserve to be judged, but that will not be your lot, for there are not more than two or three in 140 million competent. And of these I, alas, am not one. I am the tired salmon, a worn and scraggy fish, making fishy-goggle eyes at the moby-blubber blunderer, the Whale. The skinny salmon swoons and makes his little leaps, the Whale squirts, rolls, belches, moans and groans and finally, with one horrendous subterranean phart, moves a mountain, an inch.

Blitz-burrp, blitz-burrp, phone, fone – phucka-doodle-dandyo.
Bungho, old chap, see you tomorrow. Splendid weather, wot? (Fair
split my sides!)

[unsigned]

[P.S.] Jan 10. When do you arrive in N.Y.? A room will be got for you
somehow; you are by no means unknown by this date. The city buzzes
with your name. I'm told Aiken has just arrived from Eire. Who else do
you know here?

1950 *This addendum to Malcolm Lowry's 1950 contract with Ernst Klett for the
German translation and rights on* Under the Volcano *has been translated by
Gabriele Helms. See Lowry's 8 December 1951 letter (**484**) to Harold Matson.*

Ernst Klett Verlag
   Contract

ADDENDUM
to contract dated 30 October 1950

Mr Malcolm Lowry, c/o Harold Matson, 30 Rockefeller Plaza, New
York 10, N.Y.

and the Ernst Klett Verlag, Stuttgart-W, Rotebuhlstr. 77, licence
number US-W-1023.

hereby agree to adopt the following amendment to the contract dated
October 30, 1950:

Mr Malcolm Lowry also tranfers the film rights to the book 'Under the
Volcano' to the publishing house. Both parties will participate equally
in any net proceeds from realization of these rights. The publishing
house undertakes to provide Mr Lowry with information pertaining to
any potential proceeds.

In the event of any claims arising under this contract, the place of
fulfillment and jurisdiction is Stuttgart.

Dollarton   Stuttgart
                                                      27 November 1950
[unsigned]   [for Ernst Klett]

1951 *In his 23 April 1951 letter* **(455)** *to Clemens ten Holder, Lowry describes his stay in Bonn in 1928 and praises his German language teacher Karlheinz Schmidthüs. As fate would have it, ten Holder knew Schmidthüs, who had become an editor with Herder publishing in Freiburg. Ten Holder wrote to Schmidthüs and received the following reply, which he then sent to Lowry (UBC 1:67). The translation is by Gabriele Helms.*

7 May 1951

Mr Clemens ten Holder,
Flacht,
District of Leonberg/.. Wttbg.

Dear ten Holder!

I remember Lowry very well because among all the students I had in Bonn – and some of them were bright, intelligent, even brilliant – he was one of the most remarkable figures; he was very sullen, very confused, very unhappy, but without doubt he had a somehow ingenious talent that he was well on his way to ruining completely in those days. The greatest worry was that he drank rather a lot and as a result often sank into a state of complete mental and emotional helplessness. I knew that he was gifted as a poet and writer, but I can't remember where I knew that from. Because he did not show any of that. Only when he played jazz music at the piano could one notice something unusual. I do not know why he remembers me so well because I had little to do with him as a teacher. Of course, I was very interested in him and I would have liked to help him in the fatal situation he was in in those days. But generally he did not let anybody get very close to him. It is obvious, however, that it is never useless to take loving care of a young person in spite of all difficulties. I am happy that he became a poet in the end. Since you translate him, I assume that he must be a good writer. Please give my regards to him. I will get the book and maybe I will write to him once again when I have read it.

As to the game 'bumblepuppy,' it was an awful thing. It takes place around a three- or four-metre-long post to which a rope is attached; at the end of the rope hangs a leather ball at about the chest height of the players. There are two players who hold a piece of wood with which they hit the ball so that the rope has to twist itself around the post. The goal is to twist the rope around the post in one's own direction and to keep the other player from doing the same for himself. The game is played until everybody is dripping with sweat and completely exhausted. There is no German name for the game. The only place where I have seen it in Germany was in our garden in Bonn. [. . .]

Kind regards from your
Karlheinz Schmidthüs

1957 *John Davenport, who had come down to Ripe at Margerie's urgent request, managed the necessary business of Lowry's funeral and notified family and friends of events. The original of this letter, received by Harold Matson on 8 July 1957, is with the Matson files.*

4 Rossetti House,
Flood Street,
London, S.W. 3,
1 July 1957

Dear Mr Matson,

You will be distressed to hear of the sudden death of Malcolm Lowry, which occurred on Thursday, June 27th. I am his literary executor, and Mrs Lowry asked me to get in touch with you. She is at:

The White Cottage,
Ripe,
Nr. Lewes,
Sussex

The funeral will take place there on Wednesday, July 3rd.

I am sorry to be the medium through which you hear this grievous news.

Yours sincerely,
John Davenport

P.S. I shall be seeing Alfred Knopf within the next few days. Would you be very kind & pass this on to Conrad Aiken & Harvey Breit? They are both friends of mine, but I am overwhelmed with immediate problems connected with this business & shall write them personally later.

J.D.

Appendix 3

There are twenty miscellaneous items transcribed for this appendix. These include drafts, fragmentary letters, two late discoveries, and inscriptions by Lowry. They range, in date of composition, from at least as early as 1931 to possibly as late as 1957. Very few of these items can be dated with certainty; thus, their order here must be viewed as tentative. I have concluded the appendix with Lowry's prayer to God for dramatic reasons because it could have been written at any time during Lowry's struggle with *October Ferry to Gabriola*.

It is always possible that additional letter fragments will be located amongst Lowry's papers, although a thorough search of the manuscripts and notebooks has been conducted by myself at UBC and other archives, and by Shari Urban and Kathy Chung. Not every last scrap of possible letter draft or fragment has been transcribed. The editorial decision to include or exclude an item was determined on the basis of the following criteria: the status of the fragment or draft had to be unequivocally that of a written communication (whether in the form of a letter, a poem, or an inscription) with a clear addressee, whether or not the addressee was fully identifiable; the lack of a date, inside address, or signature did not, in itself, disqualify anything, but the item had to reveal something of literary, biographical, factual, or epistolary interest.

The following fragment was written in a hardbound notebook acquired by the Malcolm Lowry Collection in November 1994. From the context it is clear that Lowry is writing to Conrad Aiken from Cambridge and that this fragment is a

draft for or part of his 15 June 1931 letter (34), in which he mentions sending Aiken Clifford Bax's play Socrates *from* Six Plays *(1931). Lowry's allusion to 'my fixation on the sea' suggests that he was planning another voyage, which we know he made in August 1931 in the hope of meeting Nordahl Grieg in Norway.*

1: To: Conrad Aiken

P: UBC (ms)

[Cambridge]
[ca June 1931]

even though I should reach Homer

Straining at particles of light in the midst of a great darkness. Besides I can't read Homer, he's a bloody bore. I would like to *talk* to you (I very much want to at this minute), & to read you im Dauerzustand, – that means Ewigkeit; Homer may have roared in the pines, but he's not Aiken. Aiken, Keats, Shakespeare, Socrates – ah, good men all! Now I'm getting on to ground on which I can talk. You've spoiled me for nearly all the metaphysicals – I even despair of Donne just for about 5 poems, & some of the Anniversary – Hall, I like, Marvell – scarcely anyone else, Herrick is awful, Herbert, Carew, Randolph, Waller shit, Milton I can't read – Spenser, my god, what a writer: Dryden I can't read: Restoration comedy makes me sick, to like it anyway is a pose, like liking most greek tragedy: Browning, yes, to a certain extent, Rossetti sometimes, Hopkins sometimes, Pope sometimes, Peacock yes: Tolstoy, Christ what a breeze! What a bloody writer! argh! . . . I must read more Dostoievsky. I must read Dante. . . I must read, – I must read, – I must learn another language.

Of course to go a walking tour somewhere would do a hell of a lot of good, would succeed at once in doing the hardship, the finer scenes, the grander mountains etc and in your company I should move hugely towards the subtle & sophisticated: but my fixation on the sea is complete, & moreover I feel honestly I haven't extracted all the juices from it yet.

I must tell you that there has been a play written called *Socrates* by Clifford Bax which I have read & isn't at all bad, but not really good: there're too many pipes of pan, & fauns, & females playing leaden flutes: & Aristophanes gets hiccups: which reminds one that I saw The Antigone & The Lysistrata Exceedingly well done at the Festival here the other day – the Antigone's a bit of a bore, but it was bloody well produced, staged, lit, & acted: & I laughed more at the Lysistraita, which was more or less produced as a musical comedy, than I have at anything for many years. You shall have the play by Clifford Bax on Socrates

I am a little bit fearful of this letter being crossed with one of yours
which may be, deservedly, both angry and cruel.

long ago yo ho.
far away
yo hai.
Malc

hold the fort for essa cometh

2: To Unidentified [Nordahl Grieg?]

P: H(ms)

St Catharine's College,
Cambridge
[ca 1931]

I have thought of writing to you[1] for some years and I suppose this
letter is the esemplastic result of a good deal of consideration. I remember thinking at the time that I would first get something published on
my own account

[breaks off unsigned]

Annotations:

1 Lowry is probably referring to Nordahl Grieg, whom he would meet
   in September 1931 and whose novel *The Ship Sails On* he had discovered late in 1929. This letter fragment has been drafted on the verso
   of a manuscript page of *Ultramarine* and addressed from St Catharine's
   College, both of which details confirm that Lowry was not writing to
   Conrad Aiken, whom he met before going up to Cambridge.

3: To Margerie Bonner Lowry

P: H(ms)

[Dollarton]
[ca Summer 1940][a]

MARGIE
  darling
This is A Reminder
To get some suntan oil
Downtown Granville
Else we'll
be burnt to a cinder
I'll
be on my way now to the beaches,

there to contemplate the lice & leeches!
– & doom of Rays (not Sun's)[1] – & other son's
of so & so's.

LOVE
MALC

also
some pipe tobacco
of which there is a marked lacko.

Annotations:

1 A regular feature of the *Vancouver Sun* was a children's column called
the 'Sun Ray Club,' with a bedtime story and birthday greetings.

Editorial Notes:

a. Lowry has written this note on the back of a 17 June 1940 letter from
Aiken.

The following three letters (4, 5, *and* 6)*are in a special category. The only extant
copy-text for each appears to be the version transcribed into the draft material for*
Dark as the Grave *by Margerie between 1950 and 1952 so that the whole
'bolus' could be safely stored in a bank vault (UBC 9:21-22). Although the
addressee is certain for each letter and the dates can be determined for two of them,
they have not been placed in the chronological sequence of letters because of the
unusual status of the copy-texts.*

Readers of Under the Volcano *and of the general introduction to this collection in volume I will know that Lowry frequently incorporated his own and
other peoples' letters into his fiction. I would go so far as to say that letters are
important documents in the construction of his fiction, although the eventual narrative is not epistolary. Indeed, Lowry intended these letters to his father, J.D.
Smith, and Miles Went to be used as letters in* Dark as the Grave.

*The evidence for this narrative strategy lies in the notes Lowry wrote to him-
self and Margerie and that she typed up contiguously with passages of exposition,
dialogue, and raw document. For example, at one point Lowry notes (and
Margerie transcribes):*

(The following material in the form of letters may
be useful either in Dark as the Grave – perhaps in
the form of letters themselves as the abridged letter
to Conrad might be useful in (1) on the plane He read
the letter again, still not posted, or as an exposi-

tion in Eridanus, or Dark as the Grave. . . Guillaume Demares.) *[UBC 9:22, 664]*

The 'letter to Conrad' that follows this passage is, in fact, Lowry's October 1945 letter (205) to Conrad Aiken.

Regarding the letter to Mr Smith, Lowry comments: '(He [Sigbjørn] composes a letter in his head – what he ought to have said – either that or he writes it in El Paso finishes it on the plane' (UBC 9:22, 677). Then, at the end of the letter, which is unsigned, Lowry's commentary continues with the following important thematic explanation:

This letter is put in, both as evidence of the bad omens piling up, the half-affectionate, half-guilty attitude (why?) of Wilderness toward the past, the Wilderness attitude toward 'house', but above all to lend an added pathos to the situation of Primrose, and another loving reason why Sigbjørn should want her to have a good holiday. But surely there is yet another meaning for the human condition in this: it is as if

the Wildernesses were being stripped of everything

they had, preparatory to their new journey or as a punishment, or for a new birth. *[UBC 9:22, 681]*

From time to time within the text of each letter Lowry uses his characters' names, Sigbjørn and Primrose, and I have let these stand for two reasons. It is now impossible to say exactly what pronouns or nouns were used in the actual letter (assuming there were actual letters); therefore, any change from the typescript would be speculation. Moreover, by leaving the copy-text intact, it is possible to capture Lowry in the act of transforming one kind of text into another and blurring generic boundaries in the process.

4: To Arthur O. Lowry

P: UBC(ts)

[Vancouver]
[ca Fall 1939]

[Dear Father:]

. . . I do not know, naturally, what Mr Parks charged you for my journey up. But when it is considered that $85 worth of clothes – necessary, I grant you – were bought for me without a murmur last month I am forced to the conclusion that, having regard to the importance of my returning to the States at that time to wind up my affairs and collect manuscripts, which it took 5 valuable months for Mr Parks to send me only in part, you would not, had you been informed as to the true importance and slight cost – only $25 – of my trip, and to the true facts of its necessity immediately, after having obtained a visitor's visa, have objected to my going. I do not even know whether you were informed that I even received a visitor's visa, which was the only reason given me by Mr Parks for coming to Canada in the first place. It is No. 225, given me on Sept. 15, and I was told by the Consul to use it immediately. That I delayed as long as I did proved fatal, but why in the light of having been told to use it by the Consul, in the light of the fact that A.B. Carey knew perfectly well that I had it and that if it were to be any good I should have to use it, could any attempt, a failure though it was, (since you had refused to let me go on what I was certain were false grounds grounds upon which you had been misinformed) possibly be construed as ill-advised. What could I do? How could I write any longer? The objection was made on the grounds that it would cost too much, so I raised the money *myself* . . . (From Primrose, Sigbjorn thought).

Now I say that A.B. Carey is legislator over my morals, my soul, etc. because I am allowed to make absolutely no decisions for myself, – under the circumstances in which I am placed I cannot have any friends, that is I cannot accept any invitations from any worth while people for I cannot return it and cannot explain why (which seemed, Sigbjorn that, a hell of a reason) – I am so closely watched and supervised about money that I cannot even buy a toothbrush or have my hair cut without asking permission – I have received no!!! sympathy or encouragement in my work and was at one time actually held up for three weeks because they wouldn't get me supplies I needed at the stationer's and I could not get them myself because I had not sufficient money. I do not cite these things because they are important in themselves or taken separately, but it is their collective effect of constant humiliation and of being treated like a moron or a child that I feel I have a right to object to, principally because I know that however much my own actions may have contributed to my being treated this way in the past, that you would never treat me in this way, especially as I am, with all these things against me, trying to make a tremendous effort to justify myself, to you . . . (my typist even has stolen my work and I have had to bribe her with 25% of its extremely unlikely profits to get it back again)[1] And, finally, I have, immediately ahead of me the most difficult and exacting of the work that I have set myself to do in the next few months. With the situation becoming more critical, it may be that I shall have a shorter time than even I thought before joining up. The next few months are possibly the most important ones in my life and all I shall ever have in which to finish my work . . . At a time when you yourselves are making such sacrifices, however little you may think of me, you cannot think so basely of me that you would truly believe my intention was purely to be frivolous at your expense. No, and no again! The declaration of war has had the precisely opposite effect, for by limiting the extent of time at my disposal, it has grimly brought home to me the fact that if I am to prove my worth I must do so immediately and with all the energy I can command . . . Later I shall have something very decided to say about the really black news you have heard of me – in one there was a case of mistaken identity, the other was a pure 'frame up' – The only fault that attached to me was that I knew such people, but of all the other things into which my rare excursions into journalism have led me, Parks knows nothing . . . Perhaps these things were not so black, and most of them never happened as has been described to you . . . When eventually you get the whole story, which you will never be able to get from Mr Parks, or Mr Dalton (Mr Dalton was the Mexican lawyer who was so and so)[2] or anywhere else, except myself, from me, piece by piece as it really was, you will have sometimes, I am desperately afraid, to laugh . . . But it would be simply false bravado, on the other hand, a final admission of failure, not to make the most of whatever time I have. There being no possibility of enlistment in any Canadian regiment at this period it would be stupid of me, I think on mature thought, to force that possibility by joining the Foreign Legion, or some such and rushing into the battle to 'expiate all.' What, after all, have I to expiate? Wasted time, you say. I am surprised as I now arrive at the final chapter of Under the Volcano, to discover how little time has actually been wasted, how carefully I have recorded the very anguish of that feeling of wasted time, to strike some piercing chord in the reader's heart (I hope) True, I have not been a success so far. But just you wait.

[unsigned]

Annotations:

1 The typist is Carol Phillips; see Lowry's 11 August 1939 letter (**94**) to her and his unfinished letter (**342**) to her from 1948.

2 Jesse Dalton was a lawyer with the Mexico City firm of Basham & Ringe, which Arthur Lowry had hired to watch his son during the difficult months of 1938, prior to his Malcolm's departure for Los Angeles on 23 July; see Bowker (240-43).

5: To John D. Smith

P: UBC(ts)

[Dollarton]
[ca Fall 1945]

My dear Mr Smith:[1] One of those awful sad misunderstandings apparently occurred on the phone between my wife and you this evening of the kind that time and doing nothing about only makes worse so I am writing to you to clear it up since for one thing my wife seems too sad and upset and hurt after talking to you to do anything herself – First, both my wife and myself look upon you and always will as a very dear friend indeed and also our dear benefactor – a kind of guardian angel in fact (guardian angel was good after Sir Thomas Brown) so that the very last thing in the world either of us would dream of doing would be to accuse you or Angela or anyone dear to you of anything whatsoever: the idea is unthinkable and preposterous: we would as soon think of accusing each other. That is the first point. It was entirely due to the usual difficulties of speaking on the phone and mutual incredulity and bafflement if you got any such idea as that: but on calmer reflection you must have known that it was fantastic yourself. Second: the responsibility of the clothes was and is entirely *our own*. We had no right to trespass on your generosity to keep those trunks there so long anyhow, and that we did so was partly due to the fact that I have been more or less immoblized by illness, that it was a great convenience to us because we lived so primitively out here with nowhere to put them, and my wife felt the clothes would be safer with you anyhow, and partly – or mostly – due to sentiment somehow or other we didn't want to sever the connection with that summer of 1940 when, though disastrous things were happening in the world, God was good enough to let us be so happy in your house, and somehow the clothes in the trunks were symbolical of that happiness and the house and somehow we liked to feel that you didn't want to sever the connection either. This was probably a bit selfish of us since the trunks undoubtedly put you to some trouble and are now putting you to some more, but nonetheless that was how we felt about it and still do, so that I for my part am strangely sorry to see the trunks at all, because, for that sentimental reason, I liked to think of them in your house. Well this is how the human heart works. Now many waters having passed under the bridge, we are thinking of going down to Los Angeles (Mexico) to visit my wife's family there so that she thought that now she would be able to wear her clothes again and of this she has been dreaming until Monday night when the trunks arrived when – lo and behold – no clothes.'

That is to say there were some clothes, including quite a few of mine, and some too of hers, but all the clothes she had been dreaming of wearing again and which she had brought up new from Los Angeles, were gone, with the result that she was heartbroken about it, and utterly at a loss, until we realised that it was all probably susceptible of some perfectly reasonable explanation, such as that they had been very reasonably put somewhere else for safety from the damp, which was why I got her to phone you without delay – would you not have done the same? It is true that Margie brought *some* clothes back from your house from time to time but not true that she brought all or even one quarter of what she had in the trunks – that I can swear to. You remember the last time she came in and you drove her back here she had only a small bag, Angela was there and they went through the trunks together and Angela would know that she only brought a few things and left the bulk, all her *good* things there, as a matter of fact a whole wardrobe is missing and nothing but old clothes left so there must be *some* explanation, since they have been carefully sorted – perhaps if you think you can find a clue – could it have happened when you moved? Specifically what is missing is: 1 black dress trimmed with black fringe: 1 plain black silk dress, 1 black taffeta trimmed with white pearl buttons: 1 powder blue crepe: 1 American beauty crepe: 1 pale green moire with crystal buttons: 1 black silk printed with blue stars: 1 green dinner dress trimmed with gold: 2 beautiful lace blouses: 1 grey lace with a bolero jacket: 2 silk night-gowns: 1 black hat: 1 green taffeta trimmed with black lace lingerie suit. These clothes are all the pretty clothes that Margie has painstakingly collected and, since we lost nearly everything else in our fire, are about all she has: I can buy her new clothes of course, but can never replace these, as such things are virtually unpurchasable today, nearly all of the dresses being pure silk, but the point is, not their value, so much as that she is heartbroken to lose them, if they are indeed lost, which I cannot believe. But they are certainly not in the trunks and she certainly never brought them back here so, I repeat, there must be some perfectly reasonable explanation. Now, I repeat, the clothes are absolutely our responsibility. No responsibility whatsoever attaches to you for them. But I'm sure you will agree that I could scarcely do other than advise her to phone you about it, since I am supposed to keep off my feet myself just now. And though you are not obliged in the slightest to do anything about the matter yourself I would count it as the very greatest of favours if you could – in fact I implore you to try – try and find out what has happened to them, much as I hate to put you to any further trouble – Margie has written to Angela but has had as yet no reply. But you know us well enough to know that we wouldn't make up a story like this out of whole cloth, or whole silk, you know we are friends, so please do not be angry with us, as that hurts us very much. As for any accusations whatsoever, that is absurd, as you know, I was very glad to hear that your eyes were so much better, and very many congratulations on your marriage. Margie was delighted to meet your charming wife – may you both be very happy. Please forgive me again for all this rigma-role and for putting you to this trouble, but believe me, yours most faithfully –

[unsigned]

Annotations:

1 John D. Smith, a Vancouver building contractor, and his wife Hanna
met the Lowrys in May 1940 when the couple moved into a spare room
in the Smiths' West Eleventh Avenue home in Vancouver. Angela, the
Smiths' daughter, was working as a nurse in 1940; she married Alfred
McKee. The Smiths and McKees maintained their friendship and a
correspondence with the Lowrys, but no other letters appear to have
survived; see Salloum (44-51).

6: To Miles Went

P: UBC(ts)

[Dollarton]
[n.d.]

Dear old Whitey:[1] I am of the confirmed opinion that I lost, or at any
rate, mislaid my by no means good limey temper the other night and my
sense of humour (temporarily) and since I have an obscure feeling that
this may have rankled, whether you or I admit it or not, I write this to
make matters clear . . . When you say, of yourself, 'The doctor tells me
that I have not got cancer,' I say 'Good, well, you don't have that to
worry about anymore.' While I am of course, at liberty to think what I
please, it would not as a matter of fact, occur to me, nor is there any
good reason why it *should* occur to me, to think 'Well, you probably
have cancer, after all, or if not that, something else malignant': but far
less would I say, or subtly intimate – the human mind being what it is –
such a thing. But the real reason why I would not say it would surely be
because (the doctor having decided that your illness was something not
to be too alarmed about, whatever it was) there would be no earthly
point in saying it, unless I wanted to sow a pessimistic destructive and
groundless thought in your mind for reasons, conscious or unconscious,
of my own –

[breaks off unsigned]

Annotations:

1 'Whitey,' Miles Went, one of the Lowrys' friends on the beach at
Dollarton, served as the model for the character Kristbjorg in 'The
Forest Path to the Spring.' This version of the letter, within the typescript of *Dark as the Grave* (UBC 9:22, 686), breaks off without a
signature but with the following line: 'Sigbjorn abandoned the stupid
letter.'

7: To Banco Nacional, Cuernavaca

P: UBC(ms)

[Quinta Eugenia,]
[Acapulco,] [Mexico]
[20 March 1946]ᵃ

– Gentlemen –

Two weeks ago I wrote to my bank in Canada, Bank of Montreal 500 Granville St, Vancouver BC, to send me $300 Canadian to your Banco Nacional de Mexico or whatever bank you deal with here in Cuernavaca. In the meantime I have gone to Acapulco & will be very grateful if you will wire the money to me here in Acapulco at once as this is very urgent.[1]

This letter will introduce my wife who will introduce the necessary identifications.

Thanking you in advance [for your] service, I remain yours very sincerely

Malcolm Lowry

Annotations:

1 According to Day (355-65), the Lowrys settled into the Quinta Eugenia Hotel on Caleta Beach, Acapulco, on 13 March 1946, but were visited the next day by the local immigration authorities, who claimed that Lowry had an unpaid fine from 1938. This visitation marked the beginning of weeks of harassment and frustration for the Lowrys. On the twenty-first Margerie travelled back to Cuernavaca, taking a version of this letter from Malcolm as introduction, to get money from their bank and their identification papers, which they had left in their apartment.

Editorial Notes:

a. This signed pencil draft was written in one of the notebooks that Lowry kept during his 1946 trip to Mexico (UBC 10:11). Lowry intended to use it, along with several other items of actual correspondence, in 'La Mordida.' The letter is undated, but the contents suggest that it was composed on or about 20 March 1946; see annotation 1.

8: To Madame José

P: UBC(ms)

[Quinta Eugenia,] [Acapulco,] [Mexico]
[ca 3 April 1946][a]

Madame José[1]
– C'est difficile à dire en Francais. Alors. Mais nous serions bien heureux
si vous auriez – si vous voulez un cognac avec nous. Pardonnez-moi, le
cognac n'est pas cognac, c'est habanero. Je pense aussi que c'est possible
que le habanero n'est pas habanero. Malheureusement. Pero asi es la
vida. C'est la vie.

[breaks off unsigned]

Annotations:

1 Madame José may have been the owner or manager of the Hotel
Quinta Eugenia in Acapulco where the Lowrys stayed from 13 March
to 5 April 1946. Both she and her husband are mentioned by name in
the notebooks from this Mexican trip, which forms the basis for 'La
Mordida.'

Editorial Notes:

a. This letter fragment is written in pencil in a black notebook (UBC
14:18) that Lowry kept during his 1946 trip to Mexico. Most of the
entries in this notebook are dated and they are in chronological order;
the entry immediately preceding this one is dated 2–3 April. All the
material in the notebook is marked for 'La Mordida,' and this letter has
been typed, by Margerie, and included in a typescript draft of material
for that novel (UBC 14:2, 308).

9: To Mr Green

P: UBC(ms)

[Dollarton]
[1940?][a]

Dear Mr Green:[1]
– I agree with you utterly, not only as the husband & the writer, but
as the critic, but as the husband of the critic, the wife of the husband, &
also, on behalf of the writer who happens to be my wife, who agrees too.
So I may say does the writer, not to mention the protagonist.
But, my dear old fellow, my dear very good writer, the book does not
agree: that is, it will not.
In short, it is not so much a matter of telling Emily Bronte to cut
Lochwood out:[2] it is a question, rather more precisely, of Lochwood

[. . .]; who having been there for some time in necessity, refuses to take the trouble to point out to its reader that he shouldn't be there.

Read it again: & you will see its imperfections but beatify its perfection.

Think again: you don't have to, of course. Scribners brings it out this Oct.

Your suggestions might have made it a greater book.[3] But to my mind, such in part is as the author has already done it make it perfect.

Malcolm

Annotations:

1 Both the familiar tone of the letter and the informal signature suggest that Lowry is writing to someone he knows reasonably well; however, there is know way to confirm the identity of this addressee. The name 'Julian Green' has been written, possibly by Margerie, at the top right of the holograph, but this is almost certainly an error. In a message to Sherrill Grace of 28 October 1990, Julien Green said that he never received letters from Lowry and did not know him, although he was aware of Lowry's interest in his work and was particularly fond of *Under the Volcano* and Lowry's poetry. There are no Lowry letters in the Green Collection at the University of Virginia. Lowry discovered Julien Green in 1931 when he read *The Dark Journey* (1929); see his September 1931 letter (**36**) to Conrad Aiken. In his 6 September 1940 letter (**149**) to Harold Matson, he asks Matson to forward an enclosed letter for Green, and in his 6 September 1940 letter (**150**) to Aiken, Lowry mentions having suggested to Green that he contact Aiken. It is much more likely that this letter is to John Green, of Rodney Phillips & Green, whom Lowry knew at Cambridge, see letter **30** and Lowry's 1947 letter (**297**) to John Davenport.

2 Lockwood is the tenant of Thrushcross Grange to whom Ellen Dean tells the tragic story of Catherine and Heathcliff in Emily Brontë's *Wuthering Heights* (1847), and this reference suggests that Lowry is thinking of *Horse in the Sky*; see his comparison of Margerie's novel with Brontë's classic in his 7 August 1942 letter (**176**) to his sister- and mother-in-law.

3 Mr Green's suggestions for *Horse in the Sky* do not appear to have survived.

Editorial Notes:

a. The date of this letter is uncertain. 'Summer 1940' has been added at the top right of the holograph in what may be Margerie's writing. If the letter was intended for Julien Green, then it may be the one Lowry enclosed with his 6 September 1940 letter (**149**) to Matson, but see annotation 1. The reference to Margerie's novel *Horse in the Sky* suggests a spring 1947 date.

The following two letters to Vernon van Sickle were brought to my attention after Volume I had been published. They are of interest for the light they shed on the Lowrys' friendship with Vernon and Shirley van Sickle during the fall of 1946, when the Vancouver community was struggling to revive their local film society. The friendship between Malcolm and Vernon did not survive the latter's critical response to Under the Volcano *(see letter* **296-a***), but at this stage Malcolm was trying to help Vernon establish links with others in the film business. British documentary film-maker Stuart Legg (1910-88) came to Canada in 1939 to help John Grierson establish the National Film Board, and Gerald Noxon had extensive experience with films in England, Canada, and the United States; see Lowry's 15 October 1946 letter (***251***) to Noxon. My warmest thanks to Paul Tiessen who discovered these letters and put me in touch with Shirley van Sickle Allen.*

10: To Vernon van Sickle

P: private(ts)

Dollarton, B.C.,
15 October 1946

Dear Vernon:

Just a note to say I wrote to-day to Gerald Noxon telling him you would write him, itemizing the good work you were doing and mentioning some of the difficulties involved, particularly in regard to the British Institute.

By a coincidence the last time I heard from him was from Martha's Vineyard in Massachusetts, where this August he was staying with Stuart Legg, one of the co-workers on Night Mail, which by the way we both enjoyed tremendously at the Paradise on Sunday night.[1]

Thank you very much indeed for putting us up at the flat and for the fine time we had.

We are looking forward very much to seeing you and Shirley here – what about Friday? Bus leaves from ordinary terminal on Dunsmuir – I think you have to get tickets in the bus station. They are 45c and there's a slight saving on the return. Get off at Dollarton Post Office (which is Cummins' Store as Margie told you) where we'll be waiting at about 1:40 P.M. to escort you through the forest, your having taken the 1 o'clock bus, unless you let us know to the contrary.

It would be fine if you could spend the night, there is a shortage of blankets, as I think we said, so bring some if you can.

The amenities of the situation are a little difficult to explain and somewhat depend on the weather which I hope will be as heavenly as it is now: there is some space, and even another Cabinet of Dr. Caliglowry next door; but you will be able to see for yourself.[2]

At all events there are mountains, the forest, and the sea.

I think you have Noxon's address, if not, it is Gerald Noxon, P.O. Box 11, Niagara-on-the-Lake, Ontario.

Best regards to Shirley and yourself from Margerie and myself,

Hasta la vista,

Malcolm

Annotations:

1 *Night Mail* (1936), a 'film poem' about the London-Glasgow mail train, was produced by John Grierson for the British General Post Office (G.P.O.) film unit. Stuart Legg read the verse written by W.H. Auden, and the voice-over, together with the musical score composed by Benjamin Britten, was timed to match the rhythm of the train's wheels. Contemporary foreign films were screened at the downtown Vancouver Paradise Theatre.

2 This is a reference to one of Lowry's favorite German expressionist films: *The Cabinet of Dr Caligari* (1919). See Lowry's 2 November 1940 letter (**155**) to Gerald Noxon.

11: To Vernon van Sickle

P: private(ts)

[Dollarton]
[ca 25 November 1946]

Dear Vernon:

Owing to certain auxiliary and unforseen circumstances I haven't time to go into but which have bearing on a change of our plans, the state of the roof, the roofjack, and the virtual impossibility of getting any wood before we return, I'm sorry we can't at present let you have the key to the house as we promised: we're very sorry, but the total unfeasability of the idea, so roseate in gin fog, as well as the misleading-ness of it, did not become apparent until we returned to be confronted with new inundations of the high tide. I hope this does not put you and Shirley out too much but there it is. It would, in fact, only be involving you with an untenable responsibility.

Here enclosed is some more cheerful news. If Scott is mentioning therein what it would be tactless to intimate to others, try and swallow the toad after having first removed the jewel in its forehead for what it may be worth.[1]

Meantime we are writing to Herndon: perhaps we'll get in touch with Redgrave and so on.[2] It is not impossible Herndon might write you, but one ought to be more bloody careful about making promises that are dependent upon what so and so does or how they react. It gets to be a kind of progression, resembling what happened when the man with the beard in the Italian Straw Hat nudged his neighbour.[3]

We are ourselves let down at the moment in the matter of a cheque.

Please write respecting anything else to General Delivery, New Orleans.[4]

Our kindest regards to Shirley and Dorothy.[5] In haste –

Malcolm & Margerie

Annotations:

1 No enclosure is extant with this letter, but Lowry may be referring to remarks by Vancouver *Sun* columnist Jack Scott. The notion that a toad carries a jewel in its forehead derives from folklore and fable. This jewel, worn as a ring, was believed to protect its wearer against venom. Lowry could be thinking of the fairytale "Toads and Diamonds' or the lines from *As You Like It* II.1: 'Sweet are the uses of adversity; / Which, like the toad, ugly and venomous, / Wears yet a precious jewel in his head' (ll 12–14).

2 Richard Gilbert Herndon (1873-1958) was a New York theatre owner, producer, and impressario. No Lowry correspondence with him has been found to date. The English actor, Michael Redgrave, had been a friend of Lowry's at Cambridge, and he was one of the few people to whom Lowry wished to send a copy of *Under the Volcano*; see Lowry's December 1930 letter (**26**) to Conrad Aiken and his December 1946 letter (**263**) to Albert Erskine.

3 In *The Italian Straw Hat* (1927), a French film classic directed by René Clair, there is a comic wedding scene in which the guests nudge each other in what becomes a domino-like shove that sends a fat man off the end of the bench.

4 On 30 November 1946 the Lowrys left Dollarton to begin their trip to New Orleans, Haiti, and New York, where they arrived for the February 1947 publication of *Under the Volcano*; see letters **260** and **280**.

5 Dorothy Burritt (1910-63) worked for the National Film Board in Vancouver, and she and van Sickle organized the Vancouver Film Society screenings in 1946.

The following fragment is composed of 'key sentences from Malcolm Lowry's letter to Dr D.K. Kirk,' as copied into a notebook kept by Dr Kirk's brother, Lesley Kirk. The original letter has been lost, and the photocopy of the transcription of the sentences (UBC 2:11) shows four different dates in August 1947. The Kirk brothers – Downie, Lesley, and David – were all friends of Lowry's.

12: To Dr David Keith Kirk

P: UBC(c)

[Dollarton]
[8 August 1947]

Rather than make elaborate excuses I had better appeal to your sense of humour. . . . Not that I pretend to know *all* or *even any of the answers*: What I do know is that in the end all that one could be challenged with is *one's courage* or *lack of it*. . . . Be that as it may, I am glad it happened, whatever did happen.[1]

[unsigned]

Annotations:

1 A note accompanying the UBC copy says that on 11 August 1947 Lowry asked for help in translating the phrase 'article of merchandise' into French; see Lowry's 14 August 1947 letter (**316**) to Philippe Thoby-Marcelin.

13: To Alderson-Smith

P: UBC(ts)

[ca late 1949][a]

Dear Mr Alderson Smith:[1] I thought I would drop you a line to tell you how things progress here and also to ask a few questions. Quite recently I had a fall from my pier that did not seem serious. However I got no better, finally could not rise, and after repeated x-rays it was determined I had actually cracked my spine – technical phraseology, a slight wedge of the 4th dorsal body indicative of compression fracture here, with slight depression of its entero-superior margin. This fortunately means that it is the 4th vertebrae, so no lasting injury will result. On the other

[breaks off unsigned]

Annotations:

1 Alderson-Smith was one of the solicitors of Ayerton and Alderson-Smith of Dale Street, Liverpool, which represented the Lowry family. The firm had acted for Arthur O. Lowry during 1938 and 1939, when Lowry was in trouble in Mexico and Los Angeles, and there is a substantial correspondence dating from 1938-39 between the Liverpool solicitors and Benjamin Parks, the Los Angeles attorney, in the Browne, Pictou, and Hornby Libraries in Liverpool. Lowry's three surviving letters to Benjamin Parks (**93, 120,** and **126-a**) are with this collection. After Arthur Lowry's death, Alderson-Smith handled the estate.

Editorial Notes:

a. This undated fragment (UBC 22:19) is one of a set of letters included with draft materials for 'The Ordeal of Sigbjørn Wilderness.' Lowry's reference to the fall from the pier and back injury, which occurred in July 1949, suggests a late 1949 date of writing.

14: To T.R. Henn

P: UBC(ms,ts)

[nd]

Letters 1. to Mr. Henn[a]
2. to D. L. D.
3. to Frank
4. to Ayerton & Smith . . .
5. to Mother[1]

Draft of letter to Mr Henn:[2]

Points a/ You may be surprised at the contents of this letter but after a great deal of self-examination I have decided that it is my duty to write it. b/ Brief account of accident, which it first seemed was of little account, then was obviously a stretcher case. I had broken my back and three ribs – the 4th vertebrae. I was taken to the oldest hospital here – a Roman Catholic institution, predominantly Irish, and which operates

under the direct { directions
instructions of the Archbiship.[3] That is to say, not even one of the very rare nurses who are not Catholic may participate in any activity forbidden by Papal encyclical, see a film forbidden by the Catholic league of decency, or even do anything else in her private life

that is forbidden by encyclical, or even by a passing whim of the Monsignor or the chaplin such as enter a beauty contest, under pain of dismissal: it is as strict as that; in other respects it is not strict at all. { — there seemed no *lines drawn* [on] the extent of celebrations on Irish Day, among the internes at least — & who am I to blame them — } And is the only Catholic hospital I have ever been in where the law of compassion does not seem always to prevail: nor is the building entirely a hospital: it also houses a YMCA, and in one wing, the one I was in, also a club or at least apartments: since this wing { — old fashioned in other respects — } is equipped with a bran new acoustic system — atomic — in case of air raids. You can hear not only what is being said in different wards, but for as far as a block down the street, sometimes to the extreme detriment of sleep.

c/ By chance I arrived upon or on the eve of Irish Day:[4] that is, upon the day of their final independence: soon I was to think that I had been chosen to suffer or atone for all the sins and sufferings that the English had inflicted upon the Irish. In passing here, since this letter does not strictly concern myself, but one who was up at Peterhouse, *I* had thought to write to the Master of Peterhouse;[5] I hope you will not take it amiss that, without loading you with any responsibility in the matter, that I have seen fit to write you: there are many reasons for this, which range from personal respect to the fact that this is an entirely spiritual matter & that you are Irish yourself. And while I had less than no record for any particular integrity when I was at college I believe that you will recognise that I am telling the truth, or what I passionately believe to be the truth. At all events, nothing to my dying day, can shake my conviction that what happened happened as I shall describe it.

d/ a brief account of the pain, the anxiety of the ex-ray, the diagnosis, the sense also of isolation, being English, the anxiety over my wife, whose holiday I was later to spoil, but whom I could not meet at the airport, and so on.[6] I sent her a wire by one of the nurses, delayed as long as I could, & my wife wired back that she would arrive on the 14th.

e/ On the night of the 13th I asked my doctor — who did not belong to the hospital — to take me away from the hospital, because I had a prescience that something grim was going to happen:

[breaks off unsigned]

Annotations:

1 Margerie's typescript copies of the letters here numbered 1, 3, and a fragment of 4 have survived with Lowry's materials for 'The Ordeal of Sigbjørn Wilderness' (UBC 22:19). Lowry intended to use these letters within the story, and the drafts that survive all focus upon his accident and hospitalization in July 1949. D.L.D. is John Lancelot Davenport,

but it is not clear which letter to him Lowry intended to use. Likewise the letter to 'Mother,' either Mrs Bonner or his own mother, is missing. For the letters to Frank Taylor and Ayerton and Alderson-Smith, see **374** and Appendix 3 (**13**), respectively.

2 Thomas Rice Henn (1901-74), a university lecturer in English and a college fellow, was the director of English Studies at St Catharine's College, Cambridge, during Lowry's undergraduate years there, 1928 to 1932. Henn was a distinguished scholar and specialist in Anglo-Irish literature. According to Hugh Sykes Davies, Henn and Lowry did not get along well, and for this reason Henn asked Sykes Davies to help Lowry prepare for his examinations; see *Malcolm Lowry Remembered* (46) and Day (128). There is no evidence of any surviving correspondence between Lowry and Henn with the latter's papers.

3 Lowry was taken to St Paul's Hospital in downtown Vancouver. He describes his ordeals in several letters; see, for example, his 10 August 1949 letter (**374**) to Frank Taylor.

4 Lowry was hospitalized on 11 July 1949, just before Orange Day (not Irish Day) on 12 July. Orange or Orangeman's Day is an annual Protestant celebration in Northern Ireland and in cities with large Irish Protestant populations.

5 Peterhouse is a college of Cambridge University, but Lowry's exact reference is not clear.

6 Margerie was in Los Angeles at the time of Lowry's accident. When she returned to Vancouver, she found that he had been discharged from St Paul's and was being treated in the North Vancouver General Hospital.

Editorial Notes:

a. This pencil holograph (UBC 22:20) is filed with the materials for 'The Ordeal of Sigbjørn Wilderness.' It occupies the upper half of the recto of a 26-by-35-cm sheet of paper, and there is a long marginal insert, in Lowry's tiniest script, written down the right side of the page. This arrangement leaves the lower half of the recto clear, and in this space Lowry has written, then cancelled, the following lines:

> No words assess, no pencil draws
> No picture is, no music gives
> A meaning, inkling, parrallel
> To that which drew this soul from hell
> And made it thus transcend its laws.

See also Scherf (364), where 'draws' in line one is mistakenly transcribed as 'knows.'

This 'letter' to Margerie, filed with the drafts of October Ferry to Gabriola *(UBC 20:27), dates from the 1952-54 period and provides an excellent example of how Lowry worked on his manuscripts. It approximates a dialogue with himself as much as with Margerie, to whom it is addressed. As he wrestles with details in the story, he struggles to find solutions to technical problems and to create new ways of forcing language and narrative form to serve his ends. The passages of the novel under discussion in this letter occur in chapters 4 and 5, with a majority in chapter 27 of the published, heavily edited text.*

15: To Margerie Bonner Lowry

P: UBC(ms)

[Vancouver/Dollarton][a]

Harteebeeste mio. All right, take it page by page then. *P1:* o.k, wonderfully suggests all kinds of ambiguities & confluences: but perhaps also a more constantly beautiful & lyrical product than we're offering. *P.2.* The word Duncan suggests, here or elsewhere, the train of thought: Duncan . . . *Macbeth hath murdered sleep.* (Perhaps caps ie DUNCAN MACBETH HATH MURDERED SLEEP[1] . . . At bottom. It is only love & wisdom without *use*, that has no abode. Ethan can have misunderstood this bit of Swedenborg, that should have been quoted to him by his *mother*. I see his *mother* as the Swedenborgian, also as a unconscious instrument in the supposed 'murder' of Cordwainer. Ethan has tried to sell him 'real estate' in the next world, though this must come later. Otherwise ok. But what about technique? Can my new ideas support this kind of technique? *P.3.* Assume this mostly ok for the time being, but technique, bottom 3 passim is only supportable in the light of later events & reversals, if we continually remind the reader that *Ethan really thought like this,* or *thought he thought* like this. *P 4-5* To what extent does his train of thought here – which involves a kind of *false* or semi-false exposition – now come off as a series of plausible half truths & even lies to himself (mingled of course with real truths) is now the question. Actually of course there are two kinds of consciousness at work though the second one only takes over when he realises he has a hangover & perhaps the first pheno he's had that morning is wearing off, i.e not till p 32 or thereabouts. Though in fact the second consciousness would occasionally stick out a claw into the first. Both consciousnesses are of course selective & that their method of working is akin to literary composition: it is in their method of selection too that the falsities creep in. The first suppresses most of the purely damning aspects: the second, while more honest, is also more irrational, or in places completely so (both more irrational & more logical i.e more primitive) & suppresses most of the hopeful & exculpatory aspects. But how the hell can this be done without confusing the reader? *P 7* I'm not at all sold on the McCandless part of it now, unless I know how Ethan's met Jacqueline. Why not at an amateur performance of Macbeth, or a movie of Outward Bound (yes), in Toronto? Or even in England. This information to be given in middle of 7 after McCandless & before the 'exposition in common' to which most of the above remarks apply. *P 8* Again we need (perhaps last § but one) – *& still Ethan thought like this, in the bus, or thought he thought like this.* Jacqueline, up to this point, has not in any sense come alive for me, & to tell the truth I can't *see* either of them: perhaps because the real exposition (dates etc) is still undecided. *P.9.* I thought a claw should pounce here, from the second consciousness, after Mother Gettle, something like:

> *All right, go ahead & do it, my friend . . . Mother*
> *won't let you down, I'm sure. She's got a lot of*
> *friends in high office. Besides the Tibetans say you*
> *can be comfortable even in hell, if you're clever.*
> *'But Schopenhauer says that it's the one thing a man*
> *has an inviolable right to dispose of as he thinks*
> *fit.' 'All the more reason then.'*

This, of course, left unexplained here. Again in the light of later developments this must put some of the rest of this & the following pages into the category of mere goofing (something like a drug addict), which could be explained by the fact that he's had more drinks than are mentioned in the story the previous night, & also one phenobarbitol, perhaps two, already that morning. Importance of deciding the more definitive exposition becomes important here. *P 12.* There is going to be a slight alteration here of a genius nature I can't explain. But someone – say a friend of Fairhaven – is going to taunt him more profoundly (see page 2 of The Haunted Castle notes) with his romanticism. A reason for this appears later: he actually *is reading* The Haunted Castle on the bus, has the book with him that he has borrowed from that friend. This sets the stage (see page 2 again of those notes) for the Perilous Chapel motif in a way that is also thematic to the whole work. I see no reason for you to contest me on the point that Ethan hasn't any longer a car, if I decide he shouldn't have, for this is *partly* due to a failure of nerve, consequent on other things, & perfectly logical as you will later see, & it is the recovery of that nerve that is an important part of the story. You will have to leave this to me, however, if I'm to convince you. Re The Haunted Castle itself the idea could scarcely be better (A Welshman's home is his Haunted Castle. Educated in England Ethan has something of an English accent, which causes him to be taken for an Englishman in Canada, & increases his isolation.) See also p 1 of those notes & how mysteriously it parallels our passage of seeing the pub at sunset from the ferry where of course we can [have] some brief fun with it too. Here I know what I'm doing, & when it explodes in *your* mind, I'm sure you'll be delighted.

P 17 after 'temptations to suicide,' once more a claw, from the second consciousness, though Ethan is certainly covering up something here, as you will see when the second consciousness takes over. (i.e while they were in the apartment, Jacqueline has had to go to the States for a few days to see a sick aunt or something: while she is away I visualise that Ethan – who wears a scapular round his neck of the Virgin for those who have nobody them with, given him by a Spanish Friend – or perhaps Wilderness himself – actually contemplates turning on the gas but just as he [is] going to do so the bell in the Catholic church starts to ring for early morning mass. Later in Perilous Chapel scene he will supplicate Her via St Michaels *novena*, if we can find it.

P 18 after 'wreath on the door' I contemplate – for they are walking on the promenade – putting in 'They are pulling down the old houses once built with loving hands, but still the old bandstand stands where no band stands' – (Ethan, like the Consul, has taken to writing jingles: psychologically accurate, for he is suppressing his creative work of composing briefs etc.)

P 19 The material in top paragraph 'in order to bear the loss of' etc turns up again on the ferry in the guise of a new perception. This is one of the great difficulties of the story: for if we are to believe he is to change their lives, it must be a day of *new* perceptions – they may be repeated, of course, but the effect must be gradual . . . .And wouldn't she wear shorts also on the beach?

P 20 . . . . 'objective reason for Ethan's despair.' Once again we have to emphasise some such note as: And Ethan still even now, on the bus, thought like this, or thought that he was thinking like this.

Mem p 27. Interpolated pencilled note at top belongs definitely to second consciousness, I *think*, though I'm not sure: the profound purport is that the 'happy day' at the museum symbolises – to him – with one part of his mind, something intensely pathetic: . . . & the pathos of this, the brave pretense on Jacqueline's part that it was like that old life when nothing could have better symbolised their terrifying fall from Grace than those hours, enjoyable or no, for their life, as Schopenhauer – Schopenhauer? – might have said, had indeed become like a running away from nature to look at a museum of dried plants or look at a land-scape in copperplate & pretend you were enjoying it more. (Schopenhauer of course immediately strikes the suicidal chord of Cordwainer again.) This incidentally can be taken a stage further with almost diabolical effect by contrasting it with Swedenborgian thought, wherein nature herself, in herself, being but a reflection, is but as a museum of dried plants to that which she reflects. (I don't mean I agree: but Swedenborg again strikes the Cordwainer chord.)

29. There should be slight alterations round about here, of course. He drinks now more than he does in this typed version & can't be quite as dishonest as this about it. Moreover as he now approaches the second consciousness, the claws may jab harder & swifter . . . ——

Most important of these I count some such reversal in thought as:

This morning, buying the tickets (at least he had been about to buy the tickets, though it had ended with Jacqueline buying them) . . . .

This of course is symbolic of an increasing lack of responsibility & what could foreshadow a complete abdication of it if he doesn't pull himself together.

30. Claws jabbing swifter!

31. And still swifter!!

32. BINGO! Second consciousness takes over & my troubles begin. . .

ADUMBRATION OF MY TROUBLES.

1/ – & preeminently. TECHNIQUE.

2/ distribution of the material of new 'exposition' – it can't *all* come here, i.e while the bus is standing still, though the trucks provide a certain *motion*.

3/ in what order should it be distributed, which depends partly upon whether

a/ the new consciousness is initiated by sudden realisation of hang-over & that first pheno has worn off –

b/ by something objective, such as the poster of Cordwainer, Mother-Gettle (which will weaken drama & humor of scenes at the subsequent posters, where slight alterations will, alas, be in-dicated anyhow if this Cordwainer poster be used. (I am further confused now by the fact that I have sold myself on the notion that this day is the anniversary of Cordwainer's death, as well as Edgar Allan Poe's.)

c/ by a bit of both.

4/ How far to dramatise, how far to state: how far to do both. So far I've tried this abortively a couple of ways, neither of them fully success-ful; I offer you a kind of amalgam, & can only hope you will have an inspiration yourself; from what follows: (Incidentally, on rereading the following, as well as what I've already written to you, I can already see one grave error that seems due to the temporary imbalance of the author: i.e consciousness I is *not* so terribly self-deceitful as I had thought, merely certain unpleasant things are repressed, so that he need not go on at such length reflecting what a terrific contradiction of it consciousness II is: the exception to that being of course the *half*-life they have come to lead: the solution to this is perhaps or of course *more claws* in I, which I have been trying to avoid.

. . . And equally he knew it was not the desire for a drink at all, but a longing, if a longing that every day grew less – or was it more? – a longing for a swift cold sw –

These brackets are tentative: as is another idea, that this part should be done in much smaller type – (not on your typewriter of course, that would be asking too much.)

dearduck.

(Stop! Look! Listen! *Mother Gettle's Kettle* . . . It must have been there all the time, of course, on the other side of the level crossing, the advertisement looking at him: or perhaps the Scotch mist had obscured it, or the high-piled timber on the open cars trumbling tumbling by, while now there were some curiously meaningless empty cars that he could see right over and which did not obstruct the view beyond: but he felt it had been there all the time, as indeed it had been in his mind anyhow, all the time; he had been expecting it sometime or other, but not this one, not the one with Cordwainer himself on it, not this comparitively rare one: – (follows a description of Cordwainer, on the poster, aged 15, eating joyfully)

Mother Gettle's Kettle Simmered Soup, **m'mm Good.**

'Do you see what I see Jacky?' Ethan now asked. 'Yes, I've been looking at it for the last five minutes. I hoped you wouldn't see it.' 'Please don't call it it . . . It's the one with Charley on it as a boy,' he added. 'Yes, I know. They must have got wind of your coming and put it up there on purpose.' 'Don't be harsh please on that subject, I can't stand it.' 'I'm sorry.'

The exact nature of the subject was none too easy to express to oneself, the more especially since, at this point, – and as abruptly as the machinery of a phonograph with self-changing records goes into action when another disk slips itself on to the turntable and the needle grips it – it was as though, within him, – & no matter that the subject itself which was before his eyes was one major cause of this – a totally different consciousness had taken over. Since the first full awareness of a hangover (or of its total extent, its regressive downward economy & meaning, of the steps too, also no doubt downward, that are going to be taken to 'recover' from it) since this awareness is in effect often the real beginning of a new drunkenness, it might seem natural that things half repressed in that other 'cruising' state of mind should, at its onset in this intolerable interior, now leap horribly to the surface: the bestial record had been swarming up the slippery pillar all this while, had now reached the top, & struck forth stridently. (I'm not doing very well with this bloody metaphor so far dear duck, and I'm not even sure it should be here, – however I can't afford to pause just here, so will dash at all my derangements etc, & never mind the sense just for the moment.) But here, to lose the metaphor a little – and Ethan had already lost it a little – it was as if the mind of another person, coexisting with that other mind, but utterly independent of it, had begun to work: to work, to be sure, over much of the same material, but with what a completely different viewpoint, Ethan thought, a viewpoint so radically different indeed it made that other consciousness seem like a preposterous liar, or at any rate one who had glossed over most of the important truths of the situation it was pretending to reflect, and where it had punished itself by admitting a truth, had only done so that it might, a little farther on, permit itself a worse lie. Indeed there were so many obstructing lies still on the surface of his mind that it was difficult for him even now, though torn to pieces by it, to determine what the 'subject' was, or rather precisely what he had meant by 'the subject.' When he had abjured Jacqueline not to be harsh upon it. This was not strange, perhaps, for Ethan's method of thinking – that is the way he had been thinking this morning up to this point – involved a process akin to composition: less indeed as though he had been creating a brief perhaps, but had been loosely composing a mental dossier, preparatory to making a brief, of two people he proposed to defend. Being continually involved with half truths in a world where the truth itself is only of variable or relative importance, where facts indeed were often only relative finally to what they elicited in terms of a rigid code or definition, a code or definition mostly without mercy or regard to spiritual circumstances, however **the** truth or the facts might finally prevail, lawyers were perhaps more prone than those in most other walks of life to the temptation of self-deception. Spiritually, at worst, it could even become his quo warranto. By the right of my irrefragable habit of flawless self-deceit I exercise my office! Ethan had thus probably often deceived himself before . . . But the actual & frightening & certain knowledge at this moment that he had been consciously deceiving himself with his thoughts all morning, actually dislocating the very events of his life for the sake of making them fit into a bearable pattern came with the force of a shattering revelation. Not that this new & different consciousness or self was any more rational than the Jesuitical & selective one that had just abandoned him. Indeed it was far less so, & at the same time equally selective. The trouble was that the facts it selected, in so far as there was any order as yet – or the construction it was putting on the other facts – were without comfort or hope of any kind. So despairingly implacable was it indeed in its endless and voracious accusation that Ethan almost excused that other half lying & plausible consciousness for existing – or half existing, much in the manner that the heroin fiend's consciousness half exists when he is simply 'goofing', & for a not dissimilar reason – since no doubt it only maintained itself for his benefit, (and he was bound to believe now that it did maintain itself even if he could not consciously recall any of its former manifestations,) in an effort to keep him sane. For certainly no mind could stand the merciless battering imprecations of this *new* consciousness very long without giving way, if indeed the nature of its activity, or its activity at all, were not a symptom that it had long since begun to do so.

'De clock de *clack* de clock de *clack* de clonkde *clonk* de clonkety-*clack*!
– clunkety-clunkety-click! clunkety-clunkety-click! –
Mother...Gettle's...Kettle...Simmered...Soup...

Symptom! – But what if, speak harsher truth though it might, there were latent or arrested or even actually present in the remorseless and vindictive motion of this mind – washed up like driftwood tortured into obscene shapes by those waves of suffering glutting eternally some cavern within, – the symptoms, not of one, but of nearly all the most extreme types of mental sickness. How more than terrible to think that this might be actually his soul with which he was now thinking, a soul that had become sick almost to death, that perhaps had even been sold to the devil, a soul that could only plot the most merciless revenge on him for what he had done to it, and that sick though it was, spoke though it did partly with the accents of insanity, also spoke true, alas! To recover his former image, it was as if this new consciousness, this other self, this soul, played *back* to him a new record of his first thinking, his exposition of himself, of themselves, but whereas the original record was of a composition by some meretricious, if not pedestrian composer, now the same melodies, the same motifs appeared, were heard again, recorded by a musician more somber than Sibelius, sadder than Beethoven, more cruel than Alban Berg. And yet ludicrously, the besetting & tragic bass to this more than tragic composition, spelt one thing to him, as if even in direct accusation to remind him that – though it would poison that too if it could – perhaps the only valuable spiritual asset he had left was his sense of humour: For this bass, this besetting tragic & appalling bass, what did it spell out, what did it murmur to him, what profundity reiterate as refrain for him, beneath its poetic & disastrous undertones of the soul, what inded but these words:

Mother...Gettles...Kettle...Simmered...Soup m'm good.

(I've no more idea technically how to solve the following, dear duck, than I have the above of which I've made such a bloody mess, but this is the information I want to get in, & as it were the design governing posture.) (Utter muddle of imagery & just muddle period can go no further than in these passages, oh dear duck, but perhaps there is an idea latent among these arrant contradictions, oh dear, oh dear I am losing my talent, it's gone.)

At this point we ought to feel Cordwainer's presence almost palpably at the level crossing (a double symbol of suicide that could not be better.): –

It had not been till after their house in Niagara burned down that Ethan had begun to see – or imagine – a certain hideous pattern in his life, a sort of curse & even then he had connected it less with the house burning down at first, than with the bottle of gin that was left. He thought it was perhaps during that ghastly night at the police station that his obsession – could he only believe it to be an obsession! – had really begun to take hold of him. No, he did not believe that it was until then that he had really seen any 'significance' in the manner of their losing their house in Oakville. At the time the simple sorrowfulness & unhappiness of that event cancelled all else. No doubt he had remembered that Charley Cordwainer had been the only son of the advertising manager of Mother Gettle's Soups – Mother Gettles soups indeed! – from the horrible to the ridiculous is but a step, & vice versa – but that was as far as it went, or rather, that was another reason for forgetting it, least of all attaching any significance to it, for whatever the facts Charley (whenever he'd thought of him, which was, mercifully, rarely) remained a painful & ravaging memory. Now, or in this mood, it seemed inconceivable that he could ever have thought of anything else, from the day Charley died. And this, October 7th, was the anniversary of the day Charley *had* died. {Or is it October 9th we'll have to check up?} Ethan would like to have forgotten it too but was bound to remember it for a wholly irrelevant reason: it was the day Edgar Allan Poe had died too.

Ethan had often been told he looked rather like Edgar Allan Poe . . . And his reflection in the rear view window, now opposite him, leaned forward, out of the past, as if to collaborate this. Yes, yes: there was the dark, the Byronic resemblance: but he didn't like those red veins, those blood vessels that had broken in his nose – would they get worse, himself have a red nose? Jacqueline was consoling on that point. Did Edgar Poe have a red nose? In any case his was a healthier face. A compassionate, burned, dissolute, strong face, his face nodded in approval. But his face could not see those veins: had he some kind of disease perhaps? . . Perhaps? Suddenly he saw [his] whole life had been one long malignant disease since Charley's death, ever since he'd forgotten it, forgotten it deliberately like a man who assures himself after it begins to disappear that the first lesion of syphilis is simply impetigo – like Thomas Mann's Dr Faustus, in fact – forgotten it, or pretended to forget it, & carried on as if nothing had happened. The face in the rearview mirror looked at him approvingly, smiling, but with a kind of half terror. Its lips silently formed the one word:

'Murderer!'

But was he?

The circumstances surrounding Charley's death were as follows. (They are cited: you know all this, and the main question seems to be technique, & how much to put in and where; probably some of this can be sandwiched in with effect after they leave the level crossing, and some of it perhaps must be in dialogue here, else with such a long 'monologue' with Jacqueline entirely out of the picture, no matter how dramatic, what I write will have practically no existence, from one standpoint of aesthetics anyhow. I set down my thoughts now at random, as they come to me, some will contain solutions of technical problems as they stand, others, no doubt should be cut out altogether.)

The figure on the advertisement, Charley, *the watcher on the threshold* put on flesh, grew taller, the bells that now beat along the line – Aidons nous! merci! – become the bells of the old University of South Wales. The evening of October ninth, this very day all those years ago, ten years previous to which, also in England, Cordwainer – both boys are Canadians – had been his chief persecutor at school, when Ethan, deprived of a childhood altogether, had calamitous trouble with his eyes, & now, on this day, this eye trouble has broken out again & he is wearing an eye-shade. (As boys perhaps they had both been in the boy scouts together: Cordwainer the patrol leader of the Tigers, Ethan for a time perhaps his 'second'. Cordwainer was an expert on knots.) Though early autumn, it is a freezing night with a red moon, like November. Cordwainer's father had intended his son to be a mining engineer but he is in law school with Ethan. Mother Gettle – for which his father was the advertising manager – was not then also an indigenous Canadian product. It was a kind of smaller rival of Crosse & Blackwells. There was

Mother Gettle's cake mixture. Mother Gettle's assorted fish pastes. But Mother Gettle's Kettle Simmered Soup mm good & international fame throughout the world & the Commonwealth were yet to come. Both lads are in their second year at the University – & it is right at the beginning of the term: you know the story substantially, the same as a précis of Act I Sc I of In The Dark: i.e at first he stops him, then goes out & gets the bottle of gin, after that at first he still seems to be discouraging him, then so far as he can remember (perhaps there is another contributing cause, such as that Cordwainer has confessed he'd driven away after a fatal accident, or perhaps Cordwainer himself feels he's suffering from some dire disease) 'sells him real estate,' (à la Swedenborg) in the next world. – Or had he? Had in fact Cordwainer declined the gambit, but afterwards decided to do himself in anyhow, so that only faintly could Ethan's remarks be considered a contributing cause.

At midnight he had run home – being obliged to be in his lodgings by twelve – the clock struck twelve as he passed the hospital (where the inquest was to be next day) etc. Ravenously hungry after his staggering run as well as almost blind tight Ethan having stuffed himself with ham fell asleep almost immediately: once during the night he woke up with his heart pounding, decided the whole thing was a nightmare: yet once again woke up, a heart seemed beating in his ear that was growing ever fainter etc: Well, what a youthful piece of melodrama – if he roused his landlord, called the police & went back, & he was proved wrong – what a mess: – & he found himself also indulging in the most specious piece of reasoning he had ever employed in his entire life, which was that, if proved right, Cordwainer would be placed under an indictment for a crime, & possibly imprisoned, & would therefore certainly be sent down, & as a consequence would most certainly commit suicide anyhow.

Next morning Ethan finds Cordwainer's farewell letters in his room – With a shocking hangover he goes to a lecture the next morning – he notes Cordwainer is not attending it – goes to Cordwainer's rooms & finds he's dead. His landlady had made a most peculiar remark: 'It's all for the best.' she said sympathetically. . . . If Ethan had not told all the truth at the inquest, it was only partly to defend himself, & his own parents, & even spare the feelings of Cordwainer's own parents: the real point was that he did not *know* it (supposing he had encouraged him – what had Cordwainer done to *him* to elicit that attitude? This he didn't know for sure either.) vaguely he remembered turning savage & trying to sell him 'real estate in the next world': but all this was surrounded by a blank, & perhaps he never would know the degree of his culpability . . Or *did* he know' Almost everything anyhow save the 'real estate' was a blank after he'd come back with the bottle of gin which he'd bought at a pub: 'We're doing you a favour' the man had said . . . But to almost everyone else he was perfectly frank. There was nothing for it but to post the farewell letters and get another bottle of gin, as it happened, for himself. Suicide while of temporarily unsound mind was the verdict, & Ethan (as I have said) like a man who has been assured that the first lesion of a dire disease was simply impetigo decided to forget all about it & plunged into work. That his whole subsequent life was like an impassioned defense of what he secretly believed in his own heart to be a murder hadn't occurred to him. (I think much of this can only be done in dialogue.)

Thus the thing roughly. Now, what is important to convey, & I don't know in the least how to do it, is to convey the *true deterioration* of their own situation since the threat of eviction: the new obsession with destiny: the feeling that he is destined to commit suicide himself, or that she is going so to behave that she will drive him to murder her: – as a defense against his gloomier moods she has taken to reading murder stories, in fact almost has a mania for them, – & the names of some of these should be cited. The train is now going very very slowly, perhaps slowing to a signal miles ahead, the bell beating slowly, & Charley on the advertisement, while still there, seems to stop too, shrink, become the joyfully eating child again. Or the sardonically eating child.

As I say I don't know in the least how to go about what follows, but it certainly is one of the most important parts of the whole story. I want to convey that it isn't alcoholism in the true sense but a kind of death in life: or half life. They take vitamins: but then, at five o'clock, always find themselves drinking gin. At night there are barbiturates. In the morning breakfast & more vitamins & perhaps more barbiturates & perhaps even benzedrine: but each day becomes like a longing for five o'clock. The five o'clock gin: gives the meaning to the whole day. Not they had wholly abandoned their healthy habits. They still half swam. They enjoyed half ecstasies. But everything has this 'half' quality. Even their drinking when it was five o'clock partook of the general schizophrenia: persuading themselves that this was healthy they mixed it always with large quantities of orange juice. Or they would buy angostura, telling themselves that that was a constructive sign in themselves too, since it had been evolved as a stomach medicine in Venezuela. (We might even throw in I fell half in bed with you). I find that Jacqueline's attitude, however sympathetic, towards beer parlours, is a very important one too. For now even Ethans best friend, Jacqueline herself, is turned in effect into an enemy: she equates beer & gin as equally pernicious, which is of course a lie, the real reason being that she's snobbish about beer parlours & prefers gin. So she, as by force majeure, is turned into the temptress, when Ethan isn't acting the tempter. She denies him her

companionship when she won't go into a pub with him & does not see
a certain innocence & tribute to her in Ethan's attitude: – to-day Ethan
hopes to beguile her (it is more possible when travelling, though of
course he also hopes to shift up 5 o'clock, so to say, in this manner – 'the
witching hour.' The real sin, while chiefly in Ethan, is in fact in both of
them: she perhaps refuses to realise the divine quality in the gift of
Eridanus, Ethan, while realising this, increasingly that it has carried with
it certain obligations & self-sacrifices (including the acceptance of the
threat of eviction) or it too turns to poison: of course in turn things get
much worse, since Ethan is deprived of his rituals & his holy of holies.
A Welshman's home is his haunted Castle etc. And once as I have said
nearly *does* commit suicide while she's away. Also I think the Mrs Bell
thing should be thrown in in brief: he has another brush with the police
& consequently, on top of everything else, now begins to have a fear he
may get disbarred should he even return to practise. Tommy meantime
has had an accident on a swing (one of the supporting chains of a swing
broke), which makes him slightly neurotic, & in this too Ethan has seen
the workings of nemesis, as he has in the fact that Jacqueline has discovered, shortly after the fire, that she can have no more children
{Cordwainer was the only son?}: this latter draws them closer together,
as it happens, but makes their life, in its return to pure happiness as a
teleology & meaning, far more complex: also he is affected with terror
lest he is *destined* to lose Tommy as part of the curse.

Ethan now begins to see that it would be more true to say not that
their days were passing like the pages of a book blown over by the wind
but like these cars of sad snags they were watching, full of wasted & tormented lumber and writhing shapes of agony: these were like the wasted
days of his life full of anguish etc. Not that he did not make resolutions,
wake up every morning with resolutions & prayers on his lips indeed.
But when we are in evil we are in love of evils! Ethan was like a man
snatched out by a sucking wind from an accidentally opened emergency
door, at 30,000 feet, falling through space from an aeroplane into the
middle of the Pacific Ocean, turning over & over, & yet who finds time
to observe to himself, at 20,000 feet, 'Well, now, to-morrow I must do
that,' & at 10,000, 'Yes, I am really going to reform & definitely do that,
& at 9,500, 'Yes, I shall cut it out altogether', but then at 5000 says 'But
do you suppose this pleasant looking purple sea down below there really
feels as hard to fall into as they say?' & at 3000, 'Well, perhaps they'll
find some way to pick me up after all – I told myself I ought to have
done that – but, goddam, do I care! –

Against this was the sense of the tragedy to Jacqueline. Against this
were the thoughts of the last fifty yards: how shall I spare her?

But she too is prone to 'feats' & threats of suicide & hysteria etc &

sometimes he feels the nemesis at work here, for certainly she could make it look as though he were to blame etc etc. And in so far as he is abusing his freedom he is, in another sense, to blame. In short, he is in the devil's clutches & doesn't know if he wants to get out of them, though he *tries*.

And always the significance of the curse on real estate & the significance of the gin & the terrible tyranny of five o'clock.

The upshot of this scene is that Jacqueline gives Ethan a phenobarbitol. This changes his mood somewhat – & mood, & gradation of consciousness is here fearfully important.

They go through the level crossing & past a little village of clapboard houses with advertisements for a local paper – GRAVE HANGING SHORTAGE RAPPED he reads for GRAVE HOUSING SHORTAGE etc – in a little park or playground there is a child swinging & he seems to come hurtling right out of the supporting chains: this (which is associated with Tommy too) also brings him back to Sykes, & the lie he has told about that to himself: for while he has half composed a defense, he has done nothing about it, for fear the publicity will prejudice their position on the beach. I fancy that Sykes is scheduled to die on Ethan's birthday in December which might make it worse: but the part about Sykes is very brief & truncated here, or it will lose force later.

I think, if this can be done well, we will have achieved the impossible: i.e an exposition as interesting as the story & genuinely part of it into its swing between JUS CIVILE & JUS DIVINUM, so to say: but now, my dear Harteebeeste, for the dates, the dates, without the dates, I am hamstrung ——

All Love

Dearduck

Annotations:

1 Lowry's reference here is to Shakespeare's *Macbeth* II.ii. Lowry's scattered references to other writers, such as Swedenborg, Schopenhauer, or Poe, to composers, to other works such as *Outward Bound* and *The Haunted Castle*, and to the background to *October Ferry to Gabriola* and its characters, are annotated elsewhere and noted in the index to volume II.

Editorial Notes:

a. This holograph is on thirteen numbered pages of very closely written text. There are cancellations *passim*, but considering the length of the letter, surprisingly few. Marginal comments are extensive and often difficult to read. In most instances I have located them within the text of the letter according to Lowry's arrows and asterisks. Consistent with his practice in the most personal of notes and letters to Margerie, Lowry has addressed her as 'Harteebeeste.'

16: To Nikos Kazantzakis

P: UBC(ms)

[Dollarton]
[ca 1952][a]

Honored Nikos Kazantzakis – [1]
   (dear Boss)
   Honestly I don't know how to write this letter: – I thought to ask Zorba himself, but maybe he would upset some arak on my head, which would be a waste, since your correspondent would prefer it down his gullet.
   I daresay you will be a little fed up by this time at receiving encomiums upon Zorba per se when I know full well you have written so many brilliant books: – but if I go on apologising like this, I never will get my letter done, which would be a sinful waste too, now I come to think of it, for if any letter has to be written, it is this one.
   First, let me tell you that Zorba is just one of the best books in the world: no Zorba is the best book in the world, as my friend Nordahl Grieg might say; I don't know what's lost in translation, but so far as I (& my wife) is concerned it can't be much that could be lost, considering how much we enjoyed it); I haven't any idea to meet it with any normal critical opinion, & if I did, it would again be a waste of time: it is incomparable, a diamond of the first water. I don't know anything more wonderful than the sudden shocking beheading of the widow, the terrific collapse of the cable railway (the tremendous death of Hortense
[breaks off unsigned]

Annotations:

1 Nikos Kazantzakis (1883-1957) was a prolific Greek writer. His novel *Zorba the Greek* (*Alexis Zorbas*, 1946) was first published in an English translation by Carl Wildman in 1952. The hero of the novel personifies an active, Dionysian approach to life that contrasts with the contemplative approach of its narrator.

Editorial Notes:

a. This pencil fragment (UBC 3:14), of note for what it shows of Lowry's literary interests, is also intriguing because of the suggestion, in the double address, that Lowry may have been thinking of using the letter in his fiction.

17: To Harvey Burt

p: UBC(ms)

[Dollarton]
[ca April 1953]ᵃ

For Harvey:
– *give me more pasta!*¹ – & paying no attention to excursus – or is it ii –
or the cover –
     Penticton – (or man [illegible])
     with sincere love from
          the author²

oh pasta
Oh Jesus give *me more pasta!*
20 minutes is all I can stand in dat old box even if I *am* a genius which
is very [illegible]
     Pasta! Oh pasta! oh Christ! oh [illegible]
     With love from

Malcolm

[P.S.] In memory of Eridanus and of a first rate performance, for which
I give you 1st ¡**PRIZE!**³

Annotations:

1 'Give me more pasty' is a line from the one-act play *The Devil among the
   Skins* (1931) by Ernest Goodwin, which Harvey Burt directed and acted
   for the Burnaby Little Theatre in April 1953.
2 The dust-jacket of the 1947 Reynal & Hitchcock edition of *Under the
   Volcano* has an abstract pattern of thin, wavy white lines in concentric
   circles on a dark grey ground that suggests a maelstrom or, possibly, a
   web. Lowry's 'pasta' is a play on the word 'pasty' (for Cornish pastry)
   and the pasta-like design of the dust-jacket. The 'excursus' (the plural
   of which is either excursus or excursuses, not excursii) are the quotations from Alfred Kazin, Robert Penn Warren, Conrad Aiken, and
   Stephen Spender in praise of the novel.
3 *The Devil among the Skins* was entered in the British Columbia Drama
   Festival for 1953, but it did not win first prize.

Editorial Notes:

a. This note is an inscription in the copy of *Under the Volcano* that Lowry
    gave to Harvey Burt in April 1953. It is written in pencil on the inside
    of the front cover and the first page of the book, and the writing has
    been badly smudged. It is now stored with the Harvey Burt Papers
    (UBC Burt 1:1).

18: To Harvey Burt

P: UBC(ms)

[Dollarton]
[ca 1953]^a

Beloved old Harvey:
Thank you for more
than everything.
Wait.

[Malcolm]

Editorial Notes:

a.   This pencil note on a scrap of paper is filed with the Harvey Burt Papers
(UBC Burt 1:2). Margerie has written a separate note: 'All the best God
bless Margerie.'

19: To Hans Werner Henze

P: UBC(ms)

[nd]

*a dream.*¹
Sehr Gerhte Herr Hans Werner Henze: — ²
This letter may seem a sort of fantasy but if only for that reason for
heavens sake please read it, dear & honoured Sir to the end & do not
throw it away down the abyss or into that place where all letters, so they
say, answer themselves eventually. (As, perhaps, it would, though I'd
like to live to see it.) So powerful & strange & indeed overwhelming
anyway is the motivation to write you, a fellow/brother artist work-
ing/labouring in another medium at the other end of the world that I
an advocate of sweet reason & intellective judgement as I am popularly
supposed to be, am disposed to take pen in hand & give way to the
prompting to what in English is called a velleity — I would call it a
velleity but that it was not prompted on the lowest scale, but on the
highest scale of volition! Apart from that, it is not a plea to endorse my
brand of soap to sell you a magazine or an appeal for money. I have
enough of the latter: in short a super [illegible]. Take sir, instead, your
Pilsener, your Rhein Wine, your Dortmunder Union, (my favorite beer
when on a in Bonn)

[breaks off unsigned]

Annotations:

1 This rough draft pencil holograph (UBC 3:14) is a mere fragment of a letter that does not appear to have been completed or posted. The reference to '*a dream*' suggests either that Lowry was composing the letter for his fiction or that he planned to incorporate it in his fiction.
2 Hans Werner Henze (1926–) is a prolific contemporary composer of instrumental, choral, and operatic works. Lowry may have heard some early work of Henze's on the radio and been moved to write to the younger man.

20: To Unidentified

P: UBC(phc)

[The White Cottage]
[ca March 1957][a]

Also mention & give my kindest regards to his wife Naomi.[1] She was one of the managers of The Three Penny Opera (now folded) but was in The Royal Court Management or connected with it for some 15 years and *is* now Secretary-in-head of Oscar Lowenstein (spelling mine), who is frantic for plays at The Royal Court, by new authors & is one of the most important people in London.[2]

You can mention my *name* for there is a faint suggestion in his letter that Nigel Dennis – this sub rosa – might adapt Under the Volcano for the stage.[3] Margie & I would like to be on this however – & so I would like you if you have time – but my immediate thought was of your play about guilt by association Kyd Marlowe etc.[4] So send it if you have a copy – I can *guarantee* you a reading.

[breaks off unsigned]

Annotations:

1 Naomi Dunning stage-managed the production of Bertolt Brecht's *Threepenny Opera* (*Die Dreigroschenoper*, 1928; trans. 1933), which played at the Royal Court Theatre in London through the winter months, closing on 31 March 1956. She was married to Michael Rochfort.
2 Oscar Lewenstein (1917–) has been a theatre manager, director, artistic director, and producer in London for more than four decades. He was associated with some of the plays Lowry mentions in his letters from this period, such as *Nekrassov* and *The Threepenny Opera*.
3 The implication here is that Michael Rochfort wrote to Lowry suggesting that the English writer Nigel Forbes Dennis (1912–) was interested in adapting *Under the Volcano* for the stage, but the letter Lowry mentions has not been located.

4 Lowry's reference is not clear, but Harvey Burt had written a radio play about Kyd and Marlowe (see letter **711** to Burt) and Peter Churchill had written a lot for stage and film. Lowry was familiar with Burt's radio play and he had already provided a reading of a draft of *All My Sins Remembered*; see Lowry's 4 April 1956 letter (**650**) to Churchill.

Editorial Notes:

a. This transcription is from a photocopy (UBC 3:13) of an unsigned letter fragment. The addressee cannot now be confirmed, but internal evidence suggests that Lowry is writing either to Harvey Burt or Peter Churchill; see annotation 4. Michael Rochfort's name and address appear at the top of the page in Margerie's hand, and the date, 'c. Mar '57,' is in an unidentifiable hand.

21: To Dear Lord God

P: UBC(ms)

[nd]

Dear Lord God, I earnestly pray You to help me order this work,[1] ugly chaotic and sinful though it may seem to be, in a manner that is acceptable to Thy sight, thus, so it seems to my imperfect and disordered brain, at the same time fulfilling the highest canons of art, yet breaking new ground, &, where necessary old rules: it must be tumultuous, stormy, full of thunder, the exhilarating word of God must sound through it, pronouncing hope for man, yet it also must be balanced, grave, full of tenderness & compassion, & humour: the writer himself being full of sin he cannot escape occasionally false & inane concepts, following will o' the wisps down wrong paths, if left to himself: please – I feel you need writers – let me be truly that servant in making this a great and beautiful thing, & if my motives for writing it be obscure & the words at present scattered & often meaningless, please forgive me for this but I beg You, place some Muse, some Nordahl Grieg-angel of art, at my disposal to order it beautifully: please help me, or I am lost. My prayers also to St Jude, dear Saint of the Impossible!

[unsigned]

Annotations:

1 This prayer, addressed as a letter to God, is written in pencil on a 10-by-15-cm piece of paper and is filed with notes for *October Ferry to Gabriola* (UBC 20:23). It reveals the torment Lowry suffered while composing his fiction, and illustrates Lowry's need to address himself *in writing* to another being. The letter appears in part 7 of 'Forest Path to the Spring,' without the reference to Nordahl Grieg.

The following lines are not so much a poem or letter as a fitting Lowryran coda to a life of correspondences. The pencil draft is with his poetry (UBC 5:26) and it is included in Collected Poetry *(192-93).*

a marathon of gulls,
a chiming of chickadees,
a tintinnabulation of titmice
a scapaflow of grebes
a caucus of crows
an unavoidability of vultures
a phalacrocorax of capitalists
a proletariat of Peacock (Sing)
a gobbledookery of critics
a leprosy of letter writers

And a close of this correspondence.

Selected Bibliography

As a supplement to the bibliography in volume I, this list is confined to frequently cited works or items of particular interest; all other reference materials are cited fully in the annotations. For works by and about Lowry see the List of Citations and Abbreviations in volume I.

Amor, Norman. 'Malcolm Lowry: A Checklist,' *Malcolm Lowry Review* 34/ 35 (1994): 5-235 [bibliographic supplement to New and Woolmer].

Churchill, Viscount Peter. *All My Sins Remembered*. London: Heinemann, 1964.

Eco, Umberto. *Foucault's Pendulum*. Trans. William Weaver. London and New York: Harcourt Brace Jovanovich, 1989.

Ferris, Paul. *Dylan Thomas*. London: Hodder and Stoughton, 1977.

Grace, Sherrill. 'The Asperin Tree and the Volcano: Carol Phillips and Malcolm Lowry,' *Journal of Modern Literature* 17.1 (1991): 509-20.

Graves, Robert. *The Greek Myths*. London: Cassell, 1955.

Livesay, Dorothy. *Journey with My Selves: A Memoir, 1909-1963*. Vancouver: Douglas & McIntyre, 1991.

Lyons, J.B. 'Malcolm Lowry's Love Notes,' *Malcolm Lowry Review* 28 (1991): 40-49.

Melville, Herman. *Collected Poems of Herman Melville*, ed. Howard P. Vincent. Chicago: Packard, 1947.

Oates, Whitney J., and Eugene O'Neill, Jr. *The Complete Greek Drama*. 2 vols. New York: Random House, 1938.

Raymond, Michael, 'Poetic Reflections of a Psychiatrist,' *Contemporary Review* 262. 1525 (1993): 89-95.

Shields, Carol. *Swann*. Toronto: Stoddart, 1987.

Wace, A.J.B., and F.H. Stubbings. *A Companion to Homer*. London: Macmillan, 1962.

Index

Index to Addressees giving letter number

General Reference Index